The Guide to Suffolk Churches

D.P.Mortlock: Former County Librarian of Norfolk, he was born at Wixoe, Suffolk in 1927 – merely a step from the county boundary so it was a close run thing! He spent most of his young life at Mildenhall where he was a choir boy at St Mary's, one of the finest churches in the county. Grammar school was followed by war service in the Indian Grenadiers. His library career began in 1947 with the old West Suffolk County. By this time 'church crawling' was a compulsive habit, continuing in the West Riding and Derbyshire before he came back to East Anglia in 1960. He started making notes on Norfolk churches at that time and in partnership with C.V. Roberts produced the *Popular Guide to Norfolk Churches* between 1981 and 1985 (now available in a revised one-volume edition). In 1990 he was appointed librarian to the Earl of Leicester at Holkham, and in 2006 the Roxburghe Club published his *Holkham Library: A history and description.* His *Aristocratic Splendour: Money and the world of Thomas Coke, Earl of Leicester* was published in 2007.

Kersey church and street
from a painting by Michael Daley, MBE

D.P. Mortlock

The Guide to
Suffolk Churches

With an encyclopaedic glossary

2nd revised and enlarged edition

**Foreword by His Grace
the Duke of Grafton, KG**

*Best wishes from
Sam Mortlock*

Ⓛ

The Lutterworth Press

The Lutterworth Press
P.O. Box 60
Cambridge
CB1 2NT

www.lutterworth.com
publishing@lutterworth.com

First published in three volumes, 1988, 1990, and 1992
Second revised edition in one volume, 2009

ISBN: 978 0 7188 3076 2

British Library Cataloguing in Publication Data
A catalogue record is available from the British Library

Printed in the United Kingdom by

Contents

'Walk about Sion, and go round about her:
and tell the towers thereof,
Mark well her bulwarks, set up her houses,
that ye may tell them that come after.'

Psalm XLVIII

'O go your way into his gates with thanksgiving,
and into his courts with praise.'

Jubilate Deo

Foreword

Having been Chairman of Trustees both of national and local bodies concerned with historic churches, I welcome this book and believe that it will prove to be an invaluable companion for all who visit Suffolk's churches. As more and more people discover the richness of our heritage, there is a need for a guide that is authoritative but not boring, comprehensive yet accessible, and that is what Mr Mortlock has provided.

It is not only in the grand churches of Lavenham and Long Melford that things of interest and beauty may be found. Virtually every Anglican church has something to offer and this book will encourage its readers to go and see for themselves. When they do they will realise the tremendous efforts being made by hundreds of small parishes to maintain their churches, not only as places of worship, but as havens of rest and quiet refreshment for all who visit them. And having done so I hope that they too will lend their support.

His Grace the Duke of Grafton, KG

To the fragrant memory of my Suffolk forbears.

Introduction

Since my guides to Suffolk churches were published in the late 1980s and early 1990s they have been kindly received, but are now out of print and keenly sought after. I was therefore more than happy to accept my publisher's suggestion that they should be re-issued in a revised single-volume edition. It was not practicable, unfortunately, to revisit every church, but many have been seen again, and every effort has been made to mark significant changes. Where the word 'recent' occurs in a description it should be remembered that it may refer to the 1980s rather than the present century. It is notable that many of Suffolk's churches are now being used for a variety of community purposes and have installed kitchen, cloakroom and cloakroom facilities, either within the building or as an adjunct. Such developments are only noted in those cases where they have a decisive impact on the character of the building. With the invaluable help of George Pipe I have taken the opportunity to include brief details of all the ringable bells in the county, and in those cases where bells stand on the church floor their inscriptions are recorded; on the other hand silver is not listed because I have confined myself to those things which can normally be seen by the average visitor.

The churches of Suffolk are among its abiding treasures, and to study them all in depth demands a lifetime. Nonetheless, a short visit to any of them can be an adventure of discovery and delight. Because I am an enthusiast rather than an expert, technical terms are avoided where possible but, when used, they are printed in *italic* and a definition or an explanation will be found in the Glossary. There, entries will also be found for famous persons, artists, architects and craftsmen, as well as historical notes for background information. Saints' names are italicised in the text and thumbnail sketches of them will be found in Appendix I. Styles of architecture are summarised in Appendix II. The book covers all Anglican churches currently in use and those cared for by the Churches Conservation Trust which are still consecrated and used for occasional services. Post-medieval and modern churches have their own fascination and do not deserve to be ignored, and I cannot a recall a visit that did not yield something of interest.

Sir Henry Wootton, James I's writer-diplomat, might well have been thinking of churches when he wrote that the essentials of good building were 'commoditie, firmness and delight' – the delights to be experienced in discovering the glories, beauties, ornamentations and downright eccentricities that abound in our churches. They are not just buildings constructed to specific architectural patterns and designed for common worship. They have become mute witnesses to the communities they have served over the centuries, intimate parochial histories, ageless symbols of continuity whose essence has been formed by the countless good souls who have worshipped in them, loved them and have been buried within and around their walls. If one of them seems neglected (and thankfully that is rare these days), pardon human frailty and remember that this is nothing new. In 1562, *The Second Book of Homilies* talks of '…the sin and shame to see so many churches so ruinous

and so foully decayed in almost every corner…
Suffer them not to be defiled with rain and
weather, with dung of doves, owls, choughs…
and other filthiness'. The Victorians inherited a
legacy of neglect, and while many a restoration
or rebuilding may be criticised, we owe them a
debt that is not always acknowledged. In general
our churches are in better state than they have
been for centuries, thanks to the energies and
faith of local communities. The sterling work
of the Suffolk Historic Churches Trust, the
Churches Conservation Trust, and a growing
national awareness of the scale of the problem

all contribute to a substantially improved
position.

Visitors will find that binoculars are invaluable
for appreciating the often beautiful details of
roofs, wall paintings and stained glass, and a
powerful torch comes in handy if the weather is
dismal.

Once again I wish to express my warmest
thanks to all those who have helped me,
especially Andrew Anderson, Michael Daley,
James Halsall, George Pipe and Roy Tricker. The
host of kind people that I met by chance along
the way have treasure in store.

D.P.M.
Norwich, 2009

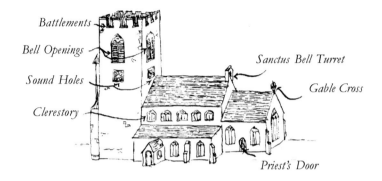

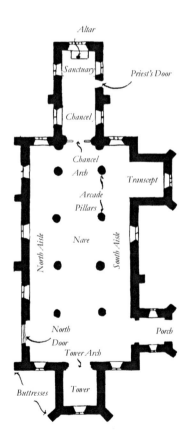

Elevation and Ground Plan of a Medieval Church

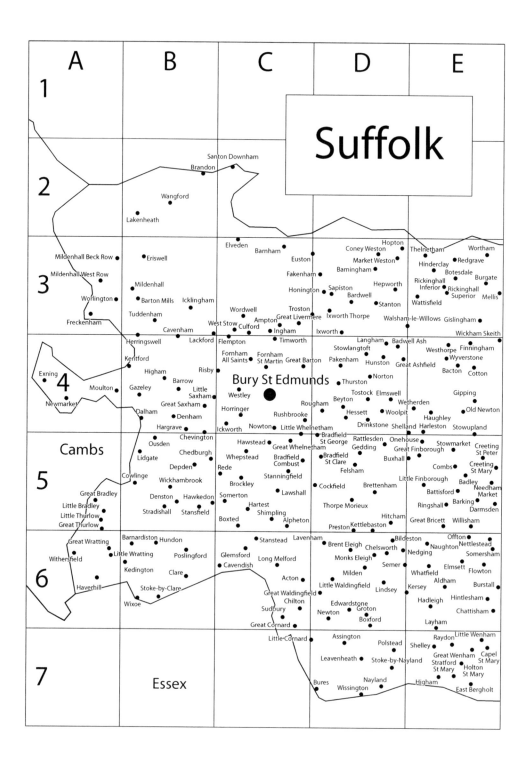

Suffolk

A
B
C
D
E

1

2

Santon Downham
Brandon
Wangford
Lakenheath

3
Elveden
Barnham
Euston
Hopton
Coney Weston
Thelnetham
Wortham
Mildenhall Beck Row
Eriswell
Market Weston
Hinderclay
Redgrave
Mildenhall West Row
Fakenham
Barningham
Botesdale
Burgate
Mildenhall
Honington
Sapiston
Hepworth
Rickinghall Inferior
Rickinghall Superior
Mellis
Worlington
Barton Mills
Icklingham
Bardwell
Stanton
Wattisfield
Freckenham
Tuddenham
Wordwell
Troston
Great Livermere
Ixworth Thorpe
Walsham-le-Willows
Gislingham
Cavenham
West Stow
Culford
Ampton
Ingham
Ixworth
Wickham Skeith

4
Herringswell
Lackford
Flempton
Timworth
Langham
Badwell Ash
Stowlangtoft
Westhorpe
Finningham
Kentford
Fornham All Saints
Fornham St Martin
Great Barton
Pakenham
Hunston
Great Ashfield
Wyverstone
Exning
Higham
Risby
Norton
Bacton
Cotton
Moulton
Gazeley
Barrow
Bury St Edmunds
Thurston
Newmarket
Little Saxham
Westley
Tostock
Elmswell
Gipping
Great Saxham
Horringer
Rougham
Beyton
Wetherden
Old Newton
Dalham
Denham
Rushbrooke
Hessett
Woolpit
Haughley
Hargrave
Ickworth
Nowton
Little Whelnetham
Drinkstone
Shelland
Harleston
Stowupland

5
Chevington
Bradfield St George
Rattlesden
Onehouse
Stowmarket
Creeting St Peter
Cambs
Ousden
Hawstead
Great Whelnetham
Gedding
Great Finborough
Lidgate
Chedburgh
Whepstead
Bradfield Combust
Bradfield St Clare
Buxhall
Creeting St Mary
Depden
Rede
Felsham
Combs
Cowlinge
Wickhambrook
Stanningfield
Little Finborough
Badley
Brockley
Cockfield
Brettenham
Battisford
Needham Market
Great Bradley
Denston
Hawkedon
Somerton
Lawshall
Ringshall
Barking
Little Bradley
Hartest
Thorpe Morieux
Hitcham
Darmsden
Little Thurlow
Stradishall
Stansfield
Shimpling
Great Bricett
Willisham
Great Thurlow
Boxted
Alpheton
Preston
Kettlebaston

6
Great Wratting
Barnardiston
Hundon
Stanstead
Lavenham
Bildeston
Offton
Nettlestead
Little Wratting
Brent Eleigh
Chelsworth
Nedging
Naughton
Somersham
Withersfield
Poslingford
Glemsford
Long Melford
Monks Eleigh
Semer
Elmsett
Flowton
Kedington
Clare
Cavendish
Milden
Whatfield
Aldham
Burstall
Haverhill
Stoke-by-Clare
Acton
Little Waldingfield
Lindsey
Kersey
Hadleigh
Hintlesham
Wixoe
Great Waldingfield
Chilton
Edwardstone
Groton
Chattisham
Sudbury
Newton
Boxford
Layham
Great Cornard

7
Little Cornard
Assington
Raydon
Little Wenham
Polstead
Shelley
Essex
Leavenheath
Stoke-by-Nayland
Great Wenham
Capel St Mary
Stratford St Mary
Holton St Mary
Bures
Nayland
Higham
Wissington
East Bergholt

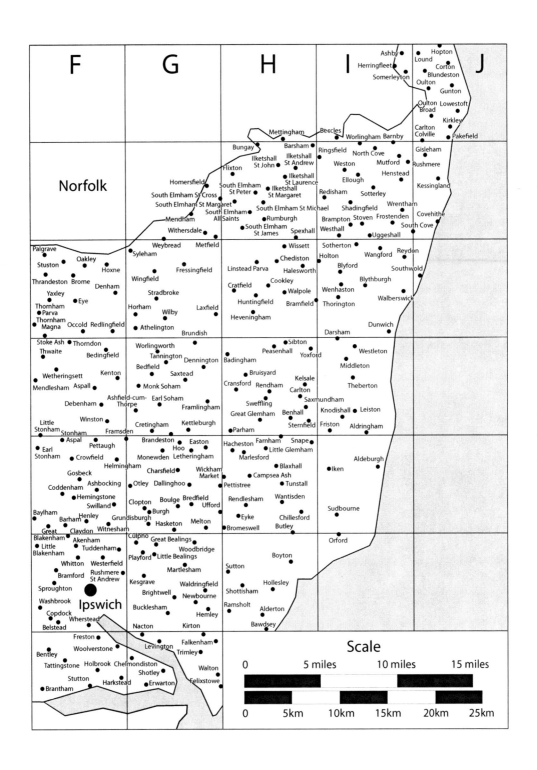

Styles of Architecture

Monarchs

An instant check-list – but see 'Appendix 2 – Styles of Architecture' for detailed background. All dates are approximate only.

Saxon – C7 to the Conquest (1066)

William I, 1066-87
William II, 1087-1100
Norman – 1066 to about 1200   Henry I, 1100-35
Stephen, 1135-54
Henry II, 1154-89
Richard I, 1189-99

John, 1199-1216
Transitional/Early English – 1200 to 1300   Henry III, 1216-72
Edward I, 1272-1307

Edward II, 1307-27
Decorated – 1300 to 1350   Edward III, 1327-77
Richard II, 1377-99

Henry IV, 1399-1413
Henry V, 1413-22
Perpendicular – 1350 to 1500   Henry VI, 1422-71
Edward IV, 1461-83
Richard III, 1483-85

Henry VII, 1485-1509
Henry VIII, 1509-47
Tudor – 1500 to 1600   Edward VI, 1547-53
Mary I, 1553-58
Elizabeth I, 1558-1603

Map references in brackets after the church names refer to the map on pp. 12-13. References to Glossary and Appendix entries in the text are printed in *italics*.

Alphabetical Guide to Churches

Acton, All Saints (C6): Placed on the western edge of the village, a long avenue of tall limes leads up to the church. The base of the tower dates from about 1300 but it became unsafe and was partly demolished in 1885 when there was an extensive restoration by W.M. Fawcett. The roofs were entirely replaced, using oak from Acton Place, the *chancel* was raised, and the e. window was restored following the style of the original. It was not until 1923 that the tower was rebuilt. The walls of the *porch* and s. *aisle* are rendered and there is an attractive *string course* decorated with a selection of tiny masks and animals. The s. aisle chapel goes beyond the chancel and the windows are blocked by the large tomb within, for which the chapel was built. The n. aisle chapel finishes level with the chancel and has a handsome C19 e. window. Its n.e. window has a late *Decorated* example of the four-petalled flower motif in the *tracery*. There is a *priest's door* on that side and a plain early-C14 n. door with signs above it of a vanished porch. There is a *stoup* by the s. door under a *cusped* arch and the remains of a *hood mould*. Within the tower, a strange relic of the more recent past is a small bomb dropped on the village by a Zeppelin in 1916. Above the tower arch is a *sanctus-bell window* and over the n. door is an exquisite set of *Hanoverian Royal Arms*, pierced and beautifully carved in limewood. They are smaller than the set at Long Melford but are so similar that the same craftsman may have been responsible. The *font* is C19 but in the s. aisle at the e. end stands the bowl of the late-C13 original which was recovered from the vicarage garden. Also at that end is an interesting C19

bier which, unlike most of that period, was made by a wheelwright in the fashion of a miniature waggon. The *nave* benches have a fine selection of *poppyheads*, including an unusual subject on the third bench-end from the w. in the s. aisle – a pair of moorhens. The s. aisle chapel doubles now as a *vestry* but was built to contain an excellent monument installed in 1761 for Robert Jennens, the Duke of Marlborough's aide-de-camp who died in 1725. He lies on a pillowed couch in long wig and sumptuous coat whose lace edgings and buttons are beautifully modelled. His wife's figure, seated pensively at his feet, was placed there at her death. The background is in pale, mottled marble, with three urns on the *pediment* and a *cartouche* of arms behind the figures. Also buried here is Jennens' son, William, who died in 1798 at the age of 98. He had been a page to George I, a life-long bachelor, and an inveterate miser who died a millionaire and intestate. The interminable case in Chancery had all the trappings of false claimants, fake family Bibles, and an unsigned will, and has been taken to be the basis for 'Jarndyce v. Jarndyce' in *Bleak House*, although Dickens did not admit it. The chancel roof is attractive in red and white, with star shapes over the *sanctuary* as a *canopy of honour*. Below are late-C17 *communion rails* with well-turned *balusters*, and the two-bay *arcade* to the s. has a good bearded *headstop* in the centre. Opposite is a lovely *ogee* arch which opens into the n. aisle chapel over a tomb. It is *cusped* and *crocketted* on both sides, though the large angel terminals to all the cusps have sadly lost their heads. There are *paterae* in the mouldings, tall side pinnacles, and two shields hang from heads above. Whose it was is not known but its magnificence and position point to an important benefactor, and it is highly likely that it was used as a base for the *Easter sepulchre*. A small doorway at the side connects with the chapel. The e. window glass is a Last Supper by *Heaton, Butler & Bayne*, with the painted faces showing signs of deterioration. The n. chapel contains the church's treasure – the finest military *brass* in the country of its period. By the n. wall, it commemorates Sir Robert de Bures who died in 1331 and it is the oldest brass in Suffolk. It is also, at 79 in., one of the largest, and is in beautiful condition. The style of armour is that of the 1300s and it may conceivably have been made for another knight. The shield is engraved as a separate plate which is most unusual. Sir Robert is dressed entirely in mail except for the elaborate knee guards and wears a surcoat over the armour. He was a distinguished servant of his country and further over is the effigy of the last of his line to live at Acton, Henry de Bures, who died in 1528. Henry wears a good example of *Tudor* armour, with a long sword hung in front of him. Also on the n. side is the brass of Alyce, widow of Sir Edmund Bryan, who probably died about 1435; she wears widows' weeds with a veil head-dress, and portions of the canopy and two shields have survived. Another Dame Alyce, widow of Sir Guy Bryan, priest, endowed a *chantry* here before the *Reformation*. There are two smaller brasses in the s.e. corner of the chapel: for Edmund and Margaret Daniel (1569 and 1589), and John Daniel (1590). A replica of the famous de Bures brass is mounted on a table for the convenience of brass rubbers. You may perhaps find a pterodactyl and its offspring lurking on the wall plate at the w. end of the n. aisle – a quirky reminder that not all church people take life seriously all the time. The church has a ground floor ring of five bells with an 8 cwt. tenor in excellent condition.

Akenham, St Mary (F6): Just n. of the Ipswich suburb of Whitton a country lane meanders down into a little valley, and from it a rough farm track strikes off for half a mile until it reaches the church. Ipswich hovers on the skyline but the setting is genuinely rural, with just a house and a farm nearby; a charming spot. A stray landmine in 1940 badly damaged the church and it lay derelict for twenty years. Then, local enthusiasm backed by grants secured its repair but sadly it was declared redundant in 1976. However, the Churches Conservation Trust assumed responsibility two years later and it is now well maintained and still used for occasional services. As at a number of churches in this area, its C14 tower is placed on the s. side of the nave and serves also as a porch. Unbuttressed, it has one set-off below a bell stage that was shortened in the C18. Full-scale restoration of the church in 1854 included a rebuilding of the top of the tower and the battlements. The belfry has cusped lancet windows and one jamb of the entrance arch is bowed with age. On walking round, you will see that there are some substantial C18 and C19 table tombs of local gentry, and in the n. wall of the nave there is a Norman lancet confirming that the church has been here since the C11. Its miniature jamb shafts are an unusual embellishment for such a small window. There is a window with Decorated tracery on the n. side of the chancel, a Perpendicular e. window, and two large late-C13 lancets with a matching priest's door on the s. side. One of the window-sills here was deeply inscribed in the C15 or C16 with a name which could be 'Jo. Suckeym'. Nave and chancel have plastered walls, but in the C17 a short s. aisle was added, built in a dark red brick with Tudor-style windows, as a chapel for the Hawys family who were Lords of the Manor.

The interior is uncomplicated, with simple furniture and brick floors, but appealing nonetheless. Below a Perpendicular w. window the C15 font has an enterprising selection of tracery patterns in the bowl panels, including a trefoil with elaborate cusps and a block of nine quatrefoils; the shaft is decorated with miniature window designs. The nave roof is cross-braced with king posts, and in front of the font there is a ledger-stone for Elizabeth Fynn who died in 1683 and her husband Robert who followed her three years later:

> For nineteen yeares I liv'd a virgin life,
> For seaventeen more beeing married liv'd a
>   wife,
> At thirty six pale death my life assail'd,
> And as I liv'd I dy'd belov'd bewail'd.

Despite the profusion of apostrophes you will see that the mason was hard put to fit all the verse in. There is a small suite of pews with traceried ends and doors which have linen-fold panels. They are C19 and may have been the work of George Drury, who was rector here. The heavily moulded pulpit stands on a shaft and dates from the late C18. Beyond a Tudor arch the chancel weeps slightly to the s., and although the ceiling is plastered the castellated wall plate of the medieval roof remains.

One would not expect such a small and humble church to be the setting for an important change in the law of the land, but in 1878 a Baptist couple in the parish sought to bury their unbaptised two-year-old son in the churchyard, having no alternative. This was refused by the rector but permission was given for the grave to be sited n. of the church where still-born infants lay. When a Baptist minister attempted to hold a short service for the mourners just outside the gate of the churchyard he was peremptorily interrupted by the Revd. Drury and an unseemly argument that came close to blows ensued. The corpse was eventually put to rest, but court proceedings followed and what became known as 'The Akenham Burial Case' was the prelude to the Burial Law Reform Act of 1880 which ensured that such a thing could not happen again. In your walk round you may have seen the solitary stone n. of the church that was raised for little Joseph Ramsey, the unwitting cause of it all, and the full story is told in Ronald Fletcher's *In a Country Churchyard*.

Aldeburgh, St Peter and St Paul (I5): The church stands proudly above the town, and, like others along our coast, it has always served as a sea-mark for mariners. The handsome C14 tower is a dappled fawn colour rather than the more familiar dark grey of flint, and a strong stair turret rises above the stepped battlements, with their paterae and gargoyles. There is a flushwork base course, and the w. doorway with its heavy label is very eroded. Above it, in the Perpendicular window, three roundels of glass by Andrew Anderson sustain the nautical theme and are lettered so that they can be read from outside – 'I saw three ships'. The church was enlarged when a broad n. aisle was added in the 1520s, its chapel dedicated to St Clement and St Catherine. The modern n.e. vestry is medieval in style to the extent of having battlements, and round the corner there is an unusually broad frontage, with chancel and aisle chapels all in line. The chancel was rebuilt in 1545 and enlarged as part of a restoration in 1853. The town's Holy Trinity guild added its chapel on the s. side of the church, and in 1535 it was lengthened to form the present s. aisle. Two years later, the unusually long porch was built, reaching to the very edge of the pavement, and pierced with side arches that enabled processions to circle the church without leaving consecrated ground.

Although the nave roof was raised when the aisles were added, there is no clerestory, and the centre is rather dark in consequence. The C18 ringing gallery was glazed in 1986, the glass boldly lettered: 'All the bells on earth shall ring', and the panels of the front are lettered with C19 texts. Their heads are filled with intricate tracery, and they probably formed part of the pre-Reformation rood loft. To the r., a large memorial in copper commemorates the loss of the crew of the lifeboat 'Aldeburgh' in December, 1899. On the other side, shapely brass plates record the gift of the church clock in 1741 and its replacement in 1901. The nave arcades are graceful, and note that the capital of the pier at the e. end of the s. aisle is decorated with small masks, marking the point where the extension began. The roofs were rebuilt in the 1930s, and the exceptionally broad nave roof faithfully reproduces the original arch-braced, king post design. Uninspired C19 benches, but the brass candle stands are nice period pieces, with barley-sugar shafts and ivy leaf scrolls. The contemporary eagle lectern is equally good, but inevitably one's eye is drawn to the excellent pulpit alongside. In 1631, the parish sent Charles Warne to study Kelsale's pulpit, and paid him £20.7.0. the following year for making this one. It stands high on a tapered shaft, and the decorative carving is well above average. The lower panels are filled with intricate arabesques, the conventional blind arches are enlivened with vine trails and centre frets, and there are lively sea creatures with sprays of fruit in the top panels; brackets support the wide book ledge, and the pulpit has been fitted with an elegant curving stair. Parts of the reading desk opposite are the same period, and on the wall above it hang the Royal Arms of Charles II, painted on board. Purchased at the Restoration, they migrated to the Moot Hall in 1840 and returned to the church a century later. A brass lies in the nave floor at the e. end – a 19in. headless figure of a man, with a plate showing his three sons; the figures of his wife and daughters have been lost, and the fragment of inscription includes the name Benet. The nave has seen many things in its time – regular ship auctions were held before the Reformation, and bands of players used it, like the Earl of Leicester's men who came in 1573. In 1597, Margaret Neale was made to do penance, with a paper lettered 'Witchcraft and Inchantment' on her breast because, poor woman, 'she taketh upon her to cure diseases by prayer'. Dowsing was here in January 1643, giving his orders about destroying a score of cherubims and lots of stained glass. He mentions the town Captain, Mr Johnson, and thought Mr Swayn the minister was a godly man, so this was probably one of the parishes where he found influential sympathisers.

The almost flat roof of the s. aisle has angel corbels, and there is a brass on the w. wall for John Bence and his family (when it lay in the n. chapel there were effigies for both his wives); he died in 1635, having been four times a bailiff of the town. Entering the s. aisle chapel, the war memorial on the l. is by Gilbert Bayes – a beautifully delicate bas-relief of a fallen captain below the rays of the sun, with angels carrying sheaf and cup in the flanking panels. The list below includes a VC – Capt. J. Fox Russell, killed while rescuing wounded in Palestine. The chapel seating incorporates C15 bench ends with poppyheads, and three of them are intricately traceried. On the s. wall looms the 1780s monument for Lady Henrietta Vernon. Backed by a dark obelisk, the large figure stands pensive by an urn, while a floating angel cavorts off-centre. The sarcophagus below is realistically masked with marble drapery, and it is surprising that such a lavish piece of London statuary should be unsigned. The hatchment that was used for the funeral of her son Leveson in 1831 hangs above the s. door. To the r. of the chapel e. window, Louisa Garrett's memorial of 1903 is a shallow alabaster relief of Faith, Hope and Charity by E.M. Rope – typically understated. The altar is a Stuart table, and the 1929 glass above is by A.K. Nicholson in C15 style. The Blessed Virgin is taught by St Anne in the centre, and SS Catherine, Ursula, Cecilia, and Margaret fill the surrounding panels. To the l., the bronze head in a roundel is a replica of Henry Fawcett's memorial in Westminster Abbey, the blind Postmaster General who died in 1884. In the floor below there are two more brasses, both for members of the Bence family who were active in C17 Aldeburgh affairs. Alexander died in 1612, having been six times bailiff, and his 25in. figure shows him in a long gown, with nine sons and two daughters (his wife's effigy has gone); William and Mary's brass of 1606 has 24in. figures and a dozen lines of verse beginning:

If to be just, religious, wise and free be
    mans,
Or his what better could there be...

The musical angels in the tracery of the n. aisle w. window are probably 1870s work by Ward & Hughes, and the glass in the next window is by Hardman & Co. It dates from the early C20, and the three lights are filled with a lively version of Christ walking on the water, all under heavy canopies. High on the wall nearby, the late-C18 tablet in demure classical style for William Sparkes is by Charles Regnart, a quality London mason whose work can be found all over the country. Further along, there is more Hardman glass – the visit of the Magi, with vignettes of St Mary Magdalene below, but the most striking window in the church is just beyond it. Its dark and vibrant colour acts like a magnet as soon as one enters, and it commemorates Benjamin Britten, whose life and work was so closely bound up with Aldeburgh. The design by John Piper, carried out by Patrick Reyntiens, illustrates Britten's Three Parables for Church Performance – 'Curlew River', flanked by 'The Prodigal Son', and 'The Burning Fiery Furnace'. The font which stands nearby is typical of the area, with lions and angels alternating in the bowl panels, but the figures supporting the shaft have gone. Two more brasses can be found in front of the entrance to the vestry. Emme Foxe died about 1570, and she is shown with her fourteen offspring, the black letter epitaph running to sixteen lines. The second brass of 1601 has little 6in. figures of John and Joan James and their children. The inscription displays his merchant's mark and ends:

Who lusts to live the world to see,
And pleasures therein crave,
At length he shall be dispossest,
And buryed in the grave.

Another name forever linked with Aldeburgh is George Crabbe, Suffolk's own 'poet of nature and truth', and the town honoured him by commissioning a bust by Thomas Thurlow. Standing on a plinth at the entrance to the n. aisle chapel, it shows how the Saxmundham mason maintained the classical tradition well into Victoria's reign, and it is one of his best pieces. The opening in the wall overhead indicates that in all probability the rood loft stretched across both aisles as well as the entrance to the chancel. The chapel is largely taken up by the organ, but a piscina remains in the corner, still with a fragment of its wooden credence shelf.

The short chancel has broad arches opening into the side chapels, and its modern roof has angel corbels. There are doorways on each side of the arch, and above it on the e. side, the apex of the original nave roof has been outlined. The deep ranges of choir stalls incorporate C15 bench ends, and a single animal carving has survived on the s. side. Two curious memorials lie in front of the sanctuary entrance. They are wooden coffin shapes, crudely lettered for 'Thomas Eliot 1654', and 'daughter of Captain Elyot 1662'. The 1911 communion rails feature excellent standing angels in Arts & Crafts style, and two more kneel at the sides, one of them armoured and holding a chalice. The broad 1950s reredos has the figure of the resurrected Christ at the centre, the church's patron saints stand at each side, and there are shields of the diocese, the borough, and the Vernon-Whitworths, patrons of the living. The 1890s Hardman glass in the e. window is a crowded Crucifixion scene spread across the five lights; below are vignettes of the Nativity, Christ with St Peter, and St Paul on the road to Damascus. The church has a lovely ring of eight bells, cast by Taylors, which were augmented from six in 1960.

The churchyard affords enticing glimpses of the sea, and there are a number of interesting memorials. The double stone for Crabbe's parents stands just to the e. of the chancel but will not be legible for much longer I fear. On the n. side you will find the grave of Elizabeth Garrett Anderson, pioneer woman doctor and the first woman to be elected mayor of a corporation in England. Lord Britten's simple headstone is towards the n. boundary.

Alderton, St Andrew (H6): A church which has seen many changes over the years. The tower is ruinous and is half its original height. The last great fall was on a Sunday in 1821, killing a cow in the churchyard but happily sparing the congregation. Lots of *septaria* was used in the walls, and there are shields in the *spandrels* of the w. doorway. Fragments of *blind arcading* can be seen above it, and the gaping w. window is shorn of all its *tracery*. An 1860s restoration by *Sir Arthur Blomfield* was so thorough that the *nave* was virtually rebuilt, and the s. wall has a dense finish of pebble flints. The window arches are outlined in flint and yellow brick, and the tracery does not repeat the original designs. Bishop Redman's Visitation notes of 1597 include: 'There is a controversy betweene the ministers & parishioners whether there be a chauncell or no, which is occasion the Easte parte is suffered to ruinate'. Thus it was that the *chancel* had gone by the C18, and Charles Archer, who was rector here for over fifty years, built a new one in 1862. The earlier walling was retained on the n. side

of the nave and it is unusually banded with brick. The C15 n. *porch* was evidently a fine piece in its heyday, but has suffered over the years. The *Blessed Virgin's* monogram features in the *flushwork* of the *base course*, and the facade is panelled with flushwork. A *woodwose* and a dragon inhabit the archway spandrels, and there are the remains of triple niches above. The side windows have been blocked, and by the inner door an C18 engraving shows a little bell-cote on the nave roof and no chancel.

Within, the very tall tower arch is backed by a blank wall, and there are C19 zinc *Decalogue* plates each side. The small-scale *font* is a curiosity, sculpted by John Luard in the 1860s. He was a retired colonel who had served under Wellington and charged with the 16th Lancers at Waterloo. No mean artist, he is best remembered for his *Sketches of India*, published in 1837. In common with Sutton, Alderton has a bell by Thomas Gardiner of Sudbury. Cast in 1740, it stands on the floor by the tower arch. A large and well-restored set of George III *Royal Arms* hangs over the s. door. Blomfield designed a slightly eccentric roof for the broad nave in pine, with two very tall *king posts* resting on slim *tie-beams*. The contemporary benches below are numbered on the n. side – a reminder that seating was often reserved in the C19. A doorway in the n. wall of the nave means that there was probably a chapel on that side before the *Reformation*. A tablet not far away commemorates Robert Biggs, vicar of Bawdsey and rector here for sixteen years until 1769. Having scratched their heads, his executors composed an engagingly candid epitaph:

> He was not distinguished by his Activity or
> literary Abilities,
> But he was what is more truly valuable,
> An honest man.

On the s. side, a C14 *piscina* shorn of its *cusping* marks the site of a nave *altar*. Above it, the Victorian rebuilding did not disturb an image niche with *crocketted* canopy at the angle of the window embrasure. The peculiar wooden lectern is presumably C19 and has a turned shaft with a large central globe, with a canted top set on twisted columns. Stevenson of Woodbridge supplied the plain tablet on the s. chancel wall for Capt. Stanley Ellis, lost at the battle of Jutland in 1916. Charles Archer, the rector who rebuilt the chancel, has his memorial over the *priest's door*, and note that the *sanctuary* arch above has bases and capitals left rough for carving but never finished.

Aldham, St Mary (E6): A lane leads only to the Hall and the church, which stands on a little knoll beyond the farm buildings, with a pond in the sunken meadow to the w. It is possible that the original church was *Saxon* and the base of the round tower may date from before the Conquest. The *quoins* at the s.w. corner of the *nave* are made up of flints and Roman bricks and this is generally taken as evidence of an early building. By the 1880s it was well-nigh ruinous and most of the tower was replaced, the s. nave wall was taken down completely, and all the windows were restored or renewed. More work followed in the 1930s when the e. wall and its window were replaced. The tower is slim, with two small *lancets* set in brick surrounds to the w. and lancet bell openings. A number of brick *put-log holes* survived the rebuilding and there is a small lead spike above the plain parapet. The C14 n. doorway was unblocked in the 1880s and on that side there is 'Y' and *Decorated tracery* in the windows. A C19 'cottage' *vestry* with a chimney juts from the n. wall of the chancel and there is a s. porch which is probably of the same vintage. One s. chancel window has 'Y' tracery of about 1300 with rather nice medieval *headstops* and another has *Perpendicular* tracery.

Before going in, have a look at the fragment of *Norman* stone embedded in the s.w. corner of the nave, carved with an interlace design. It was probably part of a *preaching cross* shaft and inside the church there is another section set in the e. jamb of the window nearest to the door. The interior is beautifully kept and redolent of wax polish. There are new doors to the C16 brick tower arch which was uncovered in 1933, and above hangs a large set of *George II Royal Arms* – painted on board and very well restored recently. The complementary set of the present Queen's arms which hang over the n. door would look even better if they were framed. The *font* is square, with octagonal shafts at the corners of the bowl, four supporting columns, and a centre shaft. It looks neither Norman nor medieval and it would be interesting to know its date. The nave roof is a late-C19 renewal of very high quality in pitch pine with *tie-beams* and *arch-braces*. The 1930s work included parquet flooring and the oak panelling which has a pierced trail along the top. Most of the benches were installed at that time and are beautifully made to match the few originals that had survived. You will find four at the w. end on the n. side which have token *poppyheads* (one with an original mask) and elbows roughly carved with roundels – a *Tudor Rose*, a star, and a *St*

Andrew's cross. There are also three medieval bench ends on the same side farther e. which have their poppyheads strangely offset and large oblong shields carved below, with a bear's head (?), a crown with spear, star and crescent, and a peculiar spike with forked ends. The lectern has a modern shaft and slope but the hexagonal base is C15 and very like the one at Kersey. The low *screen* and choir stalls in solid Perpendicular style came in with the nave benches, and the chancel arch was part of the 1880s restoration. However, the original C14 roof remains, with a tie-beam and *king post* strutted four ways, with a runner e. to w. below the plastered ceiling. The *Stuart communion rails* have thin square shafts between the balusters and there is a C13 *piscina* in a deep recess with quarter-round shafts to the moulded arch. The modern e. window has large king and queen *headstops*, the *jambs* are panelled, and there are twin niches in Decorated style each side. The 1930s glass is by Walter Wilkinson and has large figures of the Blessed Virgin and Child, Elijah, and St Paul set in pale, intricate tabernacles. As you leave, note that faint traces of medieval painting survive on the inner jambs of the door.

Aldringham, St Andrew (I4): A lane leads from the Thorpeness road down to a line of almshouses, and the tiny church is set in a fold of countryside – a lovely spot. It was built by Ralph de Glanville, the C12 Chief Justiciar who fought with Richard Coeur de Lion and died at Acre. The years took their toll on the building, and by the 1840s the tower was a shell and half the *nave* was in ruins. A w. end had been cobbled on to the thatched *chancel*, but it was obviously unsatisfactory, and rebuilding was put in hand. In 1872, a second restoration shortened the nave, rebuilt the w. end, and added a diminutive s. *porch* and a *vestry* entered through the old n. door. The new look included angle buttresses with little conical caps, a bellcote on the gable, and a three-*light* w. window. All the windows are *Perpendicular* (one with nice beast *headstops*), with the exception of an *ogee lancet* in the s. chancel wall where the narrow C13 *priest's door* has been blocked.

The entrance has two friendly medieval faces as *stops* on its arch, and within, the organ stands on a low w. *gallery* with tiered seats. The w. window contains good 1890s glass by Alexander Gibbs – Jesus healing the sick man whose friends have lowered him through the roof. Its excellent colour and assured line is much better than most of Gibbs' Suffolk work. A small painting displayed on the s. wall gives a good impression of the church as it was before the C19 rebuilding. The shaft of the C15 *font* is almost as broad as the deep bowl, and there are unusually rangy lions round it. The bowl panels have excellent *Evangelistic symbols* cleverly disposed within their frames, and the angels bearing shields are nicely varied – this is a quality example of the East Anglian type. A pair of *tie-beams* span the plastered ceiling, and below there are sturdy pine benches with *trefoil finials*. Following the alterations, neither arch nor *screen* divide nave from chancel, and the Victorian pulpit, lectern, and *reredos* are riotous exercises in *Early English* style, all beautifully made. The arch and shaft of a C13 *pillar piscina* survive in the *sanctuary*, and there is more attractive glass by Gibbs in the e. window – the miracle of the loaves and fishes, with Christ and his disciples richly robed. The only other stained glass is the 1940s figure of the church's patron saint in the s. lancet by an unidentified glazier. The churchyard is a pleasant place in which to stroll, and s.e. of the chancel Martha Taylor has a well-cut stone of 1801. In a roundel, a kneeling girl points up, her elbow on an anchor, and on the rim: 'We hope to meet in heaven'. In 2003 an extension was added to the vestry on the n. side to provide a small meeting room, kitchen and cloakroom. It is unfussy and blends well with the rest of the building. To the w. of the church there are three excellent modern headstones which show how much better the alternative to undertakers' polished black marble can be. For Marc Smith, David Willis and Peter Kemp, they are beautifully designed and lettered, and all came from Harrier Fraser's at Snape.

Alpheton, St Peter and St Paul (C5): The church is a good half mile to the w. of the village and the main road, but it is clearly signposted. The *Perpendicular* tower has a wide w. window, renewed bell openings, and part of the battlements retain some *flushwork*. The C14 *priest's door* in the s. wall of the *chancel* has slim, partially renewed attached columns and there are two ranks of *paterae* in the mouldings above worn *headstops*. The base of the chancel walls is decorated with chequer flushwork and the e. window has renewed intersected 'Y' *tracery*. There is a blocked n. door to the *nave* and on that side the windows have interesting headstops – grotesques, three crouching animals and two human heads. The wooden s. *porch* was extensively restored in 1911 and given new

doors, but the door frame and main timbers are the original C15 ones and there are exposed timbers in the sides within, some of which are moulded. The handsome inner doorway has three bands of *fleurons* in the mouldings and large king and queen headstops; over the years the soft stone has accumulated lots of graffiti. To the r. is a *stoup* under a *trefoil* arch and the oblong shape of the bowl suggests that it may once have been a *reliquary*. The nave lies under a single-framed open *roof* with *castellated wall plates*. At the w. end, the plain octagonal C14 *font* rests on a base of *Purbeck marble* which belonged to its C13 predecessor. To the w. of the n. door are the very faint remains of a large *St Christopher* and opposite hangs a set of Charles II *Royal Arms* painted on board in muted colours, with naive supporters. At the w. end of the nave there are three ranges of plain and solid *box pews*. The *rood loft* stair was on the n. side and there are niches either side of the chancel arch. For some unknown reason an aperture was cut in the wall to the l. in the C19 and the niche moved higher up. It has paterae in the moulding, a *groined* canopy, and a grinning Bacchus mask at the top. The other niche has lost its canopy but there are dear little painted heads carved as *corbels* to the miniature groining; traces of gold and blue remain and there is the outline of a figure. The *Jacobean* pulpit is decorated with conventional lozenge patterns in the lower panels and shallow carving under the rim; the base and stairs are modern, as is the low *screen*. The stall to the l. within the chancel has carved elbows, and a pair of *misericords*, with their lips chopped off, have been used very eccentrically to form a back. To the s. of the *sanctuary* a Perpendicular window was inserted in the C15, thereby mutilating what must have been a beautiful combined suite of *piscina* and *sedilia*. As it is, the piscina has a heavily *cusped ogee* arch with side pinnacles and of the stepped sedilia, only the w. stall for the sub-deacon is intact. Its canopy has an ogee arch with large *crockets* rising to a *finial* in the form of a crowned figure. There is a crouched lion in the parapet moulding, flanking pinnacles, and a triple range of paterae in the arch mouldings. The wall behind the altar was faced in the C19 with large unglazed tiles impressed with diaper work and coloured in soft pastel shades, and as a *reredos* it is quietly attractive. On the wall to the l. is a memorial to John Shepherd who, as a Royal Marines captain, served 'under the immortal Nelson in an attack on the harbour of Boulogne' in 1805 and died of his wounds ten years later. When I first visited the church in 1986 it was decked for the Harvest Festival and that, combined with oil lamps and honest brick floors, made it memorable, calling to mind Betjeman's lines:

> Light's abode celestial Salem!
> Lamps of evening,
> smelling strong...

To mark the millenium, the parish commissioned Pippa Blackall to design a new e. window which is well worth studying. It is unusual in that the central figure of Christ is shown as a beardless young man in everyday working clothes, whose outstretched arms reach into the flanking *lights*, with the stain of the wound in his side glimpsed beneath his coat and the mark of the nail on his left hand. Within a jagged containing roundel of shapes in pastel colours there are vignettes – Saints *Felix* and *Fursey* with the three crowns of East Anglia, *St Edmund's* martyrdom above the abbey of St Edmundsbury, Alpheton's original church, and little contemporary farming scenes, all flanked by two 'M's for the millenium. A fine window.

Ampton, St Peter (C3): This compact little church stands across the village street from the door in the high brick wall guarding the grounds of the Hall. It was extensively restored in the early 1840s by *Samuel Saunders Teulon*, one of the rogue architects of the period whose characteristic was complication rather than simplicity, but here he was quite restrained. The unbuttressed C14 tower has *Decorated* bell openings, large *gargoyles* at the corners, and a stair turret on the s. side that continues the line of the nave wall. Blocked *put-log holes*, outlined in red brick, show up clearly. A *vestry* was added in the C19 against the old n. door and beyond the projecting *chantry chapel* on that side there is a bricked-up portion of a window with intersecting *tracery*. The e. window is pure Teulon and on the s. side of the *chancel* is a large *lancet* with the remains of *cusping* in the head and the outline of another window. The hopper of the drain pipe at the corner is dated 1888. The s. nave windows are C19 and the *porch* has Decorated windows with deep *labels*. Within it, the steep medieval roof timbers are enhanced by small *paterae* in the mouldings and the *wall plates* have two bands of embattling. There is quite a lot of graffiti on the window *jambs*, including the date '1589' on the w. side. Through the plain and small C14 doorway is an interior that is attractive and interesting. The door to the

tower stair is medieval and on the walls overhead there are two *hatchments*, the paint on the canvas now flaking, unfortunately. That on the n. wall is for Henry, 1st Baron Calthorpe (1797), and the other is for his widow Frances (1827). A small C19 *font* stands in front of the tower arch and there is a *consecration cross* on the wall to the l. and part of another on the other side of the opening. Nearby, on the n. wall, is an unusual set of *Stuart Royal Arms* cut in thick fretwork, with exuberant mantling and faded colour. They were originally tenoned into the top of the now vanished *rood screen*, and the emblems of rose and thistle that stood with them are now hung upside down at the bottom. Further along the n. wall is a memorial to James Calthorpe designed by *John Bacon*. It is an excellent bas-relief portrait head in an oval medallion set on a grey obelisk, with a shield and crest above. To the e. is a marble tablet that reminds us that Jeremy Collier – divine, contraversialist and non-juring bishop, was rector here from 1679 to 1684. His *Short View of the Immorality and Profaneness of the English Stage*, which attacked Congreve and Vanbrugh, made a great stir a few years later. On the s. side of the nave, are the remains of a *stoup* by the door and a memorial to Dorothy Calthorpe, founder of the village almshouses, who died in 1693. There is a sweetly worded epitaph and her graceful little statue kneels within an arched niche flanked by *pilasters*, with her shield of arms above. In 1479, John Coket obtained a licence to found a perpetual chantry here, and the first chantry priest was Valentine Stabler who was given a house opposite the church. The chantry chapel is on the n. side of the nave and is entered through a late *Perpendicular* arch which has blank shields within *quatrefoils* in the *spandrels;* the cornice is *castellated* and below it, carved in relief, is the legend: 'Capella perpetue cantarie – Joh'is Coket'. Beneath the blind tracery within the arch, there are fine mosaics each side. To the w. is *St Christopher*, commemorating the use of Ampton Hall as a hospital in the 1914-18 war, when over 6000 sick and wounded were cared for there. Opposite is the figure of *St George* below the badge of the South Staffordshire Regiment, in memory of the rector's only son, Lieut. Bernard Wickham, killed at Ypres in 1917. Within the chapel there is an upright C13 grave slab against the e. wall, and on the n. wall, an oval tablet to Sir James Calthorpe and Dorothy his wife who died in 1702 – marble drapes at the sides, a profusion of richly carved flowers at the top, and a coat of arms tucked in at the bottom. There are fragments of medieval glass in the w. window and the arms of the Calthorpe, Cough, Reynolds and Yelverton families in the other windows. The square recess in the s.e. corner was probably a *piscina* for the chantry *altar*. There are a number of *brasses* in the church, and the most easily seen is that of a lady of about 1490, which is now fixed to the nave wall by the chapel entrance. At the e. end of the nave floor there are the 18in. figures of members of the Coket family, the wife wearing a veil headdress. The brass dates from about 1480 and includes a plate showing their seven daughters, all in *butterfly headdresses*, although the complementary group of sons is missing. Half of Coket's merchant mark survives. Half way down the nave is a very worn brass which probably depicts Alice, the wife of John Coket, who died in 1480. She too wears a butterfly headdress and, although the inscription has gone, her shield of arms remains. The plain, panelled pulpit is late C17 and the underside of the *tester* is decorated with a marquetry star. Above it is the blocked entry to the old *roof loft*, and the bottom doorway can be seen to the r. of the pulpit. The nave was re-roofed in the 1888 restoration and it was then that the C17 *arch-braced* chancel roof was uncovered and the boarded panels, with their painted *bosses*, recoloured. There are two important monuments on the n. side, the largest of which is for Henry Calthorpe, signed and dated in a small oval below, *John and Matthias Christmas*, 1638. The half-length figures of Calthorpe and his wife hold hands, he looking pompous in massive ruff and small Van Dyke beard, while she seems distinctly bored. Between the epitaph and the main figures, there is a panel containing little figures of their family (those that died young hold skulls), an infant and three boys on one side with a *chrysom child*, and the girls on the other. There are seven coats of arms in all, and the parents are flanked by black marble columns with a broken *pediment* above. To the e. is one of the best mural monuments carved by *Nicholas Stone* – an excellent portrait of William Whettall, Henry Calthorpe's father-in-law, who died in 1630. He wears an enormous ruff over a furred gown and the bust stands within a dished oval and finely moulded frame. Above is a *putto* and a pair of swags, a curved pediment enclosing a small coat of arms, and a full *achievement* on top. The late-C18 *communion rails* have very slender *balusters* and in the *sanctuary* there is an early and very time-worn piscina. An ironbound chest with complicated locks stands in the n.e. corner,

and just above it is a brass inscription for Edmund Coket; it is undated and the shield has gone. The e. window is filled with glass by *Burlison & Grylls*, with large figures of *Saints Edmund, Peter, Paul* and *Etheldreda*, with Christ in the centre; there is very little flesh colour but there are deep tints in the robes, and musical angels fill the tracery. The interest centres on the panel beneath the figure of Christ. There, 'In grateful memory of January 3rd, 1885' we have Shadrach, Meshach and Abednego in the rich, dark red and purple flames of the fiery furnace, commemorating the destruction of Ampton Hall by fire when all within were saved. The church has a ring of four bells with an 8 cwt. tenor, the third of which is a late-C14 casting by Thomas Potter of Norwich with a beautiful inscription; because of the condition of the frame and fittings they are seldom rung.

Ashbocking, All Saints ( ): Well away from the village, the church stands by the Hall at the end of a lane off the road to Coddenham. The broad, slightly austere tower was probably built by Edmund Bockinge in the C16 and its red brick walls are patterned with lozenges of dark blue up to belfry level. The C14 *nave* windows have *mouchette* shapes in their *tracery*, and there are examples of late-C13 *plate tracery* in the *chancel*. The e. window, with its three stepped *lights*, belongs to the same period but the wall was rebuilt in C16 (or later) red brick. A small window is rather curiously placed low in the nave s. wall and entry is by way of a lovely little *porch* in dark red brick, again with diaper patterning. It has a crow-stepped gable and the stone demi-angel below, together with the side windows, probably dates from an 1872 restoration directed by *E. C. Hakewill*. The deeply moulded C14 inner doorway has worn *headstops* and there is a *stoup* to the r.

Seen from within, the nave walls have a decided lean and the roof is the plainest of *hammerbeams*, with rustic braces rising to *collars* and *king posts* with four-way struts. The *font* shaft is modern but the bowl is an unusual *Norman* example shaped like a cauldron bulging out of a square frame. It had been encased in brick and plaster and was uncovered in 1842. The cover has a pinnacled corona at the base out of which a short *crocketted* spire rises to a *finial*. It is a handsome piece and is generally described as late C15, but parts at least are modern. The n. door is blocked and in front stands a large iron-bound C14 chest secured by four locks and a drawbar. There are some C15 bench ends at the back of the nave but the rest of the benches are C17, with heavy mouldings on the square tops and coarse triple *pilasters*. Theodore Beadle was the staunchly royalist vicar here before the Civil War and he had a set of *Royal Arms* painted on board, dated 1640, and inscribed 'God Save the King'. Restored in 1977, they still hang on the s. wall as a reminder that he 'spoke against the rebellion and Parliament' and ultimately died a prisoner in the Thames hulks for his obdurate loyalty. A little farther along is a splendid C14 tomb recess with no clue as to whose it was. The large *ogee* arch is very deeply moulded and the crockets are curiously varied so that they form strings of foliage and fruit on the l. side. The heavy *cusps* are carved, each with a terminal head, and the tall side pinnacles have two ranks of crocketted gables and shallow foliage in their front panels. The little window noticed outside lies within the arch and was obviously inserted later. A fine Elizabethan *brass* has been mounted on the opposite wall and displays the effigies of Edmund Bockinge, his wives Frances and Mary, and two daughters. Probably builder of the tower, he died in 1585 and wears typical armour of the period, while his wives have French bonnets and brocaded petticoats. The Latin of the second inscription is helpfully translated on a card below. C19 *Decalogue* boards hang at the e. end of the nave and, although there is now no *screen*, you will see that the chancel arch still has the slots in which a *tympanum* was secured. The wall plate of the roof beyond is medieval and there are late-C17 *communion rails*, a tall set which have fluted columns at the centre and against the walls. In the floor by the *priest's door* is the brass inscription for Thomas Horseman who died in 1619, and it is an interesting example of an acrostic based on his name; a note nearby supplies a translation of the verse. Within the sanctuary there is a tall and misshapen C14 piscina and the altar is a plain Stuart table which has been given a larger top. At the time of my visit in 1988 it had a lovely lime-green frontal on which the text 'Gather my saints together unto me' was lettered in gold thread and leather appliqué. Ashbocking has an excellent ground floor ring of six bells with a 10 cwt. tenor which came from the Taylor foundry in the early 1900s.

Ashby, St Mary (I1): This simple little church lies secluded, some way down a farm track, and has probably been here since well before the Conquest. It is likely that the round tower was added a little later, and at some stage the top two-thirds were replaced by an octagon. This has thin bricks at the angles, tall brick *lancets* and

matching battlements, and precise dating is impossible – late-C15 or early-C16 is likely. *Nave* and *chancel* lie under a continuous thatched roof, and in walking round you will see C13 lancets and a wide four-*light* e. window of the same period. Some simple *Perpendicular* windows were added later and the n. door is now blocked. There is a single memorial on the s. wall and the wording is curiously precise: 'Sarah Sherwood ye wife of John Sherwood who liv'd together 36 years 8 months 2 weeks. She departed this Life May ye 19 1730 between 1 & 2 of ye clock in ye morning on ye 66 year of her age.' No doubt there was a reason, but it seems odd that the memorial stone by the gate is set in the boundary fence, neither inside nor outside the churchyard. It commemorates seven men of the US 8th Air Force who were killed nearby in 1944 and 1945.

There is no porch, and watch out for the three deep steps down into the nave. The tower arch was remodelled in simple *ogee* form and this may have been done when the upper section was rebuilt. Above it, a large *sanctus-bell window* is now blocked. The outlines of the square, late C12 *Purbeck marble font* have been blurred by time and harsh usage, and the familiar *blind arcading* can barely be traced. The base shows that originally there were corner pillars round the central shaft, but these have been succeeded by stumpy, turned and carved wooden posts – probably a local improvisation for want of a mason. The nave roof is open to the underside of the thatch, with a boarded ceiling in the chancel, and all the furniture is simple C19 work. There are two *consecration crosses* on the nave walls (with another in the chancel), and if their outlines can be trusted they are interesting early examples. The stairs that led to the *rood loft* are neatly set in the s. wall, and in the *sanctuary* a C13 *piscina* lies under a deeply moulded *trefoil* arch set on *jamb shafts* that have ring *capitals* and bases; there are *dropped-sill sedilia* alongside.

Ashfield-cum-Thorpe, St Mary (G4): In 1810 it was recorded: 'the church has lain in ruins and has not been preached in these thirty years', and by 1839 there was not much more than a half of the square tower left. Although the churchyard continued in use, the people went to 'the chapel in Thorpe' for services. That may refer to St Peter's, of which the round tower remains. The present building dates from 1853 and is a simple but pleasing design in red brick with plum-coloured patterning designed by William Constable Woollard. It has a small wooden bellcote at the w. end of the *nave*, a tall

s. *porch*, and a *vestry* on the n. side. Medieval convention was followed to the extent of having a *priest's door* on the s. side of the *chancel* and there are crosses on the gables. The interior is light and airy and the short nave is lofty, with a deal *arch-brace* and *hammerbeam* roof above the brick floor. The small chamber organ has no case, giving it a rather avant-garde appearance, and the pulpit of 1939 incorporates three panels of typical *Jacobean* work. Were they perhaps salvaged from one of the earlier churches?

Aspall, St Mary of Grace (F5): There are over 150 churches in the county whose patron saint is the *Blessed Virgin* but this is the only one that particularises in this fashion. A narrow grove of holly and yew hugs the path right up to the tower, and on the n. side a path leads to cottages via an attractive *lych-gate* of 1869. The C15 tower has angle buttresses to the w. and *Perpendicular* bell openings, and the finely moulded door was blocked in the C19 with a *trefoil* window inserted in the head. The C17 n. *porch* of wood and red brick had nice barge boards added by the Victorians, and theirs is the large *vestry* and organ chamber n. of the short *chancel*. The 'Y' *tracery* of the windows and the plain *priest's door* on the s. side suggest an early-C14 date for the chancel, but the *nave* was given tall late Perpendicular windows under deep *labels* with attractive little *headstops*. To the w. of the plain C14 s. door all that is left of a *scratch dial* on the buttress is the centre hole.

The tower arch within is devoid of ornament and two *hatchments* hang on the w. wall – for the Revd. Temple Chevallier (1804, s. side) and Mary, his widow (1807). Most of the carving on the C15 *font* has been re-cut. It follows the common East Anglian pattern – profiled lions alternate with large *Tudor Roses* and an angel bearing *Passion emblems* in the bowl panels, while four more lions squat round the shaft. Overhead is a plain C15 *arch-braced* and *tie-beam* roof with stone *corbels*, and the C19 *nave* benches are excellent. They have traceried ends with *poppyheads*, and a variety of beasts and figures are carved on the elbows. On the s. side look especially for the rat at the w. end, a modern version of the *pelican in her piety*, a farmer binding a sheaf of corn, and, opposite him, the lovely little figure of a woman at her wash tub. High on the n. wall is a most attractive roundel of a naked, muscular young man sitting crouched with a dove on his knee, sculpted in deep bas-relief. It commemorates Raulin Guild, who died young in 1966, and the epitaph is a single line

from *As You Like It*: 'of all sorts enchantingly beloved'. Its gentleness seems to contrast strangely with the tablet opposite: 'Horatio Herbert Kitchener. A tribute of love and grief from countrymen overseas. Overseas Club, Kitchener Branch, Santa Barbara, California.' The World War I field marshal was not born here but his mother was, and in choosing the title 'Baron Kitchener of Khartoum and Aspall' he betrayed an affection for the place. There is another memorial to him at Lakenheath, where one of his forebears was bailiff to the Lord of the Manor. One of the s. nave windows has glass of the 1850s by *Powell & Sons* and is an example of their early work. The two oblong medallions portray Christ with children and the raising of Lazarus, the rest of the window being filled with *quarries* painted with the *Sacred monogram*. The bold chancel arch has octagonal *responds* and *capitals* and you will find that sections of a C15 *screen* (and some copies) have been used in the fronts of the Victorian choir stalls. The tracery is compressed, with *castellated transoms* and flower terminals to the *cusps*. The *altar* is a small *Stuart* table with finely turned legs which has been raised on blocks, and it stands in front of a C19 *reredos* whose panels are painted with the Creed, Lord's Prayer, and *Decalogue*. There is a large, restored *piscina* under a trefoil arch, and the e. window contains three oval panels of stained glass by Powells of the Last Supper, Christ's baptism, and the Ascension set in *grisaille*.

Assington, St Edmund (D7): A splendid setting in parkland with enough of a rise to give the church prominence. It is in essence a late-C14 to early-C15 building but by 1827 the *chancel* was ruinous and had to be rebuilt. The C14 *priest's door* was retained but is now blocked although a *low side window* was left in place nearby. In the 1860s the vicar acted as his own architect and carried out a full-scale restoration, re-roofing the *nave* and adding a *vestry* to the n. The tower was rebuilt using the original materials and following the old design, although the *sound hole* to the w. is a Norfolk type and, like the door at the base of the stair turret, is unlikely to have figured in the original. The side windows of the tall C15 *porch* were blocked with brick but the inner doors are exceptionally good. The oak has faded to a silvery grey and one of the edges retains its band of vine carving in which birds peck at the grapes. The slim panels are ridged like roofs, with slender columns running up their centres to *capitals* on which perch lions,

Athelington, St Peter: Parish stocks

eagles, and angels, and there is dense *Perpendicular tracery* above them; the bottom rail is carved with shields within *quatrefoils* reminiscent of the screen at Great Cornard, and the doorway's *hood mould* has large bishop and queen *headstops*.

Lacking a *clerestory*, the church is a little dark inside and the nave *arcades* have capitals only within the arches, like those in St Gregory's Sudbury. The blocked original door to the tower stair is at the w. end of the s. *aisle* beyond the C19 *font*, and the pine benches have decorative lamp standards, each with a brass cup at the top to house the lamp and four prickets for candles. The Gurdons were C16 Lords of the Manor and resolute Puritans during the Civil War and Commonwealth. The first of their numerous monuments to catch the eye is a handsome *cartouche* on the n. wall for the Revd. Nathaniel Gurdon, who died in 1695 secure in the family pardons granted by Charles II and James II. His *achievement of arms* at the top is backed by drapes which are caught up by cherub heads lower down, and there is a sharply carved winged skull at the base. In high contrast, a plain tablet below commemorates the life of William Warner who died at 80 in 1926, having been organist for fifty-five years. And he, like the organist at Bramford, was blind. Turning back to the s. door you will see the memorial of another clerical Gurdon – Philip, who died in 1817. It is an innocuous design by *John Bacon the Younger* but the prolix epitaph contains a peculiar phrase: 'whose gospel he had adorned and voluntarily proclaimed in this church for nearly 40 years with exemplary ability, fidelity and zeal'. Preachers seldom operate under duress, surely! A tablet to the e. of the s. aisle window is for John Gurdon who died in 1679. In his younger days he had been a Suffolk MP in the Short and Long Parliaments and a member of the

Commonwealth Council of State in the early 1650s. Just beyond is the imposing monument for Brampton Gurdon, dated 1648. His portrait bust shows him wearing a spade beard and holding what might be a pomander. On either side are the demi-figures of his wives – Elizabeth wearing a ruff, and Meriell dressed in the Puritan fashion with a broad starched cape. The women's faces, particularly, are strong and full of character. All in alabaster, there are a dozen coloured shields arranged within the handsome *pediment* and frame, and veined marble columns separate the figures.

There is a small image niche with headstops to the hood mould by the aisle e. window and in the centre of the nave lies the church's only *brass*. The two 30in. figures are likely to be Robert and Letitia Taylboys (1506) and he wears *Tudor* armour with a large sword hung frontally, while she has a lavish *kennel headdress* and a heavily ornamented tassel to her girdle. Taylboys was in the service of Thomas Rotherham, archbishop of York and Chancellor of England, and his wife had been the widow of a Corbet whose family held the manor before the Gurdons. Parts of a C15 *screen* are built into the fronts of the choir stalls and more Gurdon monuments were replaced on the walls when the chancel was rebuilt. The largest is for Robert (1577) and John (1623) and their wives. The pairs of small figures kneel and face each other across prayer desks, and two children of each marriage are shown in the panels below. There are three shields and a skull at the top above flanking obelisks and a centre column. The e. window has 1860s glass by *Clayton & Bell* – an example from perhaps their best period. The ascended Christ is flanked by groups of angels above the disciples and the *Blessed Virgin*, and the general effect is cool, with dark reds and blues contrasting well with the steely grey of frames and tabernacles. St Edmund's has a ring of six bells in fair going order with a 10 cwt. tenor.

Athelington, St Peter (G3): Money was bequeathed in the mid-C15 for the 'new tower' but it is unbuttressed and slim, which suggests that it dates from the C12 or C13 and was perhaps given a new upper storey later. Now, however, it is capped with a pyramid roof just above the bell openings – an alteration likely to date from the C19 when the stair turret was given a stone cap and exuberant finial. The w. window has *Decorated tracery* and there are plenty of *putlog holes* filled with brick. *Nave* and *chancel* lie under one C19 roof and on walking round you will see that the e. window has attractive *headstops* and intersecting 'Y' *tracery* of about 1300. Don't miss the interesting inscription cut in the sill: 'Dns Johns de Trun me fecit facere' (Master John de Trun had me made). The *porch* was built in 1873 and the village stocks have found a home here (as they have at Saxtead and at St Margaret, S. Elmham).

As with the w. door, the s. doorway was provided with new headstops when the porch was built, and one enters to find a neat, compact interior in which the separation of nave and chancel is marked only by the *rood beam*. This rests on substantial stone king and queen *corbels* which were moved to their present positions in 1873. The early-C15 *font* stands in the base of the tower, its shallow bowl decorated with nicely varied tracery patterns. The C14 *scissors-braced* roof has wide *wall plates* which are *embattled* and decorated with *fleurons* in the chancel, and there you will find a *piscina* under a *trefoil* arch, with *dropped-sill sedilia* alongside. The *altar* is a small, almost square *Stuart* table. The choir stalls and pulpit date from the 1870s restoration, and although the rest of the benches were remade then, the ends next to the centre aisle are C15 in the main and are an interesting set. The scale is small and the sides are finely traceried in the style of *Perpendicular* windows, with each *poppyhead* flanked by little upright figures. Many of them can be identified by their symbols and on the s. side from w. to e. they are: *SS Simon, Jude, Philip, James the Less (?), John, James the Great (?), Paul, Peter, Matthew (C19), Bartholomew (C19), Andrew (C19), Thomas (C19)*; on the n. side from w. to e. there are three female figures that might represent Chastity, Temperance, and Constancy or three saints whose identity is unknown, plus *SS Margaret, Barbara (C19), Catherine (C19), Agnes (C19), and the Blessed Virgin and Child (C19)*. In addition, there are bearded heads and a lion and an eagle on taller half-ends at the back of the church. The church has only three bells but they were all cast by Thomas Lawrence in the early-C16 and one bears the inscription 'O Magdalene duc nos ad gaudia plena' – O *Mary Magdalene* lead us to full joy.

Bacton, St Mary (E4): There are not many churches in the county with spires and so it is rather a pity that Bacton's had to be removed in 1935 (although it was but a modest C18 affair). The church stands back from the street behind a line of elms noisy with rooks. The C14 tower has 'Y' *tracery* bell openings e. and w., and less usual *Decorated* tracery in the others. An early-

C16 brick stair turret rises on the s. side to a conical cap at *nave* roof level. *William Butterfield* was in charge of extensive restorations in the 1860s and may have been responsible for the *Norman* shape of the w. door arch. Under the *aisle* eaves there are inscriptions cut on blocks of *ashlar* that are interesting but now very difficult to read. On the n. side, over the blocked door, one is asked to pray for the souls of Robert Goche, a C15 chaplain, and his wife, and on the s., the same request for Sir James Hobart, Margaret his wife, and their parents. Hobart was Henry VII's Attorney General. The nave has ten tall *clerestory* windows on each side and there are two ranks of *flushwork* panels between them along the entire length, with a wide range of symbols. They include the *Sacred monogram*, *Catherine* wheel, mitre, triangle for the *Trinity*, and the venerable Christian sign of the fish (4th from the w. on the n. side); the device nearest the tower on the n. side displays the tools of a shearman who will have been a donor to the church. A *sanctus-bell turret* crowns the nave gable, and the e. windows of the aisles have *reticulated* tracery.

Passing through a heavily restored s. *porch*, one reaches a fine interior with many points of interest. There is no tower arch into the nave but merely a low door, and the tower stair, with its medieval door, rises from the w. end of the s. aisle. The early C16 *font* has *paterae* and blank shields in the stem panels, with angels spreading their wings under the bowl. The bowl is carved with alternate *Tudor Roses* and angels bearing shields, and the fact that one face is blank suggests that it originally stood against an *arcade* pillar. The fine pair of benches at the w. end of the nave have varied tracery on the ends and backs, as well as good carvings on the elbows; an eagle and a monk in a pulpit on the n. side, a dog and a fierce lion on the s. The two arcade pillars here carry lovely *cartouche* memorials for George Pretyman (d.1732) on the n., and Jane Pretyman (d.1738) on the s. The lovely C15 double *hammerbeam* roof has cresting on the hammers, on the *collar beams* below the ridge, and on the *wall plates*, and there are large flowers at the intersections. Unfortunately, all the angels have gone, together with the figures that once stood under delicate canopies at the base of the *wall posts*. It is worth using binoculars to study the carvings in the *spandrels* over the clerestory windows where, with a little patience, one can find dogs fighting over a joint of meat and another seizing a rat. Butterfield found the roof in a dangerous state in the 1860s and a great deal of new timber was inserted. At the same time, the *celure* at the e. end over the *rood* was recoloured, following the original design. The work was done by a local artist by the name of Osborne and it still looks beautiful. In 1968, the *Doom* over the *chancel* arch was excellently restored and now much of it can be seen. Wearing the papal tiara and bearing his keys, *St Peter* receives the righteous as they rise from the tomb on the l., while devils consign the rest to hellfire opposite. The centre section will have shown Christ in Majesty but this did not survive. Behind the C19 pulpit is a painted memorial for Thomas Smyth and Dorothy his wife who died in 1702 and 1728 respectively and on the other side of the nave is the entrance to the *rood loft stairs*. The s. aisle chapel has the simplest form of *piscina* set in the window ledge, and it is worth noting that some of the aisle roof *bosses* incorporate figures. In the early 1500s, Richard Nix was the last Bishop of Norwich to be Lord of the Manor of Bacton, and his shield of arms is in the e. window of the s. aisle. This was once the *chantry chapel* of the Pretyman family, Lords of the Manor from 1587, and its *parclose screen* was moved (probably in the C19) to take the place of the destroyed *rood screen*, which explains the awkward joins in the tracery and absence of panels. The low-pitched chancel roof is *arch-braced* and was effectively recoloured by Butterfield, with extra decoration forming a celure over the *High altar*. At that time, the whole chancel was refurbished, complete with *encaustic tiles, reredos,* and glass in the s. windows by Alexander Gibbs. The piscina was re-set in a square recess. The e. window is a 1914-18 war memorial and the glass is by *Morris & Co.* The arrangement of figures in two ranks is typical of the firm and shows how the designs of Morris and *Burne-Jones* continued to be used long after their deaths. In the upper tier, the angels with long trumpets are adapted from a Burne-Jones design, and the figures of St Peter holding a book and *St John* are both by him. His too are the *Evangelists* in the bottom rank: from the l., *SS Matthew, Mark, Luke* and John. The Christ as saviour of the world in the top centre is by Dearle (see Appendix under Morris & Co) and the Virgin and Child below is also his – a repeat of a design he used at Bloxham near Banbury. The backgrounds are alternating blue and red drapery and the Evangelists have their symbols behind their heads; the eagle of St John pecks at his shoulder and St Matthew's foot rests on a casket containing money as a sign that he was a customs officer. It is a fine window. The church

has an excellent ground floor ring of six bells with an 8 cwt. tenor.

Badingham, St John the Baptist (H4): It is quite a steep climb up to the church from the road, and at one time peacocks sometimes appeared to surprise the visitor in the churchyard – but not for me in 2006. The unbuttressed tower has a single *string course* below the bell openings, and the attenuated *Norman lancets* at belfry level were probably reused when it was rebuilt about 1300. The tall shafts at the w. corners of the *nave* are another sign that the church was originally *Norman*. Roof lines on the nave wall show that there was a n. *porch* at one time, and there is a C13 lancet on each side halfway along. A n. window has pretty *Decorated tracery*, with a thinner version in the *chancel* further along, before one comes to a bald C19 *vestry*. In a vigorous restoration of 1879, most of the chancel was rebuilt, given new windows and *priest's door*, and smoothly faced with flint on the s. side. There are *Perpendicular* windows on the s. side of the nave, and the two *clerestory* windows in brick were probably inserted in the early 1500s to give extra light for the *rood*. The lancet at the w. end was a C19 addition, and the 1480s porch was restored in 1890. It has a facade of *flushwork*, a central canopied niche, and the arch *spandrels* contain a dragon and a *woodwose*, reminiscent of those at Cratfield and Peasenhall. On the *weathering* of the s.e. buttress there is a curious little carving which most people identify as a hound with a dish between its teeth. Others see it as a tiger with a mirror, from the *bestiary* story which said that to catch a tiger cub, one must ride off with it and elude the parents. If the tigress followed too closely, the trick was to throw down a mirror so that she would mistake the reflection for her cub and lick it while the hunter escaped. There is a similar carving on Ufford's porch, and the best known illustration of the story is on a bench end at Lakenheath. There are small sections of Norman stonework on the window sills just inside, and a pair of C12 *corbels* are set in the walls, one a grotesque and the other a rather nice cat. The large leafy *stops* of the inner archway were part of the Victorian restoration.

On entering, one's eye is drawn immediately to the *Seven Sacrament font,* one of the best of the series. It stands on a step with traceried riser, and the shaft is panelled like a smaller version of the bowl – shallow *groined* arches with *crocketted* pinnacles above a series of small figures: s. *St Edmund;* e. an angel in armour with his sword raised behind his head, his shield grounded; w. another angel with shield and (possibly) arrows; bishops in the other niches. The base of the deep bowl is similar to Laxfield's, and in the panels there is a forest of crocketted pinnacles above each broad arch. The carvings are not so badly mutilated as those on some of the other sacrament fonts, and clockwise from the e. they represent: baptism (one of three instances where a woman holds the *chrysom cloth*); marriage (the man's hat dates it as about 1485); ordination; confirmation; mass (note that the figure kneeling on the r. holds a *sacring bell* – the pouch at his waist and absence of vestments identifies him as the *clerk*; the only way that the sculptor could portray the congregation was to have two heads peering over the *reredos* either side of the *altar* candles); penance (the fleeing evil spirit is shown with horns in the top l.-hand corner); extreme unction (the sick man's shoes and hat lie under the bed and his wife weeps at his feet); baptism of Christ (an appropriate choice, considering the church's dedication – *St John the Baptist* pours water over Our Lord's head while an angel holds his cloak). Norman *jamb shafts* feature again in the wide tower arch, and beyond there are C18 or early-C19 *Decalogue* canvas panels on the walls. Five C15 bench ends with *poppyheads* are to be found near the font, and there is a puzzling section of an arch embedded low in the wall by the s. door – it looks like part of a C14 *arcade*. The superb nave roof shows C15 carpenters' skills at their best – *Cautley* called it 'the perfect example of a single *hammerbeam*', and said that 'other roofs may be more elaborate but none can surpass in technical skill and refinement of detail'. The long hammerbeams tilt slightly upwards above tall *wall posts* which rest on wooden *corbels*, and the lavish *wall plates* are pierced with *tracery*; there is more tracery above the hammers, the collars are *castellated,* and there are transverse braces to the *king posts* under the ridge. The demi-angels on the hammerbeams are modern replacements, but the smaller versions against some of the king posts are original and still have traces of their colour.

A remarkable feature of Badingham is the way in which the floor slopes upward from w. to e., with a difference of 25in. between tower and chancel. It is a prime example of medieval builders making use of an inclined site to economise on masonry. When *Dowsing* came in September 1644, apart from condemning the 'sixteen superstitious cherubims with crosses on their breasts' (roof angels?), he ordered the steps

in the chancel to be levelled. It was all to be done in a fortnight, but the steps are still there, and faced with such a formidable change in levels, one can imagine the churchwardens giving up in despair. The embrasure of the C13 lancet in the n. wall was cut away later to accommodate a large image niche under a broad, *cinquefoil* arch adorned with crockets, which has the remains of an angel above it. The lancet opposite contains attractive armorial glass of 1977 by Michael Farrar Bell, with small mounted figures of a 13th/18th Royal Hussar and a Transjordanian trooper. The glass of 1928 in the next window is by Hugh Easton and portrays the *Blessed Virgin* and Child with *St Elizabeth* and St John the Baptist as a boy – the group set against a background drape held aloft by angels. More of Easton's glass is to be found at St Peter's, Bury St Edmund's; Elveden; Stowlangtoft; and St Augustine's, Ipswich. The window opposite is a memorial for a commander of the Framlingham Volunteer Infantry, a reminder of early-C19 militia enthusiasms – figures of *St Luke* and *St John*, probably by Cox & Son. The pitchpine nave benches were made by George Grimwood of Weybread as part of the 1879 refurbishing, and he also reconstructed the chancel *screen,* making use of the old panels with their fine tracery. The excellent mid-C17 pulpit

Badingham, St John the Baptist: Seven Sacrament font – extreme unction

has *blind-arched* panels embellished with split turning and scrolly brackets to the book ledge. The back board is flanked with half-columns, and the *tester* has extraordinary brackets carved as female grotesques with cloven feet that could well disconcert the unwary preacher. The large reading desk across the nave matches the pulpit and may have stood with it originally. There is a large and shallow tomb recess in the chancel n. wall which has three helms and a line of blank shields carved above the flattened arch, and an angel holds a shield just below; the finely carved pedestals on each side are reminiscent of those in the Bardolph chapel at Dennington. It is probably the tomb of Sir John Carbonell who died in 1412, and may have served as an *Easter sepulchre*. Next to it, and encroaching a little on the *sanctuary*, is the massive tomb of William Cotton and his wife. Their lifesize recumbent figures are all in black, and he lies behind and just above her. Their heads rest stiffly on red double cushions, and the epitaph is cut on *touchstone* panels below a deep double arch and coloured cherub heads. The flanking *Corinthian* columns are painted red and faced with no fewer than twenty little shields, with two more at the top displaying all the quarterings. A painted figure holds an heraldic drape at the very top, and two children kneel at the front of the tomb chest. Overall, the effect is coarse and heavy. The C19 glass in the chancel is all rather undistinguished work, again probably by Cox & Son, but at least the e. window has a Baptist theme – the saint preaching in the wilderness, baptising Christ, and having his head presented to Herod on a charger. The church's only *brass* is on the s. wall of the chancel – a Latin verse commemorating Catherine Cornwaleis who died in childbirth in 1584. The lettering is well cut within a border of strapwork and there were once crests and shields to go with it. The church has a good ground floor ring of five bells with an 8 cwt. tenor.

Badley, St Mary (E5): Newcomers are pouring into Suffolk and its towns and villages spawn dormitories and factories, but there are still the secret places. Those who love them will notice the sign on the Stowmarket to Needham Market road which points to Badley church. A very rough track winds through fields for more than a mile and, topping a rise, there is the church set in a bowl of meadowland, with Badley Hall farm beyond it. The *Churches Conservation Trust* assumed responsibility in 1986 and within two years they had carried out a major restoration,

making the building sound and watertight; a shining example, if one were needed, of the value of their work. The church is used for occasional services and is normally open at weekends; a key is kept at the farm.

The unbuttressed tower was probably built around 1300, but in the C15 a massive five-*light* w. window was inserted which takes up the whole width of the wall. The red brick belfry stage with its plain parapet is *Tudor*, and all has been meticulously restored. One interesting feature is that the *nave* walls are extended w. under tile caps to lap the tower, and the belfry stair fits neatly above on the n. side. On walking round, you will find brick buttresses to the n. and the remnant of a *rood stair turret* with a bricked-up top door. There has been a church here since the Norman Conquest and the blocked *lancet* in the n. wall of the *chancel* dates from the early C13. All other windows are *Perpendicular* and it is strange that the e. window is rather small for the wall in contrast to the one in the tower. On the s. side a *dripstone* marks the site of a C14 window and just by it is a monument which would pass without much notice inside a church but which is unusually elaborate for an outside wall; a miniature sarcophagus and *cartouche* of arms are set within an architectural frame, and there is an urn with swags and flaming torches above the *pediment*. All trace of the epitaph has weathered away but it was for Henrietta Robins who died in 1728, and the original iron railings survive, having escaped the scrap metal drive in World War II that cleared most churchyards. The open wooden *porch* has a modern roof but the base and what remains of the barge boards are medieval, and it is guarded by a lift-gate that has to be teased out of its slots. Designed to deter farm stock, it looks as though it has always been there and I do not know another like it. The simple inner doorway is late C12, and the door itself is ancient – ridged boards in a heavy frame, with massive lock, original ironwork, and a grill window that was fitted with a shutter at one time.

One more step and you will see how important it is that this church should be preserved. In essence, nothing has been changed for two centuries; enthusiasms, doctrinaire theory, the obsession with domestic comfort, all have passed it by, and age has bestowed upon it an infinite charm. Below plastered ceilings, the three cambered *tie-beams* that support tall *king posts* with their four-way struts under the ridge may well be C14, and the *pamments* of the floor are interrupted haphazardly with *ledger-stones*. All

Badley, St Mary

the unstained oak has aged to a silvery grey, and the benches are an extraordinary mixture, made up from at least three sets. Some have fullsize ends with *poppyheads* and the pair opposite the door have the remains of animals on the elbows. The mortice holes for a book slope show that they once belonged to a choir stall, and the singleton by the n. wall with its curious disc *finial* looks like a giant's cheese board. The boards at the e. end on that side are pierced with two *elevation squints*, and all the timbers are rough and sturdy, with the occasional hole where a knot or piece of rot was taken out. The plain *Stuart* pulpit is a tiny octagon that will not serve for anyone broader than 17in. unless they slide in sideways, but there is a commodious reading desk of the early C17 alongside whose door has a prettily carved top rail. The contemporary *box pews* beyond are crude but their makers could not altogether resist the beauty of the C14 *rood screen* that they or their fathers had taken out, and two sections of its *tracery* are fixed to the fronts. The base of the screen was left to serve as a division between one set of pews and another in the chancel, and there are traces of stencil flower decoration on its plum-coloured panels. Turned finials are the box pews' only ornament, and a few were added to the old screen in a jaunty attempt to draw all together.

The furniture is so beguiling that one moves about haphazardly to examine it, but there are other things to be seen – note that the step of the tower door is 7ft. from the floor so that valuables could be kept up there with some security. A *stoup* is partly hidden by the wall panelling by the door, and the C13 *Purbeck marble font* has the usual pairs of blank arches in the sides of its deep, canted bowl. Its *ogee*-shaped panelled cover with acorn finial is probably C18. Beside it lies a C13 tomb slab with fragments

of an inscription, and in the centre of the nave is a *brass* inscription for Edmund Brewster who died in 1633. Further e. is Edmund Poley's, dated 1613 with three shields, set in a large *touchstone* slab. Part of the blocked doorway to the old rood stairs can be seen above the panelling on the n. wall. There is another brass inscription in the chancel floor for John and Dorothe Poley (1615):

Reade if thou canst & mourne not,
his name & stocke being knowne,
For they will tell what pitie twas,
he was but borne & showne.

A ledger-stone on the n. side is unusual in having marble inserts – two inscriptions and a pair of shields for Peter Scrivener who died in 1604. On the wall above is the alabaster memorial for Edmund and Myrabel Poley (1548 and 1558) which was installed by one of their descendants in 1604. It has two inscription panels and a carved frame that once had six shields. These have been defaced but a larger one survives with traces of colour in a roundel at the top. On the s. side, the Edmund Poley who died in 1714 has a deeply cut ledger-stone, and on the wall is the tall and narrow memorial of 1707 for Henry Poley, in grey and white marble. The curved pediment carries a flaming urn and torches, and a delicately draped skull is poised over the epitaph. There are large C18 *Decalogue* boards each side of the e. window, with an unusual addition above the altar: 'This do in Remembrance of me: Luke ye 22d ver. ye 19:'. The church's only medieval glass is a shield of the de Badele family in a n. window, and *Dowsing* kept himself warm on a February day in 1643 by destroying thirty-four 'superstitious pictures'; a Mr Dove promised to take down the remaining twenty-eight and to level the chancel. It seems he did this because there is no change of level now, and the *sanctuary* step probably dates from 1830 when the iron *communion rails* were installed. Those apart, the only recognisable C19 touch is the 1860s glass in the e. window by Frederick Preedy, a good glazier who was often used by *William Butterfield*. This is a dense and quite attractive design, although there is scant animation in the figure work; narrow panels illustrate the Last Supper and Christ's encounters, after His Resurrection, with *St Thomas* and *St Mary Magdalene*. Dorothe Pooley died in 1625 and her grave in the n.e. corner of the sanctuary has a singular epitaph:

Staye Passinger, reade what this Marble tells,
Stones seldom speake but utter miracles ...

Indeed they do, for in the lines that follow she, who was 'her Sexes Pride, her Ages wonder' is credited with no fewer than ten virtues. This little church seduces the senses and sticks like a burr in the memory.

Badwell Ash, St Mary (D4): In the centre of the village, it is a good looking church which resembles Ixworth, Walsham-le-Willows and Bacton in many points of detail. The handsome C15 tower and s.*porch* are richly decorated with *flushwork* panels and inscriptions. In the w.-facing puttresses at eye level, the W & R panels probably commemorate William Redelysworth who made bequests to the church in 1462. The tower has three *drip courses* with intermediate *set-offs* on the diagonal buttresses, and the stepped battlements with flushwork panelling carry the inscription: 'Pray for the good estate of John Fincham and Marget hys wyf' – she died in 1521. There are emblems set in the *base course*, and there are little foliage shapes backing the letter 'R' on the s.w. buttress. Bequests imply that work on the tower was in progress 1476-86. Big *gargoyles* punctuate the s. aisle parapet and the *clerestory*, where the window arches are relieved by thin red bricks. There are tall *Decorated* windows and a *priest's door* on the s. side of the *chancel*, and beyond the C19 *vestry* on the n. side, the absence of an aisle gives the *nave* a leggy appearance.

The doorway on that side is blocked and entry is via an attractive C15 s. *porch*. Like the tower, there are emblems in the base course, and on the s.e. buttress, a panel displays blacksmith's tools over horseshoes (like the bench end at nearby Great Ashfield). The battlements are stepped above a central canopied niche, the frontage is faced with thin panels of flushwork, and *St George* fights the dragon in the *spandrels* of the arch. Quite deep steps lead down into the church. The cream-washed interior is light and open and the tall *arcade* rests on octagonal *piers*. Overhead is a good C15 roof, with alternating *tie-beams* and *hammerbeams* that have large angels in good condition except that some of their emblems have been hacked away; a range of smaller figures in equally good condition adorns the *wall posts*. There are early-C18 churchwardens' names carved on the end tie-beams and, although it does not look like it, *Cautley* thought that the beams might have been inserted then to prevent the roof from spreading. The shields on the stem of the late-C14 *font* were once carved with coats of arms or emblems, and there is a Sacred Heart on the s.

side of the bowl which has *cusped* and *crocketted ogee* arches in the panels, heads (possibly re-cut) underneath, and a *castellated* rim. A *Jacobean* chest with a carved front stands at the w. end of the s. aisle and the window above contains some medieval glass. There is a fork-bearded head not unlike that at Whissonsett in Norfolk which is almost certainly the face of the risen Christ; the glass of the e. window is a war memorial which includes regimental badges in the *tracery*. The early-C14 angle *piscina* nearby has an arch within an arch and pretty, pierced tracery, with a blind *trefoil* above the side opening. The *rood stairs* rise to the s. of the chancel arch, with a little *quatrefoil* window in the segment that bulges out into the aisle chapel. The church was restored in the 1860s when the chancel roof was replaced and the choir stalls date from then. They are excellently done, with *poppyheads* and *Evangelistic symbols* on the elbows. The late-C13 piscina in the *sanctuary* lies within a deep trefoil arch, the cusps of which terminate in leaves. The e. window glass of 1920 is probably by the *Powells*. It has Christ the King flanked by the *Blessed Virgin* and *St Peter*, against a blue background and within inter-laced tendrils of vine – the whole set off by clear glass. There are three tablets in the chancel by Matthew Wharton Johnson, a prolific but not exciting C19 statuary. All are for members of the Norgate family and the best, in white marble on black, is for Thomas Norgate who died in 1818 – a draped urn above, coat of arms below, and frontal *acanthus* leaves as scrolls each side of the tablet. The church has a ground floor ring of five bells with a 13 cwt. tenor but is currently classified by the Suffolk Guild as being in 'poor going order'.

Bardwell, St Peter and St Paul (D3): The tall tower with its centre spike can be seen from some way off, and one climbs what amounts to a little hill in these parts to reach the churchyard. The *nave* windows have *tracery* which shows how the *ogee* arch came back into favour in the early part of the C15. The *chancel* was virtually rebuilt as part of an extensive restoration in 1853. The tower, built about 1420, has a chequer *base course*, *Perpendicular* windows, and a stair turret on the s. side. As was often the case, considerable care was lavished on the s. *porch*, and the front is decorated with *flushwork* panelling. There is a chequer base course and there are three niches around the entrance, occupied by modern figures of *St Peter* and *St Paul*, with the *Blessed Virgin* in the centre. The arch *spandrels* contain shields of arms of the de Bardwell and de Pakenham families. The arch mouldings are decorated with two ranks of *fleurons* and the tall Perpendicular windows have deep *labels*, with *transoms* cutting through the tracery.

The interior of the early-C15 nave is brightened by a colourful blaze of embroidered hassocks resting on the C19 pews, and there is a lovely *hammerbeam* and *arch-braced* roof overhead which has the unusual distinction of being dated. Only four of the angels on the hammerbeams remain, but one of them on the n. side holds a book which bears the date 1421. The two on the s. side carry *Passion emblems*, and the 30 or so painted *bosses* are carved with a lovely variety of forms; binoculars are a great help here. Much of the painted decoration still shows, including very attractive leaf trails on the rafters, coloured red on pale yellow. There is a plain octagonal *font* which probably dates from the C14, and over the tower arch is a *hatchment*, with emblems on the frame, for Charles Reade who died in 1720. The *Royal Arms* over the blocked n. door are *Hanoverian* for George II. Four *consecration crosses* may be seen on the s. wall, and one on the n., where there are fragments of what was an extensive series of wall paintings. They are C15 and show the 'Descent from the cross'; one can see part of a ladder and Christ's body, with a face (possibly *St Mary Magdalene*) on the l. Of the medieval paintings on the s. wall, only a single head can now be recognised. Sir William de Bardwell lived from 1367 to 1434 and was a great benefactor of this church, probably paying for the tower and the s. porch. A professional soldier from his youth, he entered the service of the Duke of Suffolk in 1400, was Henry V's standard bearer in the French wars, and probably served at Agincourt. The church's great treasure is the stained glass collected in the windows at the e. end of the nave on the n. side; there you will find Sir William's portrait at the bottom of the easternmost *light* and it is one of the most interesting in Suffolk. Some small parts have been replaced by mutilated remains of other figures, but it is a fine piece. He kneels in armour, bareheaded on a stool, with a small shield hung round his neck, wearing a long broadsword and with his helmet beside him. Above are his arms with helm and crest, together with the arms of de Pakenham (his wife's family) in the other light. All trace of her effigy has gone. Above him, a panel of fragments includes the *Trinity* shield on a dark red ground, one of the five flags carried by the English at Agincourt. Sir

William, known as 'the great warrior', and his wife were buried in the chancel. Before the *Reformation* there was a shrine dedicated to Our Lady of Pity, and the *Pietà* in the bottom of the l.-hand light (moved from the w. window) may have been associated with it, although the glass is continental rather than English. In the bottom of the window to the w. are two more figures which probably represent Sir Roger Drury and his wife Margery who died in 1405. His head is a modern replacement, but she wears a beautifully ornamented coif, and apart from her purple robe, the whole design is carried out in white and yellow stain. The *rood stairs* rise on the s. side of the chancel arch, and there is a *trefoil*-headed *piscina* in the corner below. There were undoubtedly *altars* on both sides of the nave because there are *squints* either side of the chancel arch which give a view of the *High altar*. Leaning against the wall on the n. side are two sections of the old *rood screen* which were rescued from the rectory attic in the 1890s. They are now a beautifully pale colour and the quality of the carving is excellent. There are some interesting memorials to members of the Crofts Reade family in the chancel. During the 1853 restoration, a tomb chest was rather eccentrically cut in half and a portion erected on each side of the *sanctuary*. On the n. side it commemorates Sir Charles Crofts who died in 1660, and on the s., his grandson, another Sir Charles; both have coloured bas-relief shields of arms in the panels. On the s. wall of the chancel is a large wall monument which still has a good deal of the original colour. The alabaster figures of Thomas Reade and his wife Bridget (daughter of the first Sir Charles Crofts) kneel facing each other across a desk. He died in 1651 and she lived a widow for over 40 years. Tiny figures of their children occupy the panel below. Those who died young hold skulls and those that survived their infancy, a red rose. The blocked doorway on the n. side of the chancel was either a *priest's door* or led to a *vestry*. To its l. is an *aumbry* hewn from a solid block of stone. Above is a tablet by Gushing of Norwich with rounded reeded sides and a sarcophagus on top for the Revd. James Whelton who died in 1772. On the s. wall of the sanctuary is a large monument for another Thomas Reade, who died in 1678. The *touchstone* panel has marbled Doric columns each side and the heavy cornice is a broken scroll with a *cartouche* of arms in the centre. The side windows have matching glass of 1869 by the O'Connors. On the s. side, the theme is 'Feed my sheep', with Christ and two disciples against a background of a fence with flowers; on the n. side the text is 'Abide with us'. (One of the disciples wears a very Victorian hat.) The 1863 glass in the e. window also looks like O'Connor's work – six scenes in two ranks, illustrating the Virtues. The tower contains a ring of six bells with an 11 cwt. tenor, but their condition is such that they can only be rung occasionally.

Private Henry Addison of HM 43ʳᵈ Light Infantry won the VC in India in 1859. His regiment was associated with Monmouthshire, but he was born and died in Bardwell and was buried here. His gravestone lies in the s.e. corner of the churchyard and people of the parish have recently cleaned it meticulously. The citation in the London Gazette of 2ⁿᵈ September, 1859 reads: 'For gallant conduct on the 2ⁿᵈ of January, 1859, near Kurrereah, in defending against a large force and saving the life of Leitenant Osborn, Political Agent, who had fallen on the ground wounded. Private Addison received two dangerous wounds and lost a leg in this gallant service.' The stone also records his last words at his death aged 66 in 1887, and commemorates his widow Charlotte.

Barham, St Mary (F5): The church stands in a generous churchyard above the busy valley where industrial Claydon competes with the busy main road to distract the eye from the calm countryside beyond. The medieval building was heavily restored in the 1860s without detracting too much from its attraction and interest, but the large meeting room which has been added recently on the n. side does not blend happily with its senior partner. This is accentuated by the fact that the tower is on the s. side so that the w. wall of the *nave* and the new work appear as a continuous facade when seen from the entrance. Beyond the annexe there is a blocked n. doorway, and although there are no *aisles*, a *clerestory* with brick windows was added in the early C16. The Middleton chapel juts out farther along, and beyond it there is an important and unusual window in the n. wall of the *vestry*. It came from Shrubland Old Hall, and the terracotta *mullions* and lintel were made from the same moulds that were used in Henley and Barking churches and are early examples of the *Renaissance* style. After the great house at Layer Marney in Essex had been finished in the 1520s, the specialist terracotta craftsmen probably dispersed to other projects, of which this may have been one. As a window it can hardly be called beautiful, despite its importance. The C19 *chancel* e. window fails on both counts. The

position of the tower makes the nave seem short in length and very tall in height when seen from the s., and this accentuates the length of the chancel. Although extensively restored, the archway, narrow belfry slits with *ogee* tops, and 'Y' *tracery* of the bell openings date the tower as early C14, and it doubles as the main entrance.

Once inside, the size of the nave reasserts itself and light floods through the large w. window – a C19 replacement with flowing tracery. The *hammerbeam* roof is handsome, but everything above the hammers is modern work (and none the worse for that). Tall *king posts* stand on collar beams that are no more than halfway up the slope of the roof, and demi-angels have been restored to the ends of the hammers. The *font* bowl is a huge octagon on a short stem, with a continuous blind tracery pattern on its sides. It is rather an anticlimax to lift the lid and find a recess the size of a washing-up bowl for the water. A Victorian oddity, but the shaft and base are C14. A new doorway leading to the meeting room has been made in the n.w. corner, and the old n. door complete with drawbar survives, despite the fact that it has been walled up outside. The nave has an attractive brick floor in *herringbone* pattern, and leaving aside some original benches with *poppyheads* at the w. end, the main seating is C19. A good sequence of *hatchments* hangs on the n. wall; from e. to w. they were used for the funerals of Lady Harriot Fowle Middleton (1852); Sir William, her husband (1829); Sir William Fowle Fowle Middleton (1860); Anne, his widow (1867); and Sir George Nathaniel Broke-Middleton (1887). Most of the Victorian stained glass is low quality, but one s. clerestory window has an 1890s figure of Christ with a child – rich robes and *tabernacle work*, set in a yellowy-green vine trail, and possibly by *Clayton & Bell*.

Beyond a pair of arches on the n. side of the nave is the Middleton chapel, approached by four steps. This change of level provides a splendid setting for one of the Anglican Church's finest sculptures of the C20. It is by Henry Moore and was commissioned in 1948 by Sir Jasper Ridley as a World War II memorial for Claydon. When that church became redundant, Moore himself supervised its removal. It was developed from the largest of the twelve models prepared for the sculptor's Madonna and Child at St Matthew's Northampton, of which he said: 'The Divine and the human must co-exist in a sacred image without the one being wholly sacrificed to the other.' The sculpture has great presence and is relaxed but calmly dominant and vibrant, with the Christ child deeply protected within the Blessed Virgin's encircling arms. The w. half of the chapel is enclosed with a *parclose screen*, part C18 panelling and part beautifully dense *Perpendicular* tracery which, with the *cusped ogee* doorway, came from the C15 *rood screen*. This has created a compact chapel in which the Blessed Sacrament is reserved for the sick, and it is excellently furnished. On the wall is a large tablet for Sir William Middleton, his wife, and son, with three painted shields which echo the hatchments in the nave. There is a pretty *cartouche* on the e. wall – C17 in style but commemorating James and Jane St Vincent, who died in the 1930s. The stairs to the vanished *rood loft* go up from the s.e. corner. Sir William Fowle Middleton is commemorated in the window glass, which has lively heraldry and rich borders. There is an inscription, 'GR 1831', in the tracery lights and the window is probably the work of S.C. Yarington, a Norwich glazier.

The pulpit with its replacement top and base has been varnished to a dark brown, but the panels and some sections of cresting probably formed part of the rood loft. When he visited in January 1643, apart from destroying images, *Dowsing* 'digged down the steps' in his passion for degrading the status of chancels. It was to no avail in the long run, because the 1860s rebuilding restored them and, ironically, modern changes in corporate worship have called for a nave *altar* below the chancel arch. Beyond the organ in the n. wall there is a heavy C15 arch above a recessed tomb which lost its *brass* to Dowsing. It commemorates Richard Booth, or possibly his son who died in the reign of Edward IV. The arch, with its slight ogee shape, is *cusped* and sub-cusped, and one angel terminal survives. Heads of hound and boar decorate the spandrels and there are oak leaves in the moulding because Richard's crest was a boar's head and his wife was an Oke. Just in front is a brass of 1514 for Robert and Cecily Southwell that survived the Civil War. The 33in. figures are curiously attenuated, he in fur-lined gown and doublet, she with a deep *kennel headdress*. The border inscription has *quatrefoils* engraved with six shields at the corners and in the centre of the sides. A second brass lies on the s. side of the chancel, this time an inscription for Frances Southwell, 1607. There is a beautiful set of *communion rails* here, Italian work dated 1700, which I presume was part of the C19 re-ordering. The heavy bottom section is carved with putti

pairing birds and dolphins, and the short *balusters* support little arches under a substantial top rail decorated with vine trails. The deep *sanctuary* is divided by a midway step, and the fussiness of the windows, with their spindly inner shafts and pierced tracery, is on a par with the outside. The early-C14 *piscina* is humble by comparison. The large recess in the opposite wall was probably an *aumbry*, and it is rather overwhelmed by the monument next door. A massive *touchstone* chest supports the life-size alabaster figures, he on his back and she beyond and turned towards him, holding a tiny skull in her hand. There are pairs of columns each side of the backing arch, and a coloured achievement on top flanked by pairs of touchstone columns – all rather bald and ill-fitting, which is perhaps explained by the inscription: 'This monument is sent over from the Cittie of Limrick in Ireland by Sr Richard Southwell, second sonne of Jo Southwell of Barham Esq. and Margrett his wife as a pious remembrance of them to be left to their posteriti 1640.' An interesting exercise in the removers' art, no doubt, and Irish at that. Barham has a ring of four bells with an 11 cwt. tenor, but they are at present unringable.

Barking, St Mary (E5): Approached by a long lane from the Needham Market road, the church stands on rising ground, with open views to the s. beyond a pair of stately cedars. The whole building is cement rendered except the e. wall and the tower, which was rebuilt in 1870 (presumably repeating the original design). It has hexagonal buttresses which taper slightly in the centre stage and the w. door has *crocketted* pinnacles carved in the upper panels, with two vine trails below; the w. window has *Decorated tracery* and there are *Perpendicular* bell openings. Both *aisles* sport a splendid series of late-C14 *gargoyles* (note those on the n. particularly), and a two-storeyed *sacristy* juts out squarely from the *chancel* n. wall. It has two small *cusped lancets* to the n. and what is probably C18 tracery in its e. window. Attractive cusped and intersected tracery of the early C14 fills the chancel e. window and below it is an odd little buttress placed centrally. The *clerestory* windows have dense Perpendicular tracery and those in the aisles are roughly the same date – except the one at the w. end of the s. aisle, which is early C14. The late-C13 s. *porch* is set at a slight angle and the inner doorway has single attached columns with ring *capitals* and small *headstops* – the skull set at the top of the arch is a later insertion. Above it is a faded and damaged C17 text from Psalm 118;

'Open to me ye Gates of Righteousness, I will go into them and praise ye Lord', reminiscent of the one at Grundisburgh. The arch of a *stoup* survives here and the early C16 door is unusual in that the upper panels are carved with the *Blessed Virgin's* monogram enclosing the individual letters of her name. These caught *Dowsing's* eye when he came in 1644 but, perhaps because 'many superstitious pictures were down afore I came', he left them alone. They are very worn and one has been renewed – as have most of the lower panels.

Within, the *nave arcades* are similar in style but the s. is earlier, and above them is an impressive C14 *arch-braced tie-beam* roof. It has that delightful washed-out colour of unstained oak, and octagonal *king posts* with four-way struts support a runner below the ridge. The e. section of this is patterned with colour and shows that there was a decorative *celure* above the *rood*. The n. aisle roof is surprisingly lavish with braces and principal timbers carved with leaf trails, traceried *spandrels* and centre *bosses*. There may be some connection between this richness and the window by the n. door. It is later than the others on that side and received very individual treatment. The *mullions* are formed from terracotta sections stamped with varying moulds, and down each side there is a running pattern of greyhounds. Sections of two unrelated patterns are inset in the I and the designs confirm that they are by the same craftsmen whose work can be found at Henley and Barham. Versed in the fashionable Italian style, the men probably came on from Layer Marney in Essex when Lord Marney's great house was finished about 1525.

The tall tower arch rests on inner-facing head *corbels*, and below the C15 *font* has fine and deeply cut *Evangelistic symbols* alternating with angels in the bowl panels; squat lions support the corners of the shaft and between them stand excellent little *woodwoses*. The charming late-C15 cover is a compact design, with pinnacles and flying buttresses rising to a heavily crocketted *finial*. On either side stand iron braziers on delicate tripod stands. Like a pair of fat, black pumpkins with perforated lids, they were filled with charcoal and are a rare example of an early form of church heating. A C19 bier stands nearby and over in the n. aisle there is a massive 9ft. C14 chest, bound with iron and fitted with three locks. A large set of C18 *Decalogue* boards in a *pedimented* frame hangs on the s. aisle wall, and moving e. you will find one of the church's best features in the form of matching C15 *parclose screens*, enclosing a Lady chapel in the s. aisle and the

Barking, St Mary: Charcoal heating brazier

chapel of *St John* in the n. aisle. The tracery of the latter is well preserved, with beautifully delicate cusping in the entrance arch and pairs of *ogees* within each light. There is an attractive C14 *piscina* and *sedile* under cusped ogee arches in the r.-hand corner of the chapel, and a doorway overhead led to the *rood loft*. Its position suggests that a walkway may have extended along the parclose screen. The Lady chapel screen retains no colour and the restored C13 piscina there is now low in the wall following changes in floor level. The e. window was blocked to accommodate the 1727 monument for John Crowley – a handsome, restrained design with a border of patterned marble to the tablet and a shaped back above to display the family arms and a cherub's head. Moving out into the nave, it is worth noticing that the parclose screens were carefully shaped at the bottom to fit the bases of the arcade piers. The pulpit is modern but a small late-C16 or early-C17 Flemish panel of the *Annunciation* has been incorporated on one face. Above it hangs the *hatchment* of Bertram, 4th Earl of Ashburnham, who lived at Barking Hall and died in 1878, a copy of which is to be found in Ashburnham church in Sussex. On the opposite wall are *Royal Arms* in pale colour inscribed 'God save King Charles the second'; below them is the door to the rood stair (although the stairs themselves have been bricked up).

The rood screen retains the skeleton of the coving that ran below the loft and its design differs from most in the area in that the main divisions are split by mullions to form tall and narrow lights. There are remains of small figures acting as corbels for the coving ribs, and the lower panels retain some of their colouring. Eagles are carved in the spandrels of the centre arch, with others in the discs at the end of the cusps, but the best carving is to be found on the e. side where normally all is blank. Birds perch on the rim of the centre arch, there is a heart pierced by two daggers in a spandrel to the s., and two excellent dragons on the n. side. The valuables in the sacristy were very well protected in unusual fashion. C15 doors with fine tracery are fitted with two locks set vertically and covered with escutcheon plates, and behind them stands the original C14 door. This one illustrates the beginning of the dominance of carpenter over smith – crude hinges right across, massive lockplate, and very wide untrimmed boards. A range of pews in the chancel is enclosed by panelling that probably came from the rood loft, and there is fine small-scale carving in the spandrels; look particularly for the pair of fishes on the e. side, each with a smaller fish in its mouth – the carver's version of the predatory pike. The *sanctuary* has a large C14 piscina under a cusped ogee arch, with *dropped-sill sedilia* alongside, and the late-C17 *communion rails* have an interesting variant of the twisted *baluster*, growing fatter as they go down. The church has an excellent ground floor ring of six bells from the Bowen foundry in Ipswich – tenor 11 cwt.

Barnardiston, All Saints (B6): The church stands high and can be seen from some distance from the w. The early-C14 tower has a heavy belfry stair turret to the s. and on that side there are deep *nave* buttresses. On the one e. of the small s. door there are two *scratch dials* which, unlike most, have Roman numerals marking the radiating lines. *Septaria* show in the walls and thin tiles, particularly in the *chancel*. The *priest's door* is on the n. side facing the rectory and there is a massive square turret for the *rood stairs*, with a battlemented top. The mansard shape of the *nave* roof appears rather strangely above the parapet and there is a very tall C15 n. *porch*. The

lovely C14 inner doorway, with deeply moulded arch, has pairs of slim shafts and vestiges of large *headstops*. There are pairs of *crocketted* pinnacles above, and a straight *castellated* cornice that fitted snugly within the old roof line. To the r. is a square-headed *Decorated* niche with the remains of headstops but no trace of a bowl, although it was presumably a *stoup*.

Enter by an *ogee*-headed *wicket door* within the medieval door, and see how the step has been worn away just below, showing the preference of countless generations of worshippers. The nave roof, with its cambered *tie-beams* and false *hammerbeams* is modern, and the recumbent figures bear shields carved with *Passion emblems*. The low C15 benches have simple *tracery* in the ends, with shallow buttresses, and there is a door to the tower stair in the s.w. corner. Close by, the large C14 *font* was badly cracked a long time ago and an iron band was clamped round the bowl. The floors are a homely mixture of bricks and *pamments*, and opposite the door stands a plain *Jacobean* chest. There are fragments of medieval glass in the top of a s. nave window, and the simple *Stuart* pulpit has a decided lean to starboard. There are very shallow blind arches in the top panels, and in the C19 the two sections that formed the door were removed and built into the reading desk that stands alongside. A C17 *hour-glass stand* juts from the wall and there is a *piscina* below, marking the site of a medieval nave *altar*. The door to the *rood loft* stairs opposite is blocked by panelling and the C15 chancel *screen* has tall double-ogee arches, *cusped* and crocketted. It was well repaired in the 1920s and fitted with a new cornice. There is Jacobean panelling behind the choir stalls on the n. side, and in the window sill opposite there is a fascinating piece of graffiti. It has been limewashed over but is clearly a drawing of a windmill and part of another. Looking out on the rolling countryside one can imagine a bored medieval priest or idle clerk sketching the familiar mill across the valley. The C17 *communion rails*, with their close-set *balusters*, were drilled in the C19 to hold triple-branched candelabra on rods – the only instance that I can recall. Beyond *dropped-sill sedilia* there is a C15 piscina under a wide arch and castellated top. It still has its wooden *credence shelf* and the little side recess that was often provided. The hole drilled in the top lefthand corner is a mystery, however. What was it for? The church has a ring of five bells with an 8 cwt. tenor which was probably cast by the Bedforshire founder John Rufford c.1350; they are unringable at the present time.

Barnby, St John the Baptist (I2): Set apart from its village by the busy main road, this charming little church dates mainly from the late C13. The unbuttressed tower has a shallow *drip course* below the bell openings and the w. window has *Decorated tracery*; a stair turret with a conical cap is set against the s. wall, and there are battlements of *flushwork* and brick. *Nave* and *chancel* lie under a single thatched roof and, apart from two *lancets* at the w. end, the small side windows have 'Y' tracery, matching the three-*light* e. window. Note the rough flint *quoins* of the chancel, and the stone halfway along the nave s. wall – the radiating lines on it show that it was a *scratch dial*. On that side, a twin lancet window in the chancel was blocked at some time, and so was the nave door.

Entry is by way of the n. *porch*, pebble-dash outside and plastered within, but with a heavy *tie-beam* exposed to show that it is medieval. The inner doorway is small and plain, and the interior has a panelled waggon roof of pine stretching the full length of the building, with no intervening chancel arch. The small C13 *font* has an octagonal bowl of *Purbeck marble*, with the pairs of shallow *blind arches* in each panel which are a common feature of this type; the centre shaft is ringed with eight gaily painted columns. To the r. of the blocked s. door is a *banner stave locker* which is the only example in the county that retains its original C15 door. The oak is pierced to form quite crude tracery, but closer inspection reveals that the surface is incised with a much more intricate pattern which, for some reason, was never carved to complete the design. The lancets at the w. end, and another window on the s. side contain delicately executed stained glass roundels with a *St John the Baptist* theme; they date from 1945 and 1952, but I have not been able to identify the artist. C19 tradesmen working in a church sometimes took the opportunity to advertise – here a window in the nave n. wall has a *quarry* which is inscribed: 'Thos. Patrick North Cove Glazier &c.' A similar example of enterprise can be found at Blyford. Above a blocked square window in the n. wall hangs a beautifully bold set of George IV *Royal Arms*, dated 1825 and signed by the painter, a Mr Hall. That in itself is uncommon, and so is the unorthodox treatment of the lion and *unicorn* supporters, although similar examples can be found at Wantisden and Nettlestead. The church has extensive early-C15 wall paintings, and Miss Ann Ballantyne carried out the first stage of a programme of restoration in 1990 which has revealed a significant amount of

additional detail. A large *St Christopher* bearing the Christ child on his r. shoulder is placed as usual so that it could be seen from the door, but note, however, the *stoup* nearby which shows that the blocked s. doorway was the principal entrance before the painting was added. Further along, a *Seven Works of Mercy* sequence is arranged round the full length figure of Christ, his hand raised in blessing, and from whose body spread the red branches of a broad-leaved tree. On the l. at the top, two men sit in stocks, with the virtues of visiting the sick and clothing the naked illustrated below; a corpse beneath Christ's feet signifies burial, and on the r. the scenes depict feeding the hungry, giving drink to the thirsty, and succouring the stranger. The whole design is framed by a border of 'R's (possibly the donor's initial). Beyond the window there is a very interesting Crucifixion in which Christ is flanked by the two thieves whose arms are hooked over the crosses; a spear pierces the Saviour's side, and the shadowy figures below were doubtless the *Blessed Virgin* and *St John*; a third figure is painted within the window splay. On the n. wall, just to the w. of where the *rood screen* will have stood, the recent work has uncovered a complete *Annunciation*. *St Mary* holds a missal, and the *angel* is finely painted with outspread wings, all against a background pattern of black *trefoils*. The small C19 bas-relief on the n. wall of the *sanctuary* of Christ and the woman of Samaria [John 4:7] must have been a stock item, for another can be found within a *piscina* at Market Weston, and it features as part of a headstone in Wrentham churchyard. The church's original *mensa* has been recovered, and is now framed on a modern *altar*. The oddly shaped recess in the e. wall probably means that an *aumbry* or a piscina was sited there. One of the last commissions carried out by *Margaret Rope* before her retirement in the 1960s was Barnby's e. window, and it is beautiful. The central figure of Christ has St John the Baptist on one side, and St John with *St Peter* on the other. A small Crucifixion is set below the main figure, and the heavenly city, girt by a river and surmounted by a cross is placed at the top. The figures are taut and strong, with an air of introspection (only the Baptist looks directly at Christ), and the window exemplifies the artist's sensitivity in the use of muted colour.

Barnham, St Gregory (C3): In 1864, the Duke of Grafton of the day added a n. *aisle* and *transept* and made sundry other improvements, so that is is now difficult to identify much of the old church with any certainty. The early-C14 buttressed tower has 'Y' *tracery* bell openings, *lancet* belfry windows, and a later *Perpendicular* w. window below. There is an outside door to the stair on the n. side and all round the tower one can see where the square *put-log holes* have been filled in and left. The *priest's door* in the s. wall of the *chancel* is C13 and part of the e. window tracery looks original.

Inside, by the door, is a plain octagonal C13 *font* with a spiky little Victorian cover. All around, the 1864 work is plain to see: plastered ceilings to *nave* and transept, simplistic *arcade*, and all the furnishings in pitchpine except for the reading desk. However, the chancel arch was undisturbed and there is a plain C17 *Holy table*. The nice C13 *piscina* has a multi-foil drain, the *hood mould* has small, worn *headstops*, and the arch is filled with tracery in a graceful combination of *trefoils*. The e. window, with intersecting 'Y' tracery, has glass of about 1912 in *Arts and Crafts* style by Archibald Keithley Nicholson. This is a fine design which portrays Christ crucified on a living tree, flanked by the *Blessed Virgin* and *St John*, with *St Mary Magdalene* kneeling below and a medieval-style concept of Jerusalem beyond. Good glass too, probably by the same artist, is in a s. nave window, with *St Gregory the Great* in papal tiara holding a missal open at the Gloria, paired with *St Genevieve* and her candle. Two roundels below illustrate episodes in their lives. The link between the two saints is the fact that the Graftons' own church at Euston is dedicated to St Genevieve. As you go, you will pass a rather coarsely painted set of *William & Mary Royal Arms* by the door. St. Gregory's has a ring of four bells with an 8 cwt. tenor which are at present unringable.

Barningham, St Andrew (D3): This is one of the few medieval churches in East Anglia that sensibly enjoys joint use by Anglicans and Methodists. The tower has *Decorated* bell openings, but according to local wills it was being called the 'new tower' in 1440 and so it is likely that, as in many other cases, it is the product of more than one period. It has a plain panelled *base course*, diagonal buttresses to the w., and a heavy stair turret on the s. side. There are prominent *put-log holes* on the w. and the battlements are stepped. The pattern of the base course recurs on the *nave* buttresses which stand between tall *Perpendicular* windows. There is a *priest's door* in the s. wall of the early-C14 *chancel*, and to its r. the two-*light* window has a *castellated transom*, forming a *low side window* at the bottom

which has one section closed by a wooden panel. There is attractive flowing *tracery* in the e. window, and on the n. side, two large sloping buttresses shore up the wall. The *Sacred monogram* appears in *flushwork* on the *porch* parapet and the remains of a *stoup* can be seen to the r. of the C14 doorway within.

Just inside the door is an octagonal early-C14 *font*. Many others in the area have window tracery patterns carved on the bowl, but on this one there are woodcarvers' designs in the small panels, rather than those of the mason. The small wooden cover is C15 or early C16 and has radiating *crocketted* braces with a turned *finial*. On the s. wall behind the font is a section of board painted white and lettered in black Gothic script with red capitals. It reads: 'Flagellatus est (Sacred monogram) Sancta Trinitas unus Deus. Sepultus est'. In referring to Christ's Passion and Entombment it is likely to be a rare survival – part of a moveable wooden *Easter sepulchre*. There is no tower arch as such – only a plain deeply recessed doorway. The roofs of nave and chancel are *arch-braced* and the latter has pendant *bosses* at the ridge, as well as demi-figures bearing shields at the bottom of the *wall posts*. One of the delights of this church is the lovely set of C15 benches in the nave. They are low, with large *poppyheads* and they stand on deep sills. The ends are carved with an extraordinary variety of blind tracery, and although the backs are not pierced, they are moulded and carved, some with leaf trails. Many of the animals and birds on the elbows are crudely carved but there is a nice camel at the e. end on the s. side next to the wall, and a sweet little owl next but one to the w. The range at the w. end on the n. side are good C19 copies. Equally fine is the C15 *rood screen*, despite having been heavily varnished 70 years ago. The *ogees* of the main lights are crocketted and *cusped*, and over the centre opening is a graceful compound ogee arch. Judging by the painted decoration on all the uprights and arches, and the remains of gilt *gesso* on the leading edges of the buttresses, it must have been magnificent in its youth. *Cautley* reported traces of figures on the lower panels (where one would expect to see them) but I could detect none. Above the buttresses there are slots which housed the brackets supporting the floor of the loft that is no longer there. The stairs leading to it rise within the window embrasure on the r. to a very narrow entrance at the top. The stump of the main beam of the loft can be seen in the wall close by and there is a *piscina* below the steps. On the n. side, the late-C17 oak pulpit has plain panels with a deep *acanthus* moulding at step level; its *tester* is *Jacobean*, with scrollwork, and turned pendants at the angles. Entry to the chancel is through a pair of doors added to the screen in the *Stuart* period. There are turned *balusters* in the top sections and panels carved with shallow strapwork beneath them. The *altar* is of the same date, with a carved top rail and a rather odd reversed baluster shape to the turned legs. One section of the *communion rails* that went with it can now be found in front of the nave benches on the n. side. The angle piscina in the *sanctuary* is very simple and there are *dropped-sill sedilia* alongside. An *aumbry* lies in the n. wall and, above it, a *brass* in good condition for Rector William Goche who died in 1499. The 13in. figure shows him in academical dress and the inscription asks us to pray for his soul. Metal-painted *Decalogue* boards flank the altar and the 1870s oak *reredos* frames a painting of the Last Supper (more or less after Leonardo da Vinci) by the rector's sister, Eliza Evelyn Edwards. The s. sanctuary window contains attractive glass – probably 1870s work by *Clayton & Bell*. It has four panels of the *Seven Works of Mercy*, with groups of figures in medieval dress and uses lots of deep red and good blue. The only medieval glass in the church consists of C15 fragments in the nave window tracery. Over the n. door, is a boldly painted set of *Royal Arms*; they are *Hanoverian,* painted before 1801 (but later given the initials 'VR' for Victoria).

Barrow, All Saints (B4): The church is the best part of a mile n. of the village centre and was extensively restored in the 1840s and 1850s. The unbuttressed tower, with its small C19 w. door, has *Decorated* bell openings and there are numerous *gargoyles* spaced out below the battlements. In the e. wall above the *nave* roof there is part of a *Norman* window showing, within which is a small slit opening. The early-C14 s. *aisle* windows have *trefoiled lights* with a *quatrefoil* above them and there is *ogee tracery* in the aisle e. window within a *label* which has *headstops*. Below the window is a curious little opening leading into a shaft behind the *altar* which possibly ventilated a small charnel chamber where bones from old burials were laid. Nearby is a selection of well-carved C18 headstones. The three-stepped *lancets* of the e. window were apparently unchanged by the 1848 restoration and the *Perpendicular* windows on the n. side have worn male and female headstops.

Entry is by the s. *porch* and although this has

been renewed, there are small C14 quatrefoil openings in the walls. The s. aisle has a lancet to the w. and within, the Decorated *arcade* rises from octagonal *piers*. The large tower arch of the same period is blocked and a small doorway has been set within it. The *chancel* arch may have matched it before it was widened to the extent that nave and chancel are virtually one. The late-C14 *font* has an attractively panelled shaft and the bowl panels are bright with a very interesting series of shields which were repainted in 1969. Clockwise from the e. they are: the See of Canterbury, the *Royal Arms* of France and England, *Passion emblems*, *St Andrew*, le Despencer, Ely (or East Anglia), *St George*, and France (modern?). The Despencer shield is charged with a five-point label and this suggests that the font is a memorial to Elizabeth, widow of Hugh, Lord le Despencer and daughter of the Earl of Gloucester. By the side of the entrance a small bell has been hung in a frame on the wall, complete with all the fittings for change ringing – wheel, stay, slider and rope. This provides an opportunity to study the mechanics of that subtle art, and ringers make use of the excellent ground floor ring of six with its 11 cwt. tenor. Beyond the doorway, the *brass* for John Crosyer has been mounted on a board. There is the bottom half of his effigy and a verse about this benefactor of the poor and 'late parson of this towne' who died in 1569 and was buried in front of the *High altar*. Next to it are replica sections of a brass now in the British Museum. The front benches in the s. aisle have roughly traceried ends and deeply cut leaf trails on the backs. This chapel was once dedicated to *St Michael* and the *piscina* (in the e. rather than the s. wall) was uncovered during the 1852 restoration. It consists of two plain lancets with trefoil heads below a pierced quatrefoil and, although there are two compartments, there is only one drain. To the r. in the corner is a C14 tomb recess with a pointed canopy decorated with flat *crockets* on the chamfer. Restored *sedilia* join on, and because all the levels in the chancel were raised two or three ft. in the C19 they are now close to the floor. Another C19 discovery was the Norman lancet in the n. wall and the deep splays are painted with two lively little figures. The reading desk has panels of medieval tracery and only the bottom boards of the *rood screen* survive, together with the centre rail. The tall bench ends of the chancel stalls have *paterae* on the chamfers and some of the *finials* have masks with their tongues hanging out. Two others sport a jolly pair of heads in medieval billycock hats and there are birds and faces carved in the *spandrels* of the stall fronts. A C15 carver of Bury, called Richard Aleyn, left money for the High altar here and could conceivably have done this work. In the *sanctuary* the mid-C13 double piscina stands next to reconstructed sedilia and both of them are now at floor level. In the e. wall there are two large *aumbries* rebated for doors and the C19 *reredos* is in *Early English*-style blind arcading. The e. window lancets are filled with glass by R.I. Colson of 1848. Roundels painted with episodes in Christ's life are effectively married with patterns and borders in which a bright green figures. The large tomb in the sanctuary n. wall may well have been used as an *Easter sepulchre*. Of *Purbeck marble*, the front of the chest is decorated with *cusped* lozenges enclosing shields, the recess is panelled, and there is a frieze cornice with a line of *quatrefoils* below. All the shields now have brightly coloured arms applied to them, painted on hardboard. The style of the monument is early-C16 but on the back wall is a brass for Sir Clement Heigham who died in 1570. MP and Governor of Lincoln's Inn, he was Queen Mary's Chief Baron of the Exchequer and one of the few knighted by Philip of Spain. His little kneeling figure wears *Tudor* armour and his gauntlets hang neatly on the prayer desk with his helm in front. His two wives are shown with him, each with her brood of daughters, and one dead son in a shroud is shown behind his father. All the shields were once inlaid with colour and the long verse epitaph is worth studying, for while Heigham's dismissal by Elizabeth is not mentioned, the reason for it is

... the feare of God he alwaies had,
fast fixte in holy hearts,
And from his prince in loyaltye
noe iote would he departe.

On the s. wall of the sanctuary is the monument to Sir John Heigham who died in 1626. This is by John Stone and very like his father Nicholas's work – a black and white marble tablet under a broken *pediment* with urn, and a *cartouche* of arms below. On the chancel s. wall is a tablet for Susan Heigham (1695); painted white, with the detail in rather startling green and purple. There are fat side scrolls and two bas-relief skulls in drapes at the bottom corners. Her husband, Clement, supplied the long epitaph and admonition to the reader. Another Clement Heigham, who died in 1634, has his monument in shocking pink and black

further along with a bold inscription, arms in strapwork above and three coloured shields of arms below – a family obviously not averse to vivid colour.

Barsham, Holy Trinity (H2): The church and the old rectory form a picturesque group beyond a wide meadow, and a thatched C19 *lych-gate* stands at the entrance to the churchyard. The round tower is almost certainly *Saxon*, the shape slightly irregular in its lower stages, and a w. window was inserted in the C14. Above that, there is a *lancet* within a moulded frame, with two more lancets at the next level. The upper stage was probably a *Tudor* rebuilding – set back a little, banded with thin red bricks, and the bell openings have been shorn of their *tracery*. The *quoins* at the w. end of the *nave* are largely flints and small boulders which, together with the flintwork in the s. wall, is more evidence of a pre-Conquest date for the building. There is another lancet in the n. wall of the nave, and the pattern of tool marks on its *jambs* is again indicative of Saxon craftsmen. The door below was inserted around 1300, and much nearer our own time the n. chapel was rebuilt in 1908. The architect was Frederick Charles Eden, and he chose here a version of late *Perpendicular*, using a chequer of flint and tile on the w. wall. Beyond the chapel there is a C19 organ chamber and *vestry*, and circling the building one comes across its unique feature – the *chancel* e. wall. It is covered with a lattice of *ashlar* strips set in *flushwork*, and the pattern is continued without a break throughout the e. window in the form of lozenge tracery. This is an extraordinarily bold concept, and difficult to date. The chancel was apparently rebuilt with old materials in the C17, but there is an important early-C16 Echingham family tomb within, and their shield bore the same pattern as the wall/window, so they can probably be credited with the idea. There is a renewed *priest's door* on the s. side of the chancel, and the large C13 lancet alongside is fitted with a *transom* to form a *low side window*. The nave roof was destroyed by fire in 1979, but it has been smartly re-thatched, and one enters the church via a diminutive *porch* and finely moulded inner doorway.

There is a *stoup* recess to the r., and ahead stands the early-C15 *font*. *Castellated* at rim and base, its heavy octagonal bowl has *quatrefoils* in roundels, and the shaft has eight attached columns with narrow window tracery between. This is very like Shadingfield's, but here the shaft is of brick plastered over, and the outline of the former *Norman* font base can be detected below. The *Purbeck marble* bowl of the Norman font was found under the nave floor, and now rests in a corner of the *sanctuary*. There is a *sanctus-bell window* above the tower arch, and a faint depression in the surrounding wall shows that originally there was an upper doorway, a feature found in a number of East Anglian round towers which suggests that they were designed partly as places of refuge. A ring of five bells (tenor 6 cwt.) is rung from the ground floor. The church has a strong Nelson connection – one of his uncles was William Suckling who was buried here in 1798, his grandfather was parson here from 1714 to 1730, and his mother was born at the rectory. Seven shields and roundels commemorating C18 and C19 Sucklings were set with garlands and sprigs in the centre nave window in 1905 to mark the Trafalgar centenary. This most attractive design was probably by the architect of the n. chapel, Frederick Eden, who was a skilled and enthusiastic designer and maker of stained glass. The window nearest the door is filled with a fine composition by Joseph Fisher, an artist who worked with Eden. It dates from the early years of the C20, and the *Blessed Virgin* and Child are grouped with two women within a *Renaissance* arch, with harbour shipping and the sea beyond; in the tracery, a lily for the Virgin, *St Catherine's* wheel, and a *Trinity* emblem. Eden again is the most likely source for the figures of *St Cecilia* and *St Luke* in the third nave window. He was insistent that the joiners should use no planes in making the furniture installed in 1908, and you will see that the nave benches with their simple fleur-de-lys *finials* are adze-finished, particularly noticeable on the backs. Opposite the entrance, on the n. wall and in the traditional place, is the vague outline of a large *St Christopher* painting. A C14 two-bay *arcade* divides the nave from the chapel, and a most attractive and unusual World War I memorial hangs at the centre, a painted oval set in a laurel and flower wreath, backed by a carved gilt frame. The chapel was rebuilt in 1908 to commemorate Nelson's mother, and a photograph of her baptismal entry in the 1725 register is displayed on a window sill. It stands on the foundations of a *chantry chapel* founded by Sir Edward Echingham in 1527, dedicated to St Catherine, which was finally demolished in the late C18. There are a few bench ends with *poppyheads* and remains of carvings on the elbows, one of which is a *pelican in her piety*. The glass in the chapel windows was all designed by Eden in Renaissance style –

wreathed ovals illustrating the Nativity, the Magi, the *Transfiguration,* and Christ's Mocking, Crucifixion and Resurrection; all embellished against clear glass with garlands of fruit and ribbons. The large painting on the n. wall of the Blessed Virgin sewing with attendant angels is possibly late-C17/early-C18 Italian. Late-C17 *communion rails* front the chapel *sanctuary*, and on the r., a *squint* pierces the wall into the nave. Its alignment shows that an *altar* stood in front of the chancel *screen* before the *Reformation*. The doorway above led to the *rood loft*, and the chapel altar is a *Jacobean* table which came from the redundant church at Ship-meadow. The *reredos* is a C16 Italian majolica panel, a bas-relief of The Blessed Virgin and Child with the infant *St John the Baptist*. It is backed by a large *trompe-l'oeil* painting of a Renaissance arch whose illusion of perspective is remarkably effective.

Back in the nave, the square *Stuart* pulpit is set against the s. wall. Its backboard and *tester* are largely new work, but the short section of stair rail backing onto the screen is worth examining. It possibly came from the chapel demolished in 1780 and '1636 T.R.' is carved on the top – rare because rails were seldom dated. A pre-1870 photo does not show rails at the High altar and they may have come from the chapel demolished in 1780. The *rood screen* is C17 too (albeit extensively renewed), and the squared uprights are carved with shallow scrolls and leaf patterns; there are turned pendants to the paired arches, and it was fitted below the original medieval *rood beam*. The rood itself will have been removed in the C16, and the present group dates from 1893 when the screen was restored. The *canopy* arch of 1919 is a real surprise and quite unlike anything normally found in an English parish church; the detail of the architectural frame is picked out prettily in soft colours, and cutout figures of the *Annunciation* with *St Elizabeth* and *St Joseph* stand within classical arches. The organ lurks behind a stone screen within an original arch on the n. side of the chancel, and there is the outline of another arch above the vestry door. Lightning struck the chancel in 1906, damaging the e. window and shattering the medieval *mensa* which had been discovered under the e. wall a few years before. The misfortune prompted a general restoration, and the work included the delightful plaster ceiling, decorated with *Sacred monograms, pomegranates*, roses, lilies, and a *pelican*. The roof itself had been rebuilt by rector Robert Fleming in 1633, and his shield is carved on a *corbel* above the organ. The unusual *ledger-stone* in the centre of the floor with coloured marble fragments in the centre is for Thomas Missenden, the rector who died in 1771. For those of us without Greek, that part of the inscription may be translated:

I've entered port. Fortune and Hope adieu!
Make game of others, for I've done with
    you.

The glass in the s.w. chancel window is signed by *Lavers, Barraud & Westlake* and the lancet has two panels in their 1870s C13 style set within rich and colourful patterning; the s.e. window was not consecrated until 1935 and is unlikely to be their work. There are *dropped-sill sedilia* in the sanctuary, and the *piscina* has a *trefoil* arch with a hint of the *ogee* shape; a large vine corbel was added (probably in 1906) to support a *credence shelf*. Sir Edward Echingham died in 1527, and his tomb stands within an arched recess on the n. side of the sanctuary, with a fragment of inscription surviving on the base. It is one of an important group of seven terracotta tombs to be found in East Anglia and the style, originating in Italy, reached England around 1500. The four front sections are identical with those at Oxburgh in Norfolk, and the tombs probably came from a centre such as Norwich. It is likely, however, that the components were made in Flanders in the 1520s. In front of the tomb lies a fine, almost complete *brass* of a knight who is identified by most as Sir Robert atte Tighe (d.1415). But Sir Robert was buried at Sotterley and so another candidate is Sir Thomas de Echingham who succeeded to the lordship in 1450. He was a courtier, and the 48in. figure wears the *collar of SS*, and the initials 'RS' on the sword scabbard may stand for 'Regius Senescallus' – Royal Seneschal or Steward. The armour is a textbook example of the period, and only a small portion has been lost, apart from the border inscription and corner quatrefoils. *Kempe's* earliest work in Suffolk, installed between 1870 and 1880, can be seen in the e. window diamond panels. The figures illustrate the 'Te Deum' canticle, with the Trinity at the top, above two Seraphim and the three archangels, leading a heavenly host of saints – an interesting selection that includes *The Blessed Virgin, SS Agnes, Lucian,* our local *SS Edmund* and *Fursey* and *St Thomas Becket*.

There will be many visitors to Barsham who cannot leave without paying homage to a man who lies s.w. of the tower under an honest stone which simply says: 'Adrian Bell, 1901-1980. Much loved'. More than any other writer, he had the gift of seizing upon the essence of Suffolk, its people and its ways. And he wrote so well – in *Men and the Fields* the description of a village church is incomparable.

Barton Mills, St Mary (B3): The pollarded limes which front the churchyard were planted in 1845 but they are still vigorous and do not betray their age. The base of the tower, with its w. door, is late C12 but the upper stages date from around 1300. The simple 'Y' *tracery* of the bell openings was altered in the C19 and the *clerestory* renewed in a debased style at the same time. Walking round, you will find human *headstops* on the s. side and animal ones on the n. The tall n.e. *vestry* has a blank window shape large enough for a *transept*. Entry is via the C14 *porch*, with a modern Virgin and Child in a niche overhead and glazed outer doors. There is a *scratch dial* to the l. of the inner door, showing that it was in use before the porch was built and just inside are the remains of a *stoup*. The bright and shining interior is beautifully kept. The C14 *arcades* have mutilated headstops – male on the n. side, female on the s. Above the tower arch, note the 'Y' tracery belfry window that will have been above and outside the line of the original roof. The tower has been recently restored, and its arch to the nave is now filled with a plain and solid no-nonsense screen which is glazed at first-floor level. *G.F. Bodley's* main range of pews has been replaced by sensible chairs. On the n. aisle wall there is a memorial to No. 3 Group RAF who first came to Mildenhall aerodrome in 1937 and were finally moved in 1967, having suffered 10,000 casualties in the war. The present *nave* roof dates from 1886 and that in the *chancel*, with its red and green panels, is modern too. The C14 *font*, on a modern shaft, provides good examples of window tracery designs adapted to suit the panels and is similar to the one at Icklingham All Saints. The long C14 oak chest bound with iron is not joined work but is hollowed out of a solid trunk. The *Decorated* tracery in the *aisle* windows is particularly pleasing, with *mouchettes* springing from the centre *mullion* and curving over in a flowing line. On a stone base, the early-C17 pulpit is country work, with very coarse and poorly laid out panels of shallow carving. There is a brass lectern of 1903, and above the chancel arch, a mural of the Good Shepherd set against a stencilled background, designed by the firm (if not the hand) of *Sir George Gilbert Scott* and painted by *Powells* of

Whitefriars. The chamber on the n. side of the chancel has been tranformed into a neat side chapel, with the bonus that the fine unglazed Decorated window on the w. side can once again be appreciated. The chancel has some interesting things: look first for two *consecration crosses*, one just inside the arch on the s. side and the other w. of the blocked door on the n. that led to the original vestry. Close to the first consecration cross is a pair of *low side windows*, rebated for shutters with the hinges still in place. To the e. there is a stylish C18 *cartouche* with heraldic *achievement* above and cherub below for William Glasscock. Beyond that are *dropped-sill sedilia* and an eroded but still attractive late-C13 or early-C14 *piscina*. It has twin drains and the centre shaft supports *cusped ogee* arches with a *quatrefoil* above, all contained within an outer arch. There is an *aumbry* in the n. wall. Bodley was in charge of restoration work in the early years of the C20 and his chancel stalls with *poppyheads* are a very solid design. The church must have been rich in C14 glass at one time, and when the nave was re-paved in 1904, innumerable fragments were found below the brick floor. Most of what is left is in the s. aisle and in the e. window there are two figures, one of *St Edmund* on the l., with the three arrows symbolising his martyrdom, and the other one of *St John the Baptist*. In their haste, the C17 image breakers thought it enough to destroy the heads only of the saints, but it is interesting that they also smashed the heads of the winged dragons in the tops of the aisle windows. Seek out the one they missed at the w. end of the s. aisle! There is, incidentally, a family likeness in the stylised churches to be seen in three of the windows. There are some C14 fragments in the chancel too but most of the glass is C19 and early-C20. The 1866 e. window by *Clayton & Bell* has lots of small scale figures – Nativity, Transfiguration, Calvary, the women at the tomb, Ascension – with the five best-known miracles in panels below – plenty of bright colour but little feeling. The 1867 window over the sedilia by *Ward & Hughes* is a vapid piece of sentimentalism but the 1907 *Heaton, Butler & Bayne* opposite is much better – two panels in *Arts and Crafts* style on the theme of charity, with cool colour and sound modelling. As you go, have a look at the two halfends of benches by the tower arch, part of what must have been a fine C15 set. Although they are unringable, Barton Mills' bells are interesting because they were cast by the Bury St Edmund's founder Roger Reve in the 1520s or 30s, and the tenor carries a rare inscription:

'Sancte Andria Apostoli ora pro nobis' (*Apostle St Andrew* pray for us), and another is dedicated to *St Barbara*.

Battisford, St Mary (E5): A minor road meanders towards nowhere in particular and the churchyard lies in a pleasant spot by the lane leading to Battisford Hall. Limes shade the paths and the plain late-C14 s. *porch* has a step made from a pair of *gargoyles* salvaged from the long-vanished tower. Within it, there are wonderfully gnarled planks for seats in front of a simple doorway of about 1300. Both *nave* and *chancel* date from this period, with most of the windows renewed and the walls partly plastered. To the n. of the nave is a C14 chapel whose *lancet* has little *headstops*. On the w. gable a substantial bellcote with tiled roof has taken the place of the tower. It is supported by an eccentric brick buttress shaped like a chimney, with no fewer than seven varying set-offs, as though the builder made it up as he went along (which he probably did).

Entering by the n. door, one finds a simple interior with *pamment* floors and stripped pitch pine pews. The w. range is likely to be C18 and above it is a raked *gallery* with a panelled and painted front. The blocked tower arch remains and the stubs of two timber joists suggest that there was an earlier gallery. It is worth climbing the stairs to view the *Royal Arms* – painted on board and placed on the w. *tie-beam*. They are for Queen Anne and have her individual motto 'Semper eadem' (Always the same), but the heraldry is not accurate. The gallery seats have panelled backs and gangway doors which, when closed, allow hinged flaps to fall and thus provide maximum accommodation – as at Thornham Parva. From here one has an excellent view of the C14 roof, with tie-beams chosen for their natural curve and *king posts* with four-way struts. The thickly whitewashed *font* carries a range of varied window shapes in the bowl panels above a reeded shaft, and nearby there are two squares of roofing lead, clamped to the walls and embossed with simple designs together with the initials of early-C18 and C19 churchwardens. The church acquired its organ in 1914 and it takes up the n. chapel which possibly served as the squire's pew in the previous century. In front, a *ledger-stone* retains one of its shields but the inscription has gone. The C18 pulpit in plain panelled oak opposite is a highly individual shape – five irregular sides set against the wall, to which the stem returns. There is an image stool resting on a demi-angel behind it, and a vestige of the *rood loft stair* can be detected above. A low door in the n. chancel wall leads to a *vestry* with a *Perpendicular* e. window, and a plain, almost-square C17 Holy table stands in the sanctuary. Behind it are the *Decalogue*, Creed and Lord's Prayer on slate panels. They were originally painted but were banished to the back of the organ some years ago; it was only in 1983 that they were salvaged, cleaned, and, with the lettering finely cut, replaced – not only restored but improved. The 1724 monuments to Edward Salter and John Lewis which flank the e. window are identical and attractive designs; standing *putti* blow gilded trumpets at the top of the obelisks and there are pretty, painted *cartouches* of arms, with side scrolls and cherub heads below. Walter Rust's tablet is interesting because it tells us that at his death in 1685 he established a charity which specified that on a particular day each year (his birthday?) bread should be given to poor people in the church porch – one of the many ways in which the porch figured in parish life.

Bawdsey, St Mary (H6): On Guy Fawkes' night 1842, some adventurous lads let off their fireworks from the top of the tower, and the unfortunate result was almost total destruction of the church by fire. It was rebuilt in diminished style the following year, and the tower was lowered by a third. Despite that reduction, the tower is still impressive in its broad solidity, with bold buttresses and a weatherworn doorway below the C14 w. window. The line of the old *nave* roof shows on the e. face, and a *sanctus-bell window* remains below it. Walking round, you will see that the early C13 *arcades* survived the fire and were incorporated into the new walls which are topped with brick. Neither *aisles* nor *chancel* were replaced, and there are heavy brick buttresses at the e. angles.

Entering from the w. under a tower gallery we find a simple interior, neatly kept. The top of the tower arch has been re-formed, and below stands a graceful C18 *baluster font*. On the s. wall a display panel contains a most interesting example of medieval embroidery. There are six oblong panels and a centre piece and they probably formed part of a C13 Flemish cope (a ceremonial cloak). In the late C19 it was cut up and the sections were mounted on brown velvet and provided with decorative surrounds, and it may have been used as part of an altar frontal. There is a *Trinity* group in the centre flanked by six saints, one of whom is a bishop. It was given to the church by the Quilter family, whose

rather splendid table tomb stands w. of the tower outside.

On the n. wall, there is a tablet for Edward Cavell who died in 1867. He was the great-uncle of nurse Edith Cavell, heroine of World War I, and a French medallion commemorating her hangs below. The square openwork pulpit presumably dates from the 1840s rebuilding and is much more interesting than the usual Victorian 'gothick' pastiche. It has ranges of slim balusters like those of a staircase ranged below a book ledge with large brass brackets.

Baylham, St Peter (F5): The church stands on a hill within a spacious churchyard and there are pleasant views to the s. The architect Frederick Barnes carried out a full-scale restoration here in 1870 when he rebuilt the *chancel* and added *transepts* to it – 'Domus Dei, porta caeli 1870' (This is the House of God, this is the gate of heaven) is cut above the s. doorway. The C14 tower has *Decorated tracery* in the w. window but the blocked n. doorway betrays the true age of the church. It has a square Norman lintel and the *tympanum* above it is incised with a pattern of lozenges. The C19 work on that side included a tall chimney in the corner between nave and transept which was given peculiar *trefoil* smoke holes at the top in a forlorn attempt to afford it some Gothic character. There is nice flowing Decorated tracery in a s. nave window and entry is via the 1870s porch and s. door.

The C15 *font* is a familiar East Anglian design, with four lions that have lost their heads round the shaft and defaced angels beneath the bowl. Six of the bowl panels are carved with two lions and four *Tudor Roses*, but the other two are of more than usual interest. When Dowsing came here, probably in August 1644, he noted that 'there was the *Trinity* in a triangle on the Font, and a cross', and although he doubtless ordered their defacement, the shields held by the angels in the n. and s. panels of the bowl can still be identified as a Trinity emblem (s.) and the *instruments of the Passion*. The *nave* roof retains its original *tie-beams* but Barnes inserted additional *king posts* and panelled out the ceiling in chestnut. A new chancel arch was part of the reconstruction and the partial door shape just w. of the transept was probably the entrance to the old *rood loft stairs*. Parts of the medieval *screen* were found when the pews were replaced and they were incorporated in the vestry screen under the tower and in the front panels of the reading desk. The C17 monument of John and Elizabeth Acton was reinstated on the n. wall of the chancel and their little alabaster figures kneel and face each other over a prayer desk, with a gruesome skeleton reared behind them; there is an *achievement of arms* above the cornice, three sons and two daughters kneel in compartments below, and a *pelican in her piety* is carved in a roundel at the bottom – there are traces of colour here and there. The *communion rails* by Hart & Co are the ingenious tubular variety in brass, with telescopic centre sections, and the e. window has the risen Christ flanked by two of the three Marys and two apostles in attractive glass by *Clayton & Bell*, with their individual red typically dominant.

St Peter's has a ground floor ring of six with a 10 cwt. tenor which are unringable at the present time.

Beccles, St Luke (I1): A growing population after the war highlighted the need for a daughter church in Beccles, but it was not until 1965 that the first phase of St Luke's was built on Rigbourne Hill. The church proper followed in 1973, and the building stands on a raised corner site, with a view across the school playing fields to the tower of St Michael's in the town centre. It is a simple structure in quiet red brick, with lead-sheathed dormers set in the cement tiled roof. A wooden gable cross establishes its identity, and there is a large panel by the entrance which combines the saint's name with a cross and a branch of vine in a pattern of coloured pebbles. First to be built was the suite of meeting rooms and kitchen, and a common foyer links them with the church. It is a plain, broad rectangular hall, with unadorned breeze block walls, under a sloping ceiling which is partially clad with pine boarding. There are domestic windows, except for three tall *lancets* in the s. wall, in front of which stands the *font*. It is a rough cast cylinder whose panels contain a Crucifixion, the Good Shepherd, the holy dove, and Christ's baptism – all in impressionistic plastic form; a series of rather strange protuberances like bursting buds feature below the rim. A low, broad podium edged with brick surrounds the *sanctuary* with its curved frontage, and all the furnishings are simple.

Beccles, St Michael (I1): From across the Waveney valley, the long roof rises like a whaleback above the clustered town, and the splendid bell tower with its 'pepperpot' turret stands alongside to make a distinctive landmark. The siting of the tower was dictated by the lie of the land, for you will see as you walk

round that the w. boundary of the churchyard overlooks a steep drop to the level of the water meadows and the river. Begun in 1500, the tower took forty years to build and, had funds allowed, it would probably have been given a parapet and pinnacles. It is entirely faced with *ashlar*, and there is a double *base course* of shaped shields, with a curving trail above – all much eroded. The buttresses have four *set-offs*, and there are elongated niches with tremendously tall image stools in the bottom stages. Niches flank the w. door, with three more above it, and there are four shields bearing the arms of the Bumstead, Garneys and Rede families, and Bury St Edmund's abbey. The w. window has a *crocketted dripstone*, with a line of *quatrefoils* below. The size of the paired bell openings seems to have been dictated by the proportions of the tower's top stage, and they might have been larger had the design been carried to its logical conclusion. The ground floor windows have been shorn of their *tracery*, and there are *sound holes* above them. A Beccles penny of 1795 set in a plaque on the e. wall was the token payment made by the town in the 1970s when the tower passed into the council's keeping, having been extensively restored. This impressive campanile houses a grand 'old style' ring of ten bells in excellent order, with a 25 cwt. tenor.

The main body of the church dates from the second half of the C14 and is straightforward in plan. *Nave* and *chancel* lie under one roof, and the n. and s. *aisles* extend to form side chapels for the chancel, with no variation in the line of their walls. An interesting addition in recent years has been an undercroft which provides meeting rooms and other facilities, below a broad, balustraded terrace at the w. end. The w. doorway has a band of tiny shields worked in the moulding, and there are hung shields in the *spandrels* against a background of leaves. Walking round, you will see that the C15 n. *porch* has a *flushwork* facade, with a tall, canopied niche above the entrance, and a prettily crested parapet. The outer archway spandrels are carved with a *woodwose* and a dragon, one of a group of examples of this pairing in n. Suffolk. The porch has an upper room, and the range of vaulting *bosses* includes some fine heads, with a dragon featured in the centre. The aisle window *tracery* is an interesting mixture of *Decorated* and *Perpendicular* styles, and on the n. side there is a bulky *rood stair* turret with a leaded *ogee* hood and spike, matching the one on the tower. Like the nave w. window, the chancel e. window is broad, with seven *lights*, but its tracery pattern is more attractive – a lively series of stepped *transoms*. Below, the emblem of *St Edmund* can still be recognised in the band of weathered shields – a reminder that the abbey of St Edmundsbury built the church in the C14. At a guess, the ring of tiny quatrefoils with centre shields once enclosed a *Sacred monogram*. The *priest's door* in the s. chancel wall has its own little C15 porch, complete with battlements and pinnacles, and there are diminutive *headstops* on the dripstone. The inner doorway, although altered, has ring *capitals* and is C13, pre-dating most of the building. The C15 s. porch is splendid, and quite the best feature. In ashlar like the tower, it rises above the aisle roof, with a bold turret at the corner. The polygonal buttresses are niched at all stages, and a leafy motif is repeated above each of the shallow canopies. There is a trio of tall niches above the wide entrance arch, and the pinnacles of their elongated canopies reach up to the richly carved parapet. That features shields and crowned 'M's for the *Blessed Virgin*, and is topped with a diamond cresting. The abbey shield can be seen again above the doorway, and the spandrels are filled with intricate tracery within a series of circles. There were *stoups* each side of the entrance, and the vaulted roof has a fine series of bosses – Nativity, Crucifixion, Resurrection, Ascension, and Christ in Glory; note that the 'gate of hell' boss to the e. of the centre takes the common medieval form of a beast's mouth.

The interior is extremely spacious, the wide hall of the nave and chancel unbroken in its length except for the wooden *screen*. The *arcades*, with their quatrefoil *piers* have eight bays in all, and the westernmost pair of arches are lower than the rest. Above, there are thirteen small *clerestory* windows a side. The somewhat bare and sombre feeling is perhaps the result of two things – a disastrous fire, and a Victorian restoration. Medieval Beccles suffered a number of fires, but the blaze of November 1586 destroyed most of the centre of the town and gutted the church. The subsequent rebuilding accounts for the style of the clerestory and some of the other windows. By the mid-C19, the church was in poor repair, and *J.H. Hakewill* directed a full-scale restoration between 1857 and 1866. The w. end of the church had previously been partitioned off to house the town's fire engine, and this was rectified; new seating, pulpit and choir stalls were installed, and the roofs were repaired. The *font* has a C13 *Purbeck marble* bowl, but the shaft is much later – probably C17. A small, heavily banded medieval chest stands against the w. wall, and alongside is the clock which was made by local blacksmith Edward Blowers around 1685. The church's only *brasses* are mounted on the wall above – inscriptions for John and Johane Denny (1620 & 1612). An interesting feature of the s. porch's upper room is the tiny 'watching window', with its beautiful miniature tracery. Half of it is angled to align with the e. end of the n. aisle, and it must have been used to keep an eye on the lights of more than one *altar*. The main town guild of Corpus Christi was founded in 1354 in honour of *St Mary*, St Edmund and *St Michael*, but there were others dedicated to the *Holy Trinity*, *St John*, and the Ascension, and each will have had its own altar. Two small, early *hatchments* hang above the s. door. The upper one of 1691 was probably used at the funeral of William Crane, and the other was for Robert Brownrigg, a local barrister and magistrate who died in 1669. The internal stairs to the undercroft are at the w. end of the s. aisle, and just to the e., some headstones displaced from the churchyard have been laid in the floor – Alexander King's of 1824 has a variation of the familiar epitaph: 'Adieu vain world, I've had enough of thee...'. The *Royal Arms* above the n. door are those of Charles I, and are attractively cut in outline, with a strapwork motto, all within a frame. They originally stood on the chancel screen and were painted on both sides, but during the Commonwealth the w. face was defaced. When they were rediscovered in the tower, the reverse side was restored, which explains why the lion supports the r. side of the shield rather than the l.

A small tablet on the n. aisle wall commemorates Thomas Pymar, organist here for 59 years until his death in 1854. Further along, an oval set against an obelisk is for Robert Davey, the master of the Free School who 'fell victim to the stone and gout'. He was a member of the Apollo lodge and there are appropriate masonic emblems. In the s. aisle, the 1783 tablet for Dr William Crowfoot has a particularly felicitous epitaph, and listed below are seven of his descendants who practised medicine in the town and neighbourhood up to the early C20. The chancel screen was a gift from the family. A doorway and the vestige of steps can be found in the wall to the w. of the s. aisle chapel screen. One might assume that this was another access to the rood loft that stretched right across from wall to wall, but the stairs apparently led to an outside pulpit – a rare feature. Although common on the continent, there are few English examples, and none of them in parish churches.

Dowsing came visiting in April 1643, and listed a number of offending items, including 'many superstitious pictures, about 40'. That is no doubt the reason why there is no medieval glass in the church, but Victorian work is found in the chancel and its aisles. Two of the windows are signed, and all the glass is likely to be by *Heaton, Butler & Bayne*. In the s. chapel, which is dedicated as the town's war memorial, the first window shows Christ with the halt, the lame, and the blind grouped around him, all in sombre, grainy colour. In the 1890s s.e. window, there is an interesting grouping of subjects; the Salutation of the Blessed Virgin flanked by Jesus with Martha and Mary on one side, and *Dorcas* on the other. All the figures have distinctly Roman noses, as do those in the aisle e. window. This dates from the 1880s and three of the *lights* illustrate the life of Christ, with the Good Samaritan story chosen for the fourth. The chapel *piscina* has a quatrefoil drain, and its pierced arch seems to have been reworked. A memorial on the s. wall is a draped sarcophagus with a shield of arms on the front, and it commemorates Joseph Arnold, a son of Beccles who became a naval surgeon and a distinguished botanist. He was appointed naturalist in Sumatra by the East India Company in 1818, but immediately 'fell victim to the pestilential climate'. Unsigned, and not memorable in itself, the memorial has been credited to Sir Francis Chantrey, one of the C19's fashionable sculptors. The n. aisle chapel houses the organ and a *vestry*, and its e. window glass displays another enterprising choice of subjects – the sacrifice of Isaac, Christ stilling the waves and raising the dead, and Jacob's dream at Bethel. The chancel e. window is the church's best example of Heaton, Butler & Bayne's work, and commemorates Queen Victoria's Jubilee of 1887. A multitude of small scenes, all with identifying texts, illustrate the life of Christ, and in the centre stand the larger figures of St Michael and Christ as the Good Shepherd. The tracery is filled with *apostles*, *angels*, and *passion emblems* – homogeneous design, good draughting and colour. The stone-panelled *reredos* below had been designed by Benjamin Ferry the year before. The tomb set in the n. wall of the *sanctuary* was moved from the n. aisle in the late C19, and is said to belong to John Rede, a mayor of Norwich who died in 1502. However, the style predates his death by at least a hundred years and casts doubt on the attribution. Ten small weepers

stand in niches under crocketted ogee arches along the front, with remains of pierced tracery above them. Churches often have incidental connections with the mainstream of history, and Beccles is no exception. In 1749 Edmund Nelson was curate here when he married Catherine Suckling, the daughter of Barsham's rector; when they moved later to Burnham Thorpe, Horatio the 'Norfolk Hero' was born. And in 1783, George Crabbe married Sarah Elmy here, the girl who was to be the inspiration for many of his poems.

Beck Row: See Mildenhall, Beck Row (B3)

Bedfield, St Nicholas (G4): The church is to be found at the end of a lane off the village street to the e. and the C14 tower was restored in the late 1980s. It has a panelled *base course* and the *Perpendicular* w. doorway has *fleurons* in the mouldings. There are three canopied niches around the w. window and *flushwork* decorates the buttresses and battlements. On walking round, you will find evidence of *Norman* origins in the form of an early-C12 n. doorway with zigzag bobbin decoration in the arch, and there is an abrupt change in the make-up of the *chancel* wall on that side where Norman coursed flints give way to random placing. There, a single C14 *lancet* contrasts with the variety of Perpendicular windows in the nave. The stonework of the e. window and the priest's door are reminders that J.K. Colling supervised the big restoration of the chancel in 1870. The C14 *porch* is simple but most attractive, with a niche over the wide outer arch and a *king-post* roof. The side lancets in their deep splays have been blocked and the homely brick floor is worn and undulating.

Within, the tall tower arch is blocked by a combination of C19 screen and painted hardboard but just below is an interesting range of C17 benches. Their ends are cut from 2in. plank and curve up to scrolls decorated with simple gouge cuts at the rear. The deep bowl of the C14 *font* is decorated with window tracery and three shields, and stands on a plain shaft, but its C17 cover is much more unusual. Over 6ft. tall, its body is panelled, with columns at the angles, and the curved strapwork brackets on top are carved with masks where they meet the centre shaft and *finial*. Its individuality lies in the way it is prepared for use. The three w. sections are lifted away in one piece, and three of the e. panels are hinged at the top so that they can be folded inwards and secured by a hook. This allows people standing on that side to watch the priest as he christens the baby. A chest with typical *Jacobean* decoration stands by the n. door and the later-C17 pulpit has plain panels and carved scroll supports to the canted book ledge. Overhead is a single-framed and braced rafter roof, and the stairs to the old *rood loft* are set in the s. window embrasure. Judging by the size of the top opening one would have crawled rather than walked onto the loft. There are image niches on both sides of the chancel arch and the base of the C15 *screen* has narrow painted panels. At least some of the subjects were Old Testament prophets for two survive on the s. side – Joel and Baruch – and there is a fragment of the donors' inscription below: 'Robert and his wife Alice'. It may be that this section was masked by a former pulpit and so escaped the fate of the rest. The chancel roof was part of Colling's restoration, together with the Caen stone *reredos* bearing painted Creed, *Decalogue* and Lord's Prayer panels. Floor levels were altered and the plain C14 *piscina* is now very low in the wall. The *altar* is a simple C17 table. Returning down the nave you will walk over Thomas Dunston's ledger-stone of 1657. It is decorated with a skull and that popular comment: 'Hodie mihi cras tibi' (My turn today, yours tomorrow). The church has a ground floor ring of six bells with a 9 cwt. tenor, but they are now in 'poor going order'.

Bedingfield, St Mary (F4): The church stands in a bosky churchyard by the village crossroads, and walking up the path you will see that the stumps of crosses crown the gables of *nave* and *chancel*. They are a reminder that *Dowsing* paid a visit in April 1643, when he gave orders for them to be taken down, having broken 'fourteen superstitious pictures, one of God the Father, and two doves, and another of St Catherine and her wheel'. The late-C13 or early-C14 tower is unbuttressed to belfry level where there are small *trefoil lancets*, with no window above the small, plain w. doorway. The bell openings have the remains of *Decorated tracery* and, at that level, there are shallow angle buttresses with three set-offs. Some of the windows in nave and chancel are square headed with Decorated tracery, there is an earlier lancet on the n. side of the chancel, and a late *Perpendicular* design, with deep *label* and stepped *embattled transoms*, in the s. wall of the nave. The e. window is C19, and so is the tracery of the round window w. of the porch. One wonders whether it was Saxon originally, possibly uncovered during restoration work. A good deal of that was done in the C19 and a *vestry* was built onto the n. wall of the nave in

1834. The C15 *porch* is intriguing because, above the heavily moulded *tie-beams* and *wall plates*, the ridge is supported lengthwise by slim *arch-braces*. They have the remains of very delicate pierced tracery in the *spandrels*, and the uprights are slotted to take transverse braces which have largely gone. It is the latter that makes one suspect that either the original roof was a different shape or the frame came from elsewhere (it is distinctly darker than the rest). The inner doorway is finely moulded and the niche high on the r. has most unusual mouldings for its size – five shallow ranks receding to a trefoil arch.

Within, the nave lies under a well-proportioned *double hammerbeam* roof which has very little ornamentation. Arch-braces rise to collars under the ridge and there were angels or shields attached to the ends of the hammers but they have all gone. Painted Victorian *Royal Arms* are framed above the tower arch, and below stands a massive chest over 7ft. long, completely sheathed and banded in iron. C14 or early C15, it is very like the one at Horham, but is divided in two, with separate lids. A visitor in 1887 found parish papers in one half and coal in the other, and apparently thought nothing of it! The plain C15 octagonal bowl of the *font* is decorated with simple tracery shapes and it stands on an earlier shaft. The nave benches are an interesting mixture. The ends against the wall are the remains of a C15 set with varied *poppyheads* and the shattered remains of a whole range of figures and beasts, while the remainder date from 1612 and are typically *Jacobean* in style. They have pairs of scrolls with rosette centres below a finial, with more scrolls on the elbows. Unlike the earlier craftsmen, the C17 joiners were content to carve only the side facing the aisle, but the backs of two ends on the s. side bear 'R.1612L.' and 'G.1612P.' (churchwardens, no doubt), and one at the w. end simply has the date. On the other side at the w. end, one back has 'B.Bond' carved in relief. The front range are C19 along with the pulpit. There is now no *screen* but remains of the stairs that led to the *rood loft* survive in the n. wall. The centre light of the Perpendicular s. nave window has glass by *William Morris & Co*, but it dates from 1929 when the firm was limply reiterating all that had gone before. The design is probably by Dearle and has the *Blessed Virgin* kneeling with a book before her which has fallen open at the words of the *Annunciation*. Gabriel holds St Mary's lily emblem, and there is a clump of foliage which has the faint echo of *pre-Raphaelite* richness. The large and brash figures of *St James the Great, St Stephen (?)*, and *St John* in the chancel e. window have much more character. The glass is probably by William Miller and dates from the 1850s, and the Bedingfield arms at the top link it with the *hatchment* that hangs on the chancel s. wall; it was used at the funeral of John James Bedingfield in 1853. The early-C17 *altar* is an oak table with austere lines but of a most interesting design. The legs are turned and four, slimmer versions are set along the single central stretcher.

Belstead, St Mary (F6): Like those of a number of churches in the Ipswich area, Belstead's tower is on the s. side of the *nave* and doubles as a *porch*. It is small scale and unbuttressed, and at some time the battlements were renewed in brick. The bell openings probably had *tracery* originally, and in the C19 a cross was outlined in flint above the little belfry *lancet*. On walking round, you will find that the large *Perpendicular* w. window has been renewed and there is a blocked n. door. A chapel was added on that side in the C16, with three-*light* windows and a doorway in brick (the latter and one of the windows have since been blocked). The *chancel* roof continues down over a n.e. *vestry* whose window has 'Y' tracery of about 1300, but the main e. window is Perpendicular. A window on the s. side of the *nave* has attractive *Decorated* tracery, and before going inside there are *scratch dials* to be found on the s.w. and s.e. quoins of the tower. The entrance arch is small but robust and the inner doorway is set within an earlier, larger arch.

Inside, C19 *Decalogue* boards stand at the w. end and the n. doorway now houses a restored charity board. The C15 *font* is in fine condition and in one of the bowl panels an angel holds a shield carved with three fishes, one of Christianity's oldest symbols. In the other panels there are *Tudor Roses*, a *Trinity* shield, the arms of Bury abbey, and those of the Norwich diocese – of which Suffolk once formed a part; demi-angels spread their wings under the bowl and fine upstanding lions support the shaft. The range of benches with square-topped ends and heavy mouldings on the s. side w. of the entrance date from the C16, and a set of George III *Royal Arms* painted on canvas hangs above the door. The tall tablet on the s. wall is for Sir Robert Harland, an admiral who died in 1784. By way of epitaph his widow composed an extraordinary thirty-line résumé of his not very distinguished career. Farther along, the sill of the window was crudely lowered to form *sedilia* and to give access to the *rood loft stairs* that rise in

the wall. The tall bottom doorway still retains its hinge hooks and the upper exit is partially framed with thin tiles which may have been filched from an earlier building. The *piscina* below served a nave *altar* nearby but the three worn heads around the arch do not belong to it. The nice *Jacobean* pulpit has an abundance of shallow carving, with a typical range of blind-arched panels; the base and steps are modern. Over by the reading desk lies the church's only *brass* and it is a good one. It commemorates John Goldingham, who died in 1518, and his wives Jane and Thomasine. He was Lord of Belstead Parva Manor and is shown wearing *Tudor* armour with his sword eccentrically slung. The women wear *kennel headdresses* and have massive rosaries, together with missals hung from their girdles. The inscription is missing but there are three shields which were originally inlaid with colour, displaying the arms of Goldingham and his wives' families. The n. chapel was built for the use of the Blosse family and is separated from the nave by a three-bay *arcade,* with one bay taken up by the organ. Just inside is a huge *ledger-stone* for Tobias Blosse, rector here for forty years until he died in 1693. His achievement is deeply cut and displays three griffins with curly tails. Over the blocked door beyond is a tablet for an earlier Tobias who died in 1630, carved by *John Stone*, son of the better-known *Nicholas Stone*. Not installed until 1656, it is a lozenge of marble which is carved as though it hung from a beribboned ring, and the epitaph is meticulously arranged. At the same time, Stone also carved the more elaborate tablet in the n.e. corner for Elizabeth Blosse, Tobias's daughter-in-law, who died in 1653. It is a slightly domed oval tablet set within an oblong frame, with an *achievement* and bunched drapes at the top, and little figures of her three sons and four daughters kneeling at the bottom. Note how the epitaph was phrased to add lustre to her in-laws' family by dwelling on the services rendered to royalty by her Darcy forebears. Partially hidden by the organ is the large tablet for Elizabeth Hunt, wife of Tobias's grandson, who died in 1727. It has chaste scrolls each side but a riotous *cartouche* was placed on top. The chapel's w. window was filled in to make space for the largest of the family monuments. Thomas Blosse died in 1722 and is commemorated there by a mottled grey marble composition which has skulls at the top on either side of a seated *putto*, while standing putti flank the large tablet, one piping his eye while resting his foot on another skull.

The C14 *scissors-braced* roof in the nave has

been restored and there is no chancel arch now, the division being marked only by a change in roof level and flushed boarding. However, the base of the *rood screen* remains below and the painted panels are interesting. The work dates from the end of the C15 and the figures are set against a continuous landscape panorama, with lakes, hills, and castles. Although badly defaced, the colours are still bright and the paintings display a strong Flemish influence. Starting from the l., the first two panels are blank, then we have good figures of *St Osyth* and *St Ursula*, and a poor *St Margaret* followed by another female saint who is probably *St Mary Magdalene*. The next two are blank and then there are two bishops, the first of whom might be *St Thomas of Canterbury*. Then comes *St Laurence*, followed by *St Stephen* and *St Edmund* robed in red trimmed with ermine and holding a spear-like arrow. The last figure is *St Sebastian* in hunting green, with fashionable epaulettes on his doublet and a feather in his hat. The chancel lies under a plastered ceiling and there is a text over the *priest's door* which may be the survivor of a sequence like the examples at Witnesham and Hemingstone. The doorway to the vestry is C14 and the door itself is contemporary, with lapped boards and strap hinges as at Capel St Mary. Within the vestry there is a section of a C17 pew fixed to the wall, with turned uprights and a line of hat pegs. There is no piscina now in the *sanctuary* and the modern oak *reredos* frames a C19 painting of Christ blessing the bread and wine of the Eucharist. The simple Holy table in front of it has '1621' carved on the inside of the top frame but, like many others, it has had extensions screwed on to the top to make it suit a C19/C20 ecclesiastical fashion.

Benhall, St Mary (H4): The situation is quietly rural, and the church in its spacious setting is surprisingly large – the result of some ambitious Victorian extensions. The churchyard is a sanctuary, managed under the guidance of the Suffolk Wildlife Trust, and it is becoming a refuge for some of the less common wayside flowers. The unbuttressed tower has *long and short work* at three of its corners, normally an indication of an early date, but the signs of wholesale C19 restoration all over the building make one cautious. The diminutive w. doorway has *stops* on its *dripstone* which are slightly unusual – shields bearing the arms of the De La Pole family. Circling the church, you will see the large n. *transept* which was added in the last century, together with an extension which looks

like a *chancel* side chapel. It appears to have been planned for use both as a *vestry* and a school-room, and is divided internally, with twin galleries and stairs. Its e. wall was designed to match that of the chancel alongside, giving the church its broad frontage to the road. An early-C19 *priest's door*, complete with shallow vestibule, was added on the s. side of the chancel, and the windows throughout the building were replaced. The arch of the C15 *porch* has *fleurons* in its mouldings, and in the *spandrels* of the niche above it, the crowned 'M' for the dedication and *St Peter's* keys are faintly incised. The inner doorway demonstrates decisively that this was a *Norman* building. Its generously proportioned arch has been re-cut, and is an unusual combination of familiar forms. The main moulding comprises two ranks of *chevrons* set at right angles to each other to form a block, and they are pierced so that a roll moulding shows between the serried points; the terminal heads are additions, and the *capitals* of the single columns have been re-cut. As was often the case in the Norman period, the doorway is sited midway in the nave wall, and thus determined the placing of the later porch.

The most striking feature inside is the excellent range of early-C19 *box pews*, with a matching *gallery*. In pine that is grained to give an oak effect, they fill the nave, with the exception of the space in front of the transept. Under the gallery, there is even a cosy little section with a lifting seat; it allows access to the tower door and, at a guess, was designed specially for the bell ringers. Their successors can still use the good ring of six with its 8 cwt. tenor. The deep gallery is raked, and its spartan benches will have been used initially by the church choir and rustic orchestra. From up there, the *Royal Arms* of George III over the s. door can be seen to advantage – a rather nice set, painted on canvas. On the s. side of the nave, the pews enclose the base of the pulpit to form a spacious compartment, complete with curving seat, from which the parson would read the service (see *three-decker pulpits* in the appendix). The pulpit itself is painted to match the pews, but is some three hundred years older – a *Jacobean* piece lacking its backboard and *tester*. Its two ranges of panels are in the conventional form of the period, but note the interesting variation in the treatment of the arches, and the shallow arabesques carved on the corner angles. A very slim C14 image niche hides behind the pulpit, no doubt marking the site of a pre-*Reformation altar*, and the chancel arch is contemporary with it. The transept now serves as an organ chamber, and to the e. there is a large arch recess in the chancel wall, with two tablets for members of the Hollond family – one of them the vicar who built the extensions (and presumably paid for the main restoration). On the r. is a grandiose monument in varieties of pale marble for Sir Edward Duke, the squire who died in 1732. He took the opportunity to memorialise his forebears, starting in 1598, including seven infants who died between 1632 and 1643, and another clutch of baby Tyrells and Sheltons. There were nine of them lost in six years of the early-C18, and note how they are all allowed a 'Mr' or a 'Mrs' in the epitaph. *Putti* recline on the *pediment*, on either side of a set of arms with a fine gilded crest. There are four shields of arms in the *Perpendicular tracery* of the e. window, all of them quartering the Duke family arms. Named shields of other family alliances can be found on the excellent *ledger-stone* in the centre of the chancel floor. It covers the grave of Sir Ambrose Duke's daughter Elizabeth, an heiress who died young in 1620. In front lies a quality *brass* of 1598, with effigies of Edward and Dorothy Duke. He wears a sober gown with slit sleeves, but his wife redresses the balance with a Paris cap and ruff, and below her pointed stomacher, the gown is drawn back to display an embroidered petticoat; there are three shields, an inscription, and separate plates engraved with the figures of ten sons and six daughters. An inscription of 1570 on the n. sanctuary wall commemorates Edward and Mary Glemham. The church's third and best brass for Ambrose and Elizabeth Duke (he who bought the manor and died in 1611) is under the *altar* platform and is now unfortunately inaccessible. The author Mary Mitford had a cousin John, and he was parson here from 1810 until his death in 1859. A learned and energetic author, he had fashionable literary friends, and created one of the best private libraries in Suffolk, finding time to edit *The Gentleman's Magazine* in the seventeen years before his death. It seems that he was not appreciated locally, and they do say his ghost prowls in Mitford Lane, but I suspect that we have him to thank for the fine suite of pews.

Bentley, St Mary (F7): The church stands about a mile n. of the village by the lane that leads to Bentley Park. A row of limes fronts the churchyard but only one of the three large cedars survived the great gale of 1987. The sturdy *Perpendicular* tower has a simple *base course*, buttresses angled to the w., and the *flushwork* in

the battlements has been partially filled with brick. The barn-like n. *aisle* under a double pitched roof was an addition of 1858 when *R.M. Phipson* carried out a major restoration. The organ chamber/*vestry* to the e. is almost as lofty, with a circular window in the gable. The *chancel* was rebuilt in the 1880s and given a new e. window with flowing tracery, but there is a *Norman lancet* in the n. wall which marks its true age. The lancets on the s. side are late-C13, with the exception of the largest, which is C19 (the old *priest's door* disappeared in the course of the rebuilding). The low s. *porch* has Victorian king and bishop *headstops* to the outer arch, and there is a modern statue in the niche above. Passing a fine upstanding pair of boot scrapers, one is confronted by a full-scale replica of a Norman doorway which, save perhaps for painted decoration, is what the original might well have looked like. The only real evidence left is a section of *chevron moulding* which rests on a windowsill. The church once had a C13 *font* of *Purbeck marble*, and its square base with the outline of shafts remains almost flush with the floor. The present font has lions round the shaft and dates from the early-C16, but it looks as though it was re-cut by the restorers. The e. panel of the bowl is carved with the *Blessed Virgin* and Child within an aureole, and is flanked by angels bearing Tollemache shields. Others hold shields bearing initials and the cross of *St George*, and the rest of the panels are carved with a *Tudor Rose*, a *pomegranate*, and a curious interlaced strap. The *Decalogue* boards on the aisle w. wall are brightly lettered in the High Victorian style, and a dark set of George III *Royal Arms* hangs above the arch at the e. end. Below, a C13 font bowl stands in the corner, but curiously enough it does not match the old base. Nearby is a single C15 bench with *poppyheads*, a lively horse carved on one elbow, and what is possibly a *cockatrice* on the other. The glass of 1900 in the s.w. *nave* window is probably by *Powells* and has the figures of Martha and Mary, with two vignettes below. In the other window the *three Marys* gather at the tomb, with the emphasis on the Magdalene with her long golden tresses; this is the work of *Heaton, Butler & Bayne*. The nave roof is a simple C15 *hammerbeam* construction, with collar beams and *king posts*, and the *rood beam* is still in place. The chancel has a panelled waggon roof which was installed at a lower level during the rebuilding. *Henry Ringham* carried out the woodwork for Phipson's restoration, but although the choir stalls are very much in his style, they date from the 1880s, long after his death. The e. window is filled with the scene of the disciples after the Ascension, with an angel host hovering above them and Jerusalem in the distance. It contrasts nicely with the other windows although it too is by Heaton, Butler & Bayne. The whole of the e. wall below is clad with mosaic panels and, unlike most modern versions, the *piscina* in a window ledge was provided with a drain.

Beyton, All Saints (D4): The thing one remembers about Beyton is that the tower (probably *Saxon*) is oval rather than round and that two heavy C15 buttresses rise almost to the top. The narrow top section was rebuilt in 1780 and there may have been a more imposing bell stage at one time. By the 1850s the rest of the church was in a parlous state and the *nave* was rebuilt to the designs of John Johnson of Bury, with the addition of a n. *aisle*. The old *Norman* doorway with its simply carved arch was re-set in the new outer wall. In 1884 the *chancel* was restored, lengthened, and given a new e. window by *Sir Arthur Blomfield* – all good quality work. The large *vestry* annexe, in flint and white brick that looms on the s. side of the chancel, was added in 1973. It has a fussy triangular oriole window jutting out of the w. wall that does nothing for it. The *porch* is at least part C15 with an earlier inner doorway, and contains a C17 plain chest. For those with an appetite for the curious there is a doorstop formed from a pony's hoof, complete with shoe. Within, all is fresh and neat as a pin. The tower arch is C15 and above and beyond it is a ceiling of the same period supported by a heavy *arch-braced tie-beam*. The nave roof is *scissors-braced* and the 1850s benches have some good carving, including a *pelican* on the n. side which is the first realistic interpretation that I have seen in a church. The C19 oak pulpit has triple columns at the angles and delicate leaf forms carved in relief on the upper panels, but the lower panels are a quiet surprise. They are formed of strips of walnut, tongued and grooved, with tiny dovetail keys at intervals across the joints, and then they are pierced by narrow slit crosses – very odd. In the n. aisle the centre window has beautiful 1960s glass from the Goddard & Gibb Studio on the theme of the Sower; he is shown in medieval dress within one circle of a Celtic scroll that links him with a harvest vignette. Pigeons, chaffinches, larks and linnets perch about and it is very diverting. To the e. is a war memorial window with excellent glass designed by Morris Meredith Williams and probably made by *Lowndes & Drury* – a kneeling

soldier bows his head over his rifle and Christ stands in the other *light*. Blomfield designed a handsome waggon roof in oak for the chancel, with arch-braces resting on stone *corbels* and demi-angels on the *wall plates*. The stalls incorporate a good deal of C15 work, notably bench ends with replacement figures and a bench back on the n. side decorated with shields carved with initials in *quatrefoils*. The *reredos* panel is a mosaic of the Last Supper, with a gold chalice on the table and a bowl and towel in front for the washing of the feet. It came from *Powells* who also provided the e. window glass – but that is poor work. For collectors of epitaphs I found an unusual example on Rosa Wright's stone to the w. of the n. aisle outside: 'he brought down my strength in my journey and shortened my days'. If that is a quotation, I have not been able to trace it. She died at 39 in 1882.

Bildeston, St Mary Magdalene (D6): This was an important village in the great days of the wool trade but, even before that, the church had been sited half a mile away on the hill to the w. The upper part of the tower collapsed onto the *nave* in 1975, but as a result of outstanding efforts by the parish and some help from the National Lottery, a new bell stage designed by Andrew Anderson was completed by 2004. Entirely constructed of wood, it is a severely plain structure, with the upper section louvred all round, carrying a slim leaded spirelet. The fine moulded Perpendicular w. doorway has triple niches under *cusped* and *crocketted ogees* above it. Following the collapse of the tower, the six bells with their 14 cwt. tenor were rehung by the Whitechapel foundry in 1997 – they had last been rung full-circle in 1919. The treble is a C15 Suffolk casting by John Daniel and bears his initials together with the *Royal Arms*, and is dedicated to *St Thomas*. The C14 *aisles* stop short just one bay from the e. end and their e. windows have *reticulated tracery*. There is more *Decorated* tracery in the n.w. window but the others are Perpendicular – very tall and *transomed*. The C15 *clerestory* continues over the *chancel*, with thin red bricks in the window arches and *gargoyles* in the parapet. On the n. side there is a C14 doorway and a projecting slab that marks the site of the *rood loft stairs*. A small *vestry* is tucked in the n.e. angle and the chancel e. window displays interesting Decorated tracery – an irregular *cinquefoil* shape above five tall ogee-headed *lights*. The s. *sanctuary* window matches it and a *priest's door* is set in the corner by the s.

aisle. The tall *porch* is very similar to Hitcham's and has an *ashlar* parapet, in the centre of which a feathery angel holds a shield. Facade and buttresses are all panelled *flushwork* and there are three particularly good niches; tall, with vaulting and the remains of angels below the stools, their crocketted canopies are formed by pairs of little ogee arches. The lower buttress faces are carved with recessed panels in ashlar and the arch has roses in the *spandrels* and lion masks with more roses in the mouldings. The inner doorway is equally impressive, with its double rank of deep mouldings set with shields and crowns rising to an angel at the apex; there are large lion *stops* to the *hood mould* and the original doors have a broad band of vines round the edge and tracery which is cut 'in the solid' (rather than applied) in the tops of the panels. The upper room was once used as a treasury and you will see that iron rods still run through the timbers of its floor.

The interior is immaculate and bears witness to the tremendous efforts of the parish in the years of repair and restoration that followed the tower's collapse. One of those deeply involved is commemorated in a new s. aisle w. lancet which has glass by Pippa Heskett (whose work can also be seen at Withersfield); the subject is *St Mary Magdalene* kneeling with her companion below an angel and it was completed in 1981. A small early-C14 doorway to the tower is blocked and high above the main arch there is a *quatrefoil sanctus-bell window* looking rather lost in the expanse of wall. Having no step, the C15 *font* seems squat, and there are battered carvings of extra-large *Evangelistic symbols* in the bowl panels alternating with angels bearing shields. On these you will find a *Trinity* emblem (e.), a chalice and wafer for the mass (n.), and possibly the three crowns of Ely (w.). Only fragments of the *woodwoses* and lions that supported the shaft remain. The large door to the porch upper room is no longer accessible but it once opened onto a gallery and stairway above the entrance. The body of the church is tall and open, with beautiful *arcades* that sweep through to the e. end uninterrupted by a chancel arch. Their quatrefoil *piers* support finely moulded arches which have angels at the top, and the *capitals* are carved either with demi-angels or oak leaves. In the roof, cambered *tie-beams* alternate with *hammerbeams* whose ends carry newly painted angels in the chancel. The stone *corbels* are carved with foliage, shields, and some more angels with strawberry-pink hands and faces. There were a number of restorations in the C19 and the

benches, pulpit, and choir stalls date from then.

In 1977 the parishes of Bildeston and Wattisham were united, and in 1980 the s. aisle chapel was re-dedicated to *St Nicholas*, patron saint of the redundant church. Some of its fittings found a home here and its chancel *screen* is now the *reredos*. With a new cresting, the buttresses have crocketted pinnacles with little mask *stops* and, below Decorated tracery, the panels have totally repainted figures of four male and four female saints. One can identify *St John* (far l.), *St Paul* (3rd from l.), possibly *St Ursula* (4th from r.), *St Agnes* (3rd from r.), possibly *St Helen* (2nd from r.), and *St Barbara* (far r.). Nearby, the square *label* of the *piscina* encloses a pair of crocketted canopies and on the wall overhead there is an 1837 *cartouche* by Gaffin of London for Richard and Percy Wilson. The plain tablet with crossed palms to the w. is by the same firm for the same family. Above it, a stark but interesting tablet commemorates Capt. Edward Rotheram, who was with Lord Howe on the 'glorious 1st of June' and commanded the Royal Sovereign, which led the battle line at Trafalgar. The window here is a good 1890s example of the characteristic style of *Kempe & Co. Censing* angels flank the Virgin and Child in the upper panels, with the *Annunciation* beneath. The bottom panels portray the *Visitation*, *Zachariah* in the Temple, and the angel in peacock robes appearing to shepherds who obviously had a talent for music. All very sumptuous. Farther w., is a tablet carved as an open book – 'This durable volume is inscribed to the memory of John Parker . . . 1831' – by J.H. Elmes, a little-known London mason. Across in the n. aisle, a slab set against the wall at the e. end carries the *brass* of Alice Wade. Her 22in. figure is dressed in a voluminous gown, parted to display a brocaded petticoat, and she wears a fashionable Elizabethan hat. The inscription dated 1599 is for her and her husband William but his effigy has gone, although little groups of sons and daughters survive at the bottom.

Because there was no chancel arch, the rood screen stretched from wall to wall and the upper doorway remains in the n. wall. *Cautley* reminds us that it survived the despoilers of the C16 only to be torn out in the C18. The stalls in the chancel are largely Victorian but incorporate C15 *poppyheads*, and behind them are stalls which came from the now vanished chapel of St Leonard in the village. They all have *misericords* in a fairly shaky state and those that could be examined have been mutilated. They were mostly human faces but there are the remains of a *pelican* on the

n. side. The late-C17 *communion rails* have clusters of four balusters to mark the entrance to the sanctuary and beyond them to the r. is a heavy C19 *piscina* and *sedilia*. William Wailes had worked with *Pugin* in the 1840s and his Newcastle firm of Wailes & Strang produced a great deal of richly coloured glass in the C19. The e. window is characteristic of his work and the large *cinquefoil* contains a scene from *St Luke's* Gospel, while the two long quatrefoils illustrate episodes from the Acts of the Apostles. For those with keen eyes (or binoculars) the text references are lettered in the borders. The main lights are filled with patterned *quarries* crossed with diagonal text labels, and at the bottom is a beautifully painted crest of a cock. This is unlikely to be Wailes's work and is the device of Admiral James Cockburn, C. in C. naval forces in India. He died in Calcutta in 1872 and the window is his memorial.

Blaxhall, St Peter (H5): An isolated church, serving a scattered village. The tower has had heavy repairs in brick, and although it is now bricked up, the w. doorway is attractive, with pairs of slim flanking shafts, and *paterae* in the mouldings. There are lion *stops*, and in one of the *spandrels* an *angel* holds the Ufford family shield, matched by a *green man* on the other side. A *vestry* was built on to the n. *nave* door in the C19, and a later organ chamber projects from the *chancel* on that side. The *nave* windows, with their simple brick *tracery* are likely to be C16 replacements. There is a C13 *lancet* in the n. wall of the chancel, and the e. window has *cusped* intersected *tracery* of the early C14, with rather nice little *headstops*. The *priest's door* in the s. wall dates from the same period, but the *porch* is C15, with *flushwork* panelling and roundels, and a crowned 'MR' for the *Blessed Virgin* on a buttress. In the porch w. window we see the first example of work by members of a talented local family – glass by *Ellen Mary Rope*. The two *lights* contain spirited groups of musical children, drawn with the sooty line that is characteristic of the *Arts & Crafts* school.

Just inside the C14 inner doorway there is a *trefoil stoup* niche, and a section of stone with interlace carving is set in the w. wall to the l. of the tower arch. *Cautley* described it as C12, but it looks more like *Saxon* work. Above it, church-warden John Ropper had his name attractively inscribed in 1711, and there is a C19 ringers' gallery within the tower. The church still has a ring of six in fair going order with an 8 cwt. tenor. The *font's* substantial octagonal bowl is

C15 and has tracery shapes and small shields in the panels, but the shaft is untypical and would appear to be a clever modern replacement. It is large and square, and fine *evangelistic symbols* stand at the corners, with dense tracery between them. The war memorial on the n. wall is another piece by Ellen Mary Rope – a bronze plaque with a bas-relief of Christ taking the hand of a fallen soldier at the top and the list of names in good repoussé lettering below. Further along there is another small bas-relief, this time in plaster. It is a memorial for Marjorie Wilson who died in 1934, and is by *Dorothy A.A. Rope*, sculptress niece of Ellen Mary. A window embrasure to the e. displays a square sculpted panel of a kneeling angel with a small child, in the style of Walter Crane; it is unsigned but is likely to be by one of the Rope family. Across the *nave*, one slips back three hundred years to the *touchstone* and alabaster memorial for Fraunces Saunders, with its coloured *achievement* of arms in a roundel at the top, and a miniature skull at the base. There are pine benches, and overhead, the excellent *hammerbeam roof* is unstained, with demi-angels holding books at the base of the *wall posts*, and pierced tracery above the *collars*.

Blaxhall, St Peter: Mary Agnes Rope e. window detail

No chancel arch or *screen* now, but the doorways of the stair that led to the *rood loft* remain in the s. wall. The memorial on the n. wall of the chancel for Alfred Aldrich Bates, who died aged seven in 1904, is another of Ellen Mary Rope's works – a lovely small scale relief panel of an angel leading a small boy by the hand. In the *sanctuary* the large C14 *piscina* lies under a *cusped ogee* arch, with *dropped-sill sedilia* alongside. For me, the church's most beautiful possession is the glass of 1912 in the e. window, work in the Arts & Crafts style by *Margaret Agnes Rope*, and the first in which she collaborated with her younger cousin *Margaret E. Aldrich Rope*. It is a dense design in dark, rich tones, with figures in two ranks, and lines from the Requiem Mass are quietly featured on bands of colour and the hem of a robe; the *Blessed Virgin*, with the Holy Child across her knees, has a shepherd and a kneeling saint on her r., and *St Luke* seated on her l; below, Christ the carpenter planes at a bench, *St John* with a bird on his shoulder to the l., *St Michael* and *St Peter* to the r. Tiny background vignettes include a mounted countryman and a ploughman, and in the tracery, angels support an empty cross with its nails. The artist often used her brother Michael as a model, and here he posed for the figure of St Michael. This is one of those rare windows that seem to yield something new every time; a particular delight.

Blundeston, St Mary (J1):

The tower is probably late *Saxon* and, with an internal diameter of 9ft., it is one of the smallest of the round towers. It tapers slightly and has a small brick w. window below small, erratically spaced *lancets*. The upper storey is likely to have been added in the C13, and the ring of brick shapes just below were no doubt the original bell openings. The size of the *nave* was vastly increased in the C14 so that it is now nearly 30ft. across; it seems that the old n. wall was retained and all the extra space added on the s. side, leaving the tower very much off-centre. The handsome *Decorated* windows on the n. side of the nave were a feature of the rebuilding, and their *ogee tracery* pattern has a miniature *quatrefoil* set within the top shape. The tall *chancel* side windows employ the same motif, and the e. window that was inserted in a mid-C19 rebuilding repeats the theme. The large expanse of carefully squared flint work in the s. wall is probably C19 as well, but the C14 *priest's door* remains untouched. The plain octagonal *font* which stands nearby came from the ruined

church of St Andrew in the neighbouring parish of Flixton, and on the other side of the path nearer the gate there is an unusual headstone. Schoolmaster George Chaston Fisk knew the habits of small boys, and before his death in 1835 he directed that three iron spikes should be added to his memorial to stop it being used for leapfrog. Two sockets and one spike on its weathered brow show that his wishes were respected. It is interesting that the pair of *Perpendicular* windows in the nave on the s. side pick up the little quatrefoil of the earlier design, and note that there is a *scratch dial* on the buttress nearest the *porch*. When the nave was rebuilt, the *Norman* n. door (now blocked) was amended, and a new one was provided on the s. side. Even that, however, made use of Norman shafts, but reversed them so that the *capitals* are now at the bottom. There are four charming little C17 Flemish figures in the side windows of the porch, and a modern sundial has been placed over the outer arch.

Just within the nave there is a *stoup to* the r., and below it is a head with a gaping mouth set in the wall. It has been suggested that it was another stoup for children, or was it perhaps a *gargoyle* originally? The *Royal Arms* of Charles II above the door are dated 1673; the painting is very worn and the heraldry remarkably confused. The supporters and half the shield are legible, but the rest displays a fragment of the arms of the Soame family. The most likely explanation is that it is an overpainted *hatchment* and, as such, is a unique reuse. The *font* is probably C12, and the sides of its deep octagonal bowl have the remains of a curious incised decoration. The tower arch is tall and narrow, with minimal *imposts*, and to the r. is a *squint* that passes through the w. wall. This puzzling feature is like the one at Lound, both in form and placement, and it has been suggested that it provided a view of the *altar* from outside. Possible but unlikely, and I suggest that it was used from inside to align with something outside. There is a similar arrangement at Thurne in Norfolk where the squint points directly to St Benet's abbey across the river. The wide nave lies under a C19 boarded waggon roof, but the old *arch-braces* are still in place and they rest on six good head *corbels*. The w. window on the n. side has glass of 1959 by Maile & Son – Christ with a family group, the figures set within clear glass (there are other windows by them at Kessingland and Somerleyton). Most of the bench ends against the wall are C15, with *poppyheads*, and halfway along the n. side there is the kneeling figure of a hooded man holding a heavy rosary. The nearest window retains fragments of its C14 glass. Blundeston is an example of the way in which small C15 Norfolk and Suffolk parishes lavished attention on their *screens*. It is an elaborate, compact design, with excellent tracery; the elongated ogee arches are *crocketted* and the thick, double *cusps* have flower terminals. The centre arch is lavish, and the screen was no doubt designed to carry a large *rood* group. The outer panels of the base are blank but the rest are painted with sixteen angels – small, slender figures, with delicate heads. Sadly faded and mutilated, every other one has a scroll: 'Passio Christi saluatoris', and so they probably bore *instruments of the Passion* like those at Hitcham, the only other known example of this subject on a screen. The nearest window on the n. side of the chancel has 1860s glass which is almost certainly by *Clayton & Bell*. The fine 1870s window opposite has as its subject Christ's Presentation in the Temple, and the excellent figures of Anna and Simeon with the Child are set against a deep blue pattern; there is colourful *tabernacle work* above, and charming flowers in the tracery – maker unknown. A grave slab in the floor on the n. side of the chancel has a faintly incised cross and probably commemorates a C13 or early-C14 priest. The deep *sanctuary* has no rails now, and *dropped-sill sedilia* lie alongside a *piscina* under its wide *trefoil* arch. There are two *brasses* on the s. side of the *altar*, for William and Bridgett Sydnor of 1613 (inscription and three shields), and for William and Ann Sidnor of 1632 (inscription only).

Visitors fresh from reading David Copperfield's vivid memories of his childhood will not find much that strikes a chord, although the grass outside is green enough and the tombstones still as quiet. The replacement pulpit would make a tolerably fine castle but the high-backed pews are no more, and I do not suppose that there ever was a 'Mr Bodgers late of this parish' – a shame, really.

Blyford, All Saints (I3): The neatly thatched Queen's Head is set back at the crossroads, and over the way stands the church. The *Perpendicular* tower has a *flushwork base course* and there is a line of *quatrefoils* below the w. window. A *drip course* breaks the outline below the bell openings, and stepped, flushwork battlements complete the picture. Circling the church, the first sign of its beginnings is the *Norman* s. doorway, simple and weathered, with *chevron* decoration and single *jamb shafts*. There are Perpendicular windows in the *nave*, but the *chancel* has C13

lancets and 'Y' *tracery* windows of about 1300, with a contemporary *priest's door* on the s. side. The chunky n. *porch* was added in the C15 and is said to have been copied from Halesworth. It has a complete flushwork facade, with a central canopied niche, and *Trinity* and *Passion* shields are carved in the *spandrels* of the outer arch. Within, there is another and more elaborate Norman doorway. Two bands of chevrons separated by a roll moulding form the arch, a beast head is set above, and there are pairs of flanking shafts; the outer pair have spiral carving, and the bottom half of the inner pair is decorated with a chequer pattern. There is a *stoup corbel* in the corner, and another stoup for good measure just inside.

In the n. wall, just to the w. of the entrance is a 12ft. *banner stave locker*, a feature seldom seen outside e. Norfolk and Suffolk. The C13 *font* stands in the s.w. corner, a plain octagon, with eight columns round the centre shaft. A single plastered ceiling covers all, with no arch or *screen* dividing nave from chancel. The benches and pulpit are C19, and on the n. wall a tablet commemorates Edmund Freeman, killed in action off Guadaloupe in 1809, 'aged 21 years, 5 weeks and 4 days' – a curious particularity. Capt. W.E. Day was killed in action in June 1916, and his Flanders cross has been brought back here, although there is another memorial for him in the chancel. A C19 tablet sets out in some detail what should be done with the interest on a £100 bequest, and one of the *quarries* in the nearby window has a little handwritten trade advertisement: 'Jas Wright Plumber, Glazier, Halesworth Suffolk 1822'. A similar piece of modest enterprise can be seen at Barnby. In the *sanctuary*, the C13 *angle piscina* has *trefoil* arches, and there are *dropped-sill sedilia* alongside. The *Holy table* is a splendid late Elizabethan example, with carved bulbous legs and skirt. No medieval glass survives, but when *Dowsing* called in April 1643, he noted 30 superstitious pictures, a crucifix, and the *four Evangelists*. He extracted a promise that the steps would be levelled, and that a cross would be removed from the chancel, together with the emblems on the porch. As we have seen, they at least escaped.

Blythburgh, Holy Trinity (I3): There was a time when Blythburgh was a lively, bustling port, and in the C15 its people rebuilt their church on a grand scale to match their prosperity. But as trade declined and moved away, their fortunes waned, and it became a struggle to keep the great building in repair. In 1597 it was reported that 'the *chancel* is in great ruin and decay and the roof is ready to fall down'. By 1663, there had been no communion service held for twelve years, in the mid-C19 the church was 'mouldering into ruin', and in 1880 the little congregation sheltered under umbrellas as rain poured through the roof. Restoration began at last and has continued steadily ever since, with the reglazing of the *clerestory* completed in 1990 – a triumph over the years for a village whose population is a mere 300.

The great rebuilding began with the chancel in about 1442 and lasted some thirty years. Meanwhile, the early-C14 tower of the earlier building was retained and a grand replacement to match the rest of the church was probably intended. Changing fortunes ruled this out, and it remains, severe and stark by comparison. It had a spire originally, but this fell in the great tempest of 1577 – of which more later. The tower's angle buttresses, panelled with *flushwork*, stop short at the bell stage, there is renewed *Decorated tracery* in the w. window, and the tall belfry windows are shuttered. Walking round, you will see that there is a turret at the n.w. corner of the n. aisle, giving access to the roof, and the n. doorway has *griffin* and lion *stops*. When medieval masons were rebuilding, they often used stones from the earlier building, and there is an example of this in the second buttress to the e. of the doorway – three sections from *Norman* window arches used as *quoins* in the internal angles. Further along, a buttress was enlarged to house the *rood loft stair,* and the *priest's door* in the n. chancel wall shelters beneath a flying buttress, with a similar arrangement on the s. side (where there is a very large *scratch dial* to be seen). The *aisles* reach to within a single bay of the e. end, and both of the *sanctuary* side windows are still blocked with brick. There is panelled flushwork on either side of the five-*light* e. window, and below it, a unique dedication inscription. In a set of 14 panels the sequence of crowned initials almost certainly stand for 'Ad nomina sancti Johannis Baptista sancta Trinitatis Marie [et] Sancte Anne his Kancellus reconstructus est' – 'In the name of St John the Baptist, [St] Mary and St Anne this chancel was rebuilt'. Using the flushwork panels as evidence the rebuilding was clearly the work of the Aldryche firm of master masons at N. Lopham in Norfolk. The sequence was restored in 1981. Note that within the 'T', the shield is a Trinity emblem, and on the gable overhead there is another symbol of the church's dedication – the figure of God the Father which now lacks the figure of the crucified Christ between his knees. As at Southwold, 18 closely spaced clerestory windows range almost the whole length of *nave* and chancel. With the main entrance on that side, the s. frontage is more lavish, and the aisle has a wonderfully bold parapet of pierced *quatrefoils*, each with a perky *finial*. This is reminiscent of Bungay St Mary, and may have been copied from there. Figures and beasts, including chained bears and a monkey, stand above the buttresses, and the parapet continues round the *porch* whose facade is simply square *knapped* flints. A fine *stoup* stands by the entrance, with traceried shaft, and bowl carved with demi-angels bearing crowns. The porch is vaulted, and its upper room has been arranged as a place of quiet retreat, with a simple *altar* and benches. At the head of its narrow, winding stair, a little *squint* allowed the priest who occupied it to watch the altar of the *chantry chapel* in the n. aisle.

The w. half of the church is cleared of benches, and this accentuates the wonderful feeling of spaciousness. The *arcades*, with their quatrefoil *piers* continue into the chancel, and the lovely roof runs without interruption from end to end. It is an *arch-braced tie-beam* construction, and the tie-beams have large demi-angels in the centre facing e. and w., with wings outstretched. Frustrated at not being able to reach them, *Dowsing*'s men fired buckshot at them as they did at Mildenhall. He left orders for 20 cherubims and 'above 200 more pictures' [i.e. stained glass] to be taken down within eight days. The church accounts record that six shillings were paid 'to Master Dowson that came with the Troopers to our church about the taking down of Images and Brasses off the stones'. Nearly all of the roof's original colouring survives and the patterns are reminiscent of contemporary altar frontals – white rafters with foliage springing from red *Sacred monograms*, the spaces between painted red with black roses. A replica of one of the angels in full colour was made by the Institute of Archaeology in 1977 and is displayed above the s. door. The arched-braces of the aisle roofs rest on stone head *corbels*, and there is attractive tracery in the inner *spandrels*. A medieval bell headstock and wheel are displayed by the entrance to the porch chamber, and in the base of the tower hang the ropes of an excellent ring of six bells with a 10 cwt. tenor. In a case at the w. end of the n. aisle you will find a copy of the 'Judas' Bible published by John Barker in 1613, so called because Matthew 26:36 reads 'Then cometh Judas [instead of Jesus] with them'. The *font* was undoubtedly one of the *Seven Sacrament* series, but its panels have been completely cleared of detail (as at Southwold and Wenhaston); there are linked demi-angels below the bowl, the shaft has niches below nodding *ogee* arches, and there are traces of colour. Parts of the bowl have been broken away, a reminder that when the spire fell in 1577 it crashed into the nave, hitting the font and killing a man and a boy in the congregation. Many others were scorched by the lightning bolt, and all were sure that it was a visit by the Devil in person: "Did he not leave his finger marks on the n. door as he left, which can be seen to this very day?" There are traces of an inscription on the font's top step, and it read: 'Orate pro animabus Johne Masin et Katerine uxoris ejus qui istum fontem fieri fecerunt' (Pray for the souls of John Masin and Katherine his wife who had this font made). The stone kneelers for priest and godparents are not to be found anywhere else in the county.

The benches in the nave and aisles were originally backless, and the carvings on the ends formed part of three different series; they have been re-arranged so that some now face w. instead of e. They date from about 1475 and are a fascinating collection. Look first at those in the s. aisle: the 2nd from the w. is the Sower, from a Seasons series, with the reaper having lost his head next but one along. On the s. side of the nave starting at the w. end, one finds a *Seven Deadly Sins* sequence, starting with Avarice seated on his treasure chest. Then comes Hypocrisy peering open-eyed over his fingers as he kneels, followed by Gluttony hugging his fat belly, and Pride smirking in his fine robes. On the n. side of the nave, the first figure is Winter (from the Seasons), followed by Autumn (?) and Spring; the next carving is an angel bearing a Trinity shield, followed by three seated figures. In the n. aisle, from the w., the first carving is one of a *Seven Works of Mercy* sequence, 'burying the dead', and shows a coffin being lowered into the grave. Next comes 'visiting the prisoners', with a man in the stocks. In the next carving, a man sits up in bed and probably signified the sin of Sloth, although it could also represent the mercy of 'visiting the sick'. One of the most interesting carvings is second from the e. end of the aisle, a priest in cassock and biretta holding a bouquet. Flowers and sprays of blossom were often carried in procession at *rogationtide*, and some 'labours of the months' series have such a figure to represent the month of May. The mid-C15 lectern is contemporary with the benches and is one of the few wooden examples

of the period to survive. With its double slope, it will have been designed for use in the choir, and it has close set buttresses reaching halfway up the octagonal shaft. A robin nested within it in the 1880s, and another did the same fifty years later, events commemorated on pieces of embroidery and the heads of the churchwardens' staves. Strangely enough, the same thing happened in a wooden lectern at Ringsfield. The 1670s pulpit has decorative shallow arabesque and flower designs in two tiers of panels, with large scroll brackets below the book ledge. Good examples of *masons' marks* can be easily identified on the pillar behind the pulpit. There were *guilds* here dedicated to *St Barbara*, *St Andrew*, *St John* and the *Blessed Virgin*, and the corbel carved with her monogram on the pier nearest to the lectern probably marks the site of her *guild altar*. A large *piscina* with a wooden *credence shelf* sited just in front of the s. aisle *screen* shows that there was another altar there. Fragments of the church's C15 stained glass have been collected in two of the aisle windows, and in the n. aisle there are panels of modern heraldic glass on either side of the memorial to Ernest Crofts, Keeper of the Royal Academy, whose tablet bears a fine bas-relief profile head in bronze by Allan G. Wyon.

Most of the centre section of the *rood screen* is modern, but the aisle ranges are original, although they have lost all of their surface decoration. The *rood loft* stretched right across the church, and the access stair lies in the n. wall just to the e. of the screen. The n. aisle chapel was originally a *chantry chapel* endowed by Lord of the Manor John Hopton in 1451, and later served for many years as the village school. In a n. window an attractive panel of stained glass by Andrew Anderson combines builders' and carpenters' tools with initials to commemorate Bill Muttitt, the craftsman who played a vital role in the 1970s roof restoration and who was churchwarden here for many years. In the tracery above there are more C15 fragments, with figures of saints, and the glass may have come from the same Kings Lynn workshop that supplied Wiggenhall St Mary Magdalene and Sandringham. They probably all had name labels originally, and one can still identify *St Eleutherius* on the l., *St Paul*, and *St Felix*. The poorbox by the door is dated 1473 and has served ever since the church was built. There is very beautiful deep tracery on its shaft, and the top is secured with a pair of C19 handcuffs. The choir stalls were moved from the n. chapel during a C19 restoration, and their front panels (earlier than the ends) probably formed part of the rood loft originally. Most of the well-carved figures have a family likeness as far as the heads are concerned, and they stand under boldly carved nodding ogee arches. The identifying emblems are particularly good, and on the n. side, from l. to r. they are: *SS Stephen*, John, *John the Baptist, Matthew, Matthias, Bartholomew, Philip*, Andrew, *Luke*. On the s. side, from l. to r.: *SS Thomas, James the Great, James the Less, Jude, Simon*, Paul, *Peter*. Tradition has it that the last two figures represent Anna, King of the East Angles and his daughter *St Etheldreda*. The king and his son were buried here in 654, after they had been killed in battle nearby, and so the attribution is not unlikely. When the stalls were used in the side chapel as desks for the village school, holes were cut in the sloping tops for inkwells, and at the e. end of the s. range, a Swedish boy cut his name in 1665: Dirck Lowersen van Stockholm. He must have been the son of one of the men who came over from the Low Countries in the C17 to cope with the silting up of the river. The canopied *Purbeck marble* tomb of John Hopton lies between the chancel and the n. chapel. The sides of the chest are traceried, with small centre shields re-coloured, and there is an unusual draped linen effect below the slab. The *groining* is closely traceried, and there is a triple frieze above on both sides; the *brass*, along with all the others in the church was filched by Dowsing. The position and form of the tomb make it fairly certain that it was used as an *Easter sepulchre*. The painted figure of a bearded man in mid-C16 armour on the other side of the chancel is a clock jack (apparently of 1682 which seems very late), designed to strike the hours of a clock. Disconnected now, and repaired so that he strikes the bell with his axe and turns his head, it is one of the few examples left in England, although another is to be found nearby at Southwold.

Botesdale, St Botolph (E3): At the top of the village street, this little church has an interesting pedigree. It was founded as a chapel of ease for Redgrave (and gave the village its name – Botolph's Dale) about the year 1500. Later, it was restored and endowed as a *chantry* chapel by John Herife, his wife, Juliana, and Bridget Wykys. Above the door is a large *flushwork* inscription which was damaged by the insertion of a window. A possible translation of the complete original might be: 'Pray for the souls of John Shreve and Juliana his wife. Pray for the soul of Margaret Wykes.' Shreve, who died c.1480 gave lands to endow the chapel, thus

financing its rebuilding by the Aldryche firm of N. Lopham, Norfolk in the 1480s. Chantries were abolished and their endowments plundered in 1547 and so this one had a relatively short life. Then, in 1576, Sir Nicholas Bacon of Redgrave took over the building as Lord of the Manor, and used it to found a Grammar School. He added the house to the r. which shares the same roof. So it continued until it reverted to being a church in 1884. There are *Perpendicular* windows under flint and red brick arches, and a single bell is perched on the roof ridge without any cover. Pass through the original door to an interior lobby which is divided from the chapel proper by a simple screen, such as would be found in substantial houses of the period. The *gallery* above was constructed at the same time and now houses a chamber organ; below is a small C19 *font*. The chapel has a plain *arch-braced* roof, with plastered ceiling between the principals and no division marking the *chancel*. There are C19 pitchpine pews and a plain, angled set of *communion rails*. The C19 glass in the e. window, by *Heaton, Butler & Bayne* is rather good. The centre panels depict the visit of the Magi, and on either side there are scenes of Christ's baptism, His teaching in the temple, the Last Supper (with Judas turning away from the table with his purse), and Gethsemane. Musical angels inhabit the top *tracery*.

Boulge, St Michael and All Angels (G5): Boulge Hall was pulled down in 1956 and the parish is a mere handful of scattered cottages and farms. There are two routes across the park, but the one from the Bredfield/Debach road is ungated and winds through the fields until it comes to a leafy tunnel of trees that leads to the churchyard. In the C13 an older building was replaced, and a modest brick tower was added in the early C16, but the character of the present church was largely determined by the Victorians. An 1858 restoration by W.G. & E. Habershon rebuilt the e. end and added a s. *aisle*, and nine years later a s. *transept* was added, the *chancel* was rebuilt, and the walls were re-faced by Habershon & Pite. Finally, in 1895, a new *vestry*/organ chamber was built on the s. side. Coming in from the s.e. corner of the churchyard one is faced with the two large flint-faced gables – the vestry with a circular window over the door, and the transept. The latter has its own door and (rather confusingly) is placed where one would expect a s. *porch* to be. The *knapped* flintwork is exceptionally good, particularly round the s. window. The C14 n. doorway was untouched by the restorations and there is one 'Y' tracery window of about 1300 on that side. The large C19 mausoleum of the Fitzgerald family stands s.w. of the tower. It has a hipped, stone-slated roof and is half submerged, with steps down to its C13-style doorway. Guarded by heavy iron railings, it is crumbling gradually to ruin, and is in no way remarkable but for the fact that the one member of the family with a claim to fame is not buried within but has his own simple grave slab alongside. Edward Fitzgerald lived most of his life in this part of Suffolk, a gentle scholar who numbered Thackeray and Tennyson among his friends. His work would have been forgotten by the world at large had he not issued a little anonymous pamphlet in 1859 entitled *The Rubáiyát of Omar Khayyám*. Few other single poems of its class have been so widely known and loved, a singular tribute to the genius of its translator. He died in 1883 and ten years later a rose was planted at the head of his grave – no ordinary rose, however, for artist William Simpson had been to Omar Khayyám's tomb at Nishapur; the seeds he took from the roses blooming there were cultivated at Kew and one of the bushes was planted here. Six more roses came from Iran in 1972 to mark the 2500th anniversary of the Persian empire.

The interior is rather dark but once the lights are switched on it is remarkably attractive. The massive *font* that stands in the tower is one of a group of only eight in England and is made of black marble quarried at Tournai in Belgium. Dating from 1150-70, the best-known ones are in Winchester and Lincoln cathedrals, but there is another in the redundant church of St Peter, Ipswich. The sides are normally sculpted with scriptural or legendary subjects but unfortunately this one has had all its decoration carefully chiselled away, save for a few fragments beneath the corners. Nearby hangs a C19 *Decalogue* board set in an oak frame, and round the corner on the w. wall is an elegant tablet of 1792 for William Whitby. Excellently lettered within a narrow beige border, it has a small urn *finial* between scrolls above and a shield of arms with palm fronds below. The glass in the nearby *lancet* celebrated Queen Victoria's Diamond Jubilee and has a profile portrait of her held aloft by a pair of youthful angels above the *Royal Arms*. A set of George IV arms painted on canvas hangs above the n. door. Farther along on that side, stained glass which may be by *Clayton & Bell* commemorates a Suffolk Regiment lieutenant and his comrades who fell near Colesberg in the Boer War; the regimental badge is in the tracery

above the figures of *St Michael* and *Gabriel*. The transept is two bays wide, and e. of it, beyond a half-arch, is a family pew which has its own arch to the nave resting on large leafy *capitals*. Stiff Victorian Gothic memorials to the Fitzgeralds abound, and the glass by *Arthur J. Dick* in the transept window dates from 1906. The centre Crucifixion is reminiscent of the one by *Kempe* at Burgh and is flanked by figures of *St Edmund* and *St Felix*. The tracery has Christ the King, an *Annunciation* and Christ's baptism, and all is very lush. The glass of 1940 in the window farther along is not particularly distinguished – figures of Justice and Charity alongside Christ as the Light of the World – but look for the sweet little vignettes slipped in under the main figures: a view of the church, a waggon being loaded, and a cow. The artist is unknown but he may also have designed the glass in the n. chancel window which commemorates Lieut. Cdr. Robert White and the ship's company of HMS *Duchess*, sunk in action in 1939. There is a figure of *St Faith* and one of *St Nicholas* carrying a model of the ship. Strangely, and apparently as an afterthought, someone has added crudely painted anchors to the front of his chasuble. There is a blocked C13 window on the n. side of the *sanctuary*, and a few C14 tiles have been re-set within its splay. They probably formed part of the floor (like those at Icklingham, All Saints, and one bears an heraldic shield. The *altar* is a simple *Stuart* table which stands in front of a white marble *reredos* of 1913 whose design is taken from the C5 sarcophagus of Valentinian III, the Western emperor at Ravenna. A lamb, with two doves perching on a cross behind it, stands in a shallow portico with twisted columns and matching arches each side.

Boxford, St Mary (D6): This was one of Suffolk's prosperous wool villages, with a population of over 400 in the early-C16, and the houses cluster attractively round its splendid church. The tower is C14 and grotesques crouch on the lowest *weatherings* of the w. buttresses (like those at Great Waldingfield). Note that the *dripstones* of the weatherings are continued up into the corners to finish with more grotesques. The C16 w. doors are panelled, with a carved border, and the *transomed Perpendicular* window overhead is flanked by remnants of niches and a *flushwork arcade*. There is a stair turret on the s. side to belfry level bearing a C19(?) slate sundial, and the tower is crowned by a pretty little wooden octagon with a ring of wooden spirelets and flying buttresses round the leaded spike on top. The main entrance was originally on the n. side where the bulk of the village lay and there one finds the county's finest example of a C14 wooden *porch*. It is tall, with an entrance arch formed from two moulded planks flanked by niches, and there are pairs of large windows each side with *Decorated tracery* cut from 2ft. wide planks laid crosswise. Within, triple-shafted columns with *ring capitals* support the skeletal ribs of a *groined* ceiling which would have been panelled out originally. Overall, it illustrates perfectly the way in which C14 carpenters copied the patterns and designs of the masons before evolving their own disciplines. The arch of the inner doorway rests on angel *headstops* with two ranks of eroded *paterae* in the mouldings and the doors have a band of *quatrefoils* at the edge. Circling the church, you will find a *vestry* rather like a little doll's house with a tall chimney tucked into the angle by the chancel, and an e. window with panel tracery above five *ogee*-headed *lights*. Just below the e. window of the s.e. chapel there is an unusual headstone of 1821 which has a cast-iron plaque of two maidens and an urn clamped to the top which bids fair to outlast the stone itself. There is a *priest's door* on this side and the main entrance is now through the splendid C15 s. porch. Money was bequeathed for it between 1441 and 1480 and there were burials there in 1465 – always a spot favoured by the medieval wealthy. Unfortunately the soft stone has perished badly but it is one of the most lavish in Suffolk, particularly in its minor details. The *jambs* of the four-light side windows, for instance, are enriched with miniature stooled and vaulted niches and the buttresses are intricately panelled. The porch has a double *base course* of shields in quatrefoils and the side parapets are panelled and pierced. The frontage is terribly worn and only parts of the *Annunciation* scene in the spandrels survive – the archangel on the l. bears a scroll and the *Blessed Virgin's* lily emblem can be seen on the r. Above, there are seven niches in a line, all groined, with a vine trail underneath. The entrance doors have some tracery and a quatrefoiled rim, and note how the step has been worn away by countless people making use of the l.-hand door only.

The body of the church was rebuilt in the C15 and the arcades rest on quatrefoil *piers* with bold *hood moulds* to the arches. The size of the chancel and its side chapels makes the nave seem short for its height, and the heavy cambered *tie-beams* of the roof have *wall posts* resting on small head *corbels*. The w. *gallery* with its moulded front beam is set just below the spring of the tower

arch and was probably installed in the early C16. Below it there is an C18 charity board and a section of roof lead embossed with the names of churchwardens, carpenter, and plumber in 1805. The *font* stands by a pillar opposite the s. door and although the bowl is modern its C15 shaft is panelled in the form of mullioned windows. What makes it special is the C17 octagonal cover, which is built like a cupboard, with two hinged doors and a graceful ogee cap. The faded green of the inside is painted with red and cream scrolls which are lettered with texts from *St John's* Gospel: 'How can a man be borne which is old?', 'Except a man be borne of water and of the spirit, he cannot enter the Kingdom', and 'If I wash thee not thou hast no part with me'. The new step has been finely cut with a text from the Beatitudes: 'Blessed are the pure in heart . . .' The iron-bound chest in the n. aisle is probably late-C14 but, unlike the majority of medieval examples, it is made of softwood rather than oak or chestnut. The C18 pulpit has a typically restrained marquetry design with the *Sacred monogram* in one panel, and the fact that capitals from *Corinthian pilasters* are strangely attached underneath suggests that its parts may have come from a *reredos*. The shaped stair rail is beautifully done, with pairs of *balusters* like old-fashioned sticks of barley sugar.

The chancel arch is tall and wide and there is no longer a *screen*. However, the upper door to the old *rood loft* is prominent on the n. side, and there is a second opening towards the n. aisle which means that it probably connected with another loft over a *parclose screen*. Above the chancel arch is a fine painting of two *censing* angels which was uncovered in 1955. They have pale blue wings and between them is a tiny Christ in Majesty. To the l. on the *clerestory* wall is another fragment and it must have formed part of a large scheme designed to complement the rood below, painted soon after the C15 clerestory was built. A shield dated 1685 on the e. tie-beam indicates that the roof was altered slightly then, partially obscuring the angels. Before the *Reformation* there were guilds of *SS John, Peter, Christopher*, and the *Trinity*, and the two chancel chapels may have been associated with them. The arcade to the s. matches the nave but the lozenge shape of the pier on the n. side indicates a slightly later date. The e. wall of the s. chapel has two niches, one above the other, on either side of the window, groined and stooled but with their canopies shorn away. Those on the l. retain a great deal of their original colour and the shadowy marks within show the size of the images that once filled them. By the window on that side is a painting of *St Edmund* clutching one of the arrows of his martyrdom. There are sections of *linen-fold panelling* behind the late-C17 *Holy table* and, to the r., a *piscina* lies below a mutilated ogee arch. A plain tablet on the s. wall of the chapel carries the singular epitaph of Elizabeth Hyam: '. . . for the fourth time widow; who by a fall that brought on a mortification was at last hastened to her end on the 4th May 1748 in her 113th year'. An earlier and equally engaging memorial is the tiny *brass* in the n.e. corner of the chapel. It is for David Birde, the rector's son, who died a few months old in 1606. The tiny engraving shows him in a cradle with rockers and turned corner posts. A larger brass at the w. end of the chancel is for John Brond, who died four years later, and the inscription is less than specific: '. . . having in his life time two wives & left behind him by either of his wives divers children'. There could be a lot felt but left unsaid behind that! The n.e. chapel is now taken up by the organ and vestry but it is worth exploring if possible because there are some more brasses – for William Birde, 'sometyme Pastor of this churche' (1599), Robert Bird, another of the rector's sons (1612), and a plate within a strapwork border for William Doggett with his wife Avis. He died in 1610 and was 'Marchant adve(n)terer, citizen and mercer of London and free of the East India Company'. There were never effigies but four shields carry the arms of the City of London (top l.), the Mercers' Company (top r.), the Merchant Adventurers (bottom l. with faulty heraldry), and the East India Company (bottom r. and also inaccurate). The shields were originally inlaid with colour and some of the lead infilling survives. The C18 *communion rails* in the chancel have elegantly turned balusters and the e. window is filled with striking 1970s glass by Rosemary Rutherford. It is a Transfiguration scene in which tremendously elongated figures of Christ flanked by Moses and Elijah tower above the crouching figures of the disciples. The red and yellow flame-like centre splinters outwards into cooler colours, and the lead lines radiate and encircle the centre. More of this artist's work can be found at Hinderclay. The sixth of Boxford's ring of eight bells was cast by Thomas Potter in Norwich in the late-C14 and has an exceptionally beautiful inscription in large Lombardic capitals; this excellent ring was fully restored by Taylor's of Loughborough in 1997.

Boxted, Holy Trinity (C5): A little church that is sweetly situated in rolling meadowland above the village in the valley. The unbuttressed C14 tower has a modern short three-*light* window beneath the *Perpendicular* w. window and there are *gargoyles* below the parapet. Although there is no s. *aisle* the *nave* has large, late Perpendicular *clerestory* windows and those below are C19 replacements. The *chancel*, with its *priest's door*, is plastered and the s.e. window projects between buttresses under a little tiled cap. On the other side of the chancel stands the C18 brick chapel of the Poley family and the brick battlements continue along the n. aisle whose C14 door is blocked. Oddly, a little round brick chimney is perched on the n.w. corner. The C19 timber *porch*, with heavy barge boards and openwork sides, is very pleasing and it leads to a charming interior. A modern wooden *gallery* and screen have been inserted in the tower and there are C19 benches with *poppyheads* in the nave (with two C16 examples enclosed at the w. end); two ranges of *box pews* at the front are matching and are presumably a late example of that comfortable form. The cambered *tie-beams* of the roof are carved with a folded leaf pattern and the angel supporters are dated 1885 – one of the signs of the lavish restorations of the C19. The narrow n. aisle lies beyond a low C14 *arcade* on octagonal *piers* and at the w. end is a plain C14 *font*. The other two bays were formed into private pews by the insertion of *Jacobean* screens with turned uprights, and one of them now houses the organ. In the other you will find the remains of a *piscina* near the floor which shows that there was an *altar* in the aisle long before the pews were made and the Poley chapel built. There is a recess to the l. of the chancel arch which shows where the stair to the *rood loft* emerged, and above the chancel arch is an open arcade of three wooden arches – a modern insertion that seems extraordinarily eccentric. The *Stuart* pulpit has shallow carved arches in the lower panels with rose roundels above, and over the backboard the *tester* has turned pendants and is dated 1618. The chancel roof is early-C17 and therefore a late example of a *hammerbeam* construction and is very similar to the nave roof at Wickhambrook; there are openwork panels above the hammers and pierced pendants below. The *sanctuary* has a very nice set of late-C17 three-sided *communion rails* with twisted *balusters*, while all around are reminders of the Poleys. *Hatchments* hang overhead dating from 1756 to 1849, and to the r. of the altar is a most interesting tomb. It is entirely black, with no inscription or decoration, and on the chest lie the oaken figures of William Poley and his wife

Alice who died in 1587 and 1579 respectively. Wooden effigies were out of fashion by about 1350 but there was a revival in the C16 and these, black like the tomb, are very good examples in beautiful condition. He wears armour over embroidered breeches and his head, with its long moustache and beard, rests on a helm. She wears a French cap, with three chains round her neck and the prayer book suspended from her girdle is carved with their joint arms. As I said, there is no inscription but round her pillow is carved 'Beati mortui qui in Domino moriuntur' (Blessed are the dead who die in the Lord) and 'A.P. 1579 Mar 7'. There are good *ledger-stones* in the chancel, including one for John Worsley of 1625 with a fine epitaph. In the n.e. corner is a *brass* inscription for Richard Poley of 1546 and the e. window is a memorial for Hugh Thomas Weller-Poley, killed at 20 in the RAF in 1942. The design is by William Aikman – the figure of Christ in bright middle-eastern robes, with rays of light springing from Him; below are vignettes of the church and Boxted Hall, with rabbits on the greensward. Through an arch is the Poley chapel which contains two excellent and important statues, both standing in arched niches. Sir John Poley died in 1638; in pink-veined alabaster, he poses hand on hip, while his helm and gloves lie behind his feet. The modelling is crisp and lively, the pose taut and convincing. Coloured arms in a *cartouche* are above the alcove, with swags of fruit picked out in gilt, and *putti* draw aside the drapes each side. A finely lettered epitaph is set within an *acanthus* frame below while wreathed skulls adorn the corners of the base. All was meticulously restored in 1986. The monument was probably not erected until 1680 and its quality has suggested to some that it is the work of John Bushnell, that eccentric C17 genius. Sir John served in France under Henry IV and in Denmark, and he wears a small golden frog in his left ear that may be the badge of a continental order of chivalry. It has been said that it denotes the Danish order of the Elephant but the Royal College of Arms in Copenhagen refute this. It does, however, provide an intriguing link with the rhyme:

The frog he would a wooing go,
With a Roley Poley Gammon and Spinach

– a probable reference to the local families, the Roleys, Poleys, Bacons and Greens. Dame Abigail died in 1652 but her statue was not installed until 1725; London work and roughly matching her husband's effigy, but the arch-itectural frame is simpler. It is perhaps the latest work in English alabaster until the C19. On the w. wall is an omnibus epitaph for the family lettered on an open book with an urn at the top, and below it the descent of the Poleys from the C14 to the C20 is displayed on two marble scrolls. In front lies a C13 coffin lid and a stone child's coffin of the same period, while the shaft of a *pillar piscina* can be found on the window sill. The window contains some medieval glass, including a king's head, and the 1930s heraldic glass is again by William Aikman.

Boyton, St Andrew (H6): A peaceful spot where the church stands apart from the village, keeping company with a graceful range of C18/19 almshouses. Except for the tower, the church was rebuilt in 1869, and William Smith's design more or less doubled it in size. The C14 tower was probably a stage higher at one time and it now has a tile cap behind a deep parapet. The angle buttresses have been repaired with brick, and there is a two-*light Decorated* window above the blocked w. doorway. Next to a heavy stair turret on the n. side you will see that the corner of the original *Norman nave* survives, the *quoins* carved with a shaft. Smith added a n. *transept* (with a chimney on the gable), and reused Norman masonry for its doorway. The outer range of carving uses *chevrons* at right angles to a roll moulding, and the two inner ranges display an unusual form of ribbed chevron. It is likely that the stones were salvaged from two doorways and then combined. The walls are faced with typically dense C19 flintwork, and all the windows are C14 style. The inner Tudor doorway of the *porch* was retained and it has leopard heads, hung shields, and *fleurons* in the mouldings.

Within, nearly everything is Victorian, including the *font*. Half of the transept is partitioned off for a *vestry* complete with fireplace, and the space in front is fitted with a low-level bench for children. The C17 table nearby may have served as the church's *altar*, and it has had two rather nasty pine stretchers screwed on to the bottom frame. Although there are pine benches in the nave, the lectern, openwork pulpit and choir stalls are in oak. In the *sanctuary* n. wall, an *aumbry* with a metal door was provided for the reservation of the sacrament. The glass in the e. window is probably by *Ward & Hughes*, and has the figure of Christ in the centre, flanked by his disciples, illustrating the concluding verses of *St Matthew's* gospel; angels fill the upper *trefoils*, and there are *crocketted* canopies and attractive vine patterns.

Bradfield Combust, All Saints (C5): The church stands by the side of the busy Bury to Sudbury road and there is a venerable cedar in the churchyard. Although you may not feel inclined to obey the charge: 'Let every real patriot shed a tear, for genius talents worth lies here', pause at the tomb of Arthur Young just e. of the *chancel*. He was not a successful farmer himself but at a time when the mould of medieval practice was being broken in agriculture, his writings played a vital part in assisting the change. In 1768 he began publishing a series of *Tours* that gave accurate accounts of farming in England, Ireland and France, and his *Farmer's Calendar* went through many editions. Young became secretary to Pitt's Board of Agriculture in 1793 and organised the publication of county surveys (writing some himself) which have never been equalled in their comprehensiveness. His last years were sadly clouded by blindness and melancholia and he died in 1820. The walls of the stubby chancel are in banded red brick and flint and there is a tiny *priest's door* in the corner. The C19 e. window has a beautiful *tracery* design based on three *trefoils* and could conceivably repeat the original. The s. *aisle* is C14 and the w. end of the nave was remodelled in the C19 when it received a new window below a quirky bellcote for three bells. Within the wooden *porch* of 1861 is a plain C14 doorway but note that the arch was re-cut and given a moulding 200 years later. In order that it may serve a variety of purposes for the village, the *nave* and aisle have been carpeted and re-seated with very comfortable chairs spaciously arranged. The interior is rather dark but the first things that catch the eye are the early-C15 paintings on the n. wall. In the corner there is a large and lovely *St George* wearing black armour and wielding both sword and lance. Long red mantling flows from his crested helm and he wears his emblem on breast and shoulders; his caparisoned charger rears over the head of the dragon. Alongside is an equally fine *St Christopher* – a huge figure in red tunic, with the Christ child wearing a red robe seated on his right shoulder. The saint holds a massive, sprouting staff; there are fishes in the river and the hermit stands by his hut on the r. Below the painting is a tall, blocked *Norman* archway and you may have noticed outside that a C14 doorway was inserted within it. The Norman *font* stands on a short drum shaft and the underside of the square bowl is scalloped; the e. face was later carved with a *quatrefoil* within an arch flanked by side panels. The C14 *arcade* has three unequal bays and in the aisle chapel there

is a double *piscina* under a pair of trefoil arches and a pierced quatrefoil; there are *dropped-sill sedilia* alongside. The C19 glass in this aisle is good. The 1899 e. window is likely to be by the *Powells* (Christ the King with grouped female saints); the pair of 1850s windows in the side wall are by *Lavers & Barraud* (an early *Westlake* design), in C13 style and glowing with deep, rich colour. It is worth noting that the figure of the risen Christ displays no wounds. There is a Victorian stone pulpit and although there is no *rood screen* now, the old stair turret shows outside to the n. The aisle and chancel roofs are C19 but the *nave* retains the medieval *tie-beams* and *arch-braces*. The glass in the chancel e. window is a memorial to Arthur Young, put in by public subscription in 1869, long after his death. By Lavers, Barraud & Westlake, it is a Crucifixion displaying unusually good colour and composition; witness the varying attitudes of the angels above the mourners, the centurion, and the weeping *St Mary Magdalene* at the foot of the cross. On the n. wall is a marble tablet below a pyramid and *cartouche* of arms for Arthur Young senior, 'who was 40 years rector here and died in 1759. There are more Young memorials in the little *vestry* and perhaps the most affecting is for Martha, Arthur's 14-year-old daughter: ' "Pray for me papa – Now! Amen" Her last words'.

Bradfield St Clare, St Clare (D5): Set in the midst of fields with only a thatched farmhouse for company, this little church, bearing a unique dedication, is ringed about by oak, Scots pine, and horse chestnuts that hang low over the churchyard gates. A great deal of careful restoration was done in the 1870s and 100 years later an ambitious programme of renewal has left the fabric in good heart. The C14 tower has strong diagonal buttresses to the w. and the other pair continues the line of the e. face. There is a flint panelled *base course* and the w. window and bell openings all have *Decorated tracery*. The *nave* and *chancel* have renewed Perpendicular windows and the s. *porch* was 'thoroughly restored' in 1921. There is, in addition, a blocked late-C12 n. door and a *Tudor priest's door* in the s. wall of the chancel. By one of those odd accidents of history, a small piece of a C13 grave slab is embedded under the eaves in the s.w. corner of the chancel, with a portion of the double omega sign showing. Inside, all is freshly lime-washed and beautifully neat. A small *stoup* is set in the wall to the r. of the door and to the l. is a C19 octagonal *font*. The tower arch is blocked with a modern door inserted, and the C19 nave roof is a copy of the C14 original; it has tall *king posts* resting on the *tie-beams*, with *scissors-bracing* under the ridge. In a s. window tracery are some pieces of C15 glass. Beyond the wide, plain chancel arch the light-coloured C15 roof has fragments of tracery above the collars of the *arch-braces* and the *wall plates* have a double *castellation*. The stalls incorporate three medieval *poppyheads* carved with leaf forms and in the *sanctuary* is a small *piscina* under a *trefoil* arch. The *Decalogue*, Creed and Lord's Prayer are painted on canvas within oak frames on the e. wall and the three kneelers in front of the rails are quite special. They have the village name writ large and a panorama of the countryside from the s.w. of the church – all embroidered by George Insley in 1976. On the n. wall is a plain marble tablet by de Carle of Bury for Robert Davers, a C19 vicar. Over the priest's door is a small *touchstone* tablet in an alabaster frame for Richard Grandorge and his family. He was priest here for 41 years, dying in 1619, and his epitaph is worth quoting:

> Greatness sounds in his name, his hart was
> lowly,
> His soule was faithful, and his life was holy.
> Here lies the man who longe this flock did
> feed,
> I know not whether more, by tonge or
> deed...

Bradfield St George, St George (D5): This is rather a coy church that hides itself w. of the village and at the end of a lane a little curving avenue of limes crosses the churchyard to the s. *porch*. The tower is C15 although the w. window and bell openings have *Decorated tracery*. There is an inscription shared between two panels at the bottom of the buttresses which reads: 'Her begynnyth John(n) Baco(n) owthe / of the fun(n)dacyon Jhu p(re)serve hym'. So John Bacon presumably paid for the beginning of the work. There is a stair turret on the s. side up to the bell stage and the battlements have been renewed. There are C13 *lancets* in the *chancel* and a variety of *Perpendicular* windows in the *nave* and n. *aisle*, but the *Norman* origin of the church is betrayed by a lancet in the s. wall of the nave. When the n. aisle was added, the walls were raised and a *clerestory* inserted. There are fine *gargoyles* in the parapets. A large C19 *vestry* abuts the chancel on the n. side and there is a *priest's door* to the s. Over the porch entrance is a handsome C18 sundial with its reminder 'Come in time'.

There are lots of graffiti on the simple arch *jambs*. A curious feature of the window embrasure on the e. side is the carving of a hand raised in blessing. This was normally a symbol of the Deity and may conceivably have been associated with a *stoup*. The delightful late-C14 inner doorway has shafts with carved *capitals* and an *ogee* arch whose deep mouldings were once beautifully enriched, although mere fragments of the decoration now remain. On the inside there is a C16 *hood mould* resting on what appear to be C19 head *corbels*. The capitals of the tall and narrow tower arch are decorated with *paterae*, and at the e. end of the Perpendicular *arcade*, with its *quatrefoil piers*, there is an additional small arch through to the n. chapel – probably inserted in the C19. There, the *altar* is a *Stuart* table with a simply carved top rail and sturdy legs. The late-C14 *font* has pairs of *trefoil* arches in the bowl panels and a Victorian *bier* stands in the n. aisle. Nearby are four medieval benches with varied tracery backs and *poppyheads*, one of them well carved in the form of a winged lion. The C16 nave roof has *arch-braced* cambered *tie-beams* and two of the *spandrels* are appropriately carved with dragons in acknowledgement of the church's dedication. The *Jacobean* pulpit on a new base has two tiers of the usual blind arches, with strapwork panels above them. Jutting from the wall by the window is the iron frame that once held the C17 *hour-glass* which timed the sermon. To the l. of the chancel arch there is a niche with trefoil head and *castellated* canopy which houses a figure of the patron saint sculpted by C. Blakeman and installed in 1949. The C19 chancel roof is plain and white except for the e. bay which is picked out effectively in red to form a *canopy of honour*. Beneath it is a handsome wooden *reredos*, gilded and coloured, with carved panels of the Shepherds and the Magi, with the Holy Family in the centre. The e. window glass of 1913 was designed by Edward Prynne and painted by John Jennings. Christ crucified is flanked by the *Blessed Virgin* and *St John*; there are attendant angels and a group of cherub heads encircle the Saviour's head – good colour and composition. The only medieval glass is now in the s. chancel window – parts of an early C16 figure of *St George* which was originally in one of the clerestory windows. The church has a ring of 5 bells with a 9 cwt. tenor, but they are unringable at the present time

Bramfield, St Andrew (H3): A small country church, but unusually interesting on a number of counts. The opposite side of the lane is lined with a crazily leaning 'crinkle crankle wall', and a modern oak *lych-gate* stands at the entrance to the churchyard. The *Norman* round tower is the only one in East Anglia which is detached, and in *Cautley's* view they were all built thus and had their churches added to them. However, there is no evidence of that here, and the ground floor doorway and *lancet* date from the late C13. The bell openings have been re-shaped below a modern brick parapet, and the tower has recently been restored. It houses a delightful ground floor ring of five bells in a minor key with a 12 cwt. tenor; three of the bells bear the mark of the Suffolk bell founder William Chamberlain who was active between 1426 and 1456. The church itself is C14, a simple *nave*, *chancel* and *porch*, with plastered walls and thatched roofs, and a *vestry* was built on to the n. door in the C19. An original, slightly damaged cross survives on the w. gable, and there is *Decorated tracery* in the chancel windows. Those on the s. side have large, interesting *stops* on the *dripstones* – one a praying figure, and another a head with a toothy grimace under a jester's cap.

Within, only two of the *tie-beams* and *king posts* of the roof remain at the w. end below plastered ceilings. The C14 *font* has attached columns round the shaft and *quatrefoil* roundels in the bowl panels, and looks as though it was re-cut in the C19. There was an extensive restoration in the early 1870s and the nave windows were reglazed by Kings (of Norwich?). The style matches the w. window at Hunting-field, and strongly resembles the slightly earlier windows by Constantine Woolnough at Dennington. He had died in the 1860s and it is possible that the Bramfield people admired his work and asked for something similar. At all events, simple materials and techniques were used very effectively, and the bold floral designs in white glass against pale green *quarries* are quite remarkable for the period. The *hatchments* on the walls all relate to members of the Rabett family, who lived at Bramfield Hall for 300 years, and whose arms make use of rabbits as a punning or 'canting' device; individually, they are for Elizabeth, 1760 (n. wall, w.), her husband Reginald, 1763 (n. wall, e.), Reginald, 1810 (s. wall w.), and his wife Mary, 1832 (s. wall, e.). The large recess in the nave n. wall contained a particularly interesting medieval painting but, alas, most of the detail has faded and it has been affected by damp. A wooden cross was superimposed, and round it, four angels held chalices and scrolls lettered with sentences from the Gloria.

We come now to one of Bramfield's treasures, a *rood screen* which, despite mutilation and the ravages of time, is among the finest in East Anglia. It dates from the early years of the C16, and much of its interest lies in the fact that it has been left largely unrestored. There is a broad *crocketted* centre arch, and the main *lights* have flattened *ogee* arches. *Groining* springs from the buttresses, and in each section of it there is a cross motif, internally *cusped*, a device found only in East Anglia. Faded though it is, the colouring is remarkably rich and diverse – ribs of white with red margins, green and purple flowers with gold blossoms, vaulting panels of deep blue studded with gold. And the painted ornaments are just as lively – flowers with daintily curved stems on the buttress sides, fleur-de-lys on the blue mouldings, blossoms with gilded centres on the ogees. All this is heightened by the use of *gesso* (another East Anglian speciality) on the face of buttresses, as medallions on the dado mouldings with a band running below, and in the base panels. On each side, a section of the screen backs against the walls that flank the chancel arch, and *altars* were placed in front there. The series of panel paintings comprised *the Evangelists* and four other saints, of which five remain. From l. to r., they are: *SS Mark, Matthew* (both repainted), *SS Luke, John, Mary Magdalene*. The Magdalen with her jar of ointment is richly dressed in a pale rose robe like a Flemish grand dame, and the paintings may well have come from the same hand as those at Yaxley and Sotherton. Again, gesso patterns feature as backgrounds for the figures, and even St Luke's name label behind his head is formed in the same medium. It would seem that the s. altar was specially honoured, because the decoration of the loft vaulting is enhanced with a host of diminutive angels on that side. A large *piscina*, with *crocketted* ogee arch and flanking pinnacles, is sited in the wall nearby. As you pass into the chancel, note that the back of the screen is vaulted as well, and that there are traces of colour.

In the chancel, one's eye is immediately drawn to the monument for Arthur and Elizabeth Coke, another of Bramfield's memorable features. Arthur's father was that great codifier and defender of English law, Sir Edward Coke, James I's Lord Chief Justice, but about the son virtually nothing is known except that he lived the life of a country gentleman at Bramfield. His wife had died in 1627 and he followed her two years later, but the monument was not installed until after the Lord Chief Justice's death in 1634. The sculptor was *Nicholas Stone*, who

Bramfield, St Andrew:
Coke memorial; detail of recumbant figure

had also provided the old lawyer's tomb at
Tittleshall in Norfolk and, considered as a whole,
it is a curiously awkward composition to come
from such a distinguished source. The black
painted niche which contains the life-size
kneeling figure of the solemn gentleman in
armour is set about with eight *cartouches* of arms.
Below, his wife reclines on the tomb chest,
cradling one of their baby daughters in her
arms, and hers is a figure of quite remarkable
distinction. The effigy is carved in an alabaster
of finer quality than that of her husband, and
it ranks as one of the finest pieces of English
sculpture of its age. Sir Sacheverell Sitwell
regarded it as one of the great treasures of
English art and thought it 'worthy of
Bernini'. Elizabeth is raised on tasselled
pillows, wearing a dainty gown, with the lace-
trimmed coverlet turned back; the delicacy of
her hands and the treatment of the fabrics is
exquisite. The restoration in 1870 changed the
levels in the chancel and the *sanctuary* is now
approached by three steps with rather attractive
green tile risers. In the early C20, A. Winter
Rose designed a ponderous screen and
panelling for the e. end in dark grey stone,
12ft. high, with canopied niches containing
statues of *SS Helen, Paul, Peter* and *Andrew*.
The *angle piscina* has been heavily restored, and
all the glass in the chancel is by *Ward & Hughes*,
none of it memorable. There is an excellent
range of *ledger-stones* in the floor, and one close
to the sanctuary steps has an epitaph that
raised the ire of the *Ecclesiological Society* in
1846. They thought it 'so very revolting and
profane' that they would not defile the pages of
their magazine by printing it. I naturally cannot
resist quoting it in full:

Between the remains of her brother
Edward and her husband Arthur, Here
lies the Body of Bridgett Applewhaite
once Bridgett Nelson. After the
Fatigues of a Married Life Born by her
with Incredible Patience for four Years
and three Quarters bating three weeks;
And after the Enjoiment of the
Glorious Freedom of an Easy and
Unblemish't Widowhood, For four
Years and Upwards, she Resolved to
run the Risk of a second Marriage-Bed
But DEATH forbad the Banns. And
having with an Apoplectick Dart (The
same instrument with which he had
Formerly Dispatch't her Mother,)
Touch't the most Vital part of her
Brain; She must have fallen Directly to
the Ground (as one Thunder-strook),
If she had not been Catch't and
Supported by her Intended Husband.
Of which the Invisible Bruise, After a
Struggle for above Sixty Hours, With
that grand Enemy to Life, (but the
certain, and Merciful Friend to Helpless
Old Age,) In Terrible Convulsions,
Plaintive Groans or Stupefying Sleep,
Without recovery of her Speech or
Senses, She dyed on ye 12th day of
Sept in ye year of Our Lord 1737, and
of her own Age 44.

One of her 'life's fatigues' was a foul father-
in-law who persuaded his son to make no
will, and all Bridgett inherited was an
interminable law suit with her brother-in-law
in which she sought to recover her own estate.
She had no kin, and one can only suppose
that the obituary was furnished by her
disconsolate intended.

Bramford, St Mary (F6): If you approach, as I
did, across the wide expanse of churchyard on
the s. side, the church seems large but unremarkable. The C14 tower has attractive
Decorated tracery in the bell openings, *quatrefoil*
belfry windows, and a wide and shallow niche
beneath the w. window. There is a triple *base
course* in flint chequerwork, and the *dripstones* on
the buttresses continue into the corners, with
grotesques on the lower *weatherings* reminiscent
of those at Boxford; a slim C18 spire rises
behind the battlements. It is not until one sees
the n. side that the richness of the C15
rebuilding can be appreciated. A continuous
parapet carved with a frieze of shields and *Tudor*

flowers links the *aisle* with the tall *porch*, and above it there are pinnacles crowned with figures. Look particularly for the figure of *St Edmund* with his arrow on the n.w. corner of the porch, and a cowled ape carrying a flask which is seated cross-legged on the pinnacle to the e. of the porch (satirising the doctors). There are more figures above the richly traceried battlements of the *clerestory*, and the aisle buttresses each have niches at high level. The substantial 1890s *vestry* projecting from the chancel was designed by Cheston & Perkin and matches the C15 work very well. The facade of the porch is in *knapped* flint and the central canopied niche contains a statue of the *Blessed Virgin* and Child which was given in 1908 (unlike many modern replacements, it is just the right size). As with the w. window of the n. aisle, the C14 e. window of the porch was reused at the rebuilding and so was the inner doorway, although this entailed offsetting the porch to the l.

Within, the very tall tower arch has leaf *stops* to the *hood mould* and for some reason it does not align with the *nave*. This is emphasised by the differing widths of the blind *ogee* arches on either side. There seems little doubt that the tower was completed before the nave was rebuilt because the w. bays of the *arcades* are halved where they meet its substantial e. buttresses. By the organ there is a huge glacial boulder below the base of the tower buttress and, like those at Shelley and other churches nearby, it may have been a pagan cult object which was cleansed and converted to the service of the new religion. Large stone *corbels* high up in the tower show that there was vaulting originally (or at least a substantial floor) and two of them are remarkably like those below the chancel arch at nearby Hintlesham. One is a handsome man with curly hair, one a devil, and the last is a mask with arms that pull the mouth wide open. There are C19 *Decalogue* boards on the walls below and the C15 *font* has been moved within the tower. The panels are carved alternately with shields and angels bearing books or crowns, and the flat underside carries *paterae* above a traceried stem. The carcase of the elaborate early-C16 cover is hinged so that it can be opened out, and the base of each panel carries triple pedestals below shallow canopies. The domed top is *crocketted* with a *finial* and the carved detail throughout is an interesting mixture of Gothic and *Renaissance* motifs. It is supported by a thick, rather crude, post at the back – I wonder whether this was always so. The nave arcades have octagonal *piers*

and the hood mould of the arch by the organ has a stop carved as a dragon biting its tail; the dove in a vine farther along is C19 but there is a nice little medieval dog opposite. It is likely that there were extensive wall paintings in the C14 but only a fragment remains on the s.e. buttress of the tower. *Dowsing* records that he broke down 841 'superstitious pictures' in 1643 and he may have been responsible for the mutilation of the angels which form the *hammerbeams* of the C15 nave roof. Some have only lost their heads but others have been replaced with roughly shaped blocks. The *arch-braced* aisle roofs have large *bosses* and in the s. aisle canopied *wall posts* carried figures, two of which are still recognisable. There are two most attractive oval bronze tablets for Rear-Admiral Sir Lambson Loraine (1950) and Sir Percy Loraine (1961) at the w. end. The arcade pier nearest the s. door has a very interesting incised inscription: 'Remember ye pore the scripture doth record what to them is geven is lent unto the Lord 1591'. There would have been an alms box below; the present one is C19. At the e. end of the s. aisle there is a plain C14 *piscina* and the tall recess in the e. wall may have been the entrance to the *rood loft stair*. The suite of choir stalls nearby was designed by *W.D. Caröe* for the chancel in 1904 and was obviously so uncomfortable that extra backboards in pine were added. The attractive late-C16 *Holy table* is now used as a nave *altar* and, to the w. of it, Thomas Sicklemore's *ledger-stone* is dated 1619. The plain Elizabethan pulpit has two ranks of *linen-fold* panelling. Across on the wall of the n. aisle is a memorial for Eliza Mee, who died in 1912 aged 87. She had been blind since birth but led the choir when it sang in the old w. *gallery* and played the church's first organ for thirty-five years. Another memorial for a blind organist can be found at Assington. Bramford's *chancel screen* is one of the rare examples in stone. Although the cresting and the pierced quatrefoils in the *spandrels* are C19, the rest has been unchanged since the late-C13 or early-C14. It has three equal arches and there are triple shafts with ring *capitals* against the outer *jambs*; more shafts face e. and w. on either side of the entrance but the centre arch is unmoulded. The chancel arch overhead was designed by *Ewan Christian* as part of the 1864 restoration, but the roof beyond is a C15 single hammerbeam and again there are defaced angels. The C13 chancel is the earliest part of the building and the window embrasure on the s. side has a moulded arch and jamb shafts. The *sedilia* are divided by octagonal detached shafts and their plain arches match the *piscina* alongside. Attractively carpeted, the chancel is now used as a chapel for small congregations, and the *reredos* is another of Caröe's designs, reminiscent of his magnum opus at Elveden. In oak, gilded and enriched with red, there are chunky canopies below four standing angels on pinnacles; painted shields with *Passion emblems* are set on the side panels and there is a beautifully carved crucifix in the centre. The five-light Perpendicular e. window is filled with 1905 glass by *Kempe*. The Blessed Virgin and Christ are flanked by *SS Edmund, Laurence,* Giles, and *Etheldreda,* with musical angels below. St Mary's has an excellent ring of six bells with a 10 cwt. tenor, five of which were cast by the outstanding Colchester founder Miles Graye in 1632.

Brampton, St Peter (I2): The church stands above a hazardous bend on the Beccles-Blythburgh road within a steeply sloping churchyard. The good-looking C15 tower has angle buttresses faced with varied *flushwork,* and a niche above the w. window has shields in the *spandrels* of its *crocketted ogee arch. Gargoyles* jut from the corners of the flushwork battlements, and there are the remains of seated figures above them. The n. door of the *nave* gives access to a C19 brick *vestry,* and there are C13 *lancets* and two *Perpendicular* windows on that side of the nave. The 'Y' *tracery* windows on the s. side of the *chancel* give a date of about 1300, and there are *scratch dials* on both sides of the *priest's door.* The e. wall was rebuilt in brick with a new three-*light* window in the C19. The diminutive *porch* has *flushwork* buttresses, a centre niche, and there are *fleurons* in the *dripstone* of the arch. The C15 door is still in use, simply traceried and with its closing ring intact.

Within, there are many signs of C19 work, and the 1860s glass in the tower w. window is a fine example of *William Warrington's* work. The panels illustrate the *Annunciation,* the angels appearing to the Bethlehem shepherds, the Nativity, and Christ's Presentation in the Temple; there are angels in the tracery, and the designs are vigorous, in strong colours. George III *Royal Arms* hang above the tower arch and carry the name of the churchwarden of the day. More unusually, they also have: 'God save the King. 1 Samuel x chap 24 ver' ('And Samuel said to all the people, See ye him whom the Lord has chosen, that there is none like him among all the people? And all the people shouted and said, God save the King'.) The *Decalogue* boards on

either side of the tower arch are a neat exercise in C18 'gothick'. The late-C15 *font* has a traceried bowl with *paterae* beneath it, and the octagonal shaft is buttressed. Ceilings are plastered, and in the nave, *arch-braces* peep through above the *castellated wall plates.* The nave furnishings are plain C19 oak, and the pulpit stands in front of a blocked *rood stair* entrance. There is now no chancel arch, and the *screen,* with its turned shafts and strange leaf tracery looks early C20. There is a second priest's door blocked in the n. wall, and the level of the *sanctuary* has been raised so that the simple *piscina* is now low in the wall. Its arch has been altered, but note that there is a stone *credence shelf* at the back, and a recess on the r. that may have been used to store a towel. The Leman family were patrons of the living, and some of them lie under fine C17 and C18 *ledger-stones* in the chancel, with deeply cut *achievements.* Others are commemorated on the walls, and there is an excellent pair of architectural tablets of 1788 and 1807, in *touchstone* and white marble, with crisp detailing. The stained glass of 1875 in the s. chancel window is the only example in Suffolk of the work of James Perry Warrington who succeeded his father William in 1869. The two scenes of Christ preaching in the Temple and His Resurrection make clever use of space, the colour is good, and the background patterning cheerful. The glass on the n. side of the chancel was probably supplied by the elder Warrington in the 1860s, and there is an Ascension medallion backed by a rich design in one window (the other is now masked by the organ). St Peter's has a ground floor ring of five bells with a 7 cwt. tenor but they are listed as being in 'poor going order' at the present time.

Brandeston, All Saints (G4): The church stands by the entrance to Brandeston Hall (now a school) and the path to the n. door is bordered snugly by rounded hedges of clipped yew. The C14 tower has a simple *flushwork base course* and the w. door has shields and crowns in the mouldings. There are shields carved with a *Trinity* emblem and the three crowns of East Anglia (or Ely) in the *spandrels,* the *headstops* are crowned and the *label* is decorated with *paterae.* The tall, late-*Perpendicular* w. window is flanked by niches with *crocketted ogee* arches, and another above it is made more elaborate by having a canopy, and a mask below the image stool (just like the arrangement at nearby Earl Soham). The bell openings have *Decorated tracery* and there is more flushwork in the stepped battlements. The walls of the *nave* and *chancel* are startlingly white, and on the s. side there is one *scratch dial* on a nave buttress with two more on the s.e. buttress of the chancel, one of which has traces of numerals. The chancel dates from the end of the C12, with a group of three *lancets* within a single arch on the s. side, but it had become ruinous by the early C17. In the 1860s *R.M. Phipson* directed a heavy restoration in which new roofs were provided, the s. porch was demolished, and a new one was provided for the n. door.

The interior is neat with a rather cool feel. A *sanctus-bell window* is tucked under the ridge above the tower arch and to the l. of the organ is a decorative and unusually interesting peal board of 1749-50. Its scrolly outline has six pendent bells and it records a peal in seven methods, two of which were composed by the local band who thought it worthwhile to list the course ends and calls on each side. The bells (tenor 7 cwt.) now have a modern frame and fittings and are in excellent order. The C13 *Purbeck marble font* has a deep, canted bowl with the usual pairs of shallow arches in the panels, and the s. door still has its original drawbar in place. A reminder that it was once the main entrance is the *stoup* recess to the l. There are two *brass* inscriptions set in the floor e. of the font, for Jane and Elizabeth Stebbing (1616 and 1621). The Perpendicular nave windows all have places for images and there are over a dozen C15 bench ends. Some of the tracery has been skimmed off and they bear heavy *poppyheads* flanked by remnants of beasts and one or two figures – one seated with an open book 3rd from back n. side, and a man astride a beast 3rd from back against the s. wall. A *piscina* in the wall farther along shows that there was an *altar* nearby in the C14. The *rood stairs* go up from a window embrasure on the n. side and the rebuilt pulpit nearby made use of C17 blind arches and the strapwork panels above them. Behind it there is an oddly placed door shape and another section of it can be seen beyond the chancel arch. It lies partly within the wall and may have some connection with the low blank arch in the chancel n. wall. At a guess there was a chapel or *sacristy* on that side. The little enclosed stall in front has two painted shields and a monogram with the date 1868, but 'A.D. 1745' is painted inside. Another C18 piece that has been reused is the panel in the reading desk on the s. side. It bears the painted shield of the Revett family and a quote from Psalm 26: 'Domine dilexi decorum domus tuee, locum habitationis gloriae tuee' (Lord, I have loved the beauty of thy house, the

place where thy glory dwelleth). The *communion rails* also have a quotation; it is lettered in gilt on the top rail and this time is from Psalm 28: 'Exaudi meam Vocem supplicem quate, Sublatis ad tuum sacrum Penetrale Manibus, Imploro'. (Hear the voice of my humble petitions, when I cry unto thee: when I hold up my hands towards the mercy-seat of thy holy temple); it ends, 'Impensis Jos. Revett Gen: A.D. 1711'. It may have been added when what were three-sided rails were altered to stretch across the chancel. They are high-quality work and the *balusters* are turned in two stages, with barley sugar twist at the top and conventional sections below. Two more C15 benches stand in the *sanctuary* and one has a man holding something astride a beast. On the wall above is the 1671 monument for John Revett. *Corinthian* columns flank a *touchstone* tablet lettered in a wilful mixture of italic and capitals which has a laurel-wreathed skull at the foot and a cherub's head at the top; a well-carved coloured *achievement* in the pediment is supported by *putti* holding reversed torches. No piscina survives for the *High altar* but there is an admirable panel in the s. sanctuary window of the head and shoulders of a bearded man which has the look of the 1890s. The window farther w. contains some very interesting early-C16 glass. There is a *Blessed Virgin* enthroned at the top, and below are the figures of a monk robed in blue (l.) and a kneeling abbot (r.). They were placed here by John de Bury who was vicar 1501-11 and the abbot may commemorate his former superior William de Coddenham, abbot of Bury. Some of the *quarries* deserve inspection too. *St Edmund's* crown and arrows occur below the monk, and below the abbot is the crown and rose with 'H.8' for Henry VIII. Just beneath is perhaps the most interesting of all, the *pomegranate* badge of his first wife Catherine of Aragon with the Latin text which translates: 'Whom God hath joined let no man put asunder.' Historic irony is nearly always accidental. The edges of the window are filled with examples of the beautifully delicate leaf and spray designs which have so often been destroyed.

There is the chilling memory of a vicar of this quiet parish who was harried to his death for supposed witchcraft. John Lowes was priest here for close on fifty years and, it must be admitted, was often at loggerheads with his flock. Then in 1646 he was accused by Matthew Hopkins, witchfinder general, of being in league with the devil and was cruelly deprived of sleep for nights on end, while his tormentors 'ran him backwards and forwards about the room, until he was out of breath; then they rested him a little, and then ran him again'. He underwent the ordeal by swimming at Framlingham and was seen to be guilty by not sinking, and finally the poor man confessed and was hanged with seventeen others, having read his own burial service.

Brandon, St Peter (B2): Set apart to the w. of the little town centre but now lapped around by new housing, the church stands in a generous churchyard fringed with limes. It is made memorable by the pair of heavy octagonal turrets, complete with spirelets, that rise above the roof line of the early-C14 *chancel*, flanking an e. window which has *Decorated tracery*. Very worn *gargoyles* jut out well below the parapets and the outline of *rood loft* staircases can be seen built into the buttresses on both sides of the church. The profile of the C14 tower is punctuated by prominent *string courses* and it has two-*light* Decorated bell openings, with a later w. window. The early-C16 n. *porch* has heavily *transomed* unglazed side windows and the original door is enlivened by worn carving of folded leaves round its edge. To the r., a substantial *stoup* is set on a traceried shaft. The interior is bright and fresh but has that rather bare feeling so often left as a legacy of heavy-handed C19 restorations which in this case spared not a single memorial from the many that were here. Behind the *High altar* is an indigestible C19 stone and marble *reredos*, but the inset roundels of Gethsemane, Entombment and the risen Christ are good. Note that there is an *aumbry* set in the n.e. turret and a door leads to the stair in its opposite number. The n. chancel windows have lovely glass of 1898 by Leonard Walker – remarkable work for a 19-year-old craftsman. They portray *SS Paul, Peter, John* and *Luke* in *Arts and Crafts* style; the faces are boldly blocked and there is a lot of movement and vivid colour in the design. Vignettes from their lives occupy the lower panels and it is interesting that St John's, unlike the others, anticipates C20 design trends. The original C16 stalls, with *poppyheads*, and the remains of winged beasts on the front buttresses, have been remade into two ranges for the choir. Apart from recolouring, the bases of the C15 *rood screen* are intact, with *ogee* tracery and twin *quatrefoils* containing shields in each panel. The panels of the s. *aisle* section retain their stencil decoration in gold on alternate red and green backgrounds. Both ranges have modern tops

and the tracery and cornice in the aisle section are very attractive. Note the blocked C16 door on the s. side which led to the *rood stairs*. The World War I memorial in the s. aisle is a *Heaton, Butler & Bayne* window of *SS George* and *Michael*, with the crowning of a knight in the centre – all in '*William Morris* medieval' style. Below, in a glass case, is a fine copy of a Bible printed by Robert Barker the year after Shakespeare died. There are some bench ends in the nave to match those in the chancel and they too have the remains of grotesques on the elbows; mixed in with them are C19 replicas in pine. The C13 *arcade* between *nave* and s. aisle has elegant quatrefoil *piers*, with bases typical of the period. The chancel arch has male and female *headstops*. Below it, on the n. side, is a C19 wooden pulpit with a very nice pair of *Ecclesiological Society*-design brass candelabra. The simple octagonal bowl of the C13 *font* stands on a central column, with a ring of shafts whose caps and bases intersect cleverly. The cover carries a modern baptismal group in blond wood by Reeve of Lawshall. The church had some more bench ends made in the C17 and their strangely clumsy poppyheads can be seen against the wall w. of the n. door. Some advertisements are timeless they say, and to prove the point, look at the lockplate of the n. porch gates – an enduring reminder that they were made by Burrells of Thetford, the firm once famous for its steam traction engines. St Peter's has an excellent ring of six bells with a 7 cwt. tenor.

Brantham, St Michael Land All Angels (F7): St Michael's has a particularly nice 1890s *lych-gate* in the *Arts and Crafts* style, designed by Edward Schroder Prior, a founder-member and sometime master of the Art Workers' Guild. Its retaining walls curve to the roadside outside the gates, and the shingle roof has gently rounded hoods n. and s. The eaves and braces are carved with a bine and leaf pattern which is echoed on the 'S'-shaped bars of the sides; an evocative period piece. The church was more or less rebuilt by *Edward Hakewill* in 1869 but the indications are that it dates from the C14. The tower has a small *Decorated* w. window, strong *string courses*, and buttresses to belfry level. Above that, the work is largely new, including the *flushwork* roundels in the parapet and the *gargoyles*. There is a *vestry* on the s. side covered by an extension of the *nave* roof, and an odd little porch-cum-mini-vestry is tucked into the angle between nave and *chancel*. There are glimpses of the Stour estuary from this side of the churchyard, and on walking round you will see that the chancel was wholly rebuilt. Hakewill added a n. *aisle* under a continuation of the nave roof, and the steep roof of his n. *porch* drops to within 5ft. of the ground.

The glass in the tower window has a look of the 1920s but I have not been able to identify the glazier. It sets *St John the Baptist* and three other figures against an attractive landscape background and is very pleasing. The good early-C15 *font* came from the redundant church of St Martin at Palace, Norwich, in 1977; its bowl has a *castellated* rim with *quatrefoil* roundels in the panels, and there is delicate Decorated tracery between the shafts of the stem. Overhead, a small and dark set of George III *Royal Arms* hangs above the tower arch. The singlebraced nave roof, with its *tie-beams* and tall *king posts*, dates from the rebuilding and so does the n. *arcade*, but there is Decorated tracery in the s. windows. Some C15 glass has survived there too – figures of an archbishop and a civilian, three initials, and some miscellaneous fragments. The C14 *angle piscina* nearby has no drain now but it would have served a nave *altar*, and the *trefoil*-headed niche by the n. aisle altar may have been removed from another piscina on that side of the nave. The oak pulpit is a striking piece of work in Arts and Crafts style. On it, a Tree of Life is carved to form a lattice across three panels with an overlaying scroll: 'From death unto life'. It was given in 1900 by a parishioner whose wife had a penchant for pokerwork, and she added her initials and the date inside. Her husband also gave the ancient bishop's chair in the *sanctuary*, but her addition of 'Rest in the Lord' on the back was tactfully removed after her death. The chancel is offset to the n. but this may merely be one of the side-effects of the rebuilding. Its C19 arch rests on stub columns above *corbels* carved with the church's patron saint on the n. and *St Gabriel* on the s. Although rebuilt, the chancel retains another C14 angle piscina, and all the glass here is by *Lavers & Barraud*, with, in the e. window, Christ the King flanked by four angels below pretty patterns in the tracery. John Constable only painted three altar pieces, one each for Nayland and Manningtree, and one for Brantham on the theme of 'Suffer little children to come unto me'. Many have come especially to see it but it is, alas, no longer here. Security has dictated that it has to be housed in the Ipswich museum, a depressing reflection upon our largely godless generation.

Bredfield, St Andrew (G5): There are fine, mature lime trees along the frontage and this compact little church stands well in its churchyard. The shortness of *nave* and *chancel* is accentuated by their height, and the smoothly uniform finish is largely the result of a full-scale restoration by *R.M. Phipson* in 1875. He repaired the nave and renewed its tall *Perpendicular* windows, gave the chancel a new roof, and added a *vestry* on the s. side. There is a pretty little e. window, and the *priest's door* to the n. has been blocked like the s. door in the nave. The *base course* of the early-C15 tower is decorated with crowned 'M's for the *Blessed Virgin* and unusual *flushwork* roundels, each enclosing a pair of *mouchettes* and a *quatrefoil*. The narrow w. doorway has roses in the *spandrels*, there is more flushwork on the buttresses, and the battlements in stepped brick have corner pillars which project to give the top of the tower a more than usual emphasis. The tall and shallow n. *porch* was restored by Phipson but its steep C15 roof is intact, a miniature *hammerbeam* construction with carved spandrels that is quite remarkable. The only other East Anglian example that I remember seeing is in a porch is at Great Bealings. Within, one finds a full-scale version above the nave that is exceptional on a number of counts. The *wall plate* is pierced with *tracery* and so is the deep cornice above it, this time in two bands. There were once angels or shields on the ends of the hammers and at the base of the *wall posts*, and two bays at the e. end (rather than the usual one) provided a *celure* for the *rood*. Faint traces of the painted decoration remain on the hammers and in chevron form on the rafters, and the sides of the upper ribs have crowned 'M's, the *Sacred monogram*, and distinctive foliage patterns. The *font* is C19 and the benches are modern. There is a *stoup* by the s. door which means that it was the principal entrance when the nave was built. At the w. end, metal *Decalogue boards* are framed on the wall, and the church has been presented with a fine array of hassocks embroidered with English and Australian flowers worked by ladies of the village and of Australia. A *brass* of 1611 has been preserved in the s. doorway and commemorates Leonard and Elizabeth Farrington; their 14in. figures show him wearing a cloak and his wife a fashionable hat, and there are groups of six sons and two daughters below. Two Arthur Jenneys have *hatchments* here, over the n. door for the one who died in 1729, and on the s. wall for Arthur of Rendlesham who died in 1742. The *Stuart* pulpit has three ranges of panels and pierced brackets below the book ledge; for a long time its *tester* hung on the wall in Bredfield House but it came back to the church eventually and now serves as a table top in the *sanctuary*. On the s. wall there is a bronze tablet for Joseph and Emily White which is an interesting period piece of *Art Nouveau* design dating from the early 1900s – swirling, languorous female angels in a vague seascape. In the chancel the e. window glass is by *Hardman* and the window on the n. side has attractive glass of 1860 by an unidentified firm; panels illustrating four of the *Seven Works of Mercy* are set in a bright blue latticed with dark red. On the s. wall a plain tablet by Stephenson of Woodbridge commemorates George Crabbe, rector here from 1835 to 1856. He was the poet's son and biographer, and a great friend of Edward Fitzgerald, who lived at nearby Boulge. Dale of Wickham Market provided the tablet for the Revd. John Dufton on the n. wall and also for his brother William on the e. wall; the latter was a Birmingham surgeon who died in 1859 having founded the Institution for the Relief of Deafness in that city. From an earlier age is the severe *touchstone* tablet and flanking columns on the other side of the *altar*. It commemorates Robert Marryot who died in 1675 and his coloured *achievement* is displayed at the top with another shield at the base. Turning back, one can just make out the tiny *sanctus-bell window* in the wall of the tower just below the roof ridge, but it is so placed that only the altar can be seen from there – a convincing proof of its original purpose. St Andrews has one of Suffolk's best rings of six bells with a tenor of just over 11 cwt. which were restored and augmented in 1949 by Gillett & Johnston of Croydon.

Brent Eleigh, St Mary (D6): To the n. of the main road and the River Brett, the church lies quiet and secluded by the Hall. Entering the churchyard from the e., one of the first things that catches the eye is the *reticulated tracery* in the *aisle* e. window. The n. windows of the *nave* also have attractive *Decorated* tracery. The *chancel* e. window dates from 1860 and a window on the n. side was blocked when a large monument was installed within. Further along is a C19 brick and flint *vestry* in lieu of a n. *porch*. The w. doorway is well-recessed and note that the placing of the tower stair forced the w. window off-centre. It is likely that the door in the s. chancel wall was originally the *priest's door* but it was

altered in the C18 or early C19 for use as a private entrance for the family at the Hall. Close by it stands the table tomb of Robert and Dionesse Colman (1730 and 1697), boldly carved with the emblems of mortality. There are many good late-C18 and early-C19 headstones and one (1813), s. of the porch, has an age-old theme:

> We daily see Death spares no son nor age,
> Sooner or later all do quit the stage.
> The old, the young, the strong, the rich, the
>   wise,
> Must all to him become a sacrifice.

The porch windows, with their Decorated tracery, are unglazed and there is a *scratch dial* to the r. of the entrance. A modern statue of the *Blessed Virgin* stands in a niche over the inner doorway and the C14 door has lovely reticulated tracery in the head and retains all its original ironwork. Now we come to a charming interior in which a medley of architectural styles and furnishings dwell comfortably together and which were not harshly disturbed by the Victorians. The s. *arcade* and the tower arch confirm that the church has not changed significantly since it was built in the late C13 or early C14. The C13 *font* stands by an arcade *pier* and has a shallow octagonal *Purbeck marble* bowl, with canted sides each carved with a pair of typical blank arches. The early-C17 cover is an unusual design – a solid pyramid with a flat top from which rise turned spindles to support a *finial*. On either side of the tall tower arch hang charity boards bearing the names of rector and churchwardens for 1830, and over the n. door is a set of dark and yet vivid *Royal Arms* painted on board. They have the post-1707 arms and motto for Queen Anne but the initials were later changed to mark the accession of one of the Georges. The church's only *hatchment* on the nave s. wall is for Dr Thomas Brown who died in 1852 and whose wife inherited the manor. There are solid *box pews* of two periods in the aisle and nave; those at the e. end have C17 shallow carved top panels and the original butterfly hinges, and some further w. enclose C17 benches with rudimentary *poppyheads*, of which there are more at the w. end of the aisle. The single remnant of the C15 seating is a bench end at the e. end of the box pews on the s. side of the nave and it has a bird and an animal carved on the poppyhead. Above the homely brick and *pamment* floors the nave roof is plastered with only the single framed wall strips

Brent Eleigh, St Mary:
Robert & Dionesse Colman's tomb

showing. On the n. wall is a faint trace of one of the improving texts beloved of the Elizabethan church. It was probably one of a series and consists of the first two verses of Psalm 72 followed by a contemporary prayer. The stairs leading to the old *rood loft* are in the n. wall and the fine *Stuart* pulpit stands on a very tall turned post, with heavy carved brackets and skirt below the body. The lower panels have quite unusual patterns within ovals and the whole of the underside of the canted book ledge is intricately carved. Across the nave stands the oak lectern given in memory of William Baldry, killed in action in 1915. The s. aisle chapel is enclosed by a fine C14 *parclose screen* which displays Decorated tracery above turned uprights and the doors to nave and aisle still have their original hinges with incised decoration. Although it has been covered over on one side, from within the chapel you can see a trefoil *elevation squint* cut in one of the boards of the w. side of the screen. It was not usual for C14 screens to be coloured but here we have a rare example which is probably the earliest in Suffolk and likely to be the only one from the C14. On the door to the aisle there is a painting of the eagle of *St John* bearing a scroll; the predominant colours are red and green and it is enclosed in a twisted wreath of thorns. On the side facing the nave there are three shields – a lily symbol of the Blessed Virgin, a cross and crown of thorns, and a coat of arms. The chapel became the Hall pew in time and a box pew was

set within it. There are a few medieval tiles in the floor and a *piscina* in the corner. The panelled chancel ceiling dates from 1684 and the three-sided *communion rails* are of that period or a little earlier; they have twisted *balusters* which are grouped in fours at the corners and the gate posts. The tomb against the n. wall dominates the chancel and is an impressive and important piece by Thomas Dunn, who as a builder-mason was employed by Nicholas Hawksmoor to build Spitalfields' Christ's Church and St Mary Woolnoth in the City. It commemorates Edward Colman who died in 1743 and the pensive, reclining figure in flowing drapery is set against a striated grey marble backing arch between *Corinthian* columns. A large *putto* offers a crown overhead and two of his chubby fellows gesture either side of the shields of arms on the *pediment*. The C18 panelling on the s. wall was fitted round the old priest's door and the *sanctuary* piscina had its canopy cut away to give a straight run to the corner. The e. window glass of 1860 is by the *O'Connors* and is a good example of their better work. It is a Crucifixion with stylised medieval figures and lots of busy ornament; the colour is sharp and well-handled. They probably also provided the s.e. window, with its patterned *quarries* and arms of the Brown family. In 1960 a very important and significant group of paintings was uncovered on the e. wall. They date from between 1270 and 1330, indicating that the chancel predates most of the rest of the building. The centre *reredos* panel of the Crucifixion, in red against a pale green background, portrays the twisted figure of Christ with overlarge feet, flanked by the Blessed Virgin and *St John* in the attitudes typical of the period. They remind one of the figures on the Thornham Parva *retable*. To the l. are two kneeling angels (one of which is complete) *censing* the space originally occupied by a statue, probably of the Virgin. The blue background has blackened with the years and is dappled with stars. On the s. side of the altar is the remnant of a life-size figure of Christ bearing the banner of the Resurrection. The painting was originally a version of the 'Harrowing of Hell' in which Christ rescues Adam from the pit. Parts of Adam can still be made out and the figure of the priest donor is plain in the bottom corner, with the inscription +RICA above him and a wine jar by his side. The modern choir stalls have panels carved to match the C17 box pews and there are some excellent *ledger-stones* with the coats of arms cut deeply enough to trip the unwary. There was once a fine parochial library here of some 1500 volumes bequeathed in 1715 by the squire Dr Henry Colman, rector of Harpley and Foulsham in Norfolk. Sadly now dispersed, these volumes were originally housed in a library built onto the e. end of the chancel which was demolished in 1859. In the summer of 2004 a fire destroyed the *High altar* and its furniture which has now been replaced, and the s. chapel has been refurnished.

Brettenham, St Mary (D5): The church is basically a C14 building and there is an interesting variety of *Decorated* window *tracery* in the *nave*, with early *Perpendicular* forms on the n. side of the *chancel*. The e. window appears to be C19 and below it are three shields of arms – Stafford, Buckingham and Sampson. The Earl of Stafford's son, Humphrey, was patron here in the 1430s and later became Duke of Buckingham. The tower doubles as a s. *porch,* with a flint panelled *base course,* a decayed niche above the entrance, and worn *headstops* to the arch of the inner doorway. There is a *stoup* to the r. and the doors themselves are medieval, with an attractively carved border of leaves. The late-C14 *font* stands on two high steps and is similar to that at Rattlesden. It has a *castellated* rim marked with incised crosses all the way round and the panels are carved with *cusped* and *crocketted ogee* arches; the heads at the angles below have been defaced. During the invasion scare of 1940, all signposts were uprooted and names of villages obliterated so that the Germans would have to rely on map and compass. In an excess of zeal the village name was painted out on the benefaction boards here, but had the visiting 'herrenvolk' looked carefully they would have found that one example had been overlooked to give the game away. The nave roof is *arch-braced* and below are C19 benches – apart from two pairs of mutilated bench ends by the pulpit. The easternmost window on the s. side has stained glass of 1866 by *Henry Hughes* of *Ward & Hughes* illustrating the miracle of the loaves and fishes – heavy colour and precious little animation for such a theme. There is a plain *piscina,* indicating that a nave *altar* stood here. Nearby is a bronze plaque for Lieut. Cornwallis John Warner who was killed in 1915; it has his arms in enamelled colour with replicas of his four medals and there is a duplicate at Thorpe Morieux. The prayer desk incorporates a pair of medieval bench ends and tracery panels. On the n. side, the blocked door and little *quatrefoil* window mark the position of the stair to the

now vanished *rood loft.* The first window on the n. side of the chancel has some fragments of C15 glass and they include a good *Trinity* shield in a roundel. There are C15 *poppyheads* and some panel tracery built into the C19 stalls and two more old bench ends that match those in the nave. The late-C17 *communion rails* have vigorously twisted *balusters,* with gates that, when closed, complete the clusters of four balusters at each side – an uncommonly clever little piece of joinery design. The late-C14 angle piscina has a cusped and crocketted ogee arch, with Buckingham and Stafford shields in the *spandrels* repeating those outside; to the r. are the *dropped-sill sedilia.* The 1882 Ward & Hughes glass on this side portrays doubting *St Thomas* and Christ with *SS Peter* and *Andrew* but it is not memorable and the rest of the chancel glass is poor. On the e. wall there are two C19 or early-C20 murals painted on metal – the Wise Men, and Christ with two disciples on the road to Emmaus. The figures stand under canopies and are reminiscent of Walter Crane's work. In the n.e. corner of the *sanctuary* is an interesting *brass* inscription for Thomas Weniffe who died in 1611: 'A gentle and modest young man who leavinge this life lefte also this verse touching the vanity thereof.'

Short was his life yet liveth he ever.
Death hath his dewe yet dyeth he never.

Ledger-stones are seldom signed, but under the stalls on the n. side Elizabeth Wenyede's stone shows that it was cut by Charles Bottomley of Bury in 1751. Before you go, have a look at the Bible by the door. Published by John Basket in 1716, it is known as the 'Vinegar Bible' because the heading for the parable of the vineyard was misprinted.

Brightwell, St John the Baptist (G6): This sweet little church is perched on the hill, away from the scattering of houses that comprise the hamlet, and Constable's painting of it from across the valley hangs in the Tate Gallery. The immaculate churchyard is open to the fields on two sides and, despite its simplicity, the church is remarkably interesting. It dates from about 1300, and walking round, you will see that the flint and rubble core of the walls is exposed at the base, below the plaster. There is a blocked n. doorway, and only the *dripstones* remain of two side *chancel* windows. Apart from a single *cusped lancet* in the s. wall and a tall lancet in the w. wall, the windows have 'Y' *tracery. Dowsing* called here in 1644, finding stained glass to break and pictures of the *apostles* to deface, and by 1656 the church had become ruinous. At that stage, the squire, Thomas Essington, took the matter in hand – one of the very few instances of a thorough restoration completed during the Commonwealth period. He placed brick obelisks with short, clasping buttresses at the four corners of the roof and on the gable, and built a brick tower on its w. end, complete with battlements and pinnacles, like an overgrown bell turret. The C19 brick *porch* shelters a C14 doorway, and the door itself is medieval, still with its original closing ring and strap hinges.

Having added a tower in 'gothick' style, the C17 architect surprises us by supporting it inside with a pair of enormous Tuscan columns and a compact arch – totally out of scale, but a most interesting link between the two mainstreams of fashion. The w. lancet contains glass which probably dates from the 1840s, possibly by the firm of *Ward & Nixon* or by *Edward Baillie*. The figure of the church's patron saint, with the dove of the Holy Spirit above, is set in bright patterning, and the window is a rare example of quality work from the period. The C14 *font* stands on a moulded base and shaft, and the rectangular bowl panels are filled with a particularly nice selection of delicate tracery patterns. The cover dates from the C17 restoration, its centre shaft supported by eight curly brackets, all picked out in maroon, white and black. Of the four *hatchments*, the one to the e. on the s. wall for Sir Samuel Barnardiston is the most interesting. In 1640 he mixed with the rioting London apprentices who wore their hair cut round; Queen Henrietta Maria picked him out and cried: 'See what a handsome Roundhead is there!', and the nickname stuck to the whole Parliamentary party. Ironically, Sir Samuel took no active part in the Civil War, but made a vast fortune as agent for the Levant Company and was appointed Suffolk's High Sheriff in 1666. He was buried here in 1707. The other hatchments are for: Samuel Barnardiston, who succeeded to the estate in 1712 and died in 1725 (n. wall w.); Arthur, his younger brother who followed him and, dying in 1737, was the last of the Brightwell branch of the family (n. wall e.); Arthur's widow, Ann, who died in 1731 (s. wall w.). With no dividing arch, a plain plastered ceiling covers *nave* and *chancel,* and the oak benches with their rudimentary *poppyheads* were installed in 1845. Although some of its panels have been replaced, the pulpit dates from the C17, with modern

base and steps. A *ledger-stone* with a roundel of arms in the floor of the nave marks the Barnardiston family vault, and in front of the *communion rails* on the s. side, there is another which has two shields at the top linked with a bow – a pretty conceit. The inscription concludes '. . . The south side of the vault in ye chancell of this church at Brightwell belong to ym [them] & there posteritie for a place of buriall to soe many of them as shall desire it. Wherein lieth ye remains of Thomas Essington 1656, Anna Essington 1660'. The reparation of his parish church was one of the last things he did, and the touching monument on the wall above is for his little boy who died in the same year. Young Thomas looks up, clasping a hand which emerges from the flanking curtains; the familiar lines from *St Paul's* Epistle to the Corinthians are featured above, but slanted across the drape is: 'His owne words Christ will rais mee'. In the year that his mother died, she had another loss to bear, for on the e. wall there is a second monument: 'The effigies of Anna, a gratious virgin. Eldest daughter of Tho: Essington Esq. & Anne his wife... 1660. The yeers of her life seventeen five moneths & seventeen dayes'. This is a fine portrait, in an oval garlanded with swags of fruit and topped by an alabaster *putto*. The girl cradles a skull in one hand, and in the other she holds a palm and a scroll which reads: 'Her dieing words. My mortal shall put on immortality' – another echo from St Paul. Arthur, last of the local Barnardistons, has an elegant architectural tablet on the n. wall; a portrait roundel adorns the upper obelisk, and there are three coloured shields at the base. The sombre Crucifixion group (artist unknown) in the e. window is set against clear glass and dates from 1911.

Brockley, St Andrew (C5): The church is picturesquely placed among open fields n. of the present village. A path runs alongside the moat of Brockley Hall farm through a meadow to the base of the late-C15 tower. This has handsome diagonal buttresses bearing *flushwork* emblems, including 'MR' for the *Blessed Virgin* and *St Andrew's* cross. The *base course* is flint panelled to the w. and on the s. side it incorporates a fine and bold inscription: 'Ig, mg Ricardus Coppynge'. In his will of 1521, Richard Copping of Brockley left money for the completion of the tower roof and the inscription shows that he probably financed the whole work. The 'Ig' doubtless recalls another donor and could refer to a number of Brockley men –

Brockley, St Andrew: C14 door furniture

perhaps John Gridge (d.1462), John Grygge (d.1472) or John Gervice (d.1529). The w. window is a later *Perpendicular* insertion and the battlements are modern. Variations in the structure show that the *chancel* was originally much shorter and may indeed have been *Norman*, but there is a window with 'Y' tracery on the n. side pointing to a rebuilding at the end of the C13, and others in both *nave* and chancel have early-C14 tracery. There was a wholesale restoration 1866-1871 when the church was re-roofed, and the *reticulated* tracery in the e. window no doubt dates from then (although it probably copied the original). There is a small *priest's door* to the s. and a large *scratch dial* can be seen high on the s.e. nave buttress. There are some particularly good C18 headstones in the churchyard and s. of the chancel is the base of a *preaching cross* that an early C19 rector moved from the nearby meadow. The s. *porch* is simple C15 timber on a brick and flint base and the entrance door is medieval, bearing exceptionally good ironwork which is probably early C14. The closing ring is pierced and there are four lizards cast on the rim – ancient emblems of good fortune that were favoured for handles. The keyhole escutcheon, in the form of a pierced crown, is of equal quality. In front of the lofty tower arch stands a plain C13 octagonal *font* on a circle of renewed shafts and base and, like the entrance, the stair to the tower still has its medieval door. The roofs and benches were part of the 1860s restoration and the C19 pulpit was remodelled in 1986. In the s. wall there is a large tomb recess under a *cusped ogee* arch rising to an excellent *finial* and if, as has been suggested, the C14 rebuilding was by Alexander de Walsham, this might be his tomb. As at nearby Whepstead, there are simple *piscinas* cut in the *dropped sills* of

the windows each side of the nave at the e. end to serve subsidiary *altars*, and on the n. side the whole sill shows traces of colour. There is now no *rood screen* or loft but the stone *corbels* that carried the *rood beam* remain high in the wall each side of the chancel arch. The chancel stalls are Victorian but they make use of C15 bench ends. In the *sanctuary* there is a small, late-C13 double piscina under two plain arches, and you will see that the centre shaft is notched at the back to house a *credence shelf*. The C19 lays heavily on this part of the church; there are Minton tiles with a particularly dense pattern in the sanctuary and the e. wall is panelled in metal and painted with stiff figures of the *Evangelists*. The vapid e. window glass of 1869 (the Good Shepherd with Faith on the l. and Hope on the r.) is by *Ward & Hughes* and shows how much their standards fell as the result of mass production. Rector James Sprigge's 1846 memorial on the n. wall is a slightly unusual plain marble shield on grey background by Reed of Bury – one of the less well-known local masons. Before leaving, have a look at the sweet little chamber organ in a plain pine case with decorative cornice. It was built in Rutland in the 1880s and brought here 100 years later.

Brome, St Mary (F3): There is a clamorous rookery e. of the church and peacocks from the farm next door emerge as startling flashes of colour among the sombre shrubberies. The church was enthusiastically rebuilt between 1859 and 1865 to the designs of Thomas Jeckyll. He was one of the C19's quirky but highly creative designer-architects who had something in common with *Pugin* and the *pre-Raphaelites*. His only complete Anglican church was Thorpe Episcopi just outside Norwich but he worked on thirteen other Norfolk churches. A man of boundless activity, he restored a number of country houses and many of his designs in metal were brilliant (like the Norwich gates at Sandringham) and won international awards. It all proved too much in the end and he died insane. Here he replaced the *nave* and *chancel* roofs, rebuilt the w. part of the n. *aisle*, added the n. *transept* and provided parapets linking the transept with the nave and chancel. He rebuilt the belfry stage of the *Norman* round tower and added a dinky staircase turret with minute 'ox-eye' windows. Jeckyll toyed with every style in the book but the s. *porch* (now a *vestry*) was altered very little.

Within, there is a heavy three-bay *arcade* which Jekyll altered in Norman style, giving the *piers* new *capitals* with exaggerated *dog-tooth* ornament. The chancel arch was embellished with foliate heads and on the chancel side he added tiny stylised clover leafs in a band below the dogtooth. That motif is picked up in the *encaustic floor tiles* and the n. transept window. The *font* has been raised on steps within the tower to form a baptistery and its familiar East Anglian style has *Evangelistic symbols* in the bowl panels, together with angels bearing shields carved with *instruments of the Passion* and a *Trinity emblem*; there are demi-angels below the bowl and four snooty lions support the base. The stone pulpit has figures of the *apostles* within open arches and was designed by Jekyll 'en suite' with a reading desk which now (surprisingly) shows signs of decay. The sculptor was James Williams of Ipswich and the *reredos* is his also. This unusual and interesting piece (again a Jekyll design) was shown at the 1881 London Exhibition and the panels are carved in deep relief – the visit of the Magi, Christ in Gethsemane, the Resurrection, and Our Lord with doubting *St Thomas*. In the central Crucifixion scene, the two thieves are tied writhing to their crosses, in sharp contrast to the calm figure nailed between them. Williams also supplied the *piscina, sedilia*, and heavy *communion rails* to match. Lady Caroline Kerrison painted much of the glass in the body of the church but the windows in the chancel contain very good work of the 1860s by *Heaton, Butler & Bayne*. The vivid panels of the e. window portray *SS George* and *Michael*, while the damned in hell cringe below the urgent hand of the avenging angel on the r., in contrast to the company of the blessed being gathered on the other side. The s. *sanctuary* window has figures of the *Blessed Virgin*, Christ, and *St John the Baptist*, while the s. chancel window contains panels illustrating Christ's baptism, His presentation in the Temple, the visit of the Magi, the miracle at Cana, and the Last Supper. There are brilliant blues and reds and the patterns are lively. Brome Hall was the ancestral home of the Cornwallis family. Charles, 1st Marquis, was patron of the living but is better remembered for his enforced surrender at Yorktown in the American War of Independence and his governor generalship of India. There is an interesting selection of family memorials in the n.e. chapel, and the tomb under the arch just n. of the sanctuary is that of Sir John Cornwallis and his wife (although he was actually buried at Berkhamstead). The stone is painted buff, picked out with gilt and colour; there are eight painted shields on the chest and a large relief *achievement*

of arms against the wall at the foot of the effigies, where two nicely individual hounds lie. The wife wears a *kennel headdress* and has a large golden locket on a long chain. Sir John is in full armour and holds the white staff which was the symbol of his office as steward in the household of the young prince who was to become Edward VI. He was knighted for bravery at Morlaix in Brittany and died in 1544. In the n.e. corner the tomb of his eldest son, Thomas, is closely modelled on his own. He too is in full armour, while his wife wears a Paris cap and scarlet gown; a large stag lies at their feet. Sir Thomas was one of the knights who put down Kett's rebellion in 1549 and he was sheriff of Norfolk and Suffolk in 1553. He was a fervent Catholic supporter of Queen Mary and comptroller of her household until her death in 1558. As treasurer of Calais he was widely accused of its loss to the French and his epitaph sums up: 'in special grace and trust of his Mistress who untimely losing her life retired him self home to this towne wher he spent the rest of his own privately and loyally all the rayne of Queen Elizabeth her sister and died heer the second yeer of King James the 26 of December 1604 in the 86 yeer of his age.'

On the wall above, a large marble cartouche carries the worn gilt epitaph of Elizabeth, Lady Cornwallis, who died in 1680. Over it, two *putti* draw aside drapes from an oval frame containing a bas-relief bust which, with its décolleté shift and pert mouth, has a hint of the voluptuous. In the s.e. corner of the chapel is a large and distinguished mural tablet for Frederick, 1st Lord Cornwallis, who died in 1661, just after Charles II's restoration. Part of the epitaph translates: for his unshaken loyalty to the King and having suffered proscription and exile by his enemies has entered into the celestial fatherland and in the bosom of a church restored has fallen peacefully asleep. The last memorial to note is on the n. wall by the organ where a small painted and gilt figure kneels within a coffered arch, with six shields displayed around. It commemorates Henry Cornwallis, Sir Thomas's brother, who lived in Norfolk and was buried here in 1598. Brome has a ring of five bells with a 7 cwt. tenor, but they are in 'poor going order' at the present time.

Bromeswell, St Edmund (H5): The C15 tower is compact, with four *set-offs* on the angle buttresses. Like the *base course*, they are decorated with *flushwork*, and there is more of it in the stepped battlements. Walking round, one finds that the n. wall of the *nave* is blank except for a single *Perpendicular* window, and a brick chimney flue has been built over the blocked n. doorway. The *chancel* was rebuilt in red brick in the C19, and a meeting room/*vestry* has recently been added on the n. side which marries with it very well. The attractive, chunky brick *porch* dates from the early C16, and the two *corbel* heads set in its facade may have belonged to a predecessor. The C12 inner doorway shows that this was a *Norman* building, and it has a triple band of *chevrons* in the arch, with an outer rim of *billet* moulding. Traces of a *scratch dial* on the r.-hand side are a relic of the time before there was a porch.

The nave, with its brick floors, lies under a steep *hammerbeam* and *arch-braced roof*. The high *collars* support *king posts*, and there is a leaf trail carved on the *wall plate*. The Victorians inserted skylights at the e. end, and one of Archdeacon Darling's last projects was to carve a pair of demi-angels to replace those lost from the end of the hammerbeams. More of his work is to be seen in his own parish church at Eyke, and here the project has been very effectively completed with fibre glass replicas of his angels on the rest of the hammers. They all bear shields, and there is a useful key to the heraldry on the n. wall. Note the *sanctus-bell window* in the w. wall, and beyond the tall, plain tower arch, there are two very odd recesses in the side walls. Some 6ft. from the floor, they are about 7in. square, and very deep; there is a roughly carved triangular C12 head below one of them, and they are reminiscent of the exterior *squints* to be found at Lound, Blundeston, and Pakefield – and just as mysterious. The C15 *font* has four defaced lions with curly manes round the shaft, and *Evangelistic symbols* alternate with angels in the deep bowl panels. The latter bear shaped shields with a crown, rose, book, and priest's stole – emblems of church and state authority in conjunction. An interesting chart giving details of the families who were Lords of the Manor is displayed in the n. doorway, and further along, a Norman window splay was used to frame the village's World War I memorial. The low, C15 benches with *poppy-heads* are very battered, and four figures survive on the elbows. The style of the modern benches at the e. end, and the choir stalls, suggest that they may have come from Darling's school of carvers at Eyke. There is now no *screen*, but the doorways of the *rood loft stair* remain in the s. wall. Opposite, the *Jacobean* pulpit stands on a slender, coved shaft, and there is a plain niche

behind it. In the chancel there is a comely set of *Stuart communion rails*, and the stocky *Holy table*, with its thick stretchers and carved apron, is the same period. The glass of about 1860 in the e. window is possibly by *William Wailes* – brightly coloured but not memorable figures of the Good Shepherd, the *Blessed Virgin*, and *St John*, plus an *Agnus Dei*, the Evangelistic symbols, and a *pelican* at the top. The glass in the s. lancet is rather better – a *St Stephen* in the centre, with a *censing* angel above, and *St Barbara* in a roundel below. Although Bromeswell's bells can only be chimed, the tenor is notable for its early-C14 date and was probably cast by the London founder Richard de Wymblis. The treble of 1530 was cast by Cornelius Waghevens of Malines and is decorated with four medallions on the waist – the *Annunciation*, the Flight into Egypt, Christ's Presentation in the Temple, and *St Michael* and the dragon.

Bruisyard, St Peter (H4): A church in a lovely situation, perched on rising ground above the bosky valley of the infant river Alde, with an avenue of limes between the *lych-gate* and the *porch*. There is no evidence to date the round tower precisely, but it is likely to be *Norman*, and it becomes abruptly slimmer halfway up. The upper stage either collapsed or was rebuilt in the C15, and the bell openings were renewed in the late 1960s. The large w. *lancet* framed in white brick probably dates from the early C19, and so does the large 'gothick' window with a wooden frame on the n. side of the *nave*. You will see signs of a blocked n. doorway and, further along, the complete frame of an earlier, Norman, doorway is embedded in the wall. In the late C16, a substantial chapel was added at right angles to the s. wall of the chancel, and two of its three *mullioned* windows were later blocked. The builder saved the old priest's door and repositioned it in the w. wall of the chapel. A bulky *rood stair* turret of brick lies in the angle between nave and chapel, and there is a handsome C16 brick mullioned window alongside. A line of tile capping shows where the walls were raised to take the new roof that was built in the C15, and w. of the small and modest porch there is another of the early-C19 windows.

The *Early English* s. doorway has unusual little rosette terminals on its *hood mould*, and one passes through to a simple interior. The coarse moulding of the tower arch fades into the *imposts*, and beyond it, the lancet window contains an attractive Good Shepherd (probably by *Jones & Willis*, installed around 1911). The small C15 *font* is the conventional East Anglian design, with lions seated round the shaft, angel heads below the bowl, and deeply cut, hung shields in the panels. It was disastrously cracked when a staple to secure the cover was driven into the stone. From within, the tall C15 n. doorway is prominent, but there is no sign of the Norman entrance that we saw outside. The nave roof has been plastered out between the *arch-braces*, and there are *bosses* at the intersections. The demi-angels perched on the high *collars* are very like those at nearby Badingham and Sibton. A set of *Hanoverian Royal Arms* is framed on the s. wall – very much an apprentice effort, painted on canvas. There are C19 benches in the nave with simple fleur-de-lys *finials*, and in front of the entrance to the rood stair stands a seemly C18 pulpit, complete with *tester*. The Victorians re-sited the early-C17 *communion rails* under the *chancel* arch, and installed a replacement rood beam overhead. Some of the C15 bench ends with *poppyheads* were saved from the nave and used in the new choir stalls, and the C19 alterations included a Minton-tiled *sanctuary* and stone-panelled *reredos*. The e. window glass by Jones & Willis dates from the early C20 – a Crucifixion flanked by figures of the *Blessed Virgin* and *St Peter*, carrying the reversed cross of his martyrdom as well as his keys. Below stands a homely *Stuart Holy table*, and the C15 *piscina* is sited within a window embrasure that was perhaps blocked when the new chapel was added alongside. The chapel is separated from the chancel by a high, panelled screen, and the turned *balusters* in its top section resemble those in the communion rails. Now used as a *vestry,* the chapel was built by Michael Hare, who died in 1611 and lies buried there with his two wives Elizabeth and Maria. Their brass is hidden under the carpet, but an adequate rubbing is displayed in the nave. Michael's effigy and two shields have disappeared, but the 25in. figures of the ladies wearing French hoods are in good condition, and the shields of the Hobert and Brudenel families survive, along with the inscription. The chapel has two other interesting items – an C18 *bier* complete with straps, and a printed set of the *Decalogue* dated 1794. They are hand coloured, and have the figures of Moses, Aaron and Joshua as supporters, with the names of all the prophets worked into the border. Very few examples of these cheap and popular productions have survived, and this one is worth preserving.

Brundish, St Laurence (G4): The church stands in a spacious churchyard by a quiet lane at the e. end of this straggling village. The unbuttressed *Norman* tower was heightened during a C14 rebuilding but the bell opening on the e. side was retained and there are outlines of *lancets* to w., s., and n. farther down. The w. doorway and the rest of the bell openings are later. There are tall *Perpendicular* windows in the *nave*, their *hood moulds* linked by a *string course*, and the date of the *chancel* restoration is cast on one of the drain-pipe hoppers. When you walk round, you will find a low granite stone almost hidden by the yew to the n.w. of the tower. It marks the grave of Reginald Livesey, a naturalist who died in 1932, having earlier in his life explored the interior of Queensland and studied birds in the Pacific. The s. *porch* was added after the nave had been rebuilt and could only be fitted on by overlapping half of one of the windows. Its facade is decorated with *flushwork* and there is a niche over the outer arch which has large roses in the *spandrels* and little *fleurons* on the *label*. The entrance door is medieval and the shaft of a stoup remains to the r.

Once inside you will see that when the window was partly blocked by the porch, the C15 builders did not bother to remove the glazing bars but merely filled the spaces between them with plaster. The outline of the old Norman w. arch shows up plainly in the tower wall, and above it is a very attractive set of George III *Royal Arms* dated 1765 in a cutout frame complete with dummy candlesticks. The church is well blessed with *biers* – there are three in the base of the tower, one of which is child-sized like the one at Mendlesham. The plain C14 *font* rests on a low drum shaft and by it stands a single stall complete with *misericord* that must have come from a chancel set somewhere. The two panels by the n. door are all that remain of the C15 *rood screen*. The nave has a homely brick floor, C18 plastered ceiling, and a low range of C15 benches with *poppyheads* and later backs. A suite of C18 plain *box pews* was installed at the e. end and most of them merely encase the old benches (as at Gislingham). The low arch in the n. wall probably marks the grave of the founder but it now shelters an interesting 28in. *brass*, that of Sire Edmound de Burnedissh. It is the earliest of the four brasses in the county illustrating priests in vestments and dates from about 1360. In the nave floor another brass commemorates John Colby (d.1540) in Elizabethan-period armour, and his wife Anne (d.1560) shown with their four sons and nine daughters; the shields were originally coloured, and with the bold and easily read inscription, it is a fine example dating from after Anne's death. The very coarse pulpit has C15 tracery in the body panels but the back panel and tester are *Jacobean*. The statue niche in the window embrasure to the l. shows traces of original colouring and there are the remains of its twin on the s. side. The chancel arch is wide, with small *headstops*, and marks show where the old rood screen was fixed. The angle *piscina* in the *sanctuary* is most attractive, with a *cusped* and *crocketted ogee* arch flanked by pinnacles. There are *dropped-sill sedilia* to the r. and to the l. two small and oddly proportioned recesses. In the n.e. corner is the brass for Sir John Colby (d.1559), the son of John & Alice whose brass we have seen in the nave; the shields on this example were originally inlaid with colour and there is a rhyming inscription. The brass in the s.e. corner shows Thomas Glemham as a kneeling youth of about 1570 and has a verse inscription and five shields. There are sections of C15 glass in the tracery of the e. window, including a very good head and shoulders of a bearded king and a devil/monster. In his autobiography Adrian Bell recalls a visit here on one of his many Suffolk dawdles with Sir Alfred Munnings: 'Munnings had become subdued. "How short life is. We toil at our art, and then we are gone. What's it all for Bell?" An indomitable sparrow in the roof chirruped an answer. We roused, reopened the heavy door; and suddenly again all the birds of heaven were singing and the sun fell on us warm'.

Bucklesham, St Mary (G6): There has been a church here since the Conquest (and possibly before), but the present building dates almost entirely from 1878. The architect was William Smith, and he reused much of the old material, choosing the *Decorated* style for his new windows. There had been a tower until the late C18 (foundations were uncovered at the w. end in 1925), but Smith contented himself with a bell-cote topped with an attractive shingled spirelet, on the w. end of the *nave*. Changes in the masonry show that he retained the n. wall of the nave up to half its height, and the blocked C13 n. doorway still has a medieval door in place. A *stoup* is set in the wall alongside. The *Perpendicular* e. window was also saved, and an *aisle* and organ chamber were added on the s. side. In 1935, a substantial *vestry* was built on to the n. side of the *chancel*. The tablet with 'John Steel, churchwarden 1822' on the e. wall of the

organ chamber probably related to a repair of the old building. The latest change was in 1968, when a s. *porch* was added, making effective use of *knapped* and squared white flints. Its outer door is largely original, and still bears its medieval closing ring, and the inner archway dates from about 1300.

The C15 *font* follows the familiar East Anglian pattern, with four lions supporting the shaft, one of them almost entirely destroyed. The deeply cut *Evangelistic symbols* in the bowl panels have also been defaced, and the shields borne by the angels in the remaining panels have had their emblems scraped away. The fragment of stone on the aisle w. windowsill was discovered in the rectory stables, and it is part of the square bowl of a *Norman* font, possibly the one that was used here in the first building. A three-bay Perpendicular-style *arcade* separates the nave from the narrow s. aisle, matched by a new chancel arch. There are pitchpine roofs and open benches, the latter with slightly unusual curved ends. The C14 *priest's door* in the n. wall of the chancel now leads to the vestry, and the framework of the door itself is old. Half of the arch of the recess in the n. wall of the *sanctuary* is original, and it may perhaps have been saved from the *piscina* that will have existed in the opposite wall.

Bungay, Holy Trinity (H2): Now that the larger church of St Mary has been declared redundant, Holy Trinity serves both parishes. Although much of the evidence is concealed inside, it seems clear that the round tower is *Saxon* and no later than the first half of the C11. It originally had a ring of eight circular windows at the top, with four more lower down. Most of the round towers have flint walls with an occasional admixture of brick, but here you will see, in addition, bands of small sandstone blocks set in *herringbone* fashion. There is one *Perpendicular* bell opening to the w., and a matching window was added below in the 1850s. When the upper level was rebuilt in 1757, a range of shields was moved up and set in the new battlements. Clockwise from the s.e. they are for: *Edward the Confessor*; East Anglia (or Ely); Montague; Thomas Brotherton (Earl of Norfolk in 1313); Henry Despencer (Bishop of Norwich in 1370); a crowned 'M' for the *Blessed Virgin*, Beauchamp; I.M. & W.P. 1757 (for churchwardens John Meen and William Pell). The *quoins* at the w. end of the *nave* are a sign that the body of the church is probably as old as the tower, and there is a blocked *Norman lancet* in the n. wall beyond the *vestry*. The latter looks as though it may have begun as a C17 *porch*, with a window inserted later in its outer arch. The flintwork below the brick gable is a good example of the Norfolk practice of 'galleting', that is embedding shards of flint in the mortar between the stones to give extra strength and stave off frost damage. By the mid-C18 the *chancel* was ruinous, and a short extension to the nave was added in lieu. This served until 1926 when the whole of the e. end was rebuilt to the design of F.E. Howard. The wide s. *aisle* was dedicated to the Blessed Virgin, and if its w. window is a replica of the original, it dates from the C14. There is a *scratch dial* to be found on the s.e. buttress, and a low turret is placed at the s.w. corner of the aisle. It probably gave access to the porch before the latter was rebuilt in 1860. The Victorians had a weakness for cast-iron, and the Incorporated Society for Promoting the Enlargement, Building, and Repairing of Churches and Chapels made use of it for their notices (with a title like that, who wouldn't?). You will see from the example inside the porch that spaces were left in the text for the number of seats 'reserved for the use of the Poorer Inhabitants of this Parish for ever'. The great fire that all but destroyed the town in 1688 came perilously close, and four men were paid a shilling each 'for helping to quench ye fire at ye church porch and to carry the rubbish out'. Until it was restored in 1860, the s. door still bore the marks of the flames. It retains the plate of its medieval closing ring and the massive lock, and a plaque records: 'Here the fire was stayed 1688'. Just within stands one of Suffolk's few C18 *fonts*, with fluted pedestal, scalloped bowl, and four vaguely pagan masks below the rim. St Mary's was provided with a similar design after the great town fire, and this may have come from the same mason. The fine C14 *arcade* has *quatrefoil piers*, and it is continued eastward by a single Perpendicular bay which links the nave with the aisle chapel. All the roofs have been renewed, and a dormer window was inserted at the w. end of the nave to give more light to the *gallery*. The centre window in the s. aisle has glass of about 1910, probably by *Powells* – a conventional but good quality illustration of the young Christ with the Elders in the Temple. The same firm provided the World War I memorial window further along. It has figures of *SS Paul, Timothy* and Eunice. She was Timothy's mother and never sanctified by the church, although the artist has given her a halo to match the others. The 1930s aisle e. window glass is again by

Powells – an elaborate Nativity, with the manger richly decked, a lantern above, and a pristine lamb below; small figures of Isaiah and *St Luke* stand on pedestals in the *tracery*. In place of *communion rails* the chapel has a very fine pair of modern oak kneelers, each with three pairs of turned *balusters*. The diminutive *piscina* was uncovered in 1852, and at the same time a *brass* was found which is now fixed to the nearest arcade pier. The two shields and inscription commemorate Lionel Throckmorton, founder of the town's grammar school, who died in 1599. The church's other brass is a most interesting inscription which can be found on the fifth pew from the w. end of the aisle. It lay originally in the floor nearby, and asks us to pray for the soul of Margaret Dalenger who died in 1497, having been Prioress of the Benedictine nunnery which stood just across the road. A plain oval tablet between fluted *pilasters* on the aisle wall at the e. end is for Gen. Robert Kelso, a veteran marine who served in many an action before retiring here to be churchwarden and die in 1823.

Moving into the nave, note the set of C18 *Decalogue* boards by the organ on the gallery, and the memorial on the n. wall for Matthias Kerrison, with its urn against a plain pyramid and a *cartouche* of arms. A child of poor parents, he prospered as a local merchant in the Napoleonic wars and died a millionaire in 1827. The window further along contains stained glass figures of the youthful David and Christ (artist unidentified), installed in 1952. The pulpit is one of the county's best C16 examples, bought by the parish in 1558. Standing on a pedestal, it features two ranks of geometrically moulded panels with simple centre ornaments, and the angle pilasters are recess-carved with attractive scrolls; there is a band of narrow panels under the rim, and the book ledge has decorative brackets. The deftly proportioned monument on the wall above, with its three urns and cherub's head set against an obelisk, commemorates William Lamb and his wife; there is no signature but it has the quality associated with the Norwich statuaries of the 1770s. The monument of 1774 on the chancel n. wall for Thomas and Catherine Wilson was sculpted by Thomas Scheemakers, son of the better known Peter (whose only Suffolk work is at Cowlinge). A weeping *putto* leans against an urn, and palm fronds curl around the edges of the backing obelisk. The modern *sanctuary* is bounded by an excellent set of communion rails which date from the mid-C17 and have balusters shaped like Indian clubs.

Bungay, St Mary (H2): The church passed into the care of the *Churches Conservation Trust* in 1981, and much has been done since by way of restoration, with sterling support provided by the Friends of St Mary's. A Benedictine nunnery was founded here in 1160, and its church was used both by the religious community and by the parishioners until the dissolution of the monasteries in the 1530s. The nuns gave permission for a splendid new tower to be built in about 1470 and it forms the church's finest feature. Standing at the w. end of the s. aisle, it is 90ft high and shares some of its characteristics with the towers of Eye and Redenhall not far away. Most of the decoration is concentrated on the w. face where the double *base course* features a line of *quatrefoils*, with shields set in cresting above them, and the lower stages of the octagonal buttresses are enlivened with delicate *flushwork*. A band of crowned 'M's for the dedication curves over the w. window arch, and in the s. wall there is a *sound hole* which has a shield set within a ring of quatrefoils. The tall, *transomed* bell openings have lovely *tracery*, and the corner turrets are crowned with *crocketted* pinnacles and weather vanes. The fire of 1688 that destroyed almost all of the town badly damaged the church, and the top of the tower had to be partially rebuilt in the years that followed. It houses a very good ring of eight bells with a 15 cwt. tenor, and the belfry has made its mark in the history of bell ringing. At the beginning of the C15, the parishioners replaced the original C12 *nave* with a much grander version, and its w. doorway will have been used as the main entrance for special and ceremonial occasions; the mighty seven-*light* window above it has an intricate, slightly restless, tracery pattern. The late-C14 n. aisle was dedicated to the Holy Cross (like the priory itself) and it faced the town's market place before later buildings intervened. Accordingly, decoration was lavished on it. The buttresses are gabled at two levels, and the top range has shallow niches; there are angled *headstops* to all the gable arches, and even the image stools have little heads and *paterae* under the rims. The parapet (restored in 1865) is a beautiful frieze pierced with quatrefoils capped with fleur-de-lys, and it may well have been the pattern for the one at Blythburgh. On its n.e. corner there is a little figure of a man in armour, legs curiously splayed, and he could represent the donor. There are excellent *gargoyles* – look particularly for the dog and the man pulling his mouth open. Built at the same time, the *porch* rises to the same height as the aisle and has its

own stair turret leading to the upper room; that was used as a school at one time, with the children moving down to the ground floor in fine weather. There is a capacious *stoup* to the r., and the arch of another, later version survives on the l. The *spandrels* of the outer arch are carved with two cleverly condensed little scenes. On the l., an armoured knight bearing a shield with *St Mary's* device poses on the lion he has slain, and on the r. a spread-eagled lioness plays tag with her tiny cub, with the head of a saint in the corner. The arch has worn, lion *stops*, and carved beasts sit on the corners of the parapet. Walking round, you will see quite extensive remains of the priory to the e. of the church, including the n. wall of the long, early-C13 *chancel* which is slightly askew with the existing church. It would seem that the stub walls jutting out from the e. wall of the nave belonged to the nun's chapel of St Mary. The s. aisle was built about the same time as the tower and received very little decoration, adjoining as it did the nun's cloister.

Entry is via the n. porch, and its windows record the heavy 1860s restoration which included replacement of the stone vaulting and some of the foliage *bosses*; however, the one in the centre is original, a *Passion* shield ringed with eight angels. Unusually, the outer arch has a queen *headstop* on the inside. The town fire of 1688 ruined the s. aisle and so badly damaged the rest of the church that extensive rebuilding was necessary. There were further restorations in 1863 and 1879, and the recent work funded by the national body and by the Friends of St Mary's has left the spacious interior in immaculate condition, beautifully kept. The graceful, early-C14 *arcades* have ridged quatrefoil *piers* and closely banded *capitals*, with a narrower arch marking the *sanctuary* at the e. end. There are small, widely spaced *Perpendicular clerestory* windows, and the nave e. window was set high in the wall to clear the nunnery roofs that lay beyond. The *font* of 1700 that was provided after the fire stands near the entrance, one of the few C18 examples in the county (although there is another at nearby Holy Trinity). It has a scalloped bowl on a fluted shaft, and there are heavy, crudely cut cherub heads and flowers carved below the rim. On the wall nearby is a very elegant 1760s monument for Henry Williams, by Thomas Rawlins, the leading Norwich statuary; the oval tablet is within a lovely architectural frame set against an obelisk of mottled brown, with urn at head and cherub at foot. When the n. aisle was re-leaded in 1792, the churchwardens and plumber added their names according to custom; that section was saved when the lead was stripped off in 1950 and is now clamped to the w. wall.

The bowl of an ancient font that may date from before the Norman Conquest stands in the corner by the stairs that lead to the porch upper room. The interesting and unusual cupboard by the entrance is likely to have been a 'dole' cupboard, used for the storage of charity bread to be dispensed at the church door. There are three naive carvings of bishops on its sides, and at the bottom of the door you will see the initials 'WB' above a large 'Q' enclosing a little rat, and 'Bungay 1675'. It is presumably a *rebus* for a cleric with those initials, although he hasn't been identified. There is another Rawlins memorial on the n. wall, but this time it is by the father of the better known son. For Peregrina Browne who died in 1743, it is in white and mottled marble, with a *cartouche* and supporting garlands above the *pediment*, and a cherub's head below. Robert Scales' memorial in the centre of the n. wall was probably supplied by a Norwich mason as well; the tablet is flanked by *Corinthian pilasters* and scrolls, and there are crossed palms with a cherub's head below the heavily ribbed ledge. When Thomas Scheemakers was in Bungay (he provided a monument in Holy Trinity), he judged the trumpeting *putto* on top of this piece as 'very well executed'. The *priest's door* further along has oak and ivy leaves nicely carved in the spandrels, and at the e. end of the aisle there is a monument for Peregrey Browne and his wife Elizabeth that was the work of William Lane the Elder, another of the Norwich masons active in the late C18. Nicely proportioned, the shaped tablet is placed below a curly scroll cornice, with a *cartouche* of arms at the bottom. The aisle e. window glass is by Charles and Alexander Gibbs, one of the firms that led the vigorous Victorian revival of the art, and it was shown at the London 1862 exhibition. There are brightly coloured scenes of four of the *Seven Works of Mercy*, using biblical settings against deep blue backgrounds; the rest of the window is filled with attractively patterned *quarries*, family initials, and arms of the donors. The aisle sanctuary has a large *piscina* that was quite lavish in its original state, but all the tracery and niches that flanked the arch have been shorn away. The panelling behind the *altar* encloses a 20in. x 12in. wooden carving of the Resurrection which was presented to the church by the author Sir Henry Rider Haggard who lived at Ditchingham just across the border in Norfolk. It is, I believe, C17 Flemish work, and portrays Christ with billowing cloak and cross staff, rising above three gesturing soldiers, while another figure kneels by the tomb.

Before the *Reformation* a *rood screen* stretched across the church, one bay from the e. end, and marks on the arcade piers show where it was fitted. The churchwardens presumed to take it down during Elizabeth's reign but were deprived of their office for their pains; the parish had to provide a replacement but nothing of it now remains. The high e. window contains, in its upper half, 1860s glass by *Powells*; below, there are oval scenes of Christ's baptism, *Transfiguration*, Crucifixion and Ascension – all fine work of the 1870s by Thomas Baillie, set in patterned quarries. The tall arcaded stone *reredos*, with its texts picked out in colour, was designed by Henry Nursey in 1863. The s. aisle had to be re-roofed after the fire, and four of the bosses at the w. end are carved with the churchwardens' initials and '1699', the date of completion. The aisle had an unusual dedication to *St Eligius*, and the chapel's C15 piscina is still to be seen behind the organ. There are a pair of *griffins* in the quatrefoils above its double arch, with a tiny bishop's head carved between them.

Bures, St Mary (D7): A handsome, chunky church in a spacious setting. The lower section of the tower is late C13 with tall, thin *lancets* to the w. and s., and there is an exterior tomb recess on the n. side below a *finialed* gable. Most of the tower was built by Sir Richard Waldegrave in the late C14 or early C15 and there are two chambers with small lancets below the bell openings with their *Decorated tracery*; a stair lies within the n.w. buttress and rises almost to the top. The late-C15 or early-C16 s. porch is very stately in red brick and the wide outer arch incorporates two earlier stone head *corbels*. There is an niche overhead above sloping steps in the brickwork reminiscent of Little Waldingfield's n. porch. The *dripstone* of the C14 inner doorway has large *headstops* and the one on the r. is a knight wearing the chainmail 'camail' to protect his head and shoulders. The *stoup* below is most unusual in that the ledge of the bowl is supported by two figures, one of which is a bishop raising his hand in blessing. The C15 doors have the remains of tracery and a border trail of vines and birds. At the e. end of the s. aisle is the bulky *chantry chapel* built in brick by Sir William

Bures, St Mary

Waldegrave in 1514, with generous windows and some *flushwork* on the e. face. The centre buttress cunningly incorporates a *priest's door* with *fleurons* in the moulding and the table tomb nearby has a barely legible inscription on the top in which the name 'Constable' can still be recognised – apparently the last resting place of the famous landscape painter's grandfather. The window of the *vestry* on the n. side of the chancel has an angel with a curly trumpet as one of the headstops while his partner bears a *Trinity* emblem shield. The C14 n. porch is lovely, its timbers grooved and worn like driftwood. The cusped barge boards are pierced with *mouchette* roundels matching those below, and the moulded entrance arch is cut from two massive planks. Sympathetically restored in 1873, there are varying Decorated forms in the tracery of the side panels.

It seems that the wide *nave* and aisles were built in one continuous operation and the C14 *arcades*, with their octagonal *piers*, are low and wide. The original nave roof was replaced when the *Perpendicular clerestory* was added and altered again in the C19. The brutal flat ceiling probably dates from an 1860s restoration by *Ewan Christian* and now houses modern recessed lighting, but below it on the walls are large corbels which once supported *wall posts*. They now carry a pair of large and very attractive banners. There are bland

angels with shields and the three interesting heads and a grotesque in the corners no doubt survive from the original roof. A vaulted ceiling was planned for the ground floor of the tower and again there are two excellent grotesques at the base of the rib stubs – one snarling and the other sticking its tongue out. Good use has now been made of the base of the tower. The arch to the nave has been glazed above a solid screen in limed oak, and a door leads through to cloakrooms and a crèche. From there a stair leads up to a fine new matching gallery which affords a splendid view through to the e. end. The tower houses an excellent ring of eight bells with a 20 cwt. tenor. The rear of the nave has been arranged for a variety of parish uses, and the s. porch is now an attractive place of retreat for prayer, with the medieval door still in place. Plans were afoot in 2005 to remove the C19 pews in the s. aisle and replace them with comfortable chairs to match those in the n. aisle. Enhanced by new lighting, the *font* stands at the e. end of the n. aisle and its traceried stem has battered *Evangelistic symbols* at the corners. The bowl is likely to be a replacement of the 1540s and has very deeply cut angels bearing shields in the panels. These are now coloured, and clockwise from the e. they are: England, De Vere, Fitzralph, Mortimer, Cornard, Waldegrave, De Bures, and Mortimer of Clare. On a tomb chest in a n. aisle window embrasure is the superb effigy carved in sweet chestnut of a knight dating from around 1330 (the only comparable piece from this period in Suffolk is at Heveningham although there is a very late C16 example at Boxted). It probably commemorates Sir Richard de Cornard, and his head rests on a pillow borne up by a pair of angels, while his crossed, spurred feet rest on a lion which has a cloth draped and tied around its neck. I wonder why. The shields of effigies like this were usually pegged on and most have vanished but this one is complete. Both pulpit and low chancel screen are C19 but on the e. of the chancel arch (s. side just below the *capital*) is a most interesting survival. *Rood lofts* occasionally carried an *altar* and there must have been one here because the *piscina* that was used for washing the *chalice* and *paten* is built into the *respond* of the arch and its fluted underside can be seen from below.

The late-C14 n.e. vestry was altered, probably in the C16, and the doorway from the chancel has fleurons and masks in the moulding, with smiling faces on the headstops of the *hood mould*. The arch between the vestry and the *sanctuary* is blocked by a massive table tomb and indents show that the top once carried a large brass. Its placing and the nature of the brass make it virtually certain that this is the tomb of Sir Richard Waldegrave, builder of much of the church, who died in 1410, and his wife Joan. It is strange that the style of the chest is C16 rather than C15 but it is possible that it was rebuilt when the vestry was altered. Above it, angels with shields jut out and under them there is a figure with a floriated cross on one side, and a chained dog on the other. Originally, the tomb had an elaborate wooden canopy and, like many in this position, it was used as an *Easter sepulchre*. The mid-C19 glass in the e. window is of poor quality and very eroded while the contemporary *reredos* is flanked by equally vapid panels of the *Annunciation*. The Waldegrave chantry on the s. side of the chancel was also known as the Jesus chapel and although its founder's tomb has disappeared, the one below the s.e. window is likely to be that of his son Sir George Waldegrave who died in 1528. The chest has lozenges with shields deeply set within them and *spandrels* carved with leaves. What was the back now lies canted at an angle on the top and shows the marks of missing brasses. *Dowsing* perhaps removed them in 1643 when he 'brake down above 600 superstitious pictures'. The chapel e. window has glass of 1946 by H.G. Wright & A.J. Dix – Christ in Majesty within a glory, trumpeting angels each side, and three panels

of script at the bottom commemorating the chantry's founder – all set in plain glass and attractive. Another William Waldegrave, who died in 1613, and his wife Elizabeth have a large free-standing tomb in the chapel. The chest is plain except for grooved *pilasters* and the upper section has pairs of *Corinthian* columns flanking coloured *achievements*, with *pediments* and balls at the corners above. Strangely, the inscription tablet is on the back and the only effigies are those of the twelve children – little kneeling figures in alabaster.

Bures, St Stephen's chapel (D7): The road to Assington climbs Cuckoo Hill out of Bures and at the top a track leads through a farmyard and open fields to a lovely hill-top site where stands the chapel. There is a firm tradition that *St Edmund* was crowned king here on Christmas Day 855, and it is certain that Stephen Langton, archbishop of Canterbury, consecrated a private chapel here on the Feast of Stephen in 1218. This is the building we see and, although it is not a parish church, at least one service is held a year so it comes within the scope of this guide. At some time it fell into disuse and over the years it was divided into cottages and then used as a barn, with a brick and timber extension added to the w. end. Its walls were breached so that waggons could be driven in and it was not until the 1930s that restoration was put in hand leading to a re-dedication in 1940. The whole building lies under thatch, with a two-storeyed *porch* on the n. side and the brick and weatherboard section to the w., but the plain oblong of the original chapel is clear. There is a simple doorway to the s., small *lancets* in the side walls, and three taller lancets grouped at the e. end.

Within, all is immaculate under single-framed roofs and the w. wall has been rebuilt. Some of the 'mock masonry' wall painting and the original *consecration crosses* have been uncovered, and the panelled shaft of a C15 *font* stands at the w. end. In a niche beyond is the fine wooden figure of a bishop which is Continental work, but the real surprise is to find three magnificent tombs. At the *Reformation*, Earls Colne priory in Essex fell into disuse and was later sold by the earl of Oxford. It contained many De Vere monuments and when the estate changed hands in the 1930s the remaining effigies were transferred here. It is likely that the three tombs incorporate sections of at least seven, but the identity of the effigies seems certain. In the n.w. corner lies the figure of Robert De Vere, 5th Earl of Oxford and Master Chamberlain of

England, who died in 1296. His sword is slung from a broad belt, his crossed feet rest on a ridge-backed hog, and the angels that support his pillow are very like those on the wooden effigy at Bures. The chest he lies on is later and has deep niches with *cusped* and *crocketted ogee* arches and shields hung in the *spandrels*; within, they are delicately *groined* and panelled and, between them, smaller shallow niches contain little figures in typically early-C14 poses which are beautiful despite their mutilation. The other two tombs carved in alabaster stand in the centre of the chapel and the westernmost is that of Richard De Vere, 11th Earl of Oxford, who died in 1412, and Countess Alice. His head rests on a hog-crested helm, there is a lion at his feet, and his wife's horned headdress lies on a pillow supported by angels; at her feet two engaging little dogs with bell collars tug at her skirts in play. The side panels of the chest have standing angels holding shields, with the arms of England at the e. end and St George's cross to the w. The last tomb carries the armoured figure of the 8th Earl, Thomas De Vere, who died in 1371 – mail-sheathed face, gloved hands, mail showing below his *jupon*, and a lion beneath his feet, all in remarkable condition. The sides of the chest are carved with nodding ogee arches over niches in which pairs of diminutive cloaked figures stand. The last monument to look for is in fact the oldest – a fragmentary C12 coffin lid in the s.w. corner carved with the stumpy feet and legs of an effigy. It probably lay on the tomb of Alberic De Vere, first Great Chamberlain and father of the 1st Earl, who died in 1141. There is a *brass* on the n. wall commemorating Isabel Badcock whose dedication was largely respon-sible for the restoration, and in the lancet alongside is a small figure of a bishop with an arrow emblem in C17 Flemish glass. Across the nave another Flemish panel portrays *St Mary Magdalene*. The *sanctuary* n. lancet displays the Scourging of Christ and on the s. side there is a Flemish or German roundel of Christ being taken from the Cross, with a kneeling C15 figure below. Most if not all of this glass came from the priory house at Earls Colne. In the e. lancets the glass is by Henry Wilkinson – small figures of *SS Edmund, Stephen, Laurence, Edward the Confessor*, and two bishops, framed by dense patterning in which a beautiful deep blue predominates. The altar and stone balustrade *communion rails* are modern but there is a heavy pre-Reformation *piscina* with a square drain under a *trefoil* arch, and an *aumbry* with a modern door in the n. wall.

Burgate, St Mary (E3): The C14 tower has an unusual window arrangement, with *quatrefoil* belfry windows and *Decorated* bell openings which have three quatrefoil openings above them on all sides. The tall s. *porch* has blocked side windows, with a plain niche over the inner door and a shallow recess to the r. which housed the *stoup*. Pause to admire the new *headstops* of the entrance arch. They are portraits of two village stalwarts, Harry Baker and Billy Garrod who, between them, logged 150 years of service to the church as choir boys, bell ringers and churchwardens. Crafted by local mason Terence Sandy, the stones celebrated an important phase in the church's restoration in 1995. *R..M. Phipson* carried out a heavy-handed restoration of the *nave* in the 1860s, giving it a new roof, and there is now no *chancel* arch; the division is marked only by an embellished *arch-brace* in the roof with *wall posts* resting on slightly fungoid *corbels*. Phipson continued with the chancel in 1872, raising the walls to take a new roof, inserting a new e. window and replacing *tracery* in the side windows. His bench designs for the nave are attractive, with chunky and varied *poppyheads*. C18 Creed and Lord's Prayer boards flank the tower arch and a little chapel dedicated to *St Edmund* was formed in the early C20 by screening the area at the side of the organ. The *font* is a common East Anglian design but the *Evangelistic symbols* have been hacked from the bowl panels, leaving only a shield held by an angel to the w. Fat lions squat round the stem and the top step carries an inscription which says that it was given by Sir William Burgate and his wife (whose tomb you will see in the chancel), which dates it around 1400. There is a modern screen across the wide nave just e. of the entrance and a set of *Royal Arms* hangs on the n. wall. They are *Stuart* but were refurbished for George II in 1735. Farther along, the *rood stairs* remain in the wall and the *piscina* of a vanished nave *altar* dedicated to the *Trinity* survives on the s. side. A headless figure labelled *St Augustine* can be found among the fragments of medieval glass in the top of a nave n. window. The square Stuart pulpit has shallow relief panels below the ledge and, beneath them, pairs of blind arches are duplicated on each side. Traces of paint inside suggest that it was made out of sections from an old *screen*. The arched recess in the chancel n. wall is in the right place for an *Easter sepulchre* but if it was it is unusually large and it is more likely to have been the entrance to a chapel. It now frames a wooden altar which has standing candlesticks and other ornaments made from shell cases and shells themselves by convalescent soldiers in Belgium in 1917. A central glass case contains the communion set used by a chaplain in France during World War I. The turned *balusters* of the choir stall fronts look as though they were part of a C17 set of *communion rails*, and on the s. side by the *priest's door* stands a large early-C15 chest whose front and sides are tinged with colour. One can just distinguish the figure of a knight on horseback and so it was probably a jousting scene or a portrait of St George. The only C19 stained glass is in a s. chancel window and is the work of *Lavers, Barraud & Westlake*. The main panels portray three of Christ's miracles of restoring life, with a Trinity emblem at the top and three angels with scrolls below. The large piscina in the *sanctuary* has had all its cresting and *cusping* chopped away, but the shields in the *spandrels* link it with Sir William Burgate, Lord of the Manor. That brings us to his tomb, the church's most interesting feature, standing proudly in the centre of the chancel. The tomb chest has close-set niches all round, with *crocketted ogee* arches and blank stone shields hung in alternate spaces, plus two Sacred Hearts at the e. end. The bevel of the *Purbeck marble* slab carries an exceptionally good inscription with a leaf design between each word. It translates: 'William de Burgate Knight of Burgate who died on the vigil of St James the Apostle 1409 and Alianora his wife daughter of Sir Thomas Vyzdelou who died . . .'. Thus one assumes that the wife installed the tomb but that her date of death was never added. The *brass* on top is possibly the best in the county for the period. The two figures lie within a double canopy which is all but intact, although four shields and Sir William's helm have gone. His armour is a fine example of the age and he wears a heavily ornamented sword belt. There is a sprightly lion beneath his feet and Lady Alianora's dog has a collar of bells. Her figure and that of Lady Margaret Drury at Rougham are so similar that the two brasses are likely to have come from the same workshop. The church has a ring of five bells with a 7 cwt. tenor but they are unringable at the present time.

Burgh, St Botolph (G5): This most attractive little church stands on a tump above the Otley/ Grundisburgh road, and like Clopton (which is just a couple of fields away) it has a tower which also serves as a s. *porch*. There was a time when it had a joint dedication of *St Botolph* and, *St Andrew* but originally it was for St Botolph alone, and it has been suggested that the rather

shadowy saint was actually buried here before being transferred to Bury St Edmunds. There is a neat parish room of 1835 by the gate and the path rises steeply to the church. The C14 unbuttressed tower has recently been restored, there are *quatrefoil* windows and a single *string course* below the *Decorated* bell openings, and deep, *flushwork* battlements. There are *Perpendicular* windows in the *nave*, the n. door is blocked, and the raised mortar round all the flints in the walls gives the building a distinctive texture which must date from a C19 or early-C20 restoration. There is one Decorated window on the s. side of the *chancel*, and the *dripstone* of the C14 *priest's door* has C19 *stops* carved with wheat and vines. A large iron bootscraper was provided for those who used to walk through the mud to church and they would then have to squeeze round the ringers, for the six bells with their 8 cwt. tenor are rung from the ground floor. Nowadays the sallies are cheerfully wasp-coloured rather than the conventional red, white, and blue. The inner door carries a closing ring set on a massive boss 10in. in diameter. It dates from the C13 and on the ring one can just discern the outlines of twin lizards, those ancient emblems of good fortune.

The interior is dark but distinctly nice. By the door is the C15 *font* and it has an interesting range of carvings in the bowl panels, despite the fact that the heads were drastically re-cut in the C19. There are the *Evangelistic symbols*, an angel holding a crown (n.), a totally feathered angel (e.), and an *Annunciation* (w. and s.) in which the *Blessed Virgin* has been given rather masculine features. Burgh has a range of late *Kempe* glass and the 1906 w. window is not his best – figures of SS George, Paul, and Stephen. The n. doorway frames a lovely painting by Anna Zinkeisen which illustrates all the birds of the Bible and is a memorial to her husband, who died in 1967. Bands of swallows swirl down from the dove of the Holy Spirit to meet swans flying upwards, and the others perch and strut within a dream landscape; there is even a realistic *pelican in her piety* in the bottom corner. The C19 *arch-braced* roofs are enlivened by demi-angels, and there is some interesting glass in the nave windows – n. side, Crucifixion and Resurrection scenes of 1817, possibly by Cox & Sons; s. side, two roundels of 1847 set in bright geometric patterns – a rare E. Anglian example of Thomas Willementt's work. The pulpit is *Jacobean* in style, with coarse carving, but there is an inscription at the base, 'John Vance 1708', which makes it about a century behind the fashion. A simple *piscina* on the s. side shows that there was once an *altar* nearby, and although there is now no *screen*, you will see that the *imposts* of the C14 chancel arch were cut back to take one in the C15. Like the nave benches, the choir stalls are C19, and the Kempe glass of 1879 in the s.w. window is much better – a Nativity with the Holy Family bathed in light on one side and the shepherds in sombre colours against a darkling landscape on the other. A tablet by Robert Brown on the n. wall commemorates three sons of the rectory, one of whom was only 23 when he died in 1827 as adjutant of a regiment of Bombay Native Infantry. Brown also provided a tablet for the parents in 1850 on which drapes partially mask the pediment. A large arch n. of the sanctuary opens into the *vestry*, and on the s. side there is a particularly good C14 chest which has recently been restored. It is completely sheathed in iron and has three hasps, a securing bar, and a lock. Above it is more Kempe glass, this time of 1902, an *Annunciation* in typical style. It was installed 'for mercies vouchsafed in an hour of great personal danger' – an instance where pious reticence merely triggers off an unholy desire to know what happened in the fullest possible detail. Kempe's e. window is a year later and has an elongated Crucifixion in the centre light which is faintly bizarre – spurts of blood from oversize nails, and a fringed carpet hung behind against a background of blue oak leaves and sprays; St Andrew to the l. and St Botolph cradling a church to the r. There is a *piscina* under *a cinquefoil* arch, and the oak altar and *reredos* of 1876 were carved by Gambier Parry. This is an interesting design because the pierced tracery of the front is backed by fabric embroidered with grapes and ears of corn, and the three reredos panels have grapes, sheaves, and the dove of the Holy Spirit in raised embroidery on cream-patterned damask. A very attractive period piece.

Burstall, St Mary (E6): The C14 unbuttressed tower has one *set-off* below the *lancet* bell openings and the *quatrefoil*/belfry windows have *dripstones*; there is a blocked lancet below the w. window. The tall and wide n. *aisle* dates from the early C14 and its windows contain a variety of beautiful *Decorated tracery*. There are small *mouchettes* and quatrefoils, and a most unusual arrangement of *trefoils* within a curved triangle in the n.e. window. Round the corner you will find that the aisle e. window displays a variation of the four-petalled flower above the three *lights*. A *string course* links the dripstones on the n.

facade and another runs below. A brick *rood stair turret* rises in the corner between aisle and *chancel* and the lancet alongside was probably used as a *low side window*. The chancel e. window has intersected 'Y' tracery of about 1300 and on the s. side there is a *priest's door* which has been brutally used to admit a large and ugly stove flue. The walls on this side are plastered and the C15 wooden *porch* stands on a brick base. The form of the outer arch suggests that it was originally constructed in the C14 but the *cusped* and carved barge boards are C15, and the centre upright had a niche which is still just recognisable by its *crocketted finial*. The open sides have cusped arches with carved *spandrels*. The inner doorway is deeply moulded, with king and queen *headstops*, and the *jambs* are a mass of graffiti. There is a C15 name cut on the e. side (it recurs in a chancel n. window embrasure) and the date 1599 can be found opposite.

On entering, one is immediately struck by the beauty of the early-C14 n. *arcade*. The fine mouldings sweep up into the steep arches and the *hood moulds* meet in fine, large headstops. There are *capitals* within the arches only, and they are adorned with two ranks of *paterae*. Some of these are intricately pierced and undercut and a number incorporate tiny masks. As with the outside, the hood moulds of the aisle windows are linked by a string course; notice how this even lifts over the finials of the niches that flank the e. window. All the interior arches are moulded, and although the builder of the aisle has not been identified, he must have been a wealthy man who was content with nothing but the best. The *parclose screen* is of the same period and the chapel it encloses on two sides may have been a *chantry* originally. The screen has a base of plain, lapped boards, with the entrance offset to the l. It has turned shafts rather than *mullions* and a fine variety of small Decorated motifs is carved on both sides of the tracery. The blocked door to the rood stair is in the corner, and the floor level of the chapel is two steps above the aisle (this change of level may date from the period when it was used as a family pew). The *ledger-stone* of William Cage is covered but a transcript of the inscription is provided, by which you can tell that he married his father's wife's daughter. Think about it! The aisle contains some C16 rugged benches with rough fleur-de-lys *poppyheads* and they were copied on those of the C19 that complete the suite. There is now a fine new organ set against the tower arch and above it you will see the outline of a quatrefoil *sanctus-bell window*. The church was extensively restored by Frederick Barnes in the 1870s, and Thomas Stopher of Ipswich carved demi-angels bearing emblems and instruments for the *hammerbeams* in the nave roof. It has a pierced *wall plate* and is very dark, and was probably stained at the same time. The *font* is not the usual East Anglian type. Instead, there are buttresses at the angles of the plain bowl which rests on a drum shaft and four octagonal pillars. The World War I memorial window in the nave is by *Heaton, Butler & Bayne*, and rather than the usual *St George*, the two panels illustrate texts from the Old Testament: Joshua 5:13-15 (Joshua and the captain of the Lord's host), and 1 Samuel 26:9 ('who can stretch forth his hand against the Lord's anointed, and be guiltless?').

The base of the C15 *rood screen* is still in place, its narrow panels placed between heavy mullions. *Cautley* apparently recommended putting the desk lectern on the top of the n. side (convenient but untypically naughty), and he may well have designed the very handsome pulpit, with its pierced *Perpendicular* tracery, which was placed at the s. end of the screen in 1945. There is a single framed, *scissors-braced* C14 roof in the chancel, effectively outlined against a blue background. The C14 *piscina* has a trefoil arch and there are *ogee* shapes cut in the embrasure of the *dropped-sill sedilia* alongside. Below, a glacial boulder or sarsen heaves up like a foreign body through the *encaustic tiles*, and was probably a pagan cult object before it was pressed into service for the new religion. It is one of a number in this area which were used in the same way. The *communion rails* and *reredos* are modern and the 1913 e. window has attractive glass which is probably by Heaton, Butler & Bayne: the *Blessed Virgin* and Child in the centre, with an *Annunciation* on the l. and *SS Mary* and *John* by the cross on the r.

Bury St Edmunds, All Saints (C4): On Park Road, in an urban situation, the church was designed by Cecil Beadsmore Smith and built in 1962 to cater for the extensive development on the w. side of town. Utilitarian and built for economy, it has faintly bizarre echoes of older things – cosmetic buttresses on the w. porch and a C14-style arch to the *sanctuary* within. In plain, mottled red brick, its only distinguishing features are a large cross in relief on the e. end and an octagonal turret sheathed in copper on the roof above, ringed with sharply pointed buttresses and carrying a cross. The building consists of a large hall, with three flat-topped dormers each side and a n.e. *vestry* block balanced

by a Lady chapel – both with flat roofs. There is a flat roof too for the large w. porch enclosed by iron gates. The inner doors have attractive dolphin handles and lead to a plain, open hall with a ceiling that follows the line of the sanctuary arch and has chunks bitten out to admit light from the dormers. There are tall side windows, all with frosted glass, and doors midway down the *nave* are fitted with crash bars. Beyond the Gothic arch, the sanctuary has a blank e. wall and is lit by pairs of glass brick windows each side; a *consecration cross*, flanked by alpha and omega signs, is cut in the centre of the step before the *altar*. The stark whiteness of the interior is relieved only by the broad swathe of plum-coloured carpet up the centre. The fittings are unadventurous but of good quality – a small octagonal *font* with alternate panels traceried, and a solid pulpit in C18 style, with split *baluster* decoration that matches the prayer desks and *communion rails*. The small oak lectern has some character. It consists of an eagle on a tapering octagonal shaft, with a Greek inscription round the base and signed 'C.J.C. 1939'. The low-ceilinged Lady chapel has nicely detailed curved rails before the altar, and as an altar piece there is a coloured plaster Nativity panel set in a carved pine frame. A boy shepherd kneels to the side of the Virgin and Child and there are three young angels to the r., with an ox beyond. This attractive design in muted colours is the work of *Ellen Mary Rope*.

Bury St Edmunds, St Edmundsbury Cathedral (C4): In the C17, Thomas Fuller wrote in his *Worthies of England*:

> This county hath no cathedral therein... but formerly it had so magnificent an abbey church in Bury, the sun shined not on a fairer, with three lesser churches waiting thereon in the same churchyard. Of these but two are extant at this day, and those right stately structures.

One was the parish church of *St James*, built by Abbot Anselm in the C12 and the stone shafts on the outside n. face of the present building are all that remain of that beginning. By the C16, the parishioners were looking enviously at the other far grander church of *St Mary's* across the churchyard, and began to rebuild St James' to keep pace. It is almost certain that the new work was designed by John Wastell, king's mason and one of the great architects of the Middle Ages.

He lived in Bury and was probably the abbey's master mason, but he ranged widely, designing part of King's College Chapel at Cambridge (the w. window here is a smaller version of the one at King's) and was master at Canterbury where he built the Bell Harry tower. Beginning in 1503 by extending the w. end to the street, the work moved eastwards, giving us a superbly proportioned *nave* which relies on simplicity rather than surface decoration for its effect. Wastell died in 1515 and the work was probably continued under Henry Semark, to be completed around 1550. In the 1860s there was a major restoration by *Sir George Gilbert Scott* under *J.D. Wyatt*. A new *chancel* was built, the nave roof replaced and the w. gable rebuilt. In 1913, the new diocese of St Edmundsbury and Ipswich was established and St James' became the new cathedral, although it was recognised at the time that it would need to be enlarged to match its new role. However, it was not until the 1960s that the new concept began to take shape under the direction of Stephen Dykes Bower. The n.w. entrance porch came first, and then Scott's chancel was replaced by a larger e. end, *crossing tower* and stub *transepts*, completing the main phase of the work in 1970. The s. frontage gives the best view of the way in which the new has been combined with the old. The walls are faced with *ashlar* and there is fine *flushwork* decoration in East Anglian style framing the arches of the tall choir windows with their *Decorated tracery*. More flushwork exists on the battlements at the e. end, and on the upper range of the s. transept, with its octagonal *sanctus-bell turret* crowned with a shapely spirelet and weathervane. Another matches it on the n. side of the building. A bronze figure of the boy martyr, King *Edmund*, by Elizabeth Frink stands in the centre of the green, and to the w. is the C12 *Norman* tower, built by Abbot Anselm as the main entrance to the abbey. It is a splendidly massive structure, having served as the bell tower for St James' since the Middle Ages, and contains a splendid ring of ten with a 27 cwt. tenor. The bells came from the Osborn foundry at Downham Market in 1785 and have since been restored and re-hung by Taylor's of Loughborough. From the new cathedral entrance, steps lead down into the first section of the glazed cloister – very plain with a flat-boarded ceiling. Memorials on the r.-hand wall include a good portrait silhouette, by J.C. Lough, of Benjamin Malkin, master of the local grammar school, who died in 1843. Arms of the province of Canterbury and of the diocese flank the entrance to the nave, and above

the door inside are the carved and gilded *Royal Arms* of Charles II. Above them, a fine gilded cherub blowing a trumpet once decorated the original organ case and was discovered in a Belgian antique shop before being returned to its home. With the new crossing and e. end, the interior is notably light and spacious and the *aisles* still have their C16 roofs. In the C18, Wastell's low-pitched roof was replaced by a poor thing of deal, as well as a *stucco* ceiling, and so it is not surprising that Scott decided to do better with a steep double *hammerbeam* design. Harsh things have been said of it and while it may not equal St Mary's, its modern colouring of green and red enlivened by gold contrives to be extraordinarily jolly. The *font* was designed by Scott in 1870 and it has a splendid traceried cover in East Anglian style which rises over 20ft. to a corona and *crocketted* spire. It was made by F.E. Howard of Oxford as a 1914-18 war memorial and, with the font, was richly coloured and gilt in 1960. The pulpit is another Scott piece of the 1870s. There are few notable memorials in the cathedral but by the w. door is the figure of James Reynolds, Chief Baron of the Exchequer and MP for the town who died in 1738. He sits, squat and rather lumpish, facing the nave, flanked by standing cherubs, one carrying a skull and wiping his eye, while another trumpets from the *pediment* above a shield of arms. The transepts have attractive panelled roofs, densely painted and gilded. The e. end is light and airy, with tall high-level windows. The good, early *Kempe* glass in the e. window came from the C19 chancel. The choir has a painted roof matching the transepts and a line of narrow arches runs below the side windows and across the bottom of the e. window, forming a narrow passageway. The bishop's throne on the n. side of the *sanctuary* was, like the font cover, made by F.E. Howard. It is an example of quality C20 woodwork in the medieval style, with buttresses capped by wolves guarding St Edmund's head and was a memorial to the first bishop of the diocese. The top of the arched recess behind the High altar is filled with a design in wrought-iron surmounted by a gilded sunburst designed by Stephen Dykes Bower. The chapel on the n. side of the choir is dedicated to St Edmund and the double-arched entrance has a handsome wrought-iron screen of silver filigree lozenges set in a framework of blue and gold. The *reredos* and *Hardman* glass of 1869 above it came from the old choir. The Lady chapel on the s. side of the choir was completed in 1970 and is entered through a wrought-iron screen in red and gold.

Bury St Edmonds, Cathedral

In 1828, such ancient glass as remained was collected together and arranged in the western-most window of the s. aisle, opposite the entrance door. The central upper *light* contains the figure of *St John* with the chalice and on either side are figures, each with its label, from a *Jesse Tree* design. In an upper *tracery* light on the r. is a rare portrayal of the Blessed Virgin's father, *St Joachim*, carrying a lamb. The lower panels are filled with Flemish C15 glass illustrating the story of Susannah and the Elders, with the heroine in a very compact tub in the centre. The r.-hand scene has some excellent figures robed in purple and reminiscent of Holbein's drawings of Sir Thomas More. The cathedral has a splendid array of C19 glass – look first at the s. aisle w. window, a *Clayton & Bell* Jesse window of 1899. This is a solid composition in very rich colouring, with meticulously detailed fur robes, brocades and curly beards, reminiscent of Kempe's work. The Hardman 1869 w. window is one of their best – quintessential Victorian quality, using clear colours and confident lines. The theme is the Last Judgement, and while the archangel weighs the souls in the bottom centre panel, the blessed and the damned gather on either side, with Christ in majesty over all. There is another bright and lively Clayton & Bell design at the w. end of the n. aisle on the theme of the Creation. Lines from Genesis run along the bottoms of the two ranks of panels, Adam and Eve are in the garden at the centre and there is a nice diversity of creatures, including a spouting whale. The glass in the rest of the nave windows is mainly by the same firm, with themes from the Old Testament on the n. and the New Testament on the s.

The Bury skyline has now been dramatically enhanced by the great new crossing tower of the cathedral. It has great presence, with pairs of tall two-light windows at high level; crowned 'E's in flushwork decorate the parapet, and the lofty corner crocketted pinnacles are topped with weather vanes. At the time of my visit the crossing within was still filled with scaffolding, over a fine new range of choir stalls in limed oak designed to serve a nave altar. On the n. side, the cloister was near completion, and stairs lead from the aisle up to a beautifully appointed treasury; apart from an excellent collection of ecclesiastical silver, there is the diocesan Jubilee cross designed by Jack Pentney and a fine C17 embroidered dossal from Polstead parish church.

Bury St Edmunds, St George (C4): Sited on Anselm Road, this church serves the Mildenhall Road Estate and is used by Roman Catholics as well as Anglicans. It was originally built as a community hall and was converted by Waring & Hastings in 1967. In the 1970s the Whitworth Partnership designed the extension at what I will call the w. end (the back of the church). Remembering its beginnings it is, as one would expect, a conservative building in grey brick, with

sash windows and pantile roofs; the main hall has two *transept*-like projections just short of the (nominal) e. end, with a matching pair at the w. end, one of which forms the entrance lobby. A slim spirelet sheathed in lead with a cross *finial* above the *sanctuary* confirms its new role to the passer-by. The interior is calm and simple and has a very nice atmosphere. There was originally a stage at the w. end and this space, combined with the extension, forms a large activities and meeting area separated by partitioned doors from the church proper. The sanctuary is defined by a simple arch and the obscured glass of the neo-Georgian e. window has a cross and border in pale yellow. The *altar*, which is placed at the front of the sanctuary, is a slightly unhappy combination of boxy, angled pedestals and a top with a deep curved apron, all in sycamore and mahogany veneers. The sturdy *communion rails* form a half circle around it and there is a small octagonal mahogany *font* to match which was the gift of the St George and Stonham Aspal Sunday Schools in 1969. The reading desk has a very lively *St George* and the dragon frontal and there is a collage on the same theme framed by the entrance which was produced by the Holiday Club children in 1985. The *chancel* arch has a *consecration cross* inset on the s. side and a door leads through to the Lady chapel which is quietly impressive in its simplicity. The plain, oak-veneered altar has an incised cross centre front, and an oil painting of the head of the sorrowing Christ with a heavy crown of thorns hangs on the wall.

Bury St Edmunds, St John (C4): With the development of the railway and the gas works, the town grew in that direction and St John's was built in 1841 to meet a need. This was before the influence of the *Ecclesiologists* had really taken hold and William Ranger's design cannot have pleased them. The building, in local Woolpit bricks that have darkened to a greenish grey, is gaunt. Its tower is foursquare to the level of the *nave* roof where large octagonal corner turrets, with conical caps, sprout short flying buttresses into a second stage. This has pairs of very tall latticed windows with sharp gables and then comes another set of corner turrets with flying buttresses to support the spire which rises to 160ft. The whole thing is a restless and uneasy affair. The base of the tower now has recessed doors and windows set in red brick and they provide effective relief to the overall drabness of the building. The interior was originally packed with pews to achieve maximum accomodation but, as rearranged, it is now light and airy, with an engaging colour scheme mouldings and attached columns of the *arcades*, w. arch and *clerestory* all picked out in egg-yolk yellow, with the *groined* wooden roof of the continuous nave and *chancel* in dark brown. The *aisle* ceilings are flat and there are open-back benches, pulpit and choir stalls in oak, all probably designed by *J.D. Wyatt*, the architect in charge of the 1870s refitting. The three large *lancets* of the e. window were originally filled with glass by Forrest & Bromley of Liverpool in 1858, but it had become decayed and a reglazing in 1960 retained only the shaped panels, now set in antique glass. In early C19 painterly style, the centre panel is a Crucifixion, with the Last Supper and Ascension on either side. Below, the carved stone *reredos* of 1876 was coloured in 1947 and statues of *SS Peter, John, Michael* and *George* were inserted in the panels. The lancet at the e. end of the s. aisle contains *Heaton, Butler & Bayne* glass, with a seated St John writing the Gospel. He has a haunting face and the style of the layered background makes it look later than its 1863 date. There is later glass by the same firm in the n. aisle – a 1902 window depicting *St Mary Magdalene* meeting the risen Christ. Next to it, a heavy *Kempe* design of 1900 – the visit of the Magi in two panels. The tower arch was fitted with an elegant glass screen to its full height in 1974 and this allows a good view of the 1903 w. window, with its tall figures of Christ as the Good Shepherd (with curiously green flesh tints). The crucifix over the pulpit is Oberammergau work and so is the figure of St Michael in the n. aisle.

Bury St Edmunds, St Mary (C4): A previous church dedicated to St Mary was demolished in the early C12 to make way for the s. *transept* of the abbey and the sacrist Godfrey sited its replacement in the s.w. corner of the cemetery. The building was designed, like St James', to serve the needs of a town parish. The late-C14 tower is offset on the n. side, aligning with the old precinct wall. The *chancel*, built in the early C14, has a later *sanctuary* projecting one bay to the e., with a crypt beneath. The main body of the church was magnificently rebuilt between about 1424 and 1446 and is a proud example of C15 work, drawing upon the riches of the burgeoning local wool trade. Most of the work was completed in the first decade and it is likely that the architect was William Layer, a local mason who was also concerned with the vanished great w. tower of the abbey. The rebuilding brought the w. front forward to the street line and the w. face of the *nave* is almost all window – *transomed Perpendicular tracery* that is matched in the great range of windows down the s. frontage to the e. end. Above is a *clerestory* with pairs of window to each bay, and *crocketted* spirelets rise from the twin *rood stair turrets* at the e. end of the nave. The n. side is interrupted by a *porch* nearly halfway down its length – an unusual position, but the siting of the tower prevented a more conventional arrangement and it aligns conveniently with the s. door of St James' across the churchyard. This fine porch was bequeathed by John Notyngham, a wealthy grocer who died in 1437. An inscription over the door invites prayers for his soul and that of his wife Isabelle. There are *stoups* in the buttresses on either side of the door, three canopied niches above and a crocketted gable. The stone ceiling within is beautifully panelled with a circle of blank arches, and the centre hub is carved and pierced as a pendant, within which is a carving of God the Father attended by angels. Entry to the church this way is via an early-C14 doorway which, like the flanking windows, has been reused. The interior of this, one of the largest parish churches in the country, is very impressive. The pillars of the nave *arcade* of ten bays are lozenge-shaped with broad, hollow mouldings and are slim for their height. Above them and the glass wall of the clerestory is one of the finest C15 roofs in England. *Hammerbeams* alternate with *arch-braced* trusses that have, themselves, nascent hammerbeams carved as grotesques and clamped to the sides. The main timbers rise from 42 splendidly carved *wall posts* representing mainly apostles and prophets, but you will find *SS Michael, Margaret* and *Walstan* on the n. side towards the w. end. The double-depth cornice is carved with demi-angels and the *spandrels* beneath the hammerbeams are pierced and carved with all manner of beasts and birds. At the e. end there is a *celure* that honoured the original rood below and the figures of the *Annunciation* are against the wall posts – the archangel *Gabriel* on the n. and the *Blessed Virgin* on the s. The hammerbeams are carved as recumbent angels, with wings partly unfurled, and they form a fascinating sequence. They are in pairs, a series of eleven each side and, instead of displaying the usual *Passion emblems* or musical instruments, they are clergy vested for mass, followed by an arch-angel, a queen and a king. Beginning from the e. end, there are the angels of the celure (with C19 colouring), incense bearers with boat container in one hand and spoon in the other, *thurifers* with *censers*, candlebearers with spiked candlesticks (the one on the s. may hold a box for flint and steel in his right hand), sub-deacons holding the Gospel book, deacons with the *chalice*, celebrants wearing chasubles, choirmasters (clearly conducting), archangels feathered overall with double wings, young women holding crowns, and crowned kings. The features of the king, particularly the version on the n. side, remind one of the National Portrait Gallery's Henry VI as a young man, and the woman could well represent Margaret of Anjou, betrothed to Henry in 1444 and crowned in May 1445. It is tempting to suppose that the roof was finished in time for Henry to see it when he held his parliament in the abbey refectory in February 1447. Apart from the nave roof, there are dozens of superb carvings in the *aisles*, in spandrels and on *bosses*, a number of which relate to medicine and disease (reflecting the importance of Bury as a medieval centre for infirmaries). All the roofs are dark and it is well worth the small fee to have the lights switched on and to go armed with binoculars.

John Baret was a wealthy clothier and official of the abbey who died in 1467 and his *chantry chapel*, at the e. end of the s. aisle, was originally the Lady chapel. The roof is splendidly decorated and has been restored so that the small convex mirrors in the centre of the painted stars gleam and twinkle. Henry VI honoured Baret with the *collar of SS* and this figures in the decoration, together with his monogram and motto in bold gothic letters: 'Grace me governe'. He had his tomb made in his lifetime as a reminder or mortality, and when the present Lady chapel was built it was moved to its present position against the wall. The hand of the emaciated cadaver on top rests on a scroll with traces of original colouring:

He that wil sadly beholde one with his ie,
May se hys owyn merowr and lerne for to
    die.

A *piscina* under a *cinquefoil* arch and *dropped-sill sedilia* remain behind the tomb from the time when the Lady chapel was here. Jankyn (John) Smyth was another wealthy Bury merchant and both chapels flanking the chancel were built at his expense; the Jesus chapel on the n. about 1460 and the Lady chapel on the s. a little later. The architect was probably Simon Clerk or John Forster, a pupil of William Layer. Smyth's chantry was at the e. end of the n. aisle, matching the position of the Baret chantry and he was

buried there. The Jesus chapel has become better known as the Suffolk chapel and houses many memorials and colours of the county regiment. Entered through wrought-iron gates, it was furnished and decorated under the direction of *Ninian Comper*. One of the best *brasses* in the church may be found under the *sanctuary* carpet here – a 36in. figure of John Fyners vested in cassock, surplice and amice, with a Latin inscription. He died in 1509 and was Archdeacon of Sudbury. The Lady chapel, too, has a number of brasses and although Jankyn Smyth was buried in his chantry in the n. aisle, his memorial seems to have migrated here, within the sanctuary on the n. side. He wears a Yorkist collar with the lion of March as a pendant over his tunic, and his wife Anne has a *butterfly headdress* and mantle. The brass for Henry and Edmund Lucas, a fine shield with mantling and a verse, has been taken from the floor and fixed to the wall on the l. of the chapel entrance. Henry Lucas was a cousin of Henry VII, his father being the king's solicitor general. The grave of Thomas and Elizabeth Heigham (1542) lies in the centre of the chapel but the effigies and inscription have gone, leaving three shields only. The painting over the *altar* here is 'The Incarnation' by John Williams – the young Virgin crouched in a swirl of cloud and light, with vignettes of Christ's birth, teaching, Crucifixion and Ascension in the corners. There are other brass inscriptions in the nave; at the w. end, Matthew and Margaret Lancaster (1634 and 1661) set on a later stone, and one for George Boldero (1609) with shield and inscription in front of the chancel screen on the n. side. The original *rood screen* is no longer here and the present one is a 1913 memorial to members of the Suffolk regiment. Note that the old *rood loft* had access stairs on both sides and that the doors remain at ground and first floor level. It is particularly interesting that the top door on the n. side is much larger than its opposite number, pointing to the fact that the deacon would enter from that side to read the Gospel during the mass. The chancel roof, excellently restored, is panelled with intricate *cusping* and carved bosses, and here again binoculars are a great help in appreciating the quality and diversity of the carvings, many of which illustrate favourite medieval themes, such as the fox preaching to chickens. The cornice is painted with angels carrying scrolls inscribed with the 'Te Deum'. The stalls below incorporate sections of tracery from the old rood screen and there are some fine and large grotesques on the arm rests. An interesting brass is to be found on the s. arcade pillar at the e. end of the choir stalls. It is for George Estye, the minister here who died in 1601. The inscription was composed by Joseph Hall, then a young Cambridge don but later to become the much harried bishop of Norwich under the Commonwealth. His initials are engraved on the plate and the guttering candle in the top corner has the words: 'Luceo et absumor' ('I give light and am consumed'). There are two large tombs at the e. end and the one on the n. side is for Sir William Carewe who died in 1501, and his wife Margaret, who followed him in 1525. The effigies are large and stiff, he in coat armour with his head on a helm and his feet on a sizable lion, she in kirtle and mantle with a pair of small dogs at her skirts. The tomb was originally canopied and there is a funeral helm placed above. Coats of arms in *quatrefoils* decorate the front of the tomb. Opposite is the tomb of Sir Robert and Lady Anne Drury. He died in 1536 and the effigies have much in common with those on the Carewe tomb, although his feet rest on a large greyhound. The brass inscription round the top is a replacement; again, a helm hangs overhead. The projecting sanctuary was another bequest of Jankyn Smyth and matches the style of the side chapels. Traces of a coloured celure can still be seen and the pulleys for the *Lenten veil* are still in position. John Reeve (or Melford), the last abbot, lies buried before the High altar, having been deprived of office in 1540, but his grave was stripped of the brass and even the stone itself was removed and used for a time as a doorstep in the C18. In the n.e. corner of the sanctuary lies a *mensa* still bearing the *consecration crosses*, and on it is cut: 'Mary, Queen of France, 1533'. This is the last resting place of the younger daughter of Henry VII, sister of Henry VIII and, briefly, wife of the old and ailing king of France, Louis XII. Charles Brandon, Duke of Suffolk, was sent to bring the widow home but married her in secret and paid heavily for the privilege when her brother found out. Wolsey conciliated and, after a court marriage ceremony at Greenwich, the couple came to live at Westhorpe. Mary Tudor was buried in the abbey in great state and at the Dissolution hers was the only body to be removed and reburied. In 1881, Queen Victoria gave the *Clayton & Bell* window in her memory, to be seen on the s. side of the sanctuary in the Lady chapel. Not great art perhaps, but it portrays six scenes in Mary's life, including the meeting with Henry VIII and her burial service.

Although the church has no medieval glass, it is extraordinarily rich in C19 windows. There was a restoration by L.N. Cottingham in 1844 when the shape of the window over the chancel arch was altered, and *Thomas Willement* supplied a Martyrdom of *St Edmund* design for it. The w. window was reconstructed at the same time, and in thanksgiving for the harvest of 1867, glass by *Heaton, Butler & Bayne* was installed. It has a harvest theme in the top centre panel, a Crucifixion below, and medallions on either side in three ranks depicting scenes from the life of Christ. Looking down the lovely vista from the chancel, the colours of the window are very reminiscent of a Victorian kaleidoscope, and there is a fine selection of Heaton, Butler & Bayne 1880s glass in the s. aisle windows. The C15 chapel of *St Walstan* is tucked in the n.w. corner of the church and there one finds, among memorials and colours of the county regiments, a *Ward & Hughes* w. window of 1869. It is rather sentimental in feeling, with lush colouring – the Last Supper across the lower panels and the Magi, the flight into Egypt, and 'no room at the inn' above. The relatively small size of the e. window, set high in the wall of the Lady chapel, indicates that it was moved from its old position in the Baret chantry and used again when the new chapel was built; in 1856 it was filled with stained glass by Alfred Gérente of Paris. The three shaped medallions depict incidents in the life of Christ and the colours, particularly the blue, are akin to *Hardman* glass of the same period. There is another Ward & Hughes window of 1884 towards the e. end of the n. aisle – a Transfiguration scene in the upper panels, with *SS James the Great, Peter* and *John* below, all in pictorial style using soft colour. Next to it, a window of 1894, probably by *Kempe*. The great surge of church building and restoration in the 1850s created a great demand for stained glass, and one artist who turned painter-glazier was Charles Clutterbuck. He is represented here with a window over the s. door of 1854 – David, Samuel and Solomon in the main *lights*, with scenes from their lives in the smaller panels beneath – the colours creamy and soft. There are two more of his windows in the chancel and the e. window there has glass of 1914 – the four archangels vividly outlined against clear panes, with angels in the bottom centre panels holding the shields of St Edmund and the Sacred Heart. This glass is unsigned but could be *Lavers & Westlake*. The great windows of this church allow very little wall space for memorials and monuments, but advantage has been taken of the interior tower wall, and there tablets are ranged almost to the roof. By the door is a memorial to those men of the Suffolk regiment who went down in the HMS Birkenhead disaster off South Africa in 1852. Round the corner is a tablet in memory of Peter Gedge, publisher of the first local newspaper, the *Bury & Norwich Post*. He died in 1818, and his epitaph reads: 'Like a worn out type he is returned to the Founder in hopes of being recast in a better and more perfect mould'. The medieval sacrist was lodged in the first floor of the tower and his watching window can be seen above the door. On the interior w. porch there is a set of post-1837 *Royal Arms* and there are two interesting pictures on the w. wall of the s. aisle. One is a view of the church interior as it was in the early C18 and the other is a lovely C19 or early-C20 painting by Rose Mead entitled, 'Friday morning at St Mary's Bury St Edmunds'. It was the custom for bread to be given every Friday to the aged poor and they gathered in the Lady chapel to receive it. The picture shows that at that time the *font* was there and not at the w. end.

St Mary's has a ring of eight bells with a 27 cwt. tenor but they are hung dead and can only be chimed.

Bury St Edmunds, St Peter (C4): This church, in Hospital Road, is one of the many built in the mid-C19 to cater for the needs of a growing population. Designed by *J.H. Hakewill* and consecrated in 1858, it is a useful example of the small town church of the period, economical in design but with little trace of local feeling. Set against the s. wall of the *nave* one bay from the w. end, the tower has stone latticed bell openings and a shingled broach spire. The nave windows have simple *Early English tracery* and the *chancel* is only marked off by the use of a pair of *lancets*. The e. window has three lancets with *quatrefoil plate* tracery over, and the wall below has a stark banding of *knapped* flints. These are also used on the side walls below the windows, with random flint and stone work above. The arch of the w. door is picked out in stone and flint and lines of dressed flints cross the w. wall, lifting over the doorway as a *label*, with a two-light window above. The interior is 'plain Jane' indeed but attractively neat and bright. The nave roof is simple boarding, with a false chancel arch in wood coming down to *colonnettes* which rest on stone angels holding the *chalice* on one side and the *paten*, piled with bread, on the other. Beyond, the barrel roof of the chancel is painted a deep blue, with small *bosses* picked out in gold.

Beyond an archway at the e. end of the nave on the n. side there is a stub *transept*, and the panels that used to flank the *altar* have been fixed to the walls there. Of metal with moulded wooden frames, they have the Lord's Prayer, *Decalogue* and Creed. The *font* is typical of the period – quatrefoils in the bowl panels carved with cross, star of David, *Agnus Dei* and the dove of the Holy Spirit. There are four coupled shafts beneath and heavy foliage carved under the bowl. Plain pitchpine pews and a stone pulpit-cum-reading desk unit which incorporates a small stone and marble lectern supported by an angel are also to be found. The choir-stalls are pitchpine with *poppyheads* and there are plain recessed stone panels across the e. wall of the *sanctuary*, backing the plain oak *reredos*. The glass of the 1902 e. window is probably by *Kempe* and has figures of *St Peter* flanked by *SS James the Great* and *John* – florid, with intricate canopy work. There is a most attractive *Annunciation* window at the e. end of the nave on the s. side of 1955, designed by Hugh Easton. The arch-angel *Gabriel* has brilliant red and gold wings, wears a scarlet robe and holds a sceptre, while the dove of the Holy Spirit hovers over the *Blessed Virgin*; in the background is a view of the cathedral's Norman tower.

Butley, St John the Baptist (H5): This trim little church, in its spacious churchyard, stands well to the s. of the village, in company with the old village school. The unbuttressed tower has a tall and narrow *Perpendicular* w. window, and there is a large niche (or blocked belfry window) above it. The small bell openings have *Decorated tracery*, and there is rough *flushwork* in the battlements. Walking round, you will see large blocks of *septaria* in the w. wall of the *nave*, and there are three *Norman lancets* in the n. wall. Two of them are blocked, and so is the simple C12 n. door, with its continuous roll moulding. It now has no *capitals* and was probably altered at some time. The *chancel* must have been rebuilt around the beginning of the C14, and it was altered fairly drastically as part of a general restoration in the 1860s when it was shortened, the e. wall rebuilt in brick, and given a replacement window. There is a large *cusped* lancet each side, with a *priest's door* to the s., and both walls lean outward, supported on the n. by heavy brick buttresses. A clear example of a *scratch dial* with Roman numerals can be found on the l. side of the s. lancet. A variety of window forms were used in the nave over the years, and the outline of another of the original Norman lancets remains in the s. wall. The nave is thatched, and the s. *porch* is attractively homely, with a frontage and arch of *Tudor* brick. The *crocketted* C13 *dripstone* which is set in the brickwork may have belonged to the original porch or have come from elsewhere. The arch of the inner Norman doorway has a very unusual moulding – a salient rib from which spring others, angled on two faces to create a stem and branch pattern; the plain inner arch matches the n. door, and there are single shafts, with slim *jamb shafts*. The entrance door of rough, keeled boards, has recently been restored, and just above the bulge of the wooden lock a joiner carved his name: 'Augustine Broore, 1571'.

The neat interior speaks strongly of the Victorian changes, although the 1840s *gallery* has been taken out and the organ now stands on the floor at the w. end. The nave has plain pine benches, and the *scissors-braced* pine roof partially masks the large *sanctus-bell window* above the tower arch. The C15 *font* follows the East Anglian style and the sharpness of the carving means that it was probably re-cut in the last century. Upright lions with heavy manes and whiskery muzzles support the shaft, and there are others in the bowl panels, between angels whose shields display *Passion emblems* (n.), *Trinity* emblem (e.), *St George's* cross (w.), and a floriated cross (s.). The stone section that now lies on the porch windowsill was found near Butley Priory, and it would fit the top of the font shaft. Two window splays in the nave have image niches, and in 1952, the *rood loft stairs* were uncovered in the n. wall. The door was installed as a memorial for Dr Montague Randall, and the inscription is particularly well cut. Open it and you will see that the C15 builders made use of the Norman lancet to light their stair. The upper doorway is still blocked, and the base panels of the C15 *screen* have no decoration now. There is panel tracery above the *cusped ogee* arches of the lights, and only the centre arch retains its *crocketting*. An Elizabethan table with chip-carved top rail and turned legs stands in front, having been used as the church's *altar* for many years. The chancel is floored with *encaustic tiles*, and in the shallow *sanctuary* the altar is set within the e. window embrasure. Perhaps as part of the 1860s restoration, *Lavers, Barraud & Westlake* supplied the glass in the side lancets – pretty patterns, with a vase of lilies on one side and a fruiting plant on the other. Theirs also is the e. window glass of about 1870, two nicely composed scenes of Christ's baptism and the Last Supper, the rest of the space filled with curly stiff-leaf patterns.

Buxhall, St Mary (E5): This is a fine church in a secluded setting, with a long walk up to the s. *porch*. It was rebuilt about 1320 and the tall two-light windows have *Decorated tracery*. There is a *scratch dial* on one of the s. *nave* buttresses and on the other is a *flushwork* flint cross which might be the first of the external *consecration crosses*. The *chancel* gable carries tall pinnacles and the *crockets* terminate in human heads and grotesques. The e. window is large and handsome, with good flowing tracery and the nave battlements are in later brick. The tower followed the main building at the end of the C14 and its base is flint panelled, with chequer work on the buttresses. The *string courses* are bold and there is a stair turret on the s. side up to the ringing chamber. Within, the ringers have the use of an excellent six (tenor 15 cwt.) which Gillet & Johnson of Croydon restored and augmented in the fifties. The large porch has a chequered parapet and the niche, with its crocketted *finial*, was provided with a small figure of the *Blessed Virgin* in 1984. The inner door has rosette *stops* to the arch, and in 1956 workmen discovered the *stoup* to the r., with its *trefoil* arch and half of the bowl hacked away. The tower arch within is very tall and the *jambs* have a mass of C16 and C17 graffiti. The *Royal Arms* of George I, painted on canvas, were well restored in 1982 and now hang over the n. door; by the entrance, a light with a time switch has been thoughtfully provided so that they may be the better seen. The early-C14 *font* with its *castellated* rim stands on a low shaft and there are crocketted gables backed by tracery in the bowl panels. The church was restored in the 1870s by the rector and the pews of oak from the Buxhall estate were carved by a daughter of the rectory, Agnes Emily Hill. She repeated the w. window tracery design in the panels of the pulpit. The nave roof was replaced in 1923 but that in the chancel is C17 and one of the *arch-braced* principals is dated 1656 with initials of the churchwardens. There was a chapel dedicated to *St Margaret* on the s. side of the nave and its *piscina* remains under a flat *ogee* arch with trefoil *cusping*. On the other side, the guild of *St John the Baptist* had its *chantry* and although there is now no screen, the stairs to the *rood loft* remain in the n. wall. Before the restoration the nave was above the level of the chancel but now steps rise to the *sanctuary* where there is a lovely C14 double piscina – two tall and narrow compartments under steep, crocketted gables with finials, and three pinnacles reaching to the full height. There are tracery *mouchettes* above the ogee arches and the springing of the canopy alongside shows that it once matched the piscina. On the sill of the sedilia is a C13 grave slab carved with a discoid cross and the familiar double omega sign of the period. The stalls incorporate four medieval bench ends with *poppyheads* and one of them is carved as a double head, with a tongue-out mask on top. The s.w. window in the chancel contains some C15 glass, including two angels, and look for the hand holding the poisoned *chalice* of *St John* which has a little grey beast crouching on top instead of the more usual devil. The next window has two cocks on red shields in the tracery, and in the sanctuary s. window is a C14 armorial shield which illustrates the care with which the artists of the day designed such things. There are more jumbled C15 fragments in the window above the n. *vestry* door and in the tracery of the s.e. nave window but the glass in the tower window is modern.

Campsea Ash, St John the Baptist (H5): Entry is through a *lych-gate*, provided by the village to mark the coronation of King George VI. The church has a well-proportioned C14 tower, with two *string courses*, and the angle buttresses to the w. each have a *flushwork quatrefoil* at the base; more flushwork in the battlements incorporates initials and the *Sacred monogram*, and there are the remains of beasts at the corners. It was probably built during the long incumbency of Alexander Inglysshe who died in 1505, whose brass is in the nave floor and who may have funded the work. The w. doorway has *paterae* and shields in the mouldings of the w. door, worn lion *stops*, blank shields in the *spandrels*, and a line of flushwork quatrefoils stretches below the three-*light* w. window. A perky spike on top, crowned with a weathervane, completes the picture. A circuit of the building reveals that the *nave* windows were renewed in the C19, and a stone high on the s. wall records an earlier rebuilding: 'King & Sutton churchwardens 1792'. An organ chamber was added to the n. side of the *chancel* in the C19, and beyond it, there is a small red brick *Tudor vestry*. The s. frontage plainly shows the effects of the 1869 restoration, when the chancel and *porch* were faced with flint and arches of squared *knapped* flints worked over the windows.

The C14 inner doorway is tall and well proportioned, with single attached shafts and fine mouldings. The tower arch rests on high, demi-angel *corbels,* and below stands an interesting late-C14 *font.* Its heavy bowl has

canted sides below a *castellated* rim, and the *tracery* in five of the panels resembles the tops of windows, with varied quatrefoils in the remainder. The shaft is finely traceried, and there are battered heads at the angles below the bowl – three of them much smaller than the rest. Pitch pine pews are ranged under a plain plastered ceiling, and on the s. wall there is a memorial for John Sheppard who died in 1824. The carefully balanced cadences of the epitaph are typical of the period: 'His life, although principally passed in retirement, yet was marked by the exercise of those social and domestic virtues which endear man to society . . .'. It is a simple oblong tablet flanked by shallow scroll *pilasters* under a decorated gable, and is only remarkable for its sculptor – *Sir Richard Westmacott.* It confirms that fashionable sculptors did not necessarily despise the small commission. The glass in the window alongside is a memorial for Frederick William Brook, 5th Baron Rendlesham, a version of Christ's Presentation in the Temple by *Powell & Son*, installed in 1914. Just beyond, a large tablet commemorates Lieut. Frederic Sheppard of the 4th Foot, and is surmounted by a flourish of martial trophies with the single word 'Badajoz' – explained by the lengthy epitaph: 'His career was short but glorious . . . anxious to distinguish himself on the field of honour, he hastened to join the army serving under Lord Wellington before Badajoz'. He fell wounded and died six days later on April 12th, 1812. The next window along has quietly attractive figures of Faith and Hope, with the rest of the space devoted to dove symbols of the Holy Spirit set within borders of vine leaves. This is one of *Henry Holiday's* fine designs for Powells and was installed in the 1880s. Henry Clutton, the Framlingham mason, was obviously asked to copy the Westmacott tablet six years later, and he did so for John Wilson Sheppard's memorial at the e. end of the nave s. wall. Opposite, the memorial for James, 1st Viscount Ullswater is a compact, high quality essay in the C17 style, with the epitaph flanked by dusky red *Ionic* columns, and a roundel *achievement of arms* on top. The church's only *brass* is a very good one, to be found in the floor at the e. end of the nave. It is one of only four Suffolk examples of priests robed in eucharistic vestments, and commemorates Sir Alexander Inglisshe who died in 1504. His 27in. effigy is shown holding the *chalice* and wafer of the mass, and there is a separate *groined canopy*, lacking its *finial* and side pinnacles. The inscription reads: 'Of your charite pray for the soule off Alexandre

Inglisshe sutyme pyche [parish] prest of thys church o[n] whose soule Jhu [Jesus] have mcy [mercy]'. The chancel arch and roof are C19 work, and so are the heavyweight marble *communion rails* and stone *reredos* lettered with the *Decalogue*. Powells' 1912 glass in the e. window is good, with an excellent feeling for colour; Christ the King has *St John the Baptist*, the *Blessed Virgin*, and *St Peter* on one side, and *SS Etheldreda, Edmund and Edward the Confessor* (?) on the other. Above is the adoring angelic host, and there are Lowther family shields in the tracery. Three C15 shields feature in the *sanctuary* side window, and some *ledger-stones* in the floor are worth examining. Edward Blenerhayset was buried on the s. side in 1641:

Not that he neede th' monements of ston
For his weil gotten fame to rest upon . . .

And in the same year on the n. side, William Glover had:

Behold in me the life of man,
Compared by David to a spann,
Let freinds & kinred weepe no more,
Here's all the odds I went afore.

Both are boldly lettered round the edge, and Mary Braham's stone of 1660 in the centre of the chancel has a fine engraved shield. The church has a useable ring of four bells with an 8 cwt. tenor.

Capel St Mary, St Mary (E7): The church stands prominently above the village street and has a robust C15 tower with a broad, three-*light Perpendicular* w. window. There are two strong *drip courses* and the surface texture is an interesting mixture which includes bands of narrow red bricks and tiles. In the *base course*, flint has replaced most of what were *ashlar* panels decorated with very finely cut blind arcades; it has a battered angel with a shield in the centre on the s. side and there is a writhing figure on the s.w. buttress. There is now a plain cement parapet and until 1818 the tower carried a spire. On walking round, you will see large Perpendicular windows on the n. side of the *nave* with *embattled transoms*, they illustrate how the *ogee* shape came back into fashion. Opposite the n. door stands the gravestone of William Manning, 'Police Constable in this county' who died in the 1870s. The stone was 'erected as a token of respect by the members of the Suffolk Constabulary' and must be one of the earliest memorials to a local

bobby in the county. At the e. end of the nave there is the shape of a round-headed door in the wall and, together with some *herringbone work* nearby, it suggests that the building is *Norman* in origin. The *chancel,* however, was built or rebuilt in the early C14 and its n. windows have two worn grotesques and two good female *headstops*. The e. end had to be given brick buttresses at some stage and the insertion of the tall, four-light Perpendicular window may have weakened the wall. The *Decorated* windows on the s. side of the chancel each have a curved triangle above two lights and the most unusual *tracery* has *cusps* that are forked. The most easterly headstop is a very good example of the pagan *green man* symbol which masons persisted in using all through the Middle Ages, and there is a lively grinning head at the other end of the sequence. One of the female headstops of the *priest's door* is partly covered by a later buttress but the *dripstone* is nicely carved with a trail of flowers. All the s. *aisle* windows are Perpendicular except the one w. of the C15 porch. A modern *Blessed Virgin* and Child occupies the niche above the entrance, and there are *quatrefoil* roundels in the arch *spandrels* with widely spaced *paterae* in the mouldings. Pale oak *arch-braces* and *wall plates* remain of the original roof and the inner doorway has pilgrim crosses scratched in the *jambs*. The door itself, with its lapped boards and long strap hinges, can be no later than C14.

The interior is bright and beautifully kept, and despite its sturdiness the four-bay *arcade* between nave and aisle leans outward. The nave roof is a compact design with diminutive *hammerbeams* and there are *collar beams* and *king posts* under the ridge. At the w. end, the organ masks the tower arch and a C19 *font* stands in the s.w. corner. The tablet on the aisle wall is for William Press who died in 1809 and has drapes bunched at the top corners and over a centred *achievement*. Its interest lies in the signature at the bottom: 'Coade & Sealy', the firm founded by that remarkable business woman Mrs Eleanor Coade. She popularised the use of artificial stone (*Coade stone*) as a cheap and effective alternative to marble, and only employed the best designers. Having said that, one has to admit that the results are always mud-coloured. Although the epitaph concludes: 'His remains are deposited in this churchyard', the Capel registers apparently contain no record of the burial – which is a mite odd. The s. aisle is designated as the chapel of *St Edmund* and the 1920s e. window glass by Frederick Eden has the Virgin and Child flanked by figures of that saint and *St Felix*; in the tracery you will see the shields of Capel, the province of Canterbury, and the dioceses of Ely, Norwich, and St Edmundsbury & Ipswich. A centre panel of the window to the s. contains a figure of the risen Christ by the Canterbury firm of Maile & Son, placed there in the 1970s. The design is naturalistic, with attractive use of colour and very clever leading. Although much restored, the aisle roof is medieval and there are original shields to be seen: the Debenham family arms above the window e. of the door, the Loudham arms opposite, Bishop Nykke's (of Norwich) above the s. door, and Ely's opposite. A fine, large statue of the Blessed Virgin in natural wood stands by the entrance to the chancel, and on the n. side the C18 pulpit is in oak on a wine-glass stem, with a *Sacred monogram* within a sunburst on one of the panels; the *tester* has been injudiciously restored. A C19 arch-braced beam spans the chancel arch, and the figures of the *rood* group on it were carved by the renowned Lang family of Oberammergau in Bavaria. Beyond it, the chancel roof was renewed in the C19 but is, for East Anglia, a rare example of the 'cradle' type. Deep coving rises each side to a longitudinal beam above which the roof is arched in a gentle curve to the ridge, with closely spaced moulded ribs overall. Some time between 1880 and 1920 large but dumpy angels playing harps, pipes, and cymbals, their feet enveloped in medieval-style clouds, were placed on the e.-w. beams. They do not suit the roof and are quite out of scale. The painted C19 *High altar reredos* came from a Belgian church and has sharply gabled arches with gold diapered backgrounds and a centre canopy over the crucifix. In 1918 the upper half of the e. window was filled with stained glass and displays the figures of the Archangels *Uriel, Michael, Gabriel,* and *Raphael* in steely colour, with dark red behind the heads and blue below the feet. The church has a ring of five bells with a 9 cwt. tenor, but they are hung dead and can only be chimed.

Carlton, St Peter (H4): A rough track leads to this isolated little church lying sweetly among open fields, a half mile s. of the village street, and prior enquiry about the key is advised. A *chantry* was founded here in 1330 with three priests to pray for the soul of Alice of Hainault, Countess of Norfolk, and it lasted until it was dissolved in 1544 by Henry VIII. The way in which the flints are closely layered in the *nave* walls suggests that the chantry made use of an earlier church building and probably added a

new, larger *chancel*. There were restorations in 1872 and 1887, renewing the e. window and inserting another in place of the nave n. door. All the other windows have early-C14 'Y' *tracery*, and there is a contemporary *priest's door* on the n. side of the chancel. The rather leggy red brick tower, with its angle buttresses and stair on the s. wall dates from the early C16. There is a little patterning in blue brick at its base and the w. doorway is now blocked. A *scratch dial* with a double rim can be found on the centre buttress of the nave, and the snug *porch* has been strangely altered so that the outer arch almost reaches the top of the gable. It is fitted with a stout but decorative outer gate, and the inner archway is again early C14.

An unsophisticated interior, in which the *chancel* seems the larger part simply because its braced roof is open, in contrast with the lower plastered ceiling of the nave. The *hatchment* in the tower was for Harriet Fuller who died in 1803; when I visited it was quietly decaying against the wall, and there was no sign of the one that was used at the funeral of Harriet's husband Osborne in 1794. Also on the floor was quite a good set of Charles II *Royal Arms*. The *font* is C19, but nearby there are two C15 benches with angled ends that must have been shaped to provide standing room round the medieval font. They have panelled ends and *poppyheads*, and one of them has a beast and a little castle on the elbows. The Victorian pine benches have quite adventurous *finials*, with *St Peter's* keys carved on one of them, and there is a custom-built pew for the *parish clerk* complete with book stand by the tower arch. The nave walls are clad to waist height with panelling that was salvaged from C17 family pews. The fine pulpit has much in common with Kelsale's, both in design and in the way in which it has been restored. It displays two ranks of the *blind-arched* panels of the period, and one of the upper strapwork panels is dated 1626. Fitted with a new base and steps, its octagonal body has been converted into a horseshoe shape. There is no *screen* now, and only a low modern wall separates nave from chancel, but marks in the arch above indicate that it was once filled with a *tympanum* above a screen. A pair of benches in the chancel match those at the w. end, and the C15 stalls with their broad book slopes are a reminder that the chantry priests will have sung their masses here. Below a low arch in the s. wall, a worn *Purbeck marble* slab is incised with an elaborate floriated cross, and a fragment of the edge inscription reads: '. . . qui fundavit cantarium tibi' (. . . who has founded a chantry for you). There seems little doubt that it is the tomb of whoever founded the chantry and rebuilt the chancel to accommodate it. It was common practice to arrange for masses to be said not only for the souls of the founder and his family, but also for specific members of the nobility, and this was no doubt the case here. When *Dowsing* came this way in January 1643, he and his men 'brake down ten superstitious pictures and tore up six popish inscriptions in brass; and gave order to level the chancel'. However, two *brasses* escaped, and they now lie in the centre of the floor. One is the 26in. figure of an unknown man, wearing a belted tunic with a massive rosary. It dates from around 1480 and there was another effigy for his wife which had an inscription originally. Alongside is the 17in. figure of a man (again unidentified) whose hair style suggests a slightly later date, wearing a long tunic with embroidered cuffs, and a heavy rosary and purse on his belt. Nearby, Thomas and Sara Coggeshall share a massive early-C18 *ledger-stone*. Carlton's *altar* is a particularly nice Elizabethan table, its bulbous legs carved with *acanthus* foliage, and top frame decorated with strapwork. It was mounted on a new base frame in 1630 and the initials on one side probably refer to the churchwardens of the day. The window above contains excellent glass by *William Wailes*, a Crucifixion in C13 mode; the *Blessed Virgin* and *St John* stand under canopies on either side, while the centurion and the man with the sponge of vinegar are grouped below the cross; ruby red backgrounds and clear, attractive colour in the figures. The church has a ring of four bells with a 6 cwt. tenor, but the condition of the frame and fittings prohibits their use at the present time.

Carlton Colville, St Peter (J1): William Dale Andrews was rector here for the last half of the C19, and in 1883 he had the church almost entirely rebuilt in early *Decorated* style at his own expense. The tower, however, does not seem to have been much affected. It has a tall C13 *lancet* w. window, a smaller version above and then, on the s. and w. sides, there are unusual *sound holes*. They are small oblongs under *labels*, each with a pair of shields within *quatrefoils*. There is Decorated *tracery* in the bell openings, and the stepped battlements are embellished with *flushwork*. Despite the C19 work, it is worth making a circuit of the building to examine one or two things. In the n. wall of the *nave* at the w. end there is a restored *Norman* lancet which may

have come to light during the rebuilding. In 1986, a square annexe was linked to the C19 *vestry*, thus providing kitchen facilities and a meeting room. It has a pyramid roof, the walls are faced with large, roughly dressed flints, and it marries well with the rest of the building. The Victorians reused some of Decorated tracery in the nave and *chancel* windows, and probably repeated the original patterns. The e. window, however, was entirely replaced by an attractive, slightly unconventional design. An organ chamber like a stub *transept* was added on to the s. side of the chancel and the *priest's door* was renewed. There are some nice C18 headstones just e. of the chancel – one with a trio of cherubs, and another in classical style with an oval tablet. A mason active at the turn of the century provided some robust stones which have a good deal of character, and there are plenty of poetic epitaphs to collect, including that favourite Victorian quote from Charlotte Norton: 'Not lost but gone before!' Within the 1880s porch you will see that the C14 inner doorway was retained; its nicely moulded arch fades into the *jambs* and there are the faint marks of a *scratch dial* on the l.-hand side.

As one enters the church, there is a *stoup* recess just inside, and on the far wall hangs an interesting little picture. It shows how the church looked before it was rebuilt, when it had *reticulated* tracery in the e. window and a C13 lancet where the organ chamber is. The late-C14 *font* is a familiar design, with lions and seated angels alternating in the bowl panels, angel heads beneath, and lions seated round the shaft – all mutilated. Roofs and benches are C19 pine, and in a window on the s. side of the nave there is good early-C20 glass by (I think) *Clayton & Bell* – Christ with a family group, and the figure of King David in the tracery. The other window on that side has 1870s glass, this time undoubtedly by *Lavers, Barraud & Westlake* – the Good Samaritan story, with *St John's* poisoned *chalice* in the tracery. The Norman lancet in the n. wall contains a little 1870s figure of *St Peter*, and further along we see *St Luke* tending the sick and visiting *St Paul* in prison. Both are by Lavers, Barraud & Westlake, and they provided the sentimental version of the Good Shepherd and 'Behold, I stand at the gate and knock' in the next window. The chancel arch and low stone screen were part of the Victorian rebuilding, and the angled doorway in the corner was discovered at that time. Its position suggests that it led to a *rood loft* stair, and it now provides a setting for a modern wooden figure of the church's patron

saint. Above the C19 pulpit there is a sarcophagus tablet with urn on top by J. Balls of
Lowestoft; it commemorates John Woodthorpe,
42 years a churchwarden until his death in 1846.
The 1870s *Annunciation* and Nativity window
on the n. side of the chancel is again by Lavers,
Barraud & Westlake, but the window alongside
has fine 1860s glass by *Powells* which is quite
different in character – two vignettes of Christ's
miracles of healing, set in heavily patterned
quarries, the blues dominant. Nearby is a plain
tablet by Bayes & Burgess of Great Yarmouth
for Thomas Woodthorpe, a shipmaster of that
town who died in 1836. Just to the w. is another
tablet by Balls of Lowestoft, this time a chaste
design for Martha Reeve who died in 1837. The
1860s glass in the s. window is likely to be the
work of *William Wailes*. He was a Newcastle
grocer-turned-glazier whose output was quite
prolific in the mid-C19; the design is a brightly
coloured version of the wise and foolish virgins,
all nicely grouped in C13-style poses beneath
matching *tabernacle work*. The Decorated *piscina*,
with its *crocketted finial* and stone *credence shelf*,
was all sharply re-cut before being replaced.
The e. window (probably Clayton & Bell)
commemorates the rector responsible for the
rebuilding. The figure of the risen Christ is
backed by a crimson glory and attendant
cherubims, with disciples in the flanking *lights*
and *passion emblems* in the tracery. Finally, there is
attractive glass of 1938 by Powell & Sons in the
n. sanctuary window; the figures of St Peter and
St Mark are in C19 mode, and there is a medieval
ship in the top quatrefoil. The little cowled figure
at the bottom is the glazier's mark and not, as
some have supposed, a reference to a medieval
monk buried here.

Cavendish, St Mary (C6): There is no more
pleasant a prospect than a broad expanse of
village green rising to the harmonious grouping
of cottages and church beyond. 'Candish' – the
old spelling and pronunciation of the village
name can be found on a *brass* in Little Bradley
church. The C14 tower has a massive s.e. stair
turret rising well above the battlements and
capped by an openwork bell frame, giving it an
unmistakable silhouette; the ringing chamber
served originally as living quarters and the
fireplace chimney still emerges at the top. There
are *lancets* at ground floor level, two-*light* belfry
windows and *Tudor* bell openings. Unlike Clare,
it measures up to the body of the church that
was rebuilt in the C15. The whole of the
clerestory and battlements of the *nave* are

beautifully finished in *flushwork* and one of the
lead rainwater hoppers carries the Tudor device
of a rose between leopards' heads. It is likely
that the s. *aisle* was designed by Reginald Ely,
Henry VI's architect who began King's College
Chapel, Cambridge. Built about 1471, the
window *tracery* shows how the four-petalled
flower motif survived well into the *Perpendicular*
period. The *chancel* was rebuilt under the will of
Sir John Cavendish, Edward III's Lord Chief
Justice who was put to death with the Prior of
Bury in 1381. There is flushwork chequer along
the base of the walls and the windows combine
the *ogee* shape with pure Perpendicular tracery in
the heads. The *priest's door* is original and niches
curve over the whole of the arch-way. The seven-
light e. window is vast and virtually fills the
whole wall. The C19 *vestry* stands on the site of
an earlier chapel and the C14 n. aisle retains its
modest doorway and unaltered buttresses; the
blocked door at the e. end was probably used as
the entrance to a private pew. The low s. *porch* is
early C14 and the outer arch has been varied above
the pairs of *Early English* shafts. There are side
arcades resting on clustered shafts above the stone
seats, and pairs of 'Y' tracery windows, one of
which is *cusped*. The C14 door still has its original
closing ring but only the rivets remain to show
that it once had lizards attached – those ancient
emblems of good fortune that can be seen at
Withersfield, Great Thurlow and Brockley.

Within, the nave is tall and wide in relation to
its length and light floods in from the *transomed*
clerestory windows and through the wall of glass
at the e. end; this, together with the delicacy of
the arcade *piers* imparts a delicious sense of space
and airiness. There are the remains of a *stoup* to
the r. of the entrance and to the l. stands a C15
font with nicely traceried shaft and the remains
of *Evangelistic symbols* in the bowl panels. The
low and sharply pointed tower arch has been re-
cut and is fitted with a modern glazed screen. It
is unusual to find a vaulted ceiling in the ground
floor of a tower and this one has the added
distinction of a large *green man* centre *boss*.
Overhead there is a *sanctus-bell window* and the
dark, cambered *tie-beam* nave roof springs from
wall-posts that bear the mutilated remains of
canopied figures. The carvings in the *spandrels*
are very similar to those at Stansfield, and with
binoculars one can see a fierce dragon at the w.
end on the n. side and a man with a spear at the
e. end to the s. There are two fine windows in
the s. aisle; the first of 1922 in memory of
Emmeline Edmonds has the *Blessed Virgin* and
Child within a niche frame, flanked by angels

bearing shields of the Sacred Heart and *St Edmund* against a background of slightly tinted quarries; the second, by Cox & Sons of 1873, displays the *Agnus Dei* and Evangelistic symbols, set in attractive, heavily patterned glass. Nearby is a *piscina* within a wide, cusped arch with a small recess off to the l., and the *altar* is a good *Stuart* table. Arguably the most beautiful thing that Cavendish possesses is a gorgeous *reredos* ablaze with gilding and colour. On a relatively small scale, it is a C16 Flemish bas-relief of the Crucifixion in painted alabaster which came from the private chapel of Athelstan Riley in London. The three crosses of Calvary rise above a crowd of animated figures carved with infinite delicacy and feeling; the rounded enclosing arch of gilded wood, deeply niched and intricately canopied, contains figures of Jonah emerging from the jaws of the whale, *St Veronica* offering Christ her kerchief, and a *pietà*. Below the main panel stands the Virgin and Child, with *St Anthony* on the l. and (probably) *St Roche* on the r. Until relatively recently it stood behind the altar in the s. aisle, but it is now fastened nakedly to the wall by the n. door; there is no altar below it and it has been downgraded to the status of an artifact. The fact that the 1870s glass in the aisle e. window can now be seen in its entirety is little consolation and one hopes that there will be second thoughts. The early-C15 n. aisle roof is interesting because it was obviously designed to fit the old building, and when the new arcades were built in the 1480s some of the spandrels had to be cut back for it to fit. Some fashionable pendants were added later and dated at each end – 1625 and 1626 (the colouring of the bosses and pendants is modern). In the n.w. window of the aisle there is a late-C14 shield of arms which probably represents the marriage of Margaret Clifton of Buckenham in Norfolk and Roger, eldest son and heir of Sir Thomas de Grey. The monument on the wall further along is an oddity of retrospective family duty. A flat obelisk with side drapes, set on mottled marble, it was made by John Soward in 1810 but commemorates Shadrach Brise who died in 1699, his widow and various children up to 1752. There is another piece by this rather mundane sculptor at Thorpe Morieux. William White carried out a wholesale restoration and rebuilding here in the 1860s and it was then that the n. aisle was extended eastwards along the side of the chancel and the vestry built. The C15 eagle lectern is like the one at Woolpit except that in this case it has lost its base and stands on a stone plinth. The church's other lectern is in

the chancel and is an interesting early-C16 design in wood, the double slope is carried on a turned stem and the cross bars and feet of the base are also turned work. The late-C14 windows of the chancel have slim *jamb shafts* and the hollowed embrasures are worked with shallow canopies. There is a C19 boarded waggon roof with bosses, and the bays over the *sanctuary* are painted to form a *celure*. The piscina, with its *crocketted* arch and large *finial*, has been sharply restored but within there are exceptionally delicate shafts that rise to *groining* which has a centre lion boss. There is a small portion of medieval glass canopy work in the centre light of the e. window and the door to the vestry is original. When it was a chapel, the small *quatrefoil squint* to the r. enabled the celebrant to see the *High altar*. Below the squint stands the tomb of Sir George Colt who died in 1570. There are three large shields carved in the side panels which retain traces of colour and an inscription is carried on the bevel of the worn *Purbeck marble* top; there are faint indentations at one end that might perhaps be the remains of a Nine Mens' Morris board. Beyond it, to the l. of the window, is a canopied niche with two crocketted finials; below, two demi-angels support a cloth in which there is the tiny figure of a soul. They would appear to have been re-cut and the niche now contains a modern statue of the Virgin and Child. St Andrew's has an excellent ring of six bells with an 11 cwt. tenor.

Cavenham, St Andrew (B4): There is an 'S' bend at the end of the village street by the entrance to the Hall and the church lies just beyond. There are one or two interesting features on the outside – look first at the ancient slab of stone, possibly C12, under the gable at the s.w. corner. The carving is of two animals rather like rabbits and at the s.e. corner of the *nave* there is another, this time of a pair of human heads. The C13 *chancel* has a pair of matching *lancets* with *Decorated tracery*, although the fine mouldings are now partly obscured by plaster. The one to the w. had a *low side window* below but the opening has been bricked up. On the l.-hand *jamb* you will find two *scratch dials* and there is another further up. Between these windows is a simple C13 *priest's door* and an earlier lancet. The e. window dates from the restoration of 1870. On the n. side of the chancel are two *Early English* lancets (one blocked) and a *trefoil*-headed C13 window. Both the w. gables of the nave have very broad caps, and there is a short length of *dogtooth* moulding under the one on the n. side. The unbuttressed tower probably dates from the late C13, its w. door blocked at the bottom and glazed at the top to form a window. The bell opening on that side has 'Y' tracery but those on the n. and s. sides are late C14. The interesting item here is the weather mould high on the w. face. It can only mean that at one time there was a two-storied extension, presumably a *galilee porch* with a chamber above it like the one at Lakenheath. The s. *porch* has developed a decided lean outwards and the Early English doorway to the church shows traces of colour on the stonework. Within, note that the archway to the tower is hardly larger than a door and in front of it stands a large *font* with a tub bowl that is likely to be C12, standing on a later stem – the whole piece heavily plastered over. The restored nave roof is lightly *scissors-braced* and the windows form an interesting selection of Decorated and *Perpendicular* designs from the C13 to the C15. At the e. end, the irregularities in the walls and window embrasures show that steps went up to the *rood loft* on both sides of the chancel arch, and not only are there image brackets on the s. side but a *piscina* in the window sill behind the pulpit. It is a reminder that before the *Reformation* there were guilds in the church dedicated to *SS Andrew, John the Baptist, Mary*, and the *Holy Trinity* – all of which would have had their individual altars. There is a fragment of C15 wall painting just w. of the lancet in the n. wall by the pulpit; suppliant figures kneel before a king who holds sceptre and scythe and wears a cloak secured at the top with a band of round brooches. There are traces of colour but the subject is unidentified. The 1914-18 memorial window at the e. end of the nave on the s. side is by *Jones & Willis – St George*, with the dragon writhing from behind him with teeth bared, and a background of dark sky and hills; two vivid red roses peep over the brocade that backs the figure. At the e. end of the nave floor is the only *brass* now in the church, an inscription for John Symunt who died in 1588. The late-C14 chancel arch has grooves above the capitals where the *tympanum* fitted behind the *rood* and there are plenty of graffiti in the mouldings low down on the e. side. The *screen* is a simple late-C16 example, square-headed, with *fleurons* in the top moulding. The stencilled decoration on the panels is likely to be a later addition and the curious tracery in the centre arch is modern. Note the lowered sill of the low side window on the s. side of the chancel just beyond the arch, and also a narrow band of yellow stained glass masked by a glazing bar at the top of the

window. It is difficult to get at, but it has a medieval inscription in French asking us to pray for Adam the vicar. This window also has a border of C14 glass in yellow stain and a roundel at the bottom. In the *sanctuary* there is a good early-C14 angle piscina; the corner pillar has a foliated *capital* and the gable is *crocketted* with a *finial*. The e. window is filled with glass of the 1870s by *William Wailes* of Newcastle. Christ stands with children in the centre *light* and there are groups of figures on either side. The background is a hard blue and the painted faces have faded. The tracery lights are taken up with figures of the *Evangelists* with their symbols, together with two angels. C19 *Decalogue boards* flank the window and there is a tiny *aumbry* lurking behind the tortoise stove on the n. side which bears faint colour on the stone surround. The same colour appears again on the low arched recess on the other side of the chancel and round the priest's door. On the n. wall is a memorial to Sir William Webb – a marble tablet with reversed scrolls each side, a *pediment* above and a *cartouche* of arms against a pyramid. To the l. is a pair of tablets one above the other, combined in one classical design, with restrained swags at the sides and made by Jackman of Bury, dated 1865. Interestingly, the design was duplicated 46 years later by Hanchet of Bury on the far side of the Webb tablet. As you leave, note the medieval wrought-iron closing ring on the centre of the door.

Charsfield, St Peter (G5): The handsome C16 brick tower, patterned overall with diamonds of darker hue, is more than usually interesting because its builder made use of parts of its C15 predecessor. The *flushwork* panelled base course was retained and on the s. side there are crossed arrows in a crown for *St Edmund* and 'MR' for the *Blessed Virgin*. To the r. of the w. door, part of an inscription survives and to the l. there is a panel carved with the *chalice* and wafer symbol of the Eucharist which has the Virgin's initial at each corner. The doorway and w. window were also saved and so were the stepped flushwork battlements with *gargoyles* below them. On the n. side of the *nave* the plain doorway has brick *jambs* and nearby, a small *Norman lancet* shows that the building has been here since the early C12. Judging by the form of its windows, the *chancel* was added or rebuilt in the C13. At some time the s. wall of the nave was heavily repaired in brick and part of another Norman lancet is still embedded there. The brick *porch* is the same age as the tower and John Gosselyn in his will of 1513 left two horses, a colt and 20s. 6d. towards its building. Like the tower, it has an older base course with symbols in *ashlar* and flushwork. The polygonal corner buttresses rise to little domes that have clumsy brick *crockets*, and there is a niche below the crow-stepped gable. There was leaf carving at one time in the arch *spandrels,* and the *paterae* in the mouldings include the badge of the Wingfields showing that they contributed to the building. The outer door is medieval and just inside stands a very interesting bell. It is badly damaged now but the inscription recalls a fierce C18 controversy: 'Sic Sacheverellus ore melos immortali olli ecclesiae defensori hanc dicat Gulielmus Leman de Chersfield Eques 1710' (Since Sacheverell's eloquence is so musical, so this [bell] is dedicated to him, the immortal defender of the church, by Sir William Leman of Charsfield 1710). Henry Sacheverell was a High Church divine and pamphleteer who was a rabid opponent of the Whig government and of all dissenters. On 5 November 1709 he preached a sermon in St Paul's before the lord mayor in which he warned in violent language of the perils of Whig toleration for nonconformists, and openly attacked Gilbert Burnet, the bishop of Salisbury. The sermon was declared a seditious libel by the House of Commons and he was impeached. But 40,000 copies were sold and all London was on his side. At his trial in March 1710 he was found guilty but was only suspended from preaching for three years and became a popular hero. The case brought down the government and when the Tories came in, Queen Anne rewarded Sacheverell with the Crown living of St Andrew's, Holborn. A contemporary sourly labelled him 'a man of much noise but little sincerity', so a bell is perhaps appropriate, but he obviously found favour here with the family who had provided London with at least one lord mayor.

Inside the tower, the little organ with decorative pipework is neatly placed on the old ringers' *gallery,* and the beam below dated 1585 came from the old rectory. The C15 *font* is the familiar East Anglian pattern, with fragments of lions and *woodwoses* around the shaft and *Evangelistic symbols* in four of the bowl panels. Three of the remainder have angels with scrolls but the n.w. panel contains a seated figure holding a cruciform church. Apart from the head it is well preserved and probably represents *St Botolph.* The *hammerbeam* and *arch-braced* nave roof has been in-filled with plaster, and there are demi-figures holding shields below the *wall posts.*

Four little shields hang on the walls and are painted with the arms of gentlemen associated with the parish, including Sir John Leman, a C17 lord mayor of London. Half of the base of the *screen* remains below the chancel arch, and the stairs that led to the *rood loft* are in the n. wall. The modern choir stalls are the work of a Framlingham craftsman, with good *poppyheads* in the local tradition and a very nice variety of subjects on the elbows – squirrel, owl, *pelican in her piety,* muzzled dog, and a small boy being punished in the stocks. The modern *communion rails* copy a good C17 pattern and the C19 stone *reredos* is painted with Creed, Lord's Prayer, and *Decalogue.* There must have been a *piscina* once but there is no trace now. On the n. wall a marble tablet of 1730 reads:

Here also mingled with his Parents' Dust
Sleeps till ye Resurrection of the Just
Of William Leman Esq. their beloved son . . .

Odd how the 'Esq.' creeps in. His parents' little *touchstone* tablet of 1690 is to the r., signed with his monogram. You will have seen a hatchment on the nave wall for Henrietta Orgill who died in 1843, and in the chancel is her husband's; he was the Revd. Naunton Thomas Orgill and died in 1837. It is an interesting example because, having assumed the name and arms of Leman by licence in 1808, the rector had two crests and the one on the l. is a pun on the name – a pelican perches in a lemon tree. St Peter's has a ring of five bells with a 9 cwt. tenor but they are hung dead and can only be chimed.

Chattisham, St Margaret and All Saints (E6): There are countless medieval churches dedicated to All Saints, and many whose patronal saint is St Margaret, but this is the only one in England that honours them jointly. Tiny belfry *lancets* probably date the tower as C13 and it seems squat now since it lost the upper stage prior to a restoration in 1770. It was repaired with brick at that time, battlements were added, and, more recently, a *Decorated*-style w. window has been inserted. On the n. side of the *nave* there is a plain C14 door and a window of the same period, while farther along there is a blocked *low side window* and a blocked *Tudor priest's door* in the *chancel.* The e. window is modern and there is a small *vestry* on the s. side. All the walls are plastered and the C19 timber *porch* stands on a flint and brick base.

The simple interior has been lime-washed and is very comely, with brick floors and walls that incline gently outwards. There is a plain tower arch and in front of it stands a neat little late-C18 chamber organ with a fine mahogany case, given to the church recently as a thank-offering. The *font* is C19, and there are pine *tie-beams* below plastered ceilings. The C18 restoration also involved removing the chancel arch, and only rough shapes in the walls betray its position. The *rood screen* was destroyed at the same time but the blocked door leading to the *rood loft* stairway remains in the n. wall. An attractive modern figure of St Margaret stands in the low side window embrasure in the chancel, sculpted by Derek Jarman from driftwood found in the River Orwell. The saint was a shepherdess and is here portrayed cradling a lamb rather than overcoming the legendary dragon that is her usual symbol. There are two heavy C17 stone frames for tablets on the chancel walls carved with crude swags and skulls, but instead of being engraved the inscriptions were painted and have all but vanished. The *communion rails* are C19 and in the *sanctuary* there is a very simple C14 angle *piscina* (minus its drain) with *dropped-sill sedilia* alongside. In the floor on the n. side is the 1592 *brass* for John and Mary Revers and their family, but only the inscription and the plate engraved with the little figures of the three sons and seven daughters are still in place. The 12in. indents for their parents' effigies are clear and you will find Mary's figure in its wide-brimmed hat fixed to the chancel s. wall. There are two more brass inscriptions in the floor of the nave: John Bennett (1608) and Daniel Meadowe (1651, with a Latin verse). As you go, have a look at the medieval octagonal poorbox set on a pedestal by the door.

Chedburgh, All Saints (B5): The church stands by the Bury-Haverhill road. The *nave* was rebuilt in 1842 using the old windows. There are C13 *lancets* with tilted *headstops* and one two-*light* window with 'Y' *tracery* of about 1300 on the s. side. This has two in-filled panels below and one wonders whether it came from the old *chancel* and was originally a *low side window*. The chancel and small s. *vestry* were built in 1842 but the early-C14 e. window, with *reticulated* tracery, was salvaged from the old building. At the same time the old n. *porch* was removed to make way for a grey brick tower and spire. There is a pleasing C14 *quatrefoil* window in the w. gable which has small headstops on the *dripstone*. Through the small wooden s. porch lies a very simple interior, with a Victorian w. *gallery* housing a small organ and deal pews in the nave.

The *font* is the same vintage and the floors are paved with East Anglian *pamments* – much less common in churches than bricks or glazed tiles. The inner arch of the re-set window with 'Y' tracery has attached *jamb shafts* with ring *capitals*, and they match those flanking the e. window of the short chancel. There you will see fragments of medieval glass in the tracery, including two little 'suns in splendour' and two sets of lions which were probably part of a shield of *Royal Arms*. The stylised 1920s glass by Frederick Charles Eden in pale colour depicts an angel catching the fluid from the side of the crucified Christ while two floating angels mask their faces above the *Blessed Virgin* and *St John*. The glass in the window on the s. side on the theme of the Good Shepherd is not signed but may be by *Heaton, Butler & Bayne*. The *sanctuary* is bounded by a delicate little set of Gothick *communion rails* with pierced *spandrels* to the arches, turned shafts, and scrolly wrought-iron supports (made no doubt for the new chancel). On your way out you will step over a *ledger-stone* in the nave that shows how varied C18 and early-C19 pluralities could be. Thomas Knowles was not only rector of Ickworth and Chedburgh, he was a prebendary of Ely and 'Preacher' of St Mary's, Bury as well.

Chediston, St Mary (H3): The plain, un-buttressed tower is probably late C13, with a bell stage and *flushwork* battlements added in the C15. The *nave* has a blocked C14 n. doorway and renewed *Perpendicular* windows, while the *chancel* appears to be largely early C14, with a small *priest's door* on the s. side. Appearances are sometimes deceptive, however, for the modern *vestry* on the n. side conceals a *Norman lancet* which you will see inside. All the walls are cement-rendered, including the early-C14 *porch*. Its entrance arch is elegantly moulded, and the *capitals* of the slim shafts are carved with foliage, with an oak leaf and an acorn on the l. The inner doorway is a matching piece, and to its r. there is a plain *stoup* recess which is duplicated within.

The C15 *font* has much in common with nearby Wissett's. The panels of the ample octagonal bowl are carved with *Evangelistic symbols* and angels with shields bearing symbols of the *Trinity* (s.w.) and *Passion* (s.e.); lions and *woodwoses* guard the shaft. The parish chest by the door is a standard *Jacobean* design, but there is a remarkable little C14 predecessor beyond the font, a 20in. cube hewn from an upended tree trunk, to which a lid, hinges and three locks were added. The chamber organ in front of the n.

door has a case rather like a manic Victorian chiffonier, with ivy tendrils swooping around the tops of the pipes. The nave roof is an *arch-braced* design, with *collars* and *king posts* below the ridge, and a pierced trail carved in the *wall plates*. The plaster has been cut back to expose the head of what must have been a huge *St Christopher* painting high in the wall beyond the n. door. It was discovered during a restoration of 1895, and had been damaged long before when one of the early-C16 windows was inserted. There are interesting remnants of C15 glass at the top of the first nave window on the s. side. To the l. is a damaged *rebus* which is probably connected with Hamon Claxton who was the church's patron in the C16 (the 'tun' [barrel] is still clear), and two roundels lettered with 'Help' and 'Mercy'. The next window has a narrow image niche in the embrasure, and the attractive glass is a memorial to an RAF wing commander killed in 1940. The roughly textured figures of *St George* and *St Felix* are boldly set against a background of ploughing and harvest scenes. It would be nice to know who the artist was. The return of St George to the church restores the historic balance, for in 1643 *Dowsing* charged the parish six shillings and eight pence to remove 'two superstitious inscriptions, and seven popish pictures, one of Christ, and another of St George'. At the e. end of the nave on the n. side there is a large recess with curious pendants in the top; it once opened onto an C18 mausoleum for the Fleetwood family which was later used as the manorial pew but which has now been demolished. The handsome pulpit with its lovely little curving stair is dated 1631 in one of the nicely carved upper panels, and the main *blind-arched* panels of the body carry split-turned decoration. Strangely, it was ejected from Cookley when that church was restored in 1894 because 'it was inharmonious with its surroundings'; only the taste of the rural dean of the day rescued it from oblivion in a loft and brought it safe to Chediston. It is the twin of Rumburgh's pulpit and must have been made by the same man. A curious feature of the chancel is the way in which the wall is cut away between the chancel arch and the priest's door to afford a little extra width up to a height of some 7ft. (the same arrangement can be found at Thorington). The early-C17 *communion rails* are an unusual design, with pendant acorn shapes above sharp obelisks as spacers between the turned shafts. The sturdy *Holy table* belongs to the same period. The C14 *angle piscina* has been so heavily restored that only the *jamb shaft*

is old stone, but it probably repeats the original design. In the window above there is a pair of early-C14 shields, one of which bears the arms of the Mowbray family, and in the e. window a C16 or early-C17 oval displays the arms of Baxter. St Mary's has a ring of six bells with a 13 cwt. tenor, but the condition of the frame and fittings prevents their being rung at the present time.

Chelmondiston, St Andrew (G7): There has been a church on this site since the middle of the C13 (and perhaps before that), and as with many Suffolk churches, it had become so ruinous by the 1860s that a full-scale restoration was necessary. *E.C. Hakewill* rebuilt the nave and the top of the tower, and added a n. *aisle* and chapel. In 1890, the *chancel* was replaced by *G.F. Bodley* and *vestries* were provided on the n. side. It was by all accounts a handsome building, but disaster struck in December 1944 when a German flying bomb landed on a nearby cottage and wrecked the majority of the church. It was to be eleven years before the new building was begun, and the architect was Basil Hatcher whose only other church in Suffolk is St Francis, Ipswich. That was an exercise in contemporary fashion, but for Chelmondiston a version of *Perpendicular* was chosen which was thought more suitable for a village setting. The budget was tight and it is a plain, rather stark building, with rendered walls; in 1980 a meeting room was added on the n. side of the nave. The 1880s figure of the church's patron saint was saved from the old *porch* and re-set in the s. wall of the tower.

The new porch is much smaller, and the nave within is bright with a display of colourful hassocks on the pew ledges. The fine organ, with its attractive case, was built by Roger Pulham of Charsfield and was installed within the tower arch in 1982. Just beyond it on the s. wall there is an oval tablet for William Cornwallis, a memorable pluralist who died in 1786, having been rector here for 49 years and at Great Waldingfield for 54 years. The *font* was salvaged from the ruined church, a heavy octagon on closely set stub shafts designed by Hakewill in 1866. The 1890s pulpit survived too, good quality work by John Groom & Son; there is a vine trail under the rim, and look for the tiny heads carved as terminals on the buttresses. The *hour-glass* stand on the wall above is one of the few reminders of the old church, and it is one of the best in Suffolk. Its *Jacobean* wall bracket is boldly carved with a woman's figure, a lion mask, and a swag of fruit. The stained glass in the chancel is by Francis Skeat (the only other example of his work in Suffolk is at Laxfield), and the e. window was installed in 1961. In the centre *light, St Mary Magdalene* kneels at the foot of the cross, to the l. a post-Resurrection Christ recovers the lost sheep from a cliff, and on the r. he stands with the flock – excellent draughting and fresh colour. The three windows in the s. wall date from 1965 and each has an attractive *Renaissance* setting. From the w.: *St Andrew* called by Christ (commemorating a bishop of Nasik and the work of the Church Missionary Society); *St Luke* with a family; the *three Marys* at the tomb. The plain recess in the s.e. corner of the *sanctuary* contains the *piscina* drain, one of the few visible relics of the medieval church.

Chelsworth, All Saints (D6): Attractively sited, the church stands s. of the street in one of Suffolk's prettiest villages. The walls are rendered and the C14 tower has a flint panelled *base course*, with 'Y' *tracery* bell openings. The w. window is a small *cusped lancet* and there is a narrow slit to light the belfry above. A major C15 rebuilding followed, with spacious *clerestoried nave* and wide *aisles*. The s. *porch* dates from the same period and is set flush with the w. end of the aisle; a carved lion and *griffin* stand at the corners of the battlements and the *dripstones* of the side windows have *headstops*. The glass in them was restored in 1966 and displays an interesting variety of mainly continental glass, including a selection of small heads, a group of men rowing a boat, and a figure of *St Nicholas*; one of the panels is dated 1637. The porch was adapted as a *vestry* in 1843 by Peter Gage, a local builder, and it was he who made the outer doors, using the inner C15 door as a model. The windows, of about 1300 with 'Y' tracery in the s. aisle, were apparently reused at the time of the rebuilding. Round the corner, on the e. wall a sheet of roofing lead is fixed bearing the names of the churchwardens of 1838 and of the plumber who did the work. The *chancel* is C14 but was extensively restored in 1866 when a new e. window was inserted, although a fragment of the wider original is embedded in the wall to the r. There was evidently a chapel n. of the chancel at one time and a roof *corbel* juts from the wall; below it is the sweet little *ogee*-headed connecting doorway, still with its medieval door. The large tomb that you will see inside was resited in the wall of the n. aisle during the rebuilding and projects slightly. There is *ball flower* under its parapet and below the battle- ments of the small circular corner turrets. This rearrangement was evidently an afterthought because 'Y' traceried windows had been reused (as on the s. side) and then they were cut into by the tomb, leaving a lancet shape visible each side. The n. porch was repaired in 1852, again by Peter Gage, and he also lettered the arch of the plain C14 doorway. Just inside stands a C14 *font* and the bowl panels are carved with attractive *crocketted* gables, each rising to a *finial* enclosing *trefoils*. The painted shields on the stem cannot now be identified. A set of George IV *Royal Arms* hangs above the tower arch within which stands the organ, and on either side there are cutout painted metal lilies with scroll texts – a favourite form of Victorian decoration. The tall nave *arcades* have *quatrefoil piers* and above them runs a prominent *string course* carved with *paterae* and demi-angels bearing shields. The *wall posts* of the cambered *tie-beam* roof rest on corbels shaped as demi-angels, two of which hold stringed instruments. The feature of the n. aisle is the magnificent early-C14 tomb – probably free-standing before it was re-sited. It is likely to have been made for Sir John de St Philibert who died in 1334. The main gable is heavily crocketted up to a large finial and the area within the main arch is covered with diaper work. Marks on the background suggest that there were once statues in the centre trefoils, and the pairs of short *Purbeck marble* columns either side of the recess have stiff-leaf *capitals*. The recess has a *groined* ceiling with a centre *boss* and the tall, elegant side pinnacles are closely crocketted. Apart from the original move, the tomb was restored in 1850. To the r. is a large trefoil *piscina* arch and it is unusual to find another close by to the r. of the e. window – a later design which belongs to the rebuilding. The 1890s glass in the aisle e. window is an Ascension by *Lavers, Barraud & Westlake*. The colours are *pre-Raphaelite* and there is a lowering sky behind the figure of Christ. It is competent without having the quality of the firm's work in the middle of the century. The e. and w. windows of the s. aisle contain C19 heraldic shields of successive Lords of the Manor which are all named and dated, and the other aisle windows have 1850s glass by a little-known Ipswich glazier, R.B. King. Text *labels* are in pink and brown against coarsely patterned *quarries* of an insipid green – not very nice. The s. aisle has a shapeless piscina recess uncovered in 1953, and below stands a heavily banded C14 waggon chest. The deep *rood loft stair* rises from the s. aisle and there are medieval tiles within the doorway, some painted heraldically. Although there is now no *screen* the upper opening of the rood stair shows that it was lofty, and the iron hook that supported the rood itself remains embedded in the top of the chancel arch. Above are extensive remains of a painted *Doom*. Re-discovered in 1849, it was ignorantly restored, particularly the central figure of Christ on the rainbow. To his l. is the large and flaming mouth of hell, with the souls of the damned chained and held captive by a demon. To the r. of *St Peter* stands a sooty devil with a long tail but beyond the figure of the *Blessed Virgin* little survives of Paradise. The *hatchment* over the n. door is for Pleasance, wife of Samuel Pocklington, who died in 1774, and over the s. door hangs Robert Pocklington's – he died in 1767. The last and most interesting is the one to the l. of the s. door. It is for Sir Robert Pocklington who died in 1840 and who was made a knight of the military order of Maria Theresa in 1794 by Francis II, last emperor of the Holy Roman Empire. Serving with the 15th Dragoons, Pocklington had saved the emperor from the French near Cambrai. The star of the order is painted on the hatchment and also figures on his memorial further along, together with plumed helmet and martial trophies. The Royal Arms and hatchments have all been recently restored. The chancel has a panelled waggon ceiling and the e. window is filled with excellent glass of 1875 by *Hardman*. It is a Crucifixion in three panels – all medieval in feeling; the figure of Christ is set against a deep red pointed oval, and the blue of the patterned backgrounds is typical of the firm; there is attractive leafwork and *Passion emblems* in the tracery. The *sanctuary* piscina lies within a simple C14 lancet, and on the s. wall of the chancel is a plain but elegant tablet for Elizabeth Fowke (1820) by Henry Rouw.

Chevington, All Saints (B4): At the end of a cul-de-sac and in a large churchyard, the church has a decidedly gawky look. This is brought on by an almost flat *chancel roof* combining with prominent brick battlements on the tall *nave* and an oddly proportioned tower. The latter was well built, conventional late C15, until Frederick Augustus, 4th Earl of Bristol and Bishop of Derry, wanted it to be viewable from Ickworth Park and added another stage – open to the sky and complete with pseudo-Gothic *lancets*, battlements and pinnacles. The lower stages of the w. buttresses have pairs of flint-filled panels with *trefoil* heads, there is a *flushwork base course*, and the angular w. window has small *headstops* to the *dripstone*. The belfry stair turret is

on the s. side but there is another access door to the tower on the n. side – probably C19. The nave shows signs of its *Norman* origin with a very plain C12 n. door and a small single lancet. Another window has *plate tracery* and a large brick buttress was added on that side in the C16 or C17. There are *Early English* lancets in the chancel, one of which is masked by a later buttress, and the e. window set high in the wall is a relatively modern insertion. There is a lancet *low side window* on the s. side and another late-C13 window with plate tracery on that side of the nave. The s. *porch* is largely a reconstruction but the outer arch of the early-C14 original survives, with *jambs* and curves cut from single pieces of timber. Three steps lead down to the late-C12 *Transitional* doorway – *dogtooth* ornament enclosing the arch and down the sides, and pairs of unequal shafts with coarse foliage *capitals*. Within, there is a modern ringers' *gallery* and above it the ring of six with its 12 cwt. tenor is currently described as being in 'poor going order'. The early-C15 *font* looks out of proportion without its step; the shaft has fin buttresses and the decoration of the bowl is unconventional, with narrow tracery panels offsetting the *quatrefoils* and shields. Some of the benches at the w. end have wide traceried ends and there is a very interesting collection of *finials*. There are five praying women by the n. wall (one with a rosary) and another on the s. side; nearest the door is a bearded man back to back with a lute player, the third from the w. on the n. side plays a double pipe, followed to the e. by players of trumpet, bagpipe and cymbals. The westernmost figure on the s. side plays a stringed instrument and next to him is a possible harp player. Thus, with a little licence, we have the full orchestral complement for Psalm 150. One of the bench backs is traceried and it may once have formed part of the old *rood loft*. By the n. door is an excellent C14 chest; the front is intricately carved with *Decorated* tracery and on the l. there are panels containing pairs of monkeys and birds, with a dragon below. The matching panels to the r. have disappeared and a later end has been grafted on. Over the s. door is a rather nice set of George I *Royal Arms* painted on board, within a square frame, and at the e. end on that side there is a *piscina* under a trefoil arch marking the site of a nave *altar*. The roof of cambered *tie-beams* has pierced and traceried *spandrels* and additional tie-beams were inserted later. Dated 1590 and 1638, they bear the names and initials of church-wardens, and have leaf trails carved on the

Chevington, All Saints: Bagpiper bench end

chamfers. The chancel arch is tall and narrow and comes down to half-round ring capitals which have curly pendants rather like pigs' tails. At each side there are subsidiary arches with plain chamfers which would have given a view of the *High altar* from the nave altars. The original chancel was much shorter than the one built in the C13 and then that was cut back in 1697 to the present dimensions. It has recently been provided with an unadorned stone altar placed centrally and a black metal tabernacle for the reserved sacrament stands on a stone column in the n.e. corner. The simplicity of this arrangement against the stark whiteness of the walls is a potent combination. Beams in the low-pitched roof overhead are carved 'Edward Grove' and 'Soli Deo' and there are some more medieval bench ends – a figure holding a shield, another trumpeter, a bird picking berries, and a woman with a fine headdress. Nearby is an epitaph in stately periods for Elizabeth White, the rector's wife, on a *ledger-stone* cut by William Steggles of Bury in 1834; he probably provided the one for the husband in 1818 as well, and they are rare examples of the mason signing work in this form. Don't overlook the excep-tionally attractive *rococo* C18 tablet for Ann Burch on the *sanctuary* s. wall – in white marble with a coloured *cartouche* of arms.

Chillesford, St Peter (H5): The church sits on its own little hill, and the steep green path skirts a deep pond to become an avenue of limes halfway to the *porch*. It may perhaps have been established before the Conquest, and certainly there was a church here at the time of the Domesday survey in 1086. The severe, unbuttressed C14 tower is built entirely of corraline crag, a distinction it shares with Wantisden, and they are the only examples in England. The beige, attractively textured limestone is full of fossilised shells and was quarried from a number of pits in the Orford peninsular – one lies just to the n. of the church. The tower has a renewed *Decorated* w. window, and the bell openings are partially bricked up, having lost their *tracery*. The buttresses at the w. corners of the *nave* show that it predates the tower, and its small C14 n. doorway has been blocked; there is a small Decorated window on that side, and the buttresses were strengthened with C18 brick. The *priest's door* in the *chancel* s. wall was probably installed as part of an enthusiastic 1860s restoration, and a n.e. *vestry*, complete with chimney, was added in 1906. Three exceptionally large late-C18 headstones stand just s. of the chancel, and there is fine letter cutting to be seen on a number of others. The tiny porch was rebuilt in 1878, and it shelters a C14 doorway.

A simple interior, bright and white, with brick floors, pine benches, and plastered ceiling. Beyond the plain tower arch, the w. window contains attractive 1880s glass by Edward Frampton. He trained with *Clayton & Bell*, and established a thriving business in the later years of the C19. This is his only identified work in Suffolk, and it employs busy patterns above and below the two panels of Christ walking on the water. The C13 *font* has a *Purbeck marble* bowl with the usual pairs of shallow arches in its panels, and the massive, moulded stem dates from the C16. Whoever blocked the n. doorway did not bother to remove the door itself, and it remains, fossilised so to speak, in its frame. It is likely that the original *Norman* chancel was entered through a narrow archway, and the C15 replacement, although taller, is no wider. The *squints* in the flanking walls were re-fashioned in the C19 but may have been there before that. A compact *piscina* in the s. wall has traces of dark colour, and it shows that a pre-*Reformation altar* was sited nearby. Above the chancel arch there is a diminutive plaster set of Victoria *Royal Arms*, coloured and gilt. Early buildings that were subsequently altered often finished up with a *weeping chancel*, and we have an example here. Its ceiling is panelled and plastered, but the *castellated wall plate* of the medieval roof shows below. In the *sanctuary*, the piscina has a deeply *cusped trefoil* arch, and an interesting *brass* is displayed in the vestry door splay. Its long Latin inscription commemorates two Agnes Claxtons, mother and daughter, and ends:

Contiguae Jaceant pia mater, filia sancta,
Audeat has cineres nulla movere manus,
Donec magna dies venit ultima qua tuba
  Caeli,
Aure cuiq/ sonet, surgite ad invicta.
  Mater ⟵   ⟶ Filia

(Let them lie beside each other,
Loving mother, holy daughter,
Let no hand dare touch their ashes,
Till the Advent Day be come.
Till the golden trumpet soundeth,
Rise, ye dead, to judgement rise.)

At a guess, the brass lay in the floor of the chancel between the two graves, so that the arrows pointed to the mother on one side and the daughter on the other.

Chilton, St Mary (C6): This little church lies in the middle of fields beyond an industrial estate on the n.e. edge of Sudbury and is now in the care of the *Churches Conservation Trust*. Access is by footpaths and it is advisable to make enquiries about the key before a visit. The building is largely C15 but the heavily buttressed tower is C16 brick, with a solid stair turret to the s. The battlements are probably C19 but the *Decorated* bell openings may have been saved from an earlier tower and reused. C16 too is the n.e. Crane *chantry chapel* and its w. window was blocked to make space for a monument inside. The n. door of the *nave* is blocked and there are two oddly proportioned windows on that side – the one to the w. of about 1500. The large late-C15 windows on the s. side are very like those in Long Melford's s. *aisle*. The s. porch is modern and entry now is normally via the chantry chapel. This has a fine late-C15 roof with heavily moulded timbers and there are some excellent monuments. The earliest is a table tomb below and to the r. of the e. window and is for George Crane who died in 1491. Despite the loss of the hands, his alabaster figure is well preserved and shows traces of colour, with the feet resting on a *unicorn*. There was a brass inscription on the bevel originally and the *quatrefoils* in the side

panels contain blank shields. Within the arch that links the chapel with the *chancel* stands a second tomb chest on which lie the alabaster effigies of Robert Crane, who died in 1500, and his wife Anne. He wears full armour, long hair lapping his helm, and again the feet rest on a unicorn. His wife was evidently of gentle birth because she wears the *Collar of SS* and the lappet of her headdress retains traces of the coloured pattern. Like the first tomb, this one had a brass inscription on the bevel of the top but the shields of Crane, Ogard, and Lovell on the sides are set within lozenges and have been re-coloured. Portraits of Robert, the founder of the chantry, and his wife can be found in the glass at Long Melford. On the w. wall is the last and best of the Crane monuments, for Sir Robert, MP for Sudbury in the Long Parliament, and his two wives. Of alabaster, it was sculpted in 1626 by *Gerard Christmas* and the three stubby figures kneel within niches separated by columns of polished *touchstone* with *Corinthian capitals*. Sir Robert faces front and his first wife, Dorothy (who was a Norfolk Hobart from Blickling), is on the l., with Susan, her successor, on the r. They are in profile, the faces aquiline and force-ful, and Dorothy has more than a passing resemblance to Queen Elizabeth I. There are three shields of arms at the top and strangely placed behind Sir Robert's head is a pencilled inscription: 'S.Brown and A.Porter restored the chancel end of this church in the month of September 1860 assisted by J.Partridge' – a little credit note from the past that is a reminder that there was a major re-ordering at that time when the position of the s. nave windows was changed, the s. wall rebuilt, the roof replaced, and *box pews* removed – all under the direction of George Grimwood of Sudbury. Two good C15 figures have survived in the *tracery* of the chapel e. window – *St Appollonia* on the l. and *St Michael* beating down a blue dragon on the r.

The door to the nave has rudimentary *linen-fold panelling* and the *jambs* retain a portion of the decoration which was applied to all the walls in 1875 (there is another fragment by the s. door). In the tower there is an C18 *Decalogue* board framed on the n. wall, with a section of its counterpart standing close by, and another C19 set leaning against the w. wall. The C15 *font* has quatrefoils in the bowl panels, a traceried stem, and *paterae* carved on the foot. The base of the late-C15 *screen* still stands in the chancel arch and the rail is carved with two heads and two dragons biting their tails. There is a similarity with Great Cornard's screen and they may have been carved by the same man. Yet another pair of Decalogue boards hang on the e. wall and, below them, a C19 or early-C20 *reredos* of mosaic panels with fleur-de-lys and centre text set in marble. The churchyard is pleasant to stroll in, and e. of the chancel lies Thomas Creaton who, after '36 years as Steward to the elder John Addison Esq. of Chilton Hall in this Parish', died in 1835. Status is status after all, even at one remove.

Clare, St Peter and St Paul (B6): A large and handsome church, it stands within a spacious churchyard in the centre of one of Suffolk's nicest small towns. The walls of the old priest's house to the s. are decorated with some of the best pargetting to be seen anywhere. The base of the tower is C13 and the w. door has pairs of shafts, with two bands of small *dogtooth* in the deep moulding. In 1899, however, the tower was rebuilt above that level reusing the majority of the old material. The *nave* was rebuilt in the 1640s and the *chancel* in 1478, and they are very tall for their length, making one wish that the tower had been altered in scale. By the beginning of the C17 the chancel was ruinous and it was effectively rebuilt again in 1617. It seems that the e. window *tracery* was used again, but in doing so the pointed arch was smoothed out to an even curve. A study of the window emphasises how the same *Perpendicular* style was in vogue with very little variation over two centuries. Prominent *rood stair* turrets are placed on each side of the nave gable and their *crocketted* spires are reminiscent of the singleton at Lavenham. There is a *Tudor priest's door* on the s. side of the chancel with an unusually good original traceried door. The n. *porch* was built around 1400 but still has *Decorated* tracery in the side windows; it now houses the C19 *bier*. The outer arch of the C14 s. porch is decayed, and above it the 1790 sundial bears the peremptory instruction 'Go about your business' – singularly apt, when one considers how much of it was traditionally transacted in the porch. Within, the ceiling is *groined* and the centre *boss* is a fine carved head (possibly Christ's). The inner doorway is decorated with three bands of *paterae* and masks, and the traceried panels of the *postern door* match the rest of the C16 door. Note that one of the effects of the C15 rebuilding was to reduce the length of the porch by a quarter. Built on to it is a C14 chapel whose interior arch was reused at the rebuilding. It was converted later by inserting a *Jacobean gallery* with nicely turned newel posts and *balusters* to the rear staircase. This was discarded in the 1880s but

providentially there were second thoughts later and it was replaced. At my last visit thought was being given to the possibility of making the undercroft a chapel for quiet meditation. On the wall overhead are two *hatchments*: on the l. for Lieut. Col. John Barker who died in 1804, and on the r. for his widow Caroline who died in 1848. An iron-bound chest stands below and by the s. door is the early-C15 *font* with *quatrefoils* and shields in the bowl panels (except one which is blank and shows that it may originally have stood against a pillar). Clare has an excellent ring of eight bells with a tenor of 28 cwt. and the 7th of 19 cwt., making it the heaviest ring of eight in the county. The 7th bell's inscription is unusual: 'Trinitas Sancta Campanum Istam Conserva' (O Holy Trinity conserve this bell) and it was probably cast by William Wodeward c.1395-1420. Until recently this was a ground floor ring,

Clare, St Peter and St Paul: Lectern

but now there is a fine ringers' gallery. Below deep coving an oak glazed screen has been inserted to form a meeting room and cloakroom in the base of the tower. Some of the pews have been removed from the w. end of the nave to provide a useful meeting space. The church is airy and spacious, full of light, and the nave *arcade* is particularly interesting because the quatrefoil *piers* of the old C14 arcade were retained by the C15 builders. They were mounted on high bases and given new *capitals;* their slimness accentuates the sense of space. There is a *sanctus-bell window* over the tower arch and a very decorative *string course* runs below the *clerestory;* it is carved with paterae and masks, and where the slim shafts that rise to the *wall posts* of the roof cross it, there are demi-angels. There are widely spaced crockets and *finials* on the arcade arches and the wide chancel arch is similarly decorated. The *rood screen* must have been unusually tall (see the doorways either side of the arch) and a section of it now stands in front of the organ at the end of the s. aisle. To the r. is the C15 *screen* of a *chantry* chapel and the beautiful cresting above the tracery incorporates a series of crowned 'M.R.'s for the *Blessed Virgin,* with *griffins* as supporters. To the l. a glass case contains the ringers' gotch or beer jug presented to the ringers by the vicar Matthew Bell in 1729, and it is a fine specimen with a bell inscribed 'campana sonant canore' ('Let the bells resound with song'). The 1880s *aisle* window, in memory of town benefactors John and Betsy Isaacson, is by *W.G. Taylor* of the *O'Connors* workshop – figures of Faith, Hope and Charity, with the rest of the window filled with amber-coloured squares. On the wall by the n. door is a very good example of a C19 *brass* and a royal one at that. It commemorates Queen Victoria's 4th son Prince Leopold, Duke of Albany and Earl of Clarence, who died in 1884 and was at that time Master of the local masonic lodge. Further along the n. aisle is a fine window by Frederick C. Eden, architect and stained glass designer. It has a Calvary flanked by the Blessed Virgin and *St John,* with *St Mary Magdalene* kneeling below. There are figures of *St Michael* and *St George* in the side *lights,* with God the Father and the dove of the Holy Spirit above. The figures are outlined against clear glass, with green as the dominant colour and the whole effect is cool and calm; more of his work can be found at Hengrave and Whepstead. In front of the chancel arch is an outstanding late-C15 lectern of the type that can be seen at Redenhall and King's Lynn, St Margaret's, in Norfolk. Like them, it has that

Clare, St Peter and St Paul: Ringers' Gotch

lovely buttery texture that brass acquires when it has been scoured and polished for centuries, but this model has three dogs as feet rather than the lions of the others. In the chancel, the arcades and the string course match those in the nave and below is a very handsome suite of *Jacobean* stalls. There are blind arches in the front, strapwork panels, and heavier carving in the seat backs. The scroll-sided *poppyheads* are carved with varied leaf forms and are so like those at Little Thurlow that they may have been carved by the same man. Some of the stalls incorporate C15 tracery that probably came from the rood screen. The late-C17 *communion rails* with twisted balusters are an excellent set and there are signs that they were originally three-sided. There is a plain *piscina* in the *sanctuary* and on the n. wall, an early-C18 tablet for Susanna Johnson and two of her children with naive carving and lopsided lettering. Unless he was exaggerating with his 'We brake down 1,000 picture super-stitions', in January 1643 *Dowsing* smashed more glass and other things here than in any other single church that he mentions. But although he ordered that 'the Sun and Moon in the East window' should be destroyed, they are still there.

Below them is an attractive series of shields commemorating the benefactors of 1617 – local magnates Sir George le Hunt, Sir John Higham, Sir Thomas Barnardiston, Sir Steven Sonnes, Sir William Storton, as well as the Haberdashers' Company. Underneath, a lot of continental glass fragments have been formed into roundels. There is a very narrow *squint* giving a view of the *High altar* from the s.e. chapel. Across in the n.e. chapel there is a piscina and on the floor the greater part of a C13 grave slab with an elaborate cross on top. The 1823 monument to Mary Sayer on the wall is by Charles Smith, the sculptor of the great fountain on the s. front at Holkham, but with this minor work his attention wandered and a spelling mistake had to be corrected plumb in the middle.

Claydon, St Peter (F6): The church stands above the village, overlooking the Gipping valley, and it is now in the care of the *Churches Conservation Trust*. In their report for 1987 the fund had this to say: 'Within sight of new housing and burgeoning prosperity the diocese left this historic church to rot for eleven years while attempts to find an alternative use came to nothing. It is one of the most conspicuous cases of neglect that we have encountered.' One can now say that the intervention of the Trust has been spectacularly successful in dragging Claydon back from the brink.

The C15 tower has *flushwork* on the angle buttresses to the w. and the stepped battlements are rendered; eight headless figures, dazzlingly white, now stand commandingly above. The original church was *Saxon* – see the *long and short work* at the w. corners of the *nave*, and some *herringbone* masonry beneath the n. and s. windows. The C15 n. *porch* has a crow-stepped gable and its doorway was sealed off with brick years ago. The church's strongest feature is the massive pair of *transepts* whose continuous roof ridge runs across above the level of the nave. They were part of an ambitious scheme of restoration in *Decorated* style which was initiated by the rector, George Drury, in 1851-2. It so happens that he was the same man who caused the rumpus over a nonconformist burial at nearby Akenham, and he had a reputation for savaging medieval buildings. Here, however, his ideas are interesting and, as we shall see, his own artistic skills were involved. His architect was *R.M. Phipson*, and the walls (which have been restored at high level) are closely packed with small flint pebbles. The rearrangement n. of the *chancel* is

confused, with a small bell turret attached to the c. face of the transept and a *vestry* at right angles to the chancel. On the s. side there is a large organ chamber, and the naive *ball flower* decoration of the *priest's door* and the *headstops* of Victoria and Prince Albert's death mask are likely to be some of Drury's work. His grave, in High Victorian style, lies under the yew tree not far away.

Entry is via a plain C14 s. doorway, and inside you will see that it was set within a tall, narrow *Norman* arch. The tower arch was reconstituted in plain style by Drury in 1849, and he designed and painted the w. window glass, with its simply patterned borders and top *lights*. The early-C15 *font* has bowl panels carved with *crocketted trefoil* arches in which crowns and angels holding shields alternate; there are large heads below the bowl and the shaft is panelled. The scale of the transepts makes the nave with its simple *arch-braced* roof seem short. There is a single C17 or early-C18 text painted within a leaf border on the n. wall which is probably the survivor from a sequence like the one at Witnesham. The glass of 1912 in the s. nave window is by Albert Moore, and other work by him can be found at Dallinghoo and Little Bealings. The spacious centre crossing has a *groined* timber ceiling with a large painted lozenge at the centre. There are further examples of Moore's glass, this time of the 1890s, in the n. and s. transept windows, and in the w. window on the n. side you will find a good example of the early work of *Lavers, Barraud & Westlake* which dates from 1867. The panelled barrel roofs of the transepts have *bosses* which were carved by *Henry Ringham*. He also contracted with Drury in 1851 for the benches and reading desk, but the diaper patterns on the pew ends are not his style at all and were probably dictated by the rector. Though the standing figures that he carved as *finials* have, alas, gone, Drury carved the gross *corbels* smothered with foliage that support the triple stub shafts of the transept arches. He is also credited with the stone pulpit – an interesting and inventive design. It stands on a low plinth and there are three large panels (the front one curved) pierced with intricate and spiky *tracery;* the two projecting niches contain figures of the *Blessed Virgin Mary* and *St John*.

The chancel reconstruction included a new arch-braced roof and Drury carved the enterprising set of roof corbels – look for the serpent, ram, owl, and *green man*. The *sanctuary's* e. wall was faced with blind *arcading*, and the *piscina* set at an angle in the corner is matched by a *credence* recess on the n. side. Drury's best glass is to be seen in the 1852 c. window. He designed and painted pointed ovals and smaller roundels for the three *lights* (including Crucifixion, Resurrection and the *Evangelistic symbols*) and filled the rest of the space with small squares rather than *quarries*, all within leafy borders. This important work by a gifted amateur came at a time when the C19 revival in stained glass was gathering momentum, and his work has now been sympathetically repaired and restored. A landmine blew in the s. sanctuary window in World War II and the figure of *St Peter* was replaced in the 1950s. The s.e. organ chamber (with no organ now) has a faded section of painted pattern on the e. wall which probably backed an *altar* originally, and there is another fragment on the w. side of the arch into the chancel. The cockerel in the high roundel window is undoubtedly another example of Drury's work. Restoration has uncovered an earlier floor – C19 glazed and patterned tiles, and a worn *touchstone* slab in the n.e. corner bears a brass border inscription for Samuel Aylemer (d.1635), the son of John Aylmer, Bishop of London 1577-95, who had bought the manor of Claydon in 1588. There is a fireplace in the corner and the flap in the priest's door obviously had a specific purpose, so was this designed as a C19 *anchorite's* cell? Drury had High Church sympathies and Father Ignatius (of Llanthony fame), together with his four monks, enjoyed the rector's hospitality in 1862 before moving on to Norwich and founding a short-lived Anglican order. Half of the small chamber on the n. side of the chancel was used as a vestry and the other half as a miniscule chapel. The C15 cornices in its roof were salvaged from the nave when the new crossing and transepts were built. Claydon's war memorial was a fine *Blessed Virgin* and Child group sculpted by Henry Moore. When the church became redundant it was moved to Barham where it remains. The man who secured its commission was Sir Jasper Nicholas Ridley, whose grave lies by the n. porch – a good stone, with a bas-relief of a bull in a roundel.

Clopton, St Mary (G5): The village is scattered, with the church well down the Grundisburgh road within hailing distance of Burgh's St Botolph. Like a number of others in the area, the C15 tower stands to the s. of the *nave* and doubles as a *porch*. It is plain and very solid, its doorway dwarfed by the expanse of blank wall above. Just to the r. and a little higher up there

is a *consecration cross* which has probably been moved from its original position. Mock *gargoyles* without spouts were sometimes used for decoration, and there is one carved as a pig's head on the s. face here, with the genuine article e. and w. On walking round, you will see *Perpendicular* windows in the nave with varying *tracery*, but one on the n. side at the e. end has 'Y' tracery of about 1300, and the coursed flints in the wall close by suggest that the fabric is at least a hundred years older than that. Only a faint outline shows where the n. door once was. The *chancel* was replaced in the early C19 and then entirely rebuilt as part of a major restoration in the 1880s. It has a very strange lean-to organ chamber and *vestry* on the n. side, built of wood and entirely sheathed in roofing felt, a 'temporary' solution that seems to have become permanent. Within the porch/tower, the late-C13 inner doorway has two exceptionally wide chamfer mouldings rather like a window splay, and on the l.-hand *jamb* there is are fine examples of medieval graffiti – a merchant's mark of a cross and flag above a heart, precisely dated '8th April 1570', and just below is a C14 'M.S.'; someone later cut a large 'T.C.' on the opposite jamb.

The interior is light and airy and the nave has a good *hammerbeam, arch-braced* roof. There are *king posts* on the *collar beams* and, when it was restored in the 1880s, excellent demi-angels with shields were placed on the hammers, those at e. and w. having gilded wings. The lower *spandrels* are carved with some variety; there is a shield of arms at the w. end n. side, a crowned 'M' for the dedication w. of the entrance and, just to the e., a distinctly indelicate figure. The plain early-C15 *font* has small shields within pointed *quatrefoils* in the bowl panels and there are quatrefoils below the step; the shaft has been renewed. The United States flag which hangs at the w. end once flew over the local air base, and below it is a panel commemorating forty-five men of the 8th Air Force who died on missions from Clopton. The small, plain *piscina* in the s. wall shows that there was an *altar* nearby, and the boldly lettered mid-C18 tablet for John and Ann Jeaffreson has a coloured *achievement* above it. The 1880s chancel arch comes down to stub jamb shafts which rest on large carved *corbels*. These are more enterprising than the usual forms of the period and portray the Good Shepherd on one side and the Good Samaritan on the other. *Balusters* from a C17 set of *communion rails* have been used to form a low screen at the chancel entrance. The austere *reredos* and altar in oak date from 1950, and the e. window has interesting glass by *Ward & Hughes* of 1887. The three main *lights* illustrate the sacrifice of Isaac, with attractive colour and sensitive modelling. St Mary's has a ring of six bells with a 13 cwt. tenor, but are at present 'in poor going order'.

Cockfield, St Peter (D5): Many parishes had church houses which were used for *guild* feasts, church ales and other community activities and Cockfield's stands by the churchyard gate – most attractive, in *herringbone* red brick and timber. The church's C14 tower has flint chequerwork on buttresses and battlements, and the s. bell opening was offset to make room for the stair turret. An C18 rector was keen on astronomy and made extra windows for his telescope below the parapet on n. and s. The outlines can still be seen, and so can the *put-log holes* which were used when the tower was built. There are *headstops* to the *dripstones* of the windows in the C14 n. *aisle* and on that side is a *vestry* which was at one time a chapel with a room above it. The early-C14 *chancel* has wonderfully fierce devil *gargoyles* and the buttresses to e. and s. contain large niches which are lavish in a quiet way. Their *crocketted ogee* dripstones bear little headstops and rest on shafts with ring *capitals*. There is a *priest's door* with worn headstops on the s. side and the *rood stair* turret nestles between chancel and s. aisle – of brick and obviously a later addition. All the windows to the s. are *Perpendicular* and the s. aisle battlements are quite showy, with crocketted pinnacles. The *porch* is in the same grand manner. Dating from the 1460s, it is panelled in *flushwork*, with three decayed niches above the entrance whose arch is decorated with *paterae*. There are more gargoyles and the blind *tracery* of the battlements differs from the pattern of the s. aisle. The inner door is C14 and there is a *stoup* to the r. Within, the tower has buttresses which jut out brutally alongside the beginning of the nave *arcades*, suggesting that the tower was built first. Above the *clerestory* there is a C15 *tie-beam* roof with *king posts* that are braced four ways. There are decorative stops on the tie-beam chamfers and until 1879 the roof was coloured. The carved stone *corbels* of earlier aisle roofs can be seen above the arcade pillars and two principals of the C16 s. aisle roof have remnants of *wall post* figures. Some of the main timbers of the roof itself are carved with a leaf trail and there are lines of paterae under the window sills on that side. There is a square *piscina* recess in the s. aisle chapel and the rood loft stair goes up to the l. of the *altar* – a long and thin *Stuart Holy*

table which has been restored. The s. aisle windows contain some good examples of C14 stained glass borders and in the window to the s. of the altar there is a nice C15 panel of *St Anne* teaching the *Blessed Virgin* to read. A plain octagonal C14 *font* stands in front of the blocked n. door and at the e. end of the n. aisle there is another – a Victorian reproduction of C15 style. Nearby in the e. wall is an intriguing C12 niche which predates the rest of the aisle. It has a moulded *trefoil* arch with an ogee top and the *spandrels* are shallow carved with tendrils bearing leaves and flowers. The shaft of a contemporary *pillar piscina* is set against the adjoining pillar. The aisle e. window contains a panel of modern stained glass (possibly by Maile & Son of Canterbury); a swirling composition of irregular outline and vivid colour, with the figures of *St George* and *St Michael*. Resting on an earlier coved pedestal, the early-C17 pulpit has blind arches crudely carved in shallow relief on the panels and a broad, canted book ledge. One side is blank which shows that it originally backed against one of the arcade pillars. The wooden lectern appears to be modern but it does incorporate a cluster of four C17 twisted *balusters* that probably formed part of a set of *altar rails* somewhere. The chancel stalls are largely C19 but they make use of medieval remnants and the w. ends are delicately traceried and feature crocketted pinnacles (note how the designs differ). There are *poppyheads*, old tracery in four of the front panels, and four mutilated *misericords* at the back. On the n. side of the chancel is a large and splendid monument to James Harvey who died of smallpox while an undergraduate at Cambridge in 1723. It is signed by N. Royce of Bury, about whom nothing is known, but who was, on this evidence, extremely skilled. A central black sarcophagus supports a bust of the young man, dressed in coat and scarf and wearing his own hair, and there are coupled *Corinthian* columns and *pilasters* each side in mottled marble. A *cartouche* of arms, supported by swags, rests on the *pediment* and the tripartite base is elegantly lettered with Latin epitaphs – the last dated 1767. Styles changed – witness one of Robert de Carle of Bury's 'plain Jane' tablets opposite for the Revd. George Belgrave and his wife, 1831. The medieval door to the old chapel is in the n. wall and beyond is a sumptuous C14 *Easter sepulchre*. Much of the detail was replaced as part of a C19 restoration but the effect is impressive. The base is a recessed tomb in roughly textured *Purbeck marble*, with four blank shield recesses. Above it there is a very tall and steeply gabled triple canopy, crocketted and topped by *finials*. Tall, thin pinnacles divide the frontage and within the gables there are *quatrefoils* enclosing leaf forms. On the other side of the *sanctuary* a matching piscina is set in the wall, and to its r. a fragment shows that the *sedilia* were originally canopied, before the Perpendicular window was inserted. The *communion rails* have modern tops and supports but the twisted balusters are late C17; it is said that they were once three-sided but I could detect no evidence of this. The 1889 glass in the e. window is by *Kempe* – an uncharacteristic design, with twelve small panels in very dark colours of post-Crucifixion scenes. It is a memorial for Churchill Babington, kinsman of Macaulay, Cambridge professor of archaeology, authority on local natural history, and vicar here for over 20 years. An earlier Cockfield parson also has his place in history, for John Knewstub convened the first large Puritan conference here, when 60 ministers met in 1582 to discuss the prayer book and to forge the basis for English Presbyterianism. The church has a ring of six bells with a 15 cwt. tenor, but they are hung dead and cannot be rung conventionally.

Coddenham, St Mary (F5): An attractive village in a valley, and the church stands well in a spacious churchyard. Its layout is unconventional, with a C14 tower at the w. end of the n. *aisle* rather than the *nave*, and a quite eccentric n. *porch* which is sharply angled to the e. It is too marked a variation to have been an error in setting out and seems to have been aligned for convenience with the path from the street. The tower is rather bald in its upper stages below *flushwork* battlements but this is more than balanced by the richness of the nave *clerestory*. It is deep, with a profusion of flushwork below the *ashlar* battlements, and at the e. end on the n. side an inscription for the C15 donors. It reads: 'Orate pro animae Johannis Frenche et Margarete' (Pray for the souls of John and Margaret French). Look also for the *Sacred monogram*, an 'M' for the dedication, and a *Trinity* roundel which makes use of the ancient Christian fish symbol. A *sanctus-bell turret* stands on the gable with a niche below it, and the line of a previous *chancel* roof shows in the wall. The chancel was partially rebuilt about 1840 with another restoration following in 1893, and there is a C19 *vestry* on the s. side, but it does retain evidence of the church's early years – a *Norman lancet* on the n. side, and a change in wall texture showing where the chancel was extended in the C14. A brick *rood turret*

nestles in the corner by the n. aisle and its insertion partially masked a *Perpendicular* window. The C14 s. aisle has very nice flowing *tracery* in its e. window and just round the corner is a large tablet for Matthias Candler who died in 1663, having been minister of the Gospel for thirty-three years, 'solid in Divinity, Laborious in ministry, Heavenly in society, a mirrour of sound piety'. The outer arch of the porch has the remains of a Trinity shield and Sacred monogram in the *spandrels*, with a decayed inscription above them, and rather fine little lion *stops*.

Passing a *stoup* by the entrance, one finds within that the tower arch to the r. has been blocked and an C18 door inserted. The interior is spacious, with robust C14 *arcades* below a lovely and exceptionally shallow *double hammerbeam* roof. It is unstained, with *king posts* on the collars under the ridge, and the hammers are adorned with demi-angels (many renewed); the *wall posts* have mutilated figures within canopied niches and they are all decorated with rosettes or stars on the underside. This is all late-C15 or early-C16 work and the aisle roofs are the same age and quality, their *wall plates* and main timbers nicely carved and studded with *bosses*. A number of *hatchments* are displayed and they belonged to: Dorothy Bacon (1758, n. aisle e.); Nicholas, her widower (1767, s. aisle e.); Revd. John Longe (1834, n. aisle w.); Anna Maria Bacon (1783, n. nave); Revd. Nicholas, her widower (1796, s. aisle w.); and an unidentified member of the Bacon family (1740s, s. nave). The stairs that led to the rood loft are entered from the n. aisle, and the painting of Christ being shown to the multitude, which hangs opposite, is probably an C18 Dutch work. There is a C14 chest sheathed in iron close by and also a crude late-C17 or C18 *bier* which now serves as a table for the children. At the w. end of the s. aisle is a well-carved C19 version of a C15 *font*, and in the corner is the mechanism of an early iron-framed clock housed in a four-post wooden frame stamped 'I.W.'. The aisle chapel has a large, handsome C14 *piscina* with leafy *crockets*, *finial*, and shallow carving in the spandrels of the *trefoil* arch. The *altar* here is a most attractive *Stuart* table whose heavy stretcher has four slender turned shafts set upon it and a deep, canted top frame. On the ledge behind stands a small C15 alabaster panel that no doubt formed part of a *reredos*. Coloured and gilt with a lettered scroll, it has Christ crucified crowded round with figures; an angel holds a chalice below His feet. The chapel's late-C17 *communion rails* are good quality, with barley sugar *balusters* in clusters of four each side of the entrance and they, together with the range under the chancel arch, originally formed a three-sided set for the *High altar*. Between the chapel and the nave is a low screen which has an interesting series of little carvings in low relief in the upper panels; they illustrate the *Annunciation*, the visits of the shepherds and wise men, the Flight into Egypt, and Christ's circumcision, baptism, and temptation. The nave seating is in modern pitch pine and the pulpit has a new stone base, although its blind-arched panels are *Jacobean*. There is no longer a *screen* and although *Cautley* commented on its remains I could not locate them. After reading the account of Bishop Redman's visitation in 1597, one is not surprised that the chancel needed so much attention in the C19: 'The chauncell is in great decay in the rooffe, pavement and glasse wyndows, in so much that beggars creep into the chauncell through the wyndows and lye in the church abusing the same to the great anoyance of the parishioners.' Now all is neat and seemly. The modern stalls incorporate a medieval pair with *misericords* on the s. side. On the n. wall is the memorial for Philip Bacon, a naval captain who helped see off the Dutch at the battle of Sole Bay and died in the North Foreland engagement of 1666. Flanked by fluted columns, the immense epitaph is replete with nautical detail. Farther along is a beautifully proportioned tablet with a large urn on the classical *pediment* and books piled at the corners. It commemorates the Revd. Baltazar Gardemau, a Frenchman who died in 1739, having fled from persecution and married Lady Catherine Bacon. Her family have a *ledger-stone* nearby inscribed 'Crypta Baconorum' with no fewer than fourteen subsidiary shields of arms. The simple C14 *angle piscina* stands next to *dropped-sill sedilia* and there is rich and attractive glass by Percy Bacon, an artist not often found in East Anglia, although there are windows by him at Tuddenham (St Martin) and Haverhill; it dates from 1894 and Bethlehem scenes fill the three *lights*, with an Annunciation in the top tracery. St Mary's has fine ring of eight bells with a tenor of 14 cwt. They were made up from six by Theodore Eccleston of nearby Crowfield Hall and were re-hung by Taylor's of Loughborough in 1992.

Combs, St Mary (E5): A grand church that still manages to preserve its sense of isolation and tranquillity, despite the suburbs of Stowmarket that have crept up from the n. A longish lane through open fields leads to the churchyard on rising ground, and note that the C14 tower is hard up against the w. boundary – which explains why there are large archways n. and s. Although blocked now, they once allowed processions to circle the church and still remain within consecrated ground. The tower has a *flushwork base course*, the arms of Ufford, earls of Suffolk, above each entrance, and the bell openings have *Perpendicular tracery*. There is 'Y' tracery of about 1300 in the s. *aisle* w. window, and the large *Tudor* brick *porch*, with its polygonal buttresses, has had the crow-step gables recently capped and the replacement arch bricked up. The s. aisle was remodelled in the late C15 and the elongated windows have stepped *transoms*. The early-C14 *chancel* is unusual in a number of ways; look first at its w. windows. They have *ogee* arches, and a low transom forms a pair of *low side windows* in both of them. The frames were rebated to take external shutters and one hinge survives in each. Beyond the blocked *priest's door* there is a large circular window with four-leaf tracery which is placed high enough to give light above the *sedilia* within. Deep, angled buttresses flank the e. window with its intersected 'Y' tracery, and a low *string course* links them. There is another priest's door on the n. side (now a *vestry*) and the *rood stair turret* shows in the angle between chancel and aisle. The Perpendicular windows on this side have no transoms and those in the C15 *clerestory* are linked by a continuous string course. The tall C14 wooden n. porch has been heavily overlaid with modern plaster but the entrance *jambs* remain, and although the door has lost its surround, the thin closing ring still serves. The early-C14 inner doorway has single shafts and a finely moulded arch rests on oak leaf *capitals*, with large *headstops* – male to the l., a queen to the r.

This is a lovely church inside – all light and height. Note that the tower buttresses obtrude to merge with the w. bays of the *arcades*, whose tall octagonal *piers* have wide capitals. There is a narrow *sanctus-bell window* and below it is the original w. door, with slots for a drawbar. The base of the tower has been enclosed to form a vestry and boiler room and, hidden behind the pipework, the *stoup* is still in place; this unusual position indicates that the principal entrance was here. The C15 *nave* roof was *arch-braced* to begin with, but some weakness developed which called for new *tie-beams*, *king posts* and arch-braces. Both aisles have arch-braced roofs with crested *wall plates* and there are heavy *bosses* at the base of the braces in the s. aisle. The deep, canted bowl of the late-C14 *font* is carved with nubbly roses, squares, and shields, and the stem has miniature replicas of complete *Decorated* windows. Three bells stand in the n.w. corner and provide a rare opportunity to study bell founders' marks and inscriptions. The largest weighs 18 cwt. and was cast by Richard Brayser (father or son) in Norwich during the C15; their shield charged with three bells is easily identified. The inscription has excellent decorated capitals and the text is unusual: 'Nos prece Baptiste salvent tua vulnera Christe' (May thy wounds, O Christ, save us, by the Baptist's prayers). The other two bells are dated 1619 and 1662 and were cast by Miles Graye and John Darbie of Ipswich. The fine C15 benches in the nave have very varied *poppyheads* on the panelled ends and a nice selection of animals on the elbows – lions, dogs, a *griffin*, a *pelican in her piety*, a chained and muzzled bear, and an engaging hare looking typically startled. A very good C19 carver made the front three ranges (*Henry Ringham?*) and there is clever replacement on some of the others (the men 4th from the e. in the aisles, for example). There is a large, plain *piscina* in the s. aisle chapel and the surrounding *parclose screen* has been extensively restored, having lost the applied mouldings and *crockets* to the tracery (another section is against the organ). The *Stuart* pulpit has the familiar style of panelling but the design is individual – instead of single blank arches, two in each panel come down to a centre fret pendant, and the book ledge is carried on outsize scroll brackets.

The loft and upper range of the *rood screen* has been destroyed but the base remains; the tracery of its broad panels is formed by pairs of flattened *ogee* arches, above which there are small triple *quatrefoils*. The chancel lies under a C19 cross-braced waggon roof, with double wall plates adorned with demi-angels and *paterae*. Some of the stall ends are C15, and again there is dexterous Victorian restoration – examine the two heads at the e. end of the n. range. The large piscina and sedilia suite was largely replaced with undecorated and clumsy sections but the crockets and *cusps* are original and the vaulting comes down at the back to three diminutive leaf *corbels*. The tall niches that flank the e. window were similarly treated but you will see that one leaf capital on the n. side still shows original colour. On the wall below is the *brass* of Katherine, wife of the Revd. Thomas Sotherbie, who died in 1624 – a shield of arms and parallel Latin and English verses in elegant italic:

Fare well deare wife, since thou art now
Absent from mortalls sight . . . .

The two plain tablets that face each other across the chancel are not inspiring but it is interesting that they match, although separated by thirty years and cut by different masons, the first of whom was local.

Combs is noted for its fine late-C15 glass, given by Sir Christopher Willoughby who was Lord of the Manor. The Stowmarket gun cotton explosion of 1871 blew in many of the windows and most of the remaining glass has been collected in the s. aisle. (binoculars are invaluable here). In the window w. of the parclose screen are panels from a life of *St Margaret*: top centre, she receives God's blessing while tending her sheep and Olybrius, the governor, in rich red robe and steeple hat, sits on his charger while an attendant points her out; in the panel below two men at arms push her forward in front of the governor, with the green and blue devil she refused to worship overhead; in the top l. panel she is chained by her neck to a prison gateway; bottom l., she stands over a cauldron of boiling oil and the warder has a vicious looking prong; the top r. panel is a composite, with the saint being swallowed by the dragon on the l. and emerging to birch it on the r. The bottom r. panel has a baptism scene with bishop, saintly mother and child, and godparents. The s. window of the chapel contains two scenes from a *Seven Works of Mercy* sequence – food for the hungry to the l. and drink for the thirsty to the r. – both with angels hovering. The upper tracery of this, the e. window, and another farther w. contain labelled figures which must originally have formed a genealogy of Christ. The names of Abraham, Isaac, Jacob, and others are easily recognised, as are Old Testament kings like Josias. The many fragments in the e. window are worth studying and there is in the centre the remains of a Christ in Majesty, the hand raised in blessing.

Coney Weston, St Mary (D3): This is one of those churches that can prove elusive; it lies a mile or so to the e. of the village on the Hopton road and, not having a tower, it cannot be seen from a distance. With a background of trees and standing above the lane, it is an attractive C14 building with a thatched *nave*. As was often the case, the frontage was given more attention than the rest and a panelled *base course* links the tall *porch* with the nave, the walls being faced with carefully dressed flints. The *dripstones* of the three s. *chancel* windows are linked and there are remains of *corbel* heads at the outer ends, thus forming a complete unit. The *Decorated tracery* is badly decayed and in one case it has been repaired in a simpler form, possibly at the time of the restorations in 1887 and 1891. Below is an arched tomb recess. At one time there was a chapel n. of the chancel and two large arches remain embedded in the wall, with fragments of two smaller ones further e. A square-headed *Perpendicular* window was inserted within one of these arches and shows that the chapel or *chantry* cannot have lasted long. The nave originally had a n. door as well but this has been blocked up. The tower fell in the early C19. By the s. door is a *stoup* under a *cinquefoiled* arch. Within is a C13 *font* with a slightly odd selection of designs in the panels of the octagonal bowl; there are window tracery patterns, a *crocketted* canopy, large square leaves, and one panel has 12 rosettes set out like cakes on a tray. On either side of the chancel arch there are pairs of niches, one set taller than the other and retaining the *hood moulds*. There will have been nave *altars* under both originally, and one small *piscina* survives in the s. wall. The niches were reused in the C19 to house a painted *Decalogue* on the n. and two quite ambitious angels on the s. – all painted on tin. The brass lectern is a good example of mid-C19 design as influenced by the *Ecclesiological Society*, and above the openwork pulpit of the same period is a graceful oval tablet. Set on a grey obelisk with a coloured shield of arms hung from a ribbon, it tells of the misfortunes of Maurice Dreyer, a London merchant who died in 1786:

> a man of warm feelings, but of strict integrity, reduced from affluence in the prime of life by the fraudulent conduct of a partner in the foreign trade, he bore the total wreck of his property with fortitude and resignation.

The chancel e. window has truncated tracery at the top, probably another part of the C19 restoration, and across the s.e. corner of the *sanctuary* are the remains of a massive image niche which rises above the spring of the window arch, still with traces of colour. Below is a fine C14 *angle piscina* with steep crocketted gables over *trefoil cusping*. The corbel heads are broken off at the angle but the hood mould continues round to form a sill for the e. window. Alongside are stepped *dropped-sill sedilia*. The C19 altar has intricately traceried panels, painted and gilded with figures of saints and even enriched with some *gesso* work, all most competently done in the manner of a C15 *screen*. The saints, l. to r., are: *SS Edward the Confessor, Paul, Barbara*, the

Blessed Virgin, Bartholomew, John, Margaret, Helen, Hugh and *Apollonia of Alexandria*.

Cookley, St Michael (H3): The church is set back from the road on rising ground, and there are tall Scots pine and yew trees in the churchyard. The slim, unbuttressed tower probably dates from the C13, and its w. window and bell openings have 'Y' *tracery* of about 1300; *ashlar* panels with shields decorate the parapet. Walking round, you will find that a very ugly modern *vestry* has been built on to the n. doorway, and there are late *Perpendicular* windows on that side of the *nave*. New tracery was inserted in the e. window as part of an 1890s restoration, but a C13 *lancet* remains undisturbed in the n. wall of the *chancel*, and there are windows with *Decorated* tracery on either side of the *priest's door* in the s. wall.

A wooden *porch* shelters the entrance, and the interior is neat and attractive. The *font* shaft has been replaced, but the bowl panels follow a traditional C15 East Anglian pattern – lions alternating with angels bearing shields with *Trinity* emblem, crossed sword & keys, *St George's* cross, and a floriated cross. Above the tower arch there is a *sanctus-bell window*, and the church's only *brass* is mounted on the w. wall. The 19in. effigies commemorate William and Margeri Browne, he in long gown and she with high crowned hat and ruff; there is an inscription, and two small plates engraved with the figures of their four sons and four daughters. It is dated 1595 and is a reused (*palimpsest*) *brass*, and although the couple must have had a local connection, they are buried elsewhere. Evidence that the church was originally *Norman* can be found by going through to the vestry and having a look at the old n. doorway. It has two bands of *chevron moulding* set at right angles in the arch, and the *jamb shafts* have leafy *capitals*. Most of the nave benches are good C19 work, but there are four C15 originals on the s. side, with beautifully varied tracery cut in the solid on the ends. Their backs are decorated with leaf trails, and there are some interesting carvings on the elbows against the wall – a man taking his ease, a defaced devil bearing a scroll, and a bear with a ragged staff. The nave roof is a C15 *hammerbeam*, with cambered *collar beams* and deep *wall plate*s; the *wall posts* rest on wooden *corbels* carved as demi-figures holding books. The head of a Decorated niche stands on a windowsill and acts as a plinth for a small statue of the church's patron saint. The restoration of 1894 was masterminded by the patron of the living, and he had been vicar of Flixton. It may be that the wholesale changes there prompted his actions here, but nothing can excuse his destruction of the *rood screen* which was dumped in Huntingfield rectory stable. *Box pews* met the same fate (except for a portion of panelling used as a tower screen), and the *Stuart* pulpit was scorned as being 'inharmonious with its surroundings'. That too would have been lost had it not found a home at Chediston. In 1935, *Cautley* found one of the screen uprights in a Huntingfield henhouse, and it now stands forlornly in the corner. Ironically, small sections of tracery from the screen were carefully worked into the fronts of the new choir stalls. A pair of C15 bench ends were also reused, and there is a simple *piscina* in the *sanctuary*, with *dropped-sill sedilia* alongside. A small historical footnote – Sir Edward Coke, the great Chief Justice and defender of the public right married his first wife Bridget Paston here on August 13th 1583.

Copdock, St Peter (F6): The suburbs of Ipswich and the busy A12 are not far away, but the churchyard within its surrounding trees is a peaceful spot. Except for minor alterations the whole building is *Perpendicular* in style, and a panelled *base course* extends round the tower and along the *nave* and n. *transept* walls. There are *flushwork* panels in the angled buttresses of the tower, with more above the w. door, and the w. window has a *crocketted dripstone* with *finial* and angel *headstops*. There are brick battlements, and the jaunty weathervane is a cutout of King David playing his harp; it was made in the 1850s by a Mr Trent, a friend of the rector. It is worth walking round to examine the n. door, which dates from the early C15. Its panels are keeled and the *tracery* at the top is overlaid rather than carved in the solid and incorporates little *mouchette* roundels. Beyond the tall, three-*light* windows of the nave there is a blocked door in the w. wall of the transept, and a large n.e. *vestry* was added in 1901. The *chancel* is almost as tall as the nave and its walls are faced with close-set flint pebbles whose shapes are emphasised by raised pointing. Don't miss a tombstone that stands s.w. of the *priest's door*. It commemorates John Marven, a celebrated bellringer who died aged only 34 in 1789. He was one of the early composers of change ringing methods and his peal of 6,000 changes in 1813 is commemorated by a peal board in Lavenham ringing chamber. The head of his stone is carved with an oval relief of a woman holding a book and leaning against a bell, which is particularly interesting

because the design was copied from one of Bartolozzi's engravings for the 'Oxford Youths'. The bells here are a ring of six with a 9 cwt. tenor but they are not, unfortunately, in ringable condition. The s. *porch* is tall to match the rest of the building but relatively shallow, and had a stepped brick gable added in the C17. A large stone sundial was placed above the entrance in 1935 bearing the legend: 'The greater light to rule the Day', and its C17 predecessor is lodged on the windowsill within. The outer arch has hung shields in the *spandrels*, with shields and crowns in the moulding, and the *stoup* by the inner door still has the whole of its bowl intact.

A deep *gallery* installed in 1901 spans the w. end of the nave and five small C16 panels have been placed on the front. The two outer ones are carved with leaf patterns, the centre is a shield of arms, a lady plays a harp on the fourth, but the best one is carved with the little figure of Edward VI on horseback. When *Dowsing* came here in January 1643 the windows must have been full of stained glass because he records having broken down 150 'superstitious pictures'. He also says that he defaced a cross on the *font* but it looks as though the bowl was comprehensively re-cut in the C19 anyway. The panels have kneeling angels holding open books (with texts), two *pomegranates*, a *Tudor Rose*, and an interlace design – all in deep relief; the shaft is Victorian. So too is the handsome cover, a design that is an elaboration of the fine late-C15 model at Barking. The nave roof was replaced in 1901 in celebration of Queen Victoria's long reign, but the C15 transept roof remains, low pitched and heavily moulded, with leaf and flower *bosses*. The transept was originally a *chantry chapel* associated with Copdock Hall, and the priest who served its *altar* will have made use of the long *squint* that cuts through the wall at an angle to emerge in the chancel aligned with the *High altar*. The tall transept arch has hung shields in the moulding, three of which have traces of painted arms, and the *jambs* of the chancel arch were cut short in the C19 to rest on new stone *corbels*. A *brass* shield below the one on the n. side displays the arms of Goldingham impaling those of the Hacon family. The organ chamber dates from 1901 and there is a large tablet carved with a floriated cross above the vestry door. It commemorates Arnald de Grey, the rector who died in 1889 and was responsible for much of the restoration. A C19 stone *reredos* in *Decorated* style stretches the full width of the e. wall, with a central Last Supper tableau sculpted in relief. It is strange that the *sanctuary* floor was later raised to such an extent that the carving is now almost at floor level and completely hidden by the altar. Somebody obviously didn't like it. The large, plain *piscina* is also well down the wall. The e. window has a crowded scene spread across three lights of Christ carrying the cross. Despite the theatrical poses it is curiously lifeless, and the paint is deteriorating here and there.

Corton, St Bartholomew (J1): From the churchyard there is a fine prospect of the North Sea with its busy shipping lanes, and Corton's ruined tower still provides a seamark for old-fashioned mariners. The building had become ruinous by the C17, and when the *nave* roof collapsed in the 1690s, the parish walled up the *chancel* arch and took to using the *priest's door* as their entrance to a much smaller church. In 1846, it was enlarged by taking in a bay of the old nave and inserting a new w. wall. So things remained until 1985 when a visitors' centre, a meeting room and *vestries* were all neatly fitted within the old nave walls, with the s. *porch* serving once again as the main entrance. Ruined though it is, and with all the *tracery* gone from the bell openings, the C15 tower is finely proportioned. It has a set of delicate *sound holes* on the Norfolk pattern, and there are stepped *flushwork* battlements. There is a deep, plain *base course*, and note the interesting variation in the wall surfaces – *knapped* flints at the bottom and pebbles further up. Separated from the church, the tower proved a useful cache for smugglers' contraband in the C18 and C19. The nave had a C14 n. door and there is one *Perpendicular* window left at the e. end on that side. The tall *Decorated* windows in the C14 chancel make use of a pretty motif also to be found at Blundeston – a little *quatrefoil* enclosed within the top roundel; the five-*light* e. window was a later Perpendicular insertion. The shapeless bulge of the *rood stair* turret shows on the s. nave wall.

The glass w. wall of the new annexe provides another view of the tower, and a garden has been established in the w. end of the nave. The way to the church proper leads through a low brick arch where a fragment of an early-C16 *brass* has been framed on the wall. A modern w. *gallery* houses the organ, and there are four decayed medieval bench ends which have the remains of grotesques on the elbows displayed against the n. wall. The rood stairs lie within the s. wall, and below them is a *piscina*, shorn of its decoration, which served a nave *altar* here. C19 slate *Decalogue* tablets flank the chancel arch, and the late-C14 *font* now stands in front. There are squat lions

round its shaft, and others alternate with angels carrying shields in the bowl panels. The shield emblems are of more than usual interest and have a *Trinity* theme: w., the three crowns of East Anglia; n., a combination of spear, crozier and key that could relate to *St Peter*; e., three *chalices* and wafers of the mass; s., three *trefoils* for the Trinity itself. This is a rare survival and the carvings were saved by being hidden under plaster from the C17 to the C19. Another remarkable relic is the C14 gable cross that was brought inside in 1891 to save it from further weathering. It now stands on a window ledge in the chancel, and although there are only remnants of the floriated decoration, it features a tall and slim figure of the *Blessed Virgin* and Child on the shaft. A mirror placed behind it reveals that the other side has the twisted figure of Christ on the cross. The piscina and *sedilia* suite in the *sanctuary* are decidedly lavish, with deeply moulded, flattened *ogee* arches, *cusped* and *crocketted* with *finials*, and divided by quatrefoil shafts. They were largely replaced in the C19, and only the piscina arch and the w. *respond* are original C14. The wide stone *reredos* is mostly work of 1913, but some of it was recovered from a house in the village, including the figures of *St Catherine* and *St Andrew*. From l. to r. the figures are: St Catherine (note particularly the rare representation of the emperor's head at her feet); St Andrew; The Blessed Virgin and Child; *St Bartholomew; St Augustine of Hippo; St Philip.*

Cotton, St Andrew (E4): This large and handsome church stands within a spacious shady churchyard and tends, perhaps, to receive less attention than it deserves. The tower shares with Wetheringsett the strange distinction of having a tall C15 open arch in its w. face, and the ground floor serves as the draughtiest ringing chamber that I have ever experienced. The eight bells with their 10 cwt. tenor are at present 'in poor going order'. Unlike Wetheringsett's, the inner wall contains a three-*light* window and it has been suggested that this was why the outer arch was left open. The *tracery* is certainly attractive and unusual, with a large *ogee* bisected by an inverted curve. Ponderous buttresses stop short at the second stage and others which are much lighter continue diagonally to the bell chamber. A group of three niches is placed above the arch, with singles n. and s., while the bell openings have *Decorated* tracery and there are *gargoyles* below the shallow battlements. The odd shape best described as a triangle with curved sides crops up in the C14 s. *aisle* windows and there is excellent *reticulated* tracery in the aisle e. window. A *string course* on the s. wall of the C14 *chancel* links the *dripstones* of the windows and another beneath them lifts to form a dripstone with a fat *finial* for the *priest's door*. At the chancel corners, gabled pinnacles decorated with *crockets* and finials have pretty little niches facing e., each with small *corbel* heads below their ogee arches. Between them is a great e. window with a singular tracery pattern over the five tall lights. Two large ogees enclose a pair of curved triangles each, plus a *quatrefoil*. This leaves a large oval at the top and two side slivers, all containing weak subsidiary divisions, and it is these that sabotage the design so that it is more interesting than beautiful. There was once a *vestry* or *sacristy* on the n. side which disturbed the window/buttress pattern, and the Decorated tracery in the aisle contains variants of that seen on the s. side. The C14 *nave* received a new roof in the late C15 and the *clerestory* was built with it. Nine windows each side, their arches emphasised with red brick, are linked by a string course, and there are *flushwork* panels between them plus a large patch at the w. end of the s. side.

Entry is through a mid-C14 s. *porch* whose windows match the aisles. The front is decorated with flushwork, including crowned 'MR's for the *Blessed Virgin* in the *spandrels* of the outer arch with its leafy *capitals*. Some of the strange mixture of patterns in the parapet would seem to be C19. The tall inner doorway is one of the finest surviving C14 examples and a remarkable amount of its colouring remains. The capitals of the triple shafts are densely carved with oak leaves and acorns, and you will discover the face and hands of a tiny *green man* among the foliage on one of them to the r. of the doorway. The *hood mould* rested on large corbels and the shape of the remains on the l. suggests that it may have been a lizard – a symbol of good fortune that was often chosen for doorways. The outer moulding of the arch is carved with roses and foliage coloured in green and yellow against red, and the centre band features bunches of blue grapes. Follow it down to the r.-hand base and you will come across a little pagan Pan with goat feet, matched by a less distinct human figure on the other side. The doors themselves are C14 with tracery at the top, and there are remains of a *stoup* to the r.

Within, the C14 *arcades* lean alarmingly outwards under the pressure of roof and clerestory, particularly to the n., and there are attractive, undulating brick floors throughout. The w. end of the s. aisle is used as a vestry but within it a stair leads to the tower, and its iron-clad door shows that parish valuables were once protected there. The C15 *font* lacks the figures that once stood at the corners of the shaft, its panels have been re-cut with strange little monks, and the bowl is modern. Nearby stands the table that served as the *High altar* in the C17. Light from the clerestory emphasises the beauty of the pale oak roof – a rich double *hammerbeam* design whose e. bay was panelled to form a *celure* above the *rood* that stood or hung below. There are demi-angels fronting the ends of the upper hammers and pendants on the range below. Huge flat flower *bosses* abound, some divided by the principal timbers. Four ranges of cresting run lengthways and along the hammerbeams, pierced tracery is set behind the posts, and *king posts* rise to the ridge above *embattled collar beams*. Similar in many ways to nearby Bacton, this is one of Suffolk's loveliest roofs. While studying it, use binoculars if you can to look at the C15 angels in the n. clerestory windows – ten are tonsured like monks and six are crowned, some have pink wings, some have blue. A pair of bench ends at the back of the church are intricately carved and one on the n. side has a most unusual representation of a door, complete with closing ring and strap hinges. The main range is completely plain, its thick ends warped to a gentle curve, and the pews with doors at the e. end probably date from the 1903 restoration. A low tomb recess lies in the n. aisle wall below an arch which has just a hint of the ogee shape.

The early-C17 pulpit is not, for a change, darkened by stain, and it is remarkable that in this case the familiar blind arches in the panels have no *pilasters* – nor had they ever. There is attractive scrollery below the canted book ledge, and the curved rail of the modern stairs carries an extraordinarily vicious *griffin* which, as a handhold, is acquiring a fine patina as successive parsons climb to preach. The *chancel* arch capitals were roughly chopped back and morticed to house the *rood screen* and the stairs which led to the loft above it are tucked behind on the e. side rather than the more usual w. At least part of the reading desk dates from the C17 and the *Stuart communion rails* are a good set with close-set *balusters*. A small recess high in the n. *sanctuary* wall indicates that the vanished sacristy (or it might have been an *anchorite's cell*) had an upper chamber. Opposite are the beautiful remains of the C14 *piscina* and *sedilia* suite. The design placed two of the sedilia seats within the window embrasure, and although these have lost their canopies, their companion to the w. is complete. Like the piscina at the other end, its ogee arch is multi-*cusped*, the crockets are very crinkly, and the tall finial is flanked by pinnacles.

Covehithe, St Andrew (J2): When it was built in the mid-C15, this must have been one of the great churches of East Anglia, but by the C17 it had become too much of a burden for a shrinking community, and in 1672 the parish asked the diocese if they could dismantle all but the tower, sell the materials, and build a smaller church within the shell. Permission was given, and today the *Churches Conservation Trust* sees to the maintenance of the tower and ruins. The stately tower had been part of an earlier C14 church and most of its walls are surfaced with small pebble flints. There are angled buttresses to the w., and their unusual feature is the gables that occur between the *set-offs*. Three strong *drip courses* define the floor levels, and the large belfry window has an *ogee* arch with *pierced tracery*; all the tracery has gone from the bell openings. The tower houses a ring of five bells with an 11 cwt. tenor. The churchyard and grassed ruins are pleasant to walk in on a summer's day, and it is worth doing so in order to appreciate what a splendid building this must have been. Lofty, with huge windows, it was spacious enough for a city parish, and the *rood loft stair* in the n. wall shows that the *screen* stretched the whole width of the building. The single bay *chancel* had a crypt below it, and when *Dowsing* came here in April 1643, he ordered that two of the four steps up to the *High altar* should be levelled. Having broken 200 images in the windows, he was foiled when it came to the roof, for his journal says 'we could not reach, neither would they help us to raise the ladders'. The *nave arcades* have gone, but the *responds* at the w. end indicate that they were *Decorated* and predated the rest of the *Perpendicular* building. The chequer and panelled *flushwork base course* still shows boldly along the s. frontage, but the two-storied s. *porch* has disappeared, save for the base of its stair turret.

The humble replacement, with its thatched roof, snuggles up against the e. wall of the tower. The walls are a mixture of flint and stone saved from the ruins and topped with red brick. A n. doorway was made up out of sections of C15 mouldings decorated with *paterae*, and although a *priest's door* was reused on the s. side, it has since been blocked. A *gargoyle* and a *corbel* head have been sited over the porch entrance, and the inner doorway was saved from the old building. The interior is simple and homely, with C19 pitchpine benches under a plastered ceiling and

tie-beams. The tower arch is boarded up, and there hang the *Royal Arms* of George III, a well painted set on canvas that warrants restoration. Three low benches with small *poppyheads* stand at the w. end, and the C15 *font* is a large scale version of the type to be found in many East Anglian churches. Its lions and *woodwoses* round the shaft have been decapitated, and there are *fleurons* and battered angels under the bowl. The panel carvings are on a generous scale, displaying mutilated *Evangelistic symbols* and musical angels with harp (s.), citterns (e. & w.), and psaltery (n.). At first glance, the handsome pulpit could be taken for a clever piece of C19 reproduction, but much of the tracery and frame seems to be genuine C15. The e. window was inserted in the C19, and the *Decalogue* boards on either side are the same vintage, in the florid style that the Victorians favoured. Below stands a plain *Stuart Holy table*, and it was probably ordered by Enoch Girling and James Gilbert, the churchwardens in 1672. After the momentous decision had been made, and their new church completed, they each had a stone set high in the walls of the *sanctuary* to record that it was they who 'put it out', that is, placed the contract for the work.

Cowlinge, St Margaret (B5): The body of the church is early C14 and there is attractive *tracery* in the *aisle* windows, ith late *Perpendicular* designs at the e. end of the s. aisle and *chancel*. A modern door has been inserted in the s. aisle and a *scratch dial* has been replaced upside-down in the centre buttress. In the C18, heavy brick buttresses were introduced to shore up the chancel, and note that under the e. window there is a small grilled opening that probably ventilated a charnel chamber. Churchyards were reused in the Middle Ages and bones from earlier burials were removed to charnels for safe keeping. The splays of the doorway in the chancel n. wall show that it once led into a chapel or *sacristy* and there is more evidence of this within. The C18 brick tower is severely plain – round arches to door and bell openings, with a circular belfry window to the w. It houses a ring of five bells with a 10 cwt. tenor. The little brick and stone n. porch is homely and there is a lot of C17 and C18 graffiti on the C14 inner arch, with its medieval door of lapped boards. The w. *gallery* is contemporary with the tower and one must climb the stairs to see the tablet which records the munificence of Francis Dickins who built the tower in 1733. It is large with well-cut lettering, and his arms are in a *cartouche* within a broken *pediment*. Overhead, the fine set of George II *Royal Arms* painted on canvas has the royal cipher, baroque scrolls above and below, and flanking *Corinthian* columns, all painted on a board surround, with the names of the churchwardens of 1731. Also on the tower wall is a set of boards painted with the *Decalogue*, Creed and Lord's Prayer. Seating was strictly regulated from the C17 onwards and at the w. end of the n. aisle is a most interesting local arrangement. Four plain, backless forms are stepped one above the other and the tablet on the wall above explains their purpose. They were installed by special permission in 1618 to accommodate the keeper of the Cowlinge House of Correction and his prisoners in what was no doubt the coldest and draughtiest corner. The *font* dates from about 1400, its bowl decorated with *quatrefoils* and roundels and there is window tracery in the panels of the short stem. The octagonal *piers* of the C14 *arcades* have masses of medieval graffiti, but individual items are not all that easy to find or decipher. Just below the *capital* of the pillar near the n. door there is a Latin inscription which translates:

> Whensoever you go by me,
> Whether man, woman or boy you be,
> Bear in mind you do not fail,
> To say in passing 'Mary Hail'.

Its position suggests that the stone was reused and was originally at eyelevel somewhere. There are many interlaced plait-work and geometric designs, as well as hands, feet, a ship, and the crude profile of a man, possibly a bishop. The C14 *nave* and chancel roofs are *tie-beam* and *king post* construction, with coved and plastered ceilings. Until about 1400, the design of woodwork followed that of masonry but the *rood screen* here shows the parting of the ways. Although the tracery is still carved in the solid, the *mullions* are moulded and the main structure is more logical in relation to the material. The doors rise to the full height and three of the original hinges are intact, with decoration on the plates. There are quatrefoil and single hole *elevation squints* like those at Dalham. The C14 *parclose screen* in the s. aisle is also interesting because, although the workmanship is crude, the bottom panels are the earliest Suffolk example of tracery which is applied rather than being carved in the solid. The main *lights* are wide but they were originally divided into three and four compartments by mullions which were later removed. The principal uprights have little tracery shapes carved at the top and the cresting is virtually complete – the design similar to that

Cowlinge, St Margaret: Charity benches

on the parclose at Dalham. On the wall nearby is a medieval painting, mainly in pale red, of the top half of a saint against a patterned background. There are the remains of a *piscina* in the chapel and on the l., a rough arch that will have led to the *rood loft*. Next to it is a long *squint* through to the chancel and in the n. aisle there is another like it behind the organ. Instead of a window the n. chapel has a tall niche in the e. wall and, although the canopy has been cut away, traces of the vaulting remain. The chancel arch is decorated in barber's pole fashion and above it there is a fascinating variation on the traditional *Doom* theme. To the r. *St Michael* holds the scales, with an orange-coloured evil spirit being weighed against the little figure representing the souls of the righteous. On the l. of the arch the *Blessed Virgin* holds a long wand, the tip of which tilts the balance against the devil and neatly illustrates her power of intercession. All is very faint and binoculars are essential to catch the detail. Beyond the modern *communion rails* in the *sanctuary*, the *High altar* is a massively solid block with a bevelled *mensa* 8ft. long and 4ft. wide. The C14 piscina and *sedilia* are as simple as can be, and in the n. wall is the door that must have led to a chapel or sacristy. The puzzling thing here is the small doorway above and to the r. It shows that the annexe was two-storied as at Hessett, but an entrance in this position is most unusual and I can only suppose that it might have afforded security for the storage of valuables. On the s. wall is a tablet for Henry Usborne who died in 1840 and his *hatchment* hangs close by. The chancel is, however, dominated by the memorial for Francis Dickins. He died in 1747 and his flowery epitaph tells us that he 'repaired and ornamented this church and built the steeple at his own expense'. The monument is the only Suffolk example of the work of Peter Scheemakers, whose bust of Shakespeare in Westminster Abbey established his reputation. The figures of Dickins and his wife in Roman dress sit either side of an urn, below which there are reversed torches with a wreath of oak leaves (a popular classical symbol of mourning). Both base and backdrop are massive. In front of the organ in the centre of the nave is a *brass* for Robert and Margaret Higham (1571 and 1599). It is in good condition, with 18in. figures of the couple – he in ruff and gown and she wearing a Paris cap. There are groups of five sons and five daughters, a shield and an inscription. Halfway down the nave is a brass inscription and verse for Thomas Dersley who died in 1614:

Here underneath this stone interred, rest
A while deare freind, so God has thought it
best . . .

Cransford, St Peter (H4): There is a *lych-gate* by the roadside, and a modest avenue of yew and cherry shades the path to the door. *Cautley's* verdict was: 'drastically and dreadfully restored and there is nothing of interest', but that is far too dismissive and, as with any small country church, a visit is worthwhile. The *Perpendicular* C15 tower has a *flushwork base course* and there are shields set in the base of the angled buttresses bearing the emblems of *St Peter* (n.) and *St Paul* (s.) – many churches favoured the dual dedication to St Peter and St Paul, and Cransford may have done so in the middle ages. There is a two-*light* w. window, and above the bell openings, the battlements are an early-C20 addition (the tower was originally a little higher). Walking round, you will see that the C14 s. *nave* doorway is blocked, and the sloping brick buttresses on that side were an early-C19 addition – a sign that the building had by then become dilapidated. A full scale restoration followed in the 1840s, directed by the Woodbridge architect William Pattisson, and the steep line of the old nave roof shows above its replacement on the e. face of the tower. The

shallow *vestry* standing at right angles to the *chancel* s. wall was probably added at the same time, and the whole of the e. wall was rebuilt in brick and flint, with a new three-light window. The n. wall was undisturbed, and on that side there is a C13 *lancet* in the chancel, two C15 windows in the nave, and the *porch* – almost entirely rebuilt in 1864.

In many ways, the interior is what one would expect, given the circumstances – the clean and scrubbed, refurbished look that was the result of many a Victorian restoration. But it is neat and well cared-for, a credit to the parish. The tower arch has a C19 'gothick' screen, and it is easy to overlook a most unusual feature. Just above ground level, the bevel of the arch is stopped with two lovely little carved heads, one bearded, and the other showing off a fine set of teeth with a grin. The *font* was made by Henry Clutten, the Framlingham mason who signed one or two tablets in the area and carved a replica *Westmacott* piece at Campsea Ash. Here, he was content to panel in C15 style, and add an *Agnus Dei* and St Peter's keys on the bowl. The other sides record the deaths of the two infants whose memorial the font is; Charles Borrett died aged three weeks in 1839, and Louisa Alston was not much older when she died in 1845. An exceptionally good chest for its period stands in front of the s. doorway. Large, with a gently curved top and substantial carrying handles, it has four moulded panels with marquetry star centres, chip-carved *pilasters*, and two drawers at the bottom; a wide band right across the top of the front is naively carved: 'Katrina Husmans Anno 1739', and it was possibly a young girl's dowry chest from the Netherlands. There is neither *screen* nor arch between nave and chancel now, and the only mark of division is a slight change in the levels of the *arch-braced* pine roofs. The pine benches have fleur-de-lys *finials* as their only ornament, although the front pair were replaced in the 1940s by an oak set which have coarsely traceried ends and *poppyheads* in C15 style. The cranes carved on the elbows are a *rebus* on the village name, but were a little too delicate for the medium and have suffered accordingly. Maj. Gen. Charles Borrett died in 1919, having lost his sailor son at Jutland three years before, and they have matching tablets on the s. wall of the nave – curiously old-fashioned and mid-C19 in style. The neat little early-C19 chamber organ in mahogany came from a house in Hawstead, and was installed here in 1953. The 1870s openwork pulpit is most peculiar – not only is it triangular, but a section of the base is hinged for no obvious reason (except perhaps to trap a deranged curate against the wall!). There was once a large C14/C15 window on the s. side of the chancel, but it was blocked to make room for Henry and Etheldreda Dammant's large memorial. He was patron of the living, dying in 1713, and his wife followed him in 1729. The tablet has a frame of veined marble, and there is an urn set between the scrolls of the *pediment*. The *sanctuary* is bounded by brass *communion rails* of the telescopic variety admired by the Victorians for their neat ingenuity, and the stone *reredos* of 1876 is a typical period piece – diapered panels set with *Sacred monograms*, *Agnus Dei*, and a *pelican in her piety*, with spiky *Decalogue* panels on the side walls. The lancet frames a figure of the church's patron saint (the style suggests *Clayton & Bell*), and the stained glass in the e. window is by *Lavers, Barraud & Westlake*. It was installed in 1874 (a good period for the firm), and the large central figure of Christ in Majesty is flanked by roundels of Sacred monograms, *Passion emblems*, and the keys of St Peter; there are bright borders, and the backing *quarries* are lightly patterned in yellow stain.

Cratfield, St Mary (H3): Seen from the w., the church is beautifully placed, embowered in trees. The C15 tower has an excellent w. doorway flanked by worn niches, with an angel at the apex of the arch, crowned 'M's for the dedication in the moulding, and lion *stops*. One sometimes finds a *St George* carved in doorway *spandrels*, but here a grinning dragon is confronted by a *woodwose* who bears a little round shield as well as his usual club. Very similar carvings occur at Peasenhall and Badingham, and the idea was probably borrowed one from another. Cratfield is fortunate in having an unusually interesting set of parish accounts covering the C16 and early C17, and from them we learn that the parish forestalled the seizure of their silver under the royal injunctions of 1547 by selling two *chalices*, two *censers* and a cross to pay for the handsome stone battlements that crown the tower. There had been a rebuilding in about 1470, and the n. *aisle* dates from then. Above it stretches a fine range of *clerestory* windows of the same period, ten a side, with arches picked out in red brick. There is a curious sunken annexe beyond the e. end of the n. aisle (was it a C19 vault?), and a tall, boxy chapel dedicated to *St Edmund* adjoins the n. side of the *chancel*. It has a small e. window with *Decorated tracery*, well defined *put-log holes*, and is now used as a *vestry*. The *priest's door* on the s. side of the chancel dates it as C14, but the

windows are *Perpendicular* replacements. The s. aisle retains two of its original Decorated windows with small *headstops*, and you will find a *scratch dial* set high on the centre buttress. A brick *rood stair* turret nestles in the angle between aisle and chancel, and entry is by way of a low and wide Perpendicular *porch* which has little embellishment save for the small niche over the entrance.

Richard Phipson was in charge of a large programme of restoration in 1879, partially re-benching the church and providing a new roof for the s. aisle. The C15 chancel *screen* had been cannibalised in 1839 and used as part of a w. gallery, but when Phipson removed the latter he saved what was left of the screen and placed it against the w. wall. It is tall, with the remains of a double rank of delicate *cusping* in the tracery, a *crocketted* central arch, and fragments of tracery in the base panels. A recent discovery in the tower has caused a re-think on the installation of a new ringing gallery and cloakroom facilities. Behind the lathe and plaster tower-arch screen there is a substantial two-storied clock case on the n. wall, and research has identified it as medieval work. Because it is built into the fabric of the tower and the church accounts show that it was repaired as early as the 1530s, it is believed to be as old as the tower itself and may represent a unique survival in the UK. The clock mechanism is no longer there. The church's treasure is the C15 *Seven Sacrament font*, perhaps the finest of the whole series in terms of detail and decoration despite its mutilation, and it is grandly set on two steps, with *quatrefoils* in the upper riser. The octagonal stem is shafted, and below each shaft are *Evangelistic symbols* alternating with seated figures, all of which have lost their heads. Between the shafts, there are groined niches under crocketted *ogee* arches, and although the figures they contain have been harshly treated, some may be identified. Clockwise from the w.: bishop or priest vested in a cope, possibly holding a church; *St James the Less?*; the *Blessed Virgin?*; a robed figure; *St Peter*; a bishop; *St Paul*; *St John* (holding the poisoned chalice). Traces of the original colour remain, particularly on the bishop, and there are patches of green under the bowl where demi-angels hold shields and scrolls. Niches at the bowl angles contain slim, headless figures, and again, some tentative identifications can be made: w.(r.) *St Dorothy?*; e.(l.) *St James the Great*; n.(l.) *St Edmund?* Clockwise from the e., the subjects of the panels are: extreme unction, Crucifixion, baptism, confirmation (note that it is a babe in

Cratfield, St Mary: Seven Sacrament font

arms as was the medieval custom), blank (the mass), blank (penance), ordination (with the candidate kneeling), marriage. Each panel has a sloping traceried moulding above it, again retaining some colour. It is unusual not to have the Crucifixion panel on the w. side, and the meticulous defacement of two of the panels may be because *Dowsing* lived in nearby Laxfield (although Cratfield does not figure in his journal). A bulky set of steps has been set against the w. face of the font; they do not enhance its intrinsic, if somewhat battered beauty. The five-bay *nave arcades* display subtle differences in the *capitals* and arch mouldings, showing that the n. range was part of the Perpendicular rebuilding. The *arch-braced* and *tie-beam* roof overhead is panelled out with centre *bosses*. The church's only *brasses* are two inscriptions set in the floor – at the w. end of the s. aisle for William Fiske (1640), and at the w. end of the nave for Robert and Elizabeth Warner (1654 with an *achievement* displaying generous mantling). Phipson salvaged quite a lot of the old seating in 1879, and there are four C15 bench ends at the back of the church which have *poppyheads* and *paterae* on the mouldings. Less common are the *Jacobean* ranges in both aisles which have scrolly versions of poppyheads that vary surprisingly, and share a family likeness with some at Laxfield. The n.

aisle roof was restored, but the *wall posts* rest on a nice selection of C15 wooden head *corbels*. You will find an amply proportioned entrance to the rood loft stair at the e. end of the s. aisle – the loft to which it led was taken down in 1561. That was four years after the parliamentary order, and one wonders whether the delay was due to religious objection, Suffolk obstinacy, or plain idleness. In 1617 the parish accounts record that Robert Freston was paid £10 in 1617 for making the pulpit, a large sum for what must have been an elaborate piece, and in 1638 it was combined with a reading pew for a further £3.1.9. A joiner's reconstruction of 1889 has left little of the original – just the *blind-arched* panels and shallow arabesque ornament.

The *chancel* was renovated in 1889, and it has a lovely C15 roof in pale oak, with triple *castellated wall plates* and arch-braces that rise to *collars* and *king posts* under the ridge. The choir stalls incorporate more C15 bench ends, two of which have elaborately buttressed and gabled ends, and the pair in front at the e. end have very unusual *Tudor Rose* roundels as *finials*. There is a Victorian version of the *Trinity* shield in one of the n. windows, matched on the s. side by an interesting variant which symbolises Christ as 'The Way, the Truth and the Life'. The window beyond the organ on the n. side contains competent but not very exciting glass of 1923 by *Jones & Willis* – Christ in the centre, with a blind man and his family on one side and a shepherd's family on the other; *Sacred monograms* and cherub heads fill the tracery. The e. window of three years later is by the same firm and a good deal better, with attractive figures of Christ, the Blessed Virgin, *St Luke* and St Paul below tall intricate canopies; vignettes of the *Annunciation*, Nativity, Christ's Presentation in the Temple, and the *three Marys* fill the spaces below. More of this firm's work can be seen at Mettingham and Ilketshall St John. There is a medieval *aumbry* in the n. wall of the *sanctuary* and, rather confusingly, its top has been overlaid by a pair of cherub heads that actually belong to the 1724 monument for Sarah Mynne above. The C14 doorway on the n. side leading to St Edmund's chapel (vestry) has paterae in the moulding, with two beast masks at the top, and its door is original, complete with centre closing ring. The fussy *reredos* dates from the 1889 facelift, but the solid, unpretentious, and wholly satisfying *Holy table* in front of it is probably the same one which the parish paid local joiner Abraham Ellis twelve shillings to make in 1625. A modern *credence* table makes use of a panel dated 1617 which matches those on the pulpit, and it probably formed part of the backboard. There is an image stool to the r. of the e. window, and note the unusual quatrefoil drain in the *piscina*. Fragments of C15 glass survive in the tops of the chancel s. windows, but of more interest is the small panel in the sanctuary window that portrays Christ carrying the cross – a sketch in black on blue glass set within a yellow and red border which is continental work of the C18 or early C19. If you did not notice it when you entered, have a look at the clock mechanism by the s. door. It has no maker's name, but dates from the first quarter of the C18, and has some points of interest which are detailed on the card below. Cratfield has a noble of ring of six with an especially fine tenor of 20 cwt..; it is worth noting that some of the bells were cast by the C15 Norwich Brasyer family of founders noted for the quality of their work. Experienced ringers may remember that these bells are extremely difficult to ring.

Creeting St Mary, St Mary (E5): At one time there were four Creeting parishes but St Olave's church had disappeared by the C17 and in 1801 All Saints, whose churchyard adjoined this one, was demolished and a n. *transept* was added to St Mary's a year later to accommodate the joint congregation. The spire and top of the tower had by this time collapsed and been replaced by a pyramid roof, but in 1885 this in turn was followed by the present bell stage and battlements. About the same time the transept was enlarged into an *aisle* and the C13 *chancel* was largely rebuilt. The w. window of the tower is tall and thin with *Decorated tracery*, and an oblong stone above it is carved with the arms of Ufford, earls of Suffolk. The whole facade of the C15 s. *porch* is covered with *flushwork* and a modern *Blessed Virgin* and Child occupies the niche over the entrance. The *dripstone* rests on worn *headstops* and beyond the half-gates there is a *stoup* which has *paterae* on the bevel of its recess. The inner *Norman* doorway reveals the true age of the church. Thoroughly restored, the arch has a roll moulding and an outer band of semi-circles, and rests on scalloped *capitals* and single shafts. The C15 *font* stands in the base of the tower and the *Evangelistic symbols* in the bowl panels alternate with angels holding shields – a *Trinity emblem* to the w. and a well-cut arms of *St Edmund* to the e.; four lions guard the shaft and above them is a prominent range of defaced angels. The *crocketted ogee* cover was restored and supplemented by a deep skirt in 1907. Nearby

are *Decalogue boards* and a memorial for Rear-Admiral Samuel Uvedale, who died in 1808 after a distinguished career in which he commanded the *Ajax* at the battle of Cape St Vincent. The roofs, *arcade*, and furnishings are modern, including a *screen* of 1902, but the *altar* is an excellent *Jacobean* table. Its substantial turned legs are carved and the very odd metal cylinder used for storing documents that was fastened underneath at one time now rests on the floor. St Mary's has a fine array of *Kempe & Co* glass dating from the late C19 and early C20 which illustrates the consistency of their style and the variations introduced by W.E. Tower. The e. window includes figures of *SS Alban* and *Olave*, the s. chancel windows have *SS Laurence, Stephen, Cecilia,* and *Agnes*, while in the nave there is an especially rich King David group dating from 1903. In the n. aisle are two Kempe & Tower designs – an *Annunciation* and *SS George* and *Edmund*, and in the lower borders of both you will find the firm's emblem of a tower within a wheatsheaf (the wheatsheaf alone figures in the chancel windows). In complete contrast, in the n.w. aisle window there is an arresting 1950s Nativity by Brian Thomas in which the Holy Family is grouped with shepherds and their dog while *putti* float overhead. The colouring is vivid and the rough outlines of the naturalistic figures have the texture of a charcoal drawing.

Creeting St Peter, St Peter (E5): Approached by a long gravelled lane from the s., this little church nestles in a grove of trees above the busy A45 which now cuts it off from the village. There was a time in the C18 when it lay derelict and roofless but now, despite all difficulties, it is well cared for and the C14 *porch* with its original roof has recently been restored. There are flint *consecration crosses* on the *nave* buttresses and a faint *scratch dial* can be found on one of them. The small doorway of the C14 tower has plain chamfers and there is no w. window, although the bell openings have *Decorated tracery* like one of the nave n. windows. The round arch of the little n. door shows that the building was *Norman* originally. The e. window and one s. window have 'Y' tracery of about 1300 and the narrow *priest's door* is the same age. The small ogee-headed windows each side of the *chancel* are slightly later and were probably *low side windows*.

There is a neat interior, and under the C19 *gallery* there is a C15 *font* in beautiful condition which does not seem to be the result of re-cutting. It is so like Earl Stonham's that they may well have been carved by the same mason. In the bowl panels there is a *pomegranate* and crown of thorns (s.e.), a lattice with fleur-de-lys terminals (n.e.), and a fat *Tudor Rose* (s.w.). Angels with shields fill the rest, others link wings underneath, and four proud lions slightly turn their heads against the shaft. The solid C19 pews have *poppyheads* and doors, and hassocks embroidered with saints' emblems make a colourful display on the ledges. Beyond the plastered-over n. door there is a most interesting *St Christopher* painting. It is faded and one of the roof braces obliterated the saint's face, but his arm and staff are clear and so is the Christ child on his l. shoulder. Behind the figures an elongated scroll carried the message: 'Christopheri sancti speciem quicumque tuetur illa nempe die nullo languore gravetur' (Whoever looks at the picture of St Christopher shall assuredly on that day be burdened with no weariness). The red background has a pale blue border on which a red and white ribbon is folded and, farther down, the head and shoulders of a mermaid holding mirror and comb were probably in the legendary river to be crossed. Instead of the more usual eight, the C15 pulpit has seven sides of which two make up the door, and each panel has a pair of *crocketted* and *finialed* ogee arches with tracery behind them. All the bevels carry *paterae* and the underside is coved, but of the original shaft only the *capital* remains. By it stands a repaired early-C17 table and in the s. wall opposite, the recess is likely to have been the entrance to the *rood loft stair*. The chancel roof is C19, as are the stalls, but they have rather nice standing figures against the walls. The *communion rails* are composed of a series of wrought-iron upright scrolls, both unusual and decorative – Victorian or C20? There is a plain *piscina* and the e. window glass dates from the formative period of the 1840s before the large firms became established. It was designed by Mr Rawnsley, the curate, and made by an Ipswich glazier. There is a central figure of the patron saint and the rest of the window is taken up with lozenge and scroll patterns in blue, red, and yellow against cross-hatched backgrounds. George Paske of the Hon. East India Company died on his way home in 1822 and was buried on St Helena; the memorial for him and his wives on the chancel wall is quintessential High Victorian Gothic of 1874. A cast-iron lamppost twisted like traditional barley sugar stands by the porch and the peaceful churchyard invites a stroll in search of epitaphs like Henry Ellis's,

twenty yards s. of the priest's door: 'O how uncertain are the days of man . . .'.

Cretingham, St Peter (G4): It is probably pure coincidence, but both Cretingham and neighbouring Earl Soham were originally dedicated to *St Andrew*, although in Cretingham's case the change of allegiance was delayed until the beginning of the C20 century and the reason for it is unknown. The present building probably dates from the early C14 but there have been gradual, piecemeal alterations over the years, and the tower has a *Decorated* w. window and slightly later bell openings. The w. door has been bricked up and there are large *flushwork quatrefoils* in the stepped battlements. A *Perpendicular* window in the n. wall of the *nave* has to make do with wooden glazing bars and there has been a good deal of patching up in brick. The e. window has intersected 'Y' *tracery* and there is a *lancet*, more 'Y' tracery and a small *priest's door* on the s. side of the *chancel*, all of around 1300. The modest *rood stair turret* to the w. has a sloping stone slab roof and little slit window, and one of the late Perpendicular nave windows on that side has recently been renewed. There are three small niches around the entrance of the C14 *porch*, and one of its timbers is secured by a massive peg on the outside of the wall. At some stage the roof was renewed at a higher level and the side windows were blocked.

The interior is charming, largely because nobody in the C19 was minded to wield a new broom and sweep away all that was old-fashioned. The n. wall leans lazily outwards (which explains the brick buttress outside) and there is a good *hammerbeam* and *arch-braced* roof with *collars* tight under the ridge. Its *spandrels* are pierced with tracery, and so is the *wall plate*, which has carved spandrels running e.-w. below it. It is worth using binoculars to study the *St George* and dragon in the 3rd bay from the e. on the n. side. There is an 'A.T.' monogram in the corner behind the dragon and the saint's long sword and large hand project from the r. The head of a man and a recumbent figure can be found in the 3rd bay from the w. on the s. side. Half a dozen C15 benches with rustic tracery and the remains of *poppyheads* stand at the w. end on either side of the chunky *font* of the same period. Plain shields and *Tudor Roses* in *cusped* squares decorate its bowl panels, with angel heads below, smiling lions round the shaft, and quite a lot of the original red and green paint survives. A little organ stands by the blocked n. door, and by its side there is one high-backed late-C16 pew with turned *finials*. The rest of the seating is in the form of plain C18 *box pews* painted black, and above them on the n. wall there is a set of C18 or early-C19 *Decalogue* boards. Opposite hang the *Royal Arms* of Charles II, dulled by age but well painted on board. Two boys' heads peep out from below the Garter roundel and *Cautley* thought that it was the work of the same artist who painted the set in St Margaret's, Ipswich. It has been discovered that the Commandments are lettered on the back, suggesting that the arms were originally for Charles I, reversed during the Commonwealth, and revised at the *Restoration*. The pulpit is a handsome *Stuart three-decker* that lost its clerk's pew when the box pews were installed. The blind-arched panels are more delicate than usual and there are pierced brackets to the steeply canted book ledge; the hexagonal *tester* is adorned with acorn pendants. Moving into the chancel, note the curious recess below the window on the s. side – possibly the remains of a *low side window*. Two more C15 benches stand farther e. and the *altar* is a small, simple C17 table, enclosed on three sides by *communion rails*. This was a late-C17 fashion but these may have come in a little later and they are painted to match the C18 box pews. A tiny parish chest no more than 2ft. by 14in. stands by the altar and the top is lettered: 'This box is for the towne evedence A.C:C.H. 1660' (i.e., the parish's official documents). On the n. wall the C16 monument to Lionel Louth retains much of its original colour. There are two shields and an *achievement* with strapwork at the top, and he kneels within a coffered arch (minus half his legs) with a helm in front. His daughter Margaret married Richard Cornwallis (brother of Sir Thomas, whose memorial can be found at Brome) and her memorial of 1603 on the s. wall of the *sanctuary* has a *touchstone* tablet within a broad surround decorated with six small coloured shields; her arms are in a coloured roundel at the top. Her son John is commemorated on the e. wall with a touch-stone tablet set in an architectural alabaster frame, achievement on top and shield below. He died in 1615 and because his second wife was related to the Wolseys, the arms of the cardinal feature in miniature on the l. The roundel painted with the head of the *Blessed Virgin* in the e. window is likely to be C19 work, and at the top there is a small but well-painted achievement of the Chenery family arms. St Peter's has a ground floor ring of five bells with a 7 cwt. tenor and three of its bells were cast in the C15 at the Brasyer foundry in Norwich.

Crowfield, All Saints (F5): Like nearby Gosbeck and Ashbocking, Crowfield's church is well away from its village that lines the old Roman road. Beautifully placed, it is masked from the s. and e. by trees and there is a substantial moat close by. The owners of the house that stood within it probably sited the church for their convenience. For most of its history it has been a daughter chapel of Coddenham and it was only in the 1920s that it was advanced to the status of a parish church. There was a restoration here in 1862 under *E.C. Hakewill* that went so far as to rebuild the C14 *nave* from the foundations, retaining the ground plan and reusing much of the material. It is unlikely that there was ever a tower but a bellcote was sited towards the centre of the nave roof. In the C18 this became an attractive cupola but Hakewill replaced it with a banal little turret, and he added a *vestry* outside the n. door. A new *lancet* and *cinquefoil* roundel were inserted in the w. wall and stone blocks carved with an animal and a grotesque head were found new homes level with the gable ends. Quite the most interesting thing about Crowfield is the C15 *chancel*. Timber-framed like a cottage, there is nothing like it in either Norfolk or Suffolk and, with its wooden *mullioned* windows and *priest's door* on the s. side, it is very pleasing. So too is the contemporary s. *porch* which has been unobtrusively glazed. Its roof is braced by cambered *tie-beams*, crested like the *wall plates*, and the *spandrels* are carved with a lively selection – an angel with a crown, a *green man*, two birds pecking grapes, and a defaced mask.

The reused C14 doorway was given new *headstops* and just inside there is a *stoup* in a new niche. The nave *hammerbeam* and *arch-braced* roof is late C15 in essence and, like Ufford chancel,

Crowfield, All Saints

the arch-braces are interrupted by a short post partway up. The *collars* under the ridge are *castellated* and all the timbers are unstained except the C19 additions. These take the form of standing angels placed in front of the hammers and smaller ones added at the bottom of the *wall posts* and halfway up the braces. There is a good shield of Victorian *Royal Arms* in the top w. window and the 1860s *font* is quite attractive, although it is cramped up right in the s.w. corner. Hakewill's instinct for sympathetic design faltered when it came to the nave windows and he inserted pairs of internal arches with bald *trefoil* tops which were surely unnecessary. The tablet on the n. wall is a grateful tenantry's tribute to Sir William Middleton of Shrubland Park and has a profile portrait at the top. He was buried at Barham and the restoration here was funded by his widow in his memory. C19 woodcarvers were often very talented and the benches here are the work of James Wormald and William Polly. Each *poppyhead* is different and they took a generous selection of tree foliage, fruit, and corn for their subjects. They also carved the two groups of standing and kneeling angels which flank the entrance to the chancel (there is more of Polly's work at Rushmere St Andrew). There is now no medieval *screen* but you will see that the arch overhead is nicked in three places where the *tympanum* once fitted. Beyond it the roof has cambered tie-beams with plain and heavy braces below them and C19 work above. Above wainscot panelling the wall timbers are exposed, and on the e. wall there is an excellent set of *Decalogue* boards painted and gilt in true High-Victorian style. The lightweight C18 *communion rails* have turning in two sections and the *altar* is a robust *Stuart* table with a carved top rail. *Brasses* were very much out of fashion in the C18 but there is an inscription of 1775 for William Middleton on the s. wall of the *sanctuary*, and two attractive mid-C19 examples opposite mark the return of this style of memorial. The church's only *hatchment* is in the chancel and was used at the funeral of Sir William Fowle Fowle Middleton in 1860; its twin is to be found at Barham. All the stained glass is by *Ward & Hughes* and the e. window has shaped panels of the Resurrection, and the raising of the widow's son and of Jairus's daughter; the rest of the space is filled with bright geometric shapes and foliage and is quite attractive at a distance.

Culford, St Mary (C3): The church lies close to the hall (Culford School), within grounds laid out by Humphrey Repton in the C18; the setting is superb. Except for the base of the tower, it was rebuilt by *Sir Arthur Blomfield* from 1856 to 1865, with a n. *aisle* added in 1908. All the work was carried out by estate craftsmen. The architect used flint pebbles throughout for facing material, except for *flushwork* battlements on the tower and dressed flint panels on the buttresses. Some interesting Blomfield touches are the *chancel* buttresses, *dogtooth* and *paterae* decoration under the eaves, and the quite eccentric placement of a clock in the e. bell opening. The general form is *Early English* with geometric *tracery*, and one feels that this is what the avant garde thought a country church should look like. Through the small s. *porch* into a High-Victorian interior dominated by dark and heavy roofs with *arch-braces* in the nave, coming down to half-octagonal *corbels* encrusted with foliage underneath, and open tracery between the top of the braces and the ridge. A four-bay *arcade* on *quatrefoil piers* separates the *nave* and aisle. There is a small wooden w. *gallery* and, within the tower, a Blomfield *font*. Above it on the s. wall is a 1668 Cornwallis family memorial – two *touchstone* panels (only one of which was used) separated and flanked by polished black marble *Corinthian* columns, the twin *pediments* topped by skulls crowned with wreaths of laurel and alabaster swags at the bottom. On the opposite wall is an excellent portrait bust of Nathaniel Bacon, the amateur painter who died in 1627. It stands within a scooped-out oval set on a black marble lozenge garnished with a pair of palettes and coats of arms. On the w. wall of the nave is a plain marble tablet topped by a draped urn commemorating Charles, 2nd and last Marquess Cornwallis who died in 1823. Considering the European reputation of its sculptor Edward Hodges Bailey, it is disappointingly ordinary. Within the rails at the e. end of the n. aisle is the large tomb chest of Beatrix Jane Craven, Countess Cadogan, who died in 1907. The life-size figure in white marble was sculpted by Feodora, Countess Gleichen, and lies with crucifix to breast, the head with its Edwardian hair style resting on a pillow. The front of the tomb has two bas-relief cherubs plucking harps and the wall behind carries a shallow design in plaster – cherubs supporting a scroll below a crucifix framed in leaf tendrils. The aisle windows are filled with fine glass by J. Dudley Forsyth (one of *Henry Holiday's* apprentices, whose work includes windows in Westminster Abbey); at the w., for Henry Arthur, Viscount Chelsea (d.1908); at centre, for Edward

George Henry, Viscount Chelsea (d.1878), in which a portrait figure kneels by a sick bed, with an angel in the other *light*; at e. end, for the Countess Cadogan, including a woman bearing a slung bowl apparently full of potatoes! The tops of all the windows are filled with canopy work and the colours of the robes are particularly rich. The nave windows are by *Lavers & Barraud* and illustrate the life of *St Peter*. On the l. side of the chancel is the delightful monument of Dame Jane, the widow of Sir Nathaniel Bacon whose bust we saw in the tower. It was ordered in 1654 during the Commonwealth and it shows a fine disregard for the contemporary belief that all such things were idolatrous. The finest work of Thomas Stanton (uncle of the more famous William), it was to be carried out 'according to the best skill of a stone-cutter, alle in whit and black marble without the addition of any other ston whatsoever', at a cost of £300 (no mean sum at the time). It seems that the chancel was rebuilt around it, leaving its base well below the present floor level, and it stands within a new arch. A stiff composition, with a stern Dame Jane sitting facing front, wearing a wide Puritan collar and coif; a little girl sits on her lap, faintly smiling, and her other grandchildren are lined up each side. To the l. are the girls, with the youngest holding a fan and her sister clasping a handkerchief; to the r., three boys, with the smallest holding a stoolball toy. Below the group, Lady Bacon's first husband, Sir William Cornwallis, lies with legs very uncomfortably one on top of the other, resting his head on his elbow, prayer book in hand with a finger keeping the place. The family is framed within a low arch and Ionic columns, with a pediment and coloured *achievement of arms* above. Only when it was finished and 'the draft compared with the monument' did Stanton receive the balance of his fee. The portrait does not belie the character of a lady who knew what she wanted and ensured that she got it. The chancel roof is a compact *hammerbeam* design, with angels on the hammers and *wall posts* resting on kingly head *corbels*. There is a 1909 *reredos* and the recesses each side contain mosaics of the *Annunciation* – the archangel on the n. and the *Blessed Virgin* on the s. The e. window glass is in memory of Emily Julia Cadogan, Baroness Lurgan and is, I think, also by Forsyth. It depicts Christ crucified, with the Virgin below supported by *St John* and *St Mary Magdalene*; the Roman soldier and followers of Christ stand each side, and there are two gorgeous attendant angels. Christ on the cross is enclosed in a pointed oval beautifully

painted with a series of small cherub heads in salmon and pale yellow. Returning to the w. end, you will see that the tower window contains a colourful array of modern heraldic glass.

Culpho, St Botolph (G6): There has never been more than a handful of houses scattered across this little parish, but a church has stood here since the Conquest and it may indeed have been one of those founded by St Botolph himself in the C7. The core of the walls is no doubt older, but most of what we see dates from about 1300, with characteristic 'Y' *tracery* in the windows, although the *lancets* in the *chancel* are probably a little earlier. The n. door has been blocked and there is a generous *priest's door* with small, worn *headstops* on the s. side of the chancel. As with a number of churches in this area, the unbuttressed tower with its tall entrance arch stands to the s. of the *nave*, its ground floor acting as a *porch;* the upper stage has been removed and it is capped with a tiled pyramid roof. There is a *scratch dial* to be found on its s.e. corner and the inner C14 doorway is finely moulded, with the unusual accompaniment of a square *label*. This is partially obscured by the outer arch, which indicates that the tower was added a little later. The builders provided a *stoup* to the r. although you will find that there was one already set in the wall just inside.

The interior is bright and neat but it was not always so. In 1602 it was described as 'exceeding ruinous' and it must have been about that time that the e. wall of the nave was rebuilt in brick and a new chancel arch inserted. There was a full-scale restoration in the 1880s and in 1976 the church was entirely re-roofed with attractive small red tiles, the tower restored and the interior re-plastered, leaving exposed flints in the window splays. The late-C15 *font* has *quatrefoils* in the bowl panels with flowers and leaves at their centres, there are large *fleurons* underneath, and the medieval staple used to secure the cover survives on the rim. The C17 framework of the present cover was found in the stable loft at Playford vicarage in 1935 and was newly panelled for use here. Floors are brick, and the pattern on the n. side shows where *box pews* once stood. Overhead, the nave roof is *arch-braced* and plastered out, with two heavy *tie-beams* set well below the top of the walls. C18 *Decalogue* texts painted on canvas hang on the walls, and over the n. door there is a banner with decorative swags of dried flowers. The small pulpit, with its acorn-cum-pineapple *finials*, dates from 1959, and the 1970s work uncovered

a late-C14 *piscina* in the s. wall, indicating that
there was at least one nave *altar*, even in a church
as small as this. A plaque on the n. wall records
that Robert Thornhagh Gurdon, 1st Baron
Cranworth, 'rebuilt and furnished the chancel'
in 1883, but the altar that was provided has been
relegated to the back of the church and the C17
communion table reinstated. The piscina in the
sanctuary matches the one in the nave and has
small-scale *dropped-sill sedilia* alongside. The plain
rectangular recess in the n. wall was no doubt an
aumbry, and although the roof is Victorian, parts
of the *wall plate* are original.

Dalham, St Mary (B4): A delightful sunken
lane leads up from the village and the church
stands on a hillock next to the Hall, with grand
views across the rolling country to the s. There
was a complete rebuilding in the C14 – two
Decorated windows remain in the s. *aisle* and the
tracery of another can be seen on the outside of
the e. end of the n. aisle. In the C15 the n. aisle
and *clerestory* were added, and some of the *chancel*
and s. aisle windows were replaced. By the 1620s
the tower had become unsafe and was rebuilt,
with a heavy stair on the n. side. There is a door
in the e. wall giving on to the *nave* roof. The w.
window has *Perpendicular* tracery but the bell
openings are reused C14 windows. The parapet
has bold *flushwork* lettering: 'Keepe my
Sabbaths', 'Reverence my Sanctuary', 'Deo Trin
Uni Sacrum', and 'Anno Domini 1625'. The w.
buttresses carry *consecration crosses* in flint and
there are two more flanking the plain C14 *porch*
entrance. In walking round you will find an
interesting series of C19 tablets on the n. and e.
walls for servants of the squire: Francis Watts, a
dairy and poultry woman; Washington Andrews,
the butler; John Keates and Joseph Brett, aged
labourers whose epitaph concludes:

Who change their places often change with
    loss,
'Tis not the Rolling Stone that gathers
    Moss.

The *vestry* abuts the n. wall of the chancel and
to the w. is a roofless C17 compartment used in
the C18 as a mausoleum for the Affleck family,
whose weathered and largely illegible tablets now
line the n. churchyard wall. At the rebuilding,
the old inner arch of the tower was retained and
there is a medieval drawing of a post mill
scratched on each *respond*. The story goes that
there was such rivalry between the two village
mills that their sails were made to turn in

opposite directions. C19 *Decalogue* panels flank
the arch and matching Creed and Lord's Prayer
boards are on the n. aisle wall. By the s. door
there is an interesting C17 *bier* with the same
type of sliding handles as the one at Little
Saxham. Above the arch is a huge and boldly
lettered inscription setting out all the details of
the tower rebuilding by the squire, the rector
and their friends, with coloured shields in the
spandrels. Dalham's *font* is one of the few C17
examples in the county and has pleasing *ogee*
curves to the bowl. There is a fine set of
Hanoverian Royal Arms over the n. door – three-
dimensional, coloured and gilt. The nave and
chancel roofs are modern reconstructions and
the 1860s benches are excellently carved – all with
poppyheads and, on the s. range, birds and animals
on the elbows, including squirrel, sheep, lion
and eagle. The s. aisle chapel has a C14 *piscina*
with *trefoil* arch and stone *credence shelf* and image
brackets flank the *altar*. The 1850s e. window
glass here is a fine example of *Thomas Willement's*
work – Christ with groups of children and
disciples against a bright blue patterned sky. The
tracery is filled with *tabernacle work* and the Affleck
family arms figure at the bottom. There are
extensive remains of wall paintings in the nave
above the n. *arcade*. The westernmost section is
a tree of the *Seven Deadly Sins* which is very similar
to the Hessett painting but not, unfortunately,
as complete. The trunk sprouts branches which
become snarling dragons' heads, three of which
remain, and the figures of the individual sins
would have issued from them. To the r. was a
Seven Works of Mercy sequence but the central
angel has faded away. However, on the l., the
faint outline remains of a figure handing clothing
to the naked, and high on the r. a woman is
giving bread to the hungry. Instead of the more
usual *Doom* over the chancel arch there were
paintings of *Passion emblems* and scenes, but all
that is left of the flagellation is a pair of feet on
the l. and a scattering of 'M's and *Sacred
monograms*. Although much has gone, binoculars
do pick up a surprising amount of detail in all
these sequences.

The base of the C15 *rood screen* remains and
its panels are decorated with highly individual
flower patterns; the gilt and coloured carvings
in the spandrels include a dragon, birds, and
grotesques. Note the three *quatrefoil elevation
squints*. Just beyond the arch on the s. side is a
tall blank arch of indeterminate age with a recess
beyond it. Outside, it has its own little lean-to
roof but its origin and purpose are obscure. In
the *sanctuary* is a simple C14 piscina with an

Dalham, St Mary: Elevation squint

original wooden credence shelf, and to the r. is the tomb of Thomas Stutevyle who died in 1571. The chest is decorated with three shields in strapwork *cartouches* and on top is a large standing tablet bearing his epitaph in front of the window. The line of defaced shields behind probably remain from the tomb of an earlier Thomas Stutvyle who died in 1468. Across the sanctuary is the memorial to Sir Martin Stutvyle, Thomas' grandson, who died in 1631. He was knighted by James I but was essentially an Elizabethan who in his youth had sailed with Drake to the Americas. The design is compact, with marble bas-relief busts of Sir Martin and his two wives set in ovals. There are *touchstone Corinthian* columns each side with gilded *capitals*, three shields under an arch on which rests a coloured *achievement of arms*, and the figures of eight little children kneel in a panel below. A funeral helm rests on a bracket overhead. The C15 s. window was replaced by *Sir Arthur Blomfield* with an awkward design but the early-C20 glass is very good. The central figure of the *Blessed Virgin* with the Christ child in a cradle is flanked by an adoring angel and a king, and surrounding panels have angels bearing symbolic disks and scrolls. In the top *lights* there are demi-figures from the Old Testament and *SS George, Etheldreda, Jerome* and *Ambrose*. The glass is by *Kempe & Co* and is much warmer in

tone than their earlier work. You will have seen a large obelisk outside by the porch commemorating Gen. Sir James Affleck who died in 1833; on the s. wall of the chancel he has a second memorial – a tablet cut by Robert de Carle the younger of Bury. The epitaph cleverly paraphrases a redundancy: '. . . having attained to a rank exempt from ordinary services, he retired to his estate . . . '. On the opposite wall is a pink veined alabaster tablet in C17 style for Col. Frank Rhodes, brother of Cecil Rhodes and a distinguished veteran of many campaigns who was wounded at Omdurman and beseiged at Ladysmith. St Mary's has an excellent ring of eight bells with a 14 cwt. tenor.

Dallinghoo, St Mary (G5): At first sight, the church seems to have been built the wrong way round with a tower at the e. end, but on walking round you will see that it was a central tower originally and that the *chancel* has been demolished. The *herringbone* patterns in the flints of the tower walls suggest that it dates from the C12, although there is C15 *flushwork* on the e. buttresses and later brick battlements. The C19 window was perhaps inserted in the e. arch when the chancel was removed. A very large brick *vestry* was added on the n. side (early C19?) and served for a time as the village school. The w. window has attractive C14 flowing *tracery* and the little Victorian *transept* on the s. side of the *nave* is actually an organ chamber. The *porch* has all the signs of C19 rebuilding, but the *spandrels* of the C15 outer arch have shields with *Trinity* and *Passion emblems*, there are *fleurons* in the mouldings, and the *stops* are lions like those often seen in font panels. The inner doorway has *headstops* and the spandrels are filled with flushwork, just as they are at Charsfield.

C19 *Decalogue* boards hang on the w. wall and there are *Royal Arms* of George III above the n. door. The *font* is C19. The nave is fairly wide and is spanned by a shallow *arch-braced* roof which has collars and short *king posts* under the ridge. Strange little cutout emblems were added to the bottom of the *wall posts* in the late C17, and between them there are carved lateral braces. The e. bay of the roof was once a *celure* for the *rood* below, and faint traces of decoration remain on the n. side. The shields in the corners repeat those on the porch but they may be modern. The mid-C17 pulpit is particularly good and rises from a short stem of bunched scrolls. The body has flattened *acanthus* scrolls at the angles, with blind-arched panels between, and the range above is carved with a fish scale and fleur-de-lys pattern. The *tester* cornice is decorated with a vine trail and turned pendants, and there are sharp gables above each face. The backboard has a double blind arch at the top, and at the bottom a very interesting panel was incorporated from elsewhere which is carved with miniature *Tudor* arms flanked by a rose and the *pomegranate* of Catherine of Aragon. The large reading desk in front has been formed by using sections of late-C16/early-C17 woodwork, including what looks like part of an Elizabethan court cupboard. The base of the tower now serves as a chancel and the C18 *communion rails* have fine twisted *balusters* and fluted gate-posts. There is a C14 *piscina* within a *trefoil* arch but this must have been moved to its present position from the old chancel. C17 panelling has been brought from elsewhere to form a *reredos*, and in front of it stands a most attractive C17 *Holy table* with a solid bottom shelf, short bulbous legs, and a deep carved top rail. The 1880s e. window glass is by Albert Moore, an artist who had been a designer for *Powell & Sons* twenty years before. The subjects are identified by Gospel texts, the colouring is pleasing, but the figures are poor. There is another of his windows at Little Bealings. Before leaving you may like to examine the figure of Hope with her anchor that stands in the n.e. churchyard. It is a typically bland piece by that prolific statuary Matthew Wharton Johnson, whose work is scattered all over England, and it must date from the 1840s. The vault in front contains the remains of Rector Ellis Walford's family and was once enclosed by railings and a gate.

Darmsden, St Andrew (E5): A sign on the road between Needham Market and Baylham points to Darmsden, and a pretty lane climbs out of the valley to the tiny hamlet; its church which lies beyond is nearly a mile from the main road. This is a quiet and peaceful spot, with spacious views across the Gipping to the Creetings and Shrubland Park, and the tiny building is an object lesson in the virtues of tenacity and faith. The diocese closed it in 1973 and declared it redundant in 1979, but parishioners and friends bought the church and formed the St Andrew's Trust which maintains it and ensures that there is a service at least once a month. The poem by one of them on the door may not be great verse but it deserves its place:

. . . Now this little church is up for sale,
Some folks say 'Well it's getting old'
But others say 'Yes so it might be
But we'll fight like mad to keep it free.
It's too beautiful to close for ever,
When so many friends get together,
Once a month on a Sunday afternoon,
To say a prayer and sing a hymn,
And thank the Lord for everything . . .'

There was a small medieval building on the same site, but by the C19 it was in poor shape and was entirely replaced in 1880. Designed by Herbert J. Green of Norwich, the successor is an excellent example of the small Victorian church, and unlike his other church at Willisham, it is distinguished by its quality. Everything is small in scale, with a continuous roof over *nave* and *chancel,* and the bell was re-hung in the bellcote on the w. gable in 1983. The flint pebble walls have stone facings, and the general style is *Decorated.* Above the w. door there is a handsome rose window enclosing four *quatrefoils* and there is a diminutive s. *porch.*

Within, everything has an extraordinary compactness. A heavy drum *font* stands on one side at the w. end, and the neat benches are not only made of oak but they have *poppyheads* excellently carved with sprays of vine, *pomegranate*, hops, roses, and thistles. This is work by Cornish & Gaymer's men and overhead the roof, again in oak, has *arch-braces* which project to curious stubs which are at right angles to the *purlins.* There is no chancel arch, but three steps mark off the *sanctuary,* flanked by open-work pulpit and reading desk. The Cornish & Gaymer oak *reredos* has pierced and *crocketted* gables in keeping with the chosen style, and below them the figure of Christ as the Good Shepherd stands flanked by *St Paul* and *St Andrew*, all well carved in deep relief within *cusped* panels. Carved sprays of corn and vine, and painted texts of the Creed and Lord's Prayer complete the range but above, on each side of the e. window, the early C19 *Decalogue* boards from the old building were replaced in their traditional position. So too, was the *piscina*, and part of its stonework looks original. All is meticulously kept, a credit to Darmsden and an example to many, in more ways than one.

Darsham, All Saints (I4): The churchyard lies within a sharp bend in the village street, and there are mature lime trees along its boundary. The C15 tower has a three-*light* w. window, *flushwork* buttresses, and attractive *tracery* in the bell openings; a band of lozenge decoration runs below the flushwork stepped battlements. Walking round, you will see that the first clue to the age of the building is part of a *Norman* door arch embedded in the n. wall, and there are *Perpendicular* windows with *embattled transoms* on that side of the *nave*. The *chancel* was rebuilt and extended during the C13 and a contemporary *lancet* remains in the n. wall. The thin triple lancets in the e. wall are C19 insertions which probably reproduce the form of the originals. The *priest's door* of about 1300 retains one of its *headstops*, and there is quite a variety of Perpendicular windows in the newly plastered s. walls. The village commemorated Queen Victoria's golden jubilee by rebuilding the *porch*, and the simple Norman doorway within was badly treated by the restorers. It has single shafts with damaged *capitals*, and a brick arch has been inserted.

The neat, attractive interior lies under an *arch-braced* roof, on stone *corbels* carved with foliage and demi-angels. The organ masks the tower arch, and in front of it there is a section of excellent late-C17 *communion rails* which have gilded *acanthus* decoration on the *balusters*. They were salvaged from a London church by an architect who then presented them to his adopted village. The *hatchment* that hangs on the n. wall behind the organ was used at the funeral of Elizabeth Purvis in 1816, and there is a nice set of George IV *Royal Arms* above the blocked n. door. HMS Darsham was adopted by the village during World War II, and when she was laid up her bell was presented to the community and hangs below the war memorial in the doorway. The C15 *font* follows the usual Suffolk pattern, with four lions guarding the shaft and more in the bowl panels. Between them, defaced angels bear shields – s., three crowns for East Anglia (or Ely); e., *Passion emblems*; n., *Trinity emblem*; w., the arms of *St Edward the Confessor*. Around the octagonal base is an interesting and clearly lettered inscription: 'Orate pro anima dni Galfri Symond rectoris de Bradwell qui istum fontem fieri fecit in honore Dei' (Pray for the soul of Geoffrey Symond, rector of Bradwell, who had this font made to the honour of God). He was inducted at Bradwell in 1404 and must have presented his native village with the new font shortly after. The font at Middleton has similarities and it is conceivable that they came from the same workshop. The cover was made by a local craftsman, Miles Martin, in celebration of King George V's coronation in 1911. The small recess in the s. wall at the w. end was probably an *aumbry* to store the various items needed for baptisms. Just by the entrance is a tablet by *Thomas Thurlow*

of Saxmundham for Lieut. George Purvis of the Hon. East India Company's Madras Native Infantry who died in 1843. Below it, R. Balls of Halesworth provided a matching tablet for the parents in 1859. Most of the benches in the nave retain their C15 bench ends, and they are unusually slim, with stubby *poppyheads*; the ends are carved in the solid in the form of three-light transomed windows, but note that some of them are blank, having been switched from wall to centre aisle when the suite was restored and augmented. The C19 *Decalogue* panels, painted on zinc in the favourite High-Victorian style, were probably displayed in the chancel before being transferred to the nave n. wall. One of the s. nave windows contains attractive figures of *St Mary Magdalene* with her casket, and Martha with a plate of cakes. The glass was supplied in 1909 by Cox & Buckley whose work can also be seen at Marlesford, Woodbridge, and elsewhere in the county. The glass in the three-light window further along may also be by them, on the theme of 'Suffer little children to come unto me' – the figures against a dark landscape background under elaborate canopies. Between the two windows, a tablet commemorates Charles Purvis and others of his family, 1808-16; it was cut by Henry Rouw, a sculptor whose work can also be found at Yoxford and Chelsworth. A n. nave window has been re-glazed as a memorial and displays a good C17 Flemish stained glass roundel, but I have not been able to identify the subject – a saint blessing a man half submerged in a river, with fishing boats beyond. The *Stuart* pulpit has a triple tier of panels, successively decorated with lozenges, *blind arches*, and strapwork. The church's second *hatchment* hangs just within the chancel and was for Elizabeth Purvis's husband Charles. They lived at Darsham House and he died in 1808. There are two early-C16 *brass* inscriptions for Marion Reve and William Garrard in the nave, but the church's best brass is in the chancel and it can be examined by carefully folding back the carpet. It commemorates Ann Bedingfield who died a few months after her 80th birthday, a fine 19in. figure in a loose gown with turned-back buttoned sleeves, wearing a widow's headdress and carrying a large purse. She was one of the Norfolk Bedingfields and may have died while visiting her kinsman Sir Thomas at the Hall. His monument on the n. wall is a sombre, intricate design – a *touchstone* tablet set within an alabaster frame flanked by *Corinthian* columns, with small reclining females on the *pediment* on either side of a garlanded *achievement*. There is no doubt where Sir Thomas's allegiance lay: '. . . made Attorney Generall of ye Dutchy of Lancaster and one of the Judges of the Court of Common Pleas by King Charles the 1st of blessed memory. Upon whose murder, he layd downe his place & all publiq imployments, retiring himselfe to this Towne'. A shame that he died a bare two months before his king returned in triumph. Nearby stands an interesting waggon chest in pine, with canted sides and metal reinforcing; well restored, it is perhaps late-C18. There is more Cox & Son glass in the chancel, with Christ as the Good Shepherd featured in the centre e. lancet, and they probably supplied the figures of *SS Peter, Paul, John* and the *Blessed Virgin* in the side windows. In one of the s. windows there is a pleasing King David playing his harp, with flanking texts and pretty patterns, maker unidentified. The level of the *sanctuary* was raised as part of an 1870s restoration so that the plain *piscina* recess is now low in the wall, and a sturdy Stuart table still serves as the *altar*. Darsham has a ring of four bells with a 7 cwt. tenor, but they cannot be rung at the present time.

Debenham, St Mary Magdalene (F4): The main village street rises to a hump with the church on the crest, its graveyard sloping gently s. towards a little open plain. The bluff and solid tower has distinctive *long and short quoins* which are normally a sure sign of *Saxon* work, but you will find that the simple *imposts* of the arch within appear to be *Norman* and it may well date from the Conquest period when the two traditions overlapped. There are small *lancets* at ground and first-floor level but the stage above is C14, with *Decorated tracery* in the bell openings. The tower was some 20ft. higher until 1667 when it was struck by lightning and had to have the top removed – which accounts for its squat appearance in relation to the *nave;* tie-bars secured by 'S' plates were used to strengthen it. A large two-storeyed *Galilee porch* was added to the w. in the C14, the upper room being a Lady chapel that was probably used by one of the two village *guilds*. Its facade is very worn, with niches in the side buttresses and another one over the entrance, and the roof has its own *gargoyle*. The spacious churchyard allows a clear view of the impressive *Perpendicular* nave and s. *aisle*; the three-*light clerestory* windows have stepped *transoms* as do the tall windows of the aisle whose buttresses are decorated with *flushwork* panels – all, that is, except two in the centre which, with a section of the wall, were replaced

in red brick. The C13 *chancel* windows on the s. side have *plate tracery* which has been partially filled in, and the *priest's door* has single shafts below a renewed arch. The bold triple-lancet e. window is C19 work but round the corner on the n. side one of the three tall lancets is original. All the nave windows look as though they were renewed in the C19 and the finely moulded n. door has large *Tudor Roses* in the *spandrels*.

Entry is normally via the Galilee porch and tower, and you will see that one of the *imposts* of the inner arch is crudely decorated with diagonal lines on the chamfer. Above it there is a tiny slit *sanctus-bell window* in the wall. The early-C15 nave arcades are beautifully proportioned, with *quatrefoil piers* whose *capitals* are decorated with angels, *acanthus* leaves, or vine trails, each within bands of narrow mouldings enriched with tiny *paterae*. The pattern is repeated on the chancel arch but all the angels have been defaced unfortunately. Overhead, the roof has alternate *tie-beams* and *hammerbeams*, all *embattled*, and tenons projecting from the hammers indicate that there were originally angels on them. Some of the small stone *corbels* below the *wall posts* have been renewed. The nave floor is patterned with a *herringbone* of local red and yellow bricks and there are small diamond rosette tiles at the intersections. Part of the restoration work in 1871, the floor was a product of Debenham's only C19 industry and is remarkably attractive. The benches date from the same time. By the s. door stands the memorial to the Revd. John Simson, who died in 1697. His handsome half-length marble effigy stands within an arched niche with one hand raised, the other on his breast. His face is full and fat, his hair falls to his shoulders, and one astonished *putto* sits on an adjoining ledge, his twin having fallen off. With a flaming urn on top, the surround displays a selection of Latin tags, and the black marble top of the table tomb below carries a long English epitaph which is worth reading as an illustration of the contemporary attitude to funeral monuments. In case the deceased's scholarship should be in doubt the base carries a line of Greek below another epitaph in Latin. Nearby stands a C14 chest with scrolled straps, and the C15 *font* is over by the n. door. It is very worn, and defaced shields alternate with *Evangelistic symbols* in the bowl panels. The candle-snuffer cover is C19. A wooden chiming drum from a clock mechanism stands by the nearest arcade pillar, together with a decayed section of C17 *communion rails*. There are fragments of medieval glass gathered together in one of the n. aisle windows, and although the *piscina* at the e. end is a jumble of bits and pieces, there is a fine bishop's head of about 1300 at the top and shields in the spandrels. Across on the s. aisle wall is an oval tablet for the Revd. John Davie who died aged 36 in 1813. His father was master of Sidney Sussex and vice-chancellor of Cambridge University, but the ambiguous wording could have you thinking the son held those posts, but for his age. A restored piscina at the e. end of the s. aisle shows that there was an *altar* here, and an C18 Lord's Prayer board stands on the windowsill. To the l., a generous doorway leads to the *rood stair*, and moving back into the nave you will see that although the top exit is blocked, the heavy, embattled *rood beam* still spans the chancel arch.

The arch itself is interesting because the C15 builders reused it by inserting extra sections of shaft and new capitals above the old caps, thus raising the whole thing to marry with their nave. Before leaving the nave, have a look at the *Stuart* pulpit. It stands on a modern stone base, but the panels are well carved with typical blind arches and strapwork. Behind it on the wall is a plain tablet by Robert Tovell whose work is not uncommon in the county. It commemorates Robert Green, a young lieutenant of marines who fell at the battle of Trafalgar while serving in the *Royal Sovereign*, and his brother Samuel of the Madras Native Infantry who succumbed in 1818. The second phase of restoration in 1883 dealt with the chancel but the floor levels remained unchanged and there is a step down from the nave. The 1909 glass in the centre s. window has figures of the *Blessed Virgin* and *St Columba* (the only representation of him in the county) The *Annunciation* panel has Our Lady dressed in red and green rather than blue, for a change, and the message comes via a ray of light instead of the usual figure of *Gabriel*. St Columba bears a dove on his shoulder, and both colour and composition are pleasing; the maker is unknown. Farther along is the large tomb of Sir Charles Framlingham, who died in 1595. He lies in full armour alongside his wife, who wears a huge ruff and bulky skirt whose voluminous folds only show at the end round her feet. There is *Renaissance* detail on the chest, with remains of two figures within shallow niches. Large shields with innumerable quarterings decorate the ends and there is a full *achievement* within an architectural frame on the wall above – no trace of colour anywhere. On the wall overhead hang two *hatchments*, that of Lady Mary Gawdy (1691), daughter of the Earl of Desmond, to the r.,

and Sir Charles Gawdy's to the l. This has attractive heraldry within a *cartouche* and, having been used at his funeral in 1650, it is one of the earliest in the county. On the wall by the priest's door is Sir Charles's coffin plate. These are seldom seen, and this one is memorable for the lengthy epitaph. He was 'blessed in the happie choice of a most vertuous wife', and he 'lived and died a zealous professor of the reformed religion settled and established in the reigne of Qu' Elizabeth by Act of Parliament'. He had 'an undaunted loyalty to his Sovereigne Charles the First which he frequently manifested by espousing his cause and quarrell to ye uttermost hazard of his life and Fortune'. The restored C13 piscina in the *sanctuary* lies under a steep gable and *trefoil* arch. Debenham's bells are some of the mellowest in Suffolk and the beauty of the 'Debenham roll' is appreciated far and wide. With a reputation of being the best eight in the county they have always been popular with ringers. They are rung from the floor of the tower and as you leave, have a look at the peal boards on the walls – an early long length of 10,080 changes of Bob Major was rung in 1767, and in 1892 there was a record peal of 16,088 Oxford Treble Bob which was rung in 10hrs. 32mins. and thoroughly deserved the stone tablet.

Denham, St John the Baptist (F3): The church is set apart from the hamlet a short way down a narrow lane in pleasant, open countryside. There is now no trace of a tower and the w. wall is of red brick plastered over, with a small *Perpendicular* window set within it. The little n. door has no *porch* and at some time heavy brick buttresses were added on that side. Further to the e. there was once a chapel and the large arch that linked it with the *nave* remains in the wall, filled with red brick. A small *vestry* was added to the n. side of the late-C13 *chancel*, possibly at the time of a major restoration in 1873, and the e. window in *Tudor* form is of the same period. The square-headed side windows have *ogee* shapes in the *tracery*, and the *priest's door* has a continuous deep roll moulding and simple *dripstone*. Two more heavy red brick buttresses were added close together where the chancel joins the nave on the s. side, and they stand on the foundations of the *rood loft* stair turret; between them you will see part of the little upper doorway that gave access to the rood. Judging by the shape of the outer arch, the tall brick *porch* dates from the C17, and that may be a clue to the age of the other brickwork. There is a *scratch dial* on the e.

jamb of the inner doorway dating from a time when there was no porch, and a C13 closing ring has survived on the door itself.

The roof of the nave has continuous *arch-braces* which rise to stub posts under the ridge, and below the w. window is a most interesting inscription. The Latin text translates: 'William de Kirksby, Prior of Norwich placed me here. On whose soul may God have mercy Amen.' He was prior from 1280 to 1290 and the parish was one of the Benedictines' benefices. The small, oblong slab of stone was originally outside in the e. wall and its new position will ensure that the inscription remains legible. There is a C15 angel in yellow stain holding a scroll in the tracery of the window above, together with a few simply patterned *quarries*. The bowl of the octagonal *font* carries an inscription recording its restoration in 1876, and across the nave you will find that the n. doorway still has its drawbar in a deep slot. Nearby stands a bell cast by John Darbie of Ipswich in 1614, and that implies that the tower was still standing in the early C17. The arch with its triple shafts that led to the C13 n. chapel shows up boldly, and just beyond, under a low arch, lies a lovely late-C13 stone effigy of a lady. She was probably a member of the Bedingfield family and her tomb may have been in the chapel originally. The figure is only 4ft. 4in. long, and she wears a typical headdress of the period graced by a chaplet decorated with little roses and shields; her hands clasp a heart to her breast, and her feet rest on a mutilated but still recognisable lion. Two small angels each support her head with a wing; see how the naked foot of the nearer one is exposed as he kneels. There is no sign of the rood stair inside the church and the medieval *screen* itself has gone. Over the chancel arch hangs a framed set of Charles I *Royal Arms*. Well painted on board, with lively mantling, it is rated the best of the five in the county from that period.

The choir stalls in the chancel are C19, but they made use of C14 bench ends with *poppyheads*, and against the wall on both sides there are three stalls with *misericords*. They have leaf supporters and plain pendant centres, and 'T.B.' inscribed his initials on one of them on the s. side in 1719. A *ledger-stone* under the *altar* shows the outline of a *brass* which commemorated Edward Bedingfield, who died in 1574. There is a rubbing displayed in the vestry which shows his 25in. figure clad in a long gown trimmed with fur above a clear inscription. It was engraved on the back of an older Flemish brass which was made for Jacobus Weghescbede,

a religious of the abbey of Bergues St Winock. The extraordinary thing is that another section of this brass was put to similar use in 1580 for a tomb in the church at Yealhampton, Devon. That displays the heads of the *Blessed Virgin, St James*, and Weghescbede. One can only assume that the original was taken from its tomb and used in a London workshop to provide the two memorials in Devon and Suffolk. The brass is not displayed but may be seen by arrangement.

Denham, St Mary (F3): Extensively C19 restorations have left the tower and the s. side of the church looking like new work, with a regular flint pebble finish, but the n. wall of the *nave* was left alone and there the blocked door has an unadorned *Norman* arch. The *chancel* e. window has simple *Decorated tracery*, matching windows in the nave and tower, while within the largely restored s. *porch* there is a C14 doorway. In the C17 a large mortuary chapel in red brick was added to the n. of the chancel and its roof is as high as the rest. Within, there is a large, plain C14 *font* and the tower arch has a tall C19 wooden screen. The modern roofs rest on stone head *corbels* which are varied and appear to be original. There is no *screen* in the wide chancel arch and the *sanctuary* walls are clad with C17 panelling which was decorated with coloured stencil patterns in the C19 or a little later. Three plain arches take up the whole of the chancel n. wall and give access to the side chapel containing two tombs of considerable interest. In 1605 Sir Edward Lewkenor and his wife Susan died within two days of each other of the smallpox, that C17 scourge, and the size of the chapel was probably dictated by their enormous tomb. The chest stands below a heavy canopy supported on six *Corinthian* columns rising from tall plinths decorated with strapwork. There are four *cartouches* of arms in the cornice and a full *achievement* above is supported by a pyramid of strapwork between tall obelisks. Figures of the family kneel in pairs on the chest – Sir Edward and his two sons bareheaded in armour, his wife and three of her daughters wearing caps with long black flaps at the back; the three younger daughters have close bonnets. All the figures are stiff, with little individual character. Much of the original colour survives but the paint of the long Latin epitaph on the bottom panels has partially worn away. In contrast, the nearby tomb of Sir Edward's grandson is beautiful. He was another Sir Edward, also falling victim to smallpox in 1635 as the last of his line, and the monument was sculpted three years later by *John and Matthias Christmas*. The side panels of the alabaster tomb chest are carved with shields set within a combination of wings and scrolls, with cherub heads over each. The heavy black slab is supported by coloured marble columns, and on it, the recumbent 5ft. effigy in gleaming, polished marble is in almost perfect condition. It is dressed in full armour with a wide lace collar and lies on a straw mat. The features are finely modelled and one hand rests limply on the breast. Behind his head is an oval *touchstone* tablet between black marble columns together with his coat of arms; two *putti* recline on the curving *pediment* above with a skull between them.

Dennington, St Mary (G4): This is a church to delight the visitor, with a host of interesting and beautiful things to discover. Its position makes it a focal point in the village, and a circuit of the spacious churchyard is a rewarding way to begin. The walls of the early-C15 tower are a pleasing mixture of mottled stone and flint, and a substantial stair turret at the n.e. corner rises above the brick battlements. Above the slim *Perpendicular* w. window, a trio of niches have *ogee* arches decorated with *crockets* and *finials*, and their proportions suggest that they may have been designed to contain a *rood* group like the one at Parham. The s. *aisle* dates from the late C14, and a fragment of *Norman chevron* carving near the s. door shows that the masons made use of material from an earlier building. There is a *scratch dial* on the buttress nearby, and note the change in the window *tracery* at the e. end of the aisle. Below the steep, leaded *nave* roof, the small *clerestory* windows are widely spaced. The long *chancel*, with its gabled buttresses, is early C14, and the windows have attractive *reticulated* tracery and worn *headstops* (the one exception is protected by the e. wall of the s. aisle). The *priest's door* is heavily moulded and has a bishop's head at the top of the arch. A two-storied *sacristy* was added to the n. side of the chancel in the late C15, plain and bluff in red brick. The n. aisle matches its partner, and entry is by way of a tall early-C15 *porch*, its archway flanked by *flushwork* panels, and with three worn niches above.

Moving to the spacious interior, there are lofty C14 *arcades* of five bays, and the 1890s 'Father Willis' organ stands in front of the tower arch; it came from Tottenham in 1967, but the Victorian case belonged to Ipswich St Margaret's until the 1870s. The early-C15 *font* now stands in front of the s. door; its shaft is panelled and

there is matching tracery in the bowl panels, alternating with shields in *quatrefoils*. The attractive C16 pyramid cover is, painted dark blue and green, with touches of gilt; its angles are *crocketted* and the splendid foliage *finial* has a dove pecking at the fruit. There is a *stoup* recess by the s. door, and overhead hangs a set of George III *Royal Arms*, with 'John Edwards Churchwarden 1785' writ large on the frame. The nave roof dates from about 1430 and is an unusual variation of the single-framed and braced design. It seems that its width prompted the designer to use two *collars* rather than one for each principal; in addition, he added a series of ribs that curve up from *wall posts* halfway to the ridge. Overall, the closely spaced frames create a lattice effect, and at the w. end one can just see the *sanctus-bell window* in the tower wall. The aisle roofs have solid *arch-braces*, unusually decorated with tracery patterns, and the rafters have been coloured and stencilled. There are *Decalogue* boards in the s. aisle, matched by a pair of charity boards on the n. side.

Dennington possesses one of the finest ranges of C15 benches in the county. They occupy the rear half of the nave and aisles, and the ends are carved with exceptionally intricate and varied tracery, crowned with handsome *poppyheads*. There are remains of animals and figures on the buttresses, and look particularly for the following: nave – 2nd and 6th on r. lions; 4th on l. *harpy*?; n. aisle – 2nd on r. *pelican in her piety*; 3rd on r. giraffe?; 5th on r. caparisoned dog or bear wearing a saddle; 1st on l. *siren?*; 5th on l. hare; 6th on l. (by wall) seated angel; s. aisle – 4th on r. mermaid; 5th on r. tortoise (rare, possibly unique example); the bench at the e. end along the wall has a stooping eagle and a double-headed eagle. The seats are gnarled, and the backs are beautifully carved with a twisted leaf motif above a deep foliage trail. The 6th bench end on the r. of the nave is the only one that is not traceried, and it is one of the church's special treasures, for it bears the only carving of a sciapod to be found in England. This fabulous creature had only one foot, but it was so large that he could use it as a sunshade, and Pliny wrote of his 'great pertinacity in leaping'. The carver obviously thought that one foot was a bit silly and so he gave him two and, in addition, carved three round objects under his arm. There have been various theories about these, but in the Westminster *bestiary* the sciapod is shown with some Brachmani, miniature cave dwellers peering out of their holes; the Dennington craftsman had probably seen a similar illustration

Dennington, St Mary: Sciapod bench end

and popped them in for good measure. The main range of *box pews* in the e. half of the nave were installed in 1765, and those with hat pegs nearest the pulpit were added in 1805. The pulpit itself cost £3.11.8d in 1625, and stands on a centre post, with four curiously angled shafts rising under the skirt. The *blind-arched* panels are decorated with split turning and sharply profiled lozenges, and there is a little strapwork. After three years the pulpit was converted into a three-decker, and the *clerk's* pew is set at an angle at floor level. The reading desk laps round the pulpit, and its book ledge is supported by scrolls (one of which continues cleverly over the entrance door).

There are some interesting items displayed in the n. aisle, including a dinky little C14 iron-clad safe with three locks and two handles. In front of it stands a fascinating relic from the days when village children were taught in the chancel. It is a sand table – a shallow tray 8ft. x 11in., on trestles, filled with fine sand in which letters could be traced and then obliterated with the boards shaped like plasterers' floats. Bob Reeve, the sexton in 1894, was the last to learn on it. The tower clock mechanism nearby served the church faithfully from 1675 until 1948, and its long pendulum which lies behind had a two-second swing. The C18 *bier* with drop handles standing alongside still has its leather securing straps. The

n. aisle windows contain interesting and attractive 1850s glass made by Mr Woolnough, a Framlingham plumber and glazier. His tulip and vine design in greenish blue is set in striated glass, with a roundel at the top of each *light* containing a *Sacred monogram* or crowned 'M' for the church's patron saint.

Dennington is renowned for its *parclose screens*, the finest and most complete in the county. Matching doorways in the aisle walls have crocketted ogee arches with slender flanking pinnacles, and the stairs lead to the lofts which are still in place around the aisle chapels. Only the base of the *rood screen* remains, but there are passages through the walls that led to its loft, and it was possible to enter the loft in one aisle and traverse the entire width of the church. The screens themselves are beautiful – pairs of ogee arches in each light, *cusped* and crocketted, with leafy terminals, and delicate tracery filling the upper spaces. The lofts are intact, and their 4ft high parapets have a variation of the same tracery design in miniature, with a line of cresting above and below. The redecoration dates from 1800, and does scant justice to the original, with fawn paint taking the place of gilding. Two wings project westward from the base of the rood screen, to form small chapels on either side of the entrance to the chancel. C18 or early-C19 panelling was added to create two manorial pews e. of the pulpit. The n. aisle chapel is dedicated to the *Blessed Virgin*, and one of its C15 benches has a crowned 'M' carved on the end. The s. aisle chapel of *St Margaret* is dominated by the Bardolph tomb, and was extended by a few feet in the 1440-50s to make room for the monument. It is entirely of alabaster, and the chest has canopied niches that once contained figures. On top lie the splendid effigies of William, Lord Bardolph and his wife Joan, with all the colouring and gilding meticulously restored. He was Henry VI's Chamberlain and died in 1441, having fought valiantly under Henry V at Harfleur and Agincourt; as a Knight of the Garter, the insignia with its well-known motto is proudly born below his knee. His head rests on a feathered helm, an eagle crouches at his feet, and note the Sacred monogram on the hilt of his sword and on the chaplet round his helmet. Lady Bardolph wears the fashionable horned headdress enhanced by jewels, and her head rests on a pillow supported by angels; her blue mantle is lined with red, and a vigorous green and gold *wyvern* lies at her feet. Both figures wear the *collar of SS*, but the lady takes the place of honour on the r. because Lord Bardolph derived his title from her. When Adrian Bell and his friend Alfred Munnings were in the church one summer's day, the artist gave a woman half a crown to wash Lord Bardolph's face, so taken was he by the beauty of the effigy. Having seen outside that the chapel s. window differed from the rest, you will find that it has a heavily cusped inner arch, blind panelling above, crowns and shields in the moulding, and handsome flanking pedestals. It forms a canopy for the tomb chest below, whose occupant remains unidentified. There is a tall image niche to the l. of the *altar,* and the wide *piscina* has an *aumbry* alongside. The Bardolphs were succeeded by the Rous family as Lords of the Manor, and high on the s. wall of the chapel is the memorial for Sir Thomas Rous who died in 1619, and his wife Parneil. Their small, well sculpted figures face each other across a prayer desk in the convention of the period, with a skull for company, three shields above the cornice, and jolly little cupid's head below the epitaph.

The early-C14 chancel windows are exceptionally good, with richly moulded arches, and inner *hood moulds* coming down to delicate *stops*; the *jamb shafts* have beautiful *capitals* – look particularly for the long-eared owls and a *green man* on the s. side, a woman bearing flowers on the n., and fighting dogs or boars on the n. side of the e. window. The priest's door has an unusual combination of stops – a bishop's head on the r., and a pope's head on the l. The latter wears the C13 form of papal tiara , and this is one of the very few pre-*Reformation* carvings of a pope that have survived. The C14 iron-banded chest nearby was formed from a solid tree-trunk, now much eaten away, and the *communion rails* have elegantly turned *balusters*. They are said to date from 1750, but joins in the top rail show that they were once three-sided, and I would call

Dennington, St Mary:
William, Lord Bardolph's effigy

them an amended late-C17 set. The original C14 piscina remains, and beside it is a second, later version which has been shorn of most of its decoration but retains tracery which matches the *sedilia* bay to the w. The latter has a sharply gabled arch, with tall, crocketted pinnacles each side and heavy finials. Dennington has yet another rarity hanging above the *High altar* – a medieval *pyx canopy,* one of only four in England. The wooden 5ft. spirelet had a lower section which contained the Blessed Sacrament reserved for the sick, and it has been restored to its original use, with the replica pyx curtained below the canopy. The s. *sanctuary* window is filled with C19 glass by the *O'Connors,* and there are considerable remains of early-C14 glass in the other chancel windows – excellent canopies, borders, lots of little window designs incorporated, and fine leaf work in the tracery. An attractive *Arts & Crafts* banner of *St George* stands in the back of the sedilia, and on the s. wall of the chancel the village memorial to the dead of World War I has three bas-relief panels in bronze by Henry Binney – 'The call', 'The response', and 'The final call'. Above the sacristy door, Anna Wright's little latin epitaph of 1621 is followed by:

This virgins love to heaven made hir aspire,
Loathing ye drosse of sinfull worlds desire.

There is a *brass* inscription in the floor nearby for Elizabeth Barker (1613), and two more lie under the matting in the nave – for John and Elizabeth Hersant (1568/85), and Henry Edgar (1619). Lastly, as you go, note the rather nice little brass plate below the n. aisle w. window; it records the charity of a London merchant, Nathan Wright, a son of the rector who died in 1654. Dennington has a grand old ring of six bells and the third was cast by the Norwich founder Richard Baxter in the early C15. The 19 cwt. tenor came from the Ipswich foundry of Alfred Bowell in the late C19 or early C20.

Denston, St Nicholas (B5): This is one of the finest of the smaller village churches in the county, a noble building, full of interest. The late-C14 tower, with its chequered *base course,* is rather overwhelmed by the magnificence of the rest – rebuilt on a larger scale in the last half of the C15. It displays the full flowering of the *Perpendicular* style, with great *transomed* windows letting the light flood in, *aisles* that match the unbroken length of *nave* and *chancel,* and buttresses of *ashlar.* There are *priest's doors* n. and

s. below truncated windows, and two *scratch dials* can be found on the buttress to the w. Another is found high on the central nave buttress still with the remains of its original pointer. On the n. side, an octagonal *rood stair* turret with battlemented top, complete with its own *gargoyle*, rises to the level of the aisle roof. It is sited two bays from the e. end, but once inside you will see that the *rood screen* is one bay further w. A bridge along the wall once connected the stair with the *rood loft*. For a building of such quality this would seem to be a surprising gaffe but it is probably because circumstances changed just before or just after the main structure was completed. In 1475 a *chantry* college was founded under the will of John Denston, with three priests living in a house, part of which is now the cottage to the w. of the church. Although the status of the parish church was not changed, the building had to be adapted so that the master of the college and his two brethren could celebrate 'for ever the divine offices day by day' for the souls of John Denston and Katherine his wife. Thus a choir of two bays was needed, arranged in collegiate fashion, and the screen separating it from the

Denston, St Nicholas: Tabard

parish church proper was placed to the w. of it. This may well have been chosen by the executors as a way of avoiding an eastward extension. There are echoes of Long Melford's opulence here – understandable because Katherine was a Clopton before her marriage, and portraits of the couple can be found in the n. aisle there. The chantry survived until 1547 when, like the rest, its assets were seized by the Crown. The *porch* is not so grand as the rest and was perhaps adapted from the old building, although its roof is beautifully *fan vaulted*, an uncommon distinction in Suffolk. To the r. of the door there is a fine *stoup* with a *castellated* top, set in the buttress angle like the one at Hawkesdon.

Passing through the original *traceried* double doors one steps into an interior where all the virtues of Perpendicular architecture are displayed, but on an intimate scale. It impresses but does not overwhelm, and stands unchanged to all intents and purposes. Tall *arcades*, their mouldings flowing uninterrupted from base to peak, march from end to end, and the wall above them is broken only by the widely spaced *clerestory* windows and a plain *string course*. The cambered *tie-beams* and heavy timbers of the low pitched roof are beautifully pale, enhancing the sense of space and light below. There is foliage on the *spandrels* and large lions, hounds and hares prance on the *wall plates*. Of all the *Seven Sacrament fonts* in East Anglia this is the only one carved in an oatmeal-coloured stone (imported from Aubigny in Normandy, according to *Cautley*) the bowl panels are compressed within plain roll mouldings. As at Woodbridge and Great Glemham, the scenes are set against rayed backgrounds, and they are of particular interest despite their harsh mutilation. From the e. clockwise, the sacraments are: mass, penance (note the C15 practice of the confessor sitting in the special shriving pew, with an attendant holding a book), confirmation, extreme unction (with the sick bed tilted so that one can look down on it), Crucifixion (Christ's figure obliterated), ordination, matrimony, and baptism (priest behind the font and parents to the l., the mother wearing a *butterfly headdress* which gives a date between 1450 and 1485). There is a medieval screen in the tower arch and above, the *Royal Arms* of Queen Anne are well-painted on board. Note that the arcade pillars stand on rubble bases that probably formed part of the old nave walls, and then turn your attention to the fine set of low C15 benches standing on substantial sills designed to keep the foot-warming straw or rushes in place. The

Denston, St Nicholas

two ranges at the front of the n. side are C19 copies but there are over 50 grotesques sitting on the castellated caps and elbows of the bench ends. Seek out the *unicorn*, the *cockatrice*, the fox and goose, and particularly the elephant, whose fan-shaped ears and long nose demonstrate a brave attempt at imagining the unbelievable. The relatively narrow aisles were designed for processions but C18 *box pews* were inserted on the s. side. Beyond them is part of a set of *altar rails* with another section in the n. aisle, near a plain *Stuart Holy table*.

The high-silled *rood screen* stretches the whole width of the church, with excellent tracery and an attractive leaf trail along the top. There would have been *altars* at each side, and overhead the massive moulded and castellated *rood beam* remains, on which stood the Calvary flanked by figures of the *Blessed Virgin* and *St John*. The pulpit is C17 and beyond the screen on the s. side there is a raised pew behind a *parclose screen*, with C17 panelling on the outer wall. Strangely, the gates by the priest's door are a C17 wooden imitation of wrought-iron. The e. window is full of myriad fragments of Norwich C15 glass

which has been restored and re-ordered in the past few years – good examples of *green man* illustrations are to be found there. The church abounds in memorials of the Robinson family, and in the s. aisle chapel there hangs a real treasure. It is the splendidly restored C15 Robinson heraldic tabard, bearing the family's arms beneath a helm topped by a gigantic stag. The lovely stalls in the chancel are arranged so that four face e. backing on to the screen, and these have *misericords*. Three of them are carved with flowers but the fourth, on the n. side, is a rare and excellent carving of a crane, recognised by the stone that it holds with one foot. The *bestiary* taught that cranes always slept with one of their number standing sentinel, with a stone clutched in its raised claw which would fall and wake it should it inadvertently drop off. The chamfers of the stalls are decorated with *paterae* and there are large *fleurons* beneath the lip of the sloping book ledge; a low and narrow ledge for boys runs along the fronts, pierced with *quatrefoils* below. The late-C17 *communion rails* have nice, twisted *balusters*, with sets of four as gate posts, and beyond them on the n. side is a large tomb with a *Purbeck marble* top from which the *brasses* have been reaved. Within the open arches lie two figures as in death, their shrouds gathered in a topknot and held by heavily tasselled cords. The man's emaciated chest is bared and although the identity of both figures has vanished with the brasses it is possible that this key position in the church was reserved for John and Katherine Denston, the founders of the chantry. Across on the s. side, Robert de Carle the younger made a tomb to match in 1822 (except that it is solid and has no grisly cadavers) for the Robinson family. It has a polished black marble top and side panels with epitaphs and a shield of arms in an oval. There is a very good and important brass in the centre of the chancel, with 26in. figures, for Henry Everard who died in 1524 and his wife Margaret. This is the only heraldic pair on separate brasses that survives in Suffolk. Henry Everard wears an heraldic tabard over his armour, and a helm with a large head as a crest lies tilted behind his head; his wife wears a *kennel headdress* and an heraldic mantle displaying her husband's and her father's arms. Two of the four shields remain and, like the tabard, they were once inlaid with enamel. In the n. chapel there is an inscription for William Bird (1591) and his wife Mirable. Note that this is fixed to a stone which still bears two of its five *consecration crosses*, showing that it was the original *High altar mensa*. There is a third brass in the centre of the nave, with an 18in. figure of a late-C15 lady in a kennel headdress (probably Felice, the wife of Roger Drury of Hawstead who died in 1481). There is some attractive modern glass in the s. aisle; in the e. window is a *St Nicholas* theme by Martin Travers of 1932. In the centre the saint cradles Denston church, on the r. is a medieval ship with sailors in modern sou'westers, and on the l. the cook flees in alarm as the saint blesses the boys in the tub. The 1914 window of Christ in Glory, with the Blessed Virgin and the two Marys, is by *Heaton, Butler & Bayne*. As you leave you will see two *hatchments* on the aisle w. walls – the n. aisle for John (or possibly William) Robinson 1818 or 1826, the s. aisle for Rebecca, the wife of Lieut. Gen. John Robinson who died in 1795.

Depden, St Mary (B5): There is no road to this church and the footpath takes off somewhat obscurely from the section of superceded main road by the junction to Depden Green. Then follows a pleasant ten-minute walk through copses and by fields but, for this reason, preliminary enquiries about the key are advised. The building was badly damaged by fire in June 1984, when the *nave* was gutted and lost its roof. Fortunately neither the *chancel* nor the tower were seriously affected and it was not long before restoration was put in hand. Under the direction of the Whitworth partnership the work was excellently done by Valient & Sons, who received a well-earned award from the Suffolk Association of Architects. The church was re-consecrated by the diocesan bishop in October 1985 and it is now a beautiful little building in a delectable setting. The body of the church is late C13 or early C14, and the chancel corner buttresses have steep ledges and oddly restored pinnacles. The plain C15 tower has a flint chequer *base course* and a stair turret to the s., and entry is by way of a wooden C17 n. *porch* whose *balustrated* sides have been boarded over. The door is medieval with close-set mouldings. Within are tiled floors and modern chairs, and the new roof is carried on pairs of clamped trusses which sweep in a Gothic curve up to the ridge, their apricot colour showing up well against the white ceilings. The s. door is *Norman*, with scallop *capitals* to the thick shafts and a zig-zag bobbin mould in the arch. You will find a *consecration cross* incised halfway up the e. *jamb*. The porch has been rebuilt as a *vestry* and is separated from the nave by a plate glass door, which is effective and attractive. Beyond the tall tower arch there are nicely restored *Hanoverian Royal Arms* of 1836 lettered with the rector's and warden's names. A charity board signed by the same warden hangs opposite. Below is a plain *Stuart Holy table* and there are a few of the old benches that were saved from the fire at the w. end, some with broad *traceried* ends. The octagonal *font* is a rare early-C18 model, and the shaped bowl has four carved *cartouches* painted with arms. The nave windows have 'Y' tracery and there is now no *screen* in the wide chancel arch. To the l. is a tall *Decorated* niche, *groined* and embellished with *paterae* on the chamfers but the canopy and pinnacles have been cut away. It now contains a framed engraved portrait of Anthony Sparrow, the late-C17 bishop of Norwich, who was born here. Nearby is a fine *brass* set within a pair of shallow arches and framed by a crested panel on the wall. There are two pairs of figures kneeling at faldstools, each with a shield above, and it is an interesting composite memorial for Anne Drury and her two husbands. The first was George Waldegrave (on the l.) who is shown with their five sons, the eldest of whom was active in Queen Mary's cause. Waldegrave died in 1528 and his widow married Sir Thomas Jermyn, High Sheriff of

Norfolk and Suffolk and rebuilder of Rush-brooke church where he was buried. The Lady Anne died in 1572 and her two effigies are similar but not identical; there is a long Gothic lettered inscription and the brass is in perfect condition. The early-C14 *piscina* in the *sanctuary* is exceptionally nice. It has a pair of tall *trefoiled lancets* with pierced *spandrels*, and a *quatrefoil* over two layers of mouldings. Although there are two compartments there is only one drain. The e. window is tall and thin, and within the *reticulated* tracery there are two fine coats of Royal Arms of Henry VII and Victoria, enamel painted in C16 style. Just below there are large C14 canopies and then two German or Flemish C16 panels in the centre. Look for the little man trudging off with the ladder in the background of the scene where Christ is lowered from the cross, and for *St Veronica* in the bottom r. of the painting of Christ carrying the cross. There are four more contemporary panels of confused fragments and some Flemish roundels. On the s. wall is a memorial by de Carle of Bury for Sarah Lloyd, the rector's wide, who died in 1838 – a sarcophagus on which a drape falls realistically over the epitaph cut below. The panels of the modern oak *altar* are pierced with C15-style tracery which is very handsome.

Drinkstone, All Saints (D4): The brick tower peeps over surrounding trees from a distance, a replacement dating from 1694 with round-headed bell openings and stepped battlements. There is a tablet on the w. face that says the minister, Thomas Cambourne, left money for its building and for the bells. Below is a tall C19 *lancet* that was probably part of the extensive 1860s restoration by *Edward Hakewill*. He re-roofed the *nave* and provided a new e. window in the C14 *chancel*. The large three-*light* window in its s. wall with flowing *tracery* and worn *headstops* may have been in the e. wall originally. The other chancel windows have single *reticulation* tracery shapes and there are *Perpendicular* windows in the *aisles*. Hakewill provided three new *quatrefoil*, *clerestory* windows on each side (which possibly repeated an original arrange-ment). There is a little C14 *priest's door* on the n. side and in the r.-hand *jamb* of the aisle door a section of a *churchyard cross* shaft has been inserted upside down. Under the eaves of the s. aisle wall is a late example of a *rebus*. Simon Cocksedge died in 1751 and a small cockerel struts on the top of his tablet. Beside it is an enterprising *cartouche* with arms, drapes and cherubs, but the inscription is worn away. The *porch* was

rebuilt in 1872 and to the r. of the C14 inner doorway there is a small *stoup* under a *cusped* and *crocketted ogee* arch. The door itself is medieval, although the plain lapped boards have been backed and repaired at the bottom.

Just inside to the l. is a single *hatchment* and the C13 *font* stands on a step against the first pillar of the s. *arcade*. Its *Purbeck marble* bowl is a worn octagon with canted sides and pairs of shallow blind arches in the panels; it rests on a central shaft within a ring of columns. The base of the tower has been re-ordered to provide a cloakroom and a vestry. The *Decorated* arcades have tall, pointed arches rising from octagonal shafts and to the l. of the wide chancel arch is the *rood stair*, with narrow doorways and a stone newel rising to the full height within. There is a *Jacobean* chest at the w. end with a simple carving and a panelled top. Nearby are some medieval benches with *traceried* backs and battered *poppyheads*, one with the vestige of an angel holding a crown. The centre range of 1860s nave benches looks like the work of *Henry Ringham*. It contains some traceried ends and fine carvings on the arm rests (including a *pelican in her piety*, the dove of the ark with its olive branch, and a crowned eagle). The openwork C19 reading desk stands on an intriguing stone platform found beneath the floor of the old pews. Its edges are carved with *mouchettes* in circles and it has been variously described as part of a tomb chest, an *Easter sepulchre* moved from the chancel, and a preaching stone. I think the last is the most likely. A section of the floor here is paved with medieval tiles; two have lion designs, one has an heraldic shield, and four are placed to form a circle with an interlaced design. Behind the C19 pulpit there is a *squint* through to the e. end of the s. aisle, with *trefoil* ogees at each end, and although there is no *piscina* now there must originally have been an *altar* there. It was once flanked by statues and the mutilated remnants of the C14 pedestals remain on either side. The church's outstanding piece is the C15 *screen* which was at one time relegated to the w. end. The ogee arches of the main lights are double cusped and the tall crocketted *finials* reach to the top, backed by close panelled tracery; the centre arch is heavily cusped and crocketted and the stubby ogees above it are backed by roundels. The coved underside of the *rood loft* once sprang from the miniature pillars at the top of the buttresses, which themselves retain some stencil decoration. Much of the colour survives and is a clear example of how the artists followed the heraldic rules of alternating tinctures and metals (gold and silver). A link with the screen is to be found in the *sanctuary* where a narrow band of flowing tracery which may well have formed part of the rood loft has been fixed in the back of the *sedilia*. The piscina is C19 and the sanctuary floor is banded with Minton tiles. There is a contemporary oak *reredos* with heavy vine and wheat borders to the panels and a central oil painting depicts the sorrowing Christ. The rest of the wall panelling is C17 style but looks a good deal less than 300 years old. The e. window is filled with *Lavers & Barraud* glass of 1865. There are bright figures of Christ as Saviour of the world, the *Blessed Virgin, St John the Baptist*, and an old man with a raven (Elias?). There is some medieval glass too. On the s. side of the chancel is a C14 Christ in Majesty with four *censing* angels and three other figures. Opposite is a much restored figure of the Virgin, in the n. aisle e. window are C14 leaf forms and in the s. aisle are some fragments. While in the chancel, have a look at the pretty pair of late-C18 tablets flanking the priest's door. For Joshua and Jane Grigby, they have concave sides rising to large bas-relief urns, with coloured coats of arms within fronds at the bottom. Nearby, Elizabeth Motham's C17 *ledger-stone* uses the old form 'Burnt Eleigh' for Brent Eleigh. On the n. wall near the screen, a son of the rectory, with the resounding name of John Peloquin Cosserat, has his memorial. Shot in the mouth by a musket ball while leading the 1st Punjab Cavalry in the Indian Mutiny, he died at Lucknow in 1858. A similar penchant for detail crops up in the s. aisle where a small sarcophagus tablet by Joseph Kendrick for Capt. George Grigby records that he perished with 233 others en route for Cadiz when his trooper was run down by the frigate 'Franchise' in 1811. Drinkstone has a ring of six bells with a 10 cwt. tenor, but their condition only allows them to be rung occasionally.

Dunwich, St James (I3): It is not what you see, but what you can no longer see, that kindles the imagination and invites philosophic reflection at Dunwich. In the C7, *St Felix* founded the diocese of East Anglia here, and by the C12 a thriving sea port covered a square mile to the e. of the present cliff edge. In its prosperity, 4000 inhabitants worshipped in ten churches and three chapels, and there were three monastic houses. Even then, a constant battle was waged against the sea's encroachment, and by the end of the C14 five of the churches had been lost. The C17 saw the medieval town reduced to a

quarter of its size, and the last service was held in 1755 in the one remaining church of All Saints before it was dismantled in 1778. Its tower lasted until 1919, and all that is left on the cliff edge now is a single stone marking the grave of John Easey who died in 1826.

The leper hospital of *St James* was well inland from the medieval town, and in 1826 its grounds were chosen as the site for a new church which retained the old dedication. It was financed by the Barne family who had bought the Dunwich estate in 1754. Originally it was a classical design by Robert Appleton, with the tower topped by a tall stage likened to a pepper pot by the Suffolk historian Elisha Davy. It was consecrated in 1832 and in 1839 Frederick Barne decided to 'gothicise' the building by cladding it in flint, disguising the brick buttresses and inserting windows in *Decorated* style. He later added the chancel in 1881, and the tower was changed from round to square – slim and unbuttressed. As a result it looks like many another small country church of the period.

Very little of medieval Dunwich survives, but one tangible reminder can be seen on the wall just inside the entrance. Thomas Cooper was a C16 shipowner and merchant, four times chosen Bailiff, and he was buried in All Saints church. His *brass* was stolen in the C18, and a fragment found its way to Strangers' Hall museum in Norwich. It was returned here in 1927 and (with missing words added) reads:

Here Thomas Cooper, sutym baly of this
   towne, inclosed is in Clay
Which is the restynge place of fleash untill
   the latter day.
Of one sonne and daughters syx the Lord
   hym parent made
Ere cruell death did worke his spight or
   fickle life did fade.
Who deceassed ye XVII of maye in the yere
   of Our Lord 1576.

The neat, well-cared-for interior is typically Victorian in feeling, and the *arch-braced* pine roof of the *nave* rests on richly carved wooden *corbels*. The oak benches below have C15 style *poppyheads* excellently fashioned, and another interesting example of the carver's art is the panel framed on the n. wall. It features a pair of cranes within *acanthus* scrolls and is probably C19 or early C20. Mercifully, the *font* avoids the mid-C19 passion for 'gothicising' everything, and there is a set of seemly *Decalogue* panels on the w. wall. Appropriately, St Felix features in the tower w.

window, and in a s. nave window there are scenes illustrating the visit of the Magi and the text 'Suffer little children to come unto me'. The latter glass dates from about 1910 and is vaguely *Arts & Crafts* in character – possibly by George Maile & Son. Michael Barne is commemorated on the n. wall of the chancel – 'by his care and principally by the aid of his liberal contribution this church was erected in the year 1830'. The tablet, with a fine patrician head in profile, is by William Behnes, a popular and prolific sculptor whose career ended in penury in the gutter outside the Middlesex Hospital. Frederick Barne, last MP for Dunwich, was the benefactor who built the tower and chancel and changed the character of the rest of the church. His memorial by Samuel Dale of Saxmundham is on the n.. side of the *sanctuary* , a white marble *trefoil lancet* in *Early English* style. The *piscina* and *sedilia* are in the same mode, and above the *communion rail* on that side there is an unusual commemoration – a diamond-shaped brass recording that Jesse Kate Thompson received her last communion there on Easter Day, 1910. The glass in the e. window is an excellent example of *Hardman's* High-Victorian style, a Last Supper displaying typical figure work and making use of his favourite reds and blues; there are vine trails with angels in the *tracery*, and roundels of wheat and vine along the bottom. Dating from about 1860, it was re-set when the new chancel was built, and Hardman then provided the glass for the side lancets – the Magi on the n. side and a Crucifixion on the s.

The churchyard is a beguiling spot, and a sizeable portion of the *Norman* hospital church remains in the s.e. corner. It accommodates a vault for the Barne family and is railed off, but one can see the arches of an *arcade* in the chancel *apse*, and a complete window survives in the n. wall of the nave. Before All Saints finally succumbed to the sea, part of the n.w. tower buttress was carefully dismantled and rebuilt here by the s. boundary in 1923. Robert Easey's well-cut stone of 1793 rests against it, and by the path to the porch a stone of the 1980s demonstrates that the art is not yet dead, and that polished marble the colour of uncooked liver is not inevitable. A minor eccentricity of the 1840s is the cast-iron pedestal complete with urn that stands mantled with rust at the e. end of the chancel.

Earl Soham, St Mary (G4): Set attractively on slightly rising ground, the church presents its w. face to the village street and the tower is one of those whose proportions seem instinctively good, with four subtly proportioned *set-offs* and *flushwork* decoration in the *base course*, buttresses, and battlements. The w. doorway has *fleurons* in the mouldings, *Tudor Roses* in the *spandrels*, a niche each side of the w. window, and another above it. The latter is distinguished by a more elaborate canopy which has a little head pendant and there is a demi-angel below the image stool. Farther up a flushwork shield carries a *St Andrew's* cross, a reminder that the church was originally dedicated to that saint. The tower was built in the 1470s and its real distinction lies in the fact that it is one of the very few that are signed both by donor and builder, with inscriptions on the w. buttresses about 12ft. up. One would need a ladder and some patience to decipher them but they read: (n.w.) 'Campanilis eius thomus edouard fuit autor huius christopher simus optimus auxiliator' (Thomas Edward built this tower with Christopher his best helper); (s.w.) 'Ranulphus Colnitt bona maxima contulit isti ecclesiae sacrae cui prosit gratia christia' (Ranulph Colnett conferred the greatest gifts upon this sacred church; may the grace of Christ advantage this). The *nave* is cement-rendered and the 'Y' *tracery* windows with their worn *headstops* on the s. side of the *chancel* point to a date around 1300. Canon Abbay was rector from 1880 to 1928 and was responsible for much restoration work – the e. window has a *corbel* head which is a portrait of him, the other being Sir Aukland Colvin, the patron. There is a *priest's door* to the s. and the s.e. nave buttress has one complete *scratch dial* and traces of two more. The low C15 s. *porch* has late *Perpendicular* side windows and the tall medieval figure holding a staff on the gable may have been a statue of St Andrew. Below it is a worn rampant lion and a modern inscription: 'Christ who died upon the rood, grant us grace, our end be good'. Just inside, the stone block on the floor may have been the shaft of a *preaching cross*, and you will see shields bearing emblems of the *Trinity* and *instruments of the Passion* set against foliage in the spandrels of the inner doorway.

Within, there is a modern screen with massive turned uprights and false gallery front in the tower arch, and beyond it is a good C17 *Holy table*. The C15 *font* is a familiar local design, with squat lions seated round the shaft, angel heads below the bowl, and angels bearing shields in the panels – all effectively defaced. A Robert Kinge was apparently the donor but the inscription round the base is no longer legible. The C17 cover is in excellent condition, with solid scrolls reaching up to a turned *finial*. The nave was rebuilt in the C15 and given a handsome double *hammerbeam roof*, with carved spandrels and cambered *collar beams* carrying *king posts* under the ridge. The *wall posts* come down to niches under *ogee* canopies, and although the carved figures remain they have nearly all lost their heads. The C15 benches below were saved from demolition by Canon Abbay and were restored by Archdeacon Darling's group of woodworkers at Eyke. They caught the spirit of the originals so well that it is quite difficult to tell old from new in some cases. The ends are 3in. thick and have window tracery deeply carved in the solid; the large, squat *poppyheads* are flanked by animals and figures. Look particularly for the C15 figures on the 5th bench from the e., s. side – a man with a log on his shoulder and a woman setting up a sheaf of corn, and there is a good standing figure with a basket 4th from the e. on the n. side. For comparison, examples of the modern work are the two heads 6th from the w., n. side and the elephant against the s. wall. Nearby hangs a fine set of Charles II *Royal Arms* painted on canvas, and Gaffin provided a characteristic early-C19 tablet for members of the Hinde family on the n. wall – deep sarcophagus with urn and drooping willow branches on top. The pulpit is a pleasing *Jacobean* piece, tall, with blind arched panels and strapwork under the canted book ledge, and a hexagonal *tester* above the backboard. There is a little *piscina* in a recess close by marking the site of a nave *altar* and, although there is no drain, the cavity in the opposite wall was probably another. The chancel arch would seem to date from the time when the nave was rebuilt, and the concave faces of the *responds* are matched by the *capitals*. There is now no *screen* and just beyond on the r. is a window in memory of Canon Abbay with beautiful glass by *Margaret E. Aldrich Rope*, one of her last commissions. In glowing colours, *St Edmund* stands against a background of oak tree and flowers, while *St Felix* has a church on a cliff behind him. The *communion rails* have turned *balusters* below a heavy top rail and are probably late C17, and the tall C14 piscina has a hint of the ogee shape in the arch and remnants of *crocket* and *cusp* decoration. The excellent Jacobean chest in the n.w. corner has typical decoration like the pulpit but is longer than usual, with four rather than three front panels. The pallid 1880s glass in the e. window is not memorable but turning back one has a good view of the w. window – a much better design which may have been provided by *Burlison & Grylls*; the Bethlehem angels and shepherds fill

the centre of the three *lights*, and two of Christ's miracles flank a little vignette of Noah's ark below. St Mary's has a fine ring of six with a 10 cwt. tenor.

Earl Stonham, St Mary (F5): This is a cruciform church with *transepts* but there is no firm evidence to show whether or not it ever had a central tower, and a single *lancet* in the *chancel* n. wall is an indication that it was begun no later than the C13. Close by, a brick *rood stair* with blocked window is set in the corner. The n. transept was rebuilt and much work was done on the e. end generally in an 1870s restoration by Cory & Ferguson of Carlisle. There are no *aisles* and the *nave* was widened in the C14; then about 1460 it was given a lavish *clerestory* entirely paneled in *flushwork* so that the new roof should be well lit. The C15 tower replaced one that had stood at the s.w. corner of the church and the old w. window of the nave, with its *reticulated tracery*, was reused. Below it are doors with their original tracery, the archway has *paterae* and crowns in the mouldings, and there is a flushwork *base course*. Nicely graduated buttresses rise to the bell stage where one of the large *Perpendicular* bell openings is offset to leave room for the stair turret. They have a line of *quatrefoils* under them and there are stepped flushwork battlements with more quatrefoils ranged below them. The latter alternate with the device that identifies the masons as the Aldryche family of N. Lopham, Norfolk. The C14 s. *porch* has remnants of barge boards above a wide *trefoil* niche and the windows are set within large blank arches.

Passing the remains of a *stoup*, one enters a lofty interior dominated by a magnificent roof. Its *hammerbeams* are carved as angels (now minus their heads) bearing shields, some of which still have recognisable *Passion emblems* – the hammer and pincers are on the s. side above the door and there is a *chalice* and wafer representing the mass at the w. end on the n. side. The hammerbeams alternate with false hammer-beams whose posts continue down to form richly carved octagonal pendants which match those below the *collar beams* and *king posts*. Heavy *wall posts* with shields at their bases carry canopied figures, and the *wall plates* with demi-angels are widened by two more ranges of decoration. All *arch-braces* are richly carved – largely with leaf forms, but look for the fox with a goose in his mouth and a large duck on the s. side above the door. The tower now has a well-designed screen and a kitchen and cloakroom have been inserted. Above is the ringers' gallery and the bells have been lowered into the old ringing chamber. The church's excellent ring of six with its 9 cwt. tenor has recently been restored by Taylor's of Loughborough. On the tower wall a 1680s tablet for Thomas Goodall says that he was a true member of the Church of England, approving its discipline and practising its doctrine, and adds that his father-in-law was 'exemplary for piety towards God and loyalty to his martyred sovereign Charles I'. No doubt the widow had the wording of it! The C15 *font* has good carvings in the bowl panels: w., a seeded *pomegranate* within a crown of thorns, and an angel with a *Trinity emblem*; s., a pierced Sacred Heart within a wreath of leaves; n., a seeded rose; e., a lattice of ribbons with fleur-de-lys terminals. These are so like those at Creeting St Peter that both fonts must have been carved by the same mason. Most of the benches at the w. end are original and the worn inscription on the front elbow n. side reads: 'Orate pro [anima] Necolai Houk' (Pray for the soul of Nicholas Hook). The nave benches with varied *poppyheads* were made by local joiner James Gibbons in 1874 and carved by Robert Godbold of Harleston, Norfolk.

The early-C14 arches to the transepts have *paterae* in the mouldings, and above the chancel arch there is a *Doom* painting which is still recognisable. (As with the roof, binoculars are helpful for appreciation of the detail.) A small window was inserted just to the r. to give extra light for both Doom and rood. On the s. transept wall there is a large fragment of a *St George* painting and in the n. transept hang sketches of two more frescoes that have been destroyed. The pulpit of the 1680s is a good example of the period and the three unique *hour-glasses* that used to stand behind it are now housed securely elsewhere in the church. They contained differing amounts of sand to record a quarter, half, and three-quarters of an hour. The iron holder that remains held a standard hour-glass. The first range of choir stalls is Victorian and carries *Evangelistic symbols* but the others are medieval, with wide book slopes, and there are figures of a bagpiper, a man with an axe, and a *pelican in her piety* on the n., with remains of a *woodwose* and a dragon on the s. Two of the poppyheads are carved with triple faces like the one at Hawkedon and three of the stall fronts were adapted at an early stage to take tracery which probably came from the *rood screen*. The roof was remodelled in the 1870s restoration to match the nave roof, as were those in the transepts. In the *sanctuary* there is a C14

piscina under a *crocketted* gable, but note that the double drain slab was part of a C13 model. The *dropped-sill sedilia* alongside are divided by a stone arm rest carved with a hound (now minus his head). Across the n. wall a plain oblong recess served either as an *Easter sepulchre* or an *aumbry* and the cross at the back of it was found in the floor of the s. transept. Nearby is a most interesting chest of the late C13. Ironwork does not play an important part (as in the C14 Icklingham chest) and the roundels of chip carving are strongly reminiscent of *Norman* stonework. Henry Hughes of *Ward & Hughes* designed the e. window in 1874 – insipid figures of the risen Christ flanked by a Nativity and the *three Marys* at the tomb. The early-C17 *altar*, with its turned and carved legs, was probably a domestic table originally and has been cut down and extended for its present role.

East Bergholt, St Mary: (E7) Constable country attracts a host of visitors and many of them come to explore this beautiful and interesting church in the village where the artist was born. One of the pleasures of a tour of the churchyard is to identify the vantage points for his various paintings and sketches – from the s.w. in 1796, the n. arch of the tower 1806, from the n.e. 1818, and his first exhibited work in oils of the *porch*, possibly in 1810. The 1818 pencil sketch includes his parents' tomb which lies in the far n.e. corner of the churchyard – a broad, low slab resting on a wide plinth. The church's unique bell cage stood to the e. of the *chancel* until the late C17 when it was moved to its present position. It dates from the C16 and was probably a compromise solution when plans for completing the tower were abandoned. It sits attractively under a tiled pyramid roof, and the bells in their heavy frame can be seen through the lattice of the timbered walls. It is the only ring in the world that is handled by ringers standing on the frame and controlling the bells with wooden stays rather than ropes. The bells are the heaviest 'full circle' five in Britain with a 26 cwt. tenor, and for those who cannot be there when they are rung but would like to know how it is managed, the church's website shows them.

Turning to the church itself, we have a fine building that is both impressive and picturesque. There was an earlier tower, but tradition has it that Cardinal Wolsey financed its replacement as a sop to local opinion when he acquired nearby Dodnash priory. It was begun about 1525 but Wolsey's death in 1530 brought things to a standstill. Judging by the polygonal buttresses, *ashlar base course*, and broad side arches, it was to have been a massive and lavish design with echoes of Dedham and Laxfield. Stubs of vaulting show within and, having been built up to the limit of consecrated ground and beyond, the arches to n. and s. would still have allowed processions to circle the church. The *aisles* date from the C16, with tall *transomed* windows on the s. side; note how the flint work varies there, with the later and better work at the w. end. Delicately canopied niches are set in the buttresses and a profusion of tiny shields in the battlements. Above them, the *clerestory* forms virtually a wall of glass. There is a sharp drop in height to the aisle chapel, and that too has canopied niches in the buttresses. The mid-C14 chancel has later windows, plastered walls, and a *flushwork* base course. The n. aisle and chapel are largely in brick and there is a substantial *rood stair* turret at the corner of the aisle. Polygonal in plan, it has two *set-offs*, and the star (the heraldic 'mullet') of the De Vere earls of Oxford is incorporated in a little window. They were Lords of the Manor and this particular 'star-on-star' badge was used by John, the 14th Earl, 1513-26. The n. aisle windows are simpler, with four plain *lights* under *Tudor* arches, but the n. doorway is quite elaborate, with initials and merchant's mark in the *spandrels* and a band of shallow niches set in the arch. Above the shell of the tower base, which is open to the sky, the *nave* w. wall is all brick, and the windows were not inserted until 1905. Above them on the gable, the clock made by Nathaniel Hedge of Colchester in 1764 is crowned with an attractive cupola. The inscription on the w. door is a copy made in 1886 of the medieval original. The initials represent a Latin text which translates: 'For Holy Church John Fine, Francis Yual and others made [this gift] in honour of Jesus and Mary'. The tall C15 s. porch has plain plastered walls, although the buttresses retain their niches and flushwork; a handsome sundial is centred below the gable. A stair turret leading to the upper room is set in the angle between porch and aisle and rises well above the *roof* line.

Within, the early-C16 nave *arcades* are tall, with elegant *quatrefoil piers* and deep hollow mouldings. The aisle roofs are largely original but the nave roof dates from 1854. A major restoration in 1870 cleared out all the *box pews* but luckily the attractive pale brick floors were not replaced by tiles. Solid oak screens enclose choir vestries at the w. end of both aisles. The *font* of 1862 is a cumbrous affair with a variety of symbols in the bowl panels. The nave w.

window contains fine *Arts and Crafts* glass by Hugh Arnold. He was one of *Christopher Whall's* pupils and was killed in 1915 after only a few years' work. Dating from 1906, there are lovely figures of the Four Virtues in the lower lights, with Patience holding an hour-glass. They are set in clear glass with simple borders, and above are displayed the shields of the province of Canterbury, Norwich and St Edmundsbury & Ipswich dioceses, and Emmanuel College, Cambridge. The n. aisle windows are filled with *Lavers & Barraud* glass commemorating members of the Hughes family – Sir Richard (1862), Sir Edward (1880), and Sir Alfred (1890). Scenes and individual figures are largely drawn from the New Testament and are very attractive. Under the centre window is the remnant of Anna Parker's tomb of 1656, a shield flanked by crests of camel and muzzled bear. To the l. is an anonymous epitaph cut in stone which probably dates from the C16 or early C17:

What ere thou art here reader see
In this pale glass what thou shalt be,
Despised wormes and putrid slime,
Then dust forgot & lost in time.
Birth, beuty, welth may gild thy east,
But ye black grave shadowes thy west.
Ther earthly glorys shorte liv'd light,
Sets in a long & unknown night.
Here till the sun of glory rise,
My dearest darke and dusty lyes,
But clothed with his morning raye,
Ther polish't dust shall shine for aye.
Reader first pay to this bedewed stone
The tribute of thy tear & then be gone.

At the e. end of the aisle stands a large late-C14 chest with a curved, worm-eaten top; the centre hasp and broad backplate were clearly designed to resist forcing. Nearby, John Mattinson's epitaph tells us that he was 'eleven years the beloved schoolmaster of this Town and then unfortunately shott' in 1723. In the corner is the door leading to the *rood stair* turret and its position shows that the medieval loft and *screens* stretched right across the church.

Over in the s. aisle there is a C19 architect's drawing of a projected tower completion design and many will be glad that nothing came of it (although Long Melford shows how successful such projects can be). The church's most interesting drawing by John Constable of the chancel as it was before the Victorian's version of the wind of change is now in Christchurch Mansion Ipswich and there should by now be a

East Bergholt, St Mary: Bell cage

digital copy on display. As at Whitby in Yorkshire, the arch was spanned by a substantial *gallery* resting on classical pillars. The 1877 glass in the centre window is Constable's memorial by the Cambridge firm of his namesake. *St Luke* sketches the *Blessed Virgin* in the centre and the Ascension spans the three lights at the top, but it is ironic that the window is the worst in the church when it should have been the best. There are C19 painted boards with the Creed and Lord's Prayer above the arch into the aisle chapel, and the modern screen below, with its coved canopy, is excellent. The chapel was at one time walled off and used as a *vestry* but it was restored to use in the mid-C19 and the roof dates from 1866. The *communion rails* incorporate sections of medieval screen work that were discovered in 1905 and some of the old choir stalls were installed as benches. The compact e. window has good glass of 1900 by Lavers & Westlake – six of the *Seven Works of Mercy* in well-painted panels, with angels in the *tracery*. The glass in the side windows of 1873 and 1892 is by the same firm but not of the same quality. There is a tall image niche to the l. of the *altar*, and a *consecration cross* roundel can be seen on the n. wall by the rails.

Moving back into the nave, have a look at the *brass* in the floor at the e. end. It is the only one that remains in the church and is most attractive; it commemorates Robert Alfounder. He was once a churchwarden here, dying in 1639, and the 23in. figure has him sporting a Van Dyck beard and wearing a cloak, high boots, and spurs. With shield and inscription, it is the only example of its period in the county, and I wonder whether it was laid after *Dowsing* came breaking things in 1641. There is no mention in his journal but it is said that he ripped up 80lb. of brasses and destroyed the parish registers. The piers of the chancel arch are mid-C14 but the arch was renewed when the nave was rebuilt,

and on either side there are ledges that lent support to the rood loft. The heavy octagonal pulpit was both carved and given by a Mr Rimmer in the 1870s, while the chancel screen with its pretty fan-vaulted coving was designed by Sir T.G. Jackson in 1920 and made by Farmer & Brindley. At one time the n.e. chapel was the preserve of the Lords of the Manor but it now houses the organ, and just beyond it, in the n. wall, is an interesting example of an *Easter sepulchre*. Restored in 1920, the red and black C15 painting at the back has the hazy outline of the resurrected Christ set within luxurious foliage (possibly of lily and pine, alluding to the prophecy in the Book of Joel). The grandfather of John Constable's intended was the Revd. Durand Rhudde, the rector, and for a while he was strongly opposed to the marriage. After Maria's death and burial at Hampstead, Constable commissioned the sculptor Alfred Stothard to cut the plain tablet on the wall above the Easter sepulchre to commemorate her and her grandparents. Next to it is a *touchstone* tablet in an alabaster frame for an earlier rector, William Jones, who died in 1636. A charming little library of books is carved on the top and painted as though they were bound in scarlet calf and vellum with gilt edges. Opposite on the s. wall is the monument to Edward Lamb, a Lord of the Manor who endowed the local school and died in 1617. It is in alabaster, with traces of colour, and two finely carved figures draw curtains aside from the niche where his little effigy kneels in flowing robes. A quirky acrostic is arranged on the brackets at the bottom (Elizabeth Bull's monument at Sproughton is similar and, as she was a relative, one mason may have carved both). The communion rails are good specimens of the brass telescopic variety that combined utility with ingenuity in the eyes of the mid-Victorians. Prior to his screen, Sir T.G. Jackson had designed the oak choir stalls and *reredos* in 1904, and the latter has a relief of the supper at Emmaus flanked by the *Annunciation* figures below a curved top and angel *finials*. The *piscina* has a thick stone *credence shelf* and there are *dropped-sill sedilia* alongside. East Bergholt has the best range of Lavers, Barraud & Westlake glass in the county, and the n. *sanctuary* window has an Annunciation paired with a *Visitation* of 1892, while on the s. side there is a full-length scene of Christ meeting the fishermen on the shore. There is a considerable contrast between the creamy tones of these designs and the much sharper colours of the e. window (the firm's first commission here in

1867), where the subjects of the five main panels are: the Nativity, Christ's baptism, the Crucifixion, the *Three Marys,* and doubting *St Thomas.*

Easton, All Saints (G5): The great house was demolished in 1923 and there are new developments within the park, but the 1830s crinkle crankle wall is largely intact and is said to be the longest in the world. A section of it lines the w. boundary of the churchyard and joins the tower, while on the n. side the *porch* was enclosed to afford a private entrance for the earls of Rochford – a nice example of noble exclusiveness. The lower stages of the unbuttressed tower are C13, but an octagonal belfry with stepped battlements decorated with *flushwork* was added some two hundred years later. The body of the church must have been built in the late C13 but a variety of *Decorated* and *Perpendicular* windows were inserted later, and a C19 *vestry* was added to the s. wall of the *chancel.* A *scratch dial* can be found low down on a *nave* buttress, and there is a small niche above the decayed outer arch of the porch.

Seen from outside, there is a variation in the roof lines of nave and chancel, but the timber framework within is uninterrupted and there are heavy *tie-beams* with *king posts* cross-braced to the rafters – all of which looks C19. There is a small *sanctus-bell window* in the tower and the C14 octagonal *font* has a bowl whose sides angle outwards slightly to a horizontal centre line. The heraldry of the *Hanoverian Royal Arms* over the n. door dates them before 1801 and, although uncoloured, they are a particularly fine set, beautifully carved and pierced in deep relief. The range of low *box pews* in stained pine was installed in 1816, and on the n. wall is the memorial for William, 5th (and last) Earl of Rochford, who, when he died in 1830, was the last of the House of Nassau who came over with William of Orange. The tall tablet has a bas-relief of a praying woman kneeling by an urn, with a shield in scrolls at the top and an epitaph panel below. The Rochfords gave way to the dukes of Hamilton, and the window opposite is a memorial for the 11th Duke, a stylised Nativity across three *lights* of 1863, possibly by *Clayton & Bell.* The window to the w. of the pulpit contains more interesting glass and at the very top there is a C14 figure of a crowned woman in a blue and brown robe; her face is now very dark. Identification is debatable but she may represent *St Helen.* Below it are

remains of C15 canopies and two delightful 1960s roundels of flower shapes with sun, moon, and other symbols. Across the nave a window has more C15 canopy work and below, the glass of 1964 by Michael Farrar Bell takes the form of two *Annunciation* panels in a modern version of C14 style. The *rood loft stairs* in the window embrasure show where the chancel arch stood, and the plain, panelled pulpit forms part of the suite of pews that extends a little to the e. of it to include a reader's desk. On the n. wall Dame Mary Wingfield's handsome memorial of 1675 is a large *touchstone* tablet flanked by matching Ionic columns with looped garlands at the base, and beyond, within a blocked window, is the Hon. George Savage Nassau's monument of 1823. This is a coarser version of the kneeling woman and is signed by William Pistell, so one wonders whether he provided both pieces. It is the only example of his work identified in the county. There are three *brasses* in front of the *sanctuary* and the one on the n. side is particularly fine. It is the 3ft. effigy of Radcliff Wingfeld (that is how she spelt it) who died in 1601. First wife of Sir Thomas Wingfield, her Christian name was her mother's maiden name, and she wears a farthingale drawn back to display a brocaded petticoat, and a pendent jewel hangs below her French bonnet. On the s. side is a smooth 26in. figure in armour of the 1420s. It probably commemorates Sir Thomas Charles whose family were Lords of the Manor before the Wingfields. Alongside is the excellent brass for John Wingfeld who died in 1584, a classic example of Elizabethan armour, with peascod breastplate, elaborate buckles, and lots of shading. The family was established in Suffolk before the Conquest and the twenty quarterings of the shield include the arms of many ancient lines. The sturdy *communion rails* are late C17 and two more sections screwed to the e. wall indicate that they were once three-sided. The late-C13 *piscina* and *sedilia* have shafts with ring bases and *capitals* but are partially masked by the family pew which occupies the corner of the sanctuary. It is one of a pair installed by Sir Henry Wingfield about 1650, and though their placing on either side of the *altar* is eccentric, they are rather attractive. They have no ceilings and the low cornices, carved with wreaths and the Wingfield badge, are supported by turned shafts, with strapwork below the book ledge; the end panels are moulded and each door has a blind-arched panel. The stone *reredos* is C19 and grouped on the chancel walls are *hatchments* which form one of the best collections in the county.

In date order they are for: Dame Susan Wingfield (1652 e. wall, l.); Dr Ralph Cotton (1705 e. wall, r.); Hon. Henry Nassau [?] (1741 s. wall top l.); Hon. George Richard Savage Nassau [?] (1823 s. wall bottom); Anne Nassau (1771 s. wall top r.); William, 5th Earl of Rochford (1830 nave n. wall); Alexander, 10th Duke of Hamilton (1852 n. wall top); Susan, Duchess of Hamilton (1859 n. wall bottom r.); William, 11th Duke of Hamilton (1863 n. wall bottom l.). The 1848 glass in the e. window is by *Thomas Willement* – there are sacred emblems in the top *lights* above C13-style grisaille glass, and it was presented by the Duke of Hamilton. All Saints has a fine ring of six bells with a 10 cwt. tenor.

Edwardstone, St Mary (D6): A rough drive leads from the gatehouse into the park and from the church there are views over rolling fields with a farmhouse nearby. Edwardstone was one of Suffolk's thriving wool villages and the handsome church, well restored both in the C19 and recently, is meticulously maintained. The C15 tower, with its flint panelled *base course*, has a renewed w. window and bell openings, and there are generous *Perpendicular* windows in the 1460s n. *aisle*. The C14 n. door was reused and the solid n.e. *vestry* under its own gabled roof is as least as old as the *chancel* of about 1300. There is a C19 e. window in Perpendicular style but those on the s. side are early C14. Two new windows have been inserted in the s. wall of the *nave* and the low brick s. *porch* is largely C19, although an old cambered *tie-beam* survives below its plastered ceiling.

The interior is lovely, with a graceful C15 n. *arcade* and a single-framed roof above the nave. *King posts* rise from the tie-beams, one of which is heavily warped, and the roof timbers are decorated with gilded stars – part of the scheme devised by *G.F. Bodley* in the 1870s. He placed *Sacred monograms* within sunbursts as *bosses* along the centre line of the n. aisle and he designed the very attractive organ case in the chapel at the e. end. In plum and gilt, it has pierced *tracery* wings and cresting with decorative stars linking it with the roof theme. The instrument itself was rebuilt at the same time around a 'Father Smith' organ of 1670 which came from the Sheldonian in Oxford. The octagonal C14 *font* stands on a new base and has a C17 panelled *ogee* cover. Beyond it on the n. wall there are *Decalogue*, Creed, and Lord's Prayer boards in triptych form matching the benefactions board over the s. door; both are likely to be Bodley designs. The *censing* angel painted high in the

Edwardstone, St Mary: Reredos

n.w. corner of the aisle seems to be C18 – period and placement are both unusual. The pews with their stepped square ends could be taken as typical of Bodley but in this case, as it happens, he merely repeated the form of the old seats to be found under the tower and at the w. end. The *linen-fold panelling* at the back of the nave range is a copy taken from a C16 screen that fronted the aisle chapel. Nave and aisle are lit by extremely handsome wrought-iron candelabra and the *Stuart* pulpit belongs to the same family as those at nearby Milden and Little Waldingfield. On a tall turned stem, it has similar scrolls and acorn pendants below the body, blind-arched panels, and heavy scroll brackets under the canted book ledge. Unlike the others, however, this one retains its backboard and *tester*. The *rood stairs* are just behind it, and across the nave stands a new double-sided lectern in oak. The square stepped column has rectangles at the base enclosing pierced *Evangelistic symbols*, and the ends of the top frame delicate pierced lily forms carved in limewood. A nice piece. An 1860s tablet with draped standards by Gaffin on the s. wall commemorates Maj. Richard Magenis of the 7th Fusiliers who saw action at Copenhagen and retired here, having lost an arm at Albuera in the Peninsular War. There are two early-C19 tablets by *John Bacon the Younger* in the n. aisle – one is commonplace for William Shepherd, and the other with a little more style is for Thomas Dawson; it has an urn with knotted drapes against a grey obelisk. Farther along is the C19 *brass* of Armar Lowry-Corry, 3rd Earl Belmore and his family, and just inside the n. chapel is a largely lettered tablet for Joseph Brand, 'a pious, prudent, charitable person' who died in 1674. Below is a brass with the family arms and John Brand's epitaph. He died in 1642, 'a freind and lover of pious & godly ministers' (in other words, a thoroughgoing Puritan). The Brands were wealthy clothiers and C17 Lords of the Manor and at the e. end of the aisle is an excellent brass of about 1620 for Benjamin and Elizabeth. They are both in ruffs and gowns and she wears the fashionable calash hood; a dozen children kneel in neatly descending order and the inscription is memorable:

> To ye precious memory of Benjamin Brand of Edwardstone Hall, Esq., and Elizabeth his wife, whom when Providence, after 35 yeares of conjunction, divided, Death, after 12 dayes divorcment, reunited; who leaveing their rare examples to 6 sonnes and 6 daughters, (All nursed with her unborrowed milk), blest with poormen's prayers, embaulmed with numerous teares, Lye here reposed.

Bodley replaced the chancel roof in 1880 and it is gilded and painted overall in striking fashion, with Sacred monograms at the panel intersections and heavy *wall plates* pierced with *quatrefoils*. The vicar, George Augustus Dawson, died in 1848 and Robert De Carle of Bury provided an austere tablet on the *sanctuary* n. wall which is effectively enlivened by a coloured shield of arms at the top. The elaborate *reredos* of 1910 in dark oak and muted gold is by C.G. Hare, Bodley's successor, and faithfully continues his style; pierced canopies range along the top and in the centre niche *St Mary Magdalene* kneels at the foot of the cross with the *Blessed Virgin* and *St John* each side, while *Annunciation* figures take up the flanking niches. The C14 *piscina* lies under a *trefoil* arch and was probably canopied originally. The modern *communion rails* in limed oak are enlivened by gilded rings. The church has some interesting modern glass in varying styles. The e. window is a fine example of *Burlison & Grylls* in C15 idiom – a Crucifixion in the tracery, the Blessed Virgin and Child and *St Edmund* in the centre *light* flanked by two bishops, *St Anne*, and *St Margaret*. By the pulpit, an 1870s window contains six scenes with identifying labels in C15 style, and to the w. a 1920s Lowry-Corry memorial window has a large figure of Melchizedek in company with a very unusual pair – Abbot Samson of Bury St Edmunds and *St Edith*. In both cases the glass is probably by Burlison & Grylls. St Mary's has an excellent ground floor ring of six bells with a 9 cwt. tenor.

Ellough, All Saints (I2): This is a windy, upland site, and the rather bare-looking church stands in a vast churchyard which is empty on the n. side. Since 1974 the building has been in the care of the *Churches Conservation Trust* and walking round you will see that it has a simple unbuttressed tower and a blocked C13 n. door. The low-pitched roofs of *nave* and *chancel* are barely visible above plain parapets, and there are tall *Perpendicular* windows in the nave. *William Butterfield* directed an extensive restoration here in the 1880s, but nothing in the work calls him particularly to mind, except perhaps its quality. He added the tall and narrow organ chamber on the n. side of the C14 chancel, and the short e. window in Perpendicular style is probably to his design. The s. *porch* dating from 1602 has been restored and the inner doorway looks like a replacement.

A rather bare interior, but a number of interesting things to see, and look first at the good copy of the 'Degrees of Marriage', published in 1756, framed on the tower wall (not many of these have survived). The C15 *font* has a replacement drum shaft, but the outline of the base shows that the original had supporters – probably lions. *Tudor Roses* alternate with hung shields in the bowl panels, and there are *paterae* on the mouldings and below the bowl. A simple C19 *bier* stands alongside. The blocked *Early English lancet* at the w. end of the n. wall probably indicates the date of the main building, while overhead there is a handsome late-C15 cambered *tie-beam* roof in unstained oak, with curved braces between the principals. Butterfield restored it and the *wall posts* rest on head *corbels* which are typically Victorian. He tiled the floor and installed plain pine benches that are redeemed from dullness by the shallow foliage carving on the elbows of the ends. His pulpit has disappeared but the stone base remains, and see how the masons asserted their individuality by carving their names where they knew they would be hidden by the woodwork. Doors to the *rood stair* remain in the n. wall, and a large, plain *piscina* recess on the s. side marks the site of a nave *altar*. There is no *rood screen* now, and the renewed arch overhead has C19 demi-angel corbels. Butterfield installed the flat panelled ceiling, but prior to that the chancel had been restored in 1877 in memory of Richard Arnold, rector here for over sixty years. Attractive little bronze portrait roundels of him and his wife Charlotte feature on the memorial tablet. *Dowsing* was here in April 1643, breaking a dozen 'superstitious pictures' in the windows, and he left orders for the steps to be levelled and a cross to be taken off the chancel. The parish promised to comply, but the steps are still there. There are *dropped-sill sedilia* and a C14 piscina with a *crocketted ogee* arch, and Butterfield's *reredos* is a harsh design in multi-coloured tiles. All the church's *brasses* are to be found nearby, and on the s. side two shields of about 1480 remain on a slab which bears the outline of a man in armour. On the n. side there is a 14in. effigy of an unidentified lady in early-C16 costume; her *kennel headdress* has long lappets marked with crosses, and she has a purse and rosary. Nearby is a shield and inscription for Anne Gostling who died in 1612, but the most interesting brass, in the n.e. corner, is for Margaret Chewtte who died aged 85 in 1607. She was a Playters of Sotterley, and her father's shield is on the l., her second husband's on the r. – both originally inlaid. The 18in. figure has her at prayer, with skull and crossbones underfoot, wearing an enormous and eccentric veiled headdress which was perhaps a whim of her old age. The inscription is an exceptional example of ingeniously compressed lettering.

Elmsett, St Peter (E6): The church lies n. of the village proper with only a farm for company, and its buttressed C13 tower has *lancet* windows and bell openings of varying sizes. 'Y' *tracery* of about 1300 and *Perpendicular* windows are to be seen on the n. side of the *nave* as well as a blocked *Norman* lancet, and a large C17 or C18 brick buttress supports the n.e. corner of the *chancel*. The flowing *Decorated* tracery of the e. window has been renewed but is likely to have repeated the original, and in the s. wall, the windows and *priest's door* are C14 too. A *scratch dial* can be found on the bottom r.-hand corner of the s.w. chancel window and a date is cut on its sill – 1625? Another blocked Norman lancet in the s. nave wall confirms the building's age and a two-*light* C14 window has *mouchettes* and a *quatrefoil* in the tracery. The C14 *porch* was well restored in the 1970s and still has its outer wooden arch and barge boards. There is a triangular *stoup* by the inner doorway and the door itself retains its closing ring and broad bands of C14 iron work decorated with curious little pieces like tenterhooks along the edges.

Within, there are *pamment* floors and the plain w. *gallery* houses the organ. Below on the n. wall hangs a late-C17 painted version of the Table of Kindred and Affinity, which was first published by Archbishop Parker in 1563 and later printed in the Book of Common Prayer. It is but right and proper that unlawful unions between close

Elmsett, St Peter: C17 Table of Kindred & Affinity

relatives should be avoided, but many of the curious conjunctions must have stemmed from a lively imagination. Examples like this one are rare and the sign-writer had a job to fit the last four of the thirty categories in at the bottom. An interesting photograph on the opposite wall shows the church decked for a Harvest Festival in the days when there were high *box pews*, and their discarded panelling now lines the nave. There is a small table placed centrally whose lovely top is a thick slice taken from an elm which blew down in 1879, and beyond it is a square Norman *font* of *Purbeck marble*. It has long been plastered over but one of the familiar blank arches shows on one corner. The plain and timeworn pyramid cover is C17 and a chest of the same period stands nearby with inlaid lozenges in the front panels. On the wall above hangs a large, handsome *Royal Arms* of Anne – subsequently dated 1758 for George II. The board is hinged so that the back can be displayed, on which is painted a Prince of Wales feathers within a spiked circle, the significance of which escapes me.

Dowsing paid a visit in August 1644 but found that a deputy had done his work for him and he had to be content with rending the parson's hood and surplice – the only mention of vestments in the sorry catalogue of vandalism that is his journal. St Mary-at-Quay, Ipswich, is now redundant but its fine early-C17 pulpit has found a home here. The small upper panels contain *Renaissance* motifs while below there are perspective arches in which centre pendants are applied. The bottom range consists of subdivided moulded panels between turned columns at the angles. Beyond it, a niche with a multi-*cusped* arch has a single hinge left in the rebate and so must once have had a door. The chancel arch is rather rudimentary and at high level each side there are strange masonry ledges that may have supported a *rood loft*. The *hatchment* on the chancel s. wall bears the arms of Skinner/Jones but is not precisely identifiable and opposite there is a fine monument for Edward Sherland, who died in 1609. Its design is conventional and his effigy in black gown kneels before a prayer desk within a square alabaster recess; there are painted ribbons on the frame pinned by hourglass, scythe, pick, shovel, and Bible, with a coloured *achievement of arms* between obelisks on top. The epitaph is thoughtful: '. . . a painted sepulchre is but a rotten trustless treasure, and a faire gate built to oblivion . . .'. Farther along, the Revd. William Talbot's 1812 memorial is a plain sarcophagus above a tablet large enough to give elbow room for an extract from his will, including the plea: '. . . I earnestly beg the parishioners of Elmset will read the inscription every time they go into the church . . .'. Did they for a while, perchance? The *altar* is enclosed by substantial and handsome three-sided *communion rails* that were made about 1670, and there are *Decalogue* boards on the e. wall. Beside the C14 *angle piscina* there are *dropped-sill sedilia* which have a little *trefoil* arch at the w. end.

A C16 rector of Elmsett achieved immortality at one remove, for his son was John Bois, one of the translators of the Authorised Version of the Bible. Thomas Fuller said: 'Whilst St Chrysostom lives, Mr Bois shall not die.' One wonders what a more recent rector felt about the stone monolith that stands defiantly across the road from the church gate: '1934. To commemorate the Tithe seizure at Elmsett Hall of furniture including baby's bed and blankets, herd of dairy cows, eight corn stacks and seed stacks valued at £1200 for tithe valued at £385.' The list apparently exaggerates a little but

nevertheless points up the harshness of a contemporary injunction.

Elmswell, St John the Divine (D4): Seen from the w., the church stands commandingly on a rise at the very edge of the village. It was built by the Benedictines of Bury and the abbot entertained Henry VI here at his grange in 1433. The beautifully proportioned C15 tower was restored in 1980 and it has a lovely selection of flint and stone *flushwork* panels in the *base course* and on the buttresses, with binoculars one can identify the arms of Bury abbey between two *chalices* on the s.e. buttress and on the panel above that, the inscription 'Syr Wyllm Maundevyl'. The upper stages of the buttresses have canopied niches and the one on the s.e. corner is embellished with a *crocketted* pinnacle. There is a band of intricate flushwork beneath the stepped battlements and the bell openings are unusually large, with pairs of two-*light* windows under a single *dripstone*. Although she was buried in St James's Bury St Edmund's, Margery Walter left money in 1476 for the building of the tower and seems to have planned all the decorative flushwork to commemorate her first husband William Hert (d.1472), her second, Edmund Walter (d.1497), and other members of her family. The *clerestory* walls are made up of an attractive mixture of flint and freestone, with red bricks spaced over the window arches. The bold pattern of flushwork on the e. wall of the s. aisle probably dates from the early C17 when a large tomb was placed against it within. High on the buttress to the l. of the *priest's door* in the *chancel* is a *scratch dial* and, unlike most, it has the remains of the metal spike (the gnomen) in the centre. Near the *porch* is a fine example of a *churchyard cross*. Although parts of it have been renewed, there are well carved panels on the square base.

Within the church, a damaged stone head *corbel* has been re-set above the s. door and the C14 *font* stands nearby. Its bowl panels are carved with multi-*cusped* circles containing shields; one is blank but the others carry initials spelling out I (or J) HEDGE (probably the donor's name) and the three scallop shells on the last shield may have been his arms. There are angels below the bowl, and at the corners of the shaft there are three eagles, on wickerwork nests, and a horned beast. A substantial gallery has recently been installed within the w. bays of the *nave* and *aisles*. Below it and in the base of the tower, meeting rooms, cloakrooms and a kitchen have been provided – facilities that are now regarded as essential if the church is to fulfil its mission in the parish. A series of C19 restorations was begun by *E.C. Hakewill* in 1862 when the s. aisle was rebuilt, and the chancel was thoroughly restored by R.J. Withers two years later. In 1867, *J.D. Wyatt* added the n. aisle, copying the *Perpendicular* s. *arcade* with its concave-faced octagonal *piers*. There are medieval benches in both aisles, with one carved back in each set. The ends, with their large *poppyheads,* have varied *tracery* cut in the solid but the square *castellated* elbows have had their carved figures chopped off. *William Dowsing* was here in 1643 and this may have been part of his work. A *string course* decorated with closely set *fleurons* runs below the clerestory and the shafts with rounded *capitals* that supported the former roof stand between the windows. One wonders why the C19 architect did not make use of them to carry *wall posts* for his replacement. Bold Victorian texts adorn the arches of the chancel tower and n. door. The e. end of the s. aisle is enclosed by a *parclose screen,* the n. section of which is original, with subtle variations in the tracery (including a mask in the head of one of the *ogees*). The w. range is a good C19 copy which repeats the carvings of birds and leaves in the *spandrels* of the panel tracery. The paintings of saints and martyrs on the n. side are modern. The chapel e. wall is taken up with a large and imposing monument to Sir Robert Gardener who was for 18 years Queen Elizabeth's Chief Justice in Ireland and her Viceroy there for two years. The epitaph mentions his valiant action against rebellious Tyrone and the Spanish at Kinsale; King James I subsequently sent him to sort out the islands of Jersey and Guernsey before he retired here. He died at a good age in 1619 and founded the almshouses e. of the church. This outstanding monument was sculpted by James I's master carver, Maximilian Colt, and the figure of Sir Robert reclines on an elbow, gloves in one hand and prayer book in the other. His heavily braided, ermine-edged gown falls open to reveal a short coat and blue waistcoat. A lovely little alabaster rhinoceros (his crest) stands at his feet, and beyond kneels his son William. Rather oddly, his splendid robes lie bundled on a ledge below, mixed up with oddments of armour. All the colour is good and the tomb is contained within a coffered arch in black and white with flanking pink marble *Corinthian* columns. To the r. is a *piscina* with a cusped ogee arch that will have served the *altar* displaced by the tomb. There is a C19 low stone chancel screen with a wrought-iron framework above, and a

fine pair of matching gates designed by J.D. Wyatt. In the *sanctuary* is a *piscina* under an ogee *trefoil* arch, and an angular C19 stone *reredos* of simple tracery shapes. The window on the s. side of the sanctuary has 1860s glass by Alexander Gibbs – a resurrection panel, and the *Three Marys* at the tomb. The e. window glass is by *Lavers & Barraud,* and the main panels depict Christ's baptism, Gethsemane, the Crucifixion and the Entombment. The stylised figures are set against a dark blue background and the tracery above contains heads in roundels against heavily patterned backgrounds.

Elveden, St Andrew and St Patrick (C3): The grounds of the hall provides a gracious, leafy backdrop to the church, compensating for the relentless traffic surging along the A11. Walking round the outside, the only visible remnant of the original *Norman* church is the small slit window low in the centre of the s. *aisle* wall (which was then the *nave*). A tower was added in the early C14 and rebuilt in its present form about 1420, using the old materials. It has *flushwork* panelling at the base and the standing figures at the battlement corners are said to represent the four shepherds who gave them. There is a 'Y' *tracery* window of about 1300 w. of the cloister walk and, beyond it to the e., the C14 *chancel* (now the s. chapel) with flowing *Decorated* tracery in both s. and e. windows. The old nave was altered again later and things remained as they were until the 1860s when the Maharajah Duleep Singh came on the scene. Heir to the Sikh Punjab, he had been forced to resign at the age of 11 and, having become a Christian, he came to England to be made much of by Queen Victoria, given princely status and encouraged to take his place among the aristocracy. *Queen Victoria's Maharajah,* by Michael Alexander and Sushila Anand tells his extraordinary and rather sad story. Having taken Elveden, he set a careful restoration of the church in hand in 1869. By 1904, the wholesale rejuvenation of the estate by the new owner, the Earl of Iveagh, demanded a larger church for his workers and it was then that the conjunction of the Guinness fortunes with the talents of the 'rogue' architect W.D. Caröe produced an astonishing building in which lushness and wilful eccentricity combine. A new nave and chancel were added to the n. dedicated to *St Patrick,* in a style which *Pevsner* labelled with some acuteness '*Art Nouveau* Gothic'. The feeling is medieval but much of the detail decoration, particularly in tracery and *finials,* has the smooth sinuous lines of the late C19. Long, reptile-like water spouts keep company with the rich cresting and seated figures of the chancel parapet, and beyond the small rose window of the n. *vestry*, a slimly buttressed chimney stack rises as though from a country house of the period. One of the angels on the vestry parapet has unfortunately lost his copper trumpet. A medieval stone coffin lies within a low arch in the n. chancel wall and the nave windows on that side are deeply recessed, with high sills. The w. front has a small corner turret and the low doorway is flanked by squat, angled buttresses topped by angels. The small figure of a bishop occupies a niche below the gable end. The medieval octagonal *font* has been relegated to the churchyard by the s. *porch* and beyond is the most satisfying of the new work – a bell tower built in 1922 as a memorial to Viscountess Iveagh, connected by a cloister walk to the s. chapel. Here, Caröe's design is closer to the traditional East Anglian style, with an octagonal stair turret rising above the batlements, pinnacled buttresses, paired bell openings and flushwork of a very high quality. The tower houses one of the best of Suffolk's octaves with a 17 cwt. tenor.

Entrance to the church is by the s. chapel door and to the r. is a C14 *angle piscina* with a new stone *credence shelf* next to *dropped-sill sedilia*. The chapel e. window, a memorial to the Maharajah and his wife, has 1894 glass by *Kempe* – the Adoration of the Magi with lots of luxurious fur-trimmed robes, attendants with banners, and the outlines of a medieval city beyond. Below is a *Jacobean altar* table, and to the l., a tablet with full armorial *achievement* for Prince Frederick Duleep Singh. Below that is a severe black tablet for his elder brother, Prince Victor Albert Jay Duleep Singh, for whom Queen Victoria stood godmother in 1866. Note the head of a small Decorated niche in the embrasure of the chapel s. window and then go through the fine modern oak screen into the fecundity of Caröe's interior. The round-headed arches of the *arcade* have chunky enrichments in the mouldings and the deep *capitals* are carved with a weird mixture of designs in layers, none of which are alike. The octagonal *piers* have shafts separated by deeply recessed traceried panels of a quite eccentric design. The s. aisle roof is overbearingly massive for the space covered and two of the *wall posts* spring from limply shaped transverse stone arches set in the embrasures of the Perpendicular windows that Duleep Singh had carefully restored – a most unhappy

arrangement. The window by the screen is a memorial to Arthur, Viscount Elveden, and has a bright *St George* design by Hugh Easton who also designed the glass in the window to the w. – a memorial to men of the USAAF 3rd Division. A serviceman kneels below an angel with mighty wings in vivid blue and the scene beyond encapsulates the transitory feeling of a wartime air base – Flying Fortresses at dispersal and the odd tent here and there. The other window on this side, a memorial of 1971 to the 2nd Earl and Countess, is by Lawrence Lee – an attractive patchwork of colour and plant stems overlaying an C18 man-of-war. Also on the s. wall is a 1786 portrait medallion of Augustus, Viscount Keppel, and there are plain early niches flanking the Norman slit window. The font dates from the Duleep Singh restoration and is in Sicilian-Norman style, with eight slim barley-sugar columns under a bowl whose panels contain demi-figures and shields. The nave w. window of 1937 commemorates Edward Cecil, 1st Earl of Iveagh. It was designed by Sir Frank Brangwyn, the most successful artist of his generation and, possibly, least appreciated in this country. He did little stained glass work but was anxious to commemorate Lord Iveagh who was both his patron and his friend. Brangwyn was commissioned to provide a window for the Protestant cathedral in Dublin and this one. In it, children crowd round a father who reads to them and a mother who comforts them, while the two dedicatory saints look benignly down from among a host of baby faces. Squirrel, hare and doves are worked into the base of this dense design, with everything in fresh pastel colours. As with all that Brangwyn did, it is lively and vibrant. Below it, the war memorial designed by *Cautley* is stiff and early-Victorian in feeling, as though in quiet protest at all around. The nave roof is a massive double *hammerbeam*, embellished with a multitude of angels and richly carved on every available surface. The effect is slightly oppresive, possibly because roofs of this stature are normally higher. Beyond the chancel arch, itself enriched with carving, is a closely panelled barrel roof with *bosses* at every intersection; the eastern ranges of panels are decorated to form a *celure*. With no chancel screen the eye is taken forward to the *reredos* which rises on both sides of the altar to the spring of the window arch. Sumptuously carved in alabaster and heightened with gilding, the supper at Emmaus at its centre, it has 14 statues of saints and East Anglian monarchs, together with a host of minor figures. The effect is extra-

ordinarily rich. The vestry door in the n. wall of
the chancel is a prime example of Caröe at his
most wilful and least effective. The choir stalls
are relatively conventional but the nave pews are
more interesting, with smooth scrolly tops to
the bench ends and low relief carving in panels.
The wolf guarding *St Edmund's* head, in a style
reminiscent of Walter Crane, can be found both
in the nave s. side and in the s. aisle. All the
woodwork is of very high quality, the organ case
and pulpit in particular. A visit here is an
experience that one should not lightly forgo.

Eriswell, St Laurence (B3): This church has a
very neat and tidy churchyard, with a little avenue
of cherry trees leading to the n. *porch*. There has
been some confusion over the dedication here
because Eriswell's church was St Peter's over a
mile away to the n., but when it became derelict
this dependant chapel of St Laurence was taken
over and was called St Peter's for some time.
Outside in the s. wall there is a low tomb recess
and this C13 *aisle* is the earliest part of the
building, and reused stones from a *Norman*
predecessor can be found in the walls. The mid-
C14 tower houses an excellent light ring of five
bells with a 3 cwt. tenor. A porch, *nave* and *chancel*
were added during the same period and what
had been the old chancel at the e. end of the s.
aisle became a *guild* chapel dedicated to *St John
the Baptist*. Once inside, the details of this
rearrangement can be seen. In the corner of the
s. chapel is an *angle piscina* with a *cusped, cinquefoiled*
arch and *dropped-sill sedilia*. When the wall screen
was put in to divide the chapel from the s. aisle,
an *altar* dedicated to the *Blessed Virgin* was placed
against it, and a small square window was added
to give it light. This has medieval glass in the
centre *quatrefoil* – a C13 figure with a C14 head.
Below is a ledge piscina (the simplest form used),
and on the dropped-sill beside it is a stone quern
that may have begun life as a *stoup*. The chancel
e. window has tiny *headstops* and *Decorated tracery*
with an oval above *ogee* arches. Across the n.e.
corner of the *sanctuary* is a large niche for a statue
which, at some later date, has had a pair of small
cupboards inserted at the bottom. The original
aumbry is the other side of the altar, by the C14
piscina under its cusped *trefoil* arch, with stepped
dropped-sill sedilia beyond. There is a medley
of medieval glass fragments in the heads of the
chancel n. windows, and before moving down
into the nave, look for Martha Turk's grave slab
below: 'She lived in the late Earl of Orford's
family 41 years greatly respected by all that knew
her'. Well yes, that is a kindly and charitable

sentiment and one way of putting it, but this
was 'Patty', the young maid at Houghton with
whom George, 3rd Earl of Orford fell in love
and set up house with in Eriswell rectory – so
convenient for Newmarket. His famous uncle,
Horace Walpole, who eventually succeeded him
in 1791, was perpetually irritated by the
unorthodox arrangement. The stone plays safe
and says 'spinster', but the parish register is a
shade closer with 'wife and companion of the
Earl of Orford'. They say that George died of a
broken heart three weeks after losing his Patty.
The chancel *screen* appears to have modern base
panels. They carry armorial shields: from l. to r.,
de Rochester, de Tudenham, the sees of
Norwich and Ely, Bedingfield and Chamberlain.
Although the shafts on the s. side are replacements, those on the n. are original C14, as is
most of the Decorated tracery. From this point
you can see the *sanctus-bell window* high in the
tower wall, with its ogee trefoiled head. The
wrought-iron lectern and openwork pulpit in
pitchpine and wrought-iron date, like the nave
roof, from the 1874 restoration. The *arcade*
between the chancel and the s. chapel has a
quatrefoil *pier* with rounded *capitals*, but the nave
pillars and capitals are octagonal. Unfortunately,
very little survives of the carved figures on the
medieval bench ends that remain, but there are
some telling graffitti cut into two seats in the s.
aisle (second from w. and third from e.). They
show crude gibbets and were no doubt a child's
reaction to the drama of having two men
hanging in chains in the village for the 1782
murder of old Frances Philips, a miserly spinster
who lies buried in the s. chapel. The solid C14
font has cusped quatrefoils in the bowl panels
and attached shafts around the stem. On going
out, you will find a modern figure of a saint in
the niche over the door which, if it is meant to
be *St Laurence*, does not have the traditional
gridiron emblem. The original did, no doubt,
and was bought with ten sheep under the will
of shepherd John de Scherlokke who was buried
in the porch. In 1649, 'The Society for the
propagation of the faith in New England',
known as 'The New England Company',
bought the manor of Eriswell. It was the first
missionary society in this country and the
members later experimented by bringing back a
14-year-old boy and apprenticing him to the
village carpenter. Alas, in 1820 he died after only
two years in the alien land, and on his tombstone just in from the path by the porch door
can still be read 'James Paul, a North American
Indian'.

Erwarton, St Mary (G7): The lane from Shotley winds past the spectacular gatehouse and frontage of Erwarton Hall to the church in its attractive setting, where a huge field slopes gently down to broad waters of the Stour estuary. The C15 tower was damaged by lightning in 1837 and the top was renewed with brick and the bell openings partially blocked. A battered angel marks the centre of the *label* over the w. doorway and there are lion *stops*; the badly weathered shields in the *spandrels* bear the arms of Heveningham (n.) and Bacon/D'Avillers (s.), two families linked by marriage in the early-C15. Walking round, you will see a lot of *septaria* in the walls, and it looks as though the *clerestory* was refaced in the C19. *Nave* and *aisles* are C15, and there are bold *ogee* shapes in the *tracery* of the *Perpendicular* windows. The s. door is blocked and the *chancel* was entirely rebuilt in 1838, having been shortened in 1782. During the rebuilding, sections of a C14 window were discovered which showed that the chancel had formed part of an earlier building. The window was rebuilt in the n. wall but one wonders why it was not opened up. The C15 *porch* has *Tudor Roses* in its outer arch spandrels, and originally it had a *hammerbeam roof*, but this was replaced in 1838, although the hammers and the *wall plates* are still there. The strange recess just inside the entrance has been called a *stoup* but its shape and position make this unlikely.

Within, a number of things combine to give an impression of spaciousness – the nave is tall for its length, with graceful three-bay *arcades*, the centre aisle is unusually wide, and the shortened chancel places all the emphasis in the centre. The shallow *tie-beam* roof is panelled out and rests on long *wall posts*, and the n. aisle roof is probably the same C15 date. The s. aisle roof, however, is later, and the date 1650 features in the very attractive wall plates carved with *pomegranate* scrolls; the initials on the n. side no doubt refer to the donor or a churchwarden of the day. A fine *Jacobean* chest stands by the tower screen, and the C15 *font* takes the familiar East Anglian form. There are two varieties of the Tudor Rose in the bowl panels, with lions, and angels bearing shields (a *Trinity emblem* to the n.e.). Three lions squat round the shaft, and a dog makes up the party – a curious variation. Nearly all the furniture in the church dates from the 1838 restoration, and is the work of William Ollett, a Norwich craftsman. The benches have tall, well-carved ends with *poppyheads*, and his pulpit stands high enough to give a preacher vertigo. All that remains of the C15 benches is a pair of ends that have been incorporated in the reading desk at the e. end of the nave (its front panels are good modern versions of medieval work). Erwarton's monuments are memorable, although they have suffered grievously over the years. Most of them predate the C15 rebuilding and have been moved and divided, perhaps more than once. At the w. end of the s. aisle a tomb chest stands in a shallow recess and there are finely carved *quatrefoils* in the front, with shields bearing the arms of Hastyngs/Valence, Fitz-Rauff, Hastyngs, and Calthorpe (with a cross in the centre). The worn figure of a knight that lies on top probably commemorates Sir Bartholomew D'Avillers who died in 1287. The family arms are superimposed on the shield, an angel once supported his head, and a comfortably fat lion lies under his feet. Further along there is a tall, early-C14 canopy with large *cusps* and a centre *trefoil;* the gable has unusual *crockets* in the form of flowers, and there are flanking pinnacles. The chest inserted below matches the previous one, and displays the shields of Fitzwalter(?), Scales, Ufford/Beck, Vere, and Ufford. It was probably made for William de Ufford, Earl of Suffolk, who died in 1382, but the effigies are more likely to be those of Sir Bartholomew Bacon and his wife Anne whose arms we saw above the tower w. doorway and who died in 1391 and 1435 respectively. He has long wavy hair held within a circlet, head resting on a massive helm, and he wears a richly chased sword belt over his armour. One of the angels that guarded Anne's head remains, and her hair is held in a beautifully detailed crespine – the net headdress that had been fashionable in the C14. She has two little hounds underfoot, and both figures retain considerable traces of original colour. To the r. of the monument Philip Parker's *brass* is framed on the wall. He died about 1560 and the verse begins and ends:

Here Philippe Parker gravèd is in Place...
A short accompte, a reconing very small,
The Seely Soule shall at his dooming finde.

The use of 'seely' meaning 'holy' is the origin of the epithet 'silly Suffolk' and crops up again in an epitaph at Little Glemham. Further to the e. is the front of a *Renaissance* tomb with fluted columns and shields between them; the large *achievement* features the arms of Calthorpe/Bacon/Wythe/St Omer, and it was probably the tomb of Sir Philip Calthorpe who was buried here in 1551. The glass of 1915 in the window above is by *Powells*, a conventional setting for *SS Alban, George*, and *Edmund*; there is a Crucifixion panel at the bottom, and the Christian's armour according to *St Paul* is illustrated in the tracery roundels. A tall image niche has been blocked in the s.e. angle, and the glass in the e. window is again by Powells – an attractive Nativity scene, with a host of angels overhead. Before quitting the s. aisle, note the C18 coffin plates displayed on the wall, items seldom seen outside vaults; they include Lady Catherine Hanmer's, Lady Chedworth's, and Sir Philip Parker Long's. Across in the n. aisle there is another tomb canopy dating from about 1300, with carved spandrels and a conventionally crocketted gable; the worn figure of a lady wearing a wimple that lies below is contemporary. The church's other brass is in the floor nearby, an inscription for Katherine, Lady Cornwallis who died in 1636. In the centre aisle there is a good *ledger-stone* of the same period for Dorothy Gawdy, and over the years its deeply cut roundel must have tripped up several of the unwary whose thoughts were on higher things. The large marble memorial of 1736 by the door commemorates Sir Philip Parker; there is a *cartouche* of arms within the broken *pediment* and remains of a dozen more coloured shields stud the frame. The absurdly detailed genealogy manages to include 'Amata Bolleyn, Aunt to Queen Anna Bolleyn', a link with the local tradition that when the queen stayed at the Hall she asked that her heart be buried here. Support for this came in 1837 when a heart-shaped lead casket was found in the wall of the chancel. The equally tenacious story that her headless body was filched from the Tower and buried at Salle in Norfolk has been disproved – but her heart? Well, who knows?

Euston, St Genevieve (C3): A charming setting deep in the park; the track to the church passes in front of the Hall to continue under a line of lime trees, some of which are huge and ancient. Henry Bennet, Earl of Arlington, was secretary of State from 1662 to 1674, a member of the Cabal ministry and close friend of Charles II. His much-loved and only daughter Arabella was the child bride of Henry Fitzroy, 1st Duke of Grafton, the most attractive and able of the king's natural sons. Arlington kept great state at Euston, but in his retirement he told his friend John Evelyn that 'his heart smote him that, after he had bestowed so much on his magnificent palace, he should see God's house in the ruins it lay'. And so, in 1676, he rebuilt this church which is one of only two classical designs in the county.

The core of the building is medieval, and the tower retains w. buttresses up to the second stage, but the entire concept is *Stuart*. *Nave* and *chancel* are of equal length and the ample *transepts* make this a cruciform building. The nave has circular *clerestory* windows and the *aisles* have simple window *tracery* – two round-headed *lights* with a circle over. The e. window also is roundheaded and so are the bell openings in the tower, which has an openwork parapet with corner pinnacles. It houses an excellent ring of six bells with an 8 cwt. tenor. The aisles have doors (now blocked), approached by a semi-circle of broad steps and, having seen inside, one wonders whether they were ever open.

Entry is by the matching w. door, and once through the tower vestibule, the richness of the interior opens up. Over the w. door is a fine and large three-dimensional set of the arms of the 1st Duke of Grafton. As he was illegitimate, the *Royal Arms* are surmounted by a baton sinister; they impale the Bennet arms of his wife and the shield is contained within the ribbon of the Garter. The *achievement* is fully coloured and gilt and is, I suspect, plaster rather than wood. Nearby is an 1880s *font*, typical of the period. The ceilings of nave, chancel, and transepts are cross vaults of plaster, with the moulded ribs picked out in tan to match the walls, and they have gilded monograms and shields for *bosses* at the intersections. One of the features here is the use of *stucco*, and the arches of the centre crossing are inset with large flowers, with *acanthus* leaves on the chancel arch and on the cornices – all in tan against a dark brown background. The aisles have unadorned flat ceilings, except for the family pew in the s. aisle. There you will see stucco work of very high quality, with coronets over blank shields at the corners of a heavy garland of flowers. This is reminiscent of similar work in the great houses of the period. The walls are panelled and the nave pews have panelled ends and doors, while those fronting the crossing are enriched with carving. The six-sided pulpit has canted floral trophies over panels with deeply moulded acanthus frames; cherubs and swags of flowers adorn the angles, with scrolls and fruit on the base. (It had a large *tester*, too, prior to 1875). Beyond, a low chancel screen rises in elegant curves at the sides, with oblong openwork panels of acanthus foliage on either side of the opening. The *reredos* is a panel of the Last Supper carved in bas-relief; surrounding swags of fruit and flowers link with a cherub's head within folded wings at the top. This finely modelled work is deeply undercut and is reminiscent of work produced by the *Grinling Gibbons'* workshop. The rest of the e. wall has enriched panelling on either side of *Corinthian pilasters.* Although the architect is unknown, there seems little doubt that he was well aware of Wren's work in London, and the excellence of the detailing, particularly of the woodwork and stucco, points to craftsmen who were well above the standard to be found in the provinces.

The church has a number of *brasses:* 1. nave: a man with his wife who wears a *butterfly headdress,* late C15; 2. nave: a lady in a *kennel headdress* (inscription missing), about 1520; 3. nave: inscription for Gerard Sothil, 1528; 4. chancel, n. side: the top half of a man and his wife (minus her head), about 1520; 5. chancel, s. side: a late brass inscription with his arms in a roundel for George Feilding, Earl of Desmond, 1665; 6. chancel, s. side: inscription for William Foster (effigy lost), 1524; 7. sanctuary, n. side: top half of a man in Yorkist armour with his head on a helm. His wife, with her head on a cushion, is wearing a kennel headdress caught up with two clasps, and has a purse and rosary hanging from her girdle. This is probably Edmund Rokewood who died in 1530, and Alice his wife. He was Lord of the Manor and his arms are below the figures with those of his two wives above, all originally inlaid with colour. At the back of the family pew there is a large but restrained memorial in white marble to Lord Arlington, the builder of the church. It has an heraldic achievement between scrolls at the top, twin cherub heads within folded wings at the sides, and acanthus supporting scrolls below. To the r. is a 'Venetian Gothic' memorial in a variety of marbles to the 6th Duke of Grafton, and on a nave s. pillar, a *St George* panel in enamelled mosiac for Lieut. Edward Fitzroy RN, who died in 1917. One seldom has the opportunity to examine coffin plates, but there are many C18 and C19 examples here, mounted on the panelling; good examples of changing fashion and taste. Before you leave, do not overlook the many fine C18 gravestones in the churchyard.

Exning, St Martin (A4): The land falls away on two sides of the large churchyard, giving St Martin's a commanding position in the centre of the village, easily visible from the bypass. *St Etheldreda* was born here in AD 630, and both Roman and *Norman* masonry have been identified in the tower, so one can assume that there has been a church here since very early days. Of the present building, the earliest part is the

chancel, where you will see two blocked slit windows in the s. wall which date from the late C12. The tower has two bell stages, one above the other, showing that the work of about 1300 up to the first set of bell openings, with their 'Y' *tracery,* was extended within the next 50 years or so up to the present battlements. A new w. window was installed at the same time, its tracery matching those in the *transepts.* The wooden cupola containing the clock bell was added in the C18. The tower houses an excellent ring of six bells with a 14 cwt. tenor. The C19 saw extensive restorations; *nave* walls were heightened and new roofs installed in the 1820s, *aisle* windows and much of the chancel replaced in the 1860s, and a new e. window was inserted quite different in style from its predecessor. However, part of the *Decorated* tracery in the n. aisle windows is original and both C14 transepts have large end windows with fine *reticulated* tracery. There is a C15 *priest's door* with *trefoils* in the *spandrels* in the s. chancel wall.

Entry is by the s. *porch,* where all is restored except the *headstops* of the outer arch. Going through the C14 inner door, note the large holes in the *jambs* where a heavy beam was set for security. The interior is well kept and spacious, with attractive splashes of colour here and there, particularly the use of blue wall hangings in the n. transept. There are C14 *arcades* with octagonal *piers,* and a *font* of the same period with foliated crosses and shields in the bowl panels. All the ceilings are plastered. The C17 *gallery* in the tower arch originally accommodated the singers, but it now houses the organ which was moved from the n. transept in 1965. Look above it for the *sanctus-bell window,* opening from the ringing chamber. There are two sets of *Royal Arms* here: a large and dark *achievement* of George II painted on board just by the s. door, and a good example of George III's dated 1817 painted on canvas and displayed on the front of the gallery. Over by the n. door is a large, badly mutilated niche, with *Perpendicular* tracery behind what was a *crocketted* canopy. It may have housed a *St Christopher* statue or one of the church's patron saint, *St Martin.* The nave benches have C16 *linenfold* panelled ends and there are a few more in the s. aisle; these are a century later than the majority of pews in East Anglia and may have replaced a very early set. One bench, with very slim *poppyheads,* remains in the n. transept from a late-C14 or early-C15 chancel set. It has a line of *quatrefoil* sound holes under the plinth and there are vestiges of animals on the front buttresses. The *altar* here is a simple but satisfying late-C16 table, and it carries a fine cross and candlesticks adorned with the emblems of *St Edmund*. On the w. wall of this transept is a most interesting early-C17 memorial for Francis Robertson. It is a framed wooden square painted with a full achievement of his arms, and may have been used as a *hatchment* at his funeral, although the verse beneath makes me doubt this:

> Stay passenger, not ev'ry Calverie Can tell thee of such Reliques as here lie, Here lies one, that besides Coat-armorie, And other Monumentall braverie, T'adorne his Tombe hath left, ye memorie . . . Of Worth and Virtue Heavens heraldrie

The s. transept was restored in 1971 when some very interesting things came to light including the *aumbry* in the e. wall, a C13 *piscina* in the s. wall, with *dogtooth* ornament in the moulding of the trefoil arch, and a rare example of a C14 double *heart burial*, also in the s. wall. This is under a defaced *ogee* canopy and is divided into two compartments, each containing a pair of hands holding a heart. The C18 pulpit is tall, with a very high backboard and *tester*. It is plainly panelled in oak and would be vastly improved if the dark and muddy varnish could be removed. A small, typically *Jacobean* chest stands in front. There is now no chancel *screen*, but the stairs of the *rood loft* remain on the n. side, and an opening on the s. side shows that the loft probably extended over a *parclose screen* in the s. transept originally, rather like the arrangement at Dennington. In the chancel there are deeply-set *Early English lancets* and you will see that one on the s. side has been cut into to make room for the C15 priest's door. The C17 *communion rails* have nicely turned *balusters* but have had the same varnish treatment as the pulpit. In the n.e. corner of the *sanctuary* is a *Purbeck marble* tomb which may, from its position, have been used to mount the *Easter sepulchre*. The late-C13 double piscina is now a pair of short lancets devoid of ornament, with the original centre shaft. The altar *reredos* consists of the *Decalogue*, Lord's Prayer and Creed painted on zinc (a common and rather nasty C19 habit). The altar *Ecclesiological Society* candlesticks are those discarded from the pulpit when it was demoted from two-decker status in 1909, and have happily found their way back to the church. They were possibly purchased originally by Thomas Frognall Dibdin, the memorable, if slightly zany

bibliophile who was vicar here in the 1820s and who is remembered both for the pioneering and beautifully produced catalogue of the Spencer library at Althorp and for his own 'Bibliomania'.

Eye, St Peter and St Paul (F3): Eye is one of Suffolk's ancient boroughs and the splendid and beautifully kept church is set attractively just to the e. of the old castle mound. The mighty tower rises to just over 100ft. and has much in common with Redenhall a few miles away over the Norfolk border – the octagonal buttresses and a w. face completely covered with a fine web of *flushwork* in elongated panels. Begun in the 1450s, it was completed when the bells were hung in 1488, and it is interesting to see how the shape of the window arches varied significantly during those thirty years. There are still bells here – a good octave with a 19 cwt. tenor. The tower's *base course* of shields is set in multifoils and the niches flanking the door have had their canopies chipped away. The bell openings are pairs of windows linked by a *label* and the deep parapet below the stepped battlements is panelled *ashlar*; on the s. side an angel holds the shield of John De La Pole, Duke of Suffolk, whose badge occurs on Redenhall tower and probably explains why the two have so much in common. In contrast to the w. face, the rest of the tower is severely plain up to the bell stage.

The majority of the church was rebuilt in the late C15 and the *aisle* windows have miniature *embattled transoms* in the *Perpendicular tracery*. There is no n. porch and on that side the battlements are boldly chequered above prominent *gargoyles*. The aisles lap the *chancel* as far as the *sanctuary* and there is a n.e. *vestry* with an upper room. The e. window was probably renewed as part of the restoration carried out by J.K. Coiling in 1868 and the buttresses with their careful flushwork were reworked then or a little later. The n. *clerestory* wall is plain but on the s. side there are flushwork panels between the windows. The s.e. chapel follows the line of the s. aisle but the brick battlements are lower and have terracotta tiles inserted in them decorated with crowned boars and lions. The *priest's door* lies snugly below a miniature flying buttress like the one at Blythurgh and another doorway has been blocked at the e. end of the aisle. The late-C15 *porch* has suffered over the years and the dressed flints within the narrow ashlar panels on the e. side were replaced with brick at some stage. The s. face is entirely of stone and the octagonal corner buttresses are blind panelled in two stages. The base course was once decorated with monograms and the De La Pole shield crops up again, along with the *Tudor portcullis badge* and the *Blessed Virgin's* monogram. Access to the porch is now from within and one enters the church through the w. door.

The ground floor of the tower has a *fan vault* set around a circular trap door and the *gallery* above is a smaller version of the one at Mildenhall. There are *hatchments* for Mary D'Eye (1749), John Sayer (1761), and Rear-Admiral Sir Charles Cunningham (1834), together with two Tudor helmets on the s. wall, and an excellent set of George III *Royal Arms* are displayed opposite. Before exploring the body of the church, have a look at the s. porch. Built into its w. wall is a dole table of brick with a stone top which was given by Henry Cutler in 1601. This is the place where debts, tithes, and church dues were traditionally paid and where bread and other charities were distributed to the poor. There is some sage advice inscribed on the tablet above:

Seale not to soone lest thou repent to late,
Yet helpe thy frende, but hinder not thy
    state.
If ought thou lende or borrow, truly pay,
Ne give, ne take advantage, though thou
    may,
Let conscience be thy guide, so helpe thy
    frend,
With loving peace and concord make thy
    end.

Corner shafts remain of the original *groined* ceiling and the C15 rebuilding thought well enough of the C13 inner doorway to use it again – and rightly, for it is a fine piece. The flanking columns have stiff-leaf *capitals*, and there is a line of *dogtooth* decoration within the deeply cut mouldings of the arch. The C19 *font* has a 1930s cover designed by *Sir Ninian Comper*, who played a decisive role in beautifying the church. Turned pillars support the octagonal base of a skeletal tabernacle and it is prettily painted and gilt. The n. door is blocked by the tomb of Nicholas Cutler (1568) and his wife Elionora (1549), which was originally in the sanctuary. The *Purbeck marble* chest has small *cusped* lozenges that once contained brass shields, and there were more above the shallow, panelled recess. There are flanking columns and collared *griffins* on the pinnacles, while the pale *St Christopher* of 1921 in the window above is another Comper design.

Farther along in the n. aisle wall is an additional reminder of the earlier building in the form of a shallow mid-C14 tomb recess. Its tall *ogee* arch is *crocketted*, the deep cusps are carved with shallow leaf patterns, and two of the head terminals survive. The crockets of the flanking pinnacles sport tiny heads at their bases and the arch provides a lovely setting for an outstanding figure of the Blessed Virgin and Child. Carved in natural wood by Lough Pendred in the 1960s, the widely flowing and swirling cloak of Our Lady shows up boldly against a dark green background. The C14 *nave arcades* have octagonal *piers* and there are minor variations in the capitals, with the *hood moulds* on the s. side coming down to small *headstops*. The C16 roof is *arch-braced* and the deep *wall posts* rest on wooden *corbels* carved as heads. The w. end of the nave angles in towards the tower and there the wall posts are longer. The roof was extensively restored in 1868 and the small recumbent figures at the base of the braces appear to be largely C19. There are generous flower *bosses*, a canted cornice decorated with demi-angels and *paterae*, and at the e. end is a *celure*. Its panels are painted with the *Sacred monogram* in red within a green wreath sprouting flowers. This is modern work but the original may well have been similar.

Below stands the church's masterpiece, the 1480s *screen* that had its loft and *rood* figures replaced by Comper in 1925. The base has deep, cusped, and crocketted ogee arches above the painted panels and there are curly leaves carved and pierced in the *spandrels*. At the base is a line of crisply carved roundels containing triple *trefoils*, and note how each one is accompanied by a little panel to take up the space between the buttresses (a similar adjustment on a larger scale is the slim panel at the l.-hand side of the screen which was inserted to take up the full width of the arch). The *mullions* are painted with red and green scrollery on a white ground, and there are traces of *gesso* which can also be found on the leaf trail along the top rail. The arch of the centre doorway is a particularly good example of intricate elaboration and sensitive design, with a triple range of cusping (the doors themselves have gone, together with the tracery in the main *lights*). To the r. of the entrance, one of the arches carries the inscription: 'Pray for John Gold' – a reference to the probable donor. The underside of the loft is groined and decorated with stars and flowers on a blue ground, and the front arches come down to tiny demi-angels. There is a *pelican in her piety* at the base of the rood cross and dragons reach out below the feet of the Virgin and *St John,* while seraphs attend on either side. The lower panels have a full range of painted figures which are by no means great art, but they have not been so badly defaced as others elsewhere and they were meticulously restored (not repainted) by Miss Pauline Plummer in the 1960s. The selection of subjects is of more than usual interest; from l. to r. they are: *SS Paul* (or a king?), *Helen* with the true cross, *Edmund, Ursula* with the virgins under her cloak, *Henry VI* (d.1471 but never canonised), *Dorothy, Barbara, Agnes, Edward the Confessor* holding the legendary ring, *John, Catherine* with large sword and tiny wheel in the bottom corner, *William of Norwich, Lucy* smiling sweetly while carrying her bloody eyes on a book, *Thomas of Canterbury (Blaize* has been suggested but there is no sign of his wool comb), and *Cecilia.*

The C19 chamber organ in the s. aisle was restored and given by the local Bach choir in 1978, and the window to the e. of it has glass of 1876 by *Heaton, Butler & Bayne*. In the s.e. chapel there is the 1569 tomb of William Honyng which matches the Cutler monument in the n. aisle, and the e. window contains 1890s glass by H.A. Hymes on the 'Suffer little children to come unto me' theme. The side chapels are separated from the chancel by two-bay C14 arcades with *quatrefoil* pillars on tall bases and the organ is enclosed on the n. side by a handsome modern limed oak screen. The C15 clerestory continues over the chancel and the braces and *wall plates* of the roof are gaily painted. The C14 doorway to the has been restored and the door itself is in lovely pale oak, still with its original lockplate. On the n. wall is a tablet by Harvey of Diss for the Revd. Thomas Wythe who died in 1835, having been vicar here for fifty years. John Brown was a naval surgeon who died in 1732 and his memorial is on the s. wall – a shapely tablet in a dark frame below a curly cornice. At the base is a lively bas-relief tableau of the Good Samaritan whose horse grazes quietly as he tends the injured man, while the two other travellers 'pass by on the other side'. After the experience of the opulence of his rood, Comper's e. window glass seems pale and vapid, with conventional figures of Christ, SS John, Peter, and Paul. It does, however, include the kneeling figure of a vicar, John Polycarp Oakey (1927), in front of *St Polycarp* whose image is rarely seen in any medium.

Eyke, All Saints (H5): The building has a slightly strange, uneven appearance, largely because it has lost its *Norman crossing tower,* and

there was no replacement at the w. end. The *nave* was rebuilt on a larger scale in the C14, and in the 1860s *Edward Hakewill* carried out an extensive restoration. Walking round, you will see that the large w. window is a C19 replacement, and the nave has a pair of unusually slim windows with *Decorated tracery.* The *Early English* n. doorway is now unused, and a *Perpendicular* window was sited within the arch that led to the Norman n. *transept.* Above it, there is the outline of one of the C12 tower windows. A simple *vestry* has been added on the n. side of the *chancel,* and a stub of masonry at the n.e. corner shows that there was a medieval extension of some sort. A *scratch dial* is to be found low down on the r. of the C14 *priest's door,* and a vestige of the s. transept remains, much altered. The line of its *quoins* can be seen to the l. of the heavy brick buttress, and a window with intersected tracery was inserted in the early C14. The *porch* is modern, but incorporates medieval windows.

The whole character of the interior is conditioned by the splendid Norman arches of the centre crossing. They are broad and low, with *chevron* decoration – one band on the w. arch, and two on the e. The C14 nave is significantly wider than the original, and its roof has high *collars* and *king posts* below the ridge. The end wall of the nave was rebuilt a little further w. in the mid-C15, and note how the roof had to be marginally extended in consequence. Hakewill removed a plaster ceiling as part of the restoration, and replaced the angels on the *wall plate.* He inserted the new w. window and filled it with glass by *Lavers & Barraud* – a delightful series of leafy roundels in C13 style, the bands of colour alternating, within *crocketted* borders. The C15 *font* follows a familiar pattern, with its squat lions round the shaft, and fat *Tudor Roses* alternating with *Evangelistic symbols* in the bowl panels. The small chapel to the s. of the crossing was a *chantry* dedicated to the *Blessed Virgin,* known sometimes as Bavants' chantry from the name of the Rendlesham manor that endowed it. Founded in the mid-C14, its last priest was pensioned off, like many another, in 1537 at the *Reformation.* The Norman window in its e. wall was uncovered in the 1860s and the glass was probably supplied by Lavers & Barraud. The blocked doorway in the wall by the entrance gave access to a *rood loft stair,* and although there is now no *screen,* traces of paint at the e. end of the nave roof show that there was once a *celure* above the rood. The nave pews are plain, stained pine, but most of the furniture in the church is the work of Archdeacon James Darling and the villagers he taught during his time here as rector from 1893 until 1939. The font cover, organ case, pulpit, chapel screen, chancel stalls, vestry door, and *reredos* were all designed and largely made by him; a remarkable achievement. The priest's stall and lectern, by another hand, are his memorial. Moving through to the chancel, note another of the tower windows above the e. arch, and in the n. window there is a C17 roundel of the arms of the borough of Great Yarmouth, and two earlier and very faint angels. The *brass* displayed on the wall nearby dates from about 1430 and almost certainly commemorates John Staverton and his wife. He was a Baron of the Exchequer under Henry VI, and this is the only Suffolk example of an effigy in judicial robes. It lay originally in the chantry chapel, and when *William Dowsing* came in January 1643 to smash the stained glass, he 'took up a superstitious inscription', no doubt the one belonging to this brass; the heads are modern replacements. A slab in the centre of the chancel floor shows the outline of another brass, and it is now displayed on the s. wall. The 23in. bearded figure is dressed in a preaching gown and ruff, and commemorates Henry Mason who died in 1619, having been vicar of Snape some years before. He did not hold the living here, but had local connections and left bequests for the poor. The Darling stalls have an interesting variety of carvings, including the family's favourite red setter on the s. side, and an owl that nested in their stable yard; on the n. side, one finds a squirrel, otter, penguin and snake. The *Laudian communion rails* are simply turned, and within the *sanctuary* there are two *piscinas*, one C14 with a stone *credence shelf*, the other C15. The vestry door is one of the best of the archdeacon's pieces, and the 1890s glass in the e. window commemorates his father who served as rector before him for 34 years. Again by Lavers, Barraud & Westlake, in mellow colour, it pictures Christ and his disciples with children across the three *lights*, and Christ as the Good Shepherd flanked by angels within intricate *tabernacle work* above; an *Annunciation* and the four *Evangelists* fill the tracery.

Fakenham, St Peter (D3): It is important to walk round the outside of this church. Only by so doing can one see that it was begun before the Conquest. At the junction between *nave* and *chancel* on both sides there are typical *Saxon long and short quoins*. The original chancel will have been narrower than the present one. There is a blocked *Norman* slit window high in the n. wall

and another is partly concealed by the *porch* roof. The doorways and the *lancets* in the chancel are C13, but apart from a modern e. window the rest are C14. So too is the tower, which has a chequerwork *base course* and angled, stepped buttresses up to the belfry stage where there are *Decorated* windows on three sides with a lancet to the e. The porch was rebuilt in 1859, reusing the old windows and restoring the *stoup* in the angle by the door. The n. door was blocked up at the same time and the church was fitted out with new roofs, floors, pews and a *vestry*, with the organ coming in ten years later. The *font* is apparently medieval, with *paterae* on the base, stem and under the bowl, but the cross carved on one side of the bowl looks like C19 work. There is now no chancel arch, except for an *arch-braced* roof member which rests on *colonnettes* with angels below. The pulpit is C19 and the lectern of 1926 date. The *screen* incorporates some C15 work, notably the *cusping* in the main *lights* retaining a little colour, and the *mullions* which have shafts and *capitals* on the front side. The top coving, centre arch and the base panels are modern, but the blending is good and the total effect very pleasing. The C19 arch to the organ chamber-cum-vestry has stiff musical angels. The restorers dealt with the *piscina* and added *sedilia* alongside. Fragments of C15 glass, including angels' and devils' heads, have been collected together and arranged on patterns in the windows on the s. side of the chancel. In the n. wall of the *sanctuary* is a reconsituted arch over a table tomb for Reynolds Taylor (d.1692). The front panels recount a lengthy genealogy and there are seven shields of arms, with swags and drapes on the *pilasters*. Have a look at the four C13 grave slabs, with their elaborate floriated crosses, set in the w. wall of the tower, and as you close the modern s. door, admire the C14 ring handle with its mask *boss*.

Falkenham, St Ethelbert (G7): Approaching from Kirton, it is easy to overshoot the church, hidden as it is by majestic limes and set back from the road. Within the churchyard the setting is delectable, with a broad vista opening up beyond the e. end across the Deben estuary to Ramsholt. The C15 tower is compact and very handsome, with a bold stair turret on the s. side. There are *fleurons* in the mouldings of the w. doorway, and its *label* rests on fine crowned lion *stops*. One of the shields in the *spandrels* bears the remains of *Passion emblems*, and there are interesting shields ranged along the top. The lion on the l. probably represents the Mowbray family, and the bear with ragged staff on the r. identifies the arms as those of Richard Neville, Earl of Warwick, known to history as 'Warwick the Kingmaker'. The shield in the centre carries the arms of England in the form first used in 1405, completing an impressive combination for a little country church. The w. window is a wayward C19 version of the four-petalled flower motif, but the paired bell openings are the tower's best feature. Their *tracery* harks back to the C14, and there is *flushwork* between the lights and in panels below them. One of the tower's three *string courses* lifts to form labels over each opening, and decorative panels are centred on each face under the stepped flushwork battlements. Within its walls hangs an excellent ground floor ring of six bells with a 5 cwt. tenor. In the early C17, the *chancel* was ruinous, and wholesale repair was required by the end of the C18. The *nave* walls were encased in white Suffolk bricks, and stones record the work of vicar John Edgar and churchwarden John Woodger on the n. side (1800), and Edgar paired with Robert Daniel on the s. side (1806). The *chancel* was not replaced, but in the mid-C19 a polygonal *apse* in red brick was added, and in 1865 new nave windows were inserted with attractive tracery. By the s. wall you will find a good headstone of 1907 for James Howell, a seafaring man who had a full-rigged ship carved above his epitaph. The C14 *porch* was comprehensively restored and converted into a *vestry* in 1890, and entry is now by way of the w. door.

Standing within, it is obvious that when the tower was built (or rebuilt) in the C15 it was set out of alignment with the rest, and the nave has something in common with *weeping chancels*. The door to the tower stair is made of rugged, keeled boards and still has its original draw latch. A copy of a drawing by the antiquarian David Davy hangs on the opposite wall and shows that the exterior of the church has changed very little since 1843. Originally the tower boasted a *gallery*, and unlike most, it had a separate stairway whose entrance survives in the n.w. corner of the nave. The broad, almost square nave has a *hammerbeam roof*, and a bequest of 1510 suggests that it dates from that period. It has a deep, moulded *wall plate*, and the *arch-braces* rise to *collar beams* from the back of the hammers; all the angel carvings are modern replacements. The recumbent figures bear shields with (mainly) *Passion emblems* – n. side, w. to e.: cross, ladder, *Agnus Dei*, crown of thorns, spear; s. side, w. to e.: hammer & pincers, nails, scourges, *Trinity* shield. The C15 *font* is a fine example of

the East Anglian type, and the carvings in the bowl panels are exceptionally well preserved. They were plastered over in the C17, either as a defence against mutilation or as an alternative to it, and are well nigh perfect except for the angels' noses. *Evangelistic symbols* alternate with angels bearing shields, and the latter display the Trinity shield (e.), *St George's* cross (s.), triple *Sacred monograms* (w.), and the emblem of *St Edmund* (n.). There are worn angel heads below the bowl and lions guard the shaft. The 1860s restoration included a new tiled floor and pitchpine benches, replacing C18 *box pews*. In 1838, *Thurlow's* of Saxmundham provided the tablet on the s. wall for George Roddam, physician to King George IV, Princess Charlotte, and Prince Leopold of Saxe Coburg. The design, with its pair of scallop shells, was copied fifty years later by Frewer of Ipswich for the doctor's widow and is placed on the opposite wall. The handsome little chamber organ that stands by the *sanctuary* steps dates from about 1760, and the *altar reredos* incorporates the front of a C14 chest. It was given to the church in 1936, and its beautiful flamboyant tracery suggests Flemish influence.

Farnham, St Mary (H5): This hilltop site was once a Roman camp guarding the river crossing in the valley below, and there is quite a sharp drop to the w., with a view across to Stratford St Andrew's church. The tower probably dates from around 1500, and is interesting because it is built mainly of the thin white Suffolk bricks, rather than the more usual red. It has a small w. window, a shallow belfry stair on the s. side, and the stumpy bell stage is in dark C18 brick, probably replacing a more generously proportioned predecessor. The church is a simple *nave* and *chancel*, and walking round it, the first signs of it's true age are the small *Norman lancets*, one in each nave wall, and the *coursed* flints which show here and there. A dire weakness in the s. wall called for thick, sloping buttresses (C18?), and part of a C14 window shape peeps out by one of them at the w. end; a modern window has taken the place of the s. doorway. The three large lancets and the *priest's door* on that side are all framed in brick and may date from the time when the tower was rebuilt. The e. window and nave n. windows have been all been renewed, probably during the 1883 restoration. An older and higher roof line shows on the tower's e. face above the attractive pantile roofs.

A shallow, modern oak *porch* shields the n.

doorway, and the pleasantly simple interior has a number of things to interest the visitor. From the inside, one can seen that the doorway itself lies within a tall Norman arch shape whose stonework has recently been uncovered. The position of the old s. doorway opposite is marked by a *stoup* recess, and the amazing outward lean of the whole s. wall explains the buttresses outside. The typically shaped recesses of the Norman lancets have had the stonework of the inner arches cleared of plaster. All that remains of the C15 *rood screen* is displayed on the w. wall – traceried sections of two of the upper panels, and they show that it was a fine example in its heyday. The *font* is C19, and the two ranges of *box pews* in the nave date from the C18. In dark painted pine, they have panelled doors, and the front pew on the s. side was amended a little later to link up with a pulpit in cheaper style, painted to match the rest. The C19 *scissors-braced* nave roof, now stripped of its plaster, is rather handsome, and there are homely brick floors throughout, unaffected by the current craze for carpeting. Although no screen now separates nave from chancel, the substantial stair that led to the *rood loft* remains in the n. wall, and you can see that some of the wooden treads are still in place on the steps. As with the nave, the chancel ceiling has been removed to expose the C16 light-weight, single-framed roof, and C19 *Decalogue* boards flank the e. window. One finds that the priest's door has been blocked, and like the main entrance, it lies within a tall Norman arch. The *piscina* arch may be contemporary, although I suspect that it has been re-set and may not have belonged there originally. The man *Dowsing* came visiting one January day in 1643, but had to content himself with 'taking up a popish inscription in brass'.

Felixstowe, St Andrew (G7): Development at the turn of the century meant that the town needed more churches, and after the establishment of St John's, attention turned to the area close to the Town station which had opened in 1898. The first St Andrew's of 1907 was a wood and corrugated iron affair that had already seen service in London, and it was not until the advent of an enthusiastic vicar in 1925 that momentum gathered. H.B. Greene was in no doubt what sort of church he wanted, and the results were, in their way, nothing short of remarkable. Having discarded a design by Henry Buxton, he chose Hilda Mason as his architect, only to find that her first effort was turned down by the Ecclesiastical Commissioners. A second

essay in collaboration with Raymond Erith was accepted, and work began in 1929. It was to be the first church in England to use ferro-concrete as the basic material, and this determined its character. Having said that, the architects astutely harnessed their uncompromising material to the East Anglian *Perpendicular* tradition, and produced a church of genuine character. It is a pity that their concept was never fully realised; apart from the stumps of two stair turrets, the splendidly bold tower remained a dream, and there were to have been pinnacles spaced along the roof lines. The harshness of the grey building is softened now by the cedars along the frontage and shrubs against the walls, but there is still an element of skeletal gauntness. The walls between the buttresses are glazed across their whole width with a series of narrow *lights,* and the theme of verticality is continued in the bulky parapets of *nave* and *aisles*. Pebble-dash infill is used on the e. walls and the porch, and there is a medieval echo in the form of a *priest's door* into the organ chamber. The foundation stone w. of the porch sums up the rigid variety of churchmanship behind the project: '. . . in humble thanksgiving for answered prayer in the rejection of the Prayer Book Measures 1927-8 by the House of Commons, & the maintenance thereby in the national church of the teaching of Holy Scripture & the principles of the Reformation'. The tall porch was to have had a conventional outer arch with *blind arcading* above it, but this was never done and it is open to its full height.

Within, the walls of glass in the aisles and the generous *clerestory* windows promote a feeling of light and airy spaciousness, and there is a strongly vertical pattern of slate grey principals. The simple *Tudor* arch shapes of the nave *arcades* have pierced *spandrels*, and the solid w. wall is broken only by the frame that would have fronted the tower gallery. The combination of grey beams and buff panels in the *chancel* is strangely reminiscent of half-timbering, and the clerestory is a continuous range of glass, with the s. wall of the *sanctuary* glazed down to the dado. Stained glass to Hilda Mason's designs was already being installed when the vicar took exception not only to what he called an 'ice cream parlour effect', but to the e. window itself. The architects refused to compromise, and Raymond Wrinch took over. The substitute glass was supplied by Pearce & Cutler, an Ascension in which Christ rises against a cloudy blue sky with the watchers stagily grouped bottom l.. The building deserved better. Wrinch designed most of the fittings, and used a variation of *linen-fold* as a theme to link the font case, massive pulpit, and its matching reading desk. The *altar* is a finely carved reproduction of an Elizabethan table, and its gilded text matches another under the e. window; C19-style *Decalogue* boards are framed on the e. wall.

Felixstowe, St Edmund (G7): When a daughter church was planned for the parish of St John the Baptist, a plot was acquired on Langer road large enough for a hall as well. The church was to stand well back from the road, but in the event, it was never built, and in 1923 the design of the hall was adapted so that it could take its place, although it faces w. rather than e. The architect was H. Clegg, and it is a small, neat building in red brick with stone dressings. The frontage has a squared-off shallow porch with side doors, and the pair of *lancets* above are separated by a blind lancet and all are grouped below a common *dripstone*. The side walls have three pairs of lancets under sharp little gables that rise to form dormers in the roof. There are flanking *vestries*, and the bell that hangs under a wooden cote over one of them belonged originally to St John's.

The *nave* is broad for its length, and its roof is quite enterprising, considering the small scale. *Arch-braces* rise to *tie-beams* halfway up the slope, and above them, *queen-posts* are braced up to *collar beams*; the dormer shapes break in to meet alternate tie-beams. Hintlesham has recently acquired a C15 *font* from the redundant church at Shipmeadow, and their own C19 model has been passed on to St Edmund's. Standing on a short, traceried stem, the panels of the octagonal bowl are carved with *quatrefoils* and a single *Sacred monogram*. The shallow *sanctuary* lies beyond a plain brick arch.

Felixstowe, St John the Baptist (G7): Standing high, on Orwell Road, its spire is a good marker for strangers to the town. A new parish for the expanding resort was created in the late C19, and St John's was begun in 1894. The architect was *Sir Arthur Blomfield*, and this is his most significant work in the county. The nave and *aisles* were completed within a year, and a second stage followed a little later, with the *chancel*, *vestries*, and Lady chapel being consecrated in 1899, the year Blomfield died. He had planned a tower, and it was added in 1914, the design slightly amended by his son Charles. H.F. Walker designed the choir vestry in 1929, and *Cautley* was responsible for the 1940s n. porch. It is a

building with great presence, in red brick highlighted with Bath stone dressings. The uniformity of the mass is broken by the pitched roof of the Lady chapel which rises sharply alongside the chancel, cutting short the low lean-to roof of the aisle. The muscular s.w. tower is focal, able to compete with the very high roof of the nave, and its s. doorway is recessed below an angular *crocketted* arch. It is well proportioned, with good detailing, although the weak profiles of the bulky corner pinnacles quarrel with the strong lines of the stone spire. The overall inspiration for the design is *Early English*, although *Decorated tracery* was chosen for the chancel e. window. The tower houses an excellent ring of eight bells with a 7 cwt. tenor.

Within, there is a feeling of dusky mystery, even on a sunny day, the red brick warm and comfortable. The *arcades* of the broad nave have generous arches, and above them the brick is relieved by bands of rough grey stone. The same motif links the small, deeply recessed clerestory windows, alternate *cinquefoils* and *sexfoils*. The nave roof is a *tie-beam* and *king post* design, and there are tie-beams again in the aisles, with transverse braces up to the *purlins*. Wrought-iron screens enclose the baptistery at the w. end of the n. aisle, and the polygonal *font* has a chunky cover in C15 style made by Harry Turner of Ipswich in 1912. With the three exceptions detailed later, all the stained glass is by *Powell & Sons*, and provides an interesting sequence of their work between the 1890s and the 1950s. The earliest are the aisle w. windows – St Felix baptising and teaching (n.), and the Holy Family with a youthful *St John the Baptist* (s.). The aisle *lancets* contain good single figures standing within elaborate *tabernacled* niches; n. aisle (1920-42), Old Testament prophets, with Christ and *St Peter* above the door as a memorial for the church's first vicar; s. aisle (1909-1958), *apostles*, with a significant contrast in treatment between *St Paul* and *St James the Great*. The Lady chapel is entered through a half-arch from the s. aisle, and there are beautiful 1920s gates made by Wippell & Co. They have flamboyant tracery in the panels, and their stepped top rails carry pairs of kneeling angels, flanked by small figures of *St Gabriel* and the *Blessed Virgin*. A chunky two-bay *arcade* separates the chapel from the chancel, and the compact *reredos* is again by Wippells. The lancets above contain 1880s figures of a young *St Edmund* and richly robed St Felix and *St Fursey*, all on elaborate pedestals. The s. *sanctuary* window has a regal 1905 *St Etheldreda*, reading her missal, and to the w., a tall and gracious *St Cecilia*. The remaining lancets are filled with glass by Goddard & Gibbs Studios, who provided an excellent window at Beyton in the 1960s. Here, we find: a gaunt St John the Baptist; *St Thomas More*, with the axe, block, and date of his martyrdom above; *St Francis* with flames curling from the stigmata, and a vignette of Assisi below.

Blomfield had intended to have a low brick and stone chancel screen, but in 1910 Gerald Cogswell designed the present *rood screen* in conformity with the Suffolk tradition, yet with a distinct character of its own. It has very slender uprights, and there is a delicate web of tracery above idiosyncratic arches, double banked above the entrance. Cogswell had previously designed the pulpit, an intricate piece of work in traditional style, with pierced tracery panels and figures of the *Evangelists* under canopies at the angles. The broad chancel arch fades gently into the walls onto shallow stone *corbels*, and the ensign draped to the r. was flown from HMS Curlew in World War I. After the nave, the chancel is decidedly rich, particularly the sanctuary, with its e. wall veneered in marble and alabaster. There are mosaic panels heightened with gilt, and the reredos is a Last Supper in matching materials, set above five panels of gilded wheat and vine patterns. The e. window, flanked by *blind arches*, contains the best of the Powell glass, installed at the turn of the century. The centre Crucifixion has the three mourning figures below, and the cross's upright sprouts branches that enclose two kneeling angels bearing the chalice and wafer; *Passion shields* hang above them, and two more angels are crowning the cross; groups of figures fill the flanking lights – Old Testament prophets above, saints below, including *St Alban* on the l. and *St Botolph* on the r.

Felixstowe, St Nicholas (G7): The road wends its way through the golf links down to Bawdsey Ferry, and the cluster of houses and boat yards is served by this modest daughter church of St Andrew's. In the 1870s, a corrugated hut became both church and schoolroom, and so it remained until 1943 when it was damaged beyond repair in an air raid. The golfers came to the rescue with another hut until a replacement was provided in 1954. A grey martello tower looms beyond as a reminder of earlier alarms and excursions, and the small, ochre-coloured church sits demurely among its holiday-home neighbours. It is a basic building of three bays, with steel domestic windows, asbestos corrugated roof, and simple recessed porch. A

plaque by the door records its short history, and the text from the prophet Haggai is well chosen: 'The glory of the latter house shall be greater than that of the former, saith the Lord of Hosts, and in this place I will give peace'. Judging by the visitors' comments, that is what many of them have found in this simple interior which has more in common with a nonconformist chapel than the average Anglican church. There are C19-style *Decalogue* boards above the trio of small rectangular windows in the e. wall, and an American organ from the earlier building is labelled 'Felixstowe Ferry Church'. Crisp curtains, fresh flowers, and an attractive appliqué lectern frontal of a ship in honour of the patron saint provide focal points of colour.

Felixstowe, St Peter and St Paul (G7): Standing at the end of Church Road, this is the town's oldest building by far, having served since Felixstowe was no more than a hamlet by the shore. A *lych-gate* of 1911 stands at the entrance, and the churchyard is bounded s. and e. by straggling Scots pine. The attractively chunky building has been repaired and altered greatly over the years. It was neglected and decayed in the C18, and by the early C19 the tower had partially collapsed and the ruined *chancel* was meanly replaced in brick. In the 1870s, a full-scale restoration and rebuilding was put in hand – the tower was heightened, the *nave* was re-roofed and its walls were raised, while *transepts* and a new chancel transformed the e. end. The tower is capped with a pyramid roof just above the ridge of the nave, and there is an early-C14 w. doorway. Much of the original *septaria* remains in the n. wall, and there are heavy C18/ early-C19 angle buttresses in red brick. In 1988, a large meeting room with associated facilities was added, linked to the nave by the early-C14 n. doorway which provided the theme for the new *lancets* and doors. By its n.w. corner, a stone flush with the ground is Robert Passiful's memorial, a Trinity House pilot for over thirty years who died at the Ferry in 1890. The work of the 1870s changed the character of the church decisively. The transepts are very tall for their mass, and their steep roofs have a common ridge which overtops the nave. The e. gable of the crossing carries a *sanctus-bell turret*, and the short chancel is *apsidal*, with muscular buttresses and C14-style windows. The most striking feature of the new work is the way in which old, multi-coloured bricks were used in the walls. They came from a martello tower at Bawdsey and are arranged in a series of swirling patterns that is quite uncharacteristic of the period. Above the entrance of the rugged little C14 *porch* there is a niche which has shields for the church's patron saints in its *spandrels*, and three steps lead down to the inner doorway.

The Victorian alterations reduced the length of the nave, and it is spanned by heavy *tie-beams* below a plastered ceiling. A blocked C14 window remains at the w. end of the n. wall, and the late-C18 oval tablet opposite was moved from the old chancel. It commemorates Adam Wood 'of the Independent Company of Invalids at Landguard Fort', leaving one wishing to know more about a body with such an intriguing name. A C16 poorbox is fixed to the pews near the entrance, square with two-way hasps, and further along one finds a simple tablet for Viscount Allenby of World War I desert fame. A tablet on the w. wall of the n. transept commemorates Sir John Spencer Login who died in 1863. He was guardian to the young Maharajah Duleep Singh (see Elveden), and the large memorial in the churchyard n.e. of the chancel was 'erected by his affectionate friend & ward, in grateful remembrance of the tender care and solicitude with which he watched over his early years' (the text from Proverbs was Queen Victoria's contribution). The 1920s armorial glass in the n. lancets is by F.C. Eden, the artist who did good work at Barsham. Here, the *Royal Arms* are accompanied by the achievements of the Login and Campbell of Kinloch families. In a recent rearrangement the *altar* stands under the crossing on a spacious podium, with the early *Stuart* pulpit to one side. That displays three ranks of good arabesque panels, but looks a little lost without the stem, backboard and *tester* that it probably had originally. It stands on a square section of a moulded column which may have come from the vanished Benedictine priory. A wide arch opens into the chancel which has become a spacious baptistery, with the *font* transferred from the w. end – a bulky octagon which has been variously described as C15 and C17, although I would split the difference. The bowl panels are slightly dished shields carved with *Passion emblems*, a crown, an angel, and a rather fine ship to the w. When the chancel was rebuilt, the C14 *piscina* was salvaged and remains in the s. wall of what was the *sanctuary*. At the same time, a few C15 bench ends with battered *poppyheads* and fragments of animals were worked into new choir stalls and some larger beasts were added. The 1880s stained glass is unusually good and although the artist has not been identified, the colouring is reminiscent of Leonard Walker's

work in the chancel at Brandon. Each light contains a single figure – *SS Edmund, Nicholas, Peter, Paul, Felix, Sigebert*, Anna, and *Luke*. They have attractive foliage settings, and there are little vignettes – Bury Abbey for St Edmund, Norwich cathedral for St Felix, and a ship with a lighthouse for the patron saint of seafarers.

Felsham, St Peter (D5): Fronting the village street opposite the Six Bells public house, with tall limes along the frontage, this church received fairly drastic treatment in the C19. Its *chancel* was rebuilt in 1873 and there was a heavy *nave* restoration in 1899. The low w. doorway of the tower has worn *headstops*, with flowing *Decorated tracery* in the window above. The bell openings have *Perpendicular* tracery and the strong *string courses* make it very attractive. A will of 1423 refers to 'the new tower' which is helpful in dating it. It houses a ground floor ring of six bells with a 15 cwt. tenor but their condition allows them only to be rung occasionally. The nave is tall, with elegant C14 windows and *flushwork* battlements and beyond the plain little s. *porch* there is a faint *scratch dial* on the first buttress. The main entrance from the street is much more impressive and the C15 porch is large and lavish. The whole front and the buttresses are embellished with flushwork and the large side windows have *transomes* within the tracery. The mouldings of the entrance arch are decorated with three ranks of *paterae* and the *dripstone* rests on carved lions accompanied (and this is unusual) by birds. There are shields in the *spandrels* and a canopied niche over the entrance is matched by a pair in the buttresses. The old staircase to the *rood loft* juts out of the nave wall on this side and there is a *priest's door* further along in the chancel. Entry is via a plain C14 doorway and over the C19 doorway opposite is a set of George III *Royal Arms* dated 1820 and painted on board. The C15 *font* is excellent, its panels filled with intricate tracery which incorporates shields on four sides. There are demi-angels below the bowl and the shaft rests on a large octagonal base. The latter has all the appearance of being the bowl of a C14 *font* which was cut down and filled in to carry its successor – a similar ploy was used at Friston. Its side panels are carved with *cusped ogee* tracery, within which are halves of *green men's* heads, sea monsters, and one half of a standing figure. All the church's fittings and roofs are C19, as is the *bier* that stands at the w. end. There are fragments of C15 glass in the tracery of two nave windows and the *reredos* in the chancel is a copy of Raphael's 'Charge to St Peter'. All is neat and well cared for, but much of the interior's character has been restored away.

Finningham, St Bartholomew (E4): Entry is now across the n. side of the churchyard, but the emphasis originally was on the s. and the lavish C15 *porch* there is very attractive. It has three fine niches around the outer arch, one with an elaborate canopy, and the arch *spandrels* contain a merchant's mark and a *Trinity* shield. The front has *flushwork* panelling overall and there is a line of *quatrefoils* under the gable, with *crocketted* pinnacles at the corners. When walking round, look for a *scratch dial* on the l. of the s. *nave* buttress about 6ft. from the ground. All the side windows of the nave and *chancel* are *Perpendicular;* but the *priest's door* on the s. side is early C14. The e. window was renewed in the C19 and there is a niche of the same period above it. The red brick, late Perpendicular n. porch has virtually no ornament and (the door having been blocked) it is now a *vestry*. The unbuttressed early-C14 tower has 'Y' *tracery* bell openings on three sides and a quatrefoil to the e.

Entering by the s. porch, note that the C19 restoration included a new roof on stone *corbels* and look for three *consecration crosses* cut in the *jamb* of the early-C14 inner doorway. The door itself is medieval and still has its original closing ring. *Sanctus-bell windows* are generally small affairs, but here there is one nearly as large as a door, and in view of the date of the tower, it is possible that it might have been designed as a secure access to the upper chamber. Below is an attractive C19 *gallery*, in front of which stands the late-C15 *font*, raised on two steps in Maltese cross form. The bowl panels are deeply carved with tracery and, instead of a flower at the centre, the n.w. panel has a mask. The contemporary cover is a beautifully compact version of the *tabernacle* type, and the radiating ribs are heavily crocketted, rising to a turned and carved *finial*. Between the ribs are pierced tracery panels with little crocketted *pediments*, and below them, a deeply moulded and crested base. To the r. of the vestry entrance, there are remains of a *stoup*, so that the C14 doorway on that side may well have been the one in common use before the advent of the new s. porch. Most of the seating in the nave is good C19 work, but there are medieval bench ends at the w. end, and the four just e. of the font have figures which face inwards, an unusual variation. Second from the w. on the s. side is the figure of gluttony which has

lost half its head but still holds a ladle over the stock pot between its knees, while clutching a rosary in the other hand. The irony was probably intentional. The *hammerbeams, wall plates*, and *collar beams* beneath the ridge of the nave roof are all embattled, and it looks as though there were angels tenoned into the ends of the hammers. The white ceiling panels between the main timbers set them off very well. The wide chancel arch has no *screen* now and a large modern crucifix hangs very effectively within it. During extensive restorations in the 1880s, the *chancel* was partially rebuilt and given a new roof, but some medieval bench ends were reused in the new choir stalls. On the n. side there is a grotesque and a castle, and on the s., a seated figure, and a tower with a portcullis which has a head poking out of the top, entirely out of scale. The rear stall on the n. side has the front of a *Jacobean* chest used as part of the back. In the *sanctuary* there is a C14 *piscina* under a wide *trefoil* arch, and in the top *lights* of the e. window, some of the C15 glass remains in the form of rather jumbled figures without heads. Two of them, however, are identified by their emblems; the second from the l. is *St Simon* holding a fish, and to his r., *St James the Great* with his scallop shell.

Finningham has some interesting monuments. Look first at Sir John Fenn's on the chancel n. wall by *John Bacon* – a delicately sculpted figure of a woman kneeling over a table tomb; set against grey, veined marble, it has the epitaph below. Sir John was a leading C18 antiquarian and the man who discovered and published the Paston letters in 1787. He lived at East Dereham in Norfolk, but his wife was a Frere and so he was buried here, the home, since 1598, of that important Suffolk family. Lady Fenn died in 1813 and her tablet, within a 'gothick' arch, is alongside:

> Though not herself a mother, she took an interest in children... hence arose the literary works which rendered her a distinguished supporter of the improved system of early education.

That refers to her rather earnest books for children under the pseudonyms of 'Mrs Teachwell' and 'Mrs Lovechild'. She was, incidentally, the model for Lady Bountiful in George Borrow's *Lavengro*. A little to the w. is a charming tablet by John Golden of Holborn whose work spans the end of the C18 and the beginning of the C19. He was fond of using coloured marbles combined with details borrowed from the brothers Adam. This tablet is a good example of the technique; pale brown mottled stone sets off the white marble epitaph tablet and the base carries motifs often seen on chimney pieces and ceilings of the period. It commemorates John Williamson, who died in 1871, a friend of the Freres and felicitously described as being 'cheerful in his social connections...'. There are, of course, a number of Frere memorials and quite the nicest is for the rector Edward Frere who died in Bath in 1841, aged 36. It is on the nave n. wall and is an oval coat of arms in coloured marble, with a swooping and heavily curved scroll beneath – much better than the average design of the period.

Flempton, St Catherine (C4): Standing at the village crossroads, this is a neat and trim church. Most of the tower collapsed in the mid-C18 and it was rebuilt in 1839. This was followed by an almost total reconstruction of the rest of the building later in the century, with a ponderous *vestry* added outside of the old n. door. A C15 timber and plaster *porch* was replaced by the present one at that time, but the heads of the C15 entrance doors have interesting *tracery* cut in the solid. The interior is light and fresh, with plain white walls, and over the tower arch is a pretty little set of George III *Royal Arms*, dated 1763 and having the distinction of being signed by the artist, a Mr Boynton of Bury. A plain octagonal early C14 *font* stands within the tower. Despite *Cautley's* slighting comment, the Victorian bench ends are attractive, their small *finials* carved with leaves and the shoulders decorated with *paterae*. A window on the s. side of the nave contains glass by G.E.R. Smith in which the figures of *SS Francis, John the Evangelist* and *Christopher* stand out effectively against clear glass, with shields of arms in the tracery. It commemorates Sir John Wood, last of the Hengrave squires, who died in 1951. Opposite is the 1927 memorial window for Lady Wood, with figures of *St Catherine of Alexandria*, with her palm and sword (rather than the more usual wheel) and *St Gertrude*, bearing a crozier and the Sacred Heart. The pulpit is a good late-C16 or early-C17 design with two tiers of blank arches in the tall panels. Although there is now no *screen*, one can see where the chancel arch was notched on the e. side to accommodate the *rood loft*. In the window just beyond on the s. side, one of the *lights* is *transomed* to form a *low side window* below. The *priest's door* is just beyond,

and above it is a tablet for John Harcourt Powell who died in 1840. It is by Matthew Wharton Johnson whose rather dull work is scattered all over England. There are plain C17 *communion rails*, but within the *sanctuary* is a very handsome double *piscina*. The arch encloses pierced tracery, with a single *reticulation* above the *cusped* arches, and there is a small opening in the side through to the window sill. The late-C17 *altar* table stands on a slab which, although it was later engraved as a grave slab, was probably the church's original *mensa*. The *Decorated* e. window has flowing tracery and is filled with 1890s glass by *Clayton & Bell* – the Crucifixion spread across three lights, with a row of small shields painted with *Passion emblems* above. There are one or two riveting Christian names to be found hereabouts – Fitz Nun Lambe (1733) lies by the priest's door, a brass plate on the s. wall mentions Zilpha Frost (1918), and you may take my word for it that behind the organ there is a memorial to an C18 rector called Blastus Godley.

Flixton, St Mary (H2): A charming situation above the Waveney valley, with glimpses of open country through the trees from the undulating churchyard. The church was almost entirely rebuilt in two phases during the C19 and is an interesting example of quality Victorian work. In 1856, the work was under the direction of Anthony Salvin (the architect who had done drastic work on parts of Norwich cathedral twenty years earlier). The tower had fallen some years before, and he replaced it with one which seems to be derived from the unique *Saxon* tower at Sompting in Sussex, with its Rhenish spire. Sompting had been restored only three years previously and may well have been fresh in Salvin's mind. In contradiction, it has been said that he copied the original, but apparently a drawing done in 1818 shows that this was not so. The tower has a small, deeply recessed w. door under a triangular arch, and Saxon-style circular windows n. and s. There are three ranges of *lancets* up to double-arched bell openings with centre pillars, and the diamond-shaped *broaches* of the spire rise directly from the walls, to be topped by a plump and gilded weathercock. In 1861, the *nave* and n. *aisle* were rebuilt in *Perpendicular* style, and the chancel followed in 1893. It had long been in ruins, and this time the *Norman* style was chosen, with bulky lancets and a heavy *corbel* table under the eaves. Walking round, note the five-sided chapel with a tiled, pyramid roof at the w. end of the aisle that was the last major addition in 1902, and also the selection of shapely C18 headstones on the s. side of the church – Francis Chamberlain's epitaph of 1788 begins:

Here lies an Honest & a generous Friend,
Peaceful in life & happy to his end.

Having entered, you will see that in rebuilding, the architect retained the C14 four-bay *arcade*, with its *quatrefoil piers* and wave mouldings in the arches. The broad nave has a good quality *arch-braced* roof, with a double bank of flat demi-angels carved on the *wall plate*. The C19 *font* is a square bowl set on a massive stem and four corner shafts. The oak benches are Victorian too, but most of them incorporate C15 ends which have good *poppyheads*. Some of the elbows are *castellated*, and the one at the front on the s. side of the nave carries a charming little gabled building. Nearby is the church's only medieval *brass*, an inscription and shield for Elizabeth Tasburgh. She was the wife of the Lord of the Manor and died in 1583. The monument re-sited on the s. wall is for William Adair who died in 1783. It displays a bas-relief of the Good Samaritan, with *pilasters* on each side carved with leafy scrolls; the drape below the oval tablet is secured by beast skulls – a curious conceit. The handsome late-C16 or early-C17 pulpit is six-sided and stands on a coved stem. Its two ranges of panels are carved with *linen-fold*, with the exception of two which have attractive shields of arms within blind arches; the one under the book slope quarters the arms of the Duke and Parker families, and in the other, Duke is partnered with Baynard. The wide chancel arch conforms to the Norman idiom we saw outside, but the windows all have *cusped* and pierced interior arches which are quite at variance. The chancel is paved with variegated marble, and the stalls, wall panelling and *reredos* are all in oak. A wide *credence* recess is inset on the n. side of the *sanctuary*, and there are two *sedilia* stalls on the other side. This all contributes to a rich effect, and so does the glass. The e. lancets and upper circular window are filled with pleasing designs by *Thomas Willement*, dating from 1857 and re-set from the earlier building. There are three bright roundels in each lancet, illustrating Christ's Nativity, Baptism, Crucifixion, Entombment, Resurrection and Acension. In the side windows, the 1890s figures of Moses, Elias, David, St Peter and St Paul are by *Burlison & Grylls*, all in their rich C16 style.

Moving to the n. aisle, there is a Perpendicular *piscina* that served the original chapel altar there, and a group of interesting monuments on the wall. At the e. end, a pair of tall tablets for Richard Tasburgh and Lettice Wybarne his daughter (1716 and 1737), with flanking candlesticks, garlanded urns on top and *cartouches* below. Next to them is a *touchstone* tablet below a ponderous scroll cornice and coloured cartouche for Margaret Tasburgh. She died in 1705, having been: 'a patient sufferer in prison with her husband during ye persecution called ye popish Plott, of which hee was accused & tryed for his life, but by a Jury of worthy Gentlemen of Suffolk had justice done him'. Accounts of the plot seldom mention the wives of the accused and I have never seen a reference to their imprisonment with their husbands. The frame that hangs on the side of the organ nearby contains a beautifully delicate embroidery in sampler style, its Latin texts and New Testament scenes surrounded by variegated borders. Is it C19? The chapel at the w. end of the aisle is a fine essay in the *Early English* style, with a triple entrance arch and a *groined* vault. It was built in 1902 as the setting for a life-size figure of Theodosia, Lady Waveney who died in 1871. With hands clasped, she kneels on a tasseled cushion decorated with her family arms and badges, the only ornament of an otherwise austere composition. The sculptor was John Bell, a Suffolk man who achieved great

Flixton, St Mary:
Theodosia, Lady Waveney by John Bell

popularity through his 'Babes in the wood' group – now in Norwich museum. Much of his work was in poor taste and slated by the critics even in his own day, but this figure is impressive.

Flowton, St Mary (E6): Except for minor alterations, repairs, and renewals, this small, attractive church has changed but little since it was built in the late C13 or early C14. The unbuttressed tower was originally a good deal higher but in the mid-C18 it was in danger of collapse and the bell chamber was removed; in its place we have a brick parapet and tiled pyramid roof complete with a little dormer door, and the *quatrefoils* that were once the belfry windows are now just below the top. It is unusual to find the ground-floor entrance in the s. wall. There is a tall w. window with 'Y' *tracery* flanked by deep niches under multi-*cusped* arches. There is a small n. door and 'Y' tracery windows on the n. side of the *nave*, and a brick *vestry* rather like a little cottage complete with a chimney and sash window was added to the n. side of the *chancel* in the C18 or early C19. The e. window is small in scale but has lovely *Decorated* tracery, with three *reticulations* enclosing four quatrefoils each. On the s. side of the nave a very large slab-shaped *rood stair* turret was added in the early *Tudor* period and the large window with brick panel tracery alongside dates from about the same time. *Scratch dials* can be found on both of the nave buttresses. The low s. *porch* stands on a renewed brick base but the timbers of its frame are medieval and the outer archway is moulded.

The interior is homely, with brick floors and original *tie-beams* and *king posts* below plaster ceilings in nave and chancel, and there is another tie-beam placed very eccentrically just in front of the e. window. A plain *gallery* is set slightly forward in the tower arch and the bowl panels of the C13 *font* are decorated with pairs of shallow blind arches typical of the period. The C17 cover has a centre *baluster* supported by gawky scroll brackets. A fragment of C14 wall decoration was uncovered on the s. side of the nave in 1973 – a scroll pattern in dark red, and farther along there is the outline of the large door that led to the rood stair. Both *screen* and loft have gone but notches below the *capitals* of the chancel arch show where they were fitted. The boxy pulpit is squeezed right into the corner and is a *Cautley* design made by Ernest Barnes, with pierced quatrefoils under the rim. A section of C17 carving forms part of the front of the priest's stall, and there are sturdy oak *communion*

rails; beyond is a C14 *lancet piscina* which still has its original wooden *credence shelf*. Before leaving the chancel, note the roof *corbel* on the n. wall carved as a devil's head with enormous ears, and back in the nave there is an interesting *ledger-stone*:

> waiting for ye Second Coming Wm. Boggis Gent. deere to his contrey by whoes free choyce he was called to be captayne of their voluntaries raysed for their defence. Pious towards God meeke & just towards men & being about 40 yeeres of age departed this life March 18 1643.

In such a fashion the Civil War touched even this little community and they thought it worthy of record.

Fornham All Saints, All Saints (C4): The broad grass verges of the village street form a pleasant approach to the church which stands on a bend in the road. The base of the plain, unbuttressed tower is early C13 but the bell stage is about 100 years later, and the pinnacles which mark it from a distance were added in the C19. The *nave* was refashioned about 1300 and the *chancel*, with *reticulated tracery* in the e. window, dates from the first quarter of the C14. The *aisles* and *porch* were added in the late C15 or early C16, with a slightly unusual layout – the aisles abutting the e. wall of the porch. The s. aisle parapet has a sequence of *flushwork* panels which can be interpreted as spelling the names of Thomas and William Edward, followed by 'Christ have mercy'. Thomas financed the building of both aisles which were completed after his death in 1497. There was a full-scale restoration in the 1860s under *Sir Arthur Blomfield*, when the roofs of chancel and s. aisle were replaced and the majority of the windows renewed to the original designs. The porch was extensively restored at that time and the parapet has a niche at the centre. Part of the roof is original and there is a good centre *boss* carved as a human face. The inner door, although restored, is a visible survivor from the C12 church. Moving inside, the restored roof of the nave is C15, as are the *arcades*, and the one on the s. side has one arch opening into the chancel. The very large and plain octagonal *font* is probably the same age. On the tower wall is an elegant C18 set of the *Decalogue*, Creed and Lord's Prayer in black and gold, hung originally on the e. wall of the chancel. There are a dozen medieval benches in the nave, and three more in the n. aisle, all with *poppyheads* and square, *castellated* elbows. The front row of benches has carved animals but at least one is a modern replacement and others are suspect. There is an image bracket with *fleurons* at the e. end of the n. arcade which carries a small modern figure of *St Edmund*. There is another bracket on the wall of the s. aisle, where the chapel has a C17 *altar* table. Beyond it, on the e. wall, are matching image stools and the one to the r. has a fine square canopy set in the corner, pierced by *quatrefoils* and flanked by *crocketted* pinnacles with a plain *piscina* nearby. A Tudor arch at the e. end of the n. aisle leads to a *transept*, and in the s.e. corner is a *squint* (although the organ now blocks the line of sight to the *High altar*). The church's collection of *brasses* has been mounted on the w. wall of the transept. The most interesting is the remaining top half of a little figure commemorating Thomas Barwick, a professor of medicine at Bury who died in 1599. He is dressed in a gown and bears a staff; the brass includes his arms, an inscription and a Latin verse. The rest of the brasses are inscriptions for Ann Adams (1607), Thomas Manock (1608), John Manock (1656 but died in 1611), Mary Manock (1656 but died in 1615) and Thomas Manock (1656), with some fulsome phrases worth reading. The remaining shield is probably for a member of the Carewe family. Over the entrance arch is a tablet for Lieut. John Cowsell, who died in 1811 while 'gallantly leading on his company to charge the enemy' in a minor action of the Peninsula War. Opposite, the church's only *hatchment* is a large one for Sarah Elizabeth Halliday who died in 1834. The chancel arch was rebuilt by Blomfield and his new roof, although of pine, is attractively painted and has oak bosses. The arch through to the s. aisle has a modern screen which incorporates sections of medieval tracery, and on the s. side is a most unusual arrangement. Normally the piscina is to the s. of the altar, with *sedilia* to the w. of it, but here the order is reversed and the C14 piscina, with its *cusped* and crocketted *ogee* arch, is set in the wall between the stepped sedilia and the priest's door. The e. window glass is by *Hardman*, appropriately illustrating Christ reigning with all his saints. All Saints has a ground floor ring of five bells with a 7 cwt. tenor.

Fornham St Martin, St Martin (C4): The s. *aisle*, with its small rose window to the w., repeated an earlier Victorian model in 1870 but, apart from that, the church is *Perpendicular* and

the tower is particularly handsome for its size. Chequerwork battlements match the *base course* and the *transomed* bell openings are unusually tall. There is a heavy stair turret on the s. side and the *string courses* are well defined, with the lowest dipping under the w. window, which has distinctly cheerful *headstops*. There are headstops in fact to all the window arches, including the belfry *lancets*. Although they are not all in use, a whole family of *gargoyles* studs the parapet and stone *put-log holes* show on the faces of the tower. Within, there is a ground floor ring of six bells with a 6 cwt. tenor. The *Tudor* brick n. *porch* has a crow-stepped gable and there is a *stoup* recessed in the r.-hand buttress.

The organ was placed sensibly at the w. end of the s. aisle and thus the view through to the e. end is not obscured for a change. The squat C14 *font* has shields within circles on four sides of the bowl and varied *tracery* on the others. Overhead, the tower arch has large, coloured king and bishop headstops and the roofs of nave and chancel are plastered. A very dark set of George II *Royal Arms* hangs over the n. door, and in a *nave* n. window is glass designed by R.F. Ashmead for the Lancaster firm of Abbot & Co on the theme of the Benedicite: 'All ye works of the Lord, bless ye the Lord'. Two angels with outflung arms rise from a fiery star below the dove of the Holy Spirit in one *light*, and the sun, moon, earth, sky and sea are pictured in the other. The church's treasure lies in two *misericord* seats with very interesting subjects which have been adapted for reuse. The first forms the front of the C19 lectern and shows *St Thomas of Canterbury* kneeling at an altar while a knight cleaves his skull with a large sword; a second knight hovers menacingly and the archbishop's chaplain holds his crozier. Unlike continental examples, English misericords nearly all have flanking scrolls, called supporters, but they have not survived on this one. The second misericord, inset in the front of the *chancel* prayer desk does, however, have supporters carved with angels bearing crozier and mitre, and the central figure is the church's patron saint, *St Martin*. He is shown on horseback in front of a doorway with pierced tracery and the figure behind holds a portion of the cloak which the saint is cutting with his sword. What may well have been a section of the old *rood screen* is made up into a stall in the chancel and the C17 *communion rails* have shapely, turned *balusters*. The two fat and gilded cherubs that sit on the posts at the back of the *altar* are likely to have come from an C18 German or Austrian altarpiece. On the n. wall of the chancel is a tablet, by Hanchet of Bury, for Sir William Gilstrap of Fornham Park who died in 1896. His *hatchment* hangs above it and there is another, more interesting example further along. It bears the arms of Bernard, 12th Duke of Norfolk, who died in 1842. The *achievement* includes the batons of the hereditary Earl Marshal, but because he divorced Lady Elizabeth Belasyse in 1794, her arms do not appear in any form. To the s. of the chancel arch on the nave side is a tablet in memory of Sir Harry St George Ord, who was the first Colonial Governor of the Straits Settlements. On the nave n. wall is a tablet for Henry Claughton, 38 years an inspector of schools in the county. The tablet is unremarkable, except that it was put there in 1924 by his wife and his hunting and cricketing friends. An HMI who rode to hounds must have brought an invigorating whiff of fresh air and the stable into dull old County Hall.

Framlingham, St Michael (G4): Set within a neat, spacious churchyard and closely encircled by the busy little town, with the castle nearby, this is a beautiful and fascinating church. Although it was founded around the time of the *Norman* Conquest, there was a comprehensive rebuilding in the later C15 and first half of the C16. The decoration of the tower is not lavish, but it has great presence and is beautifully proportioned, with six *set-offs*, and it rises to 96ft. The worn *base course* has *flushwork* roundels and stars and this is one of the churches where the flushwork patterns identify the builders as the Aldryche family of N. Lopham in Norfolk. There you will find the shield of Thomas Whiting, the castle's auditor in the 1470s (money was still being given for the completion of the top in 1520). The w. doorway has been partially renewed, and the outline of a dragon remains in one of its *spandrels*. There is more flushwork on the buttresses, and lions guard the corners of the battlements above the four-*light* bell openings. Both *aisles* are relatively narrow, and their windows, under deep, square *labels*, display interesting and unusual *tracery*. On the n. side, a multi-*foil* motif is centred over the two lights, with the same shape halved on each side, and in the s. aisle the same principal is applied to a very pretty *quatrefoil* design. The *nave clerestory* dates from the 1520s, and there are five windows a side, linked by a *string course* and a band of *ashlar* pierced with flushwork 'MR's for the *Blessed Virgin* and *Sacred monograms*. The attractive gutter cresting in lead is pierced

with a running text, punctuated with little turrets, and diminutive angel wings hover above the spouts – late C19/early C20, I suspect. Thomas Howard, 3rd Duke of Norfolk, pulled down the C14 chancel in the 1540s and completely changed the character of the e. end of the church. His replacement *chancel* is longer than the nave and is flanked by substantial aisles. They bulk large, and spread wider than the body of the church – ponderous buttresses, huge windows, and a high, plain parapet. The six-light chancel e. window is to the same generous scale, and the *priests door* on the s. side is snugly set under an arching buttress like the ones at Eye and Blythburgh. The simple s. *porch* was rebuilt about 1770, leaving the medieval inner doorway with its large *headstops* undisturbed.

Within, the first impression is of glorious spaciousness but, paradoxically, this is countered by the interaction between the two halves of the church – there is no intervening *screen* and the lavish scale of the chancel endows the nave with a feeling of compactness that it would not otherwise have. The tall C15 *arcades* have octagonal *piers*, and note how the arches at the e. end were adapted to spring from a higher level. This is not a common arrangement in East Anglia, and was dictated here by the position of the *rood loft* which stretched right across the church. The entry door and stair to the loft can be seen in the n. aisle wall, and the connecting passageways remain in the walls above and beyond the arcades. The nave roof is a lovely example of the sophistication that followed, and in some cases disguised, constructional skill. Built of chestnut rather than oak, it is a *hammerbeam* design, but only braces, *collar beams* and *king posts* are displayed. The hammers are hidden by a very substantial range of coving on each side which rises from the short *wall posts* that flank each *clerestory* window. A deep carved and pierced cornice is applied above to complete the illusion of a simple, narrow roof rising from elaborately vaulted walls. The same technique can be seen at St Peter Mancroft, Norwich, but Framlingham's vaulting is enhanced by tracery patterns centred above each window. The stone wall shafts of the 1460s roof were left in place between the clerestory windows, and a *string course* studded with demi-angels runs the full length below them.

There is a large *stoup* recess by the s. door, and one of the *consecration crosses*, painted at the time of the C15 rebuilding, has been uncovered above it. On the other side of the doorway hangs a dark but interesting set of Charles II *Royal Arms* painted on canvas. The heavy frame bears 'Vive le Roi' at the top, with churchwardens' initials and 1661 at the bottom; the 'R.G.' on the sides stands for Richard Galty who, having been appointed rector in 1630, weathered the storms of the Civil War and Commonwealth that followed, and he obviously welcomed the Restoration. The whole of the tower arch is taken up by the organ on its gallery – a most attractive ensemble. The instrument is of particular historical interest, parts of it having been made by Thamar in 1674, and it came with its case from Pembroke College, Cambridge in 1708. Augmented in size, it was moved to the chancel in the C19, but it returned to the w. end in 1969, was enlarged again, and provided with a new console. The original and charmingly detailed case has been restored, with the muted colours of the pipe decoration sympathetically renewed. Note particularly the lovely screen which masks the console, featuring trumpeting angels and *putti*. The handsome C18 *gallery*, with its double-curve corners and reeded *Ionic* columns, had migrated to the castle in the C19, but it was retrieved to house the restored organ. Facing the entrance, above an arcade pier on the n. side of the nave, is a large C14 painting symbolising the *Trinity*. Against a dull red background, God the Father sits on a wide, pinnacled throne, holding the figure of the crucified Christ between spread knees; the dove emblem of the Holy Spirit hovers dimly above Christ's halo, but the outline of the Father's head was unfortunately overlaid by the C15 string course. A *groined* and canopied niche is unusually sited in the n.w. corner of the n. aisle. The image stool is supported by a demi-angel bearing a shield with the Blessed Virgin's monogram and '*I.H.C.* help' – it could conceivably have been connected with a *guild* chapel. There is remarkably little stained glass – medieval or modern – for a church of this consequence. However, a window at the w. end of the n. aisle has a 1930s Annunciation by Horace Wilkinson whose only other Suffolk windows are at St Augustine's, Ipswich and Wilby. The C15 *font* is a squat version of the East Anglian type, with fat lions and attenuated *woodwoses* ranged around the stem; the alternate *Evangelistic symbols* and angels in the bowl panels retain traces of colour, and one of the shields has been defaced (I suspect that the others have been re-cut): s.e., a Trinity emblem; s.w., three *chalices* and wafers for the mass; n.w., *Passion emblems*. The tall, tapering cover, with its *crocketted* spines and *finial* is contemporary. Both nave and aisles have good

C19 benches, and the pulpit is a memorial for Canon Lanchester who was rector here for thirty years. It is so like Flowton's that I think it was designed by *Cautley* and made by Edward Barnes. A large dome-topped chest for housing the parish valuables, banded with iron and fitted with three hasps and a bar, stands in the s. aisle, having managed to outlast the incidental hazards of some 600 years.

The C15 builders made use of the late-C12 chancel arch, with its diminutive *capitals*, and it is the only feature of substance that remains from the earlier building. Beyond it, the chancel invokes a tremendous sense of space and dignity, accentuated by a major 1960s re-arrangement which placed the High altar at the nave end, and sited the simple *Stuart Holy Table* well forward of the *reredos*. The four-bay arcades are taller and broader than those in the nave, with minimal decoration, and there are no screens to break the continuity of space across the church. The broad expanse of wall above the arcades is painted with an olive green repeat pattern in the style of *William Morris*, and the roof is panelled out in white, with slim ribs and *wall plate* picked out in red and gold. Many visitors wonder how it was that such a large church acquired an even larger chancel, and the answer lies in the history of that powerful family, the Howards who, by marriage with a Mowbray heiress, became Dukes of Norfolk. The Cluniac priory at Thetford had become the favoured place for family burials, and in 1524 the 2nd duke had the last of the great funerals, when 900 mourners made a solemn progress all the way from Framlingham castle to Thetford. Within twenty years, the priory had been dissolved along with all the other monastic houses, and the 3rd duke started to build a new chancel at Framlingham that would become a new and splendid mausoleum for the family. It was finished sometime after his death in 1554, and the coffins were transferred from Thetford.

A development of historical and artistic importance followed soon after. Sculptor-masons, unidentified but of consummate skill, were commissioned to provide tombs which together demonstrate English early *Renaissance* work at its best – and one of them is fit for comparison with European pieces of the mid-C16. It is curious that, with so much space available, the three tombs are awkwardly placed close to the walls, for there is no doubt that they were designed to be seen from all sides. Two of them may have been made at Thetford in the hope of a revival of the priory, the sculptor

Framlingham, St Michael: Earl of Surrey's tomb

moving to Framlingham when Elizabeth came to the throne. Dealing with the tombs in chronological order of death, the first stands on the n. side of the *sanctuary* (with no effigies, although they were intended). It is for Henry Fitzroy, Duke of Richmond, a natural son of Henry VIII who married the Lady Mary Howard. He was a great favourite of his father, with a glittering future, but died young in 1536. The design of the tomb is an unusual mixture of medieval and renaissance styles. The side panels carry raised wavy shields under coronets, but the frieze above them is a purely medieval concept and illustrates scenes from the Old Testament. On the n. side, l. to r.: the birth of Eve; God giving Eve to Adam; the Temptation; expulsion from Eden; w. side l. to r.: Eve suckling Abel, with Adam digging; Cain and Abel sacrificing, and Cain killing Abel – a very rare sequence and in lovely condition; s. side l. to r.: Noah's ark (all the family but no animals!); Noah's drunkenness; Lot escaping from Sodom and Gomorrah (with his wife as a pillar of salt with a head on top, just like the illustration in the contemporary *Golden Legend*); e. side l. to r.: the

sacrifice of Isaac and the golden calf sacrifice; Moses and the tables of the law. Corner figures hold shields with passion emblems. The second tomb stands on the s. side of the sanctuary and is for Thomas Howard, 3rd Duke of Norfolk, the man who planned the new chancel. Having been a close friend of Henry VIII, he fell from favour and, with his son the Earl of Surrey, was condemned to death for high treason. Surrey was executed, but Thomas escaped, the king dying on the very eve of his execution. The duke's effigy is a stiff figure in full armour, head on helm, wearing a jutting beard. His collar bears an inscription which is a reference to his timely deliverance: 'Gracia Dei sum quod sum' (By the grace of God I am what I am). His duchess wears a ruff that became fashionable in Queen Mary's reign, so the work was probably done between 1554 and 1565. There are elaborate corner shafts and compact lions display shields above them; along the sides, a range of shallow niches with shell tops contain apostle figures – by a gifted sculptor who was probably English, and they form one of the last major displays of religious imagery to be produced in this country before the onset of the *Reformation*: n. side l. to r.: *SS Philip, Simon, Jude, Matthias*; w. side l. to r.:

St Peter, Aaron, *St Paul*, s. side l. to r.: *SS Andrew, James the Less, James the Great, Matthew*; e. side l. to r. *St Thomas*, Simeon(?), *St John*. The last tomb in the series stands in the n.e. corner, and commemorates the two wives of Thomas, the 4th duke. He was involved in a plot to put Mary Queen of Scots on the throne, and lost his head in 1571. The effigies of Lady Margaret and Lady Mary lie with a space between them for the unlucky husband, one with a hart (with real antlers) at her feet, the other with a dragon. Strangely, they have a recumbant horse and a tethered hound under their heads instead of cushions. Both wear ermine shoulder capes, and many rings adorn their heavily veined hands. The tomb chest is massive – 11ft. long, 8ft. broad, and 5ft. high; between its delicately reeded columns the panels carry large curving shields under broad coronets. Again, there are very English lions at the top corners, and all that is missing are the canopy supports that stood at the corners. Nearby, within an *ogee* arch of an earlier period, is the tomb of Elizabeth Howard, infant daughter of the 4th earl and Lady Margaret – as with the others there is no inscription, but there may have been a *brass* originally. By the n. wall stands the last and most flamboyant of the Howard tombs, for that rumbustious son of the 3rd duke, Henry Howard, Earl of Surrey – courtier and herald of the first great age of English poetry. Executed for treason in 1547 (for presuming to quarter the royal arms with own), his bones were at length brought here by his second son in 1614. The tomb, in brilliantly painted alabaster and *touchstone*, was made by William Cure II, one of the finest sculptors of his day. The effigies of the earl and his wife Frances de Vere lie with their robes folded back to display the ermine lining, he in armour, with a coronet negligently laid upon his cloak; there is a lion at his feet, a boar by hers, and their children kneel at head and foot below – all the brilliant colours of robes and heraldry freshly restored. The last large tomb stands at the e. end of the s. aisle, commemorating Sir Robert Hitcham, who bought the castle and estate from the Howards in 1635. A great benefactor to the town (as his epitaph confirms), Sir Robert was at one stage attorney-general to Anne of Denmark, King James's queen. His memorial of lustrous black marble is in table form, its ends flanked by kneeling alabaster angels, and there is an urn placed centrally below the top – all on a broad, shaped plinth. Dated 1638, it is signed by Francis Grigs, a sculptor who was probably East Anglian and known only by this

and two other pieces. Sir Robert was to enjoy his purchase for no more than a year, and he bequethed all the properties to Pembroke College, Cambridge – which accounts for the notice on the aisle wall nearby, and for the splendid organ.

These lavish tombs are the focus of attention in the chancel and its aisles, but there are a number of other points of interest. High on the s. wall above the sanctuary hangs what is traditionally known as the 'Flodden Helm'. The Lord Thomas Howard (he who had that last funeral progress to Thetford) had been the victorious commander at Flodden against the Scots in 1615, and was thought to have worn the helmet in battle. However, experts have identified it as a jousting helm of about 1500, adapted for use as a funeral device – so it could have been part of the trappings that decked the earl's bier. The imposing early-C18 wooden reredos is an excellent piece, very restrained, and with minimal decoration. The large canvas centre panel is painted with a Sacred monogram within an aurora, and pairs of Ionic columns separate it from large *Decalogue* panels each side flanked by corner *pilasters*. The side *communion rails* are probably contemporary. An excellent chandelier of 1742 hangs in the centre of the chancel, one of six surviving examples of the work of a London craftsman, John Giles. The fine double-sided bench that stands in front of Sir Robert Hitcham's tomb came from the almshouses that he endowed. His arms are painted on the finials, and the centre division is cleverly shaped in a series of alternate curves to afford individually numbered places for the old people. Louis Francois Roubiliac was probably the finest sculptor at work in C18 England, and the only Suffolk example of his work shows that in his salad days he was happy to take on a small commission. It is the memorial above the priest's door in the s. aisle for Jane Kerridge and her daughter Cecilia (1744 and 1747). Against a dull black background, two graceful urns, with shields of arms in relief, are partially covered by a marble drape secured by three simulated nails at the top; the epitaph *cartouche* below is shaped as though it were pinned back – a period conceit meticulously executed. Mrs Kerridge's *hatchment* probably came into the church in advance of the memorial, and it hangs now in the n. chancel aisle. Lastly, the other hatchment in the s. aisle, decorated with a nice gilt border, is an early example and was either for Joseph (1644) or John (1661) Alexander. Framlingham's tower houses a good ring of eight bells with a 16 cwt. tenor

Framsden, St Mary (F5): A lane from the village street crosses a stream and a picturesque *lych-gate* of 1899 gives access to the churchyard. The C15 tower was chosen as a model for the one to be built at Helmingham and it has four *set-offs* with linking *string courses*. There is a panelled *base course* and niches flank the w. doorway, which has *fleurons* in the mouldings and shields in the *spandrels* carved with *Passion emblems* and the arrows and crown of *St Edmund*. Within is a lovely ring of eight bells with a 16 cwt. tenor which were restored by the Whitechapel foundry in 1815 at the expense of the Tollemache family, and now stand in need of restoration. On walking round, one finds that the n. side of the *nave* has two tall and thin late-*Perpendicular* windows in brick, with three more at *clerestory* level. The *chancel* is C14 although the e. window is again Perpendicular, and there is a *scratch dial* on the s.e. buttress. The s. *aisle* too is C14 and its e. window has three stepped and *cusped lancets*, with 'Y' *tracery* of about 1300 in the side windows. Above the roof the clerestory range is in *Tudor* brick. The s. *porch* has a good *flushwork* facade with three niches and the condensed dragon in the r.-hand spandrel is matched by a figure with a club like those at Cratfield and Badingham. Overhead, the stepped battlements continue along the w. wall of the aisle. The inner doorway is early-C14 and the door itself is contemporary, with a closing ring combined with one of the strap hinges.

The double *hammerbeam* roof to the nave is much less heavy in appearance than most and has long top hammers, with *king posts* on the *collars* and carved spandrels. The C15 *font* is the familiar local pattern, with battered lions round the shaft, and mutilated angels bearing books and shields alternate with lions in the bowl panels. The aisle roof is apparently dated 1620 and 1676 but despite a careful look I could not confirm this. According to *Cautley*, it also has the name of William Stebbing somewhere; his memorial tablet is on the s. wall. Farther along there is an early-C14 *piscina* within a *trefoil* arch resting on half-round *jamb shafts*. C19 benches and pulpit are in the nave and the *rood loft stairs* rise in the n. wall although the upper doorway has been blocked. The chancel roof and panelled *reredos* are Victorian but, by way of contrast, an ancient carving has survived in the n.w. window surround. It is a little *Saxon* figure about 8in. long and lies on its side at the r.-hand spring of the arch. It has a triangular face, one arm is akimbo, and it wears a full-length tunic. Is this perhaps a remnant of Framsden's first church

or is it a pagan cult figure? In the *sanctuary* there is a C14 angle piscina with a *cusped ogee* arch and curly *stop* to the *hood mould*. The *altar* is a very nice table of 1628 in excellent condition which has turned columns at an angle outside each leg and pairs of *balusters* back and front; the shapely skirt is pierced and the bottom stretchers are covered by boards to form a shelf. The stalls on the n. side of the sanctuary have *misericords* with some mutilated but interesting carvings. A man holds a cruciform church with a spire, there is a crouching lion and another beast, both with very strange supporters, and possibly the bottom half of an *Annunciation*. Two good bench ends form part of the choir stalls and they have varied tracery on one side with two quite different patterns on the other. The Revd. Loder Allen and his wife Lydia have both a *ledger-stone* and a marble tablet. He died in 1811, she in 1814, and of him we learn that 'Loder had Talents for a wider Sphere', and of his wife 'Her features stampt with Virtue's ripen'd hue, Thus polishing her charms with Age'. No doubt the author knew what he meant even if we don't. The executors of Edmund and Margaret Barker cannot have been too pleased with the mason who cut the lettering on their stone by the *priest's door*. He managed to foul up both death dates.

Freckenham, St Andrew (A3): Open to the fields on the w. but virtually hidden from the village street, the church stands on rising ground at the end of a little lane. *George Edmund Street* carried out a major restoration and rebuilding here in 1867-89, and added a new *vestry*. Because the work was carefully done it is difficult to distinguish old from new. The tower collapsed in 1882 and was rebuilt in the original style two years later; with the exception of the e. and w. windows, all the windows have been handsomely reglazed in clear glass so that the attractive interior is full of light. Street added two dormer windows of different sizes at the e. end of the *nave*, and a taller one which rests on the lintel of an ugly *priest's door* in the *chancel* – eccentric and uncharacteristic alterations. The restored early-C14 *arcade* has *quatrefoil piers* and the *capitals* have a frieze of shallow blank arches. The arches into what is now the organ chamber are largely original, but whether there was ever a chancel arch is hard to say (although there is certainly a break in the wall line). The restored waggon roof of the nave is panelled, with beautifully *cusped* openwork *bosses*. The chancel roof panelling is simpler, with central bosses of leaves and one *woodwose*; the colouring is C19. The n. aisle has an *arch braced* roof, animal and human head *corbels* below the *wall posts*, with angels and leaf bosses at the main intersections. The tower arch escaped in the 1882 collapse, as can be seen from the graffiti going back to the C17. Beyond it is a ground floor ring of five bells with a 10 cwt. tenor in good going order. Many of the pews are modern but there are some good medieval bench ends, expertly repaired with replacement heads; nave s. side from the w., priest at desk, kneeling woman with rosary at desk, kneeling woman, kneeling angel, kneeling woman at desk, spotted devil thrusting a priest into hell's mouth. Opposite is a double-headed pair of birds. At the w. end there is a pair of beasts with renewed heads and on the n. side fourth from the back, a damaged *pelican* in her piety. The conventional *poppyheads* are a mixture of old and new work. The plain octagonal *font* rests on a matching shaft with nooked corners and is likely to be early C14. By the n. door is a most interesting alabaster panel which is thought to have been part of a *reredos*. It was discovered by workmen in 1776 and, although damaged, it is the tale of *St Eligius*, with the horse's owner looking distinctly doubtful. The C17 *altar* table in the n. aisle has simple decoration on the top rails. The C19 stone pulpit is typically indigestible. The chancel e. window dates from around 1300, with three stepped *lancets* (with *tracery* renewed). The deeply moulded arch has slim *jamb shafts* and the *hood mould* rests on clustered flowers. There is a moulded ledge at various levels round most of the *sanctuary*, terminating in foliage balls. Look for the tiny creatures among the leaves. The double *piscina* has *trefoil* arches set flush with the wall, but the niche has been deepened and the *sedilia* remade so there may have been outer mouldings to the arches originally. Over the sedilia is an 1899 *Annunciation* window in attractive *Arts and Crafts* style by *Horatio W. Lonsdale* and the e. window glass of 1869 is by *Hardman and Co*, Street's chosen firm of the period. The composition of Nativity, Last Supper and the *Three Marys* is characteristic, and uses strong, clear colours very effectively.

Fressingfield, St Peter and St Paul (G3): This is a lovely church, full of interest. Unlike most of the building, the C14 tower is quite plain, its outline relieved only by three *drip courses*. It houses a recently restored ring of eight bells with a 17 cwt. tenor worthy of the church. Walking round you will find a simple n. *porch*,

and a chapel which was added in the early C16 to the n. of the *chancel*. Its doorway probably belonged to the early-C14 chancel and was reused. There was an ambitious rebuilding in the late C14 to early C15 when the *aisles* were added, together with a handsome *clerestory* which includes an e. window and whose arches are enlivened with red brick. The *sanctus-bell turret* on the gable is the finest in Suffolk, its sides daintily panelled, and crowned with miniature battlements; a new sanctus bell was donated in 1496 and the turret was probably specially built to house it. One of the church's showpieces is the s. porch of about 1420, built by Catherine de la Pole in memory of her husband Michael who died of dysentry at Harfleur in 1415, and their son who fell a month later at Agincourt. Blind arcading and a pair of niches with delicate canopies flank a neat little window above the entrance, and the rest of the facade is panelled out with *flushwork*. There are crowns carved in the arch mouldings and the *headstops* may well be portraits of Henry V and Queen Catherine. The rather strange carving in the *spandrels* must be a variation of the C17 or even C18. The porch has pretty cresting in place of battlements, with a worn figure at the apex, and there are twin *gargoyles* above the stair turret on the w. side. The ceiling within is *groined*, and the *boss* immediately above the entrance displays a *green man* mask; there is an *Assumption* boss in the centre in which the *Blessed Virgin* sits within a circle of figures. The *Evangelistic symbols* at the spring of the vaulting have been renewed.

A plain octagonal font stands just inside, and the aisle w. window is filled with luscious glass by *Henry Holiday,* dating from the 1890s – languorous figures of Hope and Love, surrounded by swirling *acanthus* foliage in pale green. The interior is spacious, and above the sturdy *arcade* with its octagonal pillars there is a good *hammerbeam* roof. It is unstained, and there is pierced *tracery* above the crested hammerbeams, and dainty transverse braces stretch between the *wall posts*; the deep *wall plate* has pierced cresting above it, and there are *castellated collars* below short *king posts*. The carved angels have gone from hammers and wall posts, but a couple survive just under the ridge on two of the collar beams. The n. aisle roof is original too, with decorative tracery in the spandrels and interesting *corbel* heads below the wall posts.

The church's most splendid feature is the magnificent range of benches which are among the finest Suffolk can offer. In terms of their

Fressingfield, St Peter & St Paul:
Sanctus-bell turret

completeness and variety of decoration they bear comparison with any in England. The scale is large, with chunky *poppyheads* more than a foot high, inviting the hand to explore their intricacies. Apart from a few with *linen-fold* panelling, the ends are deeply cut with tracery of extraordinary richness and variety, and there are a few survivors of the beasts and figures that were carved on the elbows. All of them are worth studying, but look particularly for the following: s. aisle (from the w.) 2nd. seated figure of *St Paul;* 4th. *St Dorothy;* nave, s. side (from the w.) 2nd. possibly *St Cecilia* with a cithern across her knees; 3rd. *St Peter;* 5th. possibly *St Margaret;* 6th. seated man with a dog, possibly *St Roche;* nave, n. side (from the w.) 1st. angel, probably representing *St Matthew;* 5th. a seated figure in a particularly attractive pose; 6th. an animal with a castle on its back; 7th. a *griffin;* n. aisle (from the w.) 1st. the bench end is carved with a shield which has *talbot* supporters and may commemorate John Talbot, Earl of Shrewsbury who died in 1460; 7th. the bench end has the *chalice* and wafer emblem of the Blessed Sacrament, and the initials of Alicia de la Pole,

Countess of Suffolk who was Chaucer's granddaughter. The rear benches, known as the Passion and Dedication benches, are of particular interest because of their carvings. On the n. side you will find one of the most comprehensive series of *Passion emblems* to be seen anywhere – crowing cock, striking hand, vinegar pot, *Sacred monogram*, pillar, scourge, nails, cross, crown of thorns, sponge, spear, ladder, hammer, pincers, seamless coat, and dice board. The dedication bench is carved with *St Andrew's* cross, swords for St Paul, keys for St Peter and, for good measure, P.E. and a papal tiara to show that he was the first of the popes.

The s. aisle chapel has a *piscina* which lies under an arch with just the touch of an *ogee* in its shape, and to the l. of the *altar* there is the entrance to the *rood loft stairs.* A circular frame of candles known as a trendle was often suspended in front of the rood, and ropes to control it were passed through blocks. One of these can be seen in the head of the e. arch of the s. arcade, and it is interesting that the mason took the trouble to decorate it with little battlements. Another notable survival is the hole drilled in the head of the chancel arch through which the rope for the sanctus bell passed. Canon J.J. Raven (remembered for his standard work on the county's bells) was rector here in his later years, and the lectern is one of his memorials – a clever little design, with three pairs of shafts and open tracery below the book ledge, quite exuberantly carved. The base of the *screen* is still in place, well restored, with most of the original tracery but no colour. The choir stalls are a very good late-C19 set by (I think) Robert Godbold of Harleston, more of whose work can be seen at Mendham and Earl Stonham; the *sanctuary* panelling and *reredos* are equally good. There is a C15 glass *Trinity* shield in one of the chancel s. windows, and further along are four more medieval shields, rather murky and muddled. In the 1880s, the piscina and *sedilia* were imaginatively rebuilt rather than restored, and only a small part of the frame is original. The tracery of the e. window is a C19 replacement, but note that the *jamb shafts* belong to the early-C14 original. They have delicately carved capitals and inward facing corbels in addition to the headstops on the *hood mould.* Below stands a lovely early-C17 *Holy table.* It is almost square, and the turned legs are carved with a repeat design of fleur-de-lys in shallow relief. The chapel on the n. side of the chancel is now taken up by the organ and vestry, but it was specially built for the village *guild* of St Margaret. The brightly coloured figures of the church's patron saints in the n. window are by the *O'Connors* and date from the 1860s.

In an excess of zeal that is not to everybody's taste, the entire floor area of the church has been covered with fitted carpet. Other considerations aside, this means that one can no longer admire the fine and quite important C15 brass of William and Elizabeth Brewse which lies in the chancel. However, a facsimile can be seen at the e. end of the n. aisle. On your way out, you will see an imposing portrait of Archbishop William Sancroft in the s. aisle, a copy of the painting by Lens in Emmanuel College, Cambridge. Sancroft was born here, and rose to eminence after the *Restoration*, spearheading (as Dean) the rebuilding of St Paul's. He ministered to Charles II on his deathbed and crowned James II, but he was the leading 'non-juror' after the Revolution of 1688 and refused to take the oaths to William and Mary. Harried and disgraced, he retreated to his birthplace in 1691 and died here two years later. He had chosen the site for his burial twenty years earlier, and you will find his austere tomb in the angle between s. aisle and porch outside. It bears his arms deeply cut in a roundel on the top, and the epitaph he himself composed includes the words: '. . . at last deprived of all, which he could not keep with a good Conscience, returned hither to end his life where he began it, and professeth here at the foot of his Tomb that as naked he came forth so naked he must return . . .'. A gospel verse is beautifully lettered on the wall nearby. It is said that, though he was its patron, he could never bear to enter the church for Morning Prayer after his return; to do so would have been to hear the names of William and Mary in the prayer for the King's Majesty. Lastly, admire the half-timbered walls of the Fox and Goose Inn bordering the churchyard and, remembering that it was once the guild house, look for the weathered figure of St Margaret with her dragon carved in a niche on the corner post.

Freston, St Peter (F7): The church stands by itself, caught in the angle of a lane that leads off the main road. One of the two entrances to the spacious churchyard is sheltered by a fine *lych-gate* in C15 idiom; it has a statue of the church's patron saint above the entrance, and was built to celebrate Queen Victoria's diamond jubilee in 1897. The C15 tower has angle buttresses decorated with *flushwork* chequer, while *septaria* and tiles show in the n. wall. All the windows have been renewed and there are shallow modern

battlements. The church as a whole had become ruinous by the mid-C19, and there was a wholesale restoration and rebuilding in 1875 under the direction of R.T. Orr, the Ipswich architect. Polygonal projections were added on both sides of the *chancel* – *vestry* to the n. and organ chamber to the s., while the *nave* windows were all replaced. The e. window, however, retains its C14 *cusped* intersected tracery, and there is a window of the same period on the s. side of the chancel that has nice, tilted *headstops*. The C13 n. doorway is now blocked, and you will see by the mark on the e. face of the tower that the C19 tiled roof follows the line of the original. The village's war memorial stands to the s., and takes the unusual form of a life-size wooden figure of Peace, displayed on a low stone plinth. Although it is now quite weathered and has suffered some damage, the carving is vigorous and lively, and one would like to know who the artist was. Within the wooden porch, the s. doorway's only ornaments are leaf *stops*, but note its fine proportions, and the remains of a *scratch dial* below the stop on the r. The *stoup* nearby was entirely re-formed by the C19 builders.

The *font* now stands in the base of the tower, and its shaft is a modern replacement; the panels of the deep bowl are carved alternately with lions and angels bearing shields, and although there has been the usual defacement, the symbols are easily recognised: n.e. emblem of the *Trinity*; n.w. the three crowns of East Anglia (or Ely); s.w. *instruments of the Passion*; s.e. three *chalices* and wafers for the mass. The plans and elevations prepared by the architect for the 1875 work are displayed on the tower walls, and there is a *ledger-stone* in the floor for John Wright and his wife Rachell. He died in 1723, having been patron of the living, and the stone bears his arms in a roundel. The replacement roofs are *arch-braced*, and the old *sanctus-bell window* is just visible at the w. end. Below, there are pine benches, and a s. nave window has 1890s glass by *Clayton & Bell*, with figures of Christ and two of the *three Marys* in rich colours below steely canopies. The shield in the head of the window further along is probably early-C16 glass and displays the arms of the Latymers. They were Lords of the Manor from 1463 until 1553, and founded the Latymer schools in Hammersmith and Edmonton. The attractive window across the nave was a late product of *Morris & Co*, installed in 1923. Its colours are sombre, against dark foliage backgrounds, and in one light, the figure of *St Christopher* is a reversal of a *Burne Jones* design which has had a beard added; the saint bears on his sprouting staff while the Christ child leans comfortably on his head. The matching *Blessed Virgin* and Child is a John Dearle design, and an angel plays a dulcima in the tracery. It seems that the architect of the 1870s restoration retained the old *rood beam* spanning the chancel arch, and he supplied a stolid stone pulpit which has traceried panels and coloured marble shafts at the angles. The modern pulpit cloth is a fine piece of appliqué work by Miss Miller of Holbrook – a clever ship design, with a draught of multi-coloured fishes alongside. Hers too is the golden altar cloth featuring *St Peter's* keys. The chancel n. window glass is a very good example of the work of *Thomas Willement*. Installed around 1845, the design has hieratic figures of Christ and the Blessed Virgin within niches below golden *crocketted* canopies; the colours are clear and bright, there is a *Sacred monogram* in the tracery, and two Bond family shields are featured at the bottom. The chancel's C14 *piscina* remains in the *sanctuary*, although C19 changes have brought it close to the floor, and there are *dropped-sill sedilia* alongside. The e. window glass of 1860 has a centre Crucifixion panel, set within lightly patterned quarries, and this too may be Willement's work.

Friston, St Mary (I4): The path rises fairly steeply from the gate, and there is a view across to the village postmill from the churchyard. The tower was built in the early C14, but it has had a chequered career involving many alterations, and in 1900 it was taken down and completely rebuilt under the direction of Edward Bisshopp. The old materials were reused, and the new tower is a careful copy of the original. The form of the buttresses indicate that it was once a stage higher, and it was probably altered when bells were installed in the C15. There are deep niches in all four buttresses at belfry level, and the trio of broad niches grouped round the w. bell opening provide its most striking and unusual feature. They contain pedestals for statues, and I believe that they may have contained a *rood* group like the one on the tower at Parham. *Nave* and *chancel* have plastered walls below a single tile and slate roof, and walking round you will find that there is a blocked *Norman* door on the n. side. The chancel dates from the C13, but it has been shortened and given a new e. wall and brick buttresses. The s. frontage has a variety of window forms – a C13 *lancet*, 'Y' *tracery* of about 1300, one with *Decorated* tracery, and a square-headed *Perpendicular* type. The sweet little

Friston, St Mary: Font cover

C18 brick *porch* has a grave slab in the floor that once carried a *brass*, and a C13 coffin cover hides under the door mat. The inner doorway is a handsome small-scale example of the *Transitional* style, with single shafts, and a chamfered pointed arch. There are two crosses just below the l.-hand *capital*, with another further down, and their quality suggests that they are *consecration crosses* which date from the doorway's completion in the later C12.

A simple, homely interior, and at the w. end there is a deep early-C19 *gallery* which houses the organ and masks all but the top of the tower arch. The *font* underneath is C19, but it stands on what is probably the church's old font bowl, inverted to serve as a base – a similar reuse can be found at Felsham. The very attractive modern cover is like a miniature medieval market cross, with the figure of Christ for a *finial*, and charming roundels of young children within the upper frieze. The nave roof is *arch-braced*, the white plaster panels stark against the inky black of the main timbers and moulded *wall plate*. The sturdy C17 table by the entrance served as the church's *altar* for many years, and on the n. wall there is a framed charity board of 1811. Below it, the cover of what was probably the church's first Bible is displayed in a frame; it dates from about 1550 and still has its engraved brass mounts. Alongside is Friston's showpiece, the enormous *Royal Arms* of James I which *Cautley* rescued in pieces from the tower in 1935 and cleverly reassembled. Carved from 5in. thick planks and over 6ft. square, they are virtually complete, although little of the colour survives – an astonishing piece for a small church. There are *pamment* floors, and Elizabeth Bacon's *ledger-stone* of 1647 lies at the e. end of the nave. It has three engraved shields and half of the stone was left blank for her husband Sir Thomas, but he, presumably, was buried elsewhere. Like the Royal Arms, the *Jacobean* pulpit had been consigned to oblivion but, rescued and furnished with a new base and steps, it is handsome enough, with typical *blind arches* in the panels. There is no chancel arch or *screen*, and the chancel retains its C19 colour scheme untouched. The panelled ceiling has attractive leaf sprays and *Sacred monograms* within roundels, and stencilled patterns cover the pale blue walls. A low painted and gilt *reredos* of 1913 backs the altar, while above it in the 1890s stained glass, the *Blessed Virgin* and *St John* flank Christ the King – attractive figures against a dense green vine pattern, with cherub heads in the tracery; the maker is unknown.

Frostenden, All Saints (I2): The church stands in a breezy situation some little way to the w. of the A12, with just the Hall and its farm for company. It has been here since before the Conquest, and at one time the village boasted a second church and a navigable river. The lower part of the round tower is almost certainly *Saxon*, and for some mysterious reason there are two stone querns (used for grinding household corn) embedded in the wall about 3ft. from the ground. Apart from an early blocked *lancet* in the lower stage, the other windows are C13, and the tower was well restored in the 1980s. There are renewed *Perpendicular* windows in the *nave* and *chancel*, although there is evidence inside that the chancel dates from the early C13. There is a tiny image bracket just above the e. window, and a smiling head *corbel* has been set above the *priest's door* in the s. wall. The s. *aisle* and *porch* were built as a unit in the late C14 and again, the windows have been renewed. The *scratch dial* on the centre buttress is at ground level and must have been moved and used by a mason who found himself short of a *quoin*. A handsome sundial over the entrance bids us 'Vigilate et

Orate' (Watch and Pray), and the stone *groining* of the porch was restored, along with the aisle roof, as part of the recent programme. The corbels of the diagonal ribs are carved as grotesques and a head, there are worn little animals at the ends of the ridge ribs, and the centre *boss* is a fine *pelican in her piety*. A pair of C15 benches with *poppyheads* stand below, and note how one end was left uncarved to fit against a wall. The inner doorway has attracted graffiti for over 400 years – Nicholi Herns carefully added his name in gothic letters on the l., and there are late-C16/early-C17 dates and *chalice* symbols on the r.

Opening the medieval door of lapped boards, one finds a *stoup* under a *cusped* arch just inside, with its bowl renewed. The altar frontal cupboard against the w. wall incorporates six very good C17 panels that formed part of the old pulpit. They have some *renaissance* detailing, mask roundels, and stem roses – an unusual motif in this context. The tower arch is tall and narrow, and it has recently been fitted with a neat wrought-iron gate and grill to its full height. The compact C14 *font* has eight attached shafts around the stem, and there are defaced angel heads and *paterae* beneath the bowl; roses and shields are set in the tracery of the panels. The early-C15 font cover is something of a puzzle because it is significantly smaller than the base board. The squat octagonal drum has window shapes carved on each face, and the intervening buttresses project as roughly chamfered stumps. I suspect that they formed part of a lower section which would have supplied the correct proportions to balance the lofty *crocketted* spire. There are *pamment* floors throughout, and the panelled waggon roofs of nave and chancel were renewed in 1936. Apart from a new pulpit, the Victorians supplied sturdy benches with poppyheads in the nave, and the remainder of the C15 set stand in the aisle. The three-bay *arcade* has octagonal *piers* and broad, moulded *capitals*, and there is an *angle piscina* with *dropped-sill sedilia* alongside in the aisle *sanctuary*. Two *biers* stand nearby and both are worth examining. One is low, painted black, and inscribed 'Frossinton Parish 1733' on one side, and 'J.S.' on the other for James Shuckford the churchwarden. The wheeled model was given in 1925 'thus avoiding the necessity of a cart being used to bring coffins from a distance'. There is no longer a chancel *screen*, but the stairs that led to the *rood loft* remain in the s. wall, still with their wooden treads, and the stump of the *rood beam* shows below the *wall plate* on the opposite side. Two excellent bench ends have been incorporated into the priest's prayer desk. They were probably part of the original choir stalls, and have two ranks of window tracery below the large poppyheads. The stained glass in the side windows of the chancel is undistinguished work by *Arthur L. Moore*; on the s. side, the *Three Marys* and the angel at the tomb date from the 1890s, and the other is a decade later – a conventionally sentimental Christ with a family group. The wall monuments further along are much more stylish, and on the n. side we find a lively design in an architectural frame, with a *cartouche* in the *broken pediment* and skulls and bones carved below. It is for Sir William Glover, a royalist who died in March 1660, thus missing his king's return by a bare two months. A neatly lettered translation of the epitaph was provided to mark the 300th anniversary of the *Restoration*. Another William Glover is commemorated opposite, sometime patron of the church and dying in 1726. The *touchstone* tablet has shallow flanking *pilasters* and scrolls, and there are decorative coloured armorials above and below. The C13 inner frame of the e. window provides the clue to the date of the chancel. It has *jamb shafts* with ring capitals and bases, and the arch contains a double rank of pierced carving which is akin to *dogtooth* – a zigzag of small leaf forms. It occurs again in the wide arch of the *piscina*, and a section on the r. shows that the *sedilia* were originally canopied to match. The oak *reredos*, with its flamboyant tracery, was provided by Albert Moore in 1916, a reminder that a number of the established stained glass firms offered fittings and decorative schemes as part of their service. Another example of this is conveniently to hand on the n. wall of the sanctuary. It is an attractive mosaic panel with four painted cherub heads, signed by *Jones & Willis*, and forms an interesting contrast with the C18 tablet for another rector just above. Before retracing your steps, have a look at the pleasantly varied C17 and C18 *ledger-stones* in the chancel floor.

Gazeley, All Saints (B4): Standing within a spacious, open graveyard, the church is end on to the village street and slightly above it so that one has a clear view of the particularly interesting e. window in the C14 *chancel*. Dating from about 1330, its three tall and narrow *lights* have *trefoil* heads, the centre one a little lower than the others. On them rests a *cusped* triangle with curved sides and the outline dips in to follow the *tracery* instead of being contained within a conventional arch. The tower was largely rebuilt

in 1884, repeating the original C14 design and retaining the w. doorway. Within there is a ground floor ring of six bells with a 10 cwt. tenor but they cannot be rung at the present time. The C16 *nave* roof is lower and flatter than its predecessor so that the old *sanctus-bell window* can be seen outside on the e. face of the tower. *Aisles* and *clerestory* have early-C16 *Perpendicular* windows and beneath all the parapets there are *string courses* studded with little *fleurons*. The Perpendicular s. *porch* now has a pitched roof but the line of the old one can be seen and although they now serve no purpose, the *gargoyles* remain. The *jambs* of the unglazed windows have lots of C17 and C18 graffiti and the floor slopes gently down to the inner C14 doorway.

The *arcades* within show that the nave was built in the late C13; they have *quatrefoil piers* and heavily moulded *capitals* and bases matching the chancel arch. C19 angels bearing shields were added to the tower arch, and above it there is a dim set of George III *Royal Arms* painted on canvas and in poor condition. The early-C14 *font* has a deep bowl and the panels are carved with a representative selection of the simple window tracery patterns that were in vogue at the time. The centre shaft of the plain *Stuart* cover has an acorn *finial* and is supported by four brackets. The low medieval benches at the w. end of the s. aisle have *poppyheads* and one of them has a back that offers a little puzzle to the curious. Its pierced carving is in the form of attractive capitals but some pieces have broken away and one has to guess the meaning: 'Salaman Sayet' is a possibility, but if so, the 'S's are reversed. There are more pierced backs of varying design n. of the font and the two blocks of pews at the w. end of the nave appear to have been made up, using tracery panels that may have formed part of the *rood loft*. Other benches at the w. end of the n. aisle have rudimentary poppyheads and are probably C17. By the n. door is a vast oil painting of Christ's Presentation in the Temple. By Jacques Stella, it once hung in the chapel of Trinity Hall, Cambridge. The C16 nave roof has *tie-beams*, with *arch-braces* above and below and traceried *spandrels*. It was repaired in the 1880s and angels were added below the *wall posts*. It is worthwhile using binoculars to study the early-C16 glass in the clerestory windows on the n. side. Working from the w. there are: two angels and a shield of *Passion emblems*; two demi-angels; the three crowns of East Anglia or Ely; the figures of *St Faith* and *St Apollonia*; a shield representing the *Trinity*; a mitred bishop and three more angels. Set in the wall by the *altar* in the s. aisle is a tomb chest in *Purbeck marble* – now very worn and irregular. The square canopy is carved with quatrefoils and there is a band of tracery below the recess. There were once *brasses* within but they are gone and it is quite anonymous. In the floor of the aisle there are two *ledger-stones* bearing brass shields – the westernmost dates from about 1500 and bears the arms of the Heigham family, while the other is about 60 years later and has the arms of the Blennerhassets impelling those of Heigham and Francis. The glass in both aisle e. windows is by *Lavers & Barraud*, all in deep colour. The n. aisle design is by H.S. Marks and the medieval treatment of the figures is much more marked there. Standing on a new base, the early-C16 pulpit has simply traceried panels and the chancel *screen* is C19, although old tracery has been applied to three of the bottom panels. Just to the w. is a brass inscription in the floor for Robert Tailour who died in 1586. With the organ at the w. end of the church the wide chancel is made more spacious and it has a beautiful early-C16 waggon roof; a pale brown colour, its boards are covered with a grid of moulded ribs forming *cusped* panels, with small *bosses* at the intersections. There are little angels bearing scrolls, carvings and wheat ears, vine sprays and leaves, and traces of paint show that it was once coloured. The chancel windows on both sides have *transoms* forming *low side windows* below, with wide embrasures and deep sills. The frame on the s. side is rebated and the hooks for the wooden shutters are still there. It is strange that what appears to be a pair of *scratch dials* are incised in the sill. They cannot have been very effective and are perhaps doodles (or possibly that particular stone was removed from outside). There is a *priest's door* in the s. wall and a medieval door opposite leads to the *vestry*. To the w. is a *consecration cross* and to the r., a deep recess with a solid stone slab as its base. It has a *crocketted* arch with attached columns each side and the stumps of pinnacles. There is no trace of it having had a door and its position suggests that it was a small *Easter sepulchre*. In the *sanctuary* the early-C14 *piscina*, with its *cinquefoiled* arch and stone *credence shelf*, stands next to stepped *sedilia* separated by an arm rest. With a little imagination the beast on top of it could be a lion. The design of the e. window surprises again because the splays have elongated arched panels. It is filled with glass by *Burlison & Grylls* of 1886; there is Christ in Majesty at the top and six panels in the main lights; a Crucifixion with the *Blessed Virgin*

and *St John*, three scenes from the life of Christ and, at the bottom, the Garden of Eden, Moses with the serpent, and an *Annunciation.*. High on the s. wall of the chancel is a monument to Edmund Heigham and his family. He died in 1599 and his little figure kneels in armour with sword laid by his side. His wife, in Elizabethan bonnet, kneels behind him and his shield of arms is placed within strapwork on the top. In the chancel floor on the n. side is a small *chalice brass* for a priest dating from the 1530s and in front of the *communion rails*, a brass inscription for Mary Heigham who died in 1618. Before leaving the chancel look for Thomas Nuce's ledger-stone on the s. side. He was a vicar who died in 1617 and his rhyming epitaph is a good one. Next to it is one for Alice Peer:

> Unfortunate she was, yet here she lies
> At rest (secure) from all her enemies.

I wonder what lay behind those words!

Gedding, St Mary (D5): A long path leads through the large churchyard to the s. door of the church and an old boundary ditch runs parallel with it to the w. The tower was under construction in 1470 but this little church had become very dilapidated by the 1880s and the upper stage of the tower was rebuilt in thin red bricks, with *lancet* bell openings. It was given a low, tiled cap as a prelude to something more ambitious. Nothing more was done, however, and weathering has made it very attractive, with the bulge of a tower stair on the s. side. A feature of the w. buttresses are the arms in *flushwork* of the Chamberlin family who were Lords of the Manor, with crowned 'M's for the dedication above them. There is no porch and one steps straight into a homely little interior of some considerable charm. Evidence of its *Norman* origin was uncovered at the restoration in the form of two lancets (only 2in. wide and 6in. high) set in deep splays in the *nave* walls, and the one on the s. side has *chevron mouldings* outside. Either side of the wide tower arch there are stubs of buttresses which come down to arches in the corners, and roughly carved heads lie within them. The C15 *font* has shields in the panels of the deep heavy bowl, carved with the cross of *St George* and the arms of the Shelton family while the others are filled with *Perpendicular tracery*. There was once a pillar *stoup* by the door and its bowl now lies on the font step. It is in good condition with a *quatrefoil* on one face and angel heads at the lower corners. The nave roof was re-framed as part of the restoration and a *three-decker pulpit* and *box pews* were removed, but a couple of medieval benches were suffered to remain at the w. end with their low, traceried backs and timeworn *poppyheads*. The narrow *chancel* arch has plain, continuous mouldings with no *capitals* and it is flanked by two unusual openings. They are tall, only 20in. wide and have *cusped* arches. Beneath the one on the l. is a deep recess divided in two by a *-mullion*, some 20in. by 6in. overall. Judging by its position it is likely to have been a *reliquary chamber* associated with a nave *altar* and this explains the presence of the two openings: they turned the dividing wall into a form of *screen* and gave a view of the *High altar*. On the chancel side they are splayed and in the C19, *crocketted ogee* arches with *finials* and leaf *stops* were added. There is a *low side window* within an angled recess on the s. side of the chancel and a *priest's door* further along. Two more worn medieval benches are to be found here and note that the floor levels were raised to such an extent in the 1880s that the simple *piscina* in the *sanctuary* is almost at floor level. With the exception of the Norman lancets, all the windows are early-C14 and the e. window has attractive flowing tracery.

Gipping, chapel of St Nicholas (E4): A lane with broad verges leads to a pink-washed Tudor farmhouse on one side and this lovely little building on the other. Open fields lie all around and the hamlet itself is only a scattered handful of houses. Gipping has never had a parish church and, although the abbey of St Osyth provided a chapel here in the C14, this is the private chapel built in the 1480s by Sir James Tyrell, Lord of the Manor. His friendship with Edmund De La Pole, Earl of Suffolk, brought a charge of high treason and cost him his head in 1502. Until 1850 the family mansion stood a little way to the e. but only a few farm buildings and a large pond are left to mark the spot. Tombstones have not been cleared from the churchyard for, not being a parish church, there never were any (although it has been noted that Thomas Tyrell was buried here in 1585). It became a free chapel administered by trustees to cater for the local people in the C18 and so it remains today. After crossing the footbridge from the lane, it is worth a stroll to the s. boundary to view the chapel as a whole and to appreciate its remarkable beauty. It is tall for its length and no church in Suffolk has a richer variety of *flushwork*. Below the broad eaves *transomed* windows fill most of the wall space,

and there are variations in the *tracery* between nave and *chancel* with *ogee* shapes figuring in both. Doorways are centred on both sides of the nave and form a cleverly integrated design with the windows above them, a feature encountered again at Elmswell and Woodbridge. On either side of the doorway, blank arches filled with dressed flints align with two-*light* windows overhead, and the narrow space between the pairs of lights is filled with a band of dainty flushwork flanked at the top by *mouchette* roundels. Contained beneath a *dripstone* which matches the other windows, the unit merges with the whole facade. Nave and chancel buttresses are worked with small flushwork panels which have *crocketted finials* delicately cut in the *ashlar* above each. The badge of the Tyrell family is a triangular interlace of bow shapes called the 'Tyrell knot' (a *rebus* on 'tirailleur', the French for bowman). To be seen all over the building, it is matched by two interlaced hearts because Sir James married Anne, daughter of Sir John Arundell, and it was her family's badge. More puzzling is the inscription 'AMLA' carved on diagonal labels on the buttresses. Some have said that it stands for 'Ave Maria laetare alleluia' (Hail Mary, rejoice! alleluia), but another possibility is that it is some form of Anne's name – possibly Anne Morley Lanherne Arundell. Sir James's mother was a Darcy and their shield of three rosettes is to be found on a chancel s. buttress, while the shaped shields on the e. buttresses carry the arms of Tyrell (s.e.) and Arundell (n.e.). There are tiny *Sacred monograms*, crowned 'AMR's for the *Blessed Virgin*, and 'T' for Tyrell on the n.e. buttress, and round the corner is the *vestry* which, judging by its junction with the chancel, was slightly later than the rest of the building. It originally had two windows and having a fireplace it may well have been designed as quarters for a chaplain. The chimney shaft is elaborately disguised as a

Gipping, chapel of St Nicholas

blind bay window, with transomed lights filled with flushwork, and above the set-back upper section the Tyrell arms have their two panther supporters – a rare instance of a commoner being granted this distinction. Five shields in the upper panels are carved with various combinations of family arms and from e. to w. They are: Clopton/Darcy, Tyrell/Darcy, Tyrell/Arundell, Arundell/Morley, and Tyrell/Morley. Round the corner, a little doorway with the now familiar badge in the *spandrels* has 'Pray for Sir Jamys Tirell. Dame Anne his wyf' carved in the moulding, and the wording shows that it was done in their lifetime. The Tyrell motto in Norman French is also featured: 'Groyne que voudray' (Let him complain who will) Unlike many churches, the n. side equals the s. in richness, but then one comes to the tower. In brick but faced with stucco and given commonplace windows, it was probably added in the late C16 or C17 and mars the perfection of the chapel itself.

The charming interior is full of light and beautifully maintained. Looking up at the almost flat C15 ceiling, with its panels of heavily moulded timbers and folded leaf motif on the *wall plate*, you will realise that the present roof was placed above it and the e. wall heightened in consequence. There was a major restoration in 1938 and the seating and woodwork were refurbished in 1970. The oak benches at the w. end have been stripped of paint and those on the s. side are quite plain. The range opposite came in the early C19 from the Tyrell chapel in Stowmarket church and once again the family badge appears; there is a tiny face worked on the corner of a moulding on the back bench and three of the others have broad book slopes. This fact, taken with the tracery at the front, suggests that they were once part of a set of chancel stalls. Note the interesting little pattern incised on part of the leading edge. A *hatchment* for Edmund Tyrell who died in 1799 hangs in the blank tower arch and the C15 drum *font* has large *paterae* above the octagonal stem. The C18 panelled pews and matching pulpit in deal are painted pale cream, with the tops left bare – a convention continued in the churches of New England. The flattened chancel arch has token *castellated capitals* and although there is now no *screen*, the stairs to the *rood loft* remain in the s. wall. Had the Victorians carried out a reordering here, the interesting painting on the e. wall would surely not have survived. Carefully restored by Maurice Keevil in 1971, it displays olive-brown classical columns draped with gold-fringed scarlet

curtains which spread over the top of the window, their tassels hanging the length of the splays. The *balusters* of the *communion rails* are like those seen in countless C18 country house staircases and there is a small plain *piscina*. All the windows probably contained stained glass originally but the chapel suffered badly during the Civil War and Commonwealth. The remnants were restored and rearranged in the e. window in 1938. It has been suggested that the style of painting indicates work by late-C15 Westminster glaziers for there are *Renaissance* motifs and the modelling and shading are much more subtle than usual. At the bottom, Tyrell names and family arms appear again, with their crest in the l.-hand light – a splendid yellow peacock's tail issuing from a boar's mouth. The centre panel now has five *Passion emblems* on little shields held by angels' hands, and to the l. is a figure of the Blessed Virgin in exquisitely delicate colouring. Her hands are crossed against her breast and tears course down her cheeks. On the other side *St John*, wearing a matching robe, weeps with her. No doubt they were separated by a Crucifixion panel that was destroyed in the C17. Above in the centre is the figure of an archbishop in red cope and embroidered gloves (*St Thomas of Canterbury?*), to the l., a bishop (*St Nicholas*, or more probably, an abbot of St Osyth's?), to the r., a king (*St Edward the Confessor?*). Everything else is fragmentary except some fine golden canopies. When leaving this charming place, note the pilgrim cross incised on the e. *jamb* of the door.

Gisleham, Holy Trinity (J2): The church stands pleasantly, set well back from the road in a spacious churchyard. *Cautley* and *Pevsner* both classify the tower as *Norman*, but there is apparently plenty of evidence inside it to show that it is *Saxon* and built before the Conquest. A *lancet* was inserted a little later in the w. wall and, as with a number other round towers, an octagonal bell stage was added in the C15, complete with battlements and *gargoyles*. Walking round, you will find that the n. door is bricked up, and the flanking columns with their unmatched *capitals* show that it was C12 Norman. An elaborate *porch* was added some two hundred years later, only to be demolished in the early C19. Restorations followed in 1861 and 1887, and a window was inserted above the doorway. Further e., the flintwork at the base of the wall is stratified and very regular, another sign of an early foundation. New windows with *Decorated tracery* were inserted in the C14, and the brick patch at the e. end of the nave wall probably marks the site of the *rood stair*. By the C19, the *chancel* windows had been bricked up and new ones were inserted. There is a *scratch dial* to be found on the buttress nearest the substantial C15 porch, and the latter has shields in the parapet – a *Trinity* emblem for the dedication, three *chalices* and wafers for the mass on the l., *instruments of the Passion* on the r., and flanking initials which may have belonged to the donor. These recur in the mouldings of the outer arch, along with the knot of the Stafford family and an 'S', and 'MR' (Maria Regina) for the *Blessed Virgin*. The arch has worn lion *stops*, and the niche above it is flanked by the remains of *censing* angels which were callously cut away to accomodate a sundial which has itself now disappeared. The porch has a *flushwork base course*, and the side windows are C19 replacements.

There is a *stoup* by the entrance, and the door is curiously hinged down its centre line so that one half normally remains closed. Three steps down into a *nave* that lies under a plastered barrel ceiling, with only the *wall plates* and bottoms of the *arch-braces* to show that there is a medieval roof behind it. The plain tower arch is Norman in form, with rudimentary *imposts*, and it has been blocked off with a modern door inset. C19 *Decalogue* boards hang on either side. The late-C14 font stands on a new base, and there are tall lions round the shaft. The bowl panels contain tracery with centred heads which have been mutilated, alternating with shields, one of which bears the three crowns of East Anglia. Instead of the more usual angels spreading their wings below the bowl, here we find human heads, alternately male and female, linked by a most attractive vine trail. They are very like the smaller ones on the font at nearby Mutford, and the same mason may have cut both. The nearest window on the n. side contains some fragments of C15 glass, and there is a good contemporary painting of a saint on the *jamb*. She wears a cape, holds what could be an arrow (*St Ursula?*), and stands against a red background; above her, rays shine down from a demi-angel. In the next window there is a similar painting in even better condition, but in this case the saint wears a bandeau and the angel is crowned and bears a scroll. Cautley identified this as the figure of *St Dorothy*, but I think it may be an *Annunciation*. C19 alterations left only stubs of the chancel arch *responds*, but above is the original *castellated rood beam*, with the space behind it filled with a plain *tympanum*. Like the nave, the chancel has a plain plastered ceiling

but, again, the wall plates show through. Although the Victorians replaced the windows, they left the C14 *jamb shafts* in place on the s. side, and running mouldings on all of them. Like the pulpit, the choir stalls date from 1902, and at the e. end on the n. side you will find the church's only *brass* – moved a little so that it may be read. An heraldic shield and inscription commemorate Adam Bland, an Elizabethan lawyer who was the queen's Serjeant, dying in 1593. In the *sanctuary*, the angle *piscina* retains part of its arch *cusping* although the drain has disappeared, and there are *dropped-sill sedilia* alongside. Rather oddly, an early-C13 priest's coffin slab has been inserted as the seat, and it is incised with an elaborate cross. The e. window contains 1890s glass by *Kempe:* the crucified Christ flanked by *St Peter* and *St Andrew*, with the Annunciation portrayed below; the figures are backed by the maker's typical *tabernacle work*, and there are repetitive little figures in the borders.

Gislingham, St Mary (E3): This is a generously proportioned church for a small village – over 120ft. from end to end, and the distinctive red brick tower with diminishing polygonal buttresses was a relatively late addition, being built by Robert Petto of Bramford in 1639. There is a heavy stair turret to the s. with a faded sundial, and a stone in the n. wall records that John Darbie gave £100 towards the rebuilding. He may have been the Ipswich bell founder who cast two of the bells in 1671. The early-C14 *chancel* has a fine e. window with *reticulated tracery* beneath a later arch, and there is a *priest's door* in the s. wall. The *nave* was lengthened westward in the late C15 and the original tower was replaced by another which collapsed in 1598. So things remained until the advent of the new tower forty years later. The late-C15 n. *porch* is handsome and the inscription across the front translates: 'Pray for the souls of Robert Chapman and Rose his wife who built this porch to the honour of God'. There are large flat lion supporters to the outer arch, an angel holds a shield at the apex, and suspended shields are carved within the moulding and on the inner surface. The shields in the *spandrels* carry the arms of *St Edmund* and East Anglia, and there is a panelled parapet with central canopied niche. The roof was renewed in 1661 (see the churchwardens' initials over the inner door) and the principal timbers have attractive gouge-cut decoration.

There are no *aisles* and the nave is over 20ft. wide, spanned by a lovely double *hammerbeam* roof. The struts resting on the lower hammers are tall and there is plenty of space between the *collars* and the ridge. The wooden pulleys which remain on the 6th and 9th collar beams were probably used to raise and lower lights, and another to the r. of the chancel arch was possibly used for the *Lenten veil.* The new tower was offset to the n. and a murky set of George III *Royal Arms* on a shaped board hangs above the arch. Below it is a gimcrack boarded *gallery.* The C15 *font* stands in the centre of the nave and there are remnants of an inscription on the top step which showed that it, like the porch, was a gift of the Chapman family. Four fat lions guard the base and the bowl panels are carved with the *Evangelistic symbols* alternating with angels holding shields – w., a *Trinity* emblem; n., arms of St Edmund; s., *chalice* and wafer symbolising the sacrament of the mass; e., what I think is the pot and lily emblem of the *Blessed Virgin.* To the w. of the s. door are the remains of *consecration crosses* which mark the beginning of the C15 extension. The w. range of medieval benches has small *poppyheads*, and backs with turned *finials* were added in the C17. There are early-C19 plain deal *box pews* e. of the font, but on the n. side they are built round a fine C18 *three-decker pulpit*. It is severe in style and grained to represent oak; the deep and compact *tester* has small painted flower discs in its panels, there is a seat in the pulpit, and a large *hour-glass stand* is attached to the reading pew. Its position well down the nave is typical of the arrangement to be found in a *Prayer book church.* To the r. are traces of Elizabethan texts and long ranges of C18 hat pegs are to be found farther w. on both sides of the nave. The box pews conceal more medieval seating and the front bench end on the s. side has a very worn seated figure on the elbow. The nave n.e. window contains a considerable amount of C15 glass. The figure of *St Catherine* minus her face can be recognised top l., there is a fine eagle roundel, and below it are the shields of the Toppesfield, Chirche, and Clouting families. They are surrounded by lovely tendrils of the blue columbine, and white flowers which *Cautley* identified as meadow saffron. These are some of the earliest flower paintings in Suffolk.

Like the tower, the chancel is offset to the n. and there is a large square opening to the l. of the arch. Beyond is an *arch-braced* roof and the *corbels* carry figures bearing texts, books, and (possibly) musical instruments. The one over the priest's door looks like a small organ, with a lute to the w. There is a well-turned set of sturdy C17 *communion rails* and the top of the rather

nice Elizabethan melon-legged table was grained to match the pulpit. The *reredos* and *Decalogue* panels painted on zinc are C19 and there is an elaborate pair of 1890s 'gothic' niches for memorial tablets – one on each wall by the rails. The Victorian restoration apparently did away with the *piscina.* Anthony Bedingfield, who died in 1652, has a large monument on the chancel n. wall. The heavy kneeling figure, in black robes, clutches white gloves and is set in a round-headed niche with grey *Corinthian* columns each side; a *cartouche* of arms sits within the *broken pediment* and the Greek and Latin epitaph is cut in a square *touchstone* tablet below. Mary Darby's memorial on the opposite wall is much more restrained and attractive. The alabaster oval records that she died in 1646 and gave money 'for teaching poore children to reade Englishe by their exsample'.

When leaving via the tower, have a look at the record of a long-length peal rung in 1822 – 10,080 changes of Grandsire in 6hrs. 35mins. Its particular interest lies in the fact that round the edge of the board the tools of each ringer's trade are shown. The treble ringer was a sexton (spade and coffin), the 2nd and 5th were blacksmiths, the 3rd was a bricklayer, the 4th has, I believe, a turf-cutter's spade, and the ringer of the 15 cwt. tenor was probably a carpenter. Gislingham's six bells had been out of action for a long time until 2006 when they were restored and two new trebles were added. A very pleasing octave with a 15 cwt. tenor was the result and it was dedicated by the bishop of the diocese in December 2007. An overall and thorough restoration of this fine church was begun in 1987 and successfully completed in 1993.

Glemsford, St Mary (C6): The church stands on the edge of the village and commands a broad view across the valley to Stanstead. The C14 tower has an *ashlar base course*, renewed w. window, and fine three-*light* bell openings with *reticulated tracery*, The rest of the exterior is *Perpendicular.* The w. end of the early-C16 *aisle* is decorated overall with *flushwork*, while a base course of *quatrefoils* and shields continues round the s. *porch.* The windows of the *chancel* s. aisle are taller than those in the aisle and have *ogee* shapes in the tracery – a re-emergence of an earlier fashion. Above them is an inscription which records that John and Joan Goldyng were the founders of the chapel. There is more flushwork on the s. frontage, the battlements are pinnacled, and there is a *priest's door* on that side. Beyond the very broad, five-light e. window of the chapel. The chancel walls are faced with flint pebbles – probable evidence of the 1870s restoration. On the n. side there is a matching side chapel, again with an inscription in the parapet which refers to a John and Margaret Mundys, and their son John and his wives. Both n. aisle and porch are plain and the *clerestory* windows of 1475 illustrate a late use of *cusped* heads in the tracery. The s. porch has flushwork matching the aisle and over the entrance arch there are three tall, stooled and canopied niches. Its roof is lovely; all the timbers are carved with a curling leaf and there is a vine trail on the *spandrels* and *wall plate* over the inner doorway. This has king and queen *headstops* and there are tiny *fleurons* in one moulding and equally tiny niches in another. The worn, but still handsome tracery of the medieval door is cut in the solid and has a folded leaf border.

The interior is spacious with broad aisles, and the C14 *arcades* with their octagonal *piers* do not quite match – one side is higher than the other and the *capitals* differ. The *nave* roof is steep, in C19 pine, and the line of the original shows above the renewed tower arch. Within the tower there are two charity boards (painted on canvas as it happens), and the frames have the names of the rector and wardens for 1833. The traceried stem of the C15 *font* is very worn, with the remains of four figures. There are *Evangelistic symbols* in the e. and n. bowl panels, a bishop's head on the s. side, an angel with shield on the s.e., a king's head on the n.w., and on the n.e. what was probably the *Blessed Virgin* of the *Annunciation*. In the n. aisle stands a huge C14 poplar chest, its curved top eaten away with age between the iron bands. The s. aisle roof is modern but in the n. aisle there is an excellent early-C16 cambered *tie-beam* roof. All the timbers are moulded and the tie-beams are carved with leaf and scroll. There are *wall posts* at the corners and in the n.e. chapel the effect is slightly richer, with pierced *spandrels* and figures carved on the wall posts. On the aisle wall is a monument to Elizabeth Morgan who died in 1776. We are told that 'To enumerate her amiable qualifications and distinguished virtues needs no participation' and I am left wondering what that means. There are painted *Decalogue* boards above the n. aisle *altar* and the C17 pulpit has interesting variations on the stereotyped decoration of the period: the upper panels are conventional *blind arches* with compartmented panels below, but the scroll brackets of the book ledge are carved with birds whose tongues extend as flowering plants and they have perky

bird-head terminals. The s. chapel *Holy table* is roughly the same period but quite plain. The *High altar* has bulbous C16 legs but most of the rest of it has been replaced and the *reredos* behind is an oak bas- relief of the Annunciation dating from the 1880s. St Mary's has a good ring of six bells with a 13 cwt. tenor.

Gosbeck, St Mary (F5): Like neighbouring Ashbocking and Crowfield, the church is well away from its parent village and the ancient moats to the n.e. suggest that the original settlement was in that direction. It is a tiny building almost overwhelmed by the late-C14 tower that stands on the s. side and serves as a *porch*. Above the outer arch a pretty little niche has shields in the *spandrels* of its *cusped ogee* arch, and there is *Decorated tracery* in the bell openings below the *flushwork* battlements. On walking round, one finds three graves to the w. with curious humpbacked brick bodies between head and foot stones, and there is a C14 w. window in the *nave*. The body of the church, however, is a good deal older, for the plain n. doorway and the *lancet* beyond it are *Norman* or even late *Saxon*. The earlier dating is made more likely by the *long and short work* that survives in the n.e. and s.e. corners of the nave. The *vestry* and *chancel* were rebuilt in 1848 and the e. window appears to date from another restoration in 1883.

The entrance door is made of ancient lapped boards, and just inside to the l. the small iron-clad door leading to the tower is a reminder that church and parish valuables were often stored there in the Middle Ages. The *font* is C19 and a memorial screen of 1900 divides the nave behind the pitch pine benches. Overhead is a restored *hammerbeam roof* with *collars* and *king posts* under the ridge and large flowers applied to the hammers. The pulpit was reconstructed on a new stone base but the blind-arched panels at least are *Jacobean*. The chancel arch was apparently removed during one of the restorations but a section of the old *rood screen* was saved and the five panels now hang on the n. wall. They have rather an unusual pattern of tracery, with lozenges at the bottom enclosing small shields, and there are dull but extensive remains of gilt and colour. C19 metal *Decalogue* panels flank a somewhat later *reredos* which has well-painted figures within panels enriched with *gesso* backgrounds; there is a Crucifixion in the centre with the raising of Jairus's daughter on the l. and the raising of Lazarus on the r. The 1890s glass by *Heaton, Butler & Bayne* displays panels of Christ in the garden of Gethsemane, the Resurrection and Ascension above scenes of Bethlehem, Christ's presentation in the Temple and his baptism. Terribly solemn but well drawn and not unpleasing.

Great Ashfield, All Saints (D4): On the western edge of a scattered village, the church stands by the entrance to Hall Farm, and one crosses a water splash to reach the gate. The tower has a panelled *base course* to the w. where the doorway has slim attached shafts. Above it is a nice little *Decorated* window, with the remains of similar *tracery* in the bell openings. Brick *put-log holes* show in the closely set flints of the walls and there is a spirelet above the plain parapet. The door in the n. aisle is blocked and there are square-headed *Perpendicular* windows on that side. Apart from a C13 *lancet* in the n. wall, the *chancel* seems to have been largely rebuilt in the 1870s. The attractive C16 *porch* is a pleasing mixture of brick and flint, with dressed flint panels and tracery in moulded brick. At the bottom of the niche over the door there are small heads which match those on the brick pinnacles of the porch at Ixworth Thorpe a few miles away. There are remains of a sundial below the crow-stepped gable, and the *spandrels* of the arch contain the arms of the de Pakenham and Cricketot families, at one time Lords of the Manor. The porch's *arch-braced* roof has carving in the spandrels and the pillar which supported the *stoup* stands to the r. of the C13 doorway. The ancient door retains its original lockplate.

When the *nave* was rebuilt and the *aisle* added in the C15, the *arcade* pillars were placed on sections of the old n. wall and it also formed a base for the plain octagonal *font* that stands against the westernmost *pier* like the one at Worlington. The nave has a simple C15 arch-braced roof, and at the w. end there are contemporary benches with *poppyheads* and grotesques, including the remains of two mermaids on the one nearest the tower. Nearby are two chests: one is large and iron bound and is remarkable for being of walnut rather than the usual oak; the other is a small C16 example with very interesting naive carvings in the front panels. The centre is a grotesque symmetrical ram's head, to the l., a female head, and to the r., a fine portrait of a bearded shepherd. There is now no *screen* but the *rood loft* stairs can be seen to the n. of the chancel arch, with square-headed doorways facing w. On the s. side is a magnificent, square *Jacobean* pulpit – quite the best thing here. The base is supported on fat cushion legs and there are two ranges of

panelling in the body, the lower with plain lozenges and the upper with the familiar arch and *pilaster* design. The reading desk is supported by winged beasts and the backboard has another pair of arched panels, togther with the intials of the probable donor, William Fyrmage. The carved *tester* is dated 1619 and the back continues up to the flat scrolls and a crown. The whole piece is distinguished, not only by carving of high quality, but also by individual touches like the masks beneath the side ledges. In front of the pulpit stands a prayer desk which has been reconstructed. It has a fine bench end carved with the tools of a blacksmith or farrier, and the groove of the original book ledge can be seen on the inside. A unit of the U.S. 8th Air Force was stationed locally during the war and they have their own memorial in the n. *aisle*. It is an *altar*, backed by a *reredos* which is flanked by tall canopied panels – a design by *Cautley* which reflects his love and understanding of C15 woodwork. Above it is the original e. window, now lighting a C19 *vestry* beyond. A continental *chalice* veil in Bruges lace is framed on the wall. Just to the w. stands an interesting framed example of an early-C19 church terrier – an inventory of church property and parish responsibilities that is well worth reading. On the s. wall of the nave there are two *hatchments*: one with a greyhound crest for Edward, 2nd Baron Thurlow, who died in 1829, and other for Sarah, wife of the 3rd Baron, who died in 1840. Her husband's hatchment hangs on the n. wall of the chancel, alongside another for the 4th Baron, who died in 1874. Below them is a well-restored charity board in the unusual form of a long painted scroll. It records the 1620 Fyrmage charity (a link with the pulpit) and until the early C19 it was fixed to the top of the now vanished *rood screen*. On the s. wall is another hatchment which has not been dated but was probably for James Richard Bolton. In his '*Suffolk Gypsy*', Richard Cobbold, the C19 rector of Wortham, told the story of John Steggles' flight from the rigours of a Walsham-le-Willows boarding school, his rescue by gypsies and his many subsequent adventures. He came at length to serve as curate of this parish for over 50 years, and his memorial is on the s. wall above the *priest's door*. The early-C18 *communion rails*, with their spiral *balusters*, came to the church from elsewhere in 1945 and, at the same time, the early-C17 altar table was returned to its proper place. The plinth that it stands on matches the pulpit and so does the panelling of the reredos, so that it has been suggested that they formed part of a *three-decker*. If that were so, the complete unit would have been enormous and the pulpit construction makes it unlikely. In the e. wall of the sanctuary there is a C14 niche with an *ogee* which appears to have been canopied originally. The glass of 1926 in the e. window is by A.K. Nicholson – the risen Christ and two praying angels with pale yellow wings. The flesh tints are steely against deep blue backgrounds, and below there are vignettes of the sower and the angel reaper. All Saints has a decent ring of five bells with a 10 cwt. tenor, and one of the bells cast by Thomas Church in the early C16 has an inscription invoking Suffolk's own *St Edmund*:

'Meritas Edmundi Simus A Crimine Mundi' (By the merits of Edmund may we be absolved from worldly sin).

Great Barton, Holy Innocents (C4): This handsome church lies s. of the main road and most of the village and its dedication is a rare one; there are only four other medieval examples in the whole country. The mid-C15 tower is well proportioned and has a chequered *base course* and prominent *string courses*. The three-*light* bell openings have stepped *transoms*, and above the fine *flushwork* of the stepped battlements is an elegant C18 weather vane. *Nave* and *aisles* are C15 work but the *chancel* was built in the late C13. The side windows have *plate tracery* and above the three *lancets* of the e. window are deeply recessed *quatrefoils* within circles. On the s. side, the archway of the *priest's door* stands on slim shafts. To the r. is a large, gabled tomb recess with a C13 coffin lid in the base. On the other side of the doorway you will see that a former *low side window* has been blocked up. There are handsome hexagonal buttresses at the corners of the chancel, reminiscent of Brandon and Raydon, rising to gabled pinnacles, and on the n. side the octagonal *rood stair* turret rises above the roof line. The s. *porch* boasts a fine sundial with the unusual text: 'Periunt et imputantor' (They perish and are reckoned), and while we know that porches assumed a significant role in medieval church life, it is interesting to learn that in the early-C19 this one served not only as sleeping accommodation for homeless labourers but was also used for threshing corn. Over the inner door there is a pretty little niche with *crocketted* canopy and flanking pinnacles.

The feeling of spaciousness within is accentuated by the width of the chancel arch, and the whiteness of the chancel with its plastered ceiling draws the eye eastward. The early-C14 s. *arcade* has alternating octagonal and circular *piers* with *fleurons* in the *capitals*, but the n. arcade is late *Perpendicular*, with half capitals within the arches studded with fleurons. Overhead, a C15 *hammerbeam* roof has recumbent figures that have nearly all lost their heads. To the l. of the entrance, a *vestry* enclosure incorporates parts of the old *rood screen*, and beyond is a simple C13 *font* resting on four plain shafts and a centre column. The *tabernacle* cover is modern. To the r. of the tower arch is a benefactions board dated 1858. It mentions the late-C15 vicar, William Howerdly, and it is fitting that the parish's first known benefactor should be commemorated in the C19 glass of the w. window by *Heaton, Butler & Bayne*. The greater part of the benches are good quality reproductions dating from 1856, but there are six original bench ends beneath the arcades with *poppyheads* and *tracery*. The e. window of the s. aisle is early-C14 (like the arcade on that side), and there is a roughly shaped *piscina* nearby. The most interesting thing in the s. aisle is the glass. The centre window commemorates Queen Victoria's Golden Jubilee and is by Heaton, Butler & Bayne. Beneath the old queen's full face portrait roundel is a Bible held by angels, and below that, the *Royal Arms*; the tracery lights contain the stars of six orders of chivalry, but the extraordinary thing is that the two supporting full length figures are those of the Queen of Sheba and Queen Esther – a very peculiar conjunction. The window to the w. is a memorial put in by members of the Suffolk Hunt for their MFH, F.R. Smith, in 1913. It is a fine composition from *Morris & Co*, and although the artist had been dead for nearly 20 years, the designs are by *Sir Edward Burne-Jones*, with figures of the Centurion as Faith, the Good Samaritan as Charity, and Joshua as Hope. There are blue backgrounds with dense foliage, and in the tracery, seraph heads and angels with dulcimer and double pipe. Across in the n. aisle windows there are remains of C15 canopy work. The capitals of the C13 chancel arch are carved with leaves and the door to the *rood loft stair* is on the n. side. The Bunbury family were Lords of the Manor here from the C17 to the early C20 and just within the chancel on the n. side, within a Victorian Gothic arch, is the memorial to Lieut. Gen. Sir Henry Edward Bunbury, soldier, scholar, and Under Secretary of State. His was the delicate task of informing Napoleon, captive on the 'Bellerophon', that he could not hope to live in England but was to be exiled to St Helena. The soldier's father, Henry

William Bunbury, died in 1811 and was well known as a political caricaturist. His tablet is an excellent and deceptively simple design by Magnus of London – a well-lettered light tan scroll draped over a grey slab. The scroll motif is taken up again further along, where one hangs from the branches of a willow on the 1828 tablet for Lousia Emily Bunbury. It is by Thomas Milnes (the sculptor of the Nelson statue in Norwich Cathedral Close). In the *sanctuary* the C13 piscina has a crocketted gable flanked by pinnacles and within it, a pierced *trefoil* above an *ogee* arch. The heads at the base of the pinnacles are new. The level of both the piscina and the *sedilia* alongside show that the floor levels were raised in the C19. The church has an excellent ring of six bells with an 8 cwt. tenor.

Great Bealings, St Mary (G6): A row of stately limes comes up across the meadow from the bridge to line the n. side of the churchyard. They once bordered a path leading to the Hall which lay behind the high brick wall e. of the church and they help to make this a most attractive setting. There are over 150 churches in the county under the patronage of the *Blessed Virgin*, and Great Bealings is one of the few that can be precisely linked to one of her Feast Days – a will of 1523 refers to the full dedication as 'the Nativity of Our Blessed Lady'. Although there is known to have been a church here just after the Conquest, the earliest dateable work is C13, and on walking round you will see that the w. window has *reticulated tracery* of about 1330. A number of C15 bequests mention the tower, whose *flushwork* buttresses rise to stepped battlements, and there is an *ogee*-headed niche in the n. face. The nave walls are of flint pebbles but a full-scale restoration in the 1840s and 1850s rebuilt the s. side, renewed many of the windows, and faced the *chancel* with very dense dressed flint. There is a *priest's door* to the n. and, on that side of the nave, a C19 *lancet* and a late *Perpendicular* window with stepped *transoms*. Red brick was a fashionable material in the early C16 and about 1505 Thomas Seckford used it for a new n. *porch*. The inscription over the entrance is nearly all worn away now but it asked us to pray for his soul and that of his wife Margaret. There is a canopied niche above it and the flanking polygonal buttresses are crowned with stone angels. The porch roof is a delightful miniature *hammerbeam* very like the one at Bredfield, and it shelters a fine pair of carved doors in good condition – another of Seckford's gifts, in all probability. Their narrow, keeled

panels have ogee tracery and three small figures stand within niches on the uprights, the one on the r. bearing a heavy rosary. As you close the door, see how the backs of the panels were finished with an adze.

The rather dark interior lies under single-framed and braced rafter roofs with a section of panelling below the *wall plates*. It is just possible that some of the tracery in the bottom panels of the tower screen is C15, and beyond it the w. window is filled with glass by Henry Hughes of *Ward & Hughes*. This dates from 1879 and a sentimental Good Shepherd is surrounded by illustrations of four of the *Seven Works of Mercy*, an example of what mass production did for the firm. The *font* of *Purbeck marble* is another example of mass production, this time from the C13, with its typical canted bowl whose panels are decorated with pairs of shallow arches. Edward Moor, the mid-C19 rector who restored the church so effectively, was able to secure the services of *Henry Ringham*, who did wonders with the remains of the C15 benches. Using the same techniques as he did at Tuddenham St Martin, he spliced in new bottoms to the bench ends where necessary, and matched *poppyheads*, grotesques, and emblems to such good effect that it takes a keen eye to tell old from new. Look particularly for the medieval figure holding the Christian symbol of two fishes by the s. wall opposite the organ, three *pelicans in their piety* nearby, and two cocks for *St Peter*. Ringham essayed four versions of the pelican farther e. and provided both lectern and reading desk. The pulpit, however, is a C17 piece with coarse blind-arched panels and smaller foliage panels below the rim. It stands on a modern base and the octagonal *tester* has acorn pendants. The three shields in the tracery of the n. window were inserted in the 1840s and display the arms of Meadows, Henniker-Major, and Seckford. The glass in the s.e. nave window is an *Annunciation* of 1874 by *Lavers, Barraud & Westlake*, and the lower two-thirds of the window is blocked by a memorial inserted in 1583 for Thomas and Margaret Seckford by their son, who was the founder of Woodbridge School. It has a large painted *achievement* set within a classical frame beneath a portico, and the Latin inscription on the lintel is helpfully translated below. In the chancel, Ringham excelled himself with a brilliant series of *finials* on the choir stalls. They were designed by Maj. Edward Moor, author of '*Suffolk Words and Phrases*' and father of the rector, and display the crests of successive Lords of the Manor, churchwardens, and rector. On the n. side from the e., the front rank are for Moor (rector 1844-86), Morrison (James Morrison, MP for Ipswich 1832-5, a self-made man whose motto in business was 'small profits and quick returns'), Major (Sir John, Lord of the Manor 1770-1781); the back rank are Webb (Henry, Lord of the Manor 1692-1710), Meadows (Daniel, churchwarden), Cage (Seckford, Lord of Seckford Hall Manor 1673-1713). On the s. side from the e., the front rank are for Bridges (Lords of the Manor 1770-81), Clench (Lords of the Manor 1585-1680), Henniker (Lords of the Manor from 1781 and later patrons of the living); the back rank are Heard (Thomas, churchwarden), Seckford (Lords of the Manor of Seckford Hall 1185-1673), Wood (Thomas, bishop of Lichfield and Coventry, Lord of the Manor 1680-92).

The C19 glass in the chancel is of varying quality. The e. window of 1874 is by Lavers, Barraud & Westlake and flanks the Crucifixion with the Gethsemane vigil and the *three Marys* at the tomb; the panels are set as though on pedestals within canopied niches. The windows on the n. side and s. of the *sanctuary* are poor designs, but the s.w. window contains pleasing work by Mayor & Co, a Munich-based firm which was active in this country in the latter half of the C19. It portrays the young Christ in the Temple, and there is a vivid contrast between the brightness of the child and the rich, dark robes of the elders. The heavy stone *reredos* takes the form of two traceried windows flanking a central *cusped* arch, with sharply *crocketted* gables and pinnacles. It was designed by the architect William Bassett Smith in 1882 as a memorial to William Page Wood, 1st Baron Hatherley, who was Gladstone's first Lord Chancellor. To the r. is a C14 *angle piscina* with *dropped-sill sedilia* alongside, and on the wall above is an impressive monument for John Clenche, who died in 1628, and his wife Joan, who followed him a year later. Their alabaster busts face boldly forward, with closed prayer books placed before them, and quite a lot of the original colour survives. Four kneeling figures of their sons line the panel below, with skulls by two of them to show that they predeceased their parents; a coloured *achievement* and two shields on top, and a small *touchstone* tablet at the bottom complete the piece. St Mary's has a ring of five bells with a 7 cwt. tenor but they are hung dead and can only be chimed.

Great Blakenham, St Mary (F5): A small but very interesting church, beautifully kept.

Although the w. window and bell openings have *Decorated tracery*, the tower was probably *Norman* in its lower stages and the *nave* has a bricked-up Norman n. doorway, a simple s. doorway, and contemporary *lancets*. The *chancel* dates from the late C12 and there is a small round window well above the three small, widely spaced lancets in the e. wall. An early *scratch dial* with deep holes instead of lines can be found on a s.e. *quoin*, there is another above it, a third on the s.e. corner of the nave, and yet another on the r.-hand side of the nave lancet. A *vestry* and an organ chamber were added to the sides of the chancel in the C19 and the roof neatly extends to cover both. In doing so, the *priest's door* and one lancet were left undisturbed in the old s. wall. The C15 wooden *porch* with its original *arch-braced* roof has open sides and the mortices in the *mullions* show where panels of tracery once fitted. A singular survival is the shadowy remnant of a figure of the *Blessed Virgin* carved in wood beneath a crocketted canopy above the outer arch.

The shaft of the early-C15 *font* is unusually elaborate, with panelling both between and on the buttresses, and four of the bowl panels display intricate tracery. The others are carved with *Passion emblems*: the Sacred Heart within a crown of thorns (e.); the scourging pillar with a crowing cock, ropes, and sword (n.); nails and spear (w.); cross, rod, and branch of hyssop (s.). Within the tower is the table tomb of Richard Swift, a merchant who died in 1645. Kneeling putti flank the tablet and there is a notable epitaph:

Reader knowe, this narrow earth
Incloseth one, whose name and worth
Can live, when marble falls to dust,
Honoured abroad for wise, and just,
Alike the Russe, and Sweden, theis
Report his prudence with their peace,
Deare when at home, to his faith given
Steadfast as earth, devout to heaven.
Wise merchant he (some stormes endur'd)
In the best porte his soule secur'd
For feare, thou shouldst forgett his name
'Tis the first epitaph of fame.

The open-framed and braced roofs of both nave and chancel are likely to be C13 and combine with the chancel lancets in their generous splays to form a vista which is deeply impressive in its simplicity. Although there are rough projecting *jambs* there is, oddly, no chancel arch, but stairs for the *rood loft* remain in the s. wall. The *Stuart* pulpit nearby is pleasantly rustic, with shallow carved blind arches and embellished lozenges in the panels, and the *tester* has acorn pendants to its skirt. There are well-carved *poppyheads* on the C19 pews and choir stalls, and the *communion rails* make very decorative use of tracery which probably formed part of the medieval *rood screen* – pairs of roundels over *cusped ogee* arches. Within the *sanctuary*, the round-arched *piscina* is, like the rest of the chancel, late-C12.

A tombstone e. of the chancel outside caught my eye. John Haward died aged 47 in 1870, having served in the 1st Suffolk Rifle Volunteers, one of the many local units that were raised for home defence in the 1860s. His stone carries the badge of the National Rifle Association inscribed 'Wimbledon 1864' and it was at that rifle meeting that his moment of glory came. He had earned a place in the county team almost by chance but in the first stage of the Queen's Prize he swept the board against stiff opposition to take the silver medal which was, according to the association's report, 'deservedly awarded to ... an excellent shot' – a distinction that was not forgotten in his village.

Great Bradley, St Mary (A5): Set in an attractively extended open churchyard, much of the church's exterior is cement rendered including the whole tower. This is C14 and has a slim octagonal stair turret rising above the parapet as at Withersfield. The *base course* is chequered in flint and the unusual feature is that the slopes of the w. and s. buttresses are carved with heraldic devices, as they are at Hundon. Also uncommon is the large fireplace within, from which a flue emerges some way up the n. wall, protected by a heavy stone baffle slab. The early-C14 *chancel*, with its *priest's door* to the s., was shortened in the C18 and the e. end has been repaired in brick. The *nave* was originally *Norman* – see the tall n. door with its plain roll moulding and worn scallop *capitals*. The early *Tudor* s. *porch* is built of lovely, glowing red brick, with a steep crow-stepped gable and ranks of simple niches surrounding the entrance. There are *quatrefoils* pierced in the *spandrels* and the small side windows are formed from moulded bricks. The porch shelters a grand, late-Norman doorway which is tall, with a deep *chevron moulded* arch edged with a band of crosses. The capitals are carved with scrolly birds and the twist decoration on the shafts changes direction section by section. Under the lintel there are two projecting heads that turn their faces slightly outwards.

Notches show that the tower arch had a screen at one time, and in the s.w. corner of the nave there is a deep recess that is likely to have been

an *aumbry* for baptismal oils, salt, and similar items. The late-C14 *font* has a shallow bowl, carved with quatrefoils and centre *paterae*, a panelled shaft, and paterae round the base. There are traces of colour and sizeable chunks have been broken from the rim. The nave has a single-braced roof which has been renewed in part, and there are rustic *tie-beams* with *king posts* to the ridge. The 1952 stained glass in the s. window is by *Powell & Sons* – a Nativity group, with the shepherd offering a posy and an English country background complete with castle, thatched cottages and a carpet of flowers. There are roughly shaped recesses cut in the walls at the e. end of the nave and it seems that the *rood stair* was on the s. side. To the w. is a stone *corbel* which, by its position, suggests that the loft was a deep one, underneath which there would have been nave *altars* on each side. (See the remains of a *piscina* on the s. side and another behind the pulpit). The small square window on that side was probably an afterthought to give more light. The chancel arch is early-C13 and the footings have been exposed on the s. to show the original floor level. The early-C18 pulpit has a *tester* decorated with a marquetry sunburst and until recently it was a two-decker but the *clerk's* pew has been removed. There is a moulded *string course* in the chancel below the window sills and in the corner of the *sanctuary* is a tantalising remnant of early-C14 *sedilia*, with a heavy shaft and a deeply moulded *ogee* arch. They must have been beautiful in their entirety before the chancel was truncated. Great Bradley has a very early tenor bell which was cast in London by Richard de Wymbis at the end of the C13 or the beginning of the C14.

Great Bricett, St Mary and St Laurence (E5): A church with a rare dedication – one of only three medieval examples in England, and the building has a most interesting history. It began as a priory of Augustinian canons founded in 1110 and later became a cell of Saint-Léonard near Limoges. All priories controlled from abroad were suppressed in the early C15 and this one became the parish church. Although it now has a straightforward *nave* and *chancel* under one roof, it was originally more elaborate and clues can be found on the outside. Excavation has shown that there were *transepts*, each with an e. *apse*, and the chancel was probably apsidal too. In the late-C13 lateral chapels were added to the chancel and their arches remain embedded in the walls. A manor house was subsequently built directly on to the n.w. corner and covers much of the priory complex. There is a useful plan of the church displayed within which explains the layout and identifies the various building stages. The bellcote is a 1907 replacement and below it a small blocked lancet shows in the w. wall. The s. frontage displays a bewildering variety of windows, including a blocked *lancet* by the porch and several examples of 'Y' *tracery* of about 1300 – the date of the *priest's door*. To the e. of the porch is a fragment of the original *Norman* s. door and above it is a *scratch dial* cut on a large circular stone. It is likely to be the earliest in the county and has four deeply incised lines, one of which is marked with a cross. The very decorative e. window was inserted in 1868 but its tracery almost certainly repeats the pattern of the C14 original. The 1850s wooden porch has an attractive tile and pebble patterned floor and leads to an interesting Norman doorway of about 1160 that was formerly elsewhere. The arch is carved with *billet* and zigzag mouldings and the keystone has a *trefoil* pendant. The *jambs* are also decorated and an inscription runs down the whole of the l.-hand side. In it 'Leonardus' can be plainly seen. There is a smaller section below the r.-hand capital.

The interior is broad and spacious under a single roof in which *arch-braced tie-beams* support *king posts*, and the lack of a chancel arch accentuates its length. A tall blocked Norman arch at the w. end shows that there was once a tower, and in front of it a modern screen carries large *Decalogue* boards lettered in a favourite late-Victorian style of Gothic with coloured initials. The square late-C12 *font* is carved with interlaced arches e. and w. and trefoil arcades n. and s., and there is a good deal of inventive difference between them. Beyond it, a low C16 brick doorway leads to what is now a private garden. Although it does not show from inside, there was a C13 n. doorway farther along. The C15 *rood loft stair* remains in the n. wall and to the w. is a blocked Norman lancet. Just to the l. of this are two small head *corbels* which I think may have been re-sited. A s. nave window contains four unusually good C14 panels of the *Evangelists*. They came from the tracery of the e. window and are now placed so that they can be examined easily; it is a pity that they had to be surrounded by inferior patterned glass in the C19. Each winged figure is shown with pen poised, and has a name label, with his symbol cleverly introduced at the top. The tall lancet farther along contains the figures of the two patron saints in a nice uncomplicated design of 1975 by the Maile Studios of Canterbury. On

the n. wall John Bright's memorial of 1680 is an attractive composition in alabaster and *touchstone* – leafy side scrolls, urns, and an *achievement of arms* on top, swags and cherubs with a shield below. The pulpit has one tracered panel, with *quatrefoils* and shields in the rest and like the reading desk is, I think, largely Victorian. The C14 *piscina* set in a blocked chapel arch now has no drain and its *crocketted ogee* arch rises to a *finial*. By it stands a compact C17 table and there is a nice early-*Stuart* chest with blind arches in the front panels standing in the n.e. corner.

Great Cornard, St Andrew (C6): Alongside the road to Bures, the early-C14 tower carries a graceful shingled spire like those to be found in Essex on the other side of the Stour. There are very worn niches unusually placed within the angle of the buttresses on either side of the renewed w. window; they have steep gables and there are remnants of masks below the stools. The bell openings are roundels and a polygonal brick turret was added to the n. side in the C16. The s. *porch* matches it and was probably built at the same time. In the mid-C19 the body of the church was faced with flint and the s. *aisle* of 1887 joins up with the porch. By 1908 extensive repairs were necessary and the *nave* roof was replaced. On walking round, you will find that the n. aisle windows have *headstops* with exceptionally large ears, and under the e. wall there are C18 headstones carved with cherub heads.

Through the small, plain C14 doorway, one comes into a neat interior where the organ is placed on a *gallery* within the tower. The *piers* of the C14 n. *arcade* have semi-circular shafts with *capitals* towards the arch openings – a scaled-down version of those in Sudbury, St Gregory's, and the Victorian architect sensibly designed his s. arcade to match. The aisle roofs are almost flat and most of the timbers on the n. side are medieval. The stem of the *font* is C19 but the late-C15 bowl has shields within *quatrefoils* on four sides – e., the cross of *St George*, s., the arms of the Ogard (?) family, w., an unidentified shield, and n., the arms of the Crane (?) family. The two-*light* window at the e. end of the n. aisle has glass by *Jones & Willis* of 1927; the figure of *St Andrew* and a version of Holman Hunt's 'The Light of the World' are conventional enough but competently done. The parable of the sower in the s. aisle e. window is in another class altogether and quite exceptional. It is by A.J. Dix of the London firm of James Clark in strong *Arts & Crafts* style and was installed about

1920. In the small upper panels the tares are sown by a devil with glinting eye and cast at length into the flames, while below are the larger figures of Christ as the sower of good seed and the fair harvesters – sound draughtsmanship and subtle colour. The pulpit is C19 but the base of the C15 *screen* remains, with *paterae* and masks cut on the top rail. These and the shields at the bottom are very like those at Chilton and may well have been carved by the same man. The base now supports a light wrought-iron screen and, in the *chancel*/beyond, the choir stalls incorporate C15 bench ends with *poppyheads*. Overhead there is a C16 roof which is almost flat but the e. end was apparently altered in the C19 and there are shallow niches on either side of five stepped lancets. Below is a modern oak *reredos* with small shields bearing *Passion emblems*, and under the s. *sanctuary* window set in the wall is a worn tomb which has lateral moulded bands and three raised shields carved with arms that have not been identified. *William Dowsing* called here in February 1643 when he ripped up a couple of *brass* inscriptions and ordered a cross to be taken off the steeple. The interesting thing is that John Pain, the churchwarden, refused to pay the fee for this legalised vandalism and was haled before the Earl of Manchester for his temerity. St Andrew has a ring of five bells with a 9 cwt. tenor, but they are hung dead and can only be chimed.

Great Finborough, St Andrew (E5): This is a fine specimen of confident Victorian rebuilding by *R.H. Phipson* in the 1870s, using traditional materials and not having to spare expense. The style is *Decorated* (with variations) and the church's memorable feature is the tower. It rises conventionally to an average height, and then flying buttresses support a tall octagonal belfry stage which carries a stone spire boldly banded in colour and pierced by two ranges of windows. A local tradition asserts that the squire's wife had difficulty in finding her way home after hunting and persuaded her husband to provide a marker. The spire is certainly visible from as far away as Woolpit where, incidentally, the same architect designed a quite different tower and spire in the 1850s. The s. *porch* is the only part of the building that remains of the original church and although it was largely reconstructed, it has a chequer *flushwork base course* and large octagonal corner pinnacles. These are elaborately *crocketted,* and despite the decaying stone the tiny animal heads at the base of the crockets survive. Inside the porch there are corner roof *corbels* in the form of large *Evangelistic symbols* bearing scrolls.

The interior is spacious and within the tall tower arch there is a C19 *font* displaying some of the wilfulness of Victorian design – the octagonal bowl stands on a reeded classical shaft surrounded by a ring of veined marble columns in Decorated style. Beyond two C13 grave slabs are clamped to the w. wall, one with a fine floriated cross. The *nave* roof is *arch-braced* and the main timbers are surprisingly badly placed in relation to two window arches on the s. side. There are large angel corbels now painted in a variety of sickly colours. Many monuments were transferred from the old church and the first to be seen is an anonymous fragment of a large design which now rests on a window sill at the w. end of the nave; a trio of well nourished *putti* drape a garland round an urn carved with the profile of a lady. At the e. end, on the same side, is a monument to Jane, the artist wife of Sir William Hotham, who died in 1855; large *acanthus* scrolls flank the tilted *capital* of a column surrounded by mallet, chisels, a palette and brushes. The n. *transept* is now a side chancel but was built to house the memorials of the Lords of the Manor – the Pettiwards and the Wollastons. On the n. wall is a 6ft. by 4ft. bas-relief of the Good Samaritan under a *pediment* carved with the Chi Rho *Sacred monogram*. Sculpted by *Sir Robert Westmacott*, it commemorates Roger Pettiward who died in 1833, a Fellow of the Linnean Society and, in a local capacity, commandant of the militia. To the r. is a handsome marble tablet in the form of a large open book resting on a cherub's head within outstretched wings. The Latin inscription has lost most of its colour and is consequently hard to read but it is for William Wollaston and his wife. He died in 1724 and was a moral philospher whose doctrines anticipated many C20 beliefs. His major work was *The Religion of Nature Delineated*, first published in 1724 and noteable for its literary elegance. He was an ordained priest but having inherited a comfortable fortune he lived secluded, for the most part, in London. The tablet with a draped urn against a black triangle is by John de Carle of Norwich for another William Wollaston who died in 1797. On the transept w. wall are bas-relief portrait medallions of William and Elizabeth Wollaston (1769) and opposite, a large putto lets fall a scroll from his waist bearing the epitaph of Charles Wollaston who died in 1729. The *chancel screen* has angular lattice tracery and on it stands a small cross bearing an ivory figure of Christ, with attendant statues of the *Blessed Virgin* and *St John*. The *piscina* and *sedilia* are in the Decorated style and there is a satisfying range of *Clayton & Bell* glass in the chancel, s. nave and w. windows. St Andrew's has an excellent ring of six bells with a 12 cwt. tenor.

Great Glemham, All Saints (H4): A small church, but distinctly interesting. The C14 tower has been restored recently, and one hopes that time and the English weather will tone down the heavy-handed repointing. It houses a ring of five bells with a 13 cwt. tenor which was cast by the London founder Richard Hille in the 1420s or 1430s. There is a plain w. doorway, with a renewed late *Perpendicular* window above it, and a simple, capacious niche sits in the *flushwork* of the n.w. buttress. Another which is much more attractive is sited further up the w. wall, and has little shields in the *spandrels* of its *ogee* arch. There is *cusped 'Y' tracery* in the bell openings, and above them runs a *string course* decorated with delightful little heads – the jutting figures at the corners are like those at nearby Stratford St Andrew. The battlements with flushwork panelling were added in the C15, and there are small but good *gargoyles*. The diamond-shaped clock, with its single hand, was made by James Smyth of Woodbridge and has been there since 1770; time has caught up with the timekeeper, and it now runs by electricity. There were problems with the *nave* roof in the C19, and in 1856 it was reframed (note the original line on the tower e. wall). As part of the same operation, the whole of the s. *aisle* was dismantled and rebuilt, to strengthen the building on that side. Restoration of the C13 *chancel* followed in 1878, and in walking round you will see that there is a blocked *priest's door* in *Tudor* brick, and that the e. window has Perpendicular tracery. The outer arch of the compact n. *porch* has worn lion *stops*, and there is a very nice little niche overhead which has a *crocketted* ogee arch, with shields hung in the spandrels. Ceiling plaster has been removed to reveal the porch's unstained roof timbers and *embattled wall plate*, and a cusped *stoup* niche is sited by the inner door.

There are thirty eight *Seven Sacrament fonts* in England and all but two of them are in either Norfolk or Suffolk. All have been mutilated, some grievously, and opinion naturally varies as to which is the finest. Great Glemham's can certainly stake a claim, not only by reason of the unusual amount of detail that has survived in the bowl panels, but because of one particular feature – of which more in a moment. The font

Great Glemham, All Saints:
Seven Sacraments font with lily crucifix

is beautifully proportioned and stands on a high step, whose tracery encloses squat shields. The carvings in the bowl panels, with their rayed backgrounds, are so similar to those at Denston that the designs may have come from the same source. Details of costume confirm that it was made between 1450 and about 1490. Clockwise from the e., the subjects are: confirmation (the dove that represents the Holy Spirit descending is now only a blob; note the *chrismatory* held in the assistant's hand on the r.); penance (good illustration of priest and woman in the 'shriving pew' which was used for this rite; it still has traces of colour in the intricate panelling, and the winged devil representing banished sin flees above the head of the man on the l. – who was he, I wonder?); the mass (of particular interest, because the two people receiving communion hold between them a *houseling cloth*; there is a *chalice* on the *altar*, and the *reredos* behind is crested); extreme unction (the wasted body lies on an angled bed, as at Denston, and there is a perfect carving of another chrismatory); crucifixion (seldom left undamaged by the image breakers); ordination (including the third use of a chrismatory, and, as with the emblem in the first panel, the dove in the top corner was defaced); marriage; baptism (recognisable family group). Three of the deep niches in the shaft of the font contain pots of lilies, the *Blessed Virgin's* emblem, and retain quite a lot of their original paint. The fourth niche (s.w.) is quite different, for it contains the feature that gives this font its particular importance. It is a 'lily crucifix', and less than a dozen examples have survived in England. A rare and fascinating example of medieval symbolism, it illustrates the keystone of the Christian faith, the resurrection – Christ crucified placed on the lily, the symbol so often chosen to identify the *Annunciation*. As with the crucifixion panel on the bowl, it has been damaged, and for the same reason, but the shape of the figure is unmistakable. Suffolk has another, and better known, example in a window of Long Melford's Clopton chapel.

The nave roof is an attractive, unstained *arch-braced* design, the main timbers curving upwards above a wall plate carved with a folded leaf trail. Transverse braces are placed between the *wall posts* and under the ridge, and most of the square bosses are original (three with carved faces). *Henry Ringham* masterminded the restoration of the roof in 1856, but the replacement bosses and the demi-angels at the base of the wall posts were added as part of the 1870s work. The three-bay *arcade* has *Tudor* arches, but the round *piers* may well date from the C13 church. A very neat early-C19 chamber organ by Flight & Sons stands in the aisle, and the 1920s e. window glass there is by *Powells*. In derivative *pre-Raphaelite* style, it has figures of Hope (with traditional anchor) and Justice (an armed soldier as a change from the Old Bailey variety). The new chancel arch planned by J.P. St Aubyn, the 1870s architect, never materialised – instead, he inserted *corbels* below the medieval wooden braces. The *rood screen* had gone by the end of the C18, but the doorway that led to the loft stair remains in the n. wall, and its archway is adorned with crisp little *fleurons* and still has traces of colour. The dropped sill of the lancet on the s. side of the chancel means that it doubtless served as a *low side window*. A fragment of C15 *tabernacle work* is framed (upside down!) in the window, and in the opposite lancet, I suggest that the contemporary roundel illustrates a medieval *bier* (a framework which was placed over a tomb, to be covered with a pall or hung with relics). However, there is no clue as to scale, and it might be a *reliquary* frame. There are two C14 shields in the s. *sanctuary* window, one displaying the chalice and wafer of the mass within a glory, and the other a selection of *Passion emblems*. The simple

C13 *piscina* recess stands above a large projecting drain slab which may have been a later amendment. Gathorne, 3rd Earl Cranbrook died in 1915 and his well designed *brass* is on the s. wall; the glass in the flanking lights of the e. window forms a second memorial – figures of *St Michael*, armoured captain of the host with an unusual pictorial shield, and *St Gabriel*, prince of peace, bearing the lily of the *Annunciation*; the central Christ in Majesty and Nativity vignette commemorate Emilie Dove, and all the tabernacle settings are very lush. The glass is again by Powells and dates from about 1915. George Crabbe, Suffolk's best known poet and born not far away at Aldeburgh in 1754, accepted the curacies of Swefling and Great Glemham in 1792. Dudley North had earlier supported the poet and he offered him Great Glemham Hall in 1796 as a base from which to serve this church and nearby Rendham. His son recalled that when Crabbe could no longer see in the dusk to preach in the pulpit, he would stand on the seat of a pew by the window and continue from there.

Great Livermere, St Peter (C3): The church stands just within the park and the view to the w. takes in the lake and the ivy-covered ruins of Little Livermere church, with its tall tower a little distance away. The plain early-C14 tower now has a weatherboarded belfry with a pyramid top and it houses a decent ring of five bells with a 5 cwt. tenor. The *Decorated tracery* in the w. window contains the popular four-petalled motif above a pair of *ogee* arches. The plain, blocked n. doorway dates from about 1200 and all the *nave* windows have Decorated tracery. In the *chancel* there are *low side windows* on each side, also with Decorated tracery, the lower sections having been filled in. On the n. side is a heavy C19 flint and white brick *vestry*. The e. window has renewed tracery under a four-centred arch with a deep *label*, and there is a small *quatrefoil* opening over it. The blocked *lancets* in the s. wall of the chancel shows that it was built originally in the C13, although the three-*light* window is late Decorated and there is a simple *priest's door*. The whole of the outside has recently been rendered with plaster, including the battlemented s. *porch* which is quite without ornament. To the e. it stands a very interesting headstone with a curly *cartouche* edge over the grave of William Sakings. He was 'forkner [falconer] to King Charles ye 1st, King Charles ye 2nd, King James ye 2nd' and died in 1689. Alongside is a smaller and more rudimentary stone for his son Edmund, who died in 1682 aged 17. The porch has an *arch-*

braced roof, stone seats and tall *Perpendicular* side windows.

Within, the nave roof is plastered over and there are modern benches below. Three *consecration crosses* are to be found on the s. wall and there is another opposite. On the wall by the organ there are two large C14 painted figures which were probably part of a *Three Living and Three Dead* sequence and at the e. end of the nave on the s. side there is a painting which *Cautley* described as a post-*Reformation* Christ, but now only a foot and a hand can be seen. Just inside the door, a portion of the deep *stoup* bowl remains under its worn *trefoil* arch, and there is a coarsely cut wooden set of *Royal Arms* over the blocked n. door. The panels of the large C14 octagonal *font* contain one shield in a quatrefoil and a variety of tracery shapes, including a complete Decorated window design; the cover is modern. The plain niche halfway down the nave on the n. side may be the remains of a C13 lancet. Beyond it is the top half of an elaborate image niche which has an oddly shaped canopy with a *crocketted* ogee arch beneath Perpendicular tracery and small side pinnacles; there are remains of blue background colour. The *three-decker pulpit* is a solidly handsome late-C17 example in oak, with a miniscule *clerk's* enclosure facing w., and a broad band of carved *acanthus* below the canted ledge of the reading desk. The stocky pulpit has the same motif in a deep moulding round the top. On the opposite side of the nave is a Decorated *piscina* with a tiny recess to the r. It is rebated to take a door and might, therefore, be an *aumbry*, but there is a hole drilled in the bottom and another in the arch which is puzzling. The early-C15 *screen* has buttresses crocketted at rail level, those by the entrance being coloured red and gold and the bottom crockets carved as grotesque heads. The two panels on the n. side have original diaper decoration but the woodwork as a whole is fairly coarse and there has been a good deal of replacement. This, however, has not extended to the extensive worm damage on the s. side of the base. You will see where the chancel arch was drilled to hold the *tympanum*. On either side there are moulded *corbels* which supported the *rood beam*. There is another consecration cross on the s. wall of the chancel and opposite, a medieval bench with blind tracery on the ends and half *poppyheads*. In front of it, the stall has roughly carved ends and bears the initials of either the maker, the donor or the churchwarden of 1601. Like nearby Ixworth Thorpe, the *communion rails* are three-sided, but here they are a very nice

Georgian set, with turned and carved delicate spiral *balusters*, and *Corinthian capitals* to the corner shafts from which the top rails drop away in a gentle curve. What is most unusual is that both the *altar* and the *reredos* match the rails, employing spiral turning and Corinthian capitals in their designs. The chancel roof is arch-braced with *king posts*, and the very deep *wall plates* are finely pierced with tracery. Over the priest's door, on the s. side, is a length of C14 wall decoration – thin scrollwork in red and there is a faint painted shelf high on the e. wall. Below is a plain lancet piscina and to the r., a brick recess that was probably an aumbry. The e. window is flanked by large niches that were extensively renewed in the C19. The vestry door on the n. side lies within a much larger Perpendicular arch that has leaf carving in the small *spandrels*. Its position suggests that it may originally have framed an *Easter sepulchre*.

Great Saxham, St Andrews (B4): The route to the church is a delightful lane which skirts the park and winds through wooded country. The churchyard with tall red brick walls to the s. and w. is blissfully peaceful and when I was there barnyard fowls with broods of chicks were foraging among the headstones. The early-C15 unbuttressed tower has a *trefoil lancet* to the w., a narrow lancet above it, and a stair turret to the belfry on the s. side. The church was largely rebuilt by its patron Thomas Mills in 1798. In the 1820s, new windows were inserted in the *nave*, then a *vestry* on the n. side of the *chancel* and a new *Perpendicular* e. window followed. The medieval s. *porch* was not altered and the side windows have deep sills with seats below. The roof is original and there are the remains of a cross on the gable. The oldest survivals here are the *Norman* doorways – attached shafts with elementary leaf *corbels* on the n. and a perfectly plain arch on the s.

Within, the C15 *font* has a plain shaft and *cusped* lozenges with centre rosettes in the bowl panels. Over the s. door is a very dark *Royal Arms* of Queen Anne dated 1702 and painted on boards, while a Mills family *hatchment* hangs over the n. door. One of the features of Great Saxham is the continental glass collected by William Mills and installed by his father Thomas in 1815, the year of Waterloo. It originally filled the e. window and one of the s. chancel windows, but some was transferred to the tower lancet – bright little Swiss panels depicting the Virgin and Child, Christ's baptism, the *Three Marys* at the tomb, and a scourging. One of the many fragments is dated 1630 and there are bands of brilliantly coloured miniature shields. Medieval bench ends with leaf *finials* are to be found at the back of the church and the manorial pew opposite the pulpit has large *poppyheads*. The centres of the C17 front panels are carved with cherub heads and the Mills' coat of arms, while the rear seat has two *Renaissance* panels. Above it is a simple scroll tablet by Gaffin for William Mills who collected the glass and who died in 1859. The small *Stuart* pulpit has two ranges of typical blind arch panels and stands on a later base. Close by is an elegant and deeply carved stone *cartouche* in late-C17 style set against black marble for Sir Christopher Magnay who died in 1960. The chancel e. window is filled with the rest of the French and Swiss glass and there are many figures, coats of arms and fragments. Look in particular for the Swiss *Pietà* in the top of the centre *light*. In his *Principall Navigations, Voiages and Discoveries of the English Nation*, Richard Hakluyt described the travels of that fascinating Elizabethan, John Eldred, who died aged 80 in 1632. As Lord of the Manor, he lies buried here. Originally his tomb was on the s. side of the *sanctuary* but now his *brass* is in the centre of the chancel. The 20in. effigy is in perfect condition and almost certainly a portrait; he wears cap and ruff, doublet, trunk hose and fur-lined gown. There are Latin and English inscriptions and the eight shields of arms link his family with his status as a merchant. Along the top from l. to r. are the arms of Eldred, Eldred impaling Rivett, and Rivett (his wife's family who used trivets as a pun). On the l. of the slab are the arms of the City of London, on the r., his guild, the Cloth-workers. At the bottom on the l. is the East India Company (with all the ship's pennants streaming against the wind!), Levant Merchants in the centre, and the Russia Merchants Company on the r. On the s. wall of the sanctuary is a portrait bust of Eldred in a circular niche, re-coloured and gilded, with arms in an oval above and an epitaph on a separate *touchstone* tablet below. The sculptor of the bust is not known but on the basis that the border is characteristic of Maximillan Colt's work it has been attributed to him by a leading authority. Eldred was in Arabia for five years and came back in the year of the Armada bearing the first nutmegs in 'the richest ship that ever was known to this realm'.

> . . . the Holy Land so called I have seene,
> And in the land of Babilon have bene.

But the inscription on the brass by his son ends:

> But Riches can noe ransome buy
> Nor Travells passe ye destiny.

He may, I suppose, have had his fill of travellers' tales from his father!

Great Thurlow, All Saints (A5): The church stands on a rise above the infant River Stour in this attractive village. There is an outstanding collection of C18 and early-C19 headstones in the churchyard. In particular, seek out Mary Traylen's n.w. of the tower; the oval at the top is a naive carving of a corpse, with a person drawing the curtain against the skeletal figure of Death armed with a spear. To the s. of the tower Elizabeth Snazell's stone has the mortality symbol of reversed torches against a sauceboat funerary urn, and there are others nearby with reversed trumpets. The work of this rustic sculptor can be found in a number of local churchyards. The church has been very heavily restored, with all windows renewed, and the w. belfry window of the late-C14 tower is pure C19 invention. Nevertheless, it is a handsome building, with lots of *septaria* in the walls. The tower sports a lead-sheathed open bell turret topped by a pretty wrought-iron weathervane. The clue to an early foundation can be seen at the corners of the *chancel* – little *Norman* shafts carved in the *quoins*. The squared-off restored n. *porch* is very small and the C14 entrance has a medieval door with a C13 oval closing ring on which are riveted two lizards like those at Withersfield, ancient emblems of good fortune. Within, there is a *sanctus-bell window* above the tower arch, and a modern ringers' gallery in *Jacobean* style has been inserted. All Saints has an excellent ring of six bells with a 12 cwt. tenor. The Norman *font* is a massive square with slightly canted sides, carved with a varying arrangement of blank arches and there are nook shafts at the corners. The C15 *arcade* is very plain; there are no *capitals* to the lozenge-shaped *piers*, and above is a *clerestory* with four widely spaced windows on each side. The roofs are modern and three magnificent chandliers hang in the *nave*. Are they C19 Austrian or Russian? The s. *aisle* has an early-C20 window by J. Cameron – the *Blessed Virgin* and *St Elizabeth* with a young *St John the Baptist*. Beyond the very attractive modern *parclose screen* there is a C14 *piscina* in the aisle chapel, and above it the window contains four medieval glass shields with modern name labels. James Vernon's arms are in a fine baroque shield at the top of the e. window and the inscription tells us that he was Lord of the Manor and 'repaired and beautified this church in 1741'. A similar message and arms below relate to Ronald Arthur Vestey's work in 1956. To the l. there is a long *squint* through the wall giving a view of the *High altar*. To the r. is a large oval alabaster tablet for Florence Vestey, with arms at the top in coloured metal and a flighting dove below cast in polished aluminium. The octagonal pulpit is early-C17 with typical blind arches in the top panels, and modern base and steps. All the chancel fittings are modern and include a large classical *reredos* in blue and gold, with kneeling, gilded *putti* holding candlesticks on top. Beyond, the e. window has glass of 1958 by Harry Harvey of York – Christ the King, *St Michael* with his sword and scales on one side, *St Catherine* with other saints on the other side, and purple-winged cherubim aloft. All are bright and light but strangely wooden. There are restored medieval angels in the s. chancel window, as well as *Evangelistic symbols*. In the n. aisle is an early-1900s *Kempe & Co* window portraying *St Cecilia* and two musical angels. In the s.e. corner of the *sanctuary* is an interesting *brass* which probably commemorates John and Margery Gedding of about 1470. He was the Lord of the Manor and his armour is a good example of the Yorkist period. The effigy is unusual in that he wears his helmet and carries his sword slung behind him. His wife's mantle and veil headdress shows that she was left a widow; her dog crouches underfoot wearing a bell collar. On a nearby slab is the brass of Thomas Underhill who died in 1508 and who probably built the tower. Only his torso survives, dressed in *Tudor* armour with a helm behind his head, but the 18in. figure of his wife Anne is complete (She was a Drury). Two shields of arms remain, as well as a plate of nine sons (the daughters' plate has vanished). Another *ledger-stone* on the n. side of the chancel has a single shield left of four, and may mark the grave of John Blodwell (1534) and his wife Ann.

Great Waldingfield, St Laurence (D6): A handsome church which was largely rebuilt in the late C14 by John Appleton, whose family were Lords of the Manor of Little Waldingfield. The s. clerestory parapet carries an inscription which reads: 'Pray for the sowlis of thomas malchere and Jone and Anneis his wyvis & for all thoys caused this ba'hime't to be mad.' Thomas Malcher left money in his will of 1458 for the work and may perhaps have paid for the

Great Waldingfield, St Laurence: Communion rails

whole of the s. clerestory. A stair turret rises above the parapet of the tower on the s. side and a lion crouches on the lowest *weathering* of the s.w. buttress, with a matching *griffin* to the n.w. *Groined* niches with their canopies shorn away flank the w. window and a modern figure of St Laurence stands in one of them. The tower houses a ring of six bells with a 13 cwt. tenor, but their poor condition does not allow for ringing at the present time. The C15 w. doors are traceried and shields of the Boteler and Carbonell families are set in the *spandrels* of the doorway. Its mouldings are carved with large *paterae* and you will find that one of them is a *green man* and another an eagle. By the early C19 the church was in poor state and work in the 1820s included a new n. porch. Walking along that side you will see the buttressed turret of the stair that led to the *rood loft*, which must have stretched right across the church. In 1866 the chancel was entirely rebuilt by *William Butterfield* and the walls are faced with flint in which broken lines of tiles are set edgewise; the e. window repeats the outline if not the design of the original which was found embedded in the wall. Like the tower and *aisles*, the tall s. *porch* has a flint chequer *base course* and it once had an upper room whose stair turret rises well above the aisle roof. There are *fleurons* in the mouldings of the outer and inner arches and the C19 doors have an attractive figure carved at top centre. This was part of an extensive 1870s restoration under the direction of *J.H. Hakewill*; he replaced all the roofs and the window tracery and opened up the arch to the tower.

Just inside the entrance to the l. is the tiny door to the porch stair; even in an age of small men it must have been a tight squeeze for the average and impossible for the generously built. The *font* is interesting because although there are *quatrefoils* containing shields and paterae carved on all but one of the panels, the w. face has a small section of triangular patterning. This is undoubtedly *Norman* and shows that the bowl was re-cut in the C15. The graceful *tabernacle* cover commemorates a brother and sister who died in World War I. In the tower beyond is a nicely lettered Table of Fees which reveals that it paid to live in the village if you wanted to be buried there in 1882, and opposite, the updated version of 1948 is an unusually late example. The 1877 w. window glass is by Alexander Gibbs, whose workshop supplied some excellent designs to a number of Suffolk churches. Here, there are three panels of the Resurrection (with wide-awake soldiers, for a change) and musical angels in the tracery – strong reds and blues dominating. The tall nave *arcades* have quatrefoil piers and below the clerestory a *string course* is decorated with paterae and some very nice little heads with an interesting line in period hats. The pews below are from 1877 but they make use of C15 bench ends and there is a *pelican in her piety* on the n. side 4th from the w. Above the tower arch is a small gilt and coloured set of George III *Royal Arms* carved in relief, and in the n. aisle w. window, 1880s glass by *Lavers & Westlake* – Christ flanked by angels and blessing the peoples of all nations. There is more of their glass in the window by the organ – Christ expounding in the Temple as a child, with figures in the tracery of *Zachariah*, *St Elizabeth*, *St Joseph*, the *Blessed Virgin*, *St Simeon* (in a mitre, which seems a little odd for a Jewish priest), and *St Anne*. The central n. window of Christ's miracles is by Westlake and one light of the centre s. aisle window by him shows the sacrifice of Isaac within a canopied niche, with Old Testament figures in the tracery. There is a small *piscina* in the s. aisle chapel and the e. window there contains a jumble of medieval fragments in which very little of consequence can be distinguished.

There is no trace of the C15 *rood screen* that stretched from wall to wall (except the entry door to the n.), but when St Michael's, Cornhill, was being restored by *Sir George Gilbert Scott* in the C19 he discarded the altar rails, and by some happy chance they were bought by the rector for this church and placed within the chancel arch. They are a lovely set dating from the 1670s and *Pevsner* believed them to be the work of William Cleere. With centre gates, there are *acanthus* carved *balusters* which continue up in spiral form to a heavy top rail bearing an acanthus mould on both sides. Scrolls with swags of fruit support

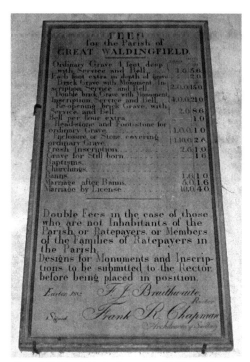

Great Waldingfield, St Laurence: Table of Fees

the gateposts; two matching ranges of balusters are worked into the fronts of the choir stalls, and more pieces were used as ends to the benches in front. Butterfield's chancel is not one of his most endearing works. The walls have a rather bald pattern of tiles and the *sanctuary* is lined with panels of marble fragments collected by two maiden ladies in an excess of zeal from the temples of Rome and Egypt (with a portion of Mount Sinai for good measure). The e. window glass of 1869 by Gibbs provides an interesting contrast with his later work at the w. end. There is no clear glass and the colours are bright and jolly. Not so the figures of the shepherds and the wise men, although their camel attempts a small smile.

Great Wenham, St John (E7): A fine cedar stands to the w. but does not mask the fine proportions of the C15 tower. The angle buttresses stop short at belfry level and they have simple *flushwork* to match the *base course*. There is a small *Perpendicular* w. window with a tiny niche above it just like the one at Little Wenham, and the bell openings have their lower sections roughly filled with flint. The rest of the building dates from about 1300 and has been rather harshly faced overall with plaster. On walking round, you will see that there is a small windowless shed in place of a n. porch and on that side of the *nave* the *rood stair* projects as a shallow slab capped with red bricks. There is a *low side window* and a pair of *lancets* in the n. wall of the *chancel*, and its e. window comprises three stepped lancets with *trefoil* heads. From the s. it seems as though a miniature porch has been added to the chancel to match the one at the s. door, but it is actually a little *vestry* which was built in the mid-C19. Above its door the tablet in memory of Spencer Fell, a rector who died in 1676, was originally on the chancel wall. The *porch* is Victorian but shelters a *stoup* by the plain C14 doorway on whose *jambs* are carved plenty of C17 graffiti.

The organ is placed in the tower and fills the arch entirely, flanked by raised C19 choir stalls with *linen-fold* panelled fronts. Rather oddly, an arch almost at floor level and five steps give access to an excavated cubby hole beneath the organ. The C19 *font* is cumbrous and by it lies a short section saved from the old roof which was replaced in 1867. Its pine successor is panelled out in waggon style, with *king posts* on *tie-beams*. A large, pale but lively set of the *Royal Arms* of George II painted on board hangs over the unused n. door, and to the r. there is a 3ft. by 2ft. 6in. recess under a *Tudor* arch. This is possibly a late example of an *aumbry* in which oil and other necessities for baptism were kept conveniently close to the font, but it could also have been designed to house a small memorial *brass* which has since disappeared. However, if so, *Dowsing* saw nothing of it when he came here in February 1643, for his journal reports that there was 'nothing to reform'. The raked metal rack with pegs that runs the whole length of the nave n. wall has been called an C18 wig rack, although I would not have thought that a parish of this size could raise as many wigs as that, even in its heyday. Perhaps hats were taken into account. The pews are Victorian and it may be that the 1860s restoration removed the chancel arch. There is now only a break in the masonry to mark the division, although a door shape in the n. wall shows where the stairs led to the old *rood loft*. Above it, a helm with a large horse crest, a short sword, and a *cartouche* of arms are mounted on a board. They were probably carried at the C17 funeral of a member of the East family. The generous pulpit matches the pews and has rather a nice bookrest with deeply cut oak leaves and acorns on the underside. The range of pews continues up to the *sanctuary*

steps where the *communion rails* are in Victorian Gothic style, with turned *balusters* like *Early English* shafts. The memorial to John and Susan Bailey on the s. wall of the chancel dates from 1813 and is by a minor sculptor, Robert Ashton the Younger. It is a small sarcophagus resting on lion paw feet, with lifting rings carved at each side, all set against a black background. The floor levels in the chancel have been changed and some C15 tiles have been relaid in the sanctuary. There are two patterns, each using four tiles, and the smaller design has crowned *Sacred monograms* in roundels about a centre *quatrefoil* (many of the tiles are good C19 copies). The small, plain C14 *piscina* has a groove in the arch where a wooden *credence shelf* once fitted and there are *dropped-sill sedilia* alongside. The panels of the C19 wooden *reredos* are painted with the *Decalogue*, Lord's Prayer, and Creed.

Great Whelnetham, St Thomas à Becket (C5): The building is finished in depressing grey pebble dash (apart from the n. *aisle* which is cement rendered). There are two *Norman lancets* under the eaves of the *nave* on the s. side and another in the n. wall at the w. end. One of the *quoins* of the s.e. corner is carved with a serpent that might well be *Saxon*. At the w. of the nave are more high-level windows, but of the C14, and there is a circular window in the w. wall enclosing a *quatrefoil*. The n. aisle, with its Gothick window *tracery*, was built in 1839, replacing an earlier chapel, and the C13 *chancel* has three of its original lancets on that side, C14 windows and *priest's door* to the s., and a C19 e. window. There was money left in 1453 for the building of a tower but the church has only a white weather-board bell turret of 1749, topped with a decorative weather-vane. The outer doors of the *porch* are ugly plywood but the roof timbers (with prominent joint pegs) are late-medieval and pieces of C14 tracery have been used to build the side window. The inner door is medieval too and the doorway has one *headstop* remaining. A C19 *sanctuary* lamp has been converted and hung overhead to light the porch.

A *Stuart Holy* table stands just inside and the blocked n. doorway frames a very decorative collage of the church's patron saint. The C14 two-bay *arcade* opens into the C19 n. aisle and the C15 *font* is sited there – octagonal, with quatrefoils, centre *paterae* and two blank shields in the bowl panels. The pulpit is modern but it makes use of panels which date from about 1520. They are similar to those in the Hawstead pulpit not far away. On the other side of the nave is a very small late-C13 double *piscina* under a single *trefoil* arch. Further w. are three rather dull C19 tablets for members of the Phillips family – two by Farrow and one by de Carle of Bury. The nave roof has simple *arch-braces* and it would seem that the chancel arch was rebuilt as part of of the C19 restoration of the chancel. The n. *vestry* is medieval and has a curiously angled entrance. The early-C18 monument for Charles Batteley on the n. wall is a peculiar design, with a mottled marble sarcophagus standing on a bulky oblong block, with draped marble behind and above it. Much nicer is the *touchstone* and alabaster memorial in the sanctuary for Richard Gipps who died in 1660; there is a *cartouche* within the broken *pediment* and a large bas-relief skull and crossbones below. On the s. side, a late-C13 double piscina under a plain arch stands next to low *sedilia* with finely moulded arches and well formed shafts. The e. window is a World War I memorial with glass by *Burlison & Grylls*. The standing figures are a slightly unusual selection – King David, *St George*, *St Nicholas* and Joan of Arc, and there are scenes from each of their stories below. The sanctuary s. window contains some interesting medieval fragments – two female heads, *quarries* painted with little birds having texts in their beaks saying 'Jhu Magi' (Lord Jesus) and 'Jhu Help', and large shields bearing the arms of Raynsford impaling Brokesborne.

Great Wratting, St Mary (A6): The church has a very attractive setting among mature trees, with a path from the handsome *lych-gate* rising over the sloping churchyard to the s. door. There is a memorable exercise in topiary along the road frontage, where bushes of the box hedge have been shaped into a chair, a church, a cross, and a diverting whirligig by the other gate. The church was subjected to rigorous restoration in the C19 and the majority of the windows, the s. door, and the *priest's door* have been renewed. The buttresses and lower walls of the *chancel* are original C13 work and there is a lot of *septaria* with thin (possibly Roman) tiles on the s. side. The tower has restored *Decorated* bell openings and it was repaired at some time at the top in red brick. There is a belfry stair to the s., and a line on the e. face shows where the original *nave* roof stretched. Sheltered by a *porch*, the handsome *Tudor* n. doorway has *quatrefoils* in the *spandrels* and the door itself is medieval.

Within, the tower arch is very tall and thin with no *imposts*, and the organ is tucked in below. The massive C14 *font* is a plain octagon with slightly canted sides. The nave benches are good-looking modern work with *linen-fold* panelling in the ends. Overhead, a modern waggon roof is separated from the *scissors-braced* chancel roof by a curious *cusped* division which has a *tie-beam* above the spandrels. The *screen* below is again good quality modern work in oak, with a coved cornice. The wide, *crocketted* arch has little heads and roses at the ends of the cusps and there are more in the *tracery* of the *lights*. A handsome wooden lectern keeps up the standard, and behind the pulpit is a *piscina* under a shaped and pierced *trefoil*. Above it and on the opposite wall there are stone *corbels* which will have supported the front of the *rood loft*. The recess beyond the pulpit is probably all that remains of the stair to the loft. In the *sanctuary* there are two large *aumbries* behind the *altar* and an attractive C13 suite of piscina and stepped *sedilia*, with triple-shafted columns and deeply moulded arches; the piscina has an unusually heavy stone *credence shelf* and a deep drain. Across on the n. side stands a good and solid late-C17 chest the colour of brown ale, decorated with marquetry vases and foliage in the front three panels. The three stepped *lancets* of the e. window are filled with 1870s glass by Constable of Cambridge – the crucified Christ in the centre, a Nativity *Blessed Virgin* and Child to the l., and the risen Lord to the r. The figures are formalised and the paint is deteriorating in places. I think the side lancets have Constable glass too, but wartime bomb damage called for extensive replacement.

Groton, St Bartholomew (D6): The churchyard is extensive and Groton Hall with its farm buildings lies along the s. boundary. The church is largely C15 but the tower has a w. window of about 1300 and below the stepped battlements the bell openings have lost their *tracery*. There are fine *gargoyles* everywhere and those on the *nave* are well above the *clerestory* windows with their cusped 'Y' tracery. The *chancel* parapet is plain and although the s. windows are *Perpendicular* the e. window has attractive C14 *reticulated* tracery. On the n. side is a brick lean-to *vestry* and, in the nave, a small blocked door. On walking round, one comes across the first indication that this church has a very special place in the hearts of Americans and the history of the United States. A table tomb in the corner between the s. *aisle* and the chancel has a modern inscription which identifies it as the grave of Adam and Anne Winthrop, the parents of John Winthrop, first governor of Massachusetts and founder of the city of Boston. A man of exceptional qualities, he was, like his father before him, Lord of the Manor here in 1618 but, at odds with Church and government, he led the Puritan exodus to New England in 1630.

Entry is by the s. *porch* and just inside there is a *stoup* with a very strange recess within it. Although blocked now, it was angled to emerge in the porch like a squint but the siting is difficult to understand. Below it stands a C14 chest with the curved top eaten away between the heavy iron bands. Under the tower two sheets of roofing lead are framed on the wall. Dated 1698, one bears the names of the churchwardens and the other: 'This done by me William Chenery Plummer'. Groton's ring of five bells with a 10 cwt. tenor are hung dead and can only be chimed. However, it is nice to find that trouble has been taken here to display casts of the interesting marks of two C15 London founders, William Chamberlain and John Keteyll. The *piers* of the tall four-bay *arcades* are a little gawky, with *capitals* only on the shafts within the arches, and overhead the pale *arch-braced* nave roof has churchwardens' initials cut at both ends and is dated 1665 (e.), 1671 (w.). Floors are *pamment* and brick, the walls are a cheerful pink, and in the heads of the aisle windows there is some mainly C18 heraldic glass which is now very worn in places. In the s. aisle (w. to e.) the shields are for: Adam Winthrop 1560, John Winthrop 1605, Winthrop/Clopton 1615, Winthrop/Tyndal 1618 (marking the second and third of John's four marriages); n. aisle (w. to e.), Anne Sears (a Winthrop girl), John Savile Halifax of Edwardstone, and John Weller Poley of Boxted. A niche in the n. aisle contains a 1950s *Blessed Virgin* and Child and the e. window (which now opens into the organ chamber) is fitted with a decorative modern iron grille which incorporates the shields of Winthrop and the state of Massachusetts. Groton was one of the cluster of prosperous Suffolk wool villages and it is notable that when Henry Dawson died in 1677 his *ledger-stone* in the centre pavement still described him as a 'Groton clothier' although the great days were long gone. There is 1870s glass by the *O'Connors* in the s. aisle e. window – a post-Resurrection Christ and *St Thomas*, with the influence of photography showing clearly in the treatment of the faces. The upper opening leading to the old *rood loft* can be seen on the n. side of the chancel arch, and although the pulpit below is Victorian, the panels and stem appear to be C15.

In the chancel the e. window is dominant, with its glass of 1875 by Cox & Sons; there are angels with scrolls in the tracery and the four main lights illustrate the text, 'I command thee this day to love the Lord thy God' (Deuteronomy), and St Paul's charge to the elders at Ephesus. It was given by John Winthrop's American descendants and in 1878 Robert Winthrop of Boston restored to the church the *brass* inscription which once lay on the tomb of his ancestor Adam Winthrop, who was the grandfather of the Puritan leader and died in 1562. It is now placed on the chancel s. wall near the *priest's door*. The *sanctuary* s. window contains 1880s glass by John Cameron (undistinguished figures of Faith and Charity). The light and golden figures of angels in the s. chancel window are much more attractive, although I have not been able to identify the maker. They are retrospective memorials for Mary and Thomasina, John Winthrop's first two wives. Before leaving, have a look at the stone in the s.e. corner of the churchyard which is claimed as the oldest (outside, that is) in Suffolk. The edge inscription identifies it as the grave of 'Lewes Kedbye whoe had to wyfe Jane Kedbye' and it is dated 1598. It once formed the top of a table tomb and there was a graven effigy and epitaph. Faint traces of the latter can still be seen and it read:

Christ is to me as life on earth
And deathe to me is gaine,
Because I trust through him alone
Salvation to obtain.

Grundisburgh, St Mary (G5): There was obviously a fashion in this part of Suffolk for putting the tower on the s. side of the *nave* and using its ground floor as the main *porch*. In Grundisburgh's case the medieval original was replaced in the C18, and one can have some sympathy with *Edward Hakewill's* comment: 'We know not whether to mourn over the fall or the restoration.' Had it been built a century earlier or later it would probably have sat more easily with the rest of the building. As it is, the outline is severe, with clasping buttresses, round-headed arches to doors and windows, and a plain parapet. The plain red brick is relieved by patterns of darker hue on the e. and w. faces, and there is an inscription above the entrance: 'This steeple was built The bells set in order And Fixt at the charge of Robert Thinge Gent. lately deceased 1731-1732.' The tower houses an excellent light ring of twelve bells with an 8 cwt. tenor. The clock has the traditional 'Tempus fugit' (Time flies) on its face, and I like the inscription on the

C18 sundial which uses the Suffolk form of the present tense: 'Life pass like a shadow.' One feels bound to echo it with: 'That that do!' The C14 s. *aisle* has *Decorated* windows with peaked arches, and there are startled *gargoyles* below the parapet. The position of the tower makes the sway-backed leaded nave roof seem low when seen from the s., and below it is a C15 *clerestory* whose windows are set within a band of lovely *flushwork*. From w. to e. one can recognise *St Edmund's* emblem, the Tudenham arms, a 'T' (Sir Thomas Tudenham?), the lily emblem of the *Blessed Virgin*, crowned letters that make up 'Ave Maria' (Hail Mary), an 'A' (Alice Tudenham?), and finally the *Sacred monogram*. At the e. end of the aisle is the chapel built by Thomas Wale in 1527. He was a London salt merchant who had property locally and lived near the church. He had no coat of arms but made up for it by decorating the chapel with the shields of the city of London and the Salters' Company (three salt cellars), and his own angular merchant's mark. The inscription is very worn in places now but reads, 'Orate p. aiabus Thome Wale et Alicie uxor eius xvcxxvii' (Pray for the souls of Thomas Wale and his wife Alice 1527), and is decorated with the rose and *pomegranate* of Henry VIII and Catherine of Aragon. The buttress below widens at the base to form a snug little porch for the *priest's door*, and a C19 Virgin and Child occupies the canopied niche. Wale's merchant's mark appears again above the doorway and there is a *scratch dial* on the plinth of the buttress to the l. After all that, the n. side is very humble, plain and plastered, with no aisle, and an ugly chimney rears up against the blocked n. door. Hakewill's full-scale restoration of 1872 included replacement e. and w. windows and he died before the work was completed. Grundisburgh's bells are well known in Suffolk and beyond, and a bell wheel serves as a wall decoration in the porch. To the r. of the C14 inner doorway is an C18 text from Leviticus which was placed there specifically to make a point: 'Ye shall keep my Sabbaths and reverence my Sanctuary. I am the Lord.' It is reminiscent of those at Hemingstone and Witnesham and may be the survivor of a sequence.

In contrast to the porch, the nave is full of light, and overhead is one of the finest roofs in the county. It is a double *hammerbeam* design, with *king posts* on the *collar beams* and pendent *bosses* below the upper hammer posts. There is a deep, richly carved cornice and the roof is all aflutter with angels – over fifty of them perch on hammers, *wall posts*, and even on the collar

beams below the ridge. They nearly all have new heads and wings which date from a restoration of 1888. The nice *pamments* of the nave floor have been replaced at the w. end by sickly yellow tiles, and the C15 *font* stands in the centre raised on steps provided by Hakewill. It is a familiar East Anglian pattern although the lions in the bowl panels are more squat than usual. Those that support the shaft sit on human heads in the same strange way as those at Helmingham and Ipswich, St Mary le Tower, but these have lost their features and only the *kennel headdresses* identify the two women. Nearby, the colourful Garter banner from St George's chapel, Windsor, serves as a memorial for Bertram Francis, Baron Cranworth, who died in 1964. On the n. wall is a C15 *St Christopher* painting which was uncovered in 1956 and restored in 1961. The huge figure in red and blue robes carries the Christ child on his shoulder and leans on a rough staff which sprouts leaves. There are buildings in the background on both sides, and the hermit fisherman stands bottom r. Fishes and eels abound and there is even a tiny mermaid to the l. of the saint's r. leg. Also on the n. wall is a good memorial in oak for Robert Brampton Gurdon, who served in the Long Range Desert Group. It is a measure of the toughness of that legendary unit that he was 38 when he was killed in 1942. Farther along, a large door led to the *rood loft* stairs, blocked now after the 4th step, and a faded C13 painting above has the remains of four figures and part of a decorative frieze. The subject is said to be Christ's appearance before the high priest.

The bulky open-work stone pulpit of 1881 stands here, and within the late-C13 chancel arch is a lovely mid-C14 *rood screen*. The deep tracery has a *crocketted ogee* arch applied to each bay, the uprights carry pinnacled buttresses, and many of the mouldings are deeply undercut. Although most of the *cusping* has been broken from the entrance arch, there is a *green man* lurking in the l.-hand *spandrel*. The low base has stencil decoration on a plum-coloured ground, and the whole screen was restored by Maurice Keevil in 1967. The plain C14 *arcade* of three bays between nave and aisle has octagonal *piers*, and the aisle roof had its angels and bosses replaced in the 1870s. On the w. wall, a tablet by Brown of Russell Street has a wreath and sword on the pediment and commemorates Lieut. Henry Freeland of the Royal Marines, who died on the Royal George off Sweden in 1854. The aisle is separated from Thomas Wale's chapel by a C15 *parclose screen* which must have belonged to an earlier chapel. It has been skilfully repaired and was restored at the same time as the rood screen. It has sharp ogee shapes in the *tracery*, and there are fleur-de-lys and roses stencilled on the uprights. The base panels have a pattern of Sacred monograms on an olive-green ground, and there are fainter 'MR's which indicate that the chapel was dedicated to the Virgin. It is largely taken up now by the organ, but there is a *piscina* under an ogee arch that belonged, like the screen, to the earlier chapel. The stone roof *corbels* again display Wale's merchant's mark and the arms of the city and his company. Three *brass* inscriptions have been taken from their slabs and mounted on the e. wall here. Two are for Anne Manocke (1610) of 'Stooke Nayland' and her son-in-law Thomas Sullyard (1612). Both families clung to the Catholic faith and suffered loss and persecution on that account. The third of 1501 begins: 'In heven God giveth everlastyng lyffe to the soulle of John Awall & Margery hys wyfe', and probably relates to the parents of Thomas, who rebuilt the chapel.

Between chapel and chancel there is a two-bay arcade with a *quatrefoil* pier and flattened arches, and although the chancel roof was lowered it still retains the medieval braced *tie-beams*. The now familiar Wale mark and Salters' arms crop up again on the s. corbels, and below is a range of choir stalls designed by Hakewill. He made good use of four C15 bench ends which have heavy *poppyheads* and a nice selection of tracery; the *Evangelistic symbols* are additions. The Blois family were Lords of the Manor for 200 years and there is a good range of their *ledger-stones* in the chancel, including one of 1631 and another of 1652 that was unfortunately masked by the C19 sanctuary step at one end. A fragment of C14 wall painting has been uncovered on the s. wall; it has a vigorous drawing of *St Margaret's* head in black line and the yellow wing of her attendant dragon. Three Blois memorials of consequence are on the n. wall. That for Martha (1645) has an oval inscription tablet set in drapes, below which man and wife face each other across a prayer desk backed by four sons and three daughters, all within an oblong frame, with an *achievement* at the top. William (1658) has a grey alabaster and *touchstone* tablet with shallow carving and five shields of arms. In a typical progression, Sir Charles's monument of 1738 is a great deal larger. It has side *pilasters* adorned with cherub heads and swags, there is a coloured *cartouche* below, and a *putto* with a golden trumpet has his own miniature portal flanked by urns on the top. In the sanctuary there is a

large piscina with a fine specimen of *dogtooth* decoration on the rim of the arch and part of an outer matching band. This confirms that the chancel was built in the late C13. The e. window glass of 1887 is by Wyndham Hughes – a slightly unusual Ascension scene, with angels in pastel shades floating on either side of Christ, above the disciples clad in sombre robes.

Gunton, St Benedict (J1): The church stands on Hollingsworth Road, just off the main Yarmouth/Lowestoft road, and it was built in 1956 to cater for the extensive housing development of the time. Designed by J.P. Chapman, the diocesan architect, to serve both as a church and a parish hall, it is a simple building in red brick, with deep pantile roof, and a slim tower at one corner. The dedication is a link with a Norwich church that was destroyed during World War II (whose war damage allowance helped to finance this project), and an Elizabethan bell cast in 1573 was salvaged from the bombed church to serve here. The building is not conventionally orientated, but at what one would normally call the e. end (i.e. the opposite end to the tower) there is a stubby extension on the side like a large porch which is gabled and rises to the level of the *nave* ridge. All the windows are domestic rather than ecclesiastical, and a flat-roofed block has been added on one side of the nave to provide meeting rooms and similar facilities. Entry is by way of the tower, and beyond the little vestibule there is a severly plain hall which has a plasterboard ceiling above curved steel roof braces. A folding screen at the far end opens on to what was originally the *sanctuary*, but everything has now been reversed so that a recessed dais at the tower end which was designed as a stage now serves as the sanctuary. A plain cross hangs on the unadorned back wall, and below it stands the *altar*, a handsome piece which has pierced carving overall in the style of *Renaissance* strapwork, with *communion rails* to match – probably late-C19 or early-C20. Although a small portable *font* is used now, the church was provided with a full-scale stone model which stands by the door beyond the folding screen.

Gunton, St Peter (J1): This trim, attractive little church stands at the end of Church Lane on the borders of the grounds of Gunton Old Hall. It probably dates from the late *Saxon* period, and the diminutive round tower has been neatly restored in recent years, displaying banded pebbles interspersed with larger flints and lumps of puddingstone; there is a C13 *lancet* to the w. and the bell openings are C15. A thoroughgoing restoration in 1899 transformed the *nave* and *chancel,* and they now lie under a single tiled roof; the e. window was replaced, and a *vestry/* organ chamber was added on the n. side of the chancel in 1903. However, it is worth a circuit of the building to examine the *Norman* n. doorway which has a roll moulding and deep chevrons in the arch, with pairs of shafts below scallop *capitals.* Recently, a substantial square meeting room, kitchen, &c., has been sited on the n. side – pyramid roof, flint pebble walls with stone dressings, and separated from the body of the church by a surround of bilious stone paving. There is a little Norman lancet in the nave n. wall, and a C13 lancet in the chancel further along. A fragment of an earlier window is embedded in the chancel s. wall, and a faint outline shows that there was a large lancet halfway down the nave. The simple s. *porch* has a C16 outer arch with a small brick niche above it, and the doorway within is another Norman example. Its wide chevron moulding differs from the version over the n. door, and the *jambs* have been varied. At an early stage, a section on the r. was cut away to house a *stoup.*

From within, you will see that the tower lancet has a very deep splay, and the arch to the nave is perhaps broader than one would expect. A single waggon roof stretches the whole length of the building, and although there is now no chancel arch, a bulge in the wall marks its original location. There will have been a *screen* too, and the tall door in the n. wall once led to the *rood loft.* As part of the 1890s restoration, all the windows were filled with that depressing pale green glass known for some reason as 'cathedral glass' but, except for one that has been left in the vestry as a sample, it has recently been replaced with clear panes which are attractively striated. They are all individual memorials, and the inscription in the s. sanctuary window is particularly interesting. It records a Dutch parishioner's grateful thanks for forty years of freedom in Holland, 1945-1985. The church's only stained glass consists of four 1960s panels set in the e. window – simplistic designs portraying Christ, the sower, the reaper, and the fishermen. There is a plain C14 *piscina,* with *dropped-sill sedilia* alongside, and a memorial tablet on the s. wall of the chancel is a little unusual. Provided by J.G. Balls of Lowestoft, it commemorates Isabella Steward who died in 1867. Conscious of her impending death, she composed her own highly charged epitaph, and

her husband dutifully had it added to the stone. His own little memorial alongside is a good example of the late-Victorian fashion for enamelled brass.

Hacheston, All Saints (H5): There was a church here in *Norman* times, but as you will discover, little evidence of it remains. The C14 tower has a small w. door, with remains of *headstops* on the *hood mould,* and the door itself is recessed in the wall, creating a little porch like the one in Parham's *chancel* – an unusual idea obviously borrowed one from the other. The bottom half of the modest w. window is blocked, and its *Decorated tracery* is matched in the bell openings. There are niches in both w. buttresses, and interesting grotesque heads (which are not true *gargoyles*) are placed at the corners of the brick parapet; the line of an earlier *nave* roof shows on the e. face. The tower houses an excellent ring of six bells with a 7 cwt. tenor. The C14 *porch* was converted to a *vestry* in 1815, and walking round, you will see that the nave n. wall had to be supported by a massive wedge buttress in the C18/19, and the chancel was given a flying buttress a little later. There is a C13 *lancet* on that side, and just beyond the buttress, a line of *quoins* marks the corner of the earlier, Norman chancel. The pattern of masonry suggests that the e. end may have been rebuilt in the C16 or early C17, and a medieval cross has survived on the gable above. The C13 *priest's door* on the s. side is now blocked, and there are faint traces of what may have been a *scratch dial* on the *jamb.* The s. *aisle* was rebuilt in the early C16; its e. window has been blocked, and the w. window has one rather fine open-mouthed headstop.

Within, there is an 1830s w. *gallery,* and the remains of the village stocks are displayed on the wall above it. The C15 *font* has mutilated lions and *woodwoses* round the shaft, and the band of *paterae* and *castellations* above them shows traces of colour. There are deeply carved *Evangelistic symbols* in the bowl panels, alternating with angels bearing shields. The latter have been defaced – when *William Dowsing* came here in October 1644, 'the Trinity on the font' was on his list, and one can just recognise the *instruments of the Passion* on the s.w. shield. Note that the angels rest on clouds which take the conventional form of the period, seen occasionally in wood carvings and stained glass. The C17 cover is a simple lid with a short, turned *finial.* The lower panels of the late-C15 *screen* now stand in the corner behind the font, the paintings terribly mutilated and in some cases destroyed entirely – they were the 'popish saints' of Dowsing's journal. From l. to r., the 3rd is a possible *St Thomas*; 4th, *St Simon* (cradling his fish); 5th, *St James the Great* (identified by the scallop shell on his wallet); 6th, *St John* (the devil above the chalice); 7th, *St Jude* with his boat; 8th, *St James the Less* (the fuller's club just identifiable). Skylights were inserted above the C19 gallery, and the front incorporates four panels saved from the *rood loft*, and old roof *bosses* (as at Parham). The door to the vestry is normally locked, so that the archway beyond is not accessible. With its simple decoration and single shafts, it is the only piece of Norman work that remains, although the inner arch does have the typical shape of the period. The entrance step is deeply worn and shows how, over the years, everyone trod to the same pattern. The C15 *hammerbeam roof* has carved *wall plates*, and the cambered *collar beams* follow the line of the *arch-braces* so that they appear to form a continuous arch well below the ridge. When the aisle was rebuilt in the early C16, the *wall posts* and lower braces on that side were dismantled to leave room for the arches of the new *arcade*, with its tall, *quatrefoil piers*. The aisle roof has some interesting bosses – look for King David with his harp over the s. door, a face with tongue stuck out, a *green man* next to it (he wears a crown, which is uncommon). The crudely carved figures under canopies on the wall posts seem to be replacements for the most part – compare them with the two originals at the w. end. The font used to stand near the s. door, and it is possible that the recess in the w. wall was originally an *aumbry* in which the necessaries for baptism such as salt and oil were stored. There are dark, canvas *Decalogue* panels nearby, and while in the aisle, do not overlook a most interesting carving in the wall near the organ. It is part of a late-C14 alabaster group illustrating 'the incredulity of St Thomas' (*St. John's* Gospel 20:27). Medieval examples are very rare, and Christ is portrayed guiding the apostle's hand to his wounded side. The C15 benches are a fine set, even though the grotesques on the elbows have been chopped down to their haunches. The ends are carved with varied and intricate tracery, there is a twisted leaf trail along the backs, and the *poppyheads* are excellent; the benches have been extensively repaired and amended, partly in softwood, and most of the ends on the n. side are replacements. One of the nave windows has 1870s glass *by Lavers & Westlake* – the story of the raising of Tabitha (better known as *Dorcas*). When the

screen was dismantled and moved to the w. end in the 1880s, the *rood beam* was left in place, and the vertical timbers above it once supported the *tympanum*. The early-C17 pulpit has decoration typical of the period, with well carved arabesques. Three *tie-beams* span the chancel at low level, inserted, like the buttresses outside, in an attempt to stop the outward lean of the n. wall. The *angle piscina* in the *sanctuary* has lost the *cusps* in its arch, and I believe the erosion of the stonework is due to the chancel having been open to the weather for quite a long period at some stage – probably calling for the rebuilding of the e. end that was noted outside. There are *dropped-sill sedilia* alongside the piscina, and the *altar* is a plain C17 table. Both the e. window and the n. sanctuary window are filled with glass by *Kempe & Tower* of the early 1920s. The former is a World War I memorial, and has the figure of Christ the King flanked by *St George* and *St Martin*, richly apparelled; there are musical angels in the tracery, and tiny figures of the *four Evangelists* occur in the borders. The side window portrays the Presentation of Christ in the Temple – his parents to the l., *Simeon* and *Anna* to the r., and a child attendant kneeling with the offering of the 'pair of turtle doves or two young pigeons'. Both windows are in the firm's instantly recognisable style. The *hatchment* on the chancel wall was used at the funeral of Andrew Arcedeckne in 1849, and the C19 mausoleum in the corner of the churchyard outside is the resting place for four of the family. In white brick, it is stylish in a quiet *Regency* fashion, with three blind arches a side, and a massive iron door at one end. Quite a number of the headstones nearby indulge in verse, and the one nearest the s. door was commissioned by the steward of the Glevering estate for John Mann, 'for many years a faithful servant':

Pope boldly says (some think the Maxim's odd)
An honest man's the noblest work of God;
If Pope's assertion is from error clear,
One of God's noblest works lies buried here.

Hadleigh, St Mary (E6): This grand church reflects the town's importance as a thriving centre of the medieval wool trade and the e. end rears majestically beyond a short cul-de-sac which leads from the High Street. Beyond, the churchyard is as spacious as a park and the ochre-coloured C15 Guildhall stands on the s. boundary. To the w.

is the glorious red brick gatehouse which survives from the Deanery built in 1495. The base of the tower may well be as early as the late C12 or early C13, but there is 'Y' *tracery* of about 1300 in the belfry windows and the bell openings have intersected tracery of the same period. In addition, there are small circular sexfoil (see *foils*) openings each side of them just below the parapet. A stair turret on the s. side has a very individual selection of windows – a pair and a trio of minute *lancets*. Suffolk has few spires and none older than this one. It is probably early-C14 and its 70ft. frame is sheathed in lead laid in attractive *herringbone* pattern. The clock bell which hangs below a little gable on the e. face was cast about 1280 and is almost certainly the oldest in the county. A major reconstruction in the C15 added a tall *clerestory* with widely separated pairs of windows which extends over the *chancel*, and the line of the *aisles* is continued by chapels at the e. end – all adding to an impression of tremendous length. The wide n. aisle has *Perpendicular* windows but the door is C14 with remnants of *headstops* and there is a massive two-storeyed *vestry* at the e. end which probably provided living accommodation for a priest. It is interesting that it was built at an acute angle to the chancel chapel to keep it within the bounds of the churchyard. The *priest's door* on the s. side cuts into the corner of the window above it and there used to be another entrance to the church (complete with two-storeyed porch) by the side of the 5th window from the e. end – conveniently placed for processions from the Guildhall opposite (Hadleigh had at least five medieval *guilds*). The early-C15 s. *porch* is wide and tall, with pairs of windows each side but with surprisingly little decoration. There are three plain niches over the entrance and within, the stumps of vaulting remain to show that there was an upper room originally. The inner doors are panelled, with a *quatrefoil* border, and the wrought-iron fittings repay some study – note particularly that the strap hinges pass underneath the mouldings.

Inside, the church is very wide and open, with sharply raked aisle roofs and a coved and boarded ceiling in the *nave* above encased *tie-beams* which have shaped iron brackets resting on *corbels*. This was all part of an 1870s restoration that changed the character of the interior significantly. The C15 *arcades* are tall and slim and the chancel arch is very wide. The mouldings of the C14 tower arch fade into the *imposts* and there is a nice oak screen below installed in 1946 which has a rich, pierced cresting. On the w. wall there are some

Hadleigh, St Mary

hatchments: top l. for Sir Henry Bunbury, 2nd Bt. (1748), top r. for David Wilkins, a rector who died in 1745, bottom l. for the Very Revd. Edward Hay-Drummond (1829), bottom r. for Mary Tanner, the wife of a rector, who died in 1779. A fine specimen of a ringers' 'gotch' or ale jug is displayed in a case nearby, with a crudely lettered inscription:

If ye love me due not lend me,
Use me often keep me clenely,
Fill me full or not at all,
And that with strong and not with small.

Today's ringers make good use of the tower's excellent octave which has a 22 cwt. tenor.

The late-C14 *font* was re-cut in the C19 but is a fine specimen; the bowl panels have pairs of shallow niches set with tiny *paterae* under *cusped* and *crocketted ogee* arches with almost flat *groining*. The stem has larger versions with gabled buttresses and there are *Tudor Roses* set at the base. The cover was made by Charles Sidney Spooner, a member of the *Arts and Crafts Movement*; it is a tall *tabernacle* with two ranks of shafts carved with overlapping feather motifs and has a range of small painted shields halfway up – anti-clockwise from the s.: the arms of the diocese; Hadleigh; 'MR' for the dedication; (unidentified); the dioceses of Norwich, Lichfield, and Ely; and the province of Canterbury. The cover was dedicated by the archbishop of Canterbury in 1925 and commemorates John Overall, who was baptised here in 1559. He was a Professor of Divinity, dean of St Paul's , bishop of Coventry and Lichfield, and finally bishop of Norwich. He drafted much of the catechism that is to be found in the Book of Common Prayer, including that memorable definition of 'Sacrament': 'an outward and visible sign of an inward and spiritual grace'. The long benches in the nave were made in 1869 and children collected wild flowers so that the carvers could use them as models for the carvings in the quatrefoils on the elbows. The 1871 pulpit was designed by Farmer & Brindley – it has a typically Victorian stone and marble base but an oak body nicely carved by John Spurgeon of Stowmarket. The nave *altar* is modern, and the lectern close by is an interesting essay in C19 Gothic style and was designed by *Hardman*.

The church has a variety of chests and the early example by the s. door has a domed lid that is formed from a half tree trunk (probably willow). Joseph Beaumont died in 1681 and his memorial is an attractive little marble *cartouche* by the n. door, with fat, trumpeting cherubs holding a heart above it. A pair of scales used by the town authorities hang over the door and there are two more waggon chests on that side. At the e. end on the wall is a *brass* for Richard and Elizabeth Glanfield (1637). Like a number of others in the church, it has been moved from its original position; it shows the couple hand in hand, he in a furred robe and she wearing a stylish wide-brimmed hat. There is now no *rood screen* but openings on either side of the chancel arch show that its loft probably continued across the aisles. Two matching C15 *parclose screens* remain. They are tall, with wide divisions, and the delicate tracery is unlike most of the period. It is cut and carved as double units out of thin board and inserted between the uprights. In the s. aisle wall is a C14 tomb recess which was left undisturbed at the rebuilding a century later. The wide ogee arch has remains of crockets and a nubbly *finial,* and the heavy cusps are carved and partially pierced. Nearby, the World War I memorial is another piece of work by Charles Spooner – finely lettered on a painted panel, with Christ crucified at the top and an oak panel below inset with little painted flowers. The n. chancel chapel houses an organ with a fine early-C18 oak case which came from Donyland Hall in Essex; there are pairs of chubby cherub heads under the corner pipe clusters and an attractive pierced *acanthus* frieze between them matches

the hoods and surrounds to the pipes above. In the floor to the w. is a brass inscription and *achievement* for William and Dorothy Foorthe (1599), and on the wall by the vestry door is another for Anne Still, the wife of a bishop of Bath and Wells, who died in 1593; the figure is worn and there is part of a curved edge inscription and a Latin epitaph. Above this brass is a memorial for Sarah Johnson who died in 1793. The obelisk above the tablet has two mourning *putti,* one reclining and one standing by an urn; it is by Charles Regnart, a competent mason whose work is found all over England, with other Suffolk examples at Mendlesham and Higham, St Mary. The large oak chest by the organ is initialled 'W.S.' below a fascinating little ball padlock. The e. window of the n. chapel contains a number of heraldic panels and roundels set in closely patterned glass. At the top from l. to r.: the shield of *St George,* the badge of Queen Elizabeth I, the arms of Tudor England, and those of England quartered with France. Lower down is a selection of arms borne by various archbishops of Canterbury – Sancroft (bottom l.), Howley (centre middle), Juxon (centre bottom), and Wareham (bottom r.).

The two-bay arcades which separate the chancel and its chapels rest on quatrefoil *piers* and at the junction of the *hood moulds* there are headstops carved as angels on the n. and devils on the s. (one would expect it to be the other way round). Unlike the nave, the chancel roof was undisturbed by restorers and is richly panelled, with *bosses* along the centre line. The mighty Perpendicular e. window is filled with glass by *Ward & Hughes* from their worst period, and to the l. is a C15 tomb set within the wall with an opening above it through to the chapel beyond. The three shields in quatrefoils along

Hadleigh, St Mary: Mock priest bench end

the front were once inlaid and there are indents for brasses on the walls above the slab. Whose it was is not known but it was obviously designed for use as an *Easter sepulchre*. The *piscina* and *sedilia* on the s. side of the *sanctuary* are C19 but three medieval *squints* remain in the wall behind them, giving a view of the *High altar* from the s. chapel. The e. window of the chapel is something which attracts the eye the moment one enters the church. It is filled with glass of 1857 by George Hedgeland, best known locally for the great w. window of Norwich cathedral. On the theme of 'Suffer little children to come unto me', it is an uncomplicated design across the three *lights* in the fashion of a large painting; the colours are clear and vivid and the artist used a great deal of textured shading both in features and drapery. The small C14 piscina to the r. is now used as a tabernacle for the Blessed Sacrament and has been fitted with a door on which is carved a gilded *Agnus Dei*. On the n. wall of the chapel sanctuary is Thomas Alabaster's brass – a kneeling figure crudely engraved within a niche. He died in 1592 'having lived in this towne a clothier about 50 yeeres'. On the s. wall John Alabaster's brass of 1637 shows him in ruff and gown within a *Renaissance* arch. Another brass to the l. of the altar and the window to the r. both commemorate the most famous of Hadleigh's rectors – Rowland Taylor, installed by Archbishop Cranmer in 1544. A diligent preacher of the new doctrine, he was arrested within six days of Queen Mary's accession and, obstinate in his refusal to recant, was sent back to Hadleigh to be burnt, meeting his end with fortitude on Aldham Common. Below his brass there are two oblong tablets commemorating Dean Francis Carter (1927) and his wife Sibella (1940); the beautiful inscriptions in red and black Roman and italic lettering were cut by Eric Gill, that modern master of typography. A bench end opposite is carved with an animal holding a human head in its mouth, and it is often identified as the wolf guarding the head of *St Edmund*. However, the creature wears a parody of priestly vestments and its back feet are cloven and so it is more likely to be a medieval carver's sardonic comment on the clergy. The windows on the s. side are again by Ward & Hughes and it is interesting to see the distinct difference in style of the three to the w. They were designed by Thomas Curtis around the turn of the century and look more like *Kempe's* work – steely grey and pale yellow, with muted colours for the robes of the *pre-Raphaelite* figures.

Halesworth, St Mary (H3): Houses and diminutive market place cluster attractively round the church in the town centre, relieved now of heavy through-traffic. There was a church on this site at least as early as the C12 (foundations of a round tower were discovered in the 1880s), and there was a rebuilding in the C14 by the Argentine family. The present tower was completed by 1430, and chapels n. and s. were added in the C15. A significant change came when the space between the n. *porch* and the n.e. chapel was filled in 1863 with an additional *aisle*, demolishing an aisle which had been added a little earlier. An outer s. aisle and *porch* were built in 1863, making the building unusually broad, an example of Victorian expansion to meet a need. The w. doorway of the tower has hung shields in the *spandrels* and mouldings, and there is a band of *quatrefoils* above it. Small niches feature underneath the belfry windows, and below the *flushwork* battlements the corner *gargoyles* have exceptionally long, slanting spouts to throw the rainwater well clear of the building. The tower houses a good ground floor ring of eight bells with an 18 cwt. tenor. The Victorian s. aisle and porch are rather dull, and the inner, medieval s. aisle reaches to within a bay of the end of the *chancel* – note the *scratch dial* on a *quoin* above the basement roof, and the *priest's door* in the chancel. There is a C15 *clerestory* of wide windows, and the five-*light* e. window has been renewed. The window of the n.e. chapel has compact and interesting *Perpendicular tracery*, and the treatment of the corner buttress is very unusual. On its e. face a panel contains eroded demi-figures of the donors, with their shields below them, and there is a canopied niche above. Round the corner, another niche shelters an original figure – again very worn, but probably the *Blessed Virgin* and Child. The n. porch has a fine flushwork panelled facade, a centre niche with modern statue, and angel figures at the corners of the parapet; the outer archway spandrels display *Passion* and *Trinity* shields.

The C19 extensions have made the interior spacious, and the architects, the Francis brothers of London, were remarkably successful in blending old with new. The C14 *nave arcade*, with its octagonal *piers* was used as the pattern for the outer arcades, and the whole church was re-benched when the s. aisle was added. The tower window contains glass by *Clayton & Bell*, an excellent example of their later, self-confident style and attractive use of colour; the main panels have figures of Faith, Hope and Charity, with the popular theme of 'Suffer little children to come unto me' below. Two of the church's surviving *brasses* are mounted on either side of the tower arch – half an effigy and an inscription for John Everard (1476) on the l., and an inscription for William Fyske (1512) on the r. The C15 *font* follows the East Anglian tradition, and particularly good *woodwoses* alternate with lions round the shaft. *Evangelistic symbols* feature in the bowl panels, together with angels whose shields bear the symbols of *St Edmund* (e.), the Trinity (n.), the mass (w.), and the Passion (s.). In 1930, a tablet was placed by the s. door to commemorate the town's connection with Sir William Jackson Hooker and his son Sir Joseph. The father was born in Norwich and settled here in 1815, consolidating his work on botany and his renowned herbarium. In 1841 he was appointed as Kew's first Director, transforming the royal gardens into the botanical showpiece of the empire, and Joseph followed in his footsteps. The 1870s glass in the centre aisle window was designed by Henry Hughes of *Ward & Hughes*. It has weathered rather badly, and the figure of Christ ascending is very pale; the disciples in dark robes are grouped below, and a host of angels with brilliant wings cluster each side. The church's third brass is clamped to the wall by the inner aisle e. window. Dated 1581, it commemorates John Browne and his wife, but unfortunately his figure has not survived and hers is cut off at the waist; two separate plates are engraved with the figures of 6 sons and 10 daughters. They were a virile stock, for when John died at the age of eighty, 54 of his 65 grandchildren were still alive. Note that a section has been hinged which, when opened, reveals that this is a *palimpsest* brass, originally engraved in Flanders in the 1530s. Its very survival is remarkable, having been dredged from the Waveney in 1825. Over in the n. aisle, part of a wooden propeller is the memorial for an RFC officer killed in Flanders in 1917. The glass in the nearby window is a typical Henry Hughes design – Christ's Presentation in the Temple, with large figures under pale canopies, again weathered. The early-C17 pulpit now stands in the corner of the aisle and has been extensively restored and rebuilt.

The Francis brothers were responsible for the roof replacements in 1889, and they inserted a new chancel arch. The s. aisle chapel is linked with the chancel by a Perpendicular arch, elaborately decorated with large *fleurons* in its broad mouldings and on the *jambs*. On the n. side of the chancel, the doorway that leads to the vestry is interesting because it records the

names of the donors (whose effigies we saw outside). Flanked by demi-angels, the inscription reads: 'Orate pro a[n]i[m]abus Thome Clement et Margarate consortis sue qui istud vestarium facerunt' (Pray for the souls of Thomas Clement and Margaret his wife who built this vestry). There are *paterae* in the deep mouldings, diminutive *headstops*, and a large beast head at the top of the arch. It dates from the end of the C15 and the contemporary door has attractive tracery. Richard Assheton died in 1641, and his memorial on the opposite wall is interesting – painted on board, with three shields above an inscription. It has been described as a *hatchment* and may have been used as such, but the inscription makes me doubt this; another very like it and of the same period can be found at Exning. When the organ was being rebuilt in the 1880s, a *piscina* was uncovered in the pillar between the aisle and the nave at the e. end. Rather than hide it again, it was moved to the n. wall of the *sanctuary* – which explains its unorthodox position. It is small but decorative, with a *cusped* and *crocketted ogee* arch, and neat panel tracery in the *spandrels*. The piscina in the conventional position on the other side is C19, but below it in the wall there are two fascinating late-C9 oblong sections of *Saxon* carving which were found under the s. aisle. In the design, hands grasp fleshy foliage stems, and the stones may have formed part of a frieze or, possibly, the shaft of a standing cross. The C18 was a period when very little church furniture was made (apart from pews and pulpits), and it is a treat to find a *High altar* which dates from the early 1700s. It has a marble top, and the cabriole legs are carved at the knee with vine and wheat emblems to distinguish it from similar domestic pieces. Above it, the glass of about 1890 in the e. window has not been positively identified but looks like *Lavers & Barraud* work. In the lower panels the Last Supper is flanked by the Nativity and Christ's Presentation in the Temple; in the centre, Christ blesses the disciples and his mother, flanked by scenes of Gethsemane and the *Three Marys*. There is much elaborate *tabernacle work*, but the figures are curiously lifeless.

By way of tailpiece, a snippet of information from Cratfield parish accounts: Christmas Day, 1594 was so cold here that the rector couldn't thaw his ink to write down the names of the communicants!

Hargrave, St Edmund (B4): Half a mile n. of Hargrave Green a long cul-de-sac of a lane leads to the Old Rectory and a farm, with the church hidden behind them. It is a quiet and peaceful place, with rabbits popping in and out of the hedges. Until relatively recently there was a s. *porch* but now the simple late-C12 doorway, with small nooks at the spring of the arch, is open to the weather. There is a *Tudor* brick window to the l. and by the *priest's door* in the *chancel*, one with *Perpendicular tracery*. The *lancets* are C19 and the n. *aisle*, with its long and low-pitched roof, was added in 1869. The tower is in Tudor red brick with a stair turret on the s. side. A Perpendicular w. window was reused and its stonework is now decayed.

Within, there is a *stoup* to the r. of the door with half its bowl gone, and to the l. there is a niche with no obvious purpose. There are two simple *box pews* at the w. end and the C15 *font* has blank shields within the *quatrefoils* of the bowl panels and long, slightly curved chamfers down to the plain shaft. With the exception of the *tie-beam* at the w. end, the roof and benches are unremarkable C19 work but the C15 *rood screen* is of considerable interest, despite its mutilation. All the *cusps* of the wide *ogee* arches are broken off and the front *crocketting* has been stripped away. There are still *paterae* on the top rail but the canopy has gone. The *spandrels* over the entrance are carved with a king's head and an eagle but the unusual feature is the carving on the e. side where there is normally little decoration. There you will see bold and interesting designs, uncommonly large – a fox with a goose in its mouth, a *wyvern*, two fish, two dragons, a *unicorn*, and the head of a man wearing a cap. Above the screen the *rood beam* remains, decorated with a line of chevron and *billet* moulding. At the e. end of the *nave*, on the s. side, there is a plain image niche in the window splay. In the *sanctuary*, the arches of the C13 *angle piscina* have been renewed and there are plain, stepped *sedilia* alongside. On the walls, the C18 *Decalogue*, Creed and Lord's Prayer boards are attractively painted in gold and two shades of grey.

Harkstead, St Mary (F7): The church is well away to the n.e. of the village, a fine upland site with glimpses of the Stour estuary, and a stately row of limes along the frontage of the churchyard. There is plenty of *septaria* in the walls of the tower, and it has a very attractive *base course*. The buttresses and the stair turret each have a large panel cut with very shallow *tracery* shaped like a window – curious additions unrelated to other decoration. The tall, *transomed*

w. window is the tower's most striking feature and its *reticulated* tracery is an interesting variation which foreshadows the *Perpendicular* style. It houses an excellent ground floor ring of six bells with an 8 cwt. tenor. Walking round, you will find evidence that this was a *Norman* church – there is a blocked n. doorway and the two nearby *lancets* were reopened and restored in 1875. The *chancel* had been largely rebuilt in 1867, its walls faced with dense black flints, and a n.e. *vestry* was added. The C14 s. *aisle* with its deep parapet was probably renovated at about the same time, along with the contemporary porch whose inner doorway has inward-turning *headstops*.

The C15 *font* now stands in the base of the tower, and it looks as though the bowl panels were extensively re-cut; angels bearing shields alternate with *evangelistic symbols* whose scrolls have had the names added. Lions guard the shaft and between them stand emaciated *woodwoses*. A most interesting fragment of C13 painting has been uncovered in the top of one of the lancet embrasures. The head had been defaced but the figure has devil's rather than angel's wings, and he holds a disc or ball in his outstretched hand; there are heads of two deer behind him, and a portion of decorative border has survived. One would love to know what legend it illustrated. A C14 *arcade* separates the *nave* from the aisle, and the nave was re-roofed in pine in the C19. The opening light of one of the aisle windows was filled with stained glass in 1990; designed and made by Anne Gray, a rainbow swirls out of the text: 'I set my bow in the cloud'. Although there is now no *altar* in the aisle chapel, the C14 *piscina* remains in the wall, with an image niche in the nearby window splay. Another shallow niche was added in the C15 to the l. of the e. window, and there are tiny headstops in its canopy. The 1860s restoration included a new chancel arch which rests on green Irish marble shafts, and the dividing wall carries a low, beautifully delicate wrought-iron screen. The stone pulpit of the same period has evangelistic symbols in roundels of coloured marble. An elaborate doorway leads to the vestry, and just beyond it is a lovely little C14 *Easter sepulchre*. Its arch is *cusped* and *crocketted*, and there are tiny grotesque heads at the base of the flanking pinnacles. A piscina was uncovered during the 1867 rebuilding, but little more than the drain was saved, and the present piscina and *sedilia* are Victorian. The glass in the e. window is good 1880s work by *Clayton & Bell*; the Crucifixion group in the centre has two of the *three Marys* on the l., and on the r., the centurion with *Joseph* of *Arimathaea* who is seldom illustrated. Some C19 stained glass firms diversified into other decorative work, and *Powells* provided the excellent tiled *reredos* here. The flanking panels are a wheat and vine design in a delicate greeny-blue, and the Greek cross in mosaic has evangelistic symbols within its arms, echoing those on pulpit and font.

Outside again, there are some worn but interesting C18 headstones to be found. Elizabeth Barker's of 1726 stands close by the chancel e. wall, and by gentle excavation I found her succinct epitaph:

Tho' Dead, Yet Dear: tho' Dear yet Dead to Me.
Dead is her Body: Dear her Memory.

As you leave you may wonder (as I did) why an elephant features on the well cut 1980s stone for Lancelot Thirkell by the path to the gate.

Harleston, St Augustine (E4): This is not a common dedication, being one of two in the county. Prettily placed outside the village by the lane that leads to Haughley, a track leads up across a meadow to the churchyard surrounded by a scattering of Scots pine. The little church has no break between *nave* and *chancel* and its thatched roof runs in an unbroken line from end to end. The small *Norman* s. doorway has a plain arch on square *imposts* and although the n. door-way is blocked, a section of its arch remains embedded in the masonry. There is a pair of renewed *lancets* and one tall, deep-set lancet in the s. wall of the nave; the C13 chancel has a *trefoil*-headed lancet on that side. The e. window is C19 and there is a single lancet on the n. side. The w. end was rebuilt in the C19 and given a pair of lancets below a *foiled* circular window, with a wooden bellcote perched on the gable.

Within, there is a plain octagonal C14 *font* below a plastered ceiling which, with two exposed *tie-beams*, runs the length of the building. The pews and openwork pulpit are Victorian, but the *screen* is C14 and a good one. The uprights between the main *lights* are turned shafts echoing the prevailing style in stone and the centre arch is a broad *ogee*. The deep *spandrels* are filled with *tracery mouchettes* within roundels and the original plain panels remain below the centre rail. The C13 *piscina* in the *sanctuary* has a simple trefoil arch, and although everything else in the chancel by way of fittings is C19, it was well done. The stall ends carry four lovely kneeling angels with their hands masking bowed

faces and their wings raised. A band of tiles decorated with alternating *Sacred monograms* and *chalices* runs under the e. window and the *sanctuary* floor of Minton tiles displays the *Evangelistic symbols* in blue roundels within large lozenges. In all, this would be a lovely place to celebrate a Harvest Festival.

Hartest, All Saints (C5): The church nestles attractively with the village in a little valley which is quite steep sided for this part of the world. The tower is C14 with a renewed w. window, but the red brick and flint mixture at the top is a reminder that it collapsed onto the *nave* and *aisles* one October Sunday in 1650, 'by which fall a great part of said church is beaten down and the rest much shaken'. Repairs were soon put in hand and the C14 *arcades* of the nave were rebuilt, the walls lowered, and a new roof provided. The n. aisle, with its *transomed Perpendicular* windows, is C15 and although the lean-to *vestry* has been restored, it has a small C13 *lancet*. To the l. of it is a small stone set in the wall which is carved with a tun (i.e. a barrel) and is probably a *rebus* for a name like Shelton – no doubt moved from elsewhere. In the churchyard not far away is a stone which is either the base of a *preaching cross* or a leftover from the C17 rebuilding. The short *chancel* and much of the s.e. Lady chapel was reconstructed in the late 1870s and the *priest's door* has recently been converted into a picture window. The C19 s. porch shelters an *Early English* doorway, and in the corner an angled *stoup* has the remains of a head *corbel* below. This was the main entrance originally but a new n. *porch* was added in the C16, probably at the behest of John Phillipson who asked to be buried there with his wife Anna in 1546 (the two small shields in the *spandrels* carry their initials). Like the s. porch, it is virtually all in squared *knapped* flints and was over-restored by the Victorians. Its cambered *tie-beam* roof is heavily carved, and note the *chalice* and wafer shield on the spandrel to the l. of the medieval door.

There is a C19 *font* just inside and the short nave, with its three-bay arcade, has a roof which is a Victorian replica of the C17 predecessor. The benches are pitch-pine but those in the n. aisle have oak *linen-fold* panels that may have been saved from an earlier set. The bench at the front of the s. range has well-carved C15 *tracery* which probably came from the old *rood screen*, but note that it is backed by C17 panelling decorated with various shallow roundels and the initials 'R.P.' (another Phillipson?). There is a tall *Stuart* pulpit with four ranges of panels which was cleaned as part of the restoration and given a new base. The simple *piscina* at the e. end of the s. aisle is Early English but the one on the n. side is C14, retaining half of its *crocketted* canopy and placed unusually on the last *pier* of the nave arcade. Before leaving the nave, note the square of C18 roofing lead on the s. wall cast with churchwardens' names and a handsome *hatchment* above the tower door. This is for Thomas Hallifax of Chadacre Hall who died in 1850 and whose monument is in the s. aisle at Shimpling. The only memorial here of consequence is by Henry Westmacott in the n. aisle – a sail carved as a drape to carry the epitaph of Lieut. James Harrington RN, who was 'entombed in a distant land' in 1812. (Not how most would describe Minorca nowadays!) There are *Tudor* arches at the e. end of the aisles and the chancel arch was rebuilt in the 1870s, along with the arch to the organ chamber on the n. side, where the rich leaf-trail carving in the roof recalls that it was once a chapel. The arch between the Lady Chapel and the chancel has been glazed to its full height so that the chapel can be used for small congragational gatherings. The *sanctuary* has a Victorian blind arcade *reredos* and the piscina, in its shapeless recess, was originally sited in a window sill. After all the chancel's vicissitudes there is still a medieval door leading to the vestry. The glass in the priest's door has made the s. chapel very light and two of the brackets from the medieval nave roof have been fixed to the wall – one supporting a *credence* table. The *altar* is starkly modern in stained black, with the top resting on a pair of box frames. All Saints has a fine ring of six bells with a 9 cwt. tenor.

Hasketon, St Andrew (G5): It is generally agreed that the round tower is *Norman*, and there are tall, thin *lancets* at belfry level. However, it was remodelled around 1300 when a w. window was inserted and a leggy octagonal bell stage added, making it the tallest round tower in Suffolk after Mutford. Perched on the brick parapet is a pretty little weathervane in the form of a ship, a replica of one on the training ship *Britannia* and presented in 1946. Despite a C14 doorway and lancet, and a *Perpendicular* window, the *herringbone* flintwork in the n. wall of the *nave* confirms that it is Norman. On walking round, you will find that the e. wall of the *chancel* was rebuilt, a *vestry* added, and the *porch* renewed in 1850. Nevertheless, there is an unusual two-*light* Perpendicular window in the chancel s. wall,

very tall and thin under a *label* shaped like a *kennel headdress* with small *headstops*. An attractive *Decorated* window on that side of the nave has *mouchettes* and a *quatrefoil* in the *tracery*, and to the w. of it there are three sections of a small lancet embedded in the wall. It is likely that this is a *Saxon* window that was reused by the Normans, and when it was uncovered in the C19 there were fragments of wood and bark in the holes drilled on the bevel. Apparently the early builders inserted sticks as part of a wattle framework for the inner splay, but if this is the explanation for the holes the stones must have been reversed in the wall. One of the porch windows has a 1960s picture of a monk playing the organ, and the early-C14 inner doorway is deeply moulded with no *capitals*.

The tower arch within is taken up by the organ, but note the doorway above it, a common feature in round towers of this period which lends substance to the theory that they served as places of refuge. St Andrew's excellent ring of six bells with a 9 cwt. tenor is rung from the ground floor of the tower. The *font* is in such good condition that I suspect it was plastered over in the C17 to protect it against the Puritan despoilers. In the bowl panels fat *Tudor Roses* alternate with angels holding shields whose heraldry is still crisp and legible. It was probably given in the 1450s by Sir Robert Brewes, one of a family who were lords of four Suffolk manors, two in Lincolnshire, and one in Norfolk. Their arms are on the w. side and those of other families linked with them by marriage are carved on the other shields: Ufford (e.), Shardelow (n.) and Stapylton (s.). The shaft has been replaced but the base shows that there were four lions around the original. There are three *embattled tie-beams* under the waggon roof of the nave, and the C19 window in the s. wall contains attractive and unusual glass of 1858. There is a thick border of holly and ivy around the lights and the tracery, two *cartouches* of arms (one with a 'hawk on hand' crest) are set within plain *quarries*, and the overall effect is Christmassy; the maker has not been identified. The blocked doorway of the *rood loft* stair is in the n. wall, and by it is a very decorative memorial in alabaster and *touchstone* for William Godwin, who died in 1663, and two of his sons, who were Smyrna merchants. A large roundel contains a coloured *achievement* on top, there are four other shields, and a cherub head is set at the bottom within a coarse garland of fruit. The C13 chancel arch with its minimal *imposts* is almost as wide as the nave, and by it stands a modern, heavy oak pulpit on a stone base. There is no *screen*. On the n. chancel wall, a tablet commemorates two young Wait brothers who were killed in 1916 – Percy, a midshipman at Jutland, and Charles, a lieutenant in the KOYLIs, who fell on the Somme. The *reredos* in C14 mode was given in their memory. On the s. wall a shaped tablet in an alabaster frame has a cherub head above, with a skull and bones below. It remembers William Farrer who died in 1635 aged 15:

Here lies his kindred's hope, his Parents' joy,
A man in manners though in years a boy.
If on his yeares you looke, hee dyd but younge,
If on his vertues, then hee lived long.

The C19 window nearby has 1860s glass by *Lavers, Barraud & Westlake*; two crowded little scenes of Christ's betrayal and the Via Dolorosa. The tall, thin window noticed outside is equally attractive within and has *jamb shafts* with moulded capitals on the splays. The Brewes arms can be seen again, this time in C15 glass, with the deep red lion's shield set on a blue ground, and there are contemporary fragments in the heads of the lights and in the borders.

Haughley, The Assumption of the Virgin (E4): The official dedication of the church is to *St Mary*, without qualification, but until 1871 there was a yearly Toy Fair in the village on 15 August, the Feast of the Assumption, and that supports the belief that the specific dedication is valid. The late-C13 tower is on the s. side and has massive *gargoyles* in the plain parapet; it houses a good ring of five bells with a 14 cwt. tenor. The ground floor frames the entrance *porch* and there is 'Y' *tracery* both in the bell openings and in the porch, with thick diagonal buttresses to the s. The s. *aisle* windows have attractive *Decorated* tracery and the aisle e. window offers an interesting variation – each *reticulation* shape is quartered, with a small lozenge in the centre. The *chancel* is early-C14 (witness the *priest's door*) but all the windows are *Perpendicular*, as are those on the n. side of the *nave* (with the exception of one with Decorated tracery at the e. end). A small *sanctus-bell turret* crowns the nave gable. Over the outer entrance arch of the porch is a wooden lintel on which is carved 'C.H. 1699 T.W.' – no doubt churchwardens' initials with the date of repairs or alterations to the tower. The handsome late-C13 inner doorway is deeply moulded and has pairs of attached columns with ring *capitals*.

Moving inside, note that the carving on the octagonal C15 *font* is exceptionally deeply cut and it is intriguing that the bowl panels are not aligned as usual to the cardinal points of the compass but placed diagonally. They contain the *Evangelistic symbols*, together with angels holding shields carved with the *Trinity* emblem, *St Edmund's* arms, three *chalices* and wafers, and the cross of *St George*. There are angel heads below the bowl, and against the shaft are lions and *woodwoses*, with no two alike. The early-C16 s. aisle roof is splendid and has angels with delicately spread wings on the *wall posts*; most of them hold books or scrolls but two, towards the e. end, are playing theorbos. The main timbers are all crested, the *spandrels* carved, there are centre *bosses*, and the *wall plates* at the e. end are carved with more angels. In the late C14, there was a chapel of the Holy Cross in the church which attracted pilgrims and the present aisle chapel has taken that dedication on the assumption that the original was there. There is a large *piscina* with a *cinquefoiled* head, and *dropped-sill sedilia* alongside. The 1860s glass in the e. window is by J. & J. King of Norwich, and the artist was the young Thomas Scott who went on to become the firm's chief designer. It is a consciously medieval design across all four panels, illustrating the raising of Jairus' daughter – pale colour with most figures in profile. The octagonal *piers* of the *arcade* rest on square bases that may have been part of the original s. wall before the aisle was built. There is a Perpendicular *clerestory* on both sides and money was left to build a n. aisle, but the will was successfully contested and the work was never done. The nave roof has alternate cambered *tie-beams* and *arch-braces*, and there are huge flower *bosses* reminiscent of snow crystals. In the large Perpendicular w. window there are two interesting medieval glass shields – the three crowns of East Anglia and the arms of Thomas Beaufort, earl of Dorset, who was John of Gaunt's son and grandson of Edward III. All the fittings are C19 and the chancel was largely reconstructed in the 1870s; it now has a barrel roof which follows the curve of the e. window arch. In the *sanctuary* is a nice square-headed piscina, the *cusped ogee* arch having blind *trefoils* in the spandrels. For those interested in heraldry there are five *hatchments*: w. wall, s. side, the Revd. Richard Ray, vicar here for 55 years, and dying at a great age in 1758; w. wall, n. side, Elizabeth Tyrell, his daughter (1826); n. wall, w. end, William Crawford of Haughley Park (1835); n. wall, e. of *vestry* door, Richard Ray (1811); over the pulpit, Sir George Wombwell (1780). Before you go, have a look at the leather fire buckets hanging on the wall at the e. end. They are dated 1725 and 1728 and at one time 30 of them hung in the porch, readily available for use in the village. In a recent ecumenical development, the United Reform church has closed its chapel and now shares the church with the Anglicans. Their communion table now serves as a nave altar.

Haverhill, St Mary (A6): On the High Street and cheek by jowl with the busy market place, the church suffered with the rest of the town in the disastrous fire of 1665 when it was reduced to a shell. Then in 1866 the *Decorated nave arcades* were rebuilt, the C14 *chancel* arches through to the Lady chapel re-opened, and other work was carried out in an attempt to restore the church to its original form. The tower, with its tall and narrow bell openings, has a prominent s.e. stair turret characteristic of the area, with *Evangelistic symbols* at the corners of the battlements. It houses a decent ring of six bells with a 12 cwt. tenor. There is a blocked C13 *lancet* in the n. wall of the chancel and, as a change from the usual grotesques, the nave *gargoyles* are good carvings of demi-figures, best seen on the s. side. There is a line of *paterae* below the s. aisle parapet and on the *porch* which is the main entrance.

Inside the church, the w. end has been adapted by inserting a low ceiling and a folding, glazed screen to form a community area. The base of the tower is now a fitted kitchen. A glazed section of the ceiling peaks up to the tower arch and the church's two *hatchments* are just visible above, but not clearly enough to describe – a pity because one of them is out of the ordinary. Entry to the church proper is from a vestibule and through a screen which is, like much of the modern work here, a product of local craftsmen. Below the flat roof of the nave there is a *Perpendicular clerestory* with four large windows each side and, over the tower arch, a *sanctus-bell window*. In the s. aisle, two of the windows have glass by Percy Bacon, a glazier active at the turn of the century – large figures of *SS John, Paul, Peter, James the Great, James the Less, Bartholomew, Simon* and *Jude*. The designs are conventional and surrounded by dense canopy work. There is a C16 chest with *linen-fold panelling* and three locks in the Lady chapel. The Mothers' Union banner is a lovely piece of work designed by Leslie Moore and made by the Wareham Guild – appliqué outlined with thread and the flesh painted. The restored late-Perpendicular *font* now stands at the e. end of the n. aisle and its cover was

designed in 1967 by Sir Frederick Gibberd, architect of Liverpool's Roman Catholic cathedral and planner of Haverhill's post-war expansion. Counterweighted, its close-set fins radiate from the centre and rise to a brass *finial*. There is another Percy Bacon window nearby, a conventional but pleasing composition of Christ with a child on his knee and other figures grouped around. Below stands a fine late-C18 headstone brought in from outside, and further to the w. is a tablet for the aged spinster Johanna Atkinson of London and bears a long and mellifluous epitaph in C18 mode. There is now no chancel *screen* but to the l. of the entrance is a small doorway with a Decorated arch which led to the original *rood loft stair*. The panelled roof of the chancel was decorated by *Heaton, Butler & Bayne* and in the sanctuary there is a restored *piscina* and a totally iron-clad chest. By the door to the *vestry* is an interesting and eccentrically designed memorial for John Ward, a C16 vicar here. There is coarse strapwork round the small panel, and within the steep gable there is a Latin epitaph which Thomas Fuller in his *Worthies of England* translated:

> Grant some of knowledge greater store,
> More learned some in preaching;
> Yet few in life did lighten more,
> None thundered more in preaching.

The little portrait in oils to the l., dated 1622, is of his eldest son Samuel who became the Puritan lecturer here, and then for many years at St Mary le Tower, Ipswich. Fuller described him as an excellent artist, divine, linguist and preacher, and the portrait, like his father's memorial, is labelled 'Watch and Warde'.

Hawkedon, St Mary (B5): The church is not large but stands quite proudly in the centre of a broad, sloping green, fringed with scattered houses and barns. In common with a number of others locally, the C14 tower, with its tall bell openings, is angular rather than graceful (an effect caused by the spread of the e. face across the buttresses and an abrupt stair turret on the n. side). It houses a decent ground floor ring of five bells with an 8 cwt. tenor. There are no *aisles* and the *nave* has a C14 n. door, *Perpendicular* windows, and a C15 brick *rood stair* to the n., covered by a little continuation of the main roof – much nicer than the gaunt C19 furnace chimney alongside. The C14 *chancel* has a later e. window and quite a lot of early graffiti can be found in the mouldings of the *priest's door*. Completing the circuit, there is a *scratch dial* on the buttress nearest the attractive s. *porch*. The entrance is very weather-worn but a *stoup* nestles under a canopy in the angle of the corner buttress (as at Denston) and a triplet of small niches fills the gable. It would seem that it was re-roofed in the C15 and given a battlemented parapet of brick, with a pretty frieze of moulded brick blind arches along the sides below. The cambered roof has a heavy carved *wall plate* over the *Early English* inner door and there is a roughly-shaped recess in the corner that housed an earlier stoup.

Within, the 1912 *gallery* at the w. end was designed by Detmar Blow (an architect better known for his houses). From it, a fragmentary wall painting on the n. wall may be examined at close quarters; it probably formed part of a *St Christopher* over the n. door, but nothing can be identified now. In its place hangs the *hatchment* of Philip Hamond of Hawkedon Hall who died in 1779, which has careless heraldry. By the stairs is another for John Oliver. The third hatchment of 1708, over the entrance, is Edmund Plume's and it has a frame roughly painted with crossed bones and skulls – an unusual addition. The square *Norman font* had two corners of the bowl removed later and the shallow carving is much more developed on the n. and w. sides. The nave roof has two *arch-braced tie-beams* and *castellated* wall plates, while below there is a fine range of C15 benches with heavy sills raised on brick ledges. The *poppyheads* are carved with a diversity of forms: to the n. of the font is a lovely little figure of a lady, and towards the front on the same side, three heavily moustached faces under conical hats combine effectively. There has been some careful restoration and the three benches at the e. end on both sides are modern. On the s. wall hangs a handsome set of *Royal Arms* painted on boards – close enough for you to see how the 'C' for Charles II was painted out and George II's 'G' substituted in 1750. In between, Queen Anne's motto had been added and removed but the parish baulked at the complications of the heraldry and the quarterings are still *Stuart*. The blocked door to the rood stair shows on the n. side and opposite is a simple *Jacobean* pulpit, with small strapwork panels under the rim. Beneath the nave carpet at the e. end is a very worn *brass* – 16in. figures of an early-C16 man and wife, he in furred gown with a large rosary, she in *kennel headdress*, with her girdle drooping with the weight of missal and rosary. There are small plates of five daughters and three sons but the inscription has gone. The mutilated base of the *rood screen*

is still in place and the outer panels seem never to have been painted, so nave *altars* doubtless stood against them. The *tracery* in the other panels was of high quality and there are shadowy figures of saints. Enough remains to identify *St Dorothy* on the far r., with another female saint beside her, and the pair on the n. side were identified as *St James* and *St John* in the late C19. It is likely that the chunky tracery fronting the s. choir stalls in the chancel came from the vanished *rood loft* and there is an unusual chained bear carved on top of the bench end – the complementary beaver opposite is modern. The late-C17 *altar rails* are excellent, with diminishing twist *balusters* closely set, and the small early-Stuart *Holy table* is now used as a *credence*. The church's ancient glass has been collected and re-set in the s. window. There are C17 continental panels at the top: from l. to r. *SS Matthew, Andrew, Paul* and *James the Great*; a fine *Royal Arms* of Richard III within the Garter is in the centre and there are three panels of fragments. It is a great pity that the C15 wall painting over the window has faded into obscurity because it was s rare representation of the Transfiguration and was injudiciously restored in 1938. A C16 priest left his mark in the embrasure to the l. of the chancel door where he wrote: 'John Lahdnge curate of Hawkedon anno 1583'. Turning w., one is confronted by the completely pagan Everard monument of 1678 in the angle by the chancel arch – a *touchstone* tablet flanked by *Corinthian* columns, urns with a *cartouche* and heavy swags on top, together with flamboyant *putti* on either side. the choirmen's hat pegs jutting out below seem to redress the balance somehow.

Hawstead. All Saints (C5): The village is small but the church is impressive, standing proudly in a large churchyard with a massive early-C16 tower whose stair turret reaches above the battlements on the s. side. Over the w. door a line of shields includes five that are charged with arms of the Drury family and their alliances by marriage. The Tau cross (like a 'T') was added to the shield by a C14 Drury after a visit to the Holy Land, and the family's history is interwoven with this building. The *base course* of the tower is panelled in *flushwork*, with stars and interlace patterns to the w. and more flushwork in the stepped battlements, and there is a *pelican* and two cocks on the e. face. W. of the tower, a sundial has been mounted on a medieval stone shaft and on the n. side stands the remains of a *preaching cross*; the base has vestiges of Drury shields and at one time it served as a step for the n. door. The *chancel* dates from about 1300 and has a variety of windows – a *lancet* and a two-*light* window with *Decorated tracery* on the n., a late-C15 e. window, and a lancet as well as a late-C13 window on the s., both of which are blocked. On that side there is also a *priest's door* and a C14 window with a *transom* that formed a *low side window* below. Like the *nave*, the s. *porch* dates from the late C15 but the *Norman* doorways, with their single shafts and *chevron mouldings*, were retained. The porch windows display an attractive selection of C19 shields of arms of local families – Drurys, Cullums and Metcalfes, and the early Drury obsession with badges even extended to the ring of the door handle.

Within, you will see that the absence of *aisles* is compensated for by the spaciousness of the nave, with its span of 30ft. The large *Perpendicular* windows give plenty of light and their sills are lowered to form seats along the walls. The tower arch is tremendously tall and narrow, and within the tower hang five C18 and C19 *hatchments* of the Metcalfe and Hammond families. Below stands a C13 *font*, a plain, deep square on a C19 base, and the coved wooden cover carries a figure of *St John the Baptist*. The set of C17 *communion rails*, complete with gate, has been moved here and its dog-defying *balusters* and intervening uprights would have pleased Archbishop *Laud*. A pale, heavily banded C14 chest is nearby and over the n. door is a fine early-C20 (?) window whose maker has not been identified. On each side of a Calvary it shows the kneeling figures of Joseph Hall, the persecuted bishop of Norwich, whose first cure of souls was the rectory here in 1601, and the Revd. Sir John Cullum, a respected local antiquary and late-C18 rector. Below, replica *brasses* are handily mounted for brass rubbers. The nave is spanned by a C16 roof which has been described as 'over restored in 1858' but which is undeniably impressive. Angels, with their new raised wings, are carved on the *hammerbeams*, the *spandrels* are pierced with tracery, and the *collars* of the *arch-braces* support *king posts* to the ridge. There are double-depth *wall plates*, dragons are carved on the braces and all the principal timbers carry a twisted roll decoration. At the w. end of the s. wall is a tablet for Claire Colville (1829) by Edward Hodges Baily, a successful sculptor whose vast output included the statues on the facade of the National Gallery. Here he is content with cleverly reproducing a crumpled sheet of paper in marble to carry a long and affecting epitaph. The nave is

Hawstead, All Saints: Original sacring bell

a good place to compare the merits of sculptor *John Bacon* with those of his son *John the Younger*. The father has a late work at the e. end of the n. side – a fine bas-relief of Benevolence for Lucy Metcalfe (1793), and the son sculpted the memorial for Mary Buckley, Viscountess Carleston (1810) on the s. side of the chancel arch – a female holding a pendent scroll while reclining on a sarcophagus. Note how the son takes the father's favourite cliché of the *pelican* to fill a space in the corner. In his later years the younger Bacon went into partnership with Samuel Manning and the firm turned out masses of rather hackneyed pieces but those for members of the Metcalfe family here are rather better than average. The *Jacobean* family pew in the s.w. corner has some marquetry inlay and used to stand in the chancel arch. Also at the w. end are a few early-C17 benches. In the corner beyond the organ is a faint C14 painting of a tall figure – probably a saint-bishop – which was discovered in the chancel and (such is the ingenuity of modern restorers) moved to its new site. The centre window on the n. side contains interesting fragments of glass. There are five shields of arms (variants of Drury), the *Evangelistic symbols* in roundels (these, however, are probably clever reproductions by the King workshop in Norwich), and two panels of continental glass (the one of the Crucifixion is enamelled, dated 1530, and signed). The roundel in the centre which shows the wolf finding *St*

Edmund's head which cries 'Heer, heer, heer!' is a modern copy by Kings of the original in the cathedral. In the wall n. of the chancel arch there is a C13 *piscina* and in the s.e. corner of the nave stands the tomb of Sir William Drury. The base is decorated with a line of *quatrefoils* with tracery panels of lozenges above. The worn *Purbeck marble* top carries a fine brass, with 2ft. figures of the nobleman and his two wives Joanne and Elizabeth, each with a Missal on a long cord. Elizabeth survived him and is shown with her eyes open. There are shields, a large inscription and a group of daughters, but the complementary clutch of sons has gone. Sir William was knighted by Edward VI and went on to serve Bloody Queen Mary as a Privy Counsellor before dying in 1557. We are lucky to see the brass because it was given to a collector in the 1860s and only returned to the church in 1909. Other brasses have been transferred to the wall behind – early-C16 figures of a boy and girl and four shields from Roger Drury's grave of 1495. On this side the s.e. and s.w. windows have excellent *Powells* glass designed by *Henry Holiday* in his own particular *pre-Raphaelite* style. The pulpit dates from about 1520 but has been over-enthusiastically restored and covered with glistening varnish. There are varying designs in the centre panels, *linen-fold* at the bottom and, at the top, the *Tudor* emblems of *pomegranate*, rose, and portcullis. There, too, are the ubiquitous

Hawstead, All Saints: Sir William Drury

arms of Drury, linked this time with Calthorpe. Sir Robert married Anne Calthorpe who died in 1513 and the couple lie buried in St Mary's Bury. Close by stands a rare example of a late-C15 wooden lectern. It has been restored but retains the simple carving on the ends below the double slope and there are rudimentary buttresses formed where the square shaft becomes an octagon. The nave benches are C19 but the front range incorporates C16 *finials* which, like the pulpit, have been unkindly varnished. There is a collared beast with long jagged horns (*ibex?*), a grotesque, and two differing versions of the pelican. The heavily restored late-C15 *screen* had a rood group added in 1906 but is remarkable for the very rare *sacring bell* that hangs on top of the s. side. It is conveniently close for the acolyte stationed by the low side window below; you will see that the latter still retains the hooks for its wooden shutter. The stained glass is a 1908 *Annunciation* in delicately pale and creamy colours by (possibly) Powells. In the quatrefoil at the top there is a small C15 Virgin and Child in yellow stain. The window opposite has glass by the A.K. Nicholson studios, with full length figures of *St George* and *St Géry*. There are low C16 stalls with a couple of *poppyheads*, and overhead the roof is coved and painted with *Sacred monograms*, the *Agnus Dei* and *chalice* emblems. The e. window glass is worth noting as the earliest surviving example of the work of *Heaton, Butler & Bayne* dating from 1856. It is a fully pictorial Ascension scene across the whole arch, well drawn and using bright (one might say virulent) colours and grainy flesh tones.

Large monuments loom everywhere in the chancel and the earliest is the effigy of a knight (reputedly Sir Eustace Fitz-Eustace who died in 1271). Very little damaged, it lies cross legged with feet on a dumpy lion. The level of the early-C14 tomb chest below shows how the floor has been raised over the years. The rounded C14 arch is decorated with encrusted foliage in a deep band. Within the arch is a disc of stone pierced at the centre and this may well be a turban finial from a Moslem grave, brought home from the Crusades as a trophy. On the n. side of the *sanctuary* is the impressive monument to Sir Robert Drury, the earliest known example of *Nicholas Stone's* work in Suffolk. It has a severe sarcophagus in polished black marble with a death's head clasp, separated from the base by lion-masked pedestals. Polished columns with alabaster *capitals* flank double alabaster arches within which are *touchstone* tablets lettered in gold. Sir Robert was knighted by the Earl of

Essex at Rouen in 1591, sailed in the Cadiz expedition of 1596, and died in 1615. The Richmond and Chester heralds saw him to his grave with ceremony and John Donne composed his epitaph. The bust in the oval at the top is of his father, Sir William (another soldier, who died after a duel in 1590). On the s. side of the sanctuary is the tomb of Sir Robert's daughter Elizabeth who died when only 14 in 1609. Donne sent her grieving parents the verses that were later called *A Funerall Elegie* and he almost certainly composed the Latin epitaph. The monument is by Gerard Christmas, carver to the Royal Navy and a sculptor of high reputation in James I's time. This is arguably the best of the effigies attributed to him. The alabaster figure of the young girl lies resting on one elbow with faintly smiling face, two collared hounds fawn at the sides of the tomb and her shield is carved within a wreath held by prancing *putti*. Had she not died young, Elizabeth would have been the bride of Henry, Prince of Wales. On the n. wall is Dudley Cullum's memorial (1720), a sensitive piece with excellent detailing by Robert Singleton of Bury and Norwich, a local mason of quality. The largest monument takes up most of the s. wall and is an extravangaza in painted plaster, mainly black. There is overblown heraldry at the top, freestanding pilasters and twin ovals with shields at each side and, at the centre, a sarcophagus – all on a stone base. It was made by Jacinthe de Courcy and was shipped by Sir Thomas Cullum from Italy to grace Hawstead Hall, and then used as his tomb in 1675 (strange that de Courcy should claim this work by scratching a little note on the n. pier of the chancel arch). It is almost a relief to return to quieter things and study the brass of Ursula Allington, a Drury daughter who died in about 1530. It is in the centre of the chancel and shows her wearing a *kennel headdress*, with a long rosary and reticule at her belt.

Helmingham, St Mary (F5): A spacious, pleasant setting, and there are glimpses of the great house across the lake to the w. The tower is attractive, with four *set-offs*, deep stepped battlements with pinnacles and *flushwork* that embodies 'MR' for the dedication and the Tollemache family arms (a family signature that will be very familiar by the time you leave). The w. doorway is flanked by niches while the flushwork above it displays a *Sacred monogram* and a crowned 'M'. The *base course* on the s. side has a bold inscription: 'scandit ad ethera virgo

puer pera virgu la Jesse' (The Virgin Mother, branch of Jesse's stem, ascends to heaven). This is one of the very few towers whose building contract still survives. In 1487 Thomas Aldryche of N. Lopham in Norfolk agreed to build a 60ft. steeple to the same design as the ones at Framsden and 'Bramston' (Brampton?). Ten years were allowed and the contract specified that it should rise at the rate of 6ft. a year, and work was only to be done between Whitsun and the beginning of September to guard against frost damage. The parish was to provide all materials and plant and no bells were to be hung until four years after completion. The whole cost was borne by the Lord of the Manor John Tollemache, his brother-in-law and two other Helmingham men. There was a proviso for making the tower higher and the battlements were not added until 1542 when John Barbour of Ipswich carried out the work. The date 1543 can be seen on the s. w. corner of the battlements. The tower holds a lovely ring of eight bells with a 19 cwt. tenor, all cast by Thomas Mears of Whitechapel in 1815. They were the gift of the Earl of Dysart who was naturally a Tollemache, and they are renowned in campanological circles. On walking round, you will find a substantial addition to the n. side of the *chancel* which covers the dank steps leading down to the Tollemache vault. The e. window has flowing *tracery* and in passing note the *scratch dial* on the s.e. buttress. There are renewed *Decorated* windows and a *priest's door* on the s. side, and the *nave* sports a curious dormer window with wooden *mullions* whose purpose will be seen within. The s. *porch* has rudimentary flushwork with a small niche above the arch whose *stops* are a little out of the ordinary, being small pendent shields. The C13 inner doorway has squared-off *capitals* and deep, ribbed mouldings, while the door itself dates from the C16 and has deep tracery cut in the solid, with two ranks of *mouchette* roundels.

First impressions inside are of a multitude of Tollemache memorials counterbalanced by a succession of bold C19 texts writ large over arches and on walls. The nave roof is either late-C16 or early-C17 and its slim *arch-braces* are interrupted by squared pendants below the *collar spandrels*, with a plastered ceiling between the main timbers. The deep *wall plate* is pierced and carved with kneeling angels holding scrolls, their wings widespread. The C15 *font* has been carefully restored and is the familiar East Anglian design, with lions and angels in the bowl panels, compact angels beneath each corner, and lions round the shaft. The latter, however, have an odd distinction because they sit on male and female human heads like the ones at Grundisburgh and Ipswich, St Mary le Tower. This little local example of symbolism must have had a particular significance and I wonder what it was. Lionel Tollemache's *ledger-stone* of 1610 has been clamped to the s.wall at the w. end and the epitaph begins:

> Wise Teare turn hither here's a stone
> Would not be left to weep alone . . .

Much grander is the monument to Maria, Countess of Dysart, on the opposite wall. Sculpted by *Nollekens* in 1804, it is a large bas-relief of a woman musing with a book on her lap, while a *putto* weeps and caresses a lamb on the other side of an urn. The figures are sharply silhouetted, beautifully modelled in high relief, and the piece illustrates how sentiment was creeping into the work of fashionable sculptors at this time. Beyond the n. door is another and quite different piece by Nollekens for Lionel Robert Tollemache, an 18-year-old ensign in the 1st Foot Guards who 'died nobly fighting for his king and country' at the siege of Valenciennes in 1793. A pile of ordnance and flags is set against a grey arch shape and there is a bas-relief bust in an oval at the top. It was set up in 1810 and the epitaph records the deaths of his father (killed in a New York duel) and two uncles (lost at sea). It understandably concludes: 'So many instance of disaster are rarely to be met with in the same family'. Flanking the s. door are two unexceptional tablets by Bedford for two early Victorian members of the family, and farther along on the n. wall is the large monument commemorating the Lionel who died in 1640. The armoured effigy lies stiffly on its side, carved in alabaster and gilt, with a painted face above a wide ruff; the backing is a double arch coffered in alabaster with *touchstone Corinthian* columns and his shields above.

Across the nave towers a multiple memorial of 1615 for four more Lionels (a confusing family fixation), starting with the one who built the tower and finishing with his great-grandson who died in 1605. They each kneel in profile within coffered arches, the senior in his judge's robes and the others in black and gilt armour. There is *Renaissance* detail on the massive frame and two vaguely pagan figures flank the upper arch; a large *achievement* within a roundel stands at the top, and a rhyming epitaph is painted below each figure. The whole thing was transferred from Bentley and its size demanded

alterations to the roof, which explains the dormer window. Some have thought that the window was originally inserted to light the *rood* but it is too far w. for that. The seating and the pulpit are C19. The chancel arch was renewed, possibly during a restoration, in the 1840s. There is no *screen* now and on the n. wall of the chancel Lieut. Gen. Thomas Tollemache has his memorial, having served in Ireland at the taking of Athlone and died in the attack on Brest harbour in 1694. The monument probably came rather later and has a large bust backed by martial trophies above a potted biography of an epitaph. To the e. is a very impressive but unsigned monument for yet another Lionel – Baron Huntingtower and Earl of Dysart, who died in 1727. The life-size muscular figure reclines in Roman costume but incongruously holds his coronet, and his mourning Countess is seated to the r. The epitaph dilates at length upon his lineage and attainments. On the opposite wall John, 1st Baron, has a bust by Thomas Mayes in a square recess flanked by touchstone columns. He died in 1890 and his memorial is a noble patrician head instinct with Victorian rectitude. To the r. one jumps back in time with a small touchstone tablet within a painted and gilt border; there is a roundel of arms with supporters topped by a little hour-glass. It commemorates Dame Catherine who died in 1620. Very decorative. Pleasing in quite a different fashion is the little kneeling figure within an alabaster niche on the n. side of the sanctuary. For Minnie, Lady Tollemache, it dates from 1918 and is signed with a monogram that I could not decipher.

Hemingstone, St Gregory (F5): Caught in the loop of a minor road that leads nowhere in particular, this charming little church is well away from its village. Fields drop away to the n. into a miniature valley, and four venerable sycamores line the grassy path up to the n. *porch*. The unbuttressed late-C14 tower has a single *string course* which lifts to form a *label* for the canopied niche on the w. face, and the *Perpendicular* window below is relatively large. There are shallow battlements and a 'G' for the dedication can be seen in the *flushwork* to the w. Two of the three bells in the tower were cast before the Reformation in Bury, and one of them carries an unusual inscription: 'Celi Det Munus Qui Regnat (Trinus) et Unus' (May He that reigns Three in One give us the gift of heaven). The first sign that this building has been here a very long time is the *long and short* *work* at the s.w. corner of the *nave*. It is a good example which reaches to the eaves and it must be *Saxon* of the C11 or earlier. Nave and *chancel* lie under one roof, with the s. door blocked up long ago and C18 glazing inserted in the head. The windows range from the 'Y' tracery of about 1300 to Perpendicular, and there is a *Tudor priest's door* on the s. side. The porch is the same age or a little later, and darker bricks pattern the walls; a niche and two small recesses are set above the outer arch. At first glance, there is duplicate porch tacked on to the nave n. wall – some 4yds. square, with the outline of a door and a high window under the gable, a chimney, a side door, and a largish window. But more about that later.

Entry is by way of a simple doorway of about 1300, still with its original door, and straight ahead is a superb C14 *font*. The Victorian tiled floor laps the step, robbing it of height, but the deep bowl panels are beautifully carved with *crocketted* gables, and there is tracery within them and in the *spandrels;* worn little heads jut out below the slim corner buttresses, and the rim is *castellated*. The base of the cover is modern – very well made to match and carry the crocketted top of the C15 original. The opening into the tower is tall and thin, and an arch of *Tudor* shape on stub *jambs* was inserted later. For those interested in heraldry and family history, there are three hatchments in the tower: n. wall, for Richard Bartholomew Martin (1865), with a nice monkey and mirror crest; for William Martin (1842); s. wall, for one of his three daughters (1842-70). On the nave w. wall is Sarah Martin's hatchment of 1841, and opposite hang the excellently restored *Royal Arms* of *William & Mary*. In the n.w. corner of the nave a plain deal cover lifts to reveal the C14 door to the tower stair. It is completely sheathed in iron and has two locks, a sure indication that the upper room was used as a safe for church and village valuables. Except for the *embattled wall plate*, all the roof timbers are hidden by a plastered ceiling, but the *rood beam* remains to mark the entrance to the chancel. The pine benches and pulpit are Victorian, and the remnants of an interesting set of painted texts in small, shaped panels on the walls can be dated by the one over the entrance. It shows that the church was repaired by a churchwarden in 1773, and the rest of the set are virtually identical to those at nearby Witnesham. They were chosen and placed to make specific points, so that the one over the s. door reads: 'This is none other than the House of God, this is the Gate of Heaven' (Genesis 28:17), and others emphasised the significance

of font, pulpit, and *altar*. The small bronze plaque of 1907 for Col. Sir Richard Martin on the s. wall of the nave is worth looking at; signed by E.A.C. Harris and E. Godwin, it has a miniature roundel portrait at the top. On the n. side is William Cantrell's tomb of 1585, a compact and fairly modest effort, with three shields on the chest, and a shell shape with flanking spikes above the back. There are dainty marble columns each side, and three more shields (coloured this time) above an epitaph:

Man here thou mayste yntombed see,
A man of honest fame
Come home to earthe, who in his life bare
Willm Cantrels name . . .

The mason rectified one mistake but missed another. See if you can spot it. All that remains of the C16 *rood screen* is a section of the base on the s. side, and that was varnished a dark brown at some time, but the piece of C14 glazing in the tracery 'eye' of the window on the n. side of the chancel is rare because it is virtually intact. The muted yellow border encloses pale green quarries decorated with delicate leaf sprays in black. The battered C14 *piscina* in the *sanctuary* has remnants of *cusping* like decayed teeth, and above is a tablet for Robert and Amelia Colvile by Humphrey Hopper, a sculptor whose genius seemed to fail him when prestigious commissions like Gen. Hay's pile of marble in St Paul's came his way. In smaller things he was always competent, and here we have a tablet of 1825 on which curtains are drawn aside between pillars to reveal the inscription, with a small coloured *achievement of arms* on top. As far as I know, his only other Suffolk work is at Worlington. Set in round-headed recesses on the opposite wall is a pair of matching sarcophagi by James Smith, another fashionable sculptor (for whom Mrs Siddons sat) but whose reputation is dogged by his largest work – the Nelson memorial in London's Guildhall, which nearly beggared him in 1810. He died in his 40s and these monuments to members of the Brand family were done in his last decade.

Now for the mysterious little annexe on the n. side of the nave. It now serves as a *vestry* and is reached by a little connecting passage from the chancel which was added later. Its fascination lies in the fact that it was built by Ralph Cantrell, a Roman Catholic who would not transfer his allegiance to the Protestant faith but who wished to avoid the penalties involved. It has always been know as 'Ralph's Hole'. By using its outer door he could attend in comfort, listen to the service, and watch it through the *squint* in the wall opposite the pulpit, but salve his conscience by not actually entering the church. Tradition does not say how he avoided taking the sacrament, but then the village had a certain reputation for awkwardness with the authorities. In 1597 the entire parish was cited in the ecclesiastical consistory court because 'their children, servants and apprentyzes [had not] come to church to be catechised for a year past'. Under the rules of 1559 they should have been there every Sunday, and the backsliding coupled with Ralph's example adds point to the wall texts of two centuries on.

When leaving it is impossible to ignore the huge 6ft. x 4ft. pair of bellows salvaged from a blacksmith's forge somewhere and now propped up in the porch – country churches often double helpfully as mini-folk museums these days.

Hemley, All Saints (G6): The lane leads only to the handful of houses and farms which, together with the church, make up the village, and there are glimpses of the Deben estuary from the churchyard. By the late C19 the church had fallen into decay, and in 1889 the *nave* and *chancel* were completely rebuilt, making use of much of the old materials. Local architects Frederick Barnes and Howard Gaye kept to the C14 *Decorated* style of the original, and the walls are a mosaic of flint, stone, and *septaria*. The weathered frame of the early-C14 n. doorway was re-set in the wall, and within the new porch, the s. doorway has a slightly later, stunted *ogee* arch, resting on replacement *corbels*. The tower was untouched by the restoration and is the church's most distinctive feature. Built of warm red brick, it dates from the late C15 or early C16, and has much in common with Waldringfield's not far away – either one man designed both, or one was copied from the other. It has the same bulky stair turret to the s., there is diaper decoration in blue brick on all faces and on the battlements, and the broad w. window is all in brick. The little belfry lancet above it is the only stone feature, and was perhaps saved from the earlier tower.

Within, the C19 pine roof in the nave has two *tie-beams* supporting *king posts* which are strutted up to a runner well below the ridge. A wooden chancel arch rests on stone wall shafts, and there is a boarded waggon roof with *bosses*, again in pine, over the chancel. The C15 benches were apparently beyond restoration, but they

were used as a pattern for the new set – quality work, with miniature *poppyheads*, although not in oak. The *font* is the oldest of the church's possessions, dating from the C13, or possibly a little earlier. It is square, of *Purbeck marble*, and there are vestiges of four blank arches on each side; the bowl rests on a stubby drum and four corner shafts, and the base is simply moulded. The George III *Royal Arms* were discarded during the 1880s restoration but, providentially rescued, they now hang on the n. wall and are a good set, painted on canvas. The *altar* is a pleasant C17 table, with turned and carved legs and a simply decorated apron. It is backed by a wooden *reredos* which is probably early or mid-C19, in a rather strange mixture of styles. The centre roundel contains a form of *Agnus Dei* in bas-relief, the lamb lying on the cross rather than carrying it, and resting on a book which has seven pendent seals or markers; swags of fruit loop out towards robust *putti* on each side, carved in the round. The churchyard is a pleasant place in which to stroll, and there are a number of good C18 stones. Rector William Cavell died in 1719 and, with his second and third wives Abigail and Martha, he is commemorated by a delicately lettered stone fixed to the e. wall of the chancel. To the s., and more or less in line, you will find the grave of Thomas Adams whose epitaph of 1775 breaks into verse:

Hark from the Tombs a doleful Sound,
My Ears attend the cry.
Ye living men come view the Ground,
Where you must shortly lie.
Princes, this Clay must be your Bed,
In spite of all your Powers,
The Tall, the Wise, the Reverend Head,
Must be as low as Ours.

Henley, St Peter (F5): Meticulously maintained and surrounded by a manicured churchyard, St Peter's is obviously appreciated by its parishioners. It has that sharp look so often associated with full-scale Victorian restoration, and indeed there were major upheavals in 1846, 1895, and 1904, but the building is welcoming and there is much of interest. The tower has angle buttresses to the w. decorated with good *flushwork*, and a panel above the w. door contains the inscription: 'Orate pro anymab: thome Sekeford et margarete uxor eius' (Pray for the soul of Thomas Seckford and Margaret his wife). He was a clothier who died in 1505 and provided most of the money for the new tower; his shield of arms and his merchant's mark of a

pair of shears feature on the panel. The little
shields in the doorway *spandrels* are interesting
because they combine, in two variations, the keys
of *St Peter* with the sword of *St Paul*. Was the
dedication shared at one time? A circuit of the
building entails a detour round a large extension
to the n., the village school of 1838, rebuilt in
1904 to serve as a *vestry* and Sunday School. It is
as big as the average cottage of the period, with
hipped gables and a generous w. window, and it
has its own diminutive porch. It fits happily
with the church and is still useful. The C15 nave
windows have been renewed but on the s. side
there is one that deserves closer attention. Square-
headed, with terracotta lintel and *mullions*, it dates
from the early 1520s and is likely to have been
taken from Shrubland Old Hall. There are large
curly dolphin heads with urns at the top, masks
on the mullions, and three shields with beasts
between below – all in what was then the new
Italian *Renaissance* style. The same moulds can
be found in windows at Barking and Barham,
and the workmen who used them probably
came up into Suffolk after they had finished
decorating the great house at Layer Marney in
Essex. A stone mask is set in the wall to the l.
and it may be a companion to the purely
ornamental *gargoyle* that keeps company with
others more active below the tower battlements.
The e. window is modern but the *chancel* as a
whole dates from the late C13 to early C14, with
lancets to the n. and *Decorated* windows to the s.
The *rood stair* turret shows as a slight projection
between *nave* and chancel on the s. side, and there
are two *scratch dials* – one on the s.w. corner of
the nave and another on the s.e. corner of the
porch.

The inner doorway could be labelled *Transitional* because its *Norman chevron* and *billet*
decorations are used in a pointed arch, but there
is an incomplete C12 *capital* on the l. and the
jambs seem to have been remade, so it may be a
case of Norman components re-assembled.
There are remains of a *stoup* to the r., and the
C14 door of lapped boards has strap hinges
right across.

Just inside, a showcase contains a copy of the
Bible printed by John Baskett in 1716 which
has become known as the 'Vinegar Bible' by
reason of a single misprint. Beyond it is an 1840s
font, and there are three *hatchments* to be seen:
over the s. door to the e., for Henrietta Sleorgin
(1808), who used her parents' arms because her
husband was but a cornet in the Horse Guards;
to the r. of it, for Mary Medows (1809), who
had no family arms of her own and made do

with her husband's; and on the n. wall for Harriet
Ibbetson (1843), the donor of the schoolroom.
Incidentally, the connecting doorway below is
the original n. entrance and is only 27in. wide.
To the r. is a well-lettered *touchstone* tablet in a
marble frame patterned with drapes and sprays;
an elegant little *cartouche* perches on top, and it
commemorates Elizabeth Vere who died in
1717, one of the De Veres who were in the
parish for over 200 years. The nave lies under a
plaster ceiling and there are substantial C19
benches with *poppyheads*. The *gallery*, with its
'Gothick' tracery balustrade, was reduced to its
present width in 1846 and in more recent times
the ringing chamber beyond has been glazed in.
From there, the ringers can make good use of
an excellent ring of eight bells with an 8 cwt.
tenor. Although heavily lime-washed, the details
of the terracotta s. window mouldings show
up clearly from within, and farther along there
are the tall and thin doorways of the rood stair.
The *rood beam*, with its plain cross, is modern
pine and goes with the waggon roof of the
chancel. The C13 *piscina* beyond *dropped-sill sedilia*
in the *sanctuary* is interesting because the bowl
previously belonged to a Norman *pillar piscina*.
Some have suggested that it came from the stoup
in the porch, but I do not think so. A small
aumbry in the opposite wall has holes drilled in
the surround that would have taken a wooden
frame for a door or an iron grille. By it stands a
very ornate C19 lectern in oak, with a turned and
carved pedestal and double book shelf. It is
rather a chaotic mixture of styles, but is
remarkable for one thing. The two slopes, with
their broad, carved borders of acanthus leaves,
were cut from a single block; I could find no
trace of a join at the ridge, which is itself carved.

Henstead, St Mary (I2): The church is isolated
w. of the village by the side of a rising bend in
the road, and car parking requires some thought.
The late-C15 tower has been well restored; there
are angle buttresses to the w. and renewed
Decorated w. window and bell openings. The
chamber below the bells has a pair of *quatrefoils*
like small *sound holes* one above the other;
gargoyles jut from the corners of the handsome
battlements, and small heads are spaced
decoratively along the moulding below. *Nave*
and *chancel* lie under one thatched roof, and
there is a textbook example of very early wall
construction (including *herringbone*) on the n.
side of the nave. The small n. doorway is *Norman*,
with a single *chevron moulding* and simple *jamb
shafts*, and *Cautley* believed that it might well be

an an instance where the Normans upgraded *Saxon* work by cutting their arch and flanking shafts out of existing masonry. The church was extensively restored in the 1840s and most of the windows were renewed then or as part of a second renovation in 1906. The rectangular *rood stair* turret, with its modern tile cap, stands proud of the chancel n. wall and is well towards the e. end. This is because fire destroyed much of the chancel in 1641 and it was rebuilt in shorter form, blocking one of the n. windows. The same disaster apparently gutted the old village grouped around the crossroads and explains the church's present isolation. There are a number of worn C18 headstones to be found s. of the chancel, and on that side of the nave the windows were fitted with large panes of glass following blast damage in World War II. The C15 *porch* has a flushwork *base course* to its facade, and there are two ranks of *fleurons* in the mouldings of the outer arch. Unusually, a *stoup* was sited just inside it, and although its bowl has gone, the shaft remains. Henstead's showpiece is the grand Norman s. doorway. The outer rim of the massive arch is formed by a triple band of *billet moulding* which encloses a broad chevron; that in turn is followed by an inner line of small beads. Triple shafts, with the centre ones spirally cut, complete the effect of massive substance. It is interesting that the inside of the arch has a continuous roll moulding enclosing a blank *tympanum* which may once have been painted.

Just inside, the 12ft. *banner stave locker* in the s. wall at the w. end is like those at Sotterley and Wrentham and the frame was rebated to take a door. Main timbers show like ribs through the plaster ceilings, and there are heavy *tie-beams* below them. The oak benches, wall panelling and pulpit came as part of the 1906 reordering, and sensible as they are, one mourns the loss of box pews and what was probably a *three-decker pulpit*. The *font* looks as though it belongs to the 1840s work. On the n. wall there is an excellent *cartouche* memorial for Laurence Eachard and his wife Anna. He was the rector, dying in 1721, and his coloured shield is displayed within a compartment which has a grotesque with lolling tongue at the bottom – a strange reversion to medieval idiom. The design is completed with a small urn on top and a winged skull below, and just above there is a *hatchment* only 18in. square which must be the smallest in Suffolk – used at the funeral of Lawrence Bence in 1746. There are two monuments on the s. wall of the nave which are interesting mainly because they are both signed 'Coade & Sealy', the firm

founded in the 1760s by that remarkable business woman Mrs Eleanor Coade. She popularised the use of artificial cast stone (*Coade stone*) as a cheap and effective alternative to marble. Having said that, one has to admit that the results are invariably mud-coloured, although the first example here is quite pleasing. A draped bas-relief oval of a mourning woman is set above a finely lettered sarcophagus, and the epitaph for George and Frances Mitchell records that they 'died in the prime of their days within six weeks of each other' in 1803. The second memorial is for William Clarke, 'late commander of HMS Iris, unfortunately slain on the eve of victory in an attack on a Dutch ship of superior force in the Indian ocean' in 1804 – a rather ponderous affair, with an overweight cherub letting his foot slip over the top of the of the tablet. The door to the rood loft stairs has been altered and given a new lintel, and the *rood beam* is modern. The recess behind the radiator in the s. wall may have been a *piscina* to serve a nave *altar* in front of the *screen*. The attractive *communion rails* were installed in 1906 and have flamboyant *tracery* roundels. The elaborate piscina in C15 style probably dates from the same time, and some C18 memorial tablets were grouped on the n. wall of the *sanctuary*. Above them is the church's second hatchment, for the rector Thomas Sheriffe of Henstead Hall. He died in 1861 and his crest is unusual – a lion's paw holding a bunch of grapes. Apart from patterning in the w. window, the church's only stained glass is in the chancel s. window, a stereotyped and typically sentimental design by *Ward & Hughes* from the 1870s.

Hepworth, St Peter (D3): The church is easily seen from the Bury-Diss road. To the n. there are wide vistas of big, open fields. It was once a thatched building, but on the Easter Monday of 1898, there was a calamitous fire that destroyed not only the roofs but almost everything else, leaving only the tower, the walls, and the s. *porch*. The architect for the rebuilding was J.S. Corder of Ipswich. The C13 tower had already suffered in 1677 when the upper stage was taken down, the stair dismantled, and the date writ large on the w. face. Some of the iron reinforcements were applied then and more, lower down, in 1828. The diagonal buttresses are very deep on the e. side and there are small, early-C14 *quatrefoil sound holes*. The C14 w. doorway has a C19 *lancet* over it, but the belfry windows were part of the C17 reconstruction, as was the little pyramid tiled roof with its perky bellcote on the side. The tower houses a ring of five bells with a 7 cwt. tenor, but they are not useable at the present time. The porch that survived the fire was two-storied (see the marks in the *nave* wall where the stair went up to it) but it had to be replaced and much of the old fabric was incorporated. The nave was given new windows in *Perpendicular* style, although the renewed *tracery* in the *chancel* windows is *Decorated* and probably repeated the old patterns. There is a separate *low side window* which is unusually small and has the distinction of being traceried. A C14 *priest's door* is also nearby, and on the n. side of the nave is another doorway of the same age, with animal *headstops* to the *dripstone*. In the porch there is the fragment of a *Norman* scallop *capital* and a section of shaft (evidence of an earlier church than the one that was burned down) and above is an image niche. The door still has its medieval closing rings and lockplate.

Just inside to the l. is the blocked doorway that led to the upper room of the porch. The tower arch is low and completely plain, pointing to an early-C13 date, and to the r. of it is the church's real treasure. One would not dare to hope that a medieval *font* cover of this size and weight would be saved from a major fire, but happily it was, and it now stands on top of an 1870s font. Originally telescopic, it is over 12ft. high, and two bottom sections are hinged for access. It is *tabernacled* and buttressed, but its individuality lies in the lower section. There, the image stools are pierced and carved in the form of miniature *castellated* towers, complete with window tracery and doorways wherein tiny men at arms come and go in lively fashion. It is perhaps unfortunate that it was not very well restored and repaired by a Mr Brooke of Hopton in the 1850s; his work can be fairly easily identified and should not distract one from the delights of the Lilliputian fortress. The nave roof of 1898 is a double *hammerbeam*, with heavy pendants on the upper hammers. Corder installed a waggon roof in the chancel and put down black and white marble paving. On the s. side of the chancel arch is a C14 *piscina* with a worn *trefoil* head, and in the n. wall is a blocked doorway that led to the *rood loft* stair. In 1998 and 2001 new memorial glass was installed in the nave s. windows. There are four square panels in pairs, taking the themes of 'The Good Shepherd', 'the Bread of Heaven, 'St Francis, of Assisi' and 'Wild birds' – each linked with a characteristic of the person commemorated. Each panel carries the little oval sign of the artist Bronwen Gordon, and her colours are refreshingly clear and used in conjunction with clever leading. The figure of St Francis is shown giving away his cloak (an incident in his life more usually associated with *St Martin of Tours*), and there is a charming vignette of a traction engine with thrashing tackle high in the corner of the 'Bread of Heaven' panel. The openwork oak pulpit of 1923 is a handsome piece of work by Sir Henry Methold, a skilled amateur craftsman who also made the litany desk in the chancel.

The choir stalls date from the fire but they incorporate medieval bench ends with castellated elbows and fine, bulbous *poppyheads*. The C18 or early-C19 *altar* is a little out of the ordinary because it is mahogany, with spiral legs and stretchers, but unfortunately it has been badly attacked by woodworm. On the s. wall of the *sanctuary* is a modern oak tabernacle for the *reserved sacrament* of unusual, if rather heavy, design. The tiny low side window, with its *ogee* tracery within a square frame, is deeply recessed and was only rediscovered after the fire. The coat of arms it contains occurs again in the window on the n. side of the chancel – a memorial for Mary Ellen Methold who died in 1903. The glass is by *Powell & Sons*, and shows the angel of the Resurrection appearing to the Two Marys – all in cool colour. The face of the *Blessed Virgin* is apparently a portrait of Mrs Methold, and her cloak is decorated with the family arms.

Herringfleet, St Margaret (I1): The round tower is faced with very regular *courses* of small flint pebbles, interrupted by two bands of *knapped flints* for decoration. Small *lancets* are spaced between the bell openings, and the latter provide an interesting example of overlapping styles – pairs of lancets with triangular heads in the *Saxon* fashion, contained within *Norman* arches which have *billet decoration*. It follows that the tower must have been built very soon after the Conquest, and there are indications that it was added to an existing church. The blocked door and tall lancet in the n. wall of the *nave* are C13, but the tiny lancet in the *chancel* on that side is *Norman*. Nearby, a group of C19 headstones shaped like exuberant *poppyheads* seem to have been a strictly local fashion. The *transomed* e. window is *Perpendicular*, and round the corner a *dripstone* shows where a window was blocked to make room for a monument within. The walls of the church are cement rendered and the nave and *porch* are both thatched. The Norman builders provided a handsome s. doorway, with bold *chevron* decoration in the arch and cross decoration on the *abaci*.

Within, the deep C19 *gallery* houses a perky little organ topped by a golden angel, and to its r. a *hatchment* bears the arms of Elizabeth Merry who died in 1824. Two more hatchments hang beneath the gallery: on the w. wall, for George Leathes of Herringfleet Hall who died in 1817, and the other for Mary his widow. The Norman tower arch has the plainest of *imposts* but there is some billet decoration on its w. face. A C19 *font* stands by the chancel arch, and the chancel itself is fitted with quite elaborate pews of the same period. They have poppyheads and there is *crocketting* down and over the elbows, with curious half-doors to match. The scheme was planned for a small congregation to sit within the chancel, and the late-C18 or early-C19 pulpit is positioned by the *sanctuary* steps. The *communion rails* with their simply turned shafts may well be C17, and there are C19 *Decalogue* boards on the e. wall. The C14 *piscina* lies below a trefoil arch. The window on that side was blocked in 1787 to make room for John Leathes' monument, a large sarcophagus and urn set against a grey background. On the n. wall, a tablet by J.G. Balls of Lowestoft commemorates Henry M. Leathes who fought with the Royal Horse Artillery at Waterloo and died in 1864, and to the e. is a tablet of 1848 by Sanders of Fitzroy Square for John Francis Leathes. He was squire, patron and, in 1827, High Sheriff of the county. It was he who provided the church with its most interesting feature – the collection of glass in the e. window.

Although there is some C15 English work, the rest is later continental glass and most of it came from the Franciscan priory at Cologne. The pieces were very attractively arranged about 1830, probably by Samuel Yarrington, the Norwich glazier, and it is worth spending some time searching for interesting items – including saints seldom encountered in England. There is a Gethsemane scene in monochrome at the bottom of the l.-hand *light* below a cardinal's arms, and in the border nearby look for the figure of *St Wolfgang*. At the top of that light there is a shield of *Passion emblems*, and at the top of the r.-hand light, a roundel illustrates the 'mass of *St Gregory*'. Close by is a monochrome figure of *St Gertrude* with mice running up her staff. The oval at the bottom of the centre light contains the contrasting figures of *St Patu* as an abbot, and *St Aimery* dressed as a legionary. The Crucifixion panel in the central upper range may be by *Robert Allen*, and there is a charming Nativity scene further down; above that and to the r., look for an excellent C14 king's

head. The two s. chancel windows also have interesting glass that was installed at about the same time. At the top of the twin lancets there are C14 figures of *St Helen* on the l. and *St Catherine* on the r. There are more miscellaneous continental pieces, but perhaps the most arresting feature is the series of lively squares and roundels by Robert Allen. The three tulip paintings right at the top may be his work as well, and provide a very rare example of this flower in stained glass. And finally, there is the little C14 figure of a saint in the n. wall lancet which apparently came from St Olave's priory. By way of a postscript, the porch benches have inscriptions that are a little out of the ordinary: 'East Anglian bull terrier club; Moatvale Sunburst of Chendor 1975-81, Crufts 1977'. Not every dog has that sort of day!

Herringswell, St Ethelbert (B3): This is one of four churches dedicated to *St Ethelbert* in the county, and in the Middle Ages there was a *guild* here dedicated to him, with a priest to celebrate a weekly mass. Walking round the outside, columns and *quoins* of the original *Norman* church can be found at the n.e. and s.e. corners of the *nave*, and this was succeeded by a C14 building. In 1869, however, a disastrous fire destroyed nearly everything and there was a rebuilding to the designs of *Sir Arthur Blomfield*. The tower had not been damaged significantly and presents a highly individual profile from almost every angle. There is a stepped buttress up the centre of the w. face as far as the belfry stage and on either side of it there are stubby blocked *lancets* that were once *traceried*. There are substantial stepped projections n. and s., the latter containing the tower stair, and the two-light bell openings are renewed below panelled battlements. The e. wall of the tower and the stair turret both show an earlier and higher roof line, indicating that the unusual design is original. Most of the exterior is new work but there is a niche above the s. *transept* window, as well as a little *trefoil* over it. Similarily, in the *porch*, there is a niche over the door, and that has very fine double mouldings, although the top has been partially obscured by the roof. A *stoup* has been re-set beside the door.

Inside, the tower continues to surprise. The arch is carried on octagonal *piers* supported by flying buttresses angled from the side walls, and behind it, tall and narrow arches open on either side. Apparantly, this arrangement is original and not part of the rebuilding. The nave roof has plain *arch-braces* and there is a waggon roof in

Herringswell, St Ethelbert:
Detail of east window by Christopher Whall

the *chancel*, panelled with *bosses* at the intersections. There is a trefoil-headed *piscina* in the s. transept and a blocked window in the e. wall. To the l. of the entrance to the transept is a blocked doorway which will have led to the old *rood loft*. Close by is a small marble statue of a

lush young maiden on a pedestal. She reclines in an attitude of langorous abandon against a crescent moon, one hand flung behind her back, with a star on her forehead and another on the diaphanous drapes that just fail to reveal all. It is an extraordinarily voluptuous piece to come across unawares. The s.w. chancel window retains its *Decorated* tracery and one of the lights is divided by a *transom*, showing that the lower section was used as a *low side window*. Beyond the stepped sill *sedilia* in the *sanctuary* is a C14 double drain piscina, but the canopy and pinnacles are C19 replacements. On either side of the e. window are tall C14 niches with trefoil *ogee* arches and *crocketted finials*. The original *vestry* door on the n. side of the chancel is deeply recessed and has devil *headstops*.

Herringswell is memorable for the outstanding series of stained glass windows designed by artists of the *Arts and Crafts movement*. The e. window of 1902, on the theme of 'The Good Shepherd', is by *Christopher Whall*. The figure of Christ, in a rich red robe lined with fur, was adapted from a design first used by him in the chapel of Fettes College, Edinburgh, in 1899. The Suffolk black-faced sheep were drawn by his sister-in-law, Alice Chaplin, better known as a distinguished sculptress patronised by Queen Victoria. The bottom of the r.-hand light portrays the biblical ram caught in a thicket, and the l.-hand light includes a distant vignette of a shepherd tending his flock. The 1904 s.w. chancel window is a memorial to the uncle of Whall's friend, Selwyn Image, and is a good example of the artist's ability to combine contemporary detail with traditional religious themes. Texts on the virtue of charity are interwoven and Christ stands as a robed king in the l.-hand light, with angel heads above and below. The other light is divided by a transom and the figures praying in the upper scene have portrait heads, while a sickbed group is shown below. Also by Whall is the Resurrection window in the s. wall of the nave and it repeats a design he used at the church of the Holy Cross at Avening, Gloucester, in 1908. As the sun rises, Christ stands within a pointed oval oriole, his hand raised to show the wound, while an angel with multi-coloured wings raises the stone; below a soldier in armour sleeps prone across the two lights. The glass in the n. chancel window of 1902 was designed by Paul Woodroffe, another member of the Arts and Crafts Movement. Mothers and children gather on the l. and Christ draws more children to Himself on the r. – one with a doll flung over her shoulder. Both lights are framed in a deep band of Celtic foliage scrolls, and the general treatment is softer and more indefinite than Whall's. The window on the s. side of the sanctuary is by Jasper Brett, a pupil of Christopher Whall. On the theme: 'Come unto me all that are weary and heavy laden . . .'.

Two of the lovliest windows here were designed by James Clark and made by A.J. Dix of Gower Street, London – memorials to Leopold Frederick Davies. The first, in the centre of the nave n. wall, takes the psalmist's text: 'All thy works praise thee O Lord', and the design spreads over both lights; there is a centre clump of Scots pine, and silver birches rise up on either side; a brilliant cock pheasant struts in the heather and swallows wheel across the sky. It is an enchanting piece. The s. transept window illustrates 'O Lord how manifold are thy works' and a brilliant landscape fills the whole of the three lights. Slender boles of laburnums and a Scots pine strike upward and in the upper branches there are pigeons and squirrels, one seeming to pause on a ledge of tracery. Rabbits sit by their burrow at the bottom and in the centre, vivid flowering cherry and lilac overhang a river where stands a heron. This is an intensely romantic concept that skilfully avoids sentimentality. Next to the pulpit in the nave is a 1950s window for Llewellyn Sidney Davies, whose enthusiasm for field sports prompted a *St Hubert* theme, designed by H.W. Luxford. The saint stands in the r.-hand light with spear, hunting horn and Gospel book, while a springer spaniel, in the likeness of one of Davies' dogs, sits at his feet. The other light has a stag at bay with a crucifix within its antlers; there are woods and hills in the middle distance and the foreground is richly carpeted with spring flowers. Lastly, a window at the w. end of the nave by James Clark shows *St Francis* scattering seed while holding a hare in the crook of his arm; a dog sits before him and flocks of birds swoop down to feed. Thin tree trunks rise through the composition to foliage at the top, and in the background is a rocky hermit's cell.

Hessett, St Ethelbert (D4): This lovely church fronts the village street against a dense background of yews and an avenue of small limes leads up to the s. *porch*. There are only 18 dedications to Ethelbert in England, four of which are understandably in Suffolk. By the gate is the shaft of a C15 *preaching cross* and the mortices cut in its sides indicate that it once had substantial arms and possibly attendant figures. The well-proportioned tower has been restored and there are new pinnacles at the corners of the pierced battlements which are moulded and set with shields bearing the initials of John Bacon who financed the late-C15 work, dying in 1513. There is a deep band of ornament under the battlements and the arches of the *Decorated* bell openings are picked out with red brick and flint with pairs of shields below. The w. window is *Perpendicular* and there is a chequerwork *base course* in flint *flush-work*. As a final touch, the tower now boasts an elegant weathervane in the form of a gilded, crowned 'E' for St Ethelbert. The parapets of the C15 *aisles* and *nave clerestory* are as richly decorated as the tower, with pinnacles at frequent intervals and openwork battlements carved with shields and roses. All the windows are Perpendicular and there is an interesting late-C15 inscription carved on the parapet of the *sacristy* n. of the *chancel*. Its medieval English translates:

> Pray for the souls of John Hoo and Katherine his wife, the which made the chapel, heightened the vestry and battlemented the aisle.

Most of the word 'souls' was hacked away by one of the Commonwealth despoilers of 'superstitious inscriptions'. The original roof line of the *vestry* is marked by the *gargoyles* still embedded in the wall. The chancel is C14 and there is attractive flowing *tracery* in the e. window which has a niche above. There is a renewed *priest's door* in the s. wall and from there one can see the strangely awkward way in which the parapet is carried over the angle of the nave roof, with the battlements at right angles to the slope. As was often the case, the C15 s. porch in stone and flint was given special attention and it has standing angels bearing scrolls at the corners of the openwork battlements. The three canopied niches over the entrance with their miniature vaults are very like those at Woolpit, while the buttresses have carved and *flushwork* panels where John Bacon's initials are a reminder that he not only built the tower but the porch as well. The carving of *St George* and the dragon in the *spandrels* of the outer arch is now very worn. The timbers of the porch roof are bleached almost white and to the r. of the small C14 inner doorway is the base of a *stoup*, whose bowl (or that of another) lies by the entrance.

The church interior is light and spacious, the slender columns of the Perpendicular *arcades* having typically wide and shallow mouldings. There is an extra bay on the n. side forming a chapel which was no doubt part of John Hoo's legacy. At the w. end stands the *font* made in Norwich in the 1450s and given by Richard and Agnes Hoo in 1500. A very worn inscription on the step asks us to pray for their souls and the sides of the wide octagonal base are traceried. The panels of the stem are carved with *paterae*, with more beneath the bowl, the panels of which are decorated with a variety of *cusped* patterns and centre ornaments. St Ethelbert's ring of five bells with a 14 cwt. tenor is handled from the ground floor of the tower, but their condition only allows for occasional ringing at the present time. Above the tower arch is a *sanctus-bell window* and the C15 *arch-braced* nave roof is flattish, with remnants of angels below the *wall posts*. Unlike most in the area, the C15 benches are low with plain, square ends, but some of them have a simple leaf twist carved on the top moulding and along the back rail; one bench end in the s. aisle has the remains of a crouching hound. There is a *piscina* in the s. aisle chapel under a finely moulded and pierced *trefoil* arch. In the n. aisle chapel the plain recess to the r. was probably another piscina originally. Nearby is a long iron-bound chest. Cromwell's commissioners were given its keys but the canny churchwardens kept back the rod that is also required to open it and so it remained inviolate. Just as well, because the unique C15 *pyx* cloth and *burse* (both now in the British Museum) were inside. Illustrations and details of them can be seen at the back of the church. A fine set of Charles II *Royal Arms* has been well restored and placed above the chest. Medieval church walls were the picture books of the people and we are fortunate that some fine examples survive here. Over the s. door is a curious painting which appears to be two figures, one superimposed over the other and differing in date. The figure on the r. has bare feet and could conceivably be *St John the Baptist*, and the other figure is winged. This might by Gabriel of an *Annunciation* scene but this is supposition. The *St Christopher* over the n. door can be recognised by the saint's legs, tunic and staff as well as two small figures and some fish in the river. Over the s. aisle piscina is a very good painting of *St Barbara* with her tower, but the most interesting subjects are on the n. aisle wall. There we see the *Seven Deadly Sins* as figures on the branches of a tree which springs from the dragon jaws of hell, with demons either side. The painting dates from the 1370s and the figures represent Pride at the top with (in descending order) on the l., Gluttony, Vanity, Avarice, and on the r., Anger, Envy and Lust. Perhaps it is just an accident of time but Lust is almost worn away. Immediately below is one of the best representations of the rare *Christ of the Trades* dating from about 1430. Our Lord is contrasted with, and perhaps neglected as a result, the common concerns of life. His faint seated figure is surrounded by pincers, hammer, scissors, chisel and gridiron, and in the top l.-hand corner is the six of diamonds – one of the earliest illustrations of 'the devil's picture books'. Below to the r. is a C15 *consecration cross*.

The *rood loft* stairs go up on the s. side of the chancel arch and the C15 *screen* remains in place. The unusually broad bottom panels have stencilled decoration and there is a shield-shaped *elevation squint* to the l. of the entrance. The *lights* have cusped and *crocketted ogee* arches with panel tracery above them. There are the remains of *gesso* work on the uprights which are impressed with a highly individual bird pattern. The wrought-iron gates are modern. The medieval choir stalls, with *poppyheads* and carved elbows, are arranged in collegiate fashion so that some of them back against the screen. Their fronts are traceried; look for a *pelican in her piety* in one of the spandrels. One bench on the n. side was almost certainly made for a private house; it is particularly fine and its back is carved with a repeat design of birds and leaves above a line of *quatrefoils* enclosing shields. Nearby is the Decorated doorway to the sacristy complete with original door. If it is open (as it sometimes is) you will find a piscina with a *cinquefoiled* arch and medieval wooden *credence shelf*. Within, a *squint* is cut through to the *sanctuary* and the low chamber must therefore have been used as a chapel or *chantry*. The upper room is reached by a ladder with triangular baulks of timber used as rungs, and it has been suggested that the whole thing was an *anchorite's* cell, with chapel below and living room above. Remember, however, that the inscription outside calls it a vestry. The squint is framed in a quatrefoil in the sanctuary wall and below it is a ledge with substantial decoration whose position suggests that it was used as a lectern from which the Gospel was read. The 1860s *reredos* is a small stone version of Leonardo da Vinci's 'Last Supper' and is flanked by the *Decalogue*, Creed and Lord's Prayer painted on stone panels. Piscina and *sedilia* are also C19. The church has a good deal of C15 glass (mostly re-set by *Warrington* about 1850), and in the s. aisle e.

window the glass depicts the Holy Kinship (as on Ranworth screen in Norfolk). One of the figures has been given a bishop's head but it is actually *St Mary Cleophas*, with her four children at her feet. One of them, the infant *St James the Less*, holds his adult emblem of a fuller's club. In the *light* to the l. the large figure is missing but the two infants below survive, holding a scallop shell and a poisoned *chalice*, and are therefore *SS James* and *John*. The missing figure would have been *St Mary Salome*, and the light on the r. would presumably have contained the *Blessed Virgin and Child* but this has been lost. In the s. aisle centre window on the l., there is an unusual panel showing the *Blessed Virgin* in front of the emperor with her parents behind and *St Joseph* to the r. In the r.-hand light is the favourite medieval way of showing Christ's Ascension – a pair of nail-pierced feet below two angels. The window to the w. has an excellent figure of *St Paul*. In the centre window of the n. aisle you will find a scourging of Christ and in the easternmost window, Christ rising from the tomb, with fragments of the sleeping soldiers. The chancel e. window tracery contains C14 glass but the main lights are by Warrington. There are three rows of good figures: top, St John, Christ, the Blessed Virgin; centre, *St Peter*, *Edward the Confessor* (or St Ethelbert), St Paul; bottom, *SS Edmund, Etheldreda* and *George*. The s. sanctuary window of 1867 is by the *O'Connors*, with two Nativity scenes. The monument in the s. aisle to Lionel and Anna Bacon (1653) is credited to *Nicholas Stone*. Draped fabric carries the inscription below a *cartouche* of arms flanked by skulls; there is an urn on top, two miniature shields below and the design terminates in a sizable pinnacle as a pendant.

Heveningham, St Margaret (H3): This little church stands proudly above the roadside, and its plain tower has a *Perpendicular* w. window over a simple doorway whose only decoration is a line of *paterae* on the *dripstone*. The *nave* was given a new roof in the early C16, and on the s. side there are six large and handsome brick *clerestory* windows of that period. Note, however, that five of the windows on the other side have moulded terracotta *mullions* and *tracery* and seem to be C17 replacements. Walking round, you will see that, in the C19, a large family pew extension was sited on the n. side of the nave, and a lean-to *vestry* was added to the C14 chancel. The *priest's door* on the s. side has an elaborately moulded arch, and there is a shallow C14 s. *aisle*.

Entry is through a low and simple s. *porch*, and the medieval door with its keeled boards opens at the top of no fewer than five steps down into the body of the church. Nearby stands a plain C18 or early-C19 *bier* with gently curved handles. The five-bay C14 *arcade* accentuates the narrowness of the aisle whose steeply angled roof dates from the early C17, a period when little roof replacement took place. It has curved braces, and there are attractive, pierced brackets on the outer wall. Beyond the plain tower arch, the w. window is filled with brightly coloured figures of the *Evangelists*, set against dark red shapes; patterned *quarries* take up the rest and the borders are lively. The glass was probably painted in 1854 by Ann Owen, the rector's wife, an artist of no mean ability. St Margaret's has a ring of five bells with a 9 cwt. tenor and they are handled from the ground floor of the tower. A C19 *font* stands at the w. end of the nave, but when Ubbeston church was made redundant, its C15 font found a home here, in front of the recess that marks the site of the old n. door. Set on a short, panelled stem, it has a *castellated* rim, and small shields within *quatrefoils* alternate with tracery shapes in the panels of the deep bowl. The early-C16 nave roof is a good double-*hammerbeam* design which has pierced tracery behind the hammers and in the *spandrels*. It is very dark, but with binoculars one can see that there are masks carved on some of the braces, and the *wall plate* is decorated with crowns and roses. Canopied niches on the *wall posts* contain figures of the apostles: n. side 2nd from w. *St Philip*; 3rd *St Jude*; 5th *St Paul*; 6th *St Andrew*; s. side 4th from w. *St John*. They appear to be in good condition, despite the fact that *William Dowsing* was here for two days in April 1643. He records the destruction of 'eight superstitious pictures, one of the *Virgin Mary*; and two inscriptions of brass, one Pray for the soul, and another orate pro animabus'. During a restoration of 1847 there was more vandalism, when the wooden effigies of Sir John Heveningham and his wife were thrown into the churchyard to be burned. The lady's perished, but the parson saved the knight's figure, and it now lies on a bench at the e. end of the aisle. Despite the cracks and mutilations and stumps for arms, the blackened effigy still impresses, with its battered features and moustaches that overlap the helmet. The head rests on a helm, and the figure wears a jupon (a padded coat that went out of fashion in the early C15), suggesting that although there was a succession of Sir Johns in the family, this was the one that died in 1379, or possibly his son who died in 1425. The only other wooden effigy of this period in Suffolk is to be found at Bures. A small *piscina* in the wall to the r. shows that an *altar* stood here before the *Reformation*, and on the window ledge is an interesting C19 painting of the church's interior which illustrates the pulpit and high *Jacobean* pew that stood next to it. Moving over to the manorial pew annexe on the n. side, you will see that sections of the panelling were incorporated in the new stalls, and that more than average comfort was ensured by having a fireplace. There is a fine image niche in the e. *respond* of the arcade, with a *crocketted ogee* arch, and tiny masks set within foliage in the spandrels, and it is notable that the *groining* is painted rather than carved. The chancel arch seems to have been re-formed, possibly at the restoration of 1847 or 1866, and there are capacious openings each side which may have been made then. Overhead hang the *Royal Arms* of George III, a pale set painted on board. The *arch-braced* chancel roof has been restored, and brightened with stencil decoration between the rafters. Like the w. window, the e. window glass was installed in 1854, and has nine vignettes from the life of Christ painted by Ann Owen. They are contained within vine patterns backed by ruby glass which was probably provided by *Ward & Hughes*. An *Agnus Dei, Trinity symbol* and dove of the Holy Spirit feature in the tracery, and the whole effect is very pleasing. The window is flanked by two good C19 paintings on canvas – large figures of *St Margaret* and *St Edmund*. The s. chancel windows with their angel medallions are probably by Ward & Hughes, although one of them is a memorial to the rector and may be the last work by Ann Owen. No glass by her has been identified elsewhere. The C14 *angle piscina* with its *cinquefoil* arch remains undisturbed, but a raised *sanctuary* floor has made the *dropped-sill sedilia* unusable. A tablet on the n. wall in memory of the Revd. Samuel Fairechough and Frances his wife is undated but is probably late-C17:

Reader Look hence, under yon marble Rest
the best of Preachers and his wife the Best
of Woemen there do their Deare Ashes lye,
Their Dearer Sowls are mounted 'bove the
    Sky
on Thrones of Glory but they'l ere long
    Returne
and reassume those Ashes From that urne.

Higham, St Mary (B4): The setting is most attractive; the church stands by the Hall and the water meadows of the Stour reach up to the edges of the churchyard. The tower is likely to have been built in the C13 but above the small w. doorway a short and broad window has *Decorated tracery* with pairs of *mouchettes* above flattened *ogees*. The bell openings are *Perpendicular* and there is a slab turret on the s. side up to the belfry. The tower houses a good ring of six bells with a 9 cwt. tenor. The s. wall of the *nave* has been recently restored and is spotted with lumps of *septaria;* like the *priest's door* farther along, the doorway has been blocked up. All the Perpendicular windows on that side have been renewed and so has the *chancel* e. window. If its intersected 'Y' tracery is a copy of the original it means that nave and chancel were probably built soon after the tower. A narrow n. *aisle* was added in the early C15 and entry now is through a C19 wooden porch and a small but substantial n. doorway.

For a little church, the four-bay *arcade* between nave and aisle is remarkably elaborate and decorative. The lobes of the *quatrefoil piers* are *ogee*-shaped and their *capitals* are carved alternately with vines and *paterae*. The *hood moulds* come down to *headstops* decorated with leaves on the n. but on the nave side there are four excellent heads, including two women wearing the net headdress known as a crespine. The roofs are C19 but the stone *corbels* in the aisle appear to be original and the nave roof incorporates medieval *arch-braces* which rest on wooden slabs that are worth studying. There is a man with his tongue out in the s.e. corner, an angel with a shield, and in the s.w. corner a cowled figure with a book grins knowingly. The simple C14 *font* has quatrefoils in the bowl panels above a traceried stem and there is another bowl on the floor nearby. Small blank shields are carved on four of its faces and it was originally set against a wall or pillar; although sometimes described as a font, it is almost certainly a large *stoup* and may have formed part of the vanished s. porch. The 1811 memorial for Robert and Marian Hoy on the n. wall is by Charles Regnart, a prolific monumental mason, some of whose work was good enough to exhibit at the Royal Academy. Here, however, he is not at his best. It is a bas-relief in which an awkwardly posed woman clasps an urn which she seems to have caught just in time, and the folds of flimsy drapery serve only to confuse the anatomy. In contrast to the stiff Victorian Gothic tablets over the n. and s. doors, there is a sweet little design on the s. wall for Helen Dawson, who died young in 1863 – an obelisk over a chaplet of flowers in relief which frames the epitaph. The glass by *Powell & Sons* in the window to the r. is a World War I memorial, with conventional regimental crests and a figure of *St George*, but it is interesting that the designer chose to pair the patron saint with Richard Coeur de Lion. In a window farther along there are two *Pre-Raphaelite* figures of Faith and Charity, with peaches-and-cream complexions and deeply coloured brocade dresses; a good turn-of-the-century period piece by Powells. Just below, a *piscina* under a *cusped* ogee arch shows that there was a nave *altar* nearby.

The chancel roof was reconstructed in the 1880s restoration but retained the old arch-braces and *castellated wall plates*. There must have been a masonry arch between nave and chancel previously but the replacement is wood and comes down to large canopied oak figures of *SS Peter* and *Paul* resting on stone corbels. The choir stalls probably date from the same time and have *Evangelistic symbols* on the elbows and two curiously flat lions at the front. The 1820s memorial in artificial *Coade stone* on the n. wall is not very attractive but it is interesting that its design is the same as a tablet in Layham church which was cut by E.J. Physick much later; this one may have been done by his father. The *sanctuary* is tiled and so is the *reredos* on either side of the alabaster centre panels. Some of the colours are fairly startling but the design includes nicely lettered *Decalogue*, Lord's Prayer and Creed. There is a plain *touchstone* tablet in the corner for Alice Dokenfielde who died in 1622, and below it is a C16 piscina with small paterae in the moulding, a wooden *credence shelf*, and an interesting drain shaped like a *Tudor Rose*. The chancel floor was probably tiled in the C14 and some examples have been found which are now embedded in the s. windowsill; two are heraldic shields and were once glazed.

Higham, St Stephen (B4): The village, with its lower, middle and upper greens was part of the parish of Gazeley but in 1861 it became a separate benefice and a new church was built, designed by *Sir George Gilbert Scott*. He had a hand in a number of C19 restorations but this is his only complete church in Suffolk and it is a stolid little building, with *nave*, *chancel* and n. *aisle* in *Early English* style. The flint walls are banded with *ashlar* and the *dripstones* have finely cut *headstops*. The round tower with its conical cap lifts the design above the ordinary and Scott let himself go on the belfry stage where tall, blind *arcading* (with bold shafts and stiff leaf *capitals*) links the bell openings.

Entry is via a s. *porch* into a dark interior under a pine roof with *tie-beams* and tall *king posts*. There is a four-bay n. arcade with *hood moulds* coming down to headstops above octagonal *piers*. As with the outside, the tower provides the interest. The ground floor was designed as a baptistry and it has a rib vault resting on shafts with stiff leaf capitals. Below them are heavy leaf *corbels*, one with a bird and another with a hound clutching at the base. The tub *font* with its cable rim rests on short, closely set marble columns and has a flat iron-scrolled cover. The C18 or early-C19 benefactions board in the n. aisle is headed 'Parish of Gazeley, Hamlet of Higham' and was transferred here in 1944. All the woodwork is plain unadorned work by Rattee & Kett of Cambridge. The pews still have their numbers which is a reminder that in the 1860s pew rents were still common and where one sat in church was determined by custom and social status. Things had begun to change, however, and it was one of the conditions of a grant by the Incorporated Church Building Society that 31 seats should be reserved for the poor of the village as part of their campaign to get rid of an iniquitous system. C19 stone pulpits are nearly always indigestible and this one is no exception; standing on polished green marble columns, it was two roundels carved with busts of *SS Peter* and *Paul* and a shaft of liverish marble supports the built-in book rest. Opposite is a wooden tablet with a coloured coat of arms at the top for members of the Barclay family spanning more than a century. The arch of the organ chamber on the n. side of the chancel has a pair of very well cut head corbels which are typical of the fine detailing in this church – something that is often ignored by those who see no virtue in Victorian buildings. The e. wall is boldly banded with ties on either side of a narrow *reredos* panel in patterned marble. All the 1870s glass is by *Clayton & Bell* and the e. window depicts the Crucifixion, with the *Two Marys* on one side and two saints on the other. The *sanctuary* s. window of the same period and almost certainly by the same makers shows the martyrdom and burial of *St Stephen* – an interesting composition, with the draped coffin being borne away on the shoulders of vested bearers preceded by cross and banner, with a young taperer by the side. Scott designed a set of altar frontals to go with his new church and it is pleasant to find them still in use more than a century later.

Hinderclay, St Mary (E3): The church is nicely situated except for the fact that on the s. side of the churchyard one is confronted with a line of black corrugated iron silos that are quite awful in their ugliness. There is a small *Decorated* w. window in the tower but it is otherwise *Perpendicular*, with bell openings that have deep *labels* over the fine *tracery*. The window shape is continued downwards below the sills in the form of panels with *cusped ogee* heads and filled with flint chequer. The tower has a plain flint *base course* and the *flushwork* in the battlements contain the letters 'SSRM' for the dedication. It is fitting that such a handsome tower houses an excellent ground floor ring of eight bells with a 10 cwt. tenor. On the n. side of the *nave* is a blocked late-C12 door of simple design and in the n. wall of the *chancel* is an early Decorated window with elongated *trefoils* in the two *lights*. The e. window has *reticulated* tracery and there is a *priest's door* with worn *headstops* round the corner on the s. side. A *quoin* on that corner (about 4ft. 6in. from the ground) has a *scratch dial* but only the hole for the centre peg can now be seen. Farther w. a window has *transoms* which formed *low side windows* at the bottom, and the tracery matches that in the e. window of the s. *aisle*. The aisle s. windows are square-headed with three lights and, like nearby Thelnetham and Rickinghall Inferior, the aisle is gabled. The w. end has been repaired in red brick but note that a C14 *gargoyle* is placed in the angle between the aisle and the nave to take water from the gulley between the roofs. Entry is by way of the s. *porch*, one of the few wooden examples in this part of Suffolk. It stands on a brick base and, although the sides have been renewed, the outer arch is C14, with the each *jamb* and half of the arch curve cut from a single piece of timber.

Through a simple and quite small doorway one passes into a pleasant little interior. There is a plain C14 font at the w. end and the tower arch is filled with an C18 screen at the bottom and the *Royal Arms* of George III on canvas above. The vestry enclosure matches the tower screen and there is a Perpendicular w. window within. The early-C13 arcade between nave and aisle is carried on low round piers and the benches are an interesting late-C17 set. The poppyheads are small and diamond-shaped, bearing mainly carved fleur-de-lys and rosettes. Those on the rear bench are lettered: 'JSK SK' and 'RL 1617 TC' – no doubt the churchwardens' initials at that time. Not all the seating is benches, for there are C18 low box pews of pine in the s. aisle and more in the eastern half of the nave, with panelled ends. The capitals of the chancel arch were cut into to accommodate the rood, and the end of the beam that supported the

front of the loft may be seen in the n. wall. There is a shadow of a niche in the window embrasure by the pulpit and this could have been the site of an altar for the guild of St Peter that was here in 1474. The square-headed chancel screen is a late example, with open tracery and moulded mullions, and looks as though it may have been re-set subsequently in another frame. To the r. you will see that the hinges of the original shutters are still set in the jambs of the low side windows. On the n. wall of the chancel is a monument for George Thompson, a rector who died in 1711. The execution is fairly coarse, with a cartouche of arms supported by garlands at the top, standing putti at each side, and cherub heads with wings and acanthus leaves below. The only other memorial of note is a well lettered oval tablet on the s. wall for Charlotte Doe who died in 1917. Behind the organ there is a very narrow plain arch connecting the aisle chapel sanctuary with the nave, and I can only think that it was to give a view across to another altar on the n. side – in other words, a very large squint. Hinderclay has some interesting modern glass designed by Rosemary Rutherford in 1973. There are three windows in the s. aisle, with simplistic figure shapes against a streaky semi-abstract design; one of the faces is treated quite differently from the rest and looks like a portrait from life. With contemporary glass, the iconography can be elusive; the *Transfiguration* and The Tree of Life were part of the artist's vision, but Moses in the bullrushes seems to figure in one of the side-windows. In the chancel e. window, the tracery alone has stained glass and there are bird, fish and flame abstracts. If you are fortunate enough to visit on a sunny day, the body of the church is filled with warm, enticing colours.

Hintlesham, St Nicholas (E6): The church stands back from the village street in a pleasant setting, and the tower has a late *Perpendicular* window above a plain w. door. There are three recently restored *clerestory* windows on the s. side, but the n. *aisle* was re-roofed at a steeper angle at some time, thus covering the upper windows on that side. The n. door is blocked and farther to the e. there is a C13 window composed of three *lancets*. There are more tall lancets in the *chancel* and a large modern brick and flint n.e. *vestry*. A small *priest's door* is set in the wall on the s. side, and the windows on that frontage have *Decorated tracery* with *mouchette* patterns like those at Washbrook; all, that is, except the one nearest the porch, which has intersected 'Y' tracery of about 1300. The s. *porch* was restored to celebrate the coronation of King George V and the inner doorway has very deep continuous mouldings.

The character of the interior is established by the simplicity and solidity of the C13 *nave arcades*. The chamfered arches rest on well-moulded *capitals* and the *piers* are circular and octagonal alternately. But it is interesting that they are not paired and one shape faces the other across the nave. The blocked clerestory windows are outlined above them on the n. side and the C19 roof has *tie-beams* and *king posts*. The *font* and the benches are Victorian too and the organ stands on a square C19 w. *gallery* which carries two *hatchments*: for Frances Burrell, who died in 1846 (1.), and Capt. Heneage Lloyd of the Coldstream Guards, who died in 1776. Fragments of a medieval wall painting survive above the n. arcade, and although nothing is left that can be recognised, its position opposite the door suggests that it was a *St Christopher*. The glass in the s. aisle windows was made and engraved at Ipswich School and there are skilfully lettered names on the clear *quarries*, recording baptisms, marriages, and deaths in a way that is both imaginative and attractive. There is a *piscina* in a square recess by the *altar* farther along, and a tall niche in the e. wall contains a large 1930s statue of the church's patron saint. Judging by the timbers, the n. aisle roof was restructured in the C15 or C16, and below the three-*light* window there is a C13 piscina within a bold *trefoil* arch. As a *retable*, the altar there has a modern, fresh-coloured painting of fisherman hauling their nets, thoughtfully combining an allusion to the disciples as fishers of men and St Nicholas's role as the patron saint of seamen. There is no chancel arch now but a cross is set on a modern, braced beam which rests on two huge stone *corbels*. They may have been elsewhere originally, but if not they are surprisingly pagan for this position. One is a devil pulling his mouth open and the other is a *green man*, although the leaves that issue from his mouth are rudimentary. The stair to the vanished *rood loft* is within the chancel on the s. side and is a late construction in *Tudor* brick. The chancel roof is apparently a C19 reconstruction and has curious pierced braces under a plastered ceiling. On the n. wall, a *touchstone* tablet for Charles Vesey (1657) is set within a lozenge like a hatchment and is engraved with his arms and crest. Farther along, there is an unusual and attractive memorial for Capt. John Timperley who died in 1629. It is a 6ft. touchstone slab engraved with his effigy in half-armour, and he

wears his hair long over a lace collar. The architectural frame contains martial trophies and his *achievement*, with all the lines emphasised by white mastic filling. The verse below has a fine disregard for the niceties of language:

> Let others tombes, which ye glad heires bestowes
> Write golde in merble, greefe affects no showes,
> There's a trew harte intombed him, & that beares
> A silent & sadd Epitaph writt in teares.

Although the vestry has been rebuilt, its door from the chancel shows that it was a medieval chapel. This is confirmed by a long *squint* which is angled up to emerge in the *sanctuary*. Across in the s. wall there is a very worn C14 piscina which has faint traces of *crockets* and pinnacles, and nearby is the dilapidated monument of Thomas Tympley, his son Nicholas, and their respective wives. Thomas died in 1593 and the little alabaster figures kneel in pairs across prayer desks, with their children grouped behind them. The plinth and cornice are inlaid in colour and there are three shields of arms on the top. The C17 *communion rails* have well-turned and very closely set *balusters* that would have earned the approval of *Archbishop Laud*. The panels that stand against the side walls of the sanctuary may well have formed part of the rood loft. Hintlesham has a ground floor ring of six bells with an 8 cwt. tenor.

Hitcham, All Saints (D5): By the sign at the s. end of the village a short lane leads past an attractive late-C15 house which was once the Guildhall to a spacious churchyard; its path rises steadily to the large, handsome church whose *Perpendicular* tower has heavy buttresses reaching almost to the top, making it seem even bulkier than it is. There is a solid stair turret to the s. and the bell stage, with its generous three-*light* windows, has the look of an addition to the original design. *Base course* and buttresses are decorated with *flushwork* chequer and the late-C14 w. doorway with small *headstops* is flanked by niches under *crocketted* canopies. The tower houses a ring of six bells with a 16 cwt. tenor, but the condition of the frame prevents their use at the present time. On walking round, you will find an early-C14 n. door and the remains of a *rood stair* just visible in the angle between the n. *aisle* and the *chancel*. The large two-storeyed *sacristy* with barred windows on that side has recently been restored, and the chancel was largely rebuilt in 1878 (look for the photograph inside which shows it minus s. and e. walls). A little to the e. there are two stones of the 1680s carved with skulls, hour-glass and death's sharp darts, while alongside is a finely lettered modern headstone – a refreshing change from most of the output of contemporary monumental masons. In the rebuilding, the C14 *priest's door* in the chancel s. wall was retained. Note the squat and curious windows of the *clerestory*. The C15 *porch* is so like Bildeston's that one suspects that the same master mason designed both – there is the same lavish flushwork on the facade and three particularly good niches; they are tall and vaulted, with angels below the stools and crocketted canopies formed by pairs of little *ogee* arches. The parapet here, however, is flushwork and instead of roses the *spandrels* contain a *Trinity* shield on the l. and *instruments of the Passion* on the r. There is no sign of an upper room here but the impressive inner doorway is again very like Bildeston's, with a double rank of deep mouldings set with shields and crowns rising to an angel at the apex; there are worn lion stops to the *hood mould* and the tracery of the doors was applied to new panels when the porch was restored in 1882.

Within, walls and C14 *arcades* are brilliantly white above pale brick floors and the narrowness of the aisles suggests that they were designed for processions rather than for additional seating. All was re-roofed in the early C17; this is interesting because the form chosen for the *nave* was a double *hammerbeam* – harking back more than a hundred years in terms of technique. The structure is familiar but the detailing reflects its age, with pineapple pendants below the *collar beams*, grotesque masks against the *arch-braces*, and *Jacobean* scrollery behind the vertical struts. Instead of the old-style angels, the hammerbeams carry oval plaques with mainly secular emblems – harp, thistle, and portcullis on the s.; rose, crossed sword and baton, and sun in splendour on the n. The date is confirmed by a crowned monogram for James I on the s. side and another for Charles I at the e. end of the s. aisle. The aisles feature interesting *bosses*, including some faces, and look for the curling *unicorn* just e. of the s. door. On the wall below is possibly the best of the county's modern *Royal Arms* – a 1937 set of George VI's, pierced and carved in gilded and painted wood. The cover of the C19 *font* in the s.w. corner has a pretty coloured and gilt Gothic cover presented

in 1943. The way in which the tower buttresses obtrude and allow the arcades to pass beyond them suggests that the tower was built separately and the nave extended to meet it. Below stands a pair of C19 churchwardens' stalls which are attractive and unusual, having hoods and desks. The medieval nave benches have fragments of beasts on the elbows and, repaired and restored, they were augmented by three C19 ranges at the e. end. A large C18 oil painting of the visit of the Magi by an unknown artist hangs on the s. wall, and in the aisle chapel the C14 *piscina* has unusual recessed *cusping* and a very deep drain. Over the n. door there is a fine and large demi-angel; I wonder whether it is a survivor from the previous roof or whether it has come from elsewhere. At the e. end of the n. aisle a tiny ogee niche is set in the *jamb* of the last arcade arch and opposite is an alabaster and touchstone memorial for Sir George Waldegrave, with fourteen lines of totally obfuscating genealogy. He died in 1636 and his wife, 'Laments her loss, and bids these lynes declare his piety . . . late faithful mate, now blissful soul (quoth she) though weeping for herself I joy for thee'. The syntax is as confused as his family tree, but it's the 'faithful mate' I rather care for.

The C18 pulpit is in plain panelled oak but its *tester* has a dark marquetry star on the underside. Close to it is the base of an early-C16 *rood screen* and there are traces of painted figures in the panels which are a little unusual – they are all angels bearing Passion emblems. Set against a stippled background pattern, they have green wings, capes of ermine, and golden crowns. Determined attempts were obviously made to disfigure them but they display from l. to r.: pincers, the pillar and cords, spear, possibly Christ's robe, (next panel half destroyed), sponge on cleft reed, nails, and a very indistinct but possible crown of thorns. The chancel is reached by no fewer than five steps, with two more into the *sanctuary*, and it is likely that such extreme changes in level were 1870s alterations in tune with 'High Church' principals that emphasised the special nature of the chancel and sanctuary. The coved and panelled ceiling above dates from the rebuilding. Three *ledger-stones* bear indents of large *brasses* and two of them had fine canopies. In the sanctuary the C14 piscina lies below a large cusped and crocketted ogee arch, complete with *finial* and leaf stops.

On the n. wall the chaste tablet of shaped marble set on a mottled dark red back is by Thomas Woolner, a Hadleigh boy who went on to achieve considerable success as a sculptor and was a friend of the *pre-Raphaelites*. It commemorates John Stevens Henslow, who was rector here from 1837 to 1861. As botanist, geologist, and chemist he had international standing, and secured for Darwin the appointment to HMS Beagle. His work at Cambridge did not mean a neglected parish, and his stand against local landowners on behalf of the poor made him powerful enemies but countless friends in the hungry 1840s. A lithograph portrait of this outstanding man hangs by the s. door and the porch was restored in his memory.

Holbrook, All Saints (F7): The stalwart C14 tower stands on the s. side and, like a number of others in s.e. Suffolk, it also serves as an entrance *porch*. A great deal of *septaria* can be seen in its walls, and there is a small niche and blocked *lancet* above the entrance; at the n.w. corner a slim stair turret rises above the shallow bell stage and altered battlements. The tower houses a good ring of six bells with an 8 cwt. tenor. The body of the church would seem to date from the first half of the C14, and the majority of its *consecration crosses* have survived (or rather, the stone discs on which they were painted). Very few exterior examples are to be found anywhere, but here there are three below the w. window and three more in the *chancel* e. wall. In 1864 *R.M. Phipson* added a n. *aisle*, complete with a little porch set in the angle with the tower. His too is the n.e. *vestry*, but in 1887 his chancel e. window was succeeded by another to celebrate the queen's jubilee. The tops of the *nave* walls had been repaired in brick, and on the s. side there is a *string course* studded with *paterae*. The brick s. aisle abuts the tower, blocking a side window, and was probably added in the late C15; its *Perpendicular* windows have high sills, and the reason why one of them is blocked will be seen within. The porch has a fine vaulted ceiling, and leaf *bosses* cluster round the octagonal trapdoor. There is a very faint *scratch dial* to the r. of the entrance, and the inner archway features unusually deep wave mouldings scored with C18 graffiti.

Inside the church, three more consecration crosses hide behind the curtains on the w. wall beyond the C19 *font*, and there are others alongside the entrance and blocked n. doorway. A string course of the same period ranges along the walls and lifts over both doorways. The *hatchment* on the n. wall bears the arms of John Reade of Holbrook House whose memorial we shall see later. An almost flat roof covers both

nave and chancel and has braced *tie-beams* and stub *king posts;* it must date from the time when the upper walls were rebuilt, probably in the C16. There is a single oblong *clerestory* window on the s. side, and another of the same period is blocked above the n. door. At the e. end of the s. aisle John Clenche's tomb masks the window we noted outside. He died in 1607, having been Ipswich's first Recorder and a Baron of the Exchequer, and his monument is a bulky affair, backed with alabaster panels and three roundels of arms. He lies in his judge's fur-lined robes, resting on one elbow, while his daughter-in-law Margerie takes up the lower level; kneeling figures of eight girls and seven boys are ranged on each side. John Reade's memorial nearby records that he too was a judge, in Madras with the East India Company, and his 1840s tablet was provided by the 'Patent Works' of Westminster. The stone pulpit and reading desk were probably Phipson's, and the lectern is an example of the sort of fittings favoured by the *Ecclesiological Society*. The church's only *brass* lies under the carpet just in front of the chancel steps, a fine 30in. figure of man, and a plate of his six sons – his wife's effigy, daughters, shields and inscription all gone. His head rests on an elaborate helm, and the exaggerated elbow pieces and other details are typical of the Yorkist fashions of the 1470s. It may conceivably commemorate William Tendryng and his wife Elizabeth who specified a brass along these lines in 1466, although the style seems too late. More sections of C14 string courses are to be found in the chancel, combined with lengths of C19 replacement, and there is a fine early-C14 *double piscina* and stepped *sedilia* suite in the *sanctuary*; a blind *quatrefoil* is centred above the arches of the piscina, and it is likely that the range had some surface ornament originally. The last of the consecration crosses will be found by the blocked *priest's door*. There is a lovely contemporary archway on th n. side of the chancel, a deeply moulded trefoil with pairs of flanking shafts. It now leads to the C19 vestry, but it probably marked the site of the founder's tomb – at a guess, Richard de Holbrook who was Lord of the Manor in the late-C13. To the l. there is a matching niche which retains a good deal of its original colour. A metal container was found within it in the C19, and it is likely to have been a heart burial, contemporary with the one at Exning. The elegant C18 chandelier with its ten branches that hangs in the chancel is very like one in Whitby church, Yorkshire, and was almost certainly made in London.

Hollesley, All Saints (H6): The mid-C15 tower has a *flushwork base course* which has been partially filled with brick, and shields occupy the *spandrels* of the w. door. Above it is a small niche, there is *Decorated tracery* in the bell openings, and the flushwork of the stepped battlements displays 'MR's for the Blessed Virgin and other devices. The tower houses a beautiful ring of eight bells with a 17 cwt. tenor cast by Taylor's of Loughborough in 1938. There were only three bells before that and the second, which lay for many years at the w. end of the nave, was moved to Moyses Hall Museum in Bury St Edmunds. The body of the church was largely rebuilt in 1886 when a narrow and slightly odd n. aisle was added. It has a *vestry* door at the w. end and there are paired *lancets*. The rest of the windows are *Perpendicular* (mainly renewed), except one with 'Y' tracery of about 1300 by the s. door. The *priest's door* in the s. wall of the chancel has headstops, and the walls are faced with a typical late-C19 *knapped* flint finish. Half a *stoup* bowl is set within a recess in the tower buttress nearest the s. door, but according to Cautley the arrangement is not original.

The s. doorway dates from about 1300, and just inside there is another stoup. The tower arch has been partitioned off, with the organ sited in front of it, and in the n.w. corner there is a large C13 slab of *Purbeck marble*. It is rather difficult to see but there are remnants of a border inscription, and the faint outline of a priest's effigy. It was used subsequently for a *brass* and has suffered a good deal over the years. There are slim buttresses round the shaft of the *font*, and its bowl panels contain *Tudor Roses* and shields within *quatrefoils*. A set of Charles II *Royal Arms* is framed and glazed on the n. wall. When the *aisle* was added, an early-C13 *arcade* with alternate round and octagonal *piers* was uncovered, showing that there had been an aisle originally. The seven C15 benches in the aisle have *poppyheads* and grotesques on the elbows, and the remainder are excellent modern replicas. Some have figures which could symbolise the *Seven Deadly Sins* – anger with a sword, vanity with a mirror, greed with money bag and chest. Those in the *nave* are equally good, and one can find a *griffin*, pelican, owl, squirrel, boar, and tortoise. On the s. side at the e. end there is even a sciapod, based on the only known medieval example at Dennington. Some of the benches are individual memorials and one commemorates the queen's coronation. The style and colours of the glass in the nave window suggest that it was supplied by *Heaton, Butler &*

Bayne. The scene of Christ with the Scribes and Pharisees is a lush grouping of figures under canopies, and vines fill the tracery, with a dove at the top. The aisle e. window contains an impressive 1980s Nativity (who is it by?) – naturalistic figures, with flowers bursting up from below and a mouse at the Blessed Virgin's feet; the background is a mesh of brilliant orange and red, and an angel with a scroll of music fills the upper quatrefoil. A cusped wooden arch in the modern roof marks the division between nave and chancel and below, the base of the C16 *screen* retains most of its attractive tracery – a dense pattern of quatrefoils. The early-C17 pulpit stands on a new stone base, and its panels are carved with lozenge shapes and blind arches. It almost hides a *piscina* which will have served a nave *altar* before the *Reformation*. The handsome *communion rails* in pine with their turned *balusters* look like an C18 set, but the *angle piscina* and *sedilia* were part of the 1880s rebuilding. The e. window glass of 1899 is by *Arthur L. Moore*, whose work can also be found at Reydon, Frostenden and Melton. Here we have a conventional Ascension scene in vivid colour, with two angels holding scrolls: 'Ye men of Galilee why stand ye gazing?'

Holton St Mary, St Mary (E7): The squat tower was no doubt a good deal taller originally and now has low brick battlements, with a perky weathervane on one corner and a flagstaff on another. There are panels of *flushwork* at the base of the buttresses and a large glacial boulder is built into the one at the n.w. This may be an example of a practice in the early church whereby a stone with a particular pagan significance was appropriated to the service of the new religion. A tall, two-*light Perpendicular* w. window was inserted later. The C14 *nave* has a n. door with worn *headstops* but it was blocked at some time and the top half glazed. The nave windows have *Decorated tracery*, and a small C19 *vestry* was added to the n. side of the C13 *chancel*, which has had all its windows renewed. Most of the *priest's door* on the s. side is apparently original and there is a Victorian s. porch whose benches incorporate medieval *poppyheads*.

The inner doorway has large king and queen headstops and within, the nave and chancel lie under modern panelled pine roofs with *tie-beams and king posts*. The C14 tower arch is tall and, beyond, the 1880s w. window glass by *Heaton, Butler & Bayne* displays better than average modelling in the Resurrection and Ascension scenes; cherub heads emerge from the angry clouds behind the figures of Christ in both. The bowl of the C15 *font* has a *Tudor Rose*, defaced shields, and a fleur-de-lys in the bowl panels, but note that there are sockets for shafts around the base, which belonged to a C13 predecessor. A dark set of George II *Royal Arms* hangs over the s. door, and to the r. is a very interesting painted wooden panel which has been well restored. It shows a youth wearing a tricorne hat, leaning on a spade, and holding a paper in one hand. The legend reads: 'Opened August 29th 1748' and flanking scrolls have: 'Not slothful in Business. Serving the Lord'. It once hung in the school (now a private house) by the churchyard gate, and the story is completed by the Revd. Stephen White's epitaph on the n. wall:

> on April 12, 1773 being Easter Monday as he was officiating in the church he was suddenly called away from his labours to receive their Reward, and expired in that School which his Piety had raised.

A chancel s. window contains glass of 1899 by Heaton, Butler & Bayne with two pale musical angels, and the windows flanking the sanctuary have glass which may be by the *O'Connors* – figures of the *Evangelists* in agreeable colour, with their symbols in the lower panels. The small C13 *piscina* has an arch with shallow *cusps* and the shafts have ring *capitals* and bases. Plain *dropped-sill sedilia* lie alongside, and in the n. wall there is an *aumbry* which was evidently fitted with a door. The odd thing is that its arch is cusped and not designed to be hidden.

Holton, St Peter (I3): A little away from the centre of the village, the church enjoys a pleasant setting on rising ground. The lower part of its slim round tower is almost certainly *Saxon*, judging from internal evidence, and there are belfry *lancets* below a complete range of lancet bell openings. The upper stage was added in the C15, the w. window is C19 and the brick battlements are modern. In 1856 there was a full-scale restoration and rebuilding by J.H. Hakewill in which he demolished a *Tudor* s. aisle and replaced it with a n. aisle which continues as an organ chamber and *vestry* to finish level with the *chancel*. It is sharply faced with *knapped* flint and has tall lancet windows. The e. window has intersected 'Y' tracery of about 1300, and the contemporary *priest's door* is flanked by C15 windows. Hakewill inserted more tall lancets in

the rebuilt s. wall of the nave and partially rebuilt the C15 *porch*. This has a rugged little figure of *St Peter* above the arch, and within there is a fine *Norman* doorway, tall, with a scalloped rim to the arch. Its single shafts have scallop *capitals*, and a separate panel above is carved with an animal in profile (perhaps a dog carrying something in its mouth).

Through to the church where an early-C15 *font* stands near the entrance, and the heavy octagonal bowl has shields and *Tudor Roses* set in the tracery of the panels; there are battered heads below and eight columns are set around the shaft. The *arch-braced* nave roof has *collar beams* cocked up close under the ridge, and Hakewill's heavy n. *arcade* rests on circular *piers* with sparingly decorated capitals. Benches and pulpit are of the same period, and nice Victorian *Decalogue* panels are framed on the s. wall. In the aisle, a small plaque commemorates all those men of the American 8th Air Force who flew from Holton during World War II. As with the nave, Hakewill reframed the chancel roof, and it has very deep *wall plates*. The e. window is filled with typical *Kempe* glass, signed with his wheatsheaf emblem in the l. border. Christ the King is flanked by the *Blessed Virgin* and St Peter, wearing pearl-encrusted robes and standing below elaborate canopies, with *censing* angels in the tracery. It dates from about 1900, and the oak *reredos* below was installed a decade later. Heightened with gilt, it has a beautiful C17 centre cross whose terminal discs carry the *evangelistic symbols*. The *altar* is a plain *Stuart* table, and to the r., the *piscina* has been shorn of all its surface ornament. The nearby window has glass of the 1860s which may have been supplied by Ward & Hughes – texts backed with a jolly pattern.

Homersfield, St Mary (G2): The village once formed part of the ancient deanery of the South Elmhams and, even now, Ordnance Survey maps mark the parish: 'St Mary South Elmham otherwise Homersfield'. Heavy-handed C19 restoration left its mark fairly decisively on the church, but it is still worth visiting. The unbuttressed tower with its single *string course* has a replacement w. window, and above it there is a tall C13 *lancet*; the bell openings have 'Y' tracery of about 1300. The *Perpendicular* windows in the nave have been renewed, and the most obvious clue to the church's early foundation is the little *Norman* lancet in the s. wall. The *billet moulding* in its arch is new work, but it may repeat the original. There are large C13 lancets in the *chancel* side walls, and although the stonework of the *priest's door* has been partly replaced, it dates from the same period. A pilgrim cross is cut in the r.-hand *jamb*, and there seem to be traces of a *scratch dial* on the other side. The *nave* gable carries a nicely floriated C14 cross. The *porch* has been comprehensively restored and given a new roof, but the shape of the blocked side windows suggests that it was added in the C15; the inner doorway has been re-formed.

Within, the plain boarded chest that stands in the base of the tower is probably C16; it still has its original lockplates and brackets, and the front corners are decorated with a delicate little chip-carved ornament. The *font* is a Victorian version of the Tournai style (as at Boulge) – a massive square with blind arcades on the sides; its attractively lettered oak cover was presented by the parishioners to mark the coronation of Edward VII. The simple interior lies under pine *arch-braced* roofs, and there are plain pine benches on *pamment* floors. The large painting of the Nativity that hangs on the n. wall was given in memory of a former rector, and the style suggests that it is C19 Italian work. The chancel dates from the C13 but, apart from the lancet windows, the only positive evidence that remains is the *double piscina* in the *sanctuary*. Except for the bases of the shafts, all its stonework has been renewed, but it is a fine design and may well be a faithful copy. There are C19 stone *Decalogue* panels on either side of the Perpendicular e. window.

Honington, All Saints (D3): Robert Bloomfield, whose pastoral poem *The Farmer's Boy* sold 26,000 copies between 1800 and 1803 and which still holds its reputation as a work of rustic genius, was born in 1766 in the cottage just across from the church. His parents' double gravestone is the one nearest to the s.w. corner of the early-C14 tower. This has a modern w. window but there is a *quatrefoil* window above, bell openings with *Decorated tracery* and a red brick stair turret to the second storey – probably added in the C16. The *chancel* and the s. side of the *nave* date from the C14 while the n. side has late *Perpendicular* windows. Because of their important role in church and village life, *porches* were favourite subjects for lavish treatment and valuable bequests, and this one is a good early-C15 example. It has a quatrefoil *flushwork base course*, step-*transomed* side windows and a battlemented parapet with stone panels carved with symbols which include a crowned 'M' for the *Blessed Virgin* and two 'J.S.' monograms which may be the initials of the donor. The s.

front has panelled flushwork, with three canopied niches, and the *dripstone* of the arch rests on weathered angels. The arch itself is enriched with leaves and shields and there are shields in the *spandrels* – one of them for *St Edmund*. Save for two ugly and obtrusive brick chimneys in the nave roof, the view from the street is most attractive. Note the line of the old roof showing above the new on the e. face of the tower. Once inside the porch, the fine *Norman* doorway betrays the real age of the building. There are three bands of decoration in the arch, with a battered head over it, as well as a carved *hood mould* coming down to beast masks on either side. Below, pairs of shafts are decorated with chevron and spiral on the l. and chevron with three carved blocks on the r. (4th shaft is a replacement). Passing through, note the shallow slot on the r. and the deep one on the l., made to house a drawbar to secure the door. C14 carvers sometimes produced the equivalent of a mason's pattern book of window tracery on *font* panels and here we have the best example in the area. In addition, the e. panel has a Crucifixion that is remarkably good. Christ is portrayed with long hair, and the Blessed Virgin and *St John* weep convincingly on either side, and both sun and moon are represented overhead. The condition of the whole piece is such that I suspect it was plastered over to shield it from the itinerent C17 image breakers. There were faint but extensive wall paintings of *St Nicholas* and *St Thomas of Canterbury* on the s. wall when *Cautley* visited before the war but not a trace can be seen now. They were all plastered over 40 years ago at the incumbent's behest which is particularly aggravating in that images of St Thomas are very rare because Henry VIII ordered their destruction in 1538. The second clue to the original Norman church is the chancel arch, entirely plain now, with small corner shafts on the nave side and fragments of carved *imposts* above them. Although the *screen* has gone you can see how a stair to the *rood loft* was cut into the n. wall. There is a large recess on that side of the chancel arch, with a plain image niche close by, the site of a nave *altar*. The handsome wooden eagle lectern of 1872 was transferred from nearby Sapiston, now in the care of the *Churches Conservation Trust*. Here, a restoration before World War I replaced the roofs and unfortunately exchanged a fine set of C15 benches for dull pitchpine pews. Some bench ends were suffered to remain and they are now part of the choir stalls. Carved on their gabled armrests are: (s. side), *unicorn, wyvern,* dog with a goose in its mouth and a hare; (n. side), monkey, two birds, and a rare example of a bagpiper that could have stepped straight out of a painting by Brueghel. On the s. wall by the *priest's door* is a 2ft. *brass* for George Duke (1594), in ruff, cloak and sword, typical dress for gentry of that period. The inscription that goes with it can be found on the e. wall behind the curtain, and another for Anne Curteis (1585) is to the l. of the altar. On the s. side of the *sanctuary* is a C14 *piscina* with a square drain under a flattened *ogee* arch, with *dropped-sill sedilia* alongside. The *Stuart communion rails* have shapely twisted *balusters* and on the n. wall is a large white marble tablet for Robert Ruskbrooke (1753). His arms are in a roundel at the top and the long inscription is cut in as fine an italic as you will see anywhere, with every stroke doubled.

Hoo, St Andrew and St Eustachius (G5): Standing by the Hall at the end of a lane, away even from the scattered houses of the hamlet, the church enjoys a memorably peaceful setting. In linking one of the *apostles* with a little known soldier-martyr, the unique dedication is one of the most curious. The leggy little brick tower dates from the early C16 and its parapet has been renewed relatively recently. It has a stair turret to the s., and makes use of an earlier w. window of about 1300 which matches the *chancel* e. window. The neat little plastered *porch* has a tiled roof, with medieval side timbers exposed within, and it shelters a C14 doorway which has a deep channel set between two mouldings.

The modest interior lies under a single plastered ceiling spanned by six heavy *tie-beams*, one of which is dated 1595. It seems likely that the body of the church needed strengthening just before the tower was built. The C15 *font* has four contented lions seated round the shaft, and in the bowl panels you will find angels holding shields which carry a *Trinity* emblem (n.e.), possible *Passion emblems* (w.), a crown, a large *Tudor Rose*, and a rampant lion. Curiously, instead of an angel the s.e. panel contains a standing figure, possibly a priest, although, like the others, it is defaced. By the n. door with its replacement drawbar stands a deep C14 chest of poplar, reinforced with narrow bands and fitted with three locks. The *Decalogue* boards above are probably early-C19 like the plain benches with their rudimentary *poppyheads*. These extend well into the chancel area, there being no division to separate it from the *nave,* but the site of the *rood screen* is marked by the stairs which gave access to the loft. They rise from a window

embrasure on the s. side and are a little unusual in that they proceed to the w. rather than the e. At first glance the niche in the chancel e. wall looks like a *piscina* but it is placed a little too high and there is no drain. Three-sided *communion rails* were a late-C17 fashion but these are very austere and have the look of the early-C18. They perform a double function on the s. side and have a book ledge which was probably for a little choir which sat on the low bench in the s.e. angle of the chancel. This is a unique arrangement in my experience. The *altar* is a small, almost square, late-C17 table with unusual turned decoration on the legs, rather like a series of napkin rings.

Hopton, All Saints (D3): The main fabric of the building is C14 but there have been a number of subsequent alterations. The tower has a pair of small *lancets* in the ground floor, an *ogee*-headed niche above, and a lancet belfry window. The upper stage, with its round-headed bell openings was attractively rebuilt in the C18 and is decorated with flint and stone chequework. The line of the original *nave* roof shows clearly on the e. face, above the handsome battlemented *clerestory* in warm, *Tudor* red brick. Its window arches and *tracery* are formed from shaped bricks and there are recessed panels at intervals. The w. end of the s. *aisle* betrays evidence of a late-C13 predecessor, not only by a lower roof line but by the *plate tracery* in the two-*light* window. There are renewed *Perpendicular* windows in the s. aisle, but the e. window there has *Decorated* tracery within a widened Tudor arch. One sometimes finds *low side windows* on both sides of a *chancel* but here, most unusually, there are two on the s. side, both divided by centre *mullions*, and a reason for the duplication eludes me. The e. window has three *trefoil* lancets and there is a *priest's door* on the n. side of the chancel. The late-C13 n. door survives, but the rest of the n. aisle is Perpendicular and its four-light e. window contains pretty curvilinear tracery under a Tudor arch. The buttress at the n.w. corner has an interesting variation – the lower stage is v-shaped before returning to a conventional angle under a gable at the top. The simple C14 s. *porch* has had angled brick buttresses added and the side windows are C19 replacements. The *dripstone* of the inner door has *headstops* and there is a niche over it. Within, the tower arch is plain and very steep, and there is a *trefoil*-headed *sanctus-bell window* in the wall above. At the w. end of the s. aisle you will see that the door to the tower stairs is heavily banded with iron – a reminder that, apart from church property, parish valuables were often kept for safety in the tower. The *font* is C19, but there is a huge and impressive C14 chest at the w. end of the n. aisle. The ends and base have suffered badly from worm, but the inset lid retains its original seven hinges and three great locks. The C14 *arcades* have octagonal *piers* and, above them, the brickwork of the clerestory has been carefully repointed and is very attractive. The low-pitched roof has alternating *hammerbeams* and *arch-braces*, and the hammers are coarsely carved figures holding books, organs, patens and chalices. The robed, seated figures on the *wall posts* have lost their heads and, above them, the double depth of *wall plate* is decorated with crudely carved flowers, painted angels, and two lines of cresting. The whole roof is painted, with red as the predominant colour, and the figures have ermine collars. They were apparently repainted by the vicar's five daughters a few generations back. The aisle roofs display delicate foliated and painted *bosses* and the bay at the e. end of the n. aisle has a carved cresting on the wall plate, possibly associated with a *celure*. There is a C14 *piscina* and *dropped-sill sedilia* in the s. aisle chapel. The inside of the chancel e. window shows more clearly than the outside that it was reconstructed in the C16. The *Stuart altar* has a carved top rail but two of its stretchers are missing. Tall niches are let into the walls at the e. end of the nave arcades and the *rood loft* stair goes up behind the pulpit; there is no lower door now but the hinges are still there. When the order came to take the rood and its loft down, the workmen sawed through the main beams but left the stumps in the wall; both ends of the *rood beam* itself can be seen and one end of the joist that supported the front of the loft. The frames of the low side windows are rebated on the inside as well as the outside for shutters (which merely adds to the mystery). In the *sanctuary* the piscina, under its trefoil arch, retains its original wooden *credence shelf*. On the n. side of the chancel there is a large tablet in memory of Thomas Raymond; he died in 1680 and was 'first sole keeper of the papers of state and council to King Charles II'. It has a *cartouche* within a broken *pediment* at the top, and a skull with crossed fronds carved in shallow relief at the bottom. The 1890s glass in the e. window is by *Ward & Hughes* (designed by *T.F. Curtis*) and displays good colour, with a nice attention to detail. Christ in Glory with his disciples, and the Crucifixion panel below is flanked by figures of the *Blessed Virgin* and *St John*. Other panels have a variety of figures, including Noah (not seen in glass anywhere else in Suffolk), *St Cecilia* and *St*

John the Baptist. The *Annunciation* window in the s. aisle is a typical *Kempe* design. All Saints has a ring of six bells with a 10 cwt. tenor.

Hopton, St Margaret (D3): The ruins of the medieval St Margaret's stand in the centre of the village, but when it was destroyed by fire in the 1860s, a site for the new church was chosen alongside the Great Yarmouth-Lowestoft road. The architect was *S.S. Teulon*, one of the 'rogue architects' of the age, and he chose a cruciform plan, and a squat central tower with an octagonal top and large bell openings. A round stair turret with conical top projects on the s.e. corner, and there are short *transepts*. The high, steep roof of the *nave* has wide eaves that rest on massive stone cantilevers, and there is a *sexfoil* window above the two tall *lancets* in the w. wall. The side windows are set within larger *carstone* blind arches, and the layout varies strangely between n. and s. (this may be because a n. *aisle* was planned but not built). The short *chancel* has a three-*light* e. window, and there is *plate tracery* throughout. The *knapped* flint of the walls is typical high quality work of the mid-C19. An octagonal meeting room in blue brick has been added recently on the n. side of the chancel.

Entry is via a s. porch, and the interior is bright and cheerful. The *font* is a period oddity, a deep sexfoil bowl resting on coloured marble shafts. Teulon used one of his favourite decorative devices to enliven the white brick walls – window and crossing arches patterned at random with red bricks, while the layout of the side windows varies as it does outside. A charity board of 1835 was moved from the old church and is now placed on the n. wall. On Sundays the parson was to give bread to 'such of the poor as he shall think most deserving objects of Charity' – a kind thought trapped in a chilling phrase. A window opposite has glass of 1981 by Paul Quail (whose work may also be seen at Somerleyton, Sweffling, and Walton St Mary). It illustrates a theme from Psalm 104: 'He sendeth the springs into the rivers: which run among the hills. All beasts of the field drink thereof' – a goat and a badger beside a stream and standing corn in one half, and a wherry with bracken fronds and fruit in the other. The n. transept houses the organ in a rather jolly case whose panelling and lattice work is decorated with gilt and stencil patterns. The s. transept is now a chapel dedicated to Mother Julian, the C14 Norwich mystic. The stone lectern has a standing angel below the book slope and is in typical High Victorian style, while in the chancel beyond there is stained glass of high quality. The e. window dates from 1882 and is a particularly rich design by *Morris & Co*. It is their best work in Suffolk, although it is from the period when Morris himself had ceased to be active and Edward Burne-Jones was the sole designer. Nevertheless, the angels in the flanking lancets are Morris's own designs, and are set against dense, dark foliage backgrounds. The lovely Resurrection panel in the centre by Burne-Jones is full of swirling movement, with Christ rising diagonally past the angel who raises the cover of the tomb while the sleeping soldiers sprawl below. Also by Burne-Jones is the centre vignette in the tracery of souls being welcomed into Paradise; the angel on the l. is also his, but the other with the mandolin is a Morris figure. In 1903, the firm provided more glass for the chancel side windows, and these are all Burne-Jones's designs; figures of Hope and Charity on the s. side in warm colour, with a cool Faith and Humility on the n. Charity holds a babe and two infants peep round her skirts, while Humility cradles a lamb and can therefore represent the church's patron saint as well. Enemy action in World War II destroyed the glass in the *sanctuary* side windows, and only a saint's head was saved in the s. lancet. The man it commemorated had his share of violent action and was a remarkable survivor too. He was Sir Thomas Troubridge who lost his right leg and left foot at the battle of Inkerman, but soldiered valiantly on propped up against a gun carriage.

Horham, St Mary (G3): The village street bends sharply to skirt the churchyard and an attractively clipped conical yew complements the handsome early-C16 tower when seen from the w. The tower (well-restored in 1984) is particularly impressive from this side, beautifully proportioned, with diagonal buttresses that have four *set-offs*, and two prominent *string courses*. The *flushwork base course* is badly mutilated to the n. and w. The w. doorway has slim attached shafts, fine moulding in the arch, and *spandrels* carved with the *Sacred monogram* and an 'M' for the dedication. The doors themselves are original, and the wear on the r.-hand side of the step shows that the entrance was heavily used for years. There are pairs of bell openings on three sides but to the s., a substantial stair turret rises to the top, leaving room only for a single, wider window. Note that the flushwork on the buttresses is doubled at that level and that there are flushwork panels worked with

emblems set below the windows. The most elaborate decoration is reserved for the battlements as if in celebration of the tower's completion, and although much of the heraldry is unidentified, with binoculars one can recognise the diamond-shaped buckles of the Jernegan family, the three boars' heads of the Borretts, crowned 'M's, and the Sacred monogram. Although the *nave* was obviously heightened, it still looks low in relation to the tower, and on the n. side is the first indication of the church's true age. The blocked n. doorway is *Norman*, with a simple roll moulding resting on shafts which have volute *capitals*. The nave walls are plastered and the late-C14 square-headed windows have simple *Decorated tracery*. By the mid-C19 the church was in a poor state and there was a full-scale restoration. The architect was Augustus Frere and in 1879-81 he virtually rebuilt the *chancel* and gave it an adventurous e. window which has three *cinquefoils* within a circle in the head. The side windows were reused, together with the *priest's door*, and above it is an interesting example of a *scratch dial*. It is incised on a square slab and the double rim is a complete circle with Roman numerals cut in the lower half. The small brick porch is probably C18 but within there is another Norman doorway, this time rather more elaborate, as befits the main entrance. There are pairs of columns with capitals matching those on the n. doorway, but here the roll moulding in the arch is joined by an outer double chevron.

The interior is attractively homely under a plastered ceiling, and the sturdy tower arch is completely panelled in. This is unusual and may have been done to reduce the draughts before the church was restored. There is a particularly interesting graffito about 6ft. up on the n. side: 'Be it knowne unto all ringers which doe assemble to this place [must] bestow somthing on the sixton'. John Darbie of Ipswich cast two of the bells in 1663 and he or an assistant added three trebles in 1672/3 making it the oldest ring of eight. The bells were restored and re-hung in 1990 and the event was commemorated by a massive oak roundel carved by Jane Quail on the nave wall. There are good examples of *consecration crosses* on either side of the tower arch – incised discoid crosses within painted circles. The C19 *Decalogue* boards on the n. wall are in good condition, and the substantial buff-coloured C15 *font* has squat, smiling lions around the shaft. Four of the bowl panels are carved with lions whose tails curl between their legs and up over their backs, and the remainder have angels holding shields. *William Dowsing* was here in August 1644, and as he specifically mentions a *Trinity* emblem that he defaced on the font, he was no doubt responsible for the rest of the damage. The contemporary spirelet cover has well-carved *crockets* on the ribs which themselves retain some colour, and the excellent *finial* still has the ring which shows that there was once a counterbalance and chain to raise it. In 1963 the remains of the church's ancient glass were rearranged in the s.e. window of the nave. The top shield in the l.-hand light is that of the Black Prince (although a lion in a roundel has been substituted for one quarter of it), and the shield below is Edward III's (with a fleur-de-lys inserted where the leopards of England should be); at the bottom is the shield of the De Veres. The Warenne shield is in the centre of the other light, with the arms of Ufford below it. Other C14 and C15 fragments include an errant leg and foot bereft of body in the l.-hand edging. *Rood* stairs lie in the n. wall and although there is now only a low C19 *screen*, the beam above it is likely to have been the original *rood beam*. The nave benches are an extraordinary mixture. At the w. end there are stubby C15 bench ends with *paterae* carved on the chamfers and *poppyheads* (some are good copies); C16 *linen-fold* panels have been inserted sideways in the backs of later benches, and there are more farther e. Although much of the main range is C19, the benches stand on the old sills that raised them above the brick floor and left room for straw covering. Quite the most intriguing item is to be found under the 4th bench from the e. end on the s. side. It is a hand-carved wooden trough which is held by a dowel so that it may be swung out. It is 14in. long, 2in. deep, and 3in. wide, with a hole drilled in the bottom. It looks a good deal older than the seat to which it is attached, and although it has been called a snuff box, I think it may once have housed long church-warden's tobacco pipes. The pulpit of 1631 is a fine piece – although much altered. The blind-arched panels have delicate strap-work and there are complementary carved panels below the canted book ledge. The door latch is a good original but the bas-relief lamb is a later addition and the base is modern. Its backboard now stands on the floor by the modern lectern and the centre panel contains a boldly carved and dated shield. Although it is tempting to describe the other panel of C17 woodwork that lies between pulpit and backboard as part of a two-decker arrangement, I think it came from another source.

A recently acquired *Royal Arms* in stained glass hangs as a panel inside the chancel n. window. The arms are Stuart, set within an oval, and although the crest and helm are missing, the painting is good. The glass in the *sanctuary* side windows is by *Ward & Hughes* and shows all the defects of the firm's early work, although the arrangement of the figures on the s. side is interesting. Christ's head in the Ascension scene probably weathered badly and was replaced. The *sanctuary* has two remarkable chairs, the backs of which belong to the *Renaissance* period, with portrait roundels. The rest is a strange amalgam, with demi-figures in heavy wigs holding lambs at the front of the arms on the n. side, while the s. side chair has naked male and female supporters holding a 'W' and an 'H'. Twisted scrolls terminating in acorns frame the backs and are C19 work (like the acorns on the font cover). There is a typical example of an early-C17 chest in the corner of the sanctuary, and a late-C14 piscina with arches that do not match. The simple C17 *altar* table has turned legs and plain stretchers; its beautiful frontal was embroidered by a retired priest, John Cowgill, who had only one arm; more of his work is to be seen at Stradbroke. The church has a fine C14 chest which is 7ft. long, totally sheathed and banded in iron, and has six locks.

Horham may well be the only church that has a couple of beehives in the churchyard – rather a nice idea, and if it helps the funds so much the better. It makes a change from sheep.

Horringer, St Leonard (C4): The church lies by the main entrance to Ickworth Park, in a very attractive setting on the village green. The top of the tower was rebuilt in 1703, and in 1818 the scale of rebuilding was such that the *Bury and Norwich Post* reported that 'nothing remains of the former edifice but the plain masonry of the walls'. A n. *aisle* with organ chamber and *vestry* was added in 1845, the *chancel* was virtually rebuilt in 1867 and most of the fittings replaced in 1883. The tower and battlements were replaced again, and this time very handsomely, in the early C20 and so was the *porch*. All of this adds up to a C14 building in which almost everything has been replaced, largely in the style of the original. What looks at first sight to be a s. aisle is in fact the C15 Horsecroft chapel; built on to the e. side of the porch, it was never a *chantry* apparently but was always associated with the hamlet of Horsecroft and particularly with the Lucas family. The outside of the church is attractive, with weathervanes on the tower pinnacles and extensive *flushwork* on porch and battlements. The w. window is unrestored *Perpendicular* and the chancel e. window, with its good *Decorated tracery*, was carefully repaired rather than replaced. There is a *stoup* to the r. of the entrance door and just inside hangs a competent late-C19 copy of the *Pietà* by Francesco Francia.

The *capitals* of the tower arch are *castellated* and carved with *fleurons*, and it is filled with a glazed screen in oak, with an elongated *lancet* motif. Beyond it is a good ground floor ring of eight with a 9 cwt. tenor. The heavy octagonal C13 *font* has repainted shields on the bowl: the abbey of Bury and the families of Brooke, Gipps, Jermyn and Lucas. The retractable cover in C17 style is hung on a counterbalance. Not far away on the w. wall of the n. aisle the C18 epitaph for Valentine Munbee says that 'he was a person of great good sense' – a comforting thought. The tablet is by Thomas Singleton who, incidentally, carved the reliefs on the outside of Bury Town Hall. Before the aisle was built Dame Elizabeth Gipps' memorial was on the n. wall and her husband lay below her. He was knighted by Charles II and died in 1681, she in 1715, and their stones were transferred first to the chancel and then to the aisle w. wall. His crest has been nearly worn away by passing feet but her arms are still sharply cut and displayed in the manner of a *hatchment*. The entry to the s. chapel is through funny little swing gates and the low screen incorporates some medieval tracery that may have come from the old *rood screen* or loft. Within the chapel there is a tablet for John Crooke who died in 1653 – wilful lettering and amateurish cherub heads, with a skull below. *Clayton & Bell* provided the glass in the s. chapel window – a *Deposition* scene and the *Three Marys* at the tomb, all in fairly virulent colour. The e. window glass of 1991 is by Michael Wiley and signed with his fish symbol. Below the text: 'The earth is the Lord's and fullness thereof'. It is a simplistic country scene, rather overpowered by the rays of the sun in shades of blue. As part of the 1880s work, the *nave* roof was stripped to reveal the original single-braced roof. The capital on the s. side of the wide chancel arch is notched where the rood screen once fitted and there are marks to show that a *tympanum* filled the space above. A hook remains in the apex of the arch and this may have been used to secure the rood itself or a *Lenten veil* over it. Beyond is a C19 waggon roof and, on the n. side, the eccentric 1860s two-bay *arcade*. The C14 entrance to the vestry has a nicely 'gothick' early-C19 door. The glass in the e.

window is by J.E. Nuttgens of High Wycombe, installed in 1946 – elongated figures of *SS Etheldreda, Leonard, Edmund* and the *Blessed Virgin* taking up the lower two-thirds, with dull blue borders for the rest of the lights and the tracery, relieved only by deep red symbols at the top. (Another of Nuttgens' windows can be seen at Kedington.) There is very little *Art Nouveau* church furniture about and the prayer desk that stands in the chancel is a rare item. The beaten metal side panels, with their characteristic shape and decoration, are lettered 'Christ Church Chester 1900' and 'Laborare et orare'; there are metal caps to the uprights and a folding kneeler – in all, a thoughtful snippet of design evocative of the period.

Hoxne, St Peter and St Paul (F3): On the evidence of place names, some would have us believe that St Edmund was martyred at Hellesdon in Norfolk, but the tradition dating from the early Middle Ages is that he met his death here at the hands of the Danes in 870. The oak against which it is claimed he was pierced by arrows finally succumbed in 1848 and some of the timber was used in the church. Recently, however, it has been suggested that, because there is a field called 'Hellesden' in the parish of Bradfield St Clare, he was martyred there. Legend has it that he was buried 'nearby' at 'Sutton', and Sutton Hall is not far off. The place of his burial at the Abbey of St Edmundsbury is only five miles away which adds some weight to the theory. A grassy walk leads from the ample *lych-gate* past weeping willow and spreading cedar to the s. *porch* and the eye is drawn inexorably to the handsome tower which, with the porch, was built in the mid-C15 by the De La Pole family. It has a delicate *base course* of foiled shields and a sturdy octagonal turret on the s. face rises above the stepped battlements. The w. door has *Tudor Roses* in the *spandrels*, small *headstops*, and shields, mitres and crowns decorate the mouldings. The pretty niches flanking the w. window are canopied, with minute heads at the end of the *cusps*, and they contain modern figures of the church's patron saints. The *put-log holes* used by the builders are outlined in brick and there are generous three-*light* bell openings.

The long *nave* is tall, with elongated *Perpendicular* windows, and just above the w. wall of the porch you will see the *quoins* that marked the end of the building before the tower was added. The n. doorway is excellent small-scale work, with shields and *paterae* in the moulding and a delightful pair of *headstops*. The *aisle* buttresses on that side were renewed in brick at some stage and a brick parapet takes a curving line along the top. The 1470s Lady chapel at the e. end is taller, and the *chancel* was largely rebuilt in 1880, with a small *vestry* set endwise against it on the n. side. This was the work of *Ewan Christian* for the Church Commissioners. A C19 embellishment was the male saint placed in a niche over the *priest's door*. The s. doorway has good king and queen headstops that have been partially re-cut, and just inside is a C13 grave slab in the floor. The nave was restored in the 1880s under the direction of J.K. Colling, who had worked at Eye, and he designed the majority of the fittings. The low-pitched roof has decayed *tie-beams* and two more were inserted later at a lower level at the e. end. The *wall plate* is now coved on the n. side only. There is a low, late-C13 *arcade* of six bays separating nave from aisle and the westernmost *hood mould* comes down to an angel bearing a shield – possibly added when the nave was extended to meet the tower. There are partially blocked *clerestory windows* on that side only. Like the *Evangelistic symbols*, the angels in the bowl of the C15 *font* have had their heads chopped away, but the heraldic shields are of more than usual interest. On the e. face are the arms of Bishop Lyhart of Norwich. He had been chaplain to William De La Pole, Duke of Suffolk, and died at his palace at Hoxne on Whitsunday 1472. The arms on the s. side are those of John De La Pole, 2nd Duke of Norfolk, who married Elizabeth Plantagenet, the sister of Edward IV and Richard III. That was in 1460 and so the font must have been installed between then and the bishop's death – a much more accurate dating than is normally possible. Seated monks and headless figures support the shaft, and the cover dates from 1879. Before moving on, note the *consecration cross* behind the font.

The wall above the arcade once displayed a most interesting range of early-C15 wall paintings but, sadly, very little can be distinguished now. However, we know what they were, and there are some things which can still be identified (a bright day and binoculars are the ideal combination). Starting from the w. end, in the traditional place opposite the main door, is *St Christopher*, recognised by his massive staff. Then we come to the tree whose fruit are the *Seven Deadly Sins*. At the bottom, the face and tail of one of a pair of devils are clear and also the saw he is using to fell the tree. The sin of envy is top l., sloth is bottom r., and lust is just above it. The dragon on that side and traces of

the red and green background can be seen. The series was balanced by the *Seven Works of Mercy* alongside in a series of panels with inscribed scrolls. There are outlines of the first six figures ministering (in order) to the naked, hungry, thirsty, imprisoned, sick, and the dead, but the end of the sequence was overlaid by an C18 memorial. The final tableau was a *Doom* of the sort more often found over a chancel arch. Only the arc of heaven remains and two massive *tie-beams* secured by wooden pins emerge just to confuse things. The n. aisle houses an excellent and varied exhibition illustrating the history of church and village. At the w. end is a huge late-C14 parish chest, 8ft. long and over 2ft. wide; heavily banded, it has securing bars as well as six hasps. A group of bench ends has been reused at the e. end of the aisle and the mutilated carving at the w. end of the range is the wolf guarding St Edmund's head, the only direct reference to the saint now to be found in the church. On the e. wall of the n. aisle chapel is the imposing memorial of Thomas Maynard who died in 1742. Its backing obelisk towers up nearly 18ft. It is one of two important monuments for the Maynard family by Charles Stanley (the other is at Little Easton in Essex and is even grander). Stanley's talents embraced stucco ceilings, chimney pieces, and even china, and here we have a life-size figure in complete Roman dress down to the sandals; he rests one arm on an urn and holds a book in his right hand. There is an exquisite bas-relief miniature of women and children on the pedestal of the urn and the front of the chest has a beautifully cut Latin epitaph.

The steps that led to the *rood loft* are exposed below the arch leading to the n. chapel and there is a statue niche behind the pulpit. Close by the lectern there are two *brass* shields and inscriptions for Thomas Thruston (1606) and John Thruston (1613); one for another John Thruston (1640) is now on the wall by the door. In the chancel you will find what is the only listed work in Suffolk by Sir Francis Chantrey, but it is not signed and it is not typical – a plain tablet and elementary sarcophagus shape against a black background as a memorial for Sir Thomas Heselrige who died in 1817. The *reredos* and *altar* date from 1907 and the church's *mensa* has been restored to its rightful place. The s. chancel windows have stiffly conventional figures of the *Evangelists* which were inserted when the chancel was restored and could possibly be the work of *Heaton, Butler & Bayne*. The e. window glass of 1853 is by Edward Baillie. There are four shapes containing scenes in blatant and sickly colour, and the rest is taken up with texts set against yellow-green patterned quarries; not very nice. It is a relief to look again at the centre nave window – a rich design of Christ subduing the waves, again, possibly by Heaton, Butler & Bayne. The window to the e. of it with the two patron saints set against deep blue, and the remainder of the space taken up by patterned quarries, may be more of Baillie's work. Nearer the door is the spiky Victorian Gothic memorial to Gen. Sir Edward Kerrison; he commanded the 7th Hussars at Waterloo and lived to remember that famous day for nigh on forty years. Hoxne's tower has a ring of five bells with a 13 cwt. tenor, but are not able to be rung at the present time.

Hundon, All Saints (B6): Approached by a little lane from the village street, the church stands in a spacious churchyard where there are many excellent C18 headstones, some carved by members of the Soane family. It was a mainly *Perpendicular* building but one Sunday evening in February 1914 it was gutted by fire, leaving little more than a charred skeleton. It was rebuilt over the next two years to the designs of Detmar Blow and Ferdinand Billeray in a conservative style that produced no surprises and largely followed the original. There is a little wooden bellcote complete with weathercock on top of the stair turret and the slopes of the buttresses to s. and w. have fine, bold carvings of grotesques which are similar to those at Great Bardley. The *nave* parapet on the s. side is a very decorative frieze of pierced *quatrefoils* with feathered *cusps* on top, reminiscent of Woolpit *porch*. There are three-*light* windows in the *aisles* dating from about 1300 and the w. windows have *Decorated tracery*. The large s. porch is very weathered and the late-C14 inner doorway has shields in the mouldings and *headstops* that do not match. There are tall niches with *crocketted* canopies each side and a band of quatrefoils along the top. It has an upper room reached by a stair whose doorway is just inside to the r. and on the window sill to the l. of the entrance stands the old gable cross – a rare opportunity to examine one at close quarters. The *font* nearby is a modern drum octagon and beyond it on the w. window sill there are remnants of what must have been a fine C13 tomb.

The interior is wide and open, with chairs used judiciously, but all the walls and *arcades* are a sad shade of grey. Two of the old *roof corbels* remain on the s. side below the *clerestory* and

there are four more in the n. aisle. The *Royal Arms* of George III painted on board hang here and on the window sill at the w. end stands a large wheatsheaf *finial* which is all that remains of a 'noble pyramid of marble' that used to be outside by the porch. It was a monument to Mrs Arethusa Vernon who died in 1728 but it became unsafe and was demolished in 1983. At the e. end of the n. aisle is the doorway to the old *rood loft* stair which emerged on the *chancel* side, and there is a *squint* through the outer wall. Close by, a small C14 *piscina* is tucked in behind the end of the rebuilt arcade, indicating that there was a medieval *altar* here. The new chancel arch is wide and the chancel has no furnishings or stalls. The *High altar* is a solid block that matches the width of the five-*light* e. window. The Decorated piscina has survived in very battered state, having had a new drain inserted (which does not happen very often). The s. chapel is at a lower level and approached through an arch from the chancel. The dark, traceried panels in the dado were in the vicarage at the time of the fire and thus were saved. A tablet on the n. wall of the chancel commemorates vicar John Norfolk who died in 1749. Below, a Latin epitaph, there are the letters: 'A.O.L.M. F.F.P.M.R.S.' which must surely be the longest acronym on record. It has been suggested that it stands for 'Adami olim lapsu mortales facti fuimus, post mortem resurrecti sumus' (By Adam's fall we became mortal, by the resurrection we live).

Hunston, St Michael (D4): This little church hides itself away, with a pond and some farm buildings for company at the end of a rough track. Its origins are *Norman*, and it is strange that, like nearby Pakenham, and despite its smallness, it has a full blown s. *transept*. There was a restoration in the 1880s and the three-stepped *lancets* in the transept s. wall were renewed then and match the main e. window. The *chancel* was given six new windows in all. Walking round, a relic of the Norman building can be seen at ground level by the n.e. corner buttress of the chancel – a very small segment of an arch, with pellet and cable ornament, that was reused to fill a space. There is a *priest's door* on that side, in company with two C13 lancets, and there is a door on the n. side of the *nave*. The unbuttressed tower has *Decorated* bell openings to the n. and s. and a matching w. window, although money was left as late as 1472 for its building. It houses a ground floor ring of five bells with a 7 cwt. tenor. Although entry is through a C19 openwork wooden *porch,* the C13 transept has its own w. door, with single shafts and renewed arch mouldings.

Within, there is a small C13 *font,* a plain drum standing on C19 columns. Beyond it, the *tester* belonging to a small *Jacobean* pulpit leans against the wall next to an attractive little chest that has both carved and panelled strapwork. On the wall above are three *hatchments*: to the r., for Maria Catherine Heigham who died in 1837; in the centre, for the Revd. Henry Heigham; to the l., for his wife Elizabeth. You will find a memorial for this couple on the s. wall of the *sanctuary.* The nave roof is a rustic form of *hammerbeam* and *arch-braced* construction and the chancel has a C19 copy of it. The blocked lancet in the s. wall was used to house a marble slab setting out the terms of an C18 village educational charity which, among other things, was to pay for 'a mistress for teaching three poor little girls to read, knit, spin and sew'. *Coade stone* was a popular late-C18 and early-C19 artificial substitute for marble and there is a good, late example of its use on the n. wall – a monument for Capt. George Heigham of the Royal Irish Dragoons (1854), and his son, Maj. George Heigham of the Royal Welsh Fusiliers, who served at Lucknow. The wide and rather shapeless arch into the transept rests on peculiar *corbels* that disappear into the walls, but between the lancets in the e. wall there is a niche with extraordinarily flamboyant decoration. The wide moulding contains large petals which rise to a centre point, like an oversize form of *dogtooth.* They vary in design and some are backed by tendrils, while the *hood mould* has little roses and two stiff-leaf forms to the r., as though the mason changed his mind or got bored. Corner *piscinas* normally jut out of an angle but the one here reverses the convention and sits in the s.e. corner, with one drain in each wall, a most unusual variation. The *trefoil* heads of the arcades have been re-cut and the r.-hand *capital* renewed. Below the lancet in the e. wall is a large *aumbrey,* and on the w. wall, a memorial for James Ellis who died in 1832. It has a small urn within the broken *pediment,* and the bold lettering marks it out as one of the better efforts of George Tovell, the Ipswich mason. The chancel arch has slim attached shafts on the outer corners and thicker, ringed shafts against the *jambs.* The *capitals* sprout very odd little leaves (rather like seedlings seeking the light), and the arch above has a thin centre groove that once held the *tympanum* behind the *rood.* The tall recess by the pulpit will have been the entry to the *rood loft*

stairs. In the chancel there is a blocked *priest's door* on the s. side with a plain round arch, and it is very curious that it lies within the embrasure of another, later arch which has a semi-circular window within the head. This has trefoil tracery with floriated *cusps,* and one wonders whether it was a tympanum originally, rather than a window. The stalls carry some attractive bench ends in good condition; on the n., two dogs (one, a collared greyhound), on the s., a monkey and a creature with long, curved horns. This is likely to be a very rare representation of the *ibex.* The two lancets on the n. side are filled with glass by *Heaton, Butler & Bayne* – one as a war memorial, with an angel bearing the palm of victory, and the other the *Blessed Virgin* and Child. Pause as you leave by the s.e. corner of the transept to read the 1846 epitaph of John Juggins which begins:

> It was so suddenly I fell,
> My neighbours started at my knell,
> Amazed that I should be no more,
> The man they'd seen the day before . . .

Huntingfield, St Mary (H3): There is *flushwork* on the bases and first stage of the angle buttresses of the C15 tower, and in walking round you will see that all the windows of the n. *aisle* are C19 replacements. It was a time of great activity here, with a restoration under the direction of J.P. St Aubyn in the late 1850s, and another between 1896 and 1906. In the C18, a chapel in red brick had been added on the n. side of the *chancel* for the Vanneck family, and two jolly heraldic greyhounds leap from the corners of the stone parapet, with an eagle and a griffin between them. Although the chancel probably dates from as early as the C13, its windows are again Victorian, displaying intricate flamboyant *tracery* on the s. side, and there is a C15 *priest's door.* Remnants of a *scratch dial* can be traced on its r. *jamb,* so the buttress that overshadows it must have been added later. The *Perpendicular* s. aisle has a flushwork parapet and corner pinnacles, a *Tudor* e. window, and a pleasant mixture of brick and flint in its walls. The C15 s. *porch* is beautifully proportioned, and its facade is panelled overall with excellent flushwork which makes use of white flints. A lion and a saint guard the corners of its parapet, and there is a pretty niche with a turreted top and *groined* canopy above the entrance; the statue of the *Blessed Virgin* and Child was given in 1907. The *spandrels* of the arch contain *Trinity* and *Passion emblem* shields, and there are angel *stops.* The inner doorway dates from the C13, and there is a *stoup* recess to the r. which seems to have had a replacement bowl inserted.

The tall tower arch is plain except for two unusually placed shields, and within the tower there are some interesting fragments of C12 stone set in the wall which were ploughed up on Chapel Hill in the early C20. The one carved with a cross may have formed part of a grave slab, and the others could be parts of a standing cross. St Mary's ring of five bells with an 8 cwt. tenor is rung from here. The *font* is the familiar East Anglian type, in very good condition, with squat lions round the shaft and angels under the bowl. Fat *Tudor Roses*, lions, and two angels with shields are carved in the bowl panels, and the heraldry suggests that the donor was the late-C14 Michael de la Pole – his arms quarter those of Wingfield on the n. side, and the other shield has the Ufford cross linked with the Beauchamp arms. The *nave* s. *arcade* is C14, but on the other side at high level there is a C12 window that identifies the wall as the original n. wall of the *Norman* church. Openings were punched through it when the aisle was built, although the Norman-style arcade is a 19C variation. There is a *clerestory* on the s. side only, with five small windows which have been refashioned. Quite the most charming thing about Huntingfield is the brilliant decoration of the *hammerbeam* and *arch-braced* roofs. Mildred Keyworth Holland was the rector's wife, and between July 1859 and February 1860 she painted the chancel roof, going on to complete the nave roof between the autumn of 1863 and September 1866. Guided by E.L. Blackburne, an acknowledged expert on medieval decoration, she aimed to recreate the splendour of a typical C15 angel roof, and the result is extraordinarily attractive. In the nave, the projecting angels bear, alternately, heraldic banners and crowns, and there are painted figures of the *apostles* between the principal timbers, with the spaces at the w. end taken by *St Anne* on the s. and *St Margaret* on the n. Every available surface is gaily patterned, and the chancel continues the theme, except that there the roof is panelled between the arch-braces, with a flat centre section displaying pairs of kneeling angels against a blue background. The gilded demi-angels with spread wings on the hammerbeams bear shields, and above the *wall plate* there are texts, *Agnus Deis* and *Sacred monograms*. Two memorials remind us of the remarkable woman who achieved all this – the

bulky, *tabernacled* font cover, and the exuberant brass lectern. The latter has, round the centre column, three linked shafts bearing lovely little copper angels with upswept wings, and winged dragons reminiscent of Notre Dame jut out below. A C15 bench survives by the tower arch, but the main seating was installed as part of the 1850s restoration, and there are some excellent carvings on the elbows of the benches: a possible St Margaret on the s. side of the nave (w. end), *Evangelistic symbols*, a kneeling angel, and two fine heads on the front corners. In the s. aisle chapel there is a *piscina* with no drain, and above it, two strange recesses are set at high level. What were they? The arms of Wingfield and de la Pole crop up again in the e. window here, and the centre light has a most interesting fragment of C15 border which contains a hound with a bell on its collar and two hares, a combination that forms a *rebus* on the village name. The *hatchment* in the n. aisle was used at the funeral of Joshua, 2nd Baron Huntingfield in 1844, and three or four more belonging to the Vanneck family are kept in the vestry.

The Vanneck chapel is now appropriated as an organ chamber and *vestry*, and above the door there is a square *touchstone* panel within an alabaster frame, set about with four shields of arms. It commemorates Anne Bedingfield who died in 1595, and the inscription is of more than usual interest. She had married three times, and Brigett, the daughter of her second marriage to John Paston, became the wife of England's first great lawyer, Sir Edward Coke. He was obviously fond of his mother-in-law because he provided the memorial and composed the epitaph to a 'godly, wise & vertuous woman', who 'kept a bountifull house in Huntingfield Hall especially for ye poore nere fifty yeares'. The Coke's second daughter Elizabeth died in her first year, 1586, and a *brass* inscription commemorates her just in front of the chancel step. There is an *Easter sepulchre* under a broad arch in the n. wall of the *sanctuary*, and faint outlines of a painting of Christ in Majesty can still be seen in the recess, with fragments of angels' wings below. The massive slab top of the tomb chest in front carries a brass for John Paston who died in 1575 which was probably transferred from elsewhere. Below his shield of arms is an inscription in gothic script which was partly enamelled in three colours by (I think) Mrs Holland:

This earthlye couloured marble stone
  behold with weeping eyes:

Under whose cold and massie weight, John
    Paston buried lies.
A gentele man by birth and deedes, the
    second sonne to one Syr William Paston,
    worthie knight, deceased long agone.
This gentle esquier in Huntingfield, a
    widow tooke to wyfe
That hight Anne Arrowsmith, with whom
    he ledde a loving lyf,
Eleven yeres space and somewhat more, by
    whom he also had
One onlye child, a virgin myld, his aged hart
    to glad.
In youthful yeres this gentleman a gallant
    cortier was,
With rarest vertues well adorned, to
    Courtiers all a glasse.
A pencioner to princes foure, Henry
    th'eight, that roye,
To Edward King, to Mary quene, to
    Elsabethe, our joye,
Which foure he served faithfullie; the Court
    lament his end,
His countrie neighboures all bewaile the
    loss of such a friend.
To poore a present remedie, to honest men
    an ayde,
A father to the fatherles, the widowes
    playnte he mayde.
Against the hongrie travailer his doores
    were never shitt,
Against the seelie needye soule his purse
    was never knitt.
When he had lived threscore yeres and
    foure, death closed up his eyes,
He lyved well, he dyed well and buryed here
    he lyes.

Note the use of 'seelie' (holy), the origin of the
phrase 'silly Suffolk', and that only one child of
the marriage is mentioned although there was a
second daughter, Elizabeth. Rector Edmund
Stubbe was Chief Justice Coke's nephew, and
his whimsical monument is over the priest's
door; the epitaph is lettered on a convex oval set
in foliage, with an *achievement* above, and the
whole is framed by an arch made up of stacked
books with a cherub on top, all coloured and
gilt. The high quality glass in the e. window must
date from the late 1860s and is probably by *Lavers,
Barraud & Westlake*; the subsidiary figures of
the central Crucifixion are unusually grouped,
with the weeping Blessed Virgin holding *St John's*
hand and a sorrowful *St Mary Magdalene* standing
behind. The *Annunciation* takes up the l.-hand
light with the *Visitation* on the other side.

Icklingham, All Saints (B3): Standing on a
little hillock above the village street, this thatched
church escaped restoration until the late C19. It
is simply beautiful, a place of quiet homeliness
and infinite charm. Now in the care of the
Churches Conservation Trust, its future is secure.
The only remains of the original early-C12
Norman building are the w. and n. walls of the
nave, where there are two blocked slit windows,
and one can see a variation in the pebble work
above the C14 windows where the walls were
heightened at the time of the rebuilding. This
took place about 1360, when a tower and s. *aisle*
were added, followed by the *chancel*, which is
probably a little longer and higher than its
predecessor. The C15 s. *porch* was then built and
lastly, a few decades later, a window was set in
the w. wall of the nave. The C14 windows have
Decorated motifs and the head of the s. aisle e.
window is filled with a splendid web of
reticulated tracery. A line of *ball flower* ornament
runs along the top of the s. nave wall and in the
chancel wall is a *low side window*.

Entry is now by the n. door and close to it is
a fine C13 stone coffin and lid that were found
under the floor nearby. There are only a few
simple C15 benches on the *pamment* floor of
the nave and this accentuates the sense of
spaciousness. At the w. end is an early-C14 *font*
with a series of tracery designs in the bowl
panels as though from a mason's pattern book;
it stands on five shafts which were at one time
encased in rubble and plaster. The w. door is
blocked and a typical late-C19 *bier* stands in front
of it. The lovely C14 chest that belongs here has
been taken down the road to St James', leaving
its plain C16 poor relation behind. Roofs of
both nave and aisle are replacements in oak,
following the original designs; the plaiting of
the underside of the thatch was copied exactly.
By the s. door is a square *Jacobean box pew* with a
canted ledge and a simple poor box fixed to the
corner. The s. aisle must have been splendid in
its youth; there are carved stone cornices tucked
under the roof and the e. window is flanked by
two large and very ornate niches: most of the r.-
hand canopy survives, the uprights are encrusted
with coloured *paterae* and the carved beasts that
supported the statue pedestal still crouch in the
stone. The design of the opposite niche is quite
different with its panelled side shafts and the
outline of a big reversed *ogee* below. There is a
contemporary *piscina* in the corner. The stairs to
the *rood loft* were cut into the wall on the l. after
the building was finished and the base of the
late-C15 *screen* remains beyond. It has a huge sill

and a centre door was added in the C17 which has bobbin shafts in the top half. Only the outer shafts of the top of the screen survive but note the four *elevation squints* bored in the tracery panels on the s. side. The arch above still has the notches for the *rood beam* and for the *tympanum* that backed it. The octagonal C17 pulpit, on a modern base, has very crude and shallow country carving in its panels which attempts to reproduce a popular Jacobean design. Behind it are *dropped-sill sedilia*, an *aumbry*, and the vestige of an image bracket, showing that there was an *altar* here, possibly for a village *guild*. The chancel e. window had become decayed and was bricked up until the late C19 or early C20; the present one is modern. On the n. side of the *sanctuary* is a double *aumbry*, rebated for doors and slotted for shelves, and to the s., a piscina with a large *trefoil* arch and its original wooden *credence shelf*; alongside are dropped-sill sedilia. The C17 *communion rails* have unusual flat serpentine uprights. An interesting feature of the church are the medieval floor tiles covering the sanctuary and the centre of the chancel. Probably laid early in the C14, the type was once common in eastern England but few examples of this magnitude remain; they compare with those in Prior Craudon's chapel in Ely cathedral. Set as mosaic, they have a variety of designs and colours; many are decorated with pairs of tiny birds in roundels reminiscent of Picasso, and there are human faces too. The remnants of C14 glass re-set in the s. chancel and s. aisle windows were recovered by a Victorian sexton from the churchyard. The arms of John of Gaunt, father of Henry IV, are to be seen in the window nearest the altar and there is a full-length figure next to it. Two more are in the next window but the heads are not original. Similarly, the heads of the demi-figures in the window in the s. aisle look like amateur replacements.

Icklingham, St James (B3): A village with two churches, and this is the one currently in use. The tower collapsed in the C18 and was rebuilt some time before 1820, using much of the old material. There was a heavy-handed restoration in the 1860s and the outside of the building reflects this. There are large expanses of *flushwork* made up of very small squared flints, and two of them on the n. side are marked 'Joseph Needham 1865' and 'H.A. 1865', possibly the churchwardens. The panelled parapets are plain and the tower has battlements in yellow brick. The *chancel* was built in the late C13 or early C14 but the *nave* is *Perpendicular*, retaining the old windows with *Decorated tracery*. The old chancel roof line is still

visible and marks on the n. wall suggest that there was once a door and perhaps a chapel here.

Enter via the original medieval n. door to find a treasure just inside, but one which does not really belong here. It is the magnificent early-C14 chest which has sadly been taken from its true home in Icklingham, All Saints, where it could be seen to much better advantage. Beautiful scrollwork, with *trefoil* terminations, covers the sides and top; there are six wrought handles and security is ensured by three long hasps. This is probably the best example of its period anywhere in England. The old hassocks of sedge, which also belong to All Saints, have been brought here and are like those at Lakenheath and Eriswell. Nowadays they are called kneelers and are often bright examples of embroidery (you can see some in the chancel), but these are their rustic ancestors; clumps of the sedge *Carex paniculata* which were cut and brought into church, either to kneel or sit on – very comforting, no doubt, in their verdant youth but harsh and prickly now. The Perpendicular nave *arcade* matches the chancel arch and is tall for its length, with *clerestory* windows above having Decorated tracery. There was another window over the chancel arch but this was blocked up by the C19 barrel roof beyond. The tower arch was entirely redone at the restoration and the simple octagonal *font* below has *quatrefoils* in the bowl panels with varied tracery on the shaft. The n. aisle e. window is C19 but there is a niche with a *cinquefoiled* head beside it and, in the n. wall, an *aumbry* still with its original door (evidence that there was an *altar* here, as there was in the s. aisle where the *piscina* remains with square drain and cinquefoiled arch). The steps up to the old *rood loft* are in the wall between the chancel arch and the s. nave arcade and there is an image bracket to the l. The pulpit is C19. The s. chancel wall has a pair of tablets, 1844 and 1879 memorials to the rector's family, one of them signed by Jackman of Bury – plain ovals with matching urns on top. The e. window of about 1300 has slim internal shafts and the *hood mould* comes down to tiny *headstops*. The glass is uninspired work by *Heaton, Butler & Bayne* and the window to the s. has *St John* and *St James the Great* in yellow and deep red that is not much better. There is a pallid C19 stone and marble *reredos* behind the plain mid-C17 altar table which has a new top. The C13 piscina has *cusped* openings on either side of a central pillar. One of the internal walls is sharply angled and was possibly altered at the time of the restoration.

Ickworth, St Mary (C4): This church has been declared redundant and sold to the Marquis of Bristol as a family memorial; it is hoped that it will continue to be accessible. The reward for a National Trust entrance fee is a pleasant drive through the park, skirting the house and discovering the church some distance to the s.w. in a splendidly pastoral setting. A mellow brick wall and tall yews surround the churchyard and the cement rendered tower abuts the track – triple coupled *lancets* as bell openings and beasts jutting from the corners below *crocketted* pinnacles. It was built by Augustus John, Earl of Bristol, in 1778 and he partially rebuilt it and added the s. *aisle* in 1833. One of St Mary's bells was cast by Thomas Gardiner in Ipswich and he used it as a trade advertisement: 'Tho Gardiner he me did cast I'll sing his praise unto the last 1711'. The *nave* and *chancel* have been extensively repaired and restructured but the lancets in the chancel are C13, as is the e. window with its three stepped lancets and the roundel above. A slanting *squint* cut through the n. wall shows that there was once a n.e. chapel. Part of a C13 grave slab with a *Lombardic* inscription lies in the n. *porch* and one passes into a very dim interior.

There is a w. *gallery* and beyond it by the w. door lies the curved head of a *Norman* lancet carved with a series of diagonal crosses. The plain C13 octagonal *font* has a late-C17 pyramid cover topped by a gilded dove, and by the window in the n. wall is the church's showpiece, an exceptionally fine double *piscina* dating from the early years of the C14. The position is unusual because it is at the w. rather than the e. end of the *dropped-window sill* and it spans the corner of the embrasure. Its steep encrusted gables rise to crocketted pinnacles, and within them are attenuated *trefoil* arches, with ledges for a *credence shelf* behind. The church has been altered to such an extent that it may have adjoined the chancel arch that was removed in the C18. The arch of the contemporary window has *headstops*, above slim shafts with ring *capitals* and bases. The chancel arch was removed in the C18 but there would have been an *altar* here, possibly dedicated to the *Blessed Virgin*. There are some fairly startling C17 Flemish roundels set in the window, including a male martyr being boiled alive, *St Nicholas* with his three boys being saved from the pickling tub and, top r., Judith triumphantly brandishing the head of Holofernes who sits up in bed bereft and spurting blood (Judith 13:15). The late-C17 *three-decker pulpit* made use of an earlier pulpit and the stair has finely turned *balusters* which match

the *communion rails*. In the chancel there are more C17 Flemish roundels, including one in a s. window of horrifying creatures straight out of the paintings of Hieronymous Bosch. The roundels are likely to have come from the same source as the much more extensive collection at Nowton and sacred mingles with secular (another roundel in the chancel illustrates the Trojan Horse). To the r. of the e. window is a tall, late-C14 or early-C15 figure of the archangel *Gabriel*, plainly outlined in reddish brown. It was uncovered in a 1911 restoration and the incomplete canopy was carefully copied and repeated. Strangely, there was no trace of an *Annunciation* scroll nor of the figure of the Virgin on the other side of the window as one would have expected. Below, the early-C14 piscina lies within a *cinquefoiled* arch with just the hint of an *ogee* shape. The good 1907 glass in the e. window by A.K. Nicholson is a memorial to the 3rd marquis from his Suffolk friends and takes the form of a *Jesse tree* spread across the three *lights*, with the Virgin and Child in the roundel above. The Hervey family has been at Ickworth since the C16 and, naturally, the evidence in *ledger-stones* and tablets is all around although, and this is a surprise, there are no monuments of distinction. The s. aisle turns out to be a family pew at high level, approached by flights of stairs at each end and boasting a separate cloakroom. There are cushioned high-backed settles with 1830s Gothick panelling at their backs and on the rear wall a marble tablet lists the burials in the vault from 1779 to 1960, including George III's unfavourite prelate, the mitred earl (whose body was shipped home from Italy in a packing case labelled as an antique statue to fool the sailors who would not have kept company with a corpse). A dull grey slab on the n. wall is all that is here to remind you of the beautiful Mary, Lady Hervey, once the toast of Pope, Gay and Voltaire. She died in 1768 and her epitaph is credited to Horace Walpole:

A while, O linger, Sacred Shade
Till every Solemn due be paid . . .

And so it goes on for nine whole verses!

Iken, St Botolph (I5): A village of houses scattered haphazardly, and the church stands at the dead end of a lane, on a bluff above the River Alde's Long Reach. There is no hint of this from the landward side until one skirts the tower to be suddenly confronted by a lovely vista of the broad estuary. The village is now confidently identified as Icanhoe and the church's patron saint became the abbot of the monastery founded here in 654. In 1977 the original timber-framed building underlying the existing building was excavated. In 1968, sparks from a churchyard bonfire caught the thatched roof of the nave and gutted it, leaving the tower, *porch* and *chancel* more or less intact. Now, the *nave* has been re-roofed, the tower restored, and the *chancel* serves as the parish church until the whole can be renewed. The C15 tower has *flushwork* in its *base course*, angled buttresses, and stepped battlements; above the w. door, the *Perpendicular* three-*light* window has stepped *transoms*, and a stair turret goes as far as the belfry on the s. wall. It houses a fine ring of five bells with an 8 cwt. tenor, cast by Thomas Bullisdon in the early 1500s.

The fire left the walls of the nave badly damaged but the windows have been reglazed. A n. door of about 1300 is blocked, and further along on that side, a brick patch identifies the site of the *rood stair* within. The chancel was entirely rebuilt in the early 1860s in *Decorated* style and given a handsome e. window with *reticulated tracery*. Most restorers of the day chose flint for Suffolk churches, but this is grey Kentish ragstone which must always have married uneasily with the rest of the building. The broad C15 porch retains its *flushwork* panels up to the head of the outer arch, with a brick gable above, and a *scratch dial* can be found on each side of the entrance.

Following the fire, the chancel was partitioned off so that it could be used separately, and by 1990 the nave had been fitted with a boarded waggon roof under its new thatch, although little else had been restored at that stage, and the C15 *font* was no longer there. The rood stair in the n. wall has been partially opened, and the remains of a wide cusped niche features in the wall to the r. of the chancel arch. The chancel is neat and takes on a greenish tinge from the s. *sanctuary* window, its quarries painted with *Sacred monograms*. There is a small replica *piscina* in the corner, and a *credence shelf* rests on an angel *corbel* on the n. wall. The roof is boldly outlined in deep red and black, and its *arch-braces* rest on riotous foliage *corbels*. The risers of the triple sanctuary steps are attractively lettered with a sacramental text, but the centre carpet effectively confuses the message. The wide bas-relief *reredos* of the Last Supper is flanked by attractive panelling in oak – small carvings of farm animals and wildfowl. In the window above,

the glass was supplied by *Powells*, and the quarries sport fleur-de-lys and oak leaves within borders of vine. *Brasses* had a revival in the C19, and there are two late examples on the walls which are interesting variations on the same theme. Ironically, the church had an alms dish made of oak and bell metal saved from the famous York Minster fire of the 1840s. Let us hope that it survived its second ordeal.

Ilketshall St Andrew, St Andrew (H2): This member of the group of villages known as 'The Saints' is no more than a sparse scattering of houses and farms across pleasant countryside, with commons dotted here and there. There is nothing specific to suggest that the round tower is *Saxon* rather than *Norman* but, like others in the area, it may date from before the Conquest. It has been smoothly repointed and has a small *Decorated* w. window. The C14 octagonal top is unusually deep, with a blank lower stage and *flushwork* window shapes between the bell openings. Walking round, you will find a blocked plain Norman n. doorway and a small *lancet* of the same period a little further along. Most of the other windows are *Perpendicular*, some of them renewed – probably as part of an 1880s restoration. The patch of brickwork on the n. side of the *nave* may mark the site of the stair which led to the old *rood loft*. The *chancel* dates from the early C14, and it is interesting that the builders found some fragments of carving from the Norman building and used them as *quoins* at the base of the chancel s. buttress. The early *Tudor porch* in brick and flint is solidly handsome, and the niche above the entrance houses a modern statue of the church's patron saint. There are C19 stained glass shields in the side windows: on the w., St Andrew's cross and the arms of the Tilney family; on the e., the three mitres of the Norwich diocese (Suffolk was once part of it) and the arms of the Ilketshall family. There is a scooped-out *stoup* recess in the corner, and the Norman doorway has a bold *chevron* moulding in the arch above single *jamb* shafts. A pilgrim cross is cut on the r.-hand jamb, and the medieval door still has its closing ring, with a drawbar socket just inside.

In 2001, having raised a great deal of money, the parish set about the redecoration of the church and, in doing so, uncovered an important series of wall paintings. Although extensive areas had been lost, what remained warranted conservation, and this was carried out in 2005. Supported by a generous grant from the Heritage Lottery Fund, layers of limewash were removed and the original paintwork stablised. The paintings are only a fraction of the decorative scheme that would have existed before the *Reformation*. The design on the n. wall shows a large church or cathedral – a double-arched *nave* with Norman *cushion capitals*, and a smaller chancel in which there is an *altar* bearing a *chalice* and *paten*. At the w. end there are fragments of a large tower with a pointed tiled roof. On the s. wall the easternmost bay has fragments of large arcades in which angels with open wings rest on a dark background. Only the female figure on the far r. has survived intact. She is dressed in a plain robe painted in vermilion and carbon black, with an indigo cloak decorated with clusters of three white dots, and she wears a wimple and a crown. Below the arcades is a band of what looks like drapery on which may be found a series of extremely curious demons – no other example of this type is known to exist in England. To the r. of the window is a unique depiction of a *Wheel of Fortune*. On the l. a figure in an ornate robe is being pulled upwards, and on top of the wheel are the remains of a seated figure which, before C15 alterations, would have been a crowned king. The basic style and technique of the painting suggests a local artist, but because of the complexity of the iconography he was probably guided by Sir James de Ilketshall who died in 1345. A detailed analysis of the paintings is displayed at the back of the church.

Ilketshall St Andrew, St Andrew:
C14 wall painting. The wheel of fortune

The shape of the tower arch suggests late-C13 and on either side there are two very interesting shields, each set within the circle of the Garter motto. The arms are those of Thomas Howard who died in 1646, with Howard alone on the l., and the quarterings of the Howard, Brotherton, Warren, Mowbray, Fitzalan, Clun, Maltravers and Widvile families on the r. He owned property in the neighbourhood, and the shields probably graced the family pew in the C17. The church has an attractively chunky set of Charles II *Royal Arms* has been restored, along with the Garter shields. The early-C15 *font* stands on a deep base, with eight shafts around the stem, and the bowl panels are carved with shields set in *quatrefoil* roundels. The early-C17 *Holy table*, with its finely turned legs and decorated top rail, now stands on the n. side of the nave. On the s. side there is an interesting C16 bench that used to be in the chancel. The back is vigorously carved with cherubs, scrolls and other Renaissance motifs, and a centre panels carries the entwined initials 'J.E.'. It also carries the name of John Bonsey. The Norman lancet contains a nice little painting of St Andrew of about 1870, and there is an image niche below. There are two more in the s. wall opposite, one of which has had its hood mould cut away. Halfway down the nave is the church's only *brass*. It commemorates John Verdon: 'which was forsaken of the soule the 28 Day of May 1624, but expects it agayne at ye Day of the resurrec-tion'. Further e. is a beautifully lettered *ledger-stone* bearing the arms of Thomas Else who died full of years in 1705, having lost his young wife Thomasine nearly half a century before. The nave roof is *arch-braced*, with lateral braces between the *wall posts* and a *tie-beam* at the junction with the chancel. The chancel roof is good C19 work which matches the nave, and fine demi-angels perch at the base of the wall posts. The lancet in the n. wall contains a *Blessed Virgin* and Child of 1910, perhaps by *Clayton & Bell*, and opposite there are the remains of a large C14 tomb – an *ogee* arch with *finial,* and flanking pinnacles closely *crocketted* at the top. The C16 *poppyheads* of the stalls match the carved bench in the nave, and there is a simple C14 *piscina* in the *sanctuary*. In front of it, the ledger-stone for a vicar's wife who died in 1772 is headed by the phrase much quoted as a comfort by the Victorians, and used by Caroline Norton as the title for her popular poem: 'Not lost but gone before'.

St Andrew's churchyard is a happy hunting

ground for botanists, with over a hundred plants identified and meticulously listed in the porch.

Ilketshall St John, St John the Baptist (H2): A modest little church that stands aside from the Bungay-Halesworth road, and its churchyard is now designated as a wildlife sanctuary, managed under the guidance of the Suffolk Wildlife Trust. Beautifully lush in the springtime, it is a particular refuge for some of the less common wayside flowers, and there are aging Scots pine along its n. and w. borders. The thin, unbuttressed C14 tower has *Perpendicular* bell openings and w. window, and there are stepped battlements. Small boulders and flints occur as *quoins* at the n.w. corner of the *nave*, and they suggest that the church was here before the Norman Conquest. Another clue to an early date is the line of quoins that shows halfway along the n. wall of the *chancel*. It must mark the e. end of the original church, and the subsequent extension can be dated by the C13 *lancet* further along. A full-scale restoration was carried out in 1860, with re-roofing and replacement of the majority of the windows. Remains of a *stoup* in the nave n. wall outside show that there was originally an entrance there, and the Victorians inserted a high-level round window at that point; it has *trefoil tracery* and a pair of rather pensive *headstops*. The e. window has stops carved with an *Agnus Dei* and the head of the church's patron saint. Someone in the parish must have had influence in high places because (as you will see from an inscription inside) the stone for the window was the gift of 'Albert Edward, Prince of Wales, September 1861'. The *Decorated* tracery of the window nearest the porch seems to be original, and the others on that side may well be copies of their predecessors. There are a number of pleasing stones in the churchyard, and one by the e. wall of the porch calls for special mention. It was beautifully cut for John Evens in 1819 and has recently been meticulously cleaned.

The porch was built (or replaced) in 1908 and, in passing, have a look at the faint *scratch dial* on the l.-hand *jamb* of the C14 inner doorway. Nave and chancel lie under a continuous plaster ceiling, but in the chancel the timbers of a waggon roof show through. There is no chancel arch, and the division is marked by a curious line of *cusps* carved on the roof timbers, terminating in pierced roundels each side. The church has a *weeping chancel* – no doubt the result of careless setting out when it was extended. The floor of

the diminutive tower is lower than the nave, and in the wall on the s. side there is a shallow recess which, if it is a *banner stave locker*, must be one of the tallest. The *Royal Arms* of William IV are rather a nice set in which the unicorn emerges most unheraldically from behind the shield. The C15 *font* is a familiar design scaled down to match the church, with lions round the shaft and *Tudor Roses* alternating with pendant shields in the bowl panels. One of the nave n. windows contains glass of 1912 by *Jones & Willis* – a romanticised figure of *St John the Baptist* wearing a blue cloak over his more usual goat skin. There is more of this firm's work at nearby Mettingham. The small C14 *piscina* has beautifully delicate, pierced cusping in its *cinquefoiled* arch, and there are *dropped-sill sedilia* alongside. *Touchstone ledger slabs* lie in the *sanctuary* floor, and Ann Gooch's of 1679 has an engraved skull within that favourite admonition: 'Hodie mihi, cras tibi' (Today, it is I; tomorrow it will be you). There are C19 *Decalogue* boards on the e. wall, and the 1860s window glass was probably provided by *Ward & Hughes* – three indifferently painted scenes relating to the church's patron saint; the shaped panels are set within a dense, multi-coloured pattern which incorporates texts and symbols, including a rather nice fish in the tracery. As you leave, spare time to read the epitaph at your feet just inside the door. It dwells at length on the virtues of Thomas Colman who: 'under the generall decays of Nature without Sigh or groan By the will of God fell asleep Feb 18th Ano Domi 1695'.

Ilketshall St Laurence, St Laurence (H2): The Roman 'Stone Street' runs between Bungay and Halesworth and, just to one side, the church stands within the outlines of one of the legions' camps that guarded the road. The early-C15 tower has buttresses to the w., restored bell openings, and a brick and flint parapet. The rough flint *quoins* at the n.e. corner of the *nave* and the regularly coursed flints nearby both suggest an early-C12 date for the church. All the windows have been renewed in *Decorated* style, possibly as part of the 1875 restoration, and they may well repeat the form of the originals. There is a *priest's door* blocked with brick in the n. wall of the *chancel*, and the whole of the e. wall was rebuilt in brick sometime in the C19. The low buttress shape between *nave* and chancel on the s. side may be the remains of a *rood stair* turret. A small *vestry* was added outside the n. door (part of the 1840 restoration?), and the s. porch too is C19 and shelters an entrance doorway of about 1300.

The plain, whitewashed interior lies under a plastered ceiling in the nave and a boarded C19 ceiling in the chancel, with no arch or *screen* now intervening. The tower arch is simply chamfered and sets abruptly into the plain *jambs*. There is a *brass* inscription of 1613 in the tower floor for Richard Beetes, nicely engraved in gothic script. In front of it, the early-C15 *font* has alternate shafts and buttresses around the stem, with angel heads minus their noses under the bowl; the hung shields in the panels will have been painted originally, and there are shallow *paterae* in the mouldings. On the wall above are the *Royal Arms* of George II, dated 1760. They are a good set in pale colour which are worth restoring. The furniture is C19 or early-C20, and the tin *Decalogue* panels on the e. wall are likely to date from the early 1800s. There is no *piscina* now in the *sanctuary*, and the small arched recess in the n. wall of about 1300 could be an *Easter sepulchre*. It is intriguing that it is sited in what appears (from the outside) to have been a priest's door and, as there is the outline of another in the s. wall, it may be that the need for an Easter sepulchre in the traditonal place prompted the priest to make himself a new door in the other wall – to be itself blocked years later. There is a memorial on the n. wall of the sanctuary for an C18 patron of the living, and you will see as you leave that one of his late-C19 or early-C20 successors is commemorated by the thatched *lych-gate* at the roadside.

Ilketshall St Margaret, St Margaret (H2): In common with one or two other 'Saints' churches, St Margaret's spacious churchyard has been designated as a Wildlife Sanctuary, organised by the Suffolk Wildlife Trust and the Nature Conservancy. The round tower tapers slightly and, although they cannot be seen from the outside, there are blocked windows below the bell stage which suggest that the tower is *Saxon* rather than *Norman*. One of the bells within is a pre-*Reformation* casting from the London foundry of John Bird, dating from the early C15. A small w. window was added in the C14, and a strengthening beam had to be inserted halfway up at some time and secured by a large wooden peg on the n. side. The line of a slightly higher *nave* roof shows towards the e., and in walking round, note the blocked n. doorway with its C19 *trefoil* window, and the *chancel* e. window of about 1300 with very worn *headstops*. The *priest's door* in the chancel s. wall has an unusually lively *cusped* arch which has shallow decoration within the deep *label*

(probably a piece of C18 exuberance), and there is a well-defined *scratch dial* on the window *jamb* to the l. The *porch* roof has two interesting grotesque masks at the base of its *arch-braces*, and the one in the s.w. corner is pulling its mouth wide.

The hood mould of the early-C14 doorway has been cut away, and within you will see that the tower arch was re-shaped at some time. The substantial C15 *font* has lost its lions from around the shaft, but the angel heads below the bowl survive more or less intact; hung shields alternate with *Tudor Roses* and square leaf shapes in the bowl panels. Above the tower arch hang the *Royal Arms* of Anne, large and pale, painted on canvas and dated 1704. Benches, pulpit and choir stalls are all modern, and the nave roof is plastered, leaving only the medieval *arch-braces* and *wall plates* exposed. The C19 boarded chancel ceiling is painted blue and enlivened by a host of gilded stars. There is a *pamment* floor, and the late-*Stuart communion rails* have closely set *balusters* and a pair of gates. A C19 restoration probably raised the *sanctuary* floor, and the *piscina* is now low in the wall. Its multi-cusped arch has a faint *ogee* shape, with *tracery* in the *spandrels* within the label. In front of it is a good *touchstone ledger-stone* of 1689 for Thomas Hunne, with a roundel of arms. There are some fine headstones to be seen among the lush grasses of the churchyard, and w. of the tower a stylish epitaph and affecting verse commemorates Sarah Owles, buried in 1810. A minor historical footnote: Chateaubriand as an emigrée fell in love with Charlotte Ives the rector's daughter in 1795. He was, alas, already married and she later became Lady Sutton.

Ingham, St Bartholomew (C3): There was a full-scale restoration and partial rebuilding here in 1861 and the *chancel* is nearly all new work. However, the tower, built about 1455, is much as it always was – tall and handsome, with diagonal buttresses to the w. and two prominent *drip courses*. The *base course* is panelled, the w. door has king and queen *headstops*, there is a *Perpendicular* w. window and the bell openings have *Decorated tracery*. *Put-log holes* framed in red brick show up clearly, and there is a stair turret on the n. side up to the second stage. It houses a ring of five bells with a 12 cwt. tenor but the condition of the frame only allows them to be rung occasionally. The arches of the large Perpendicular-style *nave* windows feature thin red bricks and there is a blocked C14 n. doorway. On that side, the churchyard has been entirely cleared of headstones.

Entry is via the w. door and the tall and narrow inner arch of the tower has head *corbels* that appear to be C19 work. The roof of the nave has been panelled in, and there are now chairs below instead of pews. The s. *porch* has been converted into a utility room but is worth exploring because it contains medieval glass in the side windows: on the e. side, a female figure with another head added, a roundel with an 'MR' monogram for the *Blessed Virgin*, and another with the eagle, symbol of *St John*; opposite, an angel and a roundel containing an eagle clutching a harp. The C19 pulpit has sections of medieval tracery let into the panels, and behind it are the stairs to the *rood loft*. There is a substantial ledge just below the upper doorway which formed part of the rood loft floor. The chancel roof was rebuilt in 1861, using the old *arch-braces* and the *spandrels* that are laid lengthwise between them. These are finely carved with *Renaissance* motifs, including two fine grotesque birds at the e. end on the s. side, and a *pomegranate* in the centre section on the n. side. The main braces now come down to angels holding books, crowns, and scrolls. Robert Lowe was rector here for 57 years and was 91 when he died in 1727. His memorial is on the n. wall of the chancel – a veined marble tablet set between fluted *pilasters*, with a *cartouche* of arms on top and all set against a dark background. To the e. is a memorial for Edward Leedes and his wife Anna – pilasters either side of the tablet, with rather coarsely carved cherubs flanking a broken *pediment*, Leedes' arms at the top, and two skulls and crossbones at the bottom. He was the master of the grammar school at Bury and died in 1707. There are C19 *Decalogue* panels either side of the e. window and the *reredos* is probably C19 too – a low relief in gold of the Virgin and Child, with *St Elizabeth* and the baby *St John the Baptist*, and side panels containing the *Evangelistic symbols*. As you retrace your steps, note the medieval *poppyheads* applied to the chancel stalls, and a tablet on the nave n. wall by William Steggles of Bury for Lieut. Col. Martin Cocksedge of the West Suffolk Local Militia who died in 1824.

Ipswich, All Hallows (F6): This, like St Thomas's and St Andrew's, was a church built in the 1930s to cater for the town's growing population. Standing on Landseer Road, it serves the area of the Gainsborough estate and was designed by *H. Munro Cautley* in 1938. Unlike his church of St Augustine, this was an economical exercise in red brick which followed a conventional contemporary line. Under a hipped roof, the *nave* has tall windows at high level and beyond the square *transepts* there is a short chancel whose blank e. wall has a cross outlined in smaller bricks. There is a *vestry* block to the s. and a slim n.e. tower, oblong in section. There are twin porches at the w. end and in the baptistery the solid octagonal *font* has a very nice cover which is arcaded like a miniature market cross and decorated with marquetry and veneers. The red brick of the walls is warm but not strident, and severity is relieved by small blind arches below the nave windows. The flat, panelled ceiling is tricked out in blue, red, and green. The transepts lie beyond two-bay *arcades*, and a miniature font stands in front of the *altar* on the s. side. Nearby on the wall is a portrait plaque of Sir William Smith, founder of the Boys' Brigade. Screened by heavy green curtains, the n. transept Lady chapel was refurnished in 1951 and its *sanctuary* lies beyond a smaller version of the chancel arch. Cautley was fond of reproducing medieval-style *piscinas* and there is one here, complete with drain and *credence shelf*, set in the brick wall. The C19 nave benches came from Ely cathedral, but pulpit, reading desk, altar, and choir stalls are all veneered in walnut banded with burr walnut in the furniture style of the period. Even the cross that hangs below the chancel arch was made to match. The barrel roof of the *chancel* matches the nave, and the altar is backed by a plain hanging against which is set a striking cross formed from polished steel rods.

Ipswich, All Saints (F6): Consecrated in 1887, the church stands on Chevallier Street, part of the w. ring road, and the architect was Samuel Wright of Morecombe, who submitted the winning design among eighty-five entries in a competition judged by *Ewan Christian*. There is a porch at the n.w. corner but the main entrance is in the base of the s.w. tower. This takes an octagonal shape at the second stage and there is a terracotta *sound hole* to the s., under tall bell openings. Above the parapet pierced with *quatrefoils* is a distinctive concave-profiled lead spirelet. The overall style is *Perpendicular* and the tall *nave* and *aisles* lie under double-pitched roofs. At the e. end of the s. aisle and on the s. wall of the *chancel* are low-level terracotta panels of intricate tracery rather like mock sound holes. There was once a medieval church dedicated to All Saints near Handford Bridge and its dedication stone is preserved in the redundant St Nicholas. A copy was made and inserted at the base of the tower here but it is now damaged and unreadable.

The architect's brief was to provide for a congregation of 800 at £7 a seat and the interior shows how successful he was in dealing with this level of economy without sacrificing aesthetics. Red brick and terracotta en masse can be overpowering but here, with plenty of light and a spacious setting, the feeling is comfortable and very pleasant. The *arcades* are particularly effective, their terracotta *quatrefoil piers* having simple *capitals* and bases, and the chamfers of the arches are slightly ridged. The nave roof is panelled out over braced *collar beams* and *tie-beams* and there are barrel roofs in the aisles, again with tie-beams. At the w. end there is a heavy stone *font* in restrained style, but a portable version in a light oak frame stands in the n. aisle. Nearby is an organ in a stripped pine case with gaily painted pipes, but the main instrument is housed to the s. of the chancel, separated from the s. aisle by a half-arch in the form of a flying buttress. This makes a distracting background for the *altar* in the Lady chapel. Wright designed the pulpit in 1905 and its rather stiff carving in conventional style incorporates two standing figures. The chancel lies under a barrel roof with a two-bay arcade each side, the easternmost bays being blind except for narrow entrance arches to *vestry* and organ and quatrefoil *clerestory* windows. Shallow *sedilia* are set in the s. wall and Wright designed the *reredos* in 1896. A cross encircled by a text from the opening of St John's Gospel is flanked by *Evangelistic symbols* and vases of lilies and roses, with shallow *tabernacle* work and cresting; the carving was by Hatch & Sons, painted panels by Jewett, and decoration by Shrigley & Hunt – all Lancaster firms. The e. window glass by Campbell of London dates from 1947 and has Christ the King with figures of the *Blessed Virgin, St John, St Edmund,* and *St Thomas of Canterbury,* with an *Agnus Dei* in the tracery.

Ipswich, Holy Trinity (F6): The church stands on rising ground above Fore Hamlet and a line of dock cranes can be seen from the churchyard. Built in 1835, it was the first of the town's C19 churches and its indeterminate design is typical of the period. The architect was Frederick Harvey, a local man, and he chose to build a *nave* that is like many a nonconformist chapel, in plain Suffolk white bricks, with round-headed windows. To it he added a spindly tower complete with battlements. At some stage, outside staircases were built at the w. end to give access to the *gallery*, and they are boxed in and glazed in domestic fashion. In 1895 a *chancel* was added by Edward Bisshopp in matching style, although we shall see inside that he was more enterprising there. A large parish hall of 1891 stands to the s. linked to the church by a passage that would have been more comely in brick.

Do not be discouraged by the dull exterior for you will find that the inside of the church is remarkably attractive. A *font* stands in the base of the tower, with *Decalogue* boards nearby, and there are replicas of the seals used by the old Holy Trinity priory reproduced in the w. window. The broad nave lies under a flat plaster ceiling pierced with round cast-iron ventilators, and the slightly raked gallery has wings which advance on each side, supported on slim iron pillars. It is Bisshopp's shining white chancel in the style of the classical revival that lifts the interior from the mundane and makes it lively. The semi-circular chancel arch has pairs of fluted *Ionic* columns each side below rich cornices, and the design is continued on the flanks by smaller, matching arches; the *sanctuary* is panelled out in white up to a deep plaster frieze decorated with foliage. In a 1960s reorganisation the organ was moved to the s. side and the narrow chancel n. aisle became a Lady chapel, using the former *High altar* and its *reredos*. This is a 1919 painting by Leonard A. Pownall of the supper at Emmaus, and the bold profiles of the two disciples with the risen Christ are characteristic of an artist whose work included stained glass design. He was related to the vicar of the time and was chosen to carry out the splendid e. window, a memorial to those who fell in World War I. Christ in Majesty stands within a ring of angels above the Tree of Life; harpists are grouped below, and in the corners stand figures of a centurion, *St George*, a C20 soldier, sailor, and a nurse below orange and *pomegranate* trees. More angels drink from the River of the Water of Life as it flows into the distance, and around the figure of Christ there is a lovely gradation of colour from lilac through orange and cerise to gold. The only other stained glass is in a nave s. window and is not in the same class, a figure of St Paul with a roundel portrait below of a vicar who died in 1917. Nearby, however, is an excellent pulpit on a tall stem in C17 style; it has strapwork in the lower panels and Ionic columns at the angles, sheathed in *acanthus* leaves at their bases.

Ipswich, St Andrew (F6): Standing just off Britannia Road, this is one of three new churches built in Ipswich in the 1930s to cater for the growing population. It was designed by *Cautley* in 1936 as a simple hall in red brick, with a shallow *chancel*, to which a w. baptistery and entrance were added in 1970. The old *nave* is used for Sunday School and youth activities, with the chancel retained as a chapel, and the main body of the new church is a large square building under a hipped roof added to the e. end in 1990. It has become a versatile church-complex designed by St Andrew's own people, with a bright and spacious entrance hall which has several rooms opening off it. The worship centre is a square auditorium with a recess behind the altar and is bright, carpeted and comfortable, seating a congregation of 400.

Ipswich, St Augustine of Hippo (F6): This is a church with a good deal of presence and it stands on a commanding site by a roundabout on the Felixstowe road. Designed by *H. Munro Cautley*, it is his one major work, carried out in the medieval style he always favoured. The walls are plain rough cast and there are tall two-*light* windows at high level in the *nave*, with gabled buttresses between them. The *aisles* are no more than narrow passages, presenting a blank wall on the s. side, with the n. aisle masked by a low slab extension which has domestic windows. A substantial tower rises above the centre crossing and there are tall *transepts*. War damage affected the s. transept and the problem was solved by adding flying buttresses down to the ground at the corners. It has a small projecting bay to the e. whose window matches the e. window of the chancel. There you will find a stone recording the gift of the site in 1926. A baptistery projects below the w. window and entry is by way of a small porch at the s.w. corner.

It has a quietly impressive interior and it is appropriate that a building in this style should give a home to a *font* that was saved from the ruined church of St Peter at Linstead Magna. This is a typical East Anglian C15 design with four lions squatting round the shaft. Four more alternate with angels in the bowl panels who carry shields carved with a *Trinity emblem, Passion emblems*, and the cross of *St George*. Old photographs of St Peter's show that the cover was transferred as well. One of the baptistery windows has stained glass of 1961 by Hugh Easton which illustrates a brightly coloured family group with the priest at the font, a guide to contemporary costume in the years to come. More of this artist's work can be seen at Bury St Edmunds (St Peter), Elveden, and

Stowlangtoft. The walls above the low arches of the *nave arcade* are blind panelled and the roof is a handsome exercise in the medieval forms that Cautley knew so well. The *tie-beams* have braces below them which rise to demi-angels, and there are *collar beams* below the ridge. Also typical of the architect are the matching pulpit and reading desk, made interesting in this case by the narrow panels of pierced foliage below the rims. The tall arches of the crossing enclose a stone vault with bosses at the rib intersections. The organ occupies the n. transept and in the *sanctuary* there are *piscina* and *sedilia* in plain recesses. The painted and gilt *reredos* has slim tracery panels, with shallow coving above the centre section. The glass in the window above by Horace Wilkinson portrays the ascended Christ with the disciples and the *Blessed Virgin* below, with miniature angels filling the tracery. The Lady chapel altar in the s. transept matches the pulpit, and in the window above there is attractive glass, again by Wilkinson, with the Blessed Virgin flanked by St Augustine and his mother *St Monica*. At the bottom of the centre panel there is a vignette of the church's great benefactor with his mother. His devotion to her explains both the dedication and the choice of subject for the chapel window. His name was Charles Bantoft and a tablet nearby reads: 'This church has been given by an Ipswich tradesman as a thank-offering to Almighty God for the blessing of a pious and affectionate mother'.

Ipswich, St Bartholomew (F6): The church stands in Newton Road, a massive building in red brick. It was designed by Charles Spooner and mainly built between 1894 and 1900, the w. end being completed in 1907. Its vast roof slopes uninterruptedly over *nave* and *aisles* and along the sides there are pairs of two-*light* windows in the *Perpendicular* style. The seven lights of the large w. window have minimal *tracery* and below it a broad and shallow porch has a wooden figure of the patron saint between the two doors. As at the town's other great red brick church of St John the Baptist, a tower was planned but never built.

Designed for Anglo-Catholic worship, the interior is spacious and beautifully appointed. Massive stone *arcade piers* continue up across the wall surface to support *tie-beams* which carry *king posts* below the waggon roof. The aisle roofs have braced tie-beams with pierced tracery in the *spandrels*. The wall below the w. window is clad with *linen-fold* panelling painted in green and white as a backing for the attractive *font* of veined alabaster and green marble. Its tall panelled oak cover was added in 1944. The pulpit matches the font and stands on tall, shaped columns, and to the l. of the chancel arch there is a brass plaque in memory of Anna Frances Spooner, who endowed the church. Her husband's memorial to the l. bearing his shield of arms is a good example of a late Victorian *brass* and is signed 'Scott, Ipswich'. George Cobbold was the church's first vicar and served the parish for over twenty years. He died in 1915 and ten years later the chapel of the Blessed Sacrament s. of the chancel was dedicated as his memorial. Designed by *H. Munro Cautley*, a two-bay arcade in *Early English* style separates it from the chancel, and there are handsome oak benches with decorative roundels on the ends. A typical Cautley touch is the medieval-style *piscina* complete with credence shelf. The *chancel* lies under a barrel vaulted roof whose ribs and *bosses* are painted, and the rood on the beam above the entrance is a memorial to a curate who fell while serving as a chaplain in Italy in 1944. The beautifully proportioned *High altar* is backed by a rich fabric hanging designed by *Morris & Co.* It falls from the base of the rose window above whose tracery is a clever combination of two pointed ovals. There is a suite of *sedilia* in oak stands on the r., excellently carved in C15 style with angel masks on the elbows and a pierced vine trail in the canopy.

Ipswich, St Francis (F6): The church stands on Hawthorn Drive and was built in 1958 to cater for the extensive development of the Chantry estate. It was designed by Basil Hatcher and is contemporary with his church at Chelmondiston. It is a tall, gaunt building under a single, shallow-pitched roof, with large, high-level windows between broad brick *pilasters*, and pebble-dash panels below. A slim, vaguely Italianate brick tower at the n.w. corner is pierced at belfry level, and the upper section is open below a double-pitched roof. With a large church hall to the l., the foyer leads into the w. end of the *nave*, a single hall under one roof, with a shallow *sanctuary* at the e. end. Concrete beams rise from the floor and arch over to carry a softboard panelled ceiling, and between them the windows form a virtual wall of glass at high level. A door in the n. wall leads in to a chapel dedicated to the Holy Cross. This is a simple room with domestic windows and a flat ceiling – unadorned except for a colourful appliqué-work *altar* frontal, but it has that essential quality of calm. In the nave there is a jolly display of

tapestry *hassocks* and the *font* is a simple bowl set in a circular oak frame. There is no division except a step between nave and *chancel*, and there the matching pulpit and lectern have that concave board cladding which seemed to be obligatory in the 1950s. The sanctuary is narrower, and its side walls have a series of vertical concrete fins with reeded glass between them from floor to ceiling. The e. wall is blind and the brickwork is painted a dark green as a backing for a large cross in black and gold above the altar. Returning to the w. end, you will see a painting of *St Francis* over the w. door which shows him bearing the mark of the nail on his hand (one of the stigmata) which he received as the result of a vision of the crucified Christ; probably C19, the artist is unknown.

Ipswich, St Helen (F6): The church gives its name to the street and houses crowd up to the e. end, leaving only a very narrow passage round to the n. side. There has been a church here since *Norman* times but although the present building is medieval in character most of it is C19 replacement. Work was done in the 1830s when *transepts* were added, and then some twelve years later the rest of the church was practically rebuilt, apart from the tower and *porch*. In 1874 the tower was replaced and the *nave* was extended westward to the limit of the churchyard. The rather battered porch is therefore the only visible survivor of the old building. It has a very worn niche above the entrance and a restored sundial is set on the apex of the gable. There are angels in the *spandrels* of the doorway, *paterae* in the mouldings, and lion *stops* on the dripstone. The inner door has a very large medieval ring handle and there are remains of a *stoup* in the corner. The tower is built onto the w. side of the porch and becomes an octagon above the belfry; the parapet is pierced with *quatrefoils* and a short, rather bald spire rises above it. The s. wall of the nave with its *Perpendicular* windows was largely undisturbed by the rebuilding and has a simple *flushwork base course*.

Entry is now via the s. transept, and a vestibule leads into what was originally the *chancel*. At this stage one tends to feel somewhat disorientated because the interior has been completely rearranged. The chancel is now a Sunday School/activities area and entry to the nave is through folding screen doors under an organ gallery. The *altar* is now placed midway along the n. wall and chairs are ranged around to centre on it. It is flanked by the lectern and C19 *font*, and the pulpit has been relegated to the n.w. corner. One of the s. windows has stained glass of 1890 which may be by *Hardman*; a Resurrection scene spans the three *lights* and there are vignettes below of the *Annunciation*, Christ's baptism, and Gethsemane. Close by is a tablet by James Drawater, a London mason of whom little is known. It is for Richard Canning, who was minister at St Lawrence's until his death in 1775. The epitaph is set in a beige frame between *pilasters* with coloured strips; the roundel at the top has three rather nice profile heads. Farther along there is a tablet of 1726 for another Richard Canning: 'who having served his country with unexceptional courage and conduct during the wars of K.William and Q.Anne retired to this town and through the resentment of Party, founded on misreported Facts died a private Captain'. I itch to know what happened to blight his career.

Ipswich, St John the Baptist (F6): The first church on Cauldwell Hall Road was built in 1857, a small building in *Perpendicular* style that never got around to being consecrated. Grander things were in store, however, and in 1899 *Sir Arthur Blomfield* designed the massive replacement that stands alongside. In rich red brick with stone dressings, it has *aisle* roofs that slope down from a *clerestory* in which triple *lancets* are set within semi-circular arches, with single lancets at each end. There is a gabled door at the e. end of the s. aisle and originally a substantial tower was planned to rise above it but was never built. The e. window has five stepped lancets under a single *dripstone* that has curly leaf *stops*, and mature cedars flank the *chancel*. There is a *vestry* at right angles on the n. side and a utilitarian extension beyond it. A polygonal baptistery projects at the w. end and, above it, the two-*light* w. window is flanked by lancets, with a double bellcote on the gable.

The interior is spacious and attractive, a prime example of the architect's skill in achieving maximum capacity with economy, without sacrificing good looks. The six-bay *nave arcades* rest on alternate octagonal and round *piers*, and the roof is a form of *hammerbeam*, with *tie-beams* and *collars*. The shaping of the main timbers and transverse braces gives an overall impression of scalloped curves. The attractive pendent light fittings in wood are reminiscent of medieval tabernacle work. The aisle roofs are quite elaborate, with *king posts* standing on the *cross-braces* and small pendent. There is a good pulpit of 1926 in C15 style and the same quality shows in the richly carved glazed screen

that forms the entrance to the chapel at the e. end of the s. aisle. The chancel lies under a waggon roof, and the centre panels of the marble *reredos* are inlaid with mosaic in a woven lattice pattern as a background for the alpha and omega signs and the *Sacred monogram*. Above it, there is attractive glass by Shrigley & Hunt, the Lancashire firm founded in 1874 and still in business today; the ten main panels contain an Ascension scene above the baptism of Christ, with surrounding figures of the *Evangelists, St Peter*, and *St Paul*.

Ipswich, St Luke (F6): This started life as a severely utilitarian low, rectangular building on Cliff Lane in 1954. Built in red brick, with corrugated asbestos roof and domestic windows, its only concession to style was a porch which continues upwards to form a substantial bellcote. However, in the mid-1980s, an extension was added to the side and rear which has made a vital difference. One now enters via a new foyer on the l. under a pyramid roof, and beyond it is a single hall which capitalises on the awkward shape dictated by the available site. It is segmental in plan, tapering towards the e., and has a roof clad in pine with substantial *arch-braces*. There are plain oblong windows to w. and n. augmented by skylights and there is a polished wood-strip floor. To the r. of the *sanctuary* a folding screen divides the new area from the old which can thus be brought into use as occasion demands. The sanctuary steps are angled in sympathy with the overall shape, and beyond the *altar* the three *lancets* of the original building have been re-sited and backlit. This is to display the glass by Francis Stephens, a contemporary artist much influenced by Martin Travers. The figure of Christ the King raises his r.-hand in blessing, with a book in the other open at the text: 'I am the Truth, the Way and the Life'. *St Paul* and *St Luke* kneel on each side, the latter bearing an ikon and a pouch to mark his traditional roles as artist and physician. This is certainly a church which cannot be judged from the outside alone and I liked it.

Ipswich, St Margaret (F6): Standing above St Margaret's Green and backed by the grounds of Christchurch Mansion, this is undoubtedly the town's most handsome church. There was a priory of the Holy Trinity here, and as the population grew around it this church was built for them to use about the end of the C13. The approach from the s. is through a manicured churchyard attractively set out with shrubs and flowers. The face of the impressive clock shows that it was made by Moore of Ipswich in 1778, although a stone below is dated 1737. The w. door is low and wide, and the belfry stage of the early-C15 tower was elegantly rebuilt in 1871 when pairs of bell openings were inserted and the parapet decorated with *flushwork*. The early-C14 n. door is unused now and the *aisle* windows on that side have typical 'Y' tracery of about 1300. The buttresses of the C16 n. *transept* are decorated with an 'MR' for the *Blessed Virgin* and the *Tudor* portcullis badge, and the s. transept is flanked by polygonal turrets with *crocketted* pinnacles. One of these housed the *rood stairs* and it has been suggested that the other served the same purpose on the n. side but was moved later purely for structural support. If that were the need, a straightforward buttress would have been as effective and much cheaper – a doubtful story, therefore. The s. aisle windows are C19 insertions but above them is a beautiful mid-C15 *clerestory*. Its windows fill most of the wall space and are separated by buttresses which rise to pinnacles between the stepped battlements. There is a good deal of shallow ornament carved in the ashlar and merchants' marks with donors' initials appear in the window *spandrels*. The solid C15 *porch* has very worn flushwork panels, with three canopied niches above the entrance, angels in the spandrels, and the remains of lion *stops*.

In a light and attractive interior, the early-C14 *arcades* have their *capitals* nicely accentuated in red and gold. The late-C15 *double hammerbeam* roof overhead is an interesting blend of faded colour. It was panelled in the 1690s and painted with a mixture of scenes and pure decoration. There are cutout *cartouches* of arms fixed to the ends of the hammers, and tie-rods were inserted in the early C19 to combat the spread of the roof. There is pierced *tracery* above the hammerbeams and the *wall posts* are carved with figures (now minus their heads) seated below canopies. Within the tower there is an C18 or early-C19 Table of Fees for the services of the Clerk and Sexton which is worth reading. Parishioners had the free use of the *bier* at their funerals but strangers had to pay for the privilege. The w. window has fine 1870s glass by *Ward & Hughes*, with figures of Faith, Hope and Charity; the same firm provided the glass in the w. window of the n. aisle where six of the *Seven Works of Mercy* are illustrated. *William Dowsing* was here in January 1643 but he relied on the promise of a churchwarden ('a godly man') to take down between twenty and thirty

'superstitious pictures'. He was probably responsible for mutilating the angels that hold scrolls in the C15 *font* panels but the text on the one facing w. is still legible. This is a rare and most fortunate survival because it refers to a pre-*Reformation* practice which was part of the sacrament of baptism. It reads: 'Sal et saliva' and reminds us that salt was placed in the child's mouth and its nose and ears were anointed with saliva during the ceremony. There is a *sanctus-bell window* under the roof ridge, and below it is a splendid *Royal Arms* of Charles II in an elaborate cutout frame. The painting is in perspective and two cherubs peer over the dais on which the supporters stand. A large painting of the Prince of Wales' feathers dated 1660 hangs above the s. door – rather strange because there was no such person at the time. Perhaps they were to flatter the young Duke of Monmouth. A C13 tomb slab is clamped to the wall nearby and it is likely to be one of the few relics of the vanished priory of Austin canons. *Box pews* were removed from the nave in 1846 and *Henry Ringham* provided the new benches. They are typical of his solid style and have nicely varied *poppyheads*. *Hatchments* hang above the n. arcade, and from w. to e. they were for: Revd. William Fonnereau (1817), Revd. Mileson Gery Edgar (1853), Mary Anne Edgar (1835), and Mileson Edgar (1830). Halfway along the s. aisle wall is a niche which seems too low for a statue and too far away from the entrance to house a *stoup*. At the e. end there is an oblong recess that may have been a *reliquary chamber*, and nearby is the entrance to the *rood stairs*. There is another like it in the n. aisle and an opening to the side of the chancel arch, so the *screen* stretched right across the church. The area in front of the chancel arch has been newly paved in textured slate to form the *sanctuary* for a nave *altar*.

The transepts open into the *chancel* and the organ takes up the n. side. Below the s. transept window a slab reaved of its *brasses* lies within a recess which has a back of panelled tracery. This was once the Lady chapel, and in his will Sir William Roskin directed that he should be buried here in 1512 so this is likely to be his tomb. There is a *piscina* to the l. and two benches in the chapel have restored sections of a screen as backs. The chancel ceiling is panelled, with a modern coloured *celure* above the *High altar*. The C19 choir stalls have their *finials* carved as *pelicans in piety*, and there is attractive *reticulated tracery* in the n.e. window. Four more hatchments hang on the walls here; s. wall e. to w.: Thomas Neale (Col. of the Ipswich Volunteers 1839), William

Charles Fonnereau (1855), Revd. Charles William Fonnereau (1840); n. wall: Revd. Dr Claudius Fonnereau (1785). Although the tracery of the e. window is C19, the inner shafts show that it dates from the C14, and it is filled with pleasant glass of 1913 by *Jones & Willis* of Birmingham – Resurrection and Ascension scenes flanked by figures of the Blessed Virgin and St John. St Margaret's has a good ring of eight bells with a 14 cwt. tenor and four of the bells were cast by Miles Gray sen. in the early C17.

Ipswich, St Mary at Stoke (F6): The church stands on Belstead Road, just above the s. bank of the river, and commands an extensive view across the docks and town. This was a simple country church dating at least from the beginning of the C14, but the expansion of C19 Ipswich flowed over the parish and major alterations were made in consequence. The building consisted simply of tower, *nave*, and *chancel*, but in the 1860s *R.M. Phipson* carried out a restoration which added a n. *transept*. Then in 1870 there was a major rebuilding by *William Butterfield*, who added a new nave and chancel, turning the old part into a n. *aisle* and Lady chapel. The unbuttressed tower is small in scale, with a *Perpendicular* window above a restored w. door. The bell openings were altered at some stage in the C19 and brick battlements were added. Beyond the large n. transept there is a *vestry* end-on to the wall of the old chancel. The Butterfield extension has bands of *ashlar* in the walls, with *flushwork* chequer in the gables of chancel and organ chamber. The flintwork is dense, of high quality, and makes use of lots of white flint. The *porch* again has chequer in the gable, with a *traceried* circular window above the entrance. Some have found the effect of the new work harsh but it is sound and competent, and while it may not be wildly exciting it marries well with the old church.

One moves in to find a light and spacious nave and chancel which make the old n. side seem dark by comparison. The *font* is a C19 replacement and the nave roof is *arch-braced* with heavy tracery below the ridge. The principal timbers rest on stone *corbels* carved with foliage and the low, five-bay *arcade* has gilded *capitals*. Immediately to the r. of the entrance is a window with very nice glass of 1905 by *Heaton, Butler & Bayne* which has been well restored recently. It illustrates the young Christ sitting among the elders in the Temple and the overall effect is golden and glowing. There is more glass by the same firm in the next window to the e., a *Blessed Virgin* and Child flanked by the *Annunciation* and St Mary with *St John* by the cross. You will see on the list on the wall between the windows that the patronage of the church has rested with the prior and covent of Ely followed by the dean and chapter since 1300, and their arms appear at the head of the second window. In the n. aisle is a good *hammerbeam* roof which was restored under Phipson's direction by *Henry Ringham*. He replaced the figures on the hammerbeams who hold shields with Passion emblems and no doubt the demi-figures at the base of the *wall posts* as well. The roof continues through unbroken over the Lady chapel but there are no replacement figures there. Phipson's transept has been blocked off with a new door in the archway and now serves as a commodious choir vestry. Phipson also replaced the e. window with a new one in *Perpendicular* style which ignored the form of the original, and it is filled with glass of 1864 by *Ward & Hughes*. This is a very pretty, dense pattern of vine and oak foliage around shapes containing texts and a centre cross, with the *Sacred monogram*, the Chi Rho (another version, based on the Greek initials), and the alpha and omega letters at the top. It is interesting that the design was by P.L. Burrell, who later became Lord Gwydyr; his brother's memorial is on the wall to the l. There is a C14 *piscina* under a *trefoil* arch to the r. With no arch between, the chancel is almost as broad as the nave. The corbels here are carved as musical angels and those over the *sanctuary* bear the *Evangelistic symbols*. There is a recess in the n. wall under an *ogee* arch, *cusped* and *crocketted*, which seems to be original C14 work; if that is so it must have been moved from elsewhere at the rebuilding. The stone *reredos* is panelled and painted with the arms of the diocese and of Ely cathedral, together with the Evangelistic symbols. The glass in the five-light e. window is fairly routine stuff by *Clayton & Bell* of 1871 – Christ's nativity, baptism, crucifixion, resurrection, and the coming of the Holy Spirit; apostles fill the tracery and there are vignettes from the life of Christ along the base.

Ipswich, St Mary at the Elms (F6): Although busy Elm Street is now right up against the *porch*, redevelopment has opened up a view of this most attractive little church from the w. There was an C11 church on this site called St Saviour's, but when it was rebuilt in the early C14 the present dedication was adopted and a reference to the nearby trees was added to identify it among the clutch of St Marys in the town. There was probably always a tower of some sort but the present one dates from the *Tudor* period, and it has been claimed that the bricks were imported by Cardinal Wolsey from the Netherlands for use in his projected college, only to be diverted here. There are patterns of darker bricks in the walls, pairs of bell openings under wide *labels*, and stepped battlements. The polygonal buttresses have shallow *set-offs* and there is a heavy stair turret on the n. side. Within is a ring of five bells with a 9 cwt. tenor that are not ringable at present. It is worth walking round to view St Mary's Cottage just n. of the churchyard. Recently restored as a meeting room with a first-floor flat, it is the oldest occupied house in Ipswich and dates from 1467. Not long after that, the brick n. *aisle* was added to the church as a chapel, but the little *transept* to the e. of it dates from the C14 or even earlier. As at a number of the town's churches, there were extensive alterations here in the C19, and in 1883 the old *chancel* was absorbed into the *nave* and a new one added; *vestries* and an organ chamber came a little later. The *priest's door* in the s. wall led into what was then the chancel and we enter by the small C14 porch. There are three niches that once had canopies above the entrance, and within is the only remaining evidence of the earlier building. It is a *Norman* doorway, with single shafts alongside very worn *jambs*, and there is a *chevron moulding* on the outer rim of the arch. The door itself may be as old and certainly its ironwork is very early.

After the strident traffic outside the interior is beautifully peaceful and meticulously ordered. The attractive little tower screen is a World War I memorial and on the walls of the *gallery* hang *hatchments* and the *Royal Arms* of Charles II. The space below is furnished as a Lady chapel and the 1870s *font* is quite an adventurous piece by a Mr Ireland of Princes Street. The small bowl panels are carved with Gospel scenes, an *Agnus Dei*, and a *Sacred monogram*, while figures of the four *Evangelists* stand round the shaft. There is a *stoup* by the entrance which is once again put to its proper use, and the 1860s restoration by *R.M. Phipson* included a good deal of *Henry Ringham's* work. The nave ceiling is C18 plaster and the first three bays of the *arcade* are C15, with the 1880s two-bay extension beyond. The aisle and transept *roofs* are C15, and at the e. end on that side is a beautiful window of 1907 by *Sir Ninian Comper* (look for his strawberry signature). It commemorates Walton Turner, who was churchwarden here; he is portrayed kneeling in his civic robes at the bottom. Above, the two

figures of the *Annunciation* flank Christ in Majesty, and there are lots of miniature angels in the borders. The nave windows are filled with glass of 1879-80 signed 'Taylor late *O'Connor*' – figures of Purity, Faith, Hope, Charity, and Mercy. The hatchment for Elizabeth Hamby hangs in the n. aisle and her memorial of 1758 is on the s. wall; an urn on a bracket and her shield of arms are set against a large oval of mottled marble. Farther along there is a *touchstone* tablet for Daniel Burrill which has an intricate alabaster frame carved with a fine selection of the emblems of mortality. The new chancel was by Edward Bisshopp, the architect of St Michael's, Ipswich, among other things, and it includes a fine arch with *paterae* and shields bearing *Passion emblems* in the mouldings. These are painted and gilt and so are the four angels at the base of the roof *arch-braces*. The monument on the n. wall is an interesting family group conceived on a small scale. William Acton died in the same year as Shakespeare and he faces his wife across a desk with a draped skeleton brandishing the arrow of death between them; a son and three daughters are ranged behind them and their daughter-in-law Alice lies in a separate compartment below, with her elbow on a skull and a book in her hand. An alabaster roundel of arms decorates the top and, as on Burrill's memorial, there are symbols of death on the frame. The e. window has been blocked in and the space is filled with a mighty figure of Christ on the cross which dominates the chancel and compels the eye from the w. end. Walking back to the door, notice how the replacement tower does not quite line up with the nave.

Ipswich, St Mary le Tower (F6): This is an impressively large church in the town centre, hemmed in by buildings, with a churchyard that is also a colourful garden of flowers and shrubs. *R.M. Phipson* directed a series of restorations between 1850 and 1870 that gave it its present character and he designed the massive replacement tower which stands on the s. side. The pairs of tall bell openings are surrounded by distinctive *flushwork* chequer, and *Evangelistic symbols* almost leap from the corners of the pierced parapet. Above it, the handsome, *crocketted* spire rises to 176ft. The tower houses one of the best rings of twelve in the country. They were cast in the main by Taylor's of Loughborough with a 35 cwt. tenor but include one cast by the elder Miles Gray of Colchester in 1610 and another by John Darbie of Ipswich in the mid-C17. Among other things, Phipson rebuilt the n. *aisle* on a larger scale, added a n. *chancel* aisle, heightened the *clerestory* and redesigned the roof. It is worth making a circuit of the building to admire the quality of the flushwork on the chancel and to examine the two niches in the e. wall, with their modern figures *of St John* and *St Mary Magdalene* sculpted by Pheifer. Like the one over the s. door, the niches were part of the medieval building. The C13 inner doorway was carefully preserved and given new *Annunciation headstops.*

An early-C15 *font* stands just within, raised on three steps which have *quatrefoils* carved in the risers. The bowl panels contain chubby lions, there are two bands of vine below, and the lions round the shaft sit on human male and female heads. These are just like those at Helmingham and Grundisburgh (but in better condition) and there must have been a reason behind this little local oddity of symbolism. As part of the Victorian upheaval, wall tablets were collected together in corners, and there is a selection by the font. Of particular interest is the painted memorial for William Smart, MP for Ipswich, who died in 1599. Framed and glazed, the first letters of its verse spell out his name, and the epitaph is set in strapwork above the kneeling figures of William and his wife. A panorama of the town is painted along the bottom and a helpful key below identifies the landmarks. Smart's *ledger-stone* is clamped to the w. wall, and nearby there are two *brass* inscriptions; one is for Robert and Grisil Clarke (he was town clerk for 40 years and died in 1697), the other is for Robert Sparowe (1594). The fifteen main panels of the w. window make up a *Jesse tree* in 1860s glass by *Clayton & Bell*. Below it there is an excellent set of Charles II *Royal Arms*, pierced and carved in relief, and they are one of the very few whose maker is known – Jonathan Reeve was paid £15 for them in 1687. On either side of the doorway there are churchwardens' pews with modern coved hoods, but the C15 bench ends with their beast *finials* and seated figures came originally from the chancel. There is attractive 1870s glass by *Lavers, Barraud & Westlake* in the aisle w. windows and in two of the n. aisle windows; episodes in the early life of Christ fill the main *lights* with vignette scenes below. Phipson linked the C15 nave *arcades* to his new chancel arch with two smaller arches, and a band of red on the *capitals* is picked up on the ledge below the clerestory. The steeply pitched roof has *tracery* above the collar beams, and there are large demi-figure *corbels* below alternate principals. *Henry Ringham* worked on the aisle roofs and they are

good solid designs, with pierced tracery in the *spandrels* and painted demi-angel corbels. The stained glass in the n. aisle is an interesting selection; from the e. end: an early design of 1844 by *William Wailes* – the figure of Christ with the text 'My beloved is gone down into his garden to gather lilies'; another window by Wailes for Herbert Cobbold, who died young on an Hon. East India Company's steamer in 1852; an attractive Transfiguration and Good Shepherd of 1862 by the *O'Connors* with features slightly eroded; Christ's first miracle illustrated above the scene with Martha and Mary, in glass of 1865 by an unidentified glazier. Phipson designed a screen for the chancel but this now stands at the e. end of the n. aisle masking the organ beyond. The pulpit is an impressive but rather ponderous late-C17 piece on an 1860s stem. Its raised marquetry panels have wreaths of flowers above them and there are coarse swags at the corners. A marquetry *Sacred monogram* decorates the backboard and the *tester* is a solid octagonal hood whose *ogee* curves rise to a gilded dove finial. The curving stairs are exceptionally nice, with delicately turned and carved *balusters*, and *acanthus* trails decorating the risers of the steps.

This has always been the town's civic church and there are two sword and mace rests on the nave pillars, with corporation pews which have the lion and ship emblems on the bench ends. The s. aisle window glass is a sequence by Clayton & Bell, and at the e. end there is a *piscina* which C19 alterations reduced to floor level. Beyond a *parclose screen* of 1906, the chapel has carved panelling to windowsill height with memorials which, in some cases, are eccentrically painted to look like pieces of parchment. The heavy *reredos* is richly coloured and gilt, and the centre triptych contains a painting in C14 mode of the supper at Emmaus, flanked by Moses and Elias. A C14 arcade separates the chapel from the chancel, and there one finds that the back ranges of the choir stalls are medieval and have simple *misericords*. The centre section of the screen in front of the organ is C16 work and the rest, together with the bulk of the choir stalls, is high quality work by Cornish & Gaymer, with statuettes by Pheifer. More monuments were collected together on the walls of the choir vestry, including a fine tablet for John and Elizabeth Robinson (1666 and 1694); nicely posed figures kneel facing each other within a frame flanked by *touchstone* columns; three children are grouped below, two of them offering the skull and posy emblems of death and rebirth. There is a brass text by the vestry door, but the church's main collection of four brasses lies under the chancel carpet and inspection is not encouraged. The *High altar* is backed by a rather splendid *reredos* of about 1900 in which the centre Crucifixion group is flanked by panels crowded with angels, all painted on a gesso ground in very slight relief. There are figures of the Evangelists with their symbols, and the panels of the sanctuary are painted with the figures of East Anglia's saints: *SS Osyth, Erkenwald, Edmund, Ethelburga, Felix, Ethelbert,* and *Etheldreda* – to these are added *SS Augustine, Edward the Confessor,* and *Alphege.* Phipson designed an exuberant suite of piscina and *sedilia,* all painted and gilt, with quatrefoil polished marble shafts and nodding ogee arches.

Ipswich, St Matthew (F6): Busy Civic Drive now runs to the e. of the church and the development has given it a more spacious setting. Like others in the town, it was considerably altered in the C19 and a *porch* disappeared when the s. *aisle* was widened in 1845. *R.M. Phipson* added the s. chapel with its small projecting porch in 1860 and the e. wall was rebuilt six years later. The n. aisle was widened and extended by *Sir George Gilbert Scott* in 1876, and in 1884 7ft. was added to the tower and the s. aisle was refaced and given new windows and buttresses. The s. wall is worth studying as an example of the very high quality of Victorian rebuilding in the medieval style.

The widening of the aisles has made them each equal to the nave and, as a result, the interior is extremely spacious. The *arcades* are superficially alike but you will see that there are differences; the s. range with small *paterae* in the *capitals* dates from the C14, while the *piers* of a century later on the n. side have concave faces. All the roofs are Victorian but those in the aisles are particularly good, with pierced *tracery* above the braced *tiebeams.* The C15 *font* stands in the n. aisle, and although considerably retouched, it is a most interesting example which differs significantly in style from the average. Six of the bowl panels have delicately carved scenes, each beneath a pair of *crocketted ogee* arches; clockwise from the n.e. they portray: the *Blessed Virgin* enthroned, her coronation, the *Assumption,* the visit of the wise men, the *Annunciation* – a sequence which matches the *Joyful Mysteries* of the rosary. Another panel has the baptism of Christ and the last pair contains a conventional *Tudor Rose* and foliage. The attractive gilded cover is modern. The w. end of the n. aisle has been curtained off to form a chapel and at the e. end

a screen incorporates six interesting panels that belonged originally to the early-C16 *rood screen.* They are painted with the figures of four bishops, and the first on the l. is probably *St Thomas of Canterbury.* The fourth may represent *St Eligius,* but *St Erasmus* is more likely because there was a *guild* here under his patronage. The remaining panels are filled with lay figures who were undoubtedly the donors and probably members of the guild. The men kneel in front and the leader has a heavy purse which may indicate that he was master or treasurer. Apart from manuscripts there is little left to illustrate guild activities and this is a rare survival. A modern *rood* group hangs within the chancel arch, and on the n. side there is a long *squint* aligned with the *High altar.* A simple *piscina* and shelf are arranged within it to serve the *altar* that stood nearby. The other openings into the chancel and s. chapel date from 1860. The good 1890s screen between the s. aisle and the chapel was designed by John Corder and made by John Groom (whose carving may be found in a number of Ipswich churches), and the *communion rails* beyond incorporate three etched glass panels illustrating India, Ethiopia, and St Matthew's. They commemorate an Indian priest who was curate here in the 1970s. The chapel e. window has an interesting example of glass from the beginning of the Victorian revival; it was designed by Frank Howard and made in 1853 by George Hedgeland, the glazier of the great w. window of Norwich cathedral whose other Suffolk windows may be found at Hadleigh. There is glass by *Ward & Hughes* in the window to the r. and more of their work can be seen in the centre window of the n. aisle. The glass in the third window from the w. end in the s. aisle is by W.H. Constable of Cambridge. The C14 chancel roof is a *hammerbeam, arch-braced* design with gilded angels below the principals, and there are two substantial monuments on the n. wall. To the w. is the memorial for Anthony Penning who died in 1630. There are reclining *putti* on top with skull and hour-glass, and the figures kneel before shallow arches flanked by polished *touchstone* columns. The similar monument alongside is for Richard Cock who died in 1629. Here the effigies are much stiffer and there are garlands on the frame with a swag of fruit below. The brass *communion rails* with a heavy square top rail came from Hart & Co in the C19, and gates were added to match in 1946. Beyond them is the *High altar* and *reredos* designed by Corder. Its three painted bas-relief panels of the Magi and the shepherds at Bethlehem are set within a richly gilded tracery frame, and figures of *St John* and St Matthew stand each side. Above, the e. window glass of 1894 by Ward & Hughes has a figure of Christ in Majesty surrounded by a host of Old and New Testament figures. St Matthew's has a fine ring of six bells with a 10 cwt. tenor

Ipswich, St Michael (F6): C19 Ipswich was thriving and so populous that the central parishes had to be subdivided, and in the 1870s the new parish of St Michael's was formed. A site was acquired in Upper Orwell Street, cleared of slum cottages, and the foundation stone of the new church was laid in 1880. The architect was Edward Fearnley Bisshopp and, although he was concerned in a number of restorations and extensions, this is his only complete church. Both site and funds were restricted but his solution was creditable. The exterior cannot be viewed as a whole although the w. front speaks for its general style – *Early English* in the main, in red brick relieved by narrow bands of terracotta and stone facings. There was not room for a tower and the centre section of the w. wall is carried up in a wide and shallow buttress to form a double bellcote on the gable. The *aisles* are lit by pairs of *lancets* and the *clerestory* takes the form of dormer windows. The *nave* was extended eastwards and *transepts* were added in 1884, with the shallow *chancel* following in 1890.

One should not be deterred by the rather downbeat exterior because within is a beautifully spacious setting for worship in the C19 Evangelical tradition. The red brick glows warmly, and bands of darker brick enliven the *arcade* arches and w. wall. The sturdy drums of the arcade *piers* are faced with Bath stone and carry square carved *capitals*, while a band of multi-coloured glazed bricks links the triple lancets of the dormer windows. Between the aisle windows there are curious little adjustable ventilators, and the *font* in the n.w. corner is particularly individual – concave panels under trefoil arches in the bowl panels, with spiral columns and leafy capitals at each angle. The s. transept window has a centre panel of *St George* with his foot on a scarlet dragon, the glass by W.H. Constable of Cambridge. There are plain pitch pine pews in the nave but the pulpit has a range of small panels which were beautifully carved by Philip Groom with foliage in which there is a beast biting its tail, another eating grapes, and a vigorous dragon. The chancel is rather more lavish than the nave, and its arch has *dogtooth* ornament and leafy capitals above triple stub *responds*. The roof is panelled out and curves to

match the line of the arch. There are large pierced *cusps* on the principal timbers, and a little arcaded cornice stretches below the plain coving. The e. window has three tall lancets contained within a single arch, each divided into three narrow traceried lights. The outer sections are filled with glass by John Underwood & Sons, and there are figures of *SS Andrew, Peter, Matthew, Luke, John,* and *Paul* set within *tabernacle work;* wreaths enclose *Passion emblems* below and a painting at the w. end of the church shows how the design should be completed. By 1903 Bisshopp had gone into partnership with *Cautley* and one or other of them designed the *altar* and *reredos*, again carved by Philip Groom. An *Agnus Dei* is set below a pendent central arch and the cornice is a thick band of vine.

Ipswich, St Peter (F6): Standing on Stoke Park Drive, this church was built in 1975 to serve the mass of new housing that has developed along the e. of the Belstead Road. It stands well, on slightly rising ground, with a view across to Bourne Park, and is clearly identified by the large wooden cross standing in front. The building was designed by Marshman, Warren & Taylor, and consists of a main hall, an ancillary block projecting on the s. side, and a two-storeyed section at the rear. The main area is wedge-shaped and the side walls are stepped to take tall, narrow windows. Viewed from the road, the long slope of the roof comes down to a heavy beam section stretching across the frontage, below which there are curtained windows across the whole width. The heavy chains which are suspended from the lintel at each end serve to direct rainwater into the concrete drums below in place of conventional fall pipes, a mildly eccentric architectural conceit. Entry is from the rear, and the foyer leads into a spacious hall that can accommodate a congregation of 250. Decoration is minimal, with white-painted brick walls under a pine boarded ceiling. The e. wall is virtually all glass, and semi-transparent curtaining serves to provide an effective backing for the *altar*. This is a large pine slab set on an iron frame, with a centre panel recess – carved with a cross and the loaves and fishes – an interesting mingling of Christian symbolism which is repeated on the lectern in front. Plans are already in hand to provide additional accomodation for church activities, and eventually there will be an extension eastward to form a *sanctuary*. St Peter's attracts people from a broad spectrum of traditions and this austere yet attractive setting seems particularly appropriate.

Ipswich, St Thomas (F6): As the town grew in the C19 and early C20 its parishes had to be divided, and in some cases divided yet again. All Saints' was carved out of St Matthew's only to prove too large itself, and a new parish of St Thomas was created alongside the Norwich road. A little corrugated iron building was used initially, but in 1937 the foundation stone for a new church was laid by the donor of a site on Bramford Lane. The architect was N.F. Cachemaille Day and his design contains faint echoes of the familiar East Anglian *Perpendicular* style. The basic material is greyish brick, but he used expanses of *knapped* flints on the w. gable and walls, and introduced *flushwork* panels round the doors and between the *aisle* windows whose arches are a rounded version of the *Tudor* shape. The church's most striking feature is the bulky four-stage tower placed at the s.e. corner. There are paired belfry windows and bell openings above them, and the clasping buttresses rise to square corner turrets which are linked by a leggy openwork parapet. Balance is maintained overall by a large n. *transept* aligned with the tower.

The interior is low key, unfussy, and quietly attractive, with all the surfaces in plain, cream-coloured plaster. The arches of the *arcades* echo the window shapes, and from the pillars, ribs rise to form smooth braces under the nave roof. On either side, a low *clerestory* wall is pierced by small rectangular two-*light* windows, while the aisles lie under flat roofs. At the e. end the organ is sited below the tower and the n. transept forms a spacious chapel, with another in the s. aisle. The ribs of the *chancel* roof are placed diagonally and the zigzag form of the e. wall is given additional emphasis by the use of exposed brickwork. Small lancets are set in the angles right at the top and their brightly coloured glass is remarkably effective. The *sanctuary* is bounded by a low brick wall which drops down in steps and curves round to meet a set of simple *communion rails*, with *sedilia* incorporated on the s. side. The *High altar* is tremendously long, but in this setting the proportions seem entirely natural and right.

Ixworth, St Mary (D3): The church is tucked away in a quiet churchyard behind the village street at the lower end, and its entrance is easily missed when driving past. For the most part, the building is late-C15 and early-C16 and the tower can be dated accurately by a stone panel on the s.e. buttress. This panel is the third above the *nave* roof, and with binoculars one can read the inscription: 'Mast Robert Schot Abot',

together with the crown and arrows badge of the abbey at Bury. Schot was abbot from 1470 to 1473 and the tower was built between 1472 and 1484. The corresponding panel on the n.e. displays masons' tools. There are emblems set in the *base course*, on the buttresses, and below the deep, stepped battlements, very like the decoration at Walsham-le-Willows. The tower houses a ring of six bells with a 16 cwt. tenor, which at the time of writing are to be restored and made up to an eight. The early-C14 *chancel* was virtually rebuilt during an 1855 restoration and the n. *aisle* was extended to form an organ chamber and *vestry* at that time. The *rood staircase* protrudes from the angle between the s. aisle and the chancel (as at Walsham-le-Willows only on the other side), and there is a *priest's door* in the s. wall of the chancel with a *stoup* in the wall beside it. There is also a blocked *low side window* to the l. In the e. wall is a wide niche with a *cusped ogee* arch that is the right shape to have contained a *rood group*; on the other side of the window is an image stool.

Entry is by way of the handsome late-C14 *porch*, with its *flushwork* front and diagonal buttresses that have grotesques lying on the slopes. Below the battlements there is a line of small heads in the moulding and there are heavy *gargoyles* at the sides. There are low stone seats within the porch and the inner early-C14 doorway has a canopied niche over it.

The ground floor of the tower was converted into a small meeting and activities room in 1980, with a glazed screen separating it from the body of the church. Three tiles that were originally set in the outer walls of the tower are now displayed here and they give further evidence of its date. One is inscribed: 'Thome Vyal gaf to the stepil iiij£', and Thomas Vyal's will was proved in 1472. He was a carpenter and is likely to have done work in this and other churches in the neighbourhood. The C15 octagonal *font* has a plain bowl, but there are shields set in the *tracery* of the shaft and two of them bear emblems that appear to be woodworkers' tools – a draw knife and two bills. The nave *arcade*, with its *quatrefoil piers*, and the *clerestory* are C15. The low pitched roof has tracery in the *spandrels* of the *arch-braces* and there are angels at the base of each brace, with more on the *wall plates*. Money was left for the leading of the roof in 1533, indicating that it was finished just before the *Reformation*. The nave benches came in at the 1855 restoration and they are now complemented by a bright array of embroidered *hassocks*. Prior to the Reformation there were *guilds* of *St Thomas* and *St John*, but apparently the n. aisle chapel (now a Lady chapel) was dedicated to *St James*. There you will find an *aumbry* in the n. wall and a small, plain *piscina* to the r. of the *altar*. The stairs to the *rood loft* can be seen at the end of the s. aisle and a modern bottom door has been fitted. The nicely traceried base of the *screen* remains, and the arch overhead shows the groove that was made to secure the *tympanum* behind the rood. The a text painted on zinc is Victorian. When the C19 vestry and organ chamber were added, a three-bay arcade was built on the n. side of the chancel. The tall priest's door and the blocked low side window can be seen on the s. side, and in the *sanctuary* is a large early-C13 piscina with a double drain below twin cusped arches. In the n.e. corner is a most interesting tomb, that of Richard and Elizabeth Codington. The chest has strapwork on the shallow *pilasters*, with three shields of arms between. At the back there is a *brass* of the couple kneeling at desks; he has medium length hair and wears a moustache and beard (note that the sleeves of his fur-trimmed gown become pockets lower down): she wears a French hood, and two children of a former marriage kneel behind her. The couple's shield of arms, together with those of his family and her first marriage were originally inlaid with colour. Codington died in 1567, and the inscription is fascinating because it tells how he was granted the manor of Ixworth by Henry VIII in 1538 in exchange for his manor of Cuddington in Surrey. It was at the time when the king was gathering in the spoils from the suppressed religious houses like Ixworth priory that he started to build the fabulous palace of Nonesuch. To do so, he swept away the village and church of Cuddington, having acquired the site by this exchange. The irony is that he never lived to see Nonesuch finished and the palace was pulled down in 1670. There are C19 painted metal *Decalogue* plates either side of the altar and on the sanctuary s. wall, a *touchstone* panel in an alabaster frame with a roundel of arms for John Norton who died in 1597. The 1944 memorial window on that side, with its figures of the sower and the Good Shepherd, was designed by *James Powell & Sons* in 1966. As you leave, have a look at the fine C17 Bible box at the w. end; it has 'H.B.' on the top and the front is richly carved.

Ixworth Thorpe, All Saints (D3): A small church, it stands on a slight rise away from the tiny village, within a churchyard ringed with trees

and affording views over gently rolling countryside. The upper part of the tower fell at some time and has been replaced by a weatherboarded bell turret, while the lower section incorporates stones from an earlier structure, particularly noticeable on the s. side. *Nave* and *chancel* are thatched, and on the n. side is a very simple blocked *Norman* doorway, square-headed *Decorated* windows and the bulge of the *rood loft* stair. There are two small C13 *lancets* on the n. side of the chancel and the e. window has wooden C18 or C19 *tracery* under a *Tudor* arch with long *labels*. On the s. side are Decorated windows, a *priest's door*, and an extraordinary collection of glaziers' graffiti scratched on the diamond *quarries* of the windows; apart from some crude modern additions, there are signatures of Edward Thibbald of Starston (1830), G. Hurrell of Ixworth (1852), Ambrose Cobb of Diss (1852), and an earlier one of 1703. This rustic form of a trade label crops up elsewhere, with examples at Stanton, Barnby and Blyford. The attractive Tudor *porch* in red brick has a crow-stepped gable and at each corner there are stumps of brick pinnacles with *crockets*, one of which is carved as a human head reminiscent of an Easter Island statue. The sides of the porch are decorated with diamond patterns in darker brick and below the battlements there is a frieze of dressed flints set in brickwork, with similar panels on the buttresses. There is a nice little *arch-braced* roof within, although the *bosses* along the ridge have disappeared.

Entry is via a plain and low Norman doorway less than 3ft. wide and a C13 grave slab has been used as a step just inside, with two more beyond it. The floors are pleasant pale yellow brick and the ceilings are plastered throughout. The plain octagonal C14 *font* has a flat board cover, decorated only by gouge cuts on the rim, and a neat set of George III *Royal Arms* painted on board hangs over the simple tower arch. The range of C15 benches has large *poppyheads* and there are grotesques and figures carved on the gabled elbows. Some of these are very good – look for a bird with a human head (w. end, s. side), the harvester (second from the door on the s. side), the mermaid with her mirror (next but one along), a *unicorn* (next along), and the lady taking her little dog for a walk (middle of the n. side). On the n. side of the nave, a small door leads to the rood loft stair and a vestige of the chancel arch juts out of the wall beyond it. On the s. side stands a tiny *Jacobean* pulpit, only 3ft. 6in. high and 2ft. 9in. across, with shallow carvings in the top panels, and there is a typical arch and *pilaster* arrangement below. Those who 'intend hereafter to enter into the State of Matrimony, Godly and agreeably to the Laws' were deflected from unholy alliances by a printed set of degrees of marriage, published in 1771 and hung in all churches; most have disappeared but there is a framed copy in good condition here on the n. wall of the chancel. Further along is a memorial to Charles Crofts who died in 1617 – a round-headed *touchstone* tablet in an alabaster frame which carries two shields of arms and two crests, still with some of their colour. Three tiny cherub heads decorate the cornice, and above is an *achievement of arms* surmounted by the small figure of a naked man minus his head, with his foot on a skull. The spelling of the epitaph is delightfully wilful. Opposite is a small marble tablet flanked by pilasters, with an attractively lettered epitaph for Sir John Crofts who died in 1640. The lancets on the n. side of the chancel have deeply splayed embrasures and there is a plain lancet *piscina* in the *sanctuary*. The Lord's Prayer, Creed, and *Decalogue* are painted on boards with marbled frames hung on either side of the *altar*. Three-sided *communion rails* are not common, but here is a late-C17 set with turned *balusters* and gates staggered to n. and s.; the front top rail is badly wormed in one section. The prayer desk in the chancel is an interesting example of a piece of furniture that has been adapted for church use. It is, I think, part of a console table – a finely carved and angry wooden eagle bearing a *Corinthian capital* on its head, now mounted on a new base and fitted with a book ledge on top.

Kedington, St Peter and St Paul (B6): This is one of the most fascinating of the county's churches but it does not wear its heart on its sleeve, presenting as it does a strange and gawky aspect to the road. The *chancel* roof is not visible above the walls, the *nave* roof has had its top sliced off, and the *porch* gable juts above the plain *aisle* parapet. There was a church here in very early times and the *Saxon* cross that you will see inside was found under the floor in the C19. The C14 tower was probably built by the Lord of the Manor, John de Novo Mercato, and there is a little gable at the foot of the s.w. buttress that shelters a lump of stone which was apparently his effigy. Above the next stage, a *trefoil* niche has a faint inscription over it which is said to read 'Dame Amicia' for John's wife. A heavy stair turret with an outside door rises to belfry level on the s. and a band of flint chequer work reaches up to the sill of the *Perpendicular*

Kedington, Saints Peter and Paul: Barnardiston pew

w. window. An original *Decorated* bell opening remains to the e., with a replacement to the n.; the others are decayed. There are early flint-filled window shapes by the side of the bell openings and on the e. face of the tower, like a strawberry birthmark, is a very strange *cinquefoil* in brick that seems to bear no relation to anything else. The line of an earlier nave roof can be seen and the clock, with its weathered octagonal face, was made in Braintree in 1729. The body of the church is late-C13 to early-C14, with two doors on the n. side, one for the convenience of the family from the Manor house which was pulled down in 1780. The chancel has tall windows with *cusped 'Y' tracery* (the soft stone is very decayed on the s. side) and a C15 e. window. To the r. of the *priest's door* there are two *scratch dials*, one of which has almost flaked away. Before moving on, have a look at William Phillips' 1690s tomb nearby, with its range of symbols of mortality. The s. porch, over a charming cobbled floor, has been repaired and altered through the years and there are lots of C18 graffiti in the window embrasures and on the deeply moulded inner door.

The low C15 *arcades* and lack of a *clerestory* must have made for a fairly dark interior until someone in 1857 was inspired to insert three skylights in the roof. Vandalism is one view and common sense another, but there is no doubt that they make a big difference and they show off the early-C16 false *hammerbeam* roof very effectively (the only parallel that comes to mind is the parish church at Whitby). To the r. of the entrance is a pillar *stoup*, its large bowl chopped away, and nearby, the remains of a *Norman piscina* are used for the same purpose today. The long and low iron-banded parish chest with divided top dates from the late C14, and there is a contemporary but unidentified area of painting on the s. aisle wall. By a n. *arcade* pillar stands the worn C15 *font*, with shields and *quatrefoils* in the bowl panels; there are traces of colour and the steps have two gridiron marks which, like others elsewhere, defy reasonable explanation. In the C17 there was an attempt to follow current fashion and the sides of the piers were painted in imitation of fluted classical columns. Kedington is one of the churches that the Victorians left alone as far as furnishings were concerned and has a wonderful conglomeration of styles and periods, a time capsule that gives a very good idea of how things were managed and how they changed between the *Reformation* and the 1840s. The mid-C18 w. *gallery* is bow-fronted and on either side, at the w. end of the aisles, are tiers of C18 children's benches: s. side (with hat pegs) for boys, n. side for girls. At the end of the nave benches there are two special seats that face w. so that the Master and Dame could keep an eye on their charges. A rare C17 *bier* (extensively restored) stands on the boys' benches and is similar in style to those at Dalham and Little Saxham but much simpler, and its C19 successor stands near the door. There is a charming irregularity about the seating in the nave and aisles. The backs of the benches at the w. end are warped and gnarled with age and have a delectable patina, while the main range is a plain, late-C15 set with *linen-fold panelling* in the ends. *Box pews* with shaped divisions face inwards all along the n. aisle, there is a high, square range at the e. end of the s. aisle, and at the front of the nave on the n. side another group evolved its own pattern of heights and widths – they date from the C17 to the C19. Beyond is the fine manorial pew built about 1610, with turned openwork above the sides and slim, turned columns supporting a flat panelled ceiling. It is divided into two compartments, each with its book box and hat pegs, and the front was formed from a 1430s *parclose screen* that stood at the e. end of the n. aisle. It has lovely Perpendicular tracery, cusped and *crocketted*, with much of the original colour revealed by a 1930s restoration. The *three-decker*

pulpit is arguably the country's best and is an early example dating from 1610, with an unusual layout – the reading pew, with *clerk's* desk in front, stands beside the pulpit. The clerk's desk, facing w., is built into the range of pews and has its own hat pegs beneath the book slope. The reading desk is long and narrow, with steps rising awkwardly right through it. There is a hinged kneeler and rough seat, and the full length book slope is carved on the underside and on the brackets, matching the upper panels on all three sides. The pulpit on its turned pedestal is tall, but a mere 26in. across, and two sides of the octagon form the door. It has a canted book ledge and above the backboard there is a square *tester*. All the carving is of high quality and there are two extras that emphasise its individuality – a turned post on the front pew on which the minister could place his wig and an *hour-glass stand* whose wrought-iron cage rests on a separate turned pole. This was the pulpit used by the Puritan, Samuel Fairclough, whose eloquence drew congregations from far and near for over 30 years. His successor was the John Tillotson who went on to become Archbishop of Canterbury in 1691. Across the aisle is a curious C14 or early-C15 alms-box formed from the trunk of a tree, bound with iron and only 15in. high. By the side door at the e. end of the n. aisle is a stairway in the wall that led to the *parclose screen loft*, and the *altar* there is a beautiful little early-C17 table; it is honeycoloured and the melon legs are delicately carved with *acanthus* leaves. Beyond it, the wall is recessed and probably housed a *reredos* for the medieval altar. The Decorated window has glass by J.E. Nuttgens of High Wycombe (see his e. window at Horringer) and portrays the risen Christ flanked by the *Two Marys*. To the l. is a portion of medieval wall painting and to the r., a narrow archway leads through to the front of the late-C13 chancel arch whose *responds* are earlier, possibly mid-C12. The *screen* is a severe *Jacobean* design and is dated 1619 in the scrolled tracery that has turned pendants in each *light*. It is one of the oldest post-Reformation screens in the country and its unusual feature is that there are two folding sections to the n. and one to the s. The fine hanging Calvary above was made in 1926 by George Jack, the well-known wood-carver, and is just the right size for the arch. The stair to the old *rood loft* was rediscovered in 1920 and can be seen within a cavity in the n. *jamb* of the arch (an uncommon, if not unique, position) and the upper exit is in the n.e. angle of the nave. A stone *corbel* and the remains of another flank the chancel arch and will have supported the original *rood beam*. The chancel now has modern chairs and benches, sensibly converting it into a convenient chapel, but the old practice of using it only to assemble the congregation for occasional communion lingered on into the C18 when a special set of communicants' pews was made. Such things were normally swept away by the Victorians to whom they were anathema but, by good fortune, some of Kedington's survive and one section stands just to the w. of the screen on the n. side. They are of deal which has been grained to look like oak and have blank 'gothick' arches before and behind. Two more ranges with high, settle backs stand by the s. door and e. of the pulpit (See also Glossary entry: *Housel bench*). The late-C13 chancel side windows have slim shafts and a *string course* below them lifts over the priest's door. The *sanctuary* is paved in the black and white chequer that was so fashionable in the C17, and the walls are deeply panelled in oak. On the s. side, a section hinges open to reveal a *piscina* which was probably shorn of its front moulding when the panelling went in. The *reredos* was painted by Professor Tristram in 1935 and above it is the church's oldest treasure, the Saxon cross. This probably formed the head of a *preaching cross* and is said to date from the early C10. The lovely set of three-sided *communion rails* fits the space to perfection and their shapely *balusters* match the legs of the *Holy table*. As his memorial on the wall in the s.e. corner tells us, they were given by Samuel Barnardiston who died in 1707. The tablet is strangely old-fashioned, in the style of 100 years earlier, and it is odd that he was actually buried at Brightwell where his *hatchment* hangs. Sir Samuel made his fortune as a Levant merchant; as a young man he demonstrated with the London apprentices in 1640 and his cropped hair prompted Queen Henrietta Maria's remark: 'See what a handsome round head is there', giving the Round-heads their name. The Barnardistons were once one of the most important families in the county and flourished here over 27 generations. In their prime they crowded some massive tombs into the e. end of the s. aisle, but before moving there, note the slab with four shields set in the n. wall of the sanctuary. It probably formed part of Sir Thomas Barnardiston's 1540s tomb which also served as an *Easter sepulchre* before it was dismantled.

The largest monument in the s. aisle is for another Sir Thomas who died in 1610 and his two wives. Standing behind tall iron railings, it rises to the roof, with polished marble *Corinthian* columns each side and twin arches at the rear, in which kneel the figures of the two wives, Mary and Katherine, the latter as a widow with veil and heavy ruff. A little tree bearing shields decorates the *pilaster* between them and a full *achievement of arms* is carved on top, flanked by a funeral helm and gauntlets on brackets; a gruesome pile of skulls with bones in their mouths rests on each corner. Sir Thomas's effigy is finely carved on the tomb chest and much of the original colour survives overall. The most extraordinary feature is the pseudo-coffin that protrudes at right-angles from the front of the tomb chest, as though the undertakers got it wrong and just gave up trying! At the e. end of the aisle is the tomb of the Sir Thomas who died in 1503 and his wife Elizabeth (some families seem to have a fixation about favourite names). Their worn effigies have been shamefully treated by generations of idle hands and the helm behind his head is broken away. An inscribed tablet set beyond their feet in the wall tells us that he was the founder of the *chantry* in the n. aisle and that after his death Elizabeth provided the new roof for the nave. To the s. of the chancel arch stands the tomb of yet another Sir Thomas, who died in 1619, and Elizabeth, his wife. Worn figures of children kneel in the side panels and the family arms are framed in stone and placed over an image niche in the wall beyond. His armour and her clothes are excellent examples of the fashions of the period. Thomas married again and had a daughter called Grissell, whose kneeling effigy, in the s.e. corner of the aisle, is perhaps the most memorable of all. She died in 1609 and her monument is of high quality, raised on the wall so that it can be seen from the nave. The figure is remarkable for the way in which the hair is mounted over a frame, with the back curls looped and knotted, and for the way the epaulettes of the sleeves extend as spikes almost to the ground. Across in the n. aisle is the monument to Sir Nathaniel and Lady Jane (1653 and 1669) – an attractive pair of alabaster demi-figures whose hands gently overlay a skull between them; he wears armour and she a very fashionable gown with slashed sleeves and a profusion of lace. A Puritan MP, he suffered imprisonment with John Hampden over the matter of ship money in 1634. Finally, the family left an excellent array of hatchments which are hung above the nave arcades. On the n. side, from w. to e., they are for Sir Thomas (1669), Sir Thomas (1700), Sir Thomas (1698), Lady Anne

(1671), Sir Robert (1728); on the s. side, from w. to e., Lady Anne (1701), Sir Samuel (1735), Sophia, Viscountess Wimbaldon (1691), Thomas (1704) and Nathaniel (1837). The church has a fine ring of six bells with an 11 cwt. tenor.

Kelsale, St Mary and St Peter (H4): A narrow twisting lane leads up to a broad, grassy space, and one enters the churchyard through one of the best modern *lych-gates* in Suffolk. It dates from the late C19 and is a lovely *Arts & Crafts* period piece, by E.S. Prior who designed a similar gate at Brantham. The tiled roof, broadly curved like a dowager's garden party hat, rises to a peak in front which frames an oval niche, above an oaken frame whose four massive ribs meet in an open vault. Over 130 lime trees border the churchyard and form avenues to the *porch* and *chance*l, so that the whole building disappears momentarily behind a leafy screen as one approaches. The church underwent two lavish C19 restorations, the first by Richard Norman Shaw in the 1870s and the second by his pupil E.S. Prior a few years later. Shaw is perhaps best remembered for his New Scotland Yard on the Embankment; here, he rebuilt the chancel (it was 'a miserable structure with a wooden e. window and flat ceiling'), added a n.e. *vestry*, and restored the chancel *aisle*. Prior followed this by

Kelsale, St Mary and St Peter: Lych-gate

restoring the *nave* and aisle, and the tower was dealt with in 1890, so that the building's character is largely determined by the work of the Victorians. As we shall see, the church was established by the *Normans*, and the first nave aligned with the tower. In the C14, a new, wider nave was added on the n. side so that the tower now stands at the s.w. corner. Its restoration included particularly attractive bell openings, their lights filled with a mesh of stone *quatrefoils* below *Decorated-style* tracery; *gargoyles* jut from the corners under *flushwork* battlements, and lions and *woodwoses* feature as pinnacles. Within the tower is a ring of eight bells with a 15 cwt. tenor. The nave has a flushwork *base course* and there is a huge w. window. Walking round, you will find that the original Norman n. door was reused when the nave was built; its broad arch has a rim of *billet moulding*, enclosing bands of irregular wedges, thin scallops, and finally, a series of worn *chevrons*. Further along, the *rood stair turret* was rebuilt during one of the restorations, and on the s. side of the chancel aisle, the Norman *priest's door* was inserted in the new work. The C15 porch has some flushwork in the facade, there are *Passion* and *Trinity* shields in the *spandrels* of the arch, and a modern St Peter stands in the central canopied niche. A *scratch dial* can just be detected on the s.e. corner, and the inner side of the arch is scored with some interesting graffiti.

Within, there is much of interest, and note first two lead roof panels by the entrance, with names of 1740 churchwardens and 1787 feoffees [charity trustees]. The C14 four-bay *arcade* has octagonal *piers*, and beyond it, the broad nave lies under a scissors-braced roof. Converted to electricity now, the pendant light fittings were once gasoliers and are one of the very few examples to have survived from the C19. The seating too is remarkable – long oak benches designed by Prior on the lines of superior garden furniture, with slatted backs, turned front posts and shaped arms that are a handsome alternative to pews or chairs. The C15 *font* follows the East Anglian tradition, but it is exceptionally broad, and so low that there is only just enough room for the lions round the shaft. Heavily mutilated angels alternate with *Evangelistic symbols* in the bowl panels. Nicely lettered C19 charity boards hang to r. and l., and the *hatchments* above them were used at the funerals of Katherine Trusson in 1785 (s.), and her son Thomas in 1809 (n.). Samuel Clouting's 1852 memorial on the s. wall is the largest and quite the best work by *Thomas Thurlow*, the Saxmundham mason. Standing

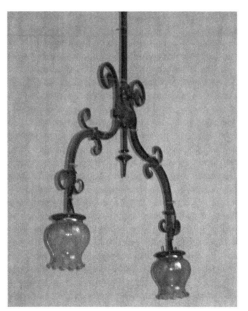

Kelsale, St Mary & St Peter: C19 gasolier

within a niche on a half-round plinth, the commanding, cloaked figure evokes memories of the Iron Duke, and while the list of bequests below his epitaph demonstrates his charity, it is ironic that his executors so blatantly ignored his instruction that there should be no memorial. The small, dark *Royal Arms* over the n. door date from the first year of Victoria's reign. Further along, a window contains excellent 1870s glass designed by the *pre-Raphaelite* Ford Madox Brown, and made by J. Aldham Heaton. The fine figures of Moses and *St John* are backed by small panes with 'Lex' (law), 'Evan' (Evangelist), and leaf sprays. Most of the other nave and aisle windows contain patterned glass which is attractively different. Supplied by *Powells*, it was probably designed by Prior as part of the second restoration. He pioneered the slab glass whose streaky texture was a favourite with the Arts & Crafts glaziers, and combined it here with bold red and green dots, keys for St Peter, and Passion symbols. Standing in front of the door to the rood stair there is an exceptionally good *Jacobean pulpit* (when Aldborough were thinking about a new one in 1631, they sent a joiner to look at this). It has intricate strapwork in the lower panels and round the *blind arches*, and winged beasts in shallow relief range below the book ledge. The latter is modern, like the base and stairs, and the original octagonal drum has been amended to a horseshoe shape.

One of the aisle windows has reticulated tracery and its glass is possibly by *Burlison & Grylls* – a 'Suffer little children to come unto me' in C15 style. The sill is lowered to form *sedilia* and there is a restored C14 *piscina* alongside, marking the site of a pre-*Reformation altar*. A two-bay arcade with quatrefoil piers links the C15 aisle chapel with the chancel, and the monument on the s. wall is an interesting piece in which a lush *cartouche* of arms is displayed against massed militaria above a severe, classical base. The epitaph relates how the younger years of Thomas Russell were 'spent in the memorable defence of Eniskillen until that Kingdom was intirely subdued by King William: the remainder of his days was spent in doing good'. Russell died in 1730 and his wife Mary in 1754. In re-jigging the pulpit, the backboard and *tester* were stupidly discarded, and the latter was used as a top for the nearby table. A number of Suffolk parishes had the same bright idea, unfortunately. An 1860s tablet by Gaffin above the priest's door commemorates Lancelot Brown, rector here for 58 years, nephew and namesake of the famous landscape gardener 'Capability' Brown. The window beyond has figures of the *Blessed Virgin and St Elizabeth* under intricate canopies and is probably by Burlison & Grylls. The style of the chapel e. window suggests the same firm, and the two ranks of panels illustrating the life of Christ are closely modelled on the Norwich C15 style. A low stone wall and a delicate C19 screen in wrought-iron and brass separate the nave and chancel, and there are matching gates leading to the side chapel. The glass in the n. chancel window has been re-set, and it contains two 1870s panels by *William Morris & Co*. The figure of the Blessed Virgin is a *Burne-Jones* design, the *St Peter* is by Morris, and both were used again in Fawley church, Berkshire. Shaw designed the sturdy choir stalls to go with his new chancel and they are much better than the average C15 reproductions. The detail is inventive, although a mite eccentric in that a little projecting shield in the back of each stall carries a letter, so that the whole range spells: 'Sing unto the Lord all ye servants of the Lord'. The 1930s *communion rails* in the style of the C17 are excellent. Although the church's medieval *mensa* has survived, it was placed underneath the *High altar* and cannot easily be seen, and the 1870s *reredos* with painted panels now stands at the w. end. The e. window glass is probably by *Heaton, Butler & Bayne*; in a vigorous Ascension panorama, the disciples are grouped across all of the five lights, with Christ in the centre; red and blue cherubim fill the tracery, and Evangelistic symbols flank the *Agnus Dei* in the bottom panels.

Kentford, St Mary (B4): The church stands well above the village street which once formed part of the main Bury to Newmarket road. It is a C14 building and the *nave* windows have flowing *Decorated tracery*. The three *lights* of the e. window have *ogee* heads, with *reticulations* above, but the single *lancet* on the n. side of the *chancel* shows that there was an earlier and simpler predecessor. The s. chancel windows are modern and much of the exterior stonework has been renewed. The memorable feature of the tower is a small and pleasing rose window just above ground floor level, with *cinquefoiled* tracery. The bell openings are small lancets on the w. and n. faces, but on the s. side there is a round-headed (possibly C18) window which appears to have been part of a reconstruction, mainly in thin red bricks, following a collapse of the upper tower on that side. The parapet is plain brick and a former roof line shows on the e. face. The C14 *porch* is badly decayed and one of the angle buttresses has been rebuilt in brick. It has a crow-stepped gable and the side windows have been blocked up, although the Decorated tracery survives in the one on the e. side. There is an C18 sundial above the entrance arch. The s. door is C18 panelled pine and there is a *trefoiled* niche above it. Until relatively recently there were remains of extensive wall paintings here, on both nave walls and at the w. end. Now, all is plain plaster except for an area on the n. wall opposite the entrance. Figures of the three young kings from the legend of the *Three Living and Three Dead* can be recognised and the figure of *St Christopher* was probably to their r. The background colour is mainly pale red with hints of green. The roofs are modern, and in the nave there is a plastered ceiling. Below is a lovely pale brick floor and a suite of C18 *box pews*, of unvarnished pine and in fine condition. The two-light window in the centre of the nave n. wall has 1902 glass – Christ as the Good Shepherd on one side, with an *Agnus Dei* within a wreath below, and the Virgin and Child alongside, a pot of lilies within a matching wreath underneath. The chancel was restored in 1877 when the arch was renewed and, possibly, the floor raised. The lancet in the n. wall contains a nice little roundel of stained glass, a 'G.G.' monogram with a bee on a tussock of grass as a crest. The window opposite contains shields of the Ely diocese and Trinity Hall, Cambridge, the patrons of the living. The glass in the e. window is a memorial to three members of the Lord family. The bottom centre panel shows Christ crucified, with a young knight kneeling before Him (obviously a portrait); there is a church in the background against a red and gold sky. On either side are scenes of Christ's presentation in the temple and the visit of the Magi, with the Resurrection and Ascension above them. A fine window. None of the stained glass artists have been identified.

Kenton, All Saints (F4): With a population of only 150, this village has done wonders in restoring its church over the past few years; it is a place of rest, refreshment, and beauty in simplicity. The w. door of the late-C14 tower is small, and the two-*light* window above it has *ogee* shapes in the *Decorated tracery*, echoed by the bell openings farther up. The curious *flushwork* roundels in the battlements may or may not be original. *Edward Hakewill* was the architect in charge of a major restoration in 1871 when all the window tracery was renewed. He designed the n. porch and rebuilt a great deal of the C13 chancel, inserting a rather harsh triple *lancet*-and-roundel e. window, and remodelling the *priest's door* on the s. side. The wide lancets in the side walls seem largely undisturbed, although the small Decorated window to the s. is partially blocked (its position suggests that it was once a *low side window*). From the e. end the line of the old *nave* roof shows up clearly above Hakewill's replacement. The s. *aisle* is entirely in mellow red brick, with an unobtrusive pattern in blue and characteristic *Tudor mullioned* windows. It was endowed as a *chantry chapel* dedicated to *St John* by Lord of the Manor John Garneys in 1524, and he made provision for a priest to serve it. The outer arch of the tall C15 s. *porch* displays fleurons and crowns in the mouldings, but despite their worn appearance, the *headstops* are likely to be C19. The roof timbers are original and one *wall plate* is carved with a little leaf trail. To the r. a handsome brick doorway with a well-worn step gives access to the Garneys chapel, but the main entrance is straight ahead and that shows that the early (possibly *Saxon*) church was rebuilt in the late C12. The style is *Transitional*, with single shafts and leaf *capitals*, one of which is a replacement; the arch has a roll moulding between deep hollows. Kenton has plenty of *scratch dials* – there are three on this doorway and you may have seen two more outside, a faint one on the centre buttress and another on the s.w. corner of the nave.

The medieval s. door still has its closing ring and opens on to a nave cheerfully enlivened with modern *hassocks*. Beyond the plain tower arch you will see attractive C19 *bosses* under the belfry ceiling, and there are sections of lead from the old tower roof framed on the n. wall. They were cast in 1714 with names, including 'W.Lord Churchwarding' and Jane Garneys (the family continuing here). Below stands an interesting Elizabethan pew, with a range of slim *balusters* at the front; the top rail has 'K.G. 1595 M.S.' There are two C15 bench ends with *poppyheads* nearby and seven *consecration cross* roundels are spaced round the walls (there is original paint on the one by the door). The octagonal bowl of the *font* is C13 *Purbeck marble*, with sharply canted sides and a traditional pattern of blind arches; the shaft and steps are by Hakewill. When he replaced the roof, one *tie-beam* across the nave was retained, and there is a plain niche in the embrasure of one of the n. windows. The other has a tall arch access to the *rood stairs,* but the medieval *screen* has gone and so has the old chancel arch – which has been replaced by a rather fussy model with multiple shafts and intricate *capitals*. The plain C17 pulpit has been largely remodelled, with Victorian Gothic tracery applied to the panels. Behind it is an attractive C15 niche which has a *Trinity shield* in one *spandrel* and *St George's* cross in the other and there may have been a nave *altar* here. A two-bay *arcade* replaced the s. wall when the chapel was built, and there are three rather odd little brackets below the capitals. The chapel has a small, plain *piscina* and the C15 shaft of the font has been moved here to carry a modern statue of the Blessed Virgin. The niche to the l. was probably designed for a statue of *St John*, and there is another with traces of stencil decoration between the side windows. The almost flat roof was undisturbed in the C19 and a blocked w. window suggests that the porch had an upper room, possibly for the *chantry priest*. John Garneys was undoubtedly buried in the chapel and there is a fine and important *brass* for him and his wife Elizabeth. He wears an heraldic *tabard*, she bears the arms of Sulyard on her cloak, and there is a rare remnant of a Crucifixion between them. Unfortunately, it can only be seen by appointment and one hopes that some day it will be placed on display. Hakewill must have enjoyed redesigning the chancel. Apart from its arch, he used a cusped arch and slim shafts to frame the e. lancets, and raised the *altar* on three steps which show off the jolly pattern of the *encaustic tiles*. The glass in the windows is by

Lavers & Barraud – small figures of the Blessed Virgin, *St Paul, St Peter, Gabriel,* two angels, and Christ the King in the top roundel.

Kersey, St Mary (E.6): In one of Suffolk's loveliest villages the steep street, followed by a flight of steps, leads up from a watersplash to the church on the hill. It is a fascinating building which shows, perhaps more clearly than most, the way in which it evolved over the years. In the C14 an ambitious reconstruction began which enlarged the *chancel*, added a sumptuous n. *aisle*, and made a start on a new tower. Then came the *Black Death* in 1349 which brought everything to a standstill. Work did not begin again until at least half a century later when the *nave* was heightened, new windows were inserted on the s. side, and the roof was rebuilt. The position of the tower shows that a s. aisle was part of the C14 plan but this was never built and the C15 s. *porch* was built directly onto the nave, with another added to the n. aisle. The tower was not finished until 1481 and the only other major alteration came in the 1860s when the chancel was rebuilt and a *vestry* added on the n. side.

The triple *base course* of the tower has squares of *flushwork* and continues round the n. aisle, confirming the unity of the C14 design. The w. doors have weathered *tracery*, a vine trail decorates the edges, and the *label* of the arch has lion *stops*. Above is a *transomed* window with slim, *cusped*, and *crocketted* niches each side within an arcade of flushwork. The two *lights* of the belfry windows are separated by a flushwork panel and there is a very deep band of flushwork at battlement level which displays a distinctly individual pattern. A stair turret on the s. side rises to the very top and, with its four set-offs and prominent *string courses*, the tower has fine proportions and is very handsome. The s. porch is lovely and has all the panache of a showpiece. The triple base course is decorated with flushwork diamonds, *quatrefoils*, and arcades, and there is more diamond embellishment on the battlements; the buttresses are stepped and gabled, with niches at the upper level, the facade is panelled with flushwork overall, and a canopied centre niche has tiny figures at the top of its flanking buttresses. The carving in the *spandrels* is intriguing but the subject is obscure. To the l. there is a tree with two fish (one with another in its mouth), and to the r. a foliage design that looks more like seaweed than anything else. The porch roof is a stunning piece of work and probably owes its fine condition to the fact that it was plastered over for ages and only uncovered in 1927. Measuring a mere 13ft. by 11ft., it is divided by heavily moulded beams into a lattice of sixteen square panels, each lined with a lacy cresting and carved with four panels of varied tracery.

The C15 alterations made the nave tall for its length but the proportions of the n. aisle are impressive and so too is its decoration. Its e. window has *Decorated* tracery, with quatrefoils within reticulations, the stepped and gabled buttresses all have niches at the upper level, and the battlements are ornamented with flushwork chequer and crocketted pinnacles. There are large *gargoyles*. The n. porch matches the s. in style but lacks the flushwork embellishment, and its roof is not in the same class. It is interesting to note, however, that mortice holes show where carved *bosses* were applied to the heavily moulded beams. The inner doorway is finely moulded with vestiges of *headstops* and the base course shows on each side as a reminder that the porch was built later than the aisle.

Within, the aisle fulfils its promise of luxuriance despite the terrible mutilations exacted after the *Reformation*. Just inside the n. door is a *stoup* which has had its *corbel* base cut away and farther along there is a large niche in the n. wall under a wide *ogee* arch with pinnacles, crockets, and *finial* shorn off; there are stumps of angels inside it which show traces of colour, and a large alabaster *Trinity* group is now displayed there. It has been defaced but the drapery-covered knees of God the Father flank the outline of a cross and remnant of Christ's figure. The wall has sections of painting in dark red and one figure is recognisable to the l. of the blocked window. Part of the stem and bowl of the early church's *font* was found doing duty as a cottage doorstep in 1927 and now stands in the aisle, and a section of the late-C15 *rood screen* is against the wall. The panels are painted with three Old Testament prophets and three kings, one of whom is *St Edmund* with his arrow emblem. Two of the prophets hold parchment scrolls and all the figures wear ermine-trimmed cloaks. The robes are curiously stiff and bulky, reminiscent of contemporary illustrations of mummers in a mystery play. The two large niches flanking the e. window were barbarously treated by the despoilers and all the frontal decoration was hacked off, but a portion of delicate *groining* with a small head corbel survives on the l. and there are traces of colour. In that niche is a headless seated figure in a golden gown holding a book, still with its lettered page, and this must

Kersey, St Mary: Squint

represent *St Anne*. To the r. stands a beautiful suite of *piscina* and *sedilia*. It is tall, with heavily cusped ogee arches, and close panelling fills the spaces below the straight top. The priest's stall was planned with a groined canopy and the deacons' stalls are decorated overhead with cusping and centred heads. You will see that the carving above the piscina and first stall was never completed; this must have been where work came to an untimely halt in 1349 or just after. There is a *squint* through to the *High altar* above the piscina bowl and the windows at the back of the sedilia were evidently renewed during the 1860s rebuilding and may have been altered. The scale and elaboration of the aisle suggest that it was perhaps planned as a parish church in miniature for use while the rest of the ambitious rebuilding went ahead. Over its *sanctuary* the roof was covered in the late C16 or early C17 with four stucco panels as a *celure* – crosses within lozenges decorated with *Tudor Roses* and the arms of the Sampson family. There are three good wooden centre bosses at the e. end and the roof itself is an interesting design. Basically a lean-to, extra timbers are framed in from the arcade side to give the impression of a cambered roof. Below it, a cornice of *clunch* was carved from end to end with figures, some of which can be recognised as angels. All is terribly mutilated but

Cautley thought that it might have a been a sequence of the *Seven Works of Mercy*. The graceful seven-bay *arcade* has tall, closely spaced arches with very attractive *hood moulds* carved as vine trails, and the octagonal *piers* have deeply moulded *capitals*. The w. bay shows again how work on the decoration was apparently interrupted. Above the arcade on the n. side are three *hatchments;* from e. to w. they are for: Sir Thomas Thorrowgood (1734), Katherine Thorrowgood (the last descendant of this important family, whose memorial you will see elsewhere), John Thorrowgood (1734).

The belfry floor in the tower is carried on heavy corbels and the bells, having been augmented to eight and lowered, are now rung from the ground floor. They are one of the best octaves in the county and have a 14 cwt. tenor. The early-C15 *font* is squat, the deep bowl panels carved with angels and circular designs; one face is blank and probably stood against an arcade pillar originally. The 1970s oak cover is thoughtfully designed, with shaped ribs rising to a finial. There is a section of painting on the s. wall of the nave which was apparently a *St George*, and within it can be seen the hook that once supported the tester of a pulpit. The C17 arrangement of box pews grouped around a pulpit well down the nave lasted here until the 1880s. Overhead, the C15 roof has alternating *hammerbeams* and *arch-braces* with the hammers carved as angels – now minus their heads. Those at the e. end carry shields carved with *Passion emblems* and the e. bay is a celure with curious bunched ribbon decoration painted in white on the main timbers. *Rood* and *screen* have gone (except for the section in the n. aisle) but the stair to the *loft* is in the s. wall and the small opening above the arcade shows that it probably connected with another screen in the n. aisle. The stem of the worn C15 wooden lectern is hexagonal (very like the one at Aldham) with little flying buttresses and miniature image stools. The handsome and very upright eagle on top is later – possibly C16. The C19 rebuilding included a wooden chancel arch resting on large stone figure corbels, and the spiky *reredos* has gabled and pinnacled side niches which have been effectively complemented by vivid little perspective paintings.

Kesgrave, All Saints (G6): The church stands by the side of the busy Ipswich-Woodbridge road and looks a conventional enough building, but there are surprises in store. The base of the tower has angled buttresses, a blocked w.

doorway, and a window above it with 'Y' *tracery* that dates from about 1300. Having collapsed or become ruinous by the early C16, it was restored to its full height in red brick patterned in dark blue and topped with stepped battlements. The large early-C14 n. *porch* has *ball flower* in the *dripstone* of the outer arch with an ample niche above it, and there are small windows at high level in the *nave* wall on either side. The C13 *chancel* is lit by side *lancets* and an unusual e. window. Its three stepped lancets lie under one arch, and in the space above them there is blind *plate tracery* – pairs of *trefoils* and *quatrefoils*, with a *sexfoil* at the top. Moving round to the s. side, one finds that the picture changes dramatically, for in 1980 a large extension designed by Derek Woodley was added that has changed the character of the church significantly. In red brick, it stands at right angles to the nave, and the sloping e. wall is hung with tiles in Kentish fashion. There is a large dormer on that side, and the shaped s. wall is broken by slit windows; *vestry*, cloakrooms, and kitchen continue back to join the tower.

The new work has transformed the interior and given it an exciting new dimension. From within, the form is like that of a giant's upturned boat attached to the old nave, with massive ribs encased in pine above exposed brickwork. The *High altar* is now placed off centre below the dormer window with the seating formed in a hollow square around it, the old nave making up one side. And what a pleasure it is to have total carpeting and comfortable chairs that are appropriate in a modern setting! The *communion rails* are of welded iron with a beech top to match the altar, and the architect's award-winning designs for lectern and candlesticks were carried out by Hector Moore. The altar is backed by a lovely appliqué hanging made by Isabel Clover on which four musical angels swirl around a golden globe, illustrating the theme of Psalm 150. Overhead, a black quadrangular cross is suspended, bearing the symbolic nails of the Crucifixion. The *hatchment* on the n. wall of the tower was used at the funeral of George Thomas, a High Sheriff of the county who died in 1820, while that for Rebecca Thomas hangs opposite and dates from 1770. Late-C18 Creed and Lord's Prayer boards flank the arch and a well-restored set of George III *Royal Arms* hangs on the s. wall. The *font* was made by a Woodbridge mason called Smythe in 1843. Overhead, the roof is a false *hammerbeam* with *king posts* above the *arch-braces*, but remedial work had to be done when the extension was built and the central timbers were replaced by steel and boxed in. When he was here in January 1643, *William Dowsing* ordered that eighteen cherubim be taken down and these would have been the carvings that once decorated the ends of the hammers. The *chancel* is now divided from the nave by a full-height glazed pine screen and has become the chapel of *St Francis*. The old *rood beam* remains just inside, and some of the C19 benches from the nave have been installed. The *Decalogue* board of the set hangs on the n. wall, and in the *sanctuary* there is a large early-C14 *piscina* with attached shafts and ring *capitals*.

Before leaving, have a look at the coffin-shaped tomb e. of the entrance to the churchyard. It was originally for Rosabella Chilcot who died in 1837 and her epitaph begins:

Stop traveller and drop the sympathetic tear . . .

Then her brother John died in 1851, also in his twenties, and the following was added:

Meek resignation did his mind display
While pale disease consum'd his life away

He had been a horse dealer, and to the r. of the verse there is a bas-relief of him displaying a likely nag to a prospective buyer (the same mason was probably responsible for the carving on Abraham Easter's stone at Woodbridge). The top of the tomb bears the epitaph of John's niece, Repronia Lee, a gypsy queen who also died young in 1862. The family evidently favoured the parting verse and this one is in the ripe tradition of Victorian sentiment:

Put your arms around me mother,
Draw your chair beside my bed,
Let me lean upon your bosom,
This poor weary aching head.
Once I thought I could not leave you,
Once I was afraid to die,
Now I feel 'tis Jesus calls me,
To his mansion in the skies.
Why should you be grieving mother,
That your child is going home,
To that land where sin and sorrow,
Pain and weakness never come.

Kessingland, St Edmund (J2): For fishing communities along this coast, a fine upstanding church tower to serve as a landmark was always an asset, and Kessingland is no exception. It is a particularly interesting example, and one whose builder can be identified with fair certainty. He

was Richard Russell, MP and master mason of Dunwich, who also built Walberswick tower, and there are some features which are common to both. This one was started in 1436 or 1437, when Walberswick was being finished, and it progressed steadily for about three years. Then, Russell died, and another mason succeeded him; the changeover level can be seen where the pattern of *flushwork* and *quoins* alters in the buttresses. Work was completed around 1449, and the tower was ready to have the bells hung in 1454. Unlike Walberswick, there is no showy parapet and apparently there never was. Above a flushwork *base course*, the w. front is rather splendid, with an interesting variety of devices in the broad mouldings of the w. doorway – look for *St Edmund's* crown and arrows, *Tudor Rose*, mitre, pierced Sacred Heart, anchor and dolphin for the fishermen, a *Trinity shield* and another with *chalices* and wafers for the mass. There are large *censing* angels in the *spandrels*, a band of *quatrefoils* with shields above the doorway and, in the centre, the figure of the church's patron saint. The w. window has *headstops* that incline inwards, and the *groined* niches each side have angels carved on the bases, each flanked by masks. The tall, three-*light* bell openings have intricate *tracery* which is nicely matched in the belfry windows below. See how one of the *string courses* lifts over the belfry windows and incorporates little angled headstops as it does so. There are prominent *gargoyles*, and a *sanctus-bell window* shows below the line of an earlier nave roof on the e. side. The present roof is thatched. A circuit of the building shows that there have been significant changes over the years. By the late C16, the C14 church was partly in ruins, and the *chancel*, a chapel, and the s. *aisle* were pulled down. The e. end of the *nave* was blanked off, the s. *arcade* was filled in to form a new outer wall, and the s. *porch* was rebuilt against it. A tall section of the aisle s. wall still stands, and a stub remains attached to the nave. There is a *priest's door* to the w. of it which may have been moved there from the old chancel, or it may have been the access doorway to a *rood stair*. Beyond the e. end, one can trace the humped outline of the C14 chancel foundations, and a new, shorter chancel was built within them in 1908, 'in memory of parishioners drowned at sea'. By the end of the C17 the church was in trouble again, with a collapsed roof and shaky n. wall. The latter was taken down and rebuilt in red brick, 3ft. inside the original line – typically patterned with darker bricks, and with one of the buttresses inscribed: 'John Campe 1695'. The well-matched brick *vestry* at the w. end was added in the early years of the present century and extended in 1980. The inscription '1578 RB' on the porch parapet probably defines the date of rebuilding, and before going in, examine the fine little grotesque on the s.w. corner who pulls his mouth wide to let his tongue loll out. There are large king and queen *corbels* (moved from elsewhere) on either side of the inner doorway, and children of another age amused themselves by drawing sailing ships on the wooden seats.

On entering, a notice high on the n. wall catches the eye: 'This church was put out and rebuilt by the care of John Campe and Thos. Godfrey Gent in the year 1694 and finished in 95'. They were the churchwardens of the day who re-roofed the nave and rebuilt the n. wall. The starkness of the rectangular windows, with their plain wooden glazing bars, is more insistent from within; the windows on the other side date from the 1871 or 1908 restorations, and they lie within the outlines of the original C14 *arcade*, as does the s. door. Above it hangs a handsome set of George II *Royal Arms*, painted on canvas, and with the distinction of the artist's signature – 'W.Cartwright 1741'. A lovely late-C14 font stands nearby, one of Suffolk's best, far superior to the standardised design seen in most of the area's churches. Its octagonal bowl is massive, and each face contains a coved niche under a *crocketted ogee* arch with flanking pinnacles. The seated figures are partly defaced, and their identification is conjectural; anti-clockwise from the s.: a queen; the *Blessed Virgin* and Child; a queen; a king; an ecclesiastic; *St Ursula* with the virgins under her cloak (?); a female saint which might be the Blessed Virgin enthroned; a king. The shaft is carved with eight niches under crocketted canopies in which bishops alternate with saints – perhaps the *Evangelists*. Above the font, an anchor has been embedded in the wall to form a striking memorial, and this seafaring theme is continued by the ship's wheel applied to the front of the pulpit. At the e. end of the n. wall a tablet commemorates Lieut. Robert Norris, a son of the rectory who was killed in the eighth Kaffir war in 1851. His fellow officers contributed the simple memorial by Gaffin further along which has a dove poised above it. The window opposite contains glass of 1929 by George Maile & Son – an attractive version of the *Three Marys* at the tomb (there are other windows by them at Blundeston and Somerleyton). The *sanctuary* of the modern chancel is backed by an oak *reredos*, and there are slate *Decalogue* panels on the e.

wall. Between them, the short, five-light window is filled with glass of 1912 by *Kempe & Tower*, with their logo in the bottom l.-hand border. The central Crucifixion, with the Blessed Virgin and *St John* has *St Edmund* on one side and *St Felix* on the other. A fine window. Looking back down the church, you will see how the alteration to the n. wall put the tower off-centre, and if you explore the vestry/chapel you will find another stained glass St Edmund, installed in 1937, maker unknown.

Kettlebaston, St Mary (D5): Winding lanes rise up to the little hamlet where the church and churchyard are blissfully peaceful. Passing through a little tunnel of yew, the first thing to catch the eye is a late-C14 niche with *dripstone* and *finial* set in the s.e. *chancel* buttress. It was originally shuttered to hide the image during Lent and was restored in 1946 when a wrought-iron grill in the form of 'M.R.' for the church's patron saint was fitted. The bas-relief within of the Coronation of the Virgin is a reproduction of one of the Kettlebaston alabasters; it was carved by Mr Green (Saunders of Ipswich) and coloured by Edith Chadwick. The *chancel* is C14 and there are interesting variations in the *Decorated tracery* of the windows; the *reticulations* in the e. window were renewed in 1902 but probably repeat the original. On the n. side there is an C18 brick *vestry* and the *rood stair* shows in the wall beyond. The *priest's door* on the s. side has *headstops* to the dripstone and there is a faint *scratch dial* still discernible on the s.e. buttress of the *nave*. The buttresses further w. are brick and so is the C18 *porch* with its rough wooden seats. The sturdy C14 tower has a belfry stair turret on the s. side, Decorated bell openings, and a later w. window. The early-C13 doorway is an excellent example of the *Transitional* style. The shafts and *capitals* are *Norman* but the arch is pointed; however, it is still decorated in the old way with a band of triangles.

Inside, this motif crops up again on the s. side of the square *font* and could mean that the same mason was involved. The rest of the bowl is carved with simple shallow patterns and there are rudimentary attached shafts at the corners. (It is odd that one of the supporting columns has been reversed at some time.) Despite the *Perpendicular* windows, the nave was originally Norman and one of the small *lancets* has been uncovered in the n. wall, its wide splays decorated with early-C14 scrolling. A plain C16 chest stands in front of the chunky tower arch and its early-C17 successor by the n. wall has bands of shallow carving and roundels in the four panels. In 1864 an important series of mid-C14 alabaster panels illustrating the *Annunciation*, Ascension, *Trinity* and Coronation of the Virgin was discovered in the chancel wall and is now in the British Museum. However, casts have been made and they are displayed in a case at the w. end. There is a section of small medieval tiles in front of the n. door but the rest of the floors are in homely brick, and it must be one of the last churches in regular use to depend on paraffin lamps and candles for evening light. Betjeman would have loved it. The nave roof has *tie-beams* and *king posts* and on the n. side the rood stair has been fitted with a wrought-iron grill designed by *Sir Ninian Comper*. In the window sill there is the simplest form of *piscina* marking the site of a medieval *altar* and now the old *Jacobean High altar* table stands there, with ponderous turned legs and prettily carved top rail and brackets.

Notches in the chancel arch show where the *tympanum* was fitted and the present screen was installed in the 1890s. Designed by the Revd. Ernest Geldart, an architectural cleric active in the Anglo-Catholic movement, it does not stretch across to the old access stairs. It has attractive tracery although the panels are too squat in relation to the overall height. The colourful decoration in medieval manner was applied by Enid Chadwick in 1950 and the figures from l. to r. are *St Felix, St Thomas More, St Thomas of Canterbury*, Cardinal John Fisher, *St Alban* and *St Fursey* – an enterprising choice to include two victims of Henry VIII's malice. Although the chancel roof is largely C19, the *wall plates* are carved with a running C17 motif, and in the n. wall below there is a C14 tomb recess under a shallow *ogee* arch topped by a replacement finial, with a repainted *consecration cross* nearby. On the s. side, the wall leans outwards and so does the handsome early-C14 suite of piscina and *sedilia*, its *trefoil* arches deeply moulded and the spaces divided by *quatrefoil* shafts. The *reredos* behind the free-standing *High altar* is another Geldart 1890s design painted by Enid Chadwick – a centre Annunciation and flanking figures of *St Peter, St Edmund*, the *Blessed Virgin* and *St Paul*. On the n. wall of the *sanctuary* is an alabaster and *touchstone* tablet for Joan, Lady Jermy 'whose arke after a passage of 87 yeres long through this deluge of teares on ye 6 Day of May Ano 1649 rested upon ye mount of joy'. Her epitaph is equally enchanting; do read it! On the floor of the chancel on that side is a *brass* inscription for a lady who was probably constrained to live as

she died, within her husband's shadow, without the courtesy of a Christian name:

The corpse of John Pricks wife lyes heere,
The pastor of this place.
Fower moneths and one and thirty yeerr
With him she ran her race.
And when some eightye yeres were past,
Her soule she did resigne
To her good God in August last,
Yeeres thrise five hundreth ninety nine.

Kettleburgh, St Andrew (G4): Church Lane winds up to finish at a pleasant pair of cottages and access is through the kissing-gate in their back yard. The C14 w. tower has a simple *base course*, *flushwork* in the buttresses, and modern stepped brick battlements. The w. window is *Perpendicular* but the bell openings have *Decorated tracery*. Within there is an excellent ring of six bells with a 7 cwt. tenor. The n. door is blocked and farther along the shape of a large archway in the wall shows where there was an entrance to a side chapel; the *trefoil piscina* that served its *altar* is still in place. The siting of the chapel may have been the reason why there are *clerestory* windows of three sizes below the eaves to give extra light for the *nave*, for strangely enough there are no other windows on that side. The *chancel* has a narrow Decorated window farther along and the e. window is Perpendicular. A heavy C18 to C19 brick buttress sits hard up against the small C14 *priest's door* and the s. facade has varied windows scattered with charming abandon. Again there is a clerestory (with no associated aisle), and the tall and wide *Tudor lancet* in the chancel is quite unusual. The low C14 *porch* has a minuscule *base course* and the inner door retains its original closing ring and strap hinges.

A rather nice set of Queen Anne *Royal Arms* stands on the tower screen; the background is a dusky pink with drapes and there are cutout acanthus scrolls each side. The C15 *font* is a familiar design, although it now lacks the lions round the shaft. There are seated lions in the bowl panels, alternating with angels bearing shields whose heraldry belongs to the Charles and Ramsey families. Sir Thomas Charles married Alice Ramsey and when she died a widow in 1463 she may have left money to provide the font. The low C17 cover is in good condition, with arched supports rising to a centre shaft and ball *finial*. There were restorations here in the 1880s and 1890s and it looks as though the *arch-braced* roof was at least partially replaced then. Steps leading to the vanished *rood loft* rise from a s. window embrasure. *Cautley* was scandalised by the screen which was installed in 1891 but I find it a light and acceptable pastiche of the *Jacobean* style, with pierced *tracery* and acorn pendants, and it happily accommodates some original C17 panels in the base. The pulpit has some more and so has the lectern. There are four low C15 benches of two sizes in the chancel, and the large pair are so like those at Earl Soham that I believe them to be from the same workshop. On the n. side there are remains of a man astride a lion, and the lower benches have parts of three small figures and a castle which has a face peeping from its tiny window. Overhead, the medieval *arch-braced* roof has its main timbers partially obscured by plaster, and the *wall plates* are embattled. The original of Murillo's The Two Trinities is in the National Gallery and the church has an C18 copy which hangs on the chancel wall. Another item of interest at an entirely different level is the little coloured map of the village on the opposite wall which was produced by the W.I. as their contribution to the Jubilee celebrations in 1977. Also on that side there is a tablet by Sanders of Fitzroy Square for George Turner who died in 1839, having been rector for thirty-two years; not in itself remarkable, but further along a Gaffin tablet commemorates another George Turner who died in 1871 and who also served the parish for thirty-two years. Like father, like son. The two sections of the *communion rails* are C17, and their style suggests that they once formed part of a three-sided set like those at Cretingham and elsewhere. The *altar* beyond is a very lightweight *Stuart* table, set on blocks with a large top added, and in the s.e. corner lies a C13 coffin slab with the double omega sign on top. A pair of excellent *Decalogue* panels painted on canvas hangs on the e. wall. They date from the early C18 and are well lettered within frames with flanking scrolls, of a standard rather higher than the similar set at Saxtead. A slab on the n. side of the *sanctuary* bears 2ft. *brass* effigies of Arthur Pennyng and one his wives (1593). He wears a ruff and gown and the lady has a fashionable hat and brocaded petticoat. The figure of the second wife is missing, as it was when Cautley made his notes in 1934, although he had seen it in the church chest some time before. He vented his feelings by supposing that 'some vile sacrilegious pilferer' had pinched it – as no doubt they had.

Kirkley, St Peter and St John (J1): The church stands on St Peter's Road, and Rectory Road aligns with the e. end to provide a glimpse of the sea beyond the cliffs. Until 1974 the dedication was to St Peter alone, but following the demolition of the Victorian Lowestoft St John's, the new title was adopted in 1974. There has been a church on this site since before the Conquest, and the C14 saw a total rebuilding, but decay and neglect followed in the C17 and the building was abandoned in 1680. Parishioners made use of nearby Pakefield until 1750 when a partial restoration was put in hand, but it was not until 1874 that a fresh start was made, and most of the work was completed within two years under the direction of J.L. Clemence. Porches were added in the late 1880s, and in 1893 the baptistery followed, designed by local architect Thomas Porter. It is a substantial church, the walls clad with high quality *knapped* flint, and although the layout is largely conventional, with *nave*, *aisles* and *chancel*, two variations give it particular interest. Firstly, the early C15 tower survived and was restored, but the main axis of the building was moved sideways so that the tower now stands at the n.w. corner. It has a *Perpendicular* w. window with small *headstops*, there is a single *sound hole* to the s., and the upper stage was rebuilt and furnished with solid corner turrets. The nave has square *clerestory* windows styled like sound holes, and the remainder of the windows are in Perpendicular style. The second and more interesting variation in the plan is the placing of the apsidal baptistery at the w. end of the s. aisle. It has a series of *lancets* with *trefoil* and *quatrefoil tracery* set in the curved wall, and the top half of a Perpendicular window was eccentrically added at high level in the e. wall. Before going in, you may like to examine some of the C18 gravestones that remain in the churchyard. One decorated with crossed bones leans against the s. aisle wall and commemorates James Meen who died in 1777.

Within, the dull white brick of the walls and octagonal *piers* is relieved with polychrome banding, and the *arcade* arches stand out in solid, rich red brick, matching the chancel arch. Overhead, the broad nave roof is *arch-braced* in pine. One enters the baptistery through a particularly fine wrought-iron screen, a modified version of a design by *Blomfield*. The *font* is a heavy octagon with inset marble roundels carved with *Agnus Deis* and a *pelican in her piety*, and there are dark marble stub shafts below. The tall openwork cover matches the screen; made by Hart & Peard, it is the only wrought-iron example in the county. One of the windows contains the figure of *St Felix*, and another has Christ with a family group in glass designed by H.J. Salisbury of St Albans in 1892 (the same firm provided the chancel window glass for Pakefield and Lowestoft, Christ Church a few years later). Fragments of the church's original font were found during the C19 rebuilding, but before that in 1750, a replacement had been obtained from All Saints, Gillingham in Norfolk. Dating from the late C14, it has *quatrefoils* and *trefoils* boldly carved in the bowl panels, and stands (minus its base) at the w. end of the nave. The clock below the w. window displays yet more elaborate ironwork in its case, painted and gilt, with two attendant angels; with a movement by Thwaite & Rees, and delightfully silvery chimes, it was installed in 1896. At the e. end of the n. aisle there is a small chapel of the Blessed Sacrament, and its *lancet* windows by an unidentified glazier contain pleasing designs. On the n. side, Christ stands within an oval holding the *chalice* and wafer, with Agnus Dei, pelican, *altar*, and two *censing* angels below; all three figures in the e. lancets are of the *Blessed Virgin*, and the figures have an attractive grainy texture. I believe that the small *reredos* below was made in 1903 for the now demolished church of St Peter's Lowestoft. It is in triptych form and was designed, carved and painted by Robert Anning Bell and Dacres Adam, two artists active in the *Arts and Crafts* movement. In the s. aisle the window at the w. end is a World War I memorial, and next along is an average example of *Ward & Hughes* glass – *St Peter* kneeling before Christ surrounded by a flock of sheep. To the e. are rather stereotyped 1920s figures *of St Cuthbert* and *St George*, and the last window on that side displays the Blessed Virgin and Child with *St John* – a quietly lush treatment (maker unknown) dating from about 1920. The aisle e. window is a painful piece of 1880s work by W.H. Constable who had enough nerve to describe himself as an artist. There are not many memorials to examine, but J. Balls (of Lowestoft?) provided a simple tablet in 1852 for Capt. Thomas Leggett who died in Rio de Janeiro. It was sited to the l. of the aisle e. window after the rebuilding, and on the s. wall there is one of the few Suffolk masonic memorials. The church boasts a pair of C19 brass eagle lecterns, and the chancel screen is another piece of high quality wrought-iron work installed in 1896, with delicate tracery painted and gilt. The *High altar* is backed by a large reredos, richly panelled, with figures of the Blessed Virgin and Child and St Peter in the upper panels; below from l. to r. are ranged *St*

Thomas of Canterbury (?), *St George*, *St Michael*, and *St Nicholas*, one of the patron saints of sailors. The window above is filled with good, C15-style glass by *Kempe* in which creamy yellow colour predominates, and Christ in Majesty is placed in the centre flanked by the archangels.

Kirton, St Mary and St Martin (G7): The church is secluded at the end of Church Lane, and it bears a dedication unique in Suffolk – there are only three pre-*Reformation* examples in England. The walls of the early-C16 tower are an attractive mixture of brick, flint pebbles, and large blocks of *septaria;* the bell openings are in brick and so are the stepped battlements above them. The body of the church is likely to date from the late C13, but there have been wholesale alterations over the years. Walking round, you will find that the C14 s. doorway has been blocked, and nearby there is a late-C18 or early-C19 window in 'gothick' style. Further along, a smooth modern replacement is in *Tudor* format, with a restored *lancet* beyond it. The *chancel* has all the appearance of a C19 restoration, and the whole e. wall was replaced in brick. The n.e. *vestry* is the same period (with a modern infill) and the n. *aisle* was added in 1858. A recent innovation is the spacious brick vestibule which fits neatly in the angle of tower and aisle. Prior to that, the w. door was the main entrance, but the organ has now been moved into the tower behind tiered benches and the whole church re-floored. It is a simple, bright interior with touches of colour, and is most attractive. Although no longer mandatory, one sometimes finds modern *Royal Arms*, and there is a 1950s set here, painted on a panel above the old s. door. The medieval *arch-braced* roof was extensively restored in the C19, and a three-bay Victorian *arcade* opens into the aisle. The oak benches form the village's World War II memorial, seven of them bearing RAF wings, one with the badge of the Suffolk Regt, and most of the of the others carved with names. The *font* now stands in the space vacated by the organ at the e. end of the aisle, and although it has been restored it is basically C13. The square bowl has nook shafts at the corners, and the four shafts have *capitals* whose foliage spreads under the bowl. Beyond, a red wall hanging displays a stylised dove of the Holy Spirit in a bright roundel. The lancet by the pulpit contains 1870s glass which is a typical commercial product of the period – maker unknown. Although it is not an extreme example, this is a *weeping chancel*, and its C15 arch-braced roof has deep, moulded *wall plates.* The *sanctuary* is bounded by simple modern *communion rails* with wrought-iron standards, and there is a C14 *piscina* with *dropped-sill sedilia* alongside. When the e. wall was rebuilt, the flanking niches were retained, and the one on the l. has miniature capitals below the arch. A door shape is outlined on the n. wall, and the original *priest's door* of about 1300 can still be seen from within the vestry.

Knodishall, St Laurence (I4): There can be few more pleasant places on a summer's day than the churchyard here, fringed by limes, a young copper beech glowing over the grass, and the stream that becomes the Hundred River tinkling under the little bridge down the lane. A church has stood here since *Norman* times and the shape of an C11 doorway can be found in the n. wall of the *nave* – blocked now, with its top half glazed. Further along, the stratified flints in the wall are typical of an early building. The *chancel* was rebuilt about 1320, a *vestry* was added in 1838, and a small organ chamber of 1907 projects on the s. side. The heavy triangular brick buttresses on the s. frontage date from 1843, and the windows on that side are an interesting mixture of styles and periods – two in restored *Tudor* brick, one with *Decorated tracery*, and a *lancet* in the chancel with amended C14 tracery; the wide lancet at the w. end is a C19 addition. The 1843 alterations removed a brick s. *porch* and blocked up the door that it sheltered, inserting a window in its place. Before the advent of the porch, *scratch dials* were cut on the door *jambs*, and there are three on the l. side (one good), and a faint one on the r. The C15 tower has angle buttresses up to the bell stage, and they have decorative *ashlar* panels just below the top. The bell openings have been restored, and above them, the *flushwork* parapet displays shields of the Jenneys, the family who held the manor from 1365 until the C18, and who built the tower. Nave and chancel have been re-tiled, but the outline of the former roof still shows on the e. face of the tower. Entry is now through the w. doorway, and there are hung shields in the *spandrels* of its arch, above worn, inward turning *headstops.*

The interior is calm and soothing – bright white walls and coved ceiling, with a C19 braced rafter roof in the chancel, and no chancel arch or screen to break the vista. It is possible that the tower gallery screen once formed part of the *rood screen.* It dates from the late C15 and has simple *tracery* above *castellated transoms.* A small set of Hanoverian *Royal Arms* in gilded cast metal perch

on top. The good C13 *font* by the n. doorway is the standard design that must have been mass produced in *Purbeck marble,* with pairs of shallow arches in its bowl panels and eight shafts ringing the centre column. The attractive glass of 1910 in the broad lancet opposite is by W.B. Simpson & Sons, a firm better known for its work on decorated tiles, often in elaborate pictorial panels. The resurrected Christ in crimson and salmon robes stands before the cross, and the broad blue border is crocketted with a golden crown at the peak. This is the only example of their work that I have identified in Suffolk. The sturdy oak benches were installed in the *nave* in 1902, and the church's only remaining piece of medieval glass can be seen in the head of the Tudor window on the s. side. The shield of arms in the window further along relates to George Whitaker, rector here for over forty years and responsible for the restoration in 1845. The *Jacobean* pulpit has three ranges of panels – lozenges, *blind arches,* and scrolls, all in shallow but good carving. The photograph on the wall above is a full scale reproduction of William Dyce's 'The meeting of Jacob and Rachel', painted in 1851. The original was given to the church in 1946, and sold in 1983 to finance a major restoration. The artist was a friend and forerunner of the *pre-Raphaelites,* and the picture was one of several versions of the subject, a charming piece of Victorian romanticism. The wooden lectern is an excellent piece of modern carving, a peregrine falcon, compact and finely carved. The church's only *brass* is a good one and is now mounted on the n. wall of the chancel. John Jenney died in 1460, having been a Norwich burgess, and as Lord of the Manor he financed the building of the tower. He is shown wearing an early version of the Yorkist style of armour, with a short sword; the plate on his right shoulder for extra protection is known as a 'moton', and this is the only example to be found in Suffolk. His wife Margaret wears a horned headdress and veil, and the grave slab (now lost) originally carried, in addition, the effigies of his first wife and three children. When working on the organ chamber, the builders uncovered the remains of the early-C14 *piscina,* and half of its *trefoil* arch can be seen to the l. There are C19 *Decalogue* boards on the e. wall, and the window is filled with 1930s glass designed by G.E.R. Smith and made by the A.K. Nicholson Studios. Christ the King is flanked by *St Laurence* and the *Blessed Virgin* – calm figures backed by tapestries within patterned borders; angel children with alpha and omega shields fill the tracery, and the shields of East Anglia and the province of Canterbury feature at the bottom.

Lackford, St Laurence (B3): The church has a delectable setting in an acre of churchyard away from the village, surrounded by mature beeches and approached by a longish track. Davy's 1829 journal says: 'I have not seen a place of religious worship so utterly neglected as this is; it is a great discredit both to the rector and to his parishioners'. Not surprising, therefore, that the 1868 restoration was on a large scale, both inside and out. The n. *aisle* had been pulled down in the C16, the *arcade* blocked up, and windows inserted, so a narrow new one was substituted, lit by a line of sharp little *lancets*. On that side, the new roof slopes in one sweep over *nave* and aisle. The mid-C14 tower has a bulging stairway up to the belfry stage on the s. side and two prominent *drip courses*. The upper level was altered in the C15, stepped brick battlements were applied in the C16, and the bell openings renewed in the C19.

The mid-C14 *porch* has stone seats along each side and inside the church is a fine *font* of the same period. Standing on a Victorian base, with stub shaft and deep bowl, the panels are carved with different foliage patterns, including ivy and roses, with more on the chamfer below. It was plastered over to protect it in the C17 and is in better condition than most. The simple *arch-braced* roofs in nave and *chancel* are C19 but the n. arcade is early-C14 and there is a matching arch further e. which has leaf decoration on the outer sections of the *capitals*. This arch leads into an extension of the n. aisle which was originally a chapel. There is a *squint* from here through to the chancel, and both ends of it have sharply gabled *trefoil* arches on *Early English* capitals and shafts – a most unusual elaboration and, what is more, a *piscina* drain is set within it at the chapel end. You will notice that there is a break in the line of the nave walls at the e. end and that they turn inwards making it safe to assume that there was a central tower early in the church's history. The chancel arch was remade at the restoration and provides no confirmation of this, but it might be significant that the squint from the chapel aligns with a point well to the w. of the *High altar* and could be evidence of an original short chancel beyond a centre tower. The C19 bench lining the aisle wall incorporates some medieval bench ends; one at the w. end has the remains of a carved animal and another is decorated with quite fine *tracery*. The C17

pulpit is in plain panelled oak, raised on a short centre stem. A window on the s. side of the nave has a dropped and stepped sill and there is a piscina on the r.-hand side, marking the site of a *guild* altar. The large C13 grave slab clamped to the s. side of the chancel arch has three discoid crosses spaced down the centre spine (there is another like it outside by the porch) and in the *sanctuary* there are C13 stepped *sedilia* under unequal restored arches separated by a pillar. Beyond is a simple piscina with a trefoil arch. There is a tomb recess in the n. wall of the sanctuary and in the e. wall nearby is a very tall niche under a *cinquefoiled* arch. The 1871 glass in the e. window was designed by *Henry Holiday* for *James Powell & Sons* of Whitefriars and is poor stuff. Christ stands in the centre blessing a mother and child on the l. and a father and babe on the r. The flesh work has lost nearly all its colour and curious tendrils of wispy foliage rise up from behind the figures, with the rest of the window taken up by close patterning. On the n. face of the chancel arch is the only list of incumbents that I have ever seen engraved on a large brass plate. Returning to the s. door, you will see a memorial in the nave to the Revd. William Greaves, a rector who died in 1806. It is one of the chaste little tablets with good lettering produced by de Carle of Norwich, a simple shallow sarcophagus standing on a pair of lion feet, set against a grey background.

Lakenheath, St Mary (B2): Standing a little above the village street, this is a church not to be missed, with lots of interest and beauty. The first thing one notices is the two-storey extension built on the w. face of the tower, in mottled brick and flint with a window above an C18 door and brick arch. This was a post-*Reformation* schoolroom built of material filched from the old church of Eriswell, St Peter. Manor business was at one time transacted there and it was still doing duty as the village school in the C19. The lower stages of the C13 tower have blocked *lancets*; above them are two-*light* bell openings with attractive *tracery*, and worn symbols of the *Four Evangelists* stand on the corner battlements around the centre spirelet. An excellent ring of six bells with a 13 cwt. tenor hangs within the tower, and two of them were cast in Cambridge before the *Reformation*. Traces of *Norman* work can be seen on the outside of the *chancel* walls – a fragment of a window or blind *arcade* on the n. side and a clear mark on the s. side where the building terminated before a C13 rebuild extended it eastwards. The evidence for this is a lancet on the n. side and the outlines of a C13 chapel which became a *vestry* before being demolished in the C18.

Within is a substantial Norman chancel arch with roll mouldings, on scalloped *capitals* and triple columns. Beyond it on the n. side of the chancel is a short column and fragment of an arch which may have been part of blank arcading round the e. end of the original building. The doorway to the old n. chapel has been re-set within the blanked-off arch that linked it with the chancel. There is a small *piscina* tucked into the s.e. corner of the chancel, with *dropped-sill sedilia* alongside. There is no *screen* now but the stairs to the old *rood loft* are within the wall on the s. side of the chancel arch. Next to them is a wall painting of the risen Christ, in monochrome. The head shows that this was fine work but much is now lost under two large obliterating patches.

The *nave* arcades have interesting variations; on the s. side cylindrical Norman sections support C13 bases which in turn carry C15 octagonal *piers* whose concave faces have *trefoil* tops. These are seen again at the w. end of the n. arcade, and e. of them is a section of wall which probably marks the w. end of the Norman church. This is directly opposite the s. door and on it is some C14 wall painting that needs to be studied with some care before the fragments make sense because part of it has been overlaid with a diaper pattern in black. At the bottom on the r., *St Edmund*, with crown and nimbus, holds three arrows in his right hand; above this, one arm and the shadowy figure of *St John* is all that is left of a Calvary. From the cross, a tree branches out with scenes from the life of Christ – the flagellation on the l. and Christ carrying his cross on the r. Above to the l., the jaws of hell have largely to be imagined, but some of the naked souls can be seen and there is a Judgement scene to the r. Further e., the arcade *spandrels* contain faint paintings of the *Annunciation* and the Resurrection, and on the pillar below are lifesize figures in dusky red that are too indistinct to identify. Across the nave above the arcade, an Elizabethan text in gothic lettering from St John's Gospel reads: 'Labour not for ye meate which perisheth'. The fine C15 octagonal pulpit, with good and varied tracery at head and foot of the panels, stands on a shapely coved stem. Across from it, on the s. side of the nave, is a *brass* with 18in. figures of an early-C16 civilian and his wife; he in a gown with high lapels, she with a turban headdress. The inscription has been lost, but the couple are likely to have been

a local farmer and his wife, John and Cecily Lacey. The C14 n. *aisle* has *reticulated tracery* in the side windows and a beautiful little roundel window over the *altar* contains glass of 1905 – a fine *Blessed Virgin* and *St Michael* flanking Christ in majesty. On the n. wall is a memorial to Lord Kitchener who went down with the cruiser *Hampshire* in 1916. By an historical coincidence one of his forebears came from Hampshire in 1666 as bailiff here to the Styward family, Lords of the Manor. There is another memorial to him at Aspall, his mother's village. The C13 octagonal *font* to the w. is the finest of its period in the county and is thought to have come from the old church of St Peter of Eriswell after the *Reformation*. The centre shaft is ringed with alternating thick and thin shafts, and each face has a sharply defined gable from which exuberant *crockets* sprout. Above are deeply recessed arches enriched with *dogtooth* ornament. The elegant cover provided in 1961 has a dove on the *finial*. At the e. end of the C15 s. aisle is a *Jacobean box pew* with panels of scroll carving, probably used by the Styward family. In the corner next to it is the tomb of Simeon Styward who died in 1568, its grey *Purbeck marble* very worn, with a battered heraldic *achievement* at the back. Everything about it is old fashioned for the period except the inscription in Roman capitals on the cornice and the bevel of the tomb

Lakenheath, St Mary: Tiger bench end

slab. Before the space was thus taken up, there was an altar to the Holy Trinity here and the piscina and dropped-sill sedilia remain. To the w. of the large tomb, an oblong panel in the wall is the memorial to Simeon's wife, Joanna, with a shield of arms hung on a tree with crossed swords below, all in shallow relief. Further w. can be seen a large *Royal Arms* of Charles II on boards, dated 1678 and rescued from neglect and decay 300 years later.

So far, very little has been said about the church's woodwork, but the lovely range of C15 benches is perhaps the one thing that draws enthusiasts to Lakenheath. Their pierced and traceried backs gleam like newly fallen chestnuts, and though many have been cruelly defaced, the range of animals and grotesques on the buttressed armrests is one of the best to be found anywhere and echoes the medieval *bestiaries* excellently. On the s. side of the nave, look for the tigress with the mirror; legend had it that to catch a tiger cub one must ride off with it and elude the parents. If the tigress followed too closely, the trick was to throw down a mirror so that she would mistake the reflection for her cub and lick it while the hunter escaped. Call the tigress 'humanity', the cub 'the soul', the hunter 'the Devil', the mirror 'sinful wordly pleasures' and there you have a sermon in a carving no bigger than your hand. On the n. side of the s. aisle is a dog licking itself because the bestiary taught that thus dogs heal their wounds. In the n. aisle at the e. end is an elongated beaver bent over itself; it was believed that it was hunted to extract certain drugs from its genitals and that, when cornered, it would bite them off to show that the whole thing was not worth it. (There is another carving very like this at nearby Wilton in Norfolk.) Further w. in the n. aisle, a whale swallows a fish (the fate of sinners at the hands of the Devil), and elsewhere you will easily identify the elephant and castle, the contortionist and the *unicorn*. The C20 also added its quota of good work in the benches at the w. end have crisp *poppyheads* and a variety of subjects on the elbows, including St Edmund, a *griffin*, a *chalice* and *paten*, and a bell and wheel. Above all this is a lovely early-C15 roof, surely designed by the master who worked at Mildenhall, Hockwold and Methwold. *Arch-braced tie-beams* have tracery in the spandrels and either side of the *queen posts*, and they alternate with *hammerbeams* bearing angels with outstretched wings. These were defaced more successfully than those at Mildenhall during the Commonwealth and the wings were not restored until the C19. *Hassocks* are

Lakenheath, St Mary: Tussocks

often marvels of meticulous embroidery, but by the n. nave pillar opposite the door you will find two of their rustic ancestors. A clump or tussock of the sedge *Carex paniculata* was known as a hassock and they were brought into church to kneel or sit on. Now harsh and prickly as a week-old beard, they must in their youth have been balm to the knees. Others like them survive at Eriswell and Icklingham.

Langham, St Mary (D4): The church is quite hidden from the road and a visit entails a quarter of a mile walk across meadowland, so a careful look at the map and an enquiry about the key are advised. The setting is a lovely one, with the Hall to the n.w. and mature trees grouped attractively round the church. The *nave* was entirely rebuilt to the design of *E.C. Hakewill* in 1877 in *Early English* style, using a great deal of material from the old building. A western double bellcote and a s. *porch* were added, and ten years later the *chancel* was rebuilt to match, together with a *vestry*-cum-organ chamber on the s. side. Although all the windows are C19 their *tracery* may well have been copied from the originals. For some obscure reason, the head of a small *lancet* was used to form a niche in the e. face of the n.w. nave buttress next to the blocked n. door.

As one would expect, the interior is largely C19 in feeling but there are some interesting things to see. The late-C14 *font* with its *castellated* rim stands on a high step, and the bowl panels contain *cusped* and *crocketted ogee* arches; an heraldic shield is repeated within four of them and there are squared-off grotesque heads in the rest; the carving is curiously crude. At the angles below the bowl there are worn human heads, but the odd thing is that one to the e. is a lamb's head. I wonder why? On the n. wall there is a *brass* recording a benefaction by John Jollye who died in 1630, leaving £100 to buy land to be let for the benefit of the poor, stipulating distributions at Christmas and on Midsummer day. The C19 benches have lozenge-shaped *poppyheads*, except for the pair at the w. end which have kneeling angels. After 100 years they have lost their arms, showing that ordinary wear and tear as well as deliberate mutilation can figure in the life cycle of an average bench end. The *rood loft* stair rises on the n. side and the C15 *screen* is a very interesting example. It is sadly mutilated but note that the openwork tracery front of the old rood loft has survived, having been moved back and placed on top of the screen itself. The base panels have been cut down so that the traceried plinth now obscures their lower sections, and although those on the l. retain their original colour and stencilled patterns, those on the r. are rough replacements. The tracery in the panels must have been fine but all the applied crocketting has been stripped away. The main *lights* have cusped ogee arches, with dense tracery above them. The clue to the unusual feature of this screen lies in the mortices cut at sill level on either side of the entrance, and the long grooves above them. They show that originally there would have been projecting wings forming bays each side of the entrance for *altars*. The same arrangement may be seen on the more elaborate screen at Ranworth in Norfolk and, like Ranworth, there would have been a coved canopy beneath the loft, probably across the entire width. In the chancel there are niches with tall crocketted *finials* each side of the altar and it is strange that, although they are of the same period, they do not match (the heights differ and the one on the n. has blank shields each side of the finial). Both have traces of colour within. The *piscina* has a reconstructed arch on which is cut 'H.K. 1875'. It is unusual to find graffiti such as this in the *sanctuary* and it may have been taken from elsewhere in the old building. The wooden *credence shelf*, however, looks original.

Lavenham, St Peter and St Paul (D6): Suffolk is rich in splendid churches but for many people Lavenham is the finest, and is remembered with affection and respect by the thousands who visit year by year. It is solidly magnificent and the exterior has a unity and strength that bears comparison with any parish church in England. Apart from the early-C14 *chancel*, with flowing *tracery* in the e. window and the unusual *trefoil* shapes in the single s. window, the building is a coherent essay in the mature *Perpendicular* style. It was raised on the wealth of the Earls of

Oxford and the Lavenham clothiers (particularly the Springs); the great rebuilding and extension began about 1470 when Thomas Spring II built the *vestry* at the e. end. Just before he died he saw the base of the tower laid in 1486 and it rose to just above the level of the belfry windows in the first phase. John de Vere, 13th Earl of Oxford, that powerful champion of the first *Tudor* king, Henry VII, counted the manor of Lavenham among his many possessions and he joined with the Springs in the new project. The *nave* was rebuilt from e. to w. and at the time of Lord Oxford's death in 1513 it was finished, together with the *aisles* and *porch*. Meanwhile, the chapel of the Holy Trinity, n. of the chancel, had been built by Simon and Elizabeth Branche about 1500. The tower was finally completed in the 1520s, using the bequests of wealthy clothiers, particularly that of Thomas Spring III. He and his wife Alice began the building of the Lady chapel s. of the chancel in about 1523.

Having generalised, let us look at the outside in detail. The splendidly proportioned tower is a landmark for miles and has substantial square projections at each corner which are themselves buttressed. *String courses* break the profile up to the top of the first building stage (where the star of the de Vere family is set in the walls), and then it sweeps up past large three-*light* bell openings to a decorated but severe parapet. It has been suggested that pinnacles and perhaps a spire were envisaged but there is little evidence for this and I do not think it likely. The design may have been the work of Simon Clerk who was the king's master mason at Eton and Cambridge. The deep *base course* is decorated with shields (many of them worn) which carry the de Vere arms and three versions of Thomas Spring's merchant's mark. By the time the tower was completed, Thomas Spring III had been knighted and the parapet repeats his arms no less than 32 times. The w. door with its worn tracery is original, and note that besides the de Vere arms there is a *chalice* and wafer carved at the top. An indent in the lowest niche on the s.w. buttress shows that there was once a *brass* placed there. Within the tower hang one of the best known rings in the world. They are an outstanding eight and the 21 cwt. tenor bell, cast by Miles Gray of Colchester in 1625, is renowned for the sweetness of its sound. It was cast in a field to the w. of the church and the anniversary of the event on 21 June is still celebrated by special ringing. There is a tradition that the benefactors threw silver coins into the

Lavenham, St Peter and St Paul

molten metal to produce its astonishing purity of tone. The battlements of nave, porch, and aisles are pierced with carvings of pointed trefoil leaves and the tall, closely spaced *clerestory* windows act as a foil to the heavier aisle windows below. The aisle buttresses are decorated with *cusped* and *crocketted ogee* arches within which leaf shapes echo the theme of the battlements. All the surfaces are *ashlar* and, as the style is reminiscent of Saffron Walden and Cambridge, Great St Mary's, it may follow that John Wastell (who followed Clerk at King's College) was the architect. The distinctive octagonal *rood stair* turret at the s.e. corner of the nave was part of the earlier church and is capped by a tall crocketted pinnacle embellished with a delicate openwork *finial*. The matching chapels that flank the chancel are slightly higher and broader than the aisles and their e. walls carry the best *flushwork* on the building. There is an inscription below the parapet of each recording their foundation, and the words asking us to pray for the souls of the donors were chiselled away during the Commonwealth. The C16 door in the s. wall has *linen-fold panelling* with the Spring arms in the *spandrels* and there are headless figures on

the parapet. There is flushwork on the e. wall of the vestry and a stone panel bears the faint marks of a brass, another instance of the unusual placing of a brass outside. Just round the corner is a gargantuan *gargoyle*, and the replica *churchyard cross* nearby is a memorial to John Croker and his wife; he was the rector largely responsible for the restorations and alterations of the second half of the C19. It is unique in my experience because not only does it carry verses of well-loved hymns but their tunes are set out as well. The s. porch was the particular gift of John, 13th Earl of Oxford, and is correspondingly lavish. The s. front has recently been cleaned and restored. Below the stepped and pierced battlements the centre canopied niche contains modern figures of the church's patron saints. On either side shallow niches contain arches with tall crocketted finials, within which are the shields of the 9th to 13th earls; they are each enclosed within the Garter which is embellished with little animals on the r.-hand side. Full details of the heraldry are displayed just within the church. The spandrels of the outer arch are carved with a weathered boar, a punning badge of the de Vere family from the Latin 'verres'. The *fan vaulting* within is likely to have been a John Wastell design and it was comprehensively restored in

1865. The fine inner doors with their linen-fold panelling are original and in the upper corners boars are carved hanging from fire jacks, another de Vere punning badge which presumes that Sir John was familiarly known as 'Sir Jack'.

A few steps down lead to an interior of great spaciousness and dignity. The openback C19 benches do not obtrude and the w. end has been largely cleared. The *piers* of the *arcades* have attached shafts on all four sides whose *capitals* vary in detail and the entire space between arches and clerestory is filled with blind tracery – blank shields in *quatrefoils* and lozenges predominating, under a line of cresting below the windows. Half-round shafts rise to carved *corbels*, on which stand the *wall post* figures. The nave roof is a restrained cambered design and the two bays at the e. end are panelled to form a *celure* for the *rood*. There you will see *bosses* freshly painted and gilded displaying the *Evangelistic symbols* in the centre, flanked by the Oxford and Neville arms and two of Thomas Spring II's merchant's marks. There are a few fragments of medieval glass in the clerestory windows and by using binoculars a medieval beacon can be identified in the sixth window from the w. end on the n. side, with another further along.

The lean-to aisle roofs have richly carved main timbers and *wall plates*, and there are seated figures on the wall posts of the s. aisle, with standing figures in the n. aisle, including *SS Simon, Jude* and *James the Less*. The recurring themes in the decoration are the de Vere stars and boars, but over the *font* the carver relented and gave us children scrambling along a vine. A vine trail can also be seen carved in stone beneath the s. aisle windows; there are corresponding *paterae* in the n. aisle. Within the tower there are seats below blind panelling at the base of the walls and the w. window has glass designed by J. Milner Allen for *Lavers & Barraud*. It won a prize at the 1862 Exhibition but unfortunately the whole window was blown in by a landmine during World War II. However, the eight main panels were salvaged and re-set and they have a *St Peter* theme: top r., he strikes off Malchus' ear and denies Christ, and bottom r., he is crucified upside down. The *Purbeck marble* C14 font now stands by the s. door and will have belonged to the earlier church. It is very worn but the design is interesting because, apart from one which has shields of the patron saints, each panel of the shallow bowl was carved with two figures. They are scarcely recognisable now but the one to the s.w. appears to be a mother and child with a satanic angel turning away. There are now only

vestiges of the four figures and the four beasts around the stem. Three sets of *Royal Arms* are grouped around the s. door: e. side, a *Hanoverian* set delicately carved in relief, coloured and gilded; w. side, a set for George II painted on canvas; overhead, a brash Queen Elizabeth II *achievement*. The w. end of the n. aisle has a solid oak screen installed in 1917 and by it on the wall is a dark brass for Alleyn Dister who died in 1534:

A clothier vertuous while he was
In Lavenham many a year,
For as in lyefe he loved best,
The poore to clothe and feede,
So with the riche and all the rest,
He neighbourlie agreed . . .

He and his wife kneel, their children behind them, his arms are in a *cartouche* at the top and the gothic lettered inscription is framed with strapwork below. Over the n. door there are traces of the painted surrounds of Elizabethan texts and in the tracery of the adjoining window two lovely little C15 angels have bandeaux adorned with large crosses. A *Sacred monogram* can be seen in the tracery of the next window, together with sections of medieval canopy work. At the e. end of the n. aisle is the *chantry chapel* of one of the church's principal benefactors, Thomas Spring III. He died in 1523 and directed that he should be buried here before the altar of *St Catherine* and arranged for a chantry priest and bedesmen to pray daily for him, his wife, Henry VIII and Queen Catherine, and Thomas Wolsey, Archbishop of York. His tombstone, reaved of its brasses, lies within and the *parclose screen* is the finest example of woodwork in the church. Dark and lustrous, the luxuriant carving is full of lively *Renaissance* detail, with foliage tracery in the lower panels, pierced main uprights, and rope-like carving with twisted chains of beads. There is openwork cresting over *groined* canopies and the tracery of the main lights is enlivened by grotesques while some of the Spring shields are supported by small figures. A small St Catherine stands within a niche at the s.w. corner and *St Blaise* can be found at the s.e. corner. The work has affinities with the screen in Henry VII's chapel in Westminster Abbey and is likely to have been the work of Flemish craftsmen. An extremely skilful restoration was carried out in 1908.

Beyond is the screen to the n.e. chapel, tall and square-headed, with dense Perpendicular tracery above ogee arches. The little angel over the entrance is, I suspect, from the hand of *Henry Ringham*. On the e. side can be seen a door which led originally to a loft above the screen. The chapel is divided from the chancel by two varying sections of Perpendicular screenwork in which are cut three *elevation squints*. The n. wall has low arcading above stone benches and the e. window glass (almost certainly by Lavers & Barraud) dates from 1864. The top half shows one of Christ's miracles of healing while below there is the first miracle at Cana, with hieratic figures in C13 dress. The *altar* here is an excellent melon-legged early-C17 table. In the s. aisle is another fine early-C16 parclose screen. It is by no means as luxuriant as the Spring chantry but the design has perhaps more clarity and grace. Pairs of main lights with dolphins in the tracery are contained within large ogee arches decorated with spaced crockets; the lower panels have Renaissance tracery and there are elevation squints to the w. The shield bearing dolphins belongs to the Spourne family and as that emblem recurs in the tracery it was probably their chantry. It now contains the tomb of clothier John Ponder (who died in 1520), which was moved in from outside in 1908. There is a *piscina* set in the wall. Across the aisle is the entrance to the rood loft stair and one of the upper doors gave access to a loft above the Lady chapel screen. The base of this is medieval and the beautifully carved top cresting is dated 1958. Within the Spring or Lady chapel the vine trail of the s. aisle is continued below the windows and there is a tiny piscina. The roof is particularly rich and one needs a bright day to appreciate it fully. On the s. side from the e. the wall posts carry figures of an angel, St Peter and St Blaise; on the n. side from the e., *SS Thomas of Canterbury, Paul* and *James the Great*. The wall plates are carved with the Spring arms and their stag's head crest, flowers and animals' heads, while the spandrels of the *arch-braces* carry *Tudor* emblems of *rose* and *pomegranate*. To the l. is a standing bronze of the *Blessed Virgin* and Child of 1983 by Neil Godfrey, and in the centre of the *sanctuary* a very good C20 heraldic brass. The chapel has three lovely windows by Lavers & Barraud, with scenes effectively arranged and in rich colours. In the s. wall you will see the stoning of *St Stephen* and the conversion of St Paul in one window and scenes from the life of Christ in the other; both are in deep, fairly sombre colours with little animation. The e. window has Christ blessing children below fruiting trees, and the lower panels contain the scene from St Luke's Gospel where *St Mary Magdalene* washes Christ's feet

with her tears and dries them with her hair. The clothes and general feeling of the composition are Renaissance and the church's principal benefactors are included in the group. The altar here is a good, early-C17 table with a carved top rail and centre pendant.

The tall and wide C14 chancel arch has very small male and female *headstops* like tragic masks on the *hood mould* and there are two more on the e. side. The hook that supported the rood still remains in the apex of the arch and below is an excellent *screen* dating from about 1330 and retained at the rebuilding. As with nearly all early screens, the lower section is plain and each panel was drilled with trefoil elevation squints. Each main light contains a heavily crocketted ogee arch divided by a slim *mullion*, with the head filled with *mouchettes* of flowing tracery, the pattern alternating. The main uprights have crocketted gables and at their bases are tiny heads of men and beasts. The screen doors were discarded during the 1861 restoration but luckily they were recovered from a stable and their hinges from a pigsty, and were replaced in 1909. Some of the clergy stalls backing on to the screen have *misericords*; the one on the s. side is carved with a man using a pig as a set of bagpipes. The three on the n. are: a *pelican in her piety;* a man playing the bellows with a pair of tongs, paired with a lady who holds a vielle (similar to a violin but fitted with a handle that turned a rosined wheel within which produced a continuous bass note. This is a rare illustration of a popular instrument which became known as the hurdy-gurdy); the two figures are backed by a dragon. Next there is a jester and, beyond him, a spoonbill and an ibis dip their beaks to the small head of a man. The stall ends have heavy tracery and *poppyheads* and there are remains of *griffins* on the n. side, with a camel and a winged lion on the s. Henry Ringham was at work here during the C19 restoration and much of his meticulous work can be recognised. In front of the sanctuary steps is a small *chrysom brass* with a Latin inscription for Clopton d'Ewes the son and heir of Sir Symonds d'Ewes who only lived ten days and died in 1631, The fine flowing tracery of the e. window is filled with an outstanding example of the stained glass of Lavers & Barraud. Designed in 1861 by James Milner Allen, the main lights contain the crucified Christ flanked by the Virgin and *St John*, with St Peter to the l. and St Paul to the r. There are Evangelistic symbols below the Christ in Majesty at the top, and while the key colour is blue, the overall effect is kaleidoscopic. Below it is an alabaster *reredos* installed in 1890; it is arcaded, with busy gables, pinnacles and standing figures. The contemporary *sedilia* to the r. is far more pleasing with its attenuated arcade and polished marble columns supporting pierced gables. High on the n. wall of the sanctuary is the large monument to Henry Copinger, rector here for over 40 years, one of whose early duties was to receive Queen Elizabeth when she visited the church. He died in 1622 and the memorial was erected by his widow. In *touchstone* and alabaster, much of the original colour survives and the couple face each other across a faldstool between *Corinthian* columns. Rather ungainly angels stand each side and the children are neatly graded in the panel below.

Lawshall, All Saints (C5): The church was rebuilt in the middle of the C15 on a fairly large scale, with *nave, aisles* and *clerestory*. The earlier tower is well-proportioned, with four strong *string courses*, angled buttresses, and *flushwork* crosses set at intervals in the *base course*, a motif used again on the nave and *porch* buttresses. The tower houses a ring of five bells with an 11 cwt. tenor which cannot be rung at the present time. *William Butterfield* rebuilt the *chancel* in restrained *Early English* style in 1857 and the random flint finish is relieved by lines of thin red tiles. These occur in the parapets too and suggest that they also were restored, along with the porch. The latter displays little beast *paterae* below the parapet and two stunted *gargoyles*. The entrance doorway is *Perpendicular*, with blank shields in the *spandrels*.

Within, there are elegant *arcades* with *piers* that are shafted on four faces and rise to *castellated capitals*. A string course runs below the clerestory and lifts over the chancel arch. It is punctuated by *fleurons* and demi-angels, from which slim shafts rise to support the *wall posts* of the closely timbered cambered roof. The *arch-braced* aisle roofs rest on *castellated corbels* that match those in the nave. The string course angels and spandrels over the chancel arch were brightly coloured some years ago, and the C15 *font* received the same treatment. It has varied *tracery* in the deep bowl panels, with defaced heads at the angles, and the underside is unusually moulded. Above the tower arch is a squat and wide *sanctus-bell window*, and to the l., an interesting memorial for Pilot Officer Johannes van Mesdag who was killed in 1945. It is a panel of cream, 3in. glazed tiles bearing a noble inscription impressed in dull gold, with a blue and gold enamelled shield at the bottom. Made at Gouda, it was designed by the eminent

typographer Jan van Krimpen. The aisles are lit by large Perpendicular windows and at the e. end on the s. side is a massive mahogany chest with filigree brass decoration and a large lockplate engraved with a double eagle, possibly C18 work from the East Indies. In the n. aisle the e. window was partially blocked when the 1850s organ chamber was added, and in front of it stands a second chest of the C17 with marquetry panels and strings, shallow bands of carving and split turnings on the front. The mid-C19 wooden lectern is a very good, high quality example of the period; the turned shaft of the desktop rises from a miniature octagonal gallery which has a sloping roof over the colonnade. The chancel is all Butterfield and a *cusped* division separates the painted waggon roof above the *sanctuary* from the rest. There are *Ecclesiological Society* candelabra, tiled fronts to the steps, and the *communion rails* are cast metal in dull red, gold and black. The tiled *reredos* has a centre cross with attractive blue enamel lobes bearing the *Evangelistic symbols* in beige. There is a mock *piscina* without a drain to match the Early English-style *lancets*. The stained glass by Alexander Gibbs is not memorable.

Laxfield, All Saints (G3): The side walls of the tower have stone facings up as far as the bell stage (something seldom seen in Suffolk), but apart from that, the design has much in common with Eye, with polygonal buttresses that are panelled with *flushwork* to the top. There is a double *base course* of worn stone roundels and flushwork panels, and above the broad, four-*light* bell openings there are finely *traceried* battlements. They bear shields of the Wingfield and Fitz-Lewes families who doubtless contributed to the cost when the tower was built in the 1450s and 1460s. The church living belonged to Eye Priory, and that may account for the similarity between this and Eye tower, particularly the overall flushwork panelling of the w. front. The w. doorway has large *paterae*, crowns and masks in the arch moulding, and there are angels in the *spandrels*, curiously swathed below the waist. Finely canopied niches flank the window above, and the n.e. buttress neatly accomodates the tower stair. Walking round, you will see a plain C14 n. door, and a variety of renewed windows, but the most noticeable feature is the mean nature of the rebuilding that took place at the e. end in the 1820s. The last bay of the *nave* and the *chancel* are mainly in white brick, and a matching porch/ *vestry* was added on the s. side after World War

II. The broad C15 s. porch must have been impressive in its youth, but the upper stage fell into decay and was repaired in brick in the C17 or C18. Niches with pretty canopies and deep stools survive on the buttresses, and the shields of East Anglia and *St Edward the Confessor* feature in the spandrels. The *stops* are worn demi-angels bearing *Trinity* and *Passion emblem* shields. The side windows are blocked, and only the stubs of the vaulted ceiling remain to show that there was an upper room.

The interior is extraordinarily spacious, a nave without *aisles* that spans 36ft., under a trussed-rafter roof augmented by scissors-bracing at the *collars*; a line of deep coving conceals the *hammerbeams*. *Cautley* believed that former aisles were absorbed in a rebuilding, but similar widths occur elsewhere in East Anglia. A *banner stave locker* is set at an angle in the s.w. corner, and the ringing chamber on the first floor of the tower has a glazed partition with an attractive stained glass panel of Christ's baptism. It has the look of the 1920s and it would be interesting to know who the artist was. The **tower** has a ring of six bells with a 15 cwt. **tenor**, but their condition only allows occasional **ringing**. The double rank of gallery rails below could be taken for early-C17 *communion rails* but they were in fact those installed when the chancel was rebuilt in the 1820s, and are a reminder that style cannot always be relied on to date church fittings. Laxfield has one of the best of the *Seven Sacrament fonts*, dating from about 1500, and its most unusual feature is the absence of a shaft, with the deep octagonal bowl resting directly on the moulded base. All the risers of the three steps are traceried, and the top level takes the form of a Maltese cross. There are mutilated carvings on four sides of the base, with a recognisable hog to the n. (a donor's badge?) and a possible *pelican* with her brood to the e. The underside of the bowl is *groined*, and the sculptured groups in each bowl panel stand within an arch below a canopy of richly *crocketted* pinnacles. All of them have been defaced but the subjects are still recognisable; (clockwise from the e.): matrimony, baptism, confirmation, ordination, mass, penance, extreme unction, baptism of Christ. The seating in the church is a fascinating mixture of periods and styles, sufficient in itself to illustrate five centuries of changing fashions. Standing on a high sill and brick floor in the s.w. corner, there is a range of *Jacobean* benches with scrolly *poppyheads* very like those at Cratfield and possibly by the same joiner. Across the way, a tiered range of C19 *box*

pews incorporate more Jacobean ends, and the door carries the notice: 'Seats for young men and boys'. The C15 benches in the body of the nave have delightful leaf trails carved along their backs, traceried ends, and poppyheads. One on the n. side has a headless, seated figure at one end, and a tower at the other which has buttresses just like the church's own tower. The bench-end in front displays the cup and wafer of the Eucharist. There are more Jacobean benches on the s. side, and those in the e. half of the nave have been encased in panelling with *Renaissance* motifs to form box pews. The Wingfield badge and a 'W' can be found on the n. side, and the front pew features a shield carved with the *Five wounds of Christ*. The *Royal Arms* of Queen Anne, in plaster relief, were displayed above the chancel arch until they fell and shattered in 1966. Beautifully restored in full colour and gilt, they are now over the n. door. Below stands the massive parish chest, iron banded, and blessed with an array of locks, one of which requires two keys to be turned in contrary directions! Across the nave, a small poor box of 1664 on a turned shaft is carved with initials which probably belonged to the churchwardens of the day. A bread charity was in operation until World War I, and the C18 shelf behind the back pew by the poor box housed the loaves that the poor took home with them on Sundays. The *Stuart* pulpit originally formed part of a *three-decker* which stood against the s. wall of the nave, but it now rests on a bracketed stem and three turned posts, and has a modern stair. The body has *blind-arched* panels decorated with split turning, and the reading desk in front carries the same form of decoration and may have been part of the original ensemble. The C15 *screen*, with crocketted *ogee* arches, has been replaced in the re-formed chancel arch, and traces of paint at the e. end of the nave roof show that there was a *celure* above the *rood*. The chancel is extremely bald, with a flat ceiling and panelled walls. The e. window contains attractive glass by Francis Skeat which was installed in 1938 – the *Blessed Virgin* and *St John* flanking Christ on the cross, with Jerusalem beyond and the heavenly city with an *Agnus Dei* above (the only other example of this artist's work in Suffolk is at Chelmondiston). The *Stuart Holy Table* was salvaged from the redundant church at Southolt and has been meticulously restored. There are three *brass* inscriptions in the floor of the nave – for John Jener (1606), John and Margaret Smyth (1597 & 1621), and William Dowsing (1614). The last may well have been the father of the notorious *William Dowsing* whose journal entry for July 17th, 1644 records the destruction of two angels on the tower, a cross on the porch, and 'many superstitious inscriptions in brass . . . a picture of Christ in glass, an eagle, and a lion with wings, for two of the *Evangelists;* and the steps in the chancel. All to be done within twenty days; the steps by William Dowsing, of the same town'. The editor of the journal took that to mean that Dowsing himself defrayed the expense involved in some of the work at his own parish church, but whether he was responsible for the mutilation of the font will never be known.

Layham, St Andrew (E6): The church dates from the late C13 or early C14 but its tower was replaced in 1742, in red brick and probably to the same scale. The w. door, belfry window, and bell openings are outlined in yellow brick, and the top stage looks as if it was rebuilt in 1861 when there was a general restoration (the date pierced in the weathervane gives the clue). There is a yew tree hard up against its s. wall reaching almost to the top which was probably planted to commemorate Queen Victoria's coronation, and a smaller one hugs the n. side. The small C14 n. door is blocked and all the windows were renewed as part of the 1860s restoration or during another in the 1880s. At that time a *vestry* was added on the n. side. The *priest's door* in the *chancel* s. wall has rather nice little male and female *headstops* and when the s.w. *nave* buttress was rebuilt a *scratch dial* was moved down almost to ground level. Just round the corner there was quite a large window in the w. wall which may have been blocked when the tower was rebuilt. Beyond the C19 s. *porch*, the wide *nave* is spanned by a new roof with *scissors-bracing* and you will see that the original w. arch was filled in and a small C18 door inserted. *Cautley* believed that the recess in the wall to the l. was a shelf where bread for the poor was placed and it may well have been used for this purpose, although it is obviously the embrasure for the blocked window. The C13 *Purbeck marble font* is unusual in being hexagonal but, apart from that, it has the typical shallow lead-lined bowl with canted sides. The pairs of arches in the panels have lost some of their detail and it rests on a centre column and six shafts. A simple *piscina* under a *trefoil* arch shows that there was a nave *altar* on the s. side and there is a *squint* cut through the *respond* of the chancel arch nearby. The odd thing is, however, that it does not align with the *High altar* but is cut e. to w. Beyond the pulpit on the other side of the nave there are four tall panels which were once part of the base of the C16 *rood screen*. The tablet above commemorates members of the Norman family and was the work of Edward J. Physick, a London sculptor and Royal Academy gold medalist – although one would not have guessed it from this design. Like the benches in the nave, the chancel stalls are Victorian but they have very elaborate *poppyheads* carved with vines, holly leaves, and thistles for the patron saint. The early-C14 *double piscina* in the *sanctuary* has no drains now and is partly obscured by the end buttress of the stone *reredos*. This dates from 1904 and is quite elaborate, with gabled and pinnacled niches each side containing roundels against a deep blue background; the centre panels have Christ in Majesty flanked by *censing* angels, St Andrew, and *St John*, all in mosaic. The 1880s e. window glass, with its heavy and intricate *tabernacle work*, may be by a pupil of *Clayton & Bell* – Christ's baptism, crucifixion, entombment, and the martyrdom of St Andrew. Anne Roane's memorial on the s. wall of the chancel is most unusual because it is in the form of a canvas *hatchment*, although I doubt if it was used as such. Her coat of arms has flourishing yellow and red mantling, the epitaph is painted on a simulated drape, and although she died in 1626 it is dated 1736.

Leavenheath, St Matthew (D7): A C19 church that is by no means typical and, for that reason, interesting in a mild way. It was designed by G. Russell French in 1835, a time when the demand was for uncomplicated buildings in economical materials and the heady passions of the *Ecclesiological Society* had not yet been kindled. And so we find a simple hall of brick like many a nonconformist chapel. Buttresses were provided to give it some respectable solidity, a wooden w. porch, and instead of the prevailing 'Gothick' *lancets*, the windows are in *Tudor* style complete with *labels* – except, that is, for a w. lancet which has lion *stops* to the *dripstone*. Its character changed in the 1880s when the architects Satchell & Edwards added a red brick *chancel*, s. *aisle* and tower, and the combination viewed from outside is faintly eccentric. The chancel has four e. lancets and its roof is carried down on the s. side to cover a *vestry;* the aisle with lancet windows has its own gabled roof and standing at its w. end is the squat and solid tower with a large w. door under a heavy arch; there are three slits for bell openings on each face and the pyramid roof is capped by a lead spike like an unfortunate afterthought.

In contrast, the simple interior is quietly attractive and the feeling is much more C20 than C19. A s. *arcade* on octagonal brick *piers* matches the chancel arch and at the e. end of the aisle an arch leads to what was presumably a family pew which opens off the chancel. The chancel fittings are solid and sensible and the *nave* gained a suite of oak pews in 1963. At the w. end stands a small octagonal *font* that would have been supplied with the original building and, ranged on the wall nearby, seven Flanders crosses with photographs of the young village men who marched away and never came back.

Leiston, St Margaret (I4): From the 1770s onwards, Leiston was gradually transformed from a sleepy village into a thriving industrial town whose prosperity stemmed from the Garrett engineering works. The population more than doubled in the following 100 years, and by 1850 the medieval church had become too small. Over the years it had been indifferently repaired, and the parish opted for a new building, retaining only the tower. Under the leadership of the Hon. Miss Sophia Thellusson, funds were raised locally, and an architect was sought to design a church that would be suitable for the large congregations being attracted by the sermons of the strongly Evangelical vicar, John Blathwayt. At a time when the *Ecclesiological Society's* influence was at its height, and countless churches were being restored and rebuilt according to their particular Gothic recipe, Edward Buckton Lamb was not at all to their taste and he ignored them totally, working against the grain of his time, and desiging some of the most unusual and original churches of the century. He delighted in complications, in contrasts between large and small, and he seemed obsessed with complicated roofs. He was not overawed by the East Anglian tradition of dense flintwork, and in choosing a combination of flint rubble, Caen stone, and Kentish ragstone, Lamb avoided the harshness of much contemporary work.

Walking round, look first at the mid-C14 tower, with its diamond *flushwork base course*, and unusual access door on the s. side. There is more flushwork in the angled buttresses and stepped battlements, and the replacement w. window has an attractive roundel of *mouchette tracery*, chosen to match the age of the tower. It houses an excellent ring of eight bells with a 20 cwt. tenor which were rung in the early C20 by ten brothers from the Bailey family – a record shared by few parish bands. Having demolished

the old *nave* and *chancel*, work began on the new building in the spring of 1853 and it was completed just over a year later. The plan is cruciform, with square projections in the angles of the cross, and the very attractive wall texture is enhanced by bands of mellow, roughly textured Kentish rag. A heavy *corbel* table runs below the immensely deep roofs, and each broad *transept* has a tall wedge-shaped buttress rising between the paired windows in the end walls. The projections each side of the chancel were planned originally as a *vestry* on the s. side and an organ chamber on the n., and they both have large rose windows with bold *tracery*. The flue for the original heating system was disguised as the strange turret with obelisk top on the s. side, and another of Lamb's foibles can be seen in the e. window. Its *flamboyant tracery* is attractive, but for some reason he thickened the centre *mullions* and buttressed them. The war memorial Calvary, with its bronze figure of Christ, stands by the n.e. corner was designed by *Dorothy A..A .Rope*, member of a talented local family, more of whose work can be found at Blaxhall. The entrance porch is on the n. side, and its wayward arch detailing is typical of Lamb – the round moulding cut brutally short to form niches whose bases slope so that they can hold nothing.

Through the porch into a vestibule area, and there stands an excellent C13 *font*, one of the few relics of the medieval church. The cauldron shape of its bowl lies within an arcade of shallow trefoil arches, and six slim columns surround the central shaft. Walking past it, one cannot but be impressed, and at the same time oppressed, by the vastness of the roof, a dark mass of timber that seems to soak up the light and bear down upon the space below. There are *hammerbeams* and *arch-braces* in the nave, and like the *wall plates*, their *spandrels* are pierced with tracery. But the eye focusses inevitably upon the crossing – on the web of struts above it that support the roofs like the spokes of an umbrella. The principals rise from four low stone piers to meet at the centre point, sprouting as they go other timbers which join to form a star. At the w. end of the nave, a raked *gallery* was provided for the children, and its front features a massive arch and gargantuan tracery. Lamb was constrained by a tight budget (which he grossly overspent) and the roofs, gallery and benches are all in pine rather than oak. The lobby space is matched by a children's corner on the s. side of the nave, and the architect signed his building in the tracery of the porthole window with his monogram, shield, and a pair of dividers, dated 1854. Below, there is a panel in coloured plaster by *Ellen Mary Rope* – the *Blessed Virgin*, with the Christ child in the manger and two children kneeling by. On the w. wall of the s. transept a stone slab details Thomas Grimsby's charity of 1755, with its positive conditions: 'I Give and bequeth to ye poor of the Parish of Leiston that Come to Church to hear Divine Service . . .'. Just below, the charming triptych of Our Lady of Leiston was painted by the Marquis D'Oisy for a lady who lived near the site of the first Leiston Abbey; the Virgin sits enthroned between monks and musical angels, with the abbey, the sea, and modern ships beyond. The organ has been transferred to the s. side of the chancel, and the original n. organ chamber is now a chapel. Its *altar* was made by Ernest Barnes and is a typical *Cautley* design. The window above contains figures of *St Edward the Confessor* and *St Elizabeth* – good glass of 1910 in C15 style by an unidentified artist. *Passion* and *Trinity* shields feature in the rose window above.

The twin windows in the n. transept contain some of the loveliest modern glass in Suffolk, an enchanting late flowering of the *Arts & Crafts* style by *Margaret E.A.. Rope* and signed with her tortoise device. Both have three bands of lively scenes separated by striated slab glass, with a larger, key figure placed centrally below. Installed in 1959, the window on the l. commemorates a local physician, with the Nativity and boyhood of Christ pictured above the Annunciation and a central St Luke. The artist's parents are commemorated in the second window, and the upper panels illustrate the Last Supper, the visit of the Magi, the youthful David, and Ruth amid the alien corn. On either side of the figure of *St Matthew* there are Suffolk scenes of springtime and harvest, recalling that Arthur Rope, a warden here for more than 40 years, farmed at Lower Abbey Farm. Nearby on the e. wall, the panel of repoussé silver is by *Dorothy Rope*, a memorial for Arthur Rope who died as a young boy in 1905 – a kneeling figure with good Arts & Crafts lettering. In complete contrast on the w. wall, we are back with Leiston's Victorian prosperity – a bust of Richard Garrett, grandson of the ironmaster, who died in 1866. It is one of *Thomas Thurlow's* best pieces, the portrait of a solid citizen with a patriarchal fringe of beard, displayed in a High Victorian Gothic niche. The whole body of the church was originally crammed with pews, but space has now been cleared in the crossing and the old church's C17 *Holy Table* brought into use again. The stone

pulpit, with its pierced tracery and raised book ledge was also made by Thurlow, and the entrance to the unusually short chancel is spanned by a rather gimcrack *rood beam*. Below it on the s. side is an excellent alabaster and mosaic panel portrait of Berney Wodehouse, vicar here for over thirty years. The architect achieved an effective change of emphasis by siting an arch, prettily decorated, at the entrance to the *sanctuary* rather than the chancel. Ridiculously small side windows provide the final eccentricity, but the e. window is filled with attractively typical *Kempe* glass of the 1890s. Christ in Majesty is surrounded by small figures of saints set against a dense blue leaf pattern studded with gold stars. The choice of subjects is a little unusual, and taking the lights from l. to r. they are: *SS Apollonia, Perpetua, Dorothy; Margaret, Cecilia, Euphemia; Catherine, Lucy, Agnes; Agatha, Prisca, Felicitas.*

Letheringham, St Mary (G5): The tower can be seen from a distance along the lane that leads from Easton to Hoo but access is a little convoluted, through the yards of Abbey farm. A priory of Augustinian canons was founded here in the 1190s and this small building is the remains of their church. Apart from the C16 gatehouse to the s.w., little else survives although there are traces of a doorway in the n. wall which may have led to the cloisters. Following the dissolution of the priory in 1537, a long sequence of neglect, spoliation, and decay set in so that when Horace Walpole visited in 1755 he found the church 'very ruinous though containing such treasures'. These were mainly the monuments and *brasses* in the spacious *chancel* and by 1780 they too were pillaged, broken, and battered. In 1789 the parish was told to put things right and, perhaps in desperation, the churchwardens gave the whole of the chancel to a Woodbridge builder in exchange for a rebuilt *nave* and new e. wall. The monuments went for road ballast, the *font* disappeared, and many of the slabs that once bore brasses were used to pave the nave. Against all odds this tiny building has emerged triumphant from its trials and is beautifully cared for by the faithful few. The C14 tower has recently been restored and there is *flushwork* on buttresses and stepped battlements which have new lions seated at the corners. The blocked w. door is partially below ground level and there is *Decorated tracery* in the w. window and bell openings. A boundary wall joins the tower at the n.w. corner so that one cannot circle the building, but there is a semi-circular sundial dated 1609 to be found at the top of a nave buttress. The low red brick *porch* also carries a date, 1685, below the quirky gable whose straight sides develop convex curves in the lower half.

The *Norman* s. doorway is almost the only visible survivor of the original building and its single attached shafts have scallop *capitals* below an arch with zigzag and *billet* mouldings. Various fragments are displayed in the porch – the body of a feathered angel, the bust of a man with a club, a defaced alabaster head of a woman, and an alabaster block carved with two female figures – possibly a mother and daughter.

The tower arch is tall and there are sections of Norman zigzag and slim *jamb shafts* that were reused by the C14 builder. On either side, rudimentary niches have been made to house the kneeling figures of William Naunton and his wife. He died in 1635 and after his monument in the chancel had been destroyed the statues were used as garden ornaments. They are of high quality and the inscriptions that were originally below them are now set in the n. wall beyond the *font*. That is a plain cauldron shape on a drum shaft and presumably came from elsewhere to replace the one that was lost at the rebuilding. A set of naively painted *Hanoverian Royal Arms* hangs above the s. door and on the n. wall is the fine brass of Sir John de Wyngefeld of 1389 set in a new wooden frame. It is just over 5ft. tall and is an excellent illustration of the armour of the period. The leather coat or jupon that was worn over the armour has the wings of the family badge, originally inlaid with colour. The stone in which it was first set has migrated to the w. end of the nave. There are no windows to the n. and those in the s. wall are early-C14 like the e. window, which was probably saved from the chancel. Floors are brick with a number of slabs reaved of their brasses, and there is a small suite of late-*Georgian box pews* in deal at the e. end to match the plain panelled pulpit. The large shield with about forty quarterings on the n. wall retains some of its colour, and below it are *touchstone* tablets for High Sheriff Thomas Wingfield who died in 1609 and Sir Anthony Wingfield who died four years earlier. The church's only other brass to survive is fixed to the e. wall. It is for Sir Thomas Wyngfeld who died in 1471 and was probably made in the same workshop as the Taylboys brass at Assington. 3ft. long, it displays a mixture of Yorkist and *Tudor* styles of armour, and was filched from the church by a collector in 1786. It eventually found its way to the Ashmolean

Museum in Oxford and by good fortune is now on permanent loan. With it is one of the shields that really belongs to Sir John's brass. On the wall above is a fragment of Sir Robert Naunton's memorial. He died in 1635 and was 'sometime principal secretarie and after Master of the Wards and Councillor of State to our late King James of happy memorie and to our now Sovereign Lord King Charles'. James, his only son and heir, had died when only two years old in 1624 and was even then given the title of esquire; his epitaph on the s. wall reflects the parents' grief at their loss:

Here lyes the Boy whose infancie was such
As promised more than parents durst
    desire.
Yea frighted them by promising to much
for earth to harbour long . . .

The *altar* is a C17 table and is set within a set of very slender three-sided *communion rails*, a late example of that fashion dating from the late C17 or early C18. The American organ may seem unremarkable but it does have the charming refinement of 'patented mouse-proof pedals', just like the one at Westley. When leaving don't overlook the group photograph of Letheringham's Home Guard in the porch. Not to be parted from their dog, they are a cheerful company with forage caps at all angles.

Levington, St Peter (G7): Part of the pleasure for visitors here is the lovely view from the churchyard across the Orwell estuary, with the neighbourly Ship Inn close by. The chunky red brick tower was built towards the end of the C15, and the w. doorway was probably salvaged from its predecessor. The eroded shield above bears the arms of the Fastolfe and Holbrooke families, a reminder that the Fastolfes were Lords of the Manor in the C15. A stone in the s. wall carries the date 1636, and this relates to the rebuilding of the upper part of the tower by Sir Robert Hitcham. A Levington man, he was at one stage attorney-general to Anne of Denmark, King James's queen; at the time of this project, he had just bought Framlingham castle from the Howards and was buried in the church there two years later. From the outside, the n. wall of the *nave* is almost entirely blank, apart from the outline of half of a *Norman* doorway and a tiny window under the eaves at the e. end which gave light to the *rood*. The *chancel* has rather an odd selection of small rectangular windows, some at high level, and there is a brick three-*light*

Tudor e. window. In addition, the s. side has a late-C14 *lancet*, and to the w., a square-headed lancet has a blocked lower section which identifies it as a *low side window*. Massive, angled brick buttresses support the chancel, and there is another Tudor window in the nave s. wall, with a replica replacement w. of the *porch*. The latter is half-timbered, and when it was converted for use as a *vestry*, the medieval inner door was moved to fill the outer arch.

Entry is by way of the w. door, passing beneath the organ gallery which was placed in the tower in 1958. The C15 *font* rests on an octagonal shaft, and the cusped panels of the bowl are carved alternately with *Tudor Roses* and shields which bear the arms of: w., East Anglia (or Ely); e., *St Edward the Confessor* (defaced); s., Sir William Brandon; n., John Garnon, grandson of the builder of Trimley St Mary tower and son-in-law of Sir William (he probably gave the font). The cover, with its *ogee*-shaped panels and *crocketted finial* is a good C19 reproduction. The original s. doorway of about 1300 now leads to the vestry. There are simple pine benches in the nave, and overhead the C14 *arch-braced* roof is plastered between the principal timbers. It was revealed and restored in 1920 when a lower ceiling was removed, and the original *rood beam* now stands clear at the junction of nave and chancel. Eaten away with age, it is unusually decorated with a line of *cusping* on the w. side. The centre light of the s. nave window is filled with an attractive figure of *St Francis* of 1954 (artist unknown), and beyond it stands a good Stuart pulpit. It is a tall octagon, with two sides forming the door, and there are three ranges of panels, with typical *blind arches* in the centre, and shallow arabesques; the shallow base is modern. The angle of the walls is very marked in the chancel, explaining the need for the huge buttresses, and they are clad with C17 panelling which came from Brightwell Hall (demolished in 1753). The style is *Renaissance*, with perspective arches in some panels, and ovals with centre bosses in others. The tall *communion rails*, with their simple, slightly swelling *balusters* date from the same period. A well-painted C19 roundel of the head of Christ hangs in front of the e. window, and note the unusual inner arch of the s. *sanctuary* window, with its slight ogee shape and pair of knobbly cusps. One of Levington's bells was from John Kebyll's foundry in London and dates from the late C15.

Lidgate, St Mary (B5): A lane leads past the large village pond up to the church which stands on what was once a fortified hill; there are still deep ditches to w. and n., and the remains of a castle to the e. The churchyard is beautifully kept and the C13 or early-C14 tower has a plain parapet. The stair lies within the s.w. buttresses so that its slit windows peep out on two sides. The *aisles* are C14 while the *lancets* and *priest's door* in the *chancel* date it as C13, with two C14 windows on the s. side and an e. window with flowing *tracery* of the same period. The brick s. *porch* is likely to be C17 and the lower roof line of its predecessor shows on the aisle wall. The inner door, with its square lintel and blank *tympanum*, is probably early *Norman* but the *jambs* have C15 mouldings. A possible *consecration cross* is incised within a circle on the r.-hand side, and Thomas Willyamson cut his name above it some time in the C17.

Inside, there are tall C14 *arcades* and the church is rather dark, mainly because there is no *clerestory*. All the floors are in pale brick and, at the w. end, the low tower arch is deeply moulded and fitted with a medieval door complete with three strap hinges and centre closing ring. There are many examples of medieval graffiti to be found in the church and they include three late-C14 fragments of music (very rare), a beautifully drawn head of the *Blessed Virgin* on a s. arcade pillar, together with inscriptions, windmills and birds. The plain C15 *font* also has its share of scribbles, and there is a curious three-pronged recess like a gridiron cut into one of the steps which has no obvious purpose. (Similar examples can be found on other fonts in the county.) The roofs are C19 but the benches below are medieval and, in their way, interesting. Unlike more flamboyant sets, they are plain and low with square ends, and seem to have been made in three blocks; those on the s. side have heavier top mouldings than the rest, and a single bench end on the n. side of the nave has tracery cut in the solid (possibly a pattern that was not accepted). In the n. aisle the ends are decorated with early-C16 *linenfold* and one of them is spectacularly warped. A C19 *bier* stands in the n. aisle and at the e. end there is a late-C15 *parclose screen* with doors to w. and s. The main *lights* have *cusped ogee* arches with attractive flowing tracery over them, and the top cresting is pierced and battlemented. Balance has been nicely achieved by a modern parclose screen enclosing the chapel in the s. aisle – solid, competent work in the medieval idiom. The chapel has a *piscina* with a *cinquefoiled* arch, and to the l. of the *altar* the *rood stair* is set squarely in the corner with a high level window. The early-C17 pulpit is an unusual design; octagonal, with strapwork panels above very plain and shallow *blind arches*, it stands on a square base with turned *finials* at the corners, and there is a carved top rail with partially carved blind arches in two panels. The C15 *rood screen* has a base of plain boards and the centre arch is a double cusped ogee, with *mouchettes* and panel tracery above it. The gates are modern. The chancel is wide and open and in the *sanctuary* is an early-C14 piscina, the arch resting on short shafts with ring *capitals* and bases. There is a small recess to the r. with a hole in the base, and one wonders whether this was an auxiliary piscina installed during the short period when two drains were the rule. In the sanctuary n. wall there is a pair of *aumbries* with C19 doors, and in front of the modern *communion rails* is an interesting late-C14 *brass*. It is the 20in. figure of a priest in eucharistic vestments, one of only four in Suffolk thus dressed. The head is a modern replacement and it was once enclosed within an octofoil cross. Although it has often been suggested, the brass has no connection with the poet-monk John Lydgate – he may have hailed from the village but the memorial dates from about 1380, some 20 years before he became a priest. It is more likely to be the brass of Thomas atte Welle who was rector here at the relevant time. John Isaacson was an early-C19 rector and his *ledger-stone* nearby has the unusual distinction of being signed by the mason, Parkinson of Newmarket. In the s. lancet is some 1860s glass by *Clayton & Bell* which has good colour and composition – a Crucifixion with the *Three Marys* in a *quatrefoil* above and the Entombment in a quatrefoil below, forming an excellent example of this firm's better work. At the time of my visit there were plans afoot to install solar panels in the hope that they will not only light the church but also produce a surplus to sell to the National Grid. This initiative must surely be a first, at least in East Anglia.

Lindsey, St Peter (D6): In a quiet upland situation, this is an unobtrusive early-C14 church with a good deal of character. By 1836 the tower had partially collapsed and it was taken down, a new window was inserted in the rebuilt w. wall, and a wooden bellcote was placed on the gable. On walking round, you will see that the *nave* has an unusually large and elaborate window on the n. side and there was another w. of the blocked n. door. The w. end of the s. *aisle* is lit by an attractive little single-*light* window with *Decorated tracery* and the *chancel* has a wide *lancet* to the n.

The e. window is C19 but may repeat an original design, and there is one with 'Y' tracery of about 1300 on the s. side. The *priest's door* with *headstops* to the *dripstone* is now blocked and a *scratch dial* can be seen on the r.-hand *jamb*. The outer arch of the open-sided C14 *porch* is gnarled and seamed like driftwood, with eroded *cusps* to the barge board of the gable, and there is a braced *tie-beam* above the small C14 doorway.

Within, there are heavy *arch-braced* tie-beams and *king posts* under plaster ceilings, and in both nave and chancel the parallel *wall plates* have a plaster cove between them. The square early-C13 *font* must have been made for an earlier building, and although it now stands close to a *pier* of the C14 *arcade*, the bowl decoration shows that it was not always so. The varying arch designs are raised in unusual fashion on flat surfaces and the C17 cover is quite unusual – a plain board carrying a centre post which is supported by eight turned struts splayed at a low angle. Creed and Lord's Prayer boards stand at the w. end, and above the outline of the blocked window in the n. wall there is a set of *Royal Arms*. They are *Hanoverian* and naively painted on board. The benches are C19 unstained pitch pine but against the n. wall there is a suite of plain C18 *box pews*. The window on that side is intriguing. It is much larger than one would expect to find in this situation and the beautiful tracery is unusually elaborate, with fragments of its original glass surviving. Not only that, but large canopied niches were formed at the inner corners of the embrasure and the one on the r. had a tall pinnacle. It must have had a special significance and may have been associated with the village *guild* of St Peter which, in the next century, was given a house so that the master and brethren could keep the annual feast in style. A small C17 chest is now used as an *altar* in the s. aisle and mortice slots in the *arcade piers* at that end show that there was once a *parclose screen* for the chapel. The piers are worth examining closely for another reason. They are thick with medieval graffiti and the bishops' heads on the s. side of the easternmost pier are of particular interest because they illustrate horned mitres of the C12, implying that the stones came from an earlier building. Above and to the l. on the s.w. face there is a lovely little *Tudor Rose* in a circle. On the pier by the font there is a scratch dial that was either drawn for fun or else indicates that the stone must have come in from the outside of the earlier church, and on the s.e. face is an elongated bird. Below it there are some very strange devices. They seem to represent basketwork objects with handles and cross *finials* and there is no way of telling their real size. Possibly related to some ancient religious ceremony, they are enigmatic and mysterious.

The stair to the *rood loft* remains in the n. wall and the base of the *screen* still stands, albeit precariously. The two panels on the n. side still have their colour and by them the pulpit is a C19 reconstruction in which the panels and three of the ledge brackets are C16. The benches on the s. side of the chancel have heavy, worn ends with remains of *poppyheads* and the front panels are likely to have formed part of the rood loft. The organ with its early-C19 case largely obscures the monument to Nicholas Hobart who died in 1606. The *touchstone* tablet has cherub heads and swags of flowers each side, there is a *cartouche* of arms in the *pediment*, and a skull nestles in a swag at the bottom. A plain lancet *piscina* lies beyond *dropped-sill sedilia* and the altar is enclosed by a very nice set of three-sided late-C17 *communion rails*. Pale in colour, they have delicately turned *balusters* with clusters of four at the corners.

Linstead Parva, St Margaret of Antioch (H3): This diminutive church is almost hidden from the road by the bulk of the horse chestnuts that flank the path up to the s. *porch*. It is the simplest of buildings, just a *nave* and *chancel*, with a weatherboarded bell-cote on the ridge of the roof. The rough and rugged flint walls were supplemented and raised in brick, probably in the early C16 when the large and handsome brick windows were inserted in the nave. Judging by the *lancet* and its flanking image niches in the w. wall, and the lancets in the chancel, the church was built in the C13, and apart from the new nave windows, little was changed until the C19. Then, in 1891 there was a heavy restoration when a *vestry* was added on the n. side, and the porch was rebuilt three years later. There is a *mason's mark* to be found on the r.-hand *jamb* of the doorway, and a C15 inscription that it remains for someone else to decipher.

The C15 *font* has four lions round the shaft, and four more alternate with angels bearing shields in the bowl panels. These are carved with a *Trinity emblem* (s.w.), *Passion emblems* (n.e.), and (possibly) the three crowns of East Anglia (s.e.). The w. side is blank, which suggests that it once stood against the w. wall. The C15 bench ends to the w. of the font were salvaged from the ruined church of St Peter at Linstead Magna in the 1920s. The rest of the benches are largely

C19, but the two ends nearest the font have nice little figures carved on the elbows, and the one by the door is medieval. The *arch-braced* nave roof has *castellated wall plates*, and the restorers boarded the ceiling between the main timbers. A heavy beam spans the chancel arch, and above it the wall is plastered and half-timbered. The chancel lies under a plastered ceiling, and the late-C13/early-C14 e. window has jamb shafts with *ring capitals*. It is flanked by C19 *Decalogue* panels in stone Gothick frames. The 1870s stained glass is interesting in that the figures of *St Peter* and *St Paul* are markedly different in style, and although the framework and incidental decoration in the two lights is similar, they seem to be by different artists. Very strange – perhaps they came from elsewhere. The plain *piscina* has a deep *cinquefoil* drain, and there are *dropped-sill sedilia* alongside. Even a humble church such as this did not escape *William Dowsing*. His journal entry for April 4th, 1643 covering this church records: 'a picture of God the Father, and of Christ, and five more superstitious in the chancel; and the steps to be levelled, which the churchwardens promised to do in twenty days, and a picture of Christ on the outside of the steeple, nailed to a cross, and another superstitious one. Crosses on the font'. Mention of a steeple makes one wonder whether there was once a tower after all. The churchyard is a pleasant spot in which to dawdle, and collectors of *scratch dials* will find one on each side of the *priest's door*, and the centre holes of two more on the s.w. nave buttress. Connoisseurs of graveyard fashion will perhaps like to record the cross in the n.w. corner that has a startlingly realistic chain wrapped round it, secured to a full-size anchor – a reassuring symbol of Hope in abundance! The final and endearing memory of Linstead Parva is the extraordinary growth of bracken on the porch roof that should not, I suppose, be there at all.

Little Bealings, All Saints (G6): This is one of a number of churches in the area which have towers to the s. of the *nave* doing duty as rather grand *porches*. All Saints' unbuttressed tower is very uncompromising, built in the C14 but with bell openings and parapet reshaped relatively recently and the s.w. corner repaired in brick at the top. Decoration is limited to *paterae* on the single *string course*. *Nave* and *chancel* date from about 1300, judging by the form of the window *tracery* and the *priest's door*, although there is one window with *Decorated* tracery on the s. side of the chancel and a late-C15 brick section with a two-*light* window was inserted in the s. wall of the nave, probably to give additional light to the *rood screen*. A n. *aisle* was added in the 1850s which has a w. window to match the nave and small brick *lancets*, and just beyond its e. end you will find the grave of James Hogger, a village blacksmith who died in 1857. He chose a version of the well-known epitaph for those of his trade, but unfortunately it has been largely masked by the footstone being moved up against it and I could only read the first two lines:

My sledges and hammers lie reclined,
My bellows too hast lost their wind . . .

The interior is plain and simple, with plastered ceilings hiding the medieval roofs, although there is still a *wall plate* to be seen in the chancel. The three-bay C19 *arcade* rests on octagonal brick pillars, and the C18 *reredos* now hangs on the aisle wall, its panels painted with the *Decalogue*, Creed, and Lord's Prayer. The C15 *font* was very roughly treated by C17 image breakers and only one of the *Evangelistic symbols* and a single angel survive in the bowl panels; the angels below the bowl and the lions round the shaft are but remnants. There was a *Stuart* pulpit, but having fallen on hard times it was skilfully reconstructed by a local carpenter in 1925 so that only a tithe of what you see is original. The glass of 1899 in the e. window is by Albert L. Moore, a designer for *Powells* in the 1860s. It is not unpleasing, with Gethsemane and Resurrection scenes flanking the Crucifixion, and trumpeting angels above the canopy work; there is another of his windows at Dallinghoo.

Little Blakenham, St Mary (F6): This little church sits attractively on a bank above a steepish lane and the garden of the old rectory reaches right up to the e. wall. In consequence, a circuit of the outside is not practicable, but just by the wicket gate into the garden there is a *scratch dial* to be found on one of the *quoins* of the s.e corner of the *Early English chancel*. All the walls are plastered and a *Perpendicular* window was added to the s. side next to the *priest's door*. The unbuttressed tower has a small w. window with *Decorated tracery* matching the bell openings and the windows in the *nave*. The s. *porch* has lost the tracery in its side windows but there is a fine modern statue of the Blessed Virgin and Child in the niche above the low C14 outer arch.
The octagonal C14 *font* has no decoration

whatsoever and within the tower a little chamber organ fits snugly onto the *gallery*. *Royal Arms* of James II hang opposite the door and they are an excellent set, vigorously painted on board and dated 1685. The solid pews with doors and the pulpit were no doubt part of the enthusiastic mid-C19 restoration. On the s. wall is a tablet for the three infant children of John and Sarah Cuthbert who died between 1841 and 1858:

My Lord hath need of these flowers gay
The reaper said, and smiled . . .

In the chancel e. wall there are three C12 stepped *lancets* within a single arch but the flanking niches with *trefoil* heads were either heavily restored or added in the C19. They once framed paintings of the *Assumption* and *St John the Baptist* but, having been repainted, they have now vanished. One wonders why. The deep splays of the lancet in the n. wall are painted with full-length figures of Christ and a woman cradling a dove; they follow the curve of the arch to the top and peer down benignly. They were repainted in 1850 and it would be interesting to know how close they are to the C13 originals. There is an undistinguished version of Holman Hunt's *Light of the World* in the e. window centre lancet with the heads of *SS Peter* and *John* in the side lights – possibly by *Ward & Hughes*. The piscina has a multi-*cusped* arch under a square head. Although I could find no trace of him, Samuel Hardy was a late-C18 rector here who was a prolific author and scholar of some standing. He published a number of works on the Eucharist and edited a Greek Testament that ran to three editions.

Little Bradley, All Saints (A5): This lovely little church is tucked away down a long lane that leads to the Hall Farm through gently undulating countryside. There are humps and hollows in the field beyond the church, marking the site of the deserted village. The *Saxon* round tower was given an octagonal belfry with stepped battlements in the mid-C15 and the arms of Underhill are displayed on a shield below the s. window. The *nave* has *Perpendicular* windows on the s. side but the masonry of the nave and w. half of the *chancel* is probably Saxon, judging by the *long and short work* at the e. angles of the nave. There is the bulge of a *rood loft* stair in the corner between nave and chancel on the s. side, and the low wall top of the original Saxon chancel and its e. corners can be seen reaching halfway along the present chancel. The extension was evidently early *Norman* because there are faint remains of little *lancets* on either side of the renewed e. window. There are two similar lancets (one blocked) on the n. side where, again, the Saxon wall can be seen. The n. side of the nave has square-headed *Decorated* windows and one of the C19 was inserted in the old n. doorway. Before going in, have a look at the fine C18 stones on the s. side, evidently by the Great Thurlow mason.

Entry is via a plain Norman doorway which has circle graffiti just inside to the r. The early Norman tower arch is low, with squared *imposts*, and a medieval door frame with carved *spandrels* was added later. By the door is a large and plain octagonal C14 *font*, and the simple interior was fitted with benches as part of a rigorous 1870s restoration. The pulpit seems to be early-C19 but the *tester*, with its marquetry star, may be a little earlier. The plain chancel arch had deep notches cut in the imposts to take the *rood screen* and beyond it on the r. is a blocked *low side window* which now contains a *brass* moved from the floor. It is the headless figure of a man in *Tudor* armour, with kneeling groups of children, and it may be for Thomas Knighton who died in 1532. Further along is the large monument in soft, pale stone for Richard le Hunt who died in 1540. It is raised up on a ledge and reaches to the roof, with two *achievements of arms* in frames on top. He, his wife and family kneel in line, and all have lost their heads except father who lacks his hands and lower legs; his helm is neatly stowed in an alcove beside him. In the *sanctuary* the *piscina* is very strangely positioned in a shapeless recess above the *dropped-sill sedilia*. Here is an excellent late brass for Thomas and Elizabeth Soame, 1612. A large plate, it shows them kneeling, he in armour with five sons, she in a variation of the Mary, Queen of Scots cap and large ruff, with her two daughters. Thomas died in 1606 but his sons are dressed in the new fashion of doublet, hose and short cloak. Like the Soame monument at Little Thurlow, there is a quotation from the Psalms, but in Latin in this case and from Psalm 88. Another brass is laid in the floor on the n. side – 18in. figures of John and Jane le Hunte (1605) – and note that in the inscription Cavendish has its old spelling of 'Candish'. On the n. wall, set within a shallow Tudor arch, is a brass of a man and woman kneeling on either side of a stone shield of arms to which they were once linked by scrolls. He wears a long fur-trimmed gown, she a *kennel headdress*, and the heraldry identifies

them as an early-C16 Underhill and his wife, though the inscription has gone. Above this memorial is a beautiful and important brass set in a moulded stone frame. It is for John Daye, the renowned Elizabethan printer, who died in 1584. Born at Dunwich in 1522, he produced the first book of church music in English, and printed Queen Elizabeth's prayer book in six languages. Works by Latimer and Archbishop Parker came from his press but he is perhaps best remembered as the printer of John Foxe's *Acts and Monuments of these Latter and Perilous Days*, that great folio of 1563 that caused an immediate sensation and was dubbed *The Book of Martyrs*. He and his second wife Alice face each other across a faldstool on which are engraved images of two *chrysom children*, and six sons kneel behind him, with five daughters ranged behind his wife. At the top, his achievement is in the centre, with the arms of the Stationers' Company (of which he was Master) on the l. He was fond of punning and used the device of a sun and 'Arise O man for it is Daye'. His wife evidently caught the habit when she composed his epitaph:

> heere lies the Daye that darkness
>   could not blynd
> When popish fogges had over cast
>   the sunne . . .

She by that time had married a Mr Stone and the temptation to have another go was too strong, for the last lines read:

> Als [Alice] was the last increase of
>   his stoore,
> Who mourning long for being left
>   alone,
> Set upp this toombe, her self turn-
>   ed to a Stone.

John probably laughed in heaven.

Little Cornard, All Saints (D7): Approached via a farmyard and a grassy track, this little church is set most attractively on the ridge above the valley of the Stour. The w. window of the tower is early C14, the bell openings have recently been renewed, and on top there is a small early-C19 circular wooden cupola; by using binoculars the names of rector and churchwardens can be picked out on the lead-covered base to the s.e. The C14 n. door is blocked but note the masses of graffiti of all ages cut in the soft stone of the *jambs*. A

C17 two-storeyed *vestry* lies alongside the *chancel* whose *Perpendicular* e. window has *headstops* turning towards each other. There is a small, plain *priest's door* on the s. side and to its l. a two-light *Decorated* window has had its *tracery* cut short at the top. The s. *porch* has large, open brick windows and the C14 inner doorway is flanked by a pair of modern plaques carved with doves set in the wall.

There is a neat interior, with modern roofs, pine pews, and pulpit. The w. window glass of the early 1920s is by *Heaton, Butler & Bayne* on the theme of the Good Shepherd, and a late-C15 *font* stands in the base of the tower. Its stem is panelled, four of the bowl panels have window tracery patterns, and the rest have shields – *St George's* cross, the chevrons of either the Cornhead or the De Grey families, the cross with serrated edges of the Peytons, and a shield with a star which was probably borne by a member of the De Vere family. A ring of five bells with a 7 cwt. tenor hangs in the tower but are not ringable at the present time. The glass in the modern window on the s. side of the *nave* featuring the figures of Christ, the *Blessed Virgin*, and *St John* looks like the work of *Clayton & Bell*, and in the window on the n. side there is a C15 roundel of an angel bearing a scroll in yellow stain. Both windows at the e. end of the nave have dropped sills and this indicates that there were probably *altars* nearby – the church certainly had one dedicated to the *Trinity* before the *Reformation*. There is no longer a *screen* within the tall chancel arch and the vestry is open to its full height on the n. side and now houses the organ. Nearby stands a C14 waggon-topped chest heavily banded with iron and fitted with four hasps. The priest's door is blocked and the window to the r. has a dropped sill; this, and its position, suggests that it was used as a *low side window*. The *piscina* in the *sanctuary* lies under a *cinquefoiled ogee* arch with a renewed base, but the interesting thing is that a C19 bas-relief of Christ presiding at the Last Supper has been set in the back (there is a similar but more elaborate treatment at Market Weston). There is a C19 stone *reredos* and a tall renewed niche by the e. window which is filled with a late example of Charles Clutterbuck's glass. With *Hardman* and the *O'Connors*, he was one of the artists who began the Victorian revival of stained glass, and having moved on from C13 forms, here he used larger figures, with a central Christ in the style of Murillo surrounded by typically Victorian angel heads. Our Lord as the Good Shepherd and the True Vine stand on either side and both are badly eroded. All are set within dense foliage patterns with texts and are by no means as pleasing as his early work.

It is surprising to find a new and very attractive parish hall in the churchyard just w. of the tower; it replaced one which was flattened by the fall of a mighty elm tree. In such a pleasant spot it is salutory to remember that once this was a place of desolation. The court rolls of one of the village manors record the first known instance of the *Black Death* in East Anglia; between January and June 1349, sixty people died and twenty-one families left no heirs to claim their goods.

Little Finborough, St Mary (E5): The short drive to Hall Farm leaves the minor road at a sharp bend, and beyond the attractive cluster of house and outbuildings the way to St Mary's is along a rough track. Tiny and unpretentious, the early-C14 church lies among open, rolling fields, with a heavy cedar to the n. and a scattering of pine and holly and a windswept hedge towards the road. There is no tower and restoration in 1856 replaced a lath and plaster w. end with a blank pebble wall banded at intervals with dressed flint. There are angle buttresses and a single bell turret sits on the gable. The *nave* was at least partially rebuilt and cement rendered, retaining two early *Perpendicular* windows to the s. and another to the n. The *chancel* is a mixture of flint and *septaria* and the e. window has intersecting 'Y' *tracery*. The set-off e. of the nave window on the n. side, combined with faint outlines on the wall within, shows that there was once a *rood loft stair* here, and just by it in the churchyard stands an old shepherd's hut on fat little cast-iron wheels. Before going in, have a look at the C18 headstones by the path. They carry *baroque* scrolls and varied cherubs, with one weeping by an urn. A double stone commemorates the four children of William and Ann Cross who died between 1789 and 1802 aged 3 years, 1 month, 2 years, and 11 months. 'Ah! why so soon just as the flower appears . . .' cries the epitaph.

Beautifully kept, the interior lies under a plaster ceiling with some of the timbers of the roof exposed, and one of the *tie-beams* has rustic *arch-braces*. Another divides nave from chancel and probably supported the *rood*. The *tympanum* above it is plastered and there hangs a handsome set of George III *Royal Arms* painted on board and dated 1767. The plain C14 *font* stands on a wide step and the sides of the bowl are slightly canted. There are no signs of original porches but, unlike the entrance, the little n. doorway retains its simple shape and leads to a C19 *vestry*. Benches and *encaustic floor tiles* date from the 1860s and so does the rather odd pulpit and reading desk. Both are square and built as a unit featuring pierced Decorated-style tracery shapes. In the *sanctuary* the cast-iron *communion rails* take the form of 'Gothick' arches and there is a *piscina* recess with no drain. The openwork *altar* has one of those Victorian eccentricities – a brass inscription set in the bevelled edge of its top to Charlotte, widow of W.M. Townsend, 1895. The *reredos* must be of about the same period and the panels are painted with sacramental sentences flanking the Lord's Prayer in a style beloved of the late C19 – florid Gothic, with multi-coloured initials. Under the soft light of candles and oil lamps, Evensong in this endearing little church must be as balm in Gilead.

Little Glemham, St Andrew (H5): A stony track leads up to the church, lying just within the park of Glemham Hall. The stages of the well-proportioned *Perpendicular* tower are defined by two *string courses*, one of which lifts over the w. window as a *label*. There is *flushwork* in the simple *base course*, buttresses, and battlements, and the stumps of figures stand at the top corners; below the *gargoyles*, a moulding is decorated with a range of tiny *paterae*. The tower houses a good ring of five bells with a 14 cwt. tenor. The w. doorway has worn lion *stops*, with shields in the *spandrels*, and the niche above it contains a modern statue of Our Lord. The blocked *nave* n. doorway is *Norman*, and interesting because the arch is decorated with beakhead shapes which were perhaps left unfinished, like those at Westhall; the *capitals* of the single shafts are scalloped simply. Beyond looms the square bulk of the early-C19 chapel of the North family, its high walls broken only by a door in the w. wall and a *lancet* on the other side. During the C18, the *chancel* was rebuilt in brick, but the windows in more conventional Perpendicular style were installed later, probably as part of the 1850s restoration carried out by J.P. St Aubyn. On the s. side, the organ chamber was added in 1884, and the whole church was re-roofed. The tall s. *porch* was rebuilt in 1858, and a medieval wooden figure of the church's patron saint was installed behind glass in the niche above the arch. The inner doorway is decorated with two ranks of *fleurons*, and its *hood mould* is borne on small male and female *headstops*. The door itself has been restored and retains the original closing ring.

There is a C19 ringers' gallery within the tower, and the stair doorway has a nice pair of headstops, with fleurons in the moulding. St Andrew's has a good ring of five bells with a 14 cwt. tenor. The C13 *Purbeck marble* font stands on a modern shaft, and a large canvas *Decalogue* is framed on the n. wall. Dating from the early C18, the painting is dulled by age, the figures of Moses, Aaron, and Joshua standing behind the tablets of the Law, with texts of the Lord's Prayer and Creed on each side. The *lancet* opposite contains bright, attractive glass by *Margaret Agnes Rope*, one of her last works, installed in 1949 – a miniature sequence of four of the Ages of Man. An instructive contrast is the glass in the three-light n. window, by her cousin, *Margaret E. Aldrich Rope*. Signed with her tortoise mark and dated 1929, it still bears the stamp of *Christopher Whall's* influence in its use of grainy line and background of streaked glass. The *Blessed Virgin* stands in the centre, upon a crescent moon, and on either side there are the two best known Gospel incidents involving St Andrew – his call by the seashore, and his role in the miracle of the loaves and fishes. The figures and structure are excellent; *St Peter* peeps out from behind his brother on the beach, and a line of heads represents the multitude standing behind Jesus and the boy. Single *quarries* are painted with the two fish and five barley loaves, an *Agnus Dei*, and a small draught of fishes in a net. As a window of quality, it exposes the rather tired conventions of the 1880/90s work opposite which is probably by *Lavers, Barraud & Westlake*. The pine benches were part of the 1858 restoration, and roofs were replaced throughout – note the *sanctus-bell window*, glimpsed through the timbers at the w. end. Moving into the chancel, the North chapel comes into view, raised up, and roughly two thirds the size of the nave. Lit by a skylight in its coffered ceiling, it has fluted Doric corner columns, and the heavy hooks at each side show that the front arch was once draped with curtains. A low, cast-iron screen separates it from the chancel, and four chairs appropriate to 'the quality' are placed in the front row. An apse was added in order that the figure of Dudley North could be properly displayed. He was born Dudley Long but took the family name when he acquired the estate. A prominent and influential Whig, he was one of the managers of the trial of Warren Hastings and died in 1829. The statue was sculpted in Rome by John Gibson in 1833, but the first effort was lost at sea, and some contemporaries did not regard the replacement as a good likeness.

Be that as it may, it is an elegant figure, with an aquiline patrician head, dressed in flowing robes and sitting entirely relaxed in a grecian chair. The effect is diminished by having chairs piled behind the statue and the chapel space given over to after-service refreshments. A tablet on the e. wall commemorates Nicholas Herbert, MP for one of the old rotten boroughs, who married a North heiress and died in 1775. It is flanked by a pair of elegant vase-shaped memorials, with drapes caught up by bas-relief urns at the top. They are for Barbara, Countess of Aldborough (1785), and heiress Ann Herbert, who died at 80 in 1789 – it was she who bequethed the estate to her nephew Dudley. These tablets will have been moved from the chancel when the chapel was built, and three *brasses* were similarly re-sited on the opposite wall. They belong to members of the Glemham family, Lords of the Manor from the early C16 until 1680 – Sir John (1535), Christopher (1549), and Thomas (1571). They share a uniform design, a shield and long verse inscription within a *blind arch*, and must have been engraved together, some time after 1571. The first line of Thomas's epitaph uses the old term for 'holy' that earned the county its title of 'silly Suffolk', (often ignorantly or wilfully misunderstood by outsiders):

This sylly grave the happy cynders hyde . . .

There are four more North monuments in the chancel, all in mottled marble, with elaborately supported *achievements of arms*, and clutches of cherub heads. The quality is uniformly high, and the largest, on the s. wall, was sculpted by William Holland to commemorate Mrs Catherine North who died in 1715. When the chancel was rebuilt, a stone carving of the *Trinity* was set in the embrasure of the *sanctuary* window, and despite some damage, the figure of Christ on the cross is clear.

Little Saxham, St Nicholas (B4): A very attractive setting at the village cross-roads. The round tower is arguably the best in Suffolk and the base may well be *Saxon*, although the belfry stage is *Norman*. There, two-*light* openings are deeply recessed and linked by an *arcade* of blank arches above a course of *billet* moulding. It has been suggested that the detailing was copied from the Norman gateway of the abbey at Bury. There is a small *lancet* lower down on the w. side within sections of *chevron moulding*. Some particularly pretty *Decorated tracery* is to be found

in one of the C14 n. *aisle* windows and the C16 Lucas chapel, with its large *Perpendicular* n. window, juts out on that side. Large three-light windows were inserted in the s. wall in the C15 and the churchyard has been cleared in front with headstones lined up – some of them C17 and C18. Within the *porch* are a small *stoup* and a Norman doorway with a plain *tympanum*. The thick roll moulding of the arch has a rim of billet decoration and the shafts have volute *capitals*.

Just inside on the l. there is a Norman archway in the w. wall, and this has been identified by some as the old n. doorway. If so, it must have been cut down and there seems to be no good reason for it being where it is. The C11 tower arch is tremendously tall and narrow and there is a doorway or large window opening above it. At the back of the aisle two base sections of the old *rood screen* rest against the wall and the buttresses have *crocketted* pinnacles at the top, while in the tracery *spandrels* you will find tiny carvings of squirrels, birds, lions, a rabbit and a pig. Nearby stands a C17 *bier* – a rarity of interesting design; it has a slatted top, rudimentary carving on the ends and, instead of the usual hinged arrangement, the handles retract into the frame. (Another example is to be found at Dalham.) Two of the church's pre-*Reformation* bells now stand at the w. end, and both were cast by the Brasyer family of Norwich in the C15. It is a good opportunity to study the shield mark of the foundry, with its three bells and ducal coronet, and to admire the characteristically splendid lettering on the crown. The treble has 'Ave Maria gratia plena Dominus tecum' (Hail Mary full of grace, the Lord is with thee) and will have been used to sound the angelus. The second is inscribed 'Missus de celis haber nomen Gabrielis' (I have the name Gabriel sent from heaven). On the n. side of the nave there are medieval benches which have birds and beasts instead of *poppyheads* and one of them is a dragon biting its tail. Near the front, one bench has traceried ends with *paterae* on the chamfers, the remains of angels on the elbows and dumpy poppyheads. Across on the s. side, one *finial* is carved as a lady in a cloak kneeling at a prayer desk on which is a large open book. The *Jacobean* pulpit has two ranges of panels with the usual blank arches; it was extensively restored in 1891 when a new *tester* was added. The stairs to the old *rood loft* are at the e. end of the n. aisle and the position of the bottom door is most unusual. With the hinge hooks still in place, it is a good 6ft. from the floor and one wonders

Little Saxham, St Nicholas: Communion rails

whether part of the loft served as a secure place for valuables. In the wall below is a *piscina*, indicating that there was a medieval *altar* here. Sir Thomas Fitz Lucas was Henry VII's Solicitor General and it was he who built the n. chapel. He died in 1531 and was buried in London but he had already prepared a tomb here, standing within an archway in the n. wall of the chancel, opening into his chapel. However, when the chapel was appropriated by the Lucas family in the C17, the panels of the tomb were piled one on another to block the arch; so they remain, with eight coloured shields bearing the arms of Lucas, Morrieux, Kent and Kemys, all set within tracery. Little Livermere church is now an abandoned ruin but its lovely set of *communion rails*, with their turned and reeded *balusters*, were salvaged and have found a home here, with the *sanctuary* floor amended to follow their elegant double curve. The *Heaton, Butler & Bayne* glass of 1902 in the s. chancel window contains large figures of *St Luke* on the l., the *Blessed Virgin*, and *St James the Great* on the r. There are three angels above them, and both the predominance of pale yellow and the texture of the painting are in strong contrast with the E.R. Suffling glass in the e. window.

The n. chapel is normally locked but it is worth making local enquiries for a key because

of the important monument within. It commemorates William Lucas, 1st (and only) Baron Crofts (1677) and his wife, and is the work of Abraham Storey, one of Wren's master masons whose monuments are of great importance. This is his finest work and takes up the full height of the chapel on the s. side. The life-size figure, in flowing robes and baron's coronet, reclines with head thrown back, his fleshy face framed by an abundant wig. In his uplifted hand he holds a folded parchment and its seal is carved with the artist's monogram. Lady Crofts lies in front and just below him, head strained back as though to catch a glimpse of her husband. The features of both are finely modelled and note the quality of his left hand. The front panel of the massive base carries the Crofts shield, *Corinthian* columns flank a large epitaph panel framed in coloured marble, and there is a coloured *achievement* set between scrolls and draped urns above the cornice. Apart from chipped noses and two missing fingers, the dazzling marble is in lovely condition. Baron Croft was a Gentleman of the Bed Chamber to Charles II and guardian to his natural son the Duke of Monmouth so that the king frequently stayed at the Hall, particularly if there was racing at Newmarket. Samuel Pepys was with the king when he stayed at Saxham in October 1668; Charles got so drunk that he could not give audience to Lord Arlington who had come over from Euston. On that occasion the royal party probably didn't make it to church, but the King was in the congregation on 17th March, 1670 to hear George Seignior of Trinity College, Cambridge preach, and he thought well enough of the sermon to have it printed. Elizabeth Crofts died in 1642 and her memorial on the e. wall is particularly interesting because few were commissioned during the Civil war, and the design is defiantly at odds with the Puritan spirit. It is possibly by Henry Boughton and the alabaster frame is carved with cherub heads in profile, while fat *putti* support a *cartouche* of arms resting on a skull in the curve of the top. Above that, a small bust of the lady displays a generous and undraped busom. By way of confirmation, her husband tells us in the epitaph that 'she had a large proportion of personal beauty and handsomeness', but hastens to add: 'ye endowments of hir minde beinge much more eminent . . . in sum a woman of extraordinary perfections'. The C18 memorial to Mrs Ann Crofts is by William Palmer, and on the w. wall there is a tablet in a simple architectural frame for William Crofts who died in 1694, his achievement within the scrolled cornice and another coloured shield at the base.

Little Stonham, St Mary (F4): Very pleasantly situated at the end of Church Lane, the church is now in the care of the *Churches Conservation Trust*. The handsome tower with sharp *drip courses* has a polygonal turret to the s. which goes right up to the stepped battlements; these are decorated with a deep band of lovely *flushwork* which features monograms of the *Blessed Virgin* and there are *Evangelistic symbols* midway between the corner pinnacles. On the e., n., & w. faces of the parapet, crowned monograms for St Mary have letter within the 'M's that spell out most of the sentence: 'Ave Maria, gratia plena, Dominus tecum' (Hail Mary, full of grace, the Lord is with thee). There is *Decorated tracery* in the twin bell openings and flushwork on the buttresses and *base course*; the w. doorway has worn lion *headstops, paterae* in the mouldings, and *quatrefoils* with arms of the Crane family above it. The doors themselves have excellent tracery – tall *crocketted* pinnacles over pairs of Decorated arches. The tower houses a ring of five bells with a 10 cwt. tenor but they cannot be rung at the present time. The *nave clerestory* is *Perpendicular* and its gable, like the *chancel's*, is crow-stepped. The C14 chancel has *reticulated tracery* in its e. window and was restored by the rector in 1886 when a new *priest's*

door was inserted beneath a buttress, like the one at Yaxley. A chapel rather like a short s. *aisle* was built onto the C15 s. *porch* and the *dripstone* of the inner doorway is carved with *paterae* and rests on large male and female headstops.

Within, an C18 *gallery* stands on very slim iron columns and the panels of the C15 *font* contain unusually interesting carvings – w., a Crucifixion; s.w., a Sacred Heart within a crown of thorns; s.e., a crowned 'MR' for the Blessed Virgin; n.e., a *Tudor Rose*; n., the Crane monogram. Four battered lions round the shaft stand below a deep band of angels with linked hands. The nave roof is quite lavish for this size of church – a *double hammerbeam* in which short *king posts* rise to the ridge from the *collar beams*, and mutilated figures sit under canopies against the *wall posts*. All the *spandrels* are carved and the ends of the hammers retain the tenons that once secured angel figures. The hammerbeam against the wall at the e. end of the s. side had to be replaced in the C17 and was decorated with scrolls and grapevines in the style of the period – a notable addition to a good roof. Over the s. door hang the *Royal Arms* of Anne painted on canvas (pre-1704 and without her usual 'Semper eadem' motto). The *touchstone* tablet, in alabaster frame with skull and hour-glass, on the n. wall is for Gilbert Mouse, sometime servant of two Lord Chancellors and one Lord Keeper of the Great Seal. He died in 1622 and was buried in St Margaret's, Westminster, but his roots were here and there are details of his local charities. It is notable for the portrait engraved at the head of the tablet as though it were a *brass*. The restrained *Stuart altar* table in the s. chapel shows how heavy timbers were no longer being used for legs – slabs were added to increase the girth before the bulky sections were turned. 'T.G. 1703' painted on the wall is probably the record of a repair with churchwarden's initials. C19 benches stand on brick and *pamment* floors and by the pulpit the wall recess may have been a *piscina* but the panelling masks any possible proof. The chancel restoration included an *arch-braced* roof which rests on stone *corbels*, four of which are carved with Evangelistic symbols. Above them are sizeable oak figures under canopies and there are two rows of demi-angels on the *wall plates*. The same bout of restoration included the angle piscina and *dropped-sill sedilia*.

As one turns w. and sees the gallery and organ again, it brings to mind the extraordinary confrontation here in 1872 between a curate and a choir – or at least one member of it. It provided plenty of juicy copy for the *Ipswich Chronicle* and ended unprofitably for all concerned at Quarter Sessions. Ronald Fletcher's *In a Country Churchyard* tells the tale.

Little Thurlow, St Peter (A5): This is a late-C13 to early-C14 church. The tower has a large w. window with *cusped*, intersected *tracery*; the tall bell openings are later, with *headstops* to the *dripstones* and the battlements are flint chequer overall. A fine ring of five bells with a 12 cwt. tenor hangs in the tower. As with other churches in this corner of the county, a lot of *septaria* show in the walls of the s. *aisle* and *chancel*. The Soame family chapel was added in the early C17 and it is as large and tall as the chancel next to it; there are blind circular windows and another on the n. side has curious tracery. The large *trefoil clerestory* windows were replaced on the n. side with plain circles in the C17. The low and simple C18 brick *porch* shelters a C14 n. door which retains one shapeless headstop.

Within, the C14 tower arch is tall and thin and the position of C17 and later graffiti in the w. window embrasure shows that there was once a gallery half way up. The square C12 *font* is large and deep; there are scrolly and very varied carvings on three sides of the bowl with a cross roundel on the s. face, and thick shafts with *chevron capitals* mark the corners. The *Jacobean* pews are very interesting, with curiously shaped tops to the ends – inverted scrolls coming to a point at the top, the outer surfaces carved with a range of flower and leaf motifs. They are so like those at Clare that they may have been carved by the same man. The roofs are modern and a lovely twelve-branched chandelier hangs in the *nave*, topped by a dove. London made, it is similar to others at Burton-on-Trent and Steyning in Sussex and dates from about 1725. The church's only *brass* is in the centre of the nave – 18in. figures of a C14 man and wife. It may be for Thomas and Anne Gedding, but he died in 1465 and the wife's early form of *kennel headdress* was not fashionable until the 1480s so there is some doubt. The late-C13 *piscina* in the s. aisle still has its wooden *credence shelf* and the e. window nearby contains 1937 glass by Geoffrey Webb – the post-resurrection scene of Christ and his disciples (John 22:15). In the corner to the l. is a fragment of large C13 *dogtooth* moulding. The very narrow doorway that led to the *rood loft* is in the n.e. angle of the nave wall and round the corner in the n. aisle is a piscina rather oddly placed within what was the stairway. There were *altars*, therefore, in both aisles. Traces of wall painting show on either side of the wide

chancel arch and the base of a C15 *screen* remains which has jumbled sections of stencilled colour on the s. side. A pedestal to the l. carries a 16in. bronze figure of *St Edmund* sculpted by Elizabeth Frink in 1974 in memory of her father. The late-C17 *communion rails* enclose the *sanctuary* on two sides and have a very shapely range of *balusters* below a heavy, smoothed-over top rail. There is a C13 double piscina here, with heavily moulded arches and centre shaft, while on the e. wall there are unusual *Decalogue* panels of slate, the lettering incised and gilded. Jacobean arches lead to the Soame chapel and two of them have strapwork decoration. The chapel was built by Sir Stephen Soame, Lord Mayor of London and local squire who died in 1619, having founded a village school and provided some almshouses. It was designed to accommodate his superb, enormous tomb whose sculptor is unknown. The magnate's bulky alabaster figure lies above and behind his wife Anne, with the armour picked out in gilt. She wears a French cap, a gilt chain is draped over her bodice, and both their heads rest on bulky, tasselled pillows. There are flanking pavilions of *Corinthian* columns and within them four sons kneel in varying attitudes, while two young daughters stand in niches behind; three daughters in long veils kneel along the front behind the iron railings and there are two more children at the sides, a bountiful quiverful. It is notable that all the family are scaled down to child size even though the sons are bearded. Small coloured shields of arms surround the large *touchstone* panel with its extended epitaph, a quotation from Psalm 144 runs along the edge of the tomb chest, while overhead lurks the figure of Old Father Time with his scythe. The large contemporary family pew, with delicately pierced panels around the top, is set in the arch behind the choir stalls and a funeral helm is placed on a bracket high in the s.w. corner of the chapel. Near to it, the circular window has C17 glass painted with the 'in coelo quies' so often found on *hatchments*; five of these hang on the walls. Those for Sir Stephen and his wife (at the w. and e. ends of the n. wall) are not contemporary but may be later copies. The hatchment in the centre of the n. wall is for Anne Soame who died in 1781, that on the chancel side at the e. end is for Stephen's grandson John (1709) and the last, over the arches to the chancel, is for Margaret Hare, the heiress wife of an C18 bishop of Chichester. Another Soame monument worth studying is floridly signed by John Walsh, a talented C18 sculptor. To the l. of the large monument, it is a large tablet for the Stephen Soame who died in 1771, with a portrait medallion of Mrs Soame and her child. There are two poignant epitaphs, one for the husband and one for the child. In the first she writes: 'Thy Frances only waits the child to rear. . .' and then she had to add the verse for her son less than a year later. Hitching rings for horses are sometimes found on church walls (Sapiston has two) but this church has a very rare C18 or C19 dog chain attached to the n.w. buttress of the tower. Have a look as you leave.

Little Waldingfield, St Laurence (D6): This was an important village in the heyday of the Suffolk wool trade and the handsome church reflects this. There was a building here at the time of the Domesday survey but this was replaced in the C14 and the tower still has *Decorated* bell openings and a stooled niche in the s. wall at ground-floor level. The buttresses have four *set-offs* and there are three well-defined *drip courses*. There are regularly spaced *put-log holes* n. and s. and below the renewed *Perpendicular* w. window the edge of the C15 door is carved with a band of *quatrefoils*; headless angels stand at the corners of the stepped battlements. The tower houses a ring of five bells with an 11 cwt. tenor but they cannot be rung at the present time. C15 and C16 wealth allowed for extensive remodelling and all the *aisle* and *clerestory* windows lie under *crocketted labels* which have a shallow *finial* at the centre and terminate in masks which are full of character. The most distinctive feature of this period is the pair of octagonal *rood stair* turrets which rise to crocketted spires on either side of the *nave* gable, and they originally gave access to the roofs. The *Tudor* brick n. *porch* is a most interesting design and has a series of steps which are *weathered* like buttresses and rise above the arch to a deep niche whose heavy octagonal pinnacle matches those at the corners. The windows are deeply moulded and now that it has become a *vestry* the outer arch is blocked. At one time there was a chapel on the n. side of the *chancel* and the outlines of *piscina, aumbry,* connecting door, and low roof remain in the outer face of the wall. The C17 five-*light* e. window has a high *transom*, and round the corner is a very small *priest's door* under a square *label*. The walls of the C15 s. porch are attractively striped in brick and flint, the windows have stepped transoms, and the *dripstone* of the inner doorway matches the aisle windows. It has angel *stops*, however, and the mouldings are

distinguished by very large *paterae* carved with masks, a centre crown, and a crowned woman's head.

Two of the charity boards under the tower specify that loads of wood are to be delivered to the poor, and by the arch stand two chests. One dates from about 1300 and its curved top is eaten away with age between the broad iron bands; the other is a C15 example whose entire front is carved with shallow Decorated *tracery* and there are four small masks in the heads of the *ogee* arches. Between stands a late-C14 *font* and all the figures round the stem have been destroyed. However, four of the panels are deeply carved with *Evangelistic symbols* and the others contain seated figures of monks. These are unusual and although they have been defaced, a lot of interesting detail remains. They are seated on benches reading, one has a pen and inkhorn by his side, two have double-sided lecterns, and one wears a cope as opposed to the capes of the others. The chancel arch and those of the elegant nave *arcades* all have crockets and finials that match the window exteriors, and the clerestory embrasures are enlivened by little headstops that angle downwards. A string course dotted with paterae is picked out in cream to match the arcades below and contrasts well with the pale blue of the plastered chancel ceiling. Overhead, a heavy cambered *tie-beam* roof with alternate *arch-braces* in unstained oak spans the nave, and in the s. aisle there is a line of centre *bosses* which includes a *green man* and a modern gridiron symbol of the church's patron saint. At the e. end you will find a small *Stuart Holy table* and there is a plain piscina nearby. Over in the n. aisle there is another in the e. wall next to the rood stair door. Fragments of medieval glass in the aisle e. window include a small crowned head and most of a monk's tonsured head. The pulpit is a good C17 example resting on a heavy turned stem. It has distinctive scrolls and acorn pendants below the body and the panels are carved with shallow *blind arches* and diagonal crosses. The canted book ledge is adventurously carved and rests on bulky scrolled brackets. It is more than likely that it was made by the same craftsman who supplied pulpits to nearby Milden and Edwardstone, and the boxy reading desk here is from the same workshop. There are three interesting *brasses* in the n. aisle: at the w. end, are the 20in. figures of Robert and Mary Appleton. He was lord of one of the local manors and died in 1526. He is shown in *Tudor* armour, with his wife wearing a *kennel headdress*, and there are also three shields, one of which bears the punning or canting device of three apples. This probably came from the same workshop as the famous De Bures brass at Acton. In the centre of the aisle is the 29in. effigy of rich clothier John Colman. This is a fine brass; he wears a cloak with heavy sleeves and has a large pouch slung at his hip. There is an inscription and separate plates showing his six sons and seven daughters. For years all the components of this brass were loose in the vestry, together with the effigy of John's wife Katherine which disappeared long ago, but in 1977 they were fixed to an unmarked slab. The third brass lies at the e. end of the aisle and is for another clothier, John Wyncoll, who died in 1544. His 'picture' (as he called it in his will) shows him wearing a flowing gown left open to display his doublet and the inscription is immediately below.

A long squint gave a view from the s. aisle chapel through to the *sanctuary* and there you will find late-C17 *communion rails* and a C19 Minton tiled floor. There is a plain piscina and *dropped-sill sedilia* and, like the door to the vanished n.e. chapel, the priest's door is blocked.

Little Wenham, All Saints (E7): Isolated churches have a fascination all their own and this is no exception. A turning off the minor road between Capel St Mary and Great Wenham soon becomes a rough farm track, but after half a mile or so the reward is to find the church perched on a hillock behind Hall farm. Although the official dedication is to All Saints, it is known locally as St Laurence's and it is now in the care of the *Churches Conservation Trust*. In such a setting, with an Elizabethan tithe barn nearby, it is easy to imagine what Suffolk was like long ago. To the s. the battlemented tower of Little Wenham Hall rears sturdily beyond the farm buildings. Built in the late C13, that is one of the earliest English country houses and the church was built at about the same time. This is most clearly seen in the *chancel* where the e. window has three plain circles of *plate tracery* above three *lancets* separated by delicate *mullions*. The tracery actually has shallow, pierced *cusping* but it is visible only from inside. The tall lancet in the n. wall has a *low side window* below it in the form of a plain slit. Other windows have 'Y' tracery, there is a *priest's door* on the s. side, and the buttresses are gabled. The one on the *nave* wall not only has an old sundial pointer but below it are three earlier *scratch dials*. The C15 tower has a *base course*, a *Perpendicular* w. window with a small niche above it, and little belfry slits.

The bell stage was rebuilt in brick, probably in the early C16. The C15 s. *porch* has a brick base but the upper framework is attractively weathered timber, with three simple niches cut in the planks above the outer arch; turned *balusters* were inserted in the open sides early in the C17. Slots in the frame indicate that there was a lift gate to keep out stock at one time (like the one at Badley, another isolated church in the care of the Churches Conservation Trust).

On entering, notice the deep drawbar holes in the stonework of the doorway and the small *stoup* recess just inside. A late-C18 or early-C19 bier stands in the tower, and on the wall is a delightful photograph of a man in a billycock hat who may well have been a sexton who used the bier later in the century. Two *tie-beams* span the nave under the *single-braced* roof, and a *sanctus-bell window* lies behind the rafters at the w. end. The early-C14 *font* is a large, plain octagon resting on a centre drum and eight polygonal shafts. At least half of it has been replaced by new stone but the rest shows that it was painted originally. An C18 Lord's Prayer board hangs on the n. wall opposite, and below it are displayed a door and section of panelling from a *Jacobean* pew. In the traditional place opposite the main entrance are the remains of a large C15 *St Christopher* painting. The head of the saint with its curly chestnut hair is clear, and the Christ child with hand upraised has a dark halo, but the rest has gone except for part of the lozenge border. The rear benches have good *linen-fold* backs, and beyond the large late-Perpendicular window, the brick steps up to the vanished *rood loft* remain complete in the n. wall. In the s. wall of the nave there is an elaborate late-C14 tomb. Its chest has four shields within *quatrefoils* on the front, and the tall recess lies under a multi-cusped arch; above that, a *crocketted ogee* flanked by blind panelling and pinnacles reaches up to an elaborate *finial* at roof level. All is in very good condition and probably restored. The *screen* consists now of solid 5ft. walls, over 1ft. thick, and one wonders whether it was like Bramford's originally. There are oblong plastered panels each side which no doubt framed painted *reredoses* for nave *altars*, and one of the *piscinas* for them remains on the s. side (the shapeless recess by the stair doorway on the n. may be the remains of the other). The C18 pulpit has a rudimentary marquetry *Sacred monogram* in one of its panels, and the little curving stair with its twisted balusters is very attractive.

On the s. side of the chancel there is a section of medieval glazed tiles which were probably saved by having a C17 box pew placed over them, and in the centre is one of the church's treasures. It is the *brass* commemorating Thomas Brewse and his wife Jane. He died in 1514 and the remains of the inscription begin: '. . . Brewse Esquyer onetyme lord of this maner and patron of this churche . . .'. The brass measures 87in. by 36in., with 28in. effigies, and has the only complete and undamaged double canopy in Suffolk. His armour is an excellent example of the *Tudor* period and his wife's dress is opulent, with fur collar and cuffs, a long veil over her *kennel headdress*, and a pomander at the end of her girdle. There are separate plates engraved with the little figures of two sons and three daughters, the latter with hair down to their waists showing that they were unmarried at the time. A most unusual feature of the design is the pair of portrait heads within roundels in the canopies which may represent the *Blessed Virgin* and *St John*. The four shields were originally inlaid and all feature the Brewse heraldic lion coupled with families connected by marriage. Pride of lineage even extended to his great-grandfather's wife's family of Stapleton! A late-C13 or early-C14 burial slab rests against the n. wall and note that the low side window has a deep sill that could be used as a seat. Over the priest's door there is a fine marble cartouche for Alice Walker who died in 1683; cherub heads rest in a garland at the top but the verse below the Latin epitaph is very roughly lettered. The late-C17 *communion rails* are sturdy, with twisted balusters, and in the s. wall of the *sanctuary* one section of the *Early English sedilia* remains, with a trefoil arch and attached shafts. The rest of the space on that side was appropriated for John Brewse's monument in 1585. In stone and multi-coloured marble, it has a classical pediment and flanking *Corinthian* columns above the tomb chest, with a small round-headed niche at the back. This contains a little kneeling figure in perfect condition, the armour completed by large metal spurs. Colour has been well restored and there are four shields of arms and an *achievement* at the top. On the n. side of the sanctuary there is a tomb chest with shields in lozenges on the front, and the late Tudor arch above has two ranges of *paterae* and is panelled within. Above it there are shallow blind panels with six shields left blank and, in the centre, a vigorous bas-relief of the Brewse arms on a tilted shield, with helm and Saracen's head crest. The recess may well have been used for an *Easter sepulchre* originally, but in 1785 a tablet was placed there for John Brewse, Col. Commandant of the Corps of Engineers.

When *William Dowsing* was here in 1643 he broke down 26 'superstitious pictures' (stained glass, one assumes) and left orders about six more, but although he says that one of them was of the Virgin Mary, the remarkable thing is that there is a painting of her on the e. wall which has survived. It is part of an important series on either side of the e. window which date, from the time that the church was built, and it is possible that in Dowsing's day it had been covered up. The Virgin and Child stand on the n. side and the robes are now blue-green and pale brown, with hands and faces oxidised to black. The chestnut hair is thick and curly, and the infant Christ reaches across his mother for the branch she holds in her right hand. Above them there was an elaborate canopy of which only the green leaves of the crockets show clearly. On the s. side of the window there are three tall figures in attitudes typical of the late C13. They stand within painted niches which have cusped and crocketted arches, above which are steep gables; across the top, a line of two-light windows under sharp gables and a roof line give the effect of a church facade. Again, the colours are blue-green and pale brown for the robes but more detail of the folds has survived. Here we have three favourite female saints, each with brown hair peeping out from under a veil: on the l., *St Margaret* (see the dragon's head at the bottom), in the centre *St Catherine*, on the r. *St Mary Magdalene*. This was work of high quality and the artist may well have belonged to the Colchester abbey group.

Little Whelnetham, St Mary Magdalene (C4): The church is attractively sited, with fields falling away to the w., and e. of the *chancel* there is an enigmatic circle of low flint ruins. It has been variously described as an *anchorite's* cell or the *apse* of a *Saxon* or *Norman* church, but the more likely solution is that it was a C10 watchtower that may have had a small church added to it. The unbuttressed tower of the present church has a C14 w. window but is likely to be older and there are bands of Roman tiles embedded in the fabric. The *nave* windows are *Perpendicular* but the corner *quoins* look C12 or C13 and there is a *scratch dial* at the s.e. corner which has recently been provided with a metal gnomen or pointer. There is a C14 *priest's door* on the s. side of the chancel, and by it, a *low side window* still fitted with its original grill. The C16 red brick *porch* has a crow-stepped gable and there is a niche above the handsome outer arch. The inner doorway is of the same period and has the unusual addition of a scroll-bearing angel at the apex of the arch. Although the door itself is modern, a medieval floriated cross has been retained in the centre.

The C15 *font* has *quatrefoils* with centre *paterae* in the bowl panels, one blank shield and a shield bearing the cross of *St George* to the e. Its interesting feature, however, is the shields below the bowl, two with *Passion emblems* and one with the *Trinity* device. The C15 nave *roof* is both handsome and unusual. It has *hammerbeams* and *arch-braces* but instead of the usual layout wherein the forms alternate, here we have hammerbeams separated by two sets of arch-braces. The other individual feature is that, unlike their fellows in the body of the nave, the large individual figures carved on the hammerbeams against the e. and w. walls lie on their sides and face each other. All were badly mutilated during the C17 and restored as part of a major restoration in 1842. At least two of the crowned heads are new, but if there were once wings these were not replaced. The grotesques at the base of the *wall posts* are an excellent sample and include two devils and a lion with foliage sprouting from his jaws like a *green man*. The tower screen is modern and incorporates two ranges of *traceried* panels that may well have formed part of the *rood loft*. The C15 benches have large *poppyheads* and a pleasing variety of tracery on the ends. You will find a coarsely carved bull and the initials 'I.B.' on a bench near the front on the s. side which means that the donor was likely to have been a John or James Bull. Four of the benches on the n. side are good C19 copies. Below the easternmost window on the s. side is a Norman *pillar piscina* – another indication of the church's early origin. To the e. of it there are two Perpendicular image brackets decorated with paterae under *castellated* rims and the larger may have had a demiangel below. Over the *Decorated* chancel arch is a *sexfoiled* circular window of the same period. The base of the C15 *screen* has good tracery in the panels, with a band of carving along the bottom. The lectern is intriguing. Given by a C19 rector, it is a great eagle excellently carved in wood and standing on a ball (the base is modern). It has had a book ledge added but the stance is so upright that one wonders whether it was not originally a purely decorative piece of the C17 or early C18 from Europe. There is a deep embrasure to the low side window and the piscina in the *sanctuary* has a plain C12 arch, with a small image bracket to the l. In the n. wall is a tiny C13 *aumbry* and if you care to look under the *altar* you will find the church's original *mensa* which was recovered from the churchyard

during one of the C19 restorations. There is a pleasant variety of late-C17 and early-C18 *ledger-stones* in the chancel and it is worth recording that the church depends entirely on candlelight for evening services, surely one of the very few that remain. The rowel-style candelabra in the nave were designed and made by Sydney Peters, craftsman and churchwarden.

Little Wratting, St Mary (A6): This diminutive church is ringed by trees and there are two distinct levels separated by a curving bank which means that it may stand in a rare example of a circular churchyard. Large pebbles, stones laid with wide joints, and rough *herringbone* work in the *nave* walls and part of the *chancel* point to an early-C11 date. The plain rectangular doorways bear this out, and the lintel of the s. entrance is carved with an inscription whose faint but unmistakable letter shapes mark it as *Saxon*. It has been suggested that the few words that can be deciphered form part of a dedication but the whole has defied an acceptable translation. There are two large floriated 'C's and three straps of late-C12 wrought-iron on the door which may well be as old.

As you enter, note the draw-bar hole to the r.; it is over 5ft. deep. There is no tower and the C19 bellcote with its shingled spire is supported within the church by C15 *arch-braced wall posts* resting on huge floor plates – a unique arrangement in Suffolk but common in Essex. The plain octagonal C14 *font* has a Victorian cover and the C15 low benches have unusual *tracery* in the end panels which is more akin to screenwork. The three front rows on the s. side are modern copies, but part of the wall panelling with its *castellated* top is original. A *box pew* at the w. end has been craftily converted to house a modern organ console. A deep *rood loft* staircase is built on to the n. wall and there are matching stone *corbels* each side of the nave which carried the front of the loft, with a ledge showing in the n.e. corner. They are only about 6ft. up but the floor level was probably raised during the C19 restoration. There were nave *altars* beneath the loft and larger windows were inserted to give more light (fragments of original glass remain in the one to the n.). The C15 *screen* was removed when the wider brick and stone chancel arch was inserted in 1895, and the chancel was partially rebuilt and re-roofed at that time. The shallow stone sink built into the n. *jamb* of the arch was found in the churchyard near the porch and it may once have been a *reliquary* associated with an altar. A chapel for the Turnour family was built on to the n. side of the chancel in the early C16 but it decayed and was demolished in 1710. All that is left is a section of the connecting *arcade* embedded in the wall just beyond the chancel arch, and a fragment from one of the tombs. This is an early-C17 kneeling woman in ruff and voluminous gown which now stands on the ledge of one of the early C16 s. windows. Another possible survivor from the chapel is an armorial plaque inserted alongside a roof corbel on the n. side of the chancel. The C14 *piscina* was rebuilt into the *sanctuary* wall and has a deeply moulded *ogee* arch, with vestiges of *headstops, crockets* and a *finial.*

Long Melford, Holy Trinity (C6): Apart from Lavenham, Suffolk has nothing that can compare with the grandeur of Long Melford, standing in solid magnificence above the broad sweep of village green. At the turn of the century the unsatisfactory C18 tower was at last encased to a design by *George F. Bodley* which, with its west country bell openings and Norfolk *sound holes*, is not locally inspired but which nevertheless matches the scale and character of the building. The quality is impeccable; note particularly the tall *flushwork* panels at the base. The tower houses a good ring of eight bells with a 15 cwt. tenor. The whole of the rest of the building is an epitome of the *Perpendicular* style and the s. front is one continuous series of verticals thrusting up through *transomed aisle* windows, buttresses and deeply recessed *clerestory*. All that is lacking are the pinnacles on parapet and battlements. The rest of the wall surfaces are meshed with flushwork and a continuous *base course* of shields in *quatrefoils* runs the length of the building. One of the remarkable features is that an unbroken band of inscriptions is cut in the parapet of *porch* and aisle and below the clerestory battlements, identifying those who paid for the building and dating the work between the 1460s and the 1490s. There is no linear break or change in height but the chapel at the e. end of the s. aisle, built in 1484, has two windows with the four-petalled flower motif in the *tracery*, a style of 30 years earlier. They may well have been reused to allow the original glass to remain in place. This is the chapel of the Martyn family and the merchants' marks of Roger and Lawrence Martyn can be seen on shields below the *string course* of the *chancel* parapet at the e. end. The chancel extends one bay beyond the aisles with deeper windows, with a bridging *vestry* at lower level below. Originally there was a Lady Chapel outside the

main building but in 1496 a new one was added to the e. end under three long, steeply gabled roofs, which, for all its splendour, does not combine happily with the rest. The windows are shorter and the entire wall surface is filled with flushwork; again, there is a continuous parapet inscription. Although the n. clerestory has flushwork and inscription, the aisle is wholly without decoration and there is an unadorned n. door; a brick *rood stair* turret rises on that side. The outer arch of the lofty s. porch is decayed, with a niche on either side, and overhead there are three stooled and canopied niches linked by blind-arched panels.

Within this great church the *arcades* march in a splendid unbroken line from end to end, although the *piers* of the five w. bays are the C14 originals and the rest adaptations of the same style. The wall space between arches and clerestory is filled with blind panelling that matches the windows, and the *arch-braces* of the almost flat roof meet in a continuous curve beneath the *tie-beams*. All the roof timbers are moulded, the *spandrels* are pierced with tracery, and dumpy figures in heavy robes stand beneath canopies on the *wall posts*. Looking eastward, the silhouetted gables of the off-centre Lady chapel appear awkwardly beyond the e. window, making one regret that it no longer has stained glass. By the door stands a C15 *Purbeck marble font*, with shields in the traceried panels and a deep mould beneath the bowl. The counter-weighted cover dates from 1935. Turning back, you will see over the door one of the finest sets of *Royal Arms* in the county; they are probably for George I, and are beautifully delicate, and carved three-dimensionally in limewood. To the w. of the door hangs the oldest diamond-shaped *hatchment* in the county and one of the earliest in England; it is for Thomas, Viscount Savage, who died in London in 1635 of 'the running gout' and was buried at Macclesfield. In 1997 the base of the tower was splendidly reordered; behind a solid screen, the ground floor accommodates cloak rooms, and a stair leads to a gallery where the tower arch is glazed to its full height. The hatchments grouped on the n. and s. walls, with names and dates on the frames, can now be studied at close quarters, and it's worth going up to the gallery to enjoy the breathtaking view of the full length of the church.

Long Melford is justly famous for its C15 glass. In the C19 it was collected in the e. window and in the aisles, but in the 1960s Christopher Woodforde directed a complete rearrangement by Kings of Norwich and it is now excellently displayed in the n. aisle. There you will find a unique series of medieval portraits, together with saints and martyrs. Name labels have been helpfully inserted under the major figures. John Clopton was the church's principal benefactor and he included portraits not only of himself and his family but political colleagues and powerful national figures. You will find Chief Justice Sir William Howard (third window from w.), Sir Ralph Joscelin, the Lord Mayor who defended London Bridge against the rebels in 1471 (fifth window from w.), and Elizabeth Howard, Countess of Oxford, wife of the 12th Earl beheaded in 1461 (third window from w.). *St Apollonia* with her pincers is in the first window and over the n. door is a lovely *Pietà*, with *St Peter Martyr* alongside. Below the Pietà is the tiny roundel of the three rabbits who share three ears. The only other known version of this *Trinity* symbol is on a roof *boss* at South Tawton in Devon, and while it is familiarly known as 'the Trinity rabbits', there is some doubt about its religious significance. In the eighth window from the w. is a fine *St Edmund* with an abbot of Bury kneeling before him. Further along there is another St Edmund, with *St George* and *St Martin*, in the *Kempe* window of 1903. The portrait of Elizabeth Talbot, Duchess of Norfolk (second window from the w.) is said to have inspired Sir John Tenniel's illustration of the Duchess in *Alice in Wonderland*. At the e. end of the n. aisle is a beautiful mid-C14 alabaster panel of the Nativity. In almost perfect condition, it was recovered from beneath the chancel floor in the C18 and is an early example of a *reredos* panel. The *Blessed Virgin* lies on a couch with the Child, the Magi are ranged with their gifts, and an attendant woman stands on one side while *St Joseph* dozes in a chair; the heads of two oxen peep out improbably from under the bed. The angular stone pulpit of 1884 is interesting in that its panels contain the figures of saints to whom altars were dedicated in the medieval church: the Virgin and Child (for the Jesus chapel and the Lady chapel), SS *Anne, James, Edmund* and *John*. Through the screen from the n. aisle is the n. chancel aisle or Kentwell aisle, as it is called, where there are a number of *brasses*, some relaid. The first one is for William Clopton (1420), and beyond it is one for a lady of his family of the same period. Beyond the organ, there are three more: nearest the outer wall, for Alice Harleston (1440), half-sister of John Clopton; she wears an heraldic mantle with her husband's arms, her kirtle bears the arms of

Clopton, and a fragment of the elaborate canopy remains. In the centre is the effigy of Francis Clopton (1578) wearing Elizabethan armour with a vestigial codpiece. Beyond him is the brass of Margery Clopton (1424), mother of the church's great benefactor. Like Alice Harleston she wears a *butterfly headdress* with transparent veil over the plucked forehead, and an heraldic mantle. Again there is a portion of the canopy work and both brasses must, on the evidence of costume, have been commissioned by John in the 1480s; both were inlaid with colour. The door in the n. wall was the private entrance from Kentwell Hall and alongside is a *consecration cross*. Beyond it is the tomb of John's father, Sir William Clopton (1446). It has been extensively restored and, apart from the freshly coloured shields, is a uniform and shiny beige. The effigy lies in armour under a low arch on the tomb chest which has a *stoup* built into it by the door. Within the recess is a lengthy Latin inscription on brass, and a helpful, beautifully lettered translation is provided. On the floor in front there is another inscription for Thomas Clopton who died in 1597. There is a *piscina* in this chapel and a most unusual *squint*. By cutting through two walls it gives a view across the corner of the Clopton *chantry* next door to the *High altar* beyond. The chantry chapel is entered through a vestibule which is only 5ft. across but which

Long Melford, Holy Trinity: The Lily Crucifix

Long Melford, Holy Trinity

contains a fireplace and has an intricate little *fan vault* which is almost flat. The chapel is a beautiful room lit by a seven-*light* e. window in which is set the late-C14 or early-C15 'lily crucifix'. Less than a dozen examples are recorded of this most interesting form – the resurrection implied by Christ crucified on the lily of the *Annunciation*. The rear of the chapel has a low ceiling, like a *gallery*, but which is glazed above, and there are remnants of verses on the w. wall. The *wall plate* is decorated with as a folded scroll through which is threaded a vine, and a hand is carved in the s.e. corner as though opening it out. It is painted with two poems attributed to John Lydgate, the monk of Bury, and the ceiling rafters carry little painted scrolls of 'I.H.U. mercy' and 'Gramercy'. There are the remains of a piscina and two *sedilia* to the r. of the *altar*, a line of Clopton shields in quatrefoils above them, and below the ceiling, twelve niches with exquisitely pinnacled canopies designed no doubt for statues of the apostles. In 1990 the chapel was handsomely refurbished by the Clopton family Association of America. A low arch connects the chapel with the *sanctuary* and within it stands the tomb of John Clopton, the church's principal benefactor, who died in 1497. A large figure of Christ holding a cross and displaying his wounds is painted on the underside of the arch, and on the top of the tomb was placed the painted timber frame of the *Easter sepulchre*. An angled mirror allows the painting to be more easily studied. In the sanctuary, the High altar is backed by a large 1870s reredos of the Crucifixion under heavy canopy work by Farmer and Brindley in dun coloured Caen stone. It is a pity that Bodley, having done so well with the tower,

could not have provided a reredos on the lines of his work at St Margaret's, King Lynn, or Sudbury, St Peter's. On the s. side is the massive tomb of Sir William Cordell who died in 1581, having been Speaker of the House of Commons under Queen Mary and Elizabeth's Master of the Rolls. Fuller in his *Worthies of England* says of him: 'great offices he had and good offices he did to posterity'; he founded the Trinity Hospital almshouses close by the church. It is highly likely that the monument is by Cornelius Cure, master mason to the Crown in the closing years of the C16, and it is in beautiful condition. He lies in armour on a rolled straw mat below two deeply coffered arches supported by polished marble *Corinthian* columns. Against his feet is his *cockatrice* crest and the four figures of Prudence, Justice, Fortitude and Temperence stand in shallow niches at the back. Such was the influence of the *Renaissance* that the head of Bacchus enlivens the scrollwork at the top. Returning to the s. aisle, there is 1880s glass by *Ward & Hughes* in one window, (six Resurrection scenes), and at the e. end, a small *trefoil*-arched piscina and *dropped-sill sedilia*. Beyond the modern screen is the Martyn chapel or chapel of the Jesus *guild*; parts of the screen dividing it from the chancel are original. There is an iron-bound chest in one corner and against the e. wall, a fine C15 settle which came from Granada cathedral; it has Gothic tracery on the back and bottom, and bears the arms of Ferdinand V of Castile and Isabella. There is a *Purbeck marble* tomb chest reaved of its brasses, with shields in lozenges along the sides and beyond it there is a piscina in the corner. There are two fine brasses here: Roger Martyn and his wives Ursula and Margaret (1615); the ladies have French hoods and ruffs and there are two groups of children. The second is for Richard Martyn and his three wives (1624); he is in doublet, hose and gown, his wives are in Paris caps, and there is a group of two sons (one bearing a skull to show that he died before his parents); in addition, there are two *chrysom children* and there was originally another group of children and another baby. The Lady chapel is entered by a door in the s. wall and is a charming building in its own right. It centres on a three-bay sanctuary which has a stone screen at the w. end and a solid wall behind the altar; around it on all four sides is an ambulatory or processional way. The centre chapel has canopied niches above the piers together with blind arcading under a cambered tie-beam roof. The lovely ambulatory roofs also have cambered tie-beams with canopied niches in the corners. There are stubby figures bearing emblems on the wall posts and the wall plates are similar to those in the Clopton chantry chapel. The floors are pale brick and in the n.e. corner a multiplication table is painted on the wall – a reminder that the chapel served as a schoolroom from 1670 until the early C19.

Lound, St John the Baptist (J1): The round *Norman* tower is plain, with a lot of brick in it, and it is likely that it was rebuilt and heightened in the C14. The *nave* has windows with 'Y' tracery of around 1300 but the *chancel* is later, with a *Perpendicular* e. window which looks as though it may have been renewed. The outline of a *scratch dial* can be traced on the buttress e. of the *priest's door*. The outer arch of the C15 *porch* has hung shields in the *spandrels* and lion *stops*, and there is a deeply moulded inner doorway with a large niche above it.

The door opens to reveal a lovely surprise, a church that glows and glistens with gilt and colour, beautifully maintained in the Anglo-Catholic tradition. It is no wonder that Lound is known as 'the golden church'. The rector in the early years of the C20 was Booth Lynes and his generosity, coupled with the talents of *Sir John Ninian Comper*, transformed the interior between 1912 and 1914. The tower arch is filled with a good screen and doors, and above it is the Comper organ case in pale green and gold, with two trumpeting cherubs dashing out from behind the pipes. It is a pleasure to report that Comper's gilded work has recently been beautifully restored to its original brilliance by Miss Pauline Plummer. The early-C15 *font* is a familiar design often found in Norfolk and Suffolk, with lions round the shaft and *Evangelistic symbols* alternating with angels in the bowl panels. The latter bear shields which were repainted as part of the restoration: w. *Trinity* shield; n. the arms of Henry Despencer, bishop of Norwich when the font was installed; e. *Instruments of the Passion*; s. the shield of the Bartlett family in recognition of the donor. The inscription on the base reads: 'Orate pro anima domini Johannis Bertelot rectoris ecclesiae de Lound qui fecit fieri hunc fontem baptismalem' (Pray for the soul of Sir John Bertelot, rector of Lound church, who had this baptismal font made). Comper designed a lovely new cover, a tall *tabernacle* with pierced vine panels and a host of slim, *crocketted* pinnacles; it is suspended from a painted *tie-beam* overhead. Just to the e. is Daniel Nave's *ledger-stone* of 1775 and it employs a version of that well known epitaph which begins: 'Adieu vain world, I've known enough of thee . . .'. There is a *stoup* once again in use by the door, and for the n. wall opposite Comper designed a large and lively *St Christopher* for modern travellers. A labourer takes a sack of corn to the water mill at the bottom, and Comper himself dashes uphill in a touring Rolls Royce. When the painting was restored in 1964, a Britannia jetliner was added in the sky overhead. Nearby stands a simple table which was used as the *altar* in the C17, but the nave benches date from an 1890s restoration. Fragments of medieval glass remain in the tops of the nave s. windows, and of the two shields on the n. side, only the plain black cross of Norwich cathedral priory has been identified. The *Stuart* pulpit has simple carving in the panels below the rim, and its base is the upended bowl of the original Norman font. The door to the l. leads to the medieval *rood loft stair*, and now one turns to Comper's major reconstruction, the *screen* with its loft and rood. It was first installed in the C14, and the turned shafts, the *ogee* arches, and the spiky *tracery* survive from the original. They have been left unpainted, but the rest is alive with gilt and colour, all renewed in 1976. The architect chose not to follow the C14 design but employed a pastiche of early-C16 forms which is typical of his style. The decorated *linen-fold* panels of the base have a band of pierced work above them – lion heads with fishy tails, and crowned initials for King George V and Queen Mary whose shields of arms are set in the gates. The underside of the loft is coved, and decorated with *Agnus Deis* and *Sacred monograms* within the vaulting; from l. to r. the shields are for: Gibson (patron of the living), the diocese, Edward III, bishop Pollock, Lynes. Twin cherubim flank the rood group, and the cross

Lound, St John the Baptist: Comper's St Christopher

bears down on dragons of evil each side of a *pelican in her piety*. To the r. is the Lady altar, and its lovely *reredos* has a figure of the *Blessed Virgin* and Child flanked by *St Elizabeth* with *St John the Baptist*, and *St Mary Salome* with *St John*, set against patterned gesso backgrounds. The exquisite frontal was embroidered by a Miss Bucknall in 1914 and restored in 1980. The chancel had been restored in 1875, and Comper provided a new *High altar* backed by curtains of Spanish silk dyed to his favourite dusky pink; the embroidery by the Sisters of Bethany displays the figures of Christ and the two St Johns. A C15 *piscina* is set in the splay of the

sanctuary s. window whose sill is lowered to form *stepped sedilia*. The e. window glass of 1875 is unremarkable, but the two chancel side windows are exceptionally good examples of the work of *Henry Holiday*; on the n. side, 1893, Christ with Mary and Martha, illustrating a text from St John's Gospel; on the s. side, 1906, Christ's Presentation in the Temple. Both windows embody excellent colour and composition, and there is dense acanthus leaf infill above and below the panels. Before leaving, have a look at the curious *squint* in the w. wall on the n. side. There is another like it at nearby Blundeston, and it has been suggested that it was designed to provide a view of the altar from outside. This is possible but seems unlikely, and it may have been used from inside to align with something outside. There is a similar arrangement in the tower of Thurne in Norfolk where the squint points directly to St Benet's abbey across the river.

Lowestoft, St Andrew (J1): The church stands on Roman Road and was planned as a memorial for the men of the district who fell in World War I. The design by Edwin J. Tench of Norwich was prepared in 1920, but lack of funds delayed the project until 1934. Its brick walls have been rendered and painted grey, and this, coupled with rectangular windows filled with obscured glass, gives it a somewhat gaunt and bleak character. There is no tower, and the single-bay chancel is defined simply by a reduction in width. A parish hall was added to the w. end in 1968, and the common vestibule gives access to a small suite of community accomodation that was completed in 1986. Within the church itself, the feeling is much less forbidding, and the simple *nave* has a parquet floor and lies below a gently cambered roof. The only discordant feature is the forest of light fittings and electric heaters suspended from the ceiling. A double-glazed panel allows anxious mothers in the congregation to keep an eye on their infants in the crèche on the other side of the w. wall. A low masonry screen divides the chancel from the nave, and a brick pulpit is built into it on the n. side. The organ is housed within a recess on the s. side of the chancel, and the *communion rails* are the telescopic tubular brass variety that some Victorian restorers favoured. Did they, I wonder, come from the same C19 church that provided the set of pitchpine benches in the nave?

Lowestoft, Christ Church (J1): The Beach industrial estate has taken the place of dense housing along Whapload Road where Christ Church was built in 1868 specifically to cater for the needs of the fishing community. With Ness Point only a quarter of a mile away, it is the most easterly church in Britain, and it is aligned n.-s. rather than the conventional e.-w. The building was designed by H. Oldham Chambers and consists of a *nave, aisles, chancel, porch*, and a tower at the s.e. corner; there is a *vestry* on one side of the chancel, and an organ chamber was added on the other side in 1879. The white brick walls are banded in red, and the modest tower has *broaches* below an octagonal bell stage and a lead-sheathed spire. The tower doorway was designed as the main entrance and has foliage decoration on the *capitals* in the *Early English* style, with *paterae* in the arch mouldings. The architect chose simple forms of that period for the whole building, and the windows have *quatrefoil* and *trefoil* shapes in the *tracery*.

The interior is surprisingly spacious, with a wide nave and compact chancel. There is a four-*light* w. window, and the roofs are arch and cross-braced in pine. The Victorians were not averse to using cast-iron structurally; Chambers made use of it here in the *piers* of the nave *arcade*, with their exuberant foliage capitals, and the form is repeated in the arcade of the organ chamber. On the e. aisle wall there are three separate memorials for men who died in World War I, and on the opposite wall there is an interesting plaque which was installed to mark the 100th anniversary of the first service to be held in the church. It lists those men ordained into the ministry from the congregation between 1932 and 1985. The wooden lectern with its muscular eagle is probably C19, but the octagonal *font*, also in wood, dates only from 1952. Above the pulpit, a brass commemorates Samuel Farrer 'late of the East India Merchant Service' who died in 1899, and his wife Rosanna. The panels of the stone 'gothick' *reredos* are painted with the *Decalogue* and Creed, and the window above has glass of about 1910 by H.J. Salisbury. It portrays the Ascension, with the disciples in statuesque poses below Christ, and there are two angels with the dove of the Holy Spirit in the tracery. More of this firm's work can be seen at nearby Kirkley and Pakefield.

Lowestoft, St Margaret (J1): The church is set well back from the town centre on rising ground, a large and impressive building which was, with the exception of the tower, almost totally rebuilt

in the 1480s. It would, perhaps, have been more satisfactory had the tower been replaced in scale at the same time, for it lacks the weight of the rest of the building. Probably dating from the mid-C13, it has a small w. window with 'Y' *tracery* of about 1300. Its walls are decorated with blind arcading below the bell openings, and at the time of the great C15 rebuilding the height was increased, with the slim spire added to bring the total height to 120ft. Walking round, you will see *Tudor Roses* in the *spandrels* of the n. door, and note the interesting tracery in the five-*light* e. window. It has a whole series of stepped *transoms*, and below the bottom range of *ogee* arches there are tiny demi-angels as pendants. The chancel buttresses are faced with delicate *ashlar* tracery incorporating shields, and the squared flint infill is recessed, giving the work great liveliness. Seen as a whole, the s. facade is rather austere, with a chequered *base course*, plain parapets, and widely spaced *clerestory* windows that, strangely enough, are of three types. The s. wall gave trouble in the late C18, and in 1871 the whole of the s. aisle was dismantled and rebuilt. The s. *porch* is massive, and its frontage is decorated overall with narrow *flushwork* panels; there are three niches containing 1890s statues of *St Margaret, St Felix* (l.), and Herbert de Losinga, bishop of Norwich, cradling his cathedral (r.). The arch below has large lion *stops*, and angels hold shields in the spandrels; the carvings are now very weathered but *emblems of the passion* can be recognised on the l. shield. The porch vaulting has prominent *bosses*, and the large room above is traditionally known as 'the Maids' chamber', having been the cell of Elizabeth and Catherine, two pre-*Reformation anchoresses*.

The interior of the church is spacious, with an uninterrupted vista, and a single roof extends over nave and chancel. The gracious *arcades* have lozenge-shaped *piers*, and slim shafts rise to the bases of the *wall posts*. The low-pitched roof is spanned by heavy *tie-beams* above braces which rest on stubby *hammerbeams*, and it was all reconstructed in the early 1890s. The gilded angels were added to the hammers by Ketts of Cambridge in 1897, and in 1899 *George Frederick Bodley* gave the roof its rich mulberry and gilt decoration, with 'M's for the dedication painted between the rafters. The small, robust tower arch of the previous century was left undisturbed by the C15 rebuilding, and sections of C18 lead roofing with churchwardens' names have been mounted on the walls each side. In the n.w. corner is one of the largest *banner stave lockers* to be found in this part of East Anglia; it has a decorative stonework panel at the head and has been fitted with a pierced replacement door. The C14 *font* stands on three steps, two of which have *quatrefoils* carved in the risers, and it must have been an exceptionally fine piece until 1644 when Francis Jessop mutilated it. He was a native of Beccles and one of *William Dowsing's*: 'a wretched commissioner not able to read or find out that which his commission injoined him to remove'. Until he came, the font had pairs of figures in each of the eight bowl panels, with more in deep niches round the shaft, but all of them were grievously defaced; the *paterae* carved on the mouldings give some indication of the quality of the work. The lovely cover was designed by *Sir Ninian Comper* in 1940 and is significantly different from his earlier piece at nearby Lound. Pairs of gilded columns rise from the angles of the bowl to support a skeletal *tabernacle* and panelled spirelet; a dove is carved in a sunburst on the underside above the bowl, and the decoration is in gilt and blue.

The aisle w. windows contain lovely figures of the *Evangelists* by *Christopher Whall*, with their symbols displayed on a large scale beneath. They date from about 1903 and came from the nearby church of St Peter which was demolished in the 1970s. Colour, texture and composition are typical of the artist, and there is more of his work in the westernmost side window in the n. aisle. There, Christ in Majesty sits holding a globe, with his feet resting on the firmament, flanked by the *Blessed Virgin* and *St Peter*; the group is set within a framework of vine branches, tall sheaves of corn rise from the bottom of the centre light, and there are interesting patterns on some of the *quarries*. The next window along has a centre panel of 1960s glass (who is it by?). The angular figure of St Andrew, premier patron saint of fishermen, with net and draught of fishes, is particularly appropriate here because the panels on the wall below record the names of: 'fishermen from this coast who have lost their lives while pursuing their calling', 1860-1923. The next window contains attractive class of 1906 by *Heaton, Butler & Bayne* – the *Three Marys* at the tomb, in a typically lush setting with soft olive green, cream, and dark red the predominant colours. The *Clayton & Bell* window of 1875 next to it is poor by contrast, in sentimental mode, with the colour eroded in places. The last window on that side is from the same period and is probably by the same firm. There is no pictorial glass in the s. aisle, but the decorated quarries (probably by *Powells*) are arranged in an pleasing pattern and date from the 1870s rebuilding; new pews, pulpit and choir stalls were provided at the same time. Outlines on the many *ledger-stones* show where Francis Jessop ripped up the majority of the *brasses*, but a few remain (or were added later), and at the e. end of the s. aisle there are two examples of *shroud brasses* of about 1500, albeit without their heads. Further w. there are headless 16in. figures of a merchant and his wife which date from about 1540; a shield shows that he was a member of the salt fishmongers' company and his initials form a merchant's mark. The last brass in the aisle is an inscription for William Coby who died in 1534. In the nave floor from w. to e., the brasses are: an inscription for Dame Margaret Parker, 1507; two large late-C15 scrolls (effigies of a couple, their children, shields and epitaph all gone); a six line verse in graceful script for Marye Wylde who died in 1651; alongside, John Wylde's epitaph of 1644 is worth reading:

The Cropp full ripe appears,
To stoope to th'earth:
And from its ears,
A numerous birth . . .

The bold and lovely eagle lectern dates from 1504; its heavy, turned base rests on three squat lions that turn their heads enquiringly, and the brass has that buttery texture that antiquity and the polishing of centuries imparts. One of a mere handful that survive from the pre-Reformation period, it probably came from the same East Anglian workshop as Oxburgh's in Norfolk, and the maker sent others as far afield as Newcastle and Urbino cathedrals.

Doors in the n. aisle wall which led to the *rood loft* show that the *screen* spanned the whole width of the church. In 1932 a section was reconstructed across the entrance to the n. aisle chapel as part of a restoration that commemorated the dead of World War I. The 1870s stained glass is probably all by Clayton & Bell, and the e. window is particularly interesting. The painting has a grainy texture, and the four large figures of Barzillai, Abijah, Melchizedek, and Simeon stand above vignette scenes from their lives; Old and New Testament figures fill the tracery. The window commemorates Dame Pleasance Smith who died in 1877 aged 104. She was the widow of Sir James Edward Smith, founder and first president of the Linnean Society, and she 'preserved to the last the bright intelligence of a cultured mind'. Just in front of the *sanctuary* is the ledger-stone of Joseph Hudson who was vicar here from 1677 to 1691; he was obviously minded to continue his instruction from beyond the grave:

Here lie your pain full minister, lament!
You must account how you this light have
    spent.

Moving into the chancel, the eye is naturally attracted by the lovely glass in the e. window, installed by Heaton, Butler & Bayne in 1891. It is an outstanding design by Edward Frampton, based on the themes of the Te Deum and Benedicite, and there is a bold grouping of figures round the throne of Christ; a descriptive diagram, with a letter from the makers, is displayed on the n. wall by the sanctuary steps. The new arrangement displaced glass which had been painted by *Robert Allen* in 1819. It was his only major work, carried out in enamels on white glass, and he received an inscribed silver cup by way of appreciation. Some of the panels were salvaged and placed in the s. sanctuary window. Two scenes at the bottom illustrate Christ healing the blind man and meeting the woman at the well, and in the centre there are four squares with decorative borders around paintings of *St Andrew, St James the Great, St Peter* and *St Matthias*. Above are larger Crucifixion and Ascension panels, and the painting can perhaps best be described as an enthusiastic but crude example of folk art. It must be remembered, however, that stained glass of any description was extremely rare in this country at that period, and any examples are valuable. The arch of the *piscina* below has been mutilated, but there is an attractive line of carving above the *dropped-sill sedilia* alongside. The *High altar*, with its riddel posts topped by angels, was designed by Comper in 1905. There is an unusual little tablet of 1720 above the *vestry* door which records that Queen Anne's Bounty gave £200 to purchase the living for the benefit of the vicar. A ledger-stone in front of the sanctuary steps on the s. side marks the grave of Samuel Pacy, a prominent dissenter who died in 1680. In 1664 he had accused two widows, Rose Cullender and Amy Drury, of bewitching his daughters, and the unfortunate women were tried by Sir Matthew Hale at Bury St Edmunds before being condemned to death. It is perhaps worth remembering that Sir Thomas Browne, that wise and civilised Norwich physician, was a fervent believer in witchcraft and gave evidence for the prosecution in this case. Retracing one's steps, there are one or two more memorials of note:

in the nave, Maj. Thomas Wild lies under the third slab w. of the chancel steps, and his epitaph is now rather difficult read, but interesting nonetheless. A Dutch privateer came close inshore in 1665 and the major was killed as he led the townsfolk to defend the harbour shipping. Another major, Thomas Walker Chambers, fell at Waterloo, and has a chaste tablet by Robert Atkins, adorned with martial trophies on the n. aisle wall. Thomas Shippe of Yarmouth provided a well-lettered tablet for Thomas Arnold of the Royal Navy who died in 1737; it has mottled marble *Corinthian* columns each side, and a clutch of maritime emblems is arranged with a cherub's head at the bottom. For those with a little more time, the churchyard offers an interesting selection of epitaphs. Look particularly for the tomb of Francis Cunningham near the *priest's door* in the chancel – he married Richenda Gurney, Elizabeth Fry's sister. The oldest surviving stone is just in front, by the edge of the path – for Michael Fowler, a fisherman who died in 1678.

Market Weston, St Mary (D3): Some way beyond the village street to the n., the church lies with open fields about it. The early-C14 tower has a panelled *base course*, diagonal buttresses to the w. with four *set-offs*, and two *drip courses*. Both w. window and bell openings have *Decorated tracery* and there is a plain C19 parapet. The line of a much steeper original roof shows on the e. face. The tower houses a ring of five bells with a 15 cwt. tenor and although they cannot be rung at the present time it is worth recording that the 4th is one of Suffolk's earliest bells, cast by Thomas Potter of Norwich in the late C14. There was a major restoration by L.N. Cottingham in 1846 and the *chancel* was entirely rebuilt. The s. *porch*, however, is *Perpendicular*, although the outer arch has been re-cut, with crowns and *fleurons* in the mouldings. There are niches either side in the *flushwork* front, with another under a canopy above, and it is lit by tall, two-*light* windows. Stone seats line the walls below them and the deeply moulded inner C14 doorway has worn *headstops*. Above it is a delightful niche, with *crocketted* canopy and nodding *ogees* that terminate in tiny heads, containing a fine statue of the Virgin and Child. As you enter, note that the door is medieval, complete with closing ring and key escutcheon.

Within, the hand of the C19 lies heavy, but there are interesting things to see. The small tower arch is fitted with a medieval door, and on the n. wall hangs a large, pale set of *Hanoverian*

Royal Arms painted on canvas. In the tracery of the westernmost window on the n. side there are two small roundels; the smaller of the two contains a kneeling figure robed in red with his name 'Thomas Asbi' inscribed underneath, and the other has the eagle symbol of *St John* in yellow stain. Above them is a small coat of arms. On the wall by the C19 *font* is a length of oak carved with pierced roundels that was found in the local post office after wartime bomb damage. In the 1840s the parish clerk was also the postmaster, and it may be that he found it when the building work was going on and took it home. If so, it could well have formed part of the *rood screen* or the loft. The *nave* has dark pine benches with rounded and pierced tops to the ends, and the roof overhead is a crude version of the double *hammerbeam*. On past the massive pine pulpit and reading desk to the chancel, where there is a small marble tablet on the s. wall to John and Margaret Thruston (1849) by de Carle of Bury. By the *priest's door* there is a much more elegant memorial signed by *John Bacon the Younger*, with a shapely urn on a pale grey background. It is for Framingham Thruston who died in 1789. This makes it a very early work of Bacon's, for it was only in that year that he entered the Royal Academy Schools, and a decade before he took over his father's business. Further e. is an 1858 memorial to another Framingham Thruston, by Bower of Highgate, which shows just how much the trade's design sense had faltered in those 70 years. On the opposite wall is a shapely unsigned tablet for Dr John Thruston who, when he died in 1776, was honoured by his friend Samuel Peck as one who was 'many years Lord of this Manor and a blessing to this neighbourhood'. On the subject of memorials, there are four good *ledger-stones* before the *communion rails*, spanning the years 1692 to 1743, with deeply cut armorial roundels for members of the Bokenham family. The e. window tracery is filled with mid-C19 glass painted with patterns of vine leaves and scrolls, and in the *sanctuary* s. wall is an intriguing *pillar piscina* of the same vintage. It has a cluster of slim shafts under a semicircular bowl, and on the wall behind is a small, framed bas-relief of Christ and the woman of Samaria (John 4:7), just like those at Barnby and Wrentham.

Marlesford, St Andrew (H5): A spacious setting, with mature trees and meadowland around the churchyard. The tower has a w. window of about 1300, and sturdy angle buttresses rise up to a *string course* below the bell

openings. The battlements, with their diamond *flushwork* pattern, have been restored, and there is a nice selection of heads at the corners and midpoints. The tower houses an excellent ring of six bells with a 9 cwt. tenor. Walking round, you will find that there are small, late-*Perpendicular* windows in the n. wall of the *nave*, and that the n. door has been obscured by a breeze block heating chamber. Further along, a variation in the masonry of the wall identifies the position of the *rood loft stair*. It looks as though the *chancel* was partially rebuilt as part of an 1880s restoration, although the *priest's door* and the *Decorated* window alongside do not seem to have been disturbed. There is a *sanctus-bell turret* on the nave gable, and except for the top of the arch, all its stonework has been recently renewed. The short and tall s. *aisle* is a late-C15/early-C16 replacement which abuts the C15 *porch*. The latter has a finely moulded entrance arch, and there are worn shields bearing *Trinity* and *Passion emblems* in the spandrels. The beautifully detailed niche above has tiny panels of blind *tracery* above its *ogee* arch, flanked by *crocketted* pinnacles. A stone tracery trail runs below the plain parapet, and the little *Agnus Dei* at the apex is still recognisable, despite the loss of its head. There are remains of flushwork panelling on the front, and most of the w. wall has been replaced in brick.

Within, the tower arch is taken up by the organ on its gallery. Below, the C15 *font* has very simple tracery in the bowl panels, vaguely reminiscent of the decoration on the mass-produced C13 *Purbeck marble* type. The slender *arch-braces* of the C15 nave roof curve up to meet under *castellated collar beams*, and the faint traces of colour at the e. end may be the remains of a *celure*. The nave walls were raised to carry the new roof, and the *aisle arcade* was rebuilt, reducing the number of its bays. One of the round, late-*Norman piers* was set on a new base and reused, to carry the broad Perpendicular arches. The handsome aisle roof is ridged, but with a very low pitch. The two roughly cut niches in the s. wall will have contained statues, and at the w. end there is a *box pew* in panelled oak. Fitted with five stalls, it was installed by the Shuldhams of Marlesford Hall, and William Shuldham's *hatchment* hangs on the wall above; he died, aged 102, in 1845. The glass of the window alongside is engraved as a memorial for John Shuldham Schreiber who died in 1968, having been squire here since the turn of the century – and he must have been one of the last country gentlemen to be described as such. The pair of pastoral scenes below the epitaph are in the style of Laurence Whistler but are not signed. The *altar* in the aisle chapel has kneeling attendant angels, nicely carved in pine and placed on wrought-iron brackets each side of the e. window. Grants for C19 church restorations were sometimes conditional on the provision of free seats at a time when pew renting was common, and this may be why the benches here are numbered. The two windows in the nave are filled with quite dreadful 1880s glass by *Ward & Hughes*, and show only too clearly what mass production did for the firm, and for the reputation of C19 stained glass generally. Between them is a memorial by James Cundy of Pimlico, perhaps better known for his work with Rundell & Bridge, the big silversmiths of the day. The plain tablet is greatly enlivened by a flourish of martial trophies on top around the name 'Waterloo'. It commemorates Lemuel Shuldham, a cornet in the Scots Greys who fell 'far in advance, within the right of the French lines. His body was found next morning and buried on the spot'. The other memorial nearby is for William Shuldham who died in 1850 – a simple marble tablet, with an *achievement of arms* in relief, by *Thomas Thurlow*. The *Jacobean* pulpit appears to have been reconstructed, and the upper range of panels are a little suspect. A solid and competent reading desk was made to match in 1948 by Robert Thompson of Kilburn, Yorkshire; it has his 'mouse' signature and is the only example of his work that I have found in Suffolk. The chancel window on the s. side has a sill lowered to form a seat, and this suggests that it was used as a *low side window*. On the n. wall there is a 1640s monument in alabaster and *touchstone* for William Alston and his wife. The busts are framed in oval wreaths of laurel, and their faintly tinged faces bear an apprehensive look; there are skulls and a *cartouche* of arms on top, and note the variation in the style of the ruffs that the couple wear. The 1880s restoration probably accounts for the absence of a *piscina* in the *sanctuary*, and the e. window glass dates from the same period. It is by Cox & Son, a firm which produced a host of windows over a thirty year period. It is one of their best designs, and while the choice of subject is familiar, the style is unusual – a combination of heavily formalised figures and vivid colours. The *Decalogue* panels that hang either side are particularly interesting because they are not only a very late example, but are also signed: 'Gilbert B. Sully, Chiswick, March 1903'. Painted on zinc, in buff, pale green and blue, with outlined

lettering and emphasised capitals, the style is typical of the *Arts and Crafts Movement*. John Edward Carew was the artist who sculpted the great bronze relief of the death of Nelson in Trafalgar Square, and it is something of an anti-climax to find that he also put his name to tablets like the one for Henry Williams and his wife on the n. wall, its only embellishment a phoenix crest. Opposite, another matches it for Edward Williams, and together they illustrate a little piece of church history. Edward was rector for 35 years, and when he died in 1775, his widow presented the living to their son Henry – who outdid his father by serving 48 years in the parish. One must always be prepared for surprises in a country church, and here it is the brass plaque for Flora Sandes Yudenitch on the s. wall of the chancel. She was a daughter of the rectory who served as a ranker in the Serbian army in World War I. Badly wounded in action, she was promoted, decorated for bravery, and in 1919 became the first woman to hold a Serbian commission. She died, full of years, at Wickham Market.

Martlesham, St Mary (G6): A lovely situation, apart from the village at the end of a lane, with glimpses of the Deben estuary from the e. end of the churchyard. The handsome C15 tower has a *base course* to the w. which displays crowned 'MR' and 'IS' monograms for the *Blessed Virgin* and Jesus in *flushwork*. More emblems decorate the buttresses, including *St Catherine's* wheel high on the n.w. buttress. The w. doorway has battered lion *stops*, and the small, worn shields in the *spandrels* carry the arms of the Noone Family, who were Lords of the Manor from 1412 to 1639 and doubtless paid for the tower. The stepped battlements are panelled with flushwork, and there is a niche with a *cusped ogee* arch in the centre of the parapet on the s. side. This is an unusual addition, and it is interesting that nearby Newbourne has one like it – an example of the way in which villages adopted each other's ideas. Walking round, you will see that the C14 *nave* n. doorway is blocked and the windows have 'Y' tracery of about 1300 on that side. One s. nave window has *Decorated tracery*, and the slab of the *rood stair* projects to the e. of it. The *chancel* was entirely rebuilt in 1835 and then, in 1905, subsidence called for a replacement e. wall and a handsome new window, with heavy buttresses projecting to the e. The 1830s work included the strange, gabled and buttressed addition on the s. side, designed to accommodate a special rectory pew.

The broad, plastered *porch* has a modern half-timbered gable and prettily pierced barge boards, and the C14 inner arch retains its medieval door.

The organ is sited on a gallery within the tower arch, and the space below is fitted with an excellent plate glass screen, engraved with the dedicatory monogram and backed by heavy curtains (the church's remaining medieval glass is a head of Christ which, with other fragments, is set in the w. window and can only be seen from outside). The bulky C15 *font* stands by the door, and although it follows the common East Anglian pattern, two of the beasts round the shaft are not conventional lions but most unusual variations. The one on the s. side has a medieval cape in place of a mane, and to the n. there is a dog with a bell collar. In the bowl panels, shields alternate with a variety of flower shapes, and traces of colour remain. The panelled nave roof dates from 1902, and the C15 *castellated wall plates* were retained. The C15 waggon chest, with its poplar lid, that stands in the n. doorway was used for a long time in the C19 as a corn bin in the rectory stables. The nicely carved C16 chest by the entrance is a more recent addition and came from Seckford Hall. The *St Christopher* painting is in its traditional place opposite the main door, and dates from about 1400. It lay hidden under limewash until 1902, and against a dull red background, the main outlines are clear, with the Christ child raising his hand in blessing behind the saint's head; the tiny niche below will have been used for votive candles. An excellent set of Charles II *Royal Arms* hangs above the s. door, and the nave windows are filled with very attractive compositions of 1903 by Walter J. Pearce, one of the leading *Arts & Crafts* glaziers. With a nice variety of texture and sympathetic leading, they illustrate particular texts with scenes of alms giving, shepherds, the sower and the harvesters, the Good Samaritan, and the prodigal son. Inscriptions in copper repoussé work under each window are a typical period touch, and this is the only example of Pearce's work in Suffolk. Most of the seating is modern, but at both ends of the nave there are C15 benches with *poppyheads*, traceried ends, and seated animals on the buttresses. The pulpit is boldly dated 1614, and the *blind arched* panels are a standard early-C17 design. Note, however, that two sides form a double-hinged door whose panels are markedly narrower (the base is modern). There are *piscinas* in both walls, showing that there were two nave *altars*, and the *rood stair* lies behind the door on the r. The chancel arch formed part of the C19 rebuilding,

and the C15 roof, with its very short *hammerbeams* and *king posts* was reconstructed. Panels salvaged from the old *rood screen* were used to make a front and door for the rectory pew in the s. wall, and two more C15 benches stand nearby. The church has a selection of *hatchments* for those interested in heraldry: nave s. wall (w.) Anne Sharpe, 1843; nave s. wall (e.) Mary Capper, 1837 (she built Beacon Hill House and was buried at Bushey, Herts); chancel n. wall, John Goodwin, Lord of the Manor, 1758; chancel s. wall (w.) John Goodwin, 1742; chancel s. wall (e.) Mary, his widow, 1769; chancel s. wall bottom, an unusually small and early example of 1663/4 for William Goodwin who is buried at Hasketon – where he apparently officiated at civil marriages for Martlesham couples during the Commonwealth. Most of the memorial tablets produced by Thomas and Edward Gaffin were plain dull, but they managed to be mildly eccentric for the memorial to three Doughty girls on the n. wall, a *crocketted* marble diamond on a black background. There were Doughty rectors here for seven generations from the C18 to the C20, and George, who died in 1832, has a stiff Gothic tablet in stone and marble by Thomas Denman, a prolific statuary, most of whose work is as turgid as this. The stained glass in the chancel is all by *Heaton, Butler & Bayne*, and is a lovely example of their work. The e. window of 1905 is a panorama of Calvary's rocky hill, with Christ crucified alone in the centre; a plume of fire rises from the temple in Jerusalem in the background against a stormy sky, and the colours are dramatic. The slightly later *lancets* contain figures of Moses, Christ as the Man of Sorrows, the centurian of the crucifixion, and a weeping *St Mary* backed by a thunderous sky.

Mellis, St Mary (E3): The village greens are extensive and the church lies on the edge of them to the w. of the main railway line. There was a tower originally but it collapsed in 1730 and two large buttresses were roughly shaped from the remains. Between them is a large window outline above a modern lean-to shelter. The wide *nave* and *chancel* have a continuous *flushwork base course* and at the e. end a frieze of flushwork panels continues across the *vestry* wall on the n. side. Extensive repairs to the chancel were evidently necessary in the C17 or C18 and large red brick buttresses support the e. end. It was probably then that the side windows were blocked up. The *rood stair turret* shows externally between the chancel and the nave on the n. side.

Entry is by way of the early-C14 s. *porch* and note that although they are blocked, the side windows still display attractive *Decorated tracery*. The nave is spacious and the tall *Perpendicular* windows have stepped *transoms* and shafts at the inner corners of the embrasures. The w. doorway is small, with a plain round arch, and this suggests that the tower was either *Saxon* or *Norman* and may have been round. The C15 *font* is similar to nearby Thrandeston's, with its *Evangelistic symbols* and fat *Tudor Roses* in the bowl panels and dumpy lions squatting round the shaft. One point of difference here is the *quatrefoil* tracery on the step. The *Royal Arms* on the w. wall are painted on board and dated 1634; one of five sets in the county from the reign of Charles I, they are well designed and worth restoring. A door in the s.w. corner opens to reveal a stair which one would have thought led to an upper chamber in the porch – but it turns the other way and presumably gave access to the tower. By the C19 pulpit there is a tomb which once had *brasses* on top and an inscription on the bevel. It is anonymous now but the shields in the lozenges along the front would have been painted with the arms of Richard Yaxley who was buried here in 1570 together with his wife. An unidentified tomb of the same period is set in the wall nearby, and overhead the window contains quite a lot of C15 glass. There is a range of eight figures but the paint is very worn and only *St Jude* can be recognised by his boat emblem (3rd from l., lower rank). A C17 chair was placed by the pulpit when I visited; it had a lively carving of the sacrifice of Isaac in the back panel, complete with the ram caught in a wispy thicket. The handsome C15 *rood screen* has been repainted and gilded and the flattened *ogee* arches of the main *lights* are backed by panel tracery. The coving has been restored and has three attractive tracery panels. The chancel has a low-pitched cambered *tie-beam* roof and the stalls below are fronted with ranges of C17 *balusters* which were the original *communion rails*. The *altar* table is of the same period and has nicely fretted top rails. There is a plain *piscina* and in the opposite corner a most interesting *Easter sepulchre* recess. The arch is decorated with *paterae* and below there are five blank and shallow niches which were once *groined* and canopied. *Cautley* suggested that they symbolise the *Five wounds of Christ* and this is not unlikely.

Melton, St Andrew (G5): In the 1860s, the old church's isolation prompted a fresh start, with a new building in the centre of the village,

designed by Frederick Barnes the Ipswich architect. He carried out a number of restorations in the county and built the handsome railway stations in *Tudor* style at Stowmarket and Needham Market. St Andrew's has little affinity with other Suffolk churches, and the main material is heavily mortared Kentish rag stone, so that all the walls resemble expanses of crazy paving. All the window *tracery* is late-C13 style. The steep slate roof of the *nave* continues down with a slight change of angle to cover the n. *aisle*, and there are *vestries* on both sides of the chancel. The tower doubles as a s. *porch*, and is divided boldly into three by narrow bands of *blind arcading* and *trefoils*. It has shallow buttresses, and there is no parapet below the stone *broach* spire with its prominent, gabled *lancets*.

The interior is fairly dark and the window arrangement on the n. side is decidedly eccentric. There are two dormers in the nave, with main timbers of the *hammerbeam/arch-braced* roof striking through them, and the aisle has a broad dormer in the lean-to roof; below it, the low wall is pierced by widely spaced roundel windows. The fine C15 *Seven Sacrament font* was moved from the old church, and although its bowl panels have been sadly mutilated, their subjects are, for the most part, easily recognised. Clockwise from the e. they are: baptism, matrimony, ordination, the mass, martyrdom of St Andrew (appropriate and unique feature), extreme unction, confession, confirmation. An intricate band of foliage decorates the underside of the bowl, and the shaft carries *Evangelistic symbols* separated by niches containing defaced figures; the lower section of the shaft has been replaced, and there is C18 graffiti on the step. The church has some good modern stained glass and the w. window probably came from *Heaton, Butler & Bayne* – an accomplished Ascension across the three *lights*. The first nave window is an excellent *Kempe* work of 1903, signed with his wheatsheaf in the l. border. In a luscious, compacted setting, St Andrew stands with *St Etheldreda*, she with a model of Ely cathedral whose Dean and Chapter are patrons of the living. The window is a memorial for Hugh Stowell Scott, better known as Henry Seton Merriman, author of popular adventure stories like *Barlasch of the Guard* and *In Kedar's tents*. The next window is an attractive 1910 piece by A.L. Moore – the *Three Marys* with the angel at the tomb, a confident piece of draughting and assured use of soft colour. Far better than the vapid 1870s window by *Ward & Hughes* further along. The *rood screen* was installed in 1934 and is a very good interpretation of C15 style, albeit without colour; there is panel tracery above *ogee* arches with spiky *cusping,* and a double rank of foliage trails in West Country fashion runs above the coving. The figures of the *Blessed Virgin* and *St John* do not stand with Christ on the cross, but are set under canopies on each side. Another large dormer window features on the n. side of the chancel, and the e. window has much more acceptable Ward & Hughes glass. Shaped panels illustrating Christ's Passion are set against a bright interlace of redand blue patterns which are continued in the upper three roundels. Blind arcading under heavily crocketted gables flanks the altar and provides a setting for the *Decalogue* panels.

Melton, Old St Andrew (G5): A long lane from the village winds past a new golf course down to this tiny church in the Deben valley. After the new St Andrew's had been built in the 1860s, the old building was converted into a cemetary chapel. Together with the C17 *porch*, the C14 *chancel* was demolished, two of its windows were inserted in place of the n. and s. *nave* doors, and an *apsidal sanctuary* with a lean-to *vestry* was built on to the e. end. The church was declared redundant in 1977 and plans to convert it into a study centre were approved. The parish, however, felt strongly about losing its first church, and the Melton Old Church Society was formed in 1980; a new scheme was approved and two years later the Society took charge as a charity to use the building for Christian, community and educational purposes. Since then, extensive repairs have been carried out, and apart from a regular programme of events, the annual All Souls' day Evensong has become a tradition.

In its truncated form, it is a tiny building, and the visit should begin with a stroll round the spacious churchyard. It is likely that there was a church here before the Conquest, but of that there is no trace. The nave windows have *Perpendicular tracery,* and the vestry extension to the apse has now been removed. The walls of the C14 tower are rendered, and there is *flushwork* in its *base course*, buttresses, and battlements. The bell openings have lost their tracery, but the fine three-*light* w. window has *reticulated tracery.* The w. doorway is now the only entrance, and *fleurons* stud its mouldings and *dripstone.* Some of the crosses that marked the battlefield graves of Melton men in World War I are preserved just inside, and one in the n.w. corner of the nave for a pilot is part of his aircraft's propellor

(there is another like it at Halesworth). In the floor below it there is an unusually interesting *brass* dating from about 1430, with the 3ft. effigy of a priest beside a man and a woman who were probably his parents. The father wears a tunic, and his wife has a veil headdress; a fragment of the triple canopy survives, but unfortunately the inscription, scrolls, and shields have been lost. The *hatchment* on the s. wall was used at the funeral of Charles Thomas Rissowe in 1821. He had apparently changed his name to Sharpe at some stage, and his widow's hatchment hangs opposite. Slim *Early English jamb shafts* with ring *capitals* flank the tall tower arch, and the *arch-braced* roof has a deep, moulded *wall plate* which continues in sections round the apse – a happy arrangement making use of salvaged material. On the s. wall the 1770s roundel tablet for Thomas and Anne Lambert bears a good verse which begins:

Ye, that in Fame's proud Titles, Wealth or State,
Unwisely deem all earthly bliss compleat . . .

Further along one finds an elegant memorial of mottled marble in an architectural frame for William Negus whose epitaph is redolent of the C18: 'Although educated in a Court he preferred the more private station of a country gentleman in which he lived beloved and esteemed and died lamented in 1773'. The austere 1880s tablet opposite for Searles V. Wood Junr. of Martlesham describes him as: 'the first geologist to undertake the detailed mapping over an extensive area of the various subdivisions of the glacial drift. A task of infinite labour and of great practical and scientific importance'. Now I didn't know that. Country churches are great educators in their quiet way.

Mendham, All Saints (G2): The village lies by the Waveney, and the river curls through water meadows w. of the church that stands in a spacious churchyard. It is a solid, well-cared for building that still bears the unmistakable signs of the restoration directed by *Richard Phipson* in 1868 and the rebuilding of the *chancel* in the 1880s. The roofs of *nave* and *aisles* needed extensive repairs, and most of the windows had to be renewed. The C14 tower has *Decorated tracery* in the bell openings, and there is a large, deep niche with a *cusped ogee* arch above the w. window. It houses an excellent ring of six bells with a 12 cwt. tenor. The body of the church was rebuilt in the C15, and above the aisles there is a tall late *Perpendicular clerestory* with four three-*light* windows a side, each with *embattled transoms* and set in walls speckled with a mixture of brick and flint. Two C17 gravestones have been salvaged from the churchyard and now stand against the s. aisle wall: Richard Dresser's of 1699 has a skull at the top, and John Green's of 1692 was once graced by a cherub's head. The C15 s. *porch* must have been very dilapidated at the time of the restoration – Phipson renewed the *flushwork* parapet and all three niches in the facade of squared flints, as well as replacing the side windows. Typically, he provided the new outer arch with a pair of unusual stops; the head of Eve on one side is matched by the serpent with the forbidden fruit on the other, reminding us to leave earthly temptations behind us as we enter. The porch's *arch-braced* roof was sound and only needed some replacement *bosses*, and although the inner door is C19, the strap hinges and boss of the closing ring are medieval.

A spacious and attractive interior. The nave *arcades* with their octagonal *piers* are similar, but they vary in the details of *capitals* and mouldings, and probably date from the late C14/early C15. The arch-braces of the low-pitched nave roof come down to *wall posts* that now rest on the series of large wooden *corbels* carved by Robert Godbold of Harleston. He was a fine craftsman (see his benches at Earl Stonham), and here his demi-angels display one of the most extensive ranges of *Passion emblems* to be found in the county, including the reed and the seamless robe on the s. side. The C14 *font* stands on a tall stem which is ringed by eight attached shafts, and there are simple *quatrefoils* in the bowl panels. The excellent set of George III *Royal Arms* that hangs above the tower arch is reminiscent of nearby Withersdale's, and I wonder whether it was painted by the same artist. A massive, heavily banded C15 parish chest stands at the w. end of the nave, and the benches are further examples of Godbold's work, the *poppyheads* carved with ears of barley and wheat, ivy, thistle, and other plants. Unusually, two in the centre range have interwoven texts, and Phipson thoughtfully designed smaller scale benches for the Sunday school at the back of the n. aisle. The organ now masks the aisle's e. window, and nearby is the memorial for William Godbold who died in 1693 (an ancestor of the wood carver perhaps?). In white and mottled marble, there are squashed scrolls each side and an urn stands within the broken *pediment* on top, with a strangely sagging drape overhanging the top of the frame. The painting of Christ's Presentation

in the Temple that hangs on the s. aisle wall is probably by a Venetian artist of about 1600. The aisle chapel has a restored C14 *piscina* and there is a blocked *squint* aligned with the *High altar*. The two memorials above the nave arcades are excellent and it is a pity they are so high. The one on the s. side is for William Rant who died in 1754, and it is signed by Thomas Rawlins, foremost Norwich statuary of his day. The other was erected eleven years earlier for James Rant, and the design is so similar that it probably came from the same workshop. The shaped tablets are set in architectural frames, with delicate side swags and small *cartouches* of arms below, and it is interesting that the epitaphs differ both in language and in type style. The e. bay of the nave roof has traces of colour on the wall plates and main timbers, all that remains of a *celure* for the *rood*. There is no longer a *screen*, but the top of the stair that led to the *loft* emerges on the n. side. Above it is a most unusual wooden chancel arch, formed by a pair of moulded arch-braces. It must date from the late C15 when the clerestory and new roof were installed, and there is one other like it in the county at Ilketshall St John. The chancel is wide, and on the s. wall is a beautifully lettered monument of 1722 for Richard Freston. It makes clever use of varied marbles and has a coloured cartouche at the base – all very decorative. In interesting contrast is the tablet for Edward Freston alongside. Although it was set up only a few years before, the style, with its huddled lettering cramped into a stone *acanthus* frame, belongs to the previous century. The Frestons were Lords of the Manor for quite some time, and their C17 genealogy is rehearsed on a large memorial in the *sanctuary*. Flanked by *pilasters*, the black tablet in a mottled marble frame is a curious affair which sags in a curve below the broken pediment, and the lettering follows the same line (more or less!) down to the curved base. The C19 choir stalls on the n. have a nice pair of carved lions, and opposite there are two faintly bizarre heads in place of conventional *poppyheads*. They represent the Lord Waveney who rebuilt the chancel and, with very little depth from back to front, it is as though he has been unkindly squashed. Some good C17 *ledger-stones* lie in front of the sanctuary steps, together with two *brasses*. On the n. side is the 19in. figure of Richard Freston dressed in gown and ruff, with *achievement* and inscription. He died in the same year as Shakespeare, and across by the *priest's door* there is the effigy of Celia Freston who died a year earlier, shown wearing the voluminous calash hood that was fashionable then. The e. window is filled with an attractive Ascension scene across the three lights. It is an 1886 Thomas Curtis design of *Ward & Hughes*, and Christ is flanked by angels who hover above the disciples posed in rich robes; the background is a deep blue, and three more angels bearing the crown and palm wait in the tracery.

Mendlesham, St Mary (F4): Fronted by limes, this lovely church stands on rising ground at the end of the village street within a large churchyard, and its noble tower can be seen from some way off. Built in the 1490s and 1515, its *base course* displays *flushwork* roundels worked in *mouchette* and *quatrefoil* patterns interspersed with shields, but those flanking the w. door are cut in stone for emphasis. There are shields of the Botecourt and Knyvet families in the *spandrels* of the doorway and the *Perpendicular* w. window, with *ogee tracery* shapes, is unusually small for such a tower. In contrast, the large double bell openings are linked by a deep *label*, with a panel of flushwork between. Above them are stepped flushwork battlements crowned with pinnacles. The s. *aisle* windows are early C14 but the porch is *Perpendicular*, with flushwork and crowned 'M's and 'MR's for the dedication set either side of a canopied niche. The entrance arch rests on decayed lion *stops* like those at Wetheringsett and there were six pinnacles on the parapet originally. The *chancel* is largely C15 and in the n. aisle you will see late-C14 windows and a *Tudor* brick *rood stair* turret. The tall *nave clerestory* has windows which match the w. window of the tower, and note how the *sanctus-bell turret* was enclosed within a later parapet on the e. gable (with a bell recently installed). Entry is via the late-Perpendicular n. *porch* and this is decidedly lavish. The elaborate flushwork facade has side niches under nodding ogee arches, and the larger version over the doorway has a beast mask below the image stool. The arch itself has an angel with a shield at the apex and decayed shields in the spandrels. The upper chamber is lit by double windows and there are unusually good crowned lions and *woodwoses* at the parapet corners. The porch builders retained the inner C13 doorway but they cut into it on the r. when constructing the stair to the room above. By it stands the little font from the redundant church at Rishangles. It was made about 1600 and it is rare to find the bowl of a post-*Reformation* example carved with *Passion emblems* and *Evangelistic symbols*, with figures in contemporary costume filling the shaft niches. Restored to the

extent that it looks quite new, it now serves as a *stoup* (it must be said that both *Cautley* and *Pevsner* had doubts about its antiquity).

The church within is bright with light and beautifully kept, a blaze of colourful *hassocks* lining the benches. Buttresses of the later tower encroach on the C13 *arcades* and its tall arch has a nice 1930s screen with turned shafts in the doors. Beyond hangs an unidentified *hatchment* bearing the arms of the Cresacre/Marshall families. Mendlesham's ring of six bells with a 15 cwt. tenor is rung from the ground floor. The arcade *piers* are circular but the easternmost bays are separated from the rest by square sections which must have either supported a central tower or marked the entrance to *transepts*. It is curious that the shape and decoration of the *corbels* on the w. faces of these piers differs – tapered fluting to the n. and oblong *dogtooth* to the s. In an 1860s restoration by *Ewan Christian*, the nave roof was replaced, the tower arch reopened, and the fine C15 benches restored. These have large *poppyheads* and an enterprising selection of tracery on all the ends, with a number of grotesques on the elbows (look for the *wyvern* at the n.w. corner of the centre range, and there is a figure holding an initialled shield at the front on the s. side). The benches in the aisles with simpler poppyheads came from Rishangles and blend well with the rest. There are other migrants on the wall of the s. aisle, this time from redundant Southolt – a good set of George III *Royal Arms*, and the *brass* of Margaret Armiger wearing a Paris cap and lacking one shoulder. Below her is an inscription for Robert Armiger, who 'departed out of this transitory world' in 1585. The s. aisle roof was untouched by the Victorian restoration and is remarkable for having *king posts* on the *tie-beams*, with traces of stencil decoration at the e. end. The s. porch was restored in 1926 and has been converted for use as a chapel of the Holy Cross. The roof has angels at the base of the braces and the large wall paintings by Cyril Fradan were commissioned in the 1970s. A fascinating miscellany has been marshalled at the w. end of the n. aisle – a C16 wooden clock weight barrel and windlass, an early-C18 clock frame, a simple late-C18 *bier* in pine, and (a rarity, but there is another at Brundish) a matching child's bier in lovely condition. The plain C15 *font* has a cover which was made by John Turner of Mendlesham in 1630, and is a remarkably fine piece. Restored in 1908, it is raised on four columns, with brief turned pendants at the other angles of the cornice, and a fat fruit trail

Mendlesham, St Mary: Font cover

runs just above the steep *broken pediments* while spiky *finials* stand in front of a second storey which repeats the first on a smaller scale. Above that, curved sea-horse brackets support the centre shaft and ball finial. The lovely pulpit is also by this gifted joiner and its style is more elaborate than most of that period, with some *Renaissance* motifs. The familiar *blind arches* in the main panels have centre pendants and they are carved with deep foliage scrolls instead of the usual strapwork. The upper range is filled with flowers and birds with seeds in their beaks and at the base the moulded panels have double-acorn bosses.

Medieval glass panels from Southolt have been hung inside the aisle windows (including a figure that has been given a lion's head!). The s. aisle e. window contains a small dove of the Holy Spirit in ruby glass inserted in 1982 and the solid *altar* block made up of medieval fragments supports the church's original *mensa* in which new consecration crosses have been cut. The *piscina* nearby lies within an ogee *trefoil* arch and there are plain *dropped-sill sedilia*. In the n. aisle Lady chapel the altar is a good early-C17 table – Doric capitals and *acanthus leaves* on the legs and

shallow carved top rail. The C14 piscina is in the windowsill to the l. and the Perpendicular e. window design is unconventional. The lower half of the centre *light* contains a niche to house a figure of the Blessed Virgin. The *cusping* of the round arch has been chopped away, along with the ogee hood mould and side pinnacles. It now contains a 1960s Virgin and Child. The glass is a World War I memorial and was designed in 1921 by T.F. Curtis of *Ward & Hughes*. To the r. are the capacious stairs that led to the vanished *rood loft* and there is now a modern rood group above the chancel arch. The limed oak altar below was designed by Jack Pentney and made by Barrie Chester in 1982. To the e. of the pulpit lies the brass of John Knyvet who died in 1417. Worn very smooth, the 4ft. 7in. figure is a fine example of the Lancastrian period; the large feet rest on a recumbent lion and there is a dragon's head crest on the helm behind the head; it is unusual to see the beard displayed outside the armour. Knyvet was Lord of the Manor and both his father and father-in-law were Lord Chancellors of England. The chancel roof and e. window date from the 1860s restoration (although the C13 shafts of the latter were retained) and the fine panelling on the e. wall came a century later.

The church has few monuments but there is one to Richard Chilton (1816) on the n. wall of the chancel which is worth studying. The shallow sarcophagus with a small flaming urn on top and Grecian ornament is by Charles Regnart, a competent sculptor whose work can be found in many counties. One of the most interesting features of Mendlesham is the parish armoury, housed since 1593 above the n. porch. All communities had to provide a stock of weapons and armour for the militia, but few collections have survived. Dating from 1470 to 1600, it includes a rare Elizabethan longbow, helmets, breastplates, and powder horns. Access is normally by appointment only.

Metfield, St John the Baptist (G2): There is a large boulder by the s.w. corner of the tower which may mark the site of pagan worship before the Christian church was established. The Cluniac priory at Mendham served the village from the C12 until 1521, and probably built the church – the *nave* in the C13, the *chancel* in the early C14. The nave was entirely rebuilt in the C15 and the s. *porch* added. There is 'Y' *tracery* of about 1300 in the tower w. window and bell openings, and the battlements (with three of their corner figures remaining) were added in 1712. The tower houses an excellent ring of six bells with a 9 cwt. tenor. In the early C18 a window was inserted in the nave n. wall to light the new gallery within, but the rest of the nave windows are handsome three-*light Perpendicular* designs that were part of the C15 rebuilding. Matching windows were inserted in the side walls of the chancel, and an unusual feature of all them is that crown-glass was used in the tracery. This may have been after *William Dowsing's* visit in 1644 when he played such havoc with the e. window that it had to be rebuilt (the wooden glazing bars date only from the late C18 or early C19). The low *priest's door* is a survivor from the early-C14 chancel, and there is a *scratch dial* on the e. nave buttress. Note the pair of brick tombs nearby which were apparently used as dole tables for the distribution of a bread charity, and there are a number of good late-C18 and early-C19 tombstones to be found. Beyond the chancel e. wall, for example, there is a well-cut stone of 1839 for William Curtis 'whose valuable Life (upon Earth) was terminated by an accident . . .', and s. of the path there is a very broad stone for Samuel Freestone who died in 1825. The C15 *porch* is very solid, and has a fine *flushwork* facade. The original window of the upper room was blocked up and a smaller one inserted at some time, and there are flanking niches. *Tudor Roses* decorate the *spandrels*, and in the mouldings of the arch you will see lion masks, crowns, and a single bishop's head. The side windows are blocked and one of the spaces was used for an C18 memorial. The porch's most unusual feature is the use of wood rather than stone for the inner vaulting. Three of the original corner posts remain, and there is a *green man boss* above the outer arch, three good masks on the other sides, and a large, worn boss in the centre of Christ enthroned. The inner doorway has lion stops, and door itself is contemporary; as you enter, note the sockets in the jambs for a heavy security bar.

The first thing that one notices inside is the measured, remorseless ticking of a clock, and the tower door is left conveniently open to give a view of the mechanism. It is one of the few early-C17 turret clocks still in use; although it began life on the ground floor, it was moved upstairs in the C18 and was only returned after an overhaul and restoration in 1979. A year later, the verger died who had tended it for half a century, and his memorial is by the door. The *gallery* was introduced in 1719 for a choir, and was quite narrow in its original form. It was only when an organ replaced the old rustic

orchestra in 1856 that the depth was doubled. Panels from the base of the medieval *rood screen* now stand against the wall below. They have excellent late-Perpendicular tracery and retain traces of colour. The painted chest of 1638 which stands nearby has simple *Renaissance* motifs in the front panelling. The early-C15 *font* is a nicely chunky version of the familiar East Anglian style, with squat lions round the shaft. The angels under the bowl have crossed hands rather than the usual wings, and four of the bowl panels contain deeply cut lions. The other four have angels carrying the leopard shield of the Jermys who had been Lords of the Manor since the C14 and who doubtless paid for much of the rebuilding. The font bears traces of colour and was in fact painted as recently as 1841. The *Royal Arms* of George IV which hang on the s. wall date from 1826, but they may overlay an earlier version because a Mr Baldry of Framlingham was paid for repainting a set in 1715. The roof overhead has *castellated wall plates*, and the *arch-braces* rise to pendants below the ridge. The bosses they once carried were probably removed by Dowsing, and while his journal gives details of *Sacred monograms* in the roof, it is remarkable that the painted *celure* for the *rood* survived his visit. It covers the e. bay of the roof and, although decayed in places, most of the decoration is intact. The four boarded panels are quartered by ribs, with two of the gilded centre bosses still in place; within the divisions, Sacred monograms alternate with crowned 'M's for the *Blessed Virgin*, both set within wreaths that sprout foliage over the rest of the panels. The colour scheme is the favourite red and green and extends to the arch-braces on the far wall. Pulleys were often used to suspend lights before the rood and also to control the *lenten veil*, two remain here, on the e. side of the arch-brace w. of the celure. You will see where the *capitals* of the chancel arch were cut back to accomodate the *screen*, and the stair that led to the *rood loft* rises from a window embrasure on the n. side. Behind the cumbrous pulpit of 1900 there is a *piscina* in the wall that marks the site of a nave *altar*. The chancel roof is very attractive – the panels have feathery bosses, and modern decoration in the style of the celure. There is an odd tie-beam above the *sanctuary* which is just like the one at nearby Withersdale, and it was probably inserted to strengthen the e. end. The tall, early-C14 piscina has a trefoil arch which is strangely varied at the top, and dim C18 Lord's Prayer and Creed canvases hang on the e. wall. There is a blocked C14 window on the n. side, and nearby is an

1835 epitaph for a vicar which is a nice illustration of how the use of language can change. He died: 'deeply deplored by his family and universally regretted by his parishioners'.

Mettingham, All Saints (H1): A steep path leads up the hillside from the Bungay-Beccles road to this compact, interesting little church. The tower is classified as round but is distinctly oval and slightly bulbous in the lower stage. Evidence drawn from first floor window embrasures inside strongly suggests that it is *Saxon*. A two-*light* w. window was inserted in the C15 and the bell openings have been reshaped; there are *gargoyles* n. and s., and the iron band like a girth around its middle was probably applied in the C19. The tower houses a ring of four bells with a 9 cwt. tenor which cannot be used at the present time. Flints and small boulders were used to make the w. corners of the *nave* – an indication that it was begun at the same time as the tower, and there is a fine small-scale *Norman* doorway in the n. wall. Its arch has two ranges of *-chevron* moulding within a line of *billet* decoration, and a beast head is placed at the top; the scalloped *capitals* of the flanking shafts are repeated in miniature on the *jamb shafts* alongside. You will see that the top line of the original wall shows clearly some 6ft. above the doorway. Following changes in the C14-C15, the short nave became quite lofty, and the *chancel* roughly matches it both in height and length. Windows on the n. side are *Perpendicular,* but the e. window is a modern replacement, below an C18 brick gable. The *priest's door* has been blocked up in the chancel s. wall, and so too has the C15 window alongside, its *tracery* outline still showing through. The church has a s. *aisle* and there is original *Decorated* tracery in the window alongside the *vestry.* The latter seems to date from the early C19, but access from the church was only effected during the restoration of 1898.

The nave lies under an *arch-braced* roof, plastered out between the principal timbers; there are *castellated wall plates,* and small, decapitated demi-angels bearing shields perch below the braces. A sturdy early-C14 *arcade* of two bays stands between nave and s. aisle, with a lower arch at the e. end. The tower arch is screened off, and above it hangs a set of George III *Royal Arms* painted on canvas – good quality but decidedly murky. The C15 *font* is a quality example of the commonest East Anglian type, but it shares a curious distinction with those at Grundisburgh and St Mary le Tower, Ipswich,

in that the lions round the shaft sit on human heads, alternately male and female; although their legs have been broken, the beasts sport luxuriantly wavy manes. The riser of the broad step is decorated with *quatrefoils,* and another unusual feature is that miniature lions are placed at all the angles. There are two ranges of *paterae* at the head of the shaft, and instead of the more usual angels, there are more human heads below the bowl. Well-nourished lions and angels bearing shields inhabit the bowl panels, there are *crocketted* pinnacles at the corners, and tiny paterae decorate the rim. All in all, a superior piece. A nearby lectern carries a copy of the illustrated 'Self-interpreting Bible' that had quite a vogue in the C19. Known familiarly as 'Brown's Bible' (from the editor), it was printed and published in Bungay by Brightly & Childs in 1814. One of the nave windows contains attractive glass by Christopher Webb, installed in 1930. Sportive cherubs swinging bells attend *St Cecilia*, and two more hold a scroll of music above her head: 'O rest in the Lord, wait patiently for Him'. More of this artist's work can be seen at Newmarket St Mary and Tuddenham St Martin. The organ now stands in the *sanctuary* of the s. aisle chapel, but a plain early-C14 *piscina* remains in the wall, and just to the w. is a large tomb recess of the same period. It has an *ogee* arch topped by a *finial,* and is probably the resting place of the aisle's builder (a head *corbel* at the base of the window nearby may have had some connection with it). The s.w. window contains glass by *Jones & Willis* of 1916 – figures of Christ with children, and Charity (haloed like a saint!) in company with a little girl. In one of the lights of the window to the e. there is a rich little composition in C15 style entitled: 'Called to be saints'. Dating from about 1912, it portrays Christ in Glory, with the *Blessed Virgin, St John the Baptist,* a king, bishop, and commoners kneeling below. It would be nice to know who the artist was. Apart from some panels which were incorporated in the choir stalls, the *rood screen* has disappeared, but the entrance to the *rood loft* remains in the n. wall, and the *castellated rood beam* is still in place. The wall subsequently started to spread, and an extra section was added to the beam, taken through the wall, and secured on the outside with a large peg. C15 bench ends with *poppyheads* were reused in the choir stalls, and the two half-ends against the n. wall have grotesques on the elbows. In the window above them, a roundel of C15 glass displays the arms of John de Norwich, the man who built Mettingham castle in 1344 and founded a college of priests there. An unusual feature of the sanctuary is the pair of piscinas. One has a *cinquefoil* arch, and the other has the hint of an *ogee* shape. This may be a late example of the transient fashion for double piscinas (see glossary entry). The e. window glass looks like late C19. Nativity, Crucifixion, and Resurrection scenes are cutout shapes against clear glass, with a *pelican* roundel below. There is an overall greenish tinge, and a faint echo of *pre-Raphaelite* feeling about the composition – the artist is unknown. C19 *Decalogue* boards hang on either side. Retracing your steps, note an unusually late (1926) example of a floor *brass* by the lectern; boldly lettered and with no decoration, it commemorates a judge of the Bombay High Court who retired to Mettingham castle and died in 1906.

Middleton, Holy Trinity (I4): If the church-yard seems unusually spacious, one must remember that it used to serve two churches; Fordley, Holy Trinity has entirely vanished and was in ruins by the C18. In 1620, parishioners complained to the Bishop of Norwich that the churches were so close that if the times of service did not precisely coincide, the people and bells of one disturbed the congregation of the other. His solution was to have one minister serve both and for the buildings to be used alternately, an arrangement that probably hastened the closure of the one that 'was but small' anyway. The C15 tower has angle buttresses decorated with *flushwork*, its w. window has been renewed, and nearly all the *tracery* has gone from the bell openings. There is more flushwork in the stepped battlements, and the church's distinctive feature is the slim lead-sheathed spire which is almost as tall as the tower itself and very like the one at Yoxford. It had just been restored in 1955 when a disastrous fire destroyed the thatched roofs of *nave* and *chancel* and caused havoc within. After valiant efforts by the community, the damage was made good, and a new tiled roof installed. A restoration in 1864 refaced the walls in flint, renewed the buttresses, and replaced most of the windows, leaving a *Perpendicular* three-*light* window undisturbed on each side of the nave. The chancel was extended about 1300, and the e. window has intersected 'Y' tracery typical of the period. It is there that we realise that the church was originally *Norman*, for the masons who built the window used fragments of old *billet moulding* in the arch. A Norman feature which has not been altered is the slender shaft which is set on the s.w. corner of the nave. The s.

porch is a heavy-handed C19 reconstruction, but it shelters a fine Norman doorway, with pairs of shafts under scalloped capitals; the arch is decorated with a *chevron* motif used sideways and an outer roll moulding. The fluted bowl of a *stoup* has been partially uncovered in the corner of the porch.

Nave and chancel have newly panelled ceilings and limewashed walls, imparting a light and airy feeling. A C19 *gallery* spans the w. end in front of the tower arch, and the organ is disposed neatly on each side of it. The church has two *brasses* and they are both displayed on a board beneath the gallery. The first is for an unidentified late-C15 or early-C16 couple; he wears a long tunic with a pouch at his belt, she has a *kennel headdress* and a fashionable girdle. The second commemorates Anthony Pettow who died in 1610 and it unfortunately suffered in the fire, when the head was destroyed; the 21in. figure in ruff and cloak stands on a plinth casting a shadow – a feature seldom seen in brass engraving. The C15 *font* has lions and *woodwoses* guarding its shaft, and the bowl panels contain *Evangelistic symbols* and angels bearing shields – n.w., *Trinity emblem*; s.w. *Passion emblems*; n.e. *St George's* cross; s.e., floriated cross. An interesting and easily legible inscription is cut in the base: 'Cryst mote us spede, and help us alle at nede'. It so like the one at Darsham that the two fonts may have come from the same workshop. George III *Royal Arms* in painted cast-iron are displayed on the n. wall, and to the r. there is a large C15 *St Christopher* painting which also suffered in the fire, although his face and the outline of the Christ child are still quite clear. On the s. wall there is a fragment of wall painting which I believe to be a *consecration cross*, and both the Perpendicular windows have image niches in their e. splays. The door which led to the *rood loft stair* is in the n. wall, and on it there are photographs of the 1955 scene of devastation. Just beyond, another large fragment of medieval wall painting has been uncovered, suggesting that much of the wall surface was decorated before the *Reformation*. A window opposite has interesting mid-C19 glass – roundels and ovals filled with attractive ivy leaf designs within leaf and flower borders. It has all the characteristics of locally made glass, and may have come from Henry Fisk, the Yoxford plumber and glazier who did the tower window at Peasenhall. If so, he may also have provided the geometrically patterned glass in the window alongside.

Just beyond the renewed chancel arch on the s. side there is another Norman *jamb shaft*, and pieces of Norman chevron moulding were used in the arch of the window opposite. The s. window contains a pleasing and unusual version of Christ's encounter with *St Mary Magdalene*, a rich *Renaissance* setting, with no hint of the Easter garden. This is 1870s glass by *Lavers, Barraud & Westlake* and is quite unlike their normal style. Two bench ends survived the C19 reordering, and were incorporated into a new priest's stall. Traceried and unusually narrow, they are very like those at Darsham not far away. Rector's wife Constance Savery died in 1925, and her fine portrait medallion in bronze by F.M. Taubman is on the n. wall. A little further along there are two baroque ovals with scrolls and cherub heads for Frances and Sarah, the wives of Thomas Meadows. He died in 1742, having outlived them both, and his tablet fits neatly between, with paired skulls at the base and a *cartouche* of arms on the curved pediment – a pleasing ensemble. The 'gothick' *communion rails* probably date from about 1820, and *Decalogue* panels in florid, High Victorian style form a *reredos* for the simple *Stuart Holy Table*. The C13 *angle piscina* appears to have made use of Norman shafts, and there is an *ogee* arch above the *dropped-sill sedilia* alongside. Middleton has a ring of five bells with a 9 cwt. tenor, but their condition does not allow them to be rung at the present time.

Milden, St Peter (D6): This is one of the highest points in Suffolk and across the valley to the n.w. the tower of Lavenham shows proudly on the skyline. The sixty-year-old avenue of laburnums leading to the s. *porch* has recently been renewed with young saplings and should soon provide a springtime swathe of blossom once again. The tower was badly damaged by lightning in 1827 and taken down in 1840; the remains were used to rebuild the w. wall, new *lancets* were inserted and a bellcote was placed on the gable. The lancet in the s. wall of the *nave* and the s. door identifies this as a *Norman* building. The *chancel* windows are C13, with triple lancets at the e. end, and there are two large renewed windows in the nave. The small porch has a little *cusped* lancet each side and the arch of the Norman doorway is carved with a bold zigzag moulding.

The C14 n. doorway is simply moulded and, like the main entrance, it has slots cut in the jambs to house a security drawbar. In the 1860s *vestry* beyond hangs a most unusual portrait of William Burkitt, who was rector from 1678 until 1702. It is engraved but scraps of fabric have been applied to represent his surplice, gown, and bands. He crops up again on the benefactions board at the w. end of the nave, from which we learn that he left money 'for learning all the poor children to read and for buying them Bibles and Catechisms'. The square Norman *font* stands on a drum shaft and four columns with circular *capitals* and bases, and to the s. there is a range of rustic C17 benches. The end of the front one is boldly lettered 'Churchwarden' and its back has: 'August 24 1685 William Stud Junr.'. There is no chancel arch, the ceilings are plastered, and on one of the two *tie-beams* is a crude C14 *king post* with four-way struts. The plain glass of the n. window affords another fine view across the valley to Lavenham and on the s. wall there is the attractive monument for bachelor John Canham who died in 1772. His arms are displayed in a *cartouche* on the *pediment* and there is a pair of pretty cherub heads at the base; coloured marble frames the epitaph: 'His only sister Mary placed here this memorial of that sincere affection with which they were mutually endeared to each other, and happily lived together for more than 50 years.'

A whole range of C13 decorative painting was discovered on the nave walls in 1987 and there are large areas of simulated masonry, with sections of a dado on the s. side and a *consecration cross* below the Norman lancet. Standing on a modern base, the *Stuart* pulpit has a canted book ledge supported by scroll brackets and the carving of the *blind arches* in the upper panels is very shallow; those below are incised with diagonal crosses and there is so much similarity between this and the pulpits at Little Waldingfield and Edwardstone that they were probably made in the same workshop. In the *sanctuary* there are *Decalogue* panels painted on the e. wall and a plain lancet *piscina*. Against the n. wall of the chancel a modern canopy encloses the tomb of James Alington who died in 1627 and whose charity you will have noted at the w. end. It was originally much more elaborate but sections were apparently dispersed into private houses early in the C20. Luckily the fine alabaster effigy is intact, apart from the feet. He is shown in armour with left hand on breast, his frogged and taselled cloak beneath him, and his head rests, most unusually, on a Bible and prayer book. On the wall behind are his arms in a roundel and there are two *touchstone* panels in oblong alabaster frames very delicately carved with bones, coffins, pick, and spade – all interspersed with fruit.

Mildenhall, St Mary (B3): In every way this is one of the great Suffolk churches. Not only is it 168ft. by 65ft., but it abounds in richness, variety and interest. Mildenhall has sprawled since the war but the nucleus of the old town laps the spacious churchyard on three sides and the mighty tower is a landmark for miles. It is 120ft. high and must have been even more commanding before the C15 spirelet with its lantern was removed in 1831. The tower was completed by 1464 and has a plain stone *base course* with virtually no decoration on the main surfaces. Alternate stages of the gabled buttresses carry tall *crocketted* pinnacles set diagonally, but essentially it is an austere design, massive and well proportioned. By the mid-C19 there was a deep fissure in the s.e. angle and in 1864 it was refaced and the stair turret extended above the battlements. The w. door, with its ample side niches, and the great w. window were both renewed. At that time, masses of fine *dogtooth* mouldings were found reversed in the tower buttresses, remnants of the C13 predecessor. The tower houses a ring of ten bells with a 16 cwt. tenor, but structural problems only allow the front six to be rung at the present time. The large and plain s. *porch* was virtually rebuilt in 1876. The s. *aisle* is restrained, with only crocketted pinnacles to the buttresses, but the e. end of the *chancel* is another matter altogether. The great window fronting the High Street is a magnificent composition dating from about 1300 which can stand comparison with any in England. The seven *lights* are graduated in width and the outer pair are continued up and over the head as a band of *quatrefoils*. In the centre is a large *cusped* oval, itself set within a rim of tiny quatrefoils, and on either side are *tracery* shapes reminiscent of the pleated paper bells used for Christmas decorations, or so it seemed to me as a child. The chancel corner buttresses are very inventive; they begin as standard right-angled pairs, rise to *cinquefoil*-headed niches in the angles and then reduce to slim octagonal pinnacles which rise above the roof line. Four of the image stools rest on carved head *corbels*. On the s. side, the chancel windows alternate attractively between stepped *lancets* within a single arch and intersected 'Y' tracery, and on the n., matching stepped lancets. Churchyards were systematically reused in the Middle Ages and displaced bones were often placed in a charnel chapel. There was one here and its ivy covered ruins can be seen s.e. of the chancel. It was founded in 1387 by Ralph de Walsham (who had a hand in the murder of the Prior of Bury

Abbey during the Peasants' Revolt of 1381). With a crypt below for the bones, it was endowed with a priest to say masses for the dead, and the sunken depression towards the street shows its size. Although there has been a church here since the Conquest, the earliest dateable work is the early-C13 chapel built of limestone (now the *vestry*) n. of the chancel, with an e. window of three stepped lancets. Part of the chancel is the same age and you will see the break in the wall line on both sides where it was extended a few decades later. A parish often chose one side of its church on which to lavish attention and here it is the n. aisle and porch. The C14 buttresses have pleasing niches under *groined ogee* canopies, and in the early-C15 rebuilding much more was done – new windows, a parapet panelled in two tiers with small blank shields and a line of small grotesques within the moulding below. The whole of the aisle is faced with chequered *flushwork*. Built about 1420, the n. porch of two storeys is the largest in Suffolk and, as the main entrance, its decoration matches the aisle. The ground floor is stone faced and there is a line of shields over the outer arch with a window above them. Within is a ribbed stone vault with *bosses* at the intersections and the inner doorway is set within a larger arch of blind tracery. The ogees each side probably backed *stoups* that have been hacked away. Over the door is a stooled and canopied niche and the shields in the *spandrels* are those of *Edward the Confessor* and *St Edmund*. The doors themselves are original, with three ranges of fine *Perpendicular* tracery in the heads.

Once inside, the sense of size coupled with richness is intensified. The *piers* of the C15 *nave arcades* are tall and slim, with minimal enrichment, and light floods in from large aisle windows and *clerestory*. To the r. of the door is a stairway leading to the porch upper room; the spandrels of the arch have carvings of the *Annunciation*, underlining the fact that the chamber was a Lady chapel in an unusual location. There is a smaller, earlier doorway below which led to the original stairs. The early-C15 *Purbeck marble font* is very eroded and, although they are well nigh illegible now, the shields in the bowl quatrefoils bear the arms of the City of London and the donor, Sir Henry Barton, who may have been involved in the great rebuilding of the 1420s. Lord Mayor in the year after Agincourt and again in 1428, he had introduced the first street lighting in London as Sheriff in 1405. He was buried in old St Paul's but a memorial tomb was placed here at the base of the tower and is now at the w. end of the s. aisle. Sir Henry's arms are on a brass shield on one end of the tomb and those of the City were on the other. The scale of the stone w. *gallery* matches the church; set within the tall, deeply moulded tower arch, it has a line of blank shields over the arch and the parapet is pierced with closely set quatrefoils. Underneath is a beautiful *fan vault*, one of the very few to be found in Suffolk or Norfolk. It is likely to have been inserted between 1530 and 1555, and there is some evidence that it was the work of Thomas Larke, the surveyor of the final phase of King's College Chapel, Cambridge. It may well have been designed and used as a *galilee porch*.

Glass in the two small windows here commemorates church workers often overlooked: that on the n. side is by J. Dudley Forsyth of a woman in medieval dress cleaning, as did Anne Jolly here for 18 years, and on the s., *St Cecilia* and a robed lady bellringer for Mary Fordham – rare, if not unique, subjects. Above the gallery is a wall to wall w. window and to the l. what may well be the largest set of *Royal Arms* in any parish church. At least 12ft. by 9ft., they are for George II, dated 1758 and hung over the chancel arch in the C19. Over Sir Henry Barton's tomb at the w. end of the s. aisle is a modern tablet commemorating William Gregory, the second Mildenhall man to be both Sheriff and Lord Mayor of London, in 1436 and 1451. Here also is the long iron-bound C14 parish chest and a stone coffin found under the n. aisle in 1851. One of the features of the church is the magnificent suite of benches designed by *Cautley* and bequeathed by his wife in 1959. The intricately traceried bench ends and *poppyheads* are all different and the standing figures in the niches at the w. end are reminiscent of Wiggenhall St Mary in Norfolk. They portray: nave, the *Blessed Virgin* and *St Etheldreda* holding a model of Ely cathedral; n. aisle, the Virgin and Child; s. aisle, *St Anne* teaching the Virgin. The aisles now have open boarded floors and the outer walls are lined with benches.

Overhead is the glory of this church, C15 roofs which in their magnificence are unsurpassed and where everything points to a designer and craftsmen of more than local standing. The nave has moulded and richly carved *tie-beams*, whose *arch-braces* rise from deep *wall posts* to meet at the centre, the spandrels filled with tracery. Above them, *queen posts* are braced up to the ridge, flanked by tracery with demi-angels adorning the sides. Alternating with the tie-beams are *hammerbeams* carved as ten mighty angels and their

wings, spread wide and raised, are held in grooves behind the figures and have no other support; each holds a *Passion emblem*, a book, or a lute. Yet more demi-angels line the deep cornice on each side. The height of the roof saved it from the worst excesses of the C17 image breakers but in their frustration they riddled it with buckshot and blunderbuss bolts. Some of the wings had to be replaced, but in the main it is as the makers left it except that close examination has revealed traces of colour. The wide aisle roofs are fitting companions and they too have arch-braced hammerbeams, carved in the n. aisle with an astonishing array of beasts and men. Here, binoculars are invaluable in revealing the richness and vitality of the imagery. Starting from the e. end, the hammerbeams are carved as: a hideous woman in a horned headdress, a king wielding a sword followed by a lion, a lion with another behind it, a *wyvern* (the badge of Lord Bardolph), a rich merchant with his dog, and another lion. The spandrels below teem with life and, from the w., the scenes are: a pardoner blessing a lady, demons playing an organ, *St George* and the dragon (the queen's 1430s headdress dates this closely), baptism of Christ, a collared swan (Henry V's badge), the Bethlehem shepherds, a chained antelope (Henry V again), Abraham and Isaac, a huntsman with dogs, deer, hare and squirrel, the Annunciation, a *griffin, St Michael,* and a *green man*. Even then, there is a carving next to the wall that cannot easily be seen. Between the hammerbeams, large, very mutilated figures jut out that have lost their arms. Slots for wings remain and they must have been angels that matched those in the nave. The damage doubtless dates from 1651 when the parish paid a man a shilling a day to smash popish images, and the figures carved on the wall posts lost their faces too. They have angels poised protectively above them in lieu of canopies – a brilliant conception. The s. aisle is not so evocative but the work is still rich. The design of the hammerbeams, with their deep cresting, is slightly angular and blind tracery rather than carved scenes fills the spandrels. Tall figures nestle in the corners and miniature carvings abound, including, at the e. end, a man attacked by a wyvern thrusting a stick between its jaws. As in the n. aisle, mutilated angels reach out over the windows. Among the mass of carved detail, Henry V's badges appear time and time again.

At the e. end of the s. aisle is the church's only large monument, the elaborate tomb of Sir Henry North (d.1620), Lord of the Manor. He

Mildenhall, St Mary

was knighted in 1586 at Zutphen (a skirmish with the Spaniards in the Netherlands where Sir Philip Sidney fell). He lies in full armour next to his wife who wears the fashionable large hood of the period. Their heads rest on tasselled cushions and there are traces of colour. Purbeck *Corinthian* columns rise either side to obelisks on the cornice, with a coloured *achievement* above, and an inscription on two *touchstone* panels at the back under cherubs within a pair of enriched arches. The tomb was restored in 1885 and the figures of the children were replaced, although Sir Henry still lacks his feet. His funeral helm hangs above. To the r. is a handsome memorial to his son Roger North (d.1651) – oval touchstone tablet set in alabaster swags and scrolls heightened with gilt; cherub, crest and two shields over, with a skull crowned with laurel on top, a macabre conceit. Nearby is a window commemorating Sir Charles Bunbury (d.1886), one of the family that were Lords of the Manor from the C18 to the C20. The glass is by C. Elliott, with centre panels on a theme from the book of Ruth and parable panels on either side. The s. aisle chapel is dedicated to *St Margaret* and the *altar* bears a *mensa* dated 1420 which was in use as a floor slab until 1936. The glass above it is signed by *Henry Hughes* and installed in the 1870s. To the r. an *aumbry* and to the l. a clutch of Bunbury memorials. It is interesting that Thomas North's 1661 tablet was copied almost exactly for Henry Bunbury 60 years later. The 1870s brass lectern is a good solid design and came from nearby Worlington (where the loss has not been forgotten). The remains of the church's C17 pulpit can be found at Beck Row, while here we have a robust 1870s piece in oak

by *J.D. Wyatt* on a stone base and with green Irish marble *colonnettes*. For some inscrutable reason the whole thing is now mounted on runners. The n. aisle chapel is dedicated to *St John the Baptist*, patron saint of one of the six *guilds* associated with the church. There is a *pillar piscina* here with a very shallow drain. Behind it was a *squint* to the *High altar* which is now blocked. The fine *Early English* chancel arch has triple shafts with *dogtooth decoration* between them, and more is set in the *hood mould*. The stiff-leaf foliage of the *capitals* continues as a band into the corners of the wall and there are renewed *headstops*. The present *screen*, with its rather fussy tracery, was installed in 1903 but the original *rood screen* must have been very grand and in keeping with the scale of the church. The stair turret for it lies to the n. and rises to roof level. It housed the *sanctus bell* and you will see that there are three blocked doorways. This prompts the conclusion that there was a double screen or two separate lofts. The upper would have been used for maintaining the rood itself and its lights, while the lower one may well have carried an altar. If the lower loft was a deep one, the space beneath would have borrowed light through the *mullioned* opening from the s. aisle chapel. There is an interesting 1670 memorial in painted marble above this opening for Sarah North, with clasped hands above a shield of arms. Her husband, Sir Henry, was the melancholic and finally suicidal author of *Eroclea, or the Mayd of Honour*. Part of the epitaph translates: 'Dead while living, oh how hard; you are happy because your life has ended, I am desolate for I cannot die'. The C13 chancel was extended and given new windows in the C14. Note that although the choir stalls are modern, there are sections of medieval tracery in the second range on the s. side, with a *woodwose*, dragon, wyvern and mask in the spandrels. The e. window has Purbeck shafts which rise to angels at the spring of the arch. To the r. is a C13 double piscina with Purbeck shafts and stiff-leaf capitals (the whole of the upper section is new work), and stepped *sedilia* with simply shaped armrests. Look for the grave slab in the floor on the n. side, e. of the vestry door. The inscription around the edge is in *Lombardic* capitals and translates: 'Here lies Richard de Wichforde, some time vicar of the church of Mildenhall who made this new work'. He was vicar from 1309 to 1344 and so we know who to thank for the beautiful e. window. One regrets the large unsightly radiator that stands on part of the slab. The glass in the e. window is probably by *Ward & Hughes* dating from the 1880s and they no doubt furnished the glass in the chancel s. windows. There are two aumbries in the s. wall, one with a *trefoil* arch, and a brass shield and inscription for Mary Warner who died in 1601. Her husband, Sir Henry, has a *brass* on the n. wall and wears Elizabethan armour in the simplified style favoured by the *Stuarts*. He was High Sheriff in 1599, MP for Thetford in 1601 and knighted in 1603. The inscription is for father and son but the latter's effigy has gone.

Mildenhall, Beck Row, St John (B3): In 1876 this was a late entrant at a fairly low level in the great Victorian church building boom. Designed by *J.D. Wyatt* in flint, it has a faint echo of the previous decade's taste for structural colour in the form of bands of red and white bricks, with matching window arches. The windows are vaguely *Early English* but hardly consistent, with simple *plate tracery* on the s. and *trefoil*-headed *lancets* on the n. A stubby s. *transept* separates the buttressed *nave* from the *chancel* and a bellcote with shingled spire caps the w. gable.

With little but the village street to shield it from the stupefying noise of aircraft using the Americans' 'Gateway to Europe', one would not expect much calm and serenity in this little church, but it manages well enough. The interior originally had patterning in brick but now all is white, with only the stone dressings of the lancets picked out in ochre, apart, that is, from the chancel and transept arches on *colonnettes* stopping well short of the floor. They contrive to look rather splendid in the original red and white bricks. The 1863 glass in the e. window is not particularly memorable except for the fact that one *light* portrays Jesus, John and Judas at the Last Supper, an unusual combination. The glass in the roundel above the lancets at the w. end has an angel blowing a trumpet that would have liked a larger window to stretch in. The C17 octagonal pulpit has shallow carved floral panels and a canted ledge supported by coarsely carved heavy scroll brackets. Now set on a modern base, it was discarded by Mildenhall, St Mary's, in 1875 when the architect of this church designed a new one there. There is a lumpish *font* at the w. end and, in the n.w. corner, the propeller blade from a Stirling of 90 Squadron which crashed on a training flight in 1943. It has been mounted as a memorial for those on board who all, save one, lie buried outside. There, on the n. side of the church, are the ranks of graves that remind one that Mildenhall was a wartime bomber aerodrome. Only a tithe of those who

were lost lie here but they came from all over the world; R.H. Middleton VC, of the Royal Australian Air Force, was killed in 1942 aged 26 and lies closest to the n.w. corner of the church.

Mildenhall, West Row, St Peter (B3): In the mid-C19 church architects often designed schools as well and liked to use the same *Early English* style. When, therefore, this National School of 1850 came to be used as a church in 1874, all that it needed was a matching *chancel* and now one cannot tell the difference. It lies by the green at the s. end of the village and is a simple building in flint and white brick, faintly enlivened by hexagonal slates on the roof.

Inside is a *queen post* roof over the nave and a *scissors-braced* construction for the one beyond the *trefoiled* chancel arch. The stepped *lancets* at the e. end repeat those at the w. and the n. chancel lancets have 1883 glass of Christ on the waters and with *Saints Peter* and *Andrew*. The glass at the w. end is by J. Dudley Forsyth, one of *Henry Holiday's* apprentices, and is a fine composition in deep, rich colour. The group of Christ with attendant figures spreads over the three *lights* but is contained within Gothick *tabernacle work*. It has almost monochrome flesh tints, and the face of Christ is reminiscent of the young Prince Consort (there is more of Forsyth's work at Culford and Worlington). Below it is a heavy, square *font* with multiple chamfers. Equally solid is the chocolate brown organ case, with a pair of Early English-style turned shafts each side and *quatrefoils* along the front. The pulpit is not, as some guides have said, the C17 piece discarded from Mildenhall, but plain C19 pine.

Monewden, St Mary (G5): The C14 tower has a simple *base course*, a doorway with blank shields in the *spandrels*, and *Decorated tracery* in the window above. There is a nice variation in the *flushwork* of the stepped battlements. One of the county's best light rings of six bells with a 5 cwt. tenor hangs in the tower in excellent condition. Two *lancets* in the *nave* show that it dates from the *Norman* period, but the rest of the windows both in nave and *chancel* are from the early part of the C14, like the low *priest's door* on the s. side. The early-C16 brick *porch* has three small niches above the outer arch and its roof rests on a cambered *tie-beam* and *king post*.

Beyond the C14 inner doorway there is a modern waggon roof over the nave, and the chancel roof is nicely panelled out and decorated with flower *bosses* – all dating from a restoration in 1906. The unassuming C15 *font* has a panelled stem and plain shields hung on little rosettes in the bowl panels. You will see that the Norman lancets lie in deep splays and that for some reason the heads were altered to a pointed shape. The *rood loft stairs* have a handsome entrance in a n. window embrasure and hinge lugs that supported the door survive in the stonework. There is a shallow niche to the r. and over on the s. side is a much larger one. Nearby stands a wooden cross brought back from the grave of a soldier who died a prisoner in World War I. The front range of benches is plain C15 work with heavy *poppyheads* of varying designs but has the virtue of being nearly intact. There is now no *screen* and the modern wooden chancel arch comes down to pretty canopied niches which rest on stone *corbels* carved with demi-angels. The C14 *piscina* in the *sanctuary* lies below a *trefoil* arch, and there is a nice chunky *Holy Table* with shallow carving on the top rails. To the r. is a *brass* in the wall commemorating the Revd. Dr Thomas Reve, who died in 1595. It is set within a shallow stone arch on which there were once three small shields, and his *achievement* and figure are engraved on the one plate. He kneels before a small table on which an open book is set, and there is a thirteen-line inscription below. He was the son of William and Rose Reve; their brass has been moved from the nave to the e. wall on the other side of the altar. There were once effigies but now only a shield and two verse inscriptions remain. The e. window glass by E. Woore takes the form of a World War II memorial, a conventional Crucifixion group, but the shield on the l. at the top is interesting because it is medieval and displays the arms of the Black Prince. Before leaving you may like to pause at the tombstone with semi-circular top which stands e. of the chancel and rather nearer the boundary hedge. The inscription is somewhat worn but it records that William Pitts died in 1819: 'Having once sailed round this terrestrial Globe, thou little knows what I have seen. To have learnt the liberal sciences thoroughly softens such men's manners and suffers them not to be brutal.' That somewhat gnomic turn of phrase is explained by his adventures. The son of a local farmer, he travelled as assistant to William Gooch, the astronomer attached to Capt. Vancouver's expedition which surveyed the w. coast of America in 1791. Gooch was murdered by the natives of Hawaii and Pitts was eventually sent home by the commander with his despatches. In the fullness of time he

succeeded to his father's farm and rural quietude but, understandably, did not wish his circumnavigation to be forgotten.

Monks Eleigh, St Peter (D6): This handsome church stands above the village street to the n., approached by a steepish lane, and in many ways reminds me of Cavendish. What we see is largely C15 and the solid stair turret on the s. face of the tower is set back where it rises above the parapet and is crowned by a bell in an openwork metal frame. There are two tiers of *flushwork* in the battlements and large three-*light* bell openings. An unusual feature is the way in which the corner buttresses are stopped short of the top and capped by carved masks. From them, small octagonal buttresses continue up to *crocketted* pinnacles. There is a flushwork *base course* in two ranks and the w. doorway is particularly rich although very worn. Constructed of clunch, the chalk building stone, there are lion masks and crouched lions and bears in the mouldings, while the square *label* terminates in large and jovial *headstops*. Stooled niches flank the doorway and the *tracery* of the tall window above was renewed in 1845. The tower houses a ring of six bells with a 15 cwt. tenor, and the fine C14 fifth bell from a London foundry has an unusual inscription: 'Assumpta est Maria in celum' (Mary is taken up into heaven). The long *chancel* was entirely rebuilt in the 1840s and a *vestry* was added on the n. side. The *Perpendicular* n. *aisle* has a simple C14 doorway that was probably part of the older building. In walking round you will find a number of good C18 headstones, for example, Elizabeth Green's of 1734 by the e. end of the s. aisle; it has a cherub's head and skull above a skilful combination of Gothic and Roman lettering. Further to the s. is an example of quality modern stone cutting by John Green – the headstone for June-Mary Dalton who died in 1981. The C15 s. *porch*, approached by a miniature avenue of pollarded limes, has large flushwork *consecration crosses* outlined in thin red tiles on either side of the entrance, with a *scratch dial* to the l. The inner doorway is deeply moulded and there is worn tracery at head and foot of the medieval doors.

Within, you will notice that the *nave arcades* do not match and the C14 s. side probably formed part of the earlier church; the *piers* and *capitals* have concave faces as opposed to the plain octagons on the n. and the arch mouldings differ. The single-framed rafter roof of the nave had a *canopy of honour* for the *rood* at the e. end which is now a plain band of plaster. Below it

Monks Eleigh:
C19 portriature in chancel s. window

hangs a large and handsome set of Queen Anne *Royal Arms*, excellently restored recently by Anna Hulbert. At the time of my visit the organ stood in front of the tall tower arch but was due to be moved as part of a general rearrangement of furniture. Near the s. door is a plain pillar poor box dated 1636. The C13 *font*, with its C15 cover, by the n. door, has a centre shaft and four columns supporting the square bowl; there are octagonal shafts inset at the corners and a strange strapwork design on the s. side, with the remains (or the beginning) of an incised pattern on the n. A simple C16 chest stands at the w. end of the s. aisle and another at the e. end has pierced corner brackets and wrought handles. Nearby, a rectangular projection houses the stairs to the old *rood loft* and the entrance is over 6ft. from the floor. The level of the upper doorway shows that the *screen* was lofty and on the n. side another opening connects with a high level doorway in the n. aisle; a *squint* aligned with the *High altar* is sited in the intervening passage. The arrangement suggests that there were *parclose screens* round both aisle chapels and that they were connected by a walkway to the main rood loft (as at Rattlesden). The notches cut in the e. *respond* of the s. arcade are further evidence of a screen being fitted there. There is a tall and elegant image niche with a *cusped ogee* arch set crosswise in the n.e. corner of the n. aisle, and to the r. of the altar you will find a *pillar piscina*. The pre-*Reformation* pulpit rises from a coved pedestal and there is squared tracery in the bottom of the panels, with applied tracery in the tops (some of which is replacement). The choir stalls were removed in the 1990s and a set

from Wells designed by *Sir George Gilbert Scott* took their place. A chancel n. window has glass by T.F. Curtis of *Ward & Hughes*; dark and sombre colours, with the figure of *Dorcas* and her handiwork in one light. Opposite, a window illustrating the text 'But when the morning was come Jesus stood on the shore' has a Victorian gentleman's portrait head peeping out behind the disciples. The e. window glass of 1880 is by *Henry Hughes* of Ward & Hughes, an Ascension flanked by a Nativity and the *Three Marys* at the tomb, with three vignettes beneath; the figures are stilted and the colour sharp. There is an interesting suite of windows on the s. side of the chancel, all in memory of children of a late-C19 rector and all have portraits – the glass again by Ward & Hughes. The *sanctuary* has C17 panelling and there is a C19 blind arch stone *reredos*. The High altar is a fine and solid *Stuart Holy Table* which is higher than average and does not appear to have been altered as so many have.

Monk Soham, St Peter (G4): Remote from the village, the church enjoys a beautifully spacious setting. The tower with its modest w. doorway dates from about 1300 and has narrow *lancets* at ground and middle levels. There is pretty *Decorated tracery* in the bell openings and the battlements are chequered with *flushwork*. On walking round, you will find that, as at Sproughton and elsewhere, there are massive boulders used as foundation stones at the s.w. corner of the tower and under the e. buttresses of the *chancel*. They may have been pagan cult stones which were transferred to the service of the new religion. The *nave* has *Perpendicular* windows but the blocked n. door is the same age as the tower, and so is the long chancel with a *priest's door* to the s. and lancets which have pointed *trefoils* in the tracery. The wide five-*light* e. window is most attractive and has intersected tracery enlivened by *cusps*. The large C15 s. *porch* is sadly decayed, with niches each side and above the archway, which shows traces of a double row of *fleurons* in the mouldings. There are the remains of flushwork and the *ashlar* of the corner buttresses is cut with shallow patterns. Before going in, don't miss the *scratch dial* on the s. buttress of the nave.

The inner doorway is narrow by contrast and its *jambs* have recesses to take a heavy security bar. The tower screen would not be remarkable but for the fact that it makes use of two varying sections of C14 tracery which were probably saved from the *rood screen*. Beyond it, St Peter's ring of five bells with a 12 cwt. tenor are rung from the ground floor. Close by are a few medieval benches with *poppyheads* and an excellent C14 chest of quite eccentric proportions – 8ft. long but only 18in. wide; encased in iron bands, it has an abundance of locks and bars. The *font* is one of the *Seven Sacrament* versions peculiar to East Anglia and although the carvings in the deep bowl have been grievously defaced, the subjects can be identified. Clockwise from the e. they are: mass, confirmation, Crucifixion, ordination, Extreme Unction, matrimony, penance, and baptism. The bulky figures round the shaft are cowled like monks but they must have represented the *Evangelists* because their symbols stand between them. Traces of green paint remain and the overall design is so like the font at Hoxne that it is likely to date from 1460-70. At first glance the nave roof looks like a standard *hammerbeam/arch-braced* design but note that the hammerbeams are only for effect – the braces rise from the back so that it is classed as a 'false hammerbeam'. *Wall plates* and hammers are decorated (although they have lost their angels or shields) and there are *embattled collars* below the ridge. There is an additional *tie-beam* above the font and the *rood beam* remains in place at the e. end. At least, it is generally assumed to be the rood beam, but you will see that the stairs to the rood loft emerge at a lower level on the n. side and the hook for a *Lenten veil* remains embedded in the apex of the chancel arch. This makes me wonder whether the rood was at a lower level and the beam is merely a structural support like the one farther w. A simple *piscina* on the s. side shows that there was a nave *altar* and the delicious little niche in the window embrasure above would have housed a statue of the dedicatory saint. It is shallow, with curly *crockets* to the arch, flanking pinnacles, and *paterae* on the bevel moulding. The pulpit is rather odd. The upper range of its plain panels is pierced with roundels and one angle is dated '12 May 1604' - it is not at all typical of the early C17. Beyond the wide chancel arch the *hood moulds* of the side lancets are linked with a moulding, and the eye is drawn to the mighty e. window which fills virtually the whole of the 14ft. width. The contemporary piscina must have been beautiful in its youth but sadly all the arch, with its mouldings and *finial*, has been hacked away although the stone *credence shelf* remains. The church had a tradition of long-serving rectors in the C18 and C19 and one of them, Robert Hindes Groome, served for forty-four

years. He was a great friend of Edward Fitzgerald, the famous translator of *The Rubáiyát of Omar Khayyám*; his children all have bronze plaques in the chancel but I didn't come across his memorial. Like the pulpit, the *Stuart* altar table is not a typical design but has square legs with recessed panels and a modestly decorated skirt below the front rail. The *sanctuary* is peaceful enough now but on Sunday 17 April 1636 it was the scene of an extraordinary disturbance. Bishop Wren was busy enforcing the *Laudian* order that communion should be received at the rail, but Daniel Wheymond violently disagreed with the change and, backed by his family and others, paraded up and down and round the parson while he attempted to administer the sacrament. For this 'indecent, prophane and unseemly' behaviour they were haled before the high commission the following month.

Moulton, St Peter (A4): Secluded at the s. end of the village, the church stands very attractively on rising ground, with a footpath leading through the churchyard to a beech hanger beyond. The tower nestles among yews, with a few Scots pines at the w. end. Originally it was a wide and tall *Norman* building and the C12 columns marking the corners can be found in the angles where the *nave* meets the *chancel* and at the w. end. There was probably an *anchorite's* cell between the w. end of the n. *aisle* and the tower – a blocked doorway led into the aisle and there is a fragment stub of wall to the l. The late-C13 tower has a truncated w. window immediately above the door, a *corbel table* just below the battlements and heavy *gargoyles*. There are *transomed lancet* windows on either side of the bell openings on the n. and s. sides, a very unusual formation but likely to be original. The weathervane is in the form of a most distinctive and well nourished fish. St Peter's has a ground floor ring of five bells with a 6 cwt. tenor, but their present condition does not allow them to be rung. The body of the building dates from the early C16, with large *Perpendicular* windows; those in the *clerestory* have stepped transoms and a continuous *hood mould*. The whole building was heavily restored in 1850 and the s. *porch* is completely C19.

Inside, the nave, aisles and *transept* chapels are linked by arches that have a common design but which differ in detail, with the arch between the s. aisle and transept lower and heavier. All the *capitals* are battlemented and decorated with *fleurons*. The tower arch is now filled-in above a low oak screen. Above the nave *arcades* is a most attractive stone frieze, battlemented and carved with fleurons; it incorporates demi-angels from which attached columns rise to support the nave roof. All the roofs are good replacements; *hammerbeams* in nave and chancel with demi-angels carved on the *wall plates*, and the *arch-braced* aisle roofs come down to *wall posts* linked by transverse arches. The *font* is probably C19, but if not, it has been comprehensively re-cut; four of its *cusped* panels contain shields with *Passion emblems* and the others are carved with closely set fleurons, with more under the bowl and on the stem. The C16 cover is crudely carved and has been badly attacked by worm. In the curtained *vestry* at the w. end of the s. aisle there is an ancient stone panel carved with two figures; a man with his arms raised in prayer and a woman with her hands folded over her belly. It appears to have been part of a larger design and could conceivably represent Adam and Eve. The nave and aisles have C19 oak pews with rather good *poppyheads* and in the n. transept chapel there is the pillar of a *piscina* with just a fragment of the bowl. To the r., a very narrow doorway to the *rood stairs*. Nearby is a massive, heavily carved C19 wooden eagle lectern. Unless they were moved in the C19 restoration, the two stone brackets near the rood stair opening on the n. side of the chancel arch are likely to have been supports for the loft rather than image brackets. On the s. side there is a tall and slim *trefoil*-headed niche for a statue. The s. transept contains a piscina with a *cinquefoiled* arch under a square *label*, with blank *quatrefoils* in the *spandrels*. There are medieval bench ends worked into the modern choir stalls, with carvings on the elbows – a *unicorn* and a rabbit on the n. side, a deer with large antlers and a dog on the s. The chancel was raised well above the level of the nave in the 1850s and a crypt was discovered beneath the *sanctuary*. The C16 piscina to the r. of the *High altar* has a *crocketted* arch with *finial* and, although the cusping has been broken, there are large fleurons in the side mouldings. The n. wall of the chancel carries a *touchstone* tablet framed in marble, with an alabaster *cartouche* of arms within a broken *pediment* above. It is for Francis Seyliard who was rector here and died in 1676. To the l. is a very plain marble tablet on a grey surround by R. Brown of London for another rector, George Greenall, who died in 1845. There are examples of Victorian *brasses* on two *ledger-stones* in the sanctuary for Edmund Mortlock, the rector who carried out the big restoration, and his sister Mary Ann.

Mutford, St Andrew (I2): Parish determination and hard work saved this little church from redundancy in 1973, and the tower was restored two years later. At 66ft., it is the tallest of the round towers, with regularly banded flint in the walls and a tall C13 *lancet* to the w. Smaller, blocked lancets at two levels, together with internal evidence, however, show that it is *Saxon*; the round section was heightened some time before a new octagonal bell stage was added in the C14. The latter has good *Decorated flushwork* panels in the form of blind windows between the bell openings which have themselves lost their tracery, and there is more flushwork in the battlements. One of the most interesting things about Mutford is its *galilee porch*, the only one to be found in conjunction with a round tower. It has been restored and provided with a new roof relatively recently, and some commentators have called it *Norman*, partly because it is built on to the round tower, and partly because the outer arch is semi-circular. The mouldings of the arch do not sustain the argument, however, and the doorway into the tower is C14, a much more likely date. The stratified flints along the base of the *nave* n. wall are a sign that the whole building is pre-Conquest in origin, and on that side there is the outline of an earlier window between the two with *Perpendicular* tracery. In 1881, the *chancel* was restored and re-roofed, and I think that the 6ft. blind arcade of flushwork along the e. wall and round the buttresses dates from then, together with the e. window. The s. *aisle* has a brick e. wall, and a large arch into the chancel was bricked up and a domestic window inserted when a side chapel was demolished in the C19. The aisle side windows have 'Y' tracery of about 1300, and they were probably saved from the old nave s. wall when the aisle was added in the early C14, a date suggested by the w. window (although the tracery has been bricked up, it was obviously an elaborate Decorated design).

The s. *porch* is Victorian, but the inner doorway is C14 and there is a *stoup* beside it. Within, the church is paved pleasantly in pale brick, and a small set of *Royal Arms* painted on canvas hangs above the entrance. Despite the William IV label and date, I think the arms were originally late-*Stuart*. The wide aisle has an *arch-braced* roof whose *spandrels* are pierced with tracery, and the early-C14 arcade has rather spindly octagonal *piers*. The organ now stands against the e. wall of the aisle, but there must have been a splendid *sanctuary* originally, judging by the quality of the *piscina*. Its *ogee* arch is *cusped*, and the *crockets* take the form of naturalistic foliage curling upwards to the *finial*; there are flanking pinnacles, and the spandrels are filled with attractive tracery. *Dropped-sill sedilia* lie alongside. The village had a guild of St John the Baptist before the *Reformation* and it is highly likely that this was their chapel. Moving into the nave, note that the *sanctus-bell window* just below the roof ridge at the w. end has a triangular top, suggesting that it was a Saxon doorway originally. The *font* was given by Elizabeth de Hengrave in about 1380, and although some of the inscription on the top step is missing, her name is still plain on the e. side. It is a well-proportioned piece, with gabled shafts at the angles of the bowl, but the panels have had their carving completely removed (*William Dowsing* was here in April 1643, and while he does not mention the font specifically, the journal says: 'we brake down nine superstitious pictures' and so this may be his doing). Four battered lions support the shaft, and above them is an interesting ring of eight little heads, male and female alternately, somewhat like the ones at nearby Gisleham. The nave n. wall was once covered with medieval wall paintings, and *Cautley* recognised part of a large *St Christopher* before the war. I could make nothing of it. A low tomb recess at the e. end on that side lies below a Norman arch which has *chevron* moulding. It spans just over 7ft. and does not, therefore, fit the galilee entrance and cannot have come from there, but it may conceivably have been saved from a C12 chancel arch dismantled in the C14. There are seven C15 bench ends with *poppyheads* incorporated in the benches on the n. side of the nave, and look for a pretty band of pierced carving set in the front bench; like the gate panels in the C19 tower screen, it may be a remnant of the church's rood screen. The pulpit of 1968 is vaguely *Jacobean* in style, with pierced roundels drawn from the C15. The only *brass* I located lies at the e. end of the nave and is an inscription for Robert Langley who died in 1608. Like the e. window, the large C14 window in the chancel n. wall still has its *jamb shafts*, but it has been entirely blocked up. As you leave, don't overlook the charming little figure of a kneeling woman placed on the plain C16 chest at the w. end. It was carved by Michael Glasscock in 1975, from a piece of the C17 bell frame. And outside, examine the base of a *preaching cross* which lies not far from the porch, and a *scratch dial* on the s.w. corner of the galilee porch.

Nacton, St Martin (G7): The church is beautifully placed – secluded and tree-girt, yet with a view across the dip to the wooded village. A door in the corner of the high churchyard wall leads to Orwell Park, the great house of the Vernons which is now a school. The C19 and early C20 saw great changes here, beginning with a restoration in 1859 by *R.M. Phipson*, whose re-roofing was one of his minor disasters and was already giving trouble by 1866. The small Broke chapel to the s. of the *nave* was added in 1870, and then in 1906 the church was closed for two years during which a major reordering took place under the direction of Charles Hodgson Fowler, an architect better known in the north than in East Anglia. He added an *aisle*, organ chamber, and *vestry* on the n. side, together with a new s. *porch* and e. window; all the roofs were replaced for a second time, and the church was re-floored. No expense was spared and the craftsmanship is excellent – much of it by the estate staff. The C15 tower has plastered, angle buttresses and lacks its belfry stage. The '1788' stone in the w. wall may date both its removal and the addition of the plain brick parapet. The *Perpendicular* w. window has a little embattled *transom* above the centre *light*, and the deep *label* carries inward turning *headstops*. Above it, the canopy of a vanished niche remains embedded in the wall. The tower houses a ring of five bells with a 4 cwt. tenor but they are hung dead and can only be chimed.

Walking round, you will see that Fowler repositioned (and then blocked) the C14 n. doorway, and his organ chamber stands at right angles to the chancel, with a faintly eccentric (and empty) bellcote on the gable. There is a C14 *cusped* lancet and a window with 'Y' tracery of about 1300 in the s. wall of the *chancel*, with a new *priest's door* between them, and there are Perpendicular windows on that side of the nave. Two dormer windows were inserted in the nave in 1870, but for some reason, one of them was removed and the other altered when the roof was replaced. The s. doorway is C14, and the medieval door, with its keeled boards, was originally fitted with a ventilation grill.

Just inside, a *stoup* is set in the wall, and the C15 *font* stands on two broad steps at the w. end. It follows the common East Anglian pattern, and was sharply re-cut during one of the restorations; lions alternate with attenuated *woodwoses* round the shaft, and there are *Evangelistic symbols* and demi-angels in the bowl panels. Their shields display: e. *Instruments of the Passion*, n. St George's cross, w. *Sacred monogram*,

s. *Trinity* emblem. There is a *sanctus-bell window* above the tower arch, and the door to the belfry stair is set in the s.w. corner, some 12ft. from the floor – a sure sign that the upper room was used to store the church and village valuables. The low pine benches with *poppyheads* date from the Phipson restoration, and the nave roof of 1908 is an impressive *tie-beam* and *arch-braced* design constructed largely in redwood. The Broke chapel is furnished with substantial family pews in C15-style oak, with poppyheads and elbow carvings, including a *pelican in her piety*. The simple *Stuart Holy Table* once served as the church's *High altar*. The family vault lies beneath, and their monuments abound. Thomas Denman provided the pair on the s. wall, and although the tablets are typical of his rather uninspired style, one of the epitaphs at least is extraordinary. Sir Philip Bowes Vere Broke commanded the Shannon in its epic encounter with the American frigate Chesapeake during the war of 1812, and the exploit was celebrated in the song 'Brave Broke'. The unusual feature is that the inscription includes an extract from an Admiralty letter to the commander of the North American station, praising Capt. Broke's skill and gallantry in action. The matching tablet commemorates his brother, Maj. Gen. Sir Charles Broke Vere, who served in the Peninsular war and was appointed quartermaster by Wellington during the battle of Waterloo. Another family sailor was Admiral Sir George Broke-Middleton whose memorial is on the w. wall. He served at Navarino against the Turks, and at Sebastopol against the Russians; High Sheriff of the county in 1864, he died in 1887. The n. aisle w. window has good glass of 1913, possibly by *Burlisson & Grylls* – a Nativity scene across the three lights, with excellent angels in the tracery. Nearby, the large tablet is for Admiral Edward Vernon who died in 1757 'as he had lived, the Friend of man, the Lover of his Country, the Father of the Poor'. His wife had died the year before, and he squeezed her epitaph (complete with a reference to his own parliamentary plaudits) in at the top to leave ample room for his own pomposity below. In the window to the e. there are (for the period) curiously old fashioned figures of the Sower, the Good Shepherd, and St Martin, with half of his cloak around the beggar. The glass is by Christopher Charles Powell, and although his output was prolific this is the only example identified in Suffolk. The centre light of the next window is a *Clayton & Bell* St George of 1907, to which two lush archangels were added in 1920

– *St Michael* labelled 'Victory', *St Raphael* labelled 'Peace'. The broad lancet beyond contains a rather flaccid *Blessed Virgin* and Child of 1905, by *Kempe & Tower* (see their emblem in the emphatic oak leaf border) – by no means their best. In the corner, a curious late-C18 tablet commemorates a doctor, Thomas Hewett, and his son who was rector of Bucklesham: 'Their souls it is hoped were carried by the Angels into Abraham's bosom'; the reader is urged to remember his own sinful condition, and Gastrell's *Christian Institutes*, or Mapletoft's *Principles and Duties* are recommended as supplementary reading. There must be copies somewhere, even yet. Across in the nave, a window is filled with a riot of jolly heraldic glass by Clayton & Bell, with eleven variations of the Broke arms displayed, and crests in the tracery. The faintly tedious celebration of family lineage continues on a bronze plate below, engraved with the genealogy from 1545 to 1855. There are two image niches in the window embrasure, and a C14 *piscina* just beyond shows that there was a pre-*Reformation altar* here. The 1908 chancel arch is much wider than the original, and its *corbels* are carved with house martins as a reminder of the church's patron saint. The fine oak choir stalls of the same period have *linen-fold* fronts and narrow, pierced panels along the backs; they were made by Bowmans of Stamford who also provided the pulpit and *communion rails*. The church's only medieval glass is the C14 shield of *Passion emblems* at the top of the chancel s. window, and the *sanctuary* lancet contains an 1860s design which is typical of *William Wailes*. Two panels set within patterns of vine leaves illustrate Jesus's post-Resurrection encounters with *St Mary Magdalene* and *St Thomas*, all in C13 style and attractive colour. This is an example of a *weeping chancel*, and the narrow lancet in its deep splay on the n. side of the sanctuary shows that it must date from the late C12 or early C13. There is more Kempe & Tower glass of 1907 in the e. window. It is a compressed crucifixion flanked by the Blessed Virgin and *St John*, in which angels hold bowls to receive the blood from Christ's wounds, against a leafy background and above a 'gothick' version of Jerusalem; a very feathery '*pelican in her piety*' sustains her young at the bottom, between seated medieval versions of the prophets Isaiah and Jeremiah – all a mite laboured. Nacton's naval tradition is completed by the stone to be found alongside the path on the way back to the gate. It marks the grave of Lieut. Hugh Montgomery who was

Master's Mate on HMS Niad when she first made contact with the enemy at the battle of Trafalgar.

Naughton, St Mary (E6): The village green is secluded and the churchyard, ringed with trees and a secretive stream, makes a beautiful setting for this little church built about 1300. The unbuttressed tower has a single *drip course* below *Decorated* and 'Y' *tracery* bell openings; the *Perpendicular* w. window is restored. All the windows to the n. are renewed and the top half of the C13 n. door is now glazed. A *priest's door* is to be found on that side of the *chancel* and although the e. window is renewed, the one round the corner to the s. has *plate tracery*. The *cusped* outline of C14 barge boards remain above the *porch* door and a bowed, moulded *tie-beam* spans the little plastered ceiling. There are remains of *headstops* to the *hood mould* of the doorway and, beyond it, one enters a simple rustic interior.

The *nave* is brick floored with a range of pitch pine pews, but at the w. end there are clumsy low C17 benches. Some of their seats and backs are warped endearingly and one rail is carved. The nave has a C14 roof whose heavy, cambered tie-beams are braced from *wall posts*, and above them *king posts* rise to a ridge beam that runs from end to end below a plastered ceiling. The *Norman font* now stands in the n. doorway and the corners of the square shallow bowl were lopped off in the C15 or thereabouts when a moulding was worked below. Part of a *St Christopher* painting was uncovered in 1953 on the n. wall and, although indistinct, one can see that the saint had the Christ child on his right shoulder and there was a stencil decoration in the background. Another small fragment discovered over the n. door is unidentified but the shapes suggest two angels facing each other with an animal of some sort in the upper r.-hand corner. There is now no *screen* but half of a doorway and a vestige of the steps of the *rood loft stair* remain in the n. wall, and the mark of the loft shows to the l. of the chancel arch. There was also a nave *altar*, and its C14 *piscina* in the s. wall has a cusped *trefoil* arch and deep drain. Both pulpit and wooden eagle lectern are C19 and the chancel is spanned by heavy C14 tie-beams resting on moulded *wall plates*. The priest's door has been sealed off and in the *sanctuary* is a large piscina of about 1300. The chamber organ of 1777 has a very nice mahogany case and there are delicate frets enclosing the heads of the pipe clusters.

Nayland, St James (D7): In this most attractive village, houses nestle around the church on three sides, with lanes to the s. and e. so that there is open churchyard only to the n. It was one of the most important centres of the Suffolk cloth trade with a population of nearly 400, and rebuilding in the C15 and early C16 made the church large enough to hold them all. The C14 unbuttressed tower, with its two strong *string courses*, was left alone until the early C19 when the top was rebuilt, and it carries a short spire. The bell openings have 'Y' *tracery*, there is a C19 clock to the w., and lower down the belfry is lit by *lancets* under *ogee* arches with *finials* and *headstops*. Four steps lead up to the w. door and it is notable that levels vary curiously throughout the church. The tower houses an excellent ring of 6 bells with a 15 cwt. tenor. William Abell was one of Nayland's wealthy clothiers and, like others of his time and station, he chose to build a new *porch* in 1525 as his memorial, but lack of space on the s. side meant that it had to be sited at the end of the s. *aisle* facing w. – a unique arrangement, as far as I know. There are three very worn *groined* and canopied niches in the frontage with blind panelling and *crocketted* pinnacles above, and there is an angel holding a shield above the *Tudor* inner arch (the interior vaulting and panelling date from a rebuilding of 1884). Towards the e. end of the late-C15 s. aisle an octagonal brick and flint *rood stair turret* juts out, its stone cap with the remains of a finial rising above the roof line. Round the corner in the angle between aisle and *chancel* there is a *priest's door* under a little porch, and the door itself is interesting because above the *linen-fold panelling* is carved: 'John Foum'. The list of known vicars is incomplete, and this may be the name of the priest who had the door installed. The e. window of the C14 chancel has attractive flowing tracery which has been renewed, and there is a n.e. *vestry* which was originally a chapel. The n. aisle has a large niche in the n.e. buttress and although the large side windows are *Perpendicular*, the w. window retains the inter-sected tracery of the earlier C14 building. The main entrance now is through the early-C15 brick n. porch (three steps down) and there is an ogee niche over the inner C14 doorway. The doors are carved with good linen-fold panelling set within a bold vine trail and they have been sensitively renewed.

The interior is beautifully wide and open, with elegant *piers* to the six-bay *arcade*; shafts rise above them to divide the *clerestory* windows into pairs and the 'wall of glass' effect continues over the chancel. The *nave* roof is almost flat and every other *tie-beam* is braced with carved *spandrels*. There are centre *bosses* and the one w. of the pulpit is carved with the head of a *green man*. The *font* stands by the n. door and is either C19 or totally re-cut; the bowl panels are deeply carved with *Evangelistic symbols* set within rays, plus two shields and two large *chalices*. The 1940s oak cover by R.Y. Goodden is a simple design – almost flat, with gabled segments and a centre finial. The plain but stylish C18 w. *gallery* happily accommodates the organ and the area below has been neatly glazed-in as a Sunday School and meeting room. The church has two sets of *Royal Arms*: a large and rather dim one over the n. door on canvas is C18 but it had William IV's initials added later, and a lively little post-1816 *Hanoverian* set on the front of the gallery – three-dimensional, with the painting and gilding beautifully restored.

There are a number of *brasses* to see and the first two lie just within the n. door – parts of a canopy dating from about 1440, and remnants of an 1475 inscription which show that it was for a man called Sekyn and his wife Joan. Of more interest are the two in front of the gallery. The first is for a Mr Hacche and his wife and dates from about 1485 but only the upper half of her effigy and its delicate canopy survives; though worn smooth, it shows her wearing a *butterfly headdress* with a book under her arm. Alongside is a brass of the early C16, with 3ft. figures of a couple under a double canopy – he in fur-lined gown and she with a *kennel headdress*. The same style of dress is to be found on the brass in the n. aisle for Richard and Joan Davy. He was a local clothier who died in 1516 and, apart from the 18in. figures, the interest lies in his merchant's mark on a shield; it bears his initials and a pair of tenterhooks which were used to hold the cloth when it was stretched and dried. To be on tenterhooks was obviously a painful experience. Another example of them can be seen in a window at Stoke by Clare, where they figure in the arms of the Clothworkers Company. A window nearby contains a memorial for Gilbert Warwick, a vicar who died in 1960 – a tall thin panel portraying Christ holding the *chalice* and wafer, with the priest and people below celebrating the Eucharist (I have not been able to identify the artist). The aisle w. window is filled with glass of 1908 by *Kempe & Tower* (see Tower's symbol of wheatsheaf and castle low down on the l.) – a fairly standard design with typical figures of the *Blessed Virgin, St John,* and *St Luke,* but enlivened a little by the six small angels who hold up the background drapery on ribbons. A particularly lovely s. aisle window of 1930 commemorates Edith Caroline Farmiloe and her life work among women and children. The artist was James Clark and Christ the King is shown with a group of old and young villagers, some with faces that are demonstrably portraits.

Farther along is the door to the rood loft stair and from the position of the upper opening you will realise that the loft spanned the whole of the church. There is a *consecration cross* nearby, and on the wall overhead are panels which originally formed part of the late-C15 *rood screen*. They carry the outlines of canopies and are terribly defaced, but enough is left to identify most of them. From l. to r.: *St Cuthbert* with the head of *St Oswald, St Edmund, St Gregory* (who had his papal tiara and staff specifically mutilated in Henry VIII's reign), Henry VI?, *St Edward the Confessor* (the best preserved, shown with the ring he is supposed to have given to St John when the latter was in the guise of a beggar), a king who might be the Emperor Charlemagne, an unidentified king, and an archbishop who was probably *St Thomas of Canterbury*. The e. wall of the n. aisle has a window at high level and the recessed ledge behind the *altar* probably housed a *retable*. To the r. is a C14 *piscina* with a roll moulding to the arch and the curious little recess above it may have been used as an alternative to a *credence shelf*. Four steps lead up to the vestry door in the chancel and the headstops on the *hood mould* boast luxuriant moustaches. Farther along, a tabernacle for the Blessed Sacrament is set within what was originally a *squint* – proving that the vestry beyond was once a chapel. There is a heavily cusped piscina opposite but the eye is constantly drawn to the painting behind the *High altar*. Set in the centre of a C19 *reredos*, it is by John Constable and portrays Christ blessing the bread and wine of the Last Supper. Commissioned and paid for by his aunt who lived in the village, it was painted in 1810 before he became successful, and his father described his activities at the time as 'pursuing a shadow'! Patently, he was hardly doing that. It is one of three altarpieces by him, the others being painted for Brantham and Manningtree in Essex. The e. window is filled with stained glass by Baillie & Mayer of 1869; there are four panels with scenes of the life of Christ and one of the stoning of St Stephen – it has strangely ungainly figures with staring eyes and the panels are set within bright interlace designs.

Its garish restlessness points up the tranquillity of the altarpiece below.

William Jones, vicar here from 1777 to 1800, was a learned divine and a leader of the old High Church party. Known as 'Jones of Nayland', his work inspired Wesley on the one hand and the youthful Newman on the other, anticipating in many ways the work of the Oxford Movement by a generation.

Nedging, St Mary (D6): The lane climbs steeply to this pleasant spot where a few houses keep the small church company in a neat, spacious setting, and there is a view across the valley to the church of the Magdalen at Bildeston. The w. window and bell openings of the tower have *Decorated tracery*, and so too has the s.w. window of the *nave* in more elaborate form, with four *quatrefoils* centred over a pair of *ogee*-headed *lights*. The rest of the windows date from about 1300, and both doorways are *Transitional*. Their round arches contain roll mouldings punctuated with thick rings and the main entrance has an additional *dogtooth hood mould* resting on head *corbels*. The *capitals* of the plain shafts are carved with varying leaf shapes. The n. doorway is blocked, its upper half filled with an C18 'Gothick' window which matches the one in the little *vestry*, and the *chancel* parapet seems to date from the same period. The C17 brick *porch* is now plastered and although its w. window is blocked, the other is fitted with a cunning set of wooden louvres that are controlled by a centre rod.

Within, all is neat and simple. The Decorated tower arch fades into the *imposts* and below is a plain C15 *font* with canted bowl. Its low *Jacobean* cover has rustic scrolls supporting a centre post carved with rudimentary leaves. Floors are paved with humble *pamments* and the C15 benches at the w. end have *poppyheads* and crested elbows. The inner range once carried carved beasts but those by the walls are little towers, and on the n. side one has a man's head resting curiously upon a pillar. C14 roofs have survived in one or two churches in the area and this one has heavy, braced *tie-beams* supporting *king posts* which are braced four ways at the top. Above them is a boarded C19 ceiling. The main range of pews and pulpit are Victorian and, although there is now no chancel *screen*, you will see the doorway and two steps of the stair to the *rood loft* in the n. wall. The chancel ceiling is plastered and in the *sanctuary* the simple C14 *piscina* has a hint of the ogee in its arch. On the s. chancel wall a tablet records how, in the 1880s, the rector lost six of his sons in eight years, two of them at sea.

Needham Market, St John the Baptist (E5): From the outside this is a rather dull, ungainly building with scarcely a hint of the glorious surprise within. Created a parish church in 1901, it began as a chapel of ease for nearby Barking and was rebuilt between the 1480s and the end of the century. William Grey was bishop of Ely from 1454 and 1478 and he appointed his nephew John as rector of Barking in 1477. John is likely to have largely financed the rebuilding. One of the church's oddities is that it is aligned s.e. and n.w., parallel with the street, and there are lanes on the other three sides. Thus there is no graveyard and the limits were set so close that the n.e. buttress had to be pierced to allow processions to circle the chapel within consecrated ground. The bishops of Ely were patrons of the Barking living and there are two worn shields carved at the top of the *priest's door* in the *chancel* s. wall – the arms of the diocese on the l. and those of Bishop Grey on the r. (which pins down the building date). But there was evidently a local benefaction involved because a stone some 12ft. above the door is inscribed:

Pray we all for grace
For he yt hav holpe ys place
God reward he for her ded
& heve' [heaven] may be her meed.

Depending on how one interprets the English of the day, that could refer to guild members who used the church or to a single benefactress. It is interesting that C19 restoration work uncovered the foundations of an earlier chapel and the *dripstone* of the priest's door is a survival from that building. The wall line of *nave* and chancel is continuous and the buttresses on the s. side have niches under worn *crocketted* canopies with, above them, inscription panels which form: 'Crist I.H.S. have merci on us'. One of the buttresses on the n. side carries a similar legend and another combines with an exterior *rood stair turret*. The shallow *clerestory*, with its small windows, adds to the oddity of the building's appearance, looking rather like the cabin top of a large Victorian yacht. The low *vestry* at the w. end was added in 1909 but there are door and arch outlines on the wall above that suggest that there may have been a tower. In 1879 the building was declared unsafe and closed for a major restoration under *John Hakewill* and C.H. Mileham. The nave roof was reconstructed, the chancel roof lowered and replaced, and a bellcote removed from the w. gable. In 1883 H.W. Hayward designed a

Needham Market, St John the Baptist: Nave roof

replacement porch that suits the building quite well, but then went on to add a clock turret and small spire in a bizarre combination.

The s. door has *tracery* within oblong panels that are similar to Barking's w. door, and one enters a spacious nave dominated by a roof which has no parallel in England. With a span of 30ft. a double *hammerbeam* under a conventional ridge might have been expected, but here is a variation of the single hammerbeam design whose technical audacity takes the breath away and stands as a supreme example of the carpenter's art. The hammers are immensely long and half their length is masked by a coved double cornice decorated with angels and *paterae*. The posts on the hammerbeams stretch right up to the low-pitched roof and are braced, first by cambered *tie-beams* e. to w., and then by heavier tie-beams n. to s. Above that, the frame is locked together by a timber clerestory with small windows. Immediately above the cornice, vertical posts backed by boards form a false wall from which springs a canted roof so that the whole upper airy space takes on the form of a clerestoried nave with narrow aisles. Prior to the C19 restoration there was a plaster ceiling 16ft.

below the roof and all but two of the hammerbeams had been cut off. This demanded a virtual rebuilding and all of the lower timbers and the angels are new. There had originally been clerestory windows on the s. side only and those on the n. were added at that time.

Below this splendid tour de force of a roof the church is spacious but undemonstrative. Its length is broken only by the *rood screen* of 1953 which, perhaps wisely, did not attempt to fill the space with tracery but carries the figures on a false gallery front supported only by two plain central posts. There is a large unidentified Madonna and Child painting (C18?) above an *altar* at the w. end and the plain C15 *font* is painted blue, red, and gold, with an *Agnus Dei* carved in the e. bowl panel. The n. door is blocked and in front of it stands what appears to be a section of a *Jacobean* court cupboard. The doors to the original rood loft stair remain in the n. wall and there are two *aumbries* in the chancel – one in the n. wall and another in the n.e. corner. Some fragments of medieval glass have been collected in the *sanctuary* window on that side.

Nettlestead, St Mary (E6): A trim and secluded little church which was badly damaged by enemy action in 1940 and restored to use ten years later. The unbuttressed tower has a stair turret to the s. where fragments of *Norman arcading* show haphazardly in the stonework – they were found, I suspect, during restoration. Its Norman origin is confirmed by a small *lancet* in the n. wall of the *nave* which has similar decorative detail in the arch – minuscule bands of interlaced arches, scrolls, and beads. There is a blocked C14 n. door and the *Perpendicular* windows on that side have lion *stops* to their *dripstones*. The e. window has attractive renewed *Decorated tracery* with a *cinquefoil* and two *trefoils* over three *lights*. The low C16 brick *porch* has a semi-circular gable with a shield of arms above the entrance, and the mouldings of the inner doorway are embellished with large *fleurons*. The early-C15 *font* is notable in that the stem is supported by four crowned lions and the bowl is much shallower than usual; its panels are carved, not only with the familiar *Evangelistic symbols*, but also with a king, a bishop, a face with tongue rudely out, and, to the n.w., *St Catherine* crowned and seated with her wheel alongside. This is interesting because *William Dowsing* noted her specifically when he came in 1644, and although images of six apostles, *SS George, Martin*, and *Simon* have disappeared, she escaped more or less unscathed.

The nave was re-seated to celebrate Queen Victoria's Jubilee in 1897 and plain *tie-beams* span it below a coved plastered ceiling. Halfway along the s. wall there is a small puzzle to ponder over. By the side of the Perpendicular window there is a small *squint* which emerges at an angle in the embrasure. It aligns roughly with the pulpit so there may have been an *altar* there, but what was outside? It seems an unusual place for an *anchorite's cell* but nothing else comes to mind. In the centre of the nave there is a 17in. brass of a man in *Tudor* armour. The inscription has gone but the Wentworth family were Lords of the Manor in the C15 and this might mark the grave of Sir Richard – sometime-high sheriff of Norfolk and Suffolk and present at the Field of the Cloth of Gold in 1520. The *Royal Arms* of George IV are well painted and unusual because the lion and unicorn don't support the oval shield heraldically but emerge from behind it. The *Stuart* pulpit stands on a new stone base and is very compact, with conventional strapwork and blind arch carving in the panels. The position of the door and seat show that it has been turned round. There is no *chancel* arch but there was once a *screen*; the stairs to the *rood loft* remain in the s. wall. The choir benches have

poppyheads and C19 Evangelistic symbols added to the elbows on the s. side, although a lion on the n. side seems original. All the e. window tracery is moulded, the *mullions* are shafted, and there is a smaller blank arch each side painted terracotta most effectively. Stone *Decalogue* tablets flank the altar and the Creed and Lord's Prayer above them form a complete set. The square-headed *piscina* has a multi-*cusped* arch with flower and leaf in the *spandrels* and there are *dropped-sill sedilia* alongside. On the opposite wall the handsome C17 alabaster busts of Samuel and Thomasina Sayer hold hands over a skull and rest on a modern ledge; his arms are displayed in an oval overhead and their epitaphs are on a separate slab below, but the rest of the monument has gone. Stephen Jackson's memorial of 1855 in the n.e. corner of the churchyard will appeal to those with a taste for Victorian extravagence. It is like a *preaching cross* but the shaft is triangular and so is the base, with three large gables festooned with fat *crockets* and *ball flowers*.

Newbourne, St Mary (G6): The C14 tower is not particularly lofty, but the buttresses have no fewer than five *set-offs* below belfry level, imparting solidity and style. There is *Decorated tracery* in the bell openings, and the stepped battlements which were added in the C15 are faced with *flushwork*. The little niche in the s. parapet is an unusual feature, and is similar to the one at Martlesham – an example of the way in which villages adopted each other's ideas; the pinnacles and intermediate figures were replaced in 1885. In common with a score or so of churches in e. Suffolk, Newbourne's tower stands on the s. side of the building, serving as a *porch* and main entrance. A circuit of the building reveals that the w. wall of the *nave* was largely rebuilt in brick in 1810, and the church-warden who put his name to it lies buried in the railed tomb by the path to the porch. The w. window was replaced as part of a major restoration in 1857 by *Richard Phipson*. The C14 n. doorway is blocked, and there is a tiny *Tudor priest's door* on the n. side of the *chancel*. Although it has been bricked up within, the original door survives, with the remnants of a central ventilation grill. The great gale of October 1987 had disastrous consequences here, blowing out the entire e. wall, but happily it has been rebuilt as a memorial to a former churchwarden. The s. *aisle* was built on to the e. side of the tower in the C14, and stretches beyond the nave to overlap the chancel. That in itself is unusual, and is made more so by the outer casing of red brick patterned with blue diaper that was added in the early C16. The roof was replaced at the same time and is almost flat, imparting a curiously restless outline to that side of the church. Two of the Decorated windows were retained, and a new one with *Perpendicular* tracery was inserted next to the tower. By its side, an *Early English* doorway has a steep and deeply moulded arch, with canted king and queen *headstops* and single shafts. This may well have been the chancel's original priest's door, moved at the time of the rebuilding and reused to provide a separate entrance for the chapel. The *jambs* of the porch outer arch have attracted graffiti up to the 1980s, but it is worth looking for the drawing of a ship which was scratched on the inside of the l. jamb, about 4ft. from the ground. No doubt the work of a local mariner, naval historians have dated it 1450-1500, and a descriptive note and illustration are displayed inside the church.

A C15 *font* of the familiar local type stands in the nave, restored and extensively re-cut in the 1840s. Lions alternate with *woodwoses* round the shaft, and there are *Evangelistic symbols* with re-lettered scrolls in the bowl panels. Between them, angels bear shields: s.e. *Trinity emblem* (re-lettered), n.e. *Passion emblems*, n.w. crowned 'M' for the dedication, s.w. cross. The 1850s restoration stripped away plaster ceilings to reveal a fine C15 roof which has canted *hammerbeams* with carved braces, *collar beams* and *king posts* below the ridge. *Henry Ringham* carried out the necessary repairs, and he provided the simple benches below – square-topped ends with paired buttresses. Careful examination of those at the rear of the church reveals that he salvaged sections of the original set and used them as patterns for the new work. The small doorway with a Tudor arch in the n. wall is the entrance to the *rood loft stair* whose robust steps lead to the upper opening. The loft will have been at that level, but only the base of the early-C16 *screen* remains, with minimal tracery in its broad panels. Ringham made the pulpit that stands on a substantial stone base, and copied the tracery pattern in its panels from the C15 stalls in the chancel. The cumbersome reading desk is not one of his best designs by any means, although the *communion rails* are better. The C13 *lancet* just inside the chancel on the r. dates from before the building of the aisle, and its dividing *transom* shows that it was once a *low side window*. There is a C14 *piscina* set in the window jamb of the *sanctuary*, with *dropped-sill sedilia* below. The

e. window has a finely moulded arch, and is interesting because it makes use of late-C12 shafts, one with a fluted *capital*, the other with a lily leaf carving. It has been suggested that the recess behind the altar may have housed a *retable* (bearing in mind that the floor level has been raised), but in its present form it is too deep and the wrong shape for that. The s. aisle, known as the Rowley chapel, was refurnished in 1950 in memory of Cordy and Lucy Wolton. Above the dedicatory tablet on the n. wall there is a lovely bas-relief roundel of 'Monarch' – Charles Bunbury's Suffolk Punch stallion, with rosette on bridle, beribboned mane and tail, carved by H. Brown. The chapel altar is a *Cautley* design, carved by Ernest Barnes, with very delicate *linen-fold* in the front panels, and a pierced vine trail along the back. On the floor to the l. is a C13 grave slab decorated with a floriated cross, and the piscina on the other side is the same age, with *jamb shafts* and the remains of a moulding round its *trefoil* arch. As you leave, pause by the gravestone third on the l. from the porch. Although the long verse epitaph is now almost worn away, one can still see that it commemorates George Page, 'the Suffolk Giant' who died in 1870 aged 26. He was 7ft. 7in. tall and 'was exhibited in most towns in England, but his best exhibition is with his Blessed Redeemer'.

Newmarket, All Saints (A4): Built as a memorial to Lord George Manners in 1875, it replaced an earlier church and part of the original tower was incorporated. It is a heavy and uninspired building in random flint with slate roofs, designed by the Lowestoft architect, W.O. Chambers, and has a conventional layout, except that the tower is offset to the s.w. All Saints has a ring of eight bells with a 10 cwt. tenor but they cannot be rung at the present time. There is a *clerestory* of paired *lancets* alternating with *quatrefoils* and a main *porch* entrance at the w. end. Within, the smooth cylindrical columns of the *nave arcades* have *capitals* heavily carved with stiff flower forms, vaguely *Norman* in style. The *chancel* arch comes down to triple *colonnettes* whose capitals are carved with wheat and grapes, and there is a boarded waggon roof beyond. The chancel was enlarged in 1887 and a new e. window installed – three large stepped lancets, deeply splayed, with polished marble shafts. Below, the *sanctuary* is panelled in oak, with a carved and gilded surround to the *reredos*. The *sedilia* and *piscina* match the e. window. The tapestry panels of angels standing under canopies on the

n. wall of the chancel were worked by Sir George Mellers in 1940. The oak pulpit has painted panels of *SS Mark, Paul* and *Luke*. The window arrangement at the w. end is unconventional, with a row of five short lancets below the w. window proper. They have glass by C.A. Gibbs – the *Four Evangelists* with the Good Shepherd in the centre. The w. window itself has glass of 1880 – figures of *SS Peter, James the Great, Paul, Philip* and *Stephen* in the tall main *lights*, and conventional angels in the *tracery*. The westernmost window in the n. aisle has glass in somewhat virulent colours by W.H. Constable and the heads of the figures are in Victorian portrait style, now rather faded. The window in the n. side of the sanctuary is probably by the same artist. The two other windows in the n. aisle are by *Powell & Sons* – Christ with his disciples in one and the *Annunciation* in the other. The w. end of the church has been rearranged to provide a meeting room in place of the old baptistery and a general purpose area, cleared of pews, at the w. end of the nave. The church's only treasure, a *Burne-Jones* cartoon, was sold to help meet the cost of the new venture.

Newmarket, St Agnes (A4): The Bury road into Newmarket, lined with spacious houses and racing stables, is the setting and this small church lives up to it. It began as the Crawfurd memorial church, a private chapel built by the Duchess of Montrose as a burying place for her second husband, and it was consecrated as a parish church in 1887. Designed by R.H. Carpenter and built in 1885 with a lavish disregard for cost, it has happily been left alone and encapsulates late Victorian taste. Contrasted with Elveden, it is richness with restraint, devoid of eccentricity, using traditional forms to create a genuine style. In red brick with stone dressings, it has a slim octagonal tower on the n. side, the belfry stage carrying a small spire ringed with *crocketted* gables. The w. window is cut short by a lean-to baptistery below, the *chancel* rises slightly above the *nave* and its e. end has *Early English*-style *blind arcading* continuing over recesses which reach to the ground.

The interior is very dark and does not come to life until the lights are switched on, but then the impression is exciting. A simple *scissors-braced* nave roof with *cusped* braces and a waggon roof in the chancel keep the attention down, and the eye is drawn to the e. end where, instead of a window, there is a large white marble *reredos* set in a round-headed recess. Sculpted by Sir Edward Boehm, this bas-relief has *St Agnes* carrying her lamb being borne up by angels from the Colosseum, while cherubs peep from the clouds. The subject was the cause of some agitation at the time, but the Duchess (Caroline Agnes) had her way. Above is an arcade within which are mosaic figures of saints against a gold background, and this treatment is sumptuously continued up to the roof. There is another mosaic of the *Blessed Virgin, St Patrick* and *St George* on the n. wall of the *sanctuary*. A two-bay arcade on the s. side of the chancel opens on to a family pew area which has its own entrance. The nave and part of the sanctuary walls are lined with majolica tiles patterned in blue, cream and buff – again, a rich effect, but the woodwork is rather dull (oak for the chancel, pulpit and altar, pitchpine for the nave). A large painting of the Last Supper by an unknown Italian artist hangs on the n. wall but is not well enough lit to be appreciated. All the windows have stained glass, most of it by *Clayton & Bell*; there are saints (mainly women) in the nave, all with their emblems, and the w. window contains attractive figures of the angels *Gabriel, Michael, Raphael* and *Uriel*. By way of a little period postcript, the organ was designed by Sir Arthur Sullivan – what better setting for 'The Lost Chord'?

Newmarket, St Mary (A4): The church lies n.w. of the High Street in an area transformed since the war by new housing and a shopping precinct. Newmarket was part of the parish of Exning until the C16, but there was a chapel of the Blessed Mary here in the C13. It was rebuilt and extended on the s. side in the C15 but most of what we see now is the result of major rebuilding in 1857, 1867 and 1887, during which a n. *transept* was converted into an *aisle*, the *chancel* was completely rebuilt and a new *vestry* added alongside. The tower is C15, with a slim shingled spire set well back from the parapet, and has a separate bellcote on one corner. It houses an excellent ground floor ring of six bells with a 21 cwt. tenor. Within the restored s. *porch*, the doorway is C15 (now badly damaged) and has an angel with a shield set in the moulding at the top. Inside, the chancel is rather dark, but the *nave* is tall, bright and spacious. The C15 s. *arcade*, with *quatrefoil piers* and battlemented *capitals* was matched on the n. side in the rebuilding. The w. window *tracery* is original and the glass of 1930 is by Christopher Webb – an *Annunciation* set in clear glass, with a backing of *Renaissance* architectural detail. This is most attractive and there is more of his work in the n. aisle – a series of different compositions in three windows on the childhood of Christ. The set calls for completion with a Flight into Egypt in the fourth window. The wrought-iron tower screen has an interesting mixture of Gothic and *Art Nouveau* motifs, and on either side there are large benefaction boards. These are worth studying for the practical details of C17 charity – cades of herrings, stones of beef, twopenny bread, and warps of salt fish. On the w. wall of the n. aisle is a large painting of the *Blessed Virgin* and Child with *St Elizabeth* and *St John the Baptist*. It is by Giovanni Battista Caracciolo, an early-C17 follower of Caravaggio. Clamped to the wall in that corner is a section of lead from the old roof, embossed with the names of C18 churchwardens and the plumber. A small glass case on the wall at the e. end of the n. aisle contains a linen purse that was found when the *High altar piscina* was uncovered in 1857. It contained three early-C16 Nuremberg trade tokens but these are no longer on display. The screen to the n. aisle Lady chapel is a war memorial and the shafts on either side of the doorway carry small, well-carved figures of *St George* and St Joan of Arc. There is a large painting on the *sanctuary* n. wall here by James Wood of Jesus entering Jerusalem, but having been placed over an unshielded radiator it is deteriorating. There is a section of wood placed behind the *altar* which carries a medieval inscription asking us to pray for the soul of Thomas Wydon who had benches made in 1494, possibly in conjunction with the first rebuilding. To the r. is a *Decorated* piscina with foliage in the *spandrels*. The High altar is backed by an oak-panelled *reredos*, and to the r. is the C13 angle piscina rediscovered in the C19. It is *groined* within and one of the *corbel* heads is original. The C19 stone pulpit is more pleasing than most and has openwork tracery panels. The s. aisle has a number of well-lettered C18 tablets which illustrate the move from Renaissance to classical detailing. There is a C19 coarsely cut epitaph in Latin to the unfortunate (or he might have said fortunate) Robert Cook, a C17 rector who died while preaching in the pulpit. Further e., the *cinquefoiled* recess in the wall was probably a piscina, although there is now no sign of a drain. Nearby, a 1907 window by *Kempe & Tower* shows a very traditional rendering of 'Suffer little children . . .' across three *lights*, with musical angels above. The s. aisle chapel of the Blessed Sacrament has two oil paintings, both un-attributed; one is a 'Descent from the Cross' and the other 'The Blessed Virgin and St Elizabeth' in C17 Italian style. Nearby is an interesting sidelight on the social attitudes of

1886 – a masonic memorial window, with figures of Solomon and *St Etheldreda* (the name of the lodge) and innumerable and no doubt significant symbolic objects. A very minor footnote to history: Cardinal Wolsey's father was an Ipswich butcher, but he was born and buried here, although nothing marks his grave.

Newton, All Saints (D6): Nowadays the *chancel* is the parish church and the rest of the C14 building is cared for by the *Churches Conservation Trust* – a happy arrangement whereby everything is beautifully maintained. The w. window of the plain tower has been renewed but the *headstops* are interesting; one is a C14 woman and the other is a devil's mask superimposed upon a second. There is new *tracery* in one of the bell openings and the battlements are of brick. The tower houses a ring of five bells with a 7 cwt. tenor, but they are hung dead and can only be chimed. The n. door is blocked with its upper half glazed, but it was part of an earlier *Norman* building. The shafts have scalloped *capitals* and the deep roll moulding of the arch is set between bands of *chevrons*. The inner one has an unusual variation, with little truncated pyramids pointing inwards from the chevron intersections. On walking round, you will find more good C14 headstops, including a pair of jovial men on the n. side of the *nave*, a man and a snarling dragon above the modern n.e. *vestry*, and two more on the *dripstone* of the shortened window in the s. chancel wall. A stone just e. of the chancel marks the grave of Amos Todd, who died in 1822 and was an officer in the early days of the yeomanry. It reflects the zeal of the movement:

> He commanded for many years the 1st Regiment of Suffolk Yeomanry Cavalry and was so much respected by the Colonel and the Members of the Troop that they have caused this Stone to be erected as a lasting Proof thereof.

Churchyards are often blessed with fine trees and here there is a rare mature specimen of a small-leaved lime, to be found n.e. of the large oak e. of the chancel. The sides of the wooden s. *porch* are now glazed and the roof renewed, but the C14 *tie-beam* and *king post* are still in place above the contemporary doorway with its large, worn headstops and pilgrim cross cut in the r.-hand *jamb*.

Within the spacious, uncluttered nave a C15 *font* stands in front of the n. door. It has a shallow bowl with pairs of *quatrefoils* in each face and is uncharacteristically gawky. A C19 *bier* can be found under the tower and a C20 horse plough at the w. end of the nave. In 1967 an interesting sequence of large C14 wall paintings was discovered on the n. wall and was restored by Miss Eve Baker in the 1970s. The left section illustrates the *Annunciation*; the centre is badly damaged but it is the *Visitation* with an angel to the l. and the *Blessed Virgin* and *St Elizabeth* embracing to the r. The 3rd panel is the Nativity, with the babe lying between the heads of ox and ass and the studding partition of the stable showing below. In front of the painting the C15 pulpit has good tracery in the heads of the panels and an inscription cut below to com-memorate the donors: 'Orate p. aia Richi Modi et Leticie [consortis suae]' (Pray for the souls of Richard Mody and Laetitia his wife). A tomb recess in the wall opposite contains the effigy of a woman which was found under the nave floor in the C19. It is probably back in its rightful position and conceivably com-memorates Christina de Moese, whose second husband was Lord of the Manor. The face of the life-size figure has been destroyed but considering its history it is in good condition, the hands at prayer and dainty feet showing below the long gown. There are matching *piscinas* under *ogee* arches at the e. end, marking the sites of two nave *altars*, and the chancel arch is now filled with a simple glazed screen.

The parish church in miniature is now entered by the *priest's door* and an abutment e. of the nave/chancel junction may mark the position of a *rood stair.* There are solid modern oak benches and the wooden lectern is an interesting C17 example from a period when few seem to have been made. It has a turned and carved stem and the decoration of the oblong desk, with its elegant, sinuous brass candle-holder, was old-fashioned from the beginning. A *brass* inscription on the n. wall commemorates Maria Weatherall who died in childbirth in 1624. Her husband was rector here but her epitaph reminds posterity that her father, John Domelaw, was vintner to Queen Elizabeth and James I. The tomb on the n. side of the *sanctuary* is one of the finest in the county for its period and almost certainly commemorates Margaret Boteler, who was Lady of the Manor from 1393 to 1410. The effigy, in a cloak with large rose brooches, lies within a recess under a *cusped* and *crocketted arch*, and the richly panelled *spandrels* are topped by a straight frieze. There are eight shields in the spandrels, five on the chest, and an extra large one held by

an angel beyond the effigy. All have been re-coloured by members of the Suffolk Heraldry Society and a helpful key is provided. On the s. side is a handsome early-C14 suite of piscina and *sedilia*. The piscina is like a small *Decorated* two-*light* window and was obviously designed for two drains although there is only one now. The contemporary e. window has *reticulated* tracery with considerable remains of C14 glass, including a number of shields. They are: top row from l. to r., the families of Deane, Seymour (St Maure), Bottevilleyn; the bottom row has the arms of England and France in the centre, Peyton on the l. and Peach on the r. There are sections of C15 glass in the s. windows, including a lion roundel (*St Mark?*).

North Cove, St Botolph (I2): The slim, unbuttressed tower displays lots of thin red brick, particularly at the corners, and the small w. *lancet*, belfry lancets and bell openings are all in brick. An attractive thatched roof stretches over *nave* and *chancel*, and the prominent ledge below the eaves marks the original height of the walls. There are short *Perpendicular* windows in the nave, and although they were renewed in an 1870s restoration, the *Decorated* windows in the chancel probably echo the originals. The C14 s. *porch* has widely spaced *paterae* in the mouldings of its entrance arch, the roof has been renewed, and it shelters a handsome *Norman* doorway. The bulky arch has three bands of ornament – ridged bobbins, chevrons, and nailheads, and there are scalloped *capitals* and bases to the paired shafts. The well-defined *scratch dial* on the r. was naturally deprived of its function when the porch was built.

Within, the nave lies under an *arch-braced* roof which has been plastered out so that only the spines of the main timbers show through. There are *castellated wall plates*, and the *wall posts* rest on a nice selection of wooden head *corbels*, with one enjoying a quiet joke on the s. side. The early-C15 *font* is in good condition, its shaft ringed with attached columns, and the fine heads carved below the bowl are so like those at Mutford and Gisleham that the same mason probably carved all of them. The panels contain demi-angels bearing shields and curiously cramped lions, and there are traces of colour. The *hatchment* on the n. wall was carried at the funeral in 1850 of Thomas Farr of Beccles, and the C17 text roundels, with their green leaf borders and rustic capitals, were uncovered in 1937 and may have formed part of a larger series like those at Hemingstone and Witnesham. Two

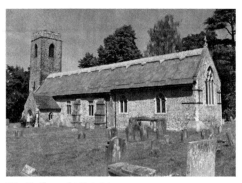

North Cove, St Botolph

of them were overlaid by later memorials – a 1790s tablet and obelisk for Lorina and John Farr, with an eight line stanza in typically period style, and a draped sarcophagus enlivened by a coloured shield of arms for another John Farr who died in 1824. The *brass* inscription on the n. wall commemorates Margaret Berney who died in 1548. It is a 'palimpsest' or reused brass, and it is held in a hinged frame so that the earlier inscription can be examined. It was originally fixed to the church's old *mensa* which lies in the nave floor, hidden (like three other brass inscriptions) under the carpet. Benches, pulpit, and *screen* are C19, and there is no chancel arch. Note, however, the pair of hooks above the screen that probably secured the *lenten veil* in front of the original *rood*. It is not known who provided the church's stained glass, but it may have been a local artist, probably during Edmund Boycott's incumbency 1873-1890. He chose the three most popular subjects of the day for the e. window panels, and the use of colour is interesting in a style that is reminiscent of C19 steel engravings; above and below, the quarries are painted with *Sacred monograms*, *chalices*, crowns of thorns and other emblems. The attractive *Evangelistic symbols* in the heads of the chancel side windows are probably by the same hand.

St Botolph's finest and most interesting feature is the series of C14 wall paintings in the chancel. Restoration has recently been completed, and they are undoubtedly the best work of the period in the county, remarkably well preserved. Unlike many others, the main subjects are easily identifiable: n. wall, w. end, Christ entering the gate of Jerusalem on an ass, with a garment being spread before him; below, Our Lord carrying his cross while being scourged and led by a rope; to the r., he is being nailed to the cross while two men ply the sponge and spear; further

to the r., Christ is taken from the cross. His tormentors, particularly those nailing him to the cross, have swinish faces, and their tunics and hose of red and yellow motley distinguish them from the other figures. Above the main scenes there is a fragmentary line of figures, with a corpse sitting up in a coffin on the l., and part of another C17 roundel has survived there. On the *sanctuary* n. wall there is a Resurrection scene at the top; only Christ's legs survive above the tomb, but the two sleeping soldiers are finely depicted below. To the r. is a gaping beast's hell's mouth, with a saint standing guard, and the rest of the space is taken up with a coarse vine pattern. Medieval artists' shorthand for the Ascension was a pair of feet disappearing into the clouds, and the painter used it on the s. wall of the sanctuary, with the twelve *apostles* grouped below. By far the largest scene is a doom which takes up most of the s. chancel wall. Christ in Majesty wears a spotted robe and is flanked by the *Blessed Virgin* and *St John*; an angel on the l. holds the cross, with the nails tucked into his belt, and another bears a spear on the other side; a third welcomes the blessed on the l., balanced by his partner who banishes the damned with a sword, while a line of the heavenly host trumpets above the dead as they rise from their coffins below.

Norton, St Andrew (D4): The church is very isolated at the end of a lane off the road to Great Ashfield. It is however a sweet situation, with a line of tall limes leading up to the s. door, and the old rectory standing foursquare beyond. Flint and stone chequerwork was a popular decoration locally in the C15 and here it can be seen on the s. *porch* parapet and in the *base course* which continues along the s. *aisle* with its large *gargoyles*. The *chancel* dates from the end of the C13 but there were restorations in the 1880s and the s. wall was rebuilt with new windows, although a *lancet* remains above the *priest's door*. On the nearby buttress, the centre hole of a *scratch dial* will be found some 3ft. from the ground. The e. window *tracery* illustrates how *Decorated* and *Perpendicular* forms may sometimes be found in charming conjunction. Round the corner, the little C15 *vestry* has been fitted with diminutive sash windows, only the second time I have found them in an East Anglian church. There is a Decorated window in the n. wall of the chancel with *headstops* on the *dripstone*. Outside the early-C14 n. door is a compact *stoup* under a *Tudor* arch. The early-C14 tower has Decorated tracery in the w. window, but it was a long time in the building because money was left for its completion in 1442. By the n.w. corner of the n. aisle, a monument topped with a draped urn for the Williams family is strong on epitaphs. For Charles (1877) we have:

Forbear dear children to mourn and weep,
While sweetly in the dust I sleep.
This toilsome world I've left behind,
A glorious crown I hope to find.

Amen to that! Like the s. aisle, the porch was added in the C15 and there is a modern *St Andrew* in the niche over the entrance.

Just inside the C15 doors is a lovely little chest, hewn out of a solid trunk whose natural curve forms rough feet at each end. Although churchwardens' initials and the date '1604' have been carved on the front, it must date from the C13. To the l. of the tower arch is a curious and interesting monument. It is a large stone block painted grey and dull pink, with an *ogee* arch forming a recess on top. There are three obelisks, painted with scroll patterns, and within the arch is the faint figure of a skeleton with hour glass and scythe and the inscription: 'As the glasse runneth, so life wasteth'. There was a *brass* plate fixed to the front which recorded the charity of Daniel Bales who, when he died in 1625, established a bread charity for the village; loaves for distribution to the poor were still being placed in the arched recess within living memory. Photographs of C19 rectors hang within the tower and the *quoins* of the former *nave* walls show up on either side of the tower arch. Idle hands have long been at work on the stonework; Robert Fuller cut his name quite elegantly in 1754 on the n. *jamb* of the arch. The early-C15 *font* is in superb condition and is highly individual; the square shaft panels contain two tiers of tracery and there are standing figures at the corners, including those two old adversaries the *woodwose* and the lion. The bowl panels are deeply carved with *Evangelistic symbols*, together with a *griffin*, a double-headed eagle, and a *pelican in her piety*. The last panel contains a *unicorn*, and although it often occurs on bench ends, it is rare on a font. It was one of the symbols of the *Blessed Virgin*, and underneath the bowl there is another, the winged hearts sprouting flowers. The octagonal *piers* of the nave *arcades* have concave faces topped with blank *trefoiled* ogee arches. The nave and aisle roofs were rebuilt in 1897 and the nave benches installed in 1907, but those in the aisles are C15. They have *poppyheads* and grotesques on the gabled elbows like the ones at Stowlangtoft (including a priest

with his rosary on the n. side). The ends, however, are not traceried and there are no poppyheads by the walls. There is a plain niche *piscina* in the s. aisle and in the n. aisle, the vestige of another – just a rough mark in the stonework with a drilled hole. There will have been *altars* by both of them and the sill of the window in the n. aisle is lowered so that it probably housed a *retable*. The stairs to the *rood loft* went up on this side (see the fragmentary steps behind the C19 pulpit and the small window above the piscina). The *hood mould* of the chancel arch comes down to small *corbel* heads and the arch itself is grooved to house the *tympanum*. To the r. is a stone block which may have served to support the rood loft, and it is pierced by a hole so that a rope may have passed through it to control the *Lenten veil* over the rood itself. Two *brass* inscriptions have been moved to the wall beneath, both for rectors – Edmund Coket (see also the Ampton entry), and John Rokewood, a member of the family who not only entertained Queen Elizabeth at Euston but provided one of the conspirators in the Gunpowder Plot (see also Stanningfield). The chancel roof is medieval, with *arch-braces* and embattled *collars* under the ridge. The bay over the *sanctuary* was painted as a *celure* and the decoration can still be seen on the deep *wall plates* and on the braces. Although they will almost certainly have come from elsewhere (perhaps even the abbey at Bury), three fine ranges of stalls with *misericords* can be found in the chancel. On the n. side, the raised seats reveal carvings of the martyrdom of St Andrew, the *pelican in her piety*, and a lovely vignette of a woman carding wool. On the s. side is a monk at his books and a martyrdom of *St Edmund* which is much more spirited than the *boss* in the Norwich cathedral cloister. In the sanctuary, the misericords are carved with three animal groups – a lion savaging a woodwose, a pretty pair of greyhounds, and the fragment of another. The elbows are carved as well, and one in the last group has a young lad being soundly birched. Overhead, the tracery of the window contains some C14 and C15 figures: from l. to r., *St Margaret*, a beautiful *St Christopher*, a saint with a palm frond, an unidentified figure, *St Etheldreda* and St Andrew. In the lancet above the priest's door is a very good panel of an angel with a *thurible* that once held the e. window, and in the top r. of the s. aisle e. window is the figure of *St Appollonia*, complete with a tooth held in massive pincers. Four C15 shields of Ashfield family arms are set in a n. aisle window. William Clarke, who was rector for the first 30 years of the C19, has a plain tablet by de Carle of Bury on the n. side of the chancel. More pleasing are the memorials for two other rectors on the e. wall – the one for Andrew Pern (1772) has a very perky shield and crest. In all this is a sweet little church.

Nowton, St Peter (C4): This little church is well away from the hamlet and stands on a rise among open fields, backed to the w. by pine trees. The building was enlarged and altered in 1843 and the *chancel* restored in 1876, all so thoroughly that the result was practically a new building, with a neo-*Norman* n. *aisle* and heavy *arcade*, windows to match on the s. side, and quaintly domestic ventilation dormers in the roof. However, the original Norman n. doorway was re-set beneath a steep little gablet and has leaf *capitals* to the columns, and there is a plain Norman s. doorway; a tiny Norman *lancet* was placed in the e. wall of the new aisle. The *chancel* retains its late-C13 or early-C14 windows with intersected *tracery* in the e. window, and the arches of the side windows betray a hint of the *ogee* shape. The C14 unbuttressed tower has two strong *string courses, Decorated* tracery in the windows, and renewed battlements with corner pinnacles. It houses a ring of six bells with a 7 cwt. tenor but they are not ringable at the present time.

The interior is rather dark and a ponderous C19 polished marble *font* stands beyond the tall tower arch. On the w. wall of the *nave* on the s. side is a small memorial by the fashionable sculptor *John Bacon the Younger*. It is for Elizabeth Oakes who died in 1811, and a mourning woman drapes herself over an angled sarcophagus. There is no chancel arch and the *arch-braced* roof is continuous, with plastered and boarded ceilings. The C19 benches are replicas of those at Little Whelnetham and there is a C19 eagle lectern, but the northern half of the *screen* is medieval. The tall C14 niches on each side of the e. window were drastically restored, probably when the panelling below was installed in the 1870s; the original *piscina* is set within it. It is most unusual to find C19 *misericords* but there are six here, and the undersides are well carved in traditional fashion with the arms and names of rectors from 1750 to 1875; all is the work of the Bury carver Henry Wormald.

What makes Nowton so special and puts it high on the list of churches not to be missed is the fabulous series of 84 continental C16 and C17 glass roundels, one of the finest in

Nowton, St Peter: Continental glass – Christ's betrayal

England. They were collected by Col. Rush-brooke in the early years of the C19 and then sold to Orbell Ray Oakes, the Lord of the Manor, who had installed them here by 1820. They are set within richly enamelled painted rosettes, borders and other decorations and these were probably the work of Samuel Yarington of Norwich. Most of the colour in fact, in the e. window particularly, derives from the setting rather than the roundels. The C19 rebuilding entailed rearrangement of the glass but the collection is virtually complete; the bottom panels of the e. window came from a collection formerly at Dagnam Park, Essex and were added in 1970. The roundels display both religious and secular scenes and are mainly from the Netherlands. Binoculars are useful when studying the e. window but one of the pleasures of the collection is that the majority of the roundels can be seen at close quarters, and they are fascinating. I found the following particularly interesting: n. aisle w. end, the nailing of Christ to the cross in chilling detail; chancel n. window, top l., a professor and students of (probably) the university of Leuven, with a little academic dog in the middle; chancel n. window, top r., Anger (one of a series on the human passions), in which a man holds another by the throat as he stabs him; chancel n. window, Job kneeling with his back to us while assorted chunks of classical architecture rain down on his unfortunate family; e. window, l.-hand *light* towards the bottom, Adam naming the animals; e. window, centre light, centre, *St Christopher* being tortured by having a red-hot helmet lowered on his head; e. window, centre light, bottom, Christ taken captive – a very vigorous scene full of movement, with Peter striking off Malchus' ear; s. chancel, bottom l., Christ carrying the Cross assisted by Simeon, while *St Veronica* holds the cloth with the imprint of Jesus' face upon it – one of the outstanding pictures here; nave, easternmost window, Christ and the woman of Samaria at the well, and the Judgement of Solomon, with the soldier about to cleave the tiny child in swaddling bands. The space at the bottom of some of the windows has been filled (rather strangely) with C19 figures of knights in the style of monumental brasses – all lying on their sides. At the w. end is a much smaller German roundel, dated 1643, of the Baptism of Christ, which is a good example of enamelled work as opposed to painted glass, and below are the C19 arms of squire Oakes, the benefactor who 'embellished and decorated' this church in such splendid fashion. For those who would like to know more, there is a full description of the glass in the Suffolk Records Office in Bury, and a shortened version by William Cole was published in *Crown in Glory* edited by Peter Moore.

Oakley, St Nicholas (F3): The church is isolated, along with the rectory, and to the n. the fields drop gently down to the Waveney, giving a pleasant prospect across to Scole and Billingford. A large oaken *lych-gate* of 1908 forms the entrance to the spacious churchyard. The buttresses of the tower extend in line with the e. face of the tower to make it seem wider, but those to the w. are angled, with a tall two-*light Decorated* window between them. There are four *set-offs* with a single *string course* below the Decorated bell openings, and the battlements are faced with *flushwork*. The tower houses a ground floor ring of six bells with a 10 cwt. tenor but they are not able to be rung at the present time. The n. wall of the *nave* is plastered, with a small blocked door and *Perpendicular* windows, and a box-like little early-C19 *vestry* is attached to the n. side of the *chancel*. The handsome Perpendicular e. window has a *castellated transom* above the *ogee tracery* of the four lights, and the *dripstone* rests on bishop and king *headstops*. The line of nave and chancel is continuous, but notice that there are *quoins* showing at the join, which proves that the

original chancel was narrower. The early-C15 s. *porch* is quite lavish and the whole of its frontage is decorated with flushwork, including the buttresses in which are set crowned initials – one of them an 'N' for the patron saint. The arch is flanked by niches and the shields in the *spandrels* bear the arms of the Crane family, who were presumably the donors. A canopied niche stands between two windows which once lit an upper room and there is a later sundial below the battlements. Prominent *gargoyles* occur on either side and there were probably standing figures on the corner pinnacles. A lozenge in the e. window of the porch contains an attractive little C15 *St Christopher* in yellow stain, and there are lots of interesting fragments of medieval glass in the window opposite, including the head of a bearded man and three heraldic hooks. Many *stoups* were smashed after the *Reformation* as symbols of superstition but Oakley's still has a complete bowl below a *trefoil* arch.

Within, the *tie-beams* of the nave roof are braced down to *wall posts*, some of which rest on tiny wooden figures. There are deep *castellated wall plates* and flower *bosses* (which were possibly renewed during the 1870s restoration, when the chancel roof was replaced). The church contains some interesting Victorian glass and the w. window is by *Heaton, Butler & Bayne*, showing the angel appearing to Cornelius the centurion in a vision (Acts 10:1). There are four bench ends with *poppyheads* at the w. end, and the one nearest the door is carved as an angry mask with its tongue out. The *font* is a very rough octagon on a short round shaft, and in the n. wall there is a very strange arrangement of two niches side by side, one taller than the other but matching in most respects. They have deeply moulded *crocketted* ogee arches, with *paterae* in the spandrels and cresting over one of them. They would have contained statues and one wonders which saints were paired thus (but perhaps one was originally elsewhere). Farther along, the *rood stair* is boldly cut in a window embrasure and continues within the wall to emerge level with the spring of the chancel arch. On the s. side there is a *piscina* under a trefoil arch, with *dropped-sill sedilia* alongside, marking the site of a nave *altar*. The wooden eagle lectern on a turned stem dates from 1908. In the s. chancel window, 1870s glass by Heaton, Butler & Bayne portrays Christ and Simeon with the *Blessed Virgin* and *St Anne*; a rich but restrained treatment of colour which is very attractive. Much less so is the glum trio of *SS Nicholas, George,* and *Edmund* opposite, but the full display of St Nicholas's symbols gives the window some interest. The s. *sanctuary* window is of the same period and portrays, with *St Stephen*, two saints rarely seen – *St Longinus* and *St Denys*. There is a large C14 angle piscina nearby and the large trefoil arch has leaf carving in the spandrels, with a smaller, matching opening to the w. There were dropped-sill sedilia originally but the space was taken in 1611 by the large tomb of Sir William Cornwallis. Unusually austere for the period, its only decoration is an alabaster *achievement of arms* in deep relief on the end; it was coloured originally. There are some well-carved modern poppyheads on the choir stalls (one displaying peasecods) and on the n. side of the sanctuary a marble *credence shelf* is backed by a gilded wooden bust of St Nicholas in low relief within a wreath; there are three cherub heads at the top, and below the shelf the saint's emblem of three golden balls lies within attractive scrollery. The 1880s e. window, probably again by Heaton, Butler & Bayne, displays scenes of the Nativity, Crucifixion, Resurrection, and the *Three Marys*, and there are *Passion emblem* shields and musical angels in the tracery. The painted stone reredos of 1882 has the scene of the Last Supper backed with gold mosaic, flanked by panels of ancient sacrifices, and the rest of the wall is filled with tiles and mosaic, mainly in a dusky pink – very pleasing.

Occold, St Michael (F3): The early-C15 tower has a panelled *base course* with flint below a shallow *ashlar arcade*. There are fragments of carving in the *spandrels* of the w. door, *fleurons* on the square *label*, and more of them along with crowns in the mouldings of the arch. There is a three-*light* w. window and the bell openings have *Decorated tracery* below the stepped *flushwork* battlements. There is a ground floor ring of five bells with an 8 cwt. tenor but they cannot be rung at the present time. On the n. side of the *nave* is a small C14 door, and the shape of a *rood stair* shows against a later brick buttress. The *sacristy* n. of the *chancel* is small in scale but had an upper room originally, and a *Norman lancet* peeps out just to the w. of it. The intersected 'Y' tracery of the early-C14 chancel e. window has been renewed, and on the s. side there is a small *priest's door*. Nearby, an early-C14 *cusped* lancet is decorated with *ball flower* ornament and the *dripstone* has shallow mask *headstops*. The simple s. *porch* has had part of its C14 outer arch encased in brick and plaster and there is a small, plain inner doorway.

Within the base of the tower you will find a very unusual painted memorial board for Stephen Humfrey who, in 1598, 'departed this life Very old and full of Daies'. His descendants are listed down to 1638 but the last two did not have their dates added – the family either died out or laid the custom aside. The n. door is blocked and above it are the *Royal Arms* of Charles II, simply painted in pale colour with no shading. The C15 *font* has plain recessed bowl panels and now stands in front of the n. door, with blue and buff C19 tiles decorated with the *Evangelistic symbols* around the base. The e. splays of two nave windows contain pretty Decorated niches which vary in design. Both have surface carving on the cusps below *crocketted ogee* arches, but the one on the s. side is flanked by pinnacles and the n. window displays delicate *jamb shafts* with miniature *capitals*. There is some *Jacobean* panelling against the n. wall and farther along you will see that the vanished *rood loft* could evidently be approached from both sides. There is the shape of a door on the n. side (where the stair shows outside) and steps lead up from the s. window embrasure through a little arch. By it stands a fine *Stuart* pulpit on a low stem. The blind arches in the panels are vigorously carved (with some careful restoration) and there are pierced brackets to the book ledge. The remains of the backboard, initialled and dated 1620, are now inside the pulpit and the *tester* has turned pendants and well-carved panels below the cornice. Behind the pulpit there is a C14 *piscina* in the s. wall and it looks as though the chancel was deliberately offset to the n. to allow enough space for a nave *altar* here. The church's only *brass* is in the centre of the nave where there are 27in. effigies of William and Joan Corbald of about 1490. Their slim figures are well worn and he has long hair and wears a fur-trimmed tunic, with a pouch and a heavy rosary. She has an early form of *kennel headdress* and the chequered pavement they stand on was once inlaid. There are large male and female head *corbels* to the chancel arch and beyond, four panels of the old *rood screen* have been incorporated in the choir stalls which have some original *poppyheads*. The lancet on the s. side contains a C14 painted figure in the embrasure and there is a trail of ivy leaves in the arch moulding – all that remains of what was probably an overall scheme of decoration. The original sacristy door survives, with ring handle and key escutcheon, and large *paterae* decorate the arch moulding. Opposite, the priest's door has a little inner porch, with *dropped-sill sedilia* and piscina to the e. The *reredos* is C19 but there is a single stall in the *sanctuary* with a good *misericord* carving of a crowned woman supported by angels. Unfortunately, there are only unidentifiable fragments of medieval glass and the reason is to be found in *William Dowsing's* journal entry for August 1644: 'Divers superstitious pictures were broke. I came, and there was Jesus, Mary and St Laurence with his gridiron and Peter's keys'. Horrid man.

Offton, St Mary (E6): The unbuttressed C14 tower has two shallow *set-offs*, with *Decorated tracery* in the small w. window and the bell openings. Below the *flushwork* of the battlements two of the *gargoyles* are purely ornamental and have no spouts. The tower houses an excellent ring of eight bells with an 8 cwt. tenor which are rung from the ground floor. The windows of *nave* and *chancel* display an interesting variety of placing and design in *lancet*, Decorated, and late *Perpendicular* forms, with a C19 e. window set in a flint wall which contrasts with the plaster of the rest of the church. There is a C15 *priest's door* on the s. side and in front of the *porch* is an interesting and unusual tomb. Robert Wyard of Castle farm was returning to the stables one morning in 1867 when he fell dead and his horse stood guard until he was found. The scene is sculpted on top of the tomb; the farmer's body lies beneath a blanket while a young woman stands at the horse's head. The late-C14 wooden porch has cusped barge boards over the entrance arch, and pierced tracery each side above *mullions* that were renewed when it was restored in 1956.

The simple inner doorway with thin *imposts* indicates that the church was begun in the C12, and within there is a fairly startling floor in a tartan pattern of red, black, and yellow tiles which was laid to celebrate the 1887 Jubilee. The w. window of 1861 is filled with richly coloured glass by *Lavers & Barraud* with figures by J.Milner Allen, illustrating Christ's presentation in the Temple, and above the arch to the nave is a small quatrefoil *sanctus-bell window*. The C15 *font* is a nice specimen of a familiar type in yellowish stone. The angels in the bowl panels have shields slung round their necks, with the arms of *St Edmund* carved on one of them, and they alternate with seeded roses, a knot of foliage, and a leaf shape; the masks of the lions round the shaft have been cleverly restored. By the s. door, the bowl of the *stoup* is quite undamaged and this is unusual, particularly as *William Dowsing* is known to have visited in 1644 and given orders for various things to be defaced – including a 'holy water font in the chancel'. Overhead, C14 *tie-beams* rest on little *wall posts*

with shafts that curl under at the base and the *spandrels* are carved; roughly moulded *king posts* with four-way struts stand below a plastered ceiling. Two nave windows inserted in the early C17 are placed high, and the undersides of their arches are panelled – one more elaborately than the other. There is no chancel arch but the *rood stair* lies hidden in the n. wall behind a C19 door. Fragments of C15 glass remain in the tracery of the s.e. nave window, and opposite you will see a C14 shield of the De Bohuns, who were Lords of the Manor from 1312 until 1377. The C17 pulpit contains familiar blind-arched panels, with scrolls in the range above, and the base is modern. The very upright wooden eagle is Victorian and so is the boarded panel ceiling of the chancel. The three-light e. window is filled with glass by *Hardman* in C13 style; parents and children are grouped under steeply gabled canopies and the girl with Christ in the centre looks uncommonly like Tenniel's Alice. There are bright angels and an *Agnus Dei* in the tracery, and some of the painting of the main figures is now grainy and fading. The n. lancet contains a figure of the *Blessed Virgin* matched by a Christ in Majesty on the s. side, and there is a pale and attractive *Annunciation* in the two-light s. window, both by Lavers, Barraud & Westlake. Half of what was the base of the *rood screen* forms the back of a bench in front of *dropped-sill sedilia* in the *sanctuary*, and the rest is similarly treated under the tower.

Old Newton, St Mary (E4): The church stands above the level of the village street and the excellent *Decorated tracery* of the C14 *nave* windows catches the eye immediately. The centre one has a single large *reticulation* shape, and the pair to the e. have the same motif tight against the *ogee* arch enclosing two *quatrefoils* and two *mouchettes*. The fine mouldings of the early-C14 doorway are uninterrupted by *capitals* and the *priest's door* in the *chancel* is a smaller version but with worn *headstops* to the *dripstone*. A *scratch dial* can be traced on the s.e. nave buttress and the s.e. corner of the chancel has an odd arrangement of two buttresses at right angles with a third diagonally between them. A heavy C17 or C18 brick buttress supports the n.e. corner so there may have been a history of structural weakness. On the n. side, there is more beautiful C14 tracery in the chancel, and on the nave a drip course runs up and over buttress and door. The tower was built around 1300 and has a small plain w. door, *lancets* n. and s. at ground level, and 'Y' tracery in the belfry windows and bell openings; there are angle buttresses to the w. and *flushwork* battlements. St Mary's has a fine ring of five bells with an 8 cwt. tenor. The porch windows have been blocked and over the inner door there is an image niche which has tiny headstops to the *crocketted hood mould*.

There were late-C19 restorations here, and the plain *tie-beam* and *king post* roof of that time lies under a coved plastered ceiling. There is a small door to the tower and over it a sharply raked C19 *gallery* rests on slim cast-iron pillars. It is worth exploring to see the mouchettes of the side windows at close quarters and to examine the seating. Apart from two crude C17 benches at the back, there are backless forms for children on each step and, by the centre rail that divided boys from girls, two spaces with rudimentary armrests were reserved for master and mistress. The *Jacobean* benches at the rear of the nave have *finials* with scrolls and rosettes and there are only moulded back rails for support. The two rear ranges are angled to provide space round the C15 *font* which has lions and angels bearing shields in the bowl panels. Headless lions and *woodwoses* support the shaft and the lack of a step makes it appear rather squat. A glass case in the blocked n. doorway contains a faintly eccentric war memorial in the form of a Moorish facade cut delicately in fretwork, with the names applied to the lower panels. The only other church fretwork that comes to mind is a Lord's Prayer which was an apprentice piece to be found at Cringleford near Norwich. A large set of George II *Royal Arms* painted on board and in good condition hangs on the n. wall and C19 pitchpine pews fill the nave – not all that attractive but a lovely timber sample. Fragments of the original C14 glass can still be seen in the heads of some of the windows. Although there is no *piscina*, *stepped sedilia* confirm that there was a nave *altar* and the C17 pulpit nearby is very plain, with shallow moulded frames to the panels and a later base. The tall chancel arch rests on half-octagon *jambs* and capitals, and in the *sanctuary* there is an attractive piscina with *cusped* ogee arches. The sedilia columns are free-standing and the mouldings appear to be later than those of the piscina. The e. window has late-C13 shafts with ring bases but the arch is later and the four *lights* have no tracery. The tall niches each side match the sedilia but have remains of crockets, finials, and pinnacles which must have made them very attractive in their salad days.

Onehouse, St John the Baptist (E5): The church is set apart from the village down a lane but is easily seen from the road. Round towers are peculiar to East Anglia and this one is likely to be *Saxon* rather than *Norman*; it has *lancet* bell openings and the later battlements are mainly brick. Extensive repairs were urgently required in the 1990s and it was reduced to one third of its height before being built up again to some two-thirds of the original. The whole has been refaced and is extremely handsome. The *nave* windows on the s. side are C19 and so is the *chancel*, with an e. window in a Victorian version of *Perpendicular*. There are rather brutal little yellow brick pedestals corbelled out below the gable ends, and on the n. side of the nave, two late-C18 or early-C19 wide lancets; however a small Norman lancet survives high in the wall beyond the small n. door. The s. *porch* is built of pleasant pale pink *Tudor* brick, with heavy angle buttresses each side of the low C16 archway. It has a simple *arch-braced* roof and there are remains of a *stoup* to the r. of the inner door.

The interior is plain and uncomplicated under a *scissors-braced* roof with *tie-beams*, and at the w. end is a C12 *font*. Its heavy bowl has become misshapen over the years and at the top corners there are shadowy outlines of heads and outstretched arms; the square plinth is later. In the tower w. window there are three small panels of continental glass painted with the figures of *SS John the Baptist, Paul* and *Matthew*. There is a fragment of stone embedded in the nave n. wall that may possibly have been an image stool, and the roughly shaped beam above the entrance to the chancel is likely to have been the original *rood beam*, with faint traces of a C19 text on the chamfer. The pews are C19 and so is the pulpit, but that is an excellent piece carved by Herbert Green in 1893. Everything is sharply cut and the tiny *crocketted* pinnacles show how much care was taken in the detail. Beyond it is the one remaining medieval bench end, with a strange web-footed creature turning its head over its shoulder.

Orford, St Bartholomew (I6): Orford was once part of the parish of Sudbourne, and until the mid-C12 it had no church. Then, Henry II decided to site a castle here, and one of his agents was the Chaplain Wimar who, as rector of Sudbourne, began to build a chapel in 1166. It matched the castle in grandeur, and a tour of the church should begin with a visit to the ruins of the *Norman chancel* at the e. end. It was six bays long, with *aisles* on each side, and enough of the *arcades* remain to show how fine it once was. The round *piers* have varied decoration in relief (a development that followed the incised patterns used in Norwich cathedral), and there are remains of intricate *chevron mouldings* in the arches. There were *transepts* and a *crossing tower*, and remnants of these will be seen inside. No one knows whether the C12 *nave* was ever completed, for everything w. of the chancel was built or rebuilt in the early C14. The chancel continued in use as a church for the nearby Augustinian priory until that was dissolved under Henry VIII, but by the beginning of the C18 it was in ruins. The massive C14 tower has a broad w. doorway, with paired shafts below the deeply moulded arch. In the 1920s a new door was fitted, designed by Hilda Mason and made by Archdeacon Darling's guild at Eyke. Above, the three-*light* window has flowing *tracery*, and there is a C14 *quatrefoil* belfry window in the n. wall. The tower was once much taller and had a large bell stage, but by the C18 it was giving trouble and in 1830 the s.w. corner collapsed. It was made weatherproof, but little more was done until 1962 when restoration was put in hand and completed in 1971. Orford now has an excellent ring of eight bells with a 10 cwt. tenor, having augmented and re-hung their original five. Nave and aisles are tall, and the windows have attractive *Decorated* tracery – some *reticulated*, others with trios of *cusped* circles above *ogee*-headed lights; the *clerestory* windows are widely spaced quatrefoils. By the 1890s, the body of the church was in such a bad state that the nave and n. aisle were unusable, and a restoration was put in hand under the direction of John Micklethwaite. All the roofs were replaced and the e. end was rebuilt, supported by a pair of flying buttresses. There is a *scratch dial* to be found on one of the aisle buttresses, and the low arch in the wall to the r. of the *porch* may have been intended for the founder's tomb although he was buried elsewhere. The C15 porch served as the village schoolroom in the C18 and by 1900 it too was dilapidated and had to be repaired and re-roofed. The *spandrels* of the outer arch contain *Passion* and *Trinity* shields, and there is a canopied niche above. The lovely C14 inner doorway has slim, single shafts, and a broad range of deeply cut mouldings; another scratch dial low down on the l. will have been in use before the porch was built.

A grand, spacious interior which, without a separate chancel, is almost square. The tall arcades have sturdy quatrefoil piers, and the modern roofs are handsome, with a particularly interesting arrangement of braces on the *tie-beams* of the wider s. aisle. A copy of Raphael's Madonna and Child in an ornate frame hangs in the blocked tower arch, and C18 paintings of Moses and Aaron are displayed on the flanking walls. Below, there are two C19 lead roof plates, and the tradition was revived for the 1972 restoration with a tablet bearing the names of the architect, rector, and churchwardens. An excellent range of modern stalls in C15 style stands in front, with carved figures in the niches; from l. to r. they are: *SS Stephen, Philip, Jude, Andrew, John*, and *Matthew*. In the floor, a large roundel commemorates Benjamin Britten, and the first performances here of his opera 'Noyes Fludde' and the three Church Parables that feature in his memorial window at Aldeburgh. C18 benefaction boards flank the s. door, and close by there is a long, low chest with a divided lid, dated 1634. A very worn set of village stocks stands alongside, and similar sets can be found at Athelington, Saxstead and S. Elmham St Margaret. The early-C15 *font* was originally in the nave but stands now in the s. aisle, and it is a prime example of the East Anglian type. The inscription on the step reads: 'Orate pro animabus Johannis Cokerell et Katerine uxoris ejis qui istam fontem in honore Dei fecerunt fieri' (Pray for the souls of John Cockerell and Katherine his wife who had this font made in honour of God). There are squat lions and *woodwoses* round the shaft, and the bowl panels are of more than usual interest. On the e. side there is a *pietà* in remarkably fine condition, and this is most unusual. The subject required delicate and vulnerable carving and was a favourite target for the C16 and C17 image breakers. *William Dowsing* was here in 1643 but although he smashed glass and reaved some *brasses*, his journal makes no mention of the font, and the carvings may have been hidden under plaster – as some others were elsewhere. The Trinity group in the w. panel is also fine, angels n. and s. hold Passion and Trinity shields, and *Evangelistic symbols* fill the remaining panels. A *piscina* nearby marks the site of a pre-*Reformation* altar.

The tall *screens* that span the church were installed in 1921. Designed in C15 style by Sidney Tugwell and made by Lawrence Turner, they have double ranks of cusped and *crocketted* ogee arches with dense panel tracery above; shallow coving runs under the parapet cresting, and there is a traditional centre *rood* group. There are some C15 bench ends with *poppyheads* in the s. aisle chapel, and the monument on the wall is for Archdeacon Francis Mason, a kneeling alabaster figure flanked by *Corinthian* columns. He was rector here 1597-1621, and chaplain to King James I. His epitaph says 'ye bookes wch he writt testifie his learninge', and they included that great defence of the English ordinal 'Of the consecration of the bishops . . . as also of the ordination of priests and deacons'. When the Norman chancel was abandoned in 1720, rector Josias Alsop had the monument moved here 'in justice to ye memory of so great a man', but then got in a muddle over his age and made it 110 instead of 55. An eagle lectern of 1900 stands nearby, and in the *sanctuary* there is a piscina, now very close to the floor. The chapel *altar* piece is a lovely Nativity by a pupil of Raphael, Raphaelino del Colle. Despite William Dowsing's efforts, Orford still has a fine selection of *brasses*, and the first is in the s. aisle chapel – a 19in. figure of a man of around 1480, with a heavy rosary at his belt. There are two more in the sanctuary: a shield and inscription for William Derehawgh, 1613, and an unusual design for Bridget Bence and her daughter Jone Wheatley. The two effigies are set one above the other on a single large stone, both wear hats, and the daughter displays a brocaded petticoat; each has a rhymed epitaph and there is a marginal inscription. The n. aisle chapel was known as the Mayor's chapel and now serves as an organ chamber and *vestry*. In its e. wall, the arch that led from the Norman chancel aisle into the n. transept can be seen plainly, with part of a transept window alongside. Above them, there are more Norman window shapes, and look for the face carved on a *capital* high on the r. It is a rare instance of the transition stage between plain Norman capitals and the imaginative sculpture of the C13. The chapel's large C14 piscina remains in the n. wall, its *trefoiled* arch notched for a *credence shelf*, and more brasses can be seen by folding back the carpet. In front of the piscina lie James and Elizabeth Coe. He died in 1591 'the firste Mayor of this Towne', and the effigies are excellent. He wears a long, fur-trimmed gown, and she a veil headdress and brocaded petticoat; there are miniature figures of their twelve children. Further over you will find another James Coe and his wife Bridget. He too was mayor of Orford and died in 1580. At the w. end, there is a very nice late brass of 1640 for John Coggishall and his wife Elizabeth. His name is cut in the stone on each side of his *achievement*, and on the large plate the couple kneel at a circular prayer desk; above them, putti hold drapes aside, and their family are grouped below. The panelling that screens the vestry from the organ formed part of the case of the church's

first organ, donated by the Marquis of Hertford in 1772.

The elegant screen in front of the organ was given by Clement Corrants in 1712; a spirited *Royal Arms* of William and Mary stands within the curved *pediment*, and pierced scrollery above the lower panels is repeated behind the s. stalls. The last arcade arches rest on the *responds* of the Norman *crossing* piers, and there is a large, rather dark altar piece on the e. wall. It is 'The Holy Family with St John and a donor' by Bernardino Luini, painted about 1520 and presented to the church in 1950. The *Blessed Virgin* sits beneath a lemon tree, with *St Joseph* to the r. and *St John the Baptist* on the l., the donor kneeling below him; beyond, a hilly, romantic landscape. The high-level e. window has 1920s glass by *Clayton & Bell* to a design by J. Clement Bell. Patterned *quarries* back the figures of *St Edmund, St Paul*, the Blessed Virgin, *St Bartholomew* and *St Nicholas*; there is bold titling below and shields for three of the saints and the diocese. As part of the 1890s restoration, late-C16 *parclose screens* were positioned on each side of the High altar sanctuary. Their *mullions* are carved like *balusters*, and the pierced cresting at the top originally had shields in each light. The remainder of the church's brasses are in the chancel, and look first for the 16in. figure of an unidentified man on the n. side in front of the steps. It dates from about 1510 and shows him in a fur-trimmed gown with voluminous sleeves, and his merchant's mark is displayed as a separate roundel. On the s. side of the sanctuary there are effigies of a couple of about 1520, he in fur-lined gown, she in *kennel headdress*; the inscription has gone but there is a beautiful little Trinity group, complete with the Dove of the Holy Spirit on Christ's shoulder. Also on the s. side is a lady of about 1500 between two men. N. of the altar is an 18in. effigy of a man, again unidentified, dating from about 1510, and nearby a 1490s lady in a veil headdress with children clustered round her skirts; the double buckle badge may perhaps be a rebus. The final brass is on the n. side step, and is a 1520s lady in a veil headdress, with groups of six sons and six daughters. Because of the number of brasses, it seems that Dowsing concentrated on destroying the inscriptions with their references to papistical prayers for the dead.

Otley, St Mary (G5): A narrow tree-lined drive leads up to the e. end of the church from a rather secretive frontage, but there are open fields to the w. and the handsome early-C15 tower can be seen from some way off in that direction. The flint work of its walls is dense and it is rather strange that the *flushwork* filling of the narrow *base course* has all disappeared. The w. door has been handsomely restored and it looks as though three of the carved figures are original. The doorway has leaves carved in the *spandrels* and a line of *tracery* shapes lies below the three-light *Perpendicular* window. The stepped battlements are in brick and the bell openings below them are one sign that a lot of money has been spent recently on restoration. On walking round, you will find a C14 n. *porch* with plain oblong windows and there is a section of brick walling in the *nave* on that side where the old *rood stair turret* was removed. The walls had to be raised in the C15 when the new roof was constructed, and the join shows just under the *clerestory* windows. The *chancel* was largely rebuilt in the C19 and a new *vestry* was added along its whole length. However, on the s. side there is a tiny little *priest's door* dating from about 1300, and there are late Perpendicular windows with deep *labels* in the s. *aisle*. Its e. wall is completely blank, but that may be the result of having the organ moved up against it inside. The canopied niche over the C14 s. porch entrance was almost hidden by rambler roses when I visited, and the moulding of the archway below is carved with hung shields, a motif that can be seen again on the inner doorway.

After passing the remains of a *stoup*, you will find that the interior gives an impression of hard whiteness – from walls and from the panels between the main timbers of the C15 roof. This is a *hammerbeam*, *arch-braced* design, but unfortunately the recumbent angels have lost their heads and have suffered the indignity of having iron tie-rods thrust into them to counteract the spread of the walls. Otley's excellent ring of six bells with a 9 cwt. tenor are rung from the ground floor. In front of the tall tower arch stands a battered C15 *font* with angels and lions alternating in the bowl panels and familiar lions round the shaft. The fine late-C14 *arcade* which separates nave and aisle has *quatrefoil piers*, and their *capitals* are carved alternately with bands of leaves and demi-angels. The arches are almost semi-circular and I wonder whether they were amended when the clerestory was built. The C19 *Decalogue* boards on the s. wall have frames enlivened with gilt rosettes, and across the nave you will see that a window and the n. door have been blocked up, together with the *rood stair* entrances farther e. The *Stuart* pulpit is a very good piece, with carvings of vines in the top panels, blind arches below, and composite mouldings in the bottom panels; the base is modern. The nave benches date from 1879 but there are some interesting survivors from earlier sets. Those ranged along the walls of the s. aisle are C15 and have excellent tracery below their *poppyheads*. Placement makes them a little difficult to see, but there are also initials that spell out the word 'Prepare', and the message may have been longer in the original layout. One bench by the entrance is C17, and there is another at the front of the nave on the n. side, its end carved from a 4in. plank, complete with fleur-de-lys *finial;* the large shield below displays the arms of Beauchamp and FitzAlan. Original C15 panels form part of the low *screen*, and beyond it on the l. a tall blank arch is filled with a bright, abstract embroidery/collage on the theme of 'Let there be light'. Just by it stands a tiny little C15 bench, again with lovely quatrefoil tracery carved in the solid on the ends, and the choir stalls incorporate more work of the same period. Although the vestry has been rebuilt, the low door of about 1300 in the n. wall shows that there was either a predecessor or a chapel on that side early on. The priest's door opposite has been plastered over, and the Victorian alterations placed the *Early English piscina* right in the corner of the *sanctuary*. The restored roof presents a very odd appearance, for, under a steeply sloping plaster ceiling, fantastically shaped braces curl up to *tie-beams* which have pairs of scrolls above, and the whole design is like a cardboard cutout when seen from the nave. The *Stuart Holy table* is particularly interesting because it has been cunningly adapted for modern use. No one would dare do it today but, probably around beginning of the 20C, a clever joiner extended it by 12in. at either end by introducing two matching legs on the front and inserting repeat sections of carving. He fooled *Cautley*. A tablet for Anne Russell on the n. wall is very delicately lettered; she died aged 87 in 1836 and the C18 convention of using Mistress (shortened to Mrs) for maiden ladies lingered on in her epitaph. On the sanctuary n. wall there is a *touchstone* tablet and flanking columns under a modest *pediment* for John Gosnold. He died in 1628, having been a minor figure at the courts of James I and Charles I; colour has been restored to the shields of arms and there is a helpful key to the heraldry below. Opposite is a plain tablet with Latin inscription which mentions nobody by name and uses only initials, but it should on no account be overlooked. It commemorates Paul Storr, probably the greatest English silversmith and goldsmith of the Regency period. He neither lived nor was buried here, but it so happened that his second son Francis was instituted as the rector in 1837 and Storr became interested in the church. He made a replica of its Elizabethan *chalice*, with a *paten* to match it, and paid for a new e. window shortly after. By way of compliment, Francis planted the avenue that leads up to it outside, and when his parents died he had them remembered here. The glass in the window is a rare and important example of the period, although the maker is unknown. Remarkably attractive, in orange, yellow, red, and sky blue enamels painted on white glass, it has three texts in the tracery, finely painted borders, and delicate leaf patterns on the *quarries*.

Oulton, St Michael (J1): The church stands in a spacious churchyard to the w. of the village development and just above the expanse of Oulton marsh. *Norman* in origin, it has a heavy central tower whose walls were replaced in the C18 and later brick above the level of the roofs. Approaching from the 1940s *lych-gate*, the s. frontage displays *Perpendicular* windows in the *nave*, and a C14 arch is outlined in the bay nearest to the tower, with another in the tower s. wall. There is the stub of a wall remaining just to the e. of it which, with the arch outlines, shows where a chapel dedicated to the *Trinity* stood in the Middle Ages. Walking round, you will find the initials 'C.K.F.' cut elegantly and on a large scale below the w. window – a particularly careful example of C18 or early-C19 graffiti. There is a small and plain Norman n. door which is now blocked, and a section of the old *rood stair* shows above the *vestry* which was added to the n. side of the tower in the C19. The *chancel* was rebuilt in the C14, and the broad, four-*light* e. window has *reticulated tracery* – a form that is repeated in two of the side windows. The *priest's door* is of the same period and there is a head *corbel* set in the wall above it, with the fragment of a *gargoyle* lying by the threshold. The outer arch of the *porch* is in brick, with a matching niche above it, and the blocked side windows are flanked by rather curious recesses inside. The inner Norman doorway is not elaborate but does have a single *chevron moulding* in the arch.

Within, a substantial w. *gallery* was 'erected at the expense of the Patron of this Rectory and some of the Principal Landowners and Inhabitants of the Parish AD 1836'. C19 alterations to the floor submerged the base of the C15 *font* but it is a good example of the

familiar local type, in prime condition; compact little lions support the shaft and two more are seated in the bowl panels, along with a pair of angels holding shields and four chunky *Tudor Roses* – all deeply cut. There are modern oak pews in the *nave*, and I imagine that the cross-braced pine roof dates from an 1850s restoration. In the window at the e. end on the n. side look for the little C14 figure of Christ at the very top. Executed in yellow stain, it portrays him wearing the crown of thorns and a cloak is draped over his outstretched arms. The doors to the *rood stair* remain in the wall beyond, and another in the tower wall shows by its position that access to the upper levels of the tower was gained from the *rood loft* – an unusual arrangement. The C14 arch on the s. side of the nave displays its *capitals* and moulding from within, and the w. tower arch has simple, shallow *imposts* and a deep chevron moulding. James II's reign was brief and, for that reason, examples of his *Royal Arms* are rare. Oulton has a fine set which hang above the chancel arch, painted on canvas and well restored, and they apparently belonged to St Margaret's Westminster originally. The organ fits neatly into the n. side of the tower, within the arch that once opened onto a *transept*. A simple *Stuart Holy table* with a new top stands against the opposite wall, and the brass lectern dates from 1879. A modern addition is the glazed screen and doors set within the e. arch of the tower which allows the chancel to be used separately. The church once owned two important *brasses* which were stolen during the 1857 restoration. Luckily, the early-C19 antiquary Henry Davy had taken careful rubbings of both, and excellent fibreglass replicas now lie in place of the originals. In the centre of the chancel floor is the 6ft. effigy of Adam Bacon, the rector who probably rebuilt the e. end of the church. Dating from about 1318, the brass was perhaps the earliest in England to illustrate vestments; the priest is tonsured, he has a stubble beard, and there is a lion at his feet. The second brass displays the 2ft. 8in. effigies of Sir John Fastolfe who fought at Agincourt and died in 1445, and Katherine his wife who died in 1478; he has a sword hung frontally and a greyhound at his feet, while she wears a *butterfly headdress*, a rope necklace and an elegant gown. The widow provided the memorial, and although one of the shields is for Fastolfe, the others belong to her first husband (Sampson), her father (Welysham) and her mother (Bedingfield). Before leaving, note that there is a *Decorated piscina* with a trefoil arch, alongside *dropped-sill sedilia,* and that the oak *reredos* had a painted *Decalogue* added in 1951 – a very late example.

There are a few early headstones s. of the church, along with a good selection of C19 examples, and look for the bulky sandstone boulder some 25yds. s.w. of the porch. Simply lettered, it commemorates George Edwards, the engineer who directed the construction of Lowestoft harbour in the late 1820s. The stone was dredged up at the time, and Edwards kept it as a memento. When the time came, he had no wish to lie in consecrated ground, but bowing to the inevitable, he stipulated that his keepsake should mark the spot rather than a conventional memorial.

Oulton Broad, St Luke (J1): Large-scale development in the parish prompted discussion on the need for an additional church as early as 1936, but it was not until 1960 that St Luke's was built on Homefield Avenue. It is a ranch-style building which employs three varieties of brick, a little cement rendering, a section of boarding below the eaves and, for good measure, a panel of flint pebbles to back the notice board. All of which were familiar conventions in house design at the time, and the church merges comfortably with its neighbours. A flat-roofed foyer projects towards the road, and an impressive, bare wooden cross rises above the side wall. Inside is a simple rectangular hall with a flat ceiling, and a meeting room, kitchen, and cloakrooms are ranged along the back wall. The opposite long wall has a wide recess, lit by concealed side windows, and it forms a *sanctuary* approached by shallow steps. There are movable *communion rails* in front, and a plain cross is displayed against a velvet curtain behind the undraped *Holy Table.*

Oulton Broad, St Mark (J1): The village has become an urban extension of Lowestoft, but until the late C19 it formed part of the parish of Carlton Colville. Then, development made an additional church necessary, and St Mark's was consecrated in 1884. It was designed by Roberts, Green & Richards, the Lowestoft architects, in basic *Early English* style as a simple hall church, capable of being extended should the need arise; Suffolk white bricks were used throughout. There is no tower, and a single bell is housed in a cote on the w. gable. Below it, the five-*light* w. window has *plate tracery,* and the *nave* is lit by groups of triple *lancets,* both at *clerestory* level and below. The short *chancel* was extended in the early 1900s, and the line of the original lean-

to roof still shows in the side walls. In 1950, an organ chamber was added to the s. side of the nave, its style matching the chancel, and a n.e. *vestry* annexe followed in 1968. Entry is via a painted wooden s. porch, and the church within is pleasantly light and lively, in contrast with the dour exterior. The architect provided Early English-style *arcades* so that *aisles* could be added as necessary, but he placed his outer walls right up against them, and that arrangement still stands. The steep pine roof has *arch-braces* that rest on tall *wall posts,* and there are two ranks of *tie-beams,* with slender *queen posts* under the ridge. The bulky *font* has crosses inset on the bowl faces, and the corners are cut back like a broach spire to form an octagon. The organ has a very stolid 'gothick' case, and nearby stands a brass eagle lectern of compact design, with the inscription: 'A Sancti Johannis theologi filiabus, alienas aegritudines allevare solitis, Jubilaeum suum concelebrantibus Deo dedicabatur haec aquila A.S. 1898' (This eagle was dedicated to God in 1898 by the daughters of *St John the Evangelist,* accustomed to relieve the sick, in celebration of their Jubilee). It was given to the church recently and the significance of the inscription – was it from the demolished Lowestoft St John? The choir stalls were installed in the 1930s to mark the church's 50th anniversary – a restrained design in very attractive timber which matches the pulpit. The wrought-iron *communion rails* are a World War II memorial, and in the *sanctuary,* a small late-C16 table with carved frame, turned legs, and a replacement top, serves as a *credence table.* The attractive stained glass in the e. window is by Abbot & Co, a Lancashire firm whose only other Suffolk work is at Fornham St Martin. Aesthetically, the figure of the *Blessed Virgin* and Child was a slightly odd choice of subject because, in this four-light window, it is necessarily offset. Nonetheless, the design is pleasing, with the Virgin's cloak and veil spread to combine with an upward swirl of wheat ears; her lily emblem is added to the l., and streaks of colour interspersed with stars rise upwards into the tracery; all is set against a background of blue striated glass.

Ousden, St Peter (B5): The church stands on rising ground at the w. end of the village and it has a central *Norman* tower which has remained virtually unaltered apart from the parapet. It is extremely simple, with attached shafts at the corners above the shallow *set-off.* The arches of the bell openings have plain roll mouldings and

there is a small *lancet* at ground floor level. There
may have been an *apse* at the e. end but a new
chancel was built about 1300 and its roof line
shows on the e. wall. This in its turn was replaced
in the late C18 and new windows were inserted
a century later. A chapel which served as a
manorial pew was added on the n. side of the
nave in the C18 and the nave was extended
westward some 20ft. in 1850, with windows
typical of the period. The main entrance used to
be on the s. side and more evidence of Norman
work is to be seen there. The blocked door (with
a modern window inserted) has three bands of
chip carving in the lintel, and within the arch of
thin Roman tiles the *tympanum* is deeply carved
with a large chequer pattern. On the l. *jamb* is the
faint outline of a very early *scratch dial* which has
holes as markers instead of radial lines. The
lancet in the nave is Norman but the larger
window with 'Y' *tracery* is C13 as is the tower
lancet; to the r. of it a window was inserted in
the early-C14, probably to give more light to the
rood. The n. *porch* is modern and the entrance
has been fitted with a well designed wrought-
iron grill. The doorway itself is an intriguing
mixture. The shaft on the l. is Norman but the
other has an *Early English capital* and the arch is
pointed – all signs of a reconstruction using
whatever came to hand.

The design of the late-C14 *font* is uncommon;
the attached columns of the tall and graceful
stem curve out to meet the bowl, the panels of
which are carved with various tracery shapes and
a single blank shield. Behind the font stands a
simple *Jacobean* chest. There are *paterae* on the
wall plates below a waggon panelled ceiling and
two *hatchments* hang on the walls; on the s., for
Thomas James Ireland of Ousden Hall who
died in 1863, and on the n., for the Revd.
Thomas Frampton, rector, who died in 1803.
Above the tower arch hangs a large set of *Royal
Arms* painted on board, with three turned *finials*
on the frame. They are *Hanoverian*, although
Cautley suspected that they were an early *Stuart*
set originally and the frame design supports this.
The n. chapel is entered through a creditable
imitation of a Norman arch and on the wall
within is a tripartite 'Victorian Gothick'
memorial for members of the Ireland family by
I.E. Thomas. To the l. of the tower arch is an
excellent memorial for Laeticia Mosley of 1619.
Two female virtues recline on the *pediment* which
encloses an hourglass, and the *touchstone* tablet
is flanked by matching *Corinthian* columns;
below, in a marble oval, a shrouded skeleton is
exquisitely carved. The inscription is gilt and

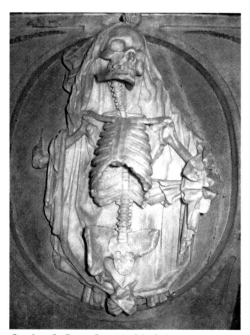

Ousden, St Peter: Laetitia Mosley's monument

although the epitaph is too long to quote, it
should not go unread. The plainness of the
C18 pulpit is subtly relieved by marquetry
banding on the panels and beyond it there is a
C13 recess which will have backed a nave *altar*.
The Norman tower arches are typically massive,
with roll mouldings, and there are two beasts
carved on the capitals of the easternmost arch.
A close look at the s. jamb of the w. arch will
reveal a roundel in low relief carved with an
interlace design. It seems to be quite isolated
and there is no clue as to its significance. There
are *Decalogue*, Creed and Lord's Prayer boards in
the *sanctuary* and the *communion rails* have clusters
of four turned *balusters*, with all the signs of
having been three-sided originally. St Peter's has
a ground floor ring of five bells with a 14 cwt.
tenor, but the present condition of the frame
prohibits ringing.

Pakefield, All Saints and St Margaret (J1):
The church stands attractively within a large
churchyard on the very edge of the low cliff.
Where there are now dunes and shingle there
were, within living memory, fields and houses,
but the sea's advance has been contained, at least
for the time being. The building has a dual
dedication because as early at the C11 it comprised
two parish churches built side by side, one
belonging to the manor of Rothenhall and the

other to the manor of Pakefield Pyes. On an April night in 1941, a German bomber dropped a stick of incendiaries across the town and two fell on the church's thatch. The rector dealt with one but could not reach the other, and the building was gutted. Most of the movable fittings were saved, and the church was the first in the country to be rebuilt and re-dedicated after the war. The walls were heightened and some minor amendments made, but it is to all intents and purposes a replica of the original, with thatched roofs that run uninterruptedly from end to end. The unbuttressed tower has a single *set-off* below the bell openings, two of which have *Decorated tracery*. Note that there are two or three changes in the masonry patterns, with flints set in *herringbone* fashion half way up. There seem to be remnants of a *stoup* by the C14 n. door, and to the l. of it is a strange *squint* at eye level. It is very similar to those at Lound and Blundeston, but in this case it gives a view across the church and will not have aligned with an *altar*. This strengthens my belief that squints like this were all used from inside, but their real purpose is obscure. The herringbone flint pattern in part of the n. wall suggests that the building dates from the *Saxon* period; the *chancel* of the n. half was extended in the C14 and its e. window has *reticulated* tracery (now mainly blocked). The window alongside matches it, and when the s. chancel was extended in the C15, a crypt was constructed below and its little windows peep out just above ground level. The brick *rood stair turret* on the s. side is lodged against a buttress, and there is a *scratch dial* on the upper section of the buttress nearest the *porch*. The latter is thatched, and there is a very worn sundial above the heavily eroded outer arch; a stoup is set in one of the angle buttresses.

The spacious interior is pleasing, and you will see that the naves of the two churches are separated by an *arcade* which replaced a solid wall in the late C14. It was bricked up again a little later and seems to have remained so for most of the time until the two parishes were united in 1748. The division made it convenient for the Independents to use one half during the Commonwealth, and Kirkley parishioners borrowed the n. side for most of the time that their own church was in ruins. Sweet reason did not always prevail, however, for in 1594 the two rectors, Mr Yowle and Mr Wincoppe, were accused of brawling in the church (in whose half, I wonder?). The *font* is a familiar East Anglian pattern, but the carving includes some interesting variations: two of the bowl panels have the

hart badge of Richard II, dating it 1377-99, and two more have lions with front paw raised for a change; there are *crocketted* pinnacles at the corners, and a band of curly leaves decorates the shaft above the seated lions. A glass case nearby displays a number of conventional trophies but perhaps the most interesting exhibit is an incendiary bomb like the one that caused all the damage. Above the large tower door there is another opening which may have provided access to a *gallery*, and a large set of Charles II *Royal Arms* hangs on the w. wall. Dated 1681 and painted on board, it is a lively design. A second set painted on a roundel may be found in the w. window of the n. aisle – post-1801 *Hanoverian* this time. In the *quatrefoil* at the top there is a little Adoration of the Magi, and the window also has a small section of foreign glass which might be part of a Holy Innocents group. On the n. wall, a *brass* of 1417 commemorates John and Agnes Bowf, the earliest civilian brass in Suffolk; there are groups of sons and daughters below the 33in. figures, and part of the marginal inscription survives. The verse is an unusually early example of English being used in place of Latin:

> All schul we ken, whedir ne when,
> May no man ken, but God above.
> For other we car, hen schul we far,
> Ful pore and bar. Thus seyd John Bowf.

(We shall all go hence, though no-one may know the time or place save God above. We provide for others [but] we must go hence quite poor and naked. Thus said John Bowf.)

A simple *Jacobean* chest stands at the e. end of the *aisle*, decorated with chip carving, and its front panels were converted to doors at some time. The chapel beyond the *screen* has a small *Stuart Holy Table* which is almost square, and above it at gallery level the whole space is filled by the organ case. Above the s. door there is a narrow recess which displays medieval stencil decoration. It was, I think, part of a window embrasure that was superseded when the porch was added, and another section of the same design has been uncovered further along. Nearby is an interesting water colour which shows the interior as it was in 1870, the font standing within the arcade, a *hatchment* on the n. wall, and a row of hatpegs on the s. wall. The restored *Early English* recess by the westernmost window in the s. wall may have been a *piscina* for a guild or *chantry* altar. Ann Cunningham's tablet of 1819 has an affecting verse by her two sons, and below the next window is a section of what was a tomb recess. The centre *light* of the window has glass of the 1960s in tones of brown and red; a child kneels between its mother's knees, with father standing by, and it was Andrew Anderson's first essay in the medium.

A passageway cut through the wall above the arcade shows that the *rood screen* stretched across the entire building, and assuming an early-C15 date, it follows that the arches were not blocked at that time. The upper parts of the screen were destroyed in the fire, but most of the base panels survived. They have carved *spandrels*, traces of colour, and there is a small section of the top rail in the n. half; note that some of the boards have been reversed so that stencilled *Sacred monograms* are now at the bottom. The nave panels have alternate red and green backgrounds, with barber's pole stringing, and a row of quatrefoils along the bottom. The roughly bored holes to the l. of the entrance into the chancel may have been *elevation squints*. The upper half of the screen was restored in 1952, carved by a Mr Cooper of Norwich. The church's other medieval brass has been set in its original position on a new slab in the chancel floor. It commemorates Richard Ffolcard who was rector of All Saints 1445-51, and the 15in. demi-figure is in academic dress, with accompanying scroll and inscription. Before his appointment to the living, Ffolcard had been the Master of Haberdashe Hall, Oxford. Further to the e. there is a rare instance of a modern portrait brass. Canon Bernard Stather Hunt was rector for 25 years until 1967, and he is shown wearing surplice and stole in the same pose as his C15 predecessor. The level of the *High altar* is dictated by the crypt below, and the s. *sanctuary* window affords a magnificent view out to sea. The small piece of stained glass is probably C17 continental work – the head and shoulders of a man with yellow hair holding a paper or piece of cloth. There is a piscina in the ledge and the little lion at the end of the graduated *sedilia* may have begun life supporting a font stem. A former rector celebrated a quarter of a century's 'Protestant and Evangelical ministry' by filling the e. window with glass by H.J. Salisbury in 1896. Christ as the Good Shepherd is portrayed with sheep and lambs against a backing of foliage and lilies in the side lights; there are patterned *quarries* and scrolls, with Sacred monograms and a dove in the tracery. More work by this firm is found at nearby Kirkley and Lowestoft, Christ Church.

Pakenham, St Mary (D4): Standing on high ground above the village street, this was originally a *Norman* church with *nave*, central tower and *chancel*. In the late C13 the chancel was rebuilt and a s. *transept* added, while in the C14 the tower was given an octagonal top with *Decorated* bell openings (the parapets are now of brick). At some time the transept was destroyed by fire and in 1849 *Samuel Saunders Teulon* carried out an extensive restoration and rebuilding. He opened up the old arch and built a new s. transept, adding another on the n. side, together with a new tower stair turret and a n. *porch*. Walking round the outside you will see the original Norman w. and s. doorways with their simple roll mouldings and scalloped *capitals*. There is a stone coffin built into the wall under a window on the s. side of the nave (unlikely to have been there originally), and there are four C13 coffin lids fixed upright on the s. wall of the chancel. Within, below the large *Perpendicular* w. window, is an excellent C15 *font*. Four of the bowl panels have *Evangelistic symbols* but on the e. there is a *pelican in her piety*, on the s., a lion with a staff topped by an encircled cross, and to the w., a *unicorn*. This is one of the symbols of the *Blessed Virgin* and is not commonly seen on fonts, although there is another example at nearby Norton. There are angels below the bowl and the *traceried* shaft has unusually good figures of seated monks at the corners: one meditating, one holding what is possibly a treasurer's satchel (n.w.), one reading his breviary and the last holding what could be a *reliquary* (s.e.). The nicely detailed *tabernacle* cover was given in 1931. Thomas Discipline died in 1752 and his *hatchment* is on the n. wall. His wife rejoiced in the name of Merelinda and her hatchment hangs opposite. The roofs were replaced in the Teulon restoration and the new nave benches, with their shapely and well carved fleur-de-lys, were modelled on those at Stanton Harcourt, Oxfordshire. Teulon presumably wished to open up the vista to the e. end and to do so, he replaced the Norman w. arch of the tower with one which is pointed and altogether larger. A modern *altar* now stands below the centre crossing, and to the r. is a small C15 chest. The original Norman e. arch of the tower was undisturbed and has simple cross decoration on the *abacus*. The plain C15 *screen* has been extensively restored and the stalls in the chancel have compact *finials* encrusted with carved foliage. The two bench ends that back on to the screen terminate in grotesque masks with tongues lolling out. There is a *priest's door* on the s. side and the *vestry* door opposite is medieval. The e. window and two of the side windows are Perpendicular but there are C13 *lancets* over the two doors and in the *sanctuary*. A window on the n. side has *Ward & Hughes* glass of 1913 designed by T.F. Curtis. It is an interesting composition in steely tints, with figures of the Sower, the Reaper, and Christ as the Lord of the Harvest. The late-C17 *communion rails* have twisted *balusters* and there is a *trefoil*-headed *piscina* in the sanctuary. The C19 *reredos* was designed by Thomas Earp – a series of low arches and roundels backed with gold mosaic. Pakenham possesses a fine ring of six bells with a 12 cwt. tenor

Palgrave, St Peter (F3): The church sits nicely in the centre of the village, and in walking round the outside, look to the s. of the *chancel* for the gravestone of John Catchpole, a waggoner who died in 1787. The top of the stone has a nice illustration of his team of six horses and the epitaph reads:

My horses have done running, my waggon
   is decay'd,
  And now in the Dust my Body is lay'd;
My whip is worn out and my work
   It is done,
  And now I'm brought here to my last
       home.

The unbuttressed tower dates from the early C14 but the *nave* was rebuilt about a century later. The chancel has rather odd round-headed windows with 'Y' *tracery* and is work of the early C18, while the n. *aisle* was rebuilt in the C19. A good deal of attention was given to the s. *porch* in the C15 rebuilding and it has an ornate front to the street, with *flushwork* panelling and battlements. *Crocketted ogee*-arched niches flank the doorway and there is another canopied niche at the gable. The doorway *spandrels* contain carvings of *St George* and the dragon, there are *fleurons* and crowns set in the mouldings, and fine lion terminals. The porch is two-storied but the upper room has now gone. To the l. of the entrance door is a fine tablet commemorating 'honest' Tom Martin, 'that able and indefatigable antiquary' who died in 1770 – placed there by Sir John Fenn, the man who first published the Paston letters in 1787.

On entering, you will see immediately above your head, one of the suits of parish armour that used to be kept in the room above the porch, and the door to that room lies to the l.

The mouldings of the tower arch fade into the *imposts* and above is a very dark set of *Royal Arms* dated 1850. The large and square late-Norman *font* is not typical of East Anglia in its decoration. It stands on a central octagonal shaft, and columns at each corner have scalloped *capitals*. There are heads at the corners and the sides are decorated with large crosses. When the n. aisle was rebuilt in the 1860s, the whole *arcade* was replaced on the original bases and the *quatrefoil piers* match the triple shafts of the early-C14 chancel arch, with its wide concave mouldings.

The joy of this church is the splendid *hammerbeam* roof. The *arch-braces* rest directly on the hammerbeams, and they sweep over in a continuous curve below the ridge. The roof retains its original decoration and there are dark tracery patterns on all the main timbers, with lighter stencilling in between. Even the spandrels and arch-braces are painted rather than carved. There are remains of delicate cresting on the hammerbeams and the *wall posts* come down to rest on head *corbels*. Below, the pitchpine pews are a legacy of the C19 and each has its little gate. There is no *screen* to the short chancel and the e. window has 1850s glass – patterned *quarries* and borders, with inset quatrefoils and roundels. The late-C17 oak *altar* table has shapely *baluster* legs, and on the n. aisle wall there is a set of painted boards bearing the Lord's Prayer, Creed and the *Decalogue*. They were carefully restored in the 1960s and look very well indeed. Over the n. door is the church's single *hatchment*, for the rector Charles Martin, who died in 1864. St Peter's has a fine ring of eight bells in the tower with a 7 cwt. tenor.

Parham, St Mary (H4): A short lane leads to the thatched *lych-gate*, built in 1897 to celebrate Victoria's jubilee, where the remains of the village stocks are housed in its roof. Like Hacheston's, only the pair of planks survive, but in Parham's case they cater for seven legs at a time! There was a church here at the time of the Norman Conquest, and records show that it was rebuilt by William de Ufford, Earl of Suffolk, about 1370. The tower has a simple *base course*, and the buttresses which rise to belfry level are decorated with *flushwork* chequer. There is a late-*Perpendicular* window over the finely moulded w. doorway, but the tower's remarkable feature is the very large niche high in the w. wall. The stone is so eroded that it is now only a crumbled shape, but there were side pinnacles, and the *cusped ogee* arch rose to a

Parham, St Mary: Rood niche

finial. The recess is as broad as the window below, and the three pedestals at the base show that it contained a *rood group* (because of its prominence, it was doubtless mutilated during the reign of Edward VI). A man's face, cradled by his hands is carved below one of the pinnacles, with a smiling woman's head below the other. Three of the bell openings are simple, cusped *lancets*, but a larger window, with *Decorated tracery*, was placed above the rood group to complete the elaboration of the w. facade. Tall, slim Perpendicular windows were inserted in the *nave* in the C15, with nicely varied tracery (some had their tracery removed later), and their deep *labels* are linked by a *string course*. All the buttresses are decorated with chequered flushwork, and at the top of the one to the r. of the s. door there is an interesting *scratch dial*. Unlike the normal half-circle layout, this one is cut on a square block, with the hours numbered on the edges, and the lines radiate from the centre of the top – a late example, designed to tell the time in sun-dial fashion, and not just to give the hours for services. There are big *gargoyles* below the plain parapets of the nave, and in the *chancel* n. wall, a porch was conjured for the *priest's door* in the C19 by fitting a new door within the thickness of the wall. Above it, the Ufford shield of the C14 founder is boldly displayed. The C15 n. *porch* was added to provide a prestigious main entrance, and is quite lavish,

although the w. side was heavily repaired in brick much later and has lost its window. The base course has flushwork roundels, and stone panels lightly carved with the crowned initials of Jesus and the *Blessed Virgin*. Slim flushwork panels cover the whole facade, and there is a central canopied niche; the archway *spandrels* have carvings of a dragon and either *St George* or a *woodwose*, and beasts sit on the corners of the parapet. It was converted for use as a *vestry* many years ago, and the tower door is now the main entrance.

Within, the fine, deeply moulded tower arch has octagonal *jamb shafts*, scratched with an unusually interesting selection of medieval graffiti, including detailed drawings of late-C14 or early-C15 ships that will have been a familiar sight in the estuaries not far away. The organ is placed on the *gallery* which has refurbished roof *bosses* displayed on the front. The early-C15 *font* has a deep, heavy bowl, and five of its panels display good tracery patterns, some harking back to the previous century. The shield of the Uffords is found on two sides, and on the e., their cross is combined with the arms of the Willoughbys, the family that succeeded to the manor in 1416. It would seem that a new nave roof was installed in the C15 (along with the windows?), and its supporting stone *corbels* remain in the walls. Five of them are carved with excellent heads, one as the eagle of *St John*, and the others as demi-angels. Some time later, probably in the late C16, an almost flat roof was installed which was restored in 1886, and again recently (but most people will need binoculars to read the commemorative disk placed at the w. end). A set of Charles II *Royal Arms* painted on canvas hangs on the n. wall, and the vestry door below is secured by an enormous heart-shaped C18 padlock that weighs 6lbs. The benches are in the *Ringham* tradition, and were made in 1888. They have fine *poppyheads* carved with a variety of flowers and fruit, and the joiner's enthusiasm led him to strike a moulding along the centre of every seat to match the one in the back – a sure way of making the congregation restless during the sermon. The chancel arch matches the tower arch, and its capitals are notched where the *rood loft* was fitted, with mortices in the curve where the *tympanum* was secured. The tall C15 *screen*, with its narrow lights remains below, rather insensitively repainted. The lower panels were removed (at the same time?) leaving the tracery intact. The steep and shallow steps that led up to the loft are beyond a tall doorway in the n. wall, and there are plain niches for statues each side of the chancel entrance. The C15 *piscina* to the r. shows that there was at least one nave *altar*; its ogee arch has neat little *headstops*, and there is a *Tudor Rose* carved at the centre of the scalloped drain.

In the chancel, the rear choir stalls incorporate C15 ends, and two of them have angels holding shields carved on the elbows. An excellent *Jacobean* chest stands nearby, the front beautifully carved, with later shields applied within the three *blind arches*. It was the gift of Mr Darby, an early-C19 curate who also devised the heraldry that decorates the *wall posts* in the roof, and was responsible for a number of alterations in the church. There are a number of fine *ledger-stones* in the chancel and, unfortunately, the chest partially hides the best of them – the memorial of Edmund Warner and his wife. Dated 1652, it has a cherub head at the top disguised as a sun in splendour, and a shrouded skeleton is engraved at the bottom, under an oval *achievement of arms*. Two *hatchments* hang on the walls: on the s., for Elizabeth Long who died in 1792 at 84; on the n., for Mary White who was 86 when she died in 1836 – both daughters of the local Corrance family. The mid-C17 *Stuart Communion rails* have widely spaced *balusters*, but it was not always so – every other one was removed at some time. An interesting little alms box is chained to one end; turned in pine, it had two hasps and cleverly contrived locks were made to fit the circumference. The box stands on the ledge of the *dropped-sill sedilia* where there is a strange series of grooves cut in the stone. Similar marks can be seen elsewhere on font steps, and some people think that they were used to sharpen arrow heads – a tempting explanation, but unlikely in the *sanctuary*. The *cusping* in the arch of the C14 piscina has been broken away, and its drain design is similar to the one in the nave. On the other side of the sanctuary there are twelve stone shields of varying sizes displayed at low level, and the crisply carved heraldry supports the tradition that they came from tombs dismantled at Butley and Campsea Ashe priories after their dissolution in the 1530s. The church's only *brass* is an inscription for Alice Wingfelde, who died in 1603. She was the wife of Thomas Wingfelde who is described as 'Feodarie of ye county of Suffolk' – an officer of the ancient Court of Wards. Nearby is a curiosity, a wooden coat hook, with 'R.H. 1716' carved on the back plate. The initials fit neither the parson nor the squire of the day – perhaps a curate's perquisite. The *reredos* is made up of sections of C16/C17 woodwork, partially gilded, with another old roof boss at the top; the 'Last Supper' is apparently a copy of a painting by a Russian artist. The e.

window contains three shapes filled with fragments of medieval glass, with four attractive C15 angels in the tracery, playing harps and psalteries.

Peasenhall, St Michael (H4): Apart from the tower, the church was almost entirely rebuilt in 1860 at the sole expense of Mr Brooke, the squire of Sibton Park. The *nave* with its deep roof, and the short *chancel*, both have *Perpendicular*-style windows, and a *vestry* was added on the s. side of the chancel. The C15 tower has *flushwork* on the bottom stage of the angle buttresses, and the w. window and bell openings were renewed as part of the restoration. The *gargoyles* were retained, and Mr Brooke added 4ft. to the height of the tower on the understanding that the villagers rebuilt the churchyard wall. Cherry trees arch over to form a tunnel between the gate and the fine C15 n. *porch* (which escaped rebuilding). It has a flushwork panelled facade, and the trio of niches over the entrance are *groined*, their delicate canopies now heavily eroded. The archway has grinning lion *stops*, and while one sometimes finds a *St George* carved in doorway *spandrels*, here the dragon is paired with a *woodwose* who bears a little shield as well as his usual club. Cratfield and Badingham have similar carvings, and the idea was probably borrowed one from another.

The interior has that particular neatness so often found in churches rebuilt by the Victorians, and the tower arch is completely masked by the organ placed on a *gallery* which has an attractive cast-iron balustrade. Beyond it there is a ground floor ring of six bells with a 10 cwt. tenor. The *font* which stands below is an unusual C12 *Norman/Transitional* design. Its heavy cylindrical body has four corner shafts with ring bases, and the bowl is squared off on four sides, with domed sections over the corner shafts; decoration is confined to a narrow band of interlace carving at the base of the bowl. A nice little etching by Henry Davy, framed on the s. wall, shows how the church looked outside in 1845. The nave seating is C19, but (at a guess) the pulpit is 1930s work, with gothic-style tracery in the panels enclosing little carved roundels, one of which has the church's patron saint putting down 'the great dragon, the old serpent, he that is called the Devil and Satan' (Revelation xii.7). The *scissors-braced* roofs are part of the 1860s work, and in the chancel, timbers were used that had been salvaged from the old nave roof. *Henry Ringham* was in charge and this was probably his doing, and he may have made the choir benches, although they are not typical of his style – the backs have large, pierced tracery roundels, and there are modest *poppyheads*. A low wooden *reredos* is painted with the *Decalogue*, Creed and Lord's Prayer, and the glass in the five-*light* e. window is by *Thomas Willement*. It was part of the 1860s scheme and is a large, simplistic Crucifixion group displayed against a red and blue backing. The outer lights have *Evangelistic symbols*, *pelican*, and *Agnus Dei* displayed within attractive roundels and *trefoils*, and the *quarries* are painted with leaves and *Sacred monograms*. Lively patterns of blue, yellow, and red fill the tracery, and the dove of the Holy Spirit hovers at the very top. In contrast, the *Ward & Hughes* glass on the n. side is a sentimental Christ healing the sick and gathering children around him – the sort of thing that has given Victorian glass such a bad name.

Pettaugh, St Catherine (F5): The stream that runs under the road to form an attractive eastern boundary to the churchyard meanders across country to join the infant River Deben. The C14 unbuttressed tower has two *string courses* and there are *Perpendicular* bell openings below the stepped *flushwork* battlements. On walking round, you will find that there is a *Decorated* w. window but no door below it, and a plain brick stair to the n. Two of the *nave* windows were replaced and others restored in 1863 (when the vicar doubled as architect), but the low n. door is C14. The plastered *chancel* has a large modern *vestry*-cum-organ chamber to the n., with new brick buttresses each side of the e. window; that has intersected 'Y' *tracery* of the early C14 and small *headstops*. The *priest's door* has been reshaped and there is a small and simple C19 *porch* in brick and flint leading to a plain C14 s. doorway.

The tan-coloured C15 *font* is the common East Anglian type – very worn lions alternating with shields in the bowl panels, battered angels underneath, and seated lions round the shaft. The plastered ceilings of nave and chancel are divided unobtrusively by the chancel arch, with no *screen* below it. The blocked n. doorway now houses a display centred on a small *brass* of about 1530. It probably commemorates Thomas Fastolfe, his wife Anne, and their daughters Pannel, Agnes, Elizabeth, and Dorothy (the inscription and the plate that pictured their sons is lost). A shield identifies the family and the women wear *kennel headdresses*. The engraving is coarse, but it is interesting because when the brass was moved it was found that part of it had once belonged to the figure of an early-C14 knight. The back of the daughters' plate is engraved with a

portion of a surcoat like that worn by Sir Roger de Trumpington on his brass at Trumpington in Cambridgeshire. The nave benches and pulpit are modern, but the prayer desk in the chancel incorporates two *Jacobean* bench ends dated 1615. Their *poppyheads* are rather like rams' horns and the carving is rudimentary. The choir stalls of 1930 were designed to match. The remains of a *pillar piscina* set below a narrow recess in the *sanctuary* suggest that the original building was *Norman*, and there was certainly a church here at the time of the Domesday survey. On the s. wall is an undistinguished tablet by Robert Wills of London for the Revd. Edmund Bellman who died in 1843, and opposite is the memorial for Charles William Tucker. He was young when he died at sea in 1861, and the models of the Crimea and Sebastopol medals sculpted at the top mean that he was a victim of that campaign.

The lovely glass in the e. window is the only work in Suffolk by *Caroline Townshend and Joan Howson*. Installed in 1936, the three scenes form a thick swathe of rich and vibrant colour across the window; Christ as the Good Shepherd stands in the centre, Lazarus rises from the dead surrounded by his family on the l., and Christ speaks to Zacchaeus in the sycamore tree on the r. Panes of striated glass fill the rest of the window, with the wheel of St Catherine at the bottom and the shields of East Anglia, St Edmundsbury, and Canterbury at the top.

Pettistree, St Peter and St Paul (G5): The churchyard is spacious and the Greyhound Inn's age and position suggest that it may have started life as the Church House where village *guilds* met and church ales were held. The C15 tower has a handsome w. frontage but the e. face extends across buttresses which project beyond the width of the *nave* and this gives it a curiously bald appearance when seen from that side. There are lozenges and chequerwork of flint in the *base course*, on the buttresses, and in a double band below the battlements, where there are corner *gargoyles*. Above the small *Perpendicular* w. window there is an unusually ornate belfry window which has *traceried ashlar spandrels* under a *label* that forms part of a *string course*. It looks as though it was designed as a niche for a statue. The tower houses an excellent ground floor ring of six bells with a 7 cwt. tenor. The nave has late Perpendicular windows but above them on each side are four *quatrefoil clerestory* windows which have been blocked. There is no sign that there were ever *aisles* and they were perhaps inserted to give additional light for the earlier C13 or C14 nave. In the tower e. wall just above the present low-pitched roof you will see a small window which was probably a *sanctus-bell window* inside the church before the roof line was lowered. The *chancel* dates from about 1300 but it was largely rebuilt in 1894 and an organ chamber was added to the n. The nave n. door is blocked and as far as one can see there have never been porches – which is unusual in a church of this size.

Within, below an almost flat plastered ceiling, most of the seating is modern but there are four low medieval bench ends with shallow tracery at the w. end on the n. side, and the *poppyhead* by the entrance is an interesting carving of a crouching lion with a mask on top. On the w. wall hangs a very decorative charity board of 1717 in black and gold, cut to a silhouette with fat flanking scrolls. Bread was to be provided for 'such poor of this parish as shall here religiously and constantly joyn with ye Congregation in ye Publick Prayers of ye Church' – wording which could, I suppose, have provided a number of excuses for being uncharitable. Half a century later the *Royal Arms* of George III were painted and they hang now on the n. wall, dark and sombre. At the e. end of the pews on the n. side is a bench made up of medieval sections. It has unmatched ends and the poppyhead next to the aisle is exceptionally well carved, while the range of panels below the seat could well have been part of the front of the *rood loft*. The stairs that led to it are still in the n. wall although the lower entrance has disappeared. Below there is a *piscina* with a *cusped* arch that would have served a nave *altar*, and there is another one to match on the s. side. Just above it the head of another arch may have been part of an image niche, although a simple recess for a statue is provided in the *jamb* of the adjoining window. There is now no *screen*, but the chancel arch has slot marks which show where a *tympanum* was fitted. The stone for Francis Bacon and his wives Elizabeth and Mary is fixed to the s. wall and bears 18in. *brass* effigies. He wears a fur-trimmed gown, both wives have Paris caps, and one displays an embroidered petticoat below her farthingale; the inscription remains although three shields have gone. There is some medieval glass on this side; look in particular for the very decorative little C15 *pelican in her piety* in the s.w. window, and the rare (albeit murky) example of C13 *grisaille* glass in the s.e. window above the C14 arms of Ufford. The C14 *angle piscina* was preserved in the restoration and the four-*light* e. window has 1880s glass by *Clayton & Bell* which is

typical of their work for the period. On the n. wall a roundel against a black ground tells how Ann Carter died in childbed in 1790:

> How dear the Purchase! how severe the Cost!
> The Fruit was sav'd, the parent Tree was lost!

Playford, St Mary (G6): The church stands on the hill above the village and the little River Fynn; there is a *lych-gate* at the bottom of a steep path and attractive steps lead up to the churchyard. Like a number of others in the area, the late-C14 tower stands to the s. of the *nave*. The substantial outer arch has large crowns in the mouldings and an angel holding a shield at the apex; judging by the shields in the *spandrels*, the tower was built by Sir George Felbrigg whose *brass* you will see inside. Just above is a nicely canopied and *groined* niche with flanking panels of *flushwork*, and the upper stage has a pair of widely spaced bell openings with a C19 cross set between them. They are *Perpendicular* in style, but the others are *Decorated* and it is likely that the arrangement on the s. side is all Victorian. On walking round, you will find that there is a three-*light* Perpendicular w. window, a blocked n. door, and a rebuilt *chancel* in early Decorated style which was designed by *R.M. Phipson* in 1873. The massive obelisk that stands s.w. of the tower commemorates Thomas Clarkson who died in 1846 and was erected eleven years later 'by a few surviving friends'. He achieved fame as 'the friend of slaves', having devoted most of his life to the cause and helping to achieve the Emancipation Bill of 1833. He lived at Playford Hall and is buried with his wife and son just outside the *priest's door* in the chancel. The grave is worth examining because not only does it retain its cast-iron railings, but they incorporate oval marble plaques set in cast-iron frames, a most unusual feature. Close by, a group of Airy family stones is enclosed within a cast-iron fence that also has distinctive components – a plaited top rail and a plate on the gate bearing a text. Within the porch the *jambs* of the inner doorway are scored with a mass of C17 and C18 graffiti, and above it within hang the *Royal Arms* of George III painted on canvas. The roof was replaced in celebration of Queen Victoria's Jubilee in 1897 and the *font* is C19 too. On the n. wall is a memorial for Sir George Biddell Airy, an Astronomer Royal who died in 1892, having restored to that office the authority and prestige it had lost in the C18. It takes the form of a fine bust by F.J. Williamson and the head is set in a dished oval with a loose collar lapping over the frame onto the grey marble surround. The chancel arch is tall, with *castellated capitals*, and beyond it on the s. wall is another bust portrait, this time in profile, of Thomas Clarkson, sculpted in 1878 by Sir Hamo Thornycroft, well known for 'The Kiss' in the Tate Gallery and his statue of Cromwell at Westminster. Fixed to the wall opposite is the fine brass of Sir George Felbrigg who died in 1400. Lord of the Manor, he was an esquire-at-arms to Edward III and lieutenant of the Court of Chivalry. Although there is now no trace of it, his tomb was in the n. wall of the nave where there was a *chantry* founded by him. The 4ft. 9in. brass is a good illustration of the armour of the period, and the heraldic lion, the helmet cords, and the sword scabbard were originally inlaid with colour; there are remnants of a canopy and marginal inscription. Above it is a lozenge-shaped panel with four coloured shields of arms and good lettering for Sir Anthony and Dame Anne Everard, placed there in 1657 by their son who 'desirous to be layd here with my parents have erected this memorial as wel for them as my selfe'. Retracing your steps, note that Sir George Felbrigg's shield occurs again (back to front!) in C15 glass in the tracery of a nave n. window.

Polstead, St Mary (D7): The church stands on a hilltop by the Hall and there are open views to the s., with a scaled-down replica of the Whitehall Cenotaph as a war memorial on the e. boundary of the churchyard. Seen from the gate, the outline of the church is a little stark, with a flat *chancel* roof behind a plain parapet and a *nave* gable that is sliced off at the top. To make amends, the early-C14 tower had an attractive spire added later which has small gabled windows at two levels – the only surviving stone medieval example in Suffolk. There is 'Y' *tracery* in the bell openings and a *lancet* is set above the small red brick w. doorway. Tie-rods with large 'S' braces are signs of a later structural problem. The tower houses an excellent ground floor ring of six bells with a 9 cwt. tenor. Although some of the windows are *Perpendicular*, the *aisles* were replaced in the C14 and the e. window of the s. aisle has *reticulated tracery*. There is a *priest's door* on that side and traces of *Norman* lancets in the chancel wall are the first indication of the true age of the building. There is a restored s. *porch* but the main entrance is on the other side and there are two steps down into the early-C14 n. porch. The side windows contain fragments of

medieval glass and, on the e. side, two roundels of C16 Flemish glass; one of them is a lively scene of Jesus being arrested, in which Judas kisses him and *St Peter* strikes at Malchus with his sword, while the other depicts the Magi. The C14 doorway has large, worn *headstops* and above is the shield of the Lambourne family, who were Lords of the Manor when it was built. The door itself still retains its original strap hinges and the remains of a central closing ring.

Once inside, the true age of the church is confirmed. The nave arcades are Norman with oblong *piers* which have pairs of shafts towards aisle and nave and varied capitals. The real interest lies in the arches which are brick with a scattering of tufa, a dark volcanic stone which was probably filched from a ruined Roman building. The bricks, however, are the wrong size and shape to be Roman and are very like those used to build Little Coggeshall abbey in Essex which have been dated about 1200. This means that these at Polstead may well be among the earliest surviving English bricks. The chancel arch matches the arcades and there are blank, roughly shaped *clerestory* windows of the same period which were covered by the roofs of the later aisles. Judging by the w. arch on the s. side of the nave, the C14 builders began to replace the arcades but the work was taken no further. Their tower, however, was placed against the Norman w. front without disturbing the original doorway and it can be seen from within the tower – fine and broad, with bands of heavy *chevrons* in the arch and three shafts in the *jambs*. The dark set of *Royal Arms* on the n. wall carries the initials of one of the Georges but it belongs to the reign of Queen Anne, although her 'Semper eadem' motto is not used. There is a C14 tomb recess below and, nearby, a fragment of wall painting that can still be recognised as the figure of a bishop. The large expanse of wall-hanging to the w. is made of crimson Italian silk velvet, embroidered with a repeat design of *Sacred monograms* within crowns of thorns. In the s. aisle, the octagonal brick bowl of the *font* is difficult to date but it rests on a C13 base with centre shaft and four columns with ring capitals and bases. The cover could, perhaps uncharitably, be described as an amorphous pancake of green fibreglass with a stylised and spiky handle representing a dove; scenes of the healing of the paralytic, the blind man, and Christ's encounter with the woman of Samaria are roughly incised on the top; it was designed by a nun of Oxford. On the wall beyond, two *consecration crosses* are placed unusually close to each other. There are a number of *hatchments* here for members of the Brand family and although the one above the arcade is unidentified, the others are for: Jacob, who probably died in the early C18 (above the font), another Jacob (w. wall, top), William, who died in 1799 (w. wall, r.), and his widow Anna Mirabella Henrietta who died in 1814 (it must have been pleasurable to call the banns!). The nave is lit by three small dormers on the s. side and below the plaster ceiling there are rough C14 *tie-beams* and heavy octagonal *king posts* which are strutted to a runner under the ridge. At the e. end of the s. aisle is a long, low C14 chest and on the wall to the r. a *touchstone* tablet framed in marble for Charles Vincent who died in 1700 – curiously old-fashioned for its period. The e. bay of the n. aisle roof is panelled with centre *bosses* and formed a *celure* for the *altar* below. It still has a lot of its C16 colouring and some of the gilded stars are cast in lead. By the pulpit is an anonymous *brass* of about 1490, with figures of a man wearing a heavy rosary, his wife with a veil headdress but with her face erased, and a group of five children. A small monument in the angle to the r. of the chancel arch is for Lord of the Manor Jacob Brand who died in 1630. It is coloured and he kneels within an arch with his hand on the head of his son Benjamin, who is said to have fallen to his death from a window in the Hall. The s. aisle has been cleared of pews to create a social gathering place.

Just within the chancel there are a pair of benches of curious design – spiral back posts and steeply cranked arms. They appear to be C18 or early-C19 and may have been used as *housel benches* like those at Shelland. The church's other brass is now fixed to the n. wall of the chancel and is a mid-C15 18in. effigy of a priest – one of only four in Suffolk which are shown wearing eucharistic vestments. *William Dowsing's* journal records a visit here in 1643 when he broke over forty 'superstitious pictures' and as a result little remains of the church's medieval glass. However, there are fragments in the s. chancel window, including a bishop holding a cross and what might be the handle of an auger. If so, it probably represents *St Leger*. The *communion rails* are a handsome three-sided set with shapely *balusters* and it is interesting that the design was varied by using twisted columns at the ends and corners. The *Stuart Holy Table* is unusual in having a thick centre stretcher which carries two slim turned posts. Behind it stands a modern oak *reredos* in *Jacobean* style but the three centre blind arches appear to be original.

Many visitors come to Polstead expecting to find some trace of poor Maria Marten but, like the Red Barn, nothing remains of her gravestone that once stood by the tower.

Poslingford, St Mary (B6): The church stands a little above the street and its solid, well-proportioned tower has *Decorated tracery* in the small w. window. Above the belfry *lancets* there are large bell openings, and on the n. side there is a long flight of steps up to an access door which was probably a C19 arrangement. Within hangs a good ring of five bells with a 9 cwt. tenor. The church was heavily restored by the Victorians but on the n. side you will find typical coursed flints, a small lancet and the *jambs* of a door, all of which are *Norman*. The windows range over a number of periods and styles: a tall late-C13 lancet (*chancel* n. side), a Decorated lancet and a two-*light* early-C14 window with *cusped* 'Y' tracery (s. chancel). Decorated windows, one with *reticulated* tracery (s. nave), and a *Perpendicular* design (n. nave); the e. window lancets are C19 but may echo what was there before. The line of an older roof shows on the e. face of the tower and it is strange to see that the restorers clad the gable wall of the nave with Kentish-style tiles. The early-C16 *porch* is very attractive in red brick and has a *stoup* inset by the outer arch. Below the crow-stepped gable there are three large and shallow niches and the side windows have *mullions* of brick. Much of the roof is original. The inner doorway is fine Norman work with sturdy shafts, and *capitals* carved with a variety of scroll patterns; the *abaci* are decorated with *chevrons* on one side and *dogtooth* on the other. Within the *tympanum*, a deep band is chip-carved with rosettes, interlace and dogtooth.

Within, the church is beautifully kept. The roofs are modern and the Decorated tower arch has been fitted with pine doors pierced by leaded *lights*. By the door stands what is probably a C12 *font* which at some time has had the corners of the bowl clipped off and then been restored to a square. On the w. wall is a mid-C17 monument for Thomas and Frances Golding which has its own endearing variety of lettering and spelling on the *touchstone* tablet; there are flanking trophies of death's sickle and spade, and at the top a coloured *achievement* is set within a broken *pediment* on which voluptuous little angels toy with skull and hour-glass. The upper *hatchment* above the arch is for Samuel Severne of Poslingford Park who died in 1865, and the lower pair are for Col. Thomas Weston and his wife Mary. It is interesting that their memorial tablets lower down are also lozenge-shaped to match the hatchments. There is a heavy C14 chest in the n.w. corner which is unusually decorated with two bands of coarse carving on the lid, which also bears centuries of graffiti. The *Royal Arms* of James I painted on board hang conveniently in front of the old n. door. The motto in rustic capitals within a strapwork surround is 'Exurgat deus dissipentur inimica' ('Let God arise and let his enemies be scattered', Psalm 68); the lion and *unicorn* are surprisingly explicit physically. An enterprising innovation is the use of two lightweight cartwheels converted to candelabra in the nave. There are remains of C14 painting in a s. nave window arch and the sill of the Perpendicular window on the n. side drops to the floor; The blocked door within it was probably the entrance to a *rood loft* stair. To the r. are the remains of what must have been a beautiful niche with a *groined* canopy. The tall C15 *screen* has *crocketted* and *cusped ogee* arches spanning two lights, with panel tracery above them. The lancet in the s. wall of the chancel retains some C13 decoration in the embrasure and the window above the stepped *sedilia* has 1880s glass by *Ward & Hughes* in sentimental mode. The early-C14 plain *piscina* has been restored and there is an *aumbry* in an uncommon position. It is round-headed, rebated for a door, and recessed in the splay above the sedilia.

Preston, St Mary (D5): By the mid-C19 the church had become very dilapidated, and when in 1868 the tower was struck for a second time by lightning and collapsed, a wholesale restoration was put in hand under *Sir Arthur Blomfield*. It was then that the tower and most of the *chancel* were rebuilt. The tall C16 *porch* is quite an eye catcher – panelled overall in *flushwork*, with three-*light Perpendicular* side windows; there are three matching niches – two in the buttresses and one over the doorway and the latter has an angel holding a shield below the stool. There are shields in the *spandrels* displaying the *Trinity* badge and *Passion emblems*, and *fleurons* stud the arch. In walking round note the *priest's door* on the s. side of the chancel and also the small angel below a stub buttress at the apex of the *nave* roof – an indication that there was probably a *sanctus-bell turret* there. Although the tower was rebuilt, the doors, niches and windows were reused and the weathervane (in the shape of a feather) is dated 1892. The tower houses a ring of six bells with an 11 cwt. tenor. It is interesting that the porch is not centred on the small C14 n. doorway but was offset to leave space for a table tomb. The

Purbeck marble top once carried a *brass* and it is likely that it commemorated the donor of the porch.

The fine C12 *font* stands just inside and the square bowl is carved with simple designs – an intersected arcade to the e., plaits and a rosette to the s., a square cabled border round a stylised Tree of Life to the w., and a floriated cross to the n.; the supporting shafts are modern. The church has one of the earliest and most interesting *Decalogue* boards to be found anywhere. Dating possibly from the time of Edward IV, it is in the form of a triptych, with the Commandments painted on the centre section and the wings inscribed with biblical texts on Sabbath-keeping and Commandment-obedience. When closed, the boards display texts on the theme of charity and the spelling is cheerfully haphazard. To match the Decalogue, Robert Ryece (of whom more later) set up one of the most splendid sets of Elizabethan *Royal Arms* in the country, again in triptych form. The wings are painted with Tudor supporters, lion and dragon, against a blue ground, with the sun and moon. Backed by strapwork, the arms are enclosed within the Garter and Ryece concocted an extraordinary collection of quarterings to display the queen's real and imaginary genealogy. Apart from the arms of England and France (reversed), he made places for Brutus; Uffa, king of the East Angles; Edward, king of the West Saxons; Swanus, king of Norway; Edward the Confessor; and even the SPQR badge of ancient Rome! 'Elizabetha Magna Regina Angliae' is lettered below, and at the top one can trace the faint outline of an 'ER' which has been overpainted. This suggests that the board may have carried Edward VI's arms originally. The back of the wings are painted with Puritan texts on an anti-imagery theme, and in 1987 the set was beautifully restored by Miss Julie Crick. They are now displayed on the n. *aisle* wall.

On that side there is a low tomb recess and the stair to the old *rood loft* rises to the l. of the chancel arch behind the pulpit, with a little window giving on to the n. aisle. There is a plain *piscina* in the s. aisle chapel and nearby, a *Ward & Hughes* 1880s window – an uninspired Nativity in muddy colours. Roofs and fittings throughout are C19, but although the *rood screen* was destroyed long before, its base was recovered and replaced with new panels inserted. The C14 piscina in the *sanctuary* has a wide *trefoiled ogee* arch, and there is a narrow opening to the *dropped-sill sedilia* alongside. *James Powell & Sons* are best

Preston, St Mary: Elizabethan Royal Arms

known for their stained glass but they undertook other work; the *reredos* here is by them – mosaic panels of the *Evangelistic symbols* and a centre inscription which informs us that the rector and his curate 'by whose exertions the church was restored in 1868' had it installed in 1883. The flanking walls are tiled and above are two large mosaic panels with the *Agnus Dei* and the *pelican in her piety* within centre lozenges. The Revd. James Dunn's tablet on the n. wall has the often-used epitaph which begins 'Adieu vain world I have seen enough of thee, and now I am careless what thou say'st of me'. The chancel glass is uniformly awful but there are two brasses in the sanctuary floor which should not be overlooked: on the s. side for Mary Ryece (1629) with four shields, an inscription and Latin verse, and on the n. for Robert Ryece. This has a lavish display of heraldry – Ryece's shield with mantling, crest and motto and eight other shields. They range widely enough in his family to include the arms of his great-great-grandfather's wife (the centre inscription is modern). Ryece, who died in 1638, was one of Suffolk's earliest antiquarians and was besotted with heraldry. He collected over 150 stained glass shields of arms dating from the C14 to the C16 and 46 of them survive in the aisle e. windows and in the *clerestory*. They figure in his *Breviary of Suffolk* written in 1618 but not published until 1902.

Ramsholt, All Saints (H6): This is one of Suffolk's lonely churches, to be found at the end of quiet lane, in a delectable setting overlooking the Deben estuary. The building was probably here before the Conquest, and the walls of the round tower are a charming mixture of *septaria*, flint, and brick. In fact it is more oval than round and has three buttresses which were probably added later like those at Beyton, the only other example of a buttressed round tower. Walking round, note the n. doorway of about 1300, and the rather strange pairs of small *lancets* at high level – C13? There is a three-*light Tudor* window in the *chancel* n. wall, and the e. window has early-C14 intersected 'Y' *tracery*. On the s. side, a *priest's door* and roughly re-formed triple lancets in the *nave* wall which are probably contemporary with those on the other side.

Entry is through a small C19 brick porch to a sweet interior. The doorway to the tower is *Norman*, with simple *imposts*, and the fine example of a C13 stone coffin which lies alongside was probably used for a priest. A *Jacobean* chest is nearby, and a simple *Stuart Holy Table* stands against the n. wall. The C15 *font* panels have small shields within *quatrefoils*, and its drum shaft came from an earlier model no doubt. Everything is seemly now, but a C19 archdeacon reported that the walls were 'as green as the grass with which they are surrounded'. There were holes in the roof, the benches were decayed, and an owl had taken up residence in the pulpit. Restoration followed, and it is most unusual to find that, as late as the 1850s, *box pews* and a *two-decker pulpit* were installed. The parish obviously clung to the traditions of its fathers and ignored the fashionable craze for Gothic. The woodwork of the pews is grained and tan-coloured, and they all have seats on two sides. A second range in the chancel reaches as far as the priest's door and its seats face the pulpit (another refusal to follow the dictates of the *Ecclesiological Society*). The square pulpit, with its heavily moulded rim, is on the s. wall, with the reading desk in front. A place was made for the *parish clerk* in the front pew, and his book slope was attached to the door. A marble tablet on the n. wall of the chancel is formed like a parchment scroll and commemorates the great-grandchildren of Robert Field, vicar here for over forty years. It also details how Field's successor ensured that the parish had a say in a subsequent appointment. Above the priest's door is a beautifully cut tablet of 1786 for John and Hannah Keeble, and in the *sanctuary* there is a capacious late-C14 *piscina*, with *dropped-sill sedilia* alongside. Outside once again, look for the excellent C18 Waller headstones s. of the nave – Mary's 1744, Jeptha's 1748, William's 1759, and one for an earlier Jeptha with the verse:

Deceas'd dear Lord, I come to thee,
Tho' now disolv'd in Grave.
In hopes the Bless'd Eternal Three,
My soul will ever save.

Rattlesden, St Nicholas (D5): This most attractive village lying in a valley has a church which stands proudly on rising ground in the centre. The C14 tower has most unusual five-sided buttresses to the w. which rise to the parapet and are gabled at the top. It has a *Decorated* w. window but the bell openings are C19 and at that time the lead on the *broach spire* was replaced by oak shingles. This was part of a major restoration in the 1880s under *Sir Arthur Blomfield* when the n. *clerestory* wall was replaced, the *porch* and s. *aisle* re-faced and many of the windows renewed. The aisles have C19 *crocketted* pinnacles at the corners, there is an early-C16 two-storied *sacristy* n. of the *chancel*, and an obtrusive chimney rises on the n.e. corner of the *nave*. The *Perpendicular* s. *clerestory* parapet has a most interesting series of sixteen *flushwork* letters and emblems. From the w. they represent: SS *Edmund, Matthew, James the Less, Philip, Thaddeus, Bartholomew, Peter*, the *Blessed Virgin*, the *Sacred monogram*, a dragon (possibly for *St John*), and SS *Paul, James the Great, Andrew, Simon,*

Thomas and *Etheldreda* (an 'A' for her popular name, St Audrey) Round the corner at the w. end are the arms of the Chamberlain and Bourchier families and on the e. face are a mitre and crossed croziers (the arms of Hervey, Bishop of Ely in the early C12). A *rood stair* turret is set in the wall of the s. aisle and the s. porch is tall and handsome. Rebuilt in the 1470s, the *ashlar* of its s. face is panelled overall, it has stepped battlements, and in the canopied niche above the doorway an 1890s figure of *St Nicholas*, vested as a bishop, sits with a child at his knee. The line of an old roof shows over the lovely inner doorway dating from about 1300 which has a deeply moulded arch resting on pairs of attached shafts; above it is a contemporary circular window inset with a *quatrefoil*.

Within are C14 *arcades* on octagonal *piers* whose concave faces are topped by blank *cusped* arches, and spread above is a superb double *hammerbeam* roof alive with the carved angels that were added when it was restored and renewed in the 1880s. There is *tracery* above the hammerbeams and on either side of the *king posts*, which rise from the *collars* to the ridge. All the angels in the aisle roofs are C19 too, with the exception of one in the n.e. corner of the s. aisle. There is a *sanctus-bell window* in the tower wall and access to the bell chamber is by way of an unusual Victorian cast-iron spiral staircase, but the church's ring of six bells with an 11 cwt. tenor is rung from the ground floor. The set of George I *Royal Arms* is dated 1714. In front of the tower arch stands a section of the C15 *rood screen*, with four-*light* tracery in its panels. The late-C14 *font* stands on a wide octagonal step and is satisfyingly solid, with a traceried shaft and a deep bowl whose panels are carved with cusped *ogee* arches flanked by flowers and leaves. Under the bowl are six varied human heads and two lion masks to the w. To the e. is a range of C17 *altar rails* which came from Kettlebaston in 1903. They are finely turned, with groups of four *balusters* at each end; other sections of the same set are placed at the e. end of the n. aisle and at the front of the nave on the s. side. Like Methwold in Norfolk, Rattlesden has a complete replica rood screen, loft, and rood, and it is a lovely reconstruction, lacking only the vivid colours that its predecessor would have had. Designed by G.F. Prynne, it was built in 1909 and in 1916 he designed the matching *parclose screen* in the s. aisle. This completes the original arrangement and its loft provides the link between the turret in the s. aisle wall and the *rood loft*, via a little curving wooden stair. All the carving is excellent, with intricate tracery roundels, cresting, and bands of ornament. The s. aisle chapel retains its *piscina*, although the canopy is chopped away, and the image niche in the e. window embrasure suffered at the same hand, which left only a portion of the vaulting. To the l., a quatrefoil *squint* once gave a view of the *High altar*. This may have been the chapel of the *guild* of *St Margaret* with the guild of *St John the Baptist* taking the n. aisle chapel where a matching image niche has been similarly defaced. The *Jacobean* pulpit stands on a new base; the bottom panels are plain but the top range of *blind arches* has better than average carving.

Through the heavy doors of the *screen* one moves into the chancel where the coved and panelled ceiling conceals a hammerbeam roof. It was extensively restored in the C19 but many of the ribs and ornaments are C16. The stalls, too, were reconstructed but, again, much is original work, including the fronts and slopes; look particularly for the four-headed *poppyhead* on the n. side and the one with six faces (all with tongues out) on the s. side. Until the 1890s the C17 *communion rails* were three-sided but they were rearranged and a section of the set now stands on the n. side of the nave at the e. end. In the n. wall is the medieval door to the sacristy. Although the upper floor has been removed, the stairs remain in the s.w. corner. The ground floor may have been used as a chapel but both windows are barred. There are traces of heavy shutters, and the door frame is slotted for a bar. On the wall hang the *Decalogue*, Creed and Lord's Prayer boards painted in 1690 for the *sanctuary*. In the n. wall of the sanctuary is a particularly fine C14 *aumbry*. It has a crocketted gable on tilted *corbel* heads, with a *trefoil* below it and flanking shafts with ringed *capitals* topped by pinnacles. The interior is grooved for a shelf and it is large enough to have served for an *Easter sepulchre* in season. Fitted with a new door it now contains the Blessed Sacrament reserved for the sick. In 1912 a wooden canopied stall was inserted into the *sedilia* and the back panels came from the original rood loft or screen. They were once painted with figures but only the faint outlines remain. There are two quite flamboyant *Art Nouveau* sanctuary lamps in copper and the e. wall is panelled in stone, with a heavy canopy over the 1890s Last Supper *reredos*. The e. window glass by *Clayton & Bell* is the same period but there are three good windows by William Aikman dating from the 1920s: on the s. side of the sanctuary, three scenes against clear glass, with lovely deep colours in the robes, of Thomas Rattlesden meeting King Henry VII at Bury, St Nicholas, and St Edmund; s. aisle, the war memorial window with *St George* flanked by scenes of the sacrifice of Isaac and David versus Goliath; s. aisle w. end, Christ gathering the children of all nations, with the church's font and altar illustrated at the bottom. The other s. aisle window has late (1913) *Hardman* glass of Christ in Glory with four *censing* angels, though it is made very dull by the tree outside. In 1897, *Heaton, Butler & Bayne* took a host of fragments from the clerestory and set them in the w. window; there is a musical angel at the top and lots of small heads in a kaleidoscope of colour. More fragments were arranged in a n. aisle window in 1901 but they are a mere jumble.

Raydon, St Mary (E7): The church was built in the late C13 to early C14 and had a tower until it collapsed in the C17, bringing down four bells with it. Now, the single bell is housed in a diminutive annexe with a tiled pyramid roof built on to the w. end. The windows have an enterprising mixture of *Decorated tracery* and there are some very good *headstops* which include two dames at the w. end. The *rood stair turret* is set within a buttress angle on the n. side, and the *chancel* is of exceptional quality for a church of this size. It is all early-C14 but the details are varied and inventive. The buttresses on the n. side are triangular (like Thorpe Morieux) with headstops on the *dripstones*, but those to the s. have very steep *weatherings* and *cusped* gables under the eaves. Each corner buttress continues upward as a traceried octagonal shaft, to finish in a flourish of densely *crocketted* gables and a pinnacle. There are quite large masks sculpted on the weatherings and little devils sprout around the gables. They were comprehensively restored in 1988; note the large dragon with a curly tail that crouches at the base of the n.e. pinnacle. The *low side windows* either side of the chancel are equally lavish in their way. Each is tall, split by a *transom*, and set within broad and shallow mouldings; the upper section is a cusped *lancet* below a *trefoil*, and the lower lancet is now blocked. The *priest's door*, with its slim shafts and large ring *capitals*, is on the s. side, and the church clock is placed above the e. window – unusual but eminently sensible. A *scratch dial* with a heavy rod in the centre hole can be seen on the s.e. nave buttress.

Passing through an open wooden porch, one enters via a plain C14 doorway which has very worn headstops to the dripstone. To the r. is the remnant of a *stoup* and a cracked C13 grave slab serves as a threshold. Within, there is a small door in the w. wall that once led to the tower, and the peculiar *font* is probably C19 – a small octagonal bowl on a baluster stem, all now picked out in brown and cream. A full-scale restoration in the 1880s provided benches, roofs, a new e. window, and the *vestry* beyond the nave n. door. This now has new doors presented by members of the 353rd Fighter Group of the American 8th Air Force, who were stationed nearby during World War II. There is no longer a *screen* between *nave* and chancel but the position of the *rood beam* is indicated by the two wooden brackets which are still in place above the arch. The steep stair to the loft can be seen in the n. wall and there is a *piscina* with a finely moulded trefoil arch on the other side of the nave marking the site of an *altar*. The remnants of two *brasses* are nearby: an inscription for Thomas Reydon, and an 8in. figure of Elizabeth Reydon which now lacks its top half and *butterfly headdress*; both date from 1479. Seen from within, the low side windows lie in deep embrasures and there are grotesques at the w. end of the arches. Behind the organ, a large tomb recess probably marks the resting place of the founder; the sharply angled arch has headstops and the deeply recessed moulding is cusped within. The bottom sections of the chancel side windows were plastered up at some time and they contain fragments of C14 and C15 glass, including some delicate leaf shapes on the n. side. The *sanctuary* floor was raised in the C19 to the detriment of the early-C14 double piscina. This is fine and large, constructed like a complete window head with all the tracery moulded and pierced. The design matches the side windows and the piscina was doubtless made along with them. On the n. wall opposite there is a *touchstone* tablet set within an alabaster frame enriched with skulls wearing wreaths of laurel. A flaming urn sits in the broken *pediment* and the memorial commemorates John Mayer, a 'faithful & laborious servant of God' who was 22 years at Little Wratting before serving 33 years here. He died at a good age in 1663 and had been no simple country parson; as the epitaph says: 'he wrote also for ye publick good these most useful books' and proceeds to list them (a rare example of a bibliography preserved in stone!). Bible expositions in many volumes were followed by an *'Antidote against Popery'*, and *'Ye history of the world from ye Creation to 1648'*, amongst other things.

Rede, All Saints (C5): There was an extensive restoration here in 1850, the *chancel* was rebuilt

in 1874 and the *porch* restored in 1877, so that much of the fabric has that sharp look of the C19. However, a good deal remains of interest and it is worth circling the outside of the building first. A round-headed *lancet* at the w. end of the *nave* on the n. side indicates that the church was originally *Norman*. The next window along has *Decorated tracery*, and C13 lancets were reused in the side walls of the chancel when it was rebuilt. The late-C13 or early-C14 tower has half-height w. buttresses, 'Y' tracery in the bell opening and lancets in the other faces. There are good *gargoyles* n. and s., with long snarling metal spouts below the recently restored battlements (in the 1830s there was no parapet at all). The s. porch is handsome in its quiet way, with a floriated cross on the gable and *crocketted* corner pinnacles. The niche above the door is richly decorated with a nodding *ogee* arch, stiff-leaf *capitals* to the little side shafts, and a carved stool on which stands a modern figure of Christ the King. Below the corner pinnacles there are jutting demi-angels and the bases of the buttresses are carved with the arms of Turner and Bullock.

The C14 s. doorway is tall and narrow and note when you use the heavy key that its wards are stamped '1850'. There is no tower arch – access is by a medieval door, and above it there is a small *sanctus-bell window* with a *cusped* arch. It is backed by a wooden traceried shutter which, if original, is a rare and unusual feature. There are some low C15 benches at the w. end that have been ravaged by woodworm and the C13 octagonal *font* is entirely plain, standing on a shaft almost as wide as the bowl. The ceilings are plastered, with two exposed *tie-beams* and, with a single exception, all the benches on the s. side are medieval, with *poppyheads*, gabled elbows, and *castellated* backs. The C17 pulpit has plain panels with coarsely carved shells applied below the rim and a canted ledge resting on plain scrolls; the square window nearby is a C19 addition. The Victorian chancel stalls have poppyheads and on the ends there are four intriguing hinged seats facing e. Their purpose is obscure and the undersides are carved rather in the fashion of *misericords* (although they have no lips to rest against and are too low anyway). The carvings are: a *pelican in her piety, Agnus Dei, Sacred monogram* with leaf supporters, and floriated cross, also with supporters. Someone obviously favoured hinged seats at toddler level because there are more fixed to the old benches by the font. The jolly little chamber organ with painted pipes held in a wrought-iron frame was built by Bevington & Sons of Soho, probably in the 1860s. The marble *reredos* set in stone panelling with alpha and omega signs is run-of-the-mill Victoriana but the e. window glass is distinctly interesting. It was the first independent commission of William Francis Dixon who had been a pupil of *Clayton & Bell* and who designed for the firm of Mayer in Munich 20 years later. His style is an individual development of the conventions adopted by Clayton & Bell and foreshadows techniques used by other artists. The choice of subjects happens to be more adventurous than usual too; the l.-hand *light* shows Cornelius the centurion kneeling before *St Peter* (Acts 10:26) and on the other side of a central Ascension is the Old Testament scene of the death of the Shunammite woman's child before Elisha restored him (2 Kings 4:20); there is a Christ in Majesty (shown as King) in the tracery and the coats of arms across the bottom are Turner on the l., *Royal Arms* in the centre, and Bullock on the r.

Redgrave, All Saints (E3): In 1897 the Revd. Holt Wilson decided that St Mary's church was too cold in winter and too far away both for him and his parishioners, so he built them a Mission Hall next to the vicarage on the village street. In 2006, when the beautiful old church was reclared redundant and passed into the care of the *CCT*, the little red brick building came into its own and was transformed into the new All Saints. With lots of local effort and some considerable skill it has become a smart, comfortable, and very efficient parish church seating just under a hundred, and is the only church in Suffolk or Norfolk that is air-conditioned. The original door has been retained on the n. side as an emergency exit, but on the s. side a sizeable extension provides an entrance vestibule, together with a kitchen and cloakrooms. The hall was gutted and fitted out afresh with comfortable seating, and the walls below the dado are neatly panelled in fresh colour. The rails of the *sanctuary* were refurbished in 1997 to celebrate the building's centenary, and the *altar* stands in a recess below an e. window which has a stylised cross faintly reminiscent of a child's plastic whirligig. To the r. is a new *font* crafted in chestnut, with a substantial bowl set on three curved and pointed slabs. Consecrated by the bishop of the diocese in September, 2008, this is a building entirely 'fit for purpose' as the politicians would have it.

Redgrave, St Mary (E3): Now cared for by the *Churches Conservation Trust*, the church stands on gently rising ground nearly a mile to the e. of the village and may have been so placed for the convenience of the Lord of the Manor. A fine building, with lots of interest, it was built in the first half of the C14, with the s. *aisle* and *clerestory* following a little later. The original tower collapsed in the C16 and was rebuilt in red brick, but late in the C18 it was cased in the local 'Woolpit whites' and the windows were remodelled. It houses a good ring of six bells with an 8 cwt. tenor. The s. aisle has a parapet of *flushwork* displaying crowned monograms and sporting large *gargoyles*. There is a two-*light* window with *Decorated tracery*, two *Perpendicular* windows, and the aisle e. window has lovely Decorated tracery, with the *ogees* of the three main lights flowing up to enclose two multi-*cusped* and pointed ovals. This design echoes what had already been used in one of the tall *chancel* windows on the s. side and shows how the Decorated and Perpendicular styles overlapped in time. There are ten windows each side of the clerestory, and a continuous *dripstone*, together with panels of flushwork, unites them in a single composition. Again, the flushwork embodies monograms, and the crowned portcullis of the House of *Tudor* can be seen at the e. end. The chancel has prominent buttresses with niches at the second stage, and there is a shapely Decorated *priest's door* complete with *crocketted finial* and *headstops*. The great e. window tracery is delicately moulded but the pattern of tracery above the seven lights is restless, with interlocking ogees enclosing a circle in the head. Above it, you will notice that the line of the original gable was much flatter. The C16 *vestry* on the n. side was altered to accommodate an C18 tomb beneath, and the outside was cased in red brick, presumably at the same time as a large egg-shaped window was introduced in the n. wall. The windows in the n. aisle have flattened Tudor arches and the door on that side has been blocked. Over the wide outer arch of the C14 *porch* is a sundial and the inner doorway is very handsome; there are pairs of shafts with leaf *capitals*, and one of the arch mouldings is enriched with *fleurons* and lion heads, coming down to large king and queen headstops. Above the arch is an image niche with a demi-angel beneath it, and to either side are head pedestals.

Inside the church one can appreciate its spaciousness. The two ranks of mouldings in the arches of the C14 *arcades* match those in the chancel arch and are very effective, but they slightly overpower the slender *quatrefoil piers* that support them. The *nave* roof, clean and light, is a warm brown colour and has alternating *hammerbeams* and *arch-braces*, with braced *queen posts* above. The *wall posts* rest on carved head *corbels*, one with his tongue sticking out. Below, on nice brick floors, there are C19 pine benches, with those in the aisles still marked 'Free', a reminder of the longstanding C17 and C18 tradition of the best pews being rented out to those who could afford them. Over the s. door is a lovely carved and painted set of *Stuart Royal Arms*; in an oval frame, it is very similar to the uncoloured example at neighbouring Wortham and was probably carved by the same man. The C14 *font* at the w. end of the n. aisle also shares a family likeness with Wortham's; the carving is not as sharp but the heads below the bowl are better and, instead of having stepped buttresses at the angles, this one has little attached columns. Beyond it on the n. wall is a huge early-C18 *reredos*, designed to stand behind the *High altar*. In wood and picked out in gilt, it has absurdly massive side scrolls, *Corinthian* columns, cherub heads, and the *Decalogue* panels are flanked by very faded paintings of Moses and Aaron. By the organ is a C15 parish chest with a divided lid, cross-banded with iron with its original padlocks. The chapel in the s. aisle contains a C14 *piscina* with a multicusped arch, *groined* within, and *dropped-sill sedilia* alongside. There is no *rood screen* now to the wide chancel and the roof is modern, but the late-C14 *sedilia* are beautiful. Divided by lozenge-shaped pillars, each seat has a vaulted canopy, and above there is an exquisitely detailed little range of Perpendicular window tracery; at each end of the straight top cresting are demi-angels holding shields. To the e. is a piscina within a cusped and crocketted arch resting on angled animal headstops. The e. window glass of 1853 is by Farrow, the local Diss glazier. There are figures of *St Peter, St Paul* and the *Evangelists* in a line across the centre, with Christ in the centre holding a chalice; below is a Crucifixion against a vivid blue background, and the rest is patterned roundels. The whole is bright and consciously medieval in feeling.

Redgrave has some uncommonly good monuments and memorials and one of the finest is in the n.e. corner of the *sanctuary*. It is for Lord Chief Justice Holt and is boldly signed by the sculptor, Thomas Green of Camberwell. Green was one of the outstanding artists of his day and this is one of his finest pieces. Daniel Defoe when he saw it called it 'that most exquisite monument'. Sir John sits in the full panoply of judicial robes, wearing the *collar of SS* and

holding the black cap in his lap. The figure of Justice, bearing the scales but without a blindfold, stands on the l., and Mercy with a coiled serpent is to the r. Corinthian columns flank the main figure and there is a *cartouche* of arms above the draped curtains in the arch behind. Three pairs of cherubs and an urn are at the top, while on the upper corners are a cock and a crane, the symbols of watchfulness and vigilance. The Latin epitaph gives his date of death as March 1709, but apparently he last sat in court in February 1710. Set in the floor of the sanctuary on the s. side is one of the most perfect post-*Reformation brasses* in England and it may well have been engraved by *Nicholas Stone*. Intended to be the top of a table tomb, it is for Mrs Anne Butts, the mother-in-law of Sir Nicholas Bacon. She died in 1609 and is shown wearing a calash (the voluminous hood that was then in vogue) and an embroidered petticoat is displayed by her parted gown. Her shield of arms is on the l. and that of her parents (the Bures) on the r. The epitaph reads:

The weaker sexes strongest precedent
Lies here belowe; seaven fayer yeares she
    spent
In wedlock sage; and since that merry age
Sixty one yeares she lived a widdowe sage
Humble as great as full of Grace as elde,
A second Anna had she but beheld
Christ in His flesh who now she glorious
    sees
Below that first in time, not in degrees.

On the wall above is an elegant oval in *touchstone*, garlanded at the sides and surmounted by a cartouche below a *pediment*. It is by Nicholas Stone and commemorates the Lady Gawdye who died in 1621. She was Sir Nicholas Bacon's second daughter and, after a first marriage of convenience, her epitaph suggests that she chose for herself and wisely. At the e. end of the n. aisle is the magnificent tomb of Sir Nicholas and Lady Anne Bacon. The massive chest, in touchstone, has lovely white marble scroll-work panels on each side, with shields of arms at the ends. It was made by Nicholas Stone's colleague Bernard Janssen, the king's engineer, but the recumbent figures on top were carved by Stone himself, for which he charged £200. The baronet wears plate armour, with the visor of his helmet raised, and his wife is in embroidered gown and bodice with a ruff. The modelling of her face is particularly good and reminiscent of Stone's effigy of Mrs Elizabeth

Coke at Bramfield (perhaps his finest anywhere). Sir Nicholas, created premier baronet by James I in 1611 and son of Elizabeth's Lord Keeper of the Great Seal, had the tomb made in 1616 when his wife died; the effigies were added after his death in 1624. The pieces of mock armour resting in the niches beyond the tomb were carried as emblems at his funeral. On the n. wall nearby is a good tablet for Robert Bacon, who died in 1652; it may be by Nicholas Stone's son, John. Nicholas himself was responsible for fitting out the w. end of the n. aisle as a Bacon chapel, including the paving and the alcoves. There you will find a severely plain tablet, finely lettered by Stone, for Lady Philippa Bacon, who died in 1626, and there is a memorial for Sir Edmund Bacon on the w. wall and a matching tablet for his wife Elizabeth to the r. in similar style. The church has an excellent array of *hatchments* for the Bacon, Holt and Wilson families, all at some time Lords of the Manor. Having been stored for many years in the vestry, they were cleaned and now make a brave show. Those in the n. aisle are for Bacon, those above the nave arcades for Holt, and those in the chancel for Wilson (including an exceptionally late one for George Rowland Holt Wilson who died in 1929). A very helpful list giving full details hangs by the font. Following the move into the care of the CCT, a local Trust has been formed which has done excellent work in improving the building's facilities. Underfloor heating has been installed under the pews which can be augmented at will by a blown air system. The base of the tower is neatly fitted with a suite of lavatories and the w. door now serves as an access point for the disabled. The C19 organ that was left unfinished when the money ran out may yet be completed by the church's local supporters.

Redisham, St Peter (I2): An unobtrusive little church, set well back from the road. When its tower collapsed in the C19, the w. wall of the *nave* was strengthened with large buttresses, twin *lancets* were inserted, and a small wooden bellcote was perched on the roof. A good deal of *septaria* shows in the walls, and a medley of flints and small boulders were used for *quoins* at the n.e. corner of the nave – often a sign of a *Saxon* building. A short section of an earlier wall (now capped with pantiles) forms part of the n. wall of the *chancel*, and suggests that the early building was shorter. The two-*light* e. window has *Decorated tracery*, and the pair of lancets on the s. side of the chancel are from the same period. C19 work included decorative barge

boards on the chancel gable – something normally seen only on porches. Even in small churches such as this, the *Normans* often made quite lavish additions, and the modest brick porch shelters a splendid doorway that is squat and immensely solid. Its arch has a triple band of mouldings, with a broad interlaced *chevron* in the centre; within it is another, shallower chevron, the under-surfaces are carved with roundels, and the outer rim is a series of disks carved with crosses. There are spiral shafts, and *billet moulding* decorates the *jambs*. A *scratch dial* shows plainly on the r.-hand *capital* and is a reminder that there was no porch in the church's early days. The n. doorway is Norman too, but simpler, with single bands of chevron and billet mouldings in the arch.

The entrance door with its closing ring is medieval, and the hinges are unusually wrought as a series of oval links. Within, the C15 *font* has blank shields and *Tudor Roses* in its cusped panels, and there are good demi-angels with crossed hands below the bowl. Brick floors and plastered ceilings feature in nave and chancel, and most of the furnishings are Victorian. However, the pulpit is a fine *Stuart* piece, apart from its base and steps. It is large and square, with two carved top panels, and its maker dated it '1619', provided handsome brackets for the book ledge, and completed it with turned *finials*. The s. wall of the nave leans gently outwards, and there you will find a small set of *Georgian Royal Arms*, painted on board and decidedly murky. The church's only stained glass is in the window by the pulpit and commemorates a late-C19 to early-C20 vicar. A post-Resurrection Christ and *St Peter* are watched by a group of fishermen in their boat beyond, and the scene is contained by a series of scrolls and set upon a bracket, all within clear glass. An effective design, with sensitive modelling – not signed, but Christopher Webb comes to mind, whose work can be seen at Brettenham, Cowlinge, Mettingham, Newmarket St Mary and Tuddenham St Martin. There is now no chancel arch, although C15 brick *responds* remain, and no *rood screen* – changes probably dating from the C18 or early-C19. There are some C15 bench ends in the chancel – a lion minus his head holds a shield on one, and on another a dragon licks from a cooking pot balanced on his back. That is particularly interesting because the same beast (albeit mutilated) can be found at nearby Weston. It was probably carved by the same man, and his inspiration may have been a *bestiary* illustration, although I have not yet identified the legend. The delightful bear with his head in a honeypot on another bench is modern. When *William Dowsing* came in April 1643, he noted: 'a crucifix and three other superstitious pictures; and gave order for Mr Barenby, the parson, to levell the steps in the chancel. He preach but once a day'. This is one of Dowsing's few snide remarks about the clergy, and it seems as though the vicar quietly got his own back by doing nothing about the steps.

On your way back to the gate, spare a thought for Eliza Westrup, a love child who was only 11 months old when she died in 1810. Her headstone stands in the second line w. of the path and the epitaph is a poignant reproach:

Remember me as you pass by,
Tho' you my Father did me deny.
Glad were you to hear the Sound
Of the Bell that passed me to the ground.
If you were as free from sin as I,
You would not be afraid to die.
As I am now so must you be,
Therefore prepare to follow me.

Was it, I wonder, the unrepentant father who reversed the headstone so that it could not be read from the path?

Redlingfield, St Andrew (F3): A small and simple church just to the s. of the hamlet, it is easily seen from the road and a footpath leads directly to it alongside Hall farm. The tower has a red brick base with fragments of blue patterning, and the second stage is plastered below a gabled roof. From the inside you will see that there is the outline of a C14 window in the w. wall of the *nave* and it is more than likely that there was no tower until the C17. A Benedictine priory was founded here in 1120, endowed with the manor, and from the outset it was assigned the parish church for its own use – an unusually early example of approp-riation. Its fortunes fluctuated and there were scandalous revelations at a bishop's visitation in 1425 when the prioress was forced to resign. Thereafter, life was blameless until its dissolution in 1536 when its prioress, seven nuns, two priests, and twenty-one servants were turned out into the world with very little to bless themselves with. It is interesting that at that time the dedication was listed as 'The Blessed Virgin and St Andrew' and the demise of the nunnery may have prompted the change. There was some rebuilding in the C14 and a blocked door of that period lies in the centre of the n.

wall; above it there is the faint outline of a *lancet* which is the only visible reminder of the original building. Farther along is a C16 brick *mullioned* window and the *chancel* appears to have been rebuilt in C18 or early-C19 brick. However, the *Decorated* e. window with its *reticulated tracery* was reused, and so was the *priest's door*. Nearby, a memorial slab with a shield of arms for Joannis Garneys who died in 1697 has been set in the wall. There are Decorated windows on the s. side of the nave and one of the *headstops* is a mask with its tongue lolling out. The angle buttresses at the w. end are another indication that the medieval building had no tower. The *porch* has blocked 'Y' tracery windows and its steeply pitched roof rests on *arch-braces*.

Moving to the simple interior, you will see the *Royal Arms* of George IV hanging on the n. wall – painted on board, with an exceptionally good unicorn. The C15 octagonal *font* is rather battered and this may be because *William Dowsing* came here in April 1643, although his diary has no direct reference to it. There are *woodwoses* and lions round the shaft, and angels below the bowl whose panels are carved with *Evangelistic symbols* alternating with angels bearing shields; the emblems of *St Edmund* (s.) and the *Passion* (n.e.) are recognisable. The nave roof is arch-braced, with *collars* under the ridge, and naive carved busts were added to the base of the wall posts, probably in the C17. The benches and pulpit are modern and may have come in when there was a restoration in 1873. A C14 *piscina* is to be found on the s. side at the e. end of the nave, and a pair of C15 bench ends survives in the chancel. Susanna Everard has a good *ledger-stone* of 1670. It lies partly under the *altar* and is a simple representation of a fashionable architectural tablet. Before you leave, note that there is an interesting modern version of a tithe map by the door. Drawn in 1977, it gives all the field names in the parish and vignettes of various buildings, and even identifies the mobile library halt.

Rendham, St Michael (H4): The main road from Framlingham to Saxmundham crosses the infant River Alde and swings to catch church and graveyard within a tight bend. The tower has a late-C14 w. window, and the unusually placed panels of *flushwork* below it are just like those at neighbouring Sweffling. The blocked window at belfry level, with its delicately *cusped ogee* arch, is more decorative than one would expect and may once have been an image niche. There is more flushwork in the angle buttresses and battlements, and the bell openings look as though they were altered in the C19. The tower houses an excellent ring of eight bells with a 10 cwt. tenor. Walking round, you will find a blocked doorway in the s. wall of the *nave*, and the coursed flints nearby suggest a C13 start for the main building. The *Decorated* window at the e. end of the nave on the s. side has good *tracery*, and the surface carving on its *cusps* includes a Sacred Heart. There is a *priest's door* in the *chancel* wall further along, and a *scratch dial* incised on a square block of stone can be found below one of the two large C13 *lancets*. At first sight, the tracery pattern of the e. window looks like early-C14, but the combination of thin *mullions* and the arch shape inside puts it much later – probably early-C17. A medieval window was reused in the Victorian *vestry*, and the patch on the n. nave wall shows where the *rood stair* projected. The substantial C15 *porch* was comprehensively restored as part of one of the two mid-C19 restorations. There are worn *headstops* to its outer arch, with a niche overhead, and parts of the original roof can be seen inside. A section from an C18 lead roof stands framed in a window recess, and note that the rebuilding included an entirely new inner doorway.

The interior bears many of the marks of enthusiastic Victorian restoration – stained pine pews with doors, and a plain replacement *font*, but there are a number of interesting things to see. A corner at the back of the nave has been converted in to a mini-museum of the village – a showcase, a fascinating selection of C19 and C20 photographs, and continuing scrapbooks; the pierced cast-iron space heater was a favourite choice for church heating about the time of the 1851 Exhibition. Homely bricks pave the floor of the nave, and a little way along it there is a good example of a *chalice brass*. These were only used for priests and are comparatively rare – the only other Suffolk example that comes to mind is at Gazeley. This one dates from 1523: 'Here lieth Thomas Kyng sutyme [sometime] vicar of this churche'. Above the tower arch there is a roundel of Victorian *Royal Arms*, and its predecessor still hangs on the s. wall – a Charles II set on canvas, with 'God Save the King' in place of the usual motto. Part of the doorway and a section of the stairs that led to the rood loft remain in the opposite wall. Another little period touch is the C19 umbrella stand and drip tray on one of the pew ends. The late-14 or early-C15 nave roof is *arch-braced*, with high *collar beams* and deep *wall plates*. The chancel roof is panelled out and may date from the time when

the e. window was renewed. The pulpit has migrated from the nave to the chancel and is the church's nicest individual feature. Its back board is inscribed: '1632 W.P.', and the initials are probably the donor's. The door is formed from two of the six sides, and while the decoration follows the familiar pattern of blind-arched panels in two ranges, the carving of the shallow arabesques is well above average; the matching *tester* has turned pendants. The reading desk in front has been made up from C17 panels, two of which display pretty *Renaissance* motifs. Richard Thurston's memorial on the n. wall of the chancel is a brass with a Latin verse, placed there by Edmund Palmer and William Curtis in the year that Shakespeare died. The simple C13 or C14 lancet *piscina* in the *sanctuary* was uncovered in 1852 and its arch was partially re-cut, and the panels of the heavy C19 stone *reredos* are painted with the *Decalogue*. Above it is good glass by *Jones & Willis*, installed in 1907 to commemorate Elizabeth, the aunt of the famous World War I heroine, Edith Cavell. The Crucifixion scene has *St John* comforting the *Blessed Virgin*, with *St Mary Magdalene* and the centurian grouped at the foot of the cross; the archangels *St Gabriel* and *St Michael* stand fiercely on either hand, and three more angels wait amid billowing clouds above a faintly *pre-Raphaelite* landscape – a lively window, with an unusual range of colour for this particular firm. George Crabbe, Suffolk's best known poet and born not far away at Aldeburgh, served four years here as a curate, pairing it with Great Glemham.

Rendlesham, St Gregory the Great (H5): A bulky stair turret gives the C14 tower a distinctive silhouette from the w., and it backs up against one of the buttresses that form extensions of the tower's e. face. The line of an earlier *nave* roof shows on that side, and just below it is the arch of a blocked *sanctus-bell window* that will have been inside originally. Flint chequer decorates the *base course* and battlements, and shields lie within *cusped* roundels in the *spandrels* of the w. doorway. There is a *stoup* outside the nave n. doorway, and a *mason's mark* shows up clearly on the l. *jamb*, level with the latch. The *Perpendicular* windows in the nave have slight variations in the *tracery*, and a shallow projection on the s. side marks the *rood loft stair*. The 1780s flamboyant tracery of the e. window is actually made of wood, and is apparently a copy of a window in a Florentine church. The nearest window on the s. side has Perpendicular tracery, also in wood and possibly installed at the same time. A stone above the renewed *priest's door* is inscribed 'John Alsop rector 1709' and may relate to restoration work. The tall, plain C15 *porch* has an external stoup, and the *hood mould* of the inner doorway is decorated with *paterae*.

Just within, a steep stair with extremely narrow treads leads to the porch's upper room. At the time of my visit it contained a small display relating to the Sutton Hoo burial not far away, and making the case that Rendlesham may have been the village of the Wuffinga royal family, and the site of their first church. Raewald, king of the East Angles who ruled from 599 to 625, set up an altar for Christian worship in his hall here, and another for pagan use to placate his wife. It is thought that the magnificent ship burial may have been for him. The tower's lofty internal arch confirms its date, and below stands a C15 *font* of the familiar East Anglian type – smiling lions supporting the shaft, and others alternating with angels in the bowl panels. The nave roof incorporates an unusual variation of the *arch-braced* design. The main ribs are split by a block where they meet the *purlins*, and originally bore angels. The braces continue down through the *wall plate* to rest on stone *corbels*. Most of these are carved as demi-angels, but there are roses above both entrances, a *green man* over the organ, and a delightful head in the s.w. corner. A fine set of George III *Royal Arms* painted on canvas hangs on the n. wall. The C18 *box pews*, painted in two tasteful shades of grey, have no doors but are a good set, with canted backs and seats. The rood stairs can be seen in the s. wall, and opposite is the large monument to Eliza Charlotte, Baroness Rendlesham, who died in 1840. It is the work of the Florentine sculptor Aristodemo Costoli, of whom it was once said: 'skilful in design and technique, but before his work the heart remains placid and the pulse is not quickened'. The noble lady's ethereal figure floats diagonally upward within a round-headed panel, and below, her monogrammed shield is set about with naturalistic roses in which a snake is sinuously entwined. Beyond a broad arch, the chancel is spacious and has lightweight, delicately crafted modern stalls. The *communion rails* are an C18 set from a London church which were reconstructed by Mr Mayn of Butley to mark the coronation of King George VI. Within the *sanctuary*, the *piscina* has a *cinquefoil* arch with rosettes very oddly distributed around the moulding; the *credence shelf* has been renewed. An unusually splendid mid-C14 tomb recess is set in the n. wall, and the recumbent figure may represent rector Sayer Sulyard, who died in 1312.

The head is supported by a pair of reclining angels, and a fat lion crouches at the feet. Above, the large and lavish *ogee* arch is cusped and sub-cusped, decorated with fat, curly *crockets,* and flanked by diapered pinnacles. Nearby, a small *touchstone* tablet in an alabaster frame commemorates Symon Mawe and his wife Margery. He bore the office of the Steward of the Liberty of St Etheldred for thirty three years, 'lived in credit to the age of 79 years', and died in peace in 1610. On the s. side of the sanctuary, John, 2nd Baron Rendlesham is remembered much more pretentiously with an 1830s piece by Humphrey Hopper in lush 'gothick' – two flanking figures under *groined* canopies, and lots of miniature details, like the crouched hounds below the groining, the sculpted heads on the parapet, and the cushioned coronet below the epitaph panel. In marked contrast, on the n. wall there is something much better for his wife, Mary Andalusia, Baroness Rendlesham. She died in 1814, and *Flaxman* supplied her memorial for £600, carving the figure of Pity himself. A marble panel, set in a gray obelisk, is carved with the lady's figure being taken up by an angel, and below there are two kneeling figures. Pity, on the r., lays her arm along the epitaph panel while shielding her face with the other hand. Apart from a piece at Tattingstone, this is Flaxman's only identified work in a Suffolk church. Three good *ledger-stones*, all with roundels of arms, lie in the chancel floor – for Dame Ann Barker, mother of Her Grace the Duchess of Hamilton (1754), John Spencer (1709), and Henry Spencer, a London merchant who died in 1731 and 'acquired a competent Estate by the Blessing of God upon his Honest Endeavours'.

Reydon, St Margaret (I3): The tower has angle buttresses to the w., and a slab-shaped stair breaks into the base of the bell opening on the s. side. The bell openings have *Decorated tracery*, but below them there are elongated belfry *lancets* which suggest a C13 beginning, and the w. window was inserted in the C15; *flushwork* battlements and small *gargoyles* complete the picture. Round the corner you will find an enterprising extension designed by Andrew Anderson that was completed in 1988. A two-level linking section clad with clapboard leads to a chunky brick and flint pebble meeting room, and it marries well with the rest of the church. There are square-headed *Perpendicular* windows in the nave, and the outline of a blocked door shows in the n. wall of the *chancel*, with the arch of another alongside. The foundations of a n.

chapel were found in 1952, and a change in the masonry pattern of the wall here suggests that the e. end may have been rebuilt. The e. window is a C19 replacement and on the s. side the *priest's door* dates from about 1300. There is a niche above the entrance of the C15 *porch,* and those on either side have been filled with dressed flints.

A typically vigorous Victorian overhaul in 1877 has left its decisive stamp on the interior – waggon roofs, pitchpine benches replacing *box pews,* and a pulpit by Cornishs taking the place of a *three-decker;* the walls were resurfaced, and the level of the chancel was raised. The latter belatedly cancelled part of *William Dowsing's* efforts. His journal entry for April 8th, 1643 reads: 'We brake down 10 superstitious pictures; and gave order to take down 2 crosses, one on the chancel, and another on the porch. Steps we digged up'. The C13 grave slab in the tower was discovered in 1988, and the late-C14 or early-C15 *font* now stands nearby. It has *quatrefoils* and four shields in the panels, and the deep bowl rests on a new shaft and base. A very nice set of Queen Anne *Royal Arms* hangs above the s. door, dated 1713 and displayed against a pale pink background. An unusual feature of the nave is that all but one of the windows have niches for images in their splays, and one on the n. side has an *ogee* arch with *paterae* in the moulding and bears traces of colour. The stairs that led to the old *rood loft* lie in the wall behind the pulpit, and they were uncovered during the 1870s restoration. A *piscina* was discovered on the opposite side of the nave, and before the *Reformation* it will have served an *altar* in front of the *rood screen,* connected no doubt with one of the two village *guilds* dedicated to *St Margaret* and *St Mary.* The stained glass in the s. nave window dates from the early years of the C20 – a pale post-resurrection Christ flanked by richly clad figures of *St Peter* and *St John;* there are angels with scrolls in the tracery, and all is in a C15 setting reminiscent of Kempe. The local fondness for window niches is seen again in the chancel, and the one on the n. side has miniature *blind arcading* above its cusped ogee arch. In the *sanctuary,* there are two niches in the s. window splay, and the lower one is handsome – a cusped and *crocketted* arch with *finial,* and tracery in the *spandrels.* A small recess in the w. splay may have housed a napkin or towel. The piscina has no *credence shelf,* but there is a recess at the back which probably served the same purpose. The 1880s *Ward & Hughes* glass in the e. window has been re-set, discarding everything except the figures – an acceptable compromise in this

instance, with the Ascension scene and four hovering angels outlined against clear glass. The s. chancel windows are from the same firm and are not particularly memorable, but there is much better glass by *Arthur L. Moore* on the n. side. Installed in the 1880s, it is the scene of Jesus with the woman at Jacob's well (John 4:6), attractively treated in painterly fashion across two *lights;* four particularly fine angels in the tracery, and two *achievements of arms* at the base. Before leaving, there is a monument in the churchyard s.e. of the chancel that should not be missed. On top, a bronze angel stands with arms flung back and head up, while the husband and a partially robed figure kneel sorrowing against the plinth – a striking piece by Paul Montford, 1921.

Rickinghall Inferior, St Mary (E3): This is a very attractive little church at the lower end of the village street. The C12 *Norman* round tower had its top remodelled into an octagon some 200 years later, and the battlements are decked with *flushwork,* with shields in *quatrefoils* and pinnacles at every angle. The bell openings have *Decorated tracery.* The C14 s. *aisle* has very large buttresses at the corners which rise to *crocketted* pinnacles whose gables terminate in grotesque heads. The windows on this side have good *headstops* and their tracery is excellent, with three quatrefoiled roundels above a pair of *trefoiled lights.* The *spandrels* of the tracery in the easternmost window of the aisle are filled with shallow carving. This most unusual feature is found again in the *Perpendicular* s. aisle e. window, as well as in a window at nearby Thelnetham. The e. window tracery of the C14 *chancel* is all renewed, dating, I suspect, from 1858 when *J.D. Wyatt* was at work here. The early-C14 *porch* was originally single storey and inside there is a low two-bay *arcade,* resting on a stubby pillar. It is lit by pairs of little windows with 'Y' tracery, as well as a centre quatrefoil. Above the outer arch is a line of flushwork containing crowned 'M's for the dedication, and the inner doorway has very big, worn headstops.

Within the church itself, one notices that the s. aisle is the same width as the *nave,* separated by a fine arcade on quatrefoil *piers,* with *hood moulds* resting on replacement heads. The *imposts* of the tower arch are plain, and there was originally an entry higher up, giving support to the theory that these early round towers were designed as places of refuge. Between the windows in the s. aisle is a blocked doorway that is rather puzzling. It is in the wrong place to give access to a *rood loft* stair or a side chapel and one wonders whether it was originally a *banner-stave locker*. The aisle chapel has *dropped-sill sedilia* and a C14 *angle piscina* that was restored in a grossly elaborate fashion in the C19 (the same hand was responsible for a similar piece at Thelnetham). The aisle e. window was originally Decorated, and the inner shafts of the earlier design remain, as well as a very decorative band of foliage along the bottom. The nave roof is a late-C16 *hammerbeam* and, beyond it, the early-C14 chancel arch retains the remains of a leaf *capital* on the n. side. Like that in the s. aisle, the *High altar* piscina was unsympathetically restored by Wyatt, who was also responsible for the Minton tiles in the *sanctuary*. The *reredos* is made up of tracery panels that will have been part of the old rood loft, and they have been painted with figures in medieval style. There are roundels and fragments of Flemish glass in the head of the window on the s. side of the sanctuary, and the 1891 glass in the s. chancel window is by *Lavers & Westlake* – scenes from the Via Dolorosa, with canopy work and two angels above. The early-C14 octagonal *font* is interesting, not because it has window tracery designs in the panels like many another in the district, but because they are incomplete; only four are totally detailed and one panel has nothing at all. One wonders why the church was content to accept half-finished work, particularly when the design on the e. side is a careful copy of the aisle w. window. Also at the w. end is a C16 chest with carved *Renaissance* panels, and an C18 *bier*. It is a simple design, with drop handles and a series of holes drilled in the bed so that pegs could be inserted to secure the coffin. Another like it can be found up the hill at Rickinghall Superior, so they probably came from the same carpenter. As you leave, note the base of an old *preaching cross* by the porch door.

Rickinghall Superior, St Mary (E3): The two Rickinghalls now share one parish church on the main road where most of the population lives. This building is in the care of the *Churches Conservation Trust*. Still used for occasional services and cared for by local people, it is well worth a visit. Standing attractively on the brow of a hill a short way to the s. of the village, it has a C14 tower with stepped *flushwork* battlements that were added in the C15 and display 'MR' for the dedication and the *Sacred monogram*. Do not overlook the *mason's mark* to be found on the s.w. buttress, some 7ft. up; it is a large try-square, with a pair of compasses in the angle, and is one of the finest examples anywhere. The *chancel*

is also early-C14 and there is an excellent *priest's door* in the s. wall with an *ogee* arch, complete with *corbel* heads and *crocketted finial*. The e. window *Decorated tracery* is quite inventive, with *ogee* heads to the main *lights* and intersected tracery above, enclosing smaller shapes. The chancel side windows, however, are later *Perpendicular*. There was a major rebuilding in the middle of the C15 and *Cautley* believed that a previous *nave* and *aisle* were absorbed into the present wide nave. This has large Perpendicular windows, with unusually good tracery, whose arches form a pleasing pattern of flint and red brick. Under the windows, a line of blank shields is set in a band of small, finely dressed flints. Judging by the way in which stone, pebbles and dressed flints are carefully arranged in the nave walls, the builders took a good deal of care to make the new work attractive. Two of the nave windows are cut short, one to allow for a n. door underneath, and the other in the s.w. corner over the entrance to a side chapel which is no longer there. It was possibly a *chantry* or a Lady chapel and filled the angle between the *porch* and the corner of the nave. The C15 porch has a room over it and there are flushwork panels above the entrance arch, again with 'MR' and the Sacred monogram. The ceiling is nicely vaulted, and a common human touch is added by the outline of a child's hand scratched in the e. window sill among other venerable graffiti.

Within, the light floods in through great windows across the 30ft. width. Low stone benches line the walls, and from them, delicate shafts rise to form transverse *arcades* over the windows. To the l. of the entrance you will see the *Tudor* arch that led to the side chapel and there also is the door to the porch upper chamber. The C14 *font* stands centrally, its panels intricately carved with tracery patterns and beyond it, high up in the tower wall, is a *quatrefoil sanctus-bell window*. Also at the w. end is a *bier* dated 1763, of the same pattern as that to be found at Rickinghall Inferior, with holes drilled in the bed for pegs to secure the coffin. The church's ring of six bells with a 9 cwt. tenor are rung from the base of the tower. In 1868 there was a major restoration directed by W.M. Fawcett of Cambridge. The roof was replaced to the old pattern but in pitchpine rather than oak, and the nave floor was lowered and tiled. At the same time, the n. door and the tower arch were reopened and the porch chamber restored. Although the *rood screen* has gone, the stairs to the loft that went with it remain in the n.e. corner of the nave; the upper opening faces w., showing that the loft will have stood forward from the chancel arch. In the C15, there were *guilds* here dedicated to *St John the Baptist*, the *Blessed Virgin*, and *St Peter*; the *piscina* at the e. end of the nave s. wall will have served an *altar* for one of them. The chancel has a C19 waggon roof and in the *sanctuary* there is a very nice C15 piscina which has a *trefoil* ogee arch, complete with flowered *cusps*. The e. window is filled with excellent 1868 glass by the Irishman *Arthur O'Connor* who, with his brother, was active in the formative period of C19 stained glass. In the centre is the Crucifixion and Our Lord as the Good Shepherd. Other panels portray Him teaching and being presented in the temple; a nice touch in the latter is the children holding the thanks-offering of two pigeons. The scenes are set in prettily patterned *quarries*, with groups of four lilies repeated. The chancel s.e. window contains two roundels, one a medieval lion, the other an C18 figure. The other window on this side has 1870s glass by *Heaton, Butler & Bayne* on a Samuel theme; it commemorates Samuel Speare, a missionary who died young in Zanzibar, and by some mischance the texts below the panels have been switched over.

Ringsfield, All Saints (I2): When I visited, the churchyard was bright with spring flowers, and a section on the s. side is being maintained as a nature reserve. By the mid-C19, in common with many others in Suffolk, the church was a little dilapidated, and the cluttered interior, with its *box pews* and *gallery*, was judged old fashioned and inconvenient. Funds were raised, and *William Butterfield* was commissioned to carry out a full-scale restoration and rebuilding. In 1883-4, he lengthened the *nave*, built a completely new *chancel* and *vestry*, and left his mark decisively on the rest of the building. It was not insensitively done, and he took pains to preserve a number of features, but the interior in particular carries the impress of his forthright views on a church's form and function. The slim C15 tower is unbuttressed, with a small *Perpendicular* w. window and brick belfry window and bell openings; the deep brick and flint parapet has sharp little corner pinnacles and weather vanes which serve to give the tower some individuality. Nave, chancel and vestry are all thatched, and there is an interesting tomb placed in the angle of the building on the n. side. It commemorates Princess Caroline Murat, grand-daughter of the King of Naples and whose great-uncle was Napoleon. Having by her second marriage become the wife of the local

squire and submerged in rural obscurity, she was accorded a faintly Gallic flourish at her death. The monument by Sanders of London would not look out of place in the Père-Lachaise in Paris, and it caught Adrian Bell's eye one day:

> The angel, with her wings in the angle of an alighting swan's, has just touched down; one delicate finger of her alabaster hand is pointing upward. She seems to be admonishing two kneeling child angels with faces of misery at either corner of the tomb, 'Now, you two, get back to heaven at once, and if I ever catch you playing around the tombs again ...' her swirling draperies, her rococo night-gown seemed actually to float and move. Her perfect face, unassailable by any human love, would be likely to send men mad. You are drawn to it by a fascination of distaste. Your eyes roam from the dramatic forefinger aloft, down the arm to the shoulders, the dragged neckline of the robe, the trumpet in the other hand parked against the thigh, to the toes, ballet-poised, and you end by liking her.

On the s. side of his chancel, Butterfield replaced a brick monument in its original position, carefully respecting its particular interest and importance. It is tall, with cornice and flanking *pilasters*, and the centre arch frames a large mermaid crest and one of the very few *brasses* to be found on the outside of a church. It commemorates Nicholas Garneys who was Suffolk's High Sheriff in 1592 and died in 1599 (although the brass was not cut until about 1620). Interestingly, the design is a copy of Garneys' great-grandfather's brass at Kenton, laid almost a century before. The armour is *Tudor*, and his wife Anne wears an heraldic mantle bearing her family's arms (the Clere's of Stokesby, Norfolk); six sons and five daughters kneel with their parents, and there are three shields at the top. The mermaid crest was granted to Sir Thomas Garneys, he having saved Henry VIII's sister Mary from drowning. The nice C16 brick *porch* has a crow-stepped gable, chunky pinnacles, and an *arch-braced* roof. The entrance was fitted with iron mesh doors in 1964, and the copper roundel with a pair of robins in relief is an attractive addition by Mrs Moore of Brandeston.

Within, the feeling of Victorian restoration is pervasive, but one of the first things to catch the eye is the C15 *font*, a compact version of the East Anglian type. Smiling lions support the shaft, with more in the bowl panels alternating with *Tudor Roses* and angels with shields. C17 churchmen liked to use biblical texts strategically, placing them in relation to the door, the pulpit and so on. They were normally painted on the walls (as at Hemingstone and Witnesham, but Ringsfield's are lettered on boards, and one remains in its proper place over the door: 'This is none other but ye hous of God, and this is the gate of Heaven. When thou seest God's hous adorned, think of his greatness that oweth it, and render thy reverence accordingly'. Most of the rest of the series have been grouped on the w. wall of the tower. The glass in the w. window is by Bell & Beckham, a firm favoured by Butterfield who exercised a firm control on all designs in his buildings. Ringsfield can claim their only work in Suffolk, and the two *Annunciation* panels, with figures in C14 mode, deploy a strong yellow and smoky blue, quite unlike their other windows that you will see here. The church has a good ring of four bells with a 3 cwt. tenor, and they are rung from here. One C15 bench with *poppyheads* survives in the tower, a predecessor of the *Stuart* range in the nave which are particularly attractive, with just enough decoration to give them interest. Quality examples of this period are not easy to find, and the square-topped ends have top panels carved in the style of a contemporary chest, every other one with a turned and carved *finial*. The 1850s tablet on the n. wall for John Garden has a plain *pediment*, flanking rustic crosses, and a sunburst below which contains a serpent biting its tail (a symbol of Time's passing). The monument came from the workshop of Charles Harriott Smith, a busy and successful sculptor who worked on the National Gallery, the Royal Exchange, and who carved the capital of Nelson's column. Two C16 Flemish roundels in yellow stain were placed in the centre s. nave window in 1967 – an interesting 'Visit of the Magi', and the *Blessed Virgin* and *St Joseph* finding Christ in the Temple. The adjoining window displays a lush version of the arms of Magdalene College, Cambridge. On the n. side, the two westernmost windows are both by *Clayton & Bell* – Moses and David in one, and the *Three Marys* in the other. The latter is a very late example of the firm's work, a rich and satisfying design. The remaining window on that side is another Bell & Beckham piece, hieratic figures of *St John the Baptist* and Elijah in a typical Butterfield setting, using bright, disciplined

colour. The early-C17 pulpit has been considerably altered, retaining blind arched panels, the tall back board, and another of the painted texts. The compact octagonal *tester*, with its vigorous brackets and top frieze, appears to be intact. The *screen* in black and gilt dates from the same period, and its two short sections have shallow carved decoration, turned balusters, and pierced pyramid finials. There are more texts neatly lettered on both sides of the rails, this time in Latin, and they no doubt reflected the views of the minister: 'Ecclesia interpres et custos veritatis' (The church, interpreter and guardian of the Truth); 'Simulata sanctitas duplex iniquitas' (Simulated holiness is a special sort of wickedness). Just beyond the screen, the wooden lectern is a typical Butterfield piece, and robins hatched in the top some years ago. The nest remains as a charming little reminder that the church achieved a momentary fame in the national press and the event is memorialised on the porch doors that you passed through. Strangely enough, precisely the same thing happened in Blythburgh lectern. A line 15in. from the base of the chancel arch nearby marks the height to which the church was flooded on August 26th 1912, that memorable day when the whole of East Anglia was deluged by 6in. of rain in 12hrs. A large C17 panel is displayed on the wall by the vestry door, and more Stuart woodwork backs the choir stalls on the s. side. There you will find a memorial for a chorister who died in Burma, but who 'Here sat and sang', and it recalls a similar remembrance on a pew at Thorndon. Under the big new *piscina* there is another Stuart panel which may well have been part of the pulpit, and Robert Shelford's memorial was re-positioned on the n. wall of the *sanctuary*. Displayed alongside is a copy of the title page of his *Five pious and learned discourses*, published in 1635. Butterfield's harsh stone *reredos* is set in the e. window embrasure, and above it the 1890s Bell & Beckham glass has been drastically treated. The figures of Christ in Majesty, *St Peter* and *St Paul*, have been taken from their original setting and backed with clear glass. From a purist point of view, this was decidedly naughty, particularly as examples of the firm's work are scarce in East Anglia, but there is no denying that the chancel has been lightened significantly.

Ringshall, St Catherine (E5): Attractively placed at the head of a little lane on rising ground, the church has a very solid *Norman* tower. A low *drip course* runs just above the tiny *lancets* set in the n. and s. walls of the ground floor and there are shallow *set-offs* farther up. The w. window of about 1300 has 'Y' *tracery*, and there are lancet bell openings and a much more recent brick parapet. The n. wall of the *nave* had to be massively supported with brick buttressing in the C18 or early C19 and there is an early-C14 doorway on that side. The side windows are all *Perpendicular* but the *chancel* e. window tracery is *Decorated*, displaying two *mouchettes* and the remains of *headstops* on the *dripstone*. The *priest's door* on the s. side dates from about 1300 and two *scratch dials* can be found on its e. *jamb*. Apart from the restored Perpendicular window on the s. side of the nave, a single Norman lancet has recently been given a new frame. Note that the line of an earlier roof is marked on the e. face of the tower and that two tie-beams emerge through the wall to be secured by large wooden pins – a most unusual feature. R.M. *Phipson* directed a restoration in 1878 and his oak porch is a very satisfactory reproduction of a C14 model. The doorway was inserted about 1300 but in going in you will see that the inner arch is round-headed and so it may have replaced a Norman original.

The tower was remodelled at that time and its arch to the nave is tall, with the plain chamfered mouldings merging into the jambs without *capitals*. Have a look beyond it at one of the little lancets and see the thickness of the walls. Octagonal C13 *fonts* in *Purbeck marble* must have been mass-produced for their design seldom varies – pairs of arches carved in low relief on each face of a canted bowl. This one has had its supporting ring of shafts replaced. There is no chancel arch, and the open roof has exceptionally low *tie-beams* on which rest two tall and slender *king posts*. They support a ridge which runs below the rafter braces and there are little *castellated* wall shafts. Hanging lamps were used at one time and their pulleys are still in place above the nave. Having seen one Norman lancet, there are two more in the n. wall, differing in size and now blocked. All the furniture dates from the 1870s restoration and Phipson repaired the roof. The *hammerbeams, wall plates* and carved *spandrels* of the C16 roof in the chancel look as if they too were restored. One normally finds a *piscina* in the s. wall of the *sanctuary* but here it is in the e. wall and has the unusual feature of a *trefoil* drain, with a wooden *credence shelf* above it. The e. and s.e. windows are filled with 1870s glass by *Clayton & Bell* in typical style – the Resurrection and Christ with *St Mary Magdalen* in the garden in one, and Christ as the Good Shepherd and the Light of the world in the other.

Risby, St Giles (C4): The approach from the street is through a *lych-gate* which snuggles delightfully between two huge horse chestnuts. There is a school of thought which maintains that the round tower is *Saxon*, built as a place of refuge, to which the *Norman* church was added later, but others are content to date it late-C11 or early-C12. Its only original windows are two tiny *lancets* some 20ft. up, capped with arches cut from a single stone. The tiers of slit openings below the parapet are later and a w. window was added in the C14. Typically large blocks of Norman masonry can be seen at the bottom of the *nave* walls but there was rebuilding and the s. nave windows with 'Y' *tracery* date from about 1300. The *chancel* was added in the early C14, with *reticulated* tracery in the e. window, and there is a large *low side window* in the s. wall. On the n. side there is a single late-C13 lancet, with a mixture of *Decorated* and *Perpendicular* tracery in the other windows. There was a C14 chapel on the n. side of the chancel and one of its roof *corbels* remains e. of the 1840s *vestry* that replaced it. The last medieval addition was the *porch* of 1435; it is plain but has an uncommonly pleasing floor of pale, narrow bricks.

Within, the tower arch is Norman, with a double roll moulding and simply carved *abaci*. Above it is an opening which lends substance to the theory that the tower was originally a Saxon refuge, for although it may have been used later as a *sanctus-bell window*, it is too large to have been designed as such and is more likely to have been the original entrance – high enough to be secure. The plaster ceiling in the nave was installed in the late C18 and covers the rough-hewn timbers of the original C13 roof. The C15 *font* is particularly interesting; four of the shaft faces are traceried and there are image stools below the rest, although the figures have gone. More damage might well have been done had not the bowl been plastered over; its fine carvings were only revealed when a lady tapped one with her parasol in the 1890s. Four of the panels contain *Evangelistic symbols*, there is a *griffin* to the n.e. and a *pelican in her piety* to the s.e. The other two panels make up an *Annunciation* scene, with the archangel on the s.w. and the *Blessed Virgin* on the n.w. face. She kneels at a prayer desk, and behind her the artist added a homely touch in the form of a little dog (contemporary tombs quite often portrayed the pets of great ladies, so why not?). Most of the nave seating dates from 1842 but there are some medieval benches at the w. end, with *poppyheads*, lightly carved back rails and signs that there were originally carvings on the squared elbows. On the s. wall are the Royal Arms of George III, still bearing the fleur-de-lys which dates them before 1800 when the claim to the French throne was finally dropped. The n. wall has an interesting but slightly confusing series of mainly early-C13 paintings. Most of them are rather faint but the following can be identified: at the w. end, a life-size outline in red of a mitred priest vested for mass, with yellow hair and beard. He bears no emblem, but the cult of *St Thomas of Canterbury* was at its height and he is a possibility; to the r. is the head of a double axe which might be one of the tools surrounding a *Christ of the Trades*; next is a clear, late-C14 outline of Christ's appearance to *St Mary Magdalene*. The sequence is then broken by the placing of the n. door, a section of Norman window arch and the C13 lancet, and it was further damaged when the walls were heightened in the C14. There was a Nativity sequence of five scenes at the top and, from the l., one can make out the faint outlines of two shepherds, the angel (very dim above the Norman window fragment and followed by a Massacre of the Innocents that has to be guessed at now), and the Flight into Egypt – shadowy figures of Joseph and the Virgin and Child on an easily recognisable donkey. There was another series below, but all that can be seen now is a faint devil which was apparently part of a *St Margaret* painting. Lower down is a *consecration cross* within a decorated roundel, and the scroll work in the lancet splays is late-C13. There are puzzling recesses by this window which suggest that the Norman nave ended here and that it was the site of an *altar*. It may well be that the first chancel became an extension of the nave, and it is obvious that when the new chancel was built about 1330, parts of the old arch were reused to form the new one, as you will see on its e. side. The mid-C17 octagonal pulpit has typical blind arches in the panels, resting on reeded shafts, with shallow carving above, and on the s. side there is a roughly contemporary altar table with a quite individual arrangement of open arches below the top rail. The nearby window has glass by *Kempe & Co* and in the sill is the simplest form of *piscina*, which shows that there was always an altar here. There are stools for images in the window splays on both sides of the nave and they have been associated with the four *guilds* known to have existed in the C15.

The entrance to the chancel is made splendid by a combination of the *rood screen* and pairs of large niches each side which formed *reredoses* for the nave altars. All were beautifully restored in 1966 with the aid of the Pilgrim Trust. Although small, the screen is fascinating in its intricacy. There are only three *lights* each side of the entrance rather than the usual four, and the base panels have stencilled patterns within their tracery; there are *crocketted* gables to the main buttresses at rail level. The main lights rise to *cusped* and crocketted *ogee* arches, and above them the space is filled with a net of cusped tracery contained within a trellis of lozenges. The centre arch has flowered cusps, with eagles and beast masks in the *spandrels*. The pairs of side niches are gorgeously coloured in red, gold and blue, the back walls rich with a lattice of diaper work framing varied flowered centres. The heads are canopied with miniature vaulting and the crocketted ogee arches rise to tall *finials*. One of the r.-hand niches has a broad image stool, and on the opposite side another contains a C19 seated figure of *St Giles*, and its clumsy plinth is the only discordant feature of the whole array. The stairs to the vanished *rood loft* are on the n. side. Passing through to the chancel, note the line of *paterae* at the top of the screen and the sections of Norman stone work in the arch above. The chancel was restored by the rector, Thomas Abrahams, in 1881 and three of the windows commemorate members of his family. His predecessor, Samuel Alderson, was obviously a woodcarver of some skill and individuality, for the profusion of heavy leaf forms on the reredos, altar, *communion rails*, and poppyheads are all his work. On either side of the altar there are large C14 niches with *trefoil* arches under ogee heads to match those in the nave, and the large piscina matches them, with canted head corbels. There are headstops on the arch of the vestry door too, and in the e. window are many fragments of C14 and C15 glass collected there by Samuel Alderson's wife in 1850. The result is rather confused, but there is a good king's head in the l.-hand light, a delicately painted *pelican in her piety* in a lozenge above the lion shield in the centre, and among the many other interesting little pieces, an *Agnus Dei*. The window to the s. received the same treatment and there are two larger figures made up of fragments, with new heads, one with an arrow emblem and the other with the wheel of *St Catherine*. Over the low side window is a tablet for John Wastell who died in 1811. He was an intimate friend of the 3rd Duke of Grafton, the famous racehorse owner, and managed his stable for him. Just in front of the communion rails is a *brass* inscription for Edward Kirke, the rector who died in 1580. He was a friend of the poet Edmund Spenser and wrote the introduction to *The Shepherd's Calendar*. A more recent rector is remembered in a nave window, Canon A.F. Webling, whose books *Risby, The Last Abbot* and *Something Beyond* are well worth seeking out.

Rougham, All Saints (D4): A number of Suffolk churches are isolated from their villages and in Rougham's case it was because the *Black Death* visitation of 1349 was so devastating that, as a desperate measure, the parishioners burnt every house to the ground and moved half a mile to the s. Now, the church has only the school, a cottage and the new rectory for company. Isolation only serves to make it more impressive and the C15 tower, with its bold angled buttresses and well-defined *string courses* is a landmark. It has a stair turret to the belfry stage on the s. side and, like Hessett, the top is lavishly decorated. The stepped battlements with corner pinnacles are set with *flushwork* and the centre panels are notable for their inscriptions – on the s. side, 'Pray for ye sowle of John Tillot', and on the n., 'Drury', in bold gothic confirms that Robert Drury and John Tillot were chiefly responsible for building the tower. The panel on the e. side carries an 'M' for the *Blessed Virgin* with her lily emblem and there are circled monograms on the w. face. A band of flushwork roundels runs below the battlements and the windows to the w. are firmly anchored in the design by the string courses. William Layer was an important C15 mason who is believed to have been the architect of the nave of St Mary's, Bury. He had property in Rougham and bequeathed 20 marks for this tower and could well have designed it. It houses a good ring of six bells with a 15 cwt. tenor, one of which was cast by John Bird in London in the early C15. There had been a large scale rebuilding in the late C13 and early C14 – new *nave, chancel* and probably the s. *aisle*. The s. *porch* was part of this work and it is notable. The three-*light* unglazed windows have sturdy columns and pierced *ogee tracery* under square tops, while the entrance arch is finely moulded. The gable shows the original roof line and there is a fat *gargoyle*, with its hands over its ears, in the e. parapet. Below the porch w. window you will find a few C13 yellow bricks and there is an angled sundial in the niche over the entrance. Two very large medieval grave slabs lie nearby and a pair of blocked arches show in the wall to the e. of the porch. They are burial recesses; one of their covers is carved with a C13

double omega and lies by the path further along. Nave and aisle parapets have pierced battlements and half way along the aisles you will see a small carved head in a roundel that is taken by some to represent *St John the Baptist's* head on a charger. The chancel was again rebuilt in 1880 and the tall square *vestry*-cum-organ chamber was added in 1900, with a large *low side window* re-sited in the s. wall; the small lean-to vestry on the n. side dates from 1856. The n. aisle was built by the Drury family and has Perpendicular windows; it can be confidently dated by inscriptions on three of the buttresses. It would be nice to think that the easternmost was put there by the workmen themselves for it reads: 'We pray you to remember us that causyde ye yle to be made thus'; on the next is the date '1514' and the third has the name of the priest John Smith.

Within, the nave has graceful C14 *arcades,* the double chamfered arches resting on *quatrefoil piers,* and the chancel arch matches. The early-C16 nave roof is beautifully solid but the decoration is restrained. *Arch-braces* rise from *hammerbeams* to thick *collars* and the eye is attracted more to the elaborate *wall plates* where two ranks of *paterae* are separated by a band of pierced tracery. The *hammerbeams* are carved as angels and although they have lost their heads they still hold shields carved with *chalices*, crowns, books and organs. Below, the *wall posts* carry canopied niches with mutilated figures and rest on stone shafts that rise from a string course that runs below the *clerestory* windows. The aisle roofs too have deep wall plates decorated with large paterae and there are stone head *corbels*. All the roofs were repaired when John Johnson of Bury carried out a restoration in 1856 and although a *Doom* was uncovered over the chancel arch, there is no trace of it now. The panels of the C14 *font* are carved with an unusual mixture of arch patterns and show traces of colour. The early-C16 nave benches are unusually good. They are low and chunky and the tracery on the ends is full of invention. There are *poppyheads* and traceried backs but, alas, all the figures have been sawn from the elbows. They are likely to have been angels because the little pads representing clouds on which they stood remain. The matching pews at the front and in the aisles were designed by Johnson in the 1850s. There are matching C14 *piscinas* at the e. end of the aisles showing that there were once *altars* there – that in the n. aisle having been resited. The *Decorated* s. aisle e. window now opens into the organ chamber and its companion on the n. side is largely blocked by a quite nasty 'Victorian

Gothick' series of panels commemorating the Bennet family. The tracery above it still has some early-C14 glass – a shield with *Passion emblems*, a shield of arms, and a tiny Virgin and Child fragment in yellow stain. Below the Bennet memorial are wooden *Jacobean* panels that came either from a chest or a pulpit. In the floor nearby is a very good *brass* with 4ft. figures of Sir Roger Drury and his wife Margery. He died in 1410 and his armour is a perfect example of the period, lacking only the helm behind the head. She died five years before her husband and wears a mantle over her gown; a little dog lies at her feet against the lion which lies under his. Lady Margery's figure is identical with Eleanor Burgate's at Burgate and shows that such memorials were produced to a standard pattern. The stained glass in the n. aisle window is an 1897 memorial for John Josselyn and his wife. His arms are in the tracery, with angels, an *Agnus Dei* and the eagle of *St John*. The main lights have figures of Christ, the Blessed Virgin, St John the Baptist and *St John the Evangelist*; at the bottom there is a small *Annunciation* panel. Behind the C19 pulpit there is a large image niche with a slight *ogee* top and on the s. side of the chancel arch is the blocked door to the *rood stairs*. *J.D. Wyatt's* reconstructed chancel is depressing rather than uplifting despite its spaciousness and the e. window glass by *Hardman* illustrates the Nativity, Annunciation, and Christ's Presentation in the Temple – all in the rich style typical of the firm. The late-C14 piscina and *sedilia* were undisturbed and form a very satisfying group.

Rumburgh, St Michael and St Felix (H2): A long path, two sets of gates, and a moat lie between the road and the church – a charming setting, with Abbey Farm nestling close to its n. wall. It began life in 1064 as the Benedictine priory of St Michael and St Felix, a cell of the abbey of St Benet's Hulme in Norfolk, and remained quietly in being until it was suppressed in 1528. The tower, *nave* and *chancel* became the parish church, and the rest of the buildings, grouped round a cloister on the n. side, made way in time for the farm. The oblong bulk of the C13 tower is impressive in its simplicity, with broad buttresses and three widely separated *lancets* in the w. wall; the doorway below is dwarfed by the dimensions of the rest of the facade. There is no way of telling whether the tower was ever completed, but it has a most attractive weatherboarded bell chamber under a hipped tile roof. The bells are an excellent ground

floor ring of six with a 7 cwt. tenor. The tall nave and chancel are the same width as the tower and lie under a single roof. Beyond the porch, the surrounds form part of the farmhouse garden. The porch walls are plastered, and the wooden outer arch is C18 or early-C19, but the *wall plate* within shows that it dates from the C15.

The simple inner doorway is probably late-C12 or early-C13, and just inside is a *stoup* recess, with a C19 *bier* standing close by. A set of George III *Royal Arms* hangs to the r. of the tall tower arch, and to the l. are the arms of the priory, discovered during a restoration of 1878. They relate to the Benedictine abbey of St Mary in York which acquired the Rumburgh property in the late C12 and was the patron of other parishes in the area. The substantial late-C14 *font* has a panelled shaft, and the bowl is carved with *quatrefoils* linked in roundels. Its early-C17 cover is almost flat, topped by a centre obelisk. The neat little organ opposite the entrance was installed at Shipmeadow in 1904, and in the wake of that church's redundancy it was transferred here and used for the first time on Christmas Eve 1986. The *arch-braced* nave roof is decorated with lacy *bosses*, and three *tie-beams* with *king posts* were inserted later, presumably to counteract movement in the walls. One large window has been bricked up in the s. wall of the nave, and the others have the unusual feature of crown glass in the tracery (like those at Metfield). The rather strange windows in the n. wall were probably inserted after the main priory buildings had gone. The bench ends carry *poppyheads*, and the rails of the rear benches have a band of shallow C17 carving (the s. range looks like a C19 copy). The floors are of homely brick, and there is a finely lettered *ledger-stone* in the nave for William Aldrich who died in 1662. A door in the n. wall leads to the *rood stair*, and beyond it stands the simply panelled Jacobean pulpit, on a tall turned shaft supported by curly brackets. The rather battered *rood screen* is unusually lofty and has intricate and quite delicate *Perpendicular* tracery, with the centre section renewed. There are still traces of *gesso* decoration on the buttresses, including miniature figures on the one nearest to the prayer desk. The *spandrels* on the e. side of the screen are decorated with flowers and leaves which proves that there was vaulting only on the w. side below the loft. There is a blocked door on the s. side of the chancel which probably led to a *sacristy*, and the door opposite was the monks' entrance. A *squint* in the *sanctuary* n. wall gave a

Rushbrooke, St Nicholas: Henry VIII Royal Arms

view of the *High altar* from a side chapel, and above it is the outline of a window which allowed the altar lights to be watched from the dormitory beyond. Eliza Davy was only 21 when she died in 1781 and her stark epitaph is cut in a ledger-stone:

> She once the fairest flower in May,
> Now turn'd to Lifeless Clay;
> Good God what can we Say,
> He calls we must Obey.

Rushbrooke, St Nicholas (C4): This church has an unbuttressed C14 tower of flint but, like the rest of the building, the walls are plastered. The bell openings have *Decorated tracery*, and a *Perpendicular* w. window, with deep *label* and *headstops*, was inserted later, probably when the *nave* and *chancel* were rebuilt by Thomas Jermyn in 1540. The new work was in red brick and many of the windows have moulded brick *mullions* and tracery. The low nave n. door and the *priest's door* on that side have been blocked up and the gables of nave, chancel and s. *porch*

are boldly crow-stepped in brick. The s. *aisle* extends half way along the chancel, with e. window and small side doorway blocked. The layout within is decidedly eccentric. The s. aisle is divided into three parts – a w. vestibule, a central *vestry* at a higher level that was once a family pew, and an eastern chapel largely given over to monuments. There is a two-bay *arcade* at the w. end, followed by an unmatched arch which is now partially walled off, and then comes a Perpendicular arch which has a separate low entrance to the r., both leading into the chapel. At the w. end of the aisle stands a C19 wooden *font* of vaguely Gothic form and on the floor is the bowl of a large C15 font which appears to have been re-cut; the panelled shaft stands close by. The C16 aisle *roof* has been extensively restored but from the nave one can see that the principal timbers in the centre section are carved. In the 1840s Col. Rushbrooke of Rushbrooke Park installed collegiate-style seating in the nave facing inwards, and at the w. end it is backed by crudely carved canopy work with steep gables; on a *gallery* there is a showy display of painted organ pipes but no sign of an actual instrument, nor is there room for one. There are medieval bench ends with *poppyheads* incorporated in the stalls and under the gallery a *hatchment* leans against the wall; it was used for Robert Rushbrooke who died in 1829. The nave roof is steep with *arch-braces* and pendants below the ridge, and in the chancel there is a lovely C16 cambered *tie-beam* roof enriched with carving on beams, *spandrels* and *wall plates*. There is no chancel arch or screen but the carved *rood beam* is still in place supported on *wall posts* bearing small figures with canopies both above and below them. Above is a *tympanum* against which is displayed a massive set of *Royal Arms*. The crowned shield is supported by carved and silhouetted dragon and greyhound, the *Tudor* badges of portcullis and rose stand alongside, and the motto with the archaic spelling of 'droict' is painted on the beam below. The form of arms was used by Henry VII and Henry VIII and the assumption is that Thomas Jermyn had them put up in 1540 when he received the manor from Henry VIII. That would make them the only example of the period in the country and a uniquely early instance of the practice. The only problem is that apparently they were not in the church in the early C19 and there is a suspicion that the antiquarian zeal of Col. Rushbrooke may have had something to do with it. A *piscina* in the s. chapel shows that there was once an *altar* there, although the e. wall was now taken up by a memorial. In 1692 Thomas, the only son of the last Lord Jermyn, died at the age of 15. 'A hopefull Youth', he was killed in a boating accident on the Thames and his monument is against the s. wall – a small marble figure in full wig, profusely buttoned coat and gown, pensively reclining with his hand on a skull, with *touchstone Corinthian* columns on either side. On the w. wall is a monument to Sir Robert Davers who died in 1722 – a dark sarcophagus backed by a tall mottled marble architectural panel with decorative garland. In the chancel, the lumpish tablet to the Countess Dowager Darlington (1763) is made interesting by the cast-metal *achievement of arms* at the base. Below it is a *brass* inscription and two shields that were once enamelled for Thomas Badby, 'one of the Quenes Maties receyvers' who died in 1583. Lower down are two C17 Jermyn tombs and across on the s. wall, a tall monument with indifferently carved cherubs for Lord Henry Jermyn, who was exiled with the Royalists in France until the *Restoration* and who died in 1672. The e. end of the chancel was rebuilt in 1885 and some medieval glass is displayed in the e.

window, including two figures and, at the top, the shield of *Edward the Confessor* with its cross and five martlets. There are other fragments in the nave and you will find rather a nice *unicorn* in a roundel in the centre window.

Rushmere St Andrew, St Andrew (I2): This is an interesting building, combining as it does ancient, Victorian, and modern work. William Cadye died in 1497, his wife Katherine in 1521, and they left money for a new tower on condition that it was built 'in like fashion, bigness and workmanship as is the steeple of Tuddenham'. Its buttresses and stepped battlements are decorated with *flushwork*, and the *Evangelistic symbols* at the corners have been renewed. The w. door and window are C19 and the latter has quite extraordinary *tracery*, with six *quatrefoils* and a centre shape around a figure of the patron saint. The tower houses an excellent ring of six bells with a 9 cwt. tenor, three of them cast by William Chamberlain in the early C15. This was part of a massive rebuilding directed by *E.C. Hakewill* in 1861 when he replaced the *nave* and *chancel* on the old foundations and added a n. *aisle*. The only sign that a church has stood here for 900 years is the fine *Norman* doorway which Hakewill retained in the s. wall. It is broad and low and has two bands of broad *chevron* moulding above flanking shafts decorated with a spiral pattern. The style of the Victorian work is *Early English*, with tall *lancets* on the s. side of the nave, and the roof slopes right down on the n. side over the aisle. Then in 1967 a major extension was added to the e. end of the chancel which, in effect, forms a second nave with aisles of unequal width. It was designed by George Pace, an architect who has several modern churches to his credit and who was responsible for the rebuilding of Llandaff cathedral. The broad slope of the C19 roof is repeated, with the addition of a dormer on the top of the ridge facing n. and a taller version on the other side lower down. There is a large hall/meeting room at right angles linked to the s. side of the chancel and a flat-roofed *vestry* block was added n.w. of the nave.

Inside it is rather dark at the w. end, with an organ blocking the tower arch; Hakewill's square block *font* stands below it. His two-bay *arcade* has a drum shaft and overweight *capital*, and there is glass by *Lavers, Barraud & Westlake* in the aisle lancets – Noah and his wife with the dove, Solomon in the Temple, and the sacrifice of Isaac. The same firm filled the nave s. lancets with scenes of Christ's baptism, His entry into Jerusalem, and the Crucifixion. Medieval timbers were reused in the nave roof and William Polley of Coggeshall provided a lovely range of benches with infinitely varied *poppyheads*. He placed delicately carved angels on the elbows and the pair at the w. end cradle models of the tower and the chancel. There are birds and beasts in the aisle and the *Evangelistic symbols* are used at the e. end. Close by them is the *ledger-stone* for William Seely who died in 1660 (note the spelling of the village name). The old chancel has become the setting for a new limed oak central *altar* flanked by elegant metal candle stands. Overhead, the roof timbers are painted a deep red and the Victorian *sedilia* have been backed with panels to match the rest of the sanctuary furniture. The window glass behind them commemorates Hakewill and he gave the carving of St Andrew bringing Simon Peter to Jesus which is now set in the wall on the n. side. The Ascension panel above dates from 1889. A s. chancel window has good glass of 1860, again by Lavers, Barraud & Westlake; jewel-like leaf patterns surround panels of Christ with St Peter and St Andrew and the martyrdom of the church's patron saint; the arms of William Schreiber are displayed below. The new e. nave has a high-pitched, cleverly braced roof whose shape and density is taken up by the wide e. window. Bulky rough-cast concrete beams provide the framework, and while these do not jar, the coarseness of the unadorned stock bricks of the walls does – simplicity should not cancel out quality. That said, and ignoring the typically uncomfortable chairs that architects delight in, this is a bold and stimulating setting for worship.

Rushmere, St Michael (I2): The church had not been in regular use since the mid-1960s and it was threatened with redundancy in 1985 when a farewell service was held. The great gale of 1987 badly damaged the thatched roof, but by that time the parochial church council had been revived, and a Trust called the 'Friends of St Michael' has been established to care for the building. In 1989 the parish became part of the Carlton Colville united benefice and plans to cope with the urgent repairs were being made. By 1994 the basic restoration had been completed with a fine new roof of Norfolk reed. Since then, a good deal of work has been done and in 2008 the interior walls were being replastered.

The round tower is probably *Saxon*, and the faint shapes of six windows no doubt mark its original upper stage. Above them, the flintwork

is more regular and there are late-C13 bell openings; the tall w. *lancet* has been renewed, and there is a brick parapet. The *nave* n. door dates from about 1300, as do all the windows except one with *Perpendicular tracery* on each side of the nave. The long *chancel* has a C13 *priest's door* in the s. wall, and a *scratch dial* can be found on the s.e. corner. Note, however, that the *quoin* has been turned on its side and the dial is now on the e. face. Unusually, the chancel is a little wider than the nave (rather than the other way round), and there is another, more interesting scratch dial on the s.w. corner. It has a large centre hole, and a cross is incised at the bottom of the quadrant. There are arches outlined in tile in the nave s. wall that do not relate to the existing windows – a strange and puzzling feature which suggests that there was once a s. *aisle*. A late-C17 *porch* in warm red brick shelters an attractively moulded doorway, with a *stoup* recess to the r.

Just within is another, complete with bowl, and it is worth remembering that *William Dowsing* 'broke down a pot for holy water' when he came here in April 1643. As usual, he destroyed stained glass and left orders for steps to be levelled, but Rushmere's is the only reference to holy water stoups in his journal. The formless tower arch has been sealed off, and there is a *banner stave locker* in the s.w. corner of the nave, with a pair of canvas *Decalogue* panels on the w. wall. The *font* is the standard C15 East Anglian design, and one of the lions round its shaft has lost his head. In the bowl panels, roses and leaves alternate with angels whose shields have been mutilated, although *Passion emblems* (s.), a *Trinity emblem* (n.), and a floriated cross (e.) can still be recognised. There is a C15 painting of a saint with staff and rosary in a s. nave window splay, and in an embrasure on the opposite side, one can make out the faint outline of a head and remnants of diaper work which is possibly C13. While preparations were being made in the *chancel* for replastering an exciting find was made in the s.w. corner of the chancel. An important fragment of late-C13 painting has been uncovered which can be linked stylistically to similar decoration that survives in the Horsham St Faith Priory near Norwich. Because the chancel is wider than the nave, there is an angled return of wall inside and fragments of painting survive both on the 'return' and on the s. chancel wall and the former appears to be later in date. It consists of a curved dark outer band and an inner band of red and is without doubt the remains of a *consecration cross*. The wall section has a series of yellow, black and red motifs against a creamy-yellow background. It is good medieval work consisting of a dado band of foliate scroll and masonry pattern in which black curving stems lead to a red rose. This part of the design can be linked with late-C13 work at Norwich cathedral as well as Horsham St Faith. When further work is done on the chancel walls it is quite likely that more fragments of wall painting will be uncovered. Although there are only remnants left in the nave and chancel, they give some idea of what must have been an extensive and very colourful scheme of decoration.

Half of the C19 pine pews in the nave have been removed and may or may not be reinstated. Meanwhile, the s. half has been cleared for use with chairs on the sound pale brick floor. The roof an *arch-braced* and *scissors-braced* construction and has been left bare so that the reed thatch shows through. The panels of the *Stuart* pulpit have pairs of arches with centre pendants, and there are narrow, carved panels below the rim. he chancel is floored with *encaustic* tiles and the sections of C17 panelling on the chancel walls partly mask the windows. The *piscina* in the *sanctuary* is unusually sited at an angle in the window splay, above *dropped-sill sedilia*,with blind tracery above its *ogee* arch and a drain carved as a leaf. Also unusual is the siting of an earlier piscina in the n. wall, with a round arch, plain drain, and faint traces of colour.

The Christmas carol service drew a capacity congregation, and the rescue of St Michael's shows what can be done when there are parishioners who care enough to pledge their time, their determination and their resources to save their church.

Santon Downham, St Mary (C2): It is more than likely that you will be able to watch grey squirrels and jays coming and going in this churchyard, set idyllically in a quiet corner of the forest. The church is small but has much of interest. Look first at the panels at the base of the C15 unbuttressed tower: n. side, a crowned 'M' for the dedication, *Sacred monogram*, two sets of initials; w. and s. sides, the names of those who gave money for its erection (reading from the w.): Sir John Downham, Margt. Reve, Jafrey Skitte, Willia' Toller; w. side: John Watt, John Reve. The *Norman* s. door of the *nave* has simple roll mouldings in the arch, set on spiral shafts, and over it is a contemporary carved panel of an animal that could be a lion, except that it has turned vegetarian and is munching a plant that matches the flourish on its own tail. Further

along in the *chancel* is a blocked *low side window* that formed part of the *lancet* above, and next to it is the *priest's door* with late-C12 *dogtooth* moulding in the arch, and shafts which may be earlier still. The doorway was originally on the n. side where the outline can still be seen. The e. window has been totally renewed and may or may not be faithful to the original. In the C14 there was a chapel on the n. side of the nave dedicated to the *Trinity* and the *piscina* for the *altar* is still embedded in the wall under a *trefoil ogee* arch.

Entering by the n. *porch*, notice that although the Norman shafts of the doorway match the s. door, the arch was replaced in the C14 to allow for a niche to be set above. The door itself is medieval with the original long strap hinges, and behind it is one of the Norman window splays that was converted to a C13 lancet. This has an 1890s stained glass figure of Faith with her shield by *Kempe & Co* and the matching windows in the C13 chancel portray the other two religious virtues – Hope with her anchor and Charity in the form of the *Blessed Virgin* and Child. Below is a C13 arched tomb recess, and a short section of Norman dogtooth moulding is found in the wall nearby, probably associated with the former priest's door. There is an *aumbry* in the n.e. corner of the *sanctuary* and the piscina opposite, under its multi-foiled ogee arch, has the remnants of the original wooden *credence shelf*. The C14 window by the priest's door has 1950s glass by Harcourt M. Doyle – *St Francis* with a colourful selection of birds and butterflies – Doyle's only work in Suffolk. *Rood screen* builders were very active in the C14 up to the time of the *Black Death* in 1349 and here is a good example from that period. The plain boards of the base have an overall stencil pattern (part of the border has been repainted) and the miniature window cut in a board on the s. side is a contemporary *elevation squint*. Much of the *tracery* and two of the shafts have been replaced, but the shafts on the n. side are original and the whole has been sympathetically treated. The early-C17 octagonal pulpit has two ranges of panels carved with simple scrolls above and lozenges below. The base and stairs are replacements and there is an image bracket on the wall beyond. Over the utilitarian stove on the s. side, a fragment of a C13 window arch is decorated with a foliage trail in dark red, showing that, like most of its contemporaries, the church was decorated overall. On the n. side of the nave is the early-C14 arch (now framing a window) which led to the lost chapel. The plain octagonal *font* has a simple pyramid cover with shallow incised carving, matching the pulpit. The lancet in the s. wall nearby contains C19 glass by *Heaton, Butler & Bayne* – a sentimental Good Shepherd with cuddly sheep. On the n. side by the tower arch is a tablet to Lieut. Col. the Hon. Henry Cadogan who fell in the Peninsular campaign at Vittoria in 1813; it is a good portrait medallion on a sarcophagus, with draped flags and a stylish shako. Penetrate the gloom of the tower to take a closer look at the good 1880s glass in the w. window by Kempe & Co. His golden wheat-sheaf emblem is right at the top and the two main *lights* contain an *Annunciation* in rich colour. The *hatchment* hanging in the tower is for William John Frederick, 3rd Duke of Cleveland, who died in 1864 (another like it is at Raby Castle, Durham). John Rous was minister here from 1623 to 1644 and although his diary contains no mention of his parish, it is well worth seeking out. Published by the *Cambridge Camden Society* in 1856, it has fascinating sidelights on the events leading up to the Civil War and the conflict itself. He saw the Parliament men ride out of Bury in 1642 bound for Lincolnshire, and their colours bore the legend 'The warre is just that is necessary'. How often have simple men heard that to their cost!

Sapiston, St Andrew (D3): Down a lane and a good half mile from the village, the church lies in meadowland by an isolated farm. We should be thankful that it is now in the care of the *Churches Conservation Trust* and is used at intervals for services. Apart from the s. doorway, the fabric is early-C14, a plain unbuttressed tower with 'Y' *tracery* bell openings, *reticulated* tracery in the e. window and *trefoil*-headed *lancets* on the n. side. There are two C13 grave slabs in the floor of the neat little *porch* but the doorway, a fine piece of *Norman* work, is what takes the eye. The scale is small, with an opening less than a yard wide between pairs of octagonal shafts under scalloped *capitals*. The arch has two bands of particularly interesting ornament, rather like a series of cloven tongues, with a carved head above. Look for the *scratch dials* on both capitals, obviously in use before the C14 porch was built.

Inside is a lovely old brick floor and, above it, a simple *hammerbeam* and *scissors-braced* roof. The *chancel* roof is boarded, with no arch between it and the *nave*. In front of the blocked n. door is a plain octagonal C13 *font;* the bowl has sloping sides and is supported by a centre shaft and four columns. The C17 black cover has large scrolls reaching up to support a turned

finial. Beyond the tall tower arch is a w. window with *Decorated* tracery, and on the n. wall, a set of *Stuart Royal Arms* with the quarterings altered to suit the *Hanoverian* dynasty. Four *consecration crosses* have been uncovered, one by each door and one each side of the nave e. end. The lancets on the n. side are set in deep embrasures with dropped sills, and over the top of a tomb arch there are tantalising traces of a large wall painting in which one figure with a sheaf of arrows can be distinguished – possibly a martyrdom of *St Edmund*. Further along there are stairs in the wall that gave access to the vanished *rood loft* and the later Decorated windows on the s. side may have been inserted to give it more light. There is a *priest's door* on the s. side of the chancel and beyond it, a lovely C14 *piscina*, its large trefoil with blind tracery in the *spandrels* set in an *ogee* arch. What gives it real individuality is the miniature replica cut in the angled side wall. On the n. chancel wall is an alabaster tablet to John Bull (1643). The name is so familiar that it is rather like meeting an old friend. It has a shield of arms in a *cartouche* over the *pediment* diminutive cherubs below, and pendant *pomegranate*s below that. A *ledger-stone* in the chancel for William Crofts (1632) is interesting and, indeed, helpful because it gives family names in the scrolls below the impaled shields of arms. Returning to the porch you will see the remains of a *stoup* inside the door, and on the outside wall below the e. window, two hitching rings remain that once secured the horses of the parson and the squire.

Saxmundham, St John the Baptist (H4): The church stands on rising ground by the Leiston road, well to the e. of the town centre. The C14 tower has strong lines, with three *set-offs* in the angle buttresses and a niche above the w. window; there is *cusped* 'Y' *tracery* in the bell openings and restored *flushwork* battlements. The tower houses a fine ring of six bells with an 8 cwt. tenor. A n. *aisle* was added in 1851, and the large organ chamber and *vestry* at its e. end was built in 1908. *R.M. Phipson* carried out a wholesale restoration and rebuilding here in 1872. He inserted a new e. window, and applied a typically hard flint finish to the whole of the s. frontage. In the process, most of the *clerestory* lost its original decoration, but two bays at the w. end retained delicate flushwork panels and two sections of an inscription which com-memorates the church reeves Thomas Norman and Robert Boteler. Phipson also dispensed with the s. porch, extended both aisles westward, and by removing an internal *gallery* he made the tower w. door the main entrance.

Saxmundham has a good ring of six bells with an 8 cwt. tenor, and two of them are C15 and may have been cast by the London founder John Sturdy. The fifth bears the emblems of the *Evangelists* which are rarely found on bells. Passing beneath the ringing chamber, one finds that the broad aisles give the interior a feeling of compactness, and overhead there is a handsome *hammerbeam nave* roof, with *castellated* hammers and wooden demi-figures as *corbels* below the *wall posts*. Until 1932 it was hidden by a plaster ceiling, and the original and replacement work can be distinguished by the variation in colour. There is a large *sanctus-bell window* above the glazed arch of the ringing chamber, and the angel in the head of the tower w. window is the only piece of medieval glass left in the church. A C15 *font* stands below, the standard East Anglian design, and the lions and *woodwoses* round the shaft were decisively re-cut in the C19. In the bowl panels, lions alternate with angels bearing shields – n., the three crowns of East Anglia; e., *Passion emblems*; s., *St George*; w., *Trinity emblem*. The agreeable little Victorian cover has a carving of the church's patron saint as a *finial*. Phipson re-benched the whole church, using New Zealand pine, a species of cedar which he also chose for Yoxford. The treatment of the e. end of the C15 clerestory is very unusual. A section of the nave roof was often decorated as a *celure* above the *rood* which stood on the chancel screen, but here, the two end windows of the clerestory are used for emphasis instead. For some reason, the treatment is varied – the n. embrasure has moulded *jamb shafts* and arch above a heavily castellated ledge, and there is a line of *paterae* below inscribed with *Sacred monograms* and 'MR' for the *Blessed Virgin*; on the s. side, the inscription: 'Sancte Johannes ora pro nobis' (*St John* pray for us) is boldly displayed within a moulded frame. The references would therefore marry up with the figures on either side of the cross in the rood group, the Blessed Virgin on Christ's r., St John on his l. The s. *arcade respond* is carved with an angel bearing a scroll (re-cut), and there is an image niche below, together suggesting that there was an *altar* nearby. The glass in the n. aisle w. window is a fairly terrible product of *Ward & Hughes* and features an outlandishly dressed centurian. The aisle e. window on the other hand is distinctly interesting. The figures of two angels displayed against patterned quarries were 'Painted and presented to this church by Mary & Bessie

McKean' in 1872, and installed by Mr Howlett, a Saxmundham glazier. It is an unusual and decorative example of local talent, and it is a pity that the organ chamber now largely obscures it. Back lighting sometime, perhaps? The single memorial of 1869 on the n. wall is for John Crampin, by the local mason *Thomas Thurlow* – a marble tablet with capitals picked out in red within a 'High Victorian Gothic' frame. The s. aisle w. window glass is a Victorian tour de force, designed by the Dowager Marchioness of Waterford, friend of John Ruskin and well known in her day as an artist and book illustrator. The glass is by *O'Connor & Taylor*, and the Ascension in brilliant colour transforms the whole aisle. Christ stands in the centre light, the disciples kneel on either side, and there are bright cherub heads against a deep blue starry sky in the tracery above. The effect is distinctly dramatic, and some of the faces would fit quite happily in any upper-class photo album of the 1870s.

The chapel on the s. side of the chancel was built in 1308 by Lord of the Manor Robert Swan as a *chantry*, and although Phipson rebuilt the two-bay arcade, he probably followed the original form. The three-*light* window in the s. wall contains glass by *Powells* based on drawings by Harry Ellis Wooldridge, a talented painter and Professor at the Slade Academy. Christ preaches in the centre, surrounded by his disciples, a family group, and the disabled. Backed by dense foliage, the design is closely knit and framed with oak leaf borders. An unusually good tiled panel below carries an epitaph and achievement for William Long, 1875. The glass in the window further along is again by Powells, using a pair of very good Wooldridge panels of Jesus and the woman of Samaria, the spaces above and below filled with a delightful vase of flowers motif. The ovals of C17 glass in the chapel e. window probably came from Innsbruck, and from l. to r. the top row contains figures of the Blessed Virgin and St John the Baptist, *St Louis*, and *St Peter*; in the centre row, *St Mark* is flanked by secular scenes. There are two more secular scenes at the bottom and, in the centre, a very interesting illustration of an alchemist tending his crucible, with the signs of Pisces, Aries and Gemini behind him. The arch *cusps* of the C14 *piscina* have suffered, and its *hood mould* has gone, but note that the moulding is dotted with unusual rosettes. The chapel was newly furnished in 1948, and the altar by Alfred Burns is a typical *Cautley* design. An image niche remains in the e. wall to the l., and to the r. a memorial with anchor and ensign draped on

Saxmundham, St John the Baptist: C17 alchemist

the obelisk commemorates George Long. As a young man in 1782 he led the storming of Trincomalee in Sri Lanka, and 'fell most honourably before that important Fortress in the Moment of Victory'. A chaste and charming tablet of 1778 over the priest's door is for Charles and Mary Long – draped urn above, garlanded oval of arms below. Another for Beeston and Sarah Long of 1785 is on the opposite wall, and they are both by William Tyler. He had studied under the famous Louis François Roubiliac and was an original member of the Royal Academy.

Phipson replaced the chancel arch and dispensed with a screen, and you will by now have noticed that Saxmundham has a *weeping chancel*. All that remains of the *rood screen* is a pair of panels which now form part of a *credence table* in the *sanctuary*. They retain virtually all of their original colour, and *gesso* features at the head of one of the panels and on the leading edges of the tracery. On this evidence, the screen must have been first class. Parts of the *piscina* have been replaced but there is *Early English dogtooth* decoration in the arch. Just to the e. of the organ there is a characteristic piece by *Nollekens* – a memorial for Charles Long who died in 1812. A fat *putto* sits with his torch reversed in mourning against the dark obelisk, and the sarcophagus below is marginally enlivened with Greek shells and fans. Thomas

Thurlow provided the tablet over the vestry door for Susanna Mayhew in 1853, with a dove in the pediment and shield of arms below. Beyond, on the sanctuary wall, Charles Long, Baron Farnborough has his memorial. He died in 1838, having been MP for Dunwich, and the tablet is by *Sir Richard Westmacott*, with a handsome profile medallion. Thurlow supplied the *reredos* in 1873, and its *blind arcades* display the *Decalogue*, Creed, and Lord's Prayer in typical period fashion. Above, there is excellent glass by *Lavers, Barraud & Westlake*, eight shaped panels linked with an interlace – Nativity, Baptism, Crucifixion and Resurrection above, and scenes from the life of St John the Baptist below. Christ in Majesty and the patron saint feature again in the tracery, and the figures are exceptionally good, particularly Zacharias in the bottom l. panel.

On your way out, note the square of C18 roofing lead with churchwardens' names on the wall under the tower, and in the churchyard look for a very unusual headstone. John Noller died in 1725, and his stone has the simplest and most invulnerable sundial imaginable. On the e. and w. faces there are small, inclined oblong recesses, and the shadow cast by the top edge marks the time on the parallel hour lines engraved within. The stone is the last of a group of four standing 8yds. to the s. of the path just w. of the church. As a relief perhaps, after his clients' choice of

Saxmundham, St John the Baptist: Unique sundial

memorials, Thomas Thurlow lies with other members of his family in a plain table tomb by the path leading to the gate.

Saxtead, All Saints (G4): For those with a taste for the precise, it is on record that Saxtead's tower fell on 8 July 1805, but whether from decrepitude or thunderbolt we know not. The w. wall was duly repaired and, typical of the period, a window with wooden *tracery* bars was inserted. A circuit of the outside reveals a C13 n. door and farther along a square window in domestic style complete with opening quarter light. There is a single *lancet* in the the n. wall of the C14 *chancel* and the lovely three-*light* e. window has *ogee* shapes in the head which enclose an oval, itself divided by tracery. There is more *Decorated* tracery in the windows on the s. side and a minuscule *Tudor priest's door* in red brick. The C15 *porch* is faced with *flushwork*, there is a small canopied niche above the entrance, and a dragon and a lion sport among writhing foliage in the *spandrels* of the arch. The *wall plates* of the roof are delicately carved and, as at Athelington and South Elmham St Margaret, the village stocks have found a home in the porch. Saxtead's, however, are a rather superior version and have a central whipping post as well. Not only that, the three sets of holes for the legs are graded in size to take both young and old, and an inscription reads 'Fear God and Honour the King' as though blasphemy and treason were the particular crimes in question.

Beyond a *Perpendicular* doorway with *fleurons* in the moulding is a neat and immaculately maintained interior which, despite its smallness, boasts a C15 *hammerbeam* roof over the *nave*. The deep *wall plates* are crested and there is pierced tracery behind the *arch-braces* and above the *collars* under the ridge. The roof was well restored in 1986 and there are interesting photographs of the work in progress displayed at the w. end. The bowl panels of the C15 octagonal *font* are decorated with plain shields within *quatrefoils* and it seems rather squat, probably because the floor level has been raised, masking the step. The C17 cover is a plain panelled pyramid. The carved seated figure on the n. side rear bench is very similar to one in the same position at Tannington, and other bench ends have traces of figures on the elbows, suggesting that the same craftsman may have been at work here. Most of the seating, however, is modern. A *consecration cross* is to be found on the nave s. wall and on the other side the *rood loft* stairs rise well to the w. of the chancel arch. Looking e.

you will see that Saxtead has an example of a *weeping chancel* – to the s. in this instance. There is a C19 pulpit and C20 choir stalls, and in the chancel with its plastered ceiling there are two more consecration crosses on the walls. The late-C17 *Decalogue* panels are rather splendid and very well preserved. On canvas, they have painted architectural surrounds and pendent swags. Also painted on canvas are the fine *Royal Arms* of George II which hang over the priest's door. The late-C17 *communion rails* are satisfyingly solid, with well-turned *balusters*, and the C14 *angle piscina* has a slender corner shaft with ring capital and base and *cusped ogee* arches. The style is repeated in the e. window which has small -*headstops* to the *hood mould*. Below stands a small *Stuart Holy Table*, and the chest with marquetry inlay which stands in the corner is probably continental work.

Semer, All Saints (D6): This little church has a captivating setting, lying as it does secluded in the valley of the Brett well away from the few houses and Manor farm. One can appreciate how it was that someone reported the C16 rector Edward Kettle to the bishop, 'because he worketh in harvest tyme in byndinge of oats without any hatt on his head, or dublett on his back, but onlie his hose and shirt'. There was a wholesale restoration here in the 1870s when the *chancel* was rebuilt and given a solid porch for the *priest's door*. A *vestry* was added beyond the n. door, and the ridge of the *nave* roof was sliced off, leaving the old line showing on the tower. Although the *Perpendicular* w. window of the tower was restored, the bell openings have fragments of *Decorated tracery* which indicate its age. The s. porch was sensitively rebuilt in 1899, making use of the original C15 barge boards and *jambs*, and the C14 inner doorway houses a medieval door which has had a whole selection of lock positions over the years.

Two *tie-beams* span the nave under a plaster ceiling and above the tower arch there is a set of George III *Royal Arms* on canvas. Within the tower is an interesting charity board, and either side of the arch hang C18 *Decalogue* boards in unusually rich frames. Oddly, they do not match in that the one to the l. has a cherub head and scrolls on top. The square and massive C14 *font* is fitted with a pleasing little *Jacobean* cover which has four scrolls against a turned and carved post, with knobs for lifting. There are C19 benches and pulpit, and a brass lectern whose inscription not only tells us that, along with the screen and reading desk, it was given by the rector in 1897, but also advises us to ponder Psalms 42, 23, and 84, and not to overlook the collect for the second Sunday in Advent. The chancel arch was part of the rebuilding and the new roof has heavy *arch-braces* resting on *corbel* angels bearing musical instruments and *Evangelistic symbols*. On the n. wall a 1660s memorial for Rector John Bruning is nicely composed in alabaster and *touchstone*. The tablet is flanked by scrolls below his arms within a broken *pediment,* and a small scrolled oval below is capped by a skull. Opposite there is a pair of tall, matching C18 tablets (and a third behind the organ) with *cartouches* of arms over them and graceful lettering, for the Revd. Thomas Cooke and his wife Sarah. The paintings of Moses and Aaron which flank the *altar* seem to have been made to accompany the Decalogue boards at the w. end, and in front stands a fine pair of brass candlestands of the type recommended by the *Ecclesiological Society*.

The setting invites a leisurely tour of the churchyard and n. of the chancel Maria Elizabeth Archer lies in a table tomb. She died aged 18 in 1786 and her epitaph is reminiscent of one of Fanny Burney's characters: 'This amiable young woman was blest with an uncommon sweetness of disposition, a refined and highly cultivated understanding, and a most striking urbanity of manner.' By the s. porch lies the recent grave of a baby boy ('our little man') and, just as one has sometimes seen favourite horses carved on an old farmer's stone, so this stone has a teddy bear – the cherished companion.

Shadingfield, St John the Baptist (I2):

The church stands by a dip and a bend in the Beccles-Saxmundham road and visitors need to take care, but there is parking space opposite. The *Perpendicular* tower has a niche above the w. window which has the remains of quite delicate pierced *tracery* in the *spandrels*. There are *gargoyles* below the parapet, and the walls were extensively patched in brick in the C18 or C19; a major restoration was completed in 1983. It is worth a circuit of the building to examine the *Transitional* n. doorway, with *dogtooth* decoration in its arch, and to note the *Norman lancets*, one in each wall at the w. end of the *nave*. There is a larger lancet in the C13 *chancel*, and a *priest's door* in its s. wall. A stone cut with initials and '1879' below the e. window probably marked the completion of a repair, although the chancel had already been heavily restored in 1841. The early-C16 *porch* has rather a grand facade for its size – in red brick, with polygonal turrets, and bands of small terracotta *quatrefoils*. The inner doorway is again Transitional, but without decoration, and this suggests that the n. door may have been the principal entrance in the early days.

The interior is a single hall, with no division now between nave and chancel, and above a *castellated wall plate*, the *arch-braces* of the nave roof disappear into a plastered ceiling. The organ which stands at the w. end was given in 1894; it has a handsome late-C18 case, painted pale grey, with cast gilt embellishments and a harp set in its broken *pediment*. Behind it in the n.w. corner you will find a tall *banner stave locker*, wedge shaped, and rebated to take a door. The worn C13 slab that lies in the floor nearby probably covered the grave of a priest. The early-C15 *font* stands on a chunky base in the form of a Maltese cross, with the four main risers hooded over panels of varied tracery; the shaft is ringed with attached columns, and the bowl panels carry *Tudor Roses* and shields. The set of *Royal Arms* boldly painted on canvas that hang on the s. wall are likely to date from the reign of Charles II. The nave benches with their *poppyheads* are late-C19 replacements of the sort to be seen in many places, but they have a very interesting variation in that the ends of the front standards are carved with two little demi-figures, one a priest and one a layman, wearing matching cloaks. They have a curiously un-English feeling and are certainly not typical of the period. Although there is now neither chancel arch nor *screen, corbels* survive in the walls to mark the division, and they too are unusual. They are carved as pairs of heads, and those on the n. side are strangely irregular in size and crudely carved, dating possibly from the early C14. Their position suggests that they supported the front beam of the *rood loft* rather than the *rood beam* itself, and there is a *castellated* base on the s. wall which no doubt carried a figure of a dedicatory saint for an *altar* in front of the screen. It is possible that the oblong ledge with a recessed top just to the w. was a *piscina* (as *Cautley* suggests), but it has no discernable drain and is suspiciously high in the wall. A base for a lamp perhaps? A *brass* inscription on the wall nearby commemorates Mary Cuddon who died in 1586. The lancet in the chancel n. wall contains a rare and beautiful example of mid-C19 glass painting, using enamels rather than stain or pot glass. Two vignettes illustrate the text 'All flesh is grass' (Peter 1.viii); the morning snowdrops, lily of the valley and meadow grasses bloom by a stream in one setting, only to lie fallen across the scythe at dusk in the other. The window is a memorial for Mary Kilner, daughter of the squire of Shadingfield Hall. She was buried at Chester in 1858, and this may therefore be the work of Evans of Shrewsbury or another of the w. country glass painters. The chancel roof is panelled, with small *bosses*, and ribs picked out in red, and there are three more brass inscriptions to be found in the floor below: in the centre for another Mary Cuddon (1640), and alongside, one for Anne Harvy who died at a great age in 1618; the inscription near the s. wall is for William Cuddon (1634). There are *dropped-sill sedilia* and a simple C13 piscina in the *sanctuary*, and the large arched recess in the e. wall will have been used as an *aumbry*. The altar is a good C17 table, its top rails and brackets nicely carved, and with a centre stretcher. The e. window is flanked by C19 stone *Decalogue* panels, and the glass is interesting. The borders make use of C16-C18 fragments, and there are enamelled roundels by various artists who were probably local. Two ovals at the bottom portray the Holy Family and the Ascension, and the latter has the texture of a sketchy line drawing. The centre panel of Christ at the Last Supper is possibly the work of John Winter, an artist and glazier who was at work in Bungay in the mid-C19. One must visit the Strangers' Hall museum in Norwich to see Shadingfield's particular treasure, an altar cloth trimmed with hand-made lace which Elizabeth, William Cuddon's wife gave to the church in 1632. The original box, complete with inscription, survives with the cloth.

Shelland, King Charles the Martyr (E4): This is a very rare dedication, there being only four others in England. It is also a church that is not marked on the average map and even the village name is elusive. However, it stands by a spacious common on the lane that runs from Harleston to Borley Green and Woolpit and is well worth seeking out. It is small, set within a spacious churchyard overlooking open fields to the s., and it is one of the very few churches in the county that the Victorians hardly touched. It had only been rebuilt in 1767 and its newness, coupled with its isolation, saved it. Outside, it is very plain and the *nave* has *lancets* and 'Y' *tracery* windows. The *chancel* is lit by a C19 e. window and there is a little *vestry* tacked on to the s. side of the nave. The w. gable boasts a substantial bellcote with an attractive *ogee* cap topped by a ball. Within the little brick n. porch there is a marble cherub's head over the inner doorway that is likely to have come from an old tomb. Inside the tiny building there is an air of peaceful

Shelland, King Charles the Martyr: Housel bench

calm and orderliness that is so often the hallmark of the C18 village church. The brick floors are laid in a herringbone pattern and the symmetry of the high *box pews* is complemented by the matching rails with elegant *balusters* that divide the nave from the chancel and isolate the *sanctuary*. All the joinery is in pine, painted and grained in pale tan, and to the r. of the brick chancel arch is a *three-decker pulpit*. The *clerk's* pew faces w., continuing the line of the pews, and one passes through it to the reading desk at the next level. This is provided with a seat and so is the pulpit just above it. Three hat pegs adorn the wall in front. The chancel ceiling has a little cornice of Gothick arches and pendants and the walls below the dado are covered with patterned uncut moquette fabric which also backs the wooden blind arcading on the e. wall. That must surely be a unique variation in wall finishes. On each side of the chancel there is a low 8ft.long *housel bench* with square tapered legs and carved top rail on which parishioners will have sat to receive communion and which must have been in parish use before the *Reformation*. It is the only one that I have identified in Suffolk. There are well-cut *ledger-stones* for the Cropley family in the floor and on the n. wall is a memorial for William Cropley who died in 1717. In white marble on pale grey, the tablet is finely lettered within an *acanthus* frame, with a *cartouche* of arms above and three shields below. Turning to the w. the vista is nicely symmetrical. Below the circular w. window an attractive little organ case rises from the musicians' pew, which has matching wings at a lower level. The organ is very rare – one of the few *barrel organs* still in use for services. It was made by Bryceson of London in 1820 and has three barrels of twelve tunes each. Cleaned and restored in 1956, Robert

Armstrong was its 'organist' from 1885 until 1935. When asked whether it was difficult to play he said: "It's not everybody who can do it; you got to have an ear". High on the w. wall is a set of George III *Royal Arms* in scale with the building and below stands the second reminder of an earlier medieval church – the C14 *font* whose panels are carved overall with a variety of leaf forms and three shields to the w. The ogee cover matches the bellcote outside but for a pineapple *finial*, and one of the curved panels is fitted with a neat little door for access. One of the memorable and endearing things about Shelland is the riotous colour scheme and I cannot resist an inventory – lilac walls in the nave with bright terracotta *tie-beams* and rafters against a white ceiling and a turqoise cornice; the chancel arch is of exposed yellow bricks with turquoise *capitals*. The walls of the chancel are lime green above the dado and the coved ceiling is deep blue. All is great fun and an excellent foil for the austere fittings. C18 churches have a fascination of their own and their devotees will not be disappointed here.

Shelley, All Saints (E7): This is a lovely situation for a country church, in the little valley of the Brett with a house or two nearby and meadowland beyond. Judging by the blocked *lancet* in the s. wall of the *chancel*, it was built in the C13 and in the early C14 a tower (which also serves as a porch) was added to the n. The s. *aisle* is of the same period and one of the windows has intersected *tracery*, although you will see that its w. window was replaced in the early C19 with a 'Gothick' model in an iron frame. Just below it a glacial boulder stone peeps through the plaster and a number were used in the foundations. They were perhaps pagan cult objects that were ritually cleansed and reused deliberately in the church. The tower bell openings are tall *cusped lancets* e. and w., with a wider one to the n. which has the remains of tracery. It was a very pleasant surprise to find that the clock not only worked but the bells chimed the quarters – a rare thing in the country these days, although the ring of five with its 8 cwt. tenor can no longer be used for change ringing. The steep entrance arch of the tower is finely moulded but now has a small wooden door set within it, and there is a straight-headed late-*Perpendicular* four-*light* window in the n. wall of the *nave*. Beyond it, the Tylney chapel in *Tudor* red brick juts out from the *chancel*, with token octagonal buttresses at the corners. A coat of arms in a small stone panel lies between two windows in the n. wall and there is the outline of a third window in the gable. It is interesting that the C16 builder still used diminutive *headstops* on the brick *dripstones*. The e. window and the *priest's door* were renewed in the 1880s and, except for the tower, all the walls are plastered. The s. *porch* has a timber frame on a brick base with stone seats and is now the principal entrance. The doorway belongs to the C13 building and has a continuous roll moulding down to the floor.

Just inside to the l. hangs a set of George III *Royal Arms* painted on canvas, and there is a small C19 *font* in the nave. The C14 *arcade*, with its octagonal *piers* and wide *capitals*, leans gently outwards. On the n. wall are two *hatchments*: one undated for Mary Kerridge to the w., and the other for Thomas Kerridge who died in 1743. There are brick floors and C19 pine benches, whose front ranks incorporate oak *linen-fold* panels that match those in the stately Elizabethan pulpit standing on a centre pedestal. At the base of the n. nave window stands the tomb of Dame Margarett Tylney who died in 1598. The chest has an alabaster epitaph panel set in strapwork and the flanking columns are made of a prettily mottled marble. The edge of the slab is moulded and picked out in yellow but her effigy is all in black, with a high-necked gown and ruff; only the nose and fingers have been mutilated. The stained glass in the aisle window is by *William Warrington* and the figures in uncomplicated colours have little animation. But it is of more than usual interest because it commemorates Henry Partridge, one of Warrington's apprentices, who died in 1864 aged 21. In the chancel, the choir stalls have two excellent *griffins* holding shields carved with the Tylney arms and a tomb chest is set in the n. wall of the *sanctuary*. There are three shields of arms within shallow niches along its front, and on the top, set in strapwork, stands a large coloured shield with many quarterings. With the two smaller shields, it really belongs to Dame Margarett's tomb, and that itself may originally have stood in the large recess in the chancel wall which is now clad with panels of linen-fold and other C16 motifs. The plain *piscina* has one drain and a dish scooped out beside it which may have been a way of providing a double version cheaply. A plain painted door in the recess on the n. side of the chancel leads into the Tylney chapel and an elaborate version of their family arms is carved in relief within a stone panel on the facing wall. Unfortunately, the supporting griffins have lost their feet but a cute little leaf trail up each side sprouts more of the beasts. The strangest thing in the chapel is the 10ft. post with a 'T' bracket at the end which stretches out from the w. wall just below the ceiling. It is carefully moulded, with a wrought-iron stay, and was used to display a tabard, a surcoat embroidered with the family arms. The C18 *Decalogue* boards below are in rather poor condition and would have been in the chancel originally, while the plain panelling came from *box pews* discarded during the 1880s restoration. On the s. wall, however, is more good C16 linenfold and (yet again) the Tylney arms carved on a panel.

Shimpling, St George (C5): An avenue of tall limes close enough to form a tunnel leads to a bridge over the Chad brook and into the churchyard at the e. end. An 1860s restoration has left its mark fairly decisively on what is largely a C14 church, and a three-stage flint and stone chimney rises on the s.e. corner of the *nave*, with another above the *vestry* which is distinctly priapic. The Hallifax mausoleum of 1841 stands by the *chancel*, rather like a superior builder's hut in stone. However, there are windows with nicely varied *Decorated tracery* in the nave, chancel and s. *aisle* and small unequal niches flank the w. window of the tower.

The rebuilt s. porch shelters a late-C13 doorway and leads to an interior made rather dark by the absence of any *clerestory* over the four-bay s. *arcade*. The C14 *font* by the door is a strange design and quite unlike others in the area; it has attached columns round the shaft and a very shallow octagonal bowl carved with *quatrefoils* and tracery panels. If Shimpling's ring of five bells with an 8 cwt. tenor were still in ringable condition they would be handled from the ground floor of the tower. Roofs, benches and the *parclose screen* in the aisle are all Victorian, and there is a very heavy-handed wooden *altar* of the same vintage in the aisle chapel. Close by is a C14 *piscina* with an exceptionally large drain. Levels were raised in the chancel so that the simple piscina there is now near the floor. Over the shallow arch of the *priest's door* there is a line of *dogtooth* decoration that one would call *Early English* except that it is very sharply cut. Victorian *Decalogue* boards flank the altar and there is a modern *brass* framed behind glass for Augustus Bolton who was rector here. Elizabeth Plampin has a memorial by *Sir Richard Westmacott* on the n. wall – a female in a rather stagey pose stands by an urn with initials and date on the plinth. The epitaph is instructive for, apart from her

extensive talents as a wife and mother, 'in epistolary correspondence she displayed a sincerity of friendship and an energy of sentiment expressed in language at once refined and natural'. A rare gift, undoubtedly. The banal 1850s monument to Thomas Hallifax in the s. aisle cannot compete with that. The stained glass at Shimpling is interesting for a number of reasons. Quite a lot of C14 *tabernacle work* remains in the tracery of the chancel side windows, and in the n.e. window of the nave there are unusual *Trinity* emblems, while shields in the centre window include that of St Edmundsbury. In the aisle the centre window has 1864 glass which was *Henry Holiday's* first design in East Anglia and his only early work in Suffolk. In strong *pre-Raphaelite* style and colouring, it shows the Presentation of Christ in the temple, with the priest vested as a medieval bishop. The *Blessed Virgin* holds two purple doves and vivid patterns are deployed in robes and background. The glass was originally planned for the aisle e. window where Holiday angels remain in the tracery; the later figures of Faith, Hope and Charity are by the *Powells*. The chancel e. window glass of 1842 is the earliest example of *Warrington's* glass in the county; *Evangelistic symbols*, central *Sacred monogram*, and the arms of Sir Thomas Hallifax are set against opaque *quarries* decorated with oak leaves and all are within pretty borders. The tower window is an instructive contrast in the High Victorian style of the 1860s – a parallel Transfiguration and Ascension by Baillie & Mayer, using dense colour and bright patterning in the tracery. Before leaving, it is worth a detour in the churchyard to view the little building in the s.w. corner. In yellow brick and slate, it has a room with fireplace, bay window and fitted seat, together with a cloakroom and closet. Restored in 1977, it was apparently designed as a 'fainting house' to which swooning C19 ladies could retire if the length or vigour of the sermon proved too much for them – unique in my experience.

Shotley, St Mary (G7): The church stands on its own little hillock with a few houses at Shotley Church End, and commands a broad view of the Orwell estuary. The tower is largely built of *septaria* which is perhaps why its upper part collapsed in the 1630s, and it received its tiled cap in the late C17. The body of the church is early-C14, but the *nave* was heightened in the late C15 when a range of closely spaced *clerestory* windows was inserted whose *dripstones* are linked. In 1745 the rector was the Hon. Henry Hervey (who later took his wife's name of Aston) and he rebuilt the *chancel* in classical style, one of the very few examples of the period in the county. It has a handsome Venetian e. window, high in the wall and deeply recessed within a semi-circular arch. The *priest's door* on the s. side has a crested and dated keystone below its *pediment*, and on the n. side there is a square brick *vestry* with sash windows (seldom used in churches). The C15 s. *porch* has had its upper parts replaced in brick, and there were once carvings in the *spandrels* of the outer arch; one of the large lion *stops* survives, there are *fleurons* in the dripstone, and a *stoup* is sited by the inner doorway.

A spacious interior, with the nave tall for its length, and note how the C14 *arcades* differ slightly, both in the shape of their arches and in their *capitals*. The tower is blanked off just beyond its arch, and a classical panelled door was inserted in 1745. Above the arch hang the *Royal Arms* of George II, dulled but well-painted on canvas. The nave has an excellent and unstained *double hammerbeam* roof, the hammers and *collar beams castellated*, and there is *tracery* on either side of the *king posts*. Its deep *wall plates* are decorated with *paterae*, and there were once demi-angels on the ends of the hammers and at the base of the *wall posts* (see where the tenons have been sawn through). Traces of paint on the timbers above the e. wall suggest that the last section formed a *celure* above the *rood*. The benches and pulpit were supplied by Robert Hawkins of Monks Eleigh in 1874, and a few years before that the rector had installed the organ which stands in its nice 'gothicky' case in the e. bay of the n. aisle. It started life as a barrel-organ and was later converted to a conventional keyboard instrument – something which was seldom done. In 1990, the n. *aisle* roof was repaired and some fine new leaf *bosses* have been carved to match the originals. A section of the wall plate at the e. end has more carving than the rest and the last bay was doubtless enhanced in honour of an *altar* below. The w. window of the s. aisle is blocked and the *font* nearby dates from 1906. Its predecessor stood near an arcade pillar further along, identified by a narrow *ogee*-headed niche whose use is uncertain. It may have housed a container for the oil and salt of baptism, or a small statue. The C17 table by the door was probably in use as an altar prior to the rebuilding of the chancel, and the simple C14 *piscina* at the e. end of the s. aisle shows that an altar originally stood under the e. window.

The chancel arch is offset to the s. and at the rebuilding it was encased in panelling with a very handsome set of the Aston family arms placed above it. To pass through into the chancel is to leave the Middle Ages behind and enter the C18 age of elegance, and a sharper contrast is not to be found anywhere. The floor is patterned with lozenges of black marble (a favourite device), and the coved, plastered ceiling has trios of cherub heads at each end, a *baroque* centre boss, and delicate cornices. The walls are panelled to shoulder height, and there are matching doors leading to the churchyard and the vestry. The high e. window allows for a tall *reredos* which extends across the whole of the wall; *Decalogue* panels are flanked by paintings of Moses and Aaron, with the Creed and Lord's Prayer beyond; the *Sacred monogram* in a glory and cherub heads are heightened with gilt, and there are urns above and swags of fruit and foliage below the panels. This provides a suitably splendid setting for the lovely altar table, a rare period example which has cabriole legs carved with large winged cherubs on the knees. The *sanctuary* is bounded by a set of three-sided *communion rails*; these are a late example of this form and their rounded corners match the curve of the step below.

The lower churchyard to the e. is a naval cemetary where many of the boys from HMS Ganges lie. An obelisk commemorates men of the 8th and 9th submarine flotillas who were lost in World War I, and it features the bronze figure of a mourning woman, with fat dolphins set at the corners. Designed by Frederick Brook-Hitch, the verse is by Rudyard Kipling:

There is but one task for all,
One life for each to give,
Who stands if freedom fall,
Who dies if England live?

Shottisham, St Margaret (H6): A steep path and steps lead up from Church Lane, and from the churchyard there is a view of the distant Deben estuary. The walls of the tower are a pleasantly mottled mixture of *septaria*, flint, and brick, and it has a bold stair turret up to belfry level on the s. side. *Edward Hakewill* carried out a major restoration in 1867, and the window above the simple w. doorway was renewed then. He added a n. *aisle*, and its deep sloping roof comes down to eaves which are only 5ft. from the ground. Walking round, you will see that a *Perpendicular* window in the n. wall of the *chancel* has been blocked, and that the whole of the e. wall was rebuilt, with triple *lancets* and a *sexfoil* roundel above them. There is a *priest's door* of about 1300 on the s. side, and the *Decorated* lancet alongside was a *low side window* which has had its bottom section filled in. The s. wall of the *nave* was re-faced during the restoration, and all the windows were replaced (with the possible exception of the lancet w. of the C19 porch).

Hakewill chose the C13 style for the new aisle *arcade*, with heavy bases and *capitals* for the *quatrefoil piers*. His nave roof is quite eccentric and has two ranges of shallow braces meeting under *collar beams*, with transverse braces and turned *wall posts*, all the timber is stained black against white plaster. C13 *Purbeck marble fonts* were nearly all made to a common pattern, and Shottisham's is no exception – pairs of shallow, pointed arches in each panel of the slightly canted bowl. The *Stuart Holy Table* has been demoted and now stands under a cloth in the tower. There no longer a *rood screen* to divide nave from chancel, but the stairs that led to its *loft* remain in the s. wall, rising from a window embrasure. The small recess below them may have been a *piscina* to serve a nave *altar*, although it no longer has a drain. A C16 chest with shallow carving all over its front stands in the chancel, and there is a restored piscina with a large *trefoil* arch next to the *dropped-sill sedilia*. The e. lancets contain a conventionally sentimental Ascension designed by Henry Hughes for *Ward & Hughes* in 1880. The church's single *brass* is a good one and lies at the e. end of the nave. It commemorates Rose, the wife of parson John Glover, and is dated 1620. A rose and a sunflower are engraved on each side of this verse:

As wither'd Rose its fragrant sent retains,
So beinge dead, her vertue still remains.
Shee is not dead, but chang'd, ye good ne'r
    dies,
But rather, shee is Sun=like, sett to rise.

Sibton, St Peter (H4): The church stands by the side of the Peasenhall to Yoxford road, and the ruins of the Cistercian abbey of the Blessed Virgin of Sibton can be seen in the valley of the Yox to the n. A *lych-gate* was added as a World War I memorial, and tall Scots pine stand in the churchyard. The spires at Yoxford and Middleton show that there was a local preference for them, and Sibton had one too until it was taken down in 1813. There is *Perpendicular tracery* in the small w. window and the bell openings of the early-C15 tower, and the battlements are decorated with *flushwork* panels above lively corner *gargoyles* like those at Yoxford; a handsome sundial of 1827 is set in the s. wall. Round about 1540, Robert Duckett left money for a n. *aisle* to be added, and the late-C12 or

early-C13 n. doorway, with its slim attached shafts, was probably saved from the old n. wall of the *nave* or pilfered from Sibton abbey (see below). All the windows on the n. side were renewed as part of a restoration in 1872, when the *chancel* was entirely rebuilt and a n.e. *vestry* added. The lancets and elaborate *priest's door* in the chancel are pure Victoriana, like the *plate tracery* in the s. nave windows. The 1870s replacement porch shelters an interesting *Transitional* doorway which still has the rounded *Norman* shape in its arch, with deep roll moulding and *dripstone*; the *jamb shafts* have carved *capitals*, and the outer shafts are banded at the base and mid-point in the later style.

The tower w. window contains 1880s glass by *Ward & Hughes*, illustrating *St Mary Magdalene's* meeting with Christ on the first Easter Day, and is typical of their later commercial style. Sibton has a ring of five bells with an 11 cwt. tenor which would be rung from the ground floor of the tower if they were restored to useable condition. The C15 *font* stands in the n. aisle on three steps, two of which have carved roundels. The shaft is set about with tall lions and *woodwoses*, and in the bowl panels there are *Evangelistic symbols*, alternating with angels holding shields – n. East Anglia (or Ely), w. *Trinity emblem*, s. *St George*, e. *Passion emblems*. The simple, attractive cover could be C17 or early-C18. Sibton abbey was sold to the Duke of Norfolk in 1536 and it is likely that the C13 four-bay *arcade* was taken in its entirety from there; with its circular *piers* and octagonal *abaci*, it now leans slightly outwards. The nave is broad for its length, and has an attractively compact *hammerbeam* roof. Cresting on the top of the hammers continues over the deep *wall plate*, and the cambered *collar beams* have centred angels facing e. and w. like those at Bruisyard. There are wooden *corbels* carved as demi-angels holding books, and the e. bay of the roof is panelled and *bossed* as a *celure*, although no colour remains. The glass in the nave s. windows is probably by *Lavers, Barraud & Westlake;* the scenes are identified by texts and there is very attractive patterning above and below. John Scrivener died in 1662, and has a handsome memorial between the windows; the well-lettered Latin epitaph is set within a chunky architectural frame in alabaster, and a coloured *achievement of arms* is integrated in the curved *pediment*. A tall, narrow door shape in the s. wall shows where the *rood loft stair* was sited. Until the Victorian restoration, the pulpit stood against the middle of the s. wall (doubtless a *three-decker* with *box pews* ranged about it). It was then reduced in size, given a new base, and moved to its present position. It has compartmented panels and there is shallow ornament carved on the angles and under the rim. By folding back the nave carpet at the e. end, you will uncover the *brass* of 1574 commemorating Edmund and Margaret Chapman. Their 15in. figures kneel facing each other, with sons and daughters ranged behind them, and there is a memorable verse:

> Here was my native soile and here I led a
>   quiet lyef,
> Full seventy yeres and here to me
> By Margaret my wyffe,
> Eight sonnes and daughters fyve were
>   borne,
> And here I yelded have,
> My dett to death, my flesh to wormes,
> My body to the grave.
> Here doe I Edmund Chapmen torne
> To that same soile againe
> Wch brought me forth and fostred me,
> Prolonging lief in vayne,
> And wish that each man could,
> This lesson learn of me,
> Here so to live, and so to die,
> To live eternally.

This is a *palimpsest* brass, and the rubbing of the reverse side displayed on the w. wall shows how it was made up from various fragments. There are inscriptions in the floor further w., for Edward Chapman (1501), and Robert Chapman (1511), and in the n. aisle, two more for John Chapman (1475), and Thomas and Ollive Copland (1595). The aisle extends one bay alongside the chancel, forming a side chapel behind the organ, and there is a pair of charming tablets for Dorothea and Marianne Scrivener, with *cartouches* of arms on the obelisks and a notable epitaph for Marianne. The pairs of niches that flank the chancel arch have been barbarously defaced, but delicate panel tracery survives above the *groined* canopies, and much of the colour also, including diaper patterning as a backgound for the vanished statues. The *rood screen* must have been exceptionally beautiful, a late and elaborate version of the normal East Anglian style; one must be grateful that the tops of the main *lights* were saved and incorporated in a low, modern replacement. The design is outstanding, and the *crocketted ogee* arches have an intricate inner fringe of *cusped tracery*, with delicate panel tracery in the spandrels; much of the original colour and gilding remains.

Two more brasses lie in the chancel, and unfortunately the one on the n. side is partially covered by the massive underframe of the choir stalls. Dating from 1626, it is for Edmond and Marryan Chapman, and they kneel facing each other across a prayer desk, with their children ranged behind them. Luckily, there is an engraving displayed by the tower that shows the whole of the brass. The final brass, for John and Julian Chapman (1582), is on the s. side, very worn and lacking his head and part of her gown; there are separate groups of children and a verse inscription. Apart from the brasses there are good *ledger-stones* with deeply cut armorials, and a quality monument for Sir Edmond Barker and his wife Mary is on the n. wall. It is a fine composition, in which their two busts incline slightly inwards within linked oval wreaths, below a curved *pediment* and shield of arms. The faces are full of character, genuine portraits. He died in 1676, having been Lord of Peasenhall Manor and Gentleman Pensioner in Ordinary to Charles II; the two infants that they lost lie below them on the ledge, the elder holding a skull. The tall *Stuart communion rails* have gates, and there are two nicely composed scenes in each of the e. lancets, with a group of angels in the top roundel – good 1870s work by Henry Hughes of Ward & Hughes. The fireplace in the vestry has: 'Peter stood and warmed himself' carved on the chimney breast, so at least one Victorian parson enjoyed a quiet jest.

Snape, St John the Baptist (H5): There was already a church here in 1085, but nothing in the present building can be dated earlier than the C13. Begun in the 1440s, the tower has three sharp *string courses*, and there are *flushwork* shields at the base of the buttresses. The *Perpendicular* w. window has a deep *label*, with inward-turning *headstops*, and there are interesting changes in the wall texture at belfry level. The stepped battlements with their flushwork shields were added as a finishing touch in about 1525. Attractive pantile roofs overall, and the *nave* n. windows have 'Y' *tracery* of about 1300. Although somewhat altered, the blocked n. door is probably the same period. Further along, the *rood stair* turret is combined with a buttress, and beyond it, a tall *Decorated lancet* now has a square head. The *chancel* has seen many changes – dilapidated in the C16, and 'very ruinous and so hath been these two or three years past' in 1602. It had to be heavily buttressed, and in 1920 the entire e. wall was rebuilt (replacing a *scratch dial* upside down and facing e. on the s.e. corner). Another square-headed lancet features in the s. wall, there is a small blocked *priest's door*, and the handsome Perpendicular windows on that side of the nave have good headstops. The late-C14 or early-C15 s. *porch* had a new roof super-imposed at some stage, although its traceried parapet is still there. The *Agnus Dei* at its centre has a scroll lettered: 'Ecce Agnus' (Behold the Lamb), echoing the words of the church's patron saint. A niche above the entrance is delicately canopied, and there are *Trinity* and *Passion emblem* shields in the *spandrels;* flushwork panelling flanks the arch and the side window which has been unblocked has Decorated tracery. The nice C15 inner doorway has two ranks of *paterae* in its mouldings, worn angel stops, and lively dragons on the spandrels. The contemporary door, with its long wrought-iron hinges has been carefully restored.

The simple, uncluttered interior has a feeling of freshness, with brick floors in the nave under a plastered ceiling which leaves the *arch-braces* exposed. They rest on stone *corbels* carved with regal heads and demi-angels, and there are *castellated wall plates*. The shallow w. *gallery* was installed in 1848, and in 2000 a new organ by Peter Bumstead of Ipswich was installed on it. The attractive case has shades designed and made by Andrew Beckwith which echo the form of the local reed beds. Below stands an excellent, unusually interesting late-C15 *font*. The step is carved with *quatrefoils*, and enough of the inscription survives to identify the donors as Ricard Mey and his family. The base has lion masks at the corners, and pairs of lizards on each side – an unusual feature, but the lizard was an emblem of good fortune often used on church door handles and this may have been its significance here. Alternatively, they could represent the powers of evil being overcome by the sacrament of baptism. Battered *Evangelistic symbols* stand at the angles of the shaft, with two kings and two bishops between them. The carving in the bowl panels is inventive, and on the s.e. face there is an easily recognisable Trinity group, even though the figure of Christ has lost its arms, and the man and woman their heads. They probably represented the donors, and above them, *censing* angels trap the ends of a scroll which laps over the angle buttresses and continues all the way round the font. The w. panel has the *Blessed Virgin* enthroned, with a kneeling figure alongside, and angels fill the remaining panels. One wears a mitre, one bears a *chalice*, and another has what I think is a lamb

in a basket – a piece of symbolism encountered on one or two other East Anglian fonts. *William Dowsing* came here in January 1643, and although he smashed some windows and removed four *brasses*, the font panels were not damaged as much as one would expect, and the carvings may have been concealed with plaster (as happened elsewhere). One of the church's *consecration crosses* has been uncovered by the entrance, and above it there are traces of an inscription which was probably one of a C16 series. There is now neither chancel arch nor *screen*, but the rood stair has been opened up in the n. wall, and the upper opening defines the height of the loft. The chancel was re-roofed in 1920, and the priest's door embrasure has been partially filled in, forming a spacious niche. This provides the setting for an elongated head of *St John the Baptist* by local sculptor Laurence Edwards which is faintly reminiscent of the enigmatic Easter Island monoliths. Another recent addition is the limed oak lectern designed by John Makepiece, with a simple cluster of rods forming the shaft. The *communion rails* with their well-turned *balusters* were made by Doves in 1932 from wood which came from Bow church. The arch of the C13 *piscina* has lost its cusping, and half of the fluted drain has been shorn away – the result of being walled up no doubt. Alterations have rendered the recess in the n. wall rather formless, but its position suggests that it once housed an *Easter sepulchre*, and there are specific references in local wills to support the theory. The *altar* frontal that was being used when I visited is a fine piece of appliqué satin embroidery by Belinda Scott, featuring the dove of the Holy Spirit within a swirl of sombre colour, and a curlew in one corner. Above, the three-light window is filled with lovely glass of 1920 by *Mary Lowndes*, the colours subtle and restrained. In the upper half, the scene is the supper at Emmaus, with a lake landscape beyond seen through an arcade. Below, Snape bridge is flanked by angel reapers, and there are angels with Trinity and Passion shields in the tracery. It is the only work by this artist in Suffolk.

One or two interesting memorials can be seen in the churchyard – look particularly for George Alabaster's of 1759 not far from the porch. He was a churchwarden and the stone is carved with those familiar emblems of mortality – spade, pick, and bones. Many C18 stones are decaying fast now, and this one has been fitted with a neat plastic cover in an effort to preserve it. S. of the nave, Jonathan Woolnough's table tomb of 1776 tells us that he 'supported 3 law suits &

secured to this parish the right of commonage excluding the tenants of Lord Strafford' – one of those cases where unauthorised enclosure was defeated by determined local effort.

Somerleyton, St Mary (I1): Sir Morton Peto, railway magnate and entrepreneur extraordinary, commissioned John Thomas to design his flamboyant country house in 1844, and ten years later he had him rebuild the church which stands within the park. By that time it was partly derelict and the *chancel* roof had collapsed. Thomas retained the early-C15 tower and part of the chancel, but rebuilt the rest (except the old n. *aisle*) in a remarkably restrained version of the East Anglian style, using quality materials and facing the walls with *knapped* whitish flint. The chancel was renovated in 1870 and extended in 1888. Walking round, you will see that stepped battlements were added to the tower and the new *nave* windows were set within broad, shallow embrasures.

There is a small s. porch, and within, a severely plain modern gallery carries the organ at the w. end. There is just room enough between it and the s. door for you to see an exceptionally interesting stone panel on the wall above. This is a *reredos* which was found in the churchyard at the time of the rebuilding, having been discarded or hidden in the C16. It is in beautiful condition and the four *Evangelistic symbols* are finely carved in deep relief; they stand within *cusped ogee* arches and the whole is set within a moulded frame. The *font,* with its alternating lions and angels in the bowl panels, and four guardian lions round the shaft, is a familiar East Anglian type which must have been mass produced in the C15. There is some interesting glass to be seen in the nave windows, with those on the s. side by Mayer & Co, the Munich firm that extended its market to England in the mid-C19. They date from the 1890s and portray the *Three Marys* at the tomb, Christ with children, and his Presentation in the Temple – competent, albeit a little sentimental, in bright colour and firm outlines. In one of the windows on the n. side there are two lovely panels of Flemish C16 glass that came from St Olave's priory and were preserved in Somerleyton Hall. One portrays *St Catherine*, and the other is the *Blessed Virgin* and Child, with her hand raised in blessing. In her role as Queen of heaven she stands on a crescent moon which has an upturned and very human face. There is 1960s glass by George Maile & Son further along – figures *of St Bridget of Kildare* (a rare appearance),

and *St Francis* in company with an English setter; more work by this firm can be found at Blundeston and Kessingland. The figure of *St Clare* which was installed in 1985 is by Paul Quail, the artist who provided windows at Hopton, Swefling, and Walton St Mary. On the wall nearby is a 1907 tablet by Gaffin which records an unusual example of historic continuity. Gen. Sir Henry de Bathe commanded his battalion of Scots Guards at Sebastapol and enjoyed a distinguished military career, but his claim to our attention is that he served as a page at Queen Victoria's coronation and survived to attend her funeral sixty-four years later.

The C15 *rood screen* has been preserved and restored, and its panels are painted with an unusually interesting range of figures. Although the decoration is not so lavish as Ranworth's in Norfolk, there are distinct similarities in some of the saints, and that more famous screen may have provided a pattern for this one. From l. to r. the paintings are: *St Michael* (raising his sword to strike the dragon under his feet), *SS Edmund, Apollonia, Laurence, Faith* (the serrated saw she holds makes the identification reasonable and there are similar figures at Horsham St Faith and Marsham in Norfolk), *Thomas of Canterbury*? (Henry VIII ordered all images of him to be defaced, and if the identification is accepted, it would explain the drastic repainting), *Anne* (wearing a white veil and resting her hand on the Blessed Virgin's shoulder who marks her place in the book with a stylus), *Andrew, John, Mary Magdalene* (pointing to her pot of ointment), an unidentified bishop, *Petronilla* (closely resembling the painting at Litcham in Norfolk which is named), *Stephen, Dorothy* (pointing to her basket), *Edward the Confessor* (holding the ring as he does in the painting at Nayland), and *George* (a very vigorous figure, considering the limitations of the panel). The screen illustrates an intriguing but unexplained relationship between St Apollonia and St Laurence. They stand side by side, as they do at Ludham in Norfolk and in seven Devon churches, and it is hardly likely to be a coincidence.

The n. wall of the chancel carries an imposing monument, boldly signed at the bottom by Anthony Ellis, for Sir John and Lady Wentworth. He died in 1651 and the piece was commissioned by the widow during the *Commonwealth,* at a time when such things were rarely contemplated. It is of high quality, with the two commanding busts set against contrasting black marble drapes between *Corinthian* columns; the *cartouche* below still has faint traces of colour, and the monument was meticulously restored in the 1960s. Sir John served on several parliamentary committees, but he appears to have had royalist sympathies and was arrested shortly after the abortive rising at Lowestoft. In that affair he was involved with Capt. Thomas Allin, a shipmaster of the town. Allin was captured, but later escaped to Holland and served Charles II with distinction after the *Restoration*, being knighted for his efforts at the battle of Lowestoft. It so happened that he bought the Somerleyton estate in 1672 and was buried here in 1686. Thus, the two squires, who were companions in arms years before, face each other across the chancel, for Allin's bust is placed high on the s. wall. It is the finer piece, with much more character than the Wentworth pair, although the sculptor is unknown. I think the 1880s e. window glass is by *Clayton & Bell*, the six panels being typical of their work during that period. The tomb of eroded *Purbeck marble* in the n.e. corner of the *sanctuary* was for Sir Thomas Gernegan who died in 1446, and its original inscription was reproduced on a brass plate in 1902 by his descendant, Sir Hubert Jerningham.

Somersham, St Mary (E6): This early-C14 church has a simple unbuttressed tower whose outline is varied only by a single *string course*. The w. window has cusped 'Y' *tracery,* and at the upper level there are *cusped lancets* n. and s. and windows with *Decorated* tracery e. and w. The top half of the blocked n. door has been glazed and a 1780s gravestone is clamped lower down – has it been there all the time? There is 'Y' tracery of about 1300 in the window farther along. Note the oblong shape of the *rood stair turret,* and beyond that, a late-*Perpendicular priest's door* with eroded *paterae* in a broad moulding. Like the e. window, those on the s. side of the *chancel* have Decorated tracery. The outer arch of the *porch* is formed from two massive slabs of timber and *Cautley* thought that it could perhaps be the earliest in the county, dating from the late C13. The open sides display prettily cusped tracery but you will see that the carving is on the inside only. This suggests that they originally formed part of the *rood screen* and were used to decorate the porch when the screen was destroyed. The modern device for housing the *bier* in the roof on hinged bearers is both neat and effective. The C14 inner doorway is simple and the door itself still has its original strap hinges and the boss of a closing ring.
The mouldings of the narrow w. arch fade

into the *imposts* and there is a modern gallery within the tower. To the l., a well-painted set of Charles II *Royal Arms* has coarse strapwork on the edge of the frame, and a single *hatchment* hangs opposite – unidentified but connected with the Bacon family. Lower on the wall, a glass case contains one of those curiosities that sometimes find a home in churches for want of a better. This one is an unexploded bomb dropped by a Zeppelin in World War I, looking rather like a small old-fashioned milk can (another is similarly preserved at Acton). There is no chancel arch and below the plastered ceilings there are four rugged *tie-beams*. The wooden pegs on the *wall plate* at the w. end may have been used to hang the garlands called crants for maidens who died young, but this is not as certain here as the example at Walsham-le-Willows. The plain octagonal *font* has a pyramid cover that probably dates from the C16, and there is a fragment of C14 wall painting on the s. wall of the *nave*, but only a pair of legs can be distinguished. Nearby, a long and shallow oblong recess in the wall is puzzling. It has a moulded frame and I can only think that it was made for a *brass* or possibly for an inscription. A second set of Royal Arms hangs above the pulpit and this time they are *Hanoverian*, cut to a silhouette. The tie-beam overhead no doubt served as the *rood beam* and the one in the chancel still carries the stocks for a *sacring bell*. This is a rare survival and the only other Suffolk example is at Hawstead. The *communion rails* are late-C17 and some panelling dated 1601 has been inserted behind the *altar*. To the r., the tall *piscina* arch is *ogee*-shaped with lightly carved cusps and a *Jacobean* chest stands in the *sanctuary*. C18 *Decalogue* panels with Lord's Prayer and Creed are framed on the side walls, and the large paintings of Moses and Aaron on the e. wall were given to the church in 1750. Painted on board, they are unusually good and are obviously the work of a competent artist – though who he or she was is not known. Apart from the usual smashing of glass, *William Dowsing's* depredations in 1644 included the removal of a *stoup* and defacing an inscription on the outside of the priest's door: 'Jesus, sancta Maria, Jesus'. He left untouched the pilgrim's cross cut in the stone just inside the doorway on the r.

Somerton, St Margaret (C5): This is a delightfully peaceful situation along the cul-de-sac at Upper Somerton, and there is a pleasant westward prospect over rolling fields and hedgerows to Hawkedon and Stansfield.

Coming in from the e. of the churchyard, the s. chapel looks like a second *chancel* and they stand side by side, with matching barge boards on the gables. The C14 tower is small but leggy, with *Decorated* bell openings, chequered *base course* and battlements, and some fearsome devil *gargoyles* The tower houses a ring of four bells with an 8 cwt. tenor but they are unringable at present. The blocked n. door, with roll moulding in the arch and simple volute *capitals*, shows that the *nave* was *Norman* although it now has C14 windows to the s. and an early-*Perpendicular* window to the n. The s. chapel juts well out and has its own w. door; low down in the angle with the nave there is part of a C13 grave slab.

Entry is via a nice little s. *porch* in thin red brick and flint, with a simple medieval roof. In front of the tower arch stands a small C16 *font* with shields in *cusped* panels and a defaced carving to the w. There are *paterae* under the bowl and it has all been heavily limewashed in cream. There are the remains of a *stoup* recess by the blocked n. door and at the e. end of the nave on the s. side is a puzzling remnant within a recess in the wall. It is the capital and beginning of an arch that is roughly contemporary with the late-C13 or early-C14 *arcade* that links the chancel and the chapel. Did the chapel once extend further w. or was there a s. *aisle*? The roofs are C19 and there being no chancel arch the division is marked by a set of early-*Stuart communion rails* which have been moved westward in place of a *screen*; they are tall and gated, with turned *balusters*. The lanky *Jacobean* pulpit is like Hartest's although not as decorative, with simple blind arches, lozenges, and grooved panels at the base (the rim and bookrests are modern). The C19 lectern is particularly graceless compared with a contemporary model at Lawshall. The chancel and chapel have Perpendicular e. windows of differing designs but in both cases the late-C13 shafts of earlier windows flank the embrasures. There is a blocked medieval door to the n.e. *vestry* and in the s. wall of the *sanctuary* is a most unusual arrangement – a *piscina* whose bowl originally projected below a triangular arch and another piscina drain which is cut within a *squint* that connects chancel with chapel. As the chapel has its own piscina in the s. wall, the drain in the squint may have been a way of providing a double piscina for the chancel when one was called for at the end of the C13. The squint is roughly shaped and there are remains of side shafts on the chapel side. The chancel e. window has 1890s glass by *Kempe & Co* of Christ in Majesty, and note that there is the bowl of a large *stoup* in the corner of the spacious chapel, while a pallid set of George III *Royal Arms* hangs on the wall.

Sotherton, St Andrew (I3): A lane leads off the main road to Church Farm, and the church is just beyond it. It was entirely rebuilt by Benjamin Ferrey and *Henry Ringham* in 1854, and despite the fact that the old materials were used, the exterior impression is essentially Victorian, neat and trim. There is no tower, and a central buttress on the w. wall rises to a stone bellcote, with a window on each side. A small *vestry*, complete with fireplace and chimney, was added on the n. side of the *chancel*, and entry is by way of a s. porch.

The C15 *font* has very upright lions round the shaft, with demi-angels under the bowl; the panels are carved with *Tudor Roses* and hung shields, and there are *paterae* in the mouldings. The early-C17 cover is an octagonal spire over 6ft. tall whose narrow base and ribs are carved, topped with a large openwork *finial*. Opposite the entrance, a simple poorbox on a shaft has been fixed to one of the C19 pitchpine benches. Overhead, the roof is unstained and handsome, with *arch-braces* meeting below *collar beams* and *king posts*. Much of it is original, including the crested *wall plate*, and Ringham added characteristic angels to the bases of the *wall posts*. There is a low, arched recess in each of the *nave* walls, and the one on the n. side contains a fine, late-C13 effigy of a knight. With surcoat belted tight at the waist and shield slung on one shoulder, he is in good condition, apart from a battered face and damaged sword. On the wall above hangs a triptych of wooden panels in a gothic frame, a crucifixion painted by Laurence Grubbe, probably around 1900. The Victorian reordering included a stone pulpit and a new chancel arch, there is a panelled waggon roof in the *chancel*, and the modern *piscina* has a quite enormous drain. The *altar* is a simple *Stuart* table. Only two panels remain of the late-C15 *rood screen* and they have been fixed to the *vestry* door, crudely overpainted but interesting for a number of reasons. The figures of *St John* and *St Mary Magdalene* have a Flemish look, like those at Yaxley and Bramfield, and the dull green background retains its *gesso* patterning. St John not only holds his usual poisoned chalice, but his eagle emblem is at his feet, the only time it appears on a painted panel in East Anglia. The 1854 rebuilding incorporated some particularly interesting stained glass, and in one of the nave s. windows there are four vignette ovals that tell the story of the wise and foolish virgins (Matthew 25:1). The groupings are quite dramatic, and the rest of the window is filled with bright red and blue patterns; the artist is unknown. The first window on that side in the chancel contains two medallions illustrating the Ascension and the gift of the Holy Spirit to the disciples, each with the tongue of flame above him – small figures closely grouped in brilliant colours; dark green quarries with a leaf pattern form the background, and the glass might perhaps be the work of Edward Baillie whose work is positively identified at Witnesham, Henley and Hoxne. The figure of the church's patron saint is set against a deep blue vine pattern in the s. sanctuary window, and the finial of the canopy opens out to carry a little Good Samaritan scene. This interesting design is by Charles Hudson of Pentonville, the only example of his work that has been positively identified in Suffolk (the glass at Uggeshall is another possibility). Opposite, there is an oval of the Transfiguration in which Moses and Elijah flank Christ against a deep blue sky while the three disciples kneel below – an effective composition, perhaps by *Ward & Hughes*.

Sotterley, St Margaret of Antioch (I2): A visit to St Margaret's involves a walk of nearly half a mile across the park from the w. gate, and there can be few more enchanting settings for a church in the entire county. It stands sequested, embowered in yew and cedar alongside the C18 Hall, with views across the lake to a little classical temple. The stub buttresses at the base of the tower were probably a much later addition, and halfway up there is a distinct break in profile, the walls tapering from that point up to the battlements and small *gargoyles*. The w. window is early-C14 and there is 'Y' *tracery* of about 1300 in the bell openings. The way in which the flints are laid at the base of the *nave* walls (particularly on the n. side) is a sure sign of *Norman* work, and it is more than likely that there was a church here before the Conquest. Walking round, you will see that, although the n. doorway has been blocked, the medieval door with one strap hinge was left in place – a curious practice encountered elsewhere locally. The *Decorated* window on that side has angled *headstops*, and beyond it, an organ chamber and *vestry* were added in the C19. The e. window may have been part of the extensive restoration carried out in 1899, but the windows and *priest's door* on the s. side date the *chancel* at around 1300. Neaby, the 1699 headstone for Ann Bell,

'relict of James Bell, sometime rector of this parish', is a lovely example of a C17 local mason's innate skills – immaculately cut and unfussy lettering and still perfectly legible after more than 300 years. *Scratch dials* abound – one on a s.e. *quoin* of the chancel, and two more on s.e. quoins of the nave. Just above the latter, one of the other quoins is the reused head of a Norman *lancet* set on its side. 'Y' tracery features again in one of the nave s. windows, and suggests that there was a total rebuilding in the late C13 or early C14. The outer arch of the small *porch* has a nice bandy-legged look, and the inner early-C15 arch frames a contemporary door with traceried head and four slim panels with scalloped bottoms. There is a *stoup* recess on the r., and yet another scratch dial can be found low down on the l. *jamb*.

A second stoup is just inside, and on the other side of the entrance a 12ft. *banner stave locker* is cut in the wall. The tower window contains two small C15 figures, a king and a bishop, in yellow stain against black backgrounds. The crossed flags above the blocked n. door are the colours of the Scots Guards presented to their colonel Sir Edward Bowater on his retirement after the Peninsular War. The C15 *font* is the standard East Anglian pattern, but its supporting lions and *woodwoses* have been hacked away and the angels under the bowl were defaced at the same time. The bowl panels, however, are relatively unharmed, and they may have been hidden under plaster. There you will find good *Evangelistic symbols* alternating with angels whose shields bear a *Trinity emblem* (w.), *Instruments of the Passion* (n.), and *St George's* cross e. The major restoration around 1900 was carried out by Sir Reginald Blomfield (not to be confused with his better known namesake Sir Arthur), and he provided stolid benches with *poppyheads* modelled on those in the chancel (the n. side is labelled 'Free' for those unable to afford a pew rent). His waggon roof has a lower pitch than its predecessor, but makes use of the old stone *corbels*, and two of them above the doors are particularly good – a bagpiper on the s. side, and a jolly fellow playing an early form of viol on the n. The *hatchments* that hang on the walls were repainted in the early C20, and from w. to e. on the n. wall they are for: Miles Barne, MP (1825); Mary Barne (c.1790); Mary Barne (1858); the singleton opposite is for another Miles Barne, MP who died in 1780. There is a shallow tomb recess in the s. wall of the nave, and opposite, it is interesting that the n.e. window is set within two thirds of a much larger *Early*

Sotterly, St Margaret of Antioch:
Ann Bell's headstone

English arch which has slim *jamb shafts*. One presumes that it opened into a side chapel, possibly a *chantry*, which was later demolished and one its windows reused. The glazing was restored by descendants of Thomas Playter in 1952 and displays: a good Flemish C16 Trinity roundel – God the Father enthroned, with the Dove of the Holy Spirit perched on his shoulder and Christ crucified resting against his knees; a shield of arms within a pretty oval garland of fruit; a piece dated 1541, and a demi-figure right at the top. There is a C15 *Agnus Dei* roundel at the top of the centre window on the s. side, and the window to the e. contains the arms of the three families who have presided at Sotterley since the C13. Roger de Soterlee was Lord of the Manor in 1309, his people having been here since before 1275, and either he or his son Edmund undoubtedly rebuilt the church. They were on the wrong side in the Wars of the Roses and their estates, seized by Edward IV, passed to Thomas Playter who died in 1479 (of whom more later). After nearly 300 years, the estate was sold to Miles Barne (whose hatchment was noted last), and it continues in the same family today. The church's *Stuart* pulpit was discarded by Blomfield but luckily survives in good condition at Framingham Earl, just outside Norwich. Its successor here is in C15 West Country style, well carved in unstained oak. The

smoothed-out recess behind it has taken the place of the *rood loft stair*, and the *screen* has been drastically restored. The heavy base, with its *castellated* top rail, still has its doors, and there are *quatrefoils* in the *spandrels* and at the bottoms of the panels. Most of the double range of delicate *cusping* survives below the replacement *rood beam*. Unfortunately, the figures in the panels were entirely repainted; they are, from l. to r.; *SS Simon, Thomas, Andrew, Peter, James the Great, Bartholomew, Stephen, Jude, James the Less, Matthew*. The *piscina* (now minus its drain) in the s. wall will have served an *altar* in front of the screen. Maj. Miles Barne of the Scots Guards died in 1917, and his Flanders cross stands nearby, with a neat memorial set in the angle above – a painted St George within a classical recess.

The choir stalls have four original C15 ends with large poppyheads, and there is some varied tracery in the front panels. Sotterley has an excellent collection of *brasses* and they are all to be found in the chancel. Firstly, within the *arcade* to the modern extension on the n. side, stands the tomb of William and Jane Playter. He died in 1512 and there is an inscription along the top edge. His little effigy was stolen in 1843, but hers remains, just 7in. high on the front of the tomb, with two of the three shields. In the centre of the chancel there is an inscription for John Playter (1609), and nearby, the 19in. effigy of Christopher Playter with its inscription and shield poses a few problems. He died in 1547, but the brass dates from about 1580 and the armour, instead of being *Tudor*, is in the style of a century earlier. It was probably an old brass reversed and engraved again. The 18in. effigy in the floor nearest the priest's door has lost its shield and inscription but probably commemorates Sir Thomas Soterley who died about 1470, the last of his family to hold the manor. The inscription in front of the centre *communion rails* is for Sir Thomas Playter (1638) 'sometime Lord & Patron of this church'. On the s. side of the *sanctuary* Thomazine Playter's brass is one of the best in the series. She died in 1578, and her neat figure is dressed in a gown divided to display a brocaded petticoat; she wears a 'Paris' headdress, and so does the tiny figure of her daughter Susan beside her. The inscription is a fine period example, and above the 24in. effigy, a large shield displays the quartered arms of the Playters and her own family, the Tyrells (see Gipping). Her husband William died in 1584 and his inscription is close by, with his *achievement* placed in the centre of the sanctuary. The effigy alongside Thomazine's is for Thomas Playter.

He died in 1572, sports a spade beard, and wears his hair short; the armour is excellent, and there is an inscription and small shield. On the n. side of the sanctuary lie Thomas and Ann Playter. He figures significantly in the Paston letters and died in 1479, having been the first of his family to live here. The armour of his 26in. effigy is typically Yorkist, with exaggerated shoulder and elbow pieces; he turns slightly to his wife who wears a huge *butterfly headdress*, a low-cut gown with train, and a long girdle complete with pomander; part of the inscription is missing and one shield remains. Two more inscriptions on the s. side of the sanctuary complete the tally – for Thomas Laci (1475), and Alice Lappage (1595). Behind them are *dropped-sill sedilia*, and the piscina has an *ogee trefoil* arch whose *capitals* have been re-cut flush with the wall. *Dowsing* came here in April 1644 and destroyed crosses on the roof and 'pictures' (probably referring to the damage to the font). The brasses probably survived because his assistant, Francis Verden, was sergeant to Sir William Playter and he may have hidden them prior to Dowsing's visit. High on the n. side is the splendid monument for Sir Thomas Playter, a particularly important piece by Edward Marshall who was Master of the Mason's Company and Royal Mason in 1660. This is his only work in Suffolk and was installed in 1658, although Sir Thomas had died 20 years before. The delay may have been caused because sculpture was frowned on in the *Commonwealth* and examples are rare, but in the same year he carved the lovely figure of Dame Frances Playter at Dickleburgh, Norfolk. The design in alabaster and *touchstone* is extremely attractive, compartmented with three niches, the modelling crisp and full of character. Thomas kneels in armour, facing forward, slightly above and between his two wives who are in profile, one in a widow's veil and one with the large and fashionable calash hood. More than a score of their children form a beautifully varied frieze below, with a *chrysom child* in the centre and one of the elder girls turning to look back at her sisters. The 1920s altar *reredos* was designed by Sir Charles Nicholson, and its three faintly coloured plaster panels of Nativity scenes are heightened with gold. Most of the e. window glass is by *Kempe*, dating from the time of the big restoration. There are good figures of *St Felix*, the *Blessed Virgin*, *St John* and *St Margaret* flanking Christ on the cross. Instead of his usual dense *tabernacle work*, Kempe used here lightly patterned *quarries* as a background for the figures, and there are bright yellow demi-angels in the

tracery. It is partially hidden by the altar curtains, but do not overlook the fine 1479 portrait of Sir William Playter in the bottom l.-hand corner of the window. He kneels at a prayer desk, wearing an heraldic tabard over his armour, and his seven sons are ranked behind him. There is a medieval head of Christ, and part of an Agnus Dei in the tops of the chancel s. windows, and the n. window contains late-C19 glass which was probably supplied by *Clayton & Bell* – a good period piece featuring *St Cornelius* and *St Phoebe*.

South Cove, St Laurence (I2): The C15 tower, restored in the 1970s, has angle buttresses up to the bell stage, and both they and the stepped battlements are decorated with *flushwork*. Walk round to the n. side and you will see that there is a very simple *Norman* doorway in the *nave*, and that the door itself is C15, with *crocketted ogee* tops to the panels and *tracery* above them. The small *Perpendicular* windows on that side of the nave are roughly contemporary, but those with 'Y' tracery in the *chancel* date from about 1300. There is a *priest's door* on the s. side, and a single thatched roof covers all. The chancel was restored in 1877, and the small porch was rebuilt three years later. The inner doorway is again Norman, and rather more elaborate, as befits the main entrance. It has *chevron moulding* in the arch, plain *imposts*, and a section of the r. *jamb* has been turned and reversed so that a *scratch dial* is now upside down and facing w.

The threshold and step look as though they were once tops of tombs, and there is a C13 grave slab in front of them. The nave has a handsome *arch-braced* roof, with *king posts* on the *collar beams*, and the transverse braces between the *wall posts* are carved with leaves and shields. In common with a number of churches in e. Suffolk and Norfolk, South Cove has a *banner stave locker* – the tall and narrow recess in the n.w. corner. The bowl of the C15 *font* has been cruelly defaced, but one can still identify angels with shields, lions, and the shield of *St Edmund* in the n.w. panel; the drum shaft and base are later amendments. The ends of the C15 benches have attractive panel tracery, and their seats and backs have been renewed. That was probably part of the 1880s refurbishing, and it is likely that the *Stuart* pulpit was dealt with at the same time. It has been heavily restored although the blind-arched panels are largely original. The church's rare if not unique feature is the tall door to the *rood loft stair* in the n. wall. It displays the pale, feathery figure of *St Michael* with sword and shield, poised above a crouching dragon, painted by an East Anglian artist about 1470. It was banished to the tower in 1877, and lay there until 1931 when it was repaired under Prof. Tristram's supervision and replaced. The gashes all over the surface show that someone had tried to deface it – possibly *William Dowsing* when he was here in April 1643. His journal talks of '42 superstitious pictures in glass and about 20 cherubims', and he is unlikely to have overlooked such a commanding and accessible figure. Of the *rood screen*, only the s. half of the base survives. The tops of the panels are painted in red and green, and there are centre emblems heightened with *gesso*. In the *sanctuary*, the attractive C14 *piscina* has a deeply moulded *trefoil* arch and there are *dropped-sill sedilia* alongside. Crudely lettered *Decalogue* boards are framed on the e. wall, and the modern oak *reredos* features rather eccentric blind tracery. Above it, the attractive 1920s glass by an unidentified artist takes the popular theme: 'Suffer little children to come unto me'; the design makes good use of the three *lights,* and a canopy of orange trees provides a backing for the text. Walking back to the churchyard gate, look for a pair of small headstones by the path, just s. of the tower. They date from the C18 and were originally parts of an *arcade pier* – probably filched from the Covehithe ruins a couple of miles away.

South Elmham All Saints and St Nicholas, All Saints (H2): Nearer St Nicholas hamlet than All Saints, a signposted lane leads to Church Farm and the church, surrounded by open fields. There are few more peaceful spots than this beautiful tree-girt churchyard, now a designated Wildlife Sanctuary, and the building has been taken into care by the *Churches Conservation Trust*. The round tower was so drastically restored that virtually all of the exterior detailing is modern, but the interior arches of the little *lancets* are of flint and so it is probably *Saxon*. The whole of the bell chamber was rebuilt and a stair with conical cap was added on the n. side in 1912. Next to it, a shaft carved in the *quoins* of the n.w. corner of the *nave* is *Norman*, and there are contemporary lancets at two levels on that side of the building – renewed, as are all the windows, although the little niche above the e. window is original. The s. *aisle* extends along the side of the *chancel*, and there is a nave *clerestory* on that side. The s. *porch* originally had an upper room, but a rebuilding of 1871 dispensed with it. However, the simple *flushwork* chequer on the lower half of the facade was retained, there are worn *headstops* on the arch, and just to the l. you

will find a *scratch dial*. The inner doorway is Norman in style but wholly C19 and probably part of the 1870s restoration.

There is a *stoup* just inside, and turning to the tower, note its Norman arch, and the doorway above which is a feature of many of the round towers in Norfolk and Suffolk. It may well have served as a *sanctus-bell window* later, but in all probability its original purpose was to provide access to a refuge. The tower arch is flanked by low C14 blind arches, and it has a wide, handsome *Jacobean* door with a profusion of carving in the panels. A C14 *arcade* of two bays separates the nave from the aisle, and a further two bays stand between aisle and chancel, with a rather odd little passage intervening between the e. and w. sections. A large, early-C13 *font* rests on a drum shaft and corner columns against the pillar nearest the door; its *Purbeck marble* square bowl has canted sides which are decorated with broad fluting rather than the more usual arcading. The e. *respond* of the arcade has been roughly chopped back and probably marks the site of an image niche. Two C15 benches at the w. end have animals on the elbows, one a dog with large and floppy ears. The main range of benches is C19, but they incorporate C15 ends with *poppyheads*. One of the nave lancets contains a little late-C15 roundel painting of *St Ursula* in yellow stain; she bears her usual arrow emblem and also a ship – an interesting addition which is not normally associated with her. At a guess, the figure with bouquet and basket in the other roundel is *St Dorothy*, although the child saint with her does not feature in her legend. Below the roundels there is a nice little bird fragment, and a window in the s. aisle contains a considerable collection of C15 fragments. Another aisle window has indifferent 1890s glass by *Jones & Willis* – Christ with children, and his baptism. In the *sanctuary*, the moulded *trefoil* arch of the *piscina* was re-cut during one of the restorations, and there is a curious recess to the r. Another and larger one to the l. is equally strange. It has a drain and therefore one may assume that it was a piscina, but it is practically at floor level.

South Elmham St Cross, St Cross (G2): The church enjoys a beautiful setting on rising ground above the little river Beck. It has a house for company, and the churchyard is set about with Scots pine, oak, lilac and laburnum. It is the only church in Suffolk dedicated to the Holy Cross, and is one of the very few anywhere to have an alternative dedication, that of *St George*.

The sturdy tower has a *Decorated* w. window and bell openings, with flint chequer in the angled buttresses and *flushwork* battlements and corner *gargoyles*. A ring of five bells with an 8 cwt. tenor hangs inside. A circuit of the building reveals a very rough, blocked C12 n. door, and although there are no *aisles*, the *nave* has a range of brick *clerestory* windows which were added when the roof was rebuilt in the C15. There is a tiny cross-shaped slit to light the *rood stair* in the n. wall, and the early-C14 *chancel* has *cusped intersected tracery* in its tall e. window. A *Tudor* brick *priest's door* is set in the chancel s. wall, and the *Perpendicular* windows on that side of the nave have small *headstops*. There were restorations here in 1841 and 1887, and the crow-stepped gables of nave and chancel seem to be no earlier than that. The C14 *porch* has a Decorated outer arch, with tiny *paterae* carved on the *capitals*, and the roof is a good C19 replacement. The inner doorway is another feature of the *Norman* church that has remained through all the subsequent changes. The capitals of the single shafts vary, with flowers on one side and scrolls on the other, and there is a simple roll moulding in the arch. The door itself is medieval, with wrought strap hinges right across the lapped boards. To the r. is a late-Perpendicular *stoup*, and partly hidden by the notice board, there is a *scratch dial*, a relic of the time when there was no porch to keep the sun off the wall.

As you enter, note the fine 'I.A. 1627' cut on the r.-hand *jamb*, and a second, simpler stoup just inside. Nearby stands a C14 waggon chest, completely banded with iron and fitted with no fewer than eleven hinges, three locks, and four rings for lifting! The noble tower arch is decorated with paterae and shields in the moulding, and there are little defaced heads on the capitals. C18 *Decalogue* panels, well painted on canvas, hang on each side, and a nicely restored painting of the raising of Lazarus hangs in the tall arch of the n. doorway. The *font* is the most common East Anglian design, and still bears traces of colour. Stumpy lions squat round the shaft, there are angel heads below the bowl, and lions alternate with angels in the panels. Three of their shields are defaced, but the fourth bears three crescents – a possible variation of William Bateman's arms, bishop of Norwich 1344-1355. If that assumption is valid the font would be a very early example of the type. The *arch-braced* roof to the nave has pendants and transverse braces under the ridge; the *wall posts* rest on painted, demi-angel *corbels*, and the *spandrels* between them are carved with painted

shields. The original decoration of the roof must have been quite lavish, and some of the *Sacred monograms* and 'M's for the *Blessed Virgin* can still be seen on the rafters. There is now no upper doorway for the rood stair, and it may have been blocked when the chancel arch was replaced in the C19 (the chancel was re-roofed at the same time). In the *sanctuary* there is a simple early-C14 *piscina* with a *trefoil* arch, and the e. window is filled with glass of the early 1900s which probably came from the *Kempe* workshop – a Crucifixion surrounded by the figures of Moses, SS John the Baptist, Paul, and John; below, Gabriel is flanked by St George and a bishop (*St Felix?*). The panels of the carved *reredos* are painted with an *Agnus Dei* flanked by the figures of the Blessed Virgin and St George. It has been said that, before repainting, they formed part of the old *rood screen*, but all the tracery, like the rest of the woodwork, is modern. Easter Gleane died in 1657 and her ledger-stone lies on the n. side of the sanctuary:

> Whoever knowes or heares whose sacred
>   bones,
> Doe rest within these monumentall stones,
> How deare a Mother, and how sweet a wief,
> If he has bowells cannot for his life,
> But on hir ashes must some teares distill,
> For if men will not weepe the marble will.

South Elmham St James, St James (H2): The unbuttressed tower has 'Y' *tracery* of about 1300 in the bell openings and a late-C14 w. window; there is a single *string course* below the bell chamber, and the battlements are decorated with flushwork, with a single *gargoyle*. The tower houses a ring of four bells with a 6 cwt. tenor but they cannot be used at present. The regular layering of the flints at the base of the *nave* n. wall is a sign of early work, and the doorway there is *Norman*, although sections of its *billet moulding* were rearranged later to form a pointed arch. *Perpendicular* windows were inserted in the nave n. wall during the C15, but there are C13 *lancets* in the *chancel* and a renewed e. window. The shape of the *rood stair* bulges out into the corner between chancel and s. *aisle*, and a *scratch dial* has been re-set on its side in the s.e. buttress. *Richard Phipson* carried out a root and branch restoration here in 1874 when he replaced all the roofs and partially rebuilt the aisle and *porch*, and I suspect that he was responsible for the extra wide buttresses on both sides of the building. Within the porch there is a *stoup* which has beautifully nubbly *crockets* on its *cusped* arch, and although the original bowl has been destroyed, there is a smaller replacement set on the ledge.

Just inside the door, sections of the church's C14 *rood screen* have been worked into a *vestry* enclosure, with turned shafts and sharply pointed *trefoil* arches. The *arcade* between nave and aisle, with its octagonal *piers* dates from about 1300, and it is slightly odd that the later w. bay is so much larger than the other three. The late-C12 *font* has a bowl of very eroded *Purbeck marble* with just a vestige of the blind arcading left on its sides, and the C15 cover is attractive, with its spirelet and pierced base frieze. It was once raised and lowered by a rope, and the gilded dove counterweight remains sitting on a wall bracket nearby. The early-C14 tower arch has no *imposts*, and above it hangs a murky set of George III *Royal Arms* painted on canvas; they would probably repay cleaning. Each side there is a curious circular recess like *Saxon* window embrasures (which I suppose they could be, if the original church had no tower). Lower down, to the l. of the tower arch, an oblong recess has a modern wooden door, and is possibly an *aumbry* for the storage of items used at the font for baptism. One of the church's *brasses* can be found on a slab in front of the n. door – a small inscription for Edmund de Ffeyvyll of about 1500. There was another halfway up the nave, where the indents show clearly in the floor, but the two 17in. effigies have been transferred to the wall opposite. They represent an unidentified man and wife, he in a tunic with a large pouch, she wearing a kennel headdress. Fragments of C15 leafy borders and a yellow stain *Tudor Rose* survive in the tops of the windows on that side, and part of a Norman lancet splay can be seen. The s. aisle chapel was dedicated to *St John the Baptist*, and the panelling behind the *altar* was part of the work carried out by villagers at evening classes. On it, a modern brass plate commemorates a C15 rector who was buried in front of the altar. During his ministry he will have made use of the *piscina* with an exceptionally deep drain set in the wall nearby. The chancel screen is a World War I memorial, and echoes the style of the old rood screen. It is another example of village work, and so is the elaborate reading desk, with its clusters of triple shafts below each corner of the wide ledge. The rood stair rises in the wall nearby, with its upper doorway blocked. The square *Stuart* pulpit is a handsome piece, with geometric panelling and bands of shallow carving below the ledge. John Green's *ledger-stone* of 1685 lies in front of the

screen, and its bold script is charming, full of character. In his new chancel roof, Phipson made quite striking use of *arch-braces* set in a continuous curve from wall to wall, meeting on a centre spine that is well below the ridge. The wall panelling is embellished with shallow carvings, and the local amateurs were given free rein to choose their own subjects – a strange selection which includes a horse, bat, serpent and fish, as well as more conventional religious symbols. The most interesting is the fenced cuckoo on the s. side of the *sanctuary* which recalls a local tradition that the men of the village tried to trap a cuckoo so that they could keep his song. Below is a beautifully solid C13 *angle piscina*, with ring *capitals* and deeply moulded trefoil arch; the stepped *sedilia* alongside have been re-worked. Phipson chose *encaustic tiles* for the sanctuary which are decorated with the staff and wallet symbols of the church's patron saint, and there is an interesting little medieval statue of him above the priest's door. It is mutilated but one can still see his pilgrim's staff and the shell badge in his hat. The church's third brass lies in front of the sanctuary step, an inscription of 1601 on the grave of William Grudgfield who gave 'ten pounde . . . for ye buying of 5 milsh kyne [milking cows] to be let out to ye use of the poore'. The e. window is flanked by stone *Decalogue* panels framed elaborately in the form of *Early English* windows with mottled marble shafts. There is a shallow *reredos* which has recessed marble panels painted with vine and wheat, separated by small green columns – all designed in 1888 by E.F. Bisshopp, the architect of Ipswich St Michael. The fine *Holy Table* in front is about the same age as the pulpit, and has *baluster* legs with heavy stretchers.

South Elmham St Margaret, St Margaret (H2): The early-C14 tower has a *flushwork* base course, varied by a shield on one of the angle buttresses and an ornament on the other. The stair turret is lit by tiny windows and the lowest takes the form of a *mouchette* roundel. At belfry level there are two small *sound holes* – a pierced *quatrefoil* to the s. and a wheel roundel to the n. The *Decorated* bell openings are generously proportioned, and although it is unusual, the plain parapet seems to suit the tower. Walking round, you will find that the small n. door has been blocked and that the *nave* windows are *Perpendicular* – except for the single *Norman* lancet on the s. side. It is a reminder, like the rough stones which were used as *quoins* at the s.e. corner of the nave, that this was an early foundation.

There is a *vestry*-cum-organ chamber on the n. side of the *chancel* which formed part of the restoration carried out by *Richard Phipson* in the 1870s. He designed the e. window, with its pretty *tracery* in Decorated style, and replaced the w. window in the tower. The tall *porch* is faced with an attractive mixture of brick and flint, and a *scratch dial* can be found on a *quoin* at the s.w. corner, with traces of two more. The entrance arch and the small lancets of the upper room were all replaced by Phipson. The village stocks have found a home inside, and they seem to have been designed for two average felons and a one-legged accomplice! More conventional models are to be found at Athelington and Saxstead. The Norman inner doorway has a plain roll moulding in the arch which rests on *imposts* scored with diagonal lines; the *capitals* of the side shafts are carved with simple scrolls against a cross-hatched background.

Just inside the doorway, a *stoup* to the r. retains the head of its *trefoil* arch, and above, the oak of the *arch-braced* roof is a lovely pale colour untouched by stain. Its short *king posts* have lateral braces, and the *wall plates* are rather oddly carved with reversed shields within a pierced foliage trail; the shields below the *wall posts* are modern. The tower has an unusually lofty Perpendicular arch, and in the window beyond there is attractive glass of 1917; foliage roundels studded with white roses frame two venerable old men bearing scrolls at the top, and the *Blessed Virgin* below, surrounded on the r. with an abundance of pears, one of the symbols of the Incarnation. The style is reminiscent of F.C. Eden whose windows may be seen at Whepstead and Clare. A small medieval door gives access to the tower stair, and John Sellynge scratched his name in a fine C16 hand on the lintel above. The church's ring of five bells with an 11 cwt. tenor are rung from here round the C15 *font* which is the familiar East Anglian type. Unlike many, however, the tall lions round the shaft have escaped mutilation; angels bearing shields alternate with *Evangelistic symbols* in the deeply cut bowl panels. The benches in the nave have *poppyheads* and the Victorian craftsman who made them followed the design of the seven originals that are at the back against the n. wall. The pulpit is modern, but above it there is a large hour-glass bracket. Nearby, the stairway in the wall led to the *rood loft*. Phipson replaced the chancel arch, stripped out the plaster and boarded the ceiling anew. In the *sanctuary* there is a compact, late-Perpendicular *Easter Sepulchre* in pristine condition; the *crocketted* arch is flanked by

pinnacles and crowned with a *finial*, with carved panels on the front of the base. On the wall to the r. is a mid-C18 mottled marble tablet set in pale stone for a member of the Carter family, with a pair of pineapples and an urn on top, and three cherub heads below the curved cornice. The 1713 memorial for John Buxton over the *priest's door* is quite striking; its tall, curved tablet stands between *Corinthian* columns of streaked marble, and *acanthus leaves* curl over the flat cornice on either side of a shapely urn. A section of the base of the *rood screen* now stands to the r. of the *altar*, badly mutilated and lacking much of the tracery. However, there are remnants of colour, and tantalising traces of the figures that were painted on the panels. Their croziers and mitres mark them as bishops, and the second from the r. can be identified as *St Hubert* by his huntsman's horn – a rare medieval illustration for East Anglia. The attractive 1880s glass in the e. window looks like the work of *Clayton & Bell*, an Ascension, with Christ ringed by a circle of deep red cherub heads against a blue background; the disciples are ranged on each side below, and between them is a vignette of *St Mary Magdalene's* meeting with Our Lord after his Resurrection. The sanctuary s. window glass of the mid-C19 may well be early work of *Ward & Hughes* – two shaped panels showing Jesus with children, and (possibly) *St Anne* teaching the Blessed Virgin to read. The rest of the space is filled with bright patterns, and there are *Evangelistic symbols* in the tracery. The glass in the s. chancel window is possibly Clayton & Bell's again, and the choice of subjects is interesting – *St Peter's* escape from prison, and the conversion of *St Paul's* jailer. To round off the visit, look for interesting C18 and early-C19 stones in the churchyard. Ann and Dan Buck's is set in the nave wall just e. of the porch, excellently lettered and with a good epitaph:

In Fine – All must to their cold Graves,
But ye Religious Actions of these two Just,
Do smell sweet in Death and blossom in ye dust.

South Elmham St Michael, St Michael (H2): The church is set back from the road beyond a swathe of meadowland, and there is an excellent oak field gate at the entrance to the churchyard. Just beyond is the grave of Frederick Aldridge who died in 1960. He was 'miller of this parish for 59 years', and the stone has a windmill carved at the top. The unbuttressed tower has a single *string course* below the bell openings, two without *tracery* and two bricked up. It is topped by stepped *flushwork* battlements, with a series of shields set within *cusped* squares. Walking round, you will see that all the windows have 'Y' tracery of about 1300, and there is a C14 *priest's door* which has a pretty little sunk moulding in the arch. The line of an earlier, much steeper *nave* roof can be seen on the e. face of the tower, and heavy repairs in brick show through the plaster below the eaves of both nave and *chancel*. The stone sundial on the nave wall has a brisk admonition – 'Why stand gazing? be about your business!' The *porch* presents a plain plastered exterior, but within, its C16 half-timbered walls are most attractive, and so is the *Norman* inner doorway. The arch has an outer band of *billet decoration*, a sequence of broad scallops, and an inner roll moulding; the edges of the *abaci* are carved, and the *capitals* of the single *jamb shafts* vary – embellished scallop on the l. and leaf with fish head on the r. The nice C18 pine door is pitted with countless pinholes, having been used as the village notice board for generations.

It is a very simple interior, with brick floors, boarded ceilings, and no arch or *screen* to divide nave from chancel, and this must be one of the last churches to be lit by oil lamps. The C15 *font* is in good condition, and the tall lions round the shaft are curiously recessed so that only their front legs, manes and heads obtrude. Four more lions in the bowl panels alternate with angels whose shields are carved with crosses of various designs and one *Trinity emblem*. The 1840s monument on the s. wall for Robert Chase is by J.J. Sanders, a prolific London mason whose rather dull work can be found in many places. Here, a sarcophagus is flanked by reversed mourning torches, with a garland of laurel at the top, and the nicest thing about it is the phrase: 'It is good to breathe the atmosphere of benevolence in pondering over the honoured ashes of those, who, when alive, were the refuge of the destitute, and the friends of the orphan'. Whoever composed it must have felt so much better afterwards. The plain panels of the pulpit are late-C17 or early-C18, and have been rearranged; they bear the marks of butterfly hinges, and I suspect that they once formed part of *box pews* (the base is C16). A C19 restoration provided *encaustic tiles* in the *sanctuary,* and note how the arch of the C14 *piscina* matches the one over the priest's door outside. There is a modern wooden *reredos*, attractively painted with the figures of *SS Michael, Felix* and *Fursey*. Before leaving, have a look at the nicely hand-lettered roll of honour by the blocked n. door in the nave. It lists eleven men who all served in minesweepers in World War I and who all came safely home – making this one of the 31 'thankful villages' of England, and the only one in Suffolk.

South Elmham St Peter, St Peter (H2): This is only a small church but there are signs here and there that it has been highly thought of in the past, and the present generation of parishioners are working hard to maintain it. The churchyard has now been designated as a sanctuary under the guidance of the Suffolk Wildlife Trust. The angled buttresses of the tower have chequered *flushwork*, there is a *Perpendicular* w. window, and a stair turret is tucked in the n. side up to belfry level; although the bell openings have lost their *tracery*, the battlements above are handsomely decorated with flushwork. There is a blocked C13 n. doorway in the *nave*, and the windows are a typical mixture of periods, with 'Y' *tracery* of about 1300 in the n. wall and in the *chancel*, and one Perpendicular and one *Decorated* on the s. side of the nave. The walls of the chancel have recently been restored, and there is a late-Perpendicular *priest's door*. The C14 *porch* has been repaired in brick and has a plastered gable. Its outer arch has worn *headstops* and is flanked by the remains of flushwork panels – look to the r. for a well-defined *scratch dial.* There is a *stoup* recess just inside, and the inner doorway is the first indication of the church's real age. It is early-*Norman*, with a plain arch and single *jamb shafts* under *capitals* carved with simple scallop decoration.

The tower arch is tall, with four wide chamfer mouldings, and below stands a C15 *font* of the familiar East Anglian variety which is in very nice condition and does not appear to have been restored. There are the usual four lions round the shaft, and the angels with crossed hands below the bowl have plenty of character; *Tudor Roses* and blank shields alternate in the panels, and little *paterae* punctuate the mouldings. The restored C17 cover has fat scrolls supporting a turned centre shaft. The *wall posts* of the *arch-braced* nave roof rest on stone *corbels*. They have been brutally defaced and most of them are demi-angels – one on the n. side has what appears to be a *Passion emblem* on his shield so they may have displayed a complete sequence. The C14 chancel arch is unusually fine for a little village church, and below the capitals the mouldings contain shallow niches with heads carved under the image stools; three of them remain on the n. side and fragments of *groining* survive at the top of one niche on the s. side. The head of the arch was filled with a *tympanum* to back the *rood*, and you can see the deep mortices that were cut to take the supporting framework.-handsome niches flank the entrance to the chancel, each with a *crocketted ogee* arch, and although the old *rood screen* has gone, there is an enterprising replacement that was installed in 1923. Carved in oak, it is a fanciful design, with three *cusped* ogee arches below a curved and pierced coving; the cornice is crisply carved and there is a rood group above. Before the *Reformation* there was a chapel dedicated to the *Blessed Virgin* on the n. side of the chancel and this is why there are no windows on that side. Low in the wall, behind the harmonium, you will find two panels carved with *quatrefoils* – all that can be seen of John Tasburgh's tomb. Member of a local family of some consequence, he died in 1493 and directed that his body should lie in the Lady chapel. In the *sanctuary*, the plain *piscina* of about 1300 has a foiled drain, and there is a curious star carved alongside – it looks heraldic and one would like to know its significance. Above the modern oak *reredos*, the e. window is filled with glass of the early 1900s in a style reminiscent of 1860. In the centre, Christ as the Good Shepherd, and quatrefoils in the flanking *lights* contain passion emblems, the bread and wine of the Eucharist, and texts – all against heavily patterned *quarries*. The artist is unknown.

Southwold, St Edmund (J3): This is a splendid church, built in one continuous operation in the C15. Its predecessor had been a small C13 chapel which was destroyed by fire, and the new church was begun about 1430 and completed with the addition of the *porch* at the close of the century. The tower in itself is a showpiece, with particularly dense flintwork, and the lavish *flushwork* of the buttresses is embellished in the first three stages. There is *blind arcading* on each side of the w. door whose broad mouldings carry double ranks of *paterae*, including a *woodwose* on the r., and dragons inhabit the *spandrels*. A dedicatory inscription with each letter crowned follows the line of the window arch: 'Sct Edmund ora p[ro] nobis' (St Edmund pray for us), and below it, weatherworn stones bear his monogram and that of the *Blessed Virgin*. From that, one may presume that the niches with their angel stools on either side of the window contained statues of Our Lady and the church's patron saint. There is a broad band of flint

chequer above the window, and in addition to the belfry windows, there is a single *sound hole* on the e. face. The bell openings are pairs of tall *transomed* windows separated by buttresses which continue up to *gargoyles* and a flushwork parapet. The absence of pinnacles and battlements serves only to emphasise the tower's character. It house a fine ring of eight bells with a 10 cwt. tenor. Walking round, you will see that there is a continuous *base course*, and an octagonal stair turret is set at the n.w. corner of the n. *aisle*. Broad mouldings with two ranks of *paterae* feature again in the n. doorway, and note that one of the buttresses on that side was broadened to house the *rood stair*. There is flushwork *blind arcading* and a line of *quatrefoils* under the e. window, and a *priest's door* is set in the s. wall. The aisles continue to within one bay of the e. end, and a *drip course* decorated with *fleurons* and demi-angels runs below their parapets – battlements on the s. side provide the only mark of difference. The *clerestory*, with 18 close-set windows each side, runs the entire length, and the distinctive feature of the roof profile is the *sanctus-bell turret* with its attractive spirelet sited halfway along the nave. A feature reminiscent of churches in the Low Countries, it was rebuilt in 1867 following the original design. The sumptuous two-storied *porch* is one of the best C15 examples that Suffolk can offer, and the flushwork of its facade is unusually delicate, featuring moulded mullions in the panels. The side walls are faced with flint chequer overall (as at Woolpit), and the Blessed Virgin's monogram decorates the base course. There are deep *ashlar* battlements, and the centre niche contains a fine St Edmund carved by Andrew Swinley in 1989. The mouldings of the outer arch are decorated with *Agnus Deis*, and the *groined* roof is set with *bosses*. Four stained glass tracery shapes have be re-set in the side windows (survivors from the wartime damage?) – figures of *SS Alban, Edward the Confessor, John the Baptist*, and Edmund, possibly by *Lavers, Barraud & -Westlake*.

The entrance door has panels typical of the early *Tudor* period, and within the church all is light, spacious, and cherished. Elegant *quatrefoil piers* support the *arcades*, and there is no chancel arch to interrupt the vista to the e. end. The roofs were reconstructed in the 1860s but their form was unchanged – *hammerbeams* carved as angels alternating with *arch-braces*; there are *castellated collars* with tracery each side of the *king posts*, and the *wall posts* rest on stone head *corbels* – some grave, some gay. The church had an excellent range of *Lavers, Barraud & Westlake*

Southwold, St Edmund

glass, but enemy action in World War II blew out a great deal, and the only complete example is the 1880 tower w. window. The two themes are the Sermon on the Mount and Christ preaching by the lakeside, with small angel figures filling the tracery. The aisle w. windows have lost their main subjects, but the tracery retains a C19 angels series which may also have been supplied by the same firm. By the tower arch is a most interesting example of a clock jack, a mechanical 4ft. warrior designed to strike the hours; no longer connected with a clock, it is operated by hand. Dressed in late-C15 armour, he strikes the bell with his reversed battle axe and has a scimitar in the other hand; the colouring is original and it is one of the finest English wooden figures of the period. The panels of the *Seven Sacrament font* have had every vestige of their carving carefully removed, and I wonder whether this was a piece of C19 vandalism like the example at Wenhaston (the average C17 defacement was much more casual). The deep bowl has shallow vaulted canopies above the panels, and the shaft niches have been cleared of their figures. When *William Dowsing*

called in April 1643, apart from the usual orgy of destruction, he ordered the font cover to be taken down, a sign that it was probably exceptional. The 1930s replacement is a worthy successor, tall and delicate, in C15 style, topped with a slender spire. Large and pale *Royal Arms* of George III are framed by the n. door, and below stands an exceptional late-C14 walnut chest. Its front is a web of beautiful *Decorated* tracery, with an oblong *St George* panel in the centre. Two charity boards are displayed by the entrance, one of them unusually handsome and featuring the arms of Capt. John Steele, 1710. Nearby, the church's only *hatchment* was used at John Robinson's funeral in 1802. There are surpringly few memorials on the walls, but one caught my eye in the s. aisle – a small 1804 tablet for Barnett Hamilton, infant son of the vicar. It has naive carving above the inscription and is signed by Branch of Halesworth, the only example of his work that I have identified. At the e. end of the aisle stands a unique example of an oval Elizabethan *Holy Table* with four drop leaves and flask-shaped legs, a most interesting piece that was still in use in the C19. In the floor not far away there are three C19 *brasses*, rare examples from before the Victorian revival – inscriptions for Mary Wayth, 1809, Francis Wayth, 1822, and Mary Hunt, 1840. Every available surface of the lovely C15 pulpit is intricately traceried, including the trumpet stem which is an unusual extravagance. A sensitive restoration and stabilization of the colour would have been more welcome than the repainting that it underwent in 1930. In the floor below there is a brass inscription for Christopher Youngs, 1626:

A good man full of fayth was Hee,
Here preacher of God's word.

Southwold is famous for its *rood screen* which spans the church from wall to wall, and despite the mutilation it is one of the most beautiful and certainly one of the most interesting in the county. The stair that led to its loft is in the n. wall, with the entrance just within the aisle chapel, but nothing of the loft remains. The screen is in three sections, spanning the two aisles and the chancel arch; the *lights* are broad and lofty, with double ranks of delicate *cusping* in the arches. All three entrances are cusped to match with the addition of *crockets*, and part of the coving of the underside of the loft has been restored on the e. side of the centre section. The panels of the n. aisle section are painted with the *nine orders of angels*, one of the very few examples to have survived from the medieval period. The figures are refined and spiritual in feeling, having much in common with those at Barton Turf in Norfolk, and it is possible that they came from the same hand. There are stars above them and flowers below, and although their faces have all been destroyed, name labels and attributes enable us to identify each order. An additional angel bearing a *Trinity emblem* begins the series on the l., and below him are the remains of the donor inscription: 'Orate p[ro] a[n]i[m]ab[u]s Johne' (Pray for the souls of John [Gueman and his wife Catherine]). Next comes *Gabriel,* and then the sequence proper: Archangels, Powers, Dominions, Cherubim, Seraphim, Thrones, Principalities, Virtues, Angels (holding little human souls in a cloth), and finally, an angel bears a shield displaying three *chalices* and wafers of the mass, symbolizing the ministry of the church on earth. The paintings of the *apostles* on the panels of the centre screen are entirely different in artistic form, and undoubtedly belong to the work of the Norwich school that produced the series at Ranworth (the figure work, robes, and backgrounds are all similar). The heads of the apostles were partially repainted by Richmond in the characteristic style of the C19, and Professor Tristram worked on the screen in the 1930s. There is much original colour, and the overall effect is particularly rich, largely because *gesso* was used lavishly, on buttresses and mouldings, and especially in the background patterns. From l. to r. the saints are: *Philip, Matthew, James the Less, Thomas, Andrew, Peter, Paul, John, James the Great (*note his shell emblem in gesso on his hat and repeated in the background*), Bartholomew, Jude,* and *Simon.* Although the design of the s. aisle screen is similar to that of the n., the decoration differs, and the figure paintings are not by the same hand. They are Old Testament prophets, a theme common in the Midlands but seldom found in East Anglia, and the style is more European than East Anglian. The figures are heavily defaced, but labels enable us to identify some of them and from l. to r. the sequence was probably: Baruch, Hosea, Nahum, Jeremiah, Elias, Moses, David, Isaiah, Amos, Jonah, and Ezekial. It has been said that the reason why the screen is so ill-fitting in relation to the walls and piers is that it was taken down and hidden before being replaced many years later. That may be so, although there was never any order banishing screens as such – only the rood that

stood on them. It seems extraordinary that in a church of this importance, the sumptuous centre section of the screen should have been made demonstrably too wide in its original form. C15 joiners were normally meticulous in such things. This fact, coupled with the significant variations in the painted panels, makes one wonder whether it came from elsewhere, perhaps from more than one source. Dunwich lost many of its churches to the sea, and the shell of Covehithe reminds us of its former glory, neither of them very far away.

The last brass to be seen is in the s. chapel *sanctuary,* an inscription of about 1500 for John and Helen Bischop. There are four simple C15 benches in the chapel, and two of the centre *bosses* are portraits of Mary Tudor and her husband Charles Brandon, Duke of Suffolk. They lived at Westhorpe and she lies buried in St Mary's Bury. Above the centre screen a section of the roof is panelled and painted as a *celure* for the rood below. The decoration was renewed in the 1860s and the original colouring was followed carefully. Each panel contains an angel displaying a scroll lettered with the words of the Benedictus, and the rest of the chancel roof is panelled and painted to match. The fine suite of late-C15 choir stalls below have traceried fronts, elaborate *poppyheads,* and polygonal buttresses topped with carved ball *finials.* They are backed by matching screens, and the rear stalls are fitted with *misericords.* The elbows between each stall are excellently carved, and some are of more than average interest. On the s. side, look for a head within a shell that is shaped like a cream horn, and next to it, a figure standing in hell's mouth. On the n. side there is a rare carving of a beaver, curled over and biting itself. It was believed that the animal was hunted to extract certain drugs from its genitals and that, when cornered, it would bite them off in an effort to dissuade the hunter. The only other illustration of this particular fable in East Anglia is at Lakenheath. The stalls stand on a pierced stone plinth, a device to improve the acoustics that can be found in a few other churches. The organ backs onto the n. aisle chapel, and its 1880s pipe case with elaborate tracery is set in an upper archway in the chancel n. wall; three trumpeting angels stand on top, and two more are corbelled out as supports below. Opposite, an 1820s tablet for infant Henrietta Crewe bears a touching epitaph:

...This star of comfort for a moment given,

Just rose on earth, then set to rise in
  heaven...

The *piscina* and *sedilia* have shallow, groined
canopies, and are framed with a plain moulding;
a row of blank shields runs below the sedilia
and there is a large *mouchette* roundel under the
piscina. Instead of a *credence shelf*, the latter has
an unusual arrangement of three recesses at the
back, graded in size, to house cruets and towel.
The centre light of the n. sanctuary window
contains a large St Edmund in ground and cut
glass by John Hutton. It was installed in 1969,
and although the figure is impressive, its effect
is curiously muted and it might have been more
effectively displayed on the s. side where sunlight
would have caught it. The painted and gilt *High
altar reredos* was designed by Fr. Benedict
Williamson in 1916, and there are five plaster
panels, with Christ blessing in the centre, and
scenes from his life on either side. Above it, the
e. window glass is by *Comper*, installed in 1954
and one of his last commissions. The four lights
illustrate Edmund as youth, king, martyr, and
saint, and they are backed with a deep blue which
is in marked contrast to the designer's usual
palette of pale colour.

Spexhall, St Peter (H2): The round tower had
fallen as long ago as 1720 but it was not until
1910 that the remains were taken down and a
new one built. It is sharply finished and has a
stair turret tucked in the angle with the *nave* on
the s. side. Walking round to the n. you will
find a blocked *Norman* doorway, with traces of
surface carving in the arch. The wall there is faced
with a multiplicity of small flints and there are
square-headed *Perpendicular* windows. The e. end
of the C14 *chancel* is dated 1713 below the gable
to mark its rebuilding, using an attractive
lozenge pattern of red brick. The e. window
was replaced in 1876 as part of a hefty restoration
by J.K. Colling, and the early-C14 *priest's door* in
the s. wall is sheltered by a buttress, as at Eye
and Blythburgh. There are larger Perpendicular
windows on the s. side of the nave, the walls of
which were raised in the mid-C15 when it was
re-roofed and the s. *porch* added. The latter has
been renovated more than once (see the 1733
stone below the gable), the label over the outer
door has been removed, and it has recently been
re-roofed. The early-C14 inner doorway has king
and bishop *headstops* inclining inwards, and there
are the remains of two *scratch dials* to be found
on the r.-hand *jamb* that were used before the
porch was built.. The soft stone of both porch

window splays provided plenty of scope for C16
and C17 graffiti artists.

Just inside, there is a *stoup* within a *trefoil* arch,
and you will see that above a new tower arch
there is the shape of an upper doorway which
suggests that the original tower was designed
as a place of refuge. Colling designed the pine
roofs, with *tie-beams* in the nave and *scissors-braces*
in the *chancel*. The early-C15 *font* has shields set
in *quatrefoils* in the bowl panels and a traceried
shaft, and early-C19 *Decalogue* boards hang on
the w. wall. The *tracery* of the n.w. window
contains fine C15 shields of the Bacon, Blagge,
Baynard, and Willoughby families. Good *Royal
Arms* of George II are displayed on the s. wall,
and further along, the church's collection of
brasses has been handsomely mounted. At the
top is the 18in. effigy of Silvester Browne
(1593), in Paris cap, ruff, and with her gown
parted to display an embroidered petticoat; six
sons are shown on a separate plate, but the figure
of husband John and another group of sons
are lost. There is an inscription for Mary
Downinge dated 1601, and the single mid-C15
shield probably relates to Robert Baynard. On
the n. wall, an impressive war memorial in
marble, brass and slate has the unusual addition
of regimental badges mounted against each
name. There is now neither chancel arch nor
rood screen but the entrance to the old *rood stair*
survives in the n. wall, blocked after the fourth
step. In the s. wall a *piscina* with a *cinquefoiled*
arch shows that there was an *altar* in front of
the screen before the *Reformation*. The Victorian
pulpit incorporates three panels of C17
strapwork, and in the chancel some C15 bench
ends with *poppyheads* have been made up into
choir stalls. During the 1870s restoration, floor
levels were raised and laid with Minton tiles,
and the large piscina and *dropped-sill sedilia* were
left undisturbed in the *sanctuary*. The e. window
commemorates the reign of Queen Victoria with
overtly sentimental but good quality figures by
Jones & Willis – Christ as the Good Shepherd
flanked by the prophetess Miriam playing her
timbrel, and the widow righteously putting the
mite she had found into the poor box.

Sproughton, All Saints (F6): The building
dates from the early C14, but there was a heavy
restoration in the 1860s and *chancel aisles* were
added shortly after. The unbuttressed tower has
two narrow *set-offs* above the belfry and the 'Y'
tracery of the bell openings points to a
completion date of about 1300. Sproughton's
excellent ring of six bells with an 8 cwt. tenor

hang within. As at nearby Washbrook and Bramford, glacial boulders can be detected in the footings and they may well have been pagan cult objects that were cleansed and reused in the service of the new religion. There is a broad *Perpendicular* window by the blocked C14 n. door, but the others on that side have angular *trefoils* in the heads of 'Y' tracery. There is a n.e. *vestry* and the Perpendicular e. window has five *ogee*-headed *lights*. There are interesting *headstops* on the *dripstone* of the chancel s. window and the C14 *priest's door* is in the s. aisle wall. Within the *porch*, there is a fine C14 doorway, with pairs of shafts set within a broad moulding under close-coupled ring *capitals*.

The C19 *reredos* has been relegated to a spot just inside, and beyond there is a *font* of the same vintage but in C15 style. The lovely C14 *arcades* match the doorway, and the *quatrefoil piers* have intermediate plain shafts. The steep chancel arch, however, with its plain chamfers fading into the *imposts*, is likely to be slightly earlier. There is a tall *clerestory*, with three windows a side and a small one over the chancel. The *nave* roof was repaired and stained as part of the C19 restoration and the angels on the alternate *hammerbeams* have had their heads and wings replaced. This may have been the work of *Henry Ringham*, who provided the excellent range of benches below. There are *embattled collars* with short *king posts* below the ridge of the roof and the braces at the e. end are painted as a *celure* for the vanished *rood*. By the s. door there is a generously proportioned tablet for Metcalfe Russell who died in 1785, and above it, a large draped urn stands against a black obelisk. This is undoubtedly the work of a London sculptor and there is a graceful epitaph provided by his 'natural and elected heir Michael Collinson' – a deliciously ambiguous phrase on which to ponder. At the e. end of the aisle is a C19 *piscina* in Gothic style but note that it was placed over an original drain, showing that there was a medieval *altar* nearby. In the n. aisle there is another but this time it is the original, beautifully proportioned and matching the arcades. There are seven C15 bench ends with *poppyheads* incorporated in the choir stalls and they were used by Ringham as his models for the rest of the seating. In the *sanctuary* the C14 piscina arch has pierced tracery which matches the aisle windows, and on the n. wall there is a large monument for Elizabeth Bull who died in 1634. Her kneeling figure is dressed in a long black cloak and two stiffly posed angels draw curtains aside. Pairs of shields and obelisks adorn the

cornice and much of the original colour remains. A similar design is used for Edward Lambe's monument at East Bergholt and, as they were relatives, one mason may have carved both. The tablet alongside commemorates Lieut. William Collinson of the Honourable East India Company's 37th Bengal Native Infantry who fell in action on 13 January 1840 (unless he survived to die again on 30 January as the omnibus family memorial above has it). The door to the vestry has small, angled headstops, and there is a *squint* to the e. of it which shows that it was originally a chapel. A small stone in the chancel floor records that Joseph Waite the rector died in 1670, and the *touchstone* tablet on the s. wall is a neatly amusing memorial for the same man. Engraved with the *Chi Rho* symbol, and a winged hour-glass on a skull, it carries the text 'Behold I come' (Revelation 16:15); below is engraved 'I. Waite' (Job 14:14), taking advantage of the fact that 'J's were always printed as 'I's in those days.

The church has an extensive array of modern glass, and apart from two windows, all of it was installed during the 1860s restoration by Alexander Gibbs, whose prolific firm supplied windows to nine Suffolk churches between 1850 and the end of the century. The e. window displays a varied colour range and the centre panel has Christ holding a *chalice* and wearing a rich purple robe; there are separate panels for each of the twelve apostles (it was probably a later repair that gave *St Philip* two left feet!). The chancel chapel s. window has glass by *Ward & Hughes* of 1881 which is a sentimental and terribly insipid version of the *Three Marys* at the tomb. For better things, move to the n. aisle where there is a fine *St Christopher* window. The central figure, in dark, sombre colours and grainy texture, is by *Christopher Whall* and was installed in the year of his death. He had used the design in a church elsewhere, and his daughter Veronica combined it with four vignettes of her own to provide an integrated composition.

Stanningfield, St Nicholas (C5): The church has a 'hunched shoulders' look because when the tower became unstable in the 1880s the upper stage was removed, and it now has a low pyramid cap. There is a square stair turret on the s. side and the *transomed* C15 w. window has been renewed. This was a *Norman* building originally, as shown by two small *lancets* in the *nave* and by the blocked n. door – very worn curly *capitals* and a *chevron moulding* which has little nodules on the inner points. The 'Y' *tracery* windows date from about 1300 and the very interesting *chancel* built by the Rokewood family followed soon after. The window tracery is exceptionally enterprising, with multi-*cusped quatrefoils* on the n. and pointed *trefoils* grouped within circles on the s. The intersected tracery of the e. window has thin trefoils in the heads of the three *lights* and contains a circled quatrefoil at the top. The s. *priest's door* is blocked and below the window to the l. is a *low side window* in the form of a small quatrefoil. A sensitive attention to detail crops up again in the s. doorway where the mouldings are carved with two runs of *fleurons* and *ball flower* decorates the *dripstone*. Just within, a *stoup* is set under a cusped arch. The heavy C15 *font* on its traceried stem has quatrefoils in the bowl panels, with the shield of *St Edmund* to the e. and Rokewood to the w. The sills of the windows at the e. end of the nave are both lowered to form *sedilia* and there will have been *altars* nearby, although only the *piscina* on the s. side remains behind the pulpit. The C15 *rood screen* is low and simple, with *mouchette* roundels in the *spandrels* of the centre arch, which has just the hint of an *ogee* shape. You may have heard of Stanningfield's fine C15 *Doom* above the chancel arch; if so, you will be very disappointed when you see that it is an expanse of sombre grey colour, with very little detail showing. It was cleaned and treated in the 1930s and was in good condition when *Cautley* saw it. There has been a sad deterioration over the years but if you have binoculars and a little patience much may still be recognised. There were almost 100 hundred figures originally and a life-size Christ is seated in the centre on a rainbow, his wounds still visible. The *Blessed Virgin* intercedes on the r. and the Passion angel, robed in red, is to the l.; each side are angels summoning the dead with long trumpets, and the myriad little figures rise naked from their shrouds and tombs. The faint figures of *St Peter* and an angel can be seen to the l. in a multistoried heaven and there are fragments of hell opposite. The s. side of the *sanctuary* has a large lancet piscina with plain sedilia alongside, and opposite is the tomb of Thomas Rokewood, who married a Clopton of Long Melford and who died in 1521. It is in fine condition, with cresting and four shields above the long, low recess; the standing angels at the corners were added in 1881. The front of the tomb chest is carved with four panels of multi-cusped quatrefoils, with shields of Rokewood and Clopton. From its position and type there seems little doubt that it served as an *Easter sepulchre*. The family were staunch Catholics and Ambrose Rokewood was a friend of Robert Catesby. Thus he was drawn into the Gunpowder Plot and met his end on the last day of January, 1606. In 2003 the chancel e. window was restored and new glass designed by Pippa Blackall was inserted. It takes the form of a pendant cross placed centrally that echoes the design of the altar cross below. A combination of broken shapes in excellent colour form a watery surround, and the Tree of Life on the l. scatters some of its leaves across the design. The dove of the Holy Spirit rests in the centre of the cross, while below there is the early Christian symbol of a fish, with another in a little vignette; small pieces of earlier glass have found a home in the tracery. Before you leave have a look at the photograph of the tower before it was shortened which hangs at the back of the nave.

Stansfield, All Saints (B5): This is a fairly large church that stands on a hill to the n. of the village and its C14 tower underwent a major restoration in 1986. The stair turret lies within the angle of the s.w. buttress, there is a double chequer *base course*, and three niches are grouped round the w. window. The tower houses a ground floor ring of six bells with a 10 cwt. tenor. There are no *aisles* and the tall *nave* dates from about 1300 with, on the n. side, a handsome octagonal *rood stair* turret. Its battlemented top, rising above the roof line, is decorated with *paterae* and tiny grotesques. The early-C14 *chancel* side windows have very pretty *tracery* reminiscent of Stanningfield, and either side of the *Perpendicular* e. window are tall *Decorated* niches, with remnants of *headstops* on the *crocketted dripstones*. The corner buttresses are angled at the second stage, there is an *Early English priest's door* on the s. side, and you will find a *scratch dial* on the centre nave buttress. The tall s. *porch* is battlemented with corner pinnacles, and there are shields within *quatrefoils* at the base of the angled buttresses. Its roof is cambered and there is a re-cut *stoup* to the r. of the late-C13 inner doorway. The door itself is modern but the medieval closing ring has been fixed in the centre.

Just inside, there is an earlier stoup in a *lancet* niche. The *font* bowl is very mutilated and once had corner shafts; it is possibly late-C13 and now stands on C19 shafts. In the n.w. corner stands a C14 chest, pale with age; it is long, low, and heavily banded with iron, and the little turned legs that were added in the C17 have probably helped to keep it dry. The nave is wide and rather bare, with C19 benches. The early-C16 roof has braced and cambered *tie-beams*; every other *wall post* is *castellated* and the deep *wall plates* have carved and pierced trails. It has been stained black and is difficult to examine, but by using binoculars some fine carving can be discovered. On the s. side, the last *spandrel* before the chancel arch has a maid peeping from the top of a castle while a sinuous dragon menaces her, and immediately opposite another dragon wields a huge pair of tongs. On the e. side of the spandrel over the s. door there is a labourer with a variety of tools, and on the n. side opposite is a group of villagers. Under the sill of the s.e. nave window is a little *piscina*, close to a tall image niche which now contains a modern Virgin and Child. This was no doubt where the *altar* of the medieval *guild* of *St Mary* was sited. A late-C16 or early-C17 *Holy Table* with a carved top rail now stands there. The early-C17 pulpit has three ranges of panels in standard designs of the period with a modern base and steps. Behind it, an iron door was fitted to the rood stair in the C19 and the upper exit blocked off. The front of the nave pews have tracery which probably came from the *rood loft* and the low *screen* has a modern frame in which is set the excellent tracery saved from the C15 original. The quality was matched by the C19 carver of the pretty trail that runs below the top rail. Similarly, the stalls are good modern work and have standing saints on the bench ends. The chancel roof is single-braced, with two rough tie-beams spanning it at wall level. In the *sanctuary* the piscina has a most attractive ogee arch with pierced *mouchettes* and a little opening to the side of the *dropped-sill sedilia*. On the e. wall there are three *consecration crosses* and the fragments of medieval glass remaining have been gathered into panels in the s. window. Francis Kedington's memorial of 1715, on the chancel n. wall, is a handsome *touchstone* slab with his arms well displayed in shallow carving; the heavy *acanthus* leaves and head in stone below would seem to be earlier work. William Steggles of Bury cut a gawky little tablet for the Revd. Beriah Brook in 1809 and it is interesting for the details it gives of how the upkeep of his tomb was to be financed. The memorial is s. of the chancel arch but there is no evidence outside, alas, that his wishes bore fruit for very long.

Stanstead, St James (C6): This small church was decisively restored by the Victorians. In the 1860s the *chancel* was restored and in the 1870s a new arch was inserted in the tower. The C14 tower has a new w. *lancet* but the very narrow little belfry lancets are original and there are *Perpendicular* bell openings. With the exception of the C19 e. window, the windows seem to be early-Perpendicular and there is a blocked C14 n. door. The n.e. *vestry* is a Victorian addition as is the tall chimney that rises at the corner of the *nave* gable. There are impressively fierce dragons at the corners of the s. *porch* parapet and a canopied *stoup* niche remains in an outside buttress.

The medieval door still has its original closing ring, and on the floor by the tower arch is a 9 cwt. bell cast by Stephen Tonni of Bury St Edmunds, one of only four from that foundry that are known to have survived. Have a look at the inscription and the maker's mark. Above the old n. door hangs a well-painted set of Queen Anne *Royal Arms*, and in the window beyond the medieval fragments include shields of Bernay and Walsham. The roofs and fittings are Victorian, the square-topped oak benches having been moulded on the original set, and there are *encaustic tile* floors. The Revd. Samuel Sheen's 1867 memorial on the chancel n. wall is a good example of High Victorian Gothic on a small scale. There is a mosaic cross in the head of the alabaster recess arch below an aggressively *crocketted* gable, with side stub shafts in green marble. The s. *sanctuary* window is a memorial to another Samuel Sheen, also rector and presumably a son. The 1907 glass is by *Heaton, Butler & Bayne* and has full length figures of *St James the Great* and the prophet Samuel as High Priest of the temple; there are drapes behind the figures and the remainder of the lights is filled with patterned squares. The *tracery* contains two angels and at the bottom two more draw out a scroll. The glass in the e. window is earlier – a centre Calvary against a deep blue ground, and roundels of the *Agnus Dei, a pelican in her piety*, alpha and omega and the *Sacred monogram*. The rest of the window is filled with opaque *quarries* and there are figures of the *Four Evangelists* in the tracery. *Decalogue* boards are framed in oak panels on either side of the *High altar*.

Stanton, All Saints (D3): The village once had two churches, and the *Churches Conservation Trust* now takes care of the empty shell of St John's (where the last service was held in 1876) by the main road. All Saints once had a fine C14 tower but it collapsed in 1906 and luckily the top two-thirds fell away from the church. In 1956, the upper portion of what remained was rebuilt and the timber belfry with its pyramid cap was added. It houses a ring of four bells with a 10 cwt. tenor but they are hung dead and can only be chimed. The *nave* and *chancel* were built about 1320 and the e. and w. windows, with their *reticulated tracery*, were replaced in 1875 as part of a major restoration. The square-headed s. *aisle* windows have *Decorated* tracery, with a compact reticulated pattern in the e. window. It would seem that the aisle was added to connect the body of the church with what had been a free-standing tower. A line of *ball flower* ornament lines the parapet. There is a *priest's door* on the s. side of the chancel and on the n. side, a heavily restored medieval *vestry*. On that side of the nave, the buttresses carry inscriptions: 'MR' for 'Maria Regina' (the Virgin) and 'Omns S' for 'Omnes Sancti' (All Saints). The n. doorway is blocked and if you look in the angle of the w. wall and the n.w. buttress there is a fragment of *Norman* masonry embedded some 6ft. from the ground. Within the *porch* there are stone seats and it is a nice touch that the builder who repaired the tower was commemorated here when he died in 1982. Within the church, one can see how the heavy corner buttresses of the tower were undisturbed when the s. aisle was built, and a large *stoup* was housed in one of them. The plain octagonal C13 *font* has a centre shaft and slim pillars at each angle. On the wall behind, two shepherd's crooks are displayed which were emblems of a Friendly Society that used to meet in the village (reminding me of those in Norfolk's Walpole St Andrew which are also relics of a similar club). The old door to the tower stair is to the l., and its position high in the wall indicates that valuables were once stored there. The *arcade* between aisle and nave has short octagonal *piers* and the *clerestory* windows are small *quatrefoils*. Floors, roofs, benches and most of the fittings date from the C19 restoration. In the wall of the aisle there is a magnificent tomb recess which almost reaches the roof. It has been terribly mutilated but is still beautiful, with a massively *cusped ogee* arch fringed with the remains of *crockets*. Only the stumps of the side pinnacles remain, but the surfaces of the arch cusps are finely carved with leaves, and some of them have tiny faces in the centre so that they resemble *green men*. This was obviously a tomb for a person of importance and that could well have been Hervey de Stanton, King Edward II's Chancellor. The main arch of the C14 *angle piscina* in the s. aisle chapel is a crocketted ogee with a *finial*, and there are *dropped-sill sedilia* alongside. The *altar* here is a very simple C17 table which came from Great Cornard (how or why I know not). In the window above are fragments of medieval glass and a nice panel of continental glass portraying *St Margaret* and *St Elizabeth*. The bottom of the *rood stair* was entered from this chapel and the upper opening faces the nave. The George III *Royal Arms* on the n. wall are painted on board and were moved here from Stanton St John's church. The simplest form of medieval piscina was one carved out of a ledge or window sill and an example can be seen here beside the pulpit – once the site of an altar. Nearby is the church's only *brass* – an inscription that was once on the *ledger-stone* of John and Elizabeth Parker who died in 1575 and 1597 respectively. The very tall chancel arch matches the nave arcade and all trace of the *rood screen* has gone except for some marks in the stonework where it was fitted. It is a fine vista through to the chancel, spoiled only by the obtrusive bulk of the C19 organ on the s. side. The *sanctuary* has a large C14 piscina under an ogee arch and the stepped sedilia alongside are separated by stone armrests, a refinement normally found only in larger churches. The centre panel of the e. window is a version of Holman Hunt's picture *'The Light of the World'*, designed by Luxford of New Barnet in 1955, but it is not a very happy translation. An oddity in the window on the s. side is the diamond cut inscription in one of the bottom *quarries*: 'John Norton glazed me for John Clarke Ixworth – Kenninghall Norf. 1891' – similar trade adverts can be found at Blyford and Barnby. The ledger slabs in the sanctuary provide an interesting contrast of lettering styles; have a look at the pair of tablets flanking the chancel arch. Rector George Bidwell employed the London mason Gaffin to cut the memorial for his wife in 1840, but his own is a carbon copy by the local mason, Sharp of Thetford, and done in 1865 after Bidwell had been rector here for 54 years.

Sternfield, St Mary Magdalene (H4): Masked by trees from the road, the church has a memorable setting, and it has seen many changes through the centuries. The early building comprised a simple *nave* and *chancel*, and the unbuttressed tower which was added in the C14 has been excellently restored recently. Michael de la Pole, Earl of Suffolk gave money to the church in 1384, and his family shield below the w. window may well record the gift. Walking round, you will see that the nave n. door of about 1300 has been bricked up, and above it, a ridge marks the height of the original walls. Square-headed *Perpendicular* windows were inserted later, and a *vestry* and organ chamber were built on to the chancel in 1877. This was part of a typically enthusiastic restoration by J.P. St Aubyn who transformed Huntingfield in the 1850s. The chancel here had already been rebuilt in 1764, but he lengthened and re-roofed it, choosing to renew in Perpendicular style, with new windows and *priest's door*. In the early C14 there was a chapel on the n. side of the chancel, and its beautiful *piscina* has survived in the outside wall just to the e. of the vestry. It has *ball flower* ornament in the *hood mould* and there is a scalloped drain. All the windows on the s. frontage were renewed in the C19, and above the nave roof, the line of its predecessor shows on the e. face of the tower. The C14 *porch* is particularly interesting. Its chunky outer arch is larger than usual and has semicircular responds, and there is a generous *trefoil*-headed niche above. A pair of *scratch dials* can be found on the s.w. *quoins*, and two more good examples lurk under the rambler rose on the s.e. corner. The centre shafts and *responds* of the broad side windows have moulded *capitals* and bases, and the *tracery* heads are shouldered. The arch of the inner doorway has the remains of leaf *stops*, there is a *stoup* to the r., and a charity board is displayed overhead. The door itself has been restored, retaining the medieval keeled boards and closing ring.

Within, St Aubyn's influence comes across fairly strongly; nevertheless, there is much of interest. The *hammerbeam* and *queen post* nave roof has some of the characteristics of the early C16 rather than the C15, but the 1870s repairs were obviously extensive and they may have changed it significantly. There is a *sanctus-bell window* above the tower arch, and two medieval stained glass shields are set in the w. window. The one on the r. belongs to the Huntingfields (Roger de Huntingfield built the church in the early C14), and the other displays the arms of Wingfield quartered with De La Pole. *Cautley* describes the late-C14 *font* as having a pair of *quatrefoils* in each bowl panel, but there are only singles now, and it looks as though the bowl was made shallower when the shaft was replaced. The church has a ring of four bells with a 6 cwt. tenor, and were they fit to ring it would be from the ground floor of the tower. Plain pine benches fill the nave, and the shape of the *rood stair* door is outlined behind the modern pulpit. On the opposite side, a taller recess could be taken for another entrance to the loft, but its size probably identifies it as a *banner stave locker*, although most if not all of the other Suffolk examples are to be found at the w. end of their churches. The chancel arch was replaced during

the 1870s restoration and new choir stalls were installed. However, the latter incorporated C15 bench ends recovered from the nave, with *poppyheads* and good tracery cut in the solid; there are seated beasts on the elbows, and the replacement hound on the n. side is a good match. You will see that the ends used in the priest's stalls have turrets rather than beasts and are carved on one side only, having stood originally against a wall. Remembering the piscina outside, there is another relic of the n.e. chapel in the n. wall of the chancel in the form of a small two-*light* window which may have served as a *squint*. True to period, the chancel flooring is Minton tiles, and there are those telescopic brass *communion rails* often favoured by the Victorians. Susanna Long who died at 102 in 1820 is commemorated over the vestry door, and there is a matching tablet for her nephew William further along. Rector here, he died in 1835 as an unabashed Trollopian pluralist, with another living at Pulham in Norfolk and a cosy canon's stall at Windsor. That piece of preferment had presumably been passed down from Montague Long who died in 1779, having been similarly blessed. He and his wife Elizabeth have matching tablets in mottled marble on the s. wall, with *cartouches* of arms sprouting surrealistically from urns on the top. St Aubyn's new *sanctuary* dispensed with a piscina, and the s. window contains 1890s glass by *Lavers, Barraud & Westlake*, a competent *Annunciation* with rather too much fussy detail. Theirs too is the glass in the e. window, where a Crucifixion is flanked by a Nativity and Christ's meeting with *St Mary Magdalene* on the first Easter Day; the slightly hieratic figures are closely compressed below canopies and set against sombre backgrounds. Below, the church is fortunate in having as an altar piece *The Blind Restored to Sight*, a painting by Benjamin West. He was an American artist who, as history painter to George III from 1772 to 1801, exerted a significant influence on artists in this country. Friend of Reynolds and President of the Royal Academy for nearly thirty years until his death in 1820, his best known painting is *The Death of Wolfe*. It is said that he was staying in the village when he painted this scene of Christ's miracle of healing, and it was given to the church by Lord Farnborough.

Stoke Ash, All Saints (F3): A neatly kept church clearly visible across a field to the e. of the A140. The bell openings of the C14 tower have *Decorated tracery*, there is a later w. window, and a substantial stair turret rises on the s. Walking round, note the flint pebbles lying in *courses* in the n. wall, and the round arches of the low, blocked nave door and *priest's door* in the *chancel* – all showing that the church was begun in the *Norman* period. The three-*light* nave window has pleasing Decorated tracery with four petals within a circle and *mouchettes* either side. The e. window is a C19 replacement and there are tall, thin *Perpendicular* windows to the s. *Flushwork* diamond crosses are worked on two nave buttresses and may have been *consecration crosses* although their high position is unusual. The homely late-C15 brick *porch* has a niche over the outer arch and there is the vestige of a *stoup* by the inner door. The windows in Decorated style were probably inserted when *R.M. Phipson* carried out a big restoration in 1868. The Norman inner doorway is entirely plain and is only 6ft. high and 3ft. 6in. wide.

Phipson stripped out plaster ceilings to reveal a *scissors-braced* roof, with heavier *arch-braces* in the *chancel* coming well down the walls; the benches are to his design and the stalls in the chancel incorporate fine medieval *poppyheads*. The tower arch is tall and thin and at the base stands the crown of a bell, affording an opportunity to examine a medieval founder's work at close quarters. It was cast at the earliest foundry that has been traced in Bury St Edmunds, between 1460 and 1480. The inscription was applied upside down and on that account it may have been one of the unknown craftsman's first efforts. The wording is apparently unique for a bell: 'Credo in Deum Patrem omni potentem' (I believe in God the Father Almighty). The church's ring of five bells with a 6 cwt. tenor is rung from the floor of the tower. Over the s. door hangs a very dark set of *Hanoverian Royal Arms*, re-labelled for William IV in 1836; they are painted on board and have a *pedimented* top. There is now no chancel arch or *screen* but the stairs which led to the *rood loft* rise within the window embrasure on the n. side. The early-C17 pulpit close by has the familiar pattern of blind arches in the panels and although the carving is shallow, it is lively, with bird beak forms in the scrolls; the lower panels are renewals. The little priest's door lies within a much larger and later pointed arch (puzzling) and in the n. wall of the *sanctuary* there is a plain and fairly large recess. Its depth suggests that it was an *aumbry* but it has chamfered edges and is therefore unlikely to have had a door – an *Easter sepulchre* is a possibility. The *Decalogue* is painted on C19 zinc plates on the e. wall and, without

its drain, the *piscina* recess is now meaningless. In the window alongside there are C15 glass fragments but a single hand in one place and a book in another are all that mean very much. The 1750s *ledger-stone* of Elizabeth Bedingfield lies before the priest's door and it is a pity that the Victorian sanctuary floor cuts short her epitaph:

> She was taken away lest wickedness should alter her understanding or deceit beguile her. . . .

Completion of it might form the basis for a cosy competition in one of the more cultivated journals.

Stoke-by-Clare, St John the Baptist (B6): The church lies in an attractive setting by the entrance to Stoke College. There had been a Benedictine priory previously but the college was founded by Edmund, Earl of March, Lord of Wigmore and Clare in 1419. Matthew Parker, who became Archbishop of Canterbury under Elizabeth, was its last Dean before the *Dissolution*. He restored the *nave* in 1535 and, being collegiate, portions of the church belonged to the priory. The handsome C14 tower has a stair set in the n.e. corner buttress with an outside door, and two worn C17 headstones rest against a n. buttress – an inscription on one and skull and crossbones on the other. The w. window has 'Y' *tracery*, with a small stooled niche above it, but the bell openings are late-*Perpendicular*. To the n. is a one-handed clock with a lozenge dial whose bell was cast by an itinerant founder around 1510, and it carries the advice 'arise early to serve God' in Latin. The tower houses a ring of six bells with a 13 cwt. tenor. Within the s. *porch*, with its stepped gable, stands a C19 *bier*, and further along a square-cut stub *transept* has yawning *gargoyles*. There is a monument of unusual design s. of the *chancel* for Edward Douglas Loch who died in 1942 – a slim oblong panel with heavy scrolls at the ends, capped with a cornice. The two-storied n.e. *vestry* has barred windows and there is a *priest's door* on that side. The three-*light* windows of *aisles* and *clerestory* are C15 and at the n.e. corner of the nave an octagonal *rood stair* turret rises to the battlements. The n. porch has a gable that matches the s., with a very worn niche over the entrance.

The interior is spacious, with pleasing brick floors, and close to the door stands an early-C14 chest, with vertical wrought-iron straps on the front which branch out like small trees. The

w. wall is blank, but note that there is the outline of an arch which is off-centre. The original church was apparently without aisles, and at the C15 rebuilding the axis moved to the n., so that what had been the old s. wall became the wall of the new s. aisle. The octagonal C15 *font* has *quatrefoils* in the panels with centre shields and *paterae*, and there are carved heads below the bowl. The nave is lofty, with tall clerestory windows, an almost flat roof, and a *castellated string course* above the *arcades*. The quatrefoil *piers*, with their castellated *capitals*, may have been saved from the C14 church and used again, as at Clare. The short s. transept is also likely to have formed part of the previous building. A plough now stands within, and there is some interesting glass in the window above it. Below the coat of arms at the top is a fine little windmill, a lozenge to the r. is painted with the white hart, and to the l. is a lozenge which has merchant marks, probably for one of the Elwes family. There are two heraldic roundels, and the one on the l. contains the arms of the Clothworkers' Company (note the teazle at the bottom used to raise a nap on woven cloth, and the two harbicks, or tenter-hooks, with points at each end which were used to fasten cloth on a tenter or drying frame). It is a reminder of the dominance of the wool and cloth trade in this part of Suffolk during the Middle Ages. The pulpit is at once one of the best that we have and the smallest, being only just over 20in. across. Money was left for its construction in 1498 and it stands on a coved and panelled stem. It has beautifully dense tracery in the panels, with an overlay of pierced work at the top. Behind it, modern doors have been fitted to the *rood loft* stair. The organ takes up virtually the whole of the n. chapel but by edging round it one can see something of the mid-C16 *Doom* painted on the e. wall. It has a pale green background and the figure of Christ is seated on a rainbow; below Him there is an angel with spread wings and hosts of subsidiary figures. This is an unusual position for a Doom and may reflect the dual use of the church by college and parish. In the wall behind the organ is the small memorial slab for William Dicons, a priest who died in 1567. The archway at high level leading into the chancel is most unusual and I can offer no reasonable explanation for it. The door to the vestry from the chancel is medieval and the benches in chancel and s. chapel have *poppyheads* carved with a fascinating variety of leaf forms, including a pair of seed pods by the s. wall. Sadly, they have all been cruelly mutilated. There is a plain *Stuart Holy table* in

the s. chapel and to the r., a small medieval statue of the Virgin and Child, given to the church some years back. The C19 stone *reredos* is boldly lettered 'This do in remembrance of me', and the *Heaton, Butler & Bayne* glass above it has not worn well. The church has a number of *brasses*: on the s. side of the nave by the lectern is an 18in. figure of a lady in *kennel headdress* dating from about 1530 (you will notice the stone was reused for 'F.C.' in 1766); nearby is the 22in. gowned figure of Edward Talkarne who died in 1597, with his coat of arms, and across by the pulpit lies his widow Alice, shown in Paris cap and ruff, who followed him eight years later. In addition, there are brass inscriptions for Ralph Turner (1600) by the pulpit, Elizabeth Sewster (1598) by the pulpit, John Croply (1584) by the lectern, and William Butcher (1611) in the n. aisle.

Stoke-by-Nayland, St Mary (D7): In one of Constable's loveliest pictures this grand church gleams atmospherically below a rainbow, standing proudly on the hill. Garden land falls sharply away from the broad sweep of gravel on the s. side which leads to the main village street and the combination of half-timbered houses, *lych-gate*, and mighty tower when viewed from the w. is irresistible. To all intents and purposes the church was rebuilt in the C15 – the *nave* and *chancel* were probably completed by 1440, the tower by 1470. And it is the tower which sticks in the mind. There seems to have been a local burst of enthusiasm for towers with corner turrets (one thinks of Eye, Redenhall, and Bungay particularly) but here the material is brick except for the *base couse* and the pinnacled parapet. A further difference is the most unusual addition of diagonal buttresses to the octagonal turrets, and at each of the four stages they are enriched with two niches under nodding *ogee* canopies. The w. facade is particularly impressive, with a broad band of grinning lion masks in the moulding of the doorway and fearsome devil *headstops* from which rise triangular shafts supporting seated beasts. Shields of the Howard and Tendring families show who paid for the work, and the arch is *crocketted* with a *finial* – a motif repeated in the four-*light* window above. The large belfry windows and the bell openings above them are set within wide, sloping embrasures. The tower houses an excellent ring of eight bells with a 22 cwt. tenor. There is a low, early C16 brick n. porch with blind arcading below its battlements and the tall *clerestory* has square-headed two-light windows which were replaced as part of an extensive restoration in 1865. There is a faint *scratch dial* to be found e. of the *priest's door* and a rather better example on a s. *aisle* buttress. The wide s. porch has windows with *Decorated tracery* and formed part of the early-C14 building. Restored in 1870, it has an upper room with a turret stair tucked in the corner to the w. and there are *bosses* on the centre line of the vaulting within (the innermost could be an *Annunciation*). The lovely C15 doors are perhaps the finest in the county for their period – silvery grey, with much of their intricate detail intact. Each has three narrow panels and, in the upper half, eight figures stand within canopied niches. Another twelve fill the niches in the border and if the worn figure carved at the top of the centre spine is the *Blessed Virgin*, the whole design may be identified as a *Jesse tree*. On that assumption, the figure top l. with a harp would be King David.

Within, the impression of spaciousness and height is sharpened by the incredibly elongated tower arch reaching to the roof. At its foot the base course decorated with shields in *foiled* circles reappears, and the high w. window seems almost lost in the vastness. It is filled with the rich, dark colours of 1860s glass by the *O'Connors* – figures of Faith, Hope, Mercy, and Charity below the *four Evangelists*, all standing in front of drapes. The superb *piers* of the nave arcades, with their tall bases, have eight miniature shafts, all with enriched *capitals*, and the *hood moulds* come down to headstops. Above the line of arches is a *string course* carved with demi-angels and *paterae*, and the *wall-posts* of the almost flat roof rest on stone *corbels*. Most of these were replaced in 1865 but eight at the w. end are original and it is worth using binoculars to study the *pelican in her piety* on the s. and what I take to be the ram caught in a thicket on the n. (the sacrifice of Isaac). The w. area has been cleared of benches and provides a generous setting for the fine C15 *font*. Its substantial base is stepped and four platforms project in the form of a cross, with shields set below them – w., the Howard/Tendring arms, s., cross of *St George*, n., *Sacred monogram*, and e., the Sun in Splendour badge of Edward IV (which gives us a date 1461-83). The short stem has nodding ogee arches reaching up to a sloping band of demi-angels, and apart from the conventional *Evangelistic symbols* and an angel, the bowl panels are carved with three mysterious figures – s.w., a woman in a cowled headdress bearing a scroll, with a tree or bush to the r., s.e., a man with a sack on his shoulder pointing to a volume standing on a bookcase with a staff

Stoke by Nayland, St Mary: C19 candelabra

resting against it, n.e., a man with a scroll by a lectern. What can they be? At the e. end of the s. aisle there is a range of late-C14 stalls, all of which had *misericords*, and there are two more single stalls – one in the s. chapel and one by the choir stalls. The large and rather murky *Hanoverian Royal Arms* over the s. door were updated by adding Queen Victoria's initials.

A small chapel dedicated to *St Edmund* which opens off the n. aisle was a *chantry* established by John de Peyton or Peydone around 1318. Its windows were replaced as part of the great C15 rebuilding but its position seems to indicate that the original church was as large as its successor. The chest which stands at the e. end of the n. aisle has four hasps and iron plates on top which are cut with two sets of initials which probably belonged to the churchwardens of the day. There is now no *rood screen* but the chapels that flank the chancel have matching screens to the w. which *Cautley* thought were not in their original position; dating from the C15, their delicate ogee arches are *cusped* and crocketted. The pulpit was part of the 1860s refurbishing and stands on a typical stone and marble base. The clerestory stops short partway along the chancel and the *sanctuary* is lit by tall side windows. Its floor is paved with black and white marble that is probably C18 and there were *communion rails* along the frontage e. of the present set. The pair of *Camden Society* standing candelabra have been beautifully cleaned and polished. The stalls on either side are interesting because their backs were once part of the original rood screen. The tracery retains some of its colour and there were painted figures originally; ends with half *poppyheads* were added and the desks in front have wide ledges, traceried fronts, and poppyheads. The tall C14 *piscina* has a cusped ogee arch but the canopy has been hacked away. The chancel roof seems to be all C19 and behind the *High altar* the 1865 *Decalogue* and Lords Prayer are on slate panels below lively Decorated-style Victorian arches resting on slim marble shafts with flowery capitals. The e. window contains more glass by the O'Connors – stagily posed figures in a Resurrection scene across the top five lights and a Crucifixion below, with heavily striated skies behind. The glass in the e. windows of the side chapels is more interesting as an example of the work in a totally different style and colour range which was imported from the Continent during the same period. Dated 1868 and 1869, it is by John B. Capronnier and is his only work in the county, although he had many commissions elsewhere, notably in Yorkshire. In the n.e. chapel there is a painterly composition of the Holy Family with *St John the Baptist* as a child and two groups of angels against a classical landscape; in the s.e chapel, the window illustrates the episode of Christ raising the widow's son to life and both designs employ canopies with riotously curly cusps and willowy angels in the upper tracery.

In the n.e. chapel there is a C13 piscina which was evidently reused; the hood mould continues down to the base and the deeply moulded arch rests on detached shafts with large ring capitals. Partially blocking a window in the n. wall is the tomb of Sir Francis Mannock who died in 1634. The base, with its heavy swags touched with gilt, is identical to one by *Nicholas Stone* elsewhere and this is likely to be his work. The effigy in pink-veined alabaster is in fine condition and there are eight coloured shields grouped round the tablet above; polished columns of *touchstone* carry small, well-carved figures each side and the semi-circular arch above is crowned with a *cartouche* of arms. If Stone was responsible for

Stoke by Nayland, St Mary

the monument he may well have provided the *brass* and *ledger-stone* for Sir Francis's wife, Lady Dorothea, which is in the floor towards the chancel. It is an excellent piece which shows her wearing the fashionable calash or voluminous hood, with elaborate lace collar and cuffs on her gown; the 7ft. stone is engraved with an architectural niche design that encloses the effigy, the large inscription plate, and a shield of arms. Next to it, all that remains of a 1590 brass commemorating an earlier Sir Francis Mannock and his family are two plates engraved with the figures of his ten children, a Latin epitaph, and two shields.

In the s.e. chapel behind the organ is the impressive brass of Sir William Tendring, the Lord of the Manor, who probably died about 1420. It is set in a stone more than 10ft. long which originally lay in front of the High altar and once had a canopy, shields, and marginal inscription; the 6ft. effigy is a good illustration of the period when chain mail gave way to plate armour and both sword and belt are highly ornamented. He is shown bare-headed, with a forked curly beard, and his helm has what is known as a 'panache' of feathers as a crest. The lion under his spurred heels is remarkably amiable – which is more than can be said for his wife Katherine's expression. Her brass is nearer the chancel and shows her wearing a cape held by a tasseled cord over a gown whose close-buttoned sleeves reach to her knuckles. Their grandson became the first Duke of Norfolk and his wife, Lady Katherine Howard, has her brass below the chapel e. window. The inscription and three of the shields are lost but it is a fine effigy engraved some eighty years after her death in 1452. That is why she wears a *kennel headdress* and heraldic mantle of the later period, The brass must have been impressive when all the inlays were coloured, and it is worth noting that she is wearing her rings – something seldom seen on brasses. She and Sir John were forebears of three queens of England – Anne Boleyn, Catherine Howard, and Elizabeth I. The large tomb on the s. side is for a later owner of the manor, Lady Anne Windsor, who died in 1615. In alabaster, with traces of colour, it shows her lying in a voluminous fur-lined cloak caught up and folded over her farthingale; she has a striking hair style of tiny curls above a steep ruff, and two daughters kneel behind her head while her fashionably dressed son kneels at her feet. The elaborate back incorporates a lengthy epitaph, a winged skull crowned with laurel, and a selection of shields. There is a helpful display of Lady Katherine Howard's armorials, and details (with translations) of the inscriptions on Lady Ann Windsor's tomb. To the w. the small alabaster wall monument is for Lady Anne's mother, Lady Waldegrave, who died in 1600. The e. end of the chapel is crowded with tablets for members of the Rowley family, of which one in the n.e. corner is by *John Bacon the Younger* for Admiral Sir William Rowley (1768) and Vice-Admiral Sir Joshua Rowley (1790); it has a sarcophagus topped by draped flags, an anchor, and a flaming urn, and two sets of arms in shallow relief on the front. On the way out of the churchyard you will pass a Calvary war memorial by W.D. Caröe – a far cry from his pyrotechnics at Elveden.

Stonham Aspal, St Mary and St Lambert (F5): A number of Suffolk churches have C14 towers which also serve as porches and this one is distinguished by a unique weatherboarded bell stage crowned by a little cupola and pointed pinnacles. Squire Theodore Eccleston was so keen a ringer that he substituted ten bells for the original five in 1742 with a 23 cwt. tenor and provided a new bell chamber large enough to house them. The *nave* w. window and those in the *aisles* are C14 and much of the *tracery* is attractive. So too is the e. window, but that was part of *E.C. Hakewill's* 1870s restoration. He provided a peculiar *priest's door* on the n. side, which has a steeply gabled porch. Niches flank the e. window and there is a *scratch dial* on the

buttress to the l. of the other priest's door in the s. wall, with two more on the next buttress – one of which has a double outer circle. The n. porch is unused now except to house a Victorian *bier*. The most striking feature outside is the *clerestory*, whose windows have *quatrefoils* in the *spandrels* and are separated by traceried buttresses; over them, a line of stepped battlements is decorated with little *flushwork trefoils*, shields, and crosses. Before going in, pause at Anthony Wingfield's tomb just s. of the *chancel*. He died in 1714 and it was sculpted by Francis Bird, a craftsman who had worked under Grinling Gibbons and whose fame rests on his 'Conversion of St Paul' in the great pediment of St Paul's cathedral. There are precious few C18 gentlemen to be found taking their ease so elegantly in a country churchyard.

Within the tower there is a *stoup* recess and one passes through red baize doors into the body of the church. The C13 *font* is an un-common design in that the bowl panels are shallow trefoil arches outlined with a roll moulding, and it stands on a shaft carved with tracery of the following century. As with the entrance, the early-C14 inner arch of the n. door is broad and shallow and above it hangs a dark set of George III *Royal Arms*. Below, the pulpit *tester* of 1616 has been made into a table and to the w. lies the *brass* of John Metcalfe who died in 1606. He was rector here for over thirty years and the 18in. effigy illustrates the preaching gown and scarf of the post-*Reformation* period; it lay originally in the chancel. The *hatchment* over the s. door is for Nathaniel Lee Acton who died in 1836. The *Jacobean* benches at the w. end have rosettes on the *finials* and bands of gouge cuts down the ends, and the main range of benches, though extensively and cleverly restored, has some interesting carvings: 4th from the w. end in the centre is a *basilisk* whose tail is itself a dragon, and on another the wolf guards *St Edmund's* head. There are praying figures too, but what is the one 2nd from the w. on the s. side holding?

According to *Cautley* the n. aisle chapel alone rather than the whole church carried the dedication to *St Lambert* and the s. chapel was dedicated to *St Anne*. There you will find a *piscina* with a deeply moulded arch, and the construction of the *arcade* at that end shows clearly how the C15 remodelling of the nave encroached on the C14 aisle. The pulpit is a nice pale golden colour, with strapwork in the top panels above conventional blind arches. It was once a *three-decker* and it is unfortunate that it was separated from its tester when it was dismantled and moved. *William Dowsing's* deputies played havoc here in 1643 and smashed most of the stained glass but some of the remains are remarkable. Apart from *Tudor Roses* in the e. clerestory windows and shields of arms in the aisles, the slivers of tracery in the e. and w. s. aisle windows contain extraordinary little beasts. Three at the e. end have secondary heads emerging from their bellies and the fourth has a pair of eyes on its rump which, with the tail, form a face; the tail continues under the body to finish with a head just like the basilisk on the bench end. The upper doorway of the *rood loft stair* is on the n. side and the tall *Decorated* windows on that side of the chancel are now unglazed and open into the organ chamber. Hakewill designed a pleasing range of choir stalls for his restored chancel and the traceried panels of the 1907 *reredos* enclose a C17 section behind the *altar*. The latter dates from about 1640 and its turned and carved legs have small volute *capitals* (the top extensions are modern). Overhead, the e. window is filled with excellent 1870s glass by *Lavers, Barraud & Westlake*. Ten panels in good clear colour illustrate scenes from the life of Christ and the figures of *St Peter, St Paul*, and the *Evangelists* stand under canopies below. Hakewill provided a large recess in the n. wall for the stone figure of a late-C14 Aspal knight. His dress of short tailored doublet and extensive chain mail is unusual and the bosses on his belt once held jewels. More or less complete to the waist, his head and the remains of his legs were found in the rood loft stair when it was reopened.

Stoven, St Margaret (I2): There was a major rebuilding here in 1849 which drew what little inspiration it had from the *Norman* s. doorway of the old church. Thankfully, that was retained unaltered and has a broad *chevron moulding* in the arch, with a *dripstone* of *billet ornament* resting on decayed beast *stops*. There are single *jamb shafts*, one of the *capitals* retains its carving, and the centre hole of a *scratch dial* can be seen on the other side. The rest of the building uses neo-Norman forms and C19 proportions in a rather depressing combination, while the thin flint tower has a vaguely Italianate bell stage. All the walls are plastered, with *pilasters* at intervals, and there is a *corbel table* of masks and beast heads. The e. window is a large *lancet*, flanked by blind lancets filled with a lozenge pattern. Although it has been almost totally masked by the C19 work, the church's medieval structure remains in the core of the walls. Although the

identity of the architect of the Victorian restoration is not recorded it is possible that it was Thomas Penrice of Lowestoft who transformed Gillingham St Mary's in Norfolk with a neo-Norman makeover in the 1850s and 1860s much more successfully. The work was funded by Thomas Orgill Leman who was the patron of the living.

Entry is by the n. door, and the interior does little to lift the spirit. Ceilings are plastered, and the huge chancel arch is inevitably neo-Norman. Curiously, the *font* is not, but is an *Early English*-style hybrid. The base of the octagonal bowl is arcaded, and there are eight shafts of polished marble round the stem. The pews, with their *trefoil finials*, follow the same trend, and the square wooden pulpit makes use of Early English forms, matching the choir stalls. There is a curious recess on the s. side of the chancel, and *Decalogue* panels are lettered in the blind arches each side of the e. window. *Encaustic tiles* feature in the *sanctuary*, enlivened a little by a mosaic panel of a *pelican in her piety* in the centre, and an inscription bears Leman's name behind the altar.

I have to confess to being less than enthusiastic about Stoven, but tell myself that beauty is in the eye of the beholder, when I remember that the church was only saved from redundancy in 1990 by a parishioners' campaign which faced up to the threat of demolition. The church reopened in 1997 and since then extensive structural repairs have been successfully completed. Like Rushmere St Michael it is a fine example of local enthusiasm and determination being successful in keeping a parish church alive.

Stowlangtoft, St George (D4): There are few country parishes that can boast such a church as this, standing tall and handsome by the street, on a hillock that was once a Roman camp. Embedded in the wall by the path that rises to the gate are fragments of *Decorated* window *tracery*, but the present building is well nigh pure *Perpendicular* and was built between about 1370 and 1400 by Robert de Ashfield. Lord of the Manor and servant of the Black Prince, he died in 1401 and was buried in the *chancel*. It had fallen on hard times by the C19 but a new chancel roof was provided in 1832 and a major restoration followed in the 1850s. It is a tall building for its size and the unity of its design is emphasised by the chequerwork that lines the plain parapets of tower, *nave*, and chancel, and is seen again on the buttresses and in the *base course* that circles the whole church. There is little difference in width between nave and chancel, and a *drip course* lifts as a *label* over the side windows whose arches are shaped like *Tudor* ladies' *kennel headdresses*. There is a small *priest's door* on the s. side of the chancel and the five-*light* e. window is able to display a wider range of panel tracery than those in the side walls. The tower has the common local feature of an e. wall made broader by the buttresses, and there are square-headed bell openings and belfry windows. A heavy stair turret rises almost to the top on the s. side, giving access to a ring of four bells with an 8 cwt. tenor. The *porch* has a deep parapet of panels and the whole of the front is covered with chequerwork. There is a lovely little niche above the entrance; it has a *crocketted ogee* arch, stiff leaf in the moulding, and a fine modern statuette of Christ as the Good Shepherd with His sheep and holding a metal crook. A simple arch spans the corner by the inner door where once was a *stoup*.

Stepping inside, one is faced by a huge painting of *St Christopher* on the n. wall, at least, there is a large area of pale brown in which some of the remains can be identified. His legs, body, one arm and a hand are clear, and there are faint traces of the fisherman hermit, wearing a deep hood, standing within the doorway of his hut on the r. Below him, more distinctly, is a smaller figure crouching with a blurred rabbit, but of the heron, otter, and lobster that *Cautley* saw I could discern no trace. In the blocked n. doorway is a gilded and coloured war memorial Calvary designed by F.E. Howard, and in the centre of the nave, a survival from the earlier church – a fine early-C14 *font*. It stands on a reeded shaft (as at Thurston), and the bowl panels contain a series of figures under *cusped pediments*. Although mutilated, they are an interesting series; clockwise from the e., the *Blessed Virgin* and Child, *St Catherine* with a small wheel held in the crook of her arm, *St George* (for the dedication of the church), with a heavy sword at rest and his emblem on his shield, *St Paul*, Christ, with both arms raised in blessing, *St Peter*, a bishop, *St Margaret* and her dragon. Note how the carvings lap over the bottom of the panels. To the w. is a long iron-banded C15 chest with a divided lid. Within the tower the stair door is completely covered with iron straps, with two locks protected by a hinged plate – a sure sign that the tower was used for a village safe deposit. Above hang two *hatchments*: at the top, for Mary Wilson, who died in the early C19; below, for Lady Anne Belasyse, first wife of Sir George Wombwell, who died in 1808. Another on the opposite wall is for Joseph Wilson, who died in 1851. The

low pitched nave roof has *tie-beams* and, unusually, the space between them and the ridge is boarded in. Note, too, that the *purlins* have little bracketed pendants coming down on either side of the tie-beams. The end bay. formed a *celure* over the *rood* and traces of decoration remain on the last tie-beam and on the purlins. The infill panels are painted with the *Sacred monogram*. There are some very dark fragments of C14 glass in the tops of the westernmost windows, with one good figure on the n. side and a tiny angel in the very top of the tracery. The rest of the nave tracery contains a range of C19 Old Testament figures, with a series of roundels set in patterned glass below them, apparently painted by a daughter of the mid-C19 rector, Samuel Rickards, who masterminded the restoration. The easternmost window on the s. side has a bold St George on a plunging steed, grappling with a psychedelic dragon. This 1934 design, by Hugh Easton, is set in clear glass, with four shields in the top *lights* and a canted *achievement* in the bottom corner. Other windows by him are found at Badingham, St Peter's Bury St Edmunds, Elvedon and Troston. At the e. end of the nave on the s. is a *piscina* under a battered, *cinquefoil* arch and opposite, a gawky stone pulpit perpetrated by William White in 1855.

The glory of the church is the woodwork, for here we have benches and stalls that vie with Wiggenhall, St Mary in Norfolk and are, perhaps, the finest to be found in any parish church. In the nave, the blind tracery on the bench ends is varied and inventive. There are large *poppyheads*, and over 60 grotesques – animals and human figures that perch on the gables of the squarely buttressed elbows. Carved to a high standard, the forms of many can be matched elsewhere but others are uncommon, and one or two unique. Look in particular for the following: n. side, next to tower, a camel and a fox with a goose in its mouth; the first beyond the n. door by the wall, a *cockatrice;* next along, an owl, then a chained monkey; next but one is a wild boar with human feet opposite a dog wearing a saddle; the next one is strangest of all, a cock with a hideous human face. On the s. side: near the font is a *unicorn*, and on the other end by the wall, a boar playing a harp; next to the e. end by the wall is the rare figure of Scandal, dipping his pen to write upon a scroll; by the door, a mermaid with her mirror, and fourth from the door eastwards, an animal dressed as a friar in a pulpit. The bench backs have varied tracery above the book ledge, and the top moulding is close carved. At the e. end, the front three benches on the n. and the front five on the s. are good C19 work to match the rest, and are likely to have been carved by *Henry Ringham*. The *rood stair* rises from a high step in the n. wall by the pulpit but only the base of the *rood screen* survives. It dates from the time the church was built and the arms of the principal benefactor, Robert de Ashfield, can be seen in the tracery *spandrel* to the l. of the entrance. The other spandrels contain leaves, birds and a cherub head. Between the panels there are deep buttresses which have tall crocketted gables terminating in tiny heads. Although most of the painted decoration is modern, the red leaf pattern showing on the sides of the buttresses next to the entrance is original. The choir stalls are quite outstanding. They form a compact unit, with six clergy seats backing onto the screen, and an L-shaped range of low benches for the choir boys in front. The seats facing e. all have *misericords* and the subjects from n. to s. are: a hawk seizing a hare, the *Evangelistic symbols* in the order of *SS Luke, Mark, John* and *Matthew*, finishing with a dragon. The broad ends of the priest's stalls are exquisitely traceried and, instead of poppyheads, the tops are crowned with small figures of priests, one in a pulpit and one at prayer (exceptionally good). The ends of the side stalls also have figures which are paired n. and s.; at the e. end, two taperers holding candlesticks; next, two vested deacons bearing the shields of Ashfield and Pêche; lastly, two acolytes with an incense boat on the s. and Gospel book on the n. Small feathered angels stand on the front edges of the stall ends and there is chunky tracery backing the boys' seats, with a line of pierced *quatrefoils* below them. Over the priest's door is a large monument for Paul d'Ewes who died in 1624 and his two wives. It is made the more interesting because details of the contract between the parish and the (otherwise unknown) stone-cutter Jan Jansen are recorded. He agreed to:

> finish and set up . . . one tomb . . . in the chancel in Stowlangtoft Church . . . three pictures statues kneeling, a full yard high, cutt graven and coloured to the life, the man to be in a gowne, the two women in vailes...also fower pictures in the base, whereof one is of a man, the second of a boy fower yeares old kneelinge, and two other being dead – whereof one of the dead was a maide of tenne yeares old, the other a

> boy of two yeares old, and fower pictures more of women on the other The oldest is married and to bee made with a vaile, the two others maidens of eighteen yeare, the fowerth a child of seven yeares.

And all this for £16 10s. (a low price even for those days) to be paid in the church porch. You may see for yourself how well Jansen carried out his brief. The small organ is a prime piece of Victoriana made by Gray & Davison and exhibited at the Great Exhibition of 1851. The ranks of pipes are painted in peacock colours, and 'Gloria in excelsis' is inlaid in marquetry below them, with the Sacred monogram and an overall dot pattern (also in marquetry) on the case. Close by, a *ledger-stone* once bore the brass figures of Robert and Alice Ashfield who died in 1550, but only the indents remain, as well as two shields. The church's other brass is an inscription in the floor of the *sanctuary* n. of the *altar* for Paul d'Ewes who died in 1630. On the s. side is a vestige of the earlier church – the drain and part of an attached column of a C13 piscina. Alongside are two *dropped-sill sedilia*, with a third under its own cusped ogee arch. To its r. is a lovely little *Jacobean* bench, just the right height for children, with vine trails on the back rail and eight carved *baluster* legs. The C19 *reredos* is a relief carving in marble of the Last Supper with, as a variation, Christ standing in front of the table; the heavy and rather overblown canopy is worked in mottled marble. Above it, the 1854 e. window glass has 15 scenes from the life of Our Lord. Carried out in clear colours with very little shading, they show sensitive grouping of figures with a medieval feel about them, and may be the work of Alexander Gibbs. Three of the side windows contain glass by A.L. Moore of 1906 – figures symbolising the virtues of Love, Loyalty, Courage, and Humility. They have heavy *tabernacle work* above and below and are rich in detail (even if they are not inspired). What is perhaps the church's finest treasure is displayed in the sanctuary. It is a series of nine early-C16 Flemish panels cut in high relief on slabs of oak 5in. thick. The groups of many figures are carved with extraordinary delicacy and the subjects are: Gethsemane; the Scourging; Bearing the Cross; *Deposition*; Preparation for Burial; Entombment; Resurrection; Ascension; the Harrowing of Hell.

Stowmarket, St Peter and St Mary (E5): For most of its life this church has had a spire which beckoned visitors from every direction. The first decayed in 1674, its successor blew down in 1703, and the third lasted until 1975 when all but the stump had to be dismantled. A splendid replacement designed by Andrew Anderson (for which he was awarded a gold medal) was set in place in 1994. The double dedication is inherited from two separate churches – the C11 St Peter's and a chapel of St Mary which stood a little to the s.e. A will of 1453 talks of 'the new tower', but it has *Decorated tracery* in the belfry windows and tall bell openings. With its heavy buttresses it stands right on the street corner and this probably explains the placing of doors n. and s. which would have allowed processions to circle the building without leaving consecrated ground. A fine ring of eight bells with a 20 cwt. tenor hangs in the tower. There are three small round windows in the w. wall of the n. *aisle* – strangely placed below a window with Decorated tracery which has *mouchettes* within two large *ogees*, and fanciful shapes in the head. The n. *porch* of the 1440s is faced with simple *flushwork* and the aisle windows continue the Decorated theme, the n.e. buttress housing a large niche. The bulky *vestry* n. of the *chancel* was extensively restored in 1986 and its second floor was originally living accommodation for a priest. The 1980s work involved stabilisation and partial rebuilding of the chancel e. wall, whose window contains *reticulated* tracery. The C14 window over the *priest's door* is very attractive and there is more interesting tracery of the period in the s. aisle windows, some of which have been replaced. Flushwork *arcading* at the base of the tall C15 s. porch reaches out across the buttresses and there are diamond chequer patterns higher up. A *stoup* is set by the outer arch, three decayed niches stand in the facade, and a large sundial is set on the gable.

The main entrance is now the tower s. door and recent cleaning and limewashing have made the spacious interior light and fresh. The *sanctus-bell window* in the tower is unusually large and its tracery is the same period as the Decorated *nave* arcades (the s. range remodelled a little later). Arches and *piers* lean outwards and above them the broad expanse of wall is pierced by tall C15 *clerestory* windows. The dark waggon roof with spindly divisions and *bosses* is part of the work carried out in the 1860s by R.M. *Phipson*, who was so determined to rid the church of its C18 fittings that he destroyed a great deal of value. A C13 grave slab is clamped by the s. aisle w. window and in front of it stands a heavy octagonal *font* whose almost flat

cover incorporates C15 cresting on the rim salvaged from a *screen*, and which uses part of a *poppyhead* as a finial. The font once stood centrally and by the entrance there is a small octagonal section of stone with C14 tracery in its panels that was probably a stoup. Dr Thomas Young was vicar here 1628-55 but is better known as one of John Milton's tutors. He introduced Milton to Latin poetry and was gratefully remembered in the poet's 4th Latin Elegy. His portrait hangs by the s. porch door, and on the other side there is a small translucent alabaster roundel of the *Blessed Virgin* and Child – probably C19. The s. aisle originally housed the Lady chapel but the *altar reredos* is now a war memorial, the work of Eleanor Gribble. The angels of Self-sacrifice, Fortitude, Victory, and Peace flank a group of the Holy Family with the Magi, and their pale colours are set against a gold ground. Details of wings, jewels, and ornaments are raised in *gesso* and, despite its harking back to the *pre-Raphaelite* style, it is fine work of high quality. A memorial *cartouche* for Charles Blosse (1724) is on the wall to the r. and the pulpit frame, lip, and panel centres are all C15 fragments salvaged from *parclose screens* that were removed in the C19. Most of the seating is pitch pine but two traceried bench ends remain at the e. end of the nave, with a well-preserved lion and monkey on the elbows. The range behind carries two angels which have been varnished and have the feel of modern work. The parish celebrated the Millenium by filling four of the s. windows with stained glass by Helen Whitaker. Taking the subject of the four seasons with appropriate quotations from the Psalms, they are spectacularly beautiful.

In the n. aisle wall there is a C14 tomb recess and, close by, an unframed *hatchment* for the Revd. Charles Tyrell, the rector of Thurston, who died in 1811. The arms have fierce leopards as supporters – a distinction seldom awarded to commoners. The Tyrell family were Lords of the Manor of Gipping and had their private chapel there, but this was their mortuary. On the wall is the monument for Margaret English of Westminster and her brother and sister, Thomas and Mary Tyrell. A crowded group of little figures kneel in a recess, with Margaret facing eight men and four women. Repainted, they front blind arches containing shields, and gold ribbons decorate the square *pilasters*; a roundel of arms from the top rests in the pew alongside. John de Carle of Norwich carved the memorial for Edmund Tyrell on the e. wall in 1799 – an urn like an Easter egg traps drapes which lap over the tablet, and the lettering is the firm's usual good quality. Ann Tyrell was only 8 when she died in 1638 and her little *shroud brass* is on the wall here. The large plate below it is engraved with a fine epitaph which is well worth reading. It begins:

Deare Virgine Child Farewell thy mothers teares
Cannot advance thy Memory . . .

The entrance to the *rood loft stairs* is to the r. and above it is a large and impressive monument of 1641 to William and Dorothy Tyrell. Their painted alabaster busts turn towards each other and his hand rests on a skull between them; *touchstone Corinthian* columns support a broken *pediment* on which mourning women lie, and below the parents are the figures of the three little children – Penelope kneels in the centre while Mary and the baby (who must have died before baptism) lie folded in gold-fringed shawls on scrolled couches.

The last bay of the n. arcade contains a tomb whose top is now at floor level but which was once just below the canopy. The brasses were probably torn up when *William Dowsing* visited in 1643 but the indents show that there was a 3ft. image surrounded by twelve 7in. figures and three shields, and it is likely to have been for Lady Margaret Tyrell, who died in the early C15. The ogee arches of the canopy are *crocketted* and panelled with *quatrefoils* and there is a crouching lion *corbel* to the e. with the remains of a dragon to the w.; *spandrels* on both faces are carved with *Sacred monograms* and 'MR's for the Blessed Virgin. The top of the rood stair is e. of the chancel arch and below it is a tablet by Robert Brown of London for Samuel Hollingsworth, C19 vicar and local historian. There is now no chancel screen but the stalls at the w. end have C15 panelled ends displaying a ram on the n. and a hound on the s. The late-C15 door to the vestry has *linen-fold* panelling and a folded leaf border, while above it Vicar Richard Shute's tablet of 1686 has fat flanking scrolls and a broken pediment and *cartouche* of arms. Dowsing broke much medieval glass in 1643 and the parish had to pay out 16 shillings the following year for re-glazing. Then in 1875 the great Stowmarket gun cotton explosion blew in the e. window and the glass was replaced by Camm Bros. of Birmingham and is their only work in Suffolk. The style is reminiscent of *Lavers, Barraud & Westlake* and the main lights contain quite good figures of Christ flanked by the *Evangelists* with their symbols below, and Our Lord in Majesty within the centre tracery. The s. window glass of 1878 is by *Clayton & Bell* – six attractive Passion scenes in C13 style under sharp, crocketted gables. The *High altar* and *reredos* are typically solid designs by *Cautley* in the C15 idiom, well carved by Edward Barnes of Ipswich. A rare example of a wig-stand hangs on the chancel wall and, unlike Kedington's, this is in wrought-iron with '1675' and 'T.B.' worked in the circular back plate. The letters stand for Thomas Blackerby who was Sheriff of London and Suffolk's High Sheriff and you will find his *ledger-stone* just in front of the sanctuary step.

Stowupland, Holy Trinity (E4): Until 1843 the village was regarded as part of Stowmarket, but then a growing population called for a separate parish and that required a new church. It was a time when the demand was for simple buildings in economic materials and the missionary fervour of the *Ecclesiological Society* had not taken hold. In consequence, the architect Thomas Marsh Nelson plumped for Woolpit white bricks and a plain rectangular *nave*, with a token *sanctuary* at the e. end flanked by twin *vestries*. A w. tower with a *broach spire* sheathed in copper, *lancet* windows throughout, and gabled buttresses were his concessions to popular notions of what a church should look like (even at the time the local press didn't think that he had quite mastered the *Early English* style!). The n.e. vestry door now leads to a small church hall completed in 1985; extending eastward, the design by Alan Noble uses window shapes and materials which blend successfully with the original.

There are stairs in the base of the tower which lead to a *gallery* resting on *quatrefoil* cast-iron columns and very shallow braces. The *Royal Arms* of Hanover (after 1816) adorn the front and are a handsome iron set in bright colour. To the r. stands a plain C14 *font* which belonged to Creeting, All Saints, a church which was demolished in 1801. By 1843 the stem was being used as a birdbath in Ringshall rectory garden but, united with its bowl once more, it was presented to Stowupland and used within a week of the consecration. The rear benches are part of the original furniture but the rest were designed by *Cautley* in the 1950s, as were the three ranks of choir stalls. Behind these, the wall panelling has cresting, *paterae*, and inset tracery panels, with an incised inscription picked out in blue. The corners of the square-topped ends are cut back to take sweet little cherub heads and the panelled, pierced fronts match the *communion rails* – a solid, typical Cautley design immaculately crafted by Edward Barnes.

The base and stem of the pulpit return to the wall in precisely the same way as Battisford's but its panels and the exuberant *caryatids* at the angles are unlike anything to be found elsewhere in the county. How they came to the church is unknown but the work is probably Flemish late-C16. The panels are carved with bas-relief scenes set within scrolls and some match incidents in the life of Christ. From the n.: the Holy Family; the Circumcision; a figure holding a cross and book that has been called *St John the Baptist* but which is demonstrably female; a group which could be the visit of the wise men except that there are only two; and on the door, a puzzling tableau of a woman proffering a child, with an elderly man at the back, while a third figure kneels and touches a vase – presentation of Christ in the Temple? The village war memorial takes the form of a painted board by the sanctuary arch, with the names excellently lettered on a natural wood insert. Its small *tympanum* contains a bas-relief of two angels supporting a stone: 'They held their lives dear' and I believe it to be the work of Ellen Mary Rope (1885-1934), who sculpted the Nativity panel in Bury St Edmunds All Saints. It is a pity that the lettering of the World War II panel is less than professional. There are doors to both vestries in the e. wall and beyond the tall arch the prevailing lancet shape is used again for pairs of *Decalogue* boards. The *altar* was made by John Pamment of Norton in 1982 and the shaped, carved skirt in yew blends very uneasily with the thick oak slab and trestle frame. Before leaving, try to fathom the symbolism of the carving on the large 1860s obelisk by the path – a snake coils round a fallen torch and dips its head over the *chalice* above.

Stradbroke, All Saints (G3): The village sign portrays a famous son of Stradbroke, Robert Grosseteste, the most formidable scholar of his day and the combative bishop of Lincoln whose diocese in the C13 stretched as far as Oxford and Hertfordshire. Despite his clashes with Henry III and the pope, he was a man whose holiness was enlivened by humanity and whose recipe for healthy living was a simple combination of food, sleep, and merriment. The church in which he was baptised was not the present building – even the font has been replaced, but the connection is worth recording. What we see in the spacious churchyard by the village street is a church whose tower, *nave*,

and *aisles* are C15, and whose *chancel* was originally C14. Over all lies the hand of *R.M. Phipson*, the architect whose restorations in the 1870s were nothing if not thorough. He was enthusiastically backed here by the vicar, Canon John Ryle, a leading Evangelical who went on to be bishop of Liverpool. The tower is impressive, with a strong stair turret rising above the battlements like the one at Hoxne. There is a narrow *base course* of shields in *cusped* squares, the angled buttresses have *flushwork* panels, and there are three *set-offs* emphasised by *string courses*. Canopied niches flank the tall and thin w. window, and the doorway mouldings are enlivened with foliage *paterae* and leopard heads – a reminder of the arms of the De La Poles, who probably financed part of the work. Above the two-*light* bell openings the battlements are panelled in flushwork. The tower houses a good ring of ten bells with a 20 cwt. tenor. The n. *porch* was restored by Phipson, but look for the initials in the doorway *spandrels* which refer to John Pype, who paid for the work in 1489. The chimney which rises from the back may be necessary but it is bald and ugly. Near the aisle wall is the grave of James Chambers who called himself an 'Itinerant Poetaster'. Born in 1748, he was a pedlar with a gift for acrostics and rustic verse, and he was buried here in 1827 and, as one would expect, his epitaph is memorable. The n.e. *vestry* was added in the 1870s and the e. window is a Phipson design of 1878, when the chancel was largely rebuilt. The *tracery* is elaborate and very attractive, with *cusps* so sharply defined that they look positively prickly. The C14 side windows were reused and so was the *priest's door*, although the new flint cladding of the s. aisle chapel partially overlaid one of the *headstops*. The high quality of the work by Grimwoods of Weybread and Vines of Eye shows on the s. aisle particularly, and also on the s. porch, which was taken down and rebuilt, using a white facing flint in meticulously *knapped* squares. There are C19 headstops to the inner doorway, but at high level it is flanked by C15 niches.

Passing over an Evangelical doormat ('Guide our feet into the way of peace'), one enters a well-kept and spacious interior. However much the passing of *box pews* and *three-decker pulpit* may be regretted, I cannot but admire the quality and integrity of Phipson's pews and other furnishings, including a tall tower screen. He carefully restored the steep nave roof and the *castellated tie-beams* are boldly lettered with texts, with another banding the new chancel arch. *Wall posts* rest on small stone *corbels* carved as angels and the arms of Canon Ryle and his wife are displayed on shields at the e. end of the roof. The *Decorated arcades* are beautifully proportioned, and above them, the *clerestory* is arranged with pairs of windows above each pillar, and singletons at each end. The tower w. window is filled with attractive glass by the *O'Connors* – grisaille patterns with centre panels of lily, rose, and grape. Having seen it, do not neglect the very good photographs below of the church in 1867, 1871, and 1874. The glass in the w. window of the n. aisle is skilful work which was moved from the previous chancel e. window and commemorated Queen Victoria's coronation. It contains several panels of stained and enamelled glass – shields and crests, with an incomplete *Royal Arms* in the centre. The C15 *font* was moved nearby in the 1870s and much of the stonework was re-cut. It is a typical East Anglian design with *woodwoses* alternating with lions round the shaft, and angels holding shields share the bowl panels with the *Evangelistic symbols*. Anti-clockwise from the n.e. are: *St Matthew*, Norwich diocese, *St Luke*, *Passion emblems*, *St John*, three *chalices*, *St Mark*, *Trinity emblem*. The beautifully clear inscription cut in the step is particularly interesting because it identifies the donors: 'Johannes Smyth et Joanne Rouse hunc fontem fieri fecerunt' (John Smith and Joan Rouse had this font made). Just by the n. door is a wide niche which by its shape suggests that it framed a *retable* or sculptured group to back an *altar*, possibly for a *guild*. Close to the font under the arcade, the *ledger-stone* of Nathaniel and Lydia Cook has a poignant text. Aged 25, they died within days of each other in 1802 'leaving two children too young to be sencible of their loss'. The benches at the e. of the n. aisle were clearly designed for children, and although it now contains the organ the n. aisle chapel retains its *piscina* and *aumbry*. In the s. aisle is a typical 1890s window by *Clayton & Bell*; Christ is flanked by *St Peter* and *St Andrew*, with three Gospel vignettes below. The upper entrance to the *rood loft* is in the wall nearby, and its position shows that it passed via a *parclose screen* round the chapel to the chancel. The s. aisle chapel roof is the only one to retain most of its original timber and a pleasing screen of 1957 separates it from the chancel. Altar frontal and hangings were exquisitely embroidered by John Cowgill, a one-armed priest who retired here and whose golden jubilee in the ministry was celebrated by the re-ordering of the chapel as a Lady chapel.

The side arches of the chancel were part of the 1871 restoration, together with the roof which rests on positively fungoid corbels. The 1878 *reredos*, altar, and pinched layout of the *sanctuary* reflect Ryle's austere taste and churchmanship, and there is a fine display of Minton floor tiles with a portcullis and rose pattern. The piscina is a replacement, but the *dropped-sill sedilia* have original and curiously placed shallow niches each side. The only remains of the late-C15 *rood screen* are two panels which are now mounted on the wall above the priest's door. They have been well restored and the painting is above average quality. They portray two seated Old Testament kings, Ahias and Abias, and their golden robes are intricately folded; a fragment of the tracery survives. The 1879 e. window glass is untypical Clayton & Bell, and the design was obviously dictated by the current churchmanship – which makes it all the more interesting. Panels portraying a helm, shield, crown, sword, and breastplate are echoed below by font, lectern, cross, pulpit, *chalice* and *paten*, thus neatly illustrating *St Paul's* message to the Ephesians listing the Christian's spiritual armour. The chancel showpiece is undoubtedly the lavish niche in the n. wall of the sanctuary. Its generous size, intricate canopy, and mock vaulting indicate that it was designed as an *Easter sepulchre* (the acanthus carving at the base is Phipson again). Note a Gaffin memorial on the n. wall which is much better than his endless and rather tedious tablets. For Elizabeth White who died in 1840, it has a graceful standing figure leaning on a sarcophagus with palm frond in hand. The epitaph is in English, but a year later her husband, the vicar, must needs have Latin for his tablet below, also by Gaffin. Passing the Phipson pulpit on the way out I was reminded that from it Sir Alfred Munnings once treated a congregation of one, Adrian Bell, to an impromptu sermon on life.

Stradishall, St Margaret (B5): A small-scale church, with *aisles* and *clerestoried nave*, set in a bosky churchyard. The tower dates from about 1300, with later brick battlements, and the line of an earlier and higher nave roof shows on the e. face. It houses a ground floor ring of five bells with a 9 cwt. tenor. The s. aisle was added and the *chancel* adapted in the C14, leaving the trace of an earlier *lancet* in the n. wall. A *Tudor* brick *rood stair* lies in the corner between the chancel and the s. aisle and there is a *priest's door* on that side. The s. *porch* is very attractive, with an openwork timber frame standing on a high brick base, and part of the original C14 timber entrance arch survives. The inner C14 doorway has worn *headstops* and there is ancient ironwork on the door – three long strap hinges with floriated ends. Within is a small C14 three-bay *arcade* with octagonal *piers* and floors of honest brick. The nave roof, with cambered *tie-beams*, is almost flat and between the clerestory windows on the n. side there are remains of an early-C17 text which had a broad painted border. The fragment of medieval painting to the r. of the n. door, mainly in red, was probably a figure of *St Christopher*. The early-C15 *font* unfortunately has no step, but there is very varied *tracery* in the bowl panels and the shaft with its line of *quatrefoils* at the bottom. The *Royal Arms* over the tower arch are too dark to be identified with certainty but could be *Stuart*. The *capitals* of the *Early English* chancel arch were chopped back when the *rood loft* was fitted. The loft stair, with its modern door, turns out to be quite roomy, with a small window to the outside. The base of the C15 *rood screen*, to the r. of the chancel entrance, has *elevation squints* bored below the tracery in the panels (the n. side is a C19 replacement). In front stands a small *Jacobean* chest, with lozenge patterns carved in the panels. The plain late-C17 pulpit stands on a coved stem and on the wall behind the lectern there is a framed section of C15 tracery which possibly belonged to the screen or loft. Some *balusters* from a set of C17 *communion rails* have been applied rather strangely to the front of the n. choir stalls and there are instructive traces of C13 wall paintings in the chancel – a band of decoration in red ties in with the lancet, and a matching section opposite has part of a larger scheme below. The e. window, with its attractive *reticulated* tracery, is filled with the sickly obscured glass that was so popular in the C19. Below the sill of the side window there is a *piscina* with a wide *cusped* arch. John de Carle was a good Norwich statuary and there are two pairs of his tablets – those for William Rayner and his wife Frances on the s. wall are par-ticularly nice – ovals set on mottled marble, with shapely little urns, all against contoured black backs.

Stratford St Mary, St Mary (E7): The A12 swoops by, and these days travellers catch only a fleeting glimpse of the church standing down by the old road at the Ipswich end of the village. The building has seen many changes over the years, and the first major alteration came in 1458–78 when the *nave* was rebuilt and a s. *aisle* was added which ran the full length of the building, together with a s. *porch*. A n. aisle was built in

1499, financed by Thomas Mors, and he also left money for the *clerestory*. The n.e. chapel was added by his son Edward and his wife in 1530 specifically to match the layout on the other side of the church. Note how the use of flint had changed between the building of the aisle and its chapel – the stones of the latter are squared and much more regular. The n. porch is the replacement built in 1532. Margaret Mors had left money for it but it bears the initials and merchant's mark of another clothier, John Smith. It extends right to the roadside and the frontage is blind panelled to the full height each side of the entrance. There is a central canopied niche and small shields decorate the parapet; the tracery of the side windows was inserted in the C19. There is an inscription around the e. and n. sides of the n.e. chapel plinth: 'Praye for the soullys of Edward Mors and Alys hys wyffe and all crysten sowles Anno Domini 1530' It continues along the aisle: 'his Maris orate pro animabus Thome Mors et Margarete uxoris ejus qui istam alam ffieri fe- [continued beyond the porch] -cerunt anno d'ni Mcccclxxxxvii' (Jesus, Mary, pray for the souls of Thomas Mors and Margaret his wife who caused this aisle to be built anno domini 1499) There are *Sacred monograms*, Mors's merchant's mark, and a crowned 'T' and 'M' with the letters 'P.B.A.E.S.'. These stand for 'Propitiemini beati ad eternam salutem' (Be propitious, ye blessed to eternal salvation), addressed to the donors' patron saints St Thomas and St Margaret. An alphabet sequence 'A' to 'Y' is carried on a horizontal band of *ashlar* along the aisle wall and buttresses. This is a unique survival and, bearing in mind that it is close to the roadside, it is probably connected with a breviary ritual used by devout travellers in the Middle Ages. When they could not pause for services they were enjoined to say the Lord's Prayer and an Ave Maria, followed by a letter of the alphabet and this prayer:

O God, who out of twenty-six letters didst will that all the sacred scriptures of this breviary should be composed, join, disjoin and accept out of these twenty-six letters, mattins with lauds, prime, terce, sext, none, vespers and compline, through Christ Our Lord, Amen.

Nothing changed very much until the 1870s when a full-scale restoration and rebuilding was put in hand under the direction of Henry Woodyer, a Guildford architect. He rebuilt the upper stage of the tower and added a rather eccentric stair turret that projects on the n.w. corner. The remainder of the tower was encased in flint to match the rest of the church, and the initials of the rector who financed the work and those of his wife can be seen on three of its walls. It houses a good ring of six bells with a 15 cwt. tenor. The whole of the s. aisle was rebuilt and the new windows in the side wall have rather wilful and untraditional *tracery*. The e. wall of the chancel and all the clerestory were also dismantled and rebuilt.

The interior is spacious, and the arches of the tall *arcades* have a vestigial *ogee* shape at the top. Shafts continue up on each side of the large clerestory windows, and the low-pitched nave roof has angels bearing scrolls in pairs along the ridge, carved by a Mr Vinnell as part of the restoration. A large w. *gallery* was removed in 1850 and the painted decoration on the smaller version in the tower arch is relatively modern. The bassoon that hangs on the wall nearby is a reminder that, like many another, the church had its own little orchestra in the C18 and early C19. The *font* below is an extraordinary confection of 1858 in stone and coloured marbles, with delicately carved little tableaux that have suffered some damage in the bowl roundels. The few remnants of the church's medieval glass were rearranged in the n. aisle w. window. There is a nice figure of *St Jude* with his ship in a centre panel, and two dark and discoloured C14 shields (one of the Black Prince's arms, the other of the De La Pole family). The little roundels at the top of the side lights contain sets of Thomas Mors's merchant's mark and initials, and the six headless figures with scrolls in the tracery seem to be Old Testament characters. The Mors family were buried as they directed in their new aisle, and the grave slabs bereft of their *brasses* must be theirs. Only two of the church's brasses have survived, and one is hidden under the nave carpet – a simple inscription for William Smithe who died in 1586, the son or grandson of the porch donor. The other, of 1558, commemorates Edward and Elizabeth Crane and is mounted on a board on the n. aisle wall. He wears a fur-trimmed gown, and it is noticeable that the 20in. figures show no signs of wear at all and can never have been walked over. They probably formed part of a wall monument. John Constable made a watercolour sketch of the church in 1798, and a reproduction is displayed by the entrance. An engraving of 1848 hangs on the s. aisle wall, and together they show what the building

looked like before Woodyer's restoration. One can but wish that he had left the tower alone.

The s. aisle chapel has modern *parclose screens* but there are fragments of the original *rood screen* tracery fixed to the wall just inside the entrance. The chapel *altar* is a time-worn *Jacobean* table with coarsely turned legs which have shallow carving to match the top rails. In the corner lies an early-C14 grave slab with a raised cross of Lorraine on the top, and above it there is an elaborate C19 gabled recess in the wall. The tall stone pulpit in Perpendicular style is a good Woodyer piece and he donated the alabaster panels between the many buttresses. His too is the chancel arch, with its purple marble triple shafts. The n.e. chapel now serves as an organ chamber and *vestry*, and although the builders matched the dimensions of the s. aisle chapel, you will see that the two arcades do not match exactly. The *piscina* with its large drain lies under an ogee arch, and on the other side of the *sanctuary* the C19 *credence shelf* is a copy of the one in All Souls' chapel, Oxford. The e. window is a memorial to Henry Palmer, the rector who restored the church, and the glass of 1898 is an excellent example of *Powell's* work. Encased in *tabernacle work*, the four scenes from l. to r. are: the *Annunciation*, the visit of the Magi, Christ's presentation in the Temple, and His being found there by His parents. The spaces below are filled with sprays of vine against red and green grounds, and angels hold shields with *Passion emblems* in the tracery. The Black Prince's shield has been repeated at the top and is matched by the arms of Queen Victoria. There is an interesting variation in decoration on the wall above the chancel n. arcade. Three large scenes are painted on canvas and portray: King Melchizedek offering Abraham bread and wine (Genesis 14:8), Moses striking the rock for water at Massah (Exodus 17:1), and the supper at Emmaus (Luke 24: 30). They date from the early C20 and were apparently painted either by the rector of the day or one of his family.

Stuston, All Saints (F3): The church stands secluded at the end of a green lane with the old rectory nearby, and the outside is trim and neat – due in large measure to the wholesale restoration, rebuilding, and extension that took place in the 1860s and 1870s. Prior to that it was described as being 'in a wretched state', and in 1861 Thomas Jekyll was brought in to oversee the new work. Here he added a n. transept with small fanciful windows but did not alter the rest of the structure significantly. Apart from the C14 octagonal belfry stage, the round tower has few distinguishing features but could possibly be *Saxon*, with its plain pointed arch within. It houses a ring of four bells with a 4 cwt. tenor but they can no longer be rung.

There is an unmutilated *stoup* in the s. *porch*, and note that the socket for the old drawbar of the door emerges in the window embrasure to the w. The n. porch was converted into a *vestry* with a window inserted in the outer arch, and both n. and s. inner doors are in medieval lapped boards. There is a plain C14 octagonal *font*, and plaster has been removed to reveal arches in narrow red bricks over the windows on the n. side of the *nave*. They can be seen again round the upper opening of the *rood stair* which climbs steeply within the wall farther along. The waggon roof and pews are Jekyll's work and the octagonal pulpit in C14 style was made by a Revd. Braham Johnson (one of a number of Suffolk parsons who were gifted amateur woodworkers). To the s. of the *chancel* step there is a *piscina* with a small, plain image niche in the window embrasure nearby – a sure sign that there was a nave *altar* although there is now no chancel *screen*. Jekyll's coloured brick voussoirs in the chancel arch are particularly intrusive with bands of pink, yellow, and black, and the same brash theme is repeated in the arches of the n. chapel, chancel windows, and *priest's door*. His open seating in the chancel and the altar rail are much more acceptable. The e. window glass by *Heaton, Butler & Bayne* is of the same period and is a fine example of their early work, using clear colours and bold design – hieratic figures of *St Peter* and *St Paul* flanking Christ with a lamb in his arms, and an *Agnus Dei* and *a pelican in her piety* in the upper *lights*. On the n. side of the *sanctuary* is the monument to Sir John Castleton and his wife Bridget. He died in 1727 and their well-modelled busts stand on a ledge above the large inscription panel, he in full wig and she in décolleté gown; their three young children are portrayed in bas-relief roundels and the architectural frame is in mottled grey marble, with two flaming urns and coloured *cartouche* of arms completing the design.

Stutton, St Peter (F7): The church lies secluded, some way to the s.e. of the village, and there is a glimpse of Holbrook Bay from the churchyard. The C15 tower doubles as a *porch*, and its sturdy buttresses reach to belfry level; there are tall *Perpendicular* bell openings, and above them the battlements are faced with *flushwork* chequer. Within hangs a good ring of six bells with an 11 cwt. tenor. There is *Decorated tracery* in the tall

and narrow w. window of the nave, and C19 brick buttresses support the n. wall. As part of an 1860s restoration by R. Hawkins, the n. doorway was replaced by a window, and a substantial *transept* was added. In 1875 the *chancel* was rebuilt and its e. window transferred to the new n.e. chapel. Two *consecration crosses* were found at this time, and one of them was set below the new chancel e. window – a floriated cross, lightly cut in a block of stone. The *vestry* that was added to the s. side of the chancel in 1879 was enlarged in 1902 to serve as an organ chamber, and the tiny *lancet* inserted by its door is a reminder that the first church here was *Norman*. It has interlace patterns above and below, and more sections of the same C12 work were built into a new buttress on the s. side of the nave. The outer arch of the tower porch is exceptionally large, and the hole drilled in one of the stones on the l. may be all that is left of a *scratch dial*. The C14 inner arch displays plenty of C17-C19 graffiti, and the original door of lapped boards retains its wrought strap hinges and boss, lacking only the closing ring.

The bowl of the C13 *Purbeck marble font* was entirely recut in 1850 and set on new shafts; the *Jacobean* style and finish of its neat cover is particularly convincing, so that the 1930 date comes as a faint surprise. The Jermy family were Lords of the Manor for generations, and two of their C17 monuments were moved from the *sanctuary* to the w. end of the nave in 1875. Forty years separate them but they have a common design in alabaster and *touchstone*, although the details vary slightly and there is an interesting contrast in the costumes. The kneeling figures of Sir Isaac and Lady Jane on the s. wall have him in armour and she with veil and ruff, while his son John opposite wears doublet and cloak, and his wife has a voluminous gown and long veil. John composed a rather laboured verse for his Mary, comparing her to Martha, Anna and Ciconia in quick succession, and his mother had to be content with an English epitaph against the superior Latin for Sir Isaac. The *nave* roof is plastered out between the main timbers, and there are demi-angels with shields at the ends of the *wall plates*. The benches date from 1842 and their bold *poppyheads* provide one of the early examples of *Henry Ringham's* work. The tablet and obelisk of 1777 on the n. wall commemorate Bridget Allan and its touching epitaph begins: 'Could all the dearest virtues...'. In a nearby window, two 1860s panels by *Ward & Hughes* illustrate the raising of Lazarus, and across the nave there is glass by *Powells* – a post-resurrection Christ by the shore with the disciples. Another window on the s. side contains interesting figures of *St Helen* and *St Peter* dating from the 1850s; the colours are strong and vivid, and the treatment of the features is not at all typical for the period – artist unknown. The wide chancel arch was part of the 1862 restoration and was carved by Frewer, the Ipswich mason, and the blocked doorway to the r. once led to the *rood loft stairs*. On the n. side, an iron hour-glass bracket marks the site of a previous pulpit, and John Smythe's mutilated *brass* inscription of 1534 can be found just in front of the chancel step. Overhead are the *Royal Arms* of George IV. The n. transept and chapel have recently been screened off very attractively with unadorned pine and glass 'gothick' partitions to form a childrens' area and chapel. The arms of Tollemache and Western feature in the w. windows, with Barrington and Mills shields in two of the n. lancets. The centre window contains glass by Charles Clutterbuck of Stratford, Essex, one of the early Victorian glaziers whose best work in Suffolk is to be found at Thwaite. These two ovals of Christ preaching and his Ascension are very badly weathered, although the *St Mary Magdalene* at the top has fared better. Anne Mills was the wife of an early-C19 rector, and before her early death in 1827 she had made significant progress on an illustrated county history, and it contains cartoons by Clutterbuck for three of the church's windows. Her *hatchment* hangs above the w. arch of the chapel, and there is a plain tablet in her memory by the e. window. In the corner below is another brass, a simple inscription of 1619 for Frances Herdson. I have not been able to identify the maker of the glass in the chapel e. window, a good Crucifixion plus some fragments of an earlier design. The chancel has recently been rearranged so that the *communion rails* are under the arch and the *altar* has been brought forward to a central position. The square-headed *screen* that stands behind it was modelled on Elmswell's in 1847 (by Ringham?), and the 1911 *reredos* now looks lost and obsolete. The Ward & Hughes Good Shepherd with angels in the e. window is typical of their 1870s designs and has weathered badly. To celebrate the Millenium, the parish engaged Thomas Denny to design a new w. window, and although he has done work in Gloucester cathedral and much elsewhere, this is his first Suffolk commission. In a rich and dense design, the artist has linked a passage from the prophet Isaiah with verses from the Revelation of St John the Divine. The tree of life in deep red straddles the bottom centre *mullion*, branching out to form a cross, and the 'rivers of water in a dry place' flow down through the upper *lights*. Listening, watching, journeying and seeking figures blend with a background full of telling details of place – dragonflies, stakes in the mudflats, and birds of the coast. The techniques of painting, staining and etching have been combined here to create a window of great beauty and subtlety.

Sudbourne, All Saints (I5): All Saints is the best part of a mile to the s.e. of the village, and it lies attractively within a broad churchyard alongside Church Farm, sheltered by a plantation to the n. The tower's sharp *string courses* combine nicely with the four *set-offs*, and the lead spirelet with its gilded weathercock completes a handsome picture; the small w. window and bell openings have *Decorated tracery*, and there are renewed panelled battlements. A thoroughgoing restoration of 1878 left its legacy of harsh wall textures on *nave* and *chancel*, characteristic of the period. The roofs were replaced, and a stub *transept* was added to each side of the chancel. The blocked *Norman* doorway discovered in the s. wall of the nave has pairs of shafts, and the *bobbin moulding* of its broad arch was partially renewed. The bulky s. *porch* has been converted to a *vestry*, but the old outer archway retains *Passion emblem* and *Trinity* shields in the *spandrels*. Most of the windows have been renewed, and you will see that a Norman lancet survives in the nave s. wall. In the C19, the n. porch had a higher roof added, rather like a cap, leaving the line of the original and flatter gable showing on the front. The shields in the arch spandrels match those on the s. porch, and there is a small canopied niche in the centre. The arch mouldings are studded with *fleurons*, and the inner doorway still has its original *hood mould* and C14 *headstops*; the one on the l. wears a bishop's mitre, and a spare head has been set above the arch.

The 1870s transformed the interior so that it is, in many ways, more like the church of a prosperous Victorian suburb than of a country parish. The roof stretches without intermission from end to end, and carved *ogee* braces support its strange *hammerbeams*; *arch-braces* meet at the ridge, and all the areas between the principal timbers are clad with tongued and grooved boards. Everything, including the benches below, is in shiny pitchpine, and all the flooring is *encaustic tile*. An interesting selection of

Devereux family *hatchments* hang at the w. end: tower s. wall, bottom, Leicester Devereux, 6th Viscount Hereford (an early example dating from 1677); s. wall, top, Price Devereux, 10th Viscount Hereford (1748); tower n. wall, bottom, Leicester Martin (1732); tower n. wall, top, Anne Martin (daughter of the 6th Viscount); nave w. wall, s. side, Francis, 2nd Marquis of Hertford (1822); nave w. wall, n. side, Frances Charles, 3rd Marquis of Hertford (1842). The *Royal Arms* of George III on canvas were well restored in 1971 and now hang over the n. door. The late-C12 *font* bowl is like a fat cauldron held within four claws, and it stands on clustered modern shafts and base. The Norman s. doorway does not feature at all from inside, but the deep splay of another contemporary lancet opens into the vestry at high level. Further along, the other lancet contains some interesting fragments of glass, including four sections of a Royal Arms which is probably early-C17 and unlike any other set in the county. The pulpit is an excellent piece of early-C18 work, and its carving is crisp and vigorous. There are raised *acanthus* panel mouldings, swags of fruit down the salient angles, and rather coarse cherub heads centred below the book ledge on each face. The transition from beige nave to chancel in duck egg blue is marked by stub columns below a pair of hammerbeams rather than an arch, and the n. transept proves to be an organ chamber. Its opposite number was designed as a family pew, and as the rather fine C18 panelling matches the pulpit, I wonder whether both were imported from elsewhere (fittings from a number of London churches did find their way into the county in the C19). The *sanctuary* walls are tiled to shoulder height, and the restoration uncovered a large C14 *piscina* with a *cusped* arch and stone *credence shelf*. Nine medieval floor tiles were also recovered and they are mounted on the wall within the piscina. The 1870s glass in the e. window is by Alexander Gibbs, whose best known (and better) work was done for *William Butterfield* in such churches as All Saints, Margaret St, London, and Keble College, Oxford. Here we have three large figures under C13-style canopies – The Good Shepherd, *St John* on the l., *St Nicholas* (or *St Clement?*) on the r.; there are pleasant patterns above and below, and a pair of angels in brilliant red robes share the tracery *trefoils* with the Dove of the Holy Spirit. The sanctuary n. wall is wholly taken up with the splendid monument for Sir Michael Stanhope, a courtier who served in Elizabeth's fleet and was a Privy Councillor in her reign and in that which followed, dying in 1621.

Everything is on a large scale, and his coloured alabaster figure kneels in profile within a shallow niche; four *touchstone Corinthian* columns are set across the frontage, and three of them are labelled 'Faythe, Hope, Charytye'. Four epitaph tablets are disposed around, and the family's arms feature on coloured shields. His widow is represented on a smaller scale in front, all in black, but only the lower halves of two daughters remain of what was a mourning trio.

Sudbury, All Saints (C6): To the s.w. of the town towards the river, the church stands at the angle of the street with the *chancel* hard up against the pavement. During the war with the Dutch in the 1660s the church was used as a prison and was somewhat damaged as a result. With the exception of the *Decorated* chancel, the whole building was rebuilt in the C15 and the tower has a stair turret at the s.e. corner not unlike Sudbury, St. Gregory. There was once a spire but it was removed in 1822. There are large, three-*light transomed* bell openings and a *string course* with *paterae* runs below the stepped battlements. The tower houses a ring of eight bells with a 26 cwt. tenor which cannot be rung at the present time. The w. doorway has worn *headstops* below the square *label* and the medieval door is *traceried*. Close to the tower on the n. side is a gravestone carved with the sun, moon, and carpenters' and masons' tools. The traceried n. door is also original and has a vine trail round the edge. Further along, the *priest's door* has good C19 carving. The two-storied n.e. *sacristy* has barred windows and is built level with the e. end of the chancel. The *aisle* battlements are set with shields and although there were once n. and s. *porches*, entry is now directly into the s. aisle.

The interior is wide and open and the *nave arcades* are unusually decorated with shields and paterae in the mouldings. Above the tall, three-light *clerestory* windows there is a fine cambered *tie-beam* roof, with large paterae on the *wall plates*; there are traces of colour overall. The wide n. aisle was rebuilt about 1460 and the cambered tie-beams have large centre *bosses*. In the n.w. corner stands the figure of a *woodwose* taken from the top of the tower. The C15 octagonal *font* has shields and *quatrefoils* in the bowl panels and a deeply traceried stem. The pews were installed as part of a restoration in 1850. The *poppyheads* are excellent work by Thomas Elliston, a local craftsman; they have great variety and those near the s. door are carved with bells showing that they were reserved for the ringers. The *rood stair* on the n. side of the chancel arch is blocked but the upper doorway is plain. Below it stands one of the best examples we have of a pre-*Reformation* pulpit. Made in 1490, it rises from a tall stem, beautifully proportioned and richly carved, with paterae below the *castellated* rim. It is in perfect condition, largely because it was boarded up and plastered, thus escaping mutilation and the accidental damage of the years. Uncovered by chance in 1850, it was restored by *Henry Ringham*; the plinth, monogram and steps are modern. Ringham may well have made the reading desks designed by C.F. Sprague which incorporate panels from the old *rood screen*. The oak lectern is in the form of a well-carved standing angel with uplifted arms and is a memorial to the men of the parish who fell in World War I. There is a *stoup* by the s. door and the remains of a *piscina* by the entrance to the s. aisle chapel. This was originally a *chantry chapel* founded by the Felton family in the C15 and its *parclose screens* are similar to those at St Peter's, Sudbury; they are tall, with *cusped* and *crocketted* arches and dense tracery above, topped by a vine trail and cresting. The chapel piscina has carving in the *spandrels* of the arch. The C14 chancel clerestory windows are blocked and the *High altar* is a Stuart *Holy table*. On the s. wall is a monument for Thomas Fenn (1818) and his family by *John Bacon the Younger* and Samuel Manning, redeemed from mediocrity by a bas-relief roundel of the Good Samaritan at the bottom. The n. aisle chapel was probably rebuilt at the same time as the aisle and was the chapel first of the Waldegrave family and then of the Edens. Thomas Eden became patron of the living at the *Dissolution* and was Clerk of the Star Chamber in 1551. Suffolk and n. Essex were Puritan strongholds and the Burkitt family, who had a vault here, were kin to Cromwell and entertained John Bunyan when he visited Sudbury. Although most of the chapel is now taken up by the organ, there is an interesting painted genealogy of the Eden family on the e. wall dating from 1622. It spans five generations and, while the names have faded away, many of the shields of arms remain. Returning to the w. end, the tower arch is wide and open and the 1880s screen incorporates two more panels from the base of the old rood screen. The glass in the w. window is one of the few Suffolk examples of the work of *Walter Tower*, successor to Charles Kempe, and was installed in 1927.

Sudbury, St Gregory (C6): Sudbury's most handsome and important church stands in a spacious churchyard beyond a triangular green on the w. side of the town. The tower is solidly impressive, with a prominent stair turret rising above the battlements at the s.e. corner. The diagonal buttresses have five *set-offs* and are linked by well-defined *string courses*. *Put-log holes* show up plainly in the walls. The tower houses a good ring of eight bells with a 15 cwt. tenor. A tomb at the base of the turret was moved from within the church, probably during the Commonwealth, and it is possible that it was once used as an *Easter sepulchre* in the *sanctuary*. The chest is decorated with shields within lozenges, and below the *traceried* hood of the shallow canopy there are indents showing that it originally carried *brasses* of two figures and an inscription (for whom, we have no means of telling). The *priest's door* on the s. of the *chancel* has leaf carvings in the *spandrels* and the square *label* drops to worn *headstops*. Nearby, the pinholes of two *scratch dials* survive in a buttress. The red brick n.e. *vestry* dates from the early-C16 and there is a deep band of chequer *flushwork* under the n. *aisle* windows. There is a large niche which has lost its *dripstone* by the side of the s. aisle w. window. The s. *porch* is interesting because the small chapel on the e. side is combined with it in a unified design rather than being added as an afterthought. They lie beneath a common gable with a medieval cross at the centre and there is an ancient sundial below it. The C15 entrance doors have attractive tracery in the heads and a very decorative band of carving outlines the edges.

The internal tower buttresses and the line of an old roof indicate that the earlier building had no *clerestory* and was probably without aisles. The n. *arcade* dates from about 1370, while that to the s. was built about 100 years later, and both have unusually heavy *piers* for the period. Simon Teobald, or Simon of Sudbury, was born in 1317 and became powerful in the service of church and state. He was appointed Papal Nuncio to Edward III in 1356 and became Archbishop of Canterbury in 1375. In 1380, as Chancellor of England, he imposed the poll tax which, necessary though it may have been, was one of the oppressive acts of government that kindled the Peasants' Revolt. Refuge with King Richard II in the Tower did not save him from the mob that beheaded him messily on Tower Hill on 14 June, 1381. Meanwhile, however, he had been making significant changes at St Gregory's. With his brother, he founded a college of canons in 1375 (of which only the gateway remains w. of the church) and built an extended chancel for their use. The n. aisle of the 1370s was also his work and a chapel dedicated to All Souls in memory of his parents now houses the organ. Just within the church stands a fine mahogany chest, with a brass plate on top bearing the arms of the borough incorporating Simon's own heraldic *talbot* badge, and engraved with the names of the churchwardens for 1785. Beyond is the lovely mid-C15 *font* cover; telescopic and raised by a counter-balance, the bottom has canopied niches, and the upper range is set back with pierced *ogee* arches. It has been beautifully restored in recent years in blue, red and gold. The shaft columns of the font curve out to meet the shallow, traceried bowl. Within the tower, sections of C18 roof lead with wardens' names are displayed on the wall. The spandrels and main timbers of the cambered roof are picked out in colour and the easternmost bay is a painted *celure*, bright in blue, red and gold. Thoughtful restoration went on here for 20 years in the mid-C19 under *William Butterfield*. The work included the aisle roofs, new seating, decorative tiling, and very elegant wrought-iron lighting brackets on the arcade piers, made for gas by Corders of Ipswich and converted to electricity in 1973. The flushwork on the outside of the n. aisle was also part of this work. The oak pulpit, designed by Paul Earee and made by E.W. Beckwith of Coggeshall, replaced a C19 stone predecessor in 1925. The chapel of *St Anne* by the s. porch was once a place of pilgrimage and may have been dedicated to the *Blessed Virgin* originally. Within is a large monument to Thomas Carter, a town benefactor who died in 1706. The rear tablet is a combined epitaph and charity list and fat cherubs recline on the *pediment*. There is a Latin epitaph within an oval on the side of the tomb:

> Traveller, I will tell a wondrous thing. On the day on which Thomas Carter breathed his last a Sudbury camel passed through the eye of a needle. If thou art wealthy go and do likewise.

In the e. wall there are three tall, shallow niches, with an *angle piscina* in the corner, indicating that there was once an *altar* here.

There is another piscina in the s. aisle under a simple arch and the first window on that side has glass by *Heaton, Butler & Bayne*, with figures of *SS Patrick, George* and *Andrew*. In the s.e. corner of the aisle is a late-C13 slab which is the grave of Segeyna, wife of Robert de Quintin, a local wool merchant. Below the e. window is the stone of William Wood, college warden and founder of the town's grammar school who died in 1491.

A window in the n. aisle in typical *Kempe & Co* style contains figures of *St Augustine, St Gregory* and the Venerable Bede, with vignettes from their lives below. There is now no *rood screen*, although one panel with a painting of *Sir John Schorne* survives in Gainsborough's house. A pity that it could not stay in the church where it belongs and has relevance. The early-C16 chancel roof is flat with angular panelling that marks the move away from Gothic forms. It was beautifully restored in 1966 following the original colour scheme – a blue background patterned with stars, the ribs in red and gold. The *wall plate* carries lovely demi-angels bearing *Passion emblems*. A reminder of Simon of Sudbury's college is the fine range of stalls with *misericords* in the chancel. His talbot badge may be found on the first stall on the s. side and there is a particularly good head midway along the n. side. A *consecration cross* is painted on the wall by the vestry door, and if there is anybody in attendance you may care to ask for a view of Simon's skull, parted from his body which is buried at Canterbury and kept in a recess in the vestry wall – a grisly relic decently concealed behind a little green door. I wonder how many choir boys have been petrified by that little surprise. The chancel e. window is high and short, and there is a small *aumbry* in the wall below. There is a larger version next to the piscina and there are traces of colour below the sills. The lower panels of the s. chancel windows are blanked off and contain figures of *SS Peter, Paul, John* (see the poisoned chalice at his feet), *John the Baptist*, Elijah and Moses. They were painted by T.L. Green, brother of a late-C19 rector; it is said that he used the parson as his model. There is no medieval glass in the church and for that we can blame *William Dowsing* who, in January 1643, 'brake down ten mighty great angels in glass'. We may mourn, understandably, but at the time the Puritan temper of Sudbury may well have been in sympathy with image breakers and government policy.

Sudbury, St Peter (C6): The church stands close to the bustle of the market place, with the statue of Gainsborough, the town's most famous son, to the w., while traffic laps the other three sides. It was a chapel of ease within the parish of St Gregory until the C16 when it acquired separate status. It was declared redundant in 1972 and four years later was vested in the *Churches Conservation Trust*. It is used for a variety of community purposes and when I visited the building was crammed with model railway enthusiasts, extensive layouts and stalls; the scent of hot dogs lay heavy on the air. Despite a credit card sellotaped to the *font* cover, it remains a consecrated building and a number of services are held there every year, both by Anglicans and Roman Catholics. There was a complete rebuilding in the late-C15 and the style is therefore homogeneous *Perpendicular*. During the Middle Ages other buildings abutted and this probably accounts for its slight irregularity and the weeping of the *chancel* to the s. The *aisles* lap the tower on both sides, with internal arches to n. and s., and there is attractive matching *tracery* in all the w. windows. There are narrow, *transomed* bell openings and stone figures on the tower corners. Within hangs an excellent ring of ten bells with a 20 cwt. tenor. The tall s. *porch* has an upper room and there was obviously a *groined* roof in prospect. There is no n. porch and the buttresses each side of the door have niches. Both n. and s. doors have worn tracery. Entry now is by way of the w. door, and to the l. is a showcase containing lovely banners of St Peter's and St Gregory's, together with mayoral and mace-bearer's robes. In the intervals of completing his showpiece. All Saints, Margaret Street in London, *William Butterfield* carried out a sensitive restoration here in the 1850s. He replaced pews with chairs, designed choir stalls, and painted the roofs. There was a restoration in 1964 and the *nave* roof, rebuilt in 1689, is beautifully tricked out, panelled and coved in pale green with gilded *bosses*. Over the chancel arch is a structural *celure* which has been renovated and repaired more than once but which is still more or less in its original form of a canopy for the old *rood*. There are traceried *spandrels* and centre bosses in the *aisle* roofs, and in the s. aisle one of the main timbers was used with its natural curve unchanged. It is quite unlike the rest, a variation that one would not expect in a church of this quality. The bowl of the mid-C15 *font* was taken by the Commonwealth mayor John Cooke to use as a horse trough but his horses refused to drink from it so he used it for pigs instead! Subsequently restored to the church, it is carved with shallow crosses. Nearby stand sections of the old *rood screen*. There are paintings of Moses and Aaron over the n. and s. doors; these were originally parts of a *reredos* which was removed during the 1850s restoration. They were painted in the 1730s by Robert Cardenall, a local artist who had studied under Kneller. There is a *piscina* at the e. end of the s. aisle and the s. aisle chapel is separated from the chancel by a beautiful *parclose screen*; it is tall, with *cusped* and *crocketted ogee* arches, with dense tracery above and delicate cresting. The complementary screen on the n. side fronts the organ. The *altar* in the s. chapel is a heavily carved piece of 1907; the *retable* under heavy canopy work is a deep bas-relief based on da Vinci's Last Supper, flanked by *St Peter, St Gregory* and the *Four Evangelists*. The front panel carving is a Nativity, with angels and Old Testament prophets on either side. There is a piscina in the corner. The chancel arch is Victorianised and painted, and the almost flat roof is splendid in green and gold, with a red and white celure; there are large leaf bosses and a line of angel bosses up the centre. The *reredos* was designed by *George F. Bodley* in 1898. It is tall, and contained within a richly carved vine border; the crucified Christ occupies the centre, flanked by the *Blessed Virgin* and *St John* in niches; there are pairs of angels below, with an *Annunciation* in the centre, a splendid thing in which dull gold and plum red predominate. On each side there are deep curtains hung from hinged filigree brackets. The 1856 e. window was designed by John Hardman Powell (*Hardman's* nephew) for Butterfield.

Sutton, All Saints (H6): The body of the church was destroyed by fire in 1616, and its ruined tower which stood at the s. entrance finally collapsed in 1642. Thus we are left with a simple *nave* and *chancel*. There was a restoration by Morgan and *Phipson* in 1859, and another by E. Low in 1876 when the porch was added. The n. door is now blocked by a heating chamber and chimney, and most of the windows have been renewed. However, the one with 'Y' *tracery* in the chancel n. wall looks authentic and would give a date of about 1300. Just to the w. of it, a tiny *quatrefoil* window lights the *rood loft stair* within. There is a *priest's door* on the s. side, and the tall, shallow Victorian porch has a triplet of niches in the gable. The *gargoyle* with a gaping mouth that lies by the entrance is perhaps the only surviving remnant of the old tower. Having lost their ring of four bells when the tower fell, in 1713 the parish ordered a single bell from Gardiner of Sudbury and hung it on a frame in the churchyard. It was stolen and then recovered in the 1990s and stood for a while in the church. The parish celebrated the Millenium by mounting the bell in a free-standing tower s. of the chancel. Four sturdy oak posts standing on a cross-frame support the louvred bell-chamber under a tiled roof, and the bell is rung electronically from within the church. It is also a memorial for the couple who had served the village faithfully for many years in the shop and post office.

Through a C14 inner doorway to a wide nave whose waggon roof is plastered out. There are C19 zinc *Decalogue* plates at the w. end. The early-C15 *font* is particularly interesting, and its scheme of ornament is unique in Norfolk and Suffolk. Anti-clockwise from the s.e., the carvings in the bowl panels represent God the Father; the ox of *St Luke; St Mary Magdalene*, with her flowing tresses and damaged box of ointment; the angel of *St Matthew; St Gabriel;* the lion of *St Mark;* the *Blessed Virgin* with her book and the angel's hand in the corner, forming an *Annunciation* pair with *St Gabriel;* the eagle of *St John.* Below the bowl, there is a sequence of heads which relate to the priestly hierarchy – a cardinal (s.), bishop, tonsured monk, two other men, a woman in hood and wimple, and a boy. Between them, there are objects associated with the mass: anti-clockwise from the s.w. – *chalice, paten, cruet,* ewer, missal, holy water pot, holy water sprinkler, napkin on a rail. The figures round the shaft are badly damaged, but a deacon holding the gospel book can be recognised at the n.e., and the figure in cassock and surplice at the n.w. possibly holds a cross. With the intervening figures, there seems little doubt that they represented all those who officiated at mass, and remind one of the similar sequence in the roof at Bury St Edmund's St Mary's. The C19 pine benches have carved and pierced roundels in the ends, and a s. nave window contains excellent 1870s glass by *Clayton & Bell,* the panels illustrate the Resurrection, Ascension, the *Three Marys,* and Christ with *St Mary Magdalene* on the first Easter Day; Christ presiding at the Last Supper is in the tracery. There is no *rood screen* now, but the stairs that led to the *loft* remain in the n. wall. It appears that when the screen was dismantled in the C19, sections of its tracery were saved and inserted in the new *communion rails.* The splay of the window just beyond the pulpit has a lovely little medieval doodle scratched in one of the stones facing the altar – a demon's head, with a long, lolling tongue. The *sanctuary* is paved with *encaustic tiles,* and the e. wall and *reredos* are in mottled marble, with vine and wheat emblems on either side of a cross. The *piscina* arch is cut into by the e. wall, which suggests that the chancel was shortened slightly as a result of the C17 fire damage. The glass in the sanctuary s. window is again by Clayton & Bell, but the 1860s e. window is by *William Warrington.* The lively design has three good panels illustrating the parable of the Good Samaritan, and lions sport on the rich canopies – all in vivid colour.

The Sutton Hoo ship burial was one of the most spectacular archaeological discoveries of the C20. The site is not far away, and Edith Pretty, who prompted the excavation, lies buried in the n. churchyard close to the single pine.

Sweffling, St Mary (H4): A spacious churchyard rises fairly steeply above the village street, setting off the church to advantage. The tower has a *Decorated* w. window, there is a blocked belfry *lancet* above it, and the bell openings and parapet have been substantially altered – in fact, the proportions of the top stage suggest that the tower may have been truncated at some time. Two tall panels of *flushwork* are very curiously placed below the w. window, and as there is a similar arrangement at nearby Rendham, the same mason may have been involved. Walking round, you will see that the tops of the *nave* walls have been replaced in brick (C18 or early-C19?), and the line of the medieval roof shows on the e. wall of the tower. A large lean-to schoolroom with 'gothick' windows was built on to the n. side in the early 1800s, and there is a slab-shaped brick *rood stair turret* further along. Beyond it, the *coursed* flints in the *chancel* n. wall and the lancets point to a C13 date. The e. window of about 1300 has intersected 'Y' *tracery,* and there is a small blocked niche above it, with the stump of a medieval cross on the gable. The chancel s. wall seems to have been rebuilt, probably when the roof was replaced in 1832, and the *priest's door* is unashamedly domestic. The *Perpendicular* nave windows have rather nice pop-eyed beast *stops,* and the late-C15 or early-C16 *porch* is quite a showpiece. There are *gargoyles* above the blocked side windows, and the parapet is decorated with good flush-work panelling, displaying crowned 'M's and 'S's for the dedication. The entrance is flanked by flushwork, and a trio of *groined* and canopied niches is set below the gable. The archway has worn lion stops, and in the *spandrels,* a dragon confronts either *St George* or a *woodwose* – the stone is too eroded to be certain which. The *Transitional* inner doorway has a rounded arch, but with a simple roll moulding, and the little *capitals* of the shafts are carved with upright leaves.

St Mary's has a good ring of six bells with a 6 cwt. tenor, and a platform for the ringers is set within the plain C14 tower arch. Underneath there is a fascinating selection of C19 and C20 village photographs. Fretwork was a popular hobby in the early years of the C20 and the Lord's Prayer, framed on the w. wall, is a typical example (there is another like it at Westleton). The schoolroom is now used as a *vestry* and one enters through the original n. doorway which is probably the same age as the main entrance. *Fonts of Purbeck marble* were mass-produced in the C13, and this one has the usual pairs of shallow arches carved on the sides of its canted bowl (shaft and base are modern). The neat, early-C19 chamber organ by Samuel Parsons (note the retractable keyboard), came to the church in 1925, and it was moved to the w. end during an overall renovation in the 1970s. The nave, with its 1880s pews, is neat and bright below a plastered ceiling, and there is an interesting early-C18 *Decalogue* painted on the n. wall. The texts are displayed within a pair of 'mock marble' arches, there are smiling cherub heads in the top corners, and a brown frame links the side panels. Look closely under the 'Amen' of the Lord's Prayer, and you will see the outlines of an earlier C17 text with a different layout. A faded but vigorous set of Queen Anne *Royal Arms* hangs above, which were displayed on the chancel *screen* until it was demolished in the 1830s. A nave window contains glass by Paul Quail, installed in 1988. The theme: 'I will make you fishers of men' (Matthew 4:19) is illustrated by an attractive beach scene, banded across the two lights, but aspects of it are a little strange. Christ is conventionally portrayed in robe and sandals, but *St Peter* wears a fisherman's slop and wellies – and where is *St Andrew*? Other windows by this artist can be seen at Hopton, Somerleyton, and Walton St Mary. The openwork triangular pulpit is the same weird design as the one at Cransford, no doubt from the same local joiner's shop. The Victorian *communion rails* are like Cransford's too – the ingeniously telescopic brass variety. In the *sanctuary*, the *cinquefoiled* arch of the *piscina* survives, but there is no drain. At some stage, the bowl of the font was let into the wall below, and that arrangement continued until the mid-C19. Strolling back down the path outside, one recalls that John Cowper Powys once wrote a sonnet in Swefling churchyard (another of that extraordinary and talented family was living at White House Farm at the time):

There is a spirit in these ancient stones,
These grassy mounds and immemorial
    trees
That scarce seem conscious of the passing
    breeze,
So deep they brood above the sleeping
    bones...

Swefling has an older poetic connection in that Suffolk's own best poet George Crabbe held a curacy here from 1795 to 1805 while living at Parham and Great Glemham.

Swilland, St Mary (F5): *Pevsner* called the top of the tower 'an extraordinary Victorian contraption' and did not at all approve, but I find it beguiling and would miss its half-timbered eccentricity, all those gables, dormers, and the perky lantern. It was designed in 1897 by John Corder, the architect who rebuilt Hepworth in much more conservative fashion the following year. Below it, the tower is in C16 brick with diamond patterns in darker colour, and the sturdy stair turret has a little window at the top shaped like a slanting oriental eye. There are small eroded shields carved with initials in the *spandrels* of the w. doorway, and on the door itself one can just trace the outline of *linen-fold panelling* that has been worn away by the weather. A brick and tile shed has been tacked onto the n. wall and part of the blocked n. doorway peeps out from behind it. There are C13 *lancets* in the *nave*, together with a single *Decorated* window on the s. side, and the roof continues uninterrupted over the *chancel* which was shortened in the C19 and given a new brick e. wall. Note that a blocked *low side window* is still set in the s. wall, and to its l. there is a *scratch dial* on the s.e. corner of the nave. The light-weight glazed wooden porch protects a *Norman* s. doorway which looks as though it lost its flanking shafts early on. The clue is that a section was cut out some time in the Middle Ages so that a *stoup* could be added. That too has gone, but it is very interesting that below it there is the original scratch dial which was replaced by another to the r. when the stoup got in the way. The outer rim of arch decoration is largely replacement, but within it is a thick *chevron*, a deep channel moulding, and a double band of diaper work. There are scalloped *capitals* but the *tympanum* has been filled with plain brick. The neatly kept interior lies under a *false hammerbeam*, arch-braced roof which has *embattled* collars, *king posts*, and a *tie-beam* at the w. end. This is matched by another at the chancel entrance which probably served as a *rood beam*. The Victorians covered the plain C14 *font* with painted patterns and texts which are now fading away and they provided the cover. The oak benches with *poppyheads* date from the same period, and their solid competence makes me wonder whether *Ringham* was responsible. The contemporary glass in the nave windows is quite pleasing, featuring the *Blessed Virgin, St Felix, St Edmund*, and *St Richard* (an unusual choice dictated by the name of the vicar commemorated). The last is possibly by *Clayton & Bell* and shows the saintly bishop richly vested. The *Royal Arms* of Queen Anne that are framed on the wall by the organ are undoubtedly the best for their period in Suffolk. Measuring only 27in. by 22in., they are carved in stained lime, pierced and deeply undercut; the detail is exquisite and apart from a little worming the condition is excellent. Nice to have them at eye level. The *Stuart* pulpit has conventional panel work of the period and may well have had a back and *tester* to match originally. A small Russian ikon stands at the centre of the *altar*, and behind it is a fine *reredos* in the *Comper* or *Bodley* manner (although I have not traced the designer). There are twenty small gilt figures of apostles and Evangelists ranged in three ranks about a centre Crucifixion, and the decoration is in muted blue and gold.

Syleham, St Mary (G3): Girt with trees, the church lies secluded in the water meadows close to the Waveney and is almost a mile from its village. It requires some effort to imagine the scene, but apparently the Baron Bigod swore submission to Henry II here in the church in 1174 and surrendered his castles of Framlingham and Bungay to the crown. The *nave* roof was replaced in the C19 at a much lower level, but the *chancel* was left alone so that a large bite seems to have been taken from the profile. The plain *Norman* round tower with its *coursed* flints seems to have earlier work at the base and there is some *long and short work* at the n.w. angle of the nave, both indications that the original church was *Saxon*. The *lancet* bell openings and the *flushwork* panels in the upper stage of the tower may date from the C19 or they may be restored C14 work. The n. doorway is blocked and two of the original lancets of the C13 chancel survive on the n. side. The e. window is a Victorian replacement and those in the nave are *Perpendicular*. Just under the eaves on the s. side there is a plate which reads: 'These leads were repeard. E. Backler churchwarden 1737.' The outer arch of the porch is decorated with *fleurons* and crowns, and the inner doorway has plain shields in the mouldings, two that bear arms in the spandrels, and the remains of seated lions as *stops*. The C13 plate for the closing ring and the keyhole escutcheon still remain on the door and there is a *stoup* recess to the r.

The tower arch within was remodelled at some time and the nearby *font* is both small and entirely plain – probably C14, but it stands on a base with heavy scrolls at the corners which belonged to a C12 predecessor. The rustic cover is like a small candle-snuffer and is dated 1667. The C13 chest is haphazardly banded with iron and has five locks. C18 *Decalogue* boards hang over the n. door, and the nave seating is C19 although there are one or two medieval bench ends in the church. Only the top panels of the C17 pulpit are carved but there was probably more decoration originally. Two tall door shapes in the n. wall close by show where stairs once led to the *rood loft* above the vanished *screen*, and a *Stuart Holy Table* stands against the chancel n. wall. The *communion rails* probably date from the late C17 and have attractive corkscrew *balusters*. C19 restoration raised the floor level of the *sanctuary* so that the wide and plain *piscina* is now low in the wall. Its drain is offset so it probably dates from the late C13 when two drains were briefly in vogue. Set in the floor below is a *brass* inscription for William Fuller who died in 1634 and his wife Anne. In the opposite corner is another, for Anthony and Elizabeth Barry, dating from 1641. There is a nice turn of phrase in the 1730s epitaph for Bridget Lambe and her sister Anne: 'They were two Worthy religious ladies and like the Wise Virgins in the Gospel had always oil in their lamps.'

Tannington, St Ethelbert (G4): Standing well back in an open churchyard, the building has rather a bald, hard look, with a continuous tiled roof over *nave* and *chancel*. The tower has a flint chequer *base course*, and although there is *Perpendicular tracery* in the bell openings the stone *mullions* of the w. window have been replaced by wooden glazing bars. There were once shields in the *spandrels* of the doorway below but they are unidentifiable now. Set in the cement-rendered n. wall of the nave you will find a *Transitional* doorway with a prominent roll moulding in the arch and single shafts (one replaced in wood) with carved *capitals*. Farther along there is a very pretty C14 *lancet* with a pair of *mouchettes* at the top. The intersected 'Y' tracery of the chancel e. window dates it at about 1300, although the side windows are C15 insertions, and a drain-pipe hopper carries the date of the full-scale restoration that took place in 1879. The facade of the attractive C15 *porch* is covered in *flushwork*, with a central niche and large roses in the spandrels of the arch.

A bright, neat interior awaits, and there is a showcase at the back of the nave full of odds and ends of memorabilia, including a village constable's staff of 1779. The bowl of the *font* is the familiar C13 *Purbeck marble* design that must have been produced on a factory basis – a shallow octagon with pairs of blind arches on the slightly canted sides. It rests on a narrow C12 shaft that probably belonged to something else altogether. The church's excellent ring of six bells with a 10 cwt. tenor are rung from the floor of the tower. The nave's waggon roof is likely to be C14 and is unusual because it has a boarded *celure* in honour of the *rood* that was once below. It has been nicely restored in red, white, and gilt, and there are *Sacred monograms* and roses painted on the panels. The church's most interesting feature is its series of C15 bench ends in the w. half of the nave. They share the distinction with those at Wilby of including parts of a 'sacraments and sins' sequence, and it is more than likely that they were carved by the same craftsman. Despite terrible mutilation, some of their subjects can be recognised. The bench at the w. end on the n. side differs from the rest in having the remains of a seated figure in the top half and an animal below. Very little is left to go on but the cloven hoofs suggest an ox, which means that the saint was probably *St Luke*. Next to the e. you will find the remnants of a Gluttony figure from the *Seven Deadly Sins* sequence, and on the other side of the *poppyhead* is the headless figure of Avarice shovelling coins (as at Wilby). Next are the remaining illustrations of the *Seven Sacraments*, that of the mass (headless priest and deacon behind an *altar)* and Penance (penitent kneeling before the priest, both lacking heads). On the s. side the rear bench has the remains of one figure by the wall and panelled tracery in the back. The 4th bench along has a little scene in which a woman pushes a man through a doorway and could perhaps stand for Lust. Beyond it there are two gaping hell's mouth masks facing upwards with the remains of figures in them. *William Dowsing* and his deputy came here in April 1643 and although he writes only of breaking pictures I suspect his hand in the damage done to these little carvings. On the s. wall of the nave are the *Royal Arms* of Elizabeth II painted by M. Moore on copper in 1966, and farther along the stairs to the old *rood loft* rise in a window embrasure. Across on the n. side the nice C14 lancet has vestiges of *headstops* to the *hood mould*, and by the modern pulpit there is a monument by Robert Blore,

who was a prolific if rather uninspired sculptor. Complete with affecting verse, it is for Jane Barker (1820) and has a mourning figure in bas-relief draped over a sarcophagus, with column and urn on top. Her *hatchment* hangs above. The two-*light* window on the n. side contains glass of 1976 (maker unidentified) in which there are consciously archaic figures of sower and reaper; birds and animals abound, with church and house in the background, and the general effect is uncomfortably close to a 'painting by numbers' exercise. The monument on the n. wall of the *sanctuary* commemorates Thomas Dade and his relations, 1612-24; in alabaster, its twin panels are flanked by no fewer than twenty coloured shields and there is a coloured *achievement* within the broken *pediment* on top. Those mentioned in the epitaph also have *brasses*, and Anne Dade's 21in. figure is just below wearing a Paris headdress and ruff. Inscriptions and shields for Thomas and Mary are on the s. side below the simple *angle piscina* of about 1300.

Tattingstone, St Mary (F7): The C14 tower has a chequered *base course*, and there is *reticulated tracery* in the three-*light* w. window; the handsome *Decorated* tracery of the bell openings features knob terminals on the *cusps*. It houses a ring of six bells with a 10 cwt. tenor. Walking round, you will see that there have been extensive repairs in brick at the s.w. corner of the *nave*, and a stone dated 1686 at the eaves probably relates to this work. The C14 s. *porch* is now a *vestry*, and the nave windows are the same period, but those in the *chancel* are tall, late-*Perpendicular* designs, with a matching *priest's door*. A good deal of brick and *septaria* show in the wall here, and on the n. side of the nave, a window with 'Y' tracery of about 1300 has attractive *headstops*. The tall C15 n. porch has a niche over the outer arch, there are fragments of medieval glass in its w. window, and traces of a *stoup* survive in the corner. Passing through the slim C14 inner doorway, you will see that the e. wall of the tower is supported by huge brick buttresses, and these may have formed part of the C17 repairs. The C13 *font* has a shallow bowl of *Purbeck marble*, with typically canted sides and pairs of shallow, pointed arches in the panels; the shaft was restored in 1850. Binoculars are needed to read the inscription on the *touchstone* tablet above the tower arch; although the style is C17, it commemorates rector Samuel Brand, who died in 1725, and has his shield at the top. The nave double *hammerbeam* roof is a late example, and the hammers at both levels are carved as recumbent figures; they had been thoroughly mutilated and new heads were roughly carved for them in the 1930s; the masks at the bottom of the braces seem to have survived unscathed. A heavy-handed restoration was directed by architect Henry Hall in 1872, and his pine benches, complete with *poppyheads*, were modelled on what remained of the C15 set. Rear-admiral Thomas Western died in 1814, having received the faintly esoteric Portuguese Order of the Tower and Sword. Apart from another at Rendlesham, his monument on the n. wall is the only Suffolk work by *John Flaxman*. Against a grey background, a beautifully modelled woman sits in profile within a shallow niche, her fingers loosely entwined, with one foot overlapping the base; a draped flag, shield and anchor are set across the top. Alongside, a young officer of the Somerset Light Infantry who fell in 1917 is commemorated by a handsome copper plaque, and the nearby window has 1890s glass – rather attractive figures of King Solomon and Zerubbabel, that shadowy character involved in the rebuilding of the Temple after the Babylonian captivity. The piece is not signed and it would be good to know who the artist was. Across the nave, there is a large *Annunciation* scene, by *Clayton & Bell*, installed in memory of Queen Victoria in 1901, with her *Royal Arms* at the top. Unfortunately, the 1870s upheaval did away with a *three-decker pulpit*, among other things, but behind its replacement there is a C14 *piscina* recess – proof that a pre-*Reformation* nave *altar* was sited there. The glass in the chancel windows forms a unified scheme supplied by Clayton & Bell, with ranks of saints in the side windows: s. *SS Thomas, James the Less, Matthias, Simon, Jude, Matthew, Peter, John, James the Great, Andrew, Philip, Bartholomew; n. Mark, Paul, Luke, Barnabas, John the Baptist, Stephen*. The e. window has two ranks of figures, with the Ascension scene across the top, and Christ's miracles of healing below. Attractive angels fill the tracery, and the handling of colour is characteristically good. The plain piscina and *dropped-sill sedilia* are contemporary with the chancel windows. Charles Elliott and his wife have matching 1850s tablets high on the e. wall. She was of Huguenot stock, and it is a pity that her interesting epitaph can only be read with the help of binoculars.

Strangers can be forgiven for thinking that the village has a second church, on the hill by the resevoir, a half mile or so to the s. Known as the 'Tattingstone Wonder', it was built as a folly in the mid-C18 by squire Thomas White (who

felt that folk ought to have something to wonder about!). With its *embattled* flint tower, nave and chancel, it was actually a pair of cottages for estate workers, and is now a bijou residence which has much in common with some real Suffolk churches which have sadly become redundant.

Theberton, St Peter (I4): An attractive church, with its decorative belfry peeping over the long expanse of thatch that covers *nave* and *chancel*. An octagonal bell stage was added to the round *Norman* tower in the C14, and the bell openings alternate with matching blind window shapes below deep C15 *flushwork* battlements. Within hang an excellent ring of six bells with a 6 cwt. tenor. A circuit of the building provides interesting clues about the way in which it has grown and changed over the years; look first at the quite intricate Norman *corbel table* below the eaves of the chancel. It stops short half way along, marking the e. end of the first building, and on the n. side a contemporary *string course* halfway up the wall is the same length. The chancel was extended around 1300, with a *priest's door* on the s. side, and there is a renewed e. window in C15 style. There were restorations and extensive alterations in 1836 and in 1846 the s. porch and aisle were rebuilt by Charles Montagu Doughty, the Lord of the Manor who had Lewis Cottingham as his architect. The original aisle was built for Sir William Jenny (d.1483) by the Aldryche masons of N. Lopham in Norfolk, identifiable by their flushwork panels. Doughty had his own initials and his 'star on a bar' crest added at the rebuilding. The aisle is high quality C19 work, with flushwork monograms on the buttresses, fantastic *gargoyles*, and a separate entrance in the e. wall. A *vestry* was built on to the nave n. door in 1870. The late-C15 *porch* has a *base course* and frontage in panelled flushwork, with a canopied niche above the entrance. The arch *spandrels* contain shields bearing keys for *St Peter*, and swords for *St Paul*, and one wonders whether the church, like many others, had a joint dedication originally. A *scratch dial* can be found on the porch's e. buttress. In 1917, a German Zeppelin was shot down not far away, and although three of its crew survived, sixteen were laid to rest here. Their bodies have since been transferred to a consolidated war graves cemetery in Staffordshire, but part of the airframe is preserved as a memorial inside the porch, and the incident is fully detailed below. The C15 entrance doors have been re-framed, but most of the original *tracery* survives, and the very worn, keeled panels have unusual fleur-de-lys *finials*.

The C15 *font* within the tower has the remains of lions and *woodwoses* round the shaft, and although they are damaged, the lions in the bowl panels are particularly well carved. They alternate with angels whose shields bear *Passion emblems* (s.w.), cross of *St George* (n.w.), *Trinity* emblem (s.e.), and three *chalices* with wafers for the mass (n.e.). Half of a C13 grave slab has been pressed into service as a step and the font cover incorporates part of a C17 conical predecessor. By entering the vestry one can examine the excellent Norman n. doorway, with its triple range of *chevron moulding* and paired shafts. The intricately traceried canopy of a C14 niche has been sited on the vestry wall, and all around there are mementoes of the village connection with Adelaide, Australia. Col. William Light surveyed the site for the future city where a suburb bears the name of Thebarton, and in 1979 the Australians restored the church's s. doors in his memory. A single plastered ceiling covers nave and chancel, through which the bottoms of the roof *arch-braces* emerge to rest on stone *corbels* carved with heads and demi-angels. The inner splay of one of the Norman windows is marked high on the n. wall of the nave by the *jamb shafts* and roll moulding of its handsome arch. There is now no chancel arch or *rood screen*, but the stair which led to the *rood loft* survives in the n. wall, still with its C15 door. The window to the l. is a memorial for Lieut. Col. Charles Hotham Montagu Doughty-Wylie VC, who died winning his decoration at Gallipoli. The design by T.F. Curtis of *Ward & Hughes* is rather laboured – St George (with a portrait head) kneeling by the slain dragon before a cross, with a classical Greek ship on the far horizon for some reason. The C15 pulpit, with simple tracery in the panels, has been fitted with a modern base and stairs. It was moved so many times in the C19 that in desperation, a churchwarden offered to fit it with castors! The C14 three-bay *arcade* is painted overall in very jolly diapered patterns of red and green, and the aisle roof is decorated to match, with *Sacred monograms* and scrolls – a creditable C19 version of a medieval practice. Cottingham may well have designed the marvellous piece of High Victorian Gothic on the w. wall, a memorial of 1843 for Frederica Doughty. The colourful profusion of *crocketted* arches, niches, pinnacles, and angels forms a frame for an intricate *brass* which has unfortunately darkened badly. The

family motto runs along the bottom and it features again in the three aisle windows. Together they celebrate the Doughty family who built the aisle, and the glass is the best example of *Thomas Willement's* work in Suffolk. The outer windows contain excellent figures of St Peter and St Paul in their centre *lights*, with beautifully designed *Evangelistic symbols* within vine-wreathed roundels on each side. The *quarries* reiterate the family monogram, and four shields of arms are displayed in the centre window. A tablet nearby provides a concise biography of the family's VC. *Cautley* records that tracery from the rood screen was used in the 1870s choir stalls but I doubt this. He called them shocking, but they are perfectly acceptable, with their massive *poppyheads* and kneeling angels on the elbows. There is a tablet by Dale, the Saxmundham mason on the n. wall which commemorates Susan Arethusa Milner-Gibson and her children. Her husband Thomas, the C19 political reformer and friend of Cobden is buried in the churchyard. On the opposite wall there is a beautifully inventive *cartouche* of 1720 in veined marble, with cherub heads and shields, for Thomas Ingram. In the C19 the chancel was paved with terrazzo, and the spacious *sanctuary* supplied with five steps which give a clue to the C19 restorers' churchmanship. The sill of the large *Perpendicular* window on the s. side was lowered to form stepped *sedilia*, and the shape of the old C13 window splay stops short on the w. side. The *piscina*, with its broad *trefoil* arch was not altered however, and it contains a wooden *credence shelf*. An *aumbry* is set in the e. wall, and there is another in the n. wall. It is fitted with a door, and although the ironwork has been renewed, the door itself may be original. The 1880s e. window glass could be by Ward & Hughes. If so, it is markedly better than most of their work in the county – Christ flanked by angels rising from the tomb while three guards sleep below, with *tabernacle work* above and below; colour and draughtsmanship are both good. The tall niches on either side were supplied by *Thomas Thurlow*.

As you leave, you may like to take up the offer cut on the top of a humble table tomb by the porch: 'Here is a stone to sitt upon, Under which lies in hope to rise, To ye day of blisse and happiness, Honest John Fenn, the Sonn of William Fenn, Clarke & late rector of this Parish, Being turned out of this liveing and sequestered for his loyalty to the late King Charles the First, Hee departed this life the 22 day of October anno Dom 1678'.

Thelnetham, St Nicholas (E3): This church has a lovely setting in park-like surroundings on the edge of the village. The building dates from the early-C14 and, like nearby Rickinghall Inferior, its s. *aisle* is gabled and sits alongside the *nave*. Its heavy corner buttresses have hoods and the window *tracery* is *Decorated*, with carved *spandrels* in the case of the s.e. window – an unusual feature which, again, can be seen at Rickinghall. There is a *priest's door* in the s. wall of the *chancel* and another is blocked on the n. side. The five-*light* e. window is remarkably wide for its height and, at the top, the intersecting tracery is contained within an outer band of oddly shaped *mouchettes* and *trefoils*. The nave n. windows also have Decorated tracery. The small tower w. window is *Perpendicular*, with a deep *label*, and above it is a niche with a *crocketted ogee* arch. The bell openings have Decorated tracery and the *sound holes* are tiny *quatrefoils*. The tower houses a ring of five bells with a 7 cwt. tenor. The battlemented *porch* is modest; its little side windows have sharply pointed arches and the inner doorway displays plain convex mouldings and leafy *headstops* with a niche overhead.

Just within is a plain C14 *font* and beyond, an equally plain tower arch with no *imposts*. This style is to be seen again in the *arcade* between the aisle and the nave, resting on octagonal *piers*. Edmund Gonville, the founder of Gonville Hall (Gonville & Caius College), Cambridge, was a rector here in the C14 and the s. aisle was built in his time. There are fragments of the original glass in the heads of the *lancets* of the e. window, with pairs of pheasants in the centre and winged grotesques at the sides. Below the sill there was once an elaborately carved *retable* but only remnants remain. The *angle piscina* in the corner has been subjected to over-elaborate and heavy-handed reconstruction, probably by R.M. *Phipson* when he carried out the general restoration in 1872, or possibly in the 1850s because it has much in common with the one at Rickinghall Inferior. On the s. wall nearby is a monument to Sir Henry Bokenham and his wife. He was High Sheriff of the county in 1630 and died in 1648. In alabaster, and still showing traces of colour, it has busts of the couple within a curtained niche, with figures of their two children in oval recesses below. Overhead is a broken *pediment* enclosed in a *cartouche* of arms with a double crest, and the frame is garlanded at the bottom – a handsome memorial for a family that were Lords of the Manor from the C14 to the C18. By the n. door in the nave there is a *stoup*, and further e. hangs an attractive C18

roundel carved in walnut of the Flight into Egypt. Probably of Italian origin, it was given to the church by a former rector in 1946. A section of stone moulding with the figure of an angel stands on a window ledge by the C19 pulpit, and one wonders whether it once formed part of the s. chapel retable. The chancel *screen* was installed in 1907 but the stairs leading to the old *rood loft* remain on the n. side (note that the bottom doorway is C14 but the upper one is *Tudor*). The chancel was restored in 1895 and given a new roof of Spanish chestnut. Apart from the fact that it has *king posts*, it is the same design as that in the nave which was probably put up in 1872. The whole of the chancel is floored with *encaustic tiles* and there is a C14 angle piscina in the *sanctuary*, the larger arch trefoiled and an ogee head to the opening at the side. A large *squint* cuts through the wall between the s. aisle chapel and the e. end of the nave, no doubt to give a view of another *altar* (the church had three *guilds* before the *Reformation*). Below the squint is the church's only *brass*, a simple gothic letter inscription asking us to pray for the soul of Anne, the wife of John Caley, who died about 1500. Nearby, a section of medieval *tabernacle work* is fixed to the wall and may have formed part of the rood loft. Two pre-Reformation *mensa slabs* were uncovered in the churchyard in the C19. They both measure some 8ft. by 4ft. and, with their *consecration crosses* re-cut, they have been replaced on modern altars in the chancel and the s. aisle chapel.

In the churchyard, e. of the chancel, lies John Middleton Murray, who died in 1957. He was one of the most controversial figures in C20 English letters and was editor of *The Athenaeum* in its last and most brilliant phase, and of *The Adelphi* in the 1920s. Husband of Katherine Mansfield, the intimate of D.H. Lawrence, he was the foremost critic of his day. The severely simple stone, designed by his brother, describes him as 'author and farmer' and adds a quotation from King Lear: 'ripeness is all'. He is perhaps better remembered in the parish for his barbed and thinly disguised portraits of local characters in his book *Community Farm*.

Thorington, St Peter (I3): The round tower is an interesting example of the form, and there are a number of reasons for classing it as *Saxon* rather than *Norman*. The tall, shallow arcading which encircles it halfway up is formed in the rubble of the wall, and the stone of the Norman *lancets* overlays typically Saxon flintwork. The height was increased and Norman bell openings were inserted – deeply recessed pairs of arches. Pretty stepped battlements were added in *Tudor* times, and the C19 contribution was a neo-Norman w. window. Victorian also is the *vestry* built on to the s. door of the *nave*, and on either side of its roof ridge you will see sections of a large Norman arch decorated with chip carving. Beyond, a small C16 sundial is set in the wall. The *chancel* was largely rebuilt in the 1860s, but *Decorated tracery* survives in some of the side windows. A pair of worn *corbel* heads in the n. wall of the nave may perhaps mark the line of the original roof level. The walls of the homely C14 n. *porch* lean outwards, and it is off-centre from the inner doorway.

Passing a C15 bench, one finds a few more inside, and there are remains of a seated angel on an elbow. The Victorians inserted a large and very brash neo-Norman tower arch, and there is no way of telling whether it bears any resemblance to the original. The opening above, uncovered in 1982, supports the claim for an early date, and suggests that the tower was used as a place of refuge. The *font* now stands within the tower and is an unusual mixture of styles and periods. The C13 *Purbeck marble* bowl has the usual pairs of *blind arches* in its panels, and it rests on a C15 shaft which is supported by seated lions and dogs. Nearby, the C17 chest is decorated with attractive chip and scroll carving. A strange and apparently unique feature of the church is the way in which the walls of the nave were hollowed out up to a height of 7ft., with a *corbel course* inserted to support the upper section – presumably to provide extra width for seating. The steep, *arch-braced* roof has pendants bearing angels below the ridge, and there are lateral braces between the *wall posts*. The 1862 rebuilding included a new chancel arch, and a very dim set of George II *Royal Arms* hangs above it. Pulpit, reading desk and stalls are C19, although the latter made use of tracery which probably came from the old *rood screen*. A large memorial on the n. wall has three Latin epitaph panels for members of the Bence family grouped below a cornice, with a coloured *cartouche* of arms at the bottom. The *priest's door* opposite has been blocked, and following C19 alterations to the floor levels, the large, late-C14 *piscina* is now low in the wall. It has a *cusped ogee* arch, there are unusual tracery designs in the *spandrels*, and traces of colour survive within. Early-C19 *Decalogue* panels are sited each side of the e. window, and the good *Stuart Holy Table* is an interesting and unusual design which features groups of four slim shafts instead of conventional legs. The

1880s oak *reredos* looks like French or Austrian work – good panels in deep relief of the Crucifixion, Christ walking on the water, and the miraculous draught of fishes. The glass in the e. window is one of the best Suffolk examples of the early work of *Heaton & Butler*. It illustrates Christ raising Lazarus, healing the sick, and his Ascension – lively design and good colour. The n. chancel window is by Thomas Baillie, whose other two Suffolk works are at St Mary's Bungay and Wissington. The family firm made windows for many churches in England, including Winchester Cathedral, and their style was based on the Georgian pictorial enamelling tradition. This window was installed in 1862 and it portrays the scene in which *St Peter* declares that Jesus is the Christ and is awarded the keys of heaven. Strangely, Christ is shown bearing the post-Resurrection sacred wounds, and sheep in the background serve only to confuse the imagery further. The strong colours and modelling are typical of the artist.

Thorndon, All Saints (F4): The early-C14 tower also serves as a s. *porch* and there are heavy buttresses up to a single *set-off* at the second stage. The bell openings have lost their *tracery* and the battlements were renewed in brick. Within the angle by the outer arch there is a *stoup* beneath a worn *trefoil* arch and overhead is a single niche. A steep wooden stair leads up to the belfry and unfortunately the church's ring of six bells with a 13 cwt. tenor cannot be rung at the present time. The porch's inner doorway shows that the tower was stitched on to a nave dating from the early-C13. Lying within a blank arch matching the entrance, it has a plain chamfered moulding and simple *capitals*. The *nave* windows, with *hoods* like a lady's headdress of the period, have stepped *embattled transoms*, and on walking round you will find a C13 tomb recess in the s. wall hiding behind a C19 table tomb. There is a grave slab in the bottom, and when it was opened in the C18 a coffin was discovered 4ft. down. This is likely to be the resting place of Nicholas de Bockland, the C14 builder of the *chancel*. The *priest's door* is flanked by a handsome pair of buttresses and the three stages of recessed *flushwork* panels have *ogee* decoration and small blank shields. There are larger, worn shields lower down and the one on the l. was carved with the arms of the Earl of Ufford (seen again on the n.w. buttress of the tower). Above the priest's doorway itself, a spacious blank niche with a *finial* is framed in lozenges of red brick. *R.M. Phipson*, architect of Great Finborough, carried out a big restoration here in 1870, and in renewing the roofs he added a characteristic conceit in the form of large *crockets* on the chancel ridge. I suspect that the e. window was his too. On the chancel n. side, the thick walls of the large *vestry* are pierced by C13 *lancets* and the blocked n. doorway is a worn version of the main entrance. The w. window had been largely bricked up but in the 1860s it was re-opened and new tracery inserted. Below it, the *Perpendicular* doorway *corbels* are seated, rather benign lions, with crowns and shields set in the moulding. There are damaged shields in the spandrels – the one on the r. looks like a *Trinity* emblem.

Within the church there is no division between nave and chancel and the line of Phipson's waggon roof is broken only by an arch-brace resting on large demi-angels above the chancel step. By the door stands the C15 *font* of the type so often found in East Anglia – four lions round the shaft, demi-angels at the angles of the bowl, and, in the panels, angels holding blank shields alternating with lions, their tails rampant. They are deeply cut; note that new faces were provided for some of the figures in the C19. One of the pews to the w. has a small brass plate in memory of A.E. Read of Bungay – an ex-chorister who obviously loved his time here: 'This is where I always sat to give my prayers and thanks to God every Sunday. My favourite hymn: "All things bright and beautiful".' A fine 1822 set of George IV *Royal Arms* on canvas hangs in the n. doorway and on the wall to the e. is a *brass* which has been moved from the redundant church at Rishangles. Comprising an inscription and two shields, it is for Edward Grimeston who died in 1599:

> By twice two kings and queens his life was gract,
> Yet one religion, held from first to last . . .

Opposite, his son's brass reads:

> The sonne paied to his fathers parts increase, wittie and wise he was . . .
> Wher truth hath writt that envie cannot blott
> The name of Grimston cannot be forgott.

A nice thought. The early-C17 pulpit, with new book ledge and base, has three ranges of panels – scrolls in the top, blind arches in the centre, and plain with centre bosses below. There is no *rood screen* now but the *rood loft stairs* remain in the n. wall. The lectern presented by a rector in 1873 is an excellent example of the Victorian woodcarver's ability to reproduce C15 styles. Its double-sided hood top is pierced with lovely tracery and three substantial lions support the triangular base.

The stained glass arranged in the n. chancel window is an interesting mixture. There is an example of a C14 heraldic border displaying the leopards of England and the castles of Castile, a tiny C15 dove of the Holy Spirit in the l.-hand *light*, with an angel holding a crown of thorns and a small *St Peter* bottom l. The C16 roundels of Flemish glass portray a Crucifixion and the stripping of Christ, in which the two thieves sit naked and bound, a carpenter bores holes in the cross with an auger, and there is a group of mourners in the background. Against the priest's door is a long, plain chest on which rests a fine Bible box. It has strapwork and leaf designs on the sides, brass lockplates, and a large 'S.B.' with flourishes carved on the lid. On the window ledge nearby stands a C19 brass-bound wooden barrel with handle, and the hoops are engraved: 'One Lord, One Faith, One Baptism'. Presumably for baptismal water, it is unique in my experience. The *sanctuary* was paved with Minton tiles as part of the restoration and their familiar *Evangelistic symbols* are set in front of the *altar*. On the e. wall are painted zinc *Decalogue* panels and Phipson designed the oak *reredos*. It was given by poet laureate Robert Bridges and it was carved by Abeloos of Louvain – a three-dimensional Last Supper under a deep, low canopy which is all spiky gables and pinnacles; the two side panels have an *Agnus Dei* and a *pelican in her piety* carved at the centre of diaper backgrounds. Like the rood stairs, the *piscina* with an *ogee* arch and slim side shafts was uncovered during the C19 restoration.

Thornham Magna, St Mary Magdelene (F3): Set just within the park and affording a pleasant view across to the big house, the church stands in a churchyard studded with sentinel evergreens. The C14 tower has a broad and flat e. face, and no window above the w. door, giving it an unusually blank appearance for its size. A stair turret rises to the bell stage on the s. side and the battlements have corner pinnacles. There was an extensive mid-C19 restoration with a number of window replacements, and a *vestry* was added beyond the old n. door. There is a *priest's door* in the s. wall of the early-C14 *chancel* and the windows of the *Perpendicular nave* retain earlier reticulated *tracery*. The tall C15 s. *porch* has *flushwork* panels, large *gargoyles*, and *crocketted ogee* niches each side of the entrance; above the arch the principal niche is more elaborate – canopied and *groined*, with a little mask below the image stool. The plain parapet has short corner pinnacles and note that there are large *consecration crosses* on the corner buttresses. Similar crosses at Stoke Ash and Wickham Skeith show that this was a local fashion, but these are formed from a pattern of shallow lozenges cut in the ashlar rather than the more common flushwork.

The nave roof is a late *hammerbeam* and *arch-brace* design and *collars* below the ridge have centre *bosses*, with others split over the main inter-sections. Tenons protruding from the ends of the hammerbeams show that they originally carried angel figures. The set of George II *Royal Arms* high on the w. wall is, I think, painted on canvas but is very dark (it is nice to hear that there is a possibility of its being cleaned and restored). The *font* is medieval in form but is either a C19 reproduction or entirely re-cut. The church possesses seven hatchments hung in the nave; they commemorate: Elizabeth, 3rd wife of the 2nd Duke of Chandos (post-1803, coronet and otter supporters); Elizabeth Major, wife of the 1st Baronet, died 1780 ('Deus major columna'); her husband John, died 1781 ('In coelo quies'); Emily, wife of 2nd Baron Henniker, died 1819 (baroness's coronet); her husband John, died 1821 ('Deus columna' on an all-black ground); John Minet, 3rd Baron Henniker, died 1832; Mary his wife, died 1837 (stag and otter supporters).

One of the most attractive things in the church is the s.w. nave window in memory of Albert Edward Henniker who died in 1902. It is by *Morris & Co*, from the period when Dearle was running the firm, but the three large figures are unaltered *pre-Raphaelite* designs by *Burne-Jones* – two versions of the *Blessed Virgin* flanking a *St John* at prayer. Set against drapery back-grounds, the rich colours alternate – blue on red, red on blue, and green on red; green foliage fills the panels below and the heads of the main *lights* above the drapery, while the tracery *quatrefoils* contain typical angels. Farther e. on the s. wall is an 1870s window which looks like the work of Cox & Son of London. Stretching across three lights in heavy colour, the picture shows the *Three Marys* at the sealed tomb before the first Easter Day. Three other nave windows may have come from the Morris workshops and have lots of patterns framing small and un-distinguished figures. Most of the furnishings

are C19 – pews with excellent *poppyheads* and *paterae* on the end chamfers, an over-fussy pulpit with openwork reading desk, and a good reproduction of a tall C15 *screen*. The stairs for the original *rood loft* remain in the n. wall. On the s. wall of the nave is a handsome wall monument of 1842 by William Frederick Woodington. He was a successful sculptor and painter, best known for the great bronze relief of the battle of the Nile at the base of Nelson's Column in Trafalgar Square and the panels in St Paul's which combine with Stevens's Wellington Monument. This one is martial too and commemorates the Hon. Major Henniker, who was a captain in the 2nd Life Guards. His plumed helmet and sword rest on a sarcophagus below an elaborate, draped cloak.

Just beyond the chancel screen on the n. side is a decorative little *cartouche* for Brig. Gen. Robert Killigrew, who fell at Alamanza in 1707 and who in his youth had been a page of honour to Charles II. The C19 roof overhead has perky angels on its short hammerbeams, and in the *sanctuary* is a fine *Decorated angle piscina*. The slim side columns have ring *capitals* but the quatrefoil corner shaft has foliage; *finials* and tightly curled crockets decorate the *trefoil* ogee arches. Opposite is the lavish memorial to John Henniker Major, Lord Henniker, and his wife Emily. Its sculptor Josephus Kendrick must take the blame for the awful tomb of Sir William Myers in St Paul's but this is one of his more restrained works. Large figures of Hope with her anchor and Piety (or Prudence) with her stork rest negligently against a pedestal carved with the family arms. All is entirely redeemed by the fine profile portrait heads in shallow relief on the large central urn.

St Mary's has a ground floor ring of six bells with an 8 cwt. tenor and if the tower is open, have a look at the peal board which celebrates a long length of Treble Bob Minor rung in just over five hours – and the photograph nearby of 'The ringers what rung the long peal'.

Thornham Parva, St Mary (F3): This is a small church of outstanding interest, beautifully maintained. *Nave* and *chancel* lie under reed thatch which was renewed in the 1970s and the pyramid cap of the little tower is thatched too – a happy conjunction. The tower dates from the 1480s and was probably based on the design at Thorpe Abbots in Norfolk. The masons were Richard Cutting and John Mason and although they were sued for defective work it has lasted well enough. As will be seen later, the church was *Saxon* originally and the regular *coursing* of

Thornam Parva, St Mary: C14 retable

the flint pebbles in the n. wall is evidence of *Norman* work, as are the doorways. The s. doorway was apparently the main entrance then and its arch, with a roll moulding, rests on single plain shafts and simple *capitals*. Farther e. on that side is a small *lancet* of the same period, followed by a *Decorated* window with curvilinear *tracery*. The *priest's door* on the n. side of the chancel has a sharply pointed arch and dates from about 1300, as do the windows each side of the *sanctuary* – although the e. window has the slightly later reticulated tracery.

Entry these days is through a tiny Norman n. doorway – less than 3ft. wide and devoid of ornament. The first thing that attracts attention is the extraordinary range of wall paintings whose restoration was begun in 1980. They are rare survivals of no later than mid-C13 and include the most extensive illustration of the legend of *St Edmund* and scenes from the life of Christ. The predominant colour is the familiar dusky red, and one needs in many cases to get as close as possible to appreciate the detail that can still be recognised. The St Edmund sequence is, at least in part, the later story of how the wolf brought the martyr's uncorrupted head to Bury

abbey, where the monks reburied it with the skeleton. The most surprising revelation is that what was for a long time taken to be the wheel emblem of *St Catherine* above the n. door actually belongs to a large farm cart, while to its r. are four small figures with a coffin. To the r. of the doorway, in faint but clear outline, is the wolf with a tip-tilted nose, and farther r., four larger monks – slightly pop-eyed and faintly smiling. To their r., two more support the king's head over a skeleton. The paintings on the s. wall were restored in 1984 and form a sequence of the infancy of Christ running from w. to e. – the *Visitation* with *St* Elizabeth and the *Blessed Virgin* embracing, the Nativity with an ox peering out above the Christ Child (the ass is to the l. but difficult to see), the Shepherds with their sheep on a green hill, the Magi, and the Presentation in the Temple. Below each panel there was a chevron border and a masonry pattern decorated with red and white roses, while scroll borders were added above and below, interrupted by *consecration crosses*, of which four can still be seen. The bow-fronted C18 *gallery* rests on two slim iron columns; access is via the r.-hand door to the tower and it should not be overlooked. The neat stair is the same period and on a platform beyond the first short flight stands the *tester* of the church's early-C17 pulpit. There are two levels of seats in the gallery; note how sections fold over both the outer door and the inner screen when they are closed in a neat arrangement that provides maximum seating (a similar thought occurred to the designer of Battisford's gallery). Once aloft, the wall paintings can be seen to advantage, particularly the heads of St Mary and St Elizabeth. The round window with its deep splay high in the w. wall is the best evidence of the church's Saxon beginnings, and either side hang *Decalogue* and Lord's Prayer boards.

The early-C14 *font* is simple but it is interesting that its bowl panels repeat some of the tracery shapes to be seen in the church. In the lower panels of the nearest nave s. window there is a memorial to Lady Osla Henniker-Major, who died in 1974, by Laurence Whistler, renowned for his engraving on domestic and celebratory glass. Birth and death dates are placed in the centre of a flower design and the second roundel displays a typically idealised Whistler landscape framed in delicate fronds of seeded grass or oats, within a finely lettered quotation from Shakespeare's 33rd sonnet:

Full many a glorious morning have I seen
Flatter the mountain tops with sovereign
eye.

The single Norman lancet is close by, with moulded jambs to the deep splay. The low pulpit is all C19 work or later but above it, note the plastered stumps in the n. wall which are the remains of the *rood loft* floor beam and the *rood beam* itself. The square-headed early-C15 *rood screen*, with its wide unadorned lower panels, has been extensively but sympathetically restored. Once through it, one's eye immediately focuses on the retable, the church's prime treasure, whose high quality and remarkable condition is outstanding. It dates from the first twenty years of the C14 and mirrors the style of the East Anglian school of manuscript illuminators. In a highly sophisticated composition, eight figures flank a Crucifixion, and apart from the outer pair, their stance and draperies undulate langorously. From l. to r. they are: *SS Dominic, Catherine, John the Baptist, Paul,* the Blessed Virgin, Christ, *SS John, Peter, Edmund, Margaret,* and *Peter Martyr.* Apart from the cleaver set in his skull which is his normal attribute, St Peter Martyr has a great wound in his chest, and St Margaret's horrid red-eyed dragon is pushed down at her feet; the Baptist

holds a large roundel with an *Agnus Dei* against a red ground. The patterned background of each panel is the best example of *gesso* work in the county; five panels are all gold and the rest are a chequerboard, with fleur-de-lys on the black squares. The designs impressed in the gesso vary – the lozenges behind St Peter and St Margaret have pairs of birds, St Paul has rampant lions, the Baptist has Agnus Deis, and the two outer figures are set against quatrefoils embossed with spread eagles. The frame is contemporary with the painting and in equally good condition; the *trefoil* arches rest on half-round columns painted in alternate sections of red and green, decorated with small fleur-de-lys and roses, while roses and oak leaves fill the *spandrels*. The history of the retable is curious. It was discovered in 1927, having come from Rookery farm, Stradbroke, owned by the Fox family in the C18. They were Catholics and had bought it in a sale. In all probability it was made for the *High altar* of the Dominican Priory at Thetford. Having been away for eight years in the hands of the expert restorers at the Hamilton Kerr Institute, this famous piece was returned in January 2003. It now looks even more splendid and is set in a massive glazed frame above the altar, effectively lit by spotlights above the rood screen. The excellent explanatory panel mounted on the s. door illustrates a frontal with which the retable was probably paired originally and which is now in the Musée de Cluny. The C17 panels below the retable are the right size to have come from the pulpit whose tester lies in the tower. In the n.e. corner of the *sanctuary* stands a plain C14 chest, with waggon top and broad iron bands, and by the priest's door a Bible of 1640 is well displayed.

Before leaving, visit the grave of Sir Basil Spence, O.M., architect of Coventry cathedral. It lies s.e. of the chancel and the two massive slabs are incised with a series of lines and arcs, as though a trace had been taken from his drawing board. Sadly, the surface of the slabs is disintegrating and the inscription is suffering.

Thorpe Morieux, St Mary (D5): In a pleasant setting off the main road, with fields around and a lake glimpsed from the churchyard to the s., the church is largely late-C13 and early-C14. The handsome tower has *Decorated* bell openings with a later *Perpendicular* w. window, *gargoyles* below the battlements, and a heavy stair turret on the s. With the exception of one *lancet* on the n. side the *nave* windows are Decorated and the V-shaped buttresses are unusual. So too are the angle buttresses to the *chancel*, with their long, steeply angled tops. A fragment of masonry on the n. side shows where the *rood stair* turret once was and there is a *priest's door* on the s. side of the chancel. The stone and flint base of the *porch* has been renewed but the open framework of wood is early-C15 and is very attractive, with its pierced barge boards and open *tracery* above the *mullions* in the sides. The medieval doors have a border of *quatrefoils* cut in the solid and the w. door carries the same style of decoration.

Down three steps into the nave is a C13 *font* standing on five columns, unadorned except for a band of cross-hatching at the bottom of the square bowl. On the n. wall is a plain 1840s tablet by Watts of Colchester for the Revd. Hezekiah Harrison (prompting the thought that Christian names are not what they were). In the centre of the s. wall is a splendid C15 image bracket that was found within the *piscina* further along when it was uncovered during a restoration. It is large, with a vine trail carved below a battlemented cresting and its original location is unknown; however, there were *altars* dedicated to the *Blessed Virgin* and *St Nicholas* in the church and it is likely to have been used near one or the other. The large C14 piscina itself has attached shafts with ring *capitals* and there are traces of *cusping* in the arch. Close by is a bronze tablet for Lieut. Cornwallis John Warner who was killed in 1915; it has his arms in enamelled colour, with replicas of his four medals and there is a duplicate at Brettenham. On the n. side the doorways and two steps of the *rood loft* stair remain in the wall. The chancel arch is sharply pointed with no capitals, and there are *hatchments* on either side; to the l., for John Haynes Harrison who died in 1839 and to the r., a modern example of 1934 for Sir Thomas Courtenay Theydon Warner. The C13 chancel is very wide and on the n. wall is a beautifully proportioned monument in grey and white of 1764 for John Fiske. The central florid *cartouche* with his arms in colour contrasts nicely with the plain background; there are small gilded torches on the *pediment*, and the lower panels carry well-lettered inscriptions for members of the family up to 1778. It would be good to know who the sculptor was. Opposite is a tall, tapering tablet of 1839 for Sarah and John Harrison, with the names of their children added for another 40 years; it has reversed mourning torches each side, a torch urn on top, and is by John Soward of London – like most of his work, it is competent but rather dull. The C13 angle piscina in the *sanctuary* has *trefoil* arches with typically nubbly

leaf *cusps* matching the foliage round the capital of the shaft, and to the r. are *dropped-sill sedilia*. The large slab of stone resting against the n. wall of the sanctuary has a bevelled edge and would appear to be the original *mensa*; measuring 5ft. 6in. by 3ft. 6in., it has lost a corner and was presumably buried at the *Reformation* and rediscovered.

Thrandeston, St Margaret (F3): The tower is handsome, with well-defined *drip courses* and *crocketted* pinnacles at the corners of the battlements. The bell openings have stepped *transoms* and the one on the n. side is offset to make room for the stair turret. Three shields are carved below the w. window – one with the Cornwallis arms and another with 'Sulyard' on the label. The tower houses a ground floor ring of six bells with an 8 cwt. tenor The C13 *chancel* has later *Perpendicular* windows and the *vestry* alongside has a tiny window high in the n. wall which suggests that it originally had an upper room. Entry is via a large s. *porch* and you will find a *scratch dial* on the e. buttress which has been moved so that it now faces s.w.

Within, there is a four-bay *nave arcade* with octagonal *piers* below a Perpendicular *clerestory*, and the roof *wall posts* rest on stone *corbels* carved with large heads that look more like C19 work than C15. The *hammerbeams* are hidden by coving decorated with painted shields and *paterae*, and there is a single *tie-beam* halfway along. A poorly painted set of Victorian *Royal Arms* hangs over the chancel arch. The C15 *font* was restored in 1846 and is in nice condition; it has *Evangelistic symbols* and fat *Tudor Roses* carved in the panels, there are demi-angels below the bowl, and four dumpy lions support the stem. The *crocketted* conical cover is of the same period.

The nave benches retain their medieval ends adorned with *poppyheads* and the range opposite the door has buttressed ends with crude figures – *St Peter* and a crouching veiled figure on the s., *St John* (identified by the *chalice* he holds) and a woman on the n. bench. At the e. end of the s. aisle is a *piscina* under a *trefoil* arch, and in the n. *aisle* wall a tall image niche has a *crocketted ogee* arch set around with paterae and houses a modern figure of the Good Shepherd. The nearby window retains a pair of C15 stained glass canopies and some miscellaneous fragments which include some vigorously crowing cocks. Farther along, the *rood stair* has a slit window on the aisle side.

The chancel arch capitals are crisply carved with vines and ears of wheat, with a dove nestling on the s. side – all C19 work. The C15 *rood screen* has had its coving chopped away above the capitals of the supporting columns and it is strange how the lower panels are out of step with the divisions above them. Looking e., you will see that here is an extreme example of a *weeping chancel*, with the centre line offset sharply to the s. The C15 choir stalls have handsome applied tracery in the heads of the front panels and there are two quite extraordinary female figures carved on the n. side stall ends, with hoods falling in waves to their feet at the back. One has her skirt rucked up to display a knee and holds what may be an owl, while her companion cradles a possible cat. It is tempting to think of them as witches. Two *hatchments* hang on the wall above, the one on the r. being for John and Elizabeth Blakeley, who died in 1810 and 1822 respectively. The other is probably for their son William who died in 1842. They look as though they were painted by the same hand. The church has two medieval *brasses* – a shield and inscription in the chancel floor for Prudence Cuppledicke who died in 1619, and an inscription for Elisabeth Cornewaleys who died in 1537; the latter was returned to the church in 1847 and is now on the chancel s. wall. A little farther to the w. is a brass inscription for Thomas Lee French who died in 1909, having been rector for sixty-four years; he was the last surviving freeman of the borough of Eye. Behind the simple *Stuart Holy Table* is a lumpish C19 stone *reredos* with the *Agnus Dei* and a *pelican in her piety* in panels, but it is redeemed by the attractive tiles on the side walls of the sanctuary. The vestry door is original and on peeping through you will see that there is now no upper floor.

Thurston, St Peter (D4): A thorough restoration was begun in 1857, but in 1860 the tower collapsed onto the *nave*, taking with it nearly everything w. of the *chancel* arch; the side walls gave way when attempts were made to salvage the windows. There was no alternative but to rebuild the body of the church and, in keeping with the spirit of the age, the work was finished within a year. The architect was *E.C. Hakewill* and, although he followed the design of the original, using all of the old materials that could be saved, the new church is 7ft. higher than it was, and the nave roof is more steeply pitched. The *Perpendicular* chancel, too, was extensively restored and given a new waggon roof. All this should not deter the visitor, for there is much of beauty and interest to see.

The interior is very tall, and above the reused Perpendicular *arcades*, Hakewill substituted *quatrefoils* for the former two-*light* windows in the *clerestory* – not an improvement. He reproduced the *blind arcading* on the *aisle* walls, but the sills of the windows are a good deal higher than they were. The C14 *font* survived and has a reeded shaft like the one at Stowlangtoft, and six of the panels of the deep octagonal bowl are carved with large leaf patterns. The remaining two (e. and s.) have *green man* masks at their centres, and another green man hides in the *poppyhead* of a medieval bench end in the *vestry* space at the w. end of the s. aisle. The *finial* on the other end of that particular bench has the figures of two women back to back, kneeling in prayer, and there is a duplicate of this lovely little carving on the bench end in the s.w. corner. The finial next to it is yet another green man, an excellent one this time, rising from between two birds with vicious beaks. The bench to the r. of the s. door has a wide *traceried* end, with more tracery on the back, and another like it stands by the n. door. By the tower arch hangs the tattered battle ensign of HMS Wren that was flown in the 1940 Narvik action, and over the n. door are the *Royal Arms* of Elizabeth II. The nave benches were designed by Hakewill and excellently carved by Farrow of Bury with varied poppyheads. The s. aisle e. window is a memorial to an infant who died in 1842, but the original glass was blown out during the war and the present design is by *Powell & Sons* – a compact group of the Virgin and Child with the Wise Men, set in striated glass with scattered symbols. Sir Walter Greene (appropriately enough, in view of the number of green men lurking about) not only restored the chancel but furnished it, and provided all the fittings. The pulpit is a very fine piece of work in oak – openwork panels with canopies and, within them, 2ft. figures of *SS Andrew, James, Peter* and *John*; the bookrest is laid upon the spread wings of a charming little angel and two more stand at the foot of the steps. Opposite is a large oaken eagle lectern on a heavy turned stem that was apparently intended for Bombay cathedral but is not out of scale here. In front of the chancel steps is a *brass* inscription for two Thomas Brights who died in 1727 and 1736 – rarely does one see C18 brasses. The tall *screen*, with its light and lacy tracery, marked Queen Victoria's Diamond Jubilee, and beyond, the stalls incorporate medieval ends, their lozenge-shaped finials carved with foliage. Four panels on the n. and five on the s. fronts of the stalls are C15 and there is good small-scale carving in the *spandrels;* look particularly on the n. side for the man in bed, opposite a woman who may be pounding something in a mortar, and on the s. side for two bats. The window on the s. side nearest the screen has beautiful painterly glass of 1895 by *Ward & Hughes* which was copied from a Norwegian church. It depicts the angel and the *Three Marys* at the tomb, with a brilliant sunrise showing up the Calvary crosses in the distance. The window on the s. of the sanctuary is also Ward & Hughes, but designed by T.F. Curtis in 1912 and in quite different style. The theme is 'Come unto me all ye that are heavy laden...' and Christ sits enthroned among the deaf, the blind and the crippled, in company with a Red Indian chief and a Chinaman – a sensitive grouping of figures below the curved and jagged rim of heaven. Opposite is another T.F. Curtis window of 1922, but nowhere near as good. The *reredos,* like all the C19 woodwork, is of high quality, richly canopied and crested. Standing angels hold the *Instruments of the Passion* (including the dice), and the centre panel is an *Annunciation* scene. All the figures are carved in limewood, stained to match the oak of the frame. To the r. is a good late C14 double *piscina* under *cinquefoiled* arches, with a heavy stone *credence shelf* half way up. The tops of the stepped *sedilia* have been restored. Thomas Gaffin cut the memorial for Admiral Sir William Hall Gage on the s. wall in 1864, and the epitaph was so long it had to go on a separate tablet underneath. Nearby is a pretty pair of ovals commemorating Robert and John Stedman (1809 and 1814). Gill Stedman, Gent, was provided with a plain and decent tablet by Thomas Farrow of Diss in 1852. Before leaving the chancel, use binoculars if possible to look at the tops of the windows nearest the screen; on the n. there are two bishops, with 'Scs Jeromus a doctor' (*St Jerome,* Doctor of the church) in C15 script above them; on the s. there are two angels bearing scrolls: 'Deo Date Gloriam' (To God give the glory), another angel and a mitred bishop. On your way out, study the medieval glass in the s. aisle w. window. Set in patterned Victorian *quarries,* you will see four good heads in the r.-hand panel and a lovely head of Christ to the l., just above a naked wanton with long, auburn hair. St. Peter's has an excellent ring of five bells with a 10 cwt. tenor.

Thwaite, St George (F4): This is a tiny church set in a bosky graveyard, with an attractive plank bridge spanning the boundary ditch on the way to the s. *porch.* The bricked-up small n. doorway is plain and, together with the tall *lancet* in the *chancel,* is evidence of the building's late-C12 origins. There is cusped 'Y' *tracery* of the early-C14 in three side windows and the w. window, with *Decorated* reticulated tracery in the e. window. Two of the *nave* windows have attractive patterns of the same period, with roll mouldings both inside and out. There was a small tower at the n.w. corner but it collapsed early in the C19 and the rubble was used to build the pair of cottages that stand at the entrance to Church Lane. The church's w. wall and much of the chancel was rebuilt in the restorations of 1846 and 1871, and a bellcote was added. With its eaves cutting into the adjacent window, the C16 *porch* in homely red brick has a tiny sundial over the arch, and its *arch-braced* roof rests on large carved wooden heads. Lolling tongues are familiar features of the period but the face on the e. side here curls his up to his nostrils for a change. It is strange that one of the *jambs* of the little inner doorway has been replaced in wood – the door itself retains one medieval strap hinge with chevron decoration.

The roof of the church is quite elaborate for its size and is an unusual mixture of *hammerbeams* and *tie-beams.* The tie-beam marking the division between nave and chancel no doubt served as a *rood beam,* and the hammerbeams to the w. show clearly the remains of tenons which secured demi-angels. However, four of the beams at the w. end do not, and one can only presume that they originally stretched across the roof space (very odd). The deep *wall plates* and the *collars* below the ridge are *castellated* and there are three grotesque wooden *corbel* heads each side. The nave benches are gnarled, and in the n.w. corner a tiny *Norman* door no more than 2ft.wide once led to the tower. In front of it on a plain shaft stands a late-C14 font, with window tracery patterns in the bowl panels as at nearby Wickham Skeith. The 1846 w. window is a memorial for Dame Letitia Sheppard and the glass is by the painter-turned-glazier Charles Clutterbuck. He was, with *Hardman* and the O'Connors, one of the artists to begin the Victorian revival of stained glass. Here, in C13 style, lozenge patterns of brilliant green and yellow enclose roundels and pointed ovals containing the figures of Christ and the *Evangelists,* with a dove at the very top. Other examples of Clutterbuck's work can be found at St Mary's, Bury, Gazeley, Great Saxham, Little Cornard and Stutton. The C15 pulpit on its coved stem is lovely. There is a crest under the lip, and each panel contains a pair of *crocketted ogee* arches with tracery behind them. At the bottom, and below a band of foliage repeats, pierced *quatrefoils* have shields at their centres, and all the angles are adorned with crocketted pinnacles. The surfaces seem to have been filled and it is likely that it was painted originally. At the base lies a *gargoyle* from the old tower which was discovered recently in the wall at the w. end. Opposite is a strange reading desk which, apart from the base and ledge, seems to have begun life as part of an early-C17 court cupboard, with *Renaissance* detailing in the panels. The chair behind it is a little older. In the *sanctuary* the *piscina* is unusual only in that it has a square raised lip, while fixed inside the bottom of the e. window is a panel of C15 glass – *St John the Baptist's* head with an *Agnus Dei*. Robert Reve's *ledger-stone* in the n.e. corner of the sanctuary has excellent, slightly idiosyncratic lettering, and his epitaph is precise to the very day about his age at death in 1688.

One should not leave Thwaite without pausing at the cast-iron cross just e. of the chancel that marks the grave of Orlando Whistlecraft, who died aged 83 in 1893. Apart from the delicious euphony of his name, he was that singular phenomenon, a 'weather prophet and poet'. A small fund was raised to enable this Suffolk worthy 'to pass his declining years in a greater degree of comfort than his needy circumstances would permit'. Originator of the enduring and no doubt invaluable Whistlecraft's Almanac, he published *The Climate of England* in 1840, a proper acknowledgement of our national obsession with the weather.

Timworth, St Andrew (C4): Timworth is a tiny hamlet, with the church quite isolated from it, and there is some reason to believe that this division dates from the *Black Death* or a subsequent fire. A narrow track winds round the edge of a field to a peaceful churchyard girt by mature trees and backed by pine forest. There was a major rebuilding here in 1868, but much of the material from the old church was reused. In particular, the C14 tower with its *Decorated* bell openings is largely original and stands on the s. side, acting as a rather splendid *porch*. Within is a ring of four bells with a 12 cwt. tenor, but their condition does not allow them to be rung at the present time. The stair turret is tucked into the n.w. angle and overlaps the *nave* roof. There is a variety of C19 windows, including one with very brash *tracery* in the w. wall, and the *priest's door* has an oddly decorated arch. The unusual thing to note on the outside

is that a *scratch dial* is incised on a special block let into the angle of the s.e. buttress of the tower, about 12ft. up and aligned to face due s.

Through a nice early-C14 doorway into a largely Victorian interior, although the small *lancets* on the n. side of the *chancel* are reminders of its C13 origin. The *font* could also be C13, or else a very restrained Victorian copy. On the s. wall there is a large set of William III *Royal Arms* painted on boards, and the pulpit is an interesting mixture. The base, with nice cherub heads at the angles, is C18, as is the *acanthus* moulding of the rim, but the panels are some 200 years older. It apparently came from St James' at Bury, and the *communion rails* may well have done so too. They have delicate twisted *balusters*, with groups of four at the ends and as supports for the central gates. There are infill panels each side which add weight to the theory that the set was designed for elsewhere.

Tostock, St Andrew (D4): Set a little apart from the e. end of the village, the church stands in a graveyard where a commendable balance is kept between manicured grass verges and natural growth with plenty of wild flowers. The *Decorated* tower has *flushwork* panelling on the buttresses and closely spaced *string courses* in the upper stages. The ring of five bells has been augmented to a six, and in 2000 the first peal on them was rung. A peal board commemorates the event on the tower wall and the old clappers are hung above it. There is an C18 or early-C19 lean-to *vestry* to the n. of the late-C13 *chancel* and the *nave* e. walls have wide, late-*Perpendicular* recesses, presumably for statuary. The C14 s. *porch* has most unusual windows which, though largely blocked, retain their *tracery*, a large *reticulation* shape with a pair of *mouchettes* above and below.

Within, the impression is spacious, largely because there are no *aisles* and a single roof spans the whole width of nearly 30ft. It is a fine late-C15 example, with *arch-braces* alternating with double *hammerbeams* whose posts continue down in the bottom range to form pendants. These have figures set within canopies, there is varied tracery above the lower hammers, and the *spandrels* are all carved (look also for the little animal on one of the arch-braces). *William Dowsing* was here in 1643, and although his journal mentions only 'superstitious pictures', he may well have been responsible for chopping off the heads of the canopied figures and removing the angels from the ends of the upper hammers. The early-C14 *font* stands on a reeded shaft and the panels of the heavy bowl are carved with a variety of leaf forms. The one on the n. side, however, is different – a pagan *green man* with tendrils curling from his mouth. There is continuous seating along the side walls and the lovely medieval benches stand clear, showing them off to good advantage. They have nicely traceried backs and there are two with traceried ends, as well as two more against the side walls. The buttressed armrests carry an interesting selection of grotesques, including a *unicorn* (third from the w. on the s. side of the centre aisle), a *pelican in her piety* (e. end of the s. wall bench), and a rare *cockatrice* (fourth from the door on the s. side). The four front ranges of benches are good modern copies and were no doubt added during the 1872 or 1889 restoration. The stair to the old *rood loft* rises on the s. side and, although the bottom door is blocked, one can see through the top opening to the little window that gave light from the outside. By the entrance is a small *aumbry*, and to the r. of the chancel arch is a plain recess that was probably associated with a *guild altar* (there were medieval guilds here dedicated to *SS Andrew, Peter*, and *John the Baptist*. It now houses a 1914-19 war memorial. Above the pulpit is a strange tablet by Gaffin for George Brown, who died in 1857; it carries a plain cross with one long scroll looped round it and another beneath. It was thought well enough of to be copied for another member of the family in 1905. The chancel arch is C13 and the attached columns on the e. side have been cut away. The mid-C17 *communion rails* have pleasing *balusters* with acorn tops and the C13 *piscina*, on the s. side of the *sanctuary*, has an *ogee* arch. The e. window tracery contains fragments of C15 glass which include, on the r., a lovely little group of animals round a tree – a stag, sheep, pig, and an owl perched in the branches.

Trimley, St Martin (G7): There were once three Trimleys, and St John's had its church at 'Alteston'. The surviving pair are sited on the very edge of their respective parishes so that they stand side by side within a common churchyard. It would seem that St Martin's was built in the C14 but a series of C19 restorations have left very little that can be recognised as original. The squat brick tower was provided with a new w. door and window and is partly cement rendered. There are heavy, wedge-shaped brick buttresses on the n. side of the *nave*, and the *Perpendicular* n. doorway has been blocked. A *chantry* dedicated to the *Holy Trinity* was founded in the early C15 by Roger Cavendish,

and its chapel on the n. side of the nave was rebuilt in the early C16 in the form of a broad brick *transept*; its w. doorway has been blocked and the windows have been renewed. The brick *chancel* has a C19/C20 *vestry* complex to the n. and a projecting organ chamber to the s., and a recent addition is the large brick and timber s. porch. The arch of the inner C14 doorway has just a hint of the *ogee* shape, just like those at nearby St Mary's, and there are tiny heads carved as *stops* within the mouldings.

The benches date from the 1860s, and the roofs of nave and chancel were replaced in 1897. The *font* with its square bowl has been described as 'late C12', but I think it is Victorian, although the minimal decoration is uncharacteristic. There is a very good set of George I *Royal Arms* above the entrance – small scale, carved three-dimensionally in oak, and picked out in gilt. The *hatchment* to the w. of the doorway was used in 1766 at the funeral of Sir John Fyton Barker of Grimston Hall, and its companion is a most interesting example. Within a wide, fluted frame, it bears the arms of the Hon. George Richard Savage Nassau who died in 1823, and is in fact a silken banner sewn on to a canvas backing. I know of no other like it in the county, although there is another hatchment in conventional style credited to George Nassau among the family collection at Easton. The altar is a handsome early C17 table, a narrow oblong, with a vine trail carved on the top rails, and bulbous *acanthus*-leafed legs. The window beyond contains glass by Hendra & Harper of Harpenden, a World War II memorial in which uncomfortably posed servicemen gaze up to a brilliantly robed figure of Christ. The e. window dates from the turn of the century and is rather better – an Ascension in creamy colours, with attendant disciples and angels, possibly by *Heaton, Butler & Bayne*. A two-bay early-C15 *arcade* forms the entrance to the Trinity chapel, and marks suggest that it was originally fitted with a *parclose screen*. The broad and shallow tomb recess in the n. wall was presumably the resting place of Roger Cavendish the founder. The glass in the pair of windows above is signed with an unidentified monogram (C.A.H.?) and the matching designs both probably date from the 1940s. On the l., the risen Christ stands in a glory above the empty tomb and sleeping soldiers; the *Three Marys* approach to one side, and the scene is spread as a band across the three *lights* under purple, crinkly clouds. The companion window uses the Adoration scene as a memorial for two servicemen whose figures act as a counterbalance to the Magi. Modelling and textures are harsh but attractive. When *William Dowsing* came visiting in August 1644, he listed the village as 'Trembly' and ordered 28 cherubims to be taken down within three days. That means that the nave probably had an angel roof, and he specifically mentions an image which may have been in a window of the Cavendish chapel: 'a Fryar with a shaven crown, praying to God, in these words "miserere mei Deus", which we brake down'.

Trimley, St Mary (G7): As an alternative to redundancy, St Mary's assumed a multi-purpose role in 1990 and the parish transformed the *nave* into a hall for a handicapped children's playgroup, with cloakrooms fitted cleverly into the tower, and the *vestry* has been equipped as an office and counselling centre – a fine example of local initiative and self-help. The *chancel* is retained for worship, and the building is still worth a visit. The tower with its rendered walls is plain and stark, but has some points of particular interest. It dates from between 1430 and 1450, and the shields in the *spandrels* of the w. doorway carry the arms of Roger Garnon on the l., and quartered with those of his wife on the r. The archway mouldings have been partially renewed recently, reproducing a particularly interesting elongated leaf motif. There are worn *headstops*, and the *dripstone* had a demi-angel at the top. Just above, another sequence of C14 shields within *quatrefoils* belonged to the earlier tower. In the centre are the arms of Thomas de Brotherton, Earl of Suffolk and Norfolk and son of Edward I. Trimley was one of his many manors and he may well have built St Mary's. The rampant lion on the l. probably stands for Sir John Mowbray, Brotherton's son-in-law, and the third shield bears the arms of Sir Walter Manny. Smaller, flanking shields display the *Blessed Virgin's* monogram and lily pot emblem. By the C19, the church had become ruinous and in 1854 there was a full-scale restoration when the w. end of the nave was rebuilt, the chancel largely reconstructed, and a large, elaborate vestry added on the n. side; more restoration followed some fifty years later. Walking round, you will see that the C14 n. doorway has just a hint of the *ogee* shape in its arch, with worn *headstops* and a head at the top. The Victorian door has an attractive and unusual two-*light* opening, fitted with wrought-iron grilles. One or two of the windows still have headstops, and the outer arch of the s. *porch* has the remains of a demi-angel at the top, shields in the spandrels, and *fleurons*

in the moulding. A gentle ogee features again in the inner arch, and there is a restored *stoup* alongside.

The nave, with its boarded waggon roof has been cleared of benches and there is stained glass in three of the windows. On the n. side the three-light window is a World War II memorial – Christ in the centre against the rising sun, with groups of figures on either side, including the boy with the loaves and fishes from the 'feeding of the five thousand' miracle; a *pelican in her piety* and a phoenix feature at the top, with alpha and omega signs. Further along there is glass in vaguely *Kempe* style (though not in his class); *St Joseph* stands with a youthful *St John the Baptist* in one light, with the *Blessed Virgin* and the Christ child in the other. Opposite, a matching window contains an *Annunciation*, with *St Gabriel* labelled to make sure no-one takes it for anything else. The *piscina* of about 1400 in the n. wall shows that there was a nave *altar* nearby before the *Reformation*. Some form of partition is planned to divide nave from chancel, and there is no trace of the original *rood screen* except the blocked doorway of the access stairs and upper window shapes. The C13 chancel arch has *responds* with broad mouldings that lap round on each side, and the pair of windows just beyond contain unusual early-C20 glass. The figures of *St Edmund* on the s. and *St George* on the n. have portrait heads of two members of the Cobbold family and, quite illogically, their walrus moustaches seem faintly incongruous. Nearby, on the s. side, hangs an interesting C18 Dutch brass sconce featuring a *Sacred monogram* and nails design but lacking its candle holders. The 1850s roof has painted ribs, and there is a two-bay *celure* enriched with *bosses* and Sacred monograms. The panelled walls of the *sanctuary* below are painted with stencilled patterns, and there is a bulky matching *reredos*. The plain piscina dates from about 1300, and the contemporary *aumbry* in the n. wall was provided with elaborate doors made by local craftsmen, a Mr Howard and a Mr Finch. The s. sanctuary window of the early 1900s contains figures of *St Felix* and *St Fursey*, but the best glass in the church is the e. 1890s window and it is a pity that its maker has not yet been identified. Christ the King stands centrally within an aureole, *censing* angels to the l., a musical ensemble to the r. There is sparkling, swirling colour in their robes, and the whole piece is distinctly attractive.

Troston, St Mary (C3): There are sound arguments for and against clearing graveyards of their stones, but there is no doubt that the church here is set off very well by the swathe of grass on the s. side. The path leads up to a fine C15 *porch*, with three canopied niches set above the arch with its foliage and blank shields in the *spandrels*. The front is faced with *flushwork* panels and there are carved stone panels in the *base course*. The battlements are decorated in flushwork and display 'M' and 'Maria' for the dedication, while the entrance arch has *fleurons* in the mouldings, both inside and out. The rather gaunt tower was built about 1300 – witness the 'Y' *tracery* in the w. window and in the bell openings. The oldest part of the building, however, is the *chancel*. Dating from the C13, it has small *lancets* in the side walls and an e. window formed of three stepped lancets. A most unusual feature of the *nave* is the way in which the roof timbers that project under the eaves have been roughly shaped and decorated with carving, a probable C17 addition.

The C14 doorway into the church has holes in the inner *jambs* for a drawbar, and one passes into a nave that was built about 1320. The window tracery employs the four-petalled flower design which was a favourite in the *Decorated* period. The sharply pointed tower arch fades into the *imposts*, and above is a *sanctus-bell window* almost hidden in the roof timbers. The *font* is a plain octagon on a cylindrical shaft and is probably C13; the cover is crude C17 work. There are some medieval bench ends at the w. end with mutilated grotesques on the elbows, but most of the benches in the nave were carved by Robert Emelyn Lofft when he had the church restored in 1869, and they are unique in their weird ugliness. There are some fine medieval paintings on the n. wall: from the w., a large-scale C15 *St George* slaying the dragon (very attractive in pale red and white); a huge C15 *St Christopher* beyond the unused n. door; an earlier and much smaller mid-C13 St George in silhouette; a C14 martyrdom of *St Edmund* which shows the king, an archer drawing a bow, and another figure beyond. Over the chancel arch are the faint remains of a painted *Doom*, and one can just make out the figure of Christ in the centre. On the s. wall of the nave is a small set of *Royal Arms* painted on board. They have been overpainted with 'G.R.' for one of the Georges, but the arms are those of James I, with the inscription 'Exurgat Deus dissipentur inimici' (Let God arise and let his enemies be scattered) – not at all common. The two-decker pulpit is a large and very odd combination. The pulpit itself is *Jacobean*, with typical panel decoration

and canted reading ledge, but a massive reading desk was added to the front which has marquetry panels and heavily scrolled pilasters – possibly C17 Dutch. A low doorway leading to the *rood stair* is blanked off behind the pulpit and the upper opening will be seen above. On the s. side, the priest's stall incorporates medieval bench ends and panelling. At the e. end of the nave on the s. side is a *piscina* with pierced tracery in the arch, and on the wall nearby is a tablet to the memory of Capel Lofft who died in Italy in 1824. Barrister, reformer, and man of letters, it was he who encouraged the local poet Robert Bloomfield, whose poem *The Farmer's Boy* had such a phenomenal success in the early 1800s. In this corner of the nave there are two *consecration crosses* and two more are on the n. wall just above the panelling. The tracery of the windows on the n. side of the nave contains many fragments of medieval glass, including some quite exotic little buildings. The mid-C15 *rood screen*, with its bulky sill across the entrance, has been crudely repainted but the arches of the main *lights* have attractive *crocketted* and *cusped ogee* arches; the cornice and cross are modern. There are some medieval bench ends in the chancel which were originally in the nave and the panelling on the walls was part of a set of C17 *box pews*. Windows in the C13 were seldom draught-proof and here one can see that the jambs of the lancets are rebated for shutters, and some of the hinge hooks remain. Another very rare survival is the original wooden shutter on the inside of the *low side window*. The iron hooks in the walls above the *sanctuary* steps supported the *Lenten veil* before the *Reformation*. The *Stuart communion rails* have simple turned *balusters*, with a scroll-carved top rail, and the riddell posts in green and gold that surround the altar were made by the Wareham guild in 1947. Behind the *altar* is a most interesting length of panelling; 4ft. high, it has crude and varying apertures cut in it, and is likely to have been the eastern front of the *rood loft*. The western front, facing the congregation, would have been as ornate as the screen below, but this would not have been thought necessary for the other side. The late-C13 double piscina on the s. side of the sanctuary has two *trefoil*-headed lancets, with a *quatrefoil* above them, and behind the pierced tracery is an original wooden *credence shelf* in an unusually high position. The e. window has glass of 1964 by Hugh Easton; in the centre is Christ at the table, with a disciple on either side. The dominant colours are a rich red, yellow, and deep blue and the composition is set in clear glass. Other windows by this artist can be found at Badingham, St Peter's Bury St Edmund's, Elvedon and Stowlangtoft. On the n. wall of the chancel there are interminable epitaphs for Fane Walker (1790) and Mrs Anne Lofft (1801); between them, an oval medallion for Henry Capel Lofft, a lieutenant in the 18th Regiment of Foot who fell in the Peninsular campaign at Albuera in 1811.

Tuddenham, St Martin (B3): It is quite a pull up the street from the bridge over the little River Finn but the effort is rewarded by a nice view over the village roofs from the churchyard. Money was left in the 1450s to build the slim tower and it was well enough thought of locally to be used as the model for the one at Rushmere. *Flushwork* decorates the buttresses and battlements, and although the bell openings have been restored, the lion *stops* and the shields of arms in the *spandrels* of the w. doorway are almost worn away. The tower houses a good ring of six bells with a 6 cwt. tenor. Coming up from the street, one's eye is taken by the fine *Norman* n. doorway which has bold *chevron moulding* in the outer arch. There are pairs of attached columns and two of them are carved in spiral form. The n.e. *vestry* dates from 1920 and was designed by John Corder, the local architect who gave us that splendidly eccentric belfry at Swilland, but here he only allowed himself decorative barge boards and a band of carving below the gable. The *chancel* e. window dates from 1861 and there is another C19 window in the s. wall. Corder also designed a comely timber s. porch for the late-C15 s. doorway.

Inside you will find that the tower arch has been blocked above the level of the ringers' gallery, which has a stolid front carved by *Henry Ringham* in 1843. Below it, the glazed screen designed by *Cautley* and probably carved by Ernest Barnes is quite lively by contrast. The *font* is one of those that can be dated by the inscription on the step. It is very worn but records that Richard and Agnes Silvester (or it might be Schuster) were the donors in 1443. The carving was aggressively re-cut in the C19 and most of the figures have new heads if nothing more, but the imagery is of more than usual interest. Round the shaft stand priest and deacons vested for the mass, with acolytes between them carrying bread, wine, a book, and a basin. Under the bowl there are carvings associated with the church's patron saint – his cloak, and a hand alongside a corpse on a bed which reminds us

that he was credited with raising a woman from the dead. The bowl panels contain the *Evangelistic symbols*, three angels, and the kneeling figure of a woman. She probably represents the *Blessed Virgin* at her devotions. There is a tiny angel squeezed into the top l.-hand corner of the panel. The *crocketted* pyramid cover with painted and carved texts is Victorian. The *nave* lies under a good C15 *hammerbeam* roof which has a ribbed coving above the *wall plate*, *castellated collar beams*, and *king posts*; there are mutilated demi-figures at the base of the *wall posts*. In the 1840s the village had its first resident vicar for many years, Mecan Thomas, and he energetically set about reversing the tide of neglect and decay. He secured the services of Henry Ringham, and the nave benches are one of the best examples in the county of that craftsman's skill in saving old work and matching it. It is very difficult to differentiate the one from the other, but you will see that he spliced on new bases for the pew ends, all the standards against the s. wall are his, and the top of the second bench end from the front on the n. side is his. The ends are carved with attractive tracery, there are lovely little sinuous beasts on most of the elbows, while others carry preachers in pulpits, *pelicans in their piety* and a cock for *St Peter* on the s. side w. of the font. The church has an interesting and attractive selection of modern glass and the first to look at is in the s.e. nave window. Dating from the early years of the C20, it is by Percy Bacon, and the figure of St Martin vested as a bishop holding a sword is flanked by *St Edmund* and *St Felix*; there are creamy colours with splashes of rich brocade. Other work by this artist can be found at St Mary's Bury St Edmund, Capel St. Mary, Coddenham, Haverhill, St Matthew's Ipswich and Long Melford. Opposite is a window of the early 1920s by Christopher Webb, who was one of *Comper's* pupils. A band of three panels across the centre illustrates the story of the prodigal son, well drawn and finely coloured. The rest is filled with obscured glass within bird and leaf borders, except for the *Agnus Dei* and *Sacred monogram* within *cartouches* and four texts. Other windows by Webb are at Brettenham, Cowlinge, Mettingham and St Mary's Newmarket. The stairs that led to the *rood loft* remain in the s. wall, and on the n. side there is a tall smoothed-out niche. This may well have contained a statue of *St John the Baptist*; there was a C14 *guild* dedicated to him here which maintained a chaplain and kept a taper burning before his image. Close by is a lovely late-C15 pulpit standing on a modern base. Its panels have crocketted *ogee* arches whose shafts are carved in a curious stepped pattern. There are miniature figures in niches at the angles and the door is formed of one-and-a-bit of the body sides. It probably stood farther away from the wall originally. The n. panel is realistically carved as a door complete with portcullis and lock. Below the plain chancel arch stands a *screen* of 1947 designed by Cautley in his typical style. It made use of timbers from Ashfield and Earl Soham windmills and was carved by Ernest Barnes. The *altar* is from the same hand, but the choir stalls are another example of Ringham's ability to match old with new. The popularity of stained glass in the mid-C19 encouraged expansion in the trade and one of the new generation of glaziers was Frederick Preedy who had worked for George Rogers at Worcester before setting up his own business. He provided the good demi-angels in C14 style in the s. chancel window, set in grey, patterned quarries within flower borders. Other windows by him are at Badley, Lieut. Thurlow and Whitton. The e. window glass of 1860 with its six brightly coloured panels is also his work and commemorates an East India Company midshipman who died aged 15. The C14 *angle piscina* is at floor level now, and although this was no doubt affected by the introduction of *sanctuary* steps by the Victorians, the original chancel may well have been below the level of the nave. On the n. wall of the sanctuary Richard Keble of Roydon Hall has his memorial of 1653. A large *touchstone* oval lies within a heavy alabaster wreath, and above it is his coloured *achievement of arms* in relief. To the l. is a brass plate recording the dedication of the vestry in 1922 'by the Lord Bishop of Suffolk' (well, we all make mistakes) and beyond there is a tablet for Sydney George Cox who died in 1948. He has his little niche in history as the solicitor who acted for Mrs Simpson in Ipswich crown court prior to the abdication of Edward VIII.

Tuddenham, St Mary (B3): This is a handsome building in a quiet way. The early-C14 tower has an attractive combination of *ogee*-headed niches flanking a *quatrefoiled* round window like the one at All Saints Icklingham. There is a vestige of another niche or window just above and the bell openings have cusped 'Y' *tracery* through which one can see the medieval bellframe. In it hang five bells with an 11 cwt. tenor but they are no longer in ringable condition. The rest of the building is mainly C14 and notice how the

Decorated tracery varies in the windows on the n. side. The e. window, with its pair of *headstops*, has *reticulated* tracery of the same period and there is an interesting variation at the top a circle enclosing *cusped* triangles. There are C15 windows on the s. side of the *chancel*, one in the s. *aisle*, and the *clerestory* is late-C14, probably designed to allow for a n. aisle that was never built.

By the mid-C19 the church was in a very poor state and in the 1870s there was a major restoration. The floor of Minton tiles, the serviceable pitch-pine pews, a renewed *chancel* arch and pine chancel roof are familiar evidence of a restoration, but the roofs of the *nave* and aisle were rebuilt extremely well on the old plan and much of the C15 timber was incorporated, together with a number of angels on the *wall posts* and *hammerbeams*. The plain C14 square *font* with heavy chamfers stands on a base with *colonnettes* at the corners which does not match it and may be C19, as is the wooden cover. On a small plaque on the n. door a verse attributed to John Maxwell Edmonds commemorates the seven members of a Stirling bomber crew lost over Kiel:

Went the day well?
We died and never knew,
But well or ill, Freedom
We died for you.

That could well stand as an epitaph for the 47,000 Bomber boys who did not return.

There is a tomb recess in the n. wall under a sharply pointed arch which may be the resting place of Richard de Freville who died in 1325. The *Jacobean* pulpit stands on a modern base and is very plain but it does have a nice pair of brass *Ecclesiological Society* design candle holders. There is no longer a chancel *screen* but the *rood stairs* still go part way up in the wall on the s. side. By the s. aisle e. window is a niche for an image, with a Decorated *piscina* in the corner. There were four village *guilds* in the C15 and this will have been the chapel for one of them. The *vestry* is a C19 replacement but its door in the chancel n. wall is medieval, with *linen-fold* carving and original ironwork. The C19 *communion rails* are an unusual combination of brass and oak and the *altar* is a plain *Stuart* table (although the top has been renewed). The e. end of the church looks even more handsome inside because it has fine and large niches on either side of the window. Carefully restored, they have the same flattened cusping under *crocketted* ogee arches that can be seen over the niches on the w. face of the tower. On the s. side is a C14 piscina under a *cinquefoiled* arch, together with *dropped-sill sedilia*. As you leave, note the *stoup* to the l. of the door and the door itself whose strap hinges have been renewed while the rest is medieval. This makes four doors in the church that have survived for over 400 years.

Tunstall, St Michael (H5): The tower is well proportioned, with angle buttresses and three *string courses*, and the windows and top were heavily repaired in brick after a lightning strike in the late C18. Its most recent restoration was completed in 1979, and it houses an excellent ring of six bells with a 7 cwt. tenor. The *stops* of the w. doorway are carved as angels bearing shields, *fleurons* stud the mouldings, and there are blank shields hung in the *spandrels*. Walking round, you will see that the *nave* n. door is partially blocked by the entrance to a stokehole, and there are brick buttresses on that side. A small C19 *vestry* in white brick adjoins the *chancel*, and the e. window has been renewed. Most of the windows and details are C15, but the *priest's door* is C14, and has a nice example of *ball flower* decoration worked into a foliage trail in the *dripstone*. The s. frontage presents an attractive, mottled mixture of stone, flint, and brick, and there is *flushwork* panelling on the front of the porch, with *Trinity* and *Passion* shields in the spandrels of the arch. The porch was drastically restored at some stage, and the ridge of its replacement roof cocks up rather strangely above the line of the original gable.

The C14 inner doorway is well proportioned, and the original weathered door of lapped boards still serves and retains its lock plate and full-width strap hinges. There is a *stoup* recess alongside, and beyond is an unpretentious interior, with pale brick floors and plastered ceilings and the w. end of the nave has been cleared . A section of the old wall surface has been preserved in the n.w. corner so that the medieval graffiti can be examined – lots of ship drawings, and their crude shapes suggest that this is children's work rather than sailors home from the sea. The *font* has a *Purbeck marble* bowl, with the familiar pairs of *blind arches* lightly carved in the bowl panels. Their tops are rounded not pointed, and the date is likely to be late-C12 rather than C13; *Tudor Roses* stud the top of the nicely traceried C16 shaft. Nearby, the fine Victorian *bier* was made by Parker Hastings and is still in use. There are some fragments of C15 glass in a n. window, and a good set of George III *Royal Arms* hangs on the s. wall, painted on

canvas and dated 1764. The nave has a no-nonsense set of C18 *box pews* painted a pale tan and the front three ranges have seats all the way round. The pulpit is squat and substantial, on a coved stem with carved flowers in the panels and a decorative hand rail with cast-iron supports. It was painted to match the pews and may have been a slightly later addition, but it has been repainted in quite jolly colours. On the s. side there is a plain *piscina*, marking the site of a nave *altar*, and there is now no *screen*. The church's only *brass* is a 1618 inscription in the floor at the e. end of the nave, for John and Mary Haughfen. The chancel has been re-paved, and the oak choir stalls were designed by W. Scott-Moncrieff in the 1950s – austere, with decoration limited to scrolled cresting inset below the top rails. Changes in level have brought the large C14 piscina in the *sanctuary* almost to the floor; its arch is embellished with *paterae*, and it has a deep *trefoil* drain. The brass telescopic *communion rails* are a typically Victorian design, but they were not installed until 1910 – which shows how misleading it can be to date things by style alone. The *Decalogue*, Creed, and Lord's prayer on the e. wall are painted on canvas, dated 1820 and bearing the rector's name. The striking figures in the e. window were designed by E. Dilworth, and painted by N. Attwood (in the 1950s?). The church's patron saint stands in the centre, weighing souls, with *St Gabriel* on his r. and *St Raphael* on his l. – all three outlined against clear glass. The churchyard has a particularly good selection of C18 and C19 gravestones – one with masons' tools carved on it s. of the *porch*, an 1851 cast-iron example for Job Sparke in the s.w. corner, and quite a number which have circular or oval inscription panels. It so happens that Tunstall has something unique in Suffolk churchyards. Some seven paces from the southern boundary wall (along the road) and fifteen paces from the eastern boundary, there is a stone in memory of two unrelated men who were buried there together on the 22nd of June 1778. Robert Debney and William Cooper were two members of the Sizewell Gap gang of smugglers and, having buried a cache of contraband gin beneath a dunghill, they were asphyxiated in trying to recover it. Debney was 28, Cooper was 18, and they were both Tunstall men. They have a joint epitaph:

All you, dear Friends that look upon this
    stone,
Oh! think how quickly both their Lives were
    gone.

Neither Age, nor Sickness brought them to
    Clay;
Death quickly took their strength and sense
    away.
Both in the Prime of Life they lost their
    breath,
And in a Sudden were cast down by Death.
A cruel Death that could no longer spare
A loving Husband nor a Child most dear.
The loss is Great to those they left behind,
But they thro' *Christ* 'tis hop'd, True Joys
    will find.

**Ufford, Assumption of the Blessed Virgin
Mary** (G5): A beautiful village, snug in its valley,
and a delectable church. The tower, begun in
the C14 and completed in the C15, is well
proportioned, with three *string courses*, and the
wall surfaces are an interesting blend of small,
densely packed flints with an admixture of brick.
It has a *base course*, flint chequer in the diagonal
buttresses, and there are *fleurons* in the *dripstone*
of the deeply moulded w. doorway. The niche
above the small *Perpendicular* w. window has
shallow *tracery* in its *spandrels*, and there is a an
unusual variation in the bell openings – three
lights to the w., and two lights on the other faces.
Within the tower hangs an excellent ring of eight
bells with a 13 cwt. tenor.Walking round, you
will see that, although there is a C15 *clerestory*,
there is no n. *aisle*, and the n. doorway is blocked.
One window on that side has 'Y' *tracery*, and
nearby, ironstone is set in a *herringbone* pattern
that dates from the C11. Further evidence that
this was a *Norman* church lies under the *chancel*
floor, where the outline of an *apsidal* e. end was
discovered. The large brick and flint *vestry* that
stands at right angles to the chancel seems to be
early-C19 and served initially as the village school.
The *priest's door*, with its cadaverous *headstops*,
has been restructured, but its form indicates that
the chancel was built in the C12. Above, a stone
shield bears the arms of the De La Pole family,
and there is a *scratch dial* on the buttress to the r.
The superb *porch* was added in the late-C15, and
it has a number of interesting details; tall
flushwork panels cover the facade and w. wall,
there are triple canopied niches above the
entrance, and note how the leaf trail in the
parapet is continued in flushwork along the
sides. The base course displays the crowned
chalice and wafer symbol of the mass (as at
Woodbridge), and intriguing carvings lie on the
upper *weatherings* of the buttresses. There is the
headless body of a man in armour on the l.,
matched by a crouching animal clutching a round

Ufford, Assumption of the Virgin

object in its jaws on the r. This possibly
illustrates the legend that in order to catch a tiger
cub, one must ride off with it and elude the
parents. If the tigress followed too closely, the
trick was to throw down a mirror so that she
would mistake the reflection for her cub, and
lick it while the hunter escaped. There is a similar
carving on Badingham's porch, and the best
known illustration is on a bench end at
Lakenheath. The porch has a good roof,
decorated with *bosses*, and someone in the C19
added stone diaper work round the plain inner
doorway. The restored *stoup* is in use again, and
the lapped boards of the C14 door still bear
their original ironwork.

Before turning to other details within, see how
the *arcade* illustrates some of the stages in the
church's history – a round *pier* and *responds* of
the early-C13 to the e., supporting Perpendicular
arches, and the two C14 w. bays with their
octagonal pier. The tall, narrow tower arch is
filled with a glazed screen, there is a *sanctus-bell
window* above it, and the *aumbry* to the l. will
probably have been used to house the things
needed for baptisms. Most of the church's C15
benches are grouped at the w. end and are a
fascinating set. They stand on *castellated* sills, and

their low backs are charmingly gnarled, with a leaf trail carved on most of them. The ends are buttressed on both sides of a tracery panel which is divided in some cases into two or three sections. Their *poppyheads* are extraordinarily varied – some with human head *finials*, some with heraldic emblems, some with fruit. The second poppyhead from the back is particularly notable, for its lobes are carved with pairs of creatures which have long sinuous necks, and hooded human faces at their rear ends. There is a fine stag on the elbow below them, its neck in a chained crown, and a lady wearing a *butterfly headdress* is carved on one of the elbows on the aisle side – which dates the benches roughly between 1450 and 1485. Just beyond the *font*, one finds *St Catherine* (l.) and *St Margaret* (r.) paired on a bench end, nicely illustrating C15 hair styles and chair styles. There are a number of animal grotesques, and the one on the s. front bench in the *nave* is a medieval carver's idea of a camel, the beast that symbolised Christ stooping to assume the burden of the world's sin.

The bowl panels of the C15 *font* have *Tudor Roses* alternating with shields that bear traces of colour, and there are large heads at the angles below, with *paterae* between. But it is the glorious cover that many people come specially to see, a breathtaking example of the C15 designer's art and woodworker's skill that has no equal in England. With its ingeniously telescopic action, it dates from about 1450, and the meticulous restoration which was completed in 1988 has revealed much of its original colour and gilding. A mass of delicate, clustered pinnacles form canopies above the stooled niches on each face, repeated in diminishing proportions in the second and third tiers, until the tall *crocketted* finial is reached, bearing on its own canopy a massive *pelican in her piety* 18ft. above the floor. Pierced buttresses at the angles of the bottom range each have a miniature niche crowned with a triplet of crocketted pinnacles, housing tiny modern figures, beautifully carved in the C15 idiom. From the w. clockwise they are: *SS Withburga, Etheldreda, Margaret, Mary Magdalene, Bernard* or *Dominic* (?), *Cecilia* (?); a modern figure of *St John* stands in the principal w. niche.

Castellated *tie-beams* and *hammerbeams* alternate in the nave roof, and there is a good deal of the original colour left on the principal timbers, including *Sacred monograms* and 'M's for the dedication. Large demi-angels have been applied to the ends of the hammers, with a full length pair floating at the e. end. *William Dowsing* ordered 'forty cherubims to be taken down of

wood' when he came here in January 1643, and having broken 'thirty superstitious pictures' and reaved six 'superstitious inscriptions in brass', he left orders for more work to be done. He was back in May and August, mutilating the chancel roof and smashing up the organ case, amongst other things, but was kept waiting two hours for the key and obviously had trouble with obstructive and obtuse churchwardens, sexton, and constable. According to villagers, he 'sent men to rifle the church', and 'went about to pull down the church, and had carried away part of the church'. Ufford has by far the longest entry in his journal, and although he describes the font cover as being glorious, 'like a pope's Triple Crown', he seems to have spared it in the main. Richard Lovekin, the rector, suffered along with his church. Having been inducted in 1631, he was stripped of all his possessions save a silver spoon that he had hidden up his sleeve, and turned out of his living. He survived, however, and came back at the *Restoration* to serve his parish until 1678, when he died aged 111, having preached the Sunday before. There are *brasses* to be seen in the nave, and look first at the one on the n. wall in memory of Richard Ballett, a London goldsmith who died in 1598. It is a finely engraved architectural design, with the shield of the Goldsmith's company in the *pediment* below a pair of dragons; a skeleton is engraved across the centre, and the verse is a variation on a popular theme:

Ufford, Assumption of the Virgin: Font cover

Thou mortall mann that wouldest attaine,
The happie havene of hevenly rest,
Prepare thy selfe of Graces all
Fayth and repentance is the best.
Like thee I was sometime,
But now am turned to dust,
As thou at leght O earth and slime,
Returne to asshes must.
I rest in hope with joye to see,
Christ Jesus that redeemed mee.

In the nave floor there is a brass for Symon Brooke and his three wives Emot, Margaret and Alice; the 18in. effigies are very worn (half of his is missing), two of the wives wear veil headdresses, and the last has a butterfly headdress, confirming the 1483 date. Only two of the mutilated *Evangelistic symbols* remain, and the inscription has gone, doubtless due to Dowsing. The third brass is a late example – a shield on Henry Groome's stone of 1634 at the e. end of the nave. *Hatchments* hang on the walls above: n. side, Robert Oneby (1753); s. side w. to e., Lady Mary Chapman (1760), Francis Brooke (1799), and his wife Anne (1772). A nave n. window contains a pale *Annunciation* , and it is interesting that, below the *Trinity* group at the top, there are kneeling figures of Erythraea and Cumana. They were two of the twelve sybils, the wise women of the classical world who were adopted by the early church as additional prophets of the events in the New Testament. This is fine glass in the manner of *Comper* at his best and one would like to know who the artist was. The pulpit is a C19 replacement, and the *hour-glass* in the recess behind it has a new housing.

A large monument spanning the w. wall of the aisle commemorates Sir Henry Wood, who died in 1671, having been Treasurer of the Household to Queen Henrietta Maria. Wreathed ox heads are placed on either side of the broad *touchstone* tablet on the front of the sarcophagus, and there is an excellent *cartouche* of arms on top which appropriately features three *woodwoses*. The bell on the floor was cast in Norwich by the Brasyers in the C15, and its inscription reads: 'Fac Margareta nobis hec munera leta' (Margaret, make these offices joyful to us). On the wall of the aisle there is an exuberant tablet for Robert Oneby (whose hatchment hangs in the nave); the domed cartouche is set in bunched drapery, weeping *putti* flank coloured arms above, and a trio of cherub heads rounds it off below. The aisle chapel is dedicated to *St Leonard*, and Sir Ninian Comper designed the fittings as a World

War I memorial. There is a simple oak screen at the entrance, and the dark green and gold *reredos* is low and broad, with a sculptured Crucifixion group in the centre. His design for the e. window is signed with his strawberry emblem and is a Via Dolorosa across the three lights, with a soldier and sailor joining with the others in helping to bear the cross. To the r. is an *Early English angle piscina*, with *dropped-sill sedilia* alongside, and a fragment of medieval stencil decoration survives on the wall above. The door leading to the *rood loft* is to the l. of the *altar*, and the stair emerges by the chancel arch.

The loft has gone, but the massive *rood beam* remains, moulded and carved, and so does the base of the *rood screen*. Its panels have intricate tracery, and the painted figures are set against a dark red background. They are primitive in style and date from 1440-60; despite terrible mutilation, those on the s. side are virgin martyrs whose names can just be read in gilded gothic script below the tracery; from l. to r. they are: *SS Agnes, Cecilia, Agatha, Faith, Bridget of Kildare, Florence*. The *arch-braced* chancel roof retains a good deal of its colour and, as in the nave, there are *Sacred monograms* and 'M's on the rafters. The pierced *wall plate* is carved with demi-angels bearing shields, and an unusual feature is the insertion of pendants halfway up the braces (as at Crowfield). These now carry a set of shields painted with *Passion emblems*. The stalls backing on to the screen have *misericords*, with the Willoughby shield on the n. side, and two cheerful masks (one a replacement) on the s. The n. chancel window contains roundels of C17/C18 continental glass, and at the bottom of the window opposite there are two survivors from a *nine orders of angels* sequence. It was believed that each order had a particular responsibility for a section of humanity, and the inscriptions identify these as the angel of Dominations (emperors and kings), and the angel of Virtues (priests). The introduction of modern steps in the *sanctuary* has put the *angle piscina* at floor level, and a few fragments of late-C14 glass, including a Passion shield, have been arranged in the window on that side. The two centre panels of the e. window contain very good C19 copies by *Clayton & Bell* of C15 figures in All Souls College, Oxford – *St Anne and St Salome*.

Uggeshall, St Mary (I2): A modern *lych-gate* in simple and sturdy oak stands at the entrance to the churchyard, and the church presents an unusual profile to the road. Having been struck by lightning, the upper stage of the tower fell in the C18, to be replaced by a clapboard belfry, and the *chancel* roof is both taller and steeper than that of the *nave*; everything is neatly thatched, including the *porch* and the lych-gate. The tower was under construction in the 1530s, and along the base of the w. window there is a worn inscription: 'Orate pro animabus Joh'is Jewle et Marione ux' ejus' (Pray for the soul of John Jewel and Marion his wife). Although there is no record to confirm it, they no doubt financed the building of the tower, and on the r. of the inscription there is a most interesting addition. Two small shields carry masons' emblems – an axe and hammer-axe on one, a square and hammer-axe on the other, and it is likely that the men who cut the inscription signed it with the recognised badges of their craft. Circling the building, you will see that there is a blocked *Norman* n. door and a mixture of *Decorated* and *Perpendicular* windows in the nave. The C14 chancel was drastically restored in 1873, with an organ chamber added, and then suffered a disaster in the 1987 gale when the entire e. end was blown out. Thankfully, it has been beautifully rebuilt in an attractive mixture of brick and flint, with an entirely new window. There is an early-C14 *priest's door* on the s. side, and further along, the line of the nave wall varies significantly. A short section is set back, and *quoins* mark the original e. end of the nave – showing that the chancel must have been rebuilt and extended around 1300. Within the dinky little porch the doorway is C14 but follows the shape of its Norman predecessor, and the arch inside shows that its position was slightly altered.

A fine, carefully restored C15 *font* stands by the entrance; its short shaft is guarded by four lions and beneath the bowl there are angels with crossed hands and overlapping wings. The panels contain *Tudor Roses,* more lions, and two angels bearing shields – one carved with *Passion emblems*; the ponderous cover with its *pelican in her piety finial* came in with the 1870s restoration. The nave roof is handsome, its *arch-braces* meeting below *collar beams* and *king posts*. The *wall posts* have demi-angels with shields at the w. end, and there are Passion and *Trinity* shields in the corners. The last bay of the roof is plastered, and enough colour remains on the braces to show that it formed a *celure* above the *rood*. The oak benches demonstrate how well Victorian craftsmen could match C15 work, and they restored the *Stuart* pulpit, placing it on a new stone base. It was probably eight-sided originally, and its tall panels have twin *blind arches* with

split-turned pendants. The 1870s restoration included a wooden replacement chancel arch, choir stalls and reading desk, and in the *sanctuary*, the e. wall was panelled to sill height in C14 style to display painted figures against a gold background – the *Evangelists, SS Peter, Paul, James the Less,* and *Jude*. The simple C14 *angle piscina* and *dropped-sill sedilia* do not appear to have been disturbed. Almost all of the 1870s glass in the e. window was recovered when the wall collapsed, and it has been re-set by Chapel Studios. The artist has not been identified, but there are similarities with a window by Charles Hudson at nearby Sotherton, and it may be his; figures of The *Blessed Virgin* and *St John* in C13 mode are set against a dark blue vine trail backing under elaborate canopies, and there are hovering angels with bright green wings. The attractive little figure of *Dorcas* with her rush basket in the n. *lancet* could also be Hudson's work, and the contemporary window opposite is likely to be by *Ward & Hughes*. High up on the e. wall there are *Evangelistic symbols* in roundels, and on either side of the window zinc squares are painted with simplistic scenes of sowers and reapers in Germanic woodcut style. To celebrate the millennium, the parish commissioned glass by Rachel Thomas for the window nearest the porch. A large roundel spreads across all three *lights* to surround the tall figure of the *Blessed Virgin* clasping the Christ Child in front of her. Geese flight beyond her head, and the swirling background is compartmented with little vignettes – two horses by a bridge, a clutch of eggs, cylindrical straw bales, the church itself, a dairy herd, a cup of tea and a spider's web. This is a lovely design which is both imaginative and pleasing.

Although Uggeshall does not feature in *William Dowsing's* journal, Lionel Playter, who was rector from 1529 to 1646, refused the Covenant and was evicted from the living by the Earl of Manchester's Committee for Scandalous Ministers on the grounds that 'he spent August 31st 1642 drinking with a papist since gone to the Royal army' and 'for eating custard after a scandalous manner'. He was a man of some spirit and announced to his flock that he had a parcel of hemp to sell and hoped it would bear a good price because if the times continued, a good many would want hanging. His royal sympathies finally saw him restored to his benefice just before his death in 1680.

Walberswick, St Andrew (I3): There was a time when this was a flourishing port, its ships trading as far away as Iceland and the Faroes but, like Dunwich and Blythburgh, it fell on hard times. The church's tithes were appropriated by Henry VIII and the loss of income compounded the town's distress. A magnificent church had been built in the C15 heyday, but within a hundred years it was in need of repair, and by the *Restoration* it had become ruinous. So much so that in 1695 the little congregation asked permission to unroof the *nave, chancel*, and n. *aisle*, sell the materials to repair the s. aisle and convert it into a smaller church. This is very much the same story that we hear at Covehithe where the parish faced a similar problem.

The town had two churches at the time of the Domesday survey, one on the marshes, and one here. The latter lacked a tower, and in 1426 the present tower was begun to make good the deficiency. It is one of the very few cases where the original contract survives, and from it we learn that master masons Richard Russell of Dunwich and Adam Powle of Blythburgh were to copy details from the towers at Tunstall and Halesworth. Similarities in structure and detail suggest that Russell moved on to begin the tower at Kessingland, and as he died in 1441, the work here was probably completed by then. The tower is beautifully proportioned, with *flushwork* in the *base course* and angled buttresses. The w. doorway has lion *stops* and hung shields in the *spandrels*, while shields and *paterae* decorate its broad mouldings. There are large belfry windows and three-*light* bell openings, and *ashlar tracery* and *gargoyles* feature below the excellent flushwork battlements. The building of a splendid church to match the tower followed quickly, and it was completed in 1493, with a n. aisle added in 1507. Enough remains to show how lavish it was, and it obviously shared a family likeness with Southwold and Blythburgh – aisles reaching to within a single bay of the e. end, and a continuous *clerestory* of eighteen windows over nave and chancel. As at Blythburgh, there was a n.w. turret giving access to the roofs, and *priest's doors* on both sides of the church. The *High altar piscina* remains in the short chancel, and there is another at the end of the s. aisle. The outline of a *sanctus-bell window* shows clearly below the roof line of the nave on the e. face of the tower. The reduced church was formed out of two thirds of the old s. aisle, and the windows on the n. side were doubtless taken from the n. aisle; sections of flushwork chequer were reused here and there, particularly in the new e. wall. A stone plaque on the n. wall of the *vestry* records

the great change: 'Edward Collins & John Taylor churchwardens in the yeare when the church was rebuilt and in the eight yeare of the reign of our sovereign Lord King William the Third AD 1696'. The *porch* has a flushwork base course, and the plain flint facade has a pretty centre niche containing a modern statue of the church's patron saint; a tall stair turret giving access to the upper room rises above the roof at the n.w. corner. The base of a *preaching cross* stands by the entrance, and the ceiling is vaulted, its *bosses* carved with demi-angels, crowns and *Tudor Roses*. There are remains of fine applied tracery on the inner door.

As one would expect, the interior is simple, and lies under an almost flat roof which has a little carved decoration on the main timbers. The *font* is the familiar C15 East Anglian type, with very battered lions and *woodwoses* round the shaft, and lions alternating with angels in the bowl panels. Half of a *pier* base is used as a step, giving one a chance to see the Roman numerals that the mason cut to match it with its other half. A *Jacobean* chest stands nearby, with typical shallow carving on the front. A tablet in a s. window sill commemorates seven fishermen who were drowned in the autumn of 1883, and on the wall a bronze plaque in the form of a palette is for Tom van Oss, killed at sea in 1941, an artist like his grandfather and uncle before him. When *William Dowsing* came here, probably in April 1643, he 'brake down 40 superstitious pictures...and we had 8 superstitious inscriptions on the grave stones'. The latter were the *brasses* that have gone from the eight slabs in the centre aisle, and the 'pictures' will have been stained glass in the windows. Hundreds of fragments have been recovered from the ruins, and some have been arranged like a mosaic in the centre light of one of the s. windows. The late-C15 or early-C16 pulpit has two tiers of panels containing large *quatrefoil* roundels separated by *castellated* moulding – an unusual design for East Anglia. The base of the *screen*, complete with doors, has a deeply moulded top rail and traceried panels, and is likely to have been adapted from a section of the larger church's *rood screen*. The bench ends of the choir stalls are C15 too, with *poppyheads*, gabled elbows, and tracery cut in the solid. Excavations in the 1930s uncovered a most interesting and rare item, a pre-*Reformation* super-*altar*. It is a small slab of stone which was consecrated, marked with crosses, and set in the top of a larger *mensa*. They were also used in some cases by itinerant priests as and when occasion demanded, and became a favourite target for the reformers. Walberswick's has been placed in a wooden frame on top of the altar, restored to its proper use after 400 years. A tomb slab reaved of its brass and mounted on a pier base provides a substantial *credence* table to the r.

Waldringfield, All Saints (G6): The church's handsome early-C16 tower is so like nearby Hemley's as to suggest that the same builder was responsible for both. Its dark red brick is enhanced by diaper patterns in blue on walls and lower buttresses, and there is a heavy stair turret to the s. The core of the *nave* and *chancel* is undoubtedly C13 to C14, but an 1865 restoration masked much of the detail. Circling the church, you will see that the *Decorated* windows in the nave have been renewed (and apparently altered), the n. doorway blocked, and the e. wall rebuilt with a new window. Between the two heavy brick buttresses on the s. side, there is a late-C13 *lancet* which has a blank section below the *transom*, showing that it originally served as a *low side window*. The small *vestry* was probably added to the n. side of the chancel in the C19. The *porch*, with its solid brick walls, has been altered, but remnants of C15 barge boards survive above the inner doorway, along with castellated *wall plates*.

Within, a single plastered ceiling lies over nave and chancel, with no intervening arch, and the s. wall leans gently outward. The broad three-*light* w. window in the tower is filled with glass of the early 1920s by *Powell & Sons* – a conventional arrangement of the Good Shepherd flanked by *St Michael* and *St Gabriel*. The massive C15 *font* stands in front of the n. doorway, and is one of the best examples of the traditional East Anglian type. In the bowl panels, excellent, deeply cut *Evangelistic symbols* alternate with angels bearing shields carved with a cross (e.), an *Agnus Dei* (n.), a *Sacred monogram* (w.), and a *Trinity emblem* (s.). The small figures round the shaft are interesting for two reasons: firstly, the cross-legged *woodwoses* are goat-legged like satyrs and wear turbans (emphasising the eastern connection); secondly, they do not in this case alternate with lions, but with figures that I would identify as women rather than priests. Was it, perhaps, to illustrate a variation of the woodwose symbolism? There are plain oak benches in the nave, and behind the modern pulpit you will see that the sill of the low side window was lowered to form a seat for whoever rang the *sanctus bell*. C19 'gothick' *communion rails* front the *sanctuary*, and there are *Decalogue* boards

of the same period on either side of the e. window. The 1860s stained glass is by *Lavers & Barraud*, a brightly coloured Crucifixion, with Christ's baptism to the l. and the Last Supper to the r.; close floral patterning abounds, with an *Agnus Dei* and musical angels in the *tracery*.

Walpole, St Mary (H3): The church stands on a hillock above the village, with a steep bluff to the w. dropping down to water meadows. The site suggests an early foundation, and the boulder stone *quoins* at the s.e. corner of the *nave*, together with shallow *pilasters* in the walls of the *chancel*, confirm that the church was built by the *Saxons*. The *Normans* added a s. doorway, its arch decorated with *chevron moulding* and an outer band of starred disks. These things aside, the whole of the exterior was transformed in 1878 by a fairly brutal restoration and rebuilding at the hands of H.M. Eyton. The base of the C14 tower, with its *base course* of *flushwork* roundels was retained, and a new belfry stage was added which has attached shafts at the corners below *broaches* and an octagonal shingled spire. All the windows employ a C19 form of *plate tracery* and those in the new n. *aisle* are particularly graceless. It is possible that the chancel was *apsidal* originally. The C14 outer arch of the *porch* survives, and there is a *scratch dial* to be found on the s.e. corner.

Within, there are one or two reminders of the church's earlier days, but the hand of the Victorian architect lies heavily overall – roofs, *arcade*, chancel arch, benches, and most of the fittings. By some chance, the C14 *font* came from St Andrew's, Norwich, when they decided to install a new one. It is a slightly unusual design, squat, with a deep range of mouldings instead of the conventional bowl panels. A small gilded set of *Hanoverian Royal Arms* in plaster hangs above the tower arch, and there is a *stoup* recess by the s. door. Above it, George Jordan's epitaph of 1813 is charming: 'Many years a resident in this Parish, where his amiable and obliging Disposition rendered him esteemed while living and his Memory respected'. The arch that led to the *rood stair* in the s. wall serves as a reminder that there was once a *rood screen* complete with loft across the entrance to the chancel. A tablet on the n. wall, more or less in the style of Adam, is for William Philpot, patron of the living, and members of his family; he died in 1814 and his coloured shield of arms is displayed below. The *priest's door* in the s. wall is now blocked, and the *cusped* arch of the C14 *piscina* has been shorn of its surface decoration.

Floor levels were raised during the restoration and both the piscina and the *dropped-sill sedilia* alongside are now low in the wall. Plenty of well-carved C18 stones can be found in the churchyard, and although it is outside the scope of this book, Walpole's Congregational Chapel of 1646 is well worth a visit but you may have to be patient over access.

Walsham-le-Willows, St Mary (D3): This is a large and handsome church for the size of the village, probably because the C11 Lord of the Manor gave the living, together with land to support it, to the Augustinian priory at Ixworth which he founded. Before the *Reformation* it was served by the canons from the priory. The building has many points of detail in common with Ixworth and it is likely that the same masons worked on both buildings. The style throughout is *Perpendicular* and the tower has well-defined *string courses*. The four *finials* on the battlements date from 1475 and they are Edward IV's armorial beasts – n.e. the Clarence bull; s.e. the *griffin*, of Edward III; and w. the Mortimer lions. The tower houses an excellent ring of six bells with an 11 cwt. tenor. Most of the decoration is concentrated on the n. side of the church facing the centre of the village and the tall *porch* is attractively chequered with *flushwork* in the style of Norwich guildhall, with a niche over the outer arch. The pattern of the *base course* continues along the length of the *aisle*. The close-set windows of the *clerestory* have arches patterned with red brick and there is a line of square panels half way up decorated with crowned 'M's, Catherine wheels (there was a *guild* of *St Catherine* here) and the *Sacred monogram*. The masons who built it have been identified as the Aldrych family of N. Lopham in Norfolk. Their mark is the second flushwork panel on the n. side and dates the work as being done in the late-1450s and 1460s. The *rood staircase* projects out of the angle between the *chancel* and the n. *aisle*, a mirror image of the arrangement at Ixworth. The s. side is much plainer and there is no porch there. Above the bench seats in the porch there is wooden panelling and the top rails are carved with: 'God's wyll be done in hevyn and erthe' from the Lord's Prayer on the e. side, and on the other (from Ecclesiasticus 3:23): 'Ejus ne fueris curiosis MCCCCCXLI' (Thou shalt not be envious of him 1541). The origin of the panelling is unknown and it was not installed until the C19.

The interior is spacious, attractive, and very well kept. Above the tall tower arch you will see a *sanctus-bell window*, and the tower w. window is filled with three panels of the Good Samaritan parable in deep, rich colour, with *tabernacle* work over them, by *Lavers, Barraud & Westlake*, installed in the 1870s. The C14 *font* is beautifully chunky, and the bowl panels are carved with *crocketted* and *cusped ogee* arches, with leaves in the *spandrels* and pinnacles at the angles. There are worn heads beneath and the shaft has deeply cut *tracery* on all sides. An unusual feature is that crosses have been drilled at intervals around the rim. The octagonal pillars of the nave *arcades* have concave faces which are carved with ogee-shaped *trefoils* below the *capitals*, a feature repeated in the *jambs* of the outer porch arch. At the w. end of the s. aisle there is a range of oak panelling dated 1620 which came from the churchwardens' pew that stood there, and over the s. door is a good set of George III *Royal Arms*. The C13 iron-bound parish chest, with its three locks and three old padlocks, stands nearby. There are medieval bench ends in the s. aisle and at the w. end of the nave which have *poppyheads*, but the figures or grotesques that were carved on the squared elbows have been cut away. At the w. end of the n. aisle, an *altar* is backed by a triptych in oils by Rosemary Rutherford, with the Last Supper flanked by Christ washing the disciples' feet and the vigil in Gethsemane. On the wall to the r. is an interesting old photograph of the wall paintings that were discovered and unfortunately plastered over again in the C19 – a series of *Christ of the Trades*. The nave roof is perhaps the most splendid thing here. It has a flattish pitch and *hammerbeams* alternate with *arch-braced tie-beams*. Originally, the hammerbeams carried angels and the drilled tenons that held them can still be seen. They rose up to fit as braces into the timbers above, a most uncommon arrangement. The roof is a lovely pale golden colour and everywhere the faded vermillion painted decoration survives. Each spandrel above the long *wall posts* is carved with Edward IV's 'sun in splendour' and there is a double band of ornament on tie-beams, hammers, and on the *wall plate*. Hanging above the arcade on the s. side of the nave is a crants – the virgin's garland which is not uncommon in the south-west but unique in Suffolk. What remains here is the elm wood disk, the thickness of a coffin board, perhaps cut for Mary Boyce whose name is carved on it. She was a maiden who died aged 20 in 1685, they say of a broken heart, and below her name is a heart pierced by an arrow. On the anniversary of her death it was decorated with a wreath of flowers but the

Walsham-le-Willows, St Mary: The crants

custom died out in the middle of the C18. In Shakespeare's *Hamlet*, the priest says over Ophelia's grave: 'Yet here she is allowed her virgin crants'.

The stair to the *rood loft* rises from a door at the e. end of the n. aisle and divides at the top to a doorway facing the nave and another facing the chancel. This suggests that the loft was wide enough to have a walkway back and front. There is an image stool above the lower door. The *rood* screen can be precisely dated by a will of 1448 and the panels of the base have blind four-*light* tracery. The main lights have shapely, cusped and crocketted ogee tops and the remains of the vaulting, that rose to the underside of the loft, spring from delicate shafts above the buttresses. The entrance arch has a double ogee, coming down to a reversed poppyhead of the sort so often seen on bench ends of the period, but I do not remember having seen one used like this before. The top of the screen and the cross are modern. In front is a good example of an *Ecclesiological Society* design brass lectern, and beyond the cumbersome and ugly pulpit of 1878 is the s. aisle chapel. It has a *piscina* with a trefoil ogee arch and there are *dropped-sill sedilia* alongside. The altar here is a nice C17 table, with a carved and moulded edge, rails and stretchers. The e. window and that to the s. have glass of the 1880s by W.G. Taylor of Berners Street. A

little to the w. is an image niche which once had a canopy or hood; the stumps of iron supports can be seen in the stonework, and it probably contained a statue connected with one of the pre-Reformation guilds – the *Trinity, St John the Baptist* or St Catherine. In the base of the niche is a *cresset* that was found in a local garden. To the l. of the altar is a C13 grave slab and nearby a small patch of C14 tiles, two of which carry the profile of a man with an enormous nose. The window in the n. wall of the chancel is a memorial to Rosemary Rutherford, the stained glass artist, and is one of her own designs (you will have seen her tryptych over in the n. aisle). The figure of the *Blessed Virgin* is surrounded by simple flower designs in a typically broad variety of pastel colours (more of her glass can be found at Boxford and Hinderclay). There is a *priest's door* on this side and also the deeply recessed doorway to the medieval *vestry*. It is sheathed with leather, banded with iron, and has two locks. Churches were often used as safe deposits for their villages and you may have noticed that the vestry window outside is barred for extra security. The piscina in the *sanctuary* has been renewed, probably at the 1878 restoration when the chancel received a new roof. The terracotta *reredos* of 1883 was commissioned by John Martineau, the patron of the living and it is by George Tinworth (1843-1913). A craftsman of humble birth, he spent his whole working life with Doulton of Lambeth, and his talents were recognised by Ruskin, G.E. Street and others. His best known work is the reredos in St Stephen's chapel at York Minster, but all of it reflects his passionate sincerity and knowledge of the Bible. Here we have a fairly conventional setting of the Last Supper, but the theme is 'Is it I?', and the figures of the disciples are full of urgency and puzzlement as they ask the question of the calm central figure. Only Judas turns away. As was his curious habit, Tinworth scratched in the names of all the figures and the relevant text reference in semi-illiterate lettering – strange contrast to the excellent modelling of the composition. The figure on the far r. is a self-portrait of the artist. In 1878 *Hardmans* arranged fragments of medieval glass in the e. window, collected in a series of octagonal panels set in the main lights, and in the tracery there are angels and delicate designs in yellow stain. On the s. wall of the chancel is an elegant monument in marble to John Hunt who died in 1725. It has good lettering on the *touchstone* panel which is flanked by Ionic columns; a coloured *cartouche* of arms is on the *pediment* supported by delicate swags, and olive and palm fronds cross below within a curly frame. The chancel reading desk embodies two medieval bench ends and there are two more at the e. end of the choir stalls, as well as three panels of C15 work. The Ascension scene in the s. chancel window is by Lavers, Barraud and Westlake.

Walton, St Mary (G7): There has been a church here since the Conquest (and possibly before), but the character of the building stems from the major reconstructions in the C19. It had become increasingly dilapidated – the tower was ruinous by the 1740s and the w. and e. walls of *nave* and *chancel* were rebuilt in brick towards the end of the century. By 1840, the s. *aisle* had largely disappeared, the w. bay of the nave had gone, and only fragments of the tower remained. Rebuilding began in 1857 under Frederick Barnes, the Ipswich architect who was then at work at Melton. The aisle was replaced, with a new *arcade*, a *vestry* was added, and the n. nave windows were installed. A second stage followed some ten years later when the w. end of the nave was rebuilt, and the chancel was restored and re-roofed. An organ chamber was added in 1897, and the tower was rebuilt in 1899 to a design by the Brown & Burgess Ipswich partnership.

A preliminary circuit of the church is worthwhile to identify the remains of the C14 building. A sizeable piece of the tower's s.w. buttress still stands, and the fact that it is largely built of friable *septaria* probably explains its collapse. There is more of the same stone in the chancel walls, and the position of the *priest's doorway* shows that the chancel was shortened when the new e. wall was built. The doorway's *dripstone* has worn *headstops*, and one of them can still be recognised as a *green man*. There is a lot more septaria in the mixed rubble of the nave n. wall, and the massive wedge-shaped C18 buttresses remain in place. Barnes' rebuilding was in C14 style – dense flintwork, with sharp and quirky window *tracery*. The tower changes character in the shallow bell stage, and has sturdy little corner turrets and orderly *flushwork* decoration. To use old headstones for paving slabs must often seem a good idea, but surely not when they have well cut, interesting inscriptions – like Colour Sgt. Thomas Smith's close to the aisle wall.

Passing through the tower *porch*, one finds that the roof of the w. end of the nave is higher than the rest. There was a plan to rebuild it all but it was not pursued, and the C14 roof is hidden behind a plaster ceiling, with heavy beams inserted below it. The *font* is a standard C15 East Anglian design in buff-coloured stone, and lions alternate with angels in the bowl panels. Apart from chipped noses, they are in fine condition, having been plastered over in the C17; there are defaced demi-angels and *fleurons* below the bowl, and the lions and *woodwoses* that guard the shaft suffered too. The 1960s glass in the nearby windows takes the three most popular themes of Christ's ministry and treats them conventionally. A slab in the floor e. of the font once bore the *brasses* of William Tabard and his wife, and the worn 18in. effigies with an inscription are now displayed on the wall by the door 'for better preservation and conspicuity' (a choice phrase). He died in 1459, and his wife wears a horned headdress and veil. The tablet on the n. wall embellished with a small open book is for Capt. Bynon RN who died in 1865. It is signed by Edward J. Physick, a successful Victorian sculptor who was not above bread and butter work. A second tablet by him further along commemorates William Boby whose main memorial is the e. window. The middle nave window contains 1970s glass by Paul Quail, a simply blocked Nativity in which the Christ Child offers an ear of wheat to his mother; a cross is worked symbolically into the stable cladding and the animal kingdom is well represented although *St Joseph* is offstage. Other work by Quail can be found at Hopton, Somerleyton and Sweffling, but the only Suffolk example of John Hayward's work is the last n. window here. It is a good 1960s design symbolising the teaching of the Old and New Testaments with strong figures of Moses and an *Evangelist*, using a smoky line firmly in the *Arts & Crafts* tradition. Displayed below is a lectern Bible 'presented to Walton in July 1619 by the desire of his Majesty King James I' – unusual distinction for a humble seaside hamlet. The outer windows in the s. aisle each have one light with stained glass by the same maker, and the centre window is a lively picture across the whole width. In it, a lifeboat surges past carrying a prayerful survivor from the barque driven ashore in the background, while Christ stands on the nearer bank displaying his wounds. The interior has been transformed by removing the old pitchpine pews and replacing them with comfortable chairs. The walls have been painted cream and the *arcade* enlivened with delicate lines of gold. The early-C14 chancel arch has no *capitals*, and the panels of the C15 *rood screen* have been placed on each side. Their details are a little unusual – triple *quatrefoils* enclosing shields at the top, large quatrefoils with shields at the bottom, and curious, arrow-shaped mouldings in between. The choir stalls have been banished and the chancel has been re-ordered to provide an attractive small worship space. The church's second brass is fixed to the wall by the organ, a 10in. by 6in. plate engraved with the kneeling figure of William Simond who died aged 11 in 1612. Except for the initial letters of his name, the acrostic verse below had quite worn away before the brass was lifted from the floor. The 1850s e. window glass may be by *Ward & Hughes*, although it is reminiscent of work by Alexander Gibbs – a dense, attractive pattern of lilies and vine leaves against strong red and blue backing; the centre panel of the *Three Marys* is undistinguished and eroded.

Wangford, St Denis (I3): Small and vulnerable in more ways than one, the church lies on the edge of Lakenheath air base, lonely among the heaths; a sure candidate for redundancy but for the fact that, by chance, it has fulfilled a need. It is now the Tabernacle Missionary Baptist church and is used regularly by a group of American Christians. It was originally *Norman* and both n. and s. doors are C12, with scalloped *capitals* on plain shafts and later arches. The C14 tower has angle buttresses to the w. and tall *Decorated* bell openings. The *chancel w*as pulled down in the C19 and subsequent restorations did not replace it. The e. window with its pretty C14 style *tracery* must, therefore, be modern. Inside, it is as plain and bare as any church could be and has a resigned dignity. The C19 pulpit and *altar* have been relegated to the tower and jostle the square C13 *font*, with its wide corner chamfers on bowl and shaft. A small niche by the n. door has an *ogee* arch and on the chancel n. wall there is a *brass* inscription for Dorothe Francklyn, with the shield of arms missing. She died in 1596 and was the sister of Sir Edward Coke, Queen Elizabeth's Attorney General. The e. wall carries early-C19 boards with the Creed, *Decalogue* and Lord's Prayer, and the modern roof has one set of *cusped arch-braces* on *colonnettes* to mark off part of the *nave* as a new chancel. Not an exciting building but be thankful that it is still used as the founders intended.

Wangford, St Peter (I3): Restoration and additions by C19 Earls of Stradbroke have determined the dominant characteristics of this fine church, but it began as part of a Cluniac Priory, a cell of the mother house at Thetford. Founded in 1160, it served both monks and villagers until the priory was dissolved in 1528. A circuit of the building is useful to identify the old and the new, and look first at the C15 *nave*, with its large, four-*light* w. window. It was restored and altered in 1863, when three flying buttresses were added to strengthen the s. wall. The *chancel* was entirely rebuilt in 1875 under the direction of A.L. Blackburne, and he designed the tower at the e. end of the n. *aisle*. At the same time, a large *vestry* was added on the s. side, eccentrically placed so that it partially masks a nave window. The tall chancel has octagonal corner turrets, and there is bold *flushwork* below the e. window, with an inscription to mark the rebuilding. The sturdy tower has heavy buttresses to belfry level, and *gargoyles* jut from the corners below stepped flushwork battlements and pinnacles. It houses an unringable five with an 8 cwt. tenor. The n. aisle, with flushwork *base course*, formed part of the medieval church, and there is an interesting variation in its windows. Two have *Perpendicular tracery*, but the third uses a form of the *Decorated* four-petalled flower, above lights with triangular tops. The aisle thus marks the transition from one style to the other, late in the C14. Churches are visited for a variety of reasons, and some readers may like to know that this side of the church is noted for the quality of its lichens – judged the best in the county. The plain *porch* abuts the end of the aisle, and with a window blocked on that side, one assumes that it was there first.

A broad and spacious interior, and again the first impression is one of solid Victorian quality – new stonework, *encaustic tiles*, good stained glass, and the low open benches so often seen in town churches of the period. There is a recess by the entrance which may have housed a *stoup*, and ahead is the late-C14 *font*. Eight columns ring the shaft, with window tracery between them, and the bowl has linked circles containing *quatrefoils*, with *castellations* above and below; the cover is modern. The tall aisle *arcade* has quatrefoil *piers*, and a rather strange low level arch intervenes between the second and third bays. One would expect to find a tomb beneath it, but there is none, and the arch appears to have been reworked so it may have suffered a change in the C19. The nave roof has castellated *tie-beams* and *wall plates*, it is plastered between the principal timbers, and there are *bosses* along the ridge. The 1880s glass in the w. window is by Gibbs &

Howard whose only other work in the county is at Haverhill. In the l.-hand light Jesus scatters money and pigeons in all directions as he banishes the Temple traders, the centre spread illustrates the building of the Temple, and on the r., the Israelites carry the ark of the Covenant through the wilderness. All bright and lavish under canopies, with *Evangelistic symbols* and a pair of red-winged seraphim in the tracery. At the w. end of the nave s. wall there is an attractive memorial for Sir John Rous who died in 1730; in veined marble, with a lively *cartouche* set against the upper obelisk, it has shapely flanking scrolls and a trio of cherub heads below. In the C15, there were parish *guilds* of *SS Peter, George*, and *John the Baptist*, and the capacious image niche in the centre of the s. wall may well have been associated with one of them. The other stained glass in the nave is excellent work by *Clayton & Bell*, dating from the early C20. Little scenes illustrating the *Seven Works of Mercy* surround the figure of Charity. Further e. is the 1827 memorial for John, 1st earl of Stradbroke. Above the tablet, a lovely woman rests her mourning head against a draped tomb at whose foot lies a coronet upon a tasselled cushion. This is the work of William Behnes, a fine artist, much sought after in his day, whose later life was a catalogue of disaster. He ended literally in the gutter outside the Middlesex Hospital with threepence in his pocket. Moving over to the aisle, Reginald Hammond's 1750s epitaph on the w. wall has a nice turn of phrase: 'He discharged ye station of life He was long plac'd in with such Exactness, Industry and Integrity As justly Intitled him to better'. On the n. wall, the 1652 memorial for Sir John Rous and Dame Elizabeth has lost its shield of arms from the top, and further along there is an accomplished piece by John Walsh for the Sir John who died in 1771. It is a broad, well lettered tablet, with a small urn in relief against the backing obelisk which has a wide urn *finial*. Another and rather more elaborate memorial by Walsh is to be found at Little Thurlow. The aisle *altar* is a *Stuart* table, and one has to squeeze behind it to find the church's only *brass* – a shield and inscription of 1635 for Christopher Rous and his infant son John who had died a year before. The reading desk and pulpit that flank the chancel steps formed part of the large pulpit which was in the private chapel of Henham Hall before the 1773 fire. They display fine C17 Flemish work, with varied and richly carved panels, scrolls and *caryatids*. The panels are inlaid with marquetry the colour of butterscotch, with an interior

perspective and a floral design featuring on the pulpit. Blackburne designed the fittings for his broad and spacious chancel, and above the handsome oak stalls, the *arch-braced* roof has demi-angels stretching out below the *wall posts*. There is a panelled *celure* above the *sanctuary*, and the elaborate *piscina* and *sedilia* have a profusion of spindly detail and polished marble shafts. The stone *reredos* is richly carved in *Early English* style, deeply recessed, with mosaic roundels of *Evangelistic symbols* at the back. In the 1870s e. window, tall, calm figures stand under pretty canopies – SS Peter & *Paul* flanking a scene illustrating the story of *Dorcas*. This rich glass is by *Heaton, Butler & Bayne*, but the source of the s. chancel window has not been identified. There, bright, almost gaudy canopies and base panels frame two scenes – one of which might well represent *St Anne* teaching the *Blessed Virgin* to read, despite the chosen text. You may be lucky enough to see the church's beautiful *William Morris* altar frontal. It is the 1878 'Bird' design which he chose for the hangings in his Hammersmith house. Handwoven on a jacquard loom in wool double cloth, this example was probably made in the early C20.

Wantisden, St John (H5): The church lies on the very edge of Bentwaters airfield; there is a long, clearly signposted metalled track up to it, and it is sensible to make enquiries about the key before a visit. The graceless buildings of the former base are only 100yds. from the tower, but resolutely ignore them. Look instead the other way, across the rolling fields and plantations of Hall Farm, and savour the wind in the long grasses of the churchyard. The village was always scattered, and its church and first manor were probably sited close to each other originally. The medieval manor lies some way off to the s., and the advent of the airforce changed the nature of the parish irrevocably. Now, a dedicated nucleus of people maintain the church and there are regular services.

It is a compact, delightful building, and shares with Chillesford the distinction of having a tower which is built entirely of coralline crag limestone – the only examples in England. The beige, attractively textured stone is full of fossilised shells and was quarried from small pits in the Orford peninsular. The muscular C14 tower is virtually without ornament; there are angle buttresses with Caen stone *quoins* to the w., and the low doorway between them retains a crowned *headstop*. Above it, a *Perpendicular* w. window, and the small bell openings have

Decorated tracery. A n. door of about 1300 has been blocked, and the stratified flints in the wall further along are a sign of an early building – confirmed by the *Norman lancet* in the n. wall of the *chancel.* Beyond it, a change in the rubble pattern shows that the e. end was extended around the beginning of the C14. The e. window, *priest's door* and windows on the s. side belong to that stage of development. The main entrance is a Norman s. doorway which has single shafts, and its broad *dripstone* is carved with two bands of saw-tooth decoration; grotesque masks act as *stops*, and there is a third above the arch. The stone is very weathered, but at least one *scratch dial* can be found on the l.

The simple interior has changed so little that it reminds one of an C18 engraving, with its brick floors, dun-coloured walls, and rustic *tie-beams* below a plastered ceiling. The *font* is remarkable in its construction, being one of three in England that are made of small blocks of stone. It could be C11, but the base mould is late-C12, and the whole piece may date from then; a band of scallop ornament runs below the large drum bowl. A *ledger-stone* nearby carries a *brass* inscription for Robert Harvie (one of the Ickworth Herveys) who died in 1633; the achievement of arms has disappeared, and the space that was left for his wife's death date was never used. *Royal Arms* of George III hang on the n. wall and, like those at Barnby, their supporters spring most unheraldically from behind the shield. Dated 1800 and painted on canvas, they have been well restored, and note how the frame was roughly shaped to fit the top the of the chancel arch when they were first installed. Two double roundels mark the sites of *consecration crosses* on the n. wall, and there are traces of early painted wall decoration, including a diaper pattern scored into the plaster. Simple benches flank the tower arch, their ends drilled for candle prickets. The rest of the *nave* is filled with low C15 benches standing on heavy sills, and they have been adapted haphazardly over the years. The ends have *poppyheads*, most of the back rails are *castellated*, and the stumps of figures and animals remain on the elbows. Some have had rough panelling added to heighten them, and four on the n. side have simplified replacement ends. As was the fashion, all were varnish-grained in the C18 or early C19. A ledger-stone at the e. end of the nave commemorates Awnam Briani Smith who died in 1655, and its large shield of arms is set within a laurel wreath. The massive Norman chancel arch has *chevron* and roll mouldings above single

shafts; an image niche was fitted in on the l. in the C14 or C15, and small apertures were cut later in the flanking walls to improve the view into the chancel. There is no *screen* now, but the stair to the *rood loft* is complete in the s. wall, and the siting of the upper doorway shows that the screen will have masked most of the Norman arch. Late-C18 or early-C19 *Decalogue* boards are framed aloft, and the floor of the chancel beyond is bright with C19 *encaustic tiles*, one of the few significant changes of modern times. On the n. side, the Norman lancet has a typically deep splay, and nearby, Smyth of Woodbridge supplied a tablet for the parson, Thomas Comyn Clerk. His coloured shield is in an oval at the top, and the epitaph includes his wife Anne, 'who exchanged time for eternity' in 1838, a transition that seems unremarkable in this peaceful place. The church's other brass is a beautifully clear 'black letter' inscription of 1582 for Mary Wingfelde on a ledger-stone in front of the *altar*. There are *dropped-sill sedilia* below the s. window, and the *piscina* alongside has a broad *trefoil* arch; the original wooden *credence shelf* survives within.

Washbrook, St Mary (F6): This little church is hidden away in a fold of the country, remote from its village, and approached by a sunken winding lane. There is an arch of yew within the gate and the churchyard is exquisitely peaceful. Two small *Norman lancets* in the *nave* walls date its beginnings and at the base of the w. wall of the tower there is a large glacial boulder. As at Bramford and other churches in this area, stones like this were probably used in the foundations to cancel their pagan associations and secure allegiance to the new religion. The tower has a flint chequer *base course* and *Perpendicular* w. window, and its single bell was cast by the London founder Richard Hille who was active between 1423 and 1440. In the nave and *chancel* the windows have C14 *Decorated tracery* involving curved *mouchettes*. On the e. wall you will see the outline of a large window that probably matched, but a smaller version was inserted as part of a C19 restoration. At that time a n.e *vestry* was added, a baptistry was built on to the n. door, and the *priest's door* on the s. side of the chancel was replaced. There is a *scratch dial* on the buttress to its l. The Victorian open porch shelters a C14 doorway whose *dripstone* has large male and female *headstops*.

Just inside, there is a simple *stoup* recess and an C18 or C19 *bier* rests against the wall beyond the tall and plain tower arch. A decorative set of

Victorian *Royal Arms* is placed above the entrance to the baptistry, three-dimensional in coloured and gilt plaster, and the *font* beyond is an excellent C15 example. In the bowl panels there are four angels holding shields, three *pomegranate*s, and a splendid *Tudor Rose*; demi-angels decorate the underside, and snooty lions strain back against the stem. The C19 stained glass has an appropriate theme although it is badly eroded, but there is a very handsome window on the n. side of the nave. Installed in the early C20, it commemorates the life of Queen Victoria, with her arms and crest set in *quarries* decorated with the royal monogram; roses, thistles, and shamrocks form a border. A tall wrought-iron *hour-glass stand* rests on a new stone *corbel* above the monolithic C19 pulpit, and the roof overhead is a C14 *tie-beam* and *king post* construction. The chancel is a lovely, coherent essay in the Decorated style, and unusually lavish for such a small church. On both sides the walls are lined with six stalls, each in its niche below *cusped* and *crocketted ogee* arches. There are delightful miniature headstops above the shafts, and a *string course* connects the arcade with the window embrasures to the w. where there are matching blind arches. On the s. side it continues to link up with a *sedile* and *piscina*, and to the n. the scheme is completed by a beautiful *Easter sepulchre*. The arch of its tall, shallow niche is elaborately cusped and the combination of sinuous curves is quite Islamic. The 1860s *Ward & Hughes* glass in the e. window combines the sacrifice of Isaac with a Crucifixion and is badly eroded, particularly the figure of Christ. Looking w. you will see the Walsingham family arms in the tower window – again C19. The church's only medieval *brass* is an inscription for Edmund Knappe (1609) which is now in the window embrasure on the s. side of the chancel (there is another behind the organ for the Revd. Joseph Clarke who died in 1653 but it is a modern reproduction). Within the vestry, the *tester* of a *Jacobean* pulpit has been converted into a table top, and in the corner is a very strange little chest. It is wedge-shaped and heavily banded with iron, with a hinged half-lid; the top is covered with strapwork in a dense scroll pattern which is C13 in form, but whether the chest is as old as that is doubtful.

Wattisfield, St Margaret (E3): Judging by the shape of the small w. window and the interior arch, the tower must date from the end of the C13 or thereabouts. Unbuttressed, it has a *flush work base course*, a large *Decorated* belfry window,

and *Perpendicular* bell openings. It houses a ground floor ring of five bells with an 8 cwt. tenor. There was a *scratch dial* on a *quoin* of the s.w. corner, just above the plinth, but little remains of it except the centre hole. The C15 s. *porch* (now the *vestry*) has a *knapped* flint face and the diagonal buttresses are decorated with crowned 'M's and monograms. The outer arch is picked out with thin red bricks and the top was extensively repaired in the C17 or C18 in brick. Above the arch is a terracotta shield bearing remnants of the De La Pole coat of arms. Overhead is a stone sundial, unusually angled out from the wall. All the windows of the *nave* and *chancel* have Perpendicular *tracery* (much of it renewed), and you will see that the line of an earlier roof shows on the e. face of the tower. There is a *priest's door* on the n. side of the chancel. The n. porch is one of the few remaining examples in wood and probably dates from the C15 or early C16. The sides have been renewed in part, but the outer arch is formed from two large slabs of timber and simply moulded.

Within the church, the tower arch is sharp and tall, with no *capitals*. The bowl of the C15 *font* carries blank shields and the shaft panels are decorated with window tracery. The C17 cover has a turned *finial* and the radiating ribs are carved with stylised eagle heads and scrolls. Both nave and chancel have modern, *scissors-braced* roofs and there is a heavy stone pulpit of 1888. The nearby window sill is lowered and may indicate that a side *altar* was positioned here before the *Reformation*. The stairs to the *rood loft* went up on the s. side of the nave and the doorway at the bottom still has its hinge pins. Parts of the old *rood screen* have been reused in the front of the prayer desks and the lectern top. On the s. wall of the chancel, a memorial to Elizabeth Bury (d.1746) has a graceful epitaph, typical of the 'age of elegance':

...Admit thee! to the chorus of the Blest,
A willing traveller and a welcome Guest.

On the n. wall of the *sanctuary* is a small *touchstone* panel set in a plain alabaster frame. It is a C17 memorial to John Osborne, who sounds as though he was a local magistrate:

A freind to vertue, A lover of learning,
of prudence greate, of Justice a furtherer,
Redress he did the wrongs of many a
    wight,
Fatherless & widdowes by him possess
    their right,

To search & trie each cause and end all strife
With patience great he spent his mortal life.
Whom blessed we accompt (as Scripture
saith)
Who peace did make & liv'd & died i'th'
faith.

Wenhaston, St Peter (I3): The church stands above the village street and there is a splendid yew tree in the s. churchyard. Traces of the original *Saxon* building were uncovered when the *chancel* was restored in 1892, and two small *Norman lancets* are to be seen in the s. wall of the *nave*. The tower probably dates from the late C14 and there is *flushwork* in the bottom stage of its diagonal buttresses; the w. window and bell openings have *Perpendicular tracery* and there is a modern flushwork parapet. St Peter's has an excellent ground floor ring of six bells with a 12 cwt. tenor. The n. *aisle* lies under a continuation of the nave roof, its wall sustained by a series of wedge-shaped C18 brick buttresses. The e. window was renewed in 1892 but the C13 lancets in the side walls were undisturbed and there is a contemporary *priest's door* on the s. side. Perpendicular windows were inserted in the s. wall of the nave, and note the window at high level which was added to give extra light to the *rood*. The C15 *porch* was re-roofed at some stage, making its *gargoyles* redundant, and the small head *corbels* inside show that there was a *groined* ceiling originally. A *stoup* is sited by the entrance and its niche has a drain groove so perhaps the bowl came from elsewhere. The inner C15 doorway displays *Trinity* and *Passion* shields in the *spandrels*, and there are hung shields in the mouldings. The door itself is medieval and still has its C13 closing ring.

Having entered, one's attention focuses naturally on Wenhaston's celebrated *Doom* painting against the n. aisle wall. Painted about 1520 and measuring some 17ft. by 8ft., it originally filled the upper part of the chancel arch and formed a background to the rood. When the rood figures and cross were removed later in the C16, the Doom was simply whitewashed and left in place. There it remained until 1892 when the chancel arch was rebuilt as part of the restoration. Having been cast into the churchyard as fit only for burning, a providential downpour loosened some of the whitewash and it was recognised for what it was. Carefully cleaned and restored, it is the most perfect of the painted tympana that survive. Painted in oil on boards, the colours are remarkably fresh, and although *Pevsner* describes the quality as 'distressingly rustic', the scenes are fascinating. Blank shapes indicate the positions of Christ on the cross and the attendant *Blessed Virgin* and *St John*. In the top l. corner, Christ in Glory is seated on a rainbow while his mother and *St John the Baptist* kneel to the r. To the l. of the cross, *St Paul*, crowned and vested in a cope receives a royal couple, a bishop and a cardinal. They are naked except for their identifying headgear to underline the moral that all are equal before the judgement seat. To the r. of the cross, *St Michael* weighs souls against little devils in his scales, while the Devil stands by holding a scroll (note the extra head in his loins). To the r., four of his minions dispatch the damned into the gaping jaws of hell, while on the other side a red robed angel welcomes the blessed into the heavenly fortress. When tympana were no longer needed for their original purpose they were often used to display *Royal Arms* and appropriate texts. Here, a quotation from St Paul's Epistle to the Romans (13:1) was added along the bottom. Illegible now in parts, the complete text read: 'Let every soule Submyt him selfe unto the authorytye of the hygher powers for there is no power but of God. The Powers that be are ordeyned of God, but they that resest or are againste the ordinaunce of God shall receyve to them selves utter damnacion. For rulers are not fearefull to them that do good but to them that do evyll for he is the mynister of God'.

Below the Doom, the crown of a C15 bell rests against the wall. It came from the Bury St Edmunds foundry of Reignold Church, and the maker's device shows that he cast cannon as well; the inscription reads: 'Sancta Anna ora pro nobis' (*St Anne* pray for us). Just to the w. of the entrance there is a *banner stave locker* with a modern door, and a good set of George III's Royal Arms on canvas hangs by the tower arch. The C15 *Seven Sacrament font* is a relatively simple design compared with others in the county, and extraordinary though it may seem, the panel sculptures were totally destroyed in the mid-C19 – a late example of senseless vandalism. Much of the original colour remains, particularly below the bowl and in the shaft niches. The n. *arcade* dates from about 1400, and the late-C15 nave roof has *arch-braces* that rise to pendant ridge posts which are braced laterally; more braces carved with shields run between the *wall posts*. There are comfortable modern chairs throughout, but sections of *Jacobean* panelling have survived here and there from earlier pews, and there are two pairs of C15 bench ends with *poppyheads* at the e. end of the nave. The *Stuart*

Wenhaston, St Peter: Doom painting

pulpit has two ranges of panels – familiar *blind arches* above, and unusual flower designs in shallow relief below; two of the brackets below the bookshelf have had modern heads added. The wooden chancel arch and waggon roof were part of the 1890s restoration, and the glass in the e. window must have been installed at the same time. The maker has not been identified and the feeling is vaguely *Pre-Raphaelite*, with nicely judged colour – a Crucifixion group, with *St Mary Magdalene* at the foot of the cross, and *Passion emblems* with the Dove of the Holy Spirit in the tracery. To the l. is an attractive monument of 1757 for Philippa Leman; a small urn in a circular recess, cherub head above and *cartouche* on the *pediment*, with the epitaph tablet swelling gently out below. It is signed 'P.L.' but I have not been able to identify the sculptor. On the other side of the window, Eliza Rooe's 1747 memorial in varied marble is a more conventional architectural design with flanking *Ionic* columns.

Westerfield, St Mary Magdalene (F6): The tower was rebuilt in the early C15 but a fragment of *Norman* stonework survives just above the plinth at the s.e. corner. The w. doorway has *paterae* in the mouldings and roses in the *spandrels*, but its most interesting feature is the l.-hand *stop*. It is very worn, but portrays a figure kneeling alongside a mass of foliage within

which there seems to be the remains of a small head – all above a little palisade. It must once have had a quite specific significance but the other stop is too eroded to provide a clue and this remains, for me at least, an iconographical mystery. The bell openings have been much altered and there are *flushwork* battlements above. Until 1986, an 1840s schoolroom of little merit adjoined the n. side of the *nave*, but to celebrate its 900th birthday the church replaced this with a square *vestry*-cum-meeting room linked by a foyer to the n. door. With flint pebble walls and a hipped roof, it blends very well with the medieval building, and has an attractive arrangement of windows – bays to the e. and w., three bay-*lancets* to the n. The nave windows have 'Y' *tracery* of about 1300 (some are C19 replacements) and in the n. wall of the *chancel* there is a C13 lancet. The e. window, with intersecting 'Y' tracery, has bishop and queen headstops and the *corbel heads* at its base are modern replicas. Round the corner on the s. side there is a blocked lancet with a *trefoil* head next to a *priest's door* in *Tudor* brick. For some unexplained reason, a restoration in 1867 did away with a Norman s. doorway and replaced it with a window, but the *stoup* remains in the wall to mark its position.

Entry is via the w. door and the narrow base of the tower. It has a very tall arch and there are dark C18 *Decalogue* boards on the side walls.

The glass in the w. window is by *Morris & Co* and dates from 1867, a prolific period for the company. It embodies no new principle of design or composition but repeats a tried and tested formula. Apart from the red and white roses by Philip Webb in the tracery, all the figures are by Morris, with four musical angels in white patterned with gold around a central figure of *St Mary Magdalene*. She wears a yellow brocade dress, bears her traditional emblem, and her very masculine face is framed in a mass of flowing hair; an 1865 version of the same design can be found at Antingham in Norfolk. The background *quarries* are patterned with *pomegranates* and the whole window has a lukewarm feeling about it. A set of George III *Royal Arms* painted on board hangs above the tower arch. The C15 *font* displays *Evangelistic symbols* in the bowl panels, together with angels bearing shields (n.e. *Trinity* emblem, s.e. three *chalices* for the Blessed Sacrament); very upright lions guard the shaft. Pieces of *chevron moulding* from the old Norman s. doorway survive in the arch and *jambs* of the window that replaced it, and (unusually) there was another stoup in the inside wall. The roof is a rare example of a C15 *hammerbeam* design that stretches uninterruptedly over nave and chancel, the division marked only by a heavy, *castellated rood beam*. Built on a more intimate scale than most, the roof merits careful study and strategically placed spotlights are a help. Its most striking feature is the series of demi-figures on the ends of the hammers and at the base of the *wall posts*. Some are renewals dating from 1901 but the majority are original and they are remarkable survivals. *William Dowsing* does not record an image-smashing session here, and for a village church so close to Ipswich to go unscathed (at least in this respect) suggests that there was someone locally with powerful friends. In the chancel the figures are of angels but in the nave kings and queens bear shields displaying a fine set of *Passion emblems*. On the s. wall is an attractive pictorial map of the village that won the local W.I. first prize in a 1977 county competition, and one light of a window opposite contains glass by Morris & Co of 1921 – a figure of *St Michael* which is a typical production of the firm's latter days and a far cry from the *pre-Raphaelite* beginnings. There is a portion of the stairs to the vanished *rood loft* in the s. wall, and the crucifix on the pulpit came from Oberammergau in 1951. The glass in the n. chancel lancet is interesting because it is one of *Burne-Jones's* designs for Morris & Co. Although it commemorates Mary Jane Drage

who died in 1850, the figure of Christ bearing a banner dates from 1873 and is a repeat of an 1871 window in Kirkbampton church, Cumberland. Nearby is a tablet commemorating *Henry Munro Cautley*, the diocesan architect whose name occurs so often in this book, and the bas-relief roundel portrait at the top betrays more than a passing likeness to Rudyard Kipling. Cautley's father was rector here and he himself read the lessons here for most of his life. Appropriately, he designed the lectern and the *reredos*. The latter dates from 1938 and has small-scale pierced tracery, with a central canopied niche for the altar cross; small statuettes stand under canopies each side, and the rest of the e. wall is taken up with six shallow seat recesses under intricate tracery and a heavy cornice. His other work in the church is the war memorial by the n. door, which confirms me in the belief that he was never any good at this sort of thing. There are *dropped-sill sedilia* on the s. side of the *sanctuary* and a *piscina* lies within a square recess. On the n. wall there is a memorial for Maj. John Whitefoord of the 15th Hussars who was severely wounded at Waterloo and fell victim to a shooting misadventure in 1825. It is probably an exaggeration to say that the family was accident prone, but Lady Deborah Whitefoord's death in 1829 was 'occasioned by her clothes taking fire in consequence of which dreadful accident she languished in extreme agony for eight and twenty days'. The sad tale is set forth on a large tablet by Matthias John Crake of London; it has a bas-relief urn against an obelisk on top. Round your visit off by visiting Cautley's grave near the kissing-gate s.w. of the tower and remember that we would not know nearly as much about Suffolk churches without his memorable survey.

Westhall, St Andrew (I2): Away from the rest of the village down its own little lane, this most interesting church deserves careful study. It illustrates, more clearly than most, an historical sequence, and it is useful to have this firmly in mind before looking at the details. To begin with, there was a *Norman* church of *nave* and *chancel*. Then, in the late C13, a tower was built onto the w. end, and a n. *aisle* was added. The crucial change came in the C14, when a splendid new *chancel* was built, and because it masked the s. side, the old Norman chancel was dismantled. About the same time the C13 *arcade* was replaced, and then in the C15 the walls of nave and s. aisle were heightened to take larger windows, and new roofs were installed. The n. *porch* was built in the C16, and by way of completion, the tower was heightened in the C17. A circuit of the building establishes the pattern of development. The angle buttresses of the C13 tower have *flushwork* panels in the bottom stage; the w. window is a *trefoil lancet*, with another at belfry level, and there are *gargoyles* at the corners of the flushwork battlements. The date of the C13 n. aisle (which later became the nave) is confirmed by the form of its buttresses and the large blocked lancet which is partially masked by the C16 porch. The latter is substantial, with an *arch-braced* roof, and there are *Trinity* and *Passion* shields in the *spandrels* of the outer arch. The inner doorway has inward-turning, battered *headstops*, and the door itself is medieval, with keeled boards and closing ring. Like the s. aisle, the nave is thatched, and its C15 windows have *ogee tracery*. The broad and tall C14 chancel has *reticulated* tracery in the five-*light* e. window and two of the side windows. However, one window on each side displays a particularly eccentric variation in which an octofoil at the top cuts into the reticulation pattern. The handsome *priest's door* has an ogee arch, with worn headstops and *finial*, and there are traces of three *scratch dials* on the buttress to the l. If you look to the l. of the aisle e. window, you will see the *jamb* of the original Norman chancel arch, and the footings of the *apsidal* chancel lie under your feet. There are significant variations to be seen in the masonry of the s. wall. At the base is the typical Norman pattern of layered flints, while higher up you will see where the wall was raised in the C15 to take the larger windows – one of which overlays the outline of a C13 predecessor. There is a lot of variation at the e. end and *corbels* with rounded ends from the Norman *corbel table* are scattered at random. The arch of the Norman s. door has a rim of *billet* moulding and then a band of lightly carved scallops whose pattern varies below the *abaci*.

Having entered, go into the tower to see the fine Norman w. facade which was the main entrance to the old nave. The church's ring of five bells with a 10 cwt. tenor is rung from here. The broad doorway has an outer moulding of cable and billet, a succession of beast masks of which only six are carved, a wave moulding, and then a broad band decorated with four-petalled flowers. The jambs have *chevron*, nail-head, and surface decoration, and there are pairs of shafts each side. The window above has bobbin and disk ornament in its arch, and it is flanked by blind chevroned arches. It is strange that the C13 builders chose to cover up such a splendid

entrance with their tower. By the s. door there is a *consecration cross* with leafy tendrils sprouting from the disk, and the wall painting between the windows may have been a *Seven Works of Mercy* or similar sequence. There is a painted backing for an image in one of the window splays, another consecration cross nearby, and further along hangs a set of George III *Royal Arms* painted on canvas. The roof is arch-braced, and there are transverse braces between the principals carved with flowers and foliage. Nicholas Bohun died in 1602 and his tomb stands in the s.e. corner of the aisle. He married the sister of Sir Edward Coke, England's first great lawyer, and the *brass* on the wall behind sets out his genealogy in considerable detail. The *Seven Sacrament font* stands on two tall steps in the spacious nave, and is remarkable for the amount of colour that survives, particularly on vestments and details like the *altar* frontal of the mass panel. Unusual too is the use of *gesso* for the beautifully delicate niches containing saints on the buttresses, and there is even gesso ornament on the rim. Clockwise from the e., the panels are: mass; baptism of Christ; ordination (note the lettered book and *chrismatory*); baptism; confirmation; matrimony; penance; extreme unction. The penance panel is particularly interesting because a demon, large enough to have played the part of the Bad Angel in a morality play is sneaking away from the kneeling penitent, a telling example of an image taken from the contemporary stage. On the n. wall a fine *St Christopher* stands within a painted doorway, with Moses receiving the tablets of the law in the top left hand corner (he was always shown with *horns of light* by medieval artists). The nave roof has cambered *collar beams* and there is pierced tracery on either side of the *king posts*. Painted demi-angels with shields perch at the base of the *wall posts*, and all have lost their heads. The *Stuart* pulpit has a broad *blind arched* front panel and well carved brackets support the canted ledge. The *rood stair* remains in the n. wall, but there is now no upper opening, and of the *screen* only the bottom panels remain – remnants of what must have been a splendid piece. The base moulds of the chancel arch are over 4ft. from the floor and in the C14 there was probably a solid partition like the one at Little Wenham. The *capitals* of the arch were cut away to take the top of the C15 screen, but there is nothing now above the centre rail which is painted with the donors' inscription: '...Margarete uxoris euis Orate p aia Tome feltonie Orate p aia ric lore ac p bono statu Margarete alen vidue qui istud...' ([Pray for the soul of ... and] Margaret his wife. Pray for the soul of Thomas Felton. Pray for the soul of Richard Lore and for the good estate of Margaret Alen, widow, who [made this]). The base panels are badly mutilated and nearly all the tracery has gone from those on the s. side. The colour scheme follows the Norfolk convention, with wavy bands on the mouldings and naturalistic foliage but the figures are decidedly odd. They seem to form two distinct groups – those on the n. are primitive and unlike any others in East Anglia, while the s. range resemble those at Ufford, set against a background of leaded windows. From l. to r. they are: *SS James the Great, Leonard, Michael, Clement*, Moses, Christ of the Transfiguration, Elias, *Anthony, Etheldreda* (half only), *Sitha, Agnes, Bridget, Catherine, Dorothy, Margaret*, and *Apollonia*. Pictures of the *Transfiguration* are rare and this is the only one to be found on a screen. The spacious chancel was thoroughly restored in 1882 and some of the choir stalls have carved *poppyheads*. The collars of the single-framed roof carry rosettes and one in the centre has a carving of the Trinity, with God the Father holding the crucified Christ between his knees (a village guild was dedicated to the Trinity in the C14). The arch of the *piscina* has lost all its surface ornament, and there is an unusually deep drain. It is rare to find two *credence shelves* (only three other instances are known), and at the w. end of the *dropped-sill sedilia* there is a recess for a towel like the one at Reydon. C19 *Decalogue* boards flank the e. window whose tracery is filled with excellent C14 patterned glass, with more in one of the s. chancel windows.

Westhorpe, St Margaret (E4): This small but interesting church stands attractively by the village street, with a yew tree close to the s. *porch*, and when I was there in the spring, primroses carpeted the churchyard. In 1419, Dame Elizabeth Elmham left money for work on the *aisles* and steeple. Like a number of others in the neighbourhood, two of the tower buttresses are at right angles, broadening the e. face; there are four *string courses* and one of them lifts up as a *label* over the *Perpendicular* w. window, while the parapet is set out in bold, flint and stone chequerwork. The n. aisle has Perpendicular windows and the C17 brick Barrow chapel projects on that side of the *chancel*; it has battlements, octagonal corner turrets, and the outline of a classical window in the e. wall. The chancel e. window has C19 *tracery*, and in the s. wall there is a *priest's door* and windows with

Decorated tracery under deep labels. The window in the e. wall of the s. aisle is the same period but the design is unusually adventurous. The windows facing s. are Perpendicular, and when the porch was added in the C15, it was carelessly set out so that it encroaches on the window to the r. There is a niche over the outer arch and the early-C14 entrance door has simple mouldings with *headstops*. To the r., a restored niche with a traceried head probably contained a *stoup*. The door itself is medieval, with surface tracery and closing ring.

Apart from work on the chancel in the 1890s, the interior was largely undisturbed in the C19 and has a homely intimacy. The floors are an attractively uneven mixture of bricks, medieval tiles and *ledger-stones*, and there is a C13 grave slab by the wall of the n. aisle, carved with the typical discoid cross and two omega signs. By the tower arch is a C14 iron-bound chest with a domed lid, and propped up against the walls are C18 boards painted with the Lord's Prayer, Creed and *Decalogue*. The door to the tower stair is heavily banded with iron, a sign that the upper chamber was used as a secure store for village valuables. The church has a ring of five bells with an 8 cwt. tenor but they cannot be rung at the present time. A small C17 *box pew*, whose only decoration is the turned corner *finials*, stands by the n. door, and on the n. wall is a set of *Royal Arms* that was reused twice. They are lettered for George III and dated 1765, but cleaning has revealed the earlier initials of James II and Queen Anne. The plain octagonal *font* could be a C19 replacement but the cover is *Stuart*. The C15 *nave* roof is a lovely pale colour and the *tie-beams* alternate with *arch-braces* above a Perpendicular *clerestory* which has four windows each side. A large tablet is fixed to the *arcade* pillar opposite the door in memory of Nathaniel Fox, who died in 1679 – a plain *touchstone* epitaph within a marble frame, and a *cartouche* of arms at the top. Joined to it below is a smaller memorial for his sister Mary, who had died three years before. That has a marble skull and wreath underneath and there is a cherub head engraved on the panel, with this epitaph:

Heavens Voyage Doth Not over hard
    appear,
She tooke it in her Early Virgin year.

The pulpit warrants close attention because two of the panels contain Decorated tracery which make it, at least in part, one of the earliest in the county. The early-C17 top cresting is in the style of chests of the period, and the rest is modern. To the r., a small door leads to the narrow *rood loft* stairs. The octagonal *piers* of the arcade originally had painted decoration and a section remains over the pulpit which shows a traceried and *crocketted* arch. There is also part of a C17 text above the s. door. In the wall of the s. aisle is a C14 recess which has had a modern finial added to the arch. The grave slab below may well be that of Henry de Elmham who died in 1330. Beyond it is a fine example of a C14 *parclose screen*. The sturdy Decorated tracery is coloured green and red and consists of *mouchettes* within circles, resting on slender columns. Some of these are replacements but the originals are striped like barbers' poles in black and white. There are stencil patterns on the uprights, traces of colour on both sides of the base panels, and a *castellated* cornice to the w. The C14 *piscina* had its top entirely replaced in the C19 and two *rood screen* panels that hang on the e. wall were repainted with angels so that their original decoration is lost. In the n. aisle there is a board reminding us that it was to Westhorpe that Henry VIII's sister Mary Tudor came to live after she had married her second husband, Charles Brandon, Duke of Suffolk. She died at the manor house in 1533 but was buried in the abbey at Bury before resting finally in St Mary's church there. A piscina in the wall of the rood loft stairs shows that there was an *altar* at the e. end of the n. aisle but in the C17 the wall was removed to give access to the Barrow chapel. This has a heavy centre pendant to the roof timbers, and one of the original chancel windows remains unglazed on the r. There was an e. window initially but the space was taken up in 1666 by a large monument for Maurice Barrow. The back wall carries a Latin epitaph within a wreathed surround, with drapes held back by two overweight cherubs, while another pair support the family arms above a curved cornice. The object of it all reclines with fleshy head thrown back and hand to breast, and it is interesting that under the tasselled pillow there is the rolled straw mat that was a convention of monuments 100 years earlier. The whole thing was 'designed and begun by Maurice Shelton but he being sudanely snatched out of this world', it was finished by his brother Henry who was by that time Barrow's heir.

Moving into the chancel, note that the *capitals* of the arch were notched to hold the screen and that the stalls have their original front panelling and wide book ledges. On the n. wall is a small and late *brass* set in a wooden frame in memory of Richard Elcock, the 'pastor of the congregation', who died in 1630, and it has a pleasing epitaph in rhyme for 'This faithful, Learned, Humble Man of God...'. In the *sanctuary*, the altar carries a pre-*Reformation mensa*, complete with *consecration crosses*, and although the e. window is a replacement the shafts each side are original. To the l. is a fine monument for another member of the Barrow family, Sir William, who died in 1615. It has been well cleaned and his little alabaster figure dressed in armour has much of the original colour. He kneels opposite his two wives, Frances and Elizabeth, who are dressed in black and have curious flat headdresses that project beyond their foreheads. Their two children kneel behind and there are two tiny infants bearing skulls below the prayer desk (showing that they died early). On the s. side is an excellent C14 piscina with an *ogee trefoiled* arch and crocketted finial, and remains of arches either side of the *sedilia* show that they were once canopied. By the piscina on the e. wall is a small touchstone tablet framed in alabaster, with a coloured shield of arms for Maria Dandy who died in 1615.

Westleton, St Peter (I4): The church stands back a little from the village street, and one enters the spacious churchyard between two massive small-leaved limes, relatively rare trees, although I noted another at Newton. Like a number of others in the county, the churchyard is now maintained as a nature reserve under the guidance of the Suffolk Trust for Nature Conservation. The church's tower fell in 1776 and only its base with angle buttresses remains. A photograph within shows that there was a spindly successor with a pyramid cap, but that too has gone, and now there is only a brick bellcote on the gable. There was apparently an earlier church on the site, but the present substantial building dates from the late-C13 or early-C14, and both *nave* and *chancel* lie under neat thatch. Walking round, you will see that the n. door is now blocked and that nearly all the window *tracery* has been renewed (there were restorations in 1857 and 1891, and much has been done since then). The large five-*light* e. window has intersected 'Y' tracery, there is a *priest's door* in the s. wall, and the nearby *low side window* has pretty Decorated tracery.

Through the simple s. *porch* to a spacious but homely interior, with brick floors and plastered ceiling. Have a look at the early photograph of the church on the wall beyond the tower arch, and at a minor curiosity opposite – the Lord's

Prayer in fretwork. It dates from the early C20 when there was a craze for the hobby, and another like it is to be found at Sweffling. The C15 *font* is in the familiar East Anglian design, with lions around the shaft, and deeply carved bowl panels displaying angels with shields and more lions. The benches date from 1857, and although they have C15 style *poppyheads*, a more comfort-conscious age added draft-excluding doors. The little painted and numbered shields are an unusually decorative relic of the days of pew rents and strictly allocated seating. The *piscina* to serve a nave *altar* remains in the s. wall, and there is a niche for its dedicatory saint in the window embrasure close by. The sill of the window opposite is lowered, and there is blind tracery with miniature shields carved on the flanking block – probably a fragment of a tomb, but it could have been the base of an elaborate niche. The *finials* of the 1930s priest's desk in front are vigorous, attractive carvings of a sower, and a fisherman taking his catch from the net, carved it would seem by a Capt. Jackson, a retired seafarer.

The long chancel, with its boarded ceiling, has recently been restored, and there are some fine C17 and C18 *ledger-stones* in the floor. Francis Snell's has an armorial roundel, and John Wood's displays a selection of grisly symbols. The large, worn slab to the e. once carried a huge brass effigy of a priest, but only the indents remain. Part of the grave slab of one of his C13 predecessors leans against the wall nearby. The 1940s stained glass in the side windows is by Edward Woore, the only example of his work in Suffolk. The panel on the n. side is a conventional 'Light of the world', but the s. window is more interesting. It commemorates a local farmer and the three sons he lost in the war, and there are figures of St Felix and *St George*, with an attractive vignette featuring farm tools, a sheaf, rod and gun. The choir stalls on the n. side incorporate two C15 ends with small poppyheads, and the traceried front on that side is original. The church's finest feature is the C13 piscina and *sedilia*, set below a range of arches with *cusping* that disappears quite eccentrically behind the arch mouldings at the top; the columns are free-standing and have good bases and *capitals*. Backhouse of Ipswich installed a tablet for William Woods on the n. wall in 1830, but it is not as stylish as Samuel and Susanna's alongside. Boldly lettered by Thomas Burgess of Great Yarmouth, this has reversed mourning torches on each side of the tapered tablet and is crowned with a graceful urn.

Readers of Ronald Fletcher's Westleton tales in his *In a Country Churchyard* will surely want to find the headstone just to the s. of the porch which marks the resting place of William Buck. The Crimean veteran and terror of the village children in his old age, served in the RHA and had a proper military funeral, complete with gun carriage. Just to the e. of the chancel lies June Perry who died aged 80 in 1838, 'Warrener in Windsor Great Park in the reigns of our several sovereigns George 3rd, George 4th, William 4th, and her present Majesty'. Grateful as we are for the story of 'Trinity Piffney', it is sad that no stone marks the grave of such a lovely character.

Westley, St Mary (C4): A road swoops up the hill to the village from the s. and the little church at the top looks quite decorative from a distance. A very simple building, it was designed by William Ranger, the architect of St John's Bury St Edmund's. The *nave* has three stepped *lancets* at each end and the tower on the s.w. corner has *quatrefoils* in the middle stage lighting the porch within and pairs of lancets as bell openings. Ranger's eccentric spire had to be removed in 1960 and was replaced by a red tile pyramid cap but a pencil drawing within shows what it was like. All the exterior was finished with Roman cement covered with *stucco* on which the various details were cast in imitation of stone, but this has weathered badly and is falling off in many places. The sandy-coloured interior is neat and simple and the boarded roof is supported by skeletal *arch-braces* rising to *king posts*, with open tracery. Under the ridge. They rest on little *hammerbeams* with octagonal pendants and are just the right weight for this size of building. Their apparent lightness is because they are cast-iron – unusual material in a church but very popular in factory and railway architecture of the period. There is no *chancel* but the walls break back to form a shallow *sanctuary* at the e. end. On the w. wall is an uncoloured set of *Hanoverian Royal Arms* in plaster and a board states that the rebuilding provided an additional 75 seats, so the original must have been very small. The two-manual American organ is a nice period piece in good condition whose 'mouse-proof pedals', patented in 1887, are fascinating. Half way up the aisle is a large *ledger-stone* with a roundel of arms for William Brooks who died in 1795, and there are three more C18 stones in the *sanctuary*. These will have been transferred from the earlier church, like the boards painted with the *Decalogue*, Creed and Lord's Prayer on the walls. The pulpit, more or less *Jacobean* in style, is a memorial for the two Westley men who died in World War I.

Weston, St Peter (I2): A mile or so w. of Ellough, the scattered hamlet straddles the Beccles-Blythburgh road, and its name doesn't feature on some maps. There has been a church here since before the Conquest, and St Peter's is attractively placed, with a nice variety of churchyard trees. Those that know about such things say that the hedge by the road is about 800 years old. The C15 tower is well-proportioned, with angle buttresses and two sharp *drip courses*, and the battlements have been replaced with a plain brick parapet. The buttresses have stooled niches and *flushwork* panels – all now filled with red brick, and there are pairs of hung shields in the *base course* below. An earlier and higher *nave* roof line shows on the tower's e. face. The broad s. doorway is in very weathered rich red *Tudor* brick, and when it was blocked, the door itself was left in place. The *chancel* dates from the C13, and the position of the *lancets* in the side walls suggests that they were *low side windows*; two more are blocked in the n. wall, and the *priest's door* is on that side. The clearest indication of the church's true age is the blocked *Norman* lancet set in the n. wall of the nave not far from the *porch*. The latter has an *arch-braced* roof, with *castellated wall plates*, and the shield in the window above the outer arch may be medieval. There are vestiges of *headstops* on the very worn inner doorway, with a *stoup* recess to the r.

Weston has a ring of three C15 bells cast by the Norwich Brayser family. Canon Raven described them as: 'a pretty little "maiden" ring and well in tune'. It would not be allowed now, but when they were recast in the 1920s, the shoulders of two of them were sliced off and mounted on the tower wall so that their lovely inscriptions can be seen by visitors. Typically delicate decoration is cast within each capital letter, and the inscriptions read: 'Missus vero pie Gabriel fert leta Marie' (Now *Gabriel* being sent, bears joyful tidings to *Mary*), and 'Petre pro me Deo intercede' (*Peter*, intercede with God for me). A *Jacobean* chest stands nearby. The tower arch has a centre spine which rests on demi-angel *corbels*, and the inner arch of the blocked s. door shows by its shape that it was part of the Norman building. The nave has an attractive brick floor, and its steep roof is arch-braced in unstained oak, with *collars* just under the ridge, and castellated wall plates. The terribly mutilated *Seven Sacrament font* is one of the more compact

versions. It stands on two steps, the top a Maltese cross, with *tracery* set in the sides, and there are the remains of demi-angels under the bowl. The bowl panels were very harshly treated, but it is still possible to identify the subjects. Clockwise from the e., they are: mass; ordination; penance (the angel behind the penitent may be fending off a devil); extreme unction; marriage; Christ's baptism; baptism; confirmation. This is one of the four Seven Sacrament fonts in Suffolk that take Christ's baptism for the eighth subject, and although little detail remains, one can make out the legs above the water, *St John the Baptist's* cloak, an angel on the l., and the Dove of the Holy Spirit at the top. There are three faint texts within leafy borders on the nave walls, and the one on the s. wall can be identified as a verse from *St Paul's* Letter to the Galatians (6:6) in the 1560 Geneva version – a useful date guide. Above it is a fragment of early-C14 wall painting which has been identified as Christ's entry into Jerusalem, but it is not clear enough to see whether there is any link with the same scene on the chancel wall at nearby North Cove. In the window to the r. is a roundel of C17 or C18 continental enamelled glass, a vivid little vignette of Christ and the sleeping disciples at Gethsemane. The C15 benches have a nice variety of *poppyhead* designs, and the low pair at the w. end have carved and pierced backs. The one on the n. side has a particularly interesting carving on the elbow, the remains of an animal with a four-legged pot on its back. This was probably by the same man who carved a benchend at Redisham not far away. There, the beast is revealed as a dragon licking out the pot and the craftsman's inspiration may perhaps have been the *bestiary* story in which some sailors set up their cooking pot over a fire on a desert island, only to find that they had landed on a slumbering whale. Like me, the carver had never seen a whale, but he knew all about dragons. At the other end of the bench there is a post mill which still has its entrance ladder, even though the sails have gone. The rear bench on the s. side of the main range has a priest (minus most of his head) in his pulpit, holding a scroll, and at the front on the same side there is a fine *cockatrice*. James II's short reign meant that his *Royal Arms* are rarely to be found, and there are only three examples in Suffolk. Weston's set, painted on board, hang on the s. wall and are well preserved, while opposite there is an C18 *Decalogue* board. As with most churches, there was originally a *rood screen*, and the wall is cut away on the n. side of the chancel arch where a flight of stairs led to the loft. The chancel roof is arch-braced, with carved wall plates, and below there is a selection of quality *ledger-stones* spanning the whole of the C17. The stall on the n. side of the chancel has three panels with delicate tracery which may have come from the front of the rood loft, and a priest seated with a book on his lap is nicely carved on one of the ends. The chancel was restored in 1860, and the shapeless *piscina* recess no longer has a drain. The e. window was glazed as a memorial in the early 1870s, and the glass is probably by *Ward & Hughes* – attractive patterns filling all three *lights* and tracery, bold colours and lively design.

The churchyard is a pleasant place in which to stroll, and a headstone in the n.w. corner has something to say about the history of the village: Robert and Mary Sarbutt lost five children aged 18 months to thirteen years between February 21st and March 11th, 1896. I suspect that there was an outbreak of scarlet fever or something similar at that time, against which a C19 community was virtually defenceless.

West Row: *See* **Mildenhall, West Row** (B3)

West Stow, St Mary (C3): This is a church that was heavily restored in the C19. It is beautifully situated in a churchyard that must be all of four acres and which is a nice conjunction of mown and wild areas. The C14 tower has chequerwork in the *base course* and on the buttresses, and the stair turret goes right to the top on the s. side. It houses a ground floor ring of six bells with a 15 cwt. tenor. The windows on the s. side of the *nave* are Victorian, although the structure is basically C13. In the C14 *chancel*, a *string course* picks up the line of the window arches and continues round the corner buttresses. The four-light e. window has attractive *reticulated tracery* and there are C15 windows on the n. side of the nave, and one of the original C13 *lancets*. The *vestry* was added in 1903 to commemorate the reign of Queen Victoria, and if you look through the window you will be able to see the early *Norman* n. door, with the heavy roll moulding of its arch standing on rudimentary volute *capitals*.

Through the C14 s. *porch*, and to the l. is the plain *font*, with blank shields in the panels. The cover is a very stolid Victorian design, with tall, gabled, blind windows giving the impression of an octagonal chapel topped by an over-large *finial*. The tower arch is tall and narrow and above it is a *sanctus-bell window*. There are fragments of medieval glass in the w. window,

and high on the inner n. wall of the tower are two finely lettered tablets for a pair of John Edwardses who died in 1758 and 1775. I think it highly likely that they were cut by the same mason who provided the tablet for Robert Rushbrooke in Honington church. Roofs and fittings are all C19 but there is a *brass* placed in the most inconvenient position possible under the pulpit. It is a Latin inscription commemorating the priest William Boyce who died in 1591:

> ...born in Halifax, educated at Cambridge, preached in Suffolk. His heart stopped and now the grave holds his body and Christ his soul.

The Victorian chancel roof has rather fine and tall figures on the *wall posts*. They are a little difficult to see, but one angel on the s. side holds a *chalice* and one on the n. a *ciborium*. There is an *aumbry* with a modern door in the n. wall and opposite, a good C14 *angle piscina* with its gables and pinnacles heavily *crocketted*. The shallow stone *credence shelf* is unusual, having a band of leaf ornament under the edge, with a beast mask in the centre. The 1852 glass in the e. window is by *Ward & Hughes*; the four panels of Christ's miracles are brightly coloured but do not inspire.

Wetherden, St Mary (E4): This church is beautifully placed. A screen of huge limes laps the churchyard to the w. and s., while the land drops away at the e. end. The recently restored tower is early-C14 and the w. door is flanked by *ogee*-headed niches under square *labels*, with a smaller version above the arch. There are *lancet* belfry windows, *Decorated tracery* in the bell openings, and the attractive w. window has three ogee-headed *lights* with a little *transom* over the centre one. The tower houses good ring of six bells with an 11cwt. tenor. The s. *aisle* is lavish and the w. end of it forms the *porch*. You will see that the fabric of the porch and the next bay differs from the rest in having a rough pattern of stone blocks. This shows that although the work was begun by Richard II's Chief Justice, Sir John Sulyard, in the 1480s, the w. end was completed by his widow's second husband Sir Thomas Bourchier, a fact confirmed by the central position of his arms over the s. door. The *base course* has a whole series of heraldic shields set in deep-cut tracery, the buttress to the r. of the doorway is carved with a pot of lilies in honour of the *Blessed Virgin*, and there is a well-defined *scratch dial* on a buttress further along. Like the tower, the *chancel* is in the Decorated style, with *reticulated* tracery in the e. window which has a little niche over it. The corner buttresses are angled and their gables are finely traceried. Attached to the n. side of the chancel is a tiny *sacristy* under a lean-to roof and its miniscule lancet is a mere 2in. wide. A faint mark on the n. wall of the *nave* betrays the site of the *rood loft* stair and the sloping brick buttresses look like an C18 effort to combat structural weakness on that side.

Entry is via a low C14 doorway and within, the C15 roofs are outstanding. The nave has double *hammerbeams*, but note that the upper range is false and the stress is taken by *arch-braces* that rise from the back of the hammerbeams. The posts drop down to form pendants and carry finely carved C19 standing figures. This roof is rather dark but that in the s. aisle is both lighter in colour and better lit and is beautiful. The inner rafters are cranked to form a ceiling and a line of shields with the Sulyard arms forms *bosses* down the centre. All the main timbers are crested and carved in a variety of forms, and large demi-angels lift their wings at the base of the *wall posts*. The chapel at the e. end of the aisle is approached through an arch which has an angel *corbel* on the s. and a small human head on the n. A helm with a scrolled shield hangs nearby. Backing on to the chancel arch is the table tomb of Sir John Sulyard who died in 1574. His *achievement* is framed between alabaster *Corinthian* columns under a plain *pediment* and there is a line of four mutilated little figures kneeling above the heavy slab. Its bevelled edge has a finely cut inscription but note that the final words have been roughly chiselled away. They were 'Cujus animae misereatur Deus' (On whose soul may God have mercy) until *William Dowsing* came this way. He had a field day here on 5 February 1643 when he broke 100 'superstitious pictures' in this aisle alone – probably mainly stained glass in the windows. Having removed 'superstitious inscriptions' and 65lbs. of brass, he was short of time and left orders for 68 cherubim and 60 more idolatrous pictures to be removed and the steps of the chancel to be levelled. He no doubt slept soundly, conscious of having done a good day's work. The C15 *font* has ogee arches in the bowl panels, within which are four large *paterae* and four shields – the crowns of East Anglia, a cross fleury, three small *Tudor Roses*, and three scallop shells. There are large heads at the angles below the bowl and the *Jacobean* cover is a plain pyramid with a *castellated* rim. Overhead you will see a small and plain

sanctus-bell window high in the tower wall. There is a good range of C15 benches on the n. side of the nave with *poppyheads* and traceried ends with grotesques on the elbows. N. of the font a bench has a *unicorn* at each end although they have lost their horns. Further e. there is a pair of squirrels eating nuts and by the wall a fox with a goose in his mouth. All the benches on the s. side, like the front four ranges on the n., are good C19 replicas. There are two suites of C18 painted deal *box pews* in the s. aisle and some more C19 benches. Although the pulpit is Victorian it incorporates medieval panelling with two ranges of tracery. The organ is at the w. end and this leaves the short chancel nicely uncluttered. An archway matching the *Perpendicular* nave *arcade* connects it with the s. aisle chapel. The roof is a hammerbeam again, with *king posts* above the arch-braces and standing figures under canopies on the wall posts. The stone corbels on which they stand are modern and one wonders whether the whole roof was reconstructed as part of the 1860s restoration. Beyond the door to the sacristy on the n. side of the *sanctuary* is an excellent example of a small *Easter sepulchre*, with a shallow, *cusped* ogee under a pointed arch. The e. window is flanked by a pair of image niches under *crocketted* ogee arches with *finials* and pinnacles. The sill of the window is lowered and no doubt contained a *retable* originally. The C14 *piscina* on the s. side has a large finial and there is one *headstop* on the cusped ogee arch. Within it is an original wooden *credence shelf*, and to the r., *dropped-sill sedilia* with a single stone armrest. The 1860s e. window glass by Henry Hughes (of *Ward & Hughes*) is uninspired, with four large figures in the main lights, but in the tracery above there are some interesting medieval fragments. These include a large group of kneeling figures, two angels, and a C14 seated figure. The church's only remaining *brass* has been (I think) relaid in the centre of the chancel floor. It is for John Daniell (1584) and has four shields (his own, his wife's and for some odd reason those of his sons-in-law) and a rather good verse. There is more heraldry in the form of *hatchments*. s. aisle, w. wall bottom, Elizabeth Crawford (1828); w. wall, top, Dorothy Sulyard (1830); s. aisle, w. end, her husband Edward (1799); s. aisle, centre, their daughter Lucy Smythe (1830). So the family that built the aisle were still marking their presence there nearly 400 years later.

Wetheringsett, All Saints (F4): Entry to the spacious churchyard ringed with trees is by way of a footbridge from the village street. The first thing one notices is that the C15 tower has a lofty w. arch that is completely open, with dainty mouldings uninterrupted save for small half-capitals. This strange feature can be seen again at Cotton not far away, but here there is no window in the inner wall – only a stooled niche. There is no doubt that the tower was built onto an earlier nave but the reason for the open plan is obscure. *Flushwork* chequer decorates the thick w. buttresses to the top and they have stooled niches to match the one over the w. arch. The tower houses a ring of five bells with a 14 cwt. tenor but their condition only allows them to be rung occasionally. The overall style of the church is *Perpendicular*, with stepped *embattled transoms* in the aisle windows, and *clerestory* walls that are practically all glass. However, note that the s. aisle retained a *Decorated* window with *reticulated tracery* at the w. end, while the n.e. *vestry* has a lancet in its e. wall, and the C13 n. door has slim attached columns below wide and shallow ring *capitals*. The *chancel* was practically rebuilt in the C19. The face of the C15 *porch* is enhanced with minor flushwork and, as at Thorndon, the arch rests on lion *corbels* with crowns and shields in the moulding. Like that on the n. side, the s. door is part of the older building and the *dripstone's* curly *stops* match those on the *priest's door*. Note the pilgrim crosses incised on the *jambs*, and mind your head as you enter through the low wicket door.

There is a small *sanctus-bell window* at the very top of the w. wall, and the bowl panels of the *font* below contain lozenges and shields – plain except for arms on the n. side which feature the knot of the Staffords; the earlier C13 stem is ringed with shafts. This is a wide, light and airy interior where the main attraction is the late-C13 arcades, generously proportioned with *quatrefoil piers* and deep ring capitals. They were heightened in the C15 to support the new clerestory, and overhead there is a C19 roof in which the space above the *tie-beams* is filled with panel tracery between the *king* and *queen posts*. On the n. aisle wall is a large benefactions board dated 1715 which has been restored (it says rather oddly 'made & written by C.A. Dilloway of Brockford 1960'). Nearby is a small iron-clad C15 chest. The main range of pews is sound C19 work but at the w. end there are some C15 benches with wide ends and *poppyheads*. By the organ in the s. aisle there are stairs which led originally to the loft of a *parclose screen* enclosing a chapel. In 1521 there was 'an altar to Our Lady in Master Richard's chapel' and this is likely to have been the site of his *chantry*. The chancel arch matches the arcade and although there is no *screen* now, the *rood loft stairs* survive to the s. Strangely, the panels on top of the organ and the roughly formed screen behind its console appear to be remnants of the vanished *rood screen*.

The panelled roof of the chancel is almost flat, and in the *sanctuary*, handsome stepped *sedilia* line the s. wall. The *Purbeck marble* columns support *trefoil* arches whose *cusps* and *hood moulds* have leaf terminals; the short end shafts rest on male and female heads which face one another. The plain *piscina* is small and unusual only in that its drain is square (like Thwaite's but without a raised lip). Two stalls with plain *misericords* stand opposite, and in the s.e. corner of the vestry is the interesting remnant of a double piscina with stiff-leaf carving below the bowl. This proves that it was used as a chapel in the late C13 or early C14. Returning down the nave, pause to read Dorothy Sheppard's epitaph; she died aged 19 in 1752 and is buried with her mother under the black *ledger-stone*: 'Reader if aught can fix th'attentive eye . . .'.

One of Wetheringsett's rectors was that eminent Elizabethan geographer Richard Hakluyt who, like Shakespeare, died in 1616. He is said to have been assiduous in his parish duties but one must remember that, apart from being secretary to the ambassador in Paris at one stage, he held prebends at Bristol and Westminster and was much in demand for advice to adventurers when Drake's circumnavigation was the topic of the day. His *Principal Navigations, Voyages and Discoveries of the English Nation* was first published in 1589 and he came here in 1590 with an international reputation. The greatly enlarged 2nd edition of 1598-1600 is an intriguing mixture of history, diplomacy, economics, and tales of daring. He was buried in Westminster abbey.

Weybread, St Andrew (G2): The round tower is *Norman*, and the rest of the building has that sharp look that denotes a root and branch Victorian restoration. In this case it was at the hands of R.M. *Phipson* in 1865, and he went on to do a similar job at Mendham three years later. Walking round, you will see that the tower has a squared-off *lancet* in the ground floor to the w., with smaller versions in brick for the belfry, and there is a *string course* below the bell openings. The latter are *trefoil*-headed lancets, with *flushwork* replicas spaced between them; *gargoyles* pierce the plain parapet. It houses a ground floor ring of six bells with a 9 cwt. tenor. The body of the church is short and tall, and above the *aisle* roofs there are four *Perpendicular clerestory* windows a side – most of the others were renewed in the same style. The C14 n. doorway is blocked, and at the e. end of the n. aisle Phipson added a little extension which he joined awkwardly on to a new *vestry*; the *castellated* octagonal chimney is typical of him, as are the harp and organ *stops* on the vestry window. His new e. window has king and queen stops, and on the s. side of the chancel he renewed the C14 *priest's door*, although one of the windows there is original. The C15 *porch* uses flushwork lavishly, in the *base course* and over the whole of the facade and angle buttresses. The centre niche is *groined*, with *cusped, crocketted ogee* arch, and the C19 figure of the church's patron saint fits it well. Angels hold shields in the *spandrels*, there are remnants of lion stops to the arch, and the corner pinnacles probably inspired Phipson's chimney! The roof, with its castellated *wall plate* and centre foliage *boss* seems untouched, and the inner doorway is of the same period.

Just inside are three massive *ledger-stones* belonging to members of the Hobart and Astley families of the late C17 to early C18, and they have heraldic roundels cut deeply enough to trip the unwary. The bulky *font* was the 1860s work of Mr Vine of Eye – sharply cut *Evangelistic symbols* and fussy roundels in the bowl panels. The tower arch is filled with a glazed screen, and the wall above is boldly and attractively painted with the figure of Christ enthroned in Majesty; angels kneel on either side, and the figures are set within stencilled *tabernacle work* against blue backgrounds. The style is reminiscent of *Clayton & Bell*, a firm well known for their glass who also provided mural decoration on occasion. The *piers* of the C14 *arcades* sport many examples of medieval graffiti. There is reputed to be a C14 knight in armour lurking somewhere but I could not locate him, although I did find a fine eagle's head scratched on the s. side of the centre pier of the n. arcade. The 1860s restoration included a new *arch-braced* pine roof in the *nave*, and the oak roofs of the aisles were restored and given new bosses. The excellent *corbels* were cut by Mr Barrett of Norwich, and on the n. side of the nave (from w. to e.) one can identify: Noah, King David, *St Benedict?*, *St Peter*; on the s. side (from w. to e.): Abraham, Moses, and *St Paul* at the e. end. There are more good corbels in the aisles, with a fine grotesque mask above the centre pillar of the s. arcade. The s. aisle chapel has a C13 *piscina* with flanking shafts, ring *capitals*

and bases. Alongside are *dropped-sill sedilia*, and the *altar* is a plain *Stuart* table, heavily restored. Nearby stand the remains of the church's C15 *font* – panelled shaft and lower half of the bowl, and one wonders how it came to be treated thus. There is a remarkably good C15 roundel in the window painted with *St John's* symbol, and to the l., the *rood stair* rises in the wall, its upper door blocked. A tablet over the n. door commemorates Lieut. William Jennings who died in 1860 'whilst gallantly leading his men to the charge against a party of Bundelcund rebels in central India'. The 2nd Bengal European Light Cavalry, and Mayne's Horse, to whom he was seconded, were two of the many regiments of the Queen Empress's Indian Army that were raised in the full flowering of the Indian Empire, now remembered only in memorials such as this, and by a few surviving old 'Koi Hais'. The oak benches, with *poppyheads* and *paterae* on the chamfers were carved by Thomas Stopher to match the originals, and tin labels painted with 'Free' were added to all of them to mark the end of the pew rent era (Stopher also carved the angels at Burstall). The chancel arch capitals were reworked, but the unmatched niches on either side were undisturbed. There is a C14 piscina in the *sanctuary*, and the e. window is filled with glass of 1866 by *Michael and Arthur O'Connor*, a curious composition with disconcerting variations of scale and restless design. The three upper panels are an Ascension, with Christ within a glory above his footprints, a livid-coloured city beyond; the disciples are grouped on each side, backed by a bright, formalised leaf design. There is a Crucifixion in the centre below, with the *Three Marys* on the r. and the visit of the shepherds on the l. The s. chancel windows are also by the O'Connors – Christ with St Peter, a post-Resurrection illustration, and two miracles of healing. W.G. Taylor of Berners St took over the O'Connor's business, and their n. window of 1884 is much better; it portrays *St Andrew* bringing his brother to Christ, and the three richly robed figures stand within archways which have arum lilies above and below, with an *Agnus Dei* in the top *quatrefoil*. The churchyard is pleasant to explore and is one of the very few places where one may find the rare birth wort growing. It is also the resting place of Suffolk's first VC, although his grave w. of the tower is unmarked. Sgt. Alfred Ablett of the Grenadier Guards was born in Weybread, won his decoration at the seige of Sebastopol in 1855, and was among the first to be presented with it by the Queen in Hyde Park two years later. His citation in ther *London Gazette* reads: 'On the 2nd September, 1855, seeing a shell fall in the centre of a number of ammunition-cases and powder, he instantly seized and threw it outside the trench; it burst as it touched the ground.' He died in London in 1897 but his body was brought back here to lie in its native earth.

Whatfield, St Margaret (E6): There are picture-book thatched cottages in the lane that leads to the churchyard and the church itself is attractive despite cement rendering all over. The tower has a *Perpendicular* w. window under a square *label*, with a stair turret to the s., and at some time the top was reduced and capped with a tiled pyramid roof. A modern *vestry* leads off the n. door and the *chancel* on that side has one 'Y' *tracery* window of about 1300 and another with *Decorated* tracery. The e. window has been renewed but the *reticulated* tracery is likely to have repeated the original C14 design. It is flanked by large marble tablets with side scrolls and one carries a mellifluous epitaph for Mary Church who died in childbed in 1741. There are Decorated windows and a *priest's door* on the s. side; w. of them, a *rood stair turret* under a tiled roof nestles against the *nave* buttress. The outer arch of the small C16 brick *porch* is flanked by low-level recesses and the copper sundial of 1984 replaced a wooden version dated 1844; that is now above the inner doorway whose hood mould has the remains of *headstops*.

Watch for the two steps down into the nave and then have a look at the rare and lovely little C13 *stoup* just to the r. It has attached columns with ring *capitals* and there is *trefoil cusping* in the narrow arch. The early-C18 *gallery* rests on iron posts and the bobbin and *baluster* turning in the balustrade is very attractive. The organ on it was rebuilt in 1952 in memory of George VI, who is credited with the royal title 'Defender of the Faith' – normally only seen on coins and abbreviated to 'F.D.' these days. There is perhaps a connection with the plain tablet on the s. wall for Sir George Falkener who was His Britannic Majesty's ambassador to Nepal after the war. There are *pamment* and brick floors, C19 seating on the s. side, and on the n. plain C16 benches with heavy roll mouldings on the backs and square ends. The one at the back is cruder and probably earlier than the rest and has a shield on the end: 'John Wilson 1589' plus '53' – his age perhaps? Over the C13 n. doorway hangs a well-painted set of Hanoverian *Royal Arms* and C17 hat pegs line the wall. The C14 *font* is a plain octagon resting on a centre shaft and ring of octagonal pillars, while overhead is a typical C14 *tie-beam* roof. The *arch-braces* spring from little shafts on the *wall posts*, *king posts* rise and are braced to a ridge beam which runs the whole length of the nave below a plastered ceiling. At the e. end on the s. side the monument of 1699 for William Vesey is most attractive. Against a shaped black background the substantial tablet is flanked by free-standing columns in mottled marble and pierced fronds; swags of fruit support an *achievement of arms* on the front of the cornice and there is a smaller *cartouche* at the base. The square recess underneath was once part of the entrance to the *rood loft* stairs. The pulpit opposite is tall and plain but its C17 back board is carved with a blind arch, and the hexagonal *tester* has pendants and a carved skirt. There is a cambered tie-beam spanning the chancel and above it is a fine C15 waggon roof, panelled with slender ribs and flower *bosses* whose centres contain animal masks and three kingly heads along the ridge. The balusters of the late-C17 *communion rails* match the legs of the table in the vestry which means that it was the *altar* of the period. In the *sanctuary* there is a tall and deep C14 *piscina* with a multi-cusped arch, and the grave slabs of two C13 priests lie in the corners – one with a plain cross and the other with the double omega symbol.

Whepstead, St Petronilla (C5): This church carries a unique dedication and brief details of the obscure Roman maiden *St Petronilla* will be found in Appendix 1. A curving line of yews leads across to the late-C15 tower which has a very odd shape. Its upper stage was taken down and an awkwardly rebuilt heavy stair turret was set in the angle of the s.e. buttress. The tower is cut short just above it and topped by later battlements. There are three small niches around the *Perpendicular* window above the w. door. A repair date of 1582 is cut high in the face of the s.e. buttress and until 1658 there was a spire, but it fell in the great storm on the night that Cromwell died. The *nave* and *chancel* are late-C13, with windows using plate and 'Y' *tracery*, and an older and much higher roof line can be seen on the face of the tower. The chancel e. window has intersected 'Y' tracery, there is a *priest's door* to the s. with one lion *headstop*, and in 1926 a *vestry* was built against the old n. door. Entry is via a s. porch rebuilt in 1926 and the *dripstone* of the arch of the inner door has curled stops. To the r. is the remnant of a small *stoup*.

Just inside is a small Victorian *font* and an open ringers' *gallery* is set within the tower where they make use of the church's ring of five bells with its 7 cwt. tenor. Beyond, the w. window is filled with striking glass of 1931 by the *Powells* – a dense design of interlaced panels illustrating the ark and its creatures, with a beautiful deep blue predominating. The benches date from 1869 but the roofs with their coved ceilings were part of the 1926 restoration, and in the chancel the ribs have been smartly picked out in red. At the same time, the wide chancel arch was rebuilt in *Norman* fashion with bold *chevron moulding*, and this is in keeping with the *jambs* which are genuine Norman, their corners having small attached shafts on both sides. No *rood screen* remains but the steps leading to the vanished loft rise up steeply in the window embrasure in the s. wall and they continue through an archway to finish at a very small opening. Simple *piscinas* are sometimes found in windowsills (there is one by the pulpit on the n. side) but to find one cut in a step of the rood loft stair, as here, is very unusual. Early wills show that before the *Reformation* the church's main dedication was to *St Thomas* who had a tabernacle or shrine, and a light burned before a statue of *St Margaret*; the two piscinas served *altars* dedicated to *St Margaret* and *St Mary*. The pulpit is modern but it makes use of two late-C16 panels. They have blind arches with better than average scroll carving, and marquetry is a feature of the *pilasters* and edging. The panels came from Plumpton House in the parish and may have formed part of an overmantel or the front of a chest. The 1928 window on the s. contains six C19 *achievement of arms* of local families including the Drurys. In the chancel on the n. side a window has 1926 glass by Frederick Charles Eden with figures of St Petronilla and *St Peter* and there is more of his work at Barsham, Capel St Mary, Chedburgh Clare, SS Peter & Paul Felixstowe, Flempton and St Margaret's S. Elmham. The window opposite contains two tiny medieval heads at the top, three roundels with fragments, and a C17 continental roundel of *St Anthony* in yellow stain. On the s. wall there is a plain tablet flanked by *touchstone Corinthian* columns, with an achievement of arms above and stiff scroll and shell decoration below; it is by Matthew Wharton Johnson, whose rather undistinguished work is found in many churches. Here it commemorates Gen. Sir Francis Hammond who died in 1850, having been George IV's first equerry and his Clerk Marshall of the Royal Stables, a resounding title if nothing else. The piscina in the *sanctuary* stands within a *Decorated* arch which has had its *cusping* cut away. The dado of blind arches on

the walls is apparently C17 work. Above it on the n. wall is a touchstone and alabaster tablet for John Ryley (1672) whose inscription is a diverting mixture of wayward lettering styles. The 1908 glass in the e. window is by *James Powell & Sons* and it is a good Nativity scene spread across three *lights*. There are singing angels below the canopies and the colours are pleasing, but the vapid *Annunciation* in the bottom centre panel lets the rest down. Before you leave, have a look at the C17 embroidered *chalice* veil in a case by the chancel arch and note how neatly the modern organ case has been placed over the n. door.

Wherstead, St Mary (F6): Lodge gates stand at a sharp bend in the village street, and from there a road leads through the park to the church. Wherstead's vicar-historian, Foster Barham Zincke, is commemorated by the *lych-gate* designed by J.S. Corder, the Ipswich architect, and as one walks round the church, a fine panorama of the Orwell estuary opens up to the e. The handsome C15 tower has *flushwork* in its angle buttresses, quite a lot of *septaria* shows in the walls, and the pinnacles were replaced on the stepped brick battlements around 1900. The huge glacial boulders on which part of the tower rests suggest that this was one of the sites of pagan worship appropriated by the early church, like Shelley and others in the Ipswich area. The *Normans* built it anew, and the very battered outline of their n. doorway remains in the wall. A pair of small *lancets* in the *chancel* are the only signs of early-C13 work to be seen now. By 1864 the church was in poor repair, and *Richard Phipson* directed a full-scale restoration, with *Henry Ringham* as his contractor – his last work. The walls were completely refaced with flint, all the windows were replaced (except the lancets), and a new *vestry* and porch were provided. A single, tiled roof covers *nave* and chancel, and Phipson designed four huge and rather splendid *gargoyles*. The porch shelters another Norman doorway, early-C12, and more elaborate than its fellow. It has two ranks of *chevron moulding*, each doubled at right angles to form lozenges, and the outer range is unusually open; one of the two pairs of *jamb shafts* lacks *capitals*, but there are small heads carved on the others. A small *stoup* recess was later insinuated by the shaft on the r., and another can be found just inside.

The glass in the w. window is by William Holland, a Warwick glazier whose work is seldom seen in East Anglia. Installed in 1864, it draws its inspiration from the C13, and there are scenes illustrating four of the *Seven Works of Mercy*, with small figures of the four *Evangelists* in the *tracery*. The *font* is a most unusual piece which was designed by vicar Zincke in the 1860s and carved by the Ipswich mason, James Williams, whose pulpit and *reredos* can be seen at Brome. It has a shafted stem in C13 style, and the bowl panels contain bas-relief scenes of some delicacy: e. *instruments of the Passion*; n.e. *St Michael*; n. baptism of Christ; n.w. dove of the Holy Spirit; s. a group of children and their parents, with Christ in the centre (note that the two children in frilly pantaloons on the l. are the only figures in contemporary dress). The nave roof is Ringham's work, and using the one C15 bench end that remained, he designed a completely new suite to his usual high standard. The traceried ends are varied, and the compact *poppyheads* are carved with a lovely selection of foliage and fruit – blackberry, strawberry, vine, wheat, and hops. The memorial on the n. wall is for Sir Robert Harland who died in 1848, and it was supplied by the Patent Marble Works – a firm established in 1809 whose work was very variable in quality. Here we have a tablet flanked by octagonal pillars set against a black slab, with a draped bas-relief urn on top, and a shield set in palm fronds at the bottom. Also on that side is Charles Vernon's memorial of 1863, by Edward James Physick. The sculptor was a Royal Academy gold medallist who contented himself in this instance with a simple marble tablet and drape; his later memorial to the Norman family can be found at Layham. A two-*light* window on the s. side of the nave contains glass by the Norwich glazier Dennis King, installed in 1963, and the text: 'I will lift up mine eyes unto the hills' is illustrated by the two figures of David as shepherd boy and king; there is clear glass above the scenes, and a C19 Good Shepherd fills the tracery *quatrefoil*. *St Edmund* is featured in the opposite window, and the massive stone pulpit in front of it came from the Louvain workshop of M. Abeloos. Sharply carved, it has *trefoil* arches on C13-style shafts, and in one of them the figure of Christ has sheep with curiously waved fleeces at his feet; sprays of roses, lilies, and olives in stiff relief fill the rest. The doorway and lower steps of the *rood loft stair* can be seen in the s. wall, and the chancel arch is a C19 wooden replacement which has angel figures under canopies resting on the stone *corbels*. The *hammerbeams* of the C15 chancel roof are strangely moulded, and the *wall plates* are odd too – ranges of ribbed mouldings that must be all of 3ft.

deep. The chamber organ, neatly tricked out in cream and gold, was made by Russells of London in 1837. Having served at Fifield in Oxfordshire, Whittlesey in Cambridgeshire, and Field Dalling in Norfolk, it finally came to rest here in 1976. The early-C14 *piscina* in the *sanctuary* lies within a trefoil arch resting on single shafts, and the sanctuary is floored with Minton *encaustic tiles* decorated with a repeat fleur-de-lys pattern. Alexander Gibbs's 1860s glass in the e. and s. sanctuary windows has kaleidoscopic colour and very indifferent figure work. A fine *ledger-stone* was cut for Robert Gooding, a salt merchant who died in 1618, but unfortunately it has lain for years outside by the porch and is now badly cracked and damaged. Little of its long, rhymed epitaph can now be read, but it is interesting that the edge inscription in bold lettering is very similar to that found on stones in Campsea Ash sanctuary, suggesting that they may have been cut by the same mason.

Whitton, St Mary (F6): Church Lane is a turning off the old Norwich road and the church is to be found at the very end, right on the edge of the housing development. It was rebuilt almost in its entirety in 1852 under the architect Frederick Barnes, who remodelled the *chancel* and provided a *nave* and n. *aisle*. Ten years later the tower and s. aisle were added by *R.M. Phipson*, incorporating stone from the ruined church of Thurleston which had not been used since the C16, except as a barn. It is an oddly shaped building from the outside, with n. aisle and nave flush at the w. end, and the small-scale tower set at the s.w. corner, complete with stone *broach spire* reminiscent of Lincolnshire. The s. aisle is built onto the e. wall of the tower and there is a flat-roofed *vestry* at the e. end of the n. aisle. Outside, the only identifiable survivor from the old church is the doorway re-set in the tower which, although it has been restored, is largely late-C13, with ring *capitals* to the slim shafts and a deep roll moulding in the arch.

The interior is attractive and made more so by a new and sophisticated lighting scheme. For some reason Phipson did not match his *arcade* with that of Barnes, but used drum pillars instead of octagons, and the roofs of nave and aisles are all boarded, panelled, and painted above the plain brick floors. The C19 *font* has been moved from the w. end to the e. end of the n. aisle and is an attractive design using C13 forms; the drum bowl has an arcade of *trefoiled* arches, and there are four columns set around the centre shaft. A *lancet* nearby contains glass of 1922 by

Morris & Co which is quite unlike the firm's earlier style. It is a half-length *Blessed Virgin* and Child against a dark background, set within elaborate *tabernacle work*. Of more interest is the glass of about 1867 in the nave three-*light* w. window by *Hardman & Co*. A demi-figure of Christ is set at the top, and above and below three large angels across the centre there are six of the *Seven Works of Mercy* in shaped panels; Celtic scroll work fills the rest of the space and it is a fine window, C14 in feeling, with good colour. The 1860s glass in the s. aisle window is also by Hardman – a Resurrection scene in one light and the Ascension in the other. It commemorates Charles Steward 'by whom this church was mainly restored'. The e. wall of the s. aisle only has a high-level *quatrefoil* window and below it hangs a painting (probably C19) of the Virgin and Child; two mysterious figures, a man and a boy, lurk in the background. The *altar* here is a small and chunky C17 table. The C14 cross-braced framework of the chancel roof survived the restoration and the plaster behind the timbers is now painted a deep blue. Below, more medieval work may be found in the form of two *misericords* in the priest's stalls which came from a Sudbury church. The one on the n. side has a head carved below the seat, and the desk fronts have intricate and varied tracery. The choir stalls would seem to be all C19 work. There is more Hardman glass in the chancel s. window of 1865 – two mailed knights above kneeling angels, with the shield of faith in the top roundel; the e. window was supplied by the same firm a decade later – a stylised Last Supper across three lights, with demi-angels bearing the elements of the Eucharist above. Altered levels in the *sanctuary* have brought the C14 *piscina* close to the floor and the *cusps* of its arch have been broken away. In 1969 the window to the r. was reglazed and now contains figures of *St Paul* and *St Peter* in pointed ovals above larger paintings of Christ and the Blessed Virgin. The four mid-C19 panels are set in plain *quarries* and were saved from the earlier church.

Wickhambrook, All Saints (B5): In a scattered village with a deceptive pattern of lanes, the church when found stands handsomely in a broad and open churchyard. Most of what can be seen is C14 but the n. *aisle* chapel that extends halfway along the *chancel* has flintwork in its e. wall that is apparently pre-Conquest, a sign that the first small building was sited there. Another clue to the church's antiquity is the little *Saxon* figure (now protected by a glass panel) which

was later built into the s.w. corner of the s. aisle. The tower has a deep *ashlar base course*, chequer battlements, a very tall and thin *Decorated* w. window, and a square turret to the s. It houses a ring of five bells with a 15 cwt. tenor but they are not ringable at the present time. The early-C14 chancel windows have particularly attractive *tracery*, with a sexfoil in the head of the e. window and the four-petalled flower motif at the sides. There is a small *priest's door* to the s. and over the *Perpendicular* side windows of the s. aisle there are later brick battlements. The C14 n. *porch* is now plastered, and within is a very worn C13 doorway with deep mouldings edged with *dogtooth*. The side shafts have gone. Propped on the window ledge is a fine little tombstone of 1693 for Ruth Partridge, the vicar's daughter, who married a mercer – rustic swags down the sides and a curved, wavy-edged surface.

Passing the huge *stoup* by the door, one enters an interior that shows in many ways how the church was continuously altered during the C14 and C15. Although not large, it has a wide and open look, and on the n. side of the n. *arcade* there is the most curious beginning of a transverse arch. It has been suggested that this was planned as a new chancel arch on the axis of the first small building, but it may have been that a new n.e. chapel was planned but never completed when the *nave* arcades were built. The heavy C13 *font* on a modern shaft by the entrance was moved from the s. aisle in the 1950s and has a curious shape – octagonal, with triangular projections on four faces (*Cautley* thought that it had originally been square). In the n. chapel (connected by a low *Tudor* arch to the chancel) there is a lovely C13 *piscina*, its diminutive arch embellished with two bands of dogtooth, one inside and one outside the narrow moulding. The *rood stair* goes up from the chapel and note that there are two doorways at the top, showing that it led not only to the loft over the chancel *screen* but also to a *parclose screen* in the chapel. In the s. aisle at the e. end one can see where the piscina arch was lowered to allow the large C15 window to be inserted above it; the e. window here dates from about 1300. The tower arch is beautifully proportioned, tall and deeply moulded, and the arches of the nave arcade have rather unusual *hood moulds* on the n. side with mutilated *stops*. Overhead, the C14 roof was replaced by a late example of a *hammerbeam* design of the early C17. There are openwork arches above the hammers and *spandrels*, and it was stained black in an 1860s restoration – all of which gives it a leggy appearance against the white ceilings. Wickhambrook was an extreme example of C17 and C18 revolt against altar-centred worship; the parish placed a *three-decker pulpit* at the w. end and turned all the pews round so that the chancel was ignored. All was reversed in the 1860s and in 1886 came the splendidly uninhibited brass lectern. The chancel roof was heightened in the C18 and altered again later, so that the squared-off ceiling above the *arch-braces* now makes the e. window look too small. There is no screen and it is a pleasant change to explore a chancel where the Victorians did not play around with the floor levels. The *sanctuary* has a set of C18 *communion rails* with close-set *balusters*, and on the n. wall is a small-scale and neatly executed 1630s monument in alabaster and veined marble for Mirable Cradock. In the s.e. corner is something much more grand – the tomb sculpted by *Nicholas Stone* for Sir Thomas Higham, with an alabaster reclining figure of the old man, noble in countenance, curly headed and with a spade beard. The epitaph on two large *touchstone* panels is a potted biography of this 'Gentillman of Ancient Desent' who fought under Essex for Queen Elizabeth at Rouen and slew Sir Edward Stanley in single combat in the Irish rebellion. He came back here to die in contented retirement in 1630. Further along in the s. wall is a grilled recess which contains an excellent *brass* for Thomas Burrough, Elizabeth and Bridget his wives, and two groups of children behind their respective mothers. He died in 1597 and is soberly dressed, although the ladies display Paris caps and brocaded petticoats. One of the three shields has mantling and much of the original enamelling has survived.

Wickham Market, All Saints (H5): The church stands on the hilltop of the town centre, and its attenuated octagonal tower topped by a spire is a landmark. The tower is on the s. side of the *nave*, the ground floor serving as a *porch* and main entrance. There are large, *Perpendicular* bell openings, and every other one has been filled with flint. Above them, *gargoyles* mark the angles, and the battlements are decorated with *flushwork* chequer. The tower houses an excellent ring of six bells with a 12 cwt. tenor, and the bell that hangs under a little hood on the w. face of the lead-sheathed spire was probably the *sanctus bell* that was originally housed in the turret on the nave gable. The body of the church was built in the C14, and the w. doorway has a *crocketted ogee* arch flanked by the remains of pinnacles; there are widely spaced niches each side, with most of their decoration worn away. The tall three-*light*

window overhead has renewed *reticulated tracery*, and just below the gable there is a pretty little niche with *mouchettes* in its arch. The n. *aisle* was added in 1869 as part of a restoration directed by *Edward Hakewill*; two bays long and placed alongside the e. half of the nave, it has an eccentric grouping of windows in the e. wall. The windows of the *chancel* have *Decorated* tracery, and circling the building, one comes to the early *Tudor* brick s. aisle. It was built as a *chantry chapel* by Sir Walter Fulbourne, and the windows were replaced in the C19.

The outer doorway of the tower is deeply recessed, with two pairs of attached shafts, and moving through, one enters a spacious nave lying under a plain plaster ceiling. The panels of the excellent C14 *font* each contain a crocketted gable surrounded by lively tracery; there are pinnacles at the angles, and the shaft is panelled and traceried in two stages. Hakewill designed the handsome oak benches, with their decorative *poppyheads*, and one of them still has a brass umbrella holder, complete with drip tray. Recently, those at the e. end have been removed to make way for a dais. The elegant s. *arcade* with its *quatrefoil pier* is C14, and Hakewill repeated the design exactly on the n. side. The modern, openwork pulpit has a centre panel which is a carving of *St John*, seated with a paper in his hand lettered with the opening words of his gospel. His eagle stands by his knee, with an inkpot bowl slung from its beak. The carving is said to have come from the Savoy chapel in London, and has been attributed to Grinling Gibbons (as so many pieces are), although the style is by no means typical. The base of the *rood screen* remains in place, and some sections of its panel tracery are original. The openings in the wall to the r. of the chancel arch will have led to the *rood loft stair*, of which no trace remains. Beyond, there are chancel aisles whose arcades match those in the nave, although they do not align with them. The C16 s. aisle roof has large, square centre *bosses*, and the *wall posts* are heavily mutilated wooden figures. The roof continues over the chancel aisle, and a neatly designed section takes up the difference in width at the e. end. A three-*light* window in the s. wall contains indifferent 1870s glass by Henry Hughes of *Ward & Hughes*, and further along, the *piscina* arch shows how the ogee shape returned to popularity in the Tudor period. There is a combined suite of piscina and *sedilia* in the *sanctuary*, under *cinquefoil* ogee arches, with solid divisions between the seat spaces; the stone *credence shelf* appears to be a late addition. The tall, carved oak *reredos* was installed in 1881, and its panels illustrate the theme of the Te Deum. Against a dull gold background, the figures are: *St Paul* and St John (the glorious company of the *Apostles*); Ezekiel, Jeremiah and Elijah (the goodly fellowship of the prophets); *SS Stephen,Cecilia, Alban* (the noble army of martyrs); *Ambrose, Chrysostom, Augustine* (the holy church throughout all the world). The window above is well designed and has attractive colour, but the details of the figures have faded. It is probably by *Lavers, Barraud & Westlake* and illustrates the Via Dolorosa, Crucifixion, Entombment, and Resurrection; there are angels in the tracery, and a small stone figure of Christ in Majesty has been applied to the top centre.

Wickham Skeith, St Andrew (E4): A lane leads off the village street to the church and it is attractively placed. The stubby mid-C14 tower is unusually bulky and the absence of a w. window accentuates this. There is a decayed niche over the plain w. doorway and the w. buttresses, chequered with *flushwork*, have *consecration crosses* of the same size and pattern as those at Stoke Ash and Thornham Magna. The n. *porch* is tall, with side *gargoyles*, and both front and buttresses are decorated with flushwork panels. A band of crowned 'M's for the *Blessed Virgin* within stars lightly cut in *ashlar* are set above the outer arch below a central *groined* and canopied niche. The C15 nave windows have stepped, *embattled transoms* and the e. window of the *chancel* matches them. The narrow side windows of the chancel are also *Perpendicular* although the *priest's door* on the s. side was saved from the earlier building. There is a *scratch dial* on the r. side of its arch and three more can be traced on the s.e. nave buttress. A will of 1459 mentions money for the compact s. porch and it is interesting that its small side windows have Decorated tracery and are likely to have been salvaged and used again. There is flushwork up to the top of the arch and a tall *lancet* overhead once lit an upper room. The access stair shows in the angle with the nave on the w. side but the floor has been removed and the porch is open to the roof. The C16 inner door has *linenfold carving* but access is normally through the tower, past the ropes of the fine ground-floor ring of five bells with a 9 cwt. tenor.

The inner door is unusual in having tracery on the w. side. Like many others in East Anglia, the octagonal *font* has window tracery designs cut in the bowl panels, including *reticulations* to the s., but the figures round the shaft have been terribly mutilated. They were *Evangelistic symbols* at the angles with *woodwoses* between them and traces of the creatures' hairy coat survive on one only. The plain and dark *hammerbeam* roof has *embattled wall plates* and rests on interesting stone *corbels*. One on the n. side seems to hold a scourge and another opposite a Sacred Heart. The *rood stair* in the n. wall has a very tall bottom doorway and the upper opening faces w. Beneath the latter there is a triplet of niches with *trefoil* heads by the late-C18 or early-C19 pulpit. On the other side of the chancel arch is a wide niche under a *cusped ogee* arch and the chamber organ in front of it has a beautiful C18 mahogany case. The 'Gothick' detailing round the pipe clusters is excellent and there is a deep, pierced frieze below the cornice.

The chancel arch springs from large corbels which face inwards – male and female heads of considerable character. Below a plastered ceiling and heavy embattled wall plates, there are tall late-C17 *communion rails* and a simple Elizabethan *Holy Table* decorated with chip carving on rails and stretchers. On the e. wall is a C19 stone *reredos*, with Creed and Lord's Prayer on flanking panels. The tall *piscina* has flowers in the *spandrels* of the trefoil arch and in front of it is an interesting group of *ledger-stones*. Jane Harvey lies in the centre (she died in 1644 and was a Le Hunt of Little Bradley), with husband and son on either side; pairs of straps and buckles incised in the stone link the family in what seems to me to be a charming conceit. The church's seating poses interesting questions. Nine of the nave benches at the w. end are demonstrably medieval but all the bench ends in nave and chancel have *poppyheads* of early-C17 design. However, the tracery in the fronts of the chancel choir stalls matches the front of the w. *gallery* and one would judge that to be C19 – good solid work that was probably part of the 1857 restoration. Under the gallery hangs a delightful photograph of David Mayes with his scythe. He died in 1949, having been sexton for many years, and he must have often used the Victorian *bier* on its sprung undercarriage that stands close by.

Wilby, St Mary (G3): The church stands close by the village street and the beautifully proportioned tower dates from about 1460. It has four *set-offs*, with *flushwork* panels in the angle buttresses, stepped flushwork battlements and corner pinnacles. There are shields in the *spandrels* of the w. doorway, one for the *Trinity* and the other carrying *Passion emblems*. The flushwork *base course* is simple and the w. window has stepped *embattled transoms*, with a niche on each side. In the tower's n. wall, by the angle of the n.w. buttress and about 7ft. from the ground, there is a large flint which, when it was knapped, revealed the fossilised outline of a bird's head with a hooked beak – like a small eagle. The tower houses a fine ring of eight bells with a 15 cwt. tenor. On walking round, you will see that all the windows are *Perpendicular* and there is a *clerestory* on one side only above the s. *aisle*. The flintwork in the wall of the aisle is a C19 restoration. For a small church the s. *porch* is quite lavish. The angle buttresses have niches and decorative stone panelling, and the mouldings of the outer arch are studded with *fleurons* with two masks at the top, while the shield of the Wingfields is carved in the spandrels. Panels of the base course are carved with 'M's for the *Blessed Virgin* and there is a *Sacred monogram* on the e. side. Nine small niches graded in size stand over the entrance, and although the top is now squared off it was more elaborate originally. Like the w. door, the inner doorway spandrels contain Trinity and Passion emblem shields and there are lion *stops*.

Just inside the door is a large monument for members of the Green family which looks as though it has been rearranged. On the front of the large chest is a beautiful *rococo* panel with winged cherub heads in deep relief and crisp foliage, while beyond on the wall a large double panel by Bedford is surrounded by lively scrolls and commemorates members of the family 1825-76. The three black marble slabs on top of the tomb are for Thomas (1730), George (1739), and Jane (1744) Green, and although the excellent portrait bust on the l.-hand wall is not labelled it probably portrays Thomas. The nave roof was restored and re-leaded in 1966 and four old panels of 1657, 1742, and 1874 with churchwardens' initials were saved and are framed on the wall nearby. By the tower arch hang two massive Union Flag battle ensigns; they probably flew from the flagship HMS Duke of Wellington on station in the Baltic during the Crimean War. The niche in the n. wall is likely to have been an *aumbry* associated with the *font* so that the oils, salt, and cloths could be stored conveniently to hand. The font has obviously been moved because it stands partly on a *ledger-stone* of 1678. The odd thing is that another stone with the same date, age, and name lies to the e. and was presumably provided in recompense. The font's bowl panels are very deeply cut and conventional angels with shields

occupy four of them. However, the other four are more interesting because they contain figures representing the *Evangelists* (with curiously abundant hair styles) and they have their emblems at their feet. There are figures round the shaft, with *St Paul* to the w. and possibly *St James the Great* to the e. The attractive *hatchment* to the l. of the tower arch was used at the funeral of Thomas Green, a barrister who lived in the village and died in 1825. Also at the w. end of the nave is a *brass* for a man who died about 1530. The inscription has been lost so we don't know who he was, but a separate plate is engraved with a sheep so he was probably a clothier. Over the blocked n. door, in the traditional place opposite the main entrance, is a large wall painting of *St Christopher*. A good deal has been lost but fishes swim in the river round his feet, his staff is massive, and the hermit's hut is plain. An Elizabethan text on the s. wall by the door has largely gone. The simple but attractive *arch-braced nave* roof has embattled *wall plates*, small flower *bosses* at the main timber intersections, and transverse braces under the ridge. The s. aisle roof is medieval too but the fine angels at the base of the *wall posts* were carved by Archdeacon Darling in 1938 – another example of the woodworking skills to be found among the old-style clergy. A s. window in the aisle has glass of 1938 by Horace Wilkinson – figures of Christ, St Paul and *St Barnabas* in uncomplicated and conventional style. Other windows by him can be found at Framlingham and St Augustine's Ipswich. The aisle e. window glass dates from 1919 and is by *Hardman*. The presentation of Christ in the Temple is illustrated across three *lights*, with lots of steely grey tints setting off dark, rich colours. Below, the *altar* carries the church's original *mensa* set in a wooden frame. It had been demoted to a paving slab in the C16 but is now fulfilling its proper function once again. Note the thick stone *credence shelf* in the *piscina* recess close by. The pulpit is luxuriously carved, with centre rosettes in the body panels within flat-arched surrounds, elaborate tester and back to match, and the style suggests late-C17. By it stands a massive C13 iron-clad chest, much eaten away, which was originally a good deal longer. The C15 glass in the tops of the nave windows has been restored. The fragments in the n.w. window include an angel playing a lute, and in the next window there is a headless figure at the top playing a psaltery. The 3rd window contains three deep, beautiful canopies with an eagle, a sweet little lion, and an angel with a cross bandeau as finials;

above them on the r. is a headless St Catherine with a sword as well as her customary wheel. The last window has shorter canopies with tiny figures in the niches. On the l. is *St Osyth* with her keys, on the r. is an unidentified man in yellow hat and gown, and, in the centre, there are three musical angels. Binoculars are helpful here, and in the e. most clerestory window one can identify St Mary on the l. and St Barbara on the r.

Although they have been terribly mutilated, Wilby's C15 bench ends are the church's most interesting feature, mainly because they include part sequences of the *Seven Deadly Sins*, the *Seven Works of Mercy* and the *Seven Sacraments*. They are so like Tannington's benches that they were probably carved by the same man. At the e. end on the n. side of the nave the first bench illustrates penance, with Extreme Unction on the other side. The head of the priest behind the bed has gone but the scene is clear, with a *chrismatory* containing the holy oils being held by an attendant at the foot of the bed. Next to the w. you will find baptism and confirmation (a chrismatory again), and farther along an eagle stoops on its prey. *St John the Baptist* holds the *Agnus Dei* on the bench end next but one to the font, and on the 3rd to the e. *St Barbara* stands in her tower. Mutilated but still recognisable, with her hands joined in prayer, it is strange that she faces away from the aisle. At the e. end of the s. aisle are the acts of mercy of burying the dead (with a cross boldly carved on the coffin lid) and feeding the hungry, followed by the sacraments of marriage and the mass (with the stump of the priest's body behind the altar, a large *paten* upon it, and the outline of the base of the *chalice*. There is a musician on the 5th bench end from the w. end, and the last one has the sin of usury illustrated by the money-lender stuffing coins into a bag, and gluttony by a drunkard supping from a small barrel. *William Dowsing* came to the church in 1643 smashing many things, and it may be that he was responsible for the damage to the pews. The rest of the benches are good C19 work with some nice carvings on the elbows in sympathy with their medieval predecessors. The medieval shields of arms in the n. chancel window belong to the Sullyard family, including Sir John, Master of the Rolls and an active supporter of Queen Mary. The large *piscina* recess in the *sanctuary* still has its wooden credence shelf and there are *dropped-sill sedilia* alongside. Part of the large stone figure of the Blessed Virgin and Child which stands on a pedestal in the corner was

discovered in the churchyard ditch in 1935 and has been nicely restored. There are more brasses in the chancel, but inscriptions only: a Latin verse for Rector William James (1569), and another with a punning translation for one of his successors, Joseph Fletcher (1637), both on the s. wall; two with shields in the floor on the s. side of the sanctuary for Elizabeth Bayles (1588) and Joane Bayles (1620), and two more, also with shields, on the n. side for Lucy Bayles (1638) and John and Thomas Bayles (1639). The e. window glass of 1904 is a very nice example of the work of *Clayton & Bell* – Christ flanked by the Blessed Virgin and St John, with small figures of the Evangelists and angels in the tracery, and the *Three Marys* with the two apostles at the tomb in the bottom panels. The colours are rich but subtle, the drapery very involved.

Willisham, St Mary (E5): From the churchyard there is a broad vista over the rolling countryside to the s., with Offton's C14 tower emerging from trees in the valley bottom. This building, however, is purely Victorian and was designed by Herbert Green in 1878. It cost only a little less than his church at Darmsden but there is not so much to show for the money. There is no tower and a tall bellcote rises above a little triple blind arcade resting on corbels. The w. door has its own shallow gable and the formal disposition of the *lancet* and two-*light* windows is broken only by a s. porch which has pairs of *quatrefoils* each side rather like portholes.

Within, there is a roof of boarded panels and light *arch-braces* above pitch pine benches. On the n. wall an interesting engraving shows St Mary's as it was in 1844 and I wonder what became of the two C13 grave slabs that are illustrated below – very like those in the chancel at Whatfield. The C15 *font* is the only thing that was saved from the old building and it is a good example of a familiar East Anglian type. Angels with shields alternate with blank shields hung on pegs in the bowl panels and all the chamfers are decorated with *paterae;* demi-angels with partially re-cut heads spread their wings below, and four squat lions sit round the shaft gazing benignly heavenward. The openwork pulpit on its stone base, the matching reading desk, and the stalls with *poppyheads* are all in oak – possibly by Cornish & Gaymer. The *Decalogue*, Creed and Lord's Prayer on the e. wall are not the usual painted set but are engraved on brass plates framed in alabaster. A similar style is used in the two matching memorials for members of the Boby family of Willisham Hall and the e.

window has the same commemoration. The crucified Christ occupies the centre light, with two of the *Three Marys* on one side and St Peter and St James on the other. The smaller panels below portray the Nativity, *St Mary Magdalene* anointing the Lord's feet, and the women at the tomb. This is fine glass (probably by *Heaton, Butler & Bayne*), with a fruit and foliage backing to the main figures which is strongly *pre-Raphaelite*. There is a style contrast in the lower panels where the drapery detailing is particularly good and the tears on the women's cheeks remind one of the Virgin at Gipping.

Wingfield, St Andrew (G3): Although there was an earlier church on this site, the genesis of the present building was the foundation of Wingfield College under the will of Sir John de Wingfield in 1361. A provost and nine priests were to say daily masses for the repose of the soul of the founder and his heirs and they were housed in the building to the s. of the church. The church itself needed to be larger and more commodious in its new role and was rebuilt, with more additions and alterations following in the C15. A number of churches made provision for the parson's or the squire's horses in the C18 and C19, and by the n. gate there is a small brick and tile stable, with a wooden mounting platform nearby. Wingfield's tower is squat, with heavy angle buttresses, a stair turret to the s., and *Decorated tracery* in the bell opening (the w. window is a later *Perpendicular* insertion). It houses an excellent ground floor ring of six bells with a 13 cwt. tenor. On walking round, you will find that the windows of the n.e. chapel have flowing tracery with *mouchette* shapes, and the great e. window has stepped *embattled transoms*. The s.e. chapel was being built in 1415 and is an interesting example of old and new tracery forms being used together. The attractive four-petalled flower motif, used in the s. aisle fifty years earlier, reappears with the *ogee* shape alongside strong *mullions* and embattled transoms. There are Perpendicular *clerestories* over *nave* and *chancel*, the latter having seven closely-set windows a side linked by a running *label*. The s. *porch* was part of the work financed by Michael De La Pole, 1st Earl of Suffolk, who had married the Wingfield heiress, but the inner doorway is part of the C14 building. Heavily moulded, with slim attached columns, it has large *headstops* inclining inwards, the one on the r. a knight's head in helmet and the chain mail collar called a 'camail'.

Within, the mid-C14 nave *arcades* have octagonal *piers* and are neatly married with the leading edges of the tower's e. buttresses. From this one would guess that the tower was part of the earlier church. The *font* is a typical East Anglian design, with lions seated round the stem, and four more in the bowl panels alternating with angels bearing shields. It was given by the 2nd Earl of Suffolk about 1405 and the arms e. and w. are De La Pole/Wingfield, n. Wingfield, s. Stafford. The cover incorporates sections of C15 *crocketting* that perhaps came from part of the *rood screen*. By the C19 the building was in a poor state and major restorations were carried out from the 1860s to the 1880s. The nave roof was stripped of its medieval decoration and colour was even removed from the four small angels which carry shields below the *arch-braces*. The pleasantly carved benches date from 1880. The rood screen stretched right across the church and the stairs which led to the loft remain in the aisle window embrasures. On the n. side, just below the top doorway, the stump of one of the floor beams remains embedded in the wall, and the heavily restored base of the screen stands below the chancel arch. The pulpit is modern but carved *spandrels* have been used in fours to fill the square panels and they were probably part of the screen originally. The shield carries the arms of William De La Pole, Duke of Suffolk. To the s. of the chancel arch is a large blocked *squint* that aligned with the *High altar*.

What is now the organ chamber was a chapel dedicated to *St Margaret* built about 1430 and the niche high in the e. wall has *groining* and traces of colour although the canopy has been chopped off; below is a small *piscina*. The chancel roof was virtually replaced in the 1860s and all the stone *corbels* date from then. The layout of the stalls follows the usual pattern for collegiate churches, with some backing onto the screen, and they all have *misericords* – plain pendent centres with leaf supporters. The attractive *parclose screens* to n. and s. have groined coving on both sides. The large recess in the n. wall, with its handsome *cusped* and crocketted ogee arch and tall side pinnacles, was almost certainly an *Easter sepulchre* and not the original setting for the figure it now contains. This is the effigy of Sir John de Wingfield, the founder of the college and the Black Prince's Chief of Council, who died in 1361. In smooth stone, the head of the armoured figure rests on the remains of a helm, with a lion at the feet. It was once richly coloured and at the back of the neck *gesso* work resembling chain mail survives. Sir John's grandson died en route to Agincourt and his son, William De La Pole, rebuilt the chancel in his memory and extended it eastwards in the 1430s. The De La Pole *chantry* was the chapel of the *Holy Trinity* (now the *vestry*) and its upper chamber has two squints to give a view of the High altar. The vestry doorway, with its finely moulded arch, was part of the rebuilding and to the e. of it is the fine tomb of John De La Pole, Duke of Suffolk, who died in 1491. His wife was Elizabeth Plantaganet, sister of Edward IV and Richard III, and their alabaster figures were once richly coloured. Even now there are traces in the folds of her dress and on the Saracen's-head helm under his head. Both wear narrow jewelled coronets and, apart from the loss of her arms and chipped noses, the figures are complete. The buckles, straps, and rivets of his armour are meticulously detailed, one of the best examples of the period, but he has been sadly treated by graffiti addicts over the centuries – his chest has 'TS 1672' and his shoulder 'JLW 1906'. Above the tomb is a painted wooden helm with huge Saracen's-head crest and the remains of two supporters. Note how the second squint from the upper chamber beyond cuts through the cresting of the monument.

The elaboration of the chancel included the lovely arcade on the s. side. The mouldings are encrusted with little wings for the Wingfields, leopards' heads for the De La Poles, and the knots of the Staffords. The *capitals* are carved with demi-angels and on both sides the two eastern bays are linked by a cresting above. Below stands the tomb of the man in whose memory the work was done, Michael De La Pole, 2nd Earl of Suffolk. He was with Henry V on his French expedition and died of dysentery before Harfleur. The Countess Katherine was one of his executors and probably erected the monument for them both soon after his death in 1415. The beautifully sculpted effigies are not of stone but wood, a very late and unusual example of the medium. They are in remarkable condition and her figure, in kirtle and a long mantle with a deep collar, is particularly attractive; the headdress is patterned with flowers set in squares and her veil is secured by a narrow band. Unfortunately, the gilded and coloured gesso decoration was painted over in the late C18. The range of niches on the s. and w. sides of the chest once contained the figures of the Duke's children, and a most unusual feature is the *sedilia* seats that are ranged along the n. side. The chancel e. window has some medieval armorial glass and a mass of fragments in the tracery, while the High altar frontal is a fine early design by *Sir Ninian Comper* – stylised grapes against a fleur-de-lys pattern. The altar in the Lady chapel to the s. of the chancel is a small *Stuart* table, and behind it hangs a panel of cloth that was used in Westminster abbey at the coronation of Queen Elizabeth II. There are large mutilated niches r. and l. which show traces of original colour, and they now contain figures of *Gabriel* and the *Blessed Virgin* which date from the 1930s. The piscina in the windowsill is the simplest type and it is odd that such a lavish chapel should not have had something more elaborate. The massive unstained dug-out chest in the chapel may well be C12 and also to be found there is a rare example of a 'hudd', the shelter used by late-C18 and early-C19 parsons at the graveside in wet weather. The only other known example is

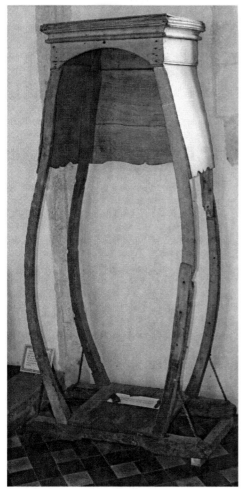

Wingfield, St Andrew: The hudd

at Walpole St Peter in Norfolk, but that is like a sentry box whereas this one has merely a boarded top fixed to curiously bandy uprights. The simple chamfer decoration is just like that used on farm waggons of the period and it would have been made by the village carpenter.

Winston, St Andrew (F4): At a sharp bend on the Debenham to Helmingham road a lane is signposted to Hall and church. It is a pleasant spot and the little church has a plain C14 tower with *quoins* of thin red bricks all the way up. The simple w. doorway has been bricked up, there is a *lancet* belfry window, bell openings with 'Y' *tracery*, and brick battlements. On walking round, 'Y' tracery is seen again in the tall windows on the n. side of the C14 *nave*, and a *vestry* was added against the n. door in the late C18 or early C19. Farther along, the old *rood stair* projects from the wall, and the *chancel* windows were probably copied from the originals when a restoration was carried out by *Phipson* in 1857. All of the outside walls were encased in flint at that time and the e. end was partially rebuilt, with a new window. There were problems of settlement, however, and in 1897 the architect *W.D. Caröe* had it rebuilt with a modest neo-*Perpendicular* window, probably because Phipson's window was overlarge. The s. nave wall is now plastered and one window has *Decorated* tracery. The diminutive *porch* is in *Tudor* red brick but makes the most of itself – a crow-stepped gable between octagonal buttresses that continue as stumpy pinnacles, and three niches above an outer arch that has deeply recessed mouldings.

Within, there is more Tudor red brick in the w. arch, and the thickness of the tower wall forms an interior porch to the little C18 door. A ring of five bells with a 5 cwt. tenor is rung from here There is a plain octagonal *font* with an C18 Creed board standing by, and a dark set of George III *Royal Arms* painted on board is framed over the n. door. The dinky vestry beyond is complete with fireplace. The nave ceiling is plastered but below it are C14 heavy *arch-braced tie-beams*, and the doorways of the rood stair can be seen in the n. wall by the C18 pulpit. This is a rather strange affair. It has a conventional body with plain bevelled panels, but it stands on three clusters of turned legs. Small monochrome panels of stained glass hang in the nave windows and are likely to be foreign C19 work. On the s. side: *St Peter* and *St Matthias*, with *St Andrew* and *St John* to the e.; n.

side: *St James the Less* and *St Jude*. A small and plain *piscina* on the s. side marks the site of a nave *altar*. There is now no *rood screen*, and in the chancel the outline of a door in the n. wall may have led to an earlier vestry. Although the waggon roof is part of Phipson's work, he retained the medieval tie-beams, and did not disturb the nice early-C13 piscina in the *sanctuary*. It is large, with detached shafts and remnants of stiff-leaf *capitals* below a *cusped* arch which has little *trefoils* on the cusps.

Wissett, St Andrew (H3): This church has one of the round towers that is often described as *Norman*, but there are three circular double-splay windows concealed in the walls to prove its *Saxon* origin. The very regular flintwork of the walls was repointed in 1977, and above the re-formed C15 bell openings there are good *gargoyles*. There was a timber n. porch at one time, but now the excellent Norman doorway on that side is exposed to the elements. Bold *chevron* and scallop mouldings decorate the arch, contained within a triple band of *billet* moulding which continues down each side of the *jambs*. The flanking shafts are carved with spirals and chevrons under varying *capitals*. The windows of the *nave* are *Perpendicular*, but if you examine the easternmost on the n. side you will see that the builder had a fine sense of economy and used small pieces of Norman stonework in the sill. The *chancel* was rebuilt in the C14, but it was ruinous by the early C17 and was eventually rebuilt again in 1848, with a little *vestry* added on the n. side. Troubles came again with the great gale of 1987 which so weakened the e. wall that it had to be entirely replaced. The C14 *priest's door* remains in the s. wall, and halfway along that side of the nave there is an interesting break in the masonry pattern, with regularly *coursed* flints to the l. and random placing to the r. It probably marks the e. end of the original nave, but it is puzzling that traces of an *apse* have been found beyond the present chancel, so that if the first nave was shorter, the corresponding chancel must have been surprisingly long. The s. *porch* was built in 1470, and there are very worn *Trinity* and *Passion emblem* shields in the door *spandrels;* plain shields flank the decorative niche above, and the blocked side windows retain remnants of *headstops*. The Norman doorway within displays a splendidly pagan range of beast heads as a rim to the arch – one is muzzled, there is a cat, a weird bird at the top, and a single human head wearing a crown completes the collection. The capitals are finely scalloped and there are good examples of *scratch dials* on each side., dating from the time when there was no porch . The C15 door has keeled boards, and note how the backplate of the closing ring is shaped like a jousting shield with a cutout for the lance.

The wide tower arch, with its simple *imposts* has remained unchanged, and there are very well-restored *Decalogue* boards on each side. In the base of the tower there are two delightfully rustic peal boards which celebrate a quarter of Grandsire in 1885, and a peal of mixed Doubles for the Queen's Jubilee in 1897. It is a pity that the ring of six bells with an 8 cwt. tenor are not in a fit state to be rung at present Local wills of the 1490s mention the *font* and confirm that it was originally painted. The panels of its deep bowl are carved with the *Evangelistic symbols*, and with curly-haired angels bearing shields, one of which has the three *chalices* of the Eucharist. Four lions guard the shaft, and between them stand excellent *woodwoses* which are like those at Chediston. There is a simple *stoup* just inside the entrance, and nearby stands the church's C19 *bier*. A fine set of George III *Royal Arms* hangs over the n. door and is one of the few that are signed – it was painted by Thomas Rounce of Halesworth in 1813 and cost £5. There is some interesting C15 glass in one of the nave n. windows – a small head of Christ in yellow stain at the top, and below, *St John the Baptist* cradles an *Agnus Dei* on a book, with his name in gothic script; alongside are three angels with beautifully drawn heads, and at the top of the window opposite there is the figure of a queen in dark yellow stain and a fragmented head of a king. The roof is *arch-braced* with *tie-beams*, and the floors are of homely brick and *pamment*. Some of the modern benches make use of C15 *poppyheads*. The *rood stair* entrance is unusually high in the wall, and the recessed space below must have had a specific use, perhaps the site of an *altar*. The two oddly placed recesses nearby, one above the other, probably survive from earlier windows. There is a fine image niche in the window embrasure on the s. side, with the remnants of a simple *piscina* below, so that there was certainly an altar there. The chancel arch was rebuilt in the C15, and although its *screen* has gone, the sawn-off stump of the *rood beam* still remains in the wall to the s. Paint splashes on the stonework of the nearby window may be a chance leftover from the reformers' zeal in obliterating the decoration they abhorred. The austere pulpit is late-C17, and it is likely that it formed a single unit with the matching reading pew opposite.

Wissington, St Mary (D7): The sign on the Bures/Nayland road points to 'Wiston church', using the local pronunciation, and the church is to be found surrounded by comfortable farm buildings in the lush valley of the Stour – a most beguiling setting. This is a *Norman* building and the restorers of 1853 decided to emphasise this by rebuilding the *apse* on the original foundations, enlarging the e. window, adding a neo-Norman *priest's door* and finishing it all off with a rib vault within. There is a glazed porch, two new windows on the s. side, a C19 w. window and n. *vestry*, but the tiny original *lancets* remain in *nave* and *chancel* and there are two ancient *corbels* projecting from the chancel walls. A large weatherboarded bell turret carries a vane pierced with the date 1722. Within the porch stands a fractured bell cast by John Thornton of Sudbury in 1719 and there is a large and lavish Norman s. doorway. It is very tall and the shaft to the l. is carved with alternating spirals up to a section of leaf carving below the *capital*. Its opposite number is cut as an octagon and decorated with *chevrons*. The deeply recessed arch has chevron, roll, and interlace mouldings and the *tympanum* is filled with chip-carved lozenges. To the l. of the doorway are two *scratch dials* and a faint but very delicate inscription is cut above the upper one. To the r. is a C15 *stoup*.

A heavy C19 *gallery* in two parts flanks the organ at the w. end and a *consecration cross* shows clearly below it on the n. wall. Overhead are the *Royal Arms* of George III in poor condition; it is interesting that 'Fear God and Honour the King' was lettered on the back, presumably for the benefit of the children who had to sit up there. Also suspended are two *hatchments*, the one on the s. side for Elizabeth Gibbons who died in 1798 and the other for a member of the Whitmore family. By going through to the vestry one can examine the n. doorway which is also Norman and has a massive rounded lintel below a plain tympanum and zigzag arch moulding. Both doorways have deep recesses in the *jambs* for security bars and the arrangement is probably as old as the church itself. While in the vestry, have a look at the pair of stalls with plain *misericords* and a nice *Jacobean* chest with some marquetry work on the front. Another stands opposite, but two of its panels have been badly damaged. Also of interest are two engravings from drawings by the antiquarian Henry Davy of the interior as it was in 1827 (i.e. before the restoration) and of the s. door. The early-C15 *font* is a fascinating and unusual example; the double-panelled stem has three very worn lions lying at its foot instead of sitting up as usual and, on the s.w. corner, a sheep lies with its lamb – a possible reference to Isaiah's prophecy of peaceful cohabitation. The rim of the bowl is *castellated* and in four of the panels angels hold shields: e., the arms of England (with the lions facing the wrong way!); s., the star of the De Veres; n.w., a *Trinity emblem*; the n.e angel holds a crown, that to the s.e. plays a psaltery, and the last one holds a rebec, one of the earliest bowed instruments.

One of the most tantalising things about Wissington is that it obviously had a complete range of wall paintings in the second half of the C13 and although enough remains to show their extent, very little can be easily distinguished now. Professor Tristram uncovered and treated them in the 1930s but they are now very faint for the most part. There was on the w. wall a *Doom* of which hardly anything is recognisable, and on the s. wall of the nave an upper range of scenes from the life of Christ. *St Michael* stands dimly above the pulpit, a Nativity scene is farther w., with the archangel appearing to the shepherds alongside, and the adoration of the Magi is discernible over the s. door. In the lower section there were scenes from the lives of *St Margaret* and *St Nicholas*, and his figure and his ship's sail are still clear. There is a huge and flamboyant red dragon over the n. door and originally the n. wall displayed incidents from the life of *St John the Baptist*, but perhaps the most interesting survival is the shadowy figure of *St Francis* high on the n. wall at the e. end. He is shown preaching to the birds which perch on a scrolly tree. This is the earliest known example of the most popular of his legends and must have been painted within a few years of his death. The nave roof is an example of *king post* and *tie-beam* construction. Below, the 1850s restorers indulged in pews with Norman-style blind arches carved in the ends and doors, plus a positively gross pulpit and matching reading desk. There are round-headed wall recesses at the end of the nave which no doubt housed *altars* and the e. arch is a grand Norman piece, wide and high with two widely separated zigzag mouldings. The supporting shafts vary, with spirals to the n. and mixed lozenge patterns to the s. It is highly likely that the original church had a tower beyond this arch like the one at Ousden. There is a large lancet above the farther arch and a beast corbel which was probably re-set when the apse was rebuilt. In the floor is a *brass* with two shields and an inscription for John

le Gris, who died in 1630, having been minister here for thirty-nine years. It was placed there by Elizabeth 'uxor amoris' (his loving wife). Beyond neo-Norman *communion rails*, the rebuilt apse has bright uncomplicated glass in C13 style by Wilmhurst & Oliphant – Crucifixion and Descent from the Cross in the e. window, the angel at the empty tomb in the n. lancet, and Christ bearing the cross to the s. This is the only example of the partnership's work in Suffolk and is very accomplished and colourful in C13 style. The other stained glass in the church consists of very conventional and flaccid designs by Thomas Baillie dating from the 1870s. The churchyard is a pleasant place in which to wander and there are some interesting headstones, including a fine modern example for Joyce Pike e. of the chancel, with excellent lettering and the *Chi Rho* symbol.

Withersdale, St Mary Magdalene (G2): This dear little church lies, with its neighbouring farm, by the side of the road in the gentle valley that runs from Withersdale Street up to Metfield. It shares its dedication with only two other churches in the county, and can be counted among the half dozen smallest, having but a modest *nave* and *chancel* and no tower. The walls are cement-rendered except for the lower half of the e. end which was replaced in C18 (or late-C17) brick, together with a wooden-framed window. The corners at the w. end are made up of large, irregular flints and glacial stones, and they point to a *Saxon* or early *Norman* beginning. The arch of a simple Norman doorway remains in the n. wall, bricked up and glazed at the top in the C18. Close by is a Norman *lancet*, matched by another on the s. side of the nave, and two square-headed windows were inserted in the C15. The chancel was an addition (or replacement) of the C13, and the 'Y' *tracery* windows were inserted about 1300. The *priest's door* on the s. side has a faint *scratch dial* on the r.-hand side which still has the remains of the metal spike in the centre. The small domestic window in the w. wall replaced a much larger C14 or C15 window at some time in the last century, and the weatherboarded bell cote on the w. gable had a little spire at one time. Although the s. *porch* is plastered to match the rest of the building, you will find that inside there are moulded wooden *mullions*, and a miniature *arch-braced tie-beam* in the roof. Apparently, both porch and bell cote were the gifts of Archbishop Sancroft, and if so, they probably date from the time when he

Withersdale, St Mary Magdalene

retreated to his native Fressingfield during the Commonwealth. Afterwards, as Dean of St Paul's he set in hand the restoration following the Great Fire when it was said that nothing was done 'without his presence, no materials bought, nor accounts passed without him'. Perhaps Withersdale gave him a taste for the greater work to come! The inner doorway dates from the early C13, and the door itself, with its lapped boards, original hinges and lock, cannot be later than the C16.

Within, little has changed since the C17, and it is a charming example of a country church that either did not need or, in their view, did not warrant, the changes that the Victorians wrought in most of our churches. The narrow C17 w. *gallery* is reached by a precipitous stair, and above it, arch-braces rise to support the bell cote. A set of George III *Royal Arms*, excellently painted on canvas, hangs on the n. wall, and below stands a Norman *font* of the late C12, its square bowl supported on a brick base. The w. face is carved with a colonnade under interlaced arches, a pair of simple arches on the n. side, and on the e. face there are three embellished arches,

with a 'Tree of Life' design on the l., a rosette above a devil mask roundel in the centre, and a crude *chevron* on the r. The corners of the bowl are recessed for rudimentary shafts, and the s. side was re-cut with a pair of *blind arches* in the C14. The nave roof has pairs of *collar beams*, and lateral curved braces under the *purlins*, with plaster infill between the principal timbers. The Norman lancets lie within deep splays, and there are two *quarries* of C15 glass in the n. window. Even the humble hymn board in this delectable church has been given a touch of elegance, with its carved and coloured roundel at the top combining *St Mary Magdalene's* two symbols – the pot of ointment and her tears. There are *pamment* floors, and the nave benches are unusual and interesting. They are a late-C16 set in unstained oak, whose ends have simple vertical mouldings and a trio of turned knobs on top; the backs are panelled, and they stand on deep sills to keep the straw in place that warmed the people's feet in winter. An anonymous visitor was of the opinion that the bench ends were pre-Jacobean and almost certainly came from the *rood screen*. There is now neither chancel arch nor screen, although the stairs that once led to the *rood loft* remain in the n. window embrasure.

When the C17 minister and parishioners wished to adapt the church to suit their consuming interest in the preaching of the Word, they used the wall of the stair as a backing for the new pulpit. Typically, it faces across the nave and is a *two-decker*, rather than a three-decker, there being no separate space for the *parish clerk*. The pulpit itself is tiny, a mere 22in. square, yet it is fitted with a narrow seat; the door still has its original butterfly hinges, catch, and *trefoil* hook. Apart from a simple chip-carved lozenge on the back board, the only embellishments are turned pendants and a little carving on the cornice of the oblong *tester*. Opposite the pulpit there are two large, plain *box pews*, one painted and earlier than the other, and the stalls on the l. of the chancel are, with the American organ, among the few C19 additions to the church furniture. On the s. side stands a C15 stall with *linen-fold panelling* in the front, strangely elongated *poppyheads*, and a broad book slope; there is the haunch of another by the priest's door. Like the nave, the chancel ceiling is plastered, with main timbers exposed, and a heavy tie-beam spans the *sanctuary* not far from the e. wall. *Cautley* thought that it might have been used for the *Lenten veil* and the *sacring bell* before the *Reformation,* but the structural weakness that eventually called for a rebuilding of the e. wall is a more likely reason. The beam is secured by pegs externally, and the same ploy was used at nearby Metfield. The C17 *communion rails* have austerely turned *balusters* and were probably installed at the same time as the pulpit; the *altar* is an early-*Stuart* table. The modern panelling on the e. wall is in C17 mode, and above it there are C18 *Decalogue* boards. The C14 glass in the head of the s. window is part of the Ufford family arms. Sometime after the Reformation, the C14 *piscina* was walled up, to be rediscovered in 1909 with the *cinquefoiled* arch shorn of its *cusps*. In all, a rustic and beguiling place.

Withersfield, St Mary (A6): Attractively sited in a village very close to the Cambridgeshire boundary, the church has a plain C15 tower with an octagonal turret at the s.e. corner. Its battlemented top rises above the parapet, a feature of a number of churches in this corner of the county. There is a yawning *gargoyle* on that side and the *Perpendicular* w. window has been renewed. The tower houses an unringable five bells with an 11 cwt. tenor. The s. *aisle* with its porch was added in 1867 and the *chancel* rebuilt, so that the frontage to the road is very trim, with lots of *septaria* showing in the walls

and heavy battlements to aisle and *nave*. The n. side has a much more subdued *stucco* finish and there is a blocked *Tudor* n. door. Within the porch, the large Tudor s. doorway (reused at the rebuilding) is decorated with *fleurons* in the mouldings and has *tracery* in the *spandrels*; above it is a battered C14 niche. The door handle is a survivor from an earlier 13C church, with a large pierced plate and an oval ring on which are riveted two lizards, those ancient symbols of good fortune that can also be found at Great Thurlow and Brockley. Just within is a *stoup* formed out of half of a *Decorated capital* that was probably saved from the original late-C13 or early-C14 *arcade*. There are pleasant brick and *pamment* floors and the *font* is an unusually late example from the C17, with three traceried panels and five shields of arms. The dark nave roof has false *hammerbeams* and bulky, roughly shaped *tie-beams* which conceal steelwork that was inserted in 1983 and which now takes the strain. Two of the hammers have the remains of small figures, and initials, together with the name of the firm that carried out the restoration, are carved on the n. *wall plate* above the *clerestory*. In contrast, the n. aisle roof is beautifully pale, with *arch-braces* rising from *wall posts*, centre *bosses,* and heavily moulded timbers. Here again there was a total reconstruction in 1974 and it was excellently done. On the wall in the n.e. corner there is a *brass* inscription which asks us to pray for the soul of Robert Wyburgh who built the aisle in 1480. The 1970s glass in the aisle e. window is by Pippa Heskett – a figure of *St Cecilia*. The C15 n. arcade, with its *quatrefoil piers*, was faithfully copied on the s. side when the C19 aisle was added. In the n.e. clerestory window you will see a *Trinity* shield. There are two differing sets of medieval benches and those on the n. have square ends with shallow buttresses. The s. range is excellent, with *paterae* on the chamfers of the shaped ends and exceptionally large *poppyheads*. At the w. end *St Michael* is weighing souls, and an arm reaches up trying to redress the balance. At the e. end there is a very vigorous *St George* who is much smaller than the dragon he is trampling; and in between you will find a *pelican in her piety* and her young, two creatures rising from a mass of vine, a collared swan, and a long-haired mermaid with her scaly bottom half just visible. The early-C17 pulpit has two ranks of blind arches with coarse, shallow carving and stands on a wooden base. *William Dowsing* was here in January 1643: 'we brake down a crucifix and sixty superstitious pictures' is the quote from his journal and he was probably referring to the *rood* and stained glass. The blocked C14 door to the *rood loft* is at the end of the s. aisle, and above the remains of a Decorated niche to the r. of the *screen* there is a fragment of what was the upper door. The C15 screen, with its original heavy doors, has deep, Perpendicular tracery and a double-*ogee* centre arch. The panel spandrels are carved with hogs, bearded heads in curly caps, birds and fish. It is a nice piece, despite a modern recolouring that ignored the basic medieval rules, and despite the addition of non-period frontal decoration, *cusps* and *crockets*. Nearby in the nave is the church's second brass – a shield and inscription for Joan Bury who died in 1579.

Witnesham, St Mary (F5): The main road dips steeply between the two halves of this straggling village and a lane leads from there to the church. The building dates largely from the late C13 or early C14, and some two hundred years later a *clerestory* under a new roof was added to the nave. Although the s. *aisle* was built in the early C14, it has no counterpart to the n., and a group of conifers overshadows the wall on that side. The late C18 was often a time of neglect and this may be why the *chancel* was shortened and partially rebuilt. You will see that the e. wall is a mixture of brick and salvaged stone, and the e. gable of the nave was renewed in brick. Nevertheless, the C13 *priest's door* with original ironwork is still there on the s. side. There was a major restoration in 1845 and the n.e. *vestry* was added in 1868. In common with a number of other churches in the area, St Mary's has a tower on the s. side which is also the main entrance. Built at roughly the same time as the aisle, it has angle buttresses up to the bell stage, *Decorated* bell openings, and *flushwork* battlements. The s. face neatly illustrates the early history of time-keeping, with a *scratch dial* which has traces of numerals by the entrance, a sundial of 1729 in the buttress angle above, and a single-hand clock with a diamond face which was installed in 1737. The inner face of the archway has a whole series of chamfer mouldings which fade into the jambs, and the C14 inner door of lapped boards still has its strap hinges and centre closing ring. The interior has a pleasant, spacious feel about it, and the *hammerbeam*, *arch-braced* roof of the nave has a plaster ceiling that masks everything above the *collar beams*. This is not uncommon but here the flat centre section is decorated with large raised roundels and diamond shapes. The placing of the tower shortens the aisle to no more than a two-bay chapel, and the

contemporary *arcade* has wide *capitals* above the slender octagonal pillar and *responds*. The church has a ring of six bells with an 11cwt. tenor, but their condition does not allow for ringing at the present time. The three-*light* e. window leans casually to one side, flanked by formless image niches, and the *piscina* with its renewed *credence shelf* shows that the aisle had its own *altar*. The floor has been newly relaid with nice bricks and there are benches ranged along the walls. These match the main suite in the nave and were made by *Henry Ringham* in the 1840s, a restrained design with good *poppyheads* and moulded top rails and ends. His skill lay in matching the remains of an original C15 set, and a careful look at those w. of the font will show how good he was. There is a medieval shield of the Weyland family arms set in the clear glass of the w. window, and although the *font* is a familiar East Anglian pattern it has been entirely re-cut. Witnesham has the best example in the county of the C18 wall texts that were the successors to the Elizabethan 'profitable sentences'. High on the walls, their small painted panels have been well preserved, and some of them are placed to make specific points of doctrine. Opposite the font over the blocked n. door you will see: 'Except a man be born of water . . .' (John 3.5); over the main entrance: '. . . this is the gate of heaven' (Genesis 28.17); and near the pulpit the preacher is reminded: '. . . woe is unto me, if I preach not the gospel' (1 Cor. 9.16). There are remains of a similar set at Hemingstone dated 1773 and it is likely that the same man painted both. In addition, there are slightly later Lord's Prayer and Creed boards in frames on either side of the chancel arch, and a matching *Decalogue* board in the aisle. The attractive little animal in the C14 glass at the top of the s.w. nave window came, it seems, from the nearby chapel of *St Thomas* which was in ruins by the C18. It has been tentatively identified as a beaver but I think that even at that time the characteristic tail was well known, and this one's is bushy. To the l. of the s. door is a memorial by *Thomas Thurlow* for Robert Carew King who died in 1842. The medallion portrait has him in profile, plump of chin and sporting sideburns. A plain tablet on the n. wall is rather odd in that it reverses the normal convention of a man boasting of his ancestry. Here we have 'Thomas Woolner (father of Thomas Woolner, RA, sculptor and poet and of Sarah Ann Meadows) was buried in this churchyard.' Presumably Thomas junior couldn't resist the advertisement when he memorialised his father. On the other side by the chancel entrance there is an extreme example of the more usual human failing. In 1824 Philip Meadows was described among other things as 'the great, great, great, grandson of William Meadows who was first seated here in 1630'. The pulpit is *Jacobean* with excellent panel work, standing on a modern base, and the shapeless chancel arch was part of the late-C18 rebuilding. Above it is a dark set of Charles II *Royal Arms*. There is another of the wall texts just beyond which relates to the Eucharist, and the Ringham choir stalls incorporate transverse C17 panels. The 'gothick' arches along the fronts match the set of *communion rails* provided at the same time. John King's memorial of 1815 on the n. wall is by *John Bacon the Younger*, a plain tablet on a black surround, with drapes falling on both sides from an urn at the top; there is a neat little *achievement* below. Opposite, two early-C19 brothers who died far apart in India and Canada are remembered on a graceful oval set on a black square. The dull and heavy stone *reredos* was designed by Robert Ireland in 1868, and the e. window is filled with 1840s glass by Edward Baillie. It is interesting historically because it precedes the flood of mass-produced glass that came later, but the colours are harsh blues, reds, and greens and Christ's figure in the Resurrection and Ascension panels seems to have strayed from a ballet. Other windows by him can be found at Henley, Hoxne and Wrentham.

Wixoe, St Leonard (B6): This small church was heavily restored in the late C19, but is not without interest. The doorways and the *coursed* flintwork in the walls show that the building is *Norman* and originally there was an *apse* at the e. end. The plain n. door is blocked and a n.e. *vestry* was added by the Victorians, together with two prominent chimneys on that side and the s. porch. The large, weatherboarded bell turret is in the Essex tradition, and there is a *priest's door* on the s. side of the *chancel*. The s. doorway is good Norman work – single shafts with scalloped *capitals*, and an arch decorated with a band of *chevrons* and bobbins.

To the l. of the door within, there is a plain octagonal C14 *font* and a *stoup* to the r. The *nave* roof is open waggon construction with two *tie-beams* and *king posts*. Below, the C19 pews have small *poppyheads* and *linen-fold* on the ends. All the windows are replacements and the 1890s e. window glass is by Cakebread, Robey & Co of Stoke Newington – the only example of their work in West Suffolk. It is an Ascension, with musical angels in the *tracery* and although

conventional, the grouping of figures and quality of colour is excellent. On the n. wall of the *sanctuary* is a memorial to Samuel Berkeley who died in 1764 – a plain tablet beneath a broken *pediment* and flanked by swags. To the w., Henry and Dorothy Berkeley have as their monument a flat obelisk against a grey background, with a *cartouche* and two flaming urns on top. A grisly winged skull is carved in the panel below, and in the centre of the chancel floor their vault is marked with curiously precise dimensions. On the s. chancel wall is a plain little tablet by Denman of Regent Street for Josias Nottidge (1844) and the memorial for William and Elizabeth Payne (1843 and 1881) on the s. wall of the nave is by Harding of Ballingdon – plain, with a mushily draped urn on top.

Woodbridge, St John (G6): The church stands on St John's Hill, a steep knoll on the e. side of the town. It was designed in the early 1840s by Alfred Lockwood, a Woodbridge builder, and the architect was his friend John Clark who built the Old Custom House in Ipswich at about the same time. He chose yellow brick as his material, and a straightforward *Early English lancet* style. To the w., the tower has three tall lancets linked by their *dripstones*, and the chamfered buttresses are gabled. The bell openings are pairs of widely spaced lancets with an arcaded frieze above them, and the parapets are gabled with corner pinnacles. In 2003, a new spire was added (the original was removed in 1982); it is slim, octagonal, and lead-sheathed, with louvers under sharp gables. Trios of lancets feature again in each bay of the *nave*, and note that their shafts are moulded brick, stone being reserved for the *capitals*, dripstones, and *headstops*. Some of the latter are surprisingly inventive – devilish characters on the n. side, and a *green man* on the s. The shallow *chancel* is *apsidal*, sturdily buttressed, and the n.e. *vestry* has a tricky little entrance; a polygonal extension to the s. was added later. Modern, single storey wings at the w. end are carefully matched to the original, providing a neat porch, foyer, and ancillary accommodation.

Beyond a new glazed screen the nave is quietly impressive – uncluttered, calm and bright. The prominent transverse ceiling ribs arch over to rest on triple wall shafts or, alternately, divide in a 'Y' to form a hood over each window. They command the colour scheme, painted white outlined in plum against a pale lilac background. The splendid *gallery* is raked, and its broad wings come forward at a shallow angle on each side. It rests on cast-iron pillars, and the front is a continuous *blind arcade* of interlaced arches, topped with a delicate cast-iron cresting. The tower arch with its dogtooth moulding has been blanked off, and the gallery still has its original pews – a fine set, all with doors and painted cream with black trim. The nave is now close-carpeted and the benches of 1901 have been replaced with comfortable chairs upholstered in a dusky pink, allowing a helpful flexibility in use. In addition, cloakrooms, an office and a kitchen have been cleverly inserted under the tower and they combine with a matching foyer. The chancel arch matches that of the tower, and the shallow *apse* has pillars with carved capitals at the angles supporting the strongly defined ceiling ribs. The lancets were filled with stained glass as individual memorials between 1891 and 1902, each a single figure. From l. to r.: the young Samuel, *Dorcas(?)*, *SS Peter, John, James the Great, Andrew*, and an interesting choice of subject from the Second Book of Kings – the Israelite serving maid that directed Naaman to Elisha to be cured of his leprosy. The last window is signed by the London glazier Ernest Suffling, and it is likely that he provided the rest. The only other example of his work in Suffolk is at Little Saxham. Below the lancets, the three e. bays contain sharply pointed blind arches, themselves enclosing a trio with free-standing slim columns. They formed a *reredos* for the original *altar*. A podium has been installed which extends into the nave and there is a range of starkly simple fittings in the chancel, including a small *font*. The elaborate 1880s stone pulpit that stood against the wall to the l. of the chancel arch has been banished, but nearby there is a tablet in typically High Victorian style for James Duningham who for 14 years was the church's 'gratuitous organist' – unpaid rather than unwarranted one assumes!

Woodbridge, St Mary (G6): Tightly lapped by the town, one way to this grand church is through a snug alleyway from the market place and down steep steps to the n. door. There has been a church here since before the Conquest, and when a priory was founded in the late C12 the old building was used by both the canons and the people. The site chosen for a new parish church was just to the n. of the priory, and work began at the beginning of the C15. The splendid tower dates from the mid-C15, and the *flushwork base course* displays crowned 'MR's for the *Blessed Virgin* and tricky roundels; there is another range below the huge w. window, and the shields of Brotherton (r.) and Segrave (l.) were transferred

from the older building to the *spandrels* of the doorway. There are paired bell openings, and a swathe of pretty flushwork is set below the battlements, themselves decorated with flushwork and inset shields; the corner pinnacles are topped with vanes, and *Evangelistic symbols* are centred on each face. All the flushwork is in the style of the Aldrych masons of N. Lopham in Norfolk and includes the device that identifies them as the builders here. For such a fine tower, the buttress arrangement is unusually gauche – polygonal at the base followed by boxy squares, then pairs at right angles and finally a diagonal form. Walking round, you will see that the flintwork of the walls is particularly dense, the only variation being the rendered wall of the s. *aisle* chapel (it may have formed a link with the priory buildings). The e. face of the church is a broad and continuous spread across the aisle chapels and the *chancel* whose e. window is set very high in the wall. The last significant addition to the building came in the 1560s when the n. aisle chapel was added. The sumptuous n. *porch* of the 1450-1460s, with its massive octagonal buttresses, is panelled overall in flushwork; there are intricate designs in the base course, *Sacred monograms*, and the *chalice* and wafer symbol of the mass. A window was inserted in the e. wall as part of the Victorian restoration, and above it on the l. you will see the badge of the *St Eligius guild*. *St George* and the dragon occupy the arch spandrels, and although the triple niches are decayed, the restorers supplied new statues – The Blessed Virgin with *St Anne* on her r. and *St Etheldreda* on her l. Charities were often dispensed in church porches, and here in 1635 John Sayer provided a handsome cupboard to store loaves. In mahogany with a classical *pediment*, it continued in use until World War I.

A spacious, stately interior, which was transformed by an *R.M. Phipson* restoration in the 1870s when the huge galleries were removed, along with the box pews. The tall *arcades* on *quatrefoil piers* stop one bay short of the tower and, above them, closely spaced *clerestory* windows stretch from end to end. The low-pitched roof has been extensively restored and runs without interruption over *nave* and chancel with *hammerbeams* alternating with strutted *tie-beams*. The s. aisle roof rests on *corbels* which are grotesques with lolling tongues, twisted noses, and cauliflower ears – except for the pair at the w. end, a man and woman of the late C14 who may be the benefactors John, Lord Segrave and his lady. *Hatchments* hang on the walls at the w. end of the nave for: n. side l., Rear Admiral

Carthew (1827); r., Ann Carthew (1758); bottom, Robert (or Thomas) Knights; s. side l., Mary Carthew (1771); r., Elizabeth Carthew (1768); bottom, Mary Knights (unusual red background). Below the hatchments on the s. side is 'The Deben Millenium Frieze' on three bright and very attractive appliqué panels. It illustrates the area's history from the time of the first Christian landing to the present day, and the names of all the contributors are worked into the design. The tower arch is closed off with a solidly substantial oak screen , coved on the e. side and supporting a new gallery for the ringers of the church's excellent ring of eight bells with a 25 cwt. tenor. The chest which stands at the w. end of the s. aisle has '1672' studded on top, but was probably made over a hundred years earlier; leather-covered, and reinforced with broad iron bands, it may well have been in domestic use originally. The *Seven Sacrament font* is a very battered example which has the Blessed Virgin's lily pot emblem carved in the shaft niches and defaced demi-angels below the bowl. The panels have rayed backgrounds like those at Great Glemham and Denston, and despite the mutilation, the subjects are recognisable and have faint traces of colour. Clockwise from the e. they are: baptism; confirmation (with the *chrismatory* on the priest's l.); penance (the priest sits in the special shriving pew, the woman kneels and the demon of sin exits l.); mass (note the chalice on the *altar*, the remains of the coloured frontal, and the rare illustration of a *houseling cloth* held by the communicants); extreme unction (sharply tilted bed and featuring another chrismatory held by the acolyte); Crucifixion; ordination; matrimony. The *butterfly headdresses* of the women in the penance and mass panels date the font as late-C15. The lovely 16-branch chandelier which hangs in the nave was given by Robert Elfreth in 1676; it shows strong Dutch influence and is one of the earliest in England. The window nearest the entrance in the n. aisle contains 1890s glass by *Arthur L. Moore*, a very restless design in which the figures of *SS Patrick, George,* and *Andrew* are closely set about with *tabernacle work*; it commemorated Queen Victoria's jubilee, and her portrait is framed in the garter at the bottom. The next window was probably made by *Powells* in the early 1900s, and features large figures of Moses, David, and Elias (?); below, Christ enthroned is flanked by the people of all nations. Nearby is an excellent tablet for Nathaniel Randall who died in 1800 – an oval with draped urn above and crossed palms below.

The C15 *rood screen* stretched right across the church, and must have been one of the most elaborate in Suffolk. It had over thirty painted panels and was given in 1444 by a weaver John Albrede and his wife Agnes. In 1631 the antiquarian Weever wrote: 'how glorious it was when it was all standing may be discerned by that which remaineth' (proving that it was defaced before the Civil War), and by the end of the C18 it had been cut down to the level of the middle rail. The present screen is a Victorian replacement, but ten of the original panels are displayed at the w. end of the s. aisle. They are fairly well preserved, and all the figures are set against green and gold stencilled backgrounds. Despite defacement, some can be identified – from the l., 1st *St Thomas*, 3rd St Andrew, 4th *St James the Great*, 6th *St Bartholomew* (?), 8th *St Jude*, 10th *St John*. The remains of the inscription that identifies the donors can be seen along the top. The glass in the window above is a painterly design by Arthur Moore on a post-resurrection theme – the *Three Marys* at the tomb in the centre, Christ with *St Mary Magdalene* on the l., and meeting the disciples on the shore on the r.; His appearance to the disciples in the upper room is illustrated below. One window in the s. aisle is full of jolly patterns in red, blue and green – 1860s glass by Cox & Sons who have windows at Badingham, Burgh, Cavendish, Darsham, Groton, Marlesford, St Mary's Newmarket and Thornham Magna. The unframed *Royal Arms* of George III now hang high on the wall nearby, painted on canvas and dated 1774. Four more panels from the old screen line the wall by the s. aisle altar; one is painted with the figure of *St Cecilia* and another with *St Ursula* and her shipload of virgins. The glass in the window above is again by Moore – a colourful, coherent design of Christ enthroned above a group of figures which includes St John the Baptist and *St Margaret*. The height of the C15 screen can be gauged by the door in the wall which led directly onto the loft. There was an altar dedicated to St Anne in the s. aisle chapel, and a *piscina* remains in the s. wall; the blocked door at low level nearby may have linked the church with the priory buildings in the early days. The splendid monument on the e. wall commemorates Geoffrey Pitman and his family. He was a Woodbridge tanner and haberdasher who died in 1627, having been Suffolk's High Sheriff two years before. It has been suggested (on stylistic grounds) that the monument came from the Janssen workshop in Southwark, those talented Dutchmen who made the

Shakespeare monument at Stratford and whose only authenticated work in Suffolk is at Redgrave. In alabaster and *touchstone*, it is in three tiers, with Geoffrey kneeling in the upper niche, his wives Alice and Anne facing each other over a prayer desk in the middle level, and his two sons in linked niches below; garnished with swags and ribbons, a roundel of arms at the top, and freshly coloured details, it is in fine condition.

The church's only remaining medieval *brass* can be found on the wall at the n. end of the *communion rails* in the *sanctuary*. John Shorland was only seven when he died in 1601, and there is a thoughtful verse below his shield and 8in. effigy:

Heaven and this stone disjoyned keepes
one double fayre in minde and face.
Heaven hath his soule, his corps here
  sleepes...

Thomas Seckford was Woodbridge's great benefactor and his name is interwoven with its history. He was Master of the Court of Requests and Elizabeth's Surveyor of the Court of Wards, and added his own chapel n. of the chancel. He was buried there in 1587, but the organ was transferred into the chapel during the C19 restoration and the Seckford tomb now stands on the n. side of the sanctuary. The chest has open arcades and has been altered so that the slab which bore the memorial brass now lies partially obscured under the tomb. The C15 ensuite piscina and stepped *sedilia* in the opposite wall are very plain, and it is likely that they once had *hood moulds*. Small figures of the *Evangelists* stand under painted canopies on the modern oak *reredos*, and in the high e. window there is very attractive glass by Martin Travers, installed in 1946 but made in 1929. An artist in the tradition of *Sir Ninian Comper* (whose pupil he was), this is his only work in Suffolk apart from a *St Nicholas* window at Denston. Here he crisply illustrates the visit of the Magi in a square panel which is slightly broader than the centre *lights* of the window – an uncomfortable arrangement; the rest of the window is largely clear glass with the occasional emblem and the shields of St George, Canterbury, the diocese, and Seckford. Before leaving, look for the humble 1640s *ledger-stone* in front of the pulpit:

Yong Henry Grome a lovely babe here lies,
Confin'd in dust under this marble stone,
Who precious was in tender parents eyes,

Yet shortly veiwd the world and now is
  gone.
Oh learne we then to draw our dearest love,
From transient treasures to the joyes above.

Woolpit, St Mary (D4): This relatively small church is rich in ornament and was highly favoured by the abbey of St Edmundsbury in whose hands it was from before the Norman Conquest until the dissolution of the monasteries. There is no trace of the earlier buildings and the s. *aisle* is early-C14 with a later brick parapet. The battlemented *chancel* is of the same period and the *priest's door* on the s. side has shafts with round *capitals*. The corner buttresses have large niches with *ogee* tops, the e. window tracery is *reticulated*, and there is an C18 lean-to *vestry* on the n. side. The *nave* is mid-C15 and has a lavish *clerestory*, with panel tracery in the two-*light* windows, linked by bands of *flushwork* emblems and monograms. The n. aisle is simpler and was built in the early years of the C16. In 1702 a gale brought down much of the C14 tower and spire and it was repaired only to be devastated by lightning in 1852. This time a completely new one was designed by *R.M. Phipson* in the Fenland *Perpendicular* style and it is interesting to compare it with the Great Finborough tower and spire not far away that he built 20 years later. Below the deep openwork parapet is a boldly lettered text, and from behind tall corner pinnacles delicately curved and pierced flying buttresses support the stone spire which is set well back and provided with the two ranges of windows called lucarnes. The tower houses a fine ring of six bells with an 8cwt. tenor. The stone s. *porch* is glorious, and of all the C15 examples in the county *Cautley* thought it was the best, and went so far as to say that its proportions and detail surpassed Northleach in Gloucestershire, making it the finest of its type in England. It towers above the s. aisle and the s. face is panelled throughout in *ashlar*. The mouldings of the outer arch are enriched by lion masks with leaves rather than tongues lolling from their mouths and, above shields bearing the three crowns of East Anglia, there are triple niches flanked by another, larger pair with flattened pinnacles above double ogee arches. These once housed statues of Henry VI and his tigress of a queen. The angle buttresses are unusually distinguished by having image stools set on the gables at three levels and the openwork parapet is reminiscent of Pulham St Mary, in Norfolk. The side windows match the entrance arch and the whole of the e. wall is faced with

Woolpit, St Mary

high quality chequerwork in flint and stone. The
inside of the porch is equally impressive and
the vaulting *bosses* are carved with an angel,
masks, and foliage. The inner doorway has a
crocketted ogee arch with its mouldings enriched
to match the entrance. The porch was a long
time in the building (from 1430 to 1473 when
the images were provided for the niches) and it
is worth searching for the merchant's marks of
three men who helped to pay for it: John
Turnour's is scratched on the stone just inside
the entrance arch on the r., John Stevyenson's is
in the corner to the r. of the inner door, and
Johannes Regnold's is to be found in the l.-
hand moulding of the inner doorway and has a
heart at the bottom containing his initials.

After such an introduction the church's interior
is no anti-climax, for it has an outstanding
double *hammerbeam* roof built in 1440-1450, pale
in colour and with a profusion of decoration
that makes it very lively. There are deep *wall posts*

with crocketted and pinnacled canopies over
figures of bishops, kings and saints; below them
are demi-angels bearing emblems and there are
more on the ends of the hammers. All the main
timbers are crested, tiny angels perch above the
collar beams under the ridge, and the deep, double
wall-plates are studded with yet more of them.
Woolpit was Suffolk's C19 master woodworker
Henry Ringham's first important commission; in
1844 he completely restored this roof and carved
new angels to replace those destroyed by *William
Dowsing's* deputy in 1644. With the exception of
the one holding an organ at the w. end, I think
they are all Ringham's work and he replaced some
of the heads of the standing figures. There is a
three-light window in the e. gable and below it
is a very intriguing construction. It consists of
five bays of delicately ribbed coving on shafts
that rise from miniature demi-angels. The cornice
is neatly mitred into the hammerbeams each side
and Cautley was convinced that it was an integral
part of the C15 design, forming a *canopy of
honour* over the rood. Another authority believed

it to be a portion of the old *rood loft*, but it was apparently installed in the 1870s and is likely to have come from another church. The C19 texts and sharp blue background colour are not congenial and tend to emphasize its alien nature. The *arch-braces* of the aisle roofs come down to wall posts on each side bearing figures in the canopied niches. Ringham carved angels for them which match those in the nave and at this level they seem overlarge. The centre rafters between the arch-braces are carved with pairs of recumbent angels, head to head with wings folded – a beautiful concept. The wall plates and centre beams are richly crested. The narrow aisles were designed as processional ways and the fine medieval benches were arranged in two main blocks reaching just beyond the *arcades*. They have *poppyheads*, traceried ends, carved backs, and grotesques on the elbows. On the n. side at the w. end is a pair of *ibex* which, in the bestiaries, are said to throw themselves over precipes and land safely on their horns. The only other East Anglian example is on a bench-end in St Nicholas Kings Lynn. Moving further along there are dogs with geese in their mouths, and a pair of *griffins*. On the s. side at the w. end there is a chained monkey and another dressed as a seated monk. Ringham carved the front six rows and in doing so duplicated some of the original animals. He must also have carved the fine pulpit on its tall granite pedestal.

Woolpit, St Mary: Hammerbeam roof

In the Middle Ages there were *guilds* of the *Holy Trinity* and the Nativity of the *Blessed Virgin*, and a shrine dedicated to 'Our Lady of Woolpit' attracted many pilgrims. It is possible that this was in the s. aisle where there is a very open C14 *piscina* under a *cinquefoiled* arch across the angle of the window embrasure. On the ledge of the *sedilia* next to it there stands part of the square shaft of a *preaching cross*, with remains of figures on three sides and a recognisable Calvary on the fourth. To the l., the outline of the *rood loft* stairs can be seen, with a little *quatrefoil* window half way up, and the bottom doorway is around the corner by the *rood screen*. Just in front of it stands the handsome C16 lectern, with that buttery texture and patina that brass achieves with age. Traditionally supposed to have been the gift of Queen Elizabeth when she visited the church; the base is supported on three dumpy lions and, as is often the case, the eagle's claws are missing. Others like it may be found at Cavendish, Upwell in Norfolk, and Corpus Christi College in Oxford. The main lights of the C15 rood screen have *cusped* and crocketted ogee arches with open tracery above them and there are patches of the original *gesso* decoration on the *mullions*. The bottom panels were repainted in the C19 and from l. to r. the figures are: *SS Withberga, Felix, Mary Magdalene, Peter, Paul*, the Blessed Virgin and Child, *St Edmund* and *St Etheldreda*. All repeat the original subjects except St Felix who supplanted *St John the Baptist*. The entrance gates are early-C17 and have a line of shaped splats below turned *balusters*, with damaged strapwork cresting the top rails. The top of the screen was altered and dated in 1750. The benches in the chancel are unlike those in the nave and have quite massive ends which are over 4in. thick. There are *green man* masks worked into the carving of three of the poppyheads and there is a seated figure on a buttress of the priest's stall. There is a collared ibex on the n. side and at the e. end of the s. range is a very interesting group of figures. Although the main figure is headless, a pot of lilies identifies her as the Blessed Virgin and there are two more women in the background. In the *sanctuary* the late-C13 or early-C14 double piscina is set within rough twin *lancets* and has a stone *credence shelf*. The e. window has shafts each side and note that although one capital is conventionally carved with stiff leaf, the other has two little crawling beasts. The glass was restored and rearranged in the 1970s and there is a fine Virgin and Child panel in the centre, with modern roundels and shields in the rest of the main lights. The tracery contains a lovely set of medieval *Evangelistic symbols*, two angels blowing long trumpets, and three more standing on wheels. There are C15 fragments in the s. chancel windows and in the top of the n. window are four small early-C19 figures of *SS Andrew, Paul, John* and *Luke*. On your way out, pause to examine the remains of a stone woodwose on the window sill in the n. aisle and note that Phipson re-set the unusual C14 circular *sanctus-bell window* in the tower wall. The glass in the tower w. window is interesting because it was made in 1848 by Mrs Lucy Marriott, the wife of the curate at Onehouse. The grisaille patterns in lively colour survived the fall of the tower to be used again in its successor. Mrs Marriott was a contempory of Lucy Rickards who was another amateur stained glass enthuiast and filled windows of her father's church at Stowlangtoft. As the only women glass painters in Suffolk at that time it would be surprising if they did not collaborate.

Woolverstone, St Michael (F7): The church enjoys a spacious setting in the grounds of Woolverstone Hall, and is a building which underwent a three-stage transformation in the C19. In 1832, Archdeacon Berners (the family were squires here for 160 years) added a n. *aisle*, and in the 1860s *Sir George Gilbert Scott* restored the *nave* and rebuilt the *chancel*. Finally, in 1888-90, the 1830s n. aisle was replaced by a new nave and chancel (making the old nave a s. aisle), with a choir *vestry* added on the n. side. It is worth a circuit of the building to see the effect of all these changes, and examine first the C15 tower. It has *flushwork* in the angle buttresses, a stair turret on the n. side to belfry level, and there are eagles at the corners below the 1880s replacement parapet. The new nave was designed in *Perpendicular* style by J.P. St Aubyn, and the flintwork is good. The n.e. vestry is as large as a chancel aisle, and its w. door and window are part of a neatly unified design. A stone at the n.e. corner of the chancel was laid by Capt. Hugh Berners RN on the feast of the church's patron saint, 1888, to mark the beginning of the grand rebuilding. The 1864 Scott chancel in *Decorated* style (now the s. aisle chapel) has dense flint facings with bands of *ashlar*. While all this was going on, the substantial *porch* was altered very little. It was built in 1492, when Roger Wolverstone, Lord of the Manor, provided half the brick and all the timber. Lozenge patterns decorate the frontage below the half-timbered gable, and the *spandrels* of the roof are carved with leaf designs springing from little vases,

with attractive terminals carved on the *wall posts*. The C14 inner doorway, with its large, timeworn *headstops*, still serves as the main entrance, and there is a restored *stoup* to the r.

A C19 *bier* in fine condition stands just inside, and the *font* belongs to the familiar C15 East Anglian family. Decidedly a poor relation, however, because although the bowl carvings have the conventional alternation of lions and demi-angels, the carving is extraordinarily crude and must have been the work of an amateur. Nevertheless, the lions falling on their noses have a curious charm. The C14 arched recess in the n. wall beyond is likely to have been an *aumbry* for the storage of vessels and other items needed for baptisms. An excellent gallery has recently been inserted in the tower, with cloakroom facilities below. Medieval poorboxes sometimes took the form of turned posts, and opposite the entrance there is a very good C19 version with wrought-iron fittings which was probably designed by Scott. The window in the s. wall is filled with 1880s glass by *Heaton, Butler & Bayne* – fine figures of *SS Martin, Agnes, Margaret*, and *Augustine*. The church's only *brass* is secured to the front of the old chancel step, and is an inscription commemorating Thomas Runtyng who was rector here and died about 1430. Except for some interesting angels in the *tracery*, the aisle e. window glass of 1862 was blown out by a flying bomb in World War II. The replacement is an Alfred Wilkinson design of 1947 – Christ the King, flanked by *St Michael* and *St Gabriel*, the figures set in clear glass. The *piscina* had its C14 *trefoil* arch refurbished in the 1860s, and the fine alabaster statue of the patron saint on the n. side of the chapel was probably installed at that stage of the rebuilding. A four-bay *arcade* was inserted in the n. wall of the old nave to link it with the extension, and there are three nice *headstops* on the n. hood moulds. Scott's roof design was repeated in the new nave – braced *tie-beams* with *king posts* under single frames. The *screen* is in C15 style, and the theme is continued with a quality *hammerbeam* roof in the chancel. A two-bay arcade and wrought-iron screen separates the new chancel from the old, and in the *sanctuary* there is a splendid piscina and *sedilia* suite in stone, groined, with heavy canopies, pinnacled shafts, and intricate *tabernacle work*. Along with the rest of the 1880s stonework, it was carved by Thomas Earp. The high-level e. window is filled with more 1880s Heaton, Butler & Bayne glass, a very pale composition centred on the Crucifixion. *St Joseph of Arimathaea* and the *Blessed Virgin* stand on one side, *St John* and *St Mary Magdalene* on the other, with a *pelican in her piety* at the top. A couple of monuments were transferred to the vestry during the rebuilding, and the older one in *touchstone* and alabaster commemorates Philip Bacon who died in 1635. It has a coloured *cartouche* of arms sporting the family boar within the broken *pediment*, and would recover its character if the inscription were highlighted once more. The other memorial is a demure tablet in the n.w. corner commemorating Mary Ann Barnard who died in 1836. A pretty chaplet of flowers overhangs the epitaph, and the memorial is one of the minor works of Robert William Sievier, a very talented sculptor whose monument to Lord Harcourt is in St George's chapel, Windsor. Of more particular interest is the excellent marble bust of Archdeacon Berners, builder of the original n. aisle. It is by *Richard Westmacott* the younger, sculptor of the relief in the pediment of London's Royal Exchange. It is a fine, four-square head, faintly smiling, and dates from 1839, well before the archdeacon's death. The vestry is comfortably appointed, complete with fireplace, and presumably the eccentric addition of a piscina in the n. wall was in case they changed their minds and used it as a chapel. In the more tempestuous climate of the 1630s, rector Timothy Dalton was suspended from his duties by Bishop Wren for helping puritans to emigrate. Dalton's brother had already fled, and he followed in 1637, to begin a new life in Dedham, Massachusetts.

Wordwell, All Saints (C3): With only a house and a farm for company,, this little church lies by the side of the Bury to Elveden road and is now in the care of the *Churches Conservation Trust*. Prior to a restoration in 1827 it had been used as a granary, and in 1857 *Samuel Saunders Teulon* directed another refurbishment, but with the declared intention of saving all features of interest; twin buttresses were placed against the w. face of the *nave*, flanking a narrow *lancet*, and a double bellcote was added. Further work was done in 1866 with less consideration and a C17 pulpit was removed amongst other things. The building is basically early-C12, as indicated by the regular *coursing* of the rubble walls on the n. side, where there is an unrestored doorway with plain arch and volute *capitals* to the columns. The *chancel* windows are C19 and the e. window has curious decoration round the arch, alternating triangles of dressed flint and *ashlar*. There is a *priest's door* on the s. side and the vestige of a *scratch dial* can just be seen on the s.e. angle of

the nave. The wooden porch, designed by Teulon, stands on a flint and stone base. The *Norman* entrance doorway has a fine, unrestored *tympanum* carved with the Tree of Life, whose branches divide in the centre and become an interlace design; two hounds bay at the base of the tree, and their tails intertwine with the foliage. At the top of the r.-hand *jamb* is a tiny carved figure of a man with his arms raised and, on entering, you will see that there is a larger version of him in the tympanum which, for some reason, faces inwards over the blocked n. door. There, the figure is accompanied by another holding a ring. The carving is much more primitive than the Tree of Life design and it may be pagan. Its meaning is a matter for conjecture, although the Sacrament of Marriage or Christ giving benediction to someone holding the crown of thorns have been suggested. The early-C12 *font* is a simple, plain drum resting on a central shaft and three rough supports, with worn heads below the bowl. The benches in the nave have large, nicely varied *poppyheads* and good blank *tracery* on the ends. Some of the grotesques on the elbows are in good condition (the one nearest the pulpit, for example) but there are replacements at the w. end on the n. side – the dog and the whole of the next bench end. The best piece of carving is on the back of the bench by the door where there are three dragons, a jester emerging from a conch shell, and an animal with a bearded human head. The small bench below the w. window incorporates an end which dates from about 1400, and there is a nicely carved dog with its head down on the elbow – another like it can be seen on a similar bench by the n. door. The prayer desk by the chancel arch is of the same period; one of its poppyheads is in the form of a bird and there is another example in the chancel where the stalls have some medieval tracery with birds in the *spandrels*. The C19 semi-circular stone replacement pulpit is quite awful, but the Norman chancel arch has a big roll moulding on the w. side, volute capitals matching the doors, and chip-carved *imposts*. Either side are large early-C14 niches which will have had *altars* below them, and the simple double *piscina* for the altar on the s. side may be found in the window sill nearby.

Worlingham, All Saints (I2): The handsome *lych-gate* is the village's memorial for the nine men lost at sea during World War I, and the churchyard wall is in C16 brick. The leggy little tower has a *Perpendicular* w. window and reshaped bell openings below stepped *flushwork* battlements pierced by *gargoyles*. *Sir Arthur Blomfield* was responsible for a thoroughgoing restoration and rebuilding in the 1870s, with new roofs, and restored windows that followed the original pattern. An unusual feature is the *aisle* that lies under a double-pitched roof on the s. side of the *chancel*. It only extends one bay further w., leaving the rest of the *nave* aisleless. There is a C14 *priest's door* with worn *headstops* in the aisle wall, and although the window alongside has been renewed, the *stops* on its *dripstone* appear to be original. The marble chest that stands against the nave s. wall is the tomb of John Felton, the builder of Worlingham Hall who died in 1703; its corners are carved with naturalistic foliage and flowers, and there is a roundel of arms on top. Felton's daughter Elizabeth married a Platers of Sotterley, and their arms are just discernible on the weathered *cartouche* in the niche above.

Entry is by way of the n. *porch*, and the interior is bright and well cared for. The tower arch rests on *corbels* carved as demi-angels bearing shields, and the window beyond has glass of 1908 on the 'Suffer little children to come unto me' theme. Like the rest of the stained glass in the church, it is almost certainly by *Clayton & Bell*. In the floor below is a *brass* inscription and shield of 1615 for Edward Duke. The church's excellent ring of six bells with an 8 cwt. tenor is rung from here. Four panels of the C15 *rood screen* have been used with new doors to form a tower screen, and a dozen C15 benchends with *poppyheads* have been worked into new benches in front of it. An interesting mid-C17 memorial hangs on the wall nearby. Painted on board, an attractive *achievement of arms* is set within a *Renaissance* arch, and there are charming epitaphs for: 'Ms Parnell Rous alias Duke' and her daughter 'the Dovelike Virgin Ms Anne Duke'. Below stands a simple, sturdy chest – late-C15 or early-C16, and the C15 *font* is placed centrally. Stunted lions buttress the shaft, and there are two ranks of angels below the bowl rather than the more usual one. Lions alternate with angels bearing shields in the panels, and all the carving has been defaced. The pine *arch-braced* roof with *king posts* was part of the Victorian restoration, and immediately below the ridge at the w. end one can just see a *sanctus-bell window*. Blomfield replaced the chancel arch and installed a new *screen*, but the door to the old *rood stair* remains in the n. wall. It is said that the lectern is made of oak that came from HMS Victory, and apart from the base it is just like the one at Nelson's

birthplace, Burnham Thorpe in Norfolk. The w. bay of the s. aisle lies alongside the nave, and the layout suggests that it may originally have been a *chantry chapel*. There are four interesting heads carved below the *capitals* of the entrance arch, with a bishop and a priest paired on the e. side (the bishop has probably been recut but the others seem untouched). The aisle w. window contains an *Annunciation* of 1906, and the s. window of 1885 illustrates the Holy Family, with groups of angels above. To the l. is a fine mural monument for Robert Sparrow who was killed in Tobago in 1805, and his grandson who died some years later. A seated, sorrowing man rests his head against the epitaph tablet which has a pair of draped urns in bas-relief on top. The work is unsigned but there is good reason to believe that it is an early work of Sir Francis Chantrey, a notable C19 sculptor whose statue of Bishop Bathurst stands in Norwich cathedral. Apart from a tablet at Hoxne and a doubtful example at Beccles, it is his only Suffolk piece. An arch leads into the choir aisle which is separated from the chancel by a two-bay arcade which has four more good heads carved below the capitals. There is a finely lettered oval tablet for rector Thomas Boyce, who died in 1793, and the 1890s window illustrates the Baptism of Christ. Half of the aisle is taken up by the organ, and at the e. end a small *vestry* is entered through a doorway with kingly headstops in the s. wall of the *sanctuary*. The *piscina* close by has renewed stops, no drain, and an inserted ledge rests on a fine figure *corbel*. The windows on the n. side of the chancel have scenes of the risen Christ with two disciples and the *Blessed Virgin*, and Christ with *St Mary Magdalene* on the first Easter morning. The e. window is the best of the Clayton & Bell designs and probably dates from the 1880s – a Crucifixion scene across the three *lights*, with angels and *Evangelistic symbols* in the *tracery*. The *altar* is notable because its wooden frame supports the church's original *mensa* which was found buried near the tower in 1925 and restored to its rightful place and function. The church's only pictorial brass, of 1511, has been re-sited on the chancel n. wall and commemorates Nicholas and Mary Wrenne. The 18in. figures are attractive – he with long hair, dressed in a girdled tunic trimmed with fur, a pouch at his belt, and she in *kennel headdress*, with an elaborate rosary and purse; both shield and inscription have been lost.

Once, the villages of Worlingham Magna and Worlingham Parva each had their own churches, dedicated to *St Mary* and *St Peter*, but by the

C15, St Peter's had fallen into disuse and the new dedication was chosen. When the Beccles bypass was being built in 1981, the graveyard of the vanished church was uncovered, and 'the mortal remains of 23 parishioners of St Peter's Parish' were re-interred in the extension of All Saints' churchyard, with a handsome stone to mark their new resting place.

Worlington, All Saints (A3): Church Lane is a cul-de-sac and the church is at the far end, n. of the village street. The base of the tower is C13, judging by the *quoins*, but the rest is C14, with *ogee*-headed niches either side of a deeply moulded w. door. The w. window has pleasing *Decorated* flowing *tracery* and above it, a small *quatrefoil* belfry window, as at nearby Tuddenham and All Saints Icklingham. On the n. side of the tower the filled-in *put-log holes* show up clearly, and within hangs a ring of five bells with a 7 cwt. tenor which are no longer in ringable condition. Although the C15 *nave* has a *clerestory* on both sides, there was evidently no call for a n. *aisle*. The C13 n. door was blocked up early in the C20 and the westernmost nave window is modern and was probably part of the 1897 restoration. The whole of the n. side has recently been brutally cement rendered, with the added blemish of a crudely executed signature and date. There is a *sanctus-bell turret* on the nave gable, although its bell is now in the museum at Bury. The iron stay and ring fixed to the wall below can only have been a rope guide and, as such, is a most unusual survival which will have been associated with the use of the blocked double *low side window* to the l. of the *priest's door* in the s. wall of the late-C13 *chancel*. That can be seen from inside the church and was an extension below the window as it exists now. The priest's door was renewed in the C19 and the niche below the corner of the nave roof looks like new work, although it may have replaced something similar. There are good C18 gravestones on this side of the church, and under the holly bush by the path to the priest's door is the base and socket of a medieval *preaching cross*. At some time a *scratch dial* has been reused as a quoin on the s.e. corner of the aisle (upside down and about 8ft. from the ground). The C18 porch in yellow brick is plain except for a stylish variation on the w. side where there are blind circular and arched recesses, one of which has been used for a memorial tablet. Inside the porch to the r. of the C13 doorway is a deep niche with three very worn heads underneath, and the stone seat is cut away below

leaving a space where the *stoup* stood. Apart from a new applied frame, the door is medieval and retains its original closing ring.

Though small, the interior is pleasing and full of interest. The early-C14 octagonal *arcade piers*, standing on earlier bases, have concave sides with *trefoil* decoration at the top (like Walsham-le-Willows). They warrant a closer look because they carry medieval graffiti of exceptional importance. Apart from compass exercises and initials of all periods, on the pillar nearest the door there are three shields clearly incised. The largest is 9in. tall and has a lion rampant within a border. It is a very early example of an armorial shield and may have been borne by a member of the Gourney family who held *Norman* manors in Norfolk and Suffolk. The other two shields are similar and are versions of the arms of the Crusaders' kingdom of Jerusalem. In addition, there is a cross with a sharpened base which may represent the wooden cross that Crusaders carried and thrust into the ground wherever they stopped. Taken together, these faint outlines could be a villager's memory of his own journeying on crusade, but it is at least possible that this small church was the meeting place of a group of knights before they set out to join Richard the Lionheart on the Third Crusade in 1190. If so, the stones will have been salvaged from the original arcade and used again. In the s.w. corner, the *vestry* is formed as a continuation of the s. aisle (an unusual position) and, judging by the slit windows, it was originally two-storied. The door is medieval and among the graffiti on the r.-hand *jamb* the name of the C15 rector Simon Bagot can just be discerned. Another rector's name was more widely known in the late C17. He was Erasmus Warren who published at least eight books. These included the texts of sermons he preached in Norwich cathedral in 1684 under the titles *Divine Rules* and *The End of Christ's Advent*. The *font* is probably early and appears to have been reshaped, with rudimentary columns cut on the corner chamfers matching four shafts below. Its base is attached to the arcade pier and there is an interesting survival built into the arch above – a pulley block carved in the shape of a hand to house the rope used for raising the cover. The present oak cover is modern.

An unusual addition to the church furniture is an *Act of Parliament clock* on the w. wall, given in the 1920s by a local landlord. The C14 bench ends in the s. aisle are square topped, with simple designs carved in the solid, three stepped *lancets* on some and large roses on others. The s. aisle chapel *altar* is a simple C17 table with carved top rail, and to the r., a very plain little *piscina*. The nave roof was restored in 1926 to the original C15 design and much of the old timber was retained. It has plain *hammerbeams* alternating with *tie-beams* which each support six tall posts, giving the whole a very open appearance. When *roods* were banned in the C16, both loft and beam were generally removed, but here the beam remains, set across the chancel arch. It is cambered and deeply moulded, and the rood, with its attendant figures and backing, will have taken up the whole of the top of the arch. Since 1973 the beam has carried a small misshapen cross carved from bog oak which might well have deep significance but which is quite wrong and out of scale in its present position. The accompanying loft has gone but the access doorway and stairs were rediscovered in the n. wall in 1901. Opposite, on the s. aisle, the *capitals* and arch of the arcade have been deeply notched and there is likely to have been a *parclose screen* round the s. aisle chapel. The C17 octagonal pulpit, complete with stem, has simple gouge carving in the small upper panels. The short *Early English* chancel still has its battlemented *wall-plates* but the ceiling was plastered, probably in the C18. There is a lancet in the n. wall set in a deep splay, and roundels and fragments of C14 glass are set in *quarries* decorated with cross motifs. The window just beyond the chancel arch on the s. side has curiously crushed Decorated tracery, and the form of the low side window can be seen at the bottom. The Early English e. window of three stepped lancets within one arch has 1909 glass by J. Dudley Forsyth. He was an apprentice of *Henry Holiday* and other work by him can be found at Mildenhall, West Row and Culford. This is a 'Suffer little children...' composition in dark and rather muddy colours, with grey flesh tints and steely canopy work. On the n. wall of the *sanctuary* is a plain tablet, white on grey, by Robert de Carle of Bury for James Gibson, aged 33 and rector here until 1850. How much nicer is the petite and elegant memorial opposite of 1738 to Martha Sankey – a shaped tablet with pendant *pomegranate*, and a pyramid over and flaming torch on top. Back in the nave, note the fragments of C14 wall paintings; above the pulpit there is a band of alternating *Tudor Roses* and *Sacred monograms*, and in a n. window embrasure, a *crocketted finial* in dark red and black. Nearby is a *brass* inscription for John Mortlock who, in 1620, bequeathed 30 shillings a year to the poor of the parish. To the w., the 1830s

memorial to the Revd. Sir William Henry Cooper is by Humphrey Hopper, a very competent London sculptor, particularly on small designs. This, in white marble on black, has a book, palm and cross above the tablet, an enamelled heraldic *achievement* on a roundel, and excellent lettering. To the e. is a good but unsigned monument for James Rice (1822) – a broad obelisk backs a well-modelled mourning woman draped over an urn in bas-relief, knotted sheaves of palms above and a colourful shield of arms at the top. On the s. side, above the arcade, is a repainted benefactions board which mentions 'in-bread'. This refers to the thirteenth, or 'vantage loaf' – that part of the baker's dozen which was included to avoid the heavy penalties for giving short weight. As you leave you will see the *Royal Arms* of George III in a gilt embellished frame.

Worlingworth, St Mary (G4): The church's display of *flushwork* is one of the most lavish in East Anglia and is found on all the buttresses, on the entire plinth and on the battlements of the tower which was completed in 1452. The shields in the *spandrels* of the w. doorway carry *Passion* and *Trinity* emblems and the w. window has stepped *embattled transoms*. Walking round you will see that the mouldings of the n. doorway are decorated with *fleurons* and masks, the buttresses of the *nave* between the large *Perpendicular* windows have flushwork designs, and that there is a flushwork *base course*. The n.e. buttress incorporates a *rood stair turret* with a tiny window, and there is a *priest's door* on the s. side of the early-C14 *chancel*. Its e. window tracery is very attractive – a pair of *trefoils* in circles and a centre sexfoil above the four main *lights*. S. of the tower you will see the base of a preaching cross and the facade of the tall C15 s. *porch* is a tour de force of flushwork, displaying *Sacred monograms* and 'M's for the dedication and covering the entire plinth. There, one finds panels of the *chalice* and *Host*, and a lily crucifix reminiscent of the stained glass at Long Melford and the font at Great Glemham. One panel is particularly important because it embodies the device of the Aldryche masons of N. Lopham in Norfolk and provides the evidence that they were the builders here. The outer archway *spandrels* are carved with *St George* and the dragon, there is a canopied niche above it, and over that, a sundial plate on the battlements dated 1663. The remains of two C15 benches (one with a dragon on the elbow) were relegated to the porch, and the inner doorway has a profusion of delicate mouldings and pairs of thin shafts.

The spacious, lofty nave has a lovely *double hammerbeam* roof which has not been stained. It has tracery each side of the *king posts* that stand on the *collars* and above the hammerbeams, and the well-restored angels at their ends bear painted shields (a key to the heraldry is helpfully provided on the w. wall). St Mary's ring of eight bells with a 12 cwt. tenor are rung from the floor of the tower, and in the w. window there is 1870s glass by *Clayton & Bell* – a scene of Moses with the tablets of the law in strong colours. By the n. door stands a fine example of a village manual fire engine. Restored in 1953, it was built by Newsham & Ragg in 1760 and was the first type to make use of compressed air, which enabled it to provide a continuous jet up to 150ft. Given by Lord of the Manor John Major, it served the village until 1930 and was last used on Guy Fawkes Night 1927. Nearby, the *Stuart* table with its turned and carved legs was used in the C17 as the altar, and is interesting because the drawer in the front shows that it was designed for domestic rather than religious use. The massive pole that rests in the n.w. corner of the nave was the spit on which an ox was roasted whole in celebration of the Jubilee of George III in 1810 (it was carried in procession for Queen Victoria's Diamond Jubilee in 1897 but there was no ox that time). The village feast is shown in a delightful painting on the s. wall of the nave which is full of homely detail. It is now paired

Worlingworth, St Mary: Parish fire engine

with a painting by John Reay of the 2002 Worlingworth Jubilee Feast. Above the tower arch is a curiously offset door. It doesn't seem quite right for an entrance to the old w. *gallery* but I can think of no other possibility. Below in the floor is a 1622 *ledger-stone* with two *brass* shields and a memorable inscription:

> James Barker to his dearest wyfe
> Susanna doth this last office of love
> for she was religious, chaste, discreet,
> loveing.

The *font* is a common East Anglian design, with deeply carved bowl panels in which the *Evangelistic symbols* alternate with angels bearing shields – n.e., Passion emblems, s.e. *St Edmund*, s.w. Trinity, n.w. St George. There are very upright lions round the stem and a clear donor's inscription round the base: 'Orate pro anima Nicholai Moni qui isti fonte fieri fecit' (Pray for the soul of Nicholas Moni who had this font made). The tall cover was originally a telescopic model like Ufford's but it was altered at some stage, and there is an unusually complete record of its fortunes over the years painted on panels at the top: 'Repaired and restored 1706', 'Removed from the gallery by the Parish Nov. 1800', 'Repaired and beautified by the Honble John Henniker Major May 1801', 'Restaur By Public Subscription 1893', 'Conserved and regilded May 1963'. It is now very jolly in red, green, white and gilt, and the two other inscriptions are easy to read. One is a Greek palindrome (the characters read the same backwards and forwards) like the one at Hadleigh which translates: 'Wash my sin and not my face only'; the other is a quotation from St Paul's Letter to the Romans (2:29): 'Circusisio cordis in spiritu non litera' (Circumcision is that of the heart, in the spirit and not in the letter). The cover is supposed to have come from the abbey at Bury although one wonders what a Benedictine foundation was doing with a font. By the door is a nice little poorbox which is dated by the worn brass plate on the top: 'W. Godbold gave me 1622'. Another plate on the front has: 'Proverbs XIX vearse XVII He that hath piti upon the poor, lendeth unto the Lord, & that which he hath given, he will pay him again 99'. Nearby, the *Royal Arms* of George III are crudely painted on board and farther along there are vestiges of a wall painting with fishes at the bottom which could have been a *St Christopher*. There are many good C15 sets of benches to be found in the Suffolk but C17 work of quality is rarer and Worlingham's suite is the best. The bench ends and the low doors are carved with blind-arched panels and there are squat *finials* supported by scrolls. At the w. end the ranges on both sides of the nave narrow to afford ample space around the font, and the front rail of the n. side is nicely carved with beast heads and strapwork together with the legend 'WGM 1630' which dates the whole range and the excellent pulpit. It has two ranks of matching panels and a six-sided *tester* suspended by a chain from the roof.

There are considerable remains of C15 glass in the tracery of the nave windows. Elizabeth Cordy died aged 11 in 1824 and her chaste tablet on the n. wall is by Smyth of Woodbridge. The one above it is by Clutten of Framlingham, who provided another on the s. wall for John Corydon who died in 1828, with a verse more C18 in style than C19. Two minor brasses lie under the nave matting; halfway along there is an inscription and verse for Jaspar Hussie who 'came to this towne after a long sicknes to take ye benefit of this aire' but died nevertheless in 1624, and at the e. end there are plates showing four sons and seven daughters – all that are left of an unidentified family group of about 1530. The *rood stair* lies in the n. wall and the small *piscina* by the pulpit shows that there was a pre-*Reformation altar* there. Only the base of the *rood screen* remains and fragments of its decoration show through a covering of dark brown paint.

The wide chancel has a C19 roof and on the n. wall is one of the better works of *John Bacon the Younger*. It is the large memorial in white marble for the Duchess of Chandos, who died in 1817. The figure of Faith with book and cross kneels by a sarcophagus, while on the other side Hope with her anchor and with her foot on a skull points upwards to the cross and crown. Farther to the e. is a memorial for Sir John and Dame Elizabeth Major provided in 1781 by a little-known sculptor, Cooper of Stratford le Bow. There is a grey obelisk at the top and the well-lettered tablet has a decorative backing in multi-coloured marbles with a coloured shield of arms inset below. On the opposite wall is a very good example of the use of Coade stone, an artificial substitute for marble popularised by that remarkable C18 businesswoman Mrs Eleanor Coade. Here we have a memorial for Dame Ann Henniker of 1792 – an epitaph panel with cherub's head below, small sarcophagus above topped by coat of arms and an urn, all crisp and attractive. Two of the windows on the s. side of the chancel have glass by Clayton

& Bell – figures of *SS Matthew, Mark, Luke* and *John*, all well drawn in good colour. The third window has glass of the 1850s – two angel medallions and coloured borders which is perhaps early work by *Ward & Hughes*. By the priest's door is a *consecration cross* and in the *sanctuary* the early-C14 angle piscina has a slim shaft and a stone *credence shelf*. In the head of the e. window the arms of John Henniker Major, 4th Baron and his wife Anna Kerrison. He was patron of the church and the glass commemorates their marriage in 1837. This is beautiful work by William Miller of London, painted in enamels on white glass and is one of his earliest pieces. Other work by him can be seen at Bedingfield, Lidgate, Thornham Magna and Thornham Parva. The *reredos* in stone and mottled marble with a pair of white marble angels is unashamedly Victorian.

John Wilson of this parish died in 1782 at the age of 116 and I searched in vain for his grave for no better reason than to ponder on the fact that his suppers for forty years were plates of roasted turnips. You may be luckier and hear the faint echo of an antique burp.

Wortham, St Mary (E3): The church stands by the side of the minor road that runs from Palgrave to Redgrave and is over a mile to the n. of Wortham itself. Its ruined round tower is the largest in England, being 29ft. across, with walls over 4ft. thick. *Cautley* was of the opinion that it was *Saxon*, dating from the early C11, and that it was built originally as a watch tower and for defence, but recent research shows that the tower and the *nave* were built at the same time around 1160. What is known as the 'Sacred Stone' lies nearby – a glacial boulder that was probably the object of pagan veneration, and which may have prompted the building of the first church here in order that Christanity might overlay the old religion. The tower roof and upper floors collapsed in 1789 and it now stands open to the sky, a most impressive ruin. Foundations of the *Norman* church were found within the present nave when the floor was relaid. There was a major rebuilding in the middle of the C14 when the *aisles* were added; they are tall and relatively narrow, with large *Perpendicular* windows. In the early C15, a fine *clerestory* was added which has a band of *flushwork* emblems between the windows on both sides including, on the s. side, the *Sacred monogram* and the letters 'S', 'T', 'S', 'M', standing for 'Sancta Trinitas Sancta Maria'. The *chancel*, with its Perpendicular windows, is of the same date, but you will see that an earlier *Decorated priest's door* was reused, with a stooled niche over it. Continuing round the outside, there is a two-storied *vestry* on the n. side of the chancel with a neat little pair of gables, and the n. door has been blocked and faced with excellent flushwork. The bells having fallen with the tower, an C18 boarded bellcote with a lead cupola and weathervane now stands at the w. end of the nave roof. There is a C13 grave slab clamped to the w. side of the tower, and over the entrance to the C14 *porch* is a sundial, with a very small niche above the inner doorway. Note as you enter that there are deep holes each side in the *jambs* to take a wooden bar for security.

Inside the door is the C14 *font* with a *castellated* rim; the panels have *crocketted* gables with fine *tracery* backing them and worn heads project at the angles below the bowl. Beyond the font are two more C13 grave slabs bearing three floriated crosses. The tower arch has been blocked up and the organ now stands in front of it. On the wall by the s. door is a very fine set of Charles I *Royal Arms* carved in wood and set in an oval frame. This is quite unusual, but there is another like it in the neighbouring church of Redgrave so they were probably carved by the same man. Above the C14 *arcades*, the nave roof has *arch-braces* alternating with *hammerbeams* and the ceiling has been plastered between the principals. The aisle roofs were rebuilt with local oak in the 1890s, and at that time new benches were made by Albert Bartrum of Wortham, who modelled them on the old ones and incorporated a number of the original bench ends. The excellent carvings on the elbows illustrate Psalm 104 and were carried out by a Mr Groom of Ipswich. Each stands on a heavy block bearing the relevant text, and one can find a tortoise, owl, walrus, bear, lion, and among the figures is a man going forth to his labour. There are also blacksmith's tools carved on a bench end by the s. door which might be a clue as to who the churchwardens were at that time. Two *hatchments* hang in the s. aisle; the one furthest e. was probably used for both Philip Vincent and his second wife Elizabeth (who died in 1724 and 1728 respectively); the other hatchment was for the Revd. George Belts, rector of Overstrand in Norfolk, who died in 1822. The window in the wall of the s. aisle at the e. end contains ornamental glass of 1820-1830, some of it painted by *Robert Allen* of Lowestoft, and probably installed by Yarington of Norwich. The s. aisle chapel has a *piscina* with a *trefoil* arch and the window over the *altar* is a memorial for two men of the Suffolk

Regiment who fell at Passchendaele and the Somme. It was possibly supplied by *Morris & Co*, and has figures of *St George* and the archangel *Michael*. To the l. is a niche with a *cinquefoiled* head. The window in the s. wall is early work by *Ward & Nixon* and is similar to work by them at Palgrave. The n. aisle chapel has a similar piscina and image niche and the altar there is a nice melon-legged C17 table. There is no screen and the chancel is very wide, with an arch-braced roof of 1904, resting on worn, heavy head *corbels*. The front of the *High altar* incorporates panels from the old *rood screen*, and round the walls of the *sanctuary* is a low range of blank arches with steep gables and tracery derived from the designs on the font. The e. wall has heavily carved stone panels, with vine trails and wheat, as well as verses from the Gospels, all dating from 1856. The C14 piscina has a *cusped* and crocketted arch, to which C19 grapevine *stops* have been added. Heavy C19 stone *Decalogue* tablets flank the fine e. window, in which *Hardman* in the 1920s re-set fragments of medieval glass, including a small scroll inscribed 'Caterina' carried by an eagle. There may be some connection between this and the Catherine wheel emblem to be found on the n. clerestory outside. Near the lectern is a memorial to Richard Cobbold who was rector here from 1824 to 1877. He was the author of the novel *Margaret Catchpole* but, more importantly, he also chronicled the lives of the ordinary humble people of his parish in illustrated diaries that are a fascinating and poignant social record. Ronald Fletcher tells the rector's story in his book *In a Country Churchyard*.

Wrentham, St Nicholas (I2): After a turnpike was built in the C18, the village gradually moved e. to the line of the A12, and the church became isolated from most of its parishioners. The churchyard is pleasantly bosky, with a tunnel of ancient yew leading up to the *porch*, and the first thing to examine is the grand C15 tower, tall enough to be used as a lookout station in the Napoleonic wars. There is a *base course* of shields and lozenges containing sacred hearts and roses within wreaths; three *set-offs* with strong *drip courses* give the tower character, and the w. doorway has shields set on sprays of leaves in the *spandrels*. It is flanked by vaulted niches and a late-*Perpendicular* window takes up most of the wall above. There are splendid *sound holes* reminiscent of Norfolk, each with a centre shield in a mesh of *quatrefoils*, and three larger shields are arranged under a *label* just above the w. sound hole. A strong stair turret rises to the *flushwork* battlements on the n. side. The boxy n. *aisle* was added in 1853, using Perpendicular and *Decorated* windows taken from the old n. wall of the *nave*. The C13 *chancel* has tall side *lancets,* and the *tracery* of the Perpendicular e. window looks as though it has been truncated at some time. Tall flying buttresses of brick were added (C19?) to support the side walls, and the *priest's door* has been blocked. A *rood stair* lies snugly in the corner between chancel and s. aisle and has been provided with a new lancet. The Perpendicular s. aisle has been cement rendered overall, and the late-C15 *porch* has seen better days. It has a flushwork facade, with most of the tracery detail missing, a badly damaged central niche, and there are the remains of flushwork lozenge patterns in the parapet. A *stoup* survives within.

The church is remarkably spacious, with a broad nave and chancel separated neither by arch nor *screen.* The church's ring of six bells with a 10 cwt. tenor are rung from the floor of the tower. The late-C14 s. *arcade* has quatrefoil *piers,* and the design was copied for the C19 n. aisle. All the roofs were restored in the 1830s, with *hammerbeams* in the nave and chancel, and crowned head *corbels* in the aisles where rough wooden posts are used in place of wall piers. Above the entrance door is an excellent 1830s Table of Fees painted on canvas, with a small gilt *Royal Arms* on the frame, and its last item prices the funeral knell at a shilling an hour. Close by the door is a 12ft. *banner stave locker,* and two *hatchments* hang to the l. of the tall tower arch; the bottom one was used for the funeral of Humphrey Brewster of Wrentham Hall in 1735, and the other for Philip Brewster thirty years later. On the opposite wall, a large case with back lighting provides a splendid setting for a particularly fine piece of stained glass, a 10ft. panel of Christ carrying his cross. Not only has it the merit of its intrinsic quality, but it was supplied by a Wrentham man, Royal William Lilly. He was born in the village in 1806 and lived here as a painter, plumber and glazier for most of his life. Apart from a window in the village hall, this is the only glass known to be connected with him, and originally it formed the centre of a *High altar reredos* installed by the rector Stephen Clissold in 1850. The panel was framed when the reredos was removed in 1932. The painting is signed both by Lilly and Clissold, but its high quality is not what one would expect from a local glazier who apparently produced nothing else. According to Birkin Haward, the best authority, it is identical with a window by

Thomas Willement in Tyldesley church, Lancashire, and is based on a C17 altarpiece by the Spanish painter Valdes Leal in Magdalen College, Oxford. It is more likely that Stephen Clissold bought the panel elsewhere for his new reredos and that Lilly installed it. A C19 *font* stands at the w. end, but its C15 predecessor was recovered from the rectory garden in the 1930s and is now at the e. end of the n. aisle. The bowl panels contain leaves, *Tudor Roses,* a *Trinity* shield (s.), and the shield on the n. side probably bore *Passion emblems* before it was defaced. There are *paterae* in the mouldings and traces of colour; the section of classical column used as a shaft came from Wrentham Hall. The e. end of the n. aisle and its window were designed as a Clissold family memorial, and the glass is a brilliant example of *Hardman* 1850s work. The Ascended Christ is richly robed, carrying a banner and blessing his disciples who are grouped below across the three *lights;* the space above is crammed with swooping *angels* blowing trumpets and clashing cymbals, and stars sparkle in the borders. Hardman probably provided glass for the centre window in the aisle wall, but only the tracery pieces remain. There is, however, a C15 figure of *St Nicholas* with a child, made up with other medieval fragments into a centre panel. The s. aisle chapel has a simple *piscina,* and the 1960s *altar* is a severe and satisfying design by Hubert Fiske – in unstained oak, with a deep skirt and exposed dovetails and tenons. The e. window above it contains a fragment of C15 *tabernacle work* and a fine C19 profile head. The tracery of the s. aisle side windows contains brilliant little vignettes in sharp colour of the Gethsemane scene with the symbolic chalice above it, and the Via Dolorosa beneath the Dove of the Holy Spirit. This is possibly 1850s work of Edward Baillie, and the windows were presumably complete originally. Examples of his glass can be seen at Witnesham and Henley.

Although there is no chancel arch, a roof brace marks the division, and just above are the Royal Arms of William IV flanked unusually by Union Jacks and white roses. The *brass* of Ele Bowet who died in 1400 lies on the n. side of the chancel and it is the earliest effigy of a lady in Suffolk. She wears a close fitting net cap, and her gown with its voluminous cuffs is buttoned from neck to foot; there are two defaced shields and an inscription. The church's other brass on the n. *sanctuary* wall commemorates Humphrey Brewster who died in 1593, his family having been Lords of the Manor since Edward VI's time. The 25in. effigy provides a good example of Elizabethan armour, and he wears a neat moustache and beard over his ruff. In 1676, his great, great, grand-daughter, Amy Skippon, was commemorated with a handsome memorial to the r. The *touchstone* tablet and flanking columns are set in a garlanded frame, with a large *cartouche* centred between scrolls on top. On the opposite wall, an attractive roundel within a laurel wreath is for Henry and Sarah Wotton and their son; dated 1679, it was cleaned and restored in 1987. C19 restoration work included raising the floor levels in the sanctuary, and the massive C13 *piscina* is now low in the wall. The church's pre-*Reformation mensa* has been framed and set on the *High altar*; it has unusually lavish *consecration crosses* and is likely to be a very early example. The e. window glass was designed by F.E. Howard for *Jones & Willis* in the 1930s; the pale figures of Christ and the *Evangelists* are set against clear glass and their symbols, together with a Trinity emblem are displayed in wreathed roundels below. The Evangelists figure again in the tracery of the side windows – good mid-C19 glass, artist unknown.

Wrentham's churchyard is maintained as a conservation area, and has one of the best collections of headstones in the area. Very few of the C17 survive nowadays, but here there are quite a number, most of them to the w. of the tower. Sarah Wotton's of 1679 just by the rectory hedge is a good, readable example. The local C18 and C19 masons were obviously skilled, and there is a wonderful variety of fine period lettering and design to be seen all over the churchyard. Under a beech, s.w. of the tower, look for Charles Wilson Tooke's stone (1859). It has a bas-relief panel of Christ and the woman of Samaria (John 4:7) which was undoubtedly a stock item to be used as required – one like it can be found behind the piscina in Market Weston church, and there is another in the sanctuary at Barnby. A couple of graveyard eccentricities for those that collect them – an 1843 cast-iron memorial for Edward Gayford s. of the chancel, and on the n. side, an 1850s vault cover on which the outline of a body lying under a pall is carved in granite.

Wyverstone, St George (E4): Like a number of churches in the area, the C14 tower has one pair of buttresses at right angles, thus extending the e. face, while the heavy w. counterparts are set diagonally. The small *Decorated* w. window matches the bell openings on the s. and w. but the other two sides have pretty, and quite individual elongated *quatrefoils*. The chequerwork battlements sport fine *gargoyles*. All other windows are *Perpendicular* and there is a *clerestory*, although no *aisles* were added to give it point. As at Hinderclay, the church has a wooden *porch* and the timbers of the outer arch are probably C14, set in a renewed frame. For some reason the porch is not centred on the C14 doorway, with its remains of head *corbels*. Within, there is a beautifully compact William and Mary *Royal Arms* on the w. wall, excellently carved in deep relief and cut to the outline of the *achievement*. Another set hangs on the n. wall, this time *Hanoverian* and dated 1812. The bowl panels of the early-C15 *font* are carved alternately with roses in quatrefoils and shields in roundels, one of which carries a possible merchant's mark. Some of the bench ends at the w. end bear *poppyheads* and there is one C17 example on the n. side which is carved with churchwardens' initials and has a scrolled top. There is not much left of the church's medieval glass but, among the fragments, look for a tiny head of Christ at the very top of the westernmost window on the n. side. In the C15 roof, *arch-braces* alternate with *hammerbeams* which, like the *wall-plates*, are embattled. The entrance to the *rood loft* stair is in the n. wall and, unusually, there is a socket in the *jamb* for a lock. Nearby stands an iron-bound chest; the sides have been renewed but the rounded top is C14. Opposite is a deep C16 pulpit with *linen-fold panelling*. Overhead, centred on one of the main roof timbers is a rare survival – the pulley block from which was hung the rowell, a ring of lights that used to hang in front of the rood before the *Reformation*. Equally interesting is the *screen*. Although the pillars of the chancel arch are drilled for supports, only the base survives but this is one of only two in Suffolk (Gislingham is the other) where the panels contain carvings rather than paintings – very rare. They were badly mutilated in the C17 but the remnants can be identified. On the n. side, from l. to r.: *St Gabriel*, with the front of his body missing; the *Blessed Virgin*, minus her head (the two panels forming an *Annunciation* group); the Nativity, with all destroyed except one sheep and a wattle hurdle at the bottom; the Magi, with two heads missing. On the s. side, l. to r.: a rare scene of the mass of *St Gregory*, where again, the fronts of the figures have been sheered off but the picture is clear; the saint kneels before an *altar* and raises the *chalice*, with the figure of Christ above and a woman to the r. The story is that, in order to sustain the faith of a sceptic, the sacred elements were transformed into a vision of the risen Christ as the pope celebrated mass. The remaining panel is carved with the *Visitation* scene from St Luke's Gospel – *St Elizabeth* with the Blessed Virgin (both obviously pregnant and one touching the other's body). The bottoms of the panels are filled with quatrefoils and the heavy Perpendicular tracery was originally *crocketted*. In the *chancel* there are early-C17 *communion rails* with turned *finials* on the posts. The floor levels were raised in the 1900 restoration and the *piscina* is now awkwardly low in the wall. The three-*light* e. window contains glass of 1926 by William Glasby – the risen Christ with angels above a panorama of Jerusalem, against a low line of purple hills. Glasby was *Henry Holidays'* principal glass painter for twenty years but the colouring here is not what one would expect from his master's studio.

Yaxley, St Mary (F3): Now that the village has been bypassed the church enjoys a tranquil setting by a sharp bend in the street. As you enter the churchyard, note the hitching ring in the wall to the r. of the gate, and look for an interesting stone on the r. of the path for Robert 'Waterloo' Bond who died on Christmas Day 1878 and was given a military funeral on New Year's Day. The C14 tower has *flushwork* and chequer on the buttresses, a deep *ogee*-headed niche in the w. wall, and tall, narrow *lancets* at ground and first-floor level. There is a s. porch of 1854 and in 1868 the *chancel* was largely rebuilt with new side windows, although the e. wall and window are mainly original. It is interesting that the restorers took the trouble to add a flying buttress over the *priest's door* in emulation of the one at Eye. The main entrance is the C15 n. *porch* and this is a splendid affair with a beautifully proportioned and detailed facade. A pair of large windows above the outer arch light the upper room and they are flanked by elaborately canopied niches. Below, a line of crowned 'M's for the dedication is set in flushwork and more tall niches occupy the corner buttresses and the spaces each side of the archway. A line of shields runs below the crested parapet whose pinnacles carry seated beasts. The *spandrels* of the arch are carved with a giant and a *woodwose* and the vault within has mutilated *bosses* of the *Evangelistic symbols*, with a possible *Annunciation* in the centre.

The *font* is a plain octagonal bowl resting on an 1860s base and columns, and nearby is a very compact iron-banded C15 chest. The tower screen has a number of medieval glass fragments inserted but they are difficult to appreciate

Yaxley, St Mary: Sexton's wheel

without access to the tower. The s. porch now serves as a vestry and over the doorway hangs Yaxley's famous sexton's wheel. In the C14 and C15 when veneration of the *Blessed Virgin* was at its height, penitents would sometimes be directed (or would choose) to observe the Lady fast – either one day a week for seven years, or 365 days continuously on bread and water. If they chose the latter, they would come to the sexton to determine the day on which to begin. There are six days in the church's calendar set aside for the honour of the Virgin, and six long threads were tied to the wheel, each one identified for a particular feast. The sexton would spin the wheel and the devotee would grasp a thread at random to decide when the fast should start. There must have been hundreds of these wheels, particularly in churches dedicated to *St Mary*, but only two have survived – one here and one at Long Stratton, just up the A140 in Norfolk. There is a *hatchment* close by for the Revd. Seymour Leeke who died in 1786 and another over the n. door for Francis Gilbert Yaxley Leeke; he was Seymour's illegitimate half-brother and heir, and died in 1836. In the s. aisle are three *brasses* – an inscription for Joan Yaxley, 1517; another for Alice Pulvertoft, 1511, at the e. end; and the 18in. figure of Andrew Feldgate, who died in 1598, in ruff and gown. On the s. wall there are wooden heraldic carvings which were once part of the tomb of William Yaxley, a Catholic Suffolk MP who married one of the Oxborough Bedingfelds and died in 1588. It stood in the s. aisle until the great upheaval of 1868. In a n. aisle window the vicar who masterminded that restoration, William Henry

Sewell, is commemorated by a *Jones & Willis* version of Holman Hunt's *The Light of the World.*

The s. aisle is separated from the nave by a three-bay *arcade* on octagonal *piers* and there is a *clerestory* on that side only. This was inserted when the new roof was built and the line of the old one still shows on the tower wall. The *arch-braces* are adorned with large flower bosses, the *wall plates* retain traces of colour, and the easternmost bay of the roof was originally decorated as a *celure* for the *rood* below. There are large patches of what was a painted *Doom* remaining on either side of the chancel arch but little detail can now be seen. The window overhead originally silhouetted the rood when the chancel roof was lower, and note that a support for the cross was slotted into the centre of the window frame. The entrance to a commodious *rood stair* is now largely masked by a superb pulpit of 1635. It has strapwork on top of the *tester* and displays the initials of churchwardens Thomas Dade and Thomas Fulcher. The back panels remind the preacher: 'Necessite is laid upon me, yea woe is me if I preach not the Gospel', (1 Cor. 9:16) and there are fine dragon scrolls on each side. The carving on the body of the pulpit is conventional for the period but unusually rich and vigorous. The nave pews date from the Victorian restoration and were supplied by Frosts of Watton in Norfolk. One of the ends on the s. side carries an interesting 1870s brass:

A stove has been placed near this bench in remembrance of a . . . widow of about four score and nine years which departed not from the temple but served God and was buried in the s.e. part of the churchyard having desired that her name should not appear on her gravestone. May it be found written in the Lamb's Book of Life. It seems like sneaking somehow to reveal that her name was Elizabeth Pretty, and judging by her engraved portrait she was a fine-looking woman.

The C15 *rood screen* is a late version of the type to be found in many East Anglian churches but is surprisingly large and elaborate for a church of this size. Although cruelly mutilated, enough remains to prove that it was once very beautiful. The *crockets* and *hoods* have been broken from the main *lights* but the centre arch still has fine triple ranks of *cusping*. The small lower panels

have paintings of saints in the Flemish style and, despite defacement, the sword and wheel of *St Catherine* can be identified just to the l. of the entrance, and a recognisable *St Mary Magdalene* on the s. side. Next to her is *St Barbara*, followed by *St Dorothy* and *St Cecilia*. The figures are backed by an interesting variety of *gesso* patterns still in good condition. Overhead, the stumps of the *rood beam* can be seen just below the *wall posts* of the nave roof. The 1860s chancel roof rests on ebullient musical angel *corbels* and the organ blower's stool has a most engaging refinement – its oval top has a massive block to match which can be lifted off its securing pegs to accommodate a smaller size of boy. A very worn C14 effigy of a priest lies within a recess in the n. wall and there is a brass inscription for Alice Yaxle, 1474, in the centre of the floor. It is worth studying the medley of medieval glass arranged in the e. window by William Sewell in the 1880s. His own minuscule profile portrait is sweetly enclosed within the letter 'P' in the inscription in the r.-hand light. There is a figure of *St John* above it, a beautiful head of Christ in the centre, a late head of St Mary in yellow stain farther down, and *St Andrew* with *St Peter* in the top *tracery*.

Yoxford, St Peter (H4): A large churchyard, with tall, pollarded limes along its w. edge, provides a spacious setting for the church, and an interesting cast-iron signpost stands at the n.w. corner; it has pierced lettering and probably dates from about 1830. The early-C14 tower has a *Perpendicular* w. window, 'Y' *tracery* bell openings, and below the *flushwork* panelled battlements there are good corner *gargoyles* like those at nearby Sibton. The tall, lead-sheathed spire is set well back from the parapet, and like Middleton's it is aggressively sharp, adding distinctive character to the tower. The body of the church dates from the early C15, and from the s. one can see C18 and C19 churchwardens' names cast in the lead of the *nave* roof, recording its periodic renewal. The blocked door in the s. *aisle* of 1500 was once the main entrance, and the Cockfield chapel, complete with *priest's door*, was added to the s. side of the *chancel* in the mid-C16. The e. window tracery was renewed in 1868, probably to the original pattern, and a previous restoration in 1837 had added a n. aisle and n.e. chapel which extends the length of the chancel, giving the church a broad e. frontage.

Within, the C14 *arcades* have octagonal *piers*, and both nave and chancel have broad, plastered ceilings; the flat n. aisle roof is plastered between the ribs, and the s. aisle has an *arch-braced* roof with tracery in the *spandrels*. The 1860s restoration was directed by *R.M. Phipson*, and he took out the galleries, blocked some dormer windows, and rebenched the whole church in New Zealand pine (a species of cedar which he also chose for Saxmundham). Just inside the n. door, a large tablet commemorates William Betts who died in 1709; mourning *putti* flank his *achievement of arms* on top, and the base is emphatically detailed. To the e. is the memorial for David Elisha Davy, that zealous antiquarian whose history of Suffolk was never published and who recorded in his journal much that has since vanished from our churches. He died in 1851, 'highly respected and deeply and sincerely regretted', and his tablet by Calver repeated the design of his parents' memorial just above – provided by Henry Rouw in 1803. The 1920s stained glass in the window further along is by Archibald Keighley Nicholson, more of whose work can be seen at Aldeburgh, Barnham, Gt. Ashfield, Hawstead and Ickworth. The subject is the visit of the Magi, and although the skin textures are faintly reminiscent of the *Arts & Crafts* style, the treatment is conventional, with monochrome landscape behind the figures and elaborate canopies. The church has one of the best arrays of *hatchments* in the area, and the earliest dates from 1669. Hanging above the n. door, it is only 2ft. square and was possibly also for his widow when she died some twenty years later. More are grouped on the tower wall for: top l., Sir Charles Blois (1850); top centre, Clara his wife (1847); bottom r., Sir John Blois (1810); bottom l., Revd. Sir Ralph Blois (1762); top r., Sir Charles Blois (1760); within the tower, s. wall, Lady Lucretia Blois (1808); n. wall, Elizabeth Clayton (1802); s. aisle, w., Elizabeth Fuller (formerly Lady Blois) (1780); s. aisle e., Thomas Bettes (1739).

The early-C15 *font* has eight attached shafts round the stem, and the bowl carvings are not at all typical. *Cusped* panels with centre crosses alternate with angels with closed wings who stand on the folded drapery that was the medieval convention for clouds; they have been defaced and originally displayed what I think were *Passion emblems* – n.w., crown of thorns; s.w., scourge?; n.e. nails? Yoxford retains a fine selection of *brasses*, and they have all been mounted on the walls. At the w. end of the s. aisle a board carries eight, and the centre 21in. effigy is that of Anthony Cooke (1613), wearing doublet and hose under his gown; below, a quirky verse:

At the due sacrifice of the Paschall Lambe,
Aprill had eayghte dayes wepte in shower he
   came,
Leane, hungry deathe who never pitty
   tooke,
And cawse ye feaste was ended slewe this
   COOKE.
On Ester Monday he lyves then no daye
   more,
But suncke to ryse with him that rose
   before.
Hees heere intombed A man of vertues
   line,
Out reche his yeares yet they were seavety
   nyne.
He left on earthe tenn Children of eleaven,
To keepe his name whilst himselfe wente to
   heaven.

On the l. from top to bottom, the inscriptions are for: Elizabeth Knyvet (1471), with two shields; William and John Tendryng (c.1480); John and Agnes Scottow (1511, 1529), with two prayer labels – 'Jesu merci' and Ladi [help]; John and Alice Coke (1522); Robert and Margery Rivet (1593). On the r. is the inscription and 18in. effigy for Christian Foxe (1618), a lady in hat, ruff, and farthingale, with the figure of her infant son Francis who died a year later. Lastly, an inscription for Francis Foxe (1612). A tablet with lively accoutrements on the s. wall commemorates Sir Charles Blois who died in 1760 – *cartouche* of arms and flaming urns above, winged cherub head below, all in varied marbles. One of the aisle windows contains an *Annunciation* in creamy colours; lush and pleasing, artist unknown. Further along, the *piscina* with a stone *credence shelf* marks the site of an *altar*. The moulded ribs of the aisle chapel roof carry an attractive display of shields – arms of the Hopton, Brooke, and Blois families, and the lion rampant device of the Norwiche family in C14 glass can be seen in the s. window. To the r. is a wall monument by *Thomas Thurlow* for Sir Charles Blois (1850) and his wife Clara. Flanked by standing angels, the oval tablet has had most of its inscription carelessly picked out in black paint. To the l. of the window, yet another Sir Charles Blois (1855) has a tablet by Charles Balls of Yoxford, with martial trophies on the *pediment* below a cartouche of arms. The window above the priest's door contains an attractive 1950s figure of the Good Shepherd, with two crests, all set in plain *quarries*, and one would like to know who did it. To its l., the rather indigestible monument in *touchstone* and marble is for Sir Robert Brooke. He was High Sheriff in 1614, MP for Dunwich in the 1620s, and died in 1646; his arms in colour feature in the broken *pediment*, and there are four small shields at the corners of the tablet. His wife Joan died in 1618, and her memorial is the brass on the e. wall, a fine 28in. figure in Paris cap, ruff, and intricately brocaded petticoat. A funeral helm hangs high on the wall, and the chapel *altar* is a sturdy mid-C17 table. The pulpit dates from around 1620, and above the two ranks of *blind arches*, narrow panels are carved with grapes. The church's best brasses are displayed on the walls of the chancel *sanctuary*. On the n. side are the effigies of John and Maud Norwiche (1428, 1418). He was Lord of Cockfield Hall manor, and dying childless, his estate was sold to pay for the completion of the church. His armour is a good example of the Lancastrian period, and her horned head-dress is the earliest example of the fashion in

Suffolk; a lion sits at his feet, and an engaging puppy with a bell collar plays round her skirts (the slab on which the brass originally lay is now clamped to the wall by the tower arch). On the s. wall there is Suffolk's best example of a *shroud brass*, the 45in. figure of Thomesine Tendryng who died in 1485, and her seven children. Two daughters outlived her, and their effigies were made by William Hayward of Norwich and added to the London brass – the only known example of a brass combining London and provincial work. The slab from which it was taken lies broken by the organ. The fine e. window glass may have been supplied by *Lavers & Westlake*, and is a World War I memorial. Christ, bearing a *chalice*, is flanked by *St George* spearing a multi-coloured dragon, and *St Edmund*; the colour is rich but not strident, there are are rich canopies, and regimental badges feature in the tracery.

Glossary of Terms & Index

Abeloos, M. of Louvain: carver; *See* Thorndon, Wherstead

Abbot & Co: stained glass; *See* Fornham St Martin, Oulton Broad St Mark

Abacus (plural, abaci): flat stone slab set on top of a pillar or *pier* to take the thrust of an arch springing from it. Most often seen in *Norman* and *Early English* architecture. (Compare with *impost* and *capital*.)

Acanthus: A stylised form of leaf decoration based on a family of plants which include Bears' Breech. Used originally by the Greeks, it became very popular in the C17 and C18, particularly for use on mouldings and scrolls.

Achievement of Arms: Heraldic arms in their full form with all or most of the following: shield of arms, crest, helm and mantling (its ornamental drapery), supporters (animals or humans), motto – as opposed to a plain shield of arms.

Act of Parliament clock: In 1797, Pitt's government levied an annual tax on all clocks and watches which so reduced the number in use that inn-keepers began to provide cheap wall clocks in their public rooms, particularly if stage-coaches called. The act was repealed the following year but the clocks were common until 1830. Some have found their way into churches and there is an example at Worlington.

Adam, Dacres: artist; *See* Kirkley

Agnus Dei (The Lamb of God): When *St John the Baptist* saw Jesus coming he said, 'Behold the Lamb of God who takes away the sin of the world'. The words were used in the mass as early as the C5 and by the C9 wax medallions were being made on Holy Saturday from remnants of the previous year's paschal candle. In the Middle Ages, the lamb bearing a cross or flag was widely used in painting and sculpture as a symbol of Our Lord.

Aikman, William: stained glass; *See* Boxted, Rattlesden

Airy, Sir George Biddell: Astronomer Royal; *See* Playford

Aisles: The parts of the church to the n. and s. of the *nave*, and sometimes of the *chancel*, under sloping roofs which give the impression of extensions to the main building. Which indeed, they often were, being added to accommodate side *altars*, (see also *chantry chapels* and *guild altars*), as well as larger congregations, and to provide processional ways – an important requirement before the *Reformation*. These are not to be confused with the 'aisle' down which the bride steps which is the centre gangway of the *nave*.

Alderson, Samuel, Revd.: carver; *See* Risby

Aldrych family: masons; *See* Bacton, Badwell Ash, Blaxhall, Blythburgh, Botesdale, Bredfield, Brockley, Campsea Ash, Charsfield, Coddenham, Cotton, Earl Stonham, Elmswell, Eye, Fornham All Saints, Framlingham,

Gedding, Great Waldingfield, Grundisburgh, Hawstead, Helmingham, Hessett, Honington, Ixworth, Knodishall, Martlesham, Mendlesham, Needham Market, Parham, Redgrave, Rickinghall Superior, Rougham, Santon Downham, Saxmundham, Southwold, Stonham Parva, Stratford St Mary, Swefling, Theberton, Troston, Walsham le Willows, Wattisfield, Woodbridge St Mary, Woolpit, Worlingworth, Wortham

Ale jug: *See* **Gotch, Ringers'**

Allen, James Milner: stained glass; *See* Lavenham, Offton

Allen, Robert (1745-1835): Stained glass worker. He began as a porcelain painter when the Lowestoft factory opened and was works manager when they closed in 1802. He began painting on glass as a hobby while still at work and built his own kiln on retirement. His major work was the e. window of St Margaret's, Lowestoft, done in 1819 as a gift to the church when he was 74. It was removed in 1891 but some panels survive in a s. chancel window. More of his glass can be seen at Herringfleet, Wortham and the Norfolk churches of Langley, Thurton and Little Plumstead.

Allin, Thomas, Capt.: *See* Somerleyton

Altar: The table used for the celebration of the Eucharist (Holy Communion or Mass), normally to be found within the *sanctuary* at the e. end of the *chancel.* Originally of wood, but stone altars (see *mensa*) became common in the early church. When the practice of celebrating private masses grew in the Middle Ages, altars were set up elsewhere in the church (see *guilds* and *chantry chapels*) and the original altar became known as the *High altar.* At the *Reformation* there was controversy over the use of stone altars; more followed in Elizabeth's reign and in the C17 over the positioning of what was then called 'the Holy table' (see also *Laudian*). In recent years the practice has grown of siting an altar at the e. end of the *nave* to emphasise corporate worship.

Altar rails: *See* **Communion rails**

Anchorite/anchoress: A religious recluse who chose to be walled up for life in a cell attached to a church in order to devote herself to prayer and meditation. A small outer window gave light and a way for food to be passed in – and for

people to receive advice from the recluse. Another small window gave a direct view of the altar so that the anchorite could watch the celebration of mass. See Cotton and Nettlestead.

Angels: *See* **Nine orders of angels**

Angle piscine: *See* **Piscina**

Anglo-Saxon: The Anglo-Saxons were the Teutonic invaders who overran Britain in the Dark Ages. Between the C5 and C7 Norfolk and Suffolk were subjugated and settled by the Angles, who gave their name to East Anglia. *Saxon* architecture, distinctive in its simplicity, existed until it was superseded by *Norman* building following the Conquest of 1066 (see Appendix 2 – Styles of Architecture).

Anna: When Christ was brought by his mother to the temple at her Purification (Luke 2.22-38), Simeon took him in his arms and spoke the words of the Nunc Dimittis. Also there was Anna, a prophetess of great age who also gave thanks to the Lord and spoke of Christ to all those who looked for redemption in Jerusalem.

Annunciation: Annunciation representations are a regular subject for stained glass scenes, as well as wood and stone carvings – the Archangel Gabriel bringing news to Mary of the Incarnation that she would conceive a child of the Holy Ghost (Luke 1: 26-38). The Feast of the Annunciation is 25 March, otherwise known as Lady Day, an important date too in the rural calendar, when tenant farmers' rents were due, and new tenancies were granted. Examples may be found in many churches.

Apostles: *See* Appendix 1 – Saints

Apse/apsidal: Rounded end of a building, usually the *chancel* at the e. end in churches. Derived from Romanesque architecture, semicircular in shape, or consisting of five sides of an octagon, and often dome-roofed or vaulted; generally associated in Britain with *Norman* churches. It is said that the apse represents the raised platform of the secular 'basilica' or public hall which in Roman times was used as law court and treasury as well as meeting hall; another theory is that it is borrowed from the platform of the meeting rooms of early Christian *guilds.*

Arcades: A series of arches supported by pillars. Sometimes arcades are 'closed', 'blind' or 'blank' – a decorative outline on a wall or tomb or furnishing; or when an aisle has been demolished and the arcade bricked up, leaving its pillars and arches outlined.

Arch-braced roof: A roof carried on a simple, braced arch. (See *Roofs*, fig. 4.)

Armour, Parish: *See* Mendlesham, Palgrave

Arnold, Hugh: stained glass; *See* East Bergholt

Art Nouveau: An ornamental style that flourished throughout Europe from 1890 to 1910, characterised by long sinuous lines mainly derived from naturalistic forms, particularly the lily, rose, and peacock. Sometimes occurring in church furniture and fittings of wood and metal, as at Bredfield, Horringer and Rattlesden, but more often seen as an influence in the stained glass of the period.

Arts & Crafts Movement: A movement active in the late C19 and early C20 which opposed the shoddy results of mass production and emphasised the value of hand crafts. One of the guiding principles was that the artist should be involved in every process, from initial design to finished work. Selwyn Image, W.R. Lethaby, *Christopher Whall*, Walter Crane and Charles Rennie Mackintosh were among the leading figures. The movement's influence in church art is mainly to be seen in stained glass (as at Blaxhall, E. Bergholt, Gt. Cornard, Herringswell, Leiston, Martlesham and Nayland), but there is a font cover at Hadleigh, a *reredos* at Kirkley, *communion rails* at Aldeburgh, and *lych-gates* at Brantham and Kelsale.

Ashlar: Square hewn stone, often used as facing for brick or rubble walls.

Ashmead, R.F.: stained glass; *See* Fornham St Martin

Ashton, Robert the Younger: sculptor; *See* Great Wenham

Assumption of the Virgin: The translation of the Virgin Mary, body and soul, into heaven – a theme often represented by medieval artists in painting and sculpture. The Feast of the Assumption is 15 August, and the Eastern Orthodox Church, with a poetic touch, celebrates it as 'The Feast of the Falling Asleep of Our Lady'. There is an Assump-

tion *boss* at Fressingfield and Flemish glass at Nowton.

Atkins, Robert: monumental mason; *See* Lowestoft St Margaret

Attwood, N.: stained glass; *See* Tunstall

Aumbry: A small cupboard or recess in which were stored the Holy oils used in baptism, confirmation, and anointing of the dying; also the sacred vessels used for the Mass. Sometimes the aumbry held the Reserved Sacrament – the consecrated bread, 'reserved' from a mass (see also *Easter sepulchre*). The aumbry is generally found on the n. side of the *chancel* (opinions vary about medieval usage), but sometimes near the *piscina* – which is almost always on the s. side – and in a few cases near the *font*. Originally, very few parish churches had *sacristies* for storing the plate and valuables. The priest robed at the *altar*, his vestments meantime being kept in a parish chest, the vessels for altar and font being placed in the aumbry. Thus chest plus aumbry equals the later *vestries*. Occasionally the aumbry was used in the C15 as a safe for documents, not only belonging to the church, but to parishioners, and it would be secured by door and lock. Very few of these wooden doors remain today, though the hinge and latch marks in the stone can often be made out. Aumbries can be found at Hacheston, Icklingham, St James (with a door), Shadingfield, Theberton (two, one with a door), Trimley St Mary, Ufford and Woolverstone.

Bacon, John (1740-1799): A mainly self-taught sculptor who first learned his skills in a porcelain factory and later worked for Wedgwood. Shortly after he was elected to the Royal Academy in 1770, he modelled a bust of George III for Christ Church, Oxford which so impressed the king that Bacon received the commission for Chatham's gargantuan monument in Westminster Abbey. Singularly apt in recognising what the public wanted, his was a career of great prosperity and his output prolific. Examples of his work may be seen at Ampton, Finningham and Hawstead.

Bacon, John, the Younger (1777-1859): Something of a child prodigy, he was sculpting figures at the age of 11. Extraordinarily prolific and successful, monuments by him are legion. A good example of his work may be seen at Worlingworth, with others at Assington,

Edwardstone, Hawstead, Market Weston, Mildenhall, Nowton, Stoke by Nayland and Witnesham.

Bacon, Percy: stained glass; *See* Bury St Mary, Capel St Mary, Coddenham, Haverhill, Ipswich St Matthew, Long Melford, Tuddenham St Martin

Bailey, Edward Hodges: sculptor; *See* Culford, Hawstead

Baillie, Edward: stained glass; *See* Henley, Hoxne, Sotherton?, Witnesham, Wrentham

Baillie, Thomas: stained glass; *See* Bungay St Mary, Thorington, Wissington

Baillie & Mayer: stained glass; *See* Nayland, Shimpling

Baker, Eve: conservator; *See* Newton

Baldry of Framlingham: painter; *See* Metfield

Ball flower: An early-C14 decorative ornament in sculpture. See *Decorated* in Appendix 2 – Styles of Architecture.

Balls, Charles: monumental mason; *See* Yoxford

Balls, J.G.: mason; *See* Carlton Colville

Balls, R.: monumental mason; *See* Darsham

Baluster: A short, decorative column, often pear-shaped, bulging at the middle and tapering at top and bottom.

Banner-stave lockers: In the late-medieval period, parish *guilds* proliferated and they had banners which were carried in the processions that were an important part of services on Sundays and Feast Days (see also *galilee porches*). Between times, the banners would be placed in the guild chapels, and the staves in their lockers, which explains the long, narrow upright niches in the walls of some churches. No one has yet explained why they are only to be found in the eastern parts of Norfolk and Suffolk. There are examples at Barnby (unique original door), Blyford, Henstead, Ilketshall St John, Laxfield, Lowestoft St Margaret, Rushmere, Shadingfield, Sotterley, Sternfield?, Wenhaston and Wrentham.

Baptismal water barrel: *See* Thorndon

Barnes, Edward: joiner; *See* Stowmarket, Stowupland

Barnes, Ernest: joiner; *See* Flowton, Framlingham, Newbourne, Tuddenham St Martin (?)

Barnes, Frederick: architect; *See* Baylham, Burstall, Melton, Walton, Whitton

Baroque: A style of architecture, music and art in the C17 and C18 which is characterised by ornate and extravagant detail.

Barrel organs: *See* Shelland, Shotley

Barrett of Norwich: carver; *See* Weybread

Bar tracery: Tracery in the heads of windows, constructed in separate pieces, as distinct from *plate tracery*, where the pattern is cut directly through the masonry. See *Early English* in Appendix 2 – Styles of Architecture.

Bartrum, Albert: carver; *See* Wortham

Base course: A horizontal layer of masonry, decorative in character, usually at the base of towers. *See* **Courses**

Basilisk: *See* **Cockatrice**

Baxter, Richard: bell founder; *See* Dennington

Bayes, Gilbert: sculptor; *See* Aldburgh

Beakhead: *Norman* ornamental device, a series of bird or beast heads with beaks that often bite into a roll moulding.

Beaver carving: *See* Lakenheath, Southwold

Beckwith, Andrew: joiner; *See* Snape, Sudbury St Gregory

Bedford, -: monumental mason; *See* Wilby

Behnes, William: sculptor; *See* Dunwich, Wangford St Peter

Bell, Adrian: author; *See* Barsham, Dennington, Ringsfield, Stradbroke

Bell, J. Clement: stained glass; *See* Orford

Bell, John: sculptor; *See* Flixton

Bell, Michael Farrer: stained glass; *See* Bedingham, Easton

Bell, Robert Anning: artist; *See* Kirkley

Bell & Beckham: stained glass; *See* Ringsfield

Bell ringer, Lady: *See* Mildenhall

Bestiary: A medieval collection of stories, each based on a description of certain qualities of an animal or plant. The stories all derive from the 'Physiologus', a C2 Greek text in which each creature is linked to a biblical text. Extremely popular in the Middle Ages, the bestiaries presented Christian allegories for moral and religious instruction, and many were illustrated, thus providing prototypes for many imaginative carvings.

Bethany, Sisters of: broderers; *See* Lound

Bevington & Sons: organ builders; *See* Rede

Beynton, -: carver; *See* Flempton

Bibliography in stone: *See* Raydon

Biers: Some churches – and particularly those with a long path between *lych-gate* and church – have a platform to carry the coffin to and from the funeral service. These curious conveyances can often be seen, discreetly tucked away at the back of the *nave* or in a side *aisle*. There are interesting C17 examples at Little Saxham, Dalham and Kedington; C18 examples at Bruisyard, Dennington, Frostenden (plus a C20 model), Mendlesham (with a matching child's bier as at Brundish) and Heveningham; C19 examples at Ellough, Rumburgh, Tunstall (made by Parker Hastings), Wissett and Woolverstone.

Bigod, Baron: *See* Syleham

Billet: Billet moulding or decoration was particularly used in *Norman* work. It was formed by cutting notches in two parallel and continuous rounded mouldings in a regular, alternating pattern.

Bird, Francis: statuary; *See* Stonham Aspal

Bird, John: bell founder; *See* Rougham, Sibton

Bisshopp, Edward: architect; *See* Friston, Ipswich Holy Trinity, Ipswich St Mary at the Elms, Ipswich St Michael, South Elmham St James

Blackburne, A.L.: architect; *See* Wangford St Peter

Black Death: Some time in the 1340s an horrific epidemic of bubonic plague ('The Black Death' is a modern expression) began, possibly in China, and by 1348 it had reached the south of France. By the end of the year it had crossed the Channel and begun the ravages which, in twelve months, would leave between a third and a half of the nation's population dead. It cut off in its prime the greatest flowering of English architectural beauty (see *Decorated* in Appendix 2 – Styles of Architecture). On 1 January 1349 the king, Edward III, issued a proclamation postponing Parliament because 'a sudden visitation of deadly pestilence' had broken out in and around Westminster, and by June the full fury of the plague had reached East Anglia. In the dreadful year ending 1350, it has been estimated that at least half, and probably more, of the population of Norfolk and Suffolk were swept away. Its first recorded appearance in East Anglia was at Little Cornard in 1349. Plague broke out again at intervals over the next three centuries until the last major outbreak, culminating in the Great Plague of London in 1665, when a quarter of the inhabitants died. What is remarkable, in considering the Black Death in relation to our churches, is that it was followed by one of the greatest ages of church building.

Blackhall, Pippa: stained glass; *See* Alpheton, Stanningfield

Blank/blind arcading: *See* **Arcades**

Blessed Virgin: *See* **Mary the Blessed Virgin** in Appendix 1 – Saints

Blomfield, Sir Arthur William (1829-1899): Son of the bishop of London and one of the successful architects of the Victorian era. He established his own practice in 1856 and was president of the Architectural Association in 1861. He carried out important cathedral restorations at Canterbury, Salisbury, Lincoln and Chichester, and designed many churches in England and abroad. He designed Felixstowe, St John the Baptist, Ipswich, St John the Baptist, and Culford is his completely; there is wrought-iron work by him at Kirkley, and he directed restorations at Alderton, Herringswell, Rattlesden, Fornham All Saints, Beyton, Dalham and Worlingham.

Blomfield, Sir Reginald: architect; *See* Sotterley

Bloomfield, Robert: poet; *See* Honington, Troston

Blore, Robert: sculptor; *See* Tannington

Blow, Detmar: architect; *See* Hawkedon

Bodley, George Frederick (1827-1907): Church architect and decorative designer, Bodley was *Sir George Gilbert Scott's* first pupil in the 1840s and established his own practice in 1860. From 1869 to 1897 he was in partnership with Thomas Garner and much of their work is indistinguishable. Bodley excelled in the use of late Gothic forms, and in furnishings his preference for rich colour enhanced by gilding shows in the many designs he provided for Watts & Co. He was also the first to commission stained glass from *Morris & Co.* The *nave* roof of Lowestoft St Margaret is a typical example of his rich decoration, as is Edwardstone, and other examples may be found at Barton Mills, Long Melford and Sudbury, St Peter.

Boehm, Edward, Sir: sculptor; *See* Newmarket St Agnes

Bosses: A boss is the carved ornamentation seen at the intersections of roof beams or of the ribs in *groined* ceilings. Usually they represent foliage or grotesque animals or figures, but may often be intricately worked with biblical scenes, portraits, heraldic arms and symbols.

Boughton, Henry: sculptor; *See* Little Saxham

Boulders, Glacial: *See* Bramford, Monk Soham, Shelley, Sproughton, Washbrook, Wherstead

Bowell, Alfred: bell founder; *See* Dennington

Bower, Stephen Dykes: architect; *See* St Edmundsbury Cathedral

Bower of Highgate: monumental mason; *See* Market Weston

Bowmans of Stamford: joiners; *See* Nacton

Box pew: Large pews panelled to waist height or higher, often with seats on three sides, and entered by a door from the *aisle*. Nicknamed 'box pews' from their similarity to horse-boxes or stalls. They came into favour in the late C17 and early C18 and were often embellished with curtains, cushions and carpets. Most disappeared in the wave of C19 restorations. There are examples at Badley (Jacobean), Benhall (good C19), Dennington, Farnham, Kedington, Kentford, Laxfield, Marlesford (squire's pew), Ramsholt, Rendlesham, Shelland, Tunstall, Withersdale and a number of other churches. See also *Prayer book churches*.

Branch of Halesworth: monumental mason; *See* Southwold

Brangwyn, Sir Frank: stained glass; *See* Elveden

Brasses: Brasses are incised memorial portraits and inscriptions, usually found set into the floor or on top of tombs, although some may be seen fixed to walls and furnishings. Brasses were made in an alloy called latten, a mixture of copper and zinc. This was chiefly manufactured at Cologne, where it was beaten into rectangular plates for export to Britain, the Low Countries and elsewhere. Such memorials were long favoured by a wide range of classes, from the nobility, through the priesthood, scholars and monks, to merchants and families of local standing. The earliest brass in England is said to be that of Sir John d'Abernon at Stoke d'Abernon in Surrey, dated 1277 in the reign of Edward I. It was not until the first half of the C17 that the fashion petered out. In the 1830s, interest stirred again, and in the 1840s *Pugin* combined with *Hardman* to design and produce brasses in the medieval manner. Effigies and inscriptions became popular, and although Hardmans were the major suppliers, many firms were at work. Very few were produced after the spate of war memorials in the 1920s. Suffolk is rich in medieval brasses, with interesting examples at Burgate, Brundish, Easton, Eyke (only judicial example), Letheringham, Orford, Pakefield (early use of English verse), Ringsfield (external), Sibton, Sotterley, Wrentham and Yoxford. But brasses are more than memorials: they are remarkable, pictorial commentaries on four centuries of our history, martial armour, manners, customs, dress and fashion. See also *chalice brass* and *shroud brass*.

Brayser family: bell founders; *See* Combs, Cratfield, Cretingham, Ufford

Braziers, Heating: *See* Barking

Bread charities: *See* Eye, Layham, Laxfield, Norton, Pettistree, Woodbridge St Mary, Worlington,

Brett, Jasper: stained glass; *See* Herringswell

Bridges, Lord Robert: poet laureate; *See* Thorndon

Britten, Lord Benjamin: composer; *See* Aldburgh, Orford

Broach spire: A spire which rises from a square base and then becomes octagonal by the insertion of triangular sections (broaches).

Broke, Philip De Vere, Capt., Sir: seaman; *See* Nacton

Brook-Hitch, Frederick: designer; *See* Shotley

Brown, Ford Madox: artist; *See* Kelsale

Brown, H.: carver; *See* Newbourne

Brown, Robert: monumental mason; *See* Moulton, Stowmarket

Brown of Russell Street: monumental mason; *See* Gunton

Bryceson of London: organ builders; *See* Shelland

Bucknall, Miss: broderer; *See* Lound

Bullisdon, Thomas: bell founder; *See* Iken

Bumstead, Peter: organ builder; *See* Snape

Bunbury, Henry William: political caricaturist; *See* Great Barton

Bunyan, John: author; *See* Sudbury All Saints

Burgess, Thomas: monumental mason; *See* Westleton

Burlison & Grylls: A firm of stained glass manufacturers founded by John Burlison and Thomas Grylls in 1868. They had trained with *Clayton & Bell* and had close links with *Sir George Gilbert Scott* and *G.F. Bodley*, for whom much of their earliest and best glass was done. Its accomplished drawing followed C15 and C16 precedents and the work was of a high technical standard. The firm closed in 1953. Excellent examples may be found at Edwardstone and Flixton, and there is more of their glass at Ampton, Earl Soham, Gazeley, Gt. Whelnetham, Nacton and Kelsale.

Burnes, Alfred: joiner; *See* Saxmundham

Butterfield, William (1814-1900): The architect and decorative designer who will always be remembered for two London churches at least – All Saints, Margaret Street, and St Matthias, Stoke Newington. His was a highly individual interpretation of the Gothic style, often characterised by structural polychromy – bands and patterns of bricks in contrasting colours, and his strong sense of craftsmanship may have stemmed from his apprenticeship in the building trade. He was a staunch Tractarian and for many years directed the *Ecclesiological Society's* scheme for the design of church furnishings. He restored Bacton, Ellough, Lawshall, Ringsfield, Sudbury St Gregory and St Peter.

Butterfly headdress: 'Butterfly' is a name given in the C16, and used ever since, for a style fashionable in the previous century, from about 1450 to 1485. Its high fashion status is indicated by its appearance on effigies of the period in brass and stone. The headdress consisted of a wire frame, fixed to a close-fitting ornamented cap, supporting a gauze veil spreading out above the head on each side like a pair of diaphanous butterfly wings.

Cambridge Camden Society: *See* **Ecclesiological Society**

Camm Bros.: stained glass; *See* Stowmarket

Campbell of London: stained glass; *See* Ipswich All Saints

Canopy of honour: *See* **Celure**

Capital: The usually decorated and ornamented top of a column/pillar, from which springs the arch which the pillar supports. (Compare with *impost* and *abacus*.)

Capronnier, John B.: stained glass; *See* Stoke by Nayland

Caracciolo, Giovanni Battista: artist; *See* Newmarket St Mary

Cardenall, Robert: artist; *See* Sudbury St Peter

Carew, John Edward: sculptor; *See* Marlesford

Caröe, W.D.: architect; *See* Elveden, Stoke by Nayland

Carpenter, R.H.: architect; *See* Newmarket St Agnes

Carstone: A soft sandstone which can be seen in the cliffs at Hunstanton, not far from the quarries at Snettisham; mainly used as a building stone in n.e. Norfolk and s. Lincolnshire.

Cartouche: Latin, 'carta', paper. Sculptural representation of a curling sheet of paper.

Caryatid: Female figure used as a pillar or pilaster.

Castellated: Decorated with miniature battlements like a castle.

Cast-iron construction: *See* Lowestoft Christ Church, Playford, Westley

Cautley, Henry Munro (1875-1959): Diocesan Surveyor from 1914 to 1947 and authority on church architecture and fittings. His only complete churches in the county are Ipswich, All Hallows, St Andrew, and St Augustine, but many others bear witness to his work, and furniture to his design may be found at Framlingham, Leiston, Newbourne and Saxmundham. His *Suffolk Churches and their Treasures* was first published in 1937 and is still essential reading for those interested in the county's medieval heritage. The fourth edition was supplemented in 1982 by Anne Riches' *Victorian Church Building and Restoration in Suffolk*, a subject that Cautley resolutely refused to contemplate. His *Royal Arms and Commandments in our Churches* was one of the first monographs on the subject. A man of parts, he farmed at Butley, specialising in Red Poll cattle, and he enjoyed the gift of water divining. His father was rector of Westerfield and Cautley himself read the lessons there for over 60 years. The superb benches at Mildenhall are an enduring memorial to his love for ancient churches and to his generosity.

Celure: Otherwise known as a 'canopy of honour'. A panelled and painted section of the roof of a church, either over the *altar*, or at the eastern end of the *nave* over the position occupied by the *rood*. There are examples at Barking, Bredfield, Bury St Mary, Cotton, Dallinghoo, Eye, Kersey, Mendham, Metfield, Monks Eleigh, Norton, Shotley, Sibton, Southwold, Sudbury St Peter & St Gregory, Trimley St Mary, Uggeshall, Woolpit and Yaxley.

Censer/Censing: *See* **Thurible**

Chadwick, Edith: artist; *See* Kettlebaston

Chalice: The goblet or cup used to contain the wine consecrated and offered to the congregation at the Eucharist or Holy Communion.

Chalice brass: A small *brass* featuring a chalice and wafer as a symbol of the Mass, found occasionally on priest's tombs. There are examples at Gazeley and Rendham.

Chamberlain, William: bell founder; *See* Bramfield, Iken, Rushmere St Andrew

Chambers, H. Oldham: architect; *See* Lowestoft Christ Church

Chambers, James: itinerant poetaster; *See* Stradbroke

Chambers, W.O.: architect; *See* Newmarket All Saints

Chancel: The e. end section of a church, containing the *altar*. Before the *Reformation* the chancel was restricted to the clergy and the celebration of mass, the people occupying the *nave*. Separating the two was a *screen* (thus the derivation of the word from the Latin cancellus – lattice). Traditionally, the parson was responsible for the repair and upkeep of the chancel while the parishioners cared for the rest, and this sometimes resulted in separate building programmes. In some cases it explains the difference in age and style between the two parts of the church. See *rood loft* and also note *weeping chancel*.

Chantrey, Sir Francis: sculptor; *See* Beccles (?), Hoxne, Worlingham

Chantry chapels: The most distinctive development in C14 and C15 church affairs was the growth of chantries. Literally, a chantry was a mass recited at an *altar* for the wellbeing of the founder during his lifetime, and for the repose of his soul after death. Instead of leaving money to monasteries or similar foundations, rich men began to favour their parish church and to endow priests to say daily masses for them and their families. By the C15 all large, and many small, churches contained a number of such chantries – often with their own chapel or altar and furnished with vestments, ornaments and sacred vessels. The endowment often provided for bedesmen to say prayers regularly at the chantry altar, and for alms to be distributed. Chantries provided light, profitable work for a priest although those less well-endowed had to make do with a part-time stipendiary chaplain. For those who could not afford the luxury of a private chantry, membership of a local *guild* often offered a substitute. Chantries were abolished by Edward VI in 1547 ostensibly on religious grounds but really to meet an acute shortage in the Exchequer.

Chapel Studios: stained glass; *See* Uggeshall

Chaplin, Alice: artist; *See* Herringswell

Charnel chamber/chapel: *See* Cowlinge, Mildenhall

Chester, Barrie: joiner; *See* Mendlesham

Chevron moulding: The chevron or zigzag is a characteristic decorative moulding of *Norman* architecture, its bold 'V' shapes being used from the early C12 around open arches and arches of windows and doors. See Appendix 2, Styles of Architecture.

Chi Rho: *See* **Sacred monogram**

Chrismatory: A container (usually with three compartments) for the holy oils used in the sacraments of baptism, confirmation and ordination, for anointing the sick, and for consecrations.

Christian, Ewan (1814-95): As architect to the Ecclesiastical Commissioners and the Church Building Society, he designed a large number of rather dull churches. None of them are in Suffolk but he also directed over 300 restorations, including Bramford, Bures, Hoxne and Mendlesham, and Lowestoft St Margaret.

Christmas, Gerard: sculptor; *See* Hawstead

Chrysom child/cloth: When a child was baptised, it was swaddled for the Christening service in the 'chrysom' cloth or sheet, which often belonged to the parish. If the child died before its mother had been churched (i.e., had been to church after the birth to receive the priest's blessing and purification) it was then buried in the chrysom cloth, thus becoming a 'chrysom child'. There is an example on a monument at Sotterley, on a *ledger-stone* at Stoke by Nayland, and the chrysom cloth features on Badingham *font*.

Church, Reignold: bell founder; *See* Wrentham

Churches Conservation Trust: It having been recognised that church and state should share responsibility for churches no longer required for regular worship and for which no suitable alternative use could be found, the Fund was set up by law in 1969. Its declared aim is to preserve churches which are of architectural, historical or archaeological importance, and it is financed jointly by the Department of the Environment (70%) and the Church Commissioners (30%), plus contributions from the general public, local authorities and other organisations. The Fund is currently caring for some 340 churches, of which 20 are in Suffolk, and many of them are used for occasional services.

Churchwardens' pipes: *See* Horham

Churchyard cross: *See* **Preaching cross**

Cinquefoils: *See* **Foils**

Clark, James: stained glass; *See* Herringswell, Nayland

Clarkson, Thomas: 'friend of the slaves'; *See* Playford

Clayton & Bell: A firm of stained glass manufacturers founded by John Richard Clayton and Alfred Bell in 1855, and still continuing under Michael Bell. Their studio was one of the largest of the Victorian period and they were notable for the brilliance of their High Victorian designs and consistency in their use of colour. Their work of the early 1860s was of a particularly high standard. There are good examples at Assington, Halesworth, Higham, Stowmarket, Tattingstone and Wangford, and among others at Carlton Colville, Harkstead,

Lowestoft St Margaret, Nacton, Ringsfield, S. Elmham St Margaret, Sutton, Ufford and Worlingham.

Cleaner, Church: *See* Mildenhall

Cleere, William: joiner; *See* Great Waldingfield

Clemence, J.L.: architect; *See* Kirkley

Clerestory: An upper storey, standing clear of its adjacent roofs, and pierced with windows which usually correspond in number with the number of arches, or bays, in the *arcade* below. Its pronunciation – 'Clear-storey' – explains the clerestory's function, namely, clear glass windows letting in light on the large covered area below.

Clerk: *See* **Parish clerk**

Clock, Turret: *See* Metfield

Clover, Isabel: broderer; *See* Kesgrave

Clutterbuck, Charles: stained glass; *See* Bury St Mary, Gazeley, Great Saxham, Little Cornard, Stutton, Thwaite

Clutton, Henry: monumental mason; *See* Cransford, Campsea Ash, Worlingworth

Coade stone: *See* Capel St Mary, Henstead, Hunsten, Worlingworth

Cobbold, Revd. Richard: author; *See* Great Ashfield, Wortham

Cockatrice: (Also known as a basilisk.) A fabulous reptile hatched by a serpent from a cock's egg. Both its breath and its look were supposed to be fatal. In medieval imagery it takes the form of a cock with a barbed serpent's tail. There are examples on bench ends at Denston, Sonham Aspal, Stowlangtoft, Troston and Weston.

Coffin plates: *See* Erwarton, Euston

Cogswell, Gerald: designer; *See* Felixstowe St John

Coke, Sir Edward: Chief Justice; *See* Cookley, Huntingfield, Wangford St Denis, Westhall

Cole, William: author; *See* Nowton

Collar beam: *See* **Roofs**

Collar of SS or Esses: A decorative collar of gold or silver composed of Ss linked together. There are many theories concerning the origin of this mark of honour and what the 'S' stood for (Sovereign, Seneschal, etc). The earliest effigy shown wearing it in this country dates from 1371 and so it cannot, as some have maintained, have been introduced by Henry IV. He did, however, issue a regulation in 1401 limiting its use to sons of the king, dukes, earls and barons and to other knights and esquires when in his presence. During the reigns of Henry IV, his son and grandson, it was a royal badge of the Lancastrian house, with a white swan as pendant rather than the more usual portcullis. It was later restricted to the Lord Chief Justice, the Lord Mayor of London, the Heralds and Kings of Arms and the Serjeants at Arms. It features on effigies at Barsham, Chilton and Dennington.

Colle, Raphaelino del: artist; *See* Orford

Collier, Jeremy: divine, author; *See* Ampton

Colling, J.K.: architect; *See* Eye, Hoxne, Spexhall

Colonnette: A small column.

Colt, Maximilian: statuary; *See* Elmswell, Great Saxham

Commonwealth: The republican period of government in Britain between the execution of Charles I in 1649 and the *Restoration* of Charles II in 1660.

Communion rails: The rails against which the congregation kneel to receive communion (often taking it for granted that this is and always was their purpose) were originally installed for quite other reasons. They were to protect the *altar* from irreverent people and even less reverent dogs – and the *balusters* were to be set close enough to ensure this. Before the *Reformation* the *chancel* was always closed off by a *screen* usually fitted with doors, and the people normally never entered it. At great festivals, they watched through the screen as the priests celebrated mass and parishioners received the sacrament. When general participation in services and the administration of the sacrament to the people became the norm, different arrangements were needed. Archbishop *Laud* ordered that the altar should be railed and not moved from its n.-s.

position, and the rails often enclosed the altar on three sides. Whether there should be rails or no, Richard Montague, Bishop of Norwich, made his position clear in a Visitation question in 1638: 'Is your communion table enclosed, and ranged about with a rail of joiners and turners work, close enough to keep dogs from going in and profaning that holy place, from pissing against it or worse?' The Bishop further ordered that 'the communicants being entered into the chancel shall be disposed of orderly in their several ranks, leaving sufficient room for the priest or minister to go between them, by whom they were to be communicated one rank after another, until they had all of them received.' This was to come into conflict with the Puritan habit of demanding that communion should be received by the congregation seated in their pews. In 1643 communion rails went the way of other 'monuments of superstition and idolatry', but at the *Restoration* in 1660 old habits were resumed and the taking of communion at the sanctuary rail became accepted practice. At that time three-sided rails like those at Cretingham, Elmsett, and Shotley were popular. Bungay Holy Trinity and Great Livermere have unusually fine rails, and there is a dated *Stuart* section at Barsham. The rails at Great Waldingfield were made by William Cleere. A unique variation can be found at Hoo where the section on the s. has a book slope, suggesting that a small village choir used the bench in the corner. Kedington also has a rare set of communicants' pews. See also *Prayer book churches* and *Housel bench*.

Comper, Sir John Ninian (1864-1960): Distinguished architect of the Gothic Revival, who in the course of 70 years built 15 churches, restored and decorated scores, and designed vestments, windows and banners for use all around the globe, for both the Roman and Anglican communions. He transformed Lound and earned it the name of 'the golden church', he designed the restored screen and much else at Eye, and left his distinctive mark at Lowestoft St Margaret, Southwold and Ufford.

Consecration crosses: Painted or carved, indicate the points at which the walls of the church, and the *altar* slab (the *mensa)* were touched with Holy oil (see *chrismatory*) by the bishop at the consecration of the building. On the altar were incised five crosses – one at each corner and one in the middle – signifying the five wounds of Christ. Medieval practice varied but normally three crosses were marked on each of the four walls, both inside and out, and spikes bearing candles were inserted below them. The bishop's procession would circle the church before he knocked to be admitted by the single deacon within. The floor was marked from corner to corner with a cross of ashes in which the bishop would inscribe the Latin and Greek alphabets before anointing the rest of the crosses and the altar. In many cases a sacred relic would be sealed within or near the altar at the same time. The crosses inside churches are not uncommon and external examples can be found at Buxhall, Dalham, Holbrook and Monks Eleigh.

Constable, John: artist; *See* Bures St Mary, East Bergholt, Nayland, Sratford St Mary

Constable, W.H.: stained glass; *See* East Bergholt, Great Wratting, Ipswich St Matthew, Ipswich St Michael, Kirkley, Newmarket All Saints

Cooke, John: mayor of Sudbury; *See* Sudbury St Peter

Cooper of Norwich: carver; *See* Pakefield

Cooper of Stratford le Bow: sculptor; *See* Worlingworth

Coralline Crag limestone: *See* Chillesford, Wantisden

Corbels: A practical item which often doubles as a very decorative one. This is the support, set firmly into the wall, to carry a weight from above (see *roofs*) and will usually be carved, either decoratively, or with heads which may or may not be reverent and are sometimes entirely fanciful.

Corbel table: A continuous row of *corbels* set into a wall to support the eaves of a roof.

Corinthian: A column of one of the classical (Grecian) orders, comprising a cushioned base, the shaft or pillar itself (usually fluted), and a *capital* enriched with *acanthus* leaves.

Corder, John: architect; *See* Hepworth, Ipswich St Matthew, Swilland, Tuddenham St Martin, Wherstead

Corders of Ipswich: ironwork; *See* Sudbury St Gregory

Cornelius: *See* Oakley, Rede

Cornish & Gaymer: joiners; *See* Darmsden, Ipswich St Mary le Tower, Reydon, Willisham

Cory & Feguson: builders; *See* Earl Stonham

Costoli, Aristodemo: sculptor; *See* Rendlesham

Cottingham, Lewis N.: architect; *See* Market Weston, Theberton

Courses: A horizontal layer of masonry. A *base course* is found at the base of the tower (and sometimes round *porches* and *aisles*) – a decorative course, a little above the ground, designed to set off the tower visually. In Suffolk, flint is often used to great effect, knapped and set flush into stone panelling to create a contrast, as well as a visual impression of vertical thrust. A *string course* is a continuous line of moulding projecting from a wall which, when used on a tower, divides it into stages. A *drip course* is a raised course doing the practical job of carrying off rain from the wall surface.

Cowgill, Revd. John: broderer; *See* Horham, Stradbroke

Cox & Buckley: stained glass; *See* Darsham, Marlesford, Woodbridge

Cox & Son: stained glass; *See* Badingham, Burgh, Cavendish, Darsham, Groton, Marlesford, Thornham Magna?

Crabbe, Revd. George: poet; *See* Great Glemham, Rendham, Swefling

Crake, Matthias John: sculptor; *See* Westerfield

Crane carving: *See* Denston

Crants: *See* Walsham-le-Willows

Credence/Credence shelf/Credence table: This is a shelf or table on which the elements of the mass or communion are placed before consecration by the priest; usually found within the niche of the *piscina* beside the *altar*, or the site of a former altar. It can sometimes occupy a niche of its own (there are niches at Southwold), and Westhall has a pair of shelves – one of only four known examples.

Crick, Julie: conservator; *See* Preston

Crinkle crankle walls: *See* Bramfield, Easton

Crockets/crocketting: An exuberant ornamentation of the *Decorated* period, in the first half of the C14, though it was to be carried through with enthusiasm into the later *Perpendicular style* (see Appendix 2 – Styles of Architecture). It is a little projecting sculpture in the form of leaves, flowers etc., used in profusion on pinnacles, spires, canopies and arches, both inside and outside the building.

Crossing/crossing tower: The crossing is the part of the church at the intersection of the cross shape of a church, where *chancel, nave,* and n. and s. *transepts* meet. The crossing tower is the central tower built over this point.

Cruet: A small vessel to hold wine or water for use in the celebration of the Eucharist. There is a carving of one on the *font* at Sutton.

Cuffling, Richard: mason; *See* Thornham Parva

Cundy, James, of Pimlico: monumental mason; *See* Marlesford

Cure, Cornelius: sculptor; *See* Long Melford

Cure, William II: sculptor; *See* Framlingham

Curtis, Thomas: stained glass; *See* Hadleigh, Pakenham, Thurston

Cusps/cusping: From the Latin 'cuspis', a point (of a spear). These are the little projecting points on the curves of window and *screen tracery*, arches etc., which give a foliated, leaf-like appearance.

Cutting, Richard: mason; *See* Thornham Parva

Dale of Saxmundham: monumental mason; *See* Theberton

Daniel, John: bell founder; *See* Bildeston

Darling, Archdeacon: Eyke woodcarving school; *See* Earl Soham, Eyke, Orford, Wilby

Davy, Henry: antiquary; *See* Oulton, Peasenhall, Yoxford

Day, N.F. Cachmaile: architect; *See* Ipswich St Thomas

Daye, John: printer; *See* Little Bradley

Decalogue: The Ten Commandments collectively. The Decalogue is a board or panel (in stone, wood, metal or canvas) upon which the Commandments are written. These became a regular part of church furnishings in the reign of Elizabeth I, when it was state policy to clear churches of the decorations and adornments which were regarded as 'popish'. In 1560, Elizabeth ordered Archbishop Parker to see 'that the tables of the Commandments be comely set or hung up in the east end of the *chancel*'. The following year more explicit instructions were given: the boards were to be fixed to the e. wall over the communion table. The Creed and Lord's Prayer were not so ordered but were felt to be 'very fit companions' for the Commandments. Decalogues were also set up on the *tympanum* – panelling which filled the curve of the chancel arch. The boards or panels have in many cases been moved from their original position, and there is a good printed and coloured set at Bruisyard which were published in the late C18, and excellent C17 sets at Kettleburgh and Saxstead. The C18 set at Badley has an additional sentence.

De Carle, John: monumental mason; *See* Great Finborough, Stowmarket

De Carle, Robert: monumental mason; *See* Cockfield, Depden, Edwardstone, Great Whelnetham, Lackford, Market Weston, Norton

De Carle, Robert the Younger: monumental mason; *See* Dalham, Denston

Decorated: This was the high point of ornamented Gothic architecture in the first half of the C14. (*See* Appendix 2 – Styles of Architecture.)

Defoe, Daniel: *See* Redgrave

Deposition, The: The taking down of Christ's body from the cross.

Denman, Thomas: statuary; *See* Martlesham, Nacton

Denny, Thomas: stained glass; *See* Sulton

Denman of Regebnt Street: monumental mason: *See* Wixoe

Dick, Arthur J.: stained glass; *See* Bures St Mary, Boulge, Great Cornard, Herringswell

Dibdin, Thomas Frognall: bibliophile; *See* Exning

Dilloway, C.A.: conservator; *See* Wetheringsett

Dilworth, E.: designer; *See* Tunstall

Dissolution of the monasteries: Wealth and a certain moral laxity had made the monasteries an object of criticism in the later Middle Ages. However, it was from personal motives that Henry VIII effected their complete abolition to replenish his treasury and to stamp his authority on the English church as its supreme head. An Act for the Dissolution of Smaller Monasteries was passed in 1536 and in 1539 the Act for the Dissolution of the Greater Monasteries completed the process.

Dixon, William Francis: stained glass; *See* Rede

Dogtooth decoration: An ornamental carving of the *Early English* period in the C12/C13 which looks like a four-leafed flower. One suggestion is that it is based on the dog's tooth violet.

D'Oisy, Marquis: artist; *See* Leiston

Dole table: *See* Eye

Donne, John: divine, poet; *See* Hawstead

Doom: A picture of the Last Judgement, normally found painted over the *chancel* arch (which symbolically separated earthly from heavenly things). Christ is often represented seated on a rainbow, with souls being weighed below before being despatched to join the blessed on his right hand or the damned on his left. One of the finest examples in England is at Wenhaston, and there are others at Bacton, Chelsworth, Cowlinge, Earl Stonham, Hoxne, North Cove, Stanningfield, Stoke by Clare, Wissington and Yaxley.

Dorcas: A woman of Joppa (also known as Tabitha) whom *St Peter* raised from the dead (Acts 9:36). She is seldom found in earlier Christian art, but the Victorians liked to use the quotation: 'this woman was full of good works and almsdeeds which she did' as a memorial inscription, and there are stained glass figures of her at Beccles, Hacheston, Uggeshall, Wangford and Woodbridge St John (?).

Double piscine: *See* **Piscina**

Doves & Co.: joiners; *See* Snape

Dowsing, William (1596?-1679?): In August 1643 Parliament ordered a general destruction of *altars*, pictures and images in all churches, and the Earl of Manchester, as general of the eastern counties, appointed William Dowsing as his visitor in Suffolk to carry out the work. Dowsing had been born at Laxfield and later lived at Coddenham and Eye. He toured the county between January and October 1644 and is the best known of the despoilers simply because he kept a diary. The original manuscript has vanished but a transcript was made in the early-C18 and it was first published in 1786 (C.H.E. White edited the best edition in 1885). Dowsing employed deputies but took a personal delight in wreaking vengeance on all that he considered 'popish', often exceeding his brief in digging up floors and disturbing tombs. An eyewitness of his work in Cambridgeshire said: 'he goes about the Country like a Bedlam breaking glasse windowes, having battered and beaten downe all our painted glasse ... and compelled us by armed soldiers to pay ... for not mending what he had spoyled and defaced, or forthwith to go to prison'. It should not be assumed that all congregations and ministers in this strongly Puritan area were averse to the purge, but some churches saved their particular treasures by guile or obstinacy. Nevertheless, Dowsing exacted a terrible reckoning. At Clare: 'we broke down 1000 Pictures superstitious; I broke down 200; 3 of God the Father and 3 of Christ and the Holy Lamb, and 3 of the Holy Ghost like a Dove with wings; and the 12 Apostles were carved in Wood, on the top of the Roof, which we gave order to take down; and 20 cherubims to be taken down; and the Sun and Moon in the East window, by the King's Arms, to be taken down'. His work done, he seems to have returned to obscurity and one of his name was buried at Laxfield in 1679. His was a very personal interpretation of the psalmist's: 'Let the righteous put their hand unto wickedness'.

Doyle, Harcourt M.: stained glass; *See* Santon Downham

Drawater, James: monumental mason; *See* Ipswich St Helen

Drip course: *See* **Courses**

Dripstone: A projecting ledge or moulding over the heads of doorways, windows etc, to carry off the rain. When the same thing is used inside a building, as a decorative feature, it is called a *hood mould*.

Dropped-sill sedilia/window: *See* **Sedilia**

Drury, Revd. George: *See* Akenham, Claydon

Early English: This is the style development of the mid-C12 which heralded the arrival of Gothic, or pointed architecture in Britain – as well as the birth of a truly native style. (*See* Appendix 2 – Styles of Architecture.)

Earee, Paul: designer; *See* Sudbury St Gregory

Earp, Thomas: designer; *See* Pakenham

Easter sepulchre: Immediately to the n. of the *High altar* a recess in the wall, ranging from the plain to the richly canopied, housed the Easter sepulchre. In some cases the top of a table tomb in the same area was used, and occasionally it was designed for this purpose. The sepulchre itself was normally a temporary structure of wood and a fragment of such a frame exists at Barningham. On Maundy Thursday, a Host was consecrated (Latin, 'hostia', victim – the bread which is the Body of Christ) and placed in the Easter sepulchre, to be consumed at the following day's Good Friday mass. This practice still continues in the Roman Catholic and some Anglican churches today, the Host being 'borne in solemn procession ... to the altar of repose', to be processed back to the High Altar the following day. Until the *Reformation*, the sepulchre would be watched over from Good Friday to Easter Day, partly from a belief that the final appearance of Christ would be early one Easter morning. Sometimes the watchers were paid. The sepulchre was often the setting for a dramatisation of the Resurrection. There are fine examples at Blythburgh, East Bergholt, Harkstead and Washbrook, with others at Ilketshall St Laurence, Mellis, S. Elmham St Margaret Stradbroke and Wingfield.

Easton, Hugh: stained glass; *See* Badingham, Bury St Peter, Elveden, Ipswich St Augustine, Stowlangtoft, Troston

Ecclesiological Society, The: The Cambridge Camden Society, later to become the

Ecclesiological Society, was founded by J.M. Neale, B. Webb, and others in 1839, and lasted until 1868. During that time it exerted an extraordinarily powerful influence on church-men, architects and laymen in laying down what it believed to be correct principles for church design, building and ornament. Its activities coincided with the great wave of church building and restoration during the mid-C19 and much of what we see now is a direct result of its activities. The preferred style was *Decorated*; anything earlier was tolerated but *Perpendicular* was stigmatised as 'debased' and classical architecture was anathema. Its critics have claimed that it destroyed more than all the Puritan iconoclasts put together, but the enthusiasm it engendered probably saved many medieval buildings that would otherwise have been lost.

Eden, Frederick Charles: stained glass; *See* Barsham, Capel St Mary, Chedburgh, Clare, Felixstowe SS Peter & Paul, Flempton, South Elmham St Margaret? Whepstead

Edmonds, John Maxwell: poet; *See* Tuddenham St Mary

Edwards, George: engineer; *See* Oulton

Elevation squint: Central to the Eucharist (mass) is the consecration of the bread and wine. During the Middle Ages, the standard practice was for the priest to raise the wafer of bread and the cup to symbolise the offering and for adoration by the people. Those kneeling close to the *chancel screen* could not gain a clear view, and the more determined sometimes bored a hole in the panel in front of their accustomed place so that they need not rise from their knees. These apertures have become known as elevation squints and there are examples at Badley, Brent Eleigh, Cowlinge, Dalham, Hessett, Lavenham, Pakefield and Stradishall. (See also *Squint*).

Eldred, John: traveller; *See* Great Saxham

Eley, Reginald: architect; *See* Cavendish

Elliott, C.: stained glass; *See* Mildenhall

Embattled: Decorated with miniature battle-ments.

Ellis, Abraham: joiner; *See* Cratfield

Ellis, Anthony: statuary; *See* Somerleyton

Emblems of the Trinity: Used extensively in wood, stone and glass to represent the idea of the three persons of the Godhead: Father, Son and Holy Spirit. The forms vary and include the equilateral triangle, the *trefoil*, three interlocking circles, and a widely used 'Trinity shield' which bears three inscribed and linked circles. Some-times the image is pictorial, with God the Father holding a miniature Christ between his knees, with a dove superimposed to represent the Holy Spirit. For good examples, see the *fonts* at Corton, Orford and Snape, a painting at Framlingham, C15 glass at Bardwell and Flemish glass at Nowton and Sotterley.

Encaustic tiles: The Victorians invented the process of burning-in different coloured clays onto tile and brick, to produce a stencil-like effect. In churches built during the C19, and in others 'restored and improved', these tiles were freely used on floors and walls.

Erith, Raymond: architect; *See* Felixstowe St Andrew

Evangelistic symbols: On *fonts* and *screens*, in stained glass etc., the symbols of the *Evangelists* are represented as man, eagle, lion and ox, all winged. The biblical sources are the vision of the prophet Ezekiel, and the four all-seeing, never-sleeping creatures around the throne of God, of *St John the Divine*: 'The first living creature was like a lion, the second was like an ox, the third had a face like a man, the fourth was like a flying eagle ...' (Revelation 4:7). The Evangelists associated with the symbols are *St John*, eagle (because he takes us directly into the Divine presence and only the eagle could gaze undazzled at the sun); *St Luke*, ox (his gospel begins with the offering of Zacharias and the ox was a sacrificial animal); *St Matthew*, man (his gospel begins with Christ's earthly descent); St *Mark*, lion (he speaks of the 'voice crying in the wilderness' – like a lion). Examples abound but Somerleyton's is particularly interesting and there is excellent C14 glass at Great Bricett.

Evangelists: *See* **Evangelistic symbols**

Evans of Shrewsbury: stained glass; *See* Shadingfield

Eyton, H.M.: architect; *See* Walpole

Fainting House: *See* Shimpling

Farmer & Brindley: joiners; *See* East Bergholt

Farrow, Thomas: monumental mason; *See* Thurston

Farrow of Bury: carver; *See* Thurston
Farrow of Diss: glazier; *See* Redgrave

Fawcett, W.M.: architect; *See* Rickinghall Superior

Fees, Table of: *See* Great Waldingfield, Ipswich St Margaret, Wrentham

Fenn, Sir John: antiquary; *See* Finningham

Ferrey, Benjamin: architect; *See* Sotherton

Finch of Trimley: joiner; *See* Trimley St Mary

Finial: A carved or moulded ornament, often in foliage or floral form, or as a particularly decorative *crocket*, completing the points of arches, pinnacles or gables. Any finishing in this sense, no matter how plain or simple, is still technically a finial

Fire engine: *See* Worlingworth

Fisher, Joseph: stained glass; *See* Barsham

Fisk, Henry: glazier; *See* Middleton

Fisk, Hubert: joiner; *See* Wrentham

Fitzgerald, Edward: author; *See* Boulge, Monk Soham

Five wounds of Christ, The: On fonts and elsewhere, the five wounds of Christ are often represented. They are the wounds of the Crucifixion – to hands, feet and side, recalling doubting Thomas': 'Except I shall ... put my finger into the print of the nails, and thrust my hand into his side, I will not believe' (John 20:25). There is an example on a pew at Laxfield. See also the *instruments of the Passion*, which often accompany representations of the wounds.

Flaxman, John (1755-1826): Sculptor. He was a sickly child, but with a great gift for drawing which brought him, when he was only eleven, a premium (repeated in 1769) from the Society of Arts. In 1767 he won the Gold Palette for modelling a statue of the actor David Garrick. At 15 he joined the Academy Schools. In 1775 he began work for Josiah Wedgwood and designed cameos and made wax models of classical friezes. Later he spent seven years in Rome on statuary and monumental work, often with aristocratic patrons which established his fame throughout Europe and ensured success when he returned to England in 1794. The poet Blake called him 'the sculptor of Eternity', and there are examples of his work at Rendlesham and Tattingstone.

Fletcher, Ronald: author; *See* Akenham, Little Stonham, Westleton, Wortham

Fleuron: A flower-shaped ornament used to decorate mouldings both in wood and stone.

Flight & Sons: organ builders; *See* Great Glemham

Flint-knapping: Flint split across the middle to achieve a shell-like fracture, and a lustrous, flat surface. (See also *Flushwork*).

Flood of 1912: *See* Ringsfield

Flushwork: This is the use of *knapped* flints, set flush in panelled patterns of brick or stone, a combination which adds visual beauty and striking impact to so many Suffolk and Norfolk churches.

Foils: From the C12, foils were a common feature in Gothic architecture. The *Early English* style produced the graceful *trefoil*, or three-leafed shape: this can represent the *Trinity*, and *St Patrick* put together three leaves of shamrock to illustrate to his converts that profound mystery. The trefoil was followed architecturally by the *quatrefoil* (four leaf), *cinquefoil* (five leaf), *sexfoil* (six leaf) and multi-foil.

Font: Receptacle for baptismal water, normally made of stone, but sometimes of wood or metal. The traditional place for the font is at the w. end of the church near to the main entrance, symbolising that baptism (christening) is the first stage in the Christian life. Medieval fonts were provided with a lockable cover to ensure the purity of the baptismal water and to guard against misuse or profanation. See also *Seven Sacrament Fonts*.

Forsyth, J. Dudley: stained glass; *See* Culford, Mildenhall, Mildenhall West Row, Worlington

Four Evangelists: *See* **Evangelistic symbols**

Four Latin Doctors: 'Doctor' here indicates one who is learned, a theologian. The Four Latin Doctors were the leading theologians of the early Christian Church in the west – *SS Ambrose, Augustine of Hippo, Jerome* and *Gregory* They feature in *Kempe* glass at Barsham. (See also Appendix 1 – *Saints*)

Fowler, Charles Hodgson: architect; *See* Nacton

Fraden, Cyril: artist; *See* Mendlesham

Frampton, Edward: stained glass; *See* Chillesford

Francis Bros.: architects; *See* Halesworth

French, G. Russell: architect; *See* Leavenheath

Frere, Augustus: architect; *See* Horham

Fretwork: *See* Old Newton, Swefling, Westleton

Frink, Elizabeth: sculptor; *See* St Edmundsbury cathedral

Frosts of Watton: joiners; *See* Yaxley

Gabriel: *See* Appendix 1 – *Saints*.

Gaffin, Thomas & Edward: monumental masons; *See* Earl Soham, Great Saxham, Kelsale, Kessingland, Kettleburgh, Martlesham, Somerleyton, Stanton, Thurston, Tostock

Gage, Peter: builder; *See* Chelsworth

Galilee porches: Where a church has a western porch it was often called the 'galilee porch' because it was the final 'station' in processions round the building. The priest at the head of the procession symbolised Christ going before his disciples into Galilee after the Resurrection. In medieval times these processions were an important part of certain services, particularly on Feast days. There are galilee porches at Debenham and Mutford. (See also *Banner-stave lockers*)

Galleries: These have a fascinating pedigree in churches. Before the *Reformation*, when every church had its *rood loft* in the *chancel* arch, singers might use the loft as a gallery, the singing being accompanied by a simple organ. In the couple of centuries that followed the Reformation and the destruction of the old rood lofts, galleries – usually at the w. end of the *nave* – became a common feature. There, a simple orchestra would sometimes assemble to accompany the singing, and village choirs were common, although the robed and surpliced variety were a mid-Victorian innovation. When organs again became popular they were sometimes placed in a western gallery, and there they can still occasionally be found. Many more galleries were installed in the C19 to accommodate the larger congregations of the period. Representative examples at: Aldeburgh and Nayland (C18), Aldringham, Benhall, Bungay Holy Trinity, Eye (C15), Framlingham (excellent C18), Friston, Hacheston, Leiston, Metfield (1719), Middleton, Oulton, Parham, Peasenhall, Snape, Withersdale (C17), Woodbridge St John. The gallery at Old Newton has school seating.

Gardiner, Thomas: bell founder; *See* Sutton

Gargoyle: A spout jutting outwards from a wall so as to throw rainwater well away from the building. But there is more to gargoyles than that. Almost always in ancient churches they are carved in all manner of fanciful forms – weird beasts, dragons, devils. This choice of subjects has a very positive aspect to it: if there is good in this world, there is assuredly evil, and to appreciate the first, one must be able to recognise the other. As medieval man also believed that evil spirits prowled around his church, what better way of keeping them at bay than putting their own kind on guard?

Gasoliers: *See* Kelsale, Sudbury St Gregory

Geldart, Ernest, Revd.: architect; *See* Kettlebaston

Gérente, Alfred: stained glass; *See* Bury St Mary

Gesso: This is a system of coating a base, usually wood, with a thick layer of plaster of Paris, or with gypsum (one of the powdered minerals used to make up plaster of Paris). When it is hard, the artist/sculptor carves into it his design, to produce an incised effect which is then painted and, in church art, almost always gilded. The best examples are the *screens* at Southwold and Bramfield and the *retable* at Thornham Parva, with others at Rumburgh, Sotherton and Westhall.

Gibberd, Sir Frederick: architect; *See* Haverhill

Gibbons, James: joiner; *See* Earl Stonham

Gibbons, Grinling: carver; *See* Wickham Market

Gibbs, Alexander: stained glass; *See* Aldringham, Bacton, Bungay St Mary, Elmswell, Great Waldingfield, Lawshall, Sproughton, Sudbourne, Wherstead

Gibbs, C.A.: stained glass; *See* Newmarket All Saints

Gibbs & Howard: stained glass; *See* Haverhill, Wangford St Peter

Gibson, John: sculptor; *See* Little Glemham

Giles, John: metalworker; *See* Framlingham

Gill, Eric: artist/typographer; *See* Hadleigh

Glasby, William: stained slass; *See* Wyverstone

Glasscock, Michael: carver; *See* Mutford

Glaziers' advertisements: *See* Barnby, Blyford, Stanton

Gleichen, Feodora, Countess: sculptress; *See* Culford

Goddard & Gibbs Studios: stained glass; *See* Beyton, Felixstowe St John

Godbold, Robert: carver; *See* Earl Stonham, Fressingfield, Mendham

Godfrey, Neil: sculptor; *See* Lavenham

Godwin, E.: artist; *See* **Harris, E.A.C. & E. Godwin**

Godynge, John: bell founder; *See* Worlington

Golden, John: monumental mason; *See* Finningham

Gonville, Edmund: college founder; *See* Thelnetham

Goodden, R.Y.: carver; *See* Nayland

Gordon, Bronwen: stained glass; *See* Hepworth

Gotch, Ringers': *See* Clare, Hadleigh

Gray & Davison: organ builders; *See* Stowlangtoft

Graye, Miles, I: bell founder; *See* Bramford, Ipswich St Mary le Tower, Lavenham, Stowmarket

Green, Herbert: carver; *See* Onehouse

Green, John: monumental mason; *See* Monks Eleigh

Green, Thomas: statuary; *See* Redgrave

Green, T.L.: artist; *See* Sudbury St Gregory

Green (Saunders of Ipswich): carver; *See* Kettlebaston

Green man: The green man is a mask, often with a devilish expression, probably representing the spirit of fertility, with tendrils of foliage sprouting from its mouth. Carved in wood or stone, it was a pagan symbol that persisted in rustic Christian art. There are particularly good examples at Capel St Mary, Dennington, Mildenhall and Woolpit, and among others, those at Fressingfield, Hacheston (crowned), Metfield, and Walton St Mary.

Gribble, Eleanor: artist; *See* Stowmarket

Griffin: Traditionally the guardian of treasure – but also used in church sculpture, carvings and paintings. The griffin, or gryphon, is a mythical monster with an eagle's head, wings and forelegs; and the body, tail and hind-legs of a lion. In Oriental folklore, a couple of griffins pulled Alexander the Great in a magic chariot up to heaven, while he was still alive that is, just to have a look around. Representative examples at Belstead, Blythburgh, Eye, Fressingfield, Huntingfield, Mildenhall, Shelley and Woolpit.

Grigs, Francis: sculptor; *See* Framlingham

Grimwood, George: builder; *See* Chilton

Grimwoods of Weybread: builders; *See* Stradbroke

Grisaille: Geometric or leaf patterns painted onto white glass.

Groining: This is the creation of a vaulted ceiling, divided into segments by raised, intersecting lines – these lines, between the angled surfaces, being the actual 'groins'. Found in carved canopies, as well as in *roofs*.

Groom, John, & Sons: cabinet makers; *See* Chelmondiston, Ipswich St Matthew

Groom, Philip: carver; *See* Ipswich St Michael, Wortham

Grosseteste, Robert, bishop: *See* Stradbroke

Guilds/guild altars: In corners of churches, in the e. ends of *aisles*, or flanking *screens*, one often finds *piscinas*, and occasionally *squints*, which indicate the presence of a guild or *chantry altar* in pre-*Reformation* times. Guilds were small local associations whose members banded together for a common charitable or practical purpose. Their religious commitment would often be shown by having their own altar in their parish church, served by a priest whom they maintained. There were two main divisions: craft or trade guilds, whose purpose was the protection of particular work, trade or skill; and religious societies or, as they are sometimes called, 'social guilds'. The split was often one of convenience rather than a real distinction. All had the same general characteristic, the principle of brotherly love and social charity, and none was divorced from the ordinary religious observances daily practised in pre-Reformation England. Broadly speaking, they were the benefit societies and provident associations of the Middle Ages – a helping hand for the sick, orphans, widows, and the needy traveller. Members were bound to support the maintenance of their guild chapel which was always dedicated to a particular saint, and their subscriptions paid for the services of a chaplain. Nearly everyone was a member of one fraternity or another. One distinct help to the parish was the provision of additional priests for the services of the church. Beccles guild of the Holy Ghost, for example, had a priest 'to celebrate in the church'. Beccles being 'a great and populous town of 800 *houseling* people ... the said priest is aiding unto the curate there, who without help is not able to discharge the said cure'. (See also *Chantry chapels*)

Gunpowder Plot: *See* Norton, Stanningfield

Hakewill, Edward Charles (1812-1872): A church architect who was one of Philip Hardwick's pupils in the 1830s and District Surveyor for St Clement Danes and St Mary-le-Strand. In 1851 he published *The Temple: an Essay on the Ark, the Tabernacle and the Temples of Jerusalem*. He carried out restorations and rebuilding at Ashbocking, Brantham, Chelmondiston, Crowfield, Drinkstone, Elmswell, Eyke, Grundisburgh, Kenton, Langham, Needham Market, Rushmere St Andrew, Shottisham, Stonham Aspal, Thurston and Wickham Market.

Hakewill, John Henry (1811-80): An architect who enjoyed an extensive practice mainly in Wiltshire, Suffolk and Essex, building many churches, schools and parsonages. He designed Bury St Peter's and was one of the consulting architects for the Incorporated Church Building Society and carried out work at Beccles and Holton and the extensive restoration at Great Waldingfield.

Haklyt, Richard: geographer; *See* Great Saxham, Wetheringsett

Hall, Henry: architect; *See* Tattingstone

Hall, Joseph, Bishop: *See* Hawstead

Hammerbeam roofs: A brilliant conception, architecturally and artistically, of the late C15-C16, in which the thrust of the roof's weight is taken on 'hammer' brackets. (See *Roofs* figs. 6, 7 and 8).

Hanchett of Bury: monumental mason; *See* Cavenham, Fornham St Martin

Hanoverian: The period during which the sovereigns were of the House of Hanover, from George I to Victoria.

Harbicks: *See* **Tenterhooks**

Harding of Ballingdon: monumental mason; *See* Wixoe

Hardman, John & Co: The family were originally button-makers in Birmingham but John Hardman (1811-67) met *Pugin* in 1837 and they became friends. The following year they were partners in a new metal-working business which set out to provide church fittings and accessories of all kinds, for which Pugin provided all the designs in medieval style. Starting with small projects, mainly in precious metals, the venture blossomed. As Hardman and Iliffe, the firm took part in the Great Exhibition in 1851 and the medieval court displayed an extraordinary range of Pugin's designs and Hardman's craftsmanship. The revival of memorial *brasses* was largely due to them and Hardman & Co became by far the largest suppliers, producing some notable designs. In the early days, Pugin's influence was pervasive and stained glass was added to the repertoire in 1845. He was the chief designer in this medium until his death in 1852 when the role passed to Hardman's nephew, John Hardman Powell who continued until 1895. The firm's early work set standards for the Gothic revival in stained glass, and despite the changes in taste that have until recently dismissed it as unworthy of serious attention, it is of high quality and beauty. They provided fine windows at Dunwich and Wrentham, and other examples are at Aldeburgh, Carlton, Chelsworth, St Edmundsbury cathedral, Fornham All Saints, Freckenham, Offton, Rattlesden, Wilby and Whitton.

Hare, C.G.: architect; *See* Edwardstone

Harpy: A ravening monster with a woman's head and body, and bird's wings and claws. There is a carving at Dennington which probably represents a harpy.

Harris, E.A.C. & E. Godwin: artists; *See* Hemingstone

Harvey, Frederick: architect; *See* Ipswich Holy Trinity

Hart & Co: church furnishings; *See* Ipswich St Matthew

Hart & Peard: wrought ironwork; *See* Kirkley

Hassocks: *See* Eriswell, Icklingham St James, Lakenheath

Hastings, Parker: joiner; *See* Tunstall

Hatcher, Basil: architect; *See* Chelmondiston, Ipswich St Francis

Hatchments: Many churches display on their walls large, diamond-shaped boards, bearing a coat of arms and either the motto of the family whose coat it is, or the word: 'Resurgam' (I shall rise again). Dating from the second half of the C17 through to the end of the C18, these boards

were carried in procession at the burial of the holder of the arms. Afterwards for some months they were hung on the dead man's house, and were later transferred to the church. Samuel Pepys had a handsome one made for a relative in 1663 which cost him four pounds. The layout followed a formalised pattern – the background is black on the l.-hand side if the dead person was a husband, black on the r. if a wife; for a bachelor, widow or widower, the whole background would be black. The earliest in the county is at Long Melford and there are other early examples at Debenham, Martlesham and Sudbourne. Blundeston's *Royal Arms* is probably a reused hatchment, Henstead has the smallest in the county, Trimley St Martin's is a silk banner, and there are good ranges at Coddenham, Easton and Yoxford.

Hawkins, Robert: joiner; *See* Shotley

Hawkins, R.: architect; *See* Stutton

Hayward, H.W.: architect; *See* Needham Market

Hayward, John: stained glass; *See* Walton

Hayward, William: brass engraver; *See* Yoxford

Headstops: Carvings, often in the form of heads at the ends of *dripstones* and *hood moulds* over arches, doors and windows.

Heart burial: If a person died away from home he sometimes requested that his heart be buried in his parish church. The chosen place was marked either by a miniature effigy or by a heart (sometimes cupped in hands). There is a good example at Exning, and Holbrook has a possible contender.

Heaton, J. Aldham: stained glass; *See* Kelsale

Heaton, Butler & Bayne: A firm of stained glass manufacturers founded by Clement Heaton and James Butler in 1855, joined by Robert Turnill Bayne in 1862. They took over the role of the most original Gothicists from *Clayton & Bell* and produced an impressively varied series of high quality windows in the 1860s which were fine examples of the High Victorian style at its most accomplished. There was significant collaboration with *Henry Holiday* and other artists of the aesthetic movement in the 1870s and the firm continued to produce glass until 1953. Their earliest surviving Suffolk window is at Hawstead and there is good work at Barton Mills, Botesdale, Brome Martlesham, Stuston and Thorington; other examples can be found at Beccles, Burstall, Eye, Gosbeck, Holton St Mary, Little Cornard, Lowestoft St Margaret, Oakley, Wangford, and Woolverstone.

Hedge, Nathaniel: clockmaker; *See* East Bergholt

Hedgeland, George: stained glass; *See* Hadleigh, Ipswich St Matthew

Hendra & Harper: stained glass; *See* Trimley St Martin

Henslow, John Stevens: botanist; *See* Hitcham

Herringbone work: A technique of positioning stones, bricks or tiles in 'arrow formation', like the bones of a fish, with alternate courses in different directions, giving a zigzag effect. Not a decorative device, but a strengthening and supporting measure. The technique goes back to Roman times, but continued through the *Saxon* period and well into the *Norman* era.

Hervey, Revd. the Hon. Henry: architect; *See* Shotley

Heskett, Pippa: stained glass; *See* Bildeston, Withersfield

High altar: *See* **Altar**

Hille, Richard: bell founder; *See* Great Glemham, Ringshall, Washbrook

Holiday, Henry (1839-1927): Artist, writer, and one of the key stained glass designers of the C19. When his friend Burne-Jones left *Powells* in 1861 he became their chief designer, and later undertook commissions for *Heaton, Butler & Bayne*. A decisive modernist who refused to ape the medieval style, he believed that the artist should be involved in every stage of stained glass production, and set up his own workshop in 1891. His *Stained glass as an art* sets out his credo as a designer, and there are lovely windows by him at Campsea Ash, Fressingfield and Lound.

Holland, Mildred Keyworth: artist; *See* Huntingfield

Holland, William: sculptor; *See* Little Glemham

Holy table: *See* **Altar**

Holy Trinity: *See* **Emblems of the Trinity**

Hood mould: *See* **Dripstone**

Hooker, Sir William Jackson: botanist; *See* Halesworth

Hopkins, Matthew: witchfinder; *See* Brandeston

Hopper, Humphrey: sculptor; *See* Rendlesham, Worlington

Horns of light: Exodus 34:30 tells us that when Moses came down from Sinai 'the skin of his face shone'. The Hebrew for 'shone' is the root of the noun meaning 'horn', which in Latin became 'facies cornuta'. Medieval artists interpreted this as 'horns', and their version of Moses can always be recognised by the horns sticking out of his head. The tradition was continued in the C17 & C18 when figures of Moses and Aaron often flanked *Decalogue boards*. There is a medieval example in a wall painting at Westhall, and C19 versions in stained glass are common.

Horse guarding his dead master: *See* Offton

Hour-glasses/stands: There was a time when long sermons were the rule rather than the exception, particularly after the *Reformation*, in the mid-C17 Puritan period, and in the C18 when preachers were renowned for their long-windedness. For their own guidance, ministers often had an hour-glass on or near the pulpit to indicate the passing time (though when the hour was up it was not unknown for sermonisers to turn the glass over and start again). Before the Reformation hour-glasses were used, though less commonly, to time private meditations. By the 1780s they were already being described as curiosities. There is a unique set of three at Earl Stonham, Cratfield installed one in 1590, and the bracket stand at Chelmondiston is one of the finest in Suffolk; other stands survive at Barnardiston, Bradfield St George, Gislingham, Kedington, South Elmham St Margaret, Stutton and Washbrook.

Houseling cloth/people: In Old English 'housel' means 'sacrifice', and was used in the English church from St Augustine to the *Reformation* to mean the Eucharist. Houseling people were those in the parish who had received communion, and a houseling cloth was held in front of them by attendants as they received the consecrated bread in order that no fragment should be lost. Housel benches were special seats placed in or near the *chancel* for them when they came up to the *altar* and there is one at Shelland – the special pews at Kedington served the same purpose. The cloth is illustrated on *fonts* at Great Glemham and Woodbridge.

Howard, Frank: stained glass; *See* Ipswich St Matthew

Howard, F.E.: carver; *See* St Edmundsbury cathedral, Stowlangtoft

Howard of Trimley: joiner; *See* Trimley St Mary

Howlett of Saxmundham: glazier; *See* Saxmundham

Howson, Joan: *See* **Townshend, Caroline and Joan Howson**

Hudd (graveside shelter): *See* Wingfield

Hudson, Charles: stained glass; *See* Sotherton, Uggeshall (?)

Hughes, Wyndham: stained glass; *See* Grundisburgh, Gunton St Peter

Hulbert, Anna: conservator; *See* Monks Eleigh

Hulton, John: stained glass; *See* Southwold

Hurdy-gurdy: *See* **Vielle**

Hymes, H.A.: stained glass; *See* Eye

IHS: *See* **Sacred monogram**

Ibex: An animal with horns that curve back along the neck. According to the *bestiaries* it was able to throw itself over precipices and land safely on its horns. There are examples at Hawstead, Hunston and Woolpit.

Ignatius, Father OSB: *See* Claydon

Impost: A simple bracket or moulding set as a 'lip' in a wall to carry a springing arch. A typical attribute of plain and massive *Saxon* architecture. (Compare with *capital* and *abacus*.)

Incendiary bomb: *See* Pakefield

Instruments of the Passion: Often used symbolically in carving and painting. They are: Christ's cross; the crown of thorns; the spear that was thrust into his side; the cup of vinegar; and the reed and sponge by which that vinegar was offered as Christ hung on the cross. The dice which were used to cast lots for his clothing and a ladder are additional symbols. The finest set is carved on a bench at Fressingfield, and there are good examples on Great Blakenham *font*, Hitcham *screen* and Westerfield roof; they occur in C14 glass at Great Glemham, and there is a good C19 range at Mendham.

Ionic: A classical column whose *capital* is characterised by corner scrolls that curl under.

Ireland, Robert: architect; *See* Witnesham

Ireland, – : mason; *See* Ipswich St Mary at the Elms

Jack, George: carver; *See* Kedington

Jackman of Bury: mason; *See* Cavenham, Icklingham St James

Jackson, T.G., Sir: architect; *See* East Bergholt

Jacobean: Style of architecture dating from the reign of James I, 1603-1625. See Appendix 2 – Styles of Architecture.

Jamb/jamb shaft: The upright of a doorway, or the side of a window opening: the 'shaft' is a decorative shaft or slim column at the angle of the window splay with the wall.

Jansen, Jan: statuary; *See* Stowlangtoft

Janssen, Bernard: statuary; *See* Redgrave, Woodbridge St Mary (?)

Jarman, Derek: sculptor; *See* Chattisham

Jarndyce v. Jarndyce (*Bleak House*): *See* Acton

Jekyll, Thomas: architect; *See* Brome, Stuston

Johnson, Revd. Braham.: joiner; *See* Stuston

Johnson, John: architect; *See* Beyton

Johnson, Matthew Wharton: statuary; *See* Dallinghoo, Flempton, Whepstead

Jones, Revd. William: divine; *See* Nayland

Jones & Willis: C19 manufacturers who set out to provide churches with everything they might need, from candlesticks to fonts and pulpits. They began to make stained glass about 1880 and supplied a number of Suffolk churches. Much of their work is plainly commercial, but Rendham e. window is an example of their better designs, a powerful piece of work. Other windows are at Bruisyard, Cavenham, Cratfield, Great Cornard, Ilketshall St John, Ipswich St Margaret, Mettingham, South Elmham All Saints, Spexhall, and Wrentham; there is a mosaic memorial by them at Frostenden.

Joyful mysteries, The five: The first chaplet of the Rosary consisting of the Annunciation, the Visitation, the Nativity, the Presentation of Christ in the Temple, and the finding of the Child Jesus in the Temple. They are seen on the *font* panels at Ipswich St. Matthew.

Jupon: A close-fitting tunic or doublet worn by knights under the hauberk; later, a sleeveless surcoat worn outside the armour (as at Bures St. Edmund).

Keevil, Maurice: conservator; *See* Gipping, Grundisburgh, Gunton

Kempe & Co. (Kempe & Tower): A firm of stained glass manufacturers founded by Charles Eamer Kempe in 1869, a designer who had worked for *Clayton & Bell*. His nephew, Walter Ernest Tower, took over in 1907 and continued until 1934. Their work is generally in C15 mode, intricate and often sentimental, with a distinctive colour range. Kempe was one of the most successful late Victorian designers and there was little change in the style he adopted, even in the C20. His windows are sometimes signed with a wheatsheaf emblem, while those of Tower often have a castle superimposed on the sheaf of corn. Good windows at Burgh, Creeting St Mary, Leiston and Melton, and other examples at Barsham, St Edmundsbury cathedral, Dalham, Gisleham, Hacheston, Holton, Kessingland, Kirkley, Nacton, Newmarket St Mary and Sotterley.

Kendrick, Josephus: sculptor; *See* Thornham Magna

Kennel headdress: A style of headdress

fashionable from about 1500 to 1540, but not in fact given its name as we know it until the C19. It appears distinctively on figures on brasses and tombs of the period, and on carved heads of corbels etc. The headdress consisted of a hood wired up to form a pointed arch over the forehead, with borders framing the face to each side. The early kind hung in folds to the shoulders behind; but after 1525 the back drapery was replaced by two long pendant flaps which hung down in front on each side of the neck. Both kinds will be seen represented. There are examples at Euston, Denston, Long Melford, Middleton and Nayland.

Kerr Institute, Hamilton: conservators; *See* Thornham Parva

Ketts of Cambridge: carvers; *See* Lowestoft St Margaret

King, Dennis: stained glass; *See* Wherstead

King, J. & J.: stained glass; *See* Haughley

King, R.B.: stained glass; *See* Chelsworth

King posts: An upright roof beam set between horizontal cross beams, or between cross beam and roof ridge, to prevent sag and give greater stability. See *roofs*, fig. 3.

Kipling, Rudyard: poet; *See* Shotley

Kitchener, Horatio, Field Marshall: *See* Aspal, Lakenheath

Knapped/knapping: *See* **Flint-knapping**

Knewstubb, John: priest; *See* Cockfield

Krimpen, Jan Van: typographer; *See* Lawshall

Label: A rectangular *dripstone* carried over a door or window enclosing the top.

Lamb, Edward Buckton: architect; *See* Leiston

Lancet: The slim, pointed window which characterises the beginnings of *Early English* architecture from about 1200. (See Appendix 2 – Styles of Architecture.)

Lark, Thomas: architect; *See* Mildenhall

Laud: *See* **Laudian**

Laudian: This refers to Archbishop William Laud, 1573-1644. His seven years as Archbishop of Canterbury, during which he tried to impose certain disciplines of worship on the English and Scottish churches, had far-reaching effects, but for him resulted in execution. Laud wanted to reform the English church in a manner compatible with Protestantism, yet without giving way to the sweeping changes and austerities called for by the increasingly powerful Puritans. Brought down to its simplicities, he wanted a disciplined order and form of worship which centred on the *altar,* placed against the e. wall of the *chancel,* with an enclosing rail around it; and with the communicants kneeling within the chancel to receive the sacrament. But these were matters of bitter and violent debate. From Elizabeth I's reign, the altar often had been placed 'table-wise', ie, e. to w. at the *nave* end of the chancel; or a temporary table was set up in the nave – the intention being in each case for the communicants to be within sight and hearing of the priest at the altar. But there were those who refused to kneel, or even to enter the chancel, and who certainly would not tolerate, in the e. end altar, what smacked to them of a popish *High altar* divorced from the people. The impression which comes down to us of the Archbishop is of a man of honest intent – but whose every action seemed to turn people against him. He was accused of 'popery' and of warmth towards Rome, and blamed for the disastrous and ineffective moves against Scotland, both judicial and military, intended to make its churches conform with his ideas. He then issued 'canons' (ie, instructions) which appeared to enshrine the absolute rule and 'divine right' of King Charles I – whose position by now was already seriously threatened. In December 1640 Parliament impeached Laud for treason, and he was imprisoned in the Tower, but it was not until March 1644 that he was put on trial. The House of Lords had decided in advance that he was guilty of trying to alter the foundations of church and state, although they hesitated to sentence him until the House of Commons threatened to set the mob on them if they didn't. On 10 January 1644, staunchly declaring his innocence and good intent, Laud died under the axe, Parliament having graciously agreed that he should be excused the usual traitor's punishment of being hung, drawn and quartered. Ironically, by the end of the century, the forms of service which developed in the Anglican church were much in sympathy with the things for which Laud fought and died. (See also *Prayer book churches, communion rails,* and *mensa slabs.*)

Lavers & Barraud (Lavers & Westlake): Stained glass manufacturers. Founded by Nathaniel Wood Lavers in 1855; he was joined by Francis Philip Barraud in 1858, both men having been with *Powell & Sons* in the 1840s. Lavers was the craftsman and business head, relying on competent artists to design his windows, but Barraud was a prolific designer for the first decade of the partnership, specialising in small figure medallions. In the 1860s the firm was much favoured by the leaders of the *Ecclesiological Society.* From then on, major commissions were designed by Nathaniel H.J. Westlake and he became a partner in 1868, doing the majority of the figure work. At that time their colouring was light and sweet, with a wide range of tints, and the leading was meticulous. Towards the end of the century there was a steady deterioration in aesthetic standards, with mass production methods being used to meet the heavy demand. Westlake was head of the firm in 1880 and continued to his death in 1921. There are good windows at Bradfield Combust, Carlton Colville, East Bergholt, Huntingfield, Lavenham and Saxmundham, and others at Barsham, Butley, Cransford, Eyke, Halesworth, Middleton, Southwold, Sternfield and Waldringfield.

Layer, William: mason; *See* Bury St Mary

Ledger-stone: When the art and use of monumental *brasses* declined in the first half of the C17, sculpture in stone began to come into its own in our churches. But while splendid monuments may catch the eye, it often pays to drop one's gaze to the ground to those dark, massive slabs in pavements, incised with arms, crests and epitaphs. These are ledger-stones, a study in themselves, and many carry quite marvellous inscriptions which can so easily be overlooked. Two signed by the mason can be found at Brettenham and Chevington.

Leal, Valdes: artist; *See* Wrentham

Lee, Lawrence: stained glass; *See* Elveden

Lehr, William: mason; *See* Rougham

Lenten veil: It was the custom in medieval times to 'curtain off' the *altar* and also the *rood* during Lent with a veil. This was suspended from *corbels,* or hooks, of which a few examples remain in Suffolk churches set in the walls, as at Monk Soham, North Cove and Troston, or in the roof, as at Bury St Mary's (pulleys) and Metfield. Some churches follow the custom today by veiling the *reredos*.

Lights: The space between the vertical divisions of a window or *screen*. So if a window has just one centre *mullion*, it is a two-light window. Not to be confused with an occasional usage of 'light' in the sense of candles or lamps kept burning before images, the *rood*, and tabernacles.

Lift-gate: *See* Badley, Little Wenham

Lilly, Royal William: stained glass; *See* Wrentham

Lily crucifix: *See* Great Glemham, Long Melford

Linen-fold panelling: This was an innovation in wood carving in the *Tudor* period – an elegant representation in wood of linen laid in crisp vertical folds. Often seen on church furnishings old and new.

Little Livermere: *See* Little Saxham

Lizard door rings: *See* Brockley, Cavendish, Great Thurlow, Withersfield

Lockwood, Alfred: architect; *See* Woodbridge St John

Lofft, Capel: reformer & man of letters; *See* Troston

Lofft, Robert Emelyn: carver; *See* Troston

Lombardic script: A calligraphic form of writing which developed in Italy after the Roman and Byzantine periods. A variant of it was used for papal documents until the early C13. From time to time it is found on tombs and memorials in English churches.

Long and short work: Distinctive of *Saxon* work, upright stone alternating with flat slabs in the *quoins* at the corners of buildings. There are examples at Benhall, Claydon, Debenham, Gosbeck and Hemingstone. (See also Appendix 2 – Styles of architecture)

Lonsdale, Horatio Walter (1844-1919): an artist in stained glass who designed much of the glass produced by W.G. Saunders, particularly for the architect William Burges. He later executed many windows of his own which illustrate

the high quality of his draughtsmanship, and some are extremely attractive, as at Freckenham.

Low, E.: architect; *See* Sutton

Lowndes, Mary (1857-1929): *Arts & Crafts* stained glass artist. A pupil of *Henry Holiday*, she designed her first window in 1885 and soon after taught herself the techniques of glass painting. She worked with, and was influenced by, *Christopher Whall*, and in 1897 in partnership with A.J. Drury she set up Lowndes & Drury. Known as 'The Glass House', their studio and workshop in Fulham became a focal point, and the staff were at the disposal of any artist who needed them. Mary Lowndes designed and made many fine windows between 1890 and the 1920s but the only example of her work in Suffolk is at Snape.

Low side windows: Almost as much nonsense has been written about low side windows as about *weeping chancels*. These small, square or oblong windows were usually low down in the s. wall of the *chancel*, just e. of the chancel arch, and fitted with shutters so that the window could be opened. It has been suggested that they were for lepers to look in and thus share in the mass – a ridiculous assertion, since not even in medieval times would lepers have been allowed to roam at leisure. Most authorities agree that they were inserted so that a bell could be rung through the open window at the point in the mass when the priest raises the consecrated bread and cup for the congregation to see. So that: 'people who have not leisure daily to be present at Mass may, wherever they are in houses or fields, bow their knees' (Archbishop Peckham, 1281). A hand bell may have been used but sometimes a bell was housed in a turret on the roof (see *sanctus bell*). Occasionally, the low side window was incorporated in a larger window but many of the separate ones have been blocked up. Interesting examples can be seen at Barsham, Combs, Great Livermere, Gazeley, Hopton (double), Levington, Newbourne, Raydon, Shottisham, Troston (original shutter), Waldringfield, Westleton, and Weston.

Luard, John: artist; *See* Alderton

Luini, Bernardino: artist; *See* Orford

Luxford, H.W.: stained glass; *See* Herringswell, Stanton

Lych-gate: The word 'lych' comes from the *Anglo-Saxon* 'lic' or 'lich', and from the German 'leiche', all meaning corpse. The purpose of the lych-gate is to provide shelter and resting place for coffin bearers on the way to the church. In former times, the lych-gate would have seats and a coffin table, on which the coffin would be set. Poor people who could not afford a coffin might be placed, temporarily, in the parish coffin; but otherwise they would be wrapped in a sheet and placed straight onto the coffin table, where they would be received by the priest, who here speaks the first sentences of the burial service. Ancient lych-gates are rare, but there are good C19 examples at Aspall, Barsham, Felixstowe St Peter & St Paul, Framsden and Sibton, with excellent *Arts & Crafts* designs at Brantham and Kelsale.

Lyhart, Walter, Bishop: *See* Hoxne

Lyne, Revd. Joseph Leycester: *See* **Ignatius, Father OSB**

McKean, Mary & Bessie: stained glass; *See* Saxmundham

Magnus, -: monumental mason; *See* Great Barton

Maile, George & Sons: stained glass; *See* Blundeston, Capel St Mary, Cockfield, Dunwich, Great Bricett, Kessingland, Somerleyton

Makepiece, John: joiner; *See* Snape

Manning, Samuel: Sculptor; *See* Stanstead, Sudbury All Saints

Marriage, Degrees of: *See* Tables of Kindred and affinity

Marriott, Lucy: stained glass; *See* Woolpit

Marshall, Edward: statuary; *See* Sotterley

Marsham, Warren & Taylor: architects; *See* Ipswich St Peter

Martin, Maria: *See* Polstead

Martin, Miles: joiner; *See* Darsham

Martin, Thomas: antiquary; *See* Palgrave

Marven, John: bell ringer; *See* Copdock

Mary Tudor, Queen of France: *See* Bury St Mary, Westhorpe

Marys: *See* **Three Marys**

Mason, Francis: divine, author; *See* Orford

Mason, Hilda: designer; *See* Orford

Mason, John: mason; *See* Thornham Parva

Mason's marks: It was the practice of medieval masons to identify their work by cutting an individual symbol on selected blocks of stone.

Mass dials: *See* **Scratch dials**

Mayer & Co: stained glass; *See* Great Bealings, Somerleyton

Mayes, Thomas: sculptor; *See* Helmingham

Mayne of Butley: joiner; *See* Rendlesham

Mead, Rose: artist; *See* Bury St Mary

Mellers, Sir George: broderer; *See* Newmarket All Saints

Mensa slabs: Before the *Reformation*, all *altars* were of stone, topped with a slab or 'mensa' (Latin for table). Each had five crosses carved upon it, one at each corner and one in the centre, representing the *five wounds of Christ*. When *chantries* were done away with, so were their altars. But stone High Altars remained, and in the reign of Edward VI (a convinced Protestant) a movement was led by two of his bishops to have them removed and replaced by wooden tables. This was realised in 1550 when every bishop was ordered to make this change in all the churches in his diocese. Some were buried in hopes of a return to the old way, others were used as paving stones, but most were destroyed. Examples survive at Barnby, Barsham, Cowlinge (huge), Denston, Flempton, Little Whelnetham, Mendlesham, Mildenhall (dated), North Cove, Thelnetham, Thorpe Morieux, Westhorpe, Wilby, Worlingham, and Wrentham. See also *consecration crosses*.

Merriman, Henry Seton: author; *See* Melton

Methold, Henry, Sir: joiner; *See* Hepworth

Micklethwaite, John: architect; *See* Orford

Middleton Murray, John: author; *See* Thelnetham

Mileham, C.H.: architect; *See* Needham Market

Miller, William: stained glass; *See* Bedingfield, Worlingworth

Milner-Gibson, Thomas: political reformer; *See* Theberton

Milnes, Thomas: sculptor; *See* Great Barton

Milton, John: author; *See* Stowmarket

Miriam: A prophetess who was Aaron's sister. After Pharaoh's host had perished in the Red Sea, Miriam led the women with timbrels and dances saying 'Sing ye to the Lord, for he hath triumphed gloriously' (Exodus 15:20). Seen in stained glass at Spexhall.

Misericords: Ancient stalls with hinged seats remain in the *chancels* of many churches. Underneath, the tip-up seats are often carved, generally with very free expression and sometimes with exuberant irreverence and humour: mythical beasts, scenes from legend, charming domestic vignettes, satirical caricature. All are worth examining closely, wherever they are found. On the leading edge of these seats is usually a smooth, hollowed surface on which, during long services, the elderly, or the just plain sleepy, could lean and rest. Thus the name, from the Latin 'misericordia', pity, compassion. There are good examples at Bildeston, Denham, Framsden, Lavenham, Norton, Southwold, Stoke by Nayland, Stowlangtoft and Ufford.

Mitford, Revd. John: author; *See* Benhall

Montford, Paul: sculptor; *See* Reyden

Moore, Albert: stained glass; *See* Claydon, Dallinghoo, Little Bealings, Melton, Stowlangtoft

Moore, Arthur Louis (1849-1939): Stained glass artist. He began in partnership with S. Gibbs in 1871 but soon set up his own firm, and his son Eustace joined him in 1896. They produced over 1000 windows, most of which are typical of the late-C19/early-C20 commercial style. Sometimes, however, there were better things – the window at Reydon, for example; more of their work can be seen at Frostenden

(where they provided a *reredos* as well), Hollesley, Melton, and Woodbridge St Mary.

Moore, Hector: metal worker; *See* Kesgrave

Moore, Henry: sculptor; *See* Barham

Moore, Leslie: designer; *See* Haverhill

Moore, M.: artist; *See* Tannington

Moorhens, Carving of: *See* Acton

More, Sir Thomas (1478-1535): Humanist, author of *Utopia*, Speaker, Lord Chancellor. The 'Man for all seasons', he was martyred by Henry VIII for refusing to accept the Act of Supremacy and acknowledge the king as head of the church. Having indicted Wolsey and succeeded him as Chancellor, he was a close friend of the king until the final rupture. On the scaffold he said that he 'died the king's good servant but God's first', and his portrait can be found in Felixstowe St John the Baptist.

Morris, William & Co: Stained glass manufacturers. William Morris (1834-96) was a designer, poet, and prolific writer on artistic and other matters. In 1861, he drew together a group of artists which included Burne-Jones, Ford Madox Brown, Rossetti and Philip Webb, to found Morris, Marshall, Faulkner & Co. The firm revolutionised British taste in furnishing and interior decoration and, from the outset, stained glass was an important part of their activities. Morris assumed responsibility for colour, and all cartoons were by the partners themselves. Rossetti dropped out in 1865 and from 1869 Burne-Jones was much more active, becoming sole designer in 1875, after which Morris gave only occasional attention to the work. Burne-Jones died two years after Morris in 1898 and thereafter John Henry Dearle was chief designer. He had worked with Morris for many years and echoed his style and that of Burne-Jones. Good design and technical excellence, combined with Morris's genius for colour, put their windows in a class apart, par-ticularly between 1865 and 1875. Although Dearle followed them faithfully, reusing and adapting many of their designs, his work in the 1920s was an empty continuation of an outdated style. The firm closed in 1940. Windows by them are to be found at Bacton, Bedingfield, Freston, Great Barton, Hopton,

Thornham Magna, Kelsale, Westerfield and Whitton.

Mouchette: A *tracery* shape or motif, used principally during the *Decorated* period early in the C14. It is a curved dagger or spearhead shape, *cusped* and arched inside.

Mouseproof organ pedals: *See* Letheringham, Westley

Mullion: Vertical bar dividing *lights* in a window.

Munnings, Sir Alfred: *See* Dennington, Stradbroke

Murat, Caroline, Princess: *See* Ringsfield

Narvic naval action: *See* Thurston

Nave: The main 'body' of a church – from the Latin 'navis', a ship. Traditionally the nave was for the congregation, the *chancel* being for the clergy. Indeed, so much was it a preserve of the people that once services were over, it was used for parish meetings, in some places as a courtroom, and sometimes for the performance of mystery plays. Its upkeep was normally the responsibility of the people, just as the chancel was maintained by the priest.

Nelson, Thomas Marsh: architect; *See* Stowupland

New England Company: *See* Eriswell

Nicholson, Archibald Keith: stained glass; *See* Barnham, Aldburgh, Great Ashfield, Hawstead, Ickworth, Knodishall, Yoxford

Nicholson, Charles, Sir: designer; *See* Sotterley

Nine Mens' Morris: *See* Cavendish (?)

Nine Orders of Angels: This theme of the heavenly hierarchy was rarely used by medieval artists, but Southwold has a fine example on its screen, Ufford has a part sequence, and there is another not far away at Barton Turf, Norfolk. The Bible references are to be found in the first chapter of Ezekiel, Isaiah 6:2, and in *St Paul's* letters to the Ephesians and Colossians. However, it was Dionysius the Areopagite, a C6 mystic, who defined the Nine Orders, and identified their mission as God's mediators. He

arranged them in three choirs, and in this order: Seraphim (who inspire man towards divine love); Cherubim (source of endless wisdom); Thrones (flaming wheels with eyes, set about God's throne); Dominions (instruments of the Almighty's will); Virtues, Powers, Principalities, Archangels, and Angels. Of these only the last two act as messengers between Earth and Heaven.

Nollekens, Joseph (1737-1823): Nollekens was to portrait sculpture what Sir Joshua Reynolds was to portrait painting – the choice of fashionable London. Having spent a decade in Italy in pursuit of his art he had a ready-made reputation on his return. Adept in every form, from chimney pieces to memorial tablets, his busts were outstanding and they made his fortune. He had a complementary genius for meanness which he shared with his wife (see Smith's *Nollekens & His Times*, the most pitiless and uncomplimentary biography imaginable). There are memorials by him at Helmingham and Saxmundham.

Norman: The Romanesque form of architecture, with its distinctive rounded arches and massive pillars, introduced to England following the Norman Conquest of 1066. See Appendix 2 – Styles of Architecture.

North, Sir Henry: author; *See* Mildenhall

Nuttgens, J.E.: stained glass; *See* Horringer, Kedington

Oberammergau work Lang family: *See* Bury St John, Capel St Mary

O'Connor, Arthur and William: Stained glass artists whose father Michael began in Dublin as an heraldic painter before moving to London in 1823. He had studied with *Thomas Willement* and worked with *Pugin* and *Butterfield*. He took his sons into partnership in the 1850s and when Arthur died in 1873, William George Taylor joined the firm and managed it from 1877 onwards. Much of the O'Connors' work is distinguished by fine colour and an effective deployment of lead lines – as at Saxmundham; there are more of their windows at Bardwell, Brent Eleigh, Fressingfield, Groton, Hessett, Ipswich St Mary le Tower, Rickinghall Superior and Stradbroke.

Ogee: This is a flowing, 'S' shaped arch or moulding – convex and concave curves combining. Usually they are not large because, by their very nature, they cannot carry heavy loads; but their grace lends them to the heads of canopies. Adorned with *crocketting*, ogee arches are still more attractive. They came into general use in the C14, particularly in the development of the sumptuous windows of the late *Decorated* period. (*See* Appendix 2 – Styles of Architecture)

Organists, Blind: *See* Assington, Bramford

Overall, John, Bishop: *See* Hadleigh

Owen, Ann: stained glass; *See* Heveningham

Pace, George: architect; *See* Rushmere St Andrew

Page, George, the Suffolk Giant: *See* Newbourne

Palimpsest brass: A memorial *brass* which has been turned over and used again by re-engraving it on its plain side. The word is also used in relation to writing material which has been re-used and comes from the Greek palimpsestos – to rub smooth.

Palmer, William: sculptor; *See* Little Saxham

Pamment: An unglazed flooring tile used widely in East Anglia; the average size is 9in. square, 2in. thick.

Pamment, John: joiner; *See* Stowupland

Parclose screen: The screens which separate *chantry* or side chapels, and/or *aisles,* from the main body of the church. See also *rood loft/screen.* The finest examples in Suffolk are at Burstall (early-C14), Dennington, Hadleigh (C15 pair) and Lavenham (C16).

Parish clerk: Not the 'clerk' to the parish council of late-Victorian local government invention, but a paid office which was for centuries of central importance in church services. The clerk lead the singing and the responses to the prayers, and was often noted for his healthy 'Amen' at the end of prayers and the sermon. Sometimes he filled the role of choirmaster; certainly he would 'give the notes' on a pitch pipe, just as the conductor gives them today to unaccompanied choirs. After the *Reformation* in the C16, the clerk continued to exercise his role; indeed, the replanning of church interiors to meet the new Protestant requirements gave him a special seat in the *three-decker pulpits* which appeared at this

time. In the C17, under James I and later Charles II, the parish clerks, who had the dignity of being a London Company, were given new Charters which stipulated that:

> every person that is chosen Clerk of the Parish should first give sufficient proof of his abilities to sing at least the tunes which are used in the parish churches.

He sang on until soon after Victoria ascended the throne, when most of his duties were given to curates (a late version of his special pew survives at Carlton). Then came the local government acts of the late C19, which finally consigned him to history and drew the line under a 700-year-old tradition.

Parish guilds: *See* **Guilds/guild altars**

Parker, Matthew, Archbishop: *See* Stoke by Clare

Parsons, Samuel: organ builder; *See* Swefling

Passion emblems: *See* **Instruments of the Passion**

Paten: a shallow dish or plate (normally of silver) used for the bread at the Eucharist.

Patent Marble Works: monumental masons; *See* Wherstead

Paterae: Ornaments in bas-relief, often used to enrich mouldings.

Pearce, Walter J.: stained glass; *See* Martlesham

Pearce & Cutler: stained glass; *See* Felixstowe St Andrew

Pediment: The low triangular gable used in classical building but often employed on classically styled monuments in churches. When the centre is cut back it is called a 'broken pediment'.

Pelican in her piety: The pelican has long had a special place in religious symbolism and may often be seen in medieval carving and embellishment. There is a legend that the bird tore its own breast to feed its young upon its own blood – the source of the idea being that the tip of the pelican's bill, which usually rests on its chest, is touched with red. In medieval art the ungainliness is transformed and its legend transmuted into a symbolism of Man's fall and redemption through the Passion of Christ. Here we find that the parent bird was said to kill its young in a moment of irritation – then, 'on the third day', to restore them to life by tearing its breast and letting its own blood pour over them. In the C18 and early C19 a female figure with the pelican signified Benevolence. Examples are plentiful.

Pendred, Lough: carver; *See* Eye

Penrice, Thomas: architect; *See* Stoven (?)

Pentney, Jack: designer; *See* St Edmundsbury cathedral, Mendlesham

Pepys, Samuel: *See* Little Saxham

Perpendicular: The great age of church building, in the second half of the C14 and through the C15, in the style characterised by soaring upward lines in great windows and majestic towers. See Appendix 2 – Styles of Architecture.

Pevsner, Sir Nikolaus: Author of the monumental and remarkable undertaking, *The Buildings of England* series – 46 volumes, written between 1951 and 1974, meticulously recording the principal buildings of every county in England, and masterminded throughout by Pevsner himself. His volume on Suffolk appeared in 1961 and another revision is expected.

Pheifer, -: sculptor; *See* Ipswich St Mary le Tower

Phipson, Richard Makilwaine (1827-84): As an architect he was not outstanding and sometimes verged on the incompetent, but he was very active in Norfolk and Suffolk from 1850 onwards. As joint diocesan surveyor from 1871 until his death, he had a hand in most of the restorations during that important period and by then had become well known, particularly for his work at St Mary le Tower, Ipswich and St Peter Mancroft, Norwich. See also Bentley, Brandeston, Burgate, Cratfield, Great Finborough, Holbrook, Ipswich (St. Mary at Stoke, St Mary at the elms and St Matthew), Mendham, Nacton, Newbourne, Playford, Ringhall, Saxmundham, S. Elmham St James, S.Elmham St Margaret, Stoke Ash, Stowmarket, Thorndon, Weybread, Wherstead, Whitton, Winston, Woodbridge, Woolpit and Yoxford.

Physick, Edward J.: sculptor; *See* Layham, Walton, Wherstead

Pier: The architectural term for a column or pillar.

Pietà: A carving or painting of the *Blessed Virgin* as Our Lady of Sorrows, seated with the dead Christ laid across her knees. There are examples at Bardwell, Cavendish, Great Saxham, Horringer, Long Melford, Nowton and Orford.

Pilaster: A miniature pillar, rectangular in section, usually based in style on one of the classical orders of architecture, and normally applied to a wall.

Pillar piscine: *See* **Piscina**

Piscina (angle/double/pillar): A stone basin near an *altar* (its presence today is sometimes the only indication that there was once altar nearby). In its simplest form it is merely a depression in a window sill but usually it is set into a niche in the wall below an arch or canopy, sometimes projecting outwards on a bowl, which in turn may be supported by a small pillar. Occasionally too a piscina may be found let into a pillar. The piscina was used for cleansing the communion vessels after mass, thus it has a drain hole in its basin, which allows the water used in the cleansing to run down into consecrated ground. It is obligatory that where water has been blessed, or has come into contact with anything consecrated, it must be returned to earth. Sometimes there is a small shelf in the piscina niche called a *credence shelf.* The angle piscina is one built into the angle of a window or *sedilia*, and opened out on two sides, often affording the opportunity for beautiful carving and design. Double piscinas (two side by side) may occasionally be found. These had but a short span of fashion in the late C13 to early C14: one was used by the priest for the cleaning of the vessels, the other for washing of his own hands. A pillar piscina is not, as the name might imply, a piscina set into a pillar; but a piscina which protrudes from a wall, its bowl and drain standing on a miniature pillar, either attached to or standing clear of the wall. A *corbel* piscina has, instead of a pillar, its bowl supported by a corbel or pendant.

Pistell, William: monumental mason; *See* Easton

Pitts, William: traveller; *See* Monewden

Plate tracery: Tracery in the heads of windows where the pattern is cut directly through the masonry; as distinct from bar tracery, which is constructed in separate pieces. See *Early English* in Appendix 2 – Styles of Architecture.
Plummer, Pauline: conservator; *See* Eye, Lound

Polley, William: joiner; *See* Crowfield, Rushmere St Andrew

Pomegranate: A pagan symbol of the return of spring and of fertility which was adopted by the church to signify immortality and resurrection. The packed seeds in a single fruit made it a convenient symbol for the church itself. There are examples at Barsham, Ewarton and elsewhere. Catherine of Aragon used it as her device, as shown by the *Tudor Royal Arms* at Dallinghoo.

Poppyheads: The boldly carved floral ornament which graces the ends of benches, said to be derived from the French 'poupée', puppet, doll or figurehead. It was during the C15 that poppyheads came into being and achieved their highest artistic expression. The carvers seem to have been given a free hand, and often worked animals, grotesques and faces into their designs. Some Victorian craftsmen like *Henry Ringham* were capable of producing poppyheads that are well up to the medieval standard.

Porches: It was not until the C14 that porches came to be regarded as an essential part of the church plan, and few are earlier than that. It explains, incidentally, why *scratch dials* will often be found beside the inner door, inside the porch, where the sun could not possibly reach them, the porch being a later addition. Once established, the porch assumed a practical importance which we tend to forget today. Services of baptism began here; sentences were spoken from the burial service, after the first pause in the *lych-gate*; part of the wedding service was conducted here; in the porch the kneeling penitent received absolution; and the porch was one of the 'stations' in the regular Sunday and Feast Day processions. Sometimes, as at Woodbridge, the porch contained a dole cupboard where bread and other charities were distributed, and it was the place where debts, tithes and church dues were traditionally paid, along with much other civil and legal business. Some porches also have an

upper room to house a priest, and some were later used to house the first village school.

Porter, Thomas: architect; *See* Kirkley

Potter, Thomas: bell founder; *See* Boxford, Market Weston

Powell, Adam: mason; *See* Walberswick

Powell, Christopher Charles: stained glass; *See* Nacton

Powell, James & Sons: Stained glass manufacturers. Founded in 1844, the business had one of the longest histories in the trade and did not close until 1973. It was among the most important and progressive firms, making a significant contribution both in technology and in the art form. Many of their designs came from artists of the calibre of Burne-Jones, *Henry Holiday* and *Christopher Whall*. Good examples may be found at Aspall, Felixstowe St John the Baptist, Higham and Saxmundham, with others at Bungay Holy Trinity and St Mary, Campsea Ash, Carlton Colville, Erwarton, Great Glemham, Hepworth, Iken, Kelsale (patterns), Shimpling, Stutton, Thurston, Waldringfield, Whepstead and Woodbridge; they also provided tiles at Harkstead.

Powell, John Hardman: stained glass; *See* Sudbury St Peter

Pownall, Leonard A.: artist; *See* Ipswich Holy Trinity

Powys, John Cowper: author; *See* Swefling

Prayer book churches: A phrase used to describe those churches where the furnishings and layout still embody the great shift of emphasis in church worship that came, first with the *Reformation* and then with the Puritans. The old, and strict, division of priest in *chancel* from people in *nave* was put away, and the English prayer book of 1549 required the laity to take part in all of the service; matins and evensong were to be conducted from the chancel and everybody had to hear the Lessons. The *altar* became 'the table' for the first time in the 1552 revision. After the Civil War, Sunday services (except on infrequent Sacrament Sundays) were conducted entirely from the reading desk, and soon the convenient reading desk-cum-pulpit became the rule (see *three-decker pulpits*). In the late C17 and C18 virtually every church in the land had its pews (often enclosed for each family – see *box pews*) arranged to focus on the reading desk and pulpit. Then, in the 1830s, a 'new wave' of churchmen were inspired by *Pugin* and John Newman's Oxford Movement, to sweep away these things. Their vision was to have truly Gothic churches again, and C18 domestic church interiors were anathema. Today, very few of the sensible and seemly furnishings of the Age of Reason are to be found, but Withersdale is a lovely example of a C17 interior, and Ramsholt is an equally charming later version.

Preaching/churchyard crosses: The medieval churchyard was also a gathering place, and sometimes a market and fairground. Most of them had a preaching cross of stone, raised on steps so that the people could gather round it to hear their priest or an itinerant friar. Sometimes the stump or just the base survives, as at Athelington, Brockley, Earl Soham, Elmswell, Hawstead, Hessett, Mutford, Rickinghall Inferior, Walberswick, Woolpit and Worlingworth. There is the head of a C10 cross above the altar at Kedington.

Preedy, Frederick: stained glass; *See* Badley, Little Thurlow, Whitton

Pre-Raphaelites: The Pre-Raphaelite Brother-hood was a group of Victorian artists who sought to go back to principles that were followed before the Italian master Raphael (d.1520) imposed his mark. The Brotherhood had only three members, Rossetti, Millais and Holman Hunt, and lasted only five years from its establishment in 1848. But its pre-occupation with biblical and literary subjects and the artists' urge for 'social realism', influenced several other artists, among them Burne-Jones. It was he who later, with *William Morris*, briefly tried to revive the Brotherhood. Inevitably the Pre-Raphaelite movement left its impression on the church art of the period, particularly in stained glass.

Pretty, Edith: *See* Sutton

Priest's door: Most *chancels* have a small door, usually on the s. side, which was the priest's 'private entrance'. Before the *Reformation*, the chancel was the priest's particular responsibility (only occasionally entered by the laity) while the parishioners looked after the *nave*. Interestingly, however, Cratfield parish records show that the parishioners made sure that they had a key.

Prior, E.S.: architect; *See* Brantham, Kelsale

Prisoners' pews: *See* Cowlinge

Prynne, Edward: stained glass; *See* Bradfield St George
Prynne, G.F.: designer; *See* Rattlesden

Pugin, Augustus Welby Northmore (1812-52): English architect and designer. After intense study of medieval buildings he established himself as an expert and designed much of the detail used on the Houses of Parliament. He had become a Roman Catholic by this time and much of his work was for that church. It was largely by his influence and through his writings that Gothic was revived as a full-blooded style. He worked with Sir Charles Barry at Westminster but illness dogged his later years and he died young.

Pulham, Roger: organ builder; *See* Chelmondiston

Purbeck marble: References to Purbeck marble are frequently in relation to *fonts*. The first wave of fonts in this material came during the *Norman* period, and it was used for long afterwards. The grey stone is not in fact marble at all, but a hard limestone full of shells. Although much of it is now eroded it originally took a high polish. It comes from strata stretching from the Isle of Purbeck, the peninsula off s.e. Dorset (famous for its quarries for a thousand years) and northwards through to Aylesbury.

Purlin: The purlin is the main horizontal supporting beam of a roof. See *Roofs*, fig. 4.

Put-log holes: The holes where the horizontal members of the (timber) scaffolding slotted into the walls during construction.

Putti (singular, putto): Little naked cherub boys first seen in that form in the work of *Renaissance* artists, and regularly in the work of C18/C19 sculptors in England on monuments and tombs. It is possible that they have their origin in the naked Eros and Mercury of classical, pagan belief – another example of the church using an older tradition for its own purposes.

Pyx/pyx canopy: The pyx is a silver container in which the consecrated bread is 'reserved' for the sick. Before the *Reformation* it was covered with a cloth and suspended above the *High altar*. No medieval example survives, and Hessett owns the only remaining pyx cloth. A C15 oak pyx canopy has been restored for use at Dennington, one of only four possible examples. Nowadays, the sacrament is usually reserved in an *aumbry* or in a tabernacle on the altar.

Quail, Jane: carver; *See* Horham

Quail, Paul: stained glass; *See* Hopton St Margaret, Somerleyton, Swefling, Walton St Mary

Quarry: A diamond-shaped pane of glass.

Quatrefoils: *See* Foils

Queen posts: Upright roof beams set in pairs on horizontal cross or *tie-beams* and thrusting up on each side to the main horizontal supporting beams, or *purlins*, of the roof. Designed, like the *king post*, to prevent sag and give greater stability. See *Roofs*.

Quoins: The outside corner stones at the angles of buildings. See also *long and short work*.

Raedwald, King of East Anglia: *See* Rendlesham

Ralph's Hole: *See* Hemingstone

Ranger, William: architect; *See* Bury St John, Westley

Rawlins, Thomas: statuary; *See* Mendham

Reay, John: artist; *See* Worlingworth

Rebus: A punning representation of a name or word by the use of symbols, normally in churches referring to the name of the place or the name of a donor.

Reeve, Jonathan: carver; *See* Ipswich, St Mary le Tower

Reformation: In particular terms, the great religious movement in western Europe during the C16, founded on a return to biblical sources and their fresh interpretation, which led to the rejection of Roman and papal authority and the establishment of Protestant churches. In England the original motivations were more basic, being political and economic, rather than theological. Firstly, a ruthless, single-minded, and wholly autocratic monarch in Henry VIII, intent on putting away one wife and taking another by whom he could beget an heir. Secondly, his calculating eye on the wealth of the monasteries

backed by his aristocracy and gentry, who were avid for land and property. Even when he had broken with Rome, however, Henry did his best to minimise the impression of any break with the tradition begun in England by St Augustine a thousand years earlier. The true religious, reforming Reformation came with his son, the boy-king Edward VI, who though young, was a fanatical Protestant

Regency: Period in English architecture 1811-1820 taking its name from George the Prince Regent.

Regnart, Charles: monumental mason; *See* Hadleigh, Higham St Mary, Mendlesham,

Reliquary/reliquary chamber: A container for relics. The bodies of saints and martyrs were venerated by the early church and wherever possible an *altar* would contain, or have housed nearby, a portion of bone or object associated with a saint. Some became famous objects of pilgrimage and a source of revenue for the church. There is a reliquary chamber at Gedding and possible examples at S. Elmham St James and Ipswich St Margaret, and a suggested illustration at Great Glemham.

Renaissance: A movement which began in Italy during the C14 in which there was a startling rebirth of culture, particularly in the arts and literature, which drew its inspiration from the classical models of Greece and Rome. It spread to the rest of Europe during the C16 and the style of architecture and decoration which originated in Florence in the early C15 gradually replaced the Gothic tradition. (See also *Jacobean* and *Caroline* in Appendix 2 – Styles of Archi-tecture)

Reyntiens, Patrick: stained glass; *See* Aldburgh

Reredos: A screening at the back of an *altar*, usually richly embellished in painting or carving. Few old examples remain, many having disappeared at the *Reformation* and in the century following, but there is a C16 majolica panel at Barsham. (See also **Retable**)

Reserved Sacrament: In some churches portions of bread and wine that have been consecrated are specially housed in a *pyx*, *aumbry* or *tabernacle* in order that they may be taken by the priest to the sick or dying without delay.

Respond: A half-pillar attached to a wall, which

supports an arch, most often seen at the ends of *arcades*.

Restoration: The period from 1660, following the restoration of the monarchy after the Civil War and Commonwealth, and the accession of Charles II.

Retable: A shelf or ledge at the back of an *altar* on which statues, lights or crosses could stand. The term can also apply to a painted or carved panel in the same position. (See also *Reredos*)

Reticulated: Latin, 'rete' a net; 'reticulum', a bag of network) A form of 'flowing' window *tracery* in a net pattern which was developed during the first half of the C14 (see Appendix 2 – Styles of Architecture, fig. 17).

Reve, Roger: bell founder; *See* Barton Mills

Reyce, Robert: antiquary; *See* Preston

Rhinoceros carving: *See* Elmswell, Great Bealings

Rickards, Lucy: stained glass; *See* Woolpit

Ringham, Henry (1806-1866): Master joiner and carver. During the C19, when so many churches were restored, the standard of crafts-manship was high and, because methods and tools had not changed significantly, many joiners and wood-carvers were able to match the work of their C15 predecessors. In this, no one excelled Henry Ringham. He came to Ipswich from Lincolnshire as an unlettered teenager, and by a mixture of perseverance and native genius made himself the master of Gothic woodwork. He devoted his life to the restoration of churches, and in 1843 was entrusted with his first big commission at Woolpit. Roofs and benches were his speciality and before he died he had worked on 83 churches in the county including Great Bealings, Great Glemham, Ipswich St Mary le Tower, Newbourne, Peasenhall, Sotherton, Stutton, Walton, and Wherstead (his last commission).

Rishangles: *See* Mendlesham, Thorndon

Roberts, Green & Richards: architects; *See* Oulton Broad, St Mark

Robins' nests: *See* Blythburgh, Ringsfield

Rococo: C18 furniture or architecture charac-terised by an elaborately ornamental style of decoration with asymmetrical patterns.

Rogationtide: *See* Blythburgh

Rood screen/loft/beam/stair: The rood (Old English for wood) is the cross with the figure of the crucified Christ, the dominant symbol of atonement. Before the *Reformation* all churches were divided in two: the *chancel* for the priests, the *nave* for the people. Between them was a wooden screen (often with a door) which stretched from pillar to pillar under the chancel arch, and in some cases right across the church. This screen is known as the rood screen because above it stood (or hung) the great crucifix, the rood itself. This sometimes stood on a separate beam (the rood beam) and was normally flanked by figures of the *Blessed Virgin* and *St John*. In many cases there was a loft built above the screen so that the images could be maintained (they sometimes had special clothes) and to carry *lights*. On occasion, the loft housed singers and during the mass the Gospel was read from there. Access to the loft was by stairs in one or both of the side walls. At the *Reformation* the rood and its images were almost universally torn down and destroyed in violent reaction against Rome and 'popery'. The fact that so many screens survive is due to Queen Elizabeth who, in a Royal Order of 1561, directed that while the great rood and its figures should go, the screens themselves should remain, and be topped with a suitable crest or with the *Royal Arms* (Cratfield's loft was taken down in that year). Where screen as well as rood had already been destroyed, a new screen – or 'partition', as the wording had it – was to be constructed: the Elizabethans thought that the church should still be divided into two distinct sections. The issue of screens and their role was to rumble on for another century. In 1638 Richard Montague, bishop of Norwich, was pointedly asking his clergy:

> Is your chancel divided from the nave or body of your church, with a partition of stone, boards, wainscot, grates or otherwise? Wherein is there a decent strong door to open and shut, (as occasion serveth) with lock and key, to keep out boys, girls, or irreverent men and women? And are dogs kept from coming to besoil or profane the Lord's table?

While rood stairs and screens are common,

rood lofts are very rare, but there are splendid reconstruction s at Eye and Lound by *Comper* and another at Rattlesden. There are remains of an external rood at Parham, and rood beams are still in place at Athelington, Barsham, Bentley, Debenham, Denston, Freston, Gisleham, Hacheston, Hargrave, Hemingstone, Kesgrave, Levington, Mettingham, Monk Soham, Onehouse, Rushbrooke, Ufford, Westerfield, Wissett (stump) and Worlington.

Roofs: The development, structural variety and embellishment of church roofs is a fascinating field. Here is a potted guide to a complex subject. Coupled rafter roofs are a simple variety, and serve to indicate the main components (fig. 1). The principal rafters, the feet of which are secured to a *wall plate*, have a *collar beam* to support them and to prevent sagging. More support is given by the collar braces, with struts lower down giving more strength. Another framing system is the scissor beam (fig. 2), which can exist with the cross beams only, or with a supporting collar. As a precaution against spreading, a tie-beam was often added between the wall plates (fig. 3); but as tie-beams have a tendency to sag in the middle a central *king-post* served to prevent this. The *arch-braced* construction is where the

roof is carried on a braced arch which incorporates 'in one' the strut, collar brace and collar beam (fig. 4). The function of the tie-beam has already been seen in fig. 3. With a low-pitched roof, it is often used simply with struts upward to the principal rafters, and downward on brace and *wall post* to a *corbel* set into the wall (fig. 5) well below the wall plates. With the advent of the *hammerbeam* development (fig. 6), a new splendour was added to the roof builder's art. Instead of a tie-beam spanning wall to wall, there are hammer-beam brackets, from which spring a vertical strut, upward to the principal rafter at its intersection with the *purlin* (fig. 4), the main horizontal

Fig. 3

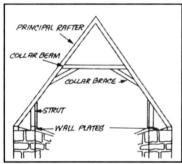

Fig. 1

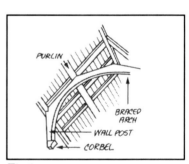

Fig. 4

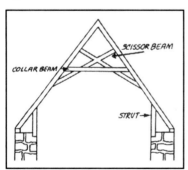

Fig. 2

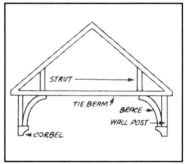

Fig. 5

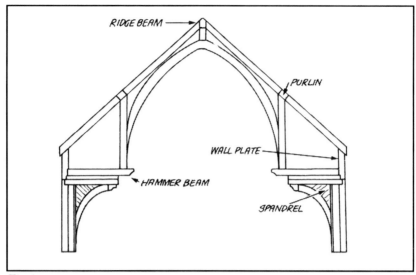

Fig. 6

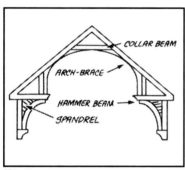

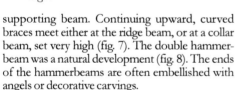

Fig. 7

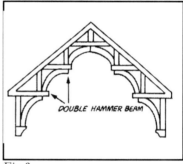

Fig. 8

supporting beam. Continuing upward, curved braces meet either at the ridge beam, or at a collar beam, set very high (fig. 7). The double hammer-beam was a natural development (fig. 8). The ends of the hammerbeams are often embellished with angels or decorative carvings.

Rope, Ellen Mary: Sculptress, one of the talented Suffolk family and aunt of Margaret E.A. Rope. She designed many memorial tablets and specialised in plaster models and bas reliefs where bronze and marble were too expensive. Her work can be found in Salisbury cathedral, Maritzburg cathedral S. Africa, and in Suffolk at Aldeburgh, Blaxhall, Bury St Edmunds All Saints, Leiston, and Stowupland.

Rope, Margaret Agnes (1882-1953): *Arts & Crafts* stained glass worker. A Roman Catholic, she studied at Birmingham and her first

commission in 1910 was the w. window of Shrewsbury R.C. cathedral. Moving to London and working in 'The Glass House' (see *Lowndes, Mary*), she collaborated with her cousin *Margaret E.A. Rope*. Their first work was a memorial window at Blaxhall in 1911. In 1923 she entered the Carmelite monastery at Woodbridge, but was able to continue with her work on stained glass. She later moved to Quidenham, Norfolk but illness prevented much further work. Apart from Blaxhall, there is a window at Little Glemham, and others may be seen in the former Franciscan convent chapel at East Bergholt and in the Roman Catholic church at Kesgrave.

Rope, Margaret Edith Aldrich: *Arts & Crafts* stained glass worker. Born of an artistic family at Leiston, she spent her childhood at Blaxhall and studied stained glass under Alfred Drury at the Central School of Arts and Crafts. She assisted her cousin *Margaret Rope* at 'The Glass House' in making the Rope memorial window for Blaxhall in 1911, and after the war she returned to Fulham and began securing independent commissions. She continued to produce work of high quality until her retirement in the 1960s. Windows by her will be found at Barnby, Leiston and Little Glemham, with others at Earl Soham and Kesgrave Roman Catholic church.

Roubiliac, Louis François: sculptor; *See* Framlingham

Rounce, Thomas: painter; *See* Wissett

Round heads: *See* Brightwell, Kedington

Rous, John: diarist; *See* Santon Downham

Rouw, Henry: monumental mason; *See* Chelsworth, Darsham, Yoxford

Royal Arms: Many churches display Royal coats of arms, usually square and framed, painted on wood or canvas; though they may also be found in carved wood or stone, cast in plaster, or set in stained glass. Occasionally the arms are set up and painted in a lozenge shape, like a *hatchment*, but this is unusual.

It was only during the reign of Henry VIII, when he assumed complete control of the English church, that Royal Arms began to come into regular use. Catholic Queen Mary was later to order their removal, and the replacement of the old *rood lofts*. But with Elizabeth's accession, they began to reappear; indeed Elizabeth directed their use and indicated that the *tympanum* (the top part of the *chancel* arch, panelled in) was the place to display them. Inevitably many disappeared during Cromwell's Commonwealth, for in 1650 his Parliamentarians ordered 'the removal of the obnoxious Royal Arms from the churches'. The *Restoration* Parliament in 1660 made Royal Arms compulsory in all our churches, ordering that 'the Armes of the Commonwealth wherever they are standing be forthwith taken down, and the Kings Majesties armes be set up instead thereof'. The practice continued generally until Victoria's accession. Royal Arms will be found throughout the county but the following are notable: Acton and Long Melford (quality carving), Dallinghoo (Tudor), Oulton and Weston (James II); Barnby, Kessingland, and Wissett (signed); Blundeston (reused *hatchment?*);

Brampton (with quote from Samuel); Friston (v. large), and Mildenhall (huge).

Royce, N.: monumental mason; *See* Cockfield

Russell, Richard: mason; *See* Walberswick

Russells of London: organ builders; *See* Wherstead

Rutherford, Rosemary: stained glass; *See* Boxford, Hinderclay, Walsham-le-Willows

Sacheverall, Henry: divine; *See* Charsfield

Sacred monogram: The two names of Christ and Jesus, originally written in Greek, were often reduced to the first two letters, or the first, second and final, or the first and last; when written in Latin they became: IH-XP, IHC-XPC, or IC-XC. For centuries the symbol XP (known as the *Chi Rho*) was used in various forms. The name came to be written IHESUS in English and IHC became IHS. This was later taken to mean (conveniently but erroneously) 'Jesus Hominum Salvator', Jesus, Saviour of mankind.

Sacring bell: A small bell rung at that point in the mass when the priest holds up the Host above the *altar* (the action known as the Elevation). There is rare example at Hawstead and the stocks for one survive at Somersham. A panel on Badingham *font* includes an illustration.

Sacristy: A room, often with specially strengthened doors and windows, where the vestments, church plate and other valuables were stored. There is a two-storied sacristy at Dennington and other examples at Barking, Rattlesden, Hessett and elsewhere.

St Aubyn, J.P.: architect; *See* Huntingfield, Little Glemham, Sternfield, Woolverstone

Salisbury, H.J.: stained glass; *See* Kirkley, Lowestoft Christ Church, Pakefield

Salvin, Sir Anthony: *See* Flixton

Samaria, Woman of: *See* Barnby, Market Weston, Nowton, Polstead, Saxmundham, Wrentham

Sancroft, William, Archbishop: *See* Fressingfield, Withersdale

Sanctuary: That part of the church containing

the *altar* (or, if there is more than one altar, the *High altar*). It is normally bounded by the *communion rails*.

Sanctus-bell/turret/window: At the point in the mass at which the priest raises the consecrated bread and the chalice of wine for the people to see, a bell was rung (and sometimes still is) so that 'people who have not leisure daily to be present at Mass may, wherever they are in houses or fields, bow their knees' – the words of Archbishop Peckham in 1281. Some churches have a small turret on the e. gable of the *nave* to house the bell used for this purpose – there are examples at Fressingfield, Marlesford, Southwold, and Wickham Market. In other cases, a sanctus-bell window is to be found in the interior wall between tower and nave, placed so that it has a clear view of the *altar*. Such an arrangement allows a ringer to use one of the tower bells for the same purpose. See also *low side windows*.

Sanders, J.J.: monumental mason; *See* Ringsfield, South Elmham St Michael

Sanders, Fitroy Square: monumental mason; *See* Herringfleet, Kettlebugh

Sash windows: *See* Norton

Satchell & Edwards: architects; *See* Leavenheath

Saxon: The period preceding the *Norman* Conquest of 1066, a vital era in the general establishment of Christianity in these islands. (*See also* in Appendix 2 – Styles of Architecture)

Scheemakers, Peter: statuary; *See* Cowlinge

Schorne, Sir John: *See* in Appendix 1 – Saints

Sciapod: *See* Dennington

Scissors-braced roofs: A roof in which the beams are crossed and interlocked diagonally in the shape of an opened pair of scissors. See *roofs*, figs. 2 and 3.

Scott, Belinda: broderer; *See* Snape

Scott, Sir George Gilbert (1811-78): One of the leading architects of the Gothic revival in England and one of the great names of the Victorian era. Stimulated by *Pugin's* enthusiasm, he designed the Martyr's Memorial in Oxford, one of the early key works of the new movement. Prolific and successful, he worked on hundreds of churches, either as designer or restorer, and subsequently much of his work attracted bitter criticism. Westminster Abbey, Ely, Salisbury and Lichfield cathedrals all bear his mark, not to mention the Albert Memorial and St Pancras station. His one complete church in Suffolk is at Higham (St Stephen), and his most extensive restoration and rebuilding was Bury, St James, before it was promoted to cathedral status. He restored the *nave* and rebuilt the *chancel* at Woolverstone.

Scott-Moncrieff, W.: architect; *See* Tunstall

Scratch dials: On or near the s. doorways of many old churches may be seen circles incised in the stone, usually about 6in. across, with lines radiating down from a centre hole. A wooden or metal peg was put in the hole and its shadow marked the time of day, a primitive sundial, but one with a specific purpose. The marks related to the times for morning mass, noon and vespers (evensong) to assist the punctuality of both priest and people in the days before clocks and watches. Sometimes the dials were divided into four 'tides' of three hours and, occasionally, the line for mass is thicker or identified with a short cross bar. There are cases where lines have been added to the top half of the circle, no doubt by mischievous young hands, and the dials at Butley and Horham are unusual in having Roman numerals. Sotterley has a total of five, and Parham's is a late, square example. The dial at Great Bricett is possibly our earliest example, Those found within a porch were in use before the porch was built.

Screen: *See* **Rood screen**

Sedilia: These are seats (usually made into decorative and architectural features, with miniature columns, arches and canopies, and detailed carvings) on the s. side of the *chancel*. Generally there are three seats. These can be all on the same level; or 'stepped', ie, on descending levels; and/or 'graduated', ie, under separate arches but contained within a composite pattern, frieze or frame. In those cases where a simple seat is created by building a low window sill, they are called *dropped-sill sedilia*. The three seats were specifically for the priest, the deacon (who read the Gospel), and the sub-deacon (who read the Epistle). Though three seats are the norm, numbers can vary between one and eight, and they may be found beside subsidiary *altars* as well as the *High altar*. In places where the seats seem impractically low, it may well be that the floor levels have been raised as part of reconstruction or restoration (the Gothic revivalists were particularly keen on the ritual significance of steps leading up to the *sanctuary* and altar, and these were often not there originally).

Seely Suffolk: *See* Ewarton, Little Glemham, Huntingfield

Septaria: Nodules of limestone or ironstone which contain other minerals, frequently used as a building material in the s.w. of the county. It does not weather well, and some towers (like Shotley) collapsed.

Serbian army: *See* Marlesford

Serpent (musical instrument): *See* Barking

Set-off: The point at which a tower buttress 'sets-off' another stage further out from the wall it is supporting.

Seven Deadly Sins: Pride, Covetousness, Lust, Envy, Gluttony, Anger, Sloth. Pride was always pre-eminent and the others encompassed other human failings; drinking went with Gluttony, suicide was linked with Anger, and spiritual idleness was seen as a form of Sloth. Pictures of them were often placed close to the *Seven Works of Mercy* to give them greater emphasis as at Dalham, and they were occasionally used to decorate bench ends as at Blythburgh, Finningham, Tannington and Wilby. There are modern examples at Hollesley.

Seven Sacraments: The sacraments of the church are: baptism, confirmation, mass (holy communion), penance, ordination to the priesthood, marriage, and extreme unction (anointing of the dying). The theme was used to decorate a fine series of *Seven Sacrament fonts* of which there are 13 in Suffolk, 23 in Norfolk and one each in Kent and Somerset. All are octagonal and the carving in the eighth bowl panel varies. Suffolk's finest example is at Cratfield and some of the others are at Great Glemham, Melton, Monk Soham, Westhall, and Woodbridge (and with totally defaced panels at Blythburgh, Southwold and Wenhaston). They are also illustrated on bench ends at Tannington and Wilby.

Seven Works of Mercy: Sometimes called the Corporal Works of Mercy, they are: to feed the hungry, to give drink to the thirsty, to shelter strangers, to clothe the naked, to visit the sick and to visit prisoners. Derived from *St Matthew's* Gospel (25: 34-9), and

listed by St Thomas Aquinas, the six works are normally augmented by a seventh, the burial of the dead. There are examples at Barnby, Blythburgh, and Wherstead; incomplete sets in medieval glass can be seen at Combs and Hoxne and part of a set survives on a bench at Wilby.

Sewell, William: stained glass; *See* Yaxley

Sexton's wheel: *See* Yaxley

Sharp of Thetford: monumental mason; *See* Stanton

Shaw, Richard Norman: architect; *See* Kelsale

Shipmeadow: *See* **Rumburgh**

Shrigley & Hunt: stained glass; *See* Ipswich St John the Baptist

Shroud brass: A brass on which the corpse is shown wrapped in a shroud ready for burial. There are two at Lowestoft St Margaret, one at Stowmarket and another fine example at Yoxford.

Shunamite woman: *See* Rede stained glass

Sievier, Robert William: sculptor; *See* Woolverstone

Simeon: The aged and devout Jew who took the infant Christ in his arms in the Temple at Jerusalem and spoke the words known as the 'Nunc Dimittis' (Luke 2.25-35) – Flemish glass at Nowton.

Simon of Sudbury (Simon Teobald), Archbishop: *See* Sudbury St Gregory

Simpson, W.B. & Sons: stained glass; *See* Knodishall

Singleton, Robert: monumental mason; *See* Hawstead

Singleton, Thomas: monumental mason; *See* Horringer

Siren: The women (or half woman/half bird) in Greek mythology who lured unwary sailors to their rocky island with enchanting songs. A bench end carving at Dennington is a possible example.

Skeat, Francis: stained glass; *See* Chelmondiston, Laxfield

Smith, Cecil Beardmore: architect; *See* Bury All Saints

Smith, Charles: sculptor; *See* Clare

Smith, Charles Harriott: sculptor; *See* Ringsfield

Smith, Father: organ builder; *See* Edwardstone

Smith, G.E.R.: stained glass; *See* Flempton, Knodishall

Smith, William Bassett: architect; *See* Great Bealings

Smugglers: *See* Tunstall

Smyth of Woodbridge: monumental mason; *See* Wantisden, Worlingworth

Solomon, Judgement of: *See* Nowton Flemish glass

Sound holes: Instead of windows at the first floor level, some towers have square, oblong or shaped openings, often treated very decoratively. These are very common in Norfolk and their purpose is not, as might be supposed from the name, to let the sound of the bells out (the bell openings higher up do that) but to light the ringing chamber and allow the ringers to hear the bells.

Southolt: *See* Mendlesham

Soward, John: sculptor; *See* Cavendish, Thorpe Morieux

Spandrels: The almost triangular space between one side of the outer curve of an arch or the supporting braces of a roof, and the wall or upright brace, and the horizontal line above. Often filled in with tracery.

Spence, Sir Basil: architect; *See* Thornham Parva

Spooner, Charles: architect; *See* Ipswich St Bartholomew

Spooner, Charles Sidney: craftsman; *See* Hadleigh

Sprague, C.F.: architect; *See* Sudbury All Saints

Spurgeon, John: carver; *See* Hadleigh

Squint (or hagioscope): An opening cut obliquely through a wall or pillar to give a view of the *High altar* from side chapels and *aisles*. During the mass, the squint made it possible for the act of consecration by a priest at a side altar to be coordinated with the celebration at the High altar. This was necessary because *chantry* and *guild* masses were not allowed to take precedence over the parish mass. Where there is a squint in the outer wall of a church it may point to the existence of a former chapel. The idea still persists that squints were provided so that lepers could watch the mass, but there is no basis for this at all. It is sometimes possible to determine the original site of the High altar by taking a line through a squint – useful in those cases where the *chancel* has been shortened or lengthened. See also *elevation squints*.

Stabling, Church: *See* Wingfield

Stanley, Charles: sculptor; *See* Hoxne

Stanton, Thomas: sculptor; *See* Culford

Stanton St John: *See* **Stanton All Saints**

Steggles, William: monumental mason; *See* Chevington, Ingham, Stansfield

Stella, Jacques: painter; *See* Gazeley

Stephens, Francis: stained glass; *See* Ipswich St Luke

Stocks: *See* Athelington, Hacheston, Orford, Parham, Saxstead, South Elmham St Margaret

Stone, Nicholas (1586-1647): Greatest sculptor of his time, he was born the son of a quarryman in Devon but soon moved to London, then to Holland to gain greater experience. By 1614 Stone was back in London and was soon employed by the king on the royal palaces. He was master mason to both James I and Charles I. His earliest work in Suffolk is at Hawstead and although there are other fine pieces at Ampton, Hessett, Redgrave and Wickhambrook, his finest is the figure of Elizabeth Coke at Bramfield. The Mannock tomb and Lady Dorothea's brass at Stoke by Nayland are probably by him.

Stone, John: statuary; *See* Belstead, Redgrave

Stopher, Thomas: carver; *See* Burstall, Weybread

Stops: *See* **Headstops**

Story, Abraham: sculptor; *See* Little Saxham

Stothard, Aldfred: sculptor; *See* East Bergholt

Stoup: In the porches of many churches, or just inside the main door, there are basins, usually recessed into the wall (often the basin has gone and only the recess remains). Usually very plain, and if there was once ornament or decoration it has often been defaced because they were one of the targets of the Puritans. This was because the stoups held holy water which was mixed once a week before mass. On entering the church, worshippers dipped their fingers into the water and crossed themselves as a reminder of their baptismal vows. To prepare the water, salt was first exorcised and then blessed; the water itself was then exorcised and blessed, the salt was sprinkled over it in the form of a cross, and then a final blessing given to the mixture.

Street, George Edward (1811-1878): One of leading C19 church architects, he worked with *Sir George Gilbert Scott* for five years before beginning his own practice in 1849. C13 Gothic was his favourite medium and of the hundreds of churches he was concerned with, St Philip and St James Oxford (1862) was the test piece for the High Victorian 'vigorous architecture' – admired and loathed in equal measure.

String course: *See* **Courses**

Stuart: The Royal House of Stuart, which inherited the Scottish throne in 1371 and the English throne, on the accession of James I, in 1603. The Stuart period covers 1603-1714 – the reigns of James I, Charles I, Charles II, James II, William and Mary, and finally Anne.

Sturdy, John: bell founder; *See* Saxmundham

Suffling, Ernest: stained glass; *See* Little Saxham, Woodbridge St John

Suffolk Giant: *See* **Page, George**

Sullivan, Sir Arthur: composer; *See* Newmarket St Agnes

Sully, Gilbert B.: artist; *See* Marlesford

Sundial inscriptions: *See* Clare, Grundisburgh, South Elmham St Michael

Sutton Hoo: *See* Rendlesham

Sybils, The: *See* Ufford

Symbols of the Evangelists: *See* **Evangelistic symbols**

Tabard, Heraldic: *See* Denston, Shelley

Tabernacle work: Representations of canopied stalls, niches and pinnacles, particularly in stained glass and wall paintings.

Tabitha: *See* **Dorcas**

Table of Kindred & Affinity: *See* Ellough, Elmsett, Ixworth Thorpe

Talbot: An heraldic hound or hunting dog, seen in the arms of a number of families, but particularly associated with the Talbots, Earls of Shrewsbury.

Taubman, F.M.: sculptor; *See* Middleton

Taylor, Rowland: divine; *See* Hadleigh

Taylor, W.G.: stained glass; *See* Walsham-le-Willows

Tenterhooks: *See* Nayland, Stoke by Clare

Teobald, Simon, Archbishop: *See* **Simon of Sudbury**

Tench, Edwin J.: architect; *See* Lowestoft St Andrew

Tester: Flat canopy above a pulpit, acting as a sounding board.

Teulon, Samuel Saunders: A C19 architect who had an established practice by the 1840s, and whose aristocratic clients included the Queen, and the Dukes of Bedford and Marlborough. He was the most strongly individualistic of the High Victorian architects, and his work is characterised by complication rather than simplicity, seeming always to strain after novelty. He carried out alterations and restorations at Ampton, Pakenham, and Wordwell, but his only complete Suffolk church is at Hopton.

Texts, C17 wall: *See* Ringsfield, Hemingstone, Witnesham

Thankful Village, Suffolk's only: *See* South Earlham St Michael

Thomas, Brian: stained glass; *See* Creeting St Mary

Thomas, I.E.: monumental mason; *See* Ousden

Thomas, John: architect; *See* Somerleyton

Thompson, Robert (mouse man): joiner; *See* Marlesford

Thorneycroft, Sir Hamo: sculptor; *See* Playford

Thornton, John: bell founder; *See* Wissington

Three-Decker Pulpits: After the Civil War, the normal Sunday service was conducted entirely from the reading desk, and only on the infrequent Sacrament Sundays would minister and people move to the *altar*. Convenience demanded that pews be grouped round a focal point, and the C17/C18 solution was a three-decker pulpit. The service was read from the second tier, and the minister climbed to the pulpit above to deliver his sermon (if the curate took the service, the rector would sit in the pulpit until sermon time). The *parish clerk* led the responses, and conducted the singing from his special pew below, and the three compartments were combined in a number of ways, often ingeniously. Some churches made do with two-deckers wherein the reading desk and pulpit were planned as a unit, or separate accommodation was found for the clerk (in 1638, Cratfield had one made by joining a desk onto its 1617 pulpit). Such arrangements, however, are occasionally the result of later alterations to suit changing needs or parsons' predilections. For decades the three-decker was the focus of congregational worship (with spasmodic acknowledgement of the altar's pre-eminence), and it gathered to itself cushions for the ledges, candlesticks, *hour-glass*, wig-stand, and the odd hat peg. The finest examples are at Dennington and Kedington, with others at Cretingham (minus clerk's pew), Gislingham, Great Livermere, Ickworth, Ramsholt (1850s two-decker), Shelland and Withersdale (2-decker). See also *Prayer book churches*.

Three Marys: In *St Mark's* Gospel *Mary Magdalene*, Mary the mother of James, and Salome visit the sepulchre to anoint Christ's body, but in some medieval accounts they were called Mary Magdalene, Mary Jacobee and Mary Salome, and in one bible text of the Middle Ages the last one becomes Maria Joseph. From this has come the convention of calling them the 'three Marys'. *St Anne* is credited with three husbands by which she had three daughters, all Marys – the *Blessed Virgin*, Mary the mother of *James the Less*, *St Simon* and *St Jude*, and Mary the mother of *St James the Great* and *St John*. These too are sometimes referred to as the 'three Marys'. The women at the tomb feature in modern glass at Bentley, Chelmondiston, Cratfield, Earl Stonham, East Bergholt, Great Bealings, Halesworth, Harkstead, Lowestoft St Margaret, Melton, Trimley St Martin, Walton, Weybread and Wilby. Mary Salome appears separately at Lound and Ufford. At Hepworth, modern glass shows the Angel of the Resurrection appearing to St Mary Magdalene and the Blessed Virgin.

Thurible: Known also as a censer, it is a pierced metal container used for the ceremonial burning of incense. The incense is burned on charcoal and the thurible is usually suspended on chains so that it can be swung in the hand of the thurifer as he censes the *altar*, the priest or the congregation, thus fanning the charcoal and directing the smoke at will. The thurifer is sometimes attended by a boy bearing a boat-shaped vessel containing incense for re-plenishing the thurible.

Thurlow, Thomas (1813-1819): A native sculptor born at Saxmundham in 1813 who spent his whole life in the county and did most of his work there. He exhibited at the Royal Academy between 1846 and 1872 and died in 1899. The best of his work is to be found at Aldeburgh, Kelsale, Leiston, and Witnesham, and there are other pieces at Darsham, Marlesford, Saxmundham, Theberton, and Yoxford.

Thwaite & Rees: clockmakers; *See* Kirkley

Tie-beam: The wall-to-wall cross beam or truss supporting a roof. See **Roofs**.

Tiger carvings: *See* Badingham, Lakenheath, Ufford

Tillotson, John, Archbishop: *See* Kedington

Tinworth, George: artist; *See* Walsham le Willows

Tonni, Stephen: bell founder; *See* Stanstead

Touchstone: A smooth, fine-grained black

stone (jasper, black marble or similar) widely used in C16-C18 for funeral monuments.

Tovell, George: monumental mason; *See* Hunston

Tovell, Robert: monumental mason; *See* Debenham

Tower, Walter: *See* **Kempe, Charles**

Townshend, Caroline & Joan Howson: stained glass; *See* Pettaugh

Tracery: Ornamental open-work in wood or stone, especially in the upper parts of windows and screens; the term also applies to similar patterns on solid panels.

Transepts: Projecting 'arms' of a church, built out to n. and s. from the point where *nave* and *chancel*/meet, to form a cross-shaped or cruciform ground plan.

Transfiguration: The appearance of Christ in glory during his earthly life, as related in the Gospels of *SS Matthew, Mark* and *Luke*. He appeared with Moses and Elijah, and tradition places the event on Mount Tabor, although Mount Hermon and the Mount of Olives have been suggested. The painting at Westhall is the only medieval example to be found on a *screen*, and there are versions in modern glass at Barsham and Hinderclay.

Transitional: Though 'transitional' can refer loosely to any change from one phase of architecture to another, it is particularly applied to the transition from the 'rounded' Norman to the 'pointed' Gothic, in the second half of the C12. (*See* Appendix 2, Styles of Architecture.)

Transoms: The horizontal crosspieces in window *tracery*, most noticeable in *Perpendicular* windows.

Travers, Martin: stained glass; *See* Denston, Woodbridge St Mary

Trefoil: *See* **Foils**

Trinity: *See* **Emblems of the Trinity**

Tristram, Prof.: conservator; *See* Kedington, South Cove, Wissington

Tudor: The dynasty founded by Henry Tudor, victor of Bosworth Field against Richard III. He

was crowned Henry VII in 1485; Henry VIII followed, then Edward VI, Mary I (Bloody Mary) and finally Elizabeth I, who died in 1603. For the church, it was a time fraught with change. Various aspects of this are dealt with under *communion rails; Laud; mensa slabs; Prayer book churches; Rood Screen*, and *Royal Arms*. Although the interiors of churches were changed decisively during this era, the Tudor influence upon church architecture as such was negligible. (See Appendix 2 – Styles of Architecture.)

Tudor Roses: A typical flower decoration of the period.

Tugwell, Sidney: designer; *See* Orford

Turner, Harry: carver; *See* Felixstowe St John

Turner, John: joiner; *See* Mendlesham

Turner, Lawrence: joiner; *See* Orford

Two-Decker Pulpits: *See* **Three-decker pulpits**

Two Marys: *See* **Three Marys**

Tyler, William: sculptor; *See* Mundham

Tympanum: Space over head of door, or in head of filled-in arch, plain (as at Gisleham), carved, or painted. See also *Royal Arms* and *Doom*. There is a *Norman* example at Wordwell.

Unicorn: A swift and fierce little animal from the *bestiary*, with a single horn on its forehead. The only way to catch it was to lay a trap with a virgin. The beast was so attracted by her purity that it would run up, lay its head in her lap, and fall asleep. Thus it became the symbol of purity and feminine chastity, and for the *Blessed Virgin* in particular. There are unicorns on bench ends at Ixworth Thorpe, Lakenheath and Wetherden, on *fonts* at Norton and Pakenham, on the *screen* at Hargrave and in glass at Rushbrooke.

Uriel: *See* Appendix 1 – Saints

Valiant & Sons: builders; *See* Depden

Vestry: That part of the church in which the vestments are kept and where the clergy robe for services. It sometimes doubles as a *sacristy* and occasionally as a choir robing area.

Victoria Cross, Holders of the: *See* Aldburgh,

Bardwell, Mildenhall, Beck Row, Theberton, Weybread

Vielle (hurdy-gurdy): *See* Lavenham

Vinegar Bible: *See* Henley

Vines of Eye: masons; *See* Stradbroke, Weybread

Vinnell, -: carver; *See* Stratford St Mary

Virgin Mary: *See* **Mary the Blessed Virgin** in Appendix 1 – Saints.

Visitation, The: Having been told by the archangel Gabriel that she would bear a son, whose name would be Jesus and whose kingdom would have no end (Luke, 1), the Virgin Mary hurried to tell the news to her cousin Elizabeth, already near her time with the child who would be *John the Baptist*. This meeting is commemorated on 2 July as the Visitation. Examples can be found at Bildeston, Newton and Thornham Parva.

Waghevens, Cornelis: bell founder; *See* Bromeswell

Wailes, William: His Newcastle firm was one of the busiest stained glass suppliers in the C19. He made glass for *Pugin* in the 1840s, and received commissions from *Scott, Butterfield* and other key architects in the 1850s and 1860s. The firm maintained a high standard, but was resolutely conservative and resisted artistic innovation. Their handling of colour and pattern is consistently good, and the style is quickly recognised. Wailes died in 1881, and the firm continued for a while under his son-in-law as Wailes & Strang. There are windows at Carlton, Carlton Colville, and Nacton, with many more elsewhere in the county.

Walker, Leonard: stained glass; *See* Brandon, Felixstowe SS Peter & Paul

Wall plate: *See* **Roofs**

Wall post: *See* **Roofs**

Walpole, Horace: poet; *See* Ickworth, Letheringham

Walsh, John: sculptor; *See* Little Thurlow, Wangford St Peter

Wall texts: *See* **Texts**

Ward & Hughes: Firm of stained glass manufacturers founded by Thomas Ward and James Henry Nixon in 1836. They traded as Ward & Nixon until 1850 when Henry Hughes became chief designer. After Hughes' death in 1883, the firm continued under Thomas Curtis until the 1920s and some later windows are signed by him. They were the largest suppliers to Norfolk and Suffolk in the C19, and their 1850s-1860s High Victorian work was well drawn and often pleasing in design and colour. In 1870, their massive production was rationalised and was often dull, repetitive, and poorly designed there-after. There is above-average work at Barton Mills, Clopton, Hopton, Long Melford, Melton, Mendham and Thurston Brightwell's w. window is possibly an example of Ward & Nixon's work.

Wareham Guild: *See* Haverhill, Troston

Warne, Charles: joiner; *See* Aldburgh

Warren, Erasmus: divine, author; *See* Worlington

Warrington, William (1833-66): He described himself as 'artist in stained glass, heraldic and decorative painter, plumber, glazier and paperhanger'. He designed in medieval styles and some of his detailing was distinctly fanciful. The firm continued under his son James until 1875. Examples of his work can be found at Brampton, Hessett, Shelley, Shimpling and Sutton.

Waterford, Dowager Marchioness of: stained glass; *See* Saxmundham

Watts of Colchester: monumental masons; *See* Thorpe Morieux

Weathering: The sloping surface of a buttress *set-off*, or a section of a wall designed to throw off rain-water.

Webb, Cristopher: stained glass; *See* Cowlinge, Mettingham, Newmarket St Mary, Redisham?, Tuddenham St Martin,

Webb, Geoffrey: stained glass; *See* Little Thurlow

Webling, A.F., Canon: author; *See* Risby

Weeping chancels: Much nonsense has been written (and is still being perpetuated in some church guide books today) about chancels which incline away from the centre line of the *nave*. The

SUFFOLK CHURCHES

popular fallacy is that this is intended to indicate the drooping of Christ's head on the cross onto his right shoulder, as he is always shown in medieval representations of the Crucifixion. As *Cautley* put it, the idea is 'too absurd to be credited by any thinking person'. In any event, there are as many chancels which 'weep' left as right. The explanation is simply that medieval buildings were seldom set out with mathematical accuracy, and the chancel being 'out of true' with the nave was often the result of a rebuilding which affected only the chancel or the nave as at Sudbury St Peter. There are examples at Chillesford, Ilketshall St John, Kirton, Nacton, Saxmundham and an extreme example at Thrandeston.

West, Benjamin: artist; *See* Sternfield

Westmacott, Henry: sculptor; *See* Hartest

Westmacott, Sir Richard (1775-1856): Sculptor. In 1793 he went to Rome, where he quickly established himself in the artistic world of Italy. He returned home in 1797 and set up his own studio, which within six years was handling commissions to the tune of a staggering £16,000 a year. His carvings lauding Nelson and Wellington are placed over the grand entrance to Buckingham Palace, and the famous Waterloo vase in the palace grounds is his work. There are memorials by him at Campsea Ash, Great Finborough, Shimpling and Saxmundham, and there is a fine bust by his son Richard at Woolverstone.

Whall, Christopher (1849-1924): *Arts & Crafts* stained glass worker. For ten years he designed for the firms of Saunders, *Hardman*, and the *Powells*, but became disenchanted with their mass production approach and the lack of opportunity to control the whole process, from cartoon to installing the window. He was fortunate in his contacts with leading architects and was able to influence others through teaching, while his high standards of craftsmanship and insistence on continuous involvement made him a leader in the movement. His book *Stained Glass Work* is still one of the best handbooks on the subject. His finest work is in Gloucester cathedral but there are outstanding windows at Herringswell, Lowestoft St Margaret, and Sproughton in this county.

Whall, Veronica: stained glass; *See* Sproughton

Whistlecraft, Orlando: weather prophet and poet; *See* Thwaite

Whistler, Laurence: artist; *See* Thornham Parva

White, William: mason; *See* Stowlangtoft

Wicket door: A small door sometimes found inserted in a larger entrance door to a church, as at Clare and Wetheringsett.

Wiley, Michael: stained glass; *See* Horringer

Wilkinson, Alfred: stained glass; *See* Woolverstone

Wilkinson, Henry: stained glass; *See* Bures St Stephen

Wilkinson, Horace: stained glass; *See* Framlingham, Ipswich St Augustine, Wilby

Wilkinson, Walter: stained glass; *See* Aldham

Willement, Thomas (1786-1871): Leading glazier of the early C19 when the art was at a low ebb. Much of his early work was heraldic and there are fine examples in St George's chapel, Windsor. He advertised himself as 'stained glass artist to Queen Victoria' and was in business from 1812 to 1865. Work by him can be found at Dalham, Flixton, Freston, Peasenhall and Theberton (the best).

William and Mary: the 'joint reign' of William III (1688-1702) and Mary II (1688-1694). He was a Dutch Protestant and she was the daughter of the deposed Catholic James II. Architecturally, a period of gracious houses and fine furniture.

Williams, James: mason; *See* Brome, Wherstead

Williamson, Benedict, Fr.: designer; *See* Southwold

Williamson, F.J.: sculptor; *See* Playford

Willis, Father: organ builder; *See* Dennington

Wills, Robert: monumental mason; *See* Pettaugh

Wilmhurst & Oliphant: stained glass; *See* Wissington

Winter, John: stained glass; *See* Shadingfield

Winthrop, John: Pilgrim Father; *See* Groton

Wippell & Co: ironwork; *See* Felixstowe St John

Witches: *See* Brandeston, Lowestoft St Margaret

Wodeward, William: bell founder; *See* Clare

Wolsey, Cardinal: *See* Ipswich St Mary at the Elms', Newmarket St Mary

Wood, James: artist; *See* Newmarket St Mary

Wood, Searles V.: geologist; *See* Melton Old St Andrew

Woodforde, Christopher: stained glass; *See* Long Melford

Woodington, William Frederick: sculptor; *See* Thornham Magna

Woodley, Derek: architect; *See* Kesgrave

Woodruffe, Paul: stained glass; *See* Herringswell

Woodwose: A wild man of the woods, bearded and hairy and usually carrying a club, to be seen in carvings on *fonts* and on woodwork. In *bestiaries* he is frequently found fighting with lions, and they alternate round the bases of many East Anglian fonts. One medieval text describes the woodwoses as wild men of India who fought the Sagittarii – they were naked until they had slain a lion, after which they wore its skin. The Sagittarius represented man's body and the woodwose his soul; as the lion was slain, so the soul overcame the vanities of the world, and this was used as an appropriate theme for a baptismal homily, with the figures round the font or in the roof overhead as illustrations. Good examples can be found at Chediston, Cratfield, Mildenhall, Peasenhall, Ufford (heraldic), and Waldringfield (satyrs with turbans).

Woodyer, Henry: architect; *See* Stratford St Mary

Wooldridge, Harry Ellis (1845-1917): Stained glass designer. As a painter, musician and critic, he had a wide influence on the educated taste of his time. He was a friend of Burne-Jones and designed many windows for the *Powells*. He worked in the *Renaissance* manner, with correct drawing and pre-determined colours. Saxmundham has a good example of his work.

Woolner, Thomas: sculptor; *See* Hitcham

Woolnough, -: glazier; *See* Dennington

Woore, Edward: stained glass; *See* Monewden, Westleton

Wormald, Henry: carver; *See* Nowton

Wormald, James: joiner; *See* Crowfield

Wright, H.G. & A.J.: stained glass; *See* Bures St Mary

Wright, Samuel: architect; *See* Ipswich All Saints

Wyatt, John Drayton (1820-1891): An architect who joined *Sir George Gilbert Scott* in 1841 and became one of his principal assistants. Akthough he set up his own practice in 1856, he continued to collaborate with Scott for many years as a draughtsman and detail designer. He was active in many churches in Suffolk, including Brandon, Clare, Freckenham, Hartest, Higham, Mildenhall, Rickinghall Inferior, Sudbury St Gregory and Thorpe Morieux.

Wymbis, Richard de: bell founder; *See* Great Bradley

Wyvern A mythical winged dragon with two eagle's feet and a snake-like barbed tail. There are examples at Dennington, Hargrave, Honington, Mendlesham and Mildenhall.

Yarington, Samuel: glazier; *See* Herringfleet, Nowton, Wortham (?)

Young, Arthur: agriculturalist; *See* Bradfield Combust

Zachariah: A Jewish priest who was *St Elizabeth's* husband and *John the Baptist's* father. Having been struck dumb for his refusal to accept the archangel's message, he praised God in the canticle known as the Benedictus when the child was named (Luke 1:64). There is a tradition that he was martyred in the Temple for refusing to tell Herod where his son was. His figure forms part of the lavish *Kempe* window in the s. aisle at Bildeston, and can also be found in a *Lavers & Westlake* window at Great Waldingfield.

Zeppelin relics: *See* Acton, Somersham, Theberton

Zincke, Revd. Foster Baham: designer; *See* Wherstead

Zinkeison, Anna: artist; *See* Burgh

588

Appendix 1 – Saints

'For all the saints, who from their labours rest ...' sings a well-loved hymn, and on *rood screens*, on *fonts*, in woodwork and stained glass, a panoply of saints is represented in Suffolk churches. Almost all of them have some identifying emblem – which adds yet another element of interest for the church visitor. The following is a list of those to be found in the county, with emblems, brief story background and some representative locations.

Agatha: Represented either with pincers in her hand or with her severed breasts upon a dish, indicating the horrid nature of her martyrdom in C6 Sicily. She vowed her virginity to Christ and refused to yield to the lust of the local governor, who took ghastly revenge. She is invoked against fire (another of her tortures) and against diseases of the breasts. Agatha is also patron saint of bell founders. She is normally shown holding a breast in a pair of pincers or with a sword thrust through her breasts. She is represented at Leiston, Nowton and Ufford.

Agnes: Her symbols are a sword, often thrust into her neck or bosom, and a lamb – Latin, 'agna', a pun on her name. Ancient Rome, about 300 AD and 13-year-old Agnes refuses to marry the prefect's son. She was publicly stripped, but her hair miraculously grew long to cover her nakedness. They tried to burn her, but the flames declined to help. So at last she was stabbed. Here characteristic emblem is the lamb. She is represented at Athelington, Barsham, Bildeston, Creeting St Mary, Eye, Leiston, Nowton, Ufford,

Westhall, and Woolverstone. Newmarket is the only Suffolk dedication.

Aimery: There was a C5 tradition (embellished in *The Golden Legend*) that St Maurice commanded a legion of 6,666 Christian knights from Egypt which joined the emperor Maximian's army on his expedition into Gaul in the year 290. At St Moritz, the emperor ordered a general sacrifice to the Roman gods, and when the Christians refused to take part, they were all martyred without offering any resistance. Aimery was one of the company, and he is shown dressed as a legionary on a piece of continental glass at Herringfleet.

Alban: Often represented with a tall cross or a sword, he was Britain's earliest martyr, a Roman knight who had been converted to Christianity here in Britain in the C3. He refused to sacrifice to pagan gods and was condemned to be executed at Verulamium, the city which became St Albans. He converted the first executioner, but the second was more successful and beheaded the saint, whereupon the man's eyes dropped out! Alban is the only saint to have enjoyed a continuous cult in England from Roman times. His emblems are various – often a tall cross or a sword. Modern illustrations at Creeting St Mary, Erwarton, Felixstowe, Kettlebaston, Southwold, and Wickham Market.

Alphege: Having been successively Abbot of Bath and Bishop of Winchester, he became Archbishop of Canterbury in 1006. Five years later the marauding Danes seized Canterbury and took Alphege prisoner. He refused to tax the poor as the price of his release and was stoned before being beheaded. Buried first in St Paul's, his remains were transferred to Canterbury in 1023. His emblems are stones or a battle axe, and there is a modern panel painting of him in the *sanctuary* at Ipswich St Mary le Tower.

Ambrose: One of the *Four Latin Doctors*. Usually represented with a beehive – allusion to the story of a swarm of bees which settled on the baby Ambrose's cradle. Also seen wearing his bishop's robes and holding whip or scourge, recalling penance he imposed on the Roman Emperor Theodosius. Ambrose became Bishop of Milan in 374. Central figure in early church with powerful influence on the Roman emperors. Seen at Dalham and with scourge at Wickham Market.

Andrew: The saltire (X-shaped cross, Scotland's part of Union Jack) and fishing net are his symbols. One of the Twelve, he was a fisherman before he became a disciple. Legends of his later life are legion, including one that he visited Scotland, thus becoming its patron saint. Martyred by crucifixion, it is said, upon an X-shaped cross – illustrated on the *font* at Melton. There is a medieval figure at Corton and his martyrdom on a *misericord* at Norton and others at Framlingham, Heveningham, Orford, Somerleyton, Southwold, and Tattingstone.

Anne: According to the apocryphal Gospel of St *James*, Anne was the mother of the *Blessed Virgin* who, after years of childlessness was told by an angel that she would bear a daughter who would become world famous. She vowed that the child would be devoted to the Lord and presented Mary to the temple at the age of three. Another tradition identifies her with the widowed prophetess Anna who was in the temple when Jesus was received (Luke 2:36-8). She is usually represented teaching the Virgin to read. Somerleyton has a fine painting, and there are other representations at Aldeburgh, Edwardstone, Felixstowe St Peter & St Paul, Huntingfield, Ufford, and Woodbridge.

Anthony of Egypt: Pigs and bells are his symbols, and occasionally a cross like the letter 'T'. Born about 251 in Egypt, he lived as a desert hermit before founding a monastery. Zealous against heresies and a miracle worker, his letters are still quoted. His bones were revered by the Hospitallers in Alexandria who attracted alms by ringing little bells. The Hospitallers' swine were allowed to roam freely, hence the alternative symbol. A painting of him is included in the interesting series on the *screen* at Westhall, and there are other examples at Cavendish, Nowton and Whepstead.

Apostles: The twelve chief disciples of Christ (the lists of names vary slightly, probably because the same person was known by more than one name). They were: *Peter, Andrew, James the Great, John, Philip, Thomas, Bartholomew, Matthew, James the Less, Simon, Jude* (Thaddaeus/Judas son of James), *Judas*. After the suicide of Judas Iscariot, his place was taken by *Matthias*. Both *Paul* and *Barnabas* are referred to as apostles in the Acts of the Apostles.

Apollonia: This poor saint is most often seen having her teeth forcibly removed with huge pincers or herself holding aloft a tooth representing the torture which preceded the martyrdom by fire of this aged and pious deaconess in Egypt in 249. Not surprisingly, she is invoked against jaw and tooth-ache. She is represented at Chilton, Coney Weston, Gazeley, Leiston, Long Melford, Norton, Somerleyton, and Westhall.

Audry: An alternative name for *Etheldreda*.

Augustine of Canterbury: In the C6 Pope *Gregory* sent Augustine, an Italian by birth, with a band of monks to convert England. King Ethelbert of Kent received him civilly and was soon won over. Augustine made Canterbury his base and built the first cathedral there, but he travelled widely as a missionary. His figure is one of the modern series in the *sanctuary* of Ipswich St Mary le Tower.

Augustine of Hippo: One of the *Four Latin Doctors* of the early church; a profound and sustaining influence through the centuries on the church's thought and teaching. Often represented holding a flaming heart in his hand or, in his bishop's robes (he was bishop of Hippo in N. Africa for 35 years to his death in 430) and carrying a pastoral staff. His saintly adulthood followed a dissolute youth, from which he was rescued by *St Ambrose*. Augustine, a man of flesh as well as spirit, is credited with the memorable prayer 'O Lord, make me chaste ... but not yet'. He can be found at Corton, Wickham Market, and Woolverstone.

Barbara: A tower, and a *chalice* with the wafer above it are her emblems. She was an early Christian convert in godless Italy, to the fury of her father, who shut her up in a high tower. When she tried to escape he beat her before handing her over to a judge who condemned her to death. She was tortured and decapitated, whereupon both father and judge were consumed by bolts of lightning. Barbara is thus patroness of architects and firearms, and also protectress from thunderbolts and lightning or any form of explosion. She is represented at Athelington, Bildeston, Bromeswell, Coney Weston, Eye, Hessett, Nowton and Yaxley.

Barnabas: The saint is described in the Acts of the Apostles as a Cypriot who sold a field and gave the proceeds to the Apostles. He was a 'prophet and teacher' in Antioch and was chosen to go with St *Paul* on his first missionary journey. They later fell out when Barnabas wished to take his cousin John Mark with them on another trip. He parted with Paul and went to Cyprus where tradition has it that he was stoned or burned to death by the Jews. Seldom seen in medieval art, there is a modern glass figure of him at Tattingstone and another at Wilby.

Bartholomew: One of the Twelve, his emblem is the butcher's flaying knife for thus, it is said, he was martyred somewhere along the Caspian Sea, being first flayed alive and then beheaded. More gruesomely, he is sometimes seen in medieval art carrying the skin of a man, with the face still attached to it. It follows that he is the patron saint of tanners. He occurs at Athelington, Blythburgh, Coney Weston, Corton, Haverhill, Orford, Rattlesden, Sotterley, Southwold, Tattingstone and Wilby.

Benedict: Usually shown as an abbot beating devils down with his crozier, or with his fingers to his lip commanding silence. A Roman noble who became a hermit and drew others to him by his example. He founded the monastery at Monte Cassino and devised the Benedictine Rule which lay down the guidelines for monasticism in Europe. He is represented at Barsham and possibly at Weybread.

Bernard: A C12 Burgundian noble who, as a young man, became a Cistercian monk. He was chosen as first abbot of Clairvaux, and his piety and sweet eloquence drew many men into the Order. A prolific theologian, he also wrote hymns which are still sung today, such as

'Jerusalem the golden'. He is seldom illustrated, but a modern figure on Ufford's *font* cover may represent him.

Blaise: During the persecutions of Christians around the year 300 by the Roman Emperor Diocletian, innumerable martyrs suffered death. Blaise, bishop of Sebaste in Armenia, was first torn with iron combs and then beheaded. A comb is thus his symbol in medieval art, and he is the patron saint of woolcombers. He can be found at Lavenham and there is a figure at Eye which has been identified as him but that is questionable.

Botolph: A shadowy C7 figure, possibly of Irish birth, he became the abbot of 'Ikanhoe'. One tradition has it that this was in Lincolnshire and that he 'dwelt in a dismal hut amidst the swamps of the fenland rivers', but his monastery may have been at Iken. The church at Burgh has been claimed as his burial place, but if so his body was transferred to Bury abbey where there was a chapel dedicated to him. He has no definite symbol although he is properly represented as an abbot, occasionally holding a church in his hand. There are five churches dedicated to him in Suffolk, including Botesdale (Botolph's Dale) Iken and North Cove; he figures in a window at Felixstowe St John the Baptist and in another at Burgh. One of the figures on Charsfield *font* probably represents him..

Bride: See *Bridget of Kildare*

Bridget of Kildare: One of Ireland's favourite saints whose picture occurs only twice in Suffolk, on Ufford's *screen*, and in a modern window at Somerleyton. After living as a consecrated virgin in her own home in C6 Ireland, Bridget founded a small community, and went on to establish several convents, notably at Kildare. Charming stories surround her. So heedless was she of material things that one day she absentmindedly hung her cloak upon a sunbeam ... but was practical enough to transform her bathwater into beer to quench the thirst of some unexpected guests.

Bridget (or Birgitta) of Sweden: Born in 1303 near Uppsala, she was a mystic whose revelations were influential in the Middle Ages. She married a provincial governor and had a large family, but after his death she retired to a life of prayer and penance. She journeyed to Rome in 1350 and, apart from pilgrimages, lived there until her death in 1373. She succoured the homeless and the sinful, and founded the Brigittine Order in 1346. Her figure is one of the interesting series on the *screen* at Westhall.

Catherine of Alexandria: The emblem of this saint is a wheel set with spikes and knives, on which she is said to have been martyred in C4 Egypt, and which in turn inspired the spinning firework that bears her name. The wheel, however, flew to pieces as she was spun on it, the knives skewering her persecutors. Her head was then cut off and from the wound flowed milk, not blood, which could explain why she is patroness of nurses. There are many images of her, but the following are notable: Herringfleet, Somerleyton, Thornham Parva (*retable*), Westhall and Wilby (C15 glass).

Cecilia: Daughter of a C3 noble Roman family, she refused to worship idols and was beheaded. Her many converts to Christianity included her husband Valerian (with whom she lived in virginal wedlock) and one of her symbols is a garland of roses or lilies because an angel is said to have brought them one each from Paradise. When she heard the organ playing at her wedding she 'sang in her heart' to God and dedicated herself to His service. Thus she is the patron saint of music and her common emblem is a harp or an organ, although this was never used in English pre-*Reformation* pictures. She is seen on *screen* panels at Ufford and Woodbridge, with modern versions at Aldeburgh, Barsham, Leiston and elsewhere.

Christopher: Patron saint of travellers pictured on many a dashboard medallion, he was probably a C3 martyr in Asia Minor. Legend describes him as a giant who wished to serve the greatest king in the world. A hermit preached the Gospel to him and suggested that he live by a dangerous river nearby and help wayfarers across. As he carried a child over one day, the waters rose and he seemed to bear the weight of the whole world on his shoulders. When they reached the other side, the child was revealed as Christ himself. The saint is invariably represented as a giant holding a huge staff as he fords the river with the Christ-child on his shoulder. He was so popular that nearly every church had a statue or painting of him. It was normally placed opposite the main door so that passers by could see it easily, for it was believed that:

If thou the face of Christopher on any
   morn shalt see,
Throughout the day from sudden death
   thou shalt preserved be.

Examples are common but note those at Bradfield Combust, Martlesham, Westhall, and modern versions at Lound and Sproughton. Nowton has the scene of his torture.

Chrysostom: See *John Chrysostom*

Clare: Clare's emblem is a *pyx*. This is the Clare of Assisi, spiritually beloved and influenced by *St Francis*, who founded the Order of Poor Clares, vowed to a life of absolute poverty. She spent her life as abbess of her convent at Assisi and never left the town. When she was old and sick, Assisi was threatened by the Saracens of the invading German Emperor Barbarossa's army. Clare was carried before him, deep in prayer and carrying a pyx containing the Blessed Sacrament, whereupon the invaders fled. Bradfield St Clare is uniquely dedicated to her.

Clement: His emblem is an anchor – one was hung round his neck when he was drowned by the Emperor Trajan in the Black Sea around 100 AD. He had been too successful in converting the heathen following his exile from his bishopric in Rome. Usually shown wearing a papal tiara. He is included in the Westhall *screen* sequence.

Columba: No special symbols. He was a prince of C6 Ireland with a talent for founding monasteries. He left Ireland in 563 when he was 41 and with a few companions headed for Scotland and the island of Iona, where he established his own monastery and lived there until his death in 597. A potent evangelist in Scotland and Northumbria, he was also a scholar and poet and work survives which is believed to be his. There is a modern glass figure of him at Debenham.

Cornelius: Pope of Rome 251-3. During that short time he was beset by controversy, persecuted, confronted with a rival pope, and driven into exile. His normal symbol is a horn (Latin 'cornu') and he occurs in modern glass at Sotterley.

Cuthbert: Born about 636, he was a Tweedale shepherd lad who, having had a vision of angels bearing the soul of St Aidan up to heaven, entered Melrose monastery. He made many missionary journeys into Scotland and in 664 was chosen prior of Lindisfarne. Retreating to even sterner self-denial on the Farne islands, he relented to become bishop of Lindisfarne for two years before returning to his cell on Farne to die in 687. He had great influence over the Northumbrian kings and his work with the sick and the poor became a legend in the north-east. His body now rests in Durham cathedral. There is a painting of him on the C15 screen at Nayland where he is shown with the head of *St Oswold*. This is because the king's head was buried at Lindisfarne and placed in St Cuthbert's coffin when the island was threatened by the Danes in 875. He is represented in modern glass at Kirkley.

Denis, or Dionysius: His symbol is a severed head. Patron saint of France and first bishop of Paris – where his missionary zeal so roused the fury of the pagans that they put him to torture from which he emerged miraculously unharmed. So they took him to Montmartre and beheaded him – only to have him rise and bear his severed head to his chosen resting place at St Denis. That is why Kings of France were traditionally buried there. He can be seen in modern glass at Oakley.

Dominic: Born of a noble Spanish family in 1170, he pursued a conventional clerical career until he became convinced of the need to reform the church in southern France. In 1218 the pope gave him authority to establish his Order of Friars Preachers and his zealous missioners became known as the Black Friars by the colour of their robes, reaching England in 1221. Illustrations of the saint are rare but a C17 roundel at Nowton shows his vision of the *Blessed Virgin*, and he features on the *retable* at Thornham Parva. He may also be represented at Ufford.

Dorothy: Usually shown holding a spray of flowers and/or a basket of fruit. During the persecution of the Emperor Diocletian in the early C4, she was threatened with terrible tortures unless she rejected her Christianity and married the prefect. Her reply, it is said, was:

> Do to me what torment thou wilt, for I am ready to suffer it for the love of my spouse, Jesu Christ, in whose garden full of delights I have gathered roses, spices and apples.

On her way to execution, she was mocked by a young lawyer who scornfully asked her to send him some of those roses and apples. After she had been beheaded, an angel appeared to the lawyer, bringing from Dorothy in Paradise the requested gift, whereupon he was converted and followed the saint to martyrdom. She is represented at Eye, Fressingfield, Hawkedon, Leiston, Somerleyton, S. Elmham All Saints, Westhall and Yaxley.

Edith: There have been two saints of this name and it is not always possible to say which is intended. St Edith of Polesworth was a sister of King Athelstan and abbess of Polesworth during the C10. St Edith of Wilton was a daughter of King Edgar and the nun Wolfrida (whom he had abducted). She took her daughter back to Wilton Abbey where she was educated. She founded the church at Wilton and died there in 984 at the age of 23. The saint (you choose) shares a C20 window at Edwardstone with Melchizedek and Abbot Samson.

Edmund, King and Martyr: Crowned at Bury, king of East Anglia from 855 until 870 when the Danes defeated him in battle and took him prisoner. He refused to renounce his faith and they tied him to a tree, shot him with arrows, and finally beheaded him. His murderers left his head in a wood to rot, but those that sought it were guided by its ability to cry 'Here! Here!' They found it guarded by a great grey wolf; the wolf followed the cortège to Bury and then returned to the wood. The great abbey church was dedicated to St Edmund and his shrine became a principal place of pilgrimage. Hoxne is the traditional site of the martyrdom although one school of thought prefers Hellesdon near Norwich. The saint's usual emblem is an arrow or arrows but the wolf's head is sometimes seen. He can naturally be found in plenty of Suffolk's churches but notably on Badingham's *font*, on Bramford's porch, on *screens* at Belstead, Eye, Kersey and Somerleyton, on wall paintings at Boxford and Thornham Parva and on a misericord at Norton.

Edward the Confessor: Usually seen in kingly crown, and holding aloft a ring. This deeply pious king of England, immediately before the *Norman* Conquest of 1066, built Westminster Abbey – the price for not having kept his vow to make a pilgrimage to the Holy Land. Confronted once by a beggar asking for alms, the king, having no money, slipped a ring from his finger and gave it to him. The beggar, it seems, was really *St*

John the Evangelist, who returned the ring to English pilgrims in Palestine and foretold the king's imminent death. This is alluded to in the paintings at Nayland and Somerleyton, and he can be found at Coney Weston, Hessett, Leiston and Southwold.

Eleutherius: A Greek C2 pope about whom little is know except that he had to battle against heresies current at the time. The Venerable Bede says that King Lucius of Britain asked him to send missionaries to convert the people and that they were successful, but there seems to be no confirmation of this. Rarely encountered, but there is a C15 figure of him in a Blythburgh window.

Eligius, or Eloy: Patron saint of farriers, his symbol is a blacksmith's hammer and tongs and occasionally a severed horse's leg. Eligius was a charitable and devoted bishop in C6 France and Flanders. His most famous exploit was to lop the leg off a difficult horse which was refusing to be shod, fix the shoe to the severed limb, and then put the leg back on again. A sign of the cross, and the beast trotted thankfully away. He is represented at Freckenham and possibly at Ipswich St Matthew; one of Bungay St Mary's aisles was dedicated to him, and he was the patron saint of a *guild* at Woodbridge.

Elizabeth: No distinguishing symbol, but usually represented at the moment of the *Visitation*, when the Virgin Mary came to tell her of the visit of the angel to announce Christ's birth, Elizabeth already being near her time with the child who would be *John the Baptist*. She is represented at Badingham, Barsham, Great Thurlow, Great Waldingfield, Huntingfield, Ingham, Kelsale, Leiston, Lound, Newmarket St Mary, Newton, Thornham Parva and Wyverstone.

Elizabeth of Hungary: Rarely represented. Daughter of a C13 king of Hungary, she married a prince and lived in great happiness with him until, to her great grief, he died on his way to the Crusades. Always a woman of immense charity and kindness, she now took to a life of poverty and to nursing the sick. She died at 24 in 1231 and was canonised four years later by Gregory XI. She can be seen in Flemish glass at Nowton.

Erasmus: His symbol is a windlass. He fled from Roman persecution, about AD 300, to a cave where he was cared for by a raven. Later,

when he resumed his preaching, his death was ordered by Emperor Maximian and he is said to have been martyred by having his entrails uncoiled and bound upon a windlass – which is why he was invoked against stomach disorders. A figure on the screen at Ipswich St Matthew may represent him.

Erkenwald: A member of the royal family of East Anglia and brother of *St Ethelburga*, he was abbot of the monastery he founded at Chersey. In 676 he became bishop of London and founded St Paul's cathedral. Little is known of his life but its sanctity is vouched for by Bede. He figures among the series of English saints in the *sanctuary* at Ipswich St Mary le Tower.

Ethelbert: He was king of East Anglia in the late C8, and was executed by King Offa of Mercia for 'political offences', say some sources; through the machinations of Offa's wife, goes a another story. He had gone to seek the hand of the king's daughter, but her mother's jealousy persuaded Offa to have him killed. Rarely represented, but four Suffolk churches are dedicated to him and there is a modern painting of him in the *sanctuary* of Ipswich St Mary le Tower.

Ethelburga: A daughter of the East Anglian royal house, she became the first abbess of the convent founded by her brother *St Erkenwald* at Barking in Essex. She lived a life of exemplary piety, experiencing prophetic visions and died in 676. There is a modern painting of her in the *sanctuary* at Ipswich St Mary le Tower.

Etheldreda: No special emblem, but generally represented as a royally crowned abbess. Daughter of a C7 king of East Anglia and born at Exning, she was twice married before becoming a nun. She founded a nunnery at Ely, became its first abbess and was known for her deep devotion and piety. After death her body remained incorrupt and its miracle-working powers made Ely a great centre of pilgrimage. She is represented at numerous Suffolk churches including Ampton, Barsham, Blythburgh, Bramford, Campsea Ash, Dalham, Felixstowe St John the Baptist, Horringer, Mildenhall, Melton, Newmarket St Mary, Norton, Ufford, and Woodbridge.

Euphemia: Seldom seen in English churches, she was a C3 virgin martyr of Constantinople. Little is known of her life but an early tradition tells of her arrest for refusing to join in pagan worship. Tortured and thrown to wild beasts who refused to maul her, she was finally beheaded. She features in the *Kempe* glass in Leiston e. window.

Eustachius, or Eustace: A saint whose name is coupled with *St Andrew's* in the unique dedication at Hoo. He was a Christian who suffered martyrdom with his wife and two sons under Emperor Hadrian about the year 120. Legend adds that he Trajan's master of horse and was converted by seeing aluminous crucifix between the horns of a stag he was hunting. A similar tale is told of St Hubert and they share the same emblem of a stag with a crucifix.

Faith (Fides): Her symbols are a palm branch and the grid-iron upon which she was roasted in France about the year 287. Occasionally, as at Gazeley, her emblem is a saw. Legend says that a thick fall of snow came to veil her body during her suffering. She features on the *screens* at Somerleyton and Ufford and in modern glass at Boulge.

Felicitas: With *St Perpetua* she, together with her seven sons, was martyred at Carthage during the C3 persecution by Severus. Tortured by gladiators and mauled by wild beasts in the arena, she was finally beheaded. In company with other female martyrs, she features in the *Kempe* window at Leiston.

Felix: Usually seen as a bishop, he came here in the C7 from France to preach the Gospel, and in 630 became the first bishop of Dunwich. For the 17 years of life that remained to him, he worked steadfastly to establish the church on the eastern seaboard, founded schools, and preached extensively, with the friendly support of the king of the East Angles. A favourite subject for C19 and C20 artists in Suffolk churches, and there are many examples.

Florence (Florentia): Two saints with this name are known: the first was a young Phrygian girl who was baptised by St Hilary of Poitiers in the C4 before devoting herself to solitary prayer and contemplation at Poitou. The second was martyred at Agde in southern France early in the C4. A *screen* panel at Ufford is the only known portrait in England, but which Florence was intended is uncertain.

Francis of Assisi: Usually seen as a friar holding a cross, often accompanied by the animals and birds with whom he is always associated; sometimes also with the 'stigmata', the wounds of Christ in hands and feet and side (as at Felixstowe St John the Baptist). Oddly this much-loved saint is only occasionally represented in medieval art, though his story is so well known – his birth in wealthy circumstances in C12 Italy; his decision as a young man to devote himself to poverty, prayer and charity; his establishment of the Franciscan Order; his healing powers; and not least, his rapport with wild animals. He died, aged only 45, in 1226, and was canonised two years later. We are fortunate in having at Wissington the earliest known example in this country of a painting which shows him preaching to the birds. Dating from the second half of the C13, it was completed not many years after his death. There is a beautiful window at Herringswell and other modern versions at Flempton, Levington and Somerleyton.

Fursey: A C7 Irish abbot who became an East Anglian saint. He came about the year 630 to Burgh castle, near Gt Yarmouth, and his mission was successful, but Mercian raiders forced him to seek refuge in Gaul. There he founded monasteries and a number of churches before he died and was buried at Peronne in about 650. There are modern stained glass portraits of him at Felixstowe St John the Baptist, Kettlebaston, S. Elmham St Michael, and Trimley St Mary.

Gabriel: One of the seven archangels mentioned in the Book of Daniel and in *St Luke's* Gospel. He is the archangel of the *Annunciation* and appears in many carvings and paintings with the *Blessed Virgin*, and alone at Barsham, Boulge, Brantham, Capel St Mary, Great Glemham, Rendham, S. Elmham St Cross, Waldringfield, and Woolverstone.

Genevieve: Rarely seen, and her emblems vary – a spinner's wheel because some say she was a shepherdess, a candle that burned throughout a night of wind and rain, or keys at her girdle to show that she is the patron saint of Paris. Born at Auxerre, she became a nun at 15 and devoted herself to a life of poverty and good works under the guidance of St German. Paris was spared the ravages of Attila the Hun in 451 through the efficacy of her prayers and, by her encouragement, the church of St Denis was built there. She died at a great age in 512. She can be found at Barnham and Euston church is dedicated to her.

George: The martial knight, England's patron saint, famed for his exploits in rescuing the beautiful maiden from the dragon, and then killing it. All this took place in Palestine, where subsequently George was horribly put to death for refusing to sacrifice to idols. It was during the Crusades that he was adopted as England's patron. King Richard Coeur-de-Lion is said to have had a vision of him, assuring him of safety and victory in a forthcoming battle against the Saracens. Commonly seen, but note the wall painting at Earl Stonham, the *spandrels* at Athelington and a modern version with a portrait head at Trimley St Mary.

Gertrude: Brought up in the palace of the C7 Frankish King Dagobert I, she was resolute in her virginity and joined her mother St Iduberga in her monastery at Nivelles. She became abbess, renowned for piety, good works and deep learning. She is sometimes shown with mice running up her crozier (as in the glass at Herringfleet), and this seems merely because her feast day, 17 March, coincides with the time when field mice emerge from hibernation and become a nuisance. She can be seen at Flempton.

Géry or St Gaugericus: He was born in the diocese of Trèves in the late-C6 and became a priest there. He was later consecrated bishop of Cambrai and Arras and governed them for 40 years. Brussels recognises him as its founder. Seldom seen in England, but there is a modern figure of him in a window at Hawstead.

Giles: His emblems are a doe or hind at his side, sometimes an arrow pierces his hand or his leg, and he is dressed as a monk or abbot. He was a hermit in C8 France, with his doe for company. One day a king hunted the doe which fled to the saint for protection. However an arrow loosed by the king by chance struck Giles. In penance the king built a monastery on that site and Giles became the first abbot. He can be found at Bramford and Risby.

Gregory (the Great): Represented as a pope, with a dove, and a roll of music in one hand. One of the *Four Latin Doctors*, he was born of noble Roman stock in 540. He became a monk and founded several monasteries, into one of which he retired. It is said he came briefly to Britain as a missionary but was recalled to be elected, much against his will, as pope. He sent *St Augustine* to these islands and gave his name to Gregorian chants (thus the symbolic roll of music). One of the best-known incidents in his life came to be called the Mass of St Gregory. It is said that, in order to sustain the faith of a sceptic, the sacred elements of bread and wine were transformed on the *altar* into a vision of the risen Christ as the Pope celebrated Mass. It is illustrated in medieval glass at Herringfleet and on the *screen* at Wyverstone, and he features at Barnham and Sudbury St Gregory. Rendlesham is dedicated to him.

Helen: Represented wearing a crown and holding a cross, sometimes an Egyptian cross, like a letter 'T'. Mother of Emperor Constantine the Great, but her own parentage is mysterious. One story says she was an inn-keeper's daughter. Another (much more colourfully) says she was the daughter of King Coel of Colchester, Old King Cole of the nursery rhyme. What is certain is that she married an emperor and bore another; and that as an old lady she set off on pilgrimage for the Holy Land, where she found fragments of the True Cross and brought them to Europe. She can be seen in C14 glass at Herringfleet and C15 glass at Wilby, in Victorian glass at Stutton and on the altar at Coney Weston.

Hubert: Born of a noble C7 French family, he was a great hunter until one day a stag confronted him with a shining crucifix between its antlers. From that moment his life was changed. He went on pilgrimage to Rome, was ordained, and quickly consecrated as bishop of Liège. He is patron saint of huntsmen and hunting. There is a rare painting of him on a C15 screen panel at S. Elmham St Margaret and a fine *Arts & Crafts* window at Herringswell.

Hugh: A C13 Carthusian monk and bishop, born in France but invited to this country by Henry II to become prior of a monastery in Somerset. The establishment flourished under his charge, so Henry chose him to be bishop of Lincoln. He is said to have been the most learned monk of his day. He rebuilt his cathedral, established schools, and was renowned for his wisdom as a judge. His reputation was for simplicity and kindness, yet wholly unmovable on matters of truth, doctrine and principle. He is represented at Coney Weston.

James the Great: Usually seen with a sword, or with the pilgrimage necessities of staff, wallet and scallop shell. One of the *apostles* closest to Christ and subsequently one of the leaders of the church, he was executed by Herod Agrippa in 44 AD (Acts, 12:2). Many traditions surround him; enough churches claim relics to make up half a dozen bodies. Strongest however is the belief that his body was put into a boat, without sails or rudder, which travelled unaided out of the Mediterranean, around Spain and fetched up at Compostella, on the northern coast, where James's shrine became throughout the medieval age one of the greatest places of pilgrimage. He features on Cratfield *font*, a tomb at Framlingham, *screens* at Southwold, Westhall and Woodbridge, on the choir stalls at Blythburgh, and there is a medieval statue at S. Elmham St James.

James the Less: His emblem is a fuller's club, a curved implement like a hockey stick, used by a fuller (a cloth cleanser) to beat cloth, with which he was killed by a blow on the head after he had survived either being stoned (one version) or being hurled from the pinnacle of the temple in Jerusalem by the Scribes and Pharisees. Representations are numerous, but note the stained glass figure at Hessett which probably represents him as a child with his emblem of martyrdom. Other examples can be found at Blythburgh, Framlingham, Hacheston, Sotterley, Southwold, Tattingstone, and Uggeshall.

Jerome: Usually seen with a cardinal's hat; sometimes with an inkhorn, and with a lion at his feet. One of the *Four Latin Doctors*, he became secretary of the Roman See about 381, after much travel and study. (this office was held by a cardinal, thus the hat). Later he travelled again, coming at last to Bethlehem, where he founded a monastery and translated the Bible from its original languages, Hebrew and Greek, into Latin (thus the inkhorn). There is a charming story that a lion came to his monastery with an injured paw. The saint healed it, and the animal stayed on as his faithful companion. He can be seen at Dalham, Nowton and Thurston.

Joachim: Traditionally the husband of *St Anne* and father of the *Blessed Virgin*. Examples are rare and although he is sometimes shown in company with the Virgin and his wife, in the medieval glass in the cathedral he stands alone, cradling a lamb, the symbol of purity and innocence.

John the Baptist: His story needs no telling in detail; the man who baptised Christ and 'led the way', and who died at a whim of Herod's daughter Salome. He figures in C17 continental glass at Saxmundham, there is a modern sculpture at Snape, and a C15 figure at Blythburgh.

John the Divine/the Evangelist: As one of the *Four Evangelists* his emblem is an eagle, but he is often shown with a cup or chalice from which a snake or devil is emerging. This is a reference to the story that he was offered poisoned drink but made it harmless by making the sign of the cross over it. John, 'the disciple whom Jesus loved', and whose figure normally stood on Christ's l. hand on the *rood*, was hurled into boiling oil in Rome but emerged unharmed. He was banished to Patmos and is said to have spent the closing years of his long life at Ephesus. He is represented in many churches, but note particularly Cratfield, Framlingham, Somerleyton, Sotherton, and Southwold.

John Chrysostom: A late-C4 lawyer of Antioch who abandoned his career to live as an ascetic in the Syrian mountains. Broken in health, he returned to be ordained, and his eloquence as a preacher earned him the nickname 'Chrysostom' (gold-mouth). Having written commentaries on all the Scriptures and revised the liturgy of the Eastern church, he was ordained bishop of Constantinople. His zeal and popularity found favour at court until he offended the empress Eudoxia, and he was eventually banished to die in the Caucasus in 407. Seldom chosen by medieval artists, he can be seen in C19 glass at Wickham Market.

Joseph: Little is written in the Gospels about St Joseph but stories abound in the literature of the early church. It is said that he was a widower chosen under divine guidance by the high priest as a husband for the *Blessed Virgin*. He continued as a carpenter until Christ saved his body from corruption at the age of 111 and entrusted his soul to the hosts of heaven. Joseph normally figures in Nativity scenes (as at Long Melford) and in the flight to Egypt, but a C15 glass panel at Hessett portrays him with the Virgin in front of the emperor. Other examples can be found at Barsham, Blaxhall, Orford, and Trimley St Mary.

Joseph of Arimathaea: The rich disciple who secured the body of Jesus and laid it in his own new sepulchre. Legend says that, with *St Philip*, he saved some of Christ's blood in a cup (the Holy Grail) and brought it to Glastonbury as our first Christian missionary. When he arrived, his staff suddenly budded and burst into flower as a sign that he had reached his journey's end. Seen in 1880s glass at Harkstead and Woolverstone.

Jude or Thaddaeus: Most often seen holding a boat, though sometimes with a club or carpenter's square. One of the Twelve, he is said to have preached in Mesopotamia, Russia and finally in Persia, where he was attacked and killed by pagan priests, says one tradition; another, that he was hung on a cross at Arat and pierced with javelins. He is seen in C15 glass at Stratford St Mary, in C19 foreign glass at Winston, and on a bench end at Athelington. Other examples can be found at Blythburgh, Framlingham, Hacheston, Heveningham, Orford, Sotterley, Southwold, Tattingstone, Uggeshall, and Woodbridge.

Lambert: Seen as a bishop holding a sword. He was bishop of his native city of Maastricht from 670. There, according to the *Golden Legend*, he shone 'by word and by example in all virtue'. But around 709 he was the victim of a revenge killing. Unknown to him, his servants had killed two brothers who looted his church, and their relatives took their revenge on the bishop. There is a picture of him at Stonham Aspal.

Laurence: He shares with *St Faith* the emblem of a grid-iron (both were martyred by being roasted on one). He is usually shown in the vestments of a deacon, an office he held under the martyred Pope Sixtus II. During the persecutions of the Emperor Valerian in the C3, Laurence was ordered to reveal the treasures of the church, whereupon he disappeared into the alleys of Rome to return with a crowd of cripples and beggars. 'These are the church's treasures,' he declared. It was an answer which earned him an agonising death. There are nine churches dedicated to him in Suffolk, and he appears on the *screens* at Belstead, Somerleyton, in C19 glass at Bramford, Bures St Stephen and Creeting and in 1930s glass at Knodishall.

Leger: Bishop of Autun in C7 France. His political partialities and involvements earned the hatred of Ebroin, a royal chamberlain. When Ebroin rebelled and sent an army against Aytun, Leger offered himself so that the inhabitants might be spared. Ebroin put his eyes out, tortured and then beheaded him. His emblem is an auger with which he was blinded. A fragment of medieval glass at Polstead may be a rare picture of him.

Longinus: Confusingly, legends assign the name both to the soldier who pierced Christ's side and to the centurian who was converted at the Crucifixion. It is said that he was later beheaded for his faith. Oakley has a picture of him in C19 glass.

Leonard: His symbols are chains or fetters in his hands. This courtier turned monk was given land near Limoges in C5 France by King Clovis, in whose court he was brought up. There he founded the monastery of Noblac and became its first abbot. Legend has it that the king also gave him the right to release any prisoner whom he visited, and he is thus the patron saint of prisoners. He features on the C15 *screen* at Westhall and at Horringer.

Louis: Louis IX, mid-C13 king of France, model Christian monarch, builder of churches and patron of friars. He twice went on Crusade to the Holy Land and died in Tunis in 1270. He was canonised only seven years later. Shown usually as a king holding a crown of thorns and a cross of three nails, recalling the sacred relics he brought back to Paris and housed in Sainte-Chapelle. Seen in C17 glass at Saxmundham and Nowton.

Lucy: Shown holding a sword, or with a sword driven through her neck; or with light issuing from her gashed throat; or holding aloft a plate or a book on which are two eyes. Martyred in Syracuse about the year 303, legend says that when she was sentenced to death nothing could move her, not even yoked oxen. So faggots were piled around her and lit, but she would not burn. At length she was killed by a sword thrust to the throat. The rays of light, and the eyes, probably refer to the similarity between her name and the latin word for light (lux). Portrayed on the *screen* at Eye and in modern glass at Leiston.

Luke: One of the *Four Evangelists*, his special symbol is an ox. *St Paul's* 'fellow worker', he was with him on his later journeys and referred to as 'the beloved physician', hence the tradition that he was a doctor. There is another story dating from the C6 that he was a painter who gained many converts by showing them portraits of

Christ and the *Blessed Virgin* – the first icons. Thus he is also the patron saint of artists. Note particularly the C15 figure on the stalls at Blythburgh, and the *Rope* stained glass at Leiston.

Margaret of Antioch: Her emblem is a dragon, which she transfixes with a cross. Thrown into prison for her Christian belief, she was tempted by the devil in the guise of a terrible dragon. Some have it that the dragon was miraculously decapitated; others that he swallowed her but burst when her cross stuck in his throat; others still that she simply made the sign of the cross and he faded away. That she is guardian of women in childbirth presumably has something to do with her 'caesarian' irruption from the dragon. To be found in fine glass at Combs, on the retable at hornham Parva and at Aldeburgh, Bury St Mary's, Coney Weston, Heveningham, Huntingfield, Leiston, Linstead Parva, Nowton, Sotterley, Ufford, Westhall, Woodbridge, and Woolverstone.

Mark: One of the *Four Evangelists*, his symbol being the winged lion. It typified the Resurrection, based on the curious idea that the lion's young were dead for three days after birth, and were then brought to life by the roaring of their parents. Mark's story as evangelist, and his missionary travels, thread through the New Testament. There is a tradition that later he went to Rome, then to Alexandria, where he became the city's first bishop, and was subsequently martyred during Nero's reign. What is certain is that in the C9 his relics were taken to Venice, whose patron saint he became, and where his lion symbol is much in evidence. Many examples, but note the C17 glass at Saxmundham.

Martin: His virtues of simplicity and charity made him a popular medieval choice, and five Suffolk churches are dedicated to him, including Trimley and Kirton (SS Mary and Martin). Born in C4 Hungary, he trained as a soldier, but after giving half of his cloak to a beggar on whom he took pity, he dreamed that he saw Christ wearing it, and was straightway baptized. He founded a monastery, and much against his will, was made bishop of Tours. To be seen at Hacheston, Nacton, Nowton (Flemish glass) and Woolverstone.

Mary the Blessed Virgin: The mother of Christ, pre-eminent among the patron saints of the medieval church. Out of the 517 in Suffolk, over 150 churches are dedicated to the

Virgin, and no other individual saint reaches a third of that. Originally, a number of them will have been associated with one of her specific feast days such as the *Assumption*, but it is now rare to find instances that can be substantiated. Acclaimed as 'the only bridge between God and man', she became the primal intercessor, 'Queen of Pity', and few churches will have been without at least an *altar* of Our Lady. The Assumption and *Annunciation* scenes were popular subjects for painting and carvings, and hers was the attendant figure on Christ's r. hand as part of the *rood* group. She figures also in some *Doom* paintings (as at Wenhaston) and is sometimes shown as a child being taught to read by her mother *St Anne*. The Blessed Virgin's usual emblem is a lily and her badge a crowned 'M' or 'MR' for 'Maria Regina', Queen of Heaven.

Mary Magdalene (Mary of Magdala): She was one of a number of women 'healed of evil spirits' mentioned in *St Luke's* Gospel, and was among those who watched the Crucifixion. Both *St Matthew* and *St John* tell how she came to the sepulchre on the first Easter day, heard from the angel that Christ was risen and hastened to tell the disciples. The first appearance of the resurrected Christ was to her as she wept by the tomb. From the earliest times, some commentators have identified her with Mary of Bethany, sister of Lazarus, and also as the unnamed woman who, as a sinner, washed Jesus' feet with her tears, dried them with her hair, and anointed them with ointment. Thus she has become the archetype of the Christian penitent and her emblem is the pot of ointment. According to an early tradition she was martyred at Ephesus, but a livelier story was current by the C9. In it, her enemies cast her adrift with Lazarus and Martha in a rudderless ship that fetched up at Marseilles where Lazarus became a bishop and Magdalene preached the Gospel. According to this version she spent the last 30 years of her life as a contemplative near Aix-en-Provence. Plentiful examples, but note especially Bramfield and Somerleyton *screens*, Sutton *font*, and the *Holiday* glass at Lound.

Mary Salome: see *The Three Marys*

Matthew: According to his own Gospel, Matthew was a customs officer in the service of Herod Antipas when he was called by Jesus to become one of the twelve *apostles*. He was the Levi at whose feast Jesus and his disciples scandalised the Pharisees and an early tradition tells of him preaching to the Hebrews. His commonest symbol is the creature that 'had a face as of a man', one of the four mentioned in Revelation. (See *Evangelistic Symbols*). He is said to have met his death by the sword for opposing a king's marriage to a consecrated virgin and so a sword is sometimes substituted. To confuse things further, he may carry an axe like St Matthias, or a carpenter's square. The commonest alternative is a money bag in reference to his early profession. Among many examples, he can be found at Blythburgh, Hawkedon, Leiston, Orford, Sotterley, and Southwold.

Matthias: Though not in the least martial, Matthias is usually shown with a weapon – axe, spear or sword, because he was beheaded in Jerusalem by the Jews. He was the disciple chosen by lot to take the place of Judas Iscariot, after the betrayer's death. He is found at Blythburgh, Framlingham, Lowestoft St Margaret, Tattingstone and Winston.

Michael: A very popular choice for medieval dedications. In the Old Testament, Michael was 'the great prince which standeth for the children of the people', the guardian angel of the Jews, and in the Revelation of St John he leads the angelic host against the devil. And so he appears as a winged angel in shining armour striking down the dragon, but his role as the weigher of souls was a popular notion and he is often seen in *Doom* paintings with the scales of justice (as at Wenhaston). Numerous other examples, but note Somerleyton *screen*, the *Rope* window at Blaxhall and a C13 painting at Wissington.

Monica: She is the saint who illustrates the ideal of a devout wife and mother. A native of North Africa, she converted her husband to Christianity, having endured rough treatment. She grieved over her son *St Augustine's* early waywardness but went with him to Milan and rejoiced in his conversion under *St Ambrose* in the year 387. She is pictured in a window at Ipswich St Augustine.

Nicholas: Very few facts are known about this C4 bishop of Myra in Asia Minor, but the legends are spectacular, and he was a popular choice for dedications. There was once a famine in the land and an innkeeper, with nothing to set before his guests, cut up three boys and put them in a pickling tub. Along came the bishop

and smartly restored them to life, providing a subject popular with medieval congregations and, incidentally, assuming the role of the patron saint of children. The sign of the three golden balls is seldom seen now in city streets but they were another of St Nicholas' symbols and he was the patron saint of pawnbrokers too. The balls stand for the bags of gold that he left secretly at the house of an impoverished nobleman in order that his three daughters should not lack dowries.'Sant Niklaus' came in time to be our own 'Santa Claus'. Having answered the prayers of some storm-tossed sailors, joined them and calmed the seas, his third role is the patron saint of mariners. He is in C13 glass at Wissington and shown with a child in C15 glass at Wrentham; and among modern illustrations see Barsham, Denston, Felixstowe St Peter & St Paul, Hessett, Kirkley, and Orford.

Olave: Patron saint of Norway. After some years fighting the Danes in England, he became a Christian and returned to his native country to defeat Earl Swayn and became king in 1016. His aggressive stance against paganism was summed up in the challenge 'Be baptized or fight'. He was killed at the battle of Stiklestad in 1030 and his shrine at Trondhjem became a focus for pilgrims in the Middle Ages. He occurs in a *Kempe* window at Creeting St Mary.

Oswald: The son of Ethelfrid, king of Northumbria, he fled to Scotland in 613 after his father's death and was converted to Christianity by the monks of Iona. He recovered his realm from Caedwalla and helped in St Aidan's missionary work. He died while fighting Penda, king of Mercia, at the battle of Maserfield and his body came at length to rest in Gloucester in 909. His hands migrated to Bamburgh and his head to Lindisfarne, but the latter journeyed on with the body of *St Cuthbert* to Durham cathedral eventually. That is why it is shown with the figure of St Cuthbert on the C15 *screen* at Nayland.

Osyth, or Sitha: She was a granddaughter of King Penda of Mercia and apparently fled from her bridal feast to take refuge at Dunwich, where she took the veil. Having founded a nunnery at Chick in Essex in 673, she was beheaded in an attack by Danish pirates. She then, as the story goes, walked to the nearest church carrying her head. She appears on the Belstead *screen*, in C15 glass at Wilby, and on a modern panel at Ipswich St Mary le Tower.

Patrick: Probably Scottish by birth, he was captured and enslaved by an Irish chieftain in the early C5. He escaped to Gaul and studied under St Germanus before returning to Ireland as a courageous and successful missionary. He converted King Liogaire at the Hill of Slane and thereafter established churches throughout the land. He is credited with banishing snakes and poisonous animals from Ireland with the help of a staff he claimed to have received from Christ. He died in 463 and was buried at Saul in County Down. He shares the dedication with *St Andrew* at Elvedon and is seen in modern glass at Woodbridge and Sudbury St Gregory.

Patu (Patto or Patten): Very little information traced. Apparently, he was a Scottish monk who became abbot of a monastery in Saxony and who died in 788. He is one of the more obscure saints illustrated in the continental glass at Herringfleet.

Paul: A sword is this apostle's symbol, usually pointing down. With this weapon his head was struck off at the order of the emperor Nero, about the year 66 in Rome, when his success in converting eminent people to Christianity became too much to tolerate. Upon his beheading, it is said, milk flowed from the wound. Paul's life story is too well related in the Acts of the Apostles, and in his own Epistles, to need retelling here. Representations of him are many.

Perpetua: The emperor Septimus Severus had forbidden any more conversions to Christianity when, in the year 203, Perpetua and some of her friends were about to be baptised in Carthage. They all persisted in their belief, and after imprisonment were thrown to wild beasts in the amphitheatre and finally beheaded. Although Perpetua is remembered in the Anglican calendar, she was not adopted as a patron saint in England. She is grouped with other female martyrs in a window at Leiston. See also *St Felicitas*.

Peter:

> Thou art Peter, and upon this rock I will build my church. ... I will give unto thee the keys of the kingdom of heaven.

And so, always, Peter's symbol is the keys. The Gospels tell his story during Christ's ministry on earth, but not his ending. He was crucified –

upside down, at his request, as he did not consider himself worthy to die in the same way as his master – in Rome by the Emperor Nero, at about the same time that *Paul* was beheaded there. Examples of Peter and his crossed keys are legion.

Peter Martyr: A Dominican friar who was born in Verona in the early C13. His eloquence and reputation as a worker of miracles led to his appointment as inquisitor to rid northern Italy of heresy. He met his death at the hands of hired assassins who cleft his head with an axe and drove a knife into his heart, and so he is normally shown with a blade in his head. There is a painting of him on the *retable* at Thornham Parva

Petronilla (Pernel): Identified only through an inscription that was found in a Roman cemetery. It gave her name as 'Aurelia Petronilla' but a misreading prompted the C5 legend that she was a daughter of *St Peter*. He was supposed to have been rebuked for not using his power to cure her paralysis but he said that it was for her own good and that she would recover to wait upon them – and she did. Thus she is sometimes shown as a serving maid holding a key (for St Peter). The Whepstead dedication is unique in England, and she is painted on one of the Somerleyton *screen* panels.

Philip: One of the Twelve, Philip is seen either with a cross, for like his Lord, he was to suffer crucifixion, at the hands of pagans in Asia Minor; or with a basket of loaves and fishes, recording his connection with the biblical story of Christ's feeding of the 5,000. Representations at Athelington, Blythburgh, Corton, Framlingham, Heveningham, Orford, Southwold, and Tattingstone.

Phoebe: Very little is known about her but she was probably one of *St Paul's* converts (Romans 16:1), and was deaconess of the church at Cenchrea. She is pictured in a window at Sotterley.

Polycarp: In his youth Polycarp was instructed by *St John*, who consecrated him bishop of Smyrna where, for forty years, he was one of the resolute leaders on the Church in Asia. In the year 167 he was arrested on a charge of atheism and the Roman authorities tried in vain to persuade him to renounce his faith. He was burnt at the stake and an eyewitness account describes how the flames seemed only to form a canopy around him so that a sword thrust was necessary to kill him. Seldom seen in English churches, but he is featured in a window at Eye.

Prisca: A C3 Roman lady condemned to be thrown to the lions in the arena. They refused to touch her, and after she had been beheaded an eagle guarded her body. Although she has been commemorated in the Anglican calendar, she never found favour as a patron saint in England. One of the female martyrs to be seen in a window at Leiston.

Raphael: One of the seven archangels. He is described in the Book of Tobit as the angel who hears the prayers of holy men and brings them before God; in the Book of Enoch, he is said to have healed the earth defiled by the sins of the fallen angels. He is represented at Capel St Mary, Nacton, Newmarket St Agnes and Tunstall(?).

Richard: Having been a brilliant student at the universities of Paris, Bologna and Oxford, Richard de Wych was appointed Chancellor of Oxford and Canterbury. After his archbishop had quarrelled with Henry III, he left for France with him and became a Dominican friar in Orleans, adding asceticism to his learning. Returning in 1244, he was elected bishop of Chichester and combined generosity to the poor with strict discipline over his clergy. He died in 1253 and his shrine at Chichester became a place of pilgrimage. He figures in C19 glass at Swilland.

Roche: Popular in the Middle Ages but all the stories come from the fanciful *Golden Legend*. He is described as a young Frenchman who used all he had to succour the poor and went on pilgrimage to Italy. There, he halted plague epidemics but was himself infected, and until he recovered, a dog brought him a daily loaf of bread. Shown as a pilgrim with marks of the plague on him. English examples are rare, but his figure is carved on the continental *reredos* at Cavendish, accompanied by the helpful dog, and one of the Fressingfield bench end figures may be him.

Salome: *See* **The Three Marys**

Sebastian: Recognisable at once, the saint riddled with arrows – or at least holding an arrow in his hand. This fate befell him in early Rome, where the saint preached and converted, and

comforted Christian prisoners – until the Emperor Diocletian had him executed in 287. He was popular in the Middle Ages as a patron against the plague which struck as quickly as an arrow. He features on the screen at Belstead.

Sigebert: Son of the C7 French king Dagobert. He was baptised by St Amandus of Maestricht and was made king of various provinces in e. France. A model Christian, he founded monasteries, and after his death in 656 his relics were preserved at Nancy. He occurs in 1880s glass at Felixstowe St Peter & St Paul.

Simon (the Zealot): He is named as one of the twelve *apostles* in the Bible but no other details are given. All stories about him come from the *Golden Legend* and he is supposed to have preached in Egypt and gone with *St Jerome* to Persia. Once there, his miracles so discredited the pagan idols that he was hacked to pieces. Later, he was identified with Simon the 'brother of the Lord' (i.e., son of Cleopas and Christ's cousin). His usual emblem is a fish to show that he was a fisherman, but confusing alternatives crop up: an oar (as at Blythburgh), an axe, or a saw. Other examples at Athelington, Finningham, Framlingham, Hacheston, Lavenham, Sotterley, Southwold, and Tattingstone.

Sir John Schorne: Rector of a Buckinghamshire parish around 1300, he is said to have wiled the devil into a boot and thereby kept him prisoner. Never formally canonised, Sir John was honoured for his piety and for his working of miracles. Sudbury St Gregory had a painting of him which is now in Gainsborough's house.

Sitha (Zita or Citha): An Italian C13 servant girl who became known for her piety and for the help given her by angels. One day, immersed in prayer, she forgot to make the bread. Hastening to the kitchen she found the loaves all ready for the oven. Thus, a loaf is sometimes her symbol. She features on Westhall *screen.*

Stephen: Shown always with a heap of stones in his hands, or on a platter or book. The first Christian martyr, he was stoned to death by the Jews of Jerusalem, when he fearlessly answered their charges of blasphemy (Acts, 6 and 7). The church tests the faithful by celebrating his martyrdom on 26 December. He can be seen on the screen at Belstead and at Blythburgh, Bromeswell, Orford, Somerleyton, Sotterley, Tattingstone, and Wickham Market.

Thomas: The *apostle* who is chiefly remembered for refusing to believe that the other disciples had seen the risen Lord, the original 'doubting Thomas', and for whom Jesus re-appeared that he might be 'not faithless but believing'. The C3 Acts of Thomas record that he was taken to India to be a carpenter for King Gundaphorus, but he spent his time preaching and working miracles, which all led to his being arrested and run through with spears. His emblem is normally a spear but it can also be a carpenter's square, and he is the patron saint of builders and masons. Note particularly Framlingham (with pointing finger), Hacheston (alabaster and *screen*), Southwold and Blythburgh.

Thomas of Canterbury (Thomas Becket): Shown always as an archbishop. Occasionally he may have a sword or an axe, a reference to his martyrdom at the hands of four of Henry II's knights in Canterbury cathedral, Christmas 1170. Thomas' shrine became a place of veneration and miracles. Four centuries later, Henry VIII branded him traitor, rather than saint, which is why representations of him are often defaced with particular savagery and thoroughness. He is found at Barsham, Fornham St Martin (the martyrdom), Eye, Kettlebaston, Lavenham and possibly at Kirkley, Nayland and Somerleyton.

Thomas More: English statesman and scholar. He did not take holy orders, and under Henry VIII he became Chancellor of the Duchy of Lancaster. On the fall of Cardinal Wolsey he was appointed Lord Chancellor but, having opposed Henry's break with Rome, he resigned. When he refused to recognise the king as head of the English Church, he was imprisoned and beheaded. He was canonised in 1923 and features in a window at Felixstowe St John.

Timothy: Born of a Gentile father and a Jewish mother at Lystra, he was the disciple to whom *St Paul* wrote two of his letters. He became bishop of Ephesus and was associated with *St John*. While protesting against a heathen festival he was killed by the mob in the year 97. He is pictured in modern glass at Bungay Holy Trinity.

Uriel: In Jewish apocryphal texts he is one of the four chief archangels who stand in the presence of God. He is represented at Capel St Mary.

Ursula: Very seldom seen, but normally portrayed crowned, with a sheaf of arrows in one hand, and young women in some profusion at her feet and under her cloak. The story has it that she was a king's daughter in early Britain who, to escape the attentions of an unwelcome suitor, set off for Rome ... accompanied by 11,000 handmaidens. This startling entourage probably stems from an early translation error because Ursula's maid was called Undecimilla – misread as a number. Be that as it may, Ursula and companions arrived in Rome where the Pope received her – and perceived in a dream that she was to suffer martyrdom. At which intelligence he put off his tiara and set off with her to Cologne. There they were beseiged by the Huns, who took the city and slew the lot – except for Ursula whom the Hun prince wanted to marry. When she refused he shot her with an arrow. She occurs in C15 glass at S. Elmham All Saints, on the screens at Belstead and Eye, at Aldeburgh, Woodbridge, and possibly at Bildeston, Gisleham and Kessingland.

Veronica: Traditionally identified as the woman who was cured by touching Jesus's robe (Matthew 9:20), she figures in the medieval *Golden Legend* as having wiped Christ's face as he carried the cross. The handkerchief or head-cloth was imprinted with his features and a portrait professing to be the original imprint has been in Rome since the C8 and at St Peter's since 1297. Competing claims are made by Genoa and Milan. Pictures of Christ's face on linen, communion *patens* etc., became known as vernicles. There is a C17 Flemish roundel at Nowton illustrating the story and another at Depden.

Walstan of Bawburgh: Norfolk's own farmer-saint, patron saint of farm workers, usually shown crowned (denoting his royal blood) and holding a scythe. The son of a prince, he chose a life of poverty, becoming a farm worker at Taverham near Norwich. After his many years of faithful service, Walstan's master wanted to make him his heir. But the saint declined and asked instead for a cart and a cow in calf. She produced two fine bulls which he trained to pull his cart. In his old age Walstan received a divine visitation foretelling his death, which came as he worked in the fields. His body was placed on his cart and, unguided, his bulls set out. They paused at Costessey, where a spring sprang up and continued to give water until the C18. At last they came to the saint's birth-place at Bawburgh, passing clean through the solid wall of the church and leaving behind them another spring which, as St Walstan's well, was famous for centuries. His shrine attracted many pilgrims until it was destroyed at the *Reformation*. He is represented at Bury St Mary.

William of Norwich: In 1144 the Jews in Norwich were accused of crucifying this 11-year old boy ad burying his body on Mousehold Heath, just outside the city. His body was found and reburied in the cathedral where is became the focus of miraculous cures and subsequent pilgrimages. The full story can be found in M.D. Anderson's *A Saint at stake*. Seldom seen outside Norfolk, there is a painting of him on the *screen* at Eye.

Withburga: Daughter of Anna, C7 king of East Anglia and sister of *St Etheldreda* and St Sexburga. After education at Holkham on the north Norfolk coast, she founded a nunnery at East Dereham and was its abbess for many years. The small community lived simply, and it is said that when they were reduced to poverty, two does appeared and provided enough milk to save the nuns from starvation. Always shown as a crowned abbess, sometimes in company with the does. Hers is one of the modern figures on the C15 *font* cover at Ufford and on the *screen* at Woolpit.

Wolfgang: Having been chaplain to the bishop of Treves, he went as a missionary to Pannonia, before being consecrated bishop of Ratisbon in 972. A holy and charitable priest, he was credited with many miracles before his death in 994. His figure is among the collection of continental glass at Herringfleet.

Appendix 2 – Styles of Architecture

From the days of the Saxons, through to the Georgians in the C18, architecture both sacred and secular has passed through many developments and details, fads and fancies, inspirations and inventions. The names we use to describe those phases – *Early English, Decorated* etc. – were coined only in the last century, and given convenient dates. But such dating can be misleading. Just as fashions in costume took time to filter through from city or court to provincial outposts, so changes in architectural ideas were only gradually assimilated. For example, the Decorated style was still being used after the *Black Death*, well into the 1360s and 1370s where, presumably, masons with the old skills had survived. Window shapes and *tracery* offer the clearest guide to individual

styles and are normally the most helpful features (although a lot of Victorian copies are now weathered sufficiently to pass for originals).

Saxon: From the C7 to the Conquest. Characterised by roughness of construction, crudely rounded arches and triangular-headed window openings (see figs. 1 and 2). Equally distinctive is their *long and short work* at corners of buildings. This is where upright stones are alternated with flat slabs. Saxon work can be seen at Barsham, Bungay Holy Trinity, Gisleham, Halesworth, Holton, Mettingham, Mutford, Walpole, and Wissett.

Norman: From the Conquest to about 1200, including the *Transitional* phase, spanning the

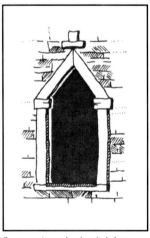

Fig. 1. Saxon triangular-headed form.

Fig. 2. Typical saxon round-headed window with crude arch.

reigns of William I and II, Henry I, Stephen, Henry II and Richard I. Massive walls and pillars are typical features, semi-circular arches and small round-headed windows, sometimes used in groups, with heavy pillar-like *mullions* between them. After the *Saxon* crudity, there is growing craftsmanship and artistry, with bold ornamentation. The small windows are usually deeply splayed (figs. 3 and 4). These would originally have been filled with parchment or oiled linen – glass came later. Good examples of Norman work are found at Orford, Theberton, and Westhall.

Transitional: This is the changeover from the rounded, Romanesque architecture of the Normans to the Gothic movement in England – the triumph of the pointed arch. It took three or four decades, to about 1200, for the change-over to take full effect. Massive pillars became slimmer and lighter, and might sometimes bear a pointed arch, carved in *Norman* character. Examples at Cookley, Friston, Shadingfield, Sibton, Sweffling, Thorington, and Walpole.

Early English: Gothic has now fully arrived, and with it the first really native English architectural style. It spans roughly the 100-year period from the end of the reign of Richard, through John and Henry II, and into the time of Edward II, to about 1300. The simple,

Fig. 3. Norman slit window – interior view of typical deep 'arrow slit' embrasure.

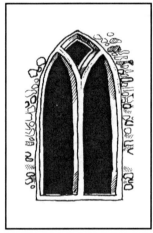

Fig. 6. The typical 'Y' traceried window of around 1300.

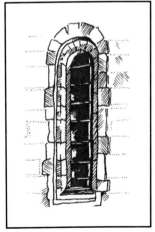

Fig. 4. Norman slit window – exterior view.

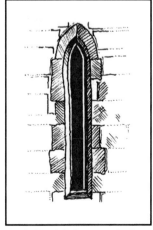

Fig. 5. Early English lancet – the first arrival in England of pointed Gothic.

Fig. 7. Early English lancets composed in a group.

Fig 9. The flowing beauty of the Decorated style's 'reticulated' form.

Fig. 8. Simple geometric 'plate' tracery.

Fig 10. Decorated artistry in imaginative flow – the butterfly motif.

elegant *lancet* made its appearance, first used singly (fig. 5) then in groups.

As ideas developed, the space between the heads of two lancets placed together was pierced with an open pattern, cut directly through the masonry: this is *plate tracery* (fig. 8). From there it was but a step to refining the tracery by constructing it in separate pieces to form *bar tracery*. About the year 1300 (and a most useful dating device) came a most distinctive phase, the 'Y' traceried window (fig. 6). A development of this was the extension of the Ys through three or four *lights* producing interlocking tracery with slim, pointed heads. Everything at this time became finer in conception: bold buttresses,

thrusting arches, beautiful foliage carving and, most distinctive of this period, the *trefoil*, decoration.

This was much used in window tracery and in decorative carving. Also popular was the *dogtooth* moulding, which looks like a square, four-leafed flower, said to be based on the dog's tooth violet.

Decorated: This supreme time of architectural achievement and marvellous confidence in the use of shape and decoration had but a half-century of full life – during the reigns of the first three Edwards – before the *Black Death* struck Europe in 1349-1350. This was the high point of ornamented Gothic. Windows grew

Fig 11. The classix Perpendicular window, its mullions thrusting to the head of the arch.

Fig 12. The Tudor contribution – a flattening of the arch over a Perpendicular window.

larger, *tracery* became progressively more flowing and adventurous: circles, *trefoils*, *quatrefoils*, and lozenges dominate the tracery, it led to *reticulated* tracery (fig. 9) and the creative beauty of form as seen in fig. 10. Rich ornamentation and carving abounded, including the distinctive *ball flower*, and there was a profusion of pinnacles and *crocketting*, both inside and outside, on gable ends to tombs. There are many Suffolk examples, but Dennington *chancel* is notable.

Perpendicular: This style takes us from the aftermath of the *Black Death*, through the reigns of Richard II, Henry IV, V and VI, Edward IV and Richard III to the time of Henry VII, until around 1500. The Perpendicular style, as its name implies, is one of soaring upward lines, drawn in great windows by vertical *mullions* (fig. 11), by majestic towers; and by meticulously panelled buttresses and parapets and the ornamented bases of walls (see also *flushwork*). Rich decoration is typical, though it usually has more of a grandly formal than of a purely aesthetic beauty. The majority of churches embody something of the style, even if it is only a window or two.

Tudor: Roughly the century to 1600 spanned by Henry VIII, Edward VI, Mary and Elizabeth.

Not so much a style as an adaptation, a flattening of the *Perpendicular* arch, while otherwise retaining the same features (fig. 12). Decoration had become stereotyped, with interminable repetitions of the royal badges, the rose and the portcullis; family heraldry followed the trend so that badges and shields of magnates and county gentry are to be found carved in wood and stone. Red brick became a fashionable alternative to stone, and in some cases it displaced the local flint as a basic material which could be laid quickly and produced locally.

Jacobean/Caroline: From the early C17 with the reign – 1603-25 – of James I (Latin, Jacobus), and continuing with the reigns of Charles I and II (Latin, Carolus). It was during James' reign that a movement towards *Renaissance* architecture began in England. It was a style which employed the principles of the Greek classical building, with classical detail and ornamentation, and as in the Elizabethan period, a copious use of bricks. The style found expression in furniture too, as will be found in many examples in churches, and the Jacobean title applies as often as not to wood carving, pulpits, and to aristocratic monuments.

Printed in the United Kingdom by
Lightning Source UK Ltd., Milton Keynes
139599UK00002B/2/P